D0982841

THE VARIORUM EDITION
OF THE PLAYS OF
W. B. YEATS

Edited by Peter Allt and Russell K. Alspach

THE VARIORUM EDITION OF THE
POEMS OF W. B. YEATS

By Russell K. Alspach

IRISH POETRY FROM THE ENGLISH
INVASION TO 1798

THE VARIORUM EDITION

OF THE PLAYS OF

W. B. YEATS

EDITED BY

RUSSELL K. ALSPACH

UNITED STATES MILITARY ACADEMY

ASSISTED BY

CATHARINE C. ALSPACH

THE MACMILLAN COMPANY · NEW YORK

1966

First Printing

Printed in Great Britain
by R. & R. Clark Ltd. Edinburgh

Library of Congress Catalog Card Number: 64-8597

CONTENTS

PREFACE

I HAVE dedicated this book to Peter Allt. Before his death in 1954 we had talked hopefully of a variorum edition of Yeats's plays that we should do after finishing our variorum edition of the poems. I hope that what I have accomplished here is worthy of the dedication.

My obligations are many. Mrs. Yeats's generosity in releasing the necessary copyrights made publication possible; and she was kind enough to read and approve a portion of the manuscript that I showed her in Dublin in the summer of 1963. Those days in Dublin were marked also by many kindnesses from Jo and Liam Miller and David Krause, professor of English at Brown University, including criticism of the manuscript and help in the overcoming of technicalities having to do with publication.

Mr. R. L. De Wilton of The Macmillan Company of New York, who was of so much assistance in the publication of the variorum poems, has been of equal assistance in the general preparation of the variorum plays. Mr. A. L. Hart, Jr., and Mr. Arthur Gregor, of the same company, were of special help a number of times. Mr. T. M. Farmiloe of Macmillan & Co. Ltd. of London was patient and helpful during the reading of proof.

Professors Marion Witt and Katherine Gatch of Hunter College read early drafts of the manuscript and gave me counsel about methods of collation and style in general. I am much indebted to them. Professor MacEdward Leach of the University of Pennsylvania made several helpful suggestions; Professor Allan Chester of the same University read critically part of the manuscript; Professor George Brandon Saul of the University of Connecticut discussed with me matters of general format; and Lieutenant-Colonels Wilfred C. Burton and George W. Tracy, associate professors of English at West Point, aided in many ways. The staff of the United States Military Academy Library, especially Miss Thelma Bedell, were prompt and efficient in granting my many requests.

The task of matching up and typing the main text and the variants was skilfully done by Miss Ann Hessian, ably assisted by Miss Genevieve Crane. Finally I want to thank the children of the late T. B. Rogers, of Birmingham, England, and Mrs. Marilyn Hogan of Detroit, for cheerfully lending me much-needed texts; and Mrs. Sally Anderson for assistance with the make-up of certain pages.

I have acknowledged on the title-page my deepest obligation.

West Point, New York   R. K. A.
March, 1964

INTRODUCTION

In 1956, shortly after completing the manuscript of *The Variorum Edition of the Poems of W. B. Yeats*, I began working on the variorum edition of the plays. My purpose here is to discuss some of the major editorial and bibliographical problems I encountered during the years of composition.

The first was that of a basic text. For the poetry this problem had been easy: shortly before his death Yeats had revised his poetry and signed pages for a de luxe edition to be published by Macmillan & Co. Ltd. But World War II intervened and it was not until 1949 that the handsome, two-volume final revised edition of the poetry was published. Ready to hand, therefore, was an authoritative basic text for the poetry variorum.

But there was no such final revised text of the plays. The best seemed to be the London Macmillan edition of *The Collected Plays of W. B. Yeats* (1952). The plays in this edition and its New York Macmillan counterpart of 1953, with the exception of 'A Full Moon in March', 'The King of the Great Clock Tower', 'The Herne's Egg', 'Purgatory', and 'The Death of Cuchulain', were reprintings with few and unimportant changes of *The Collected Plays of W. B. Yeats* (1934) that Yeats had carefully revised. The user of the present book must trust his judgment in assessing the slight textual changes between the editions of 1934 and 1952; and also between *Nine One-Act Plays* (1937)[1] and the edition of the collected plays in 1952.

The second problem was page set-up. Because the set-up of the poetry variorum had apparently met with approval, I decided to use it again, although it could not be strictly followed in all the plays (some of these I discuss below). A glance at p. 214—the first page of 'Cathleen ni Houlihan'—will make the set-up clear. The material above the line dividing the page is the basic text—*The Collected Plays of W. B. Yeats* (London, 1952)—with which the variants below the line are collated and keyed. 'Printings' lists the publications of the play; the numbers refer to the numbered bibliography on pp. xix–xxiv. The remainder of the material below the line is self-evident.

The plays are in the order of *The Collected Plays* of 1952, and are set up in a fashion generally similar to the example above, but some needed special treatment. The first such was 'The Countess Cathleen'.

The Printings[2] of 'The Countess Cathleen' begin with *The Countess*

---

[1] The textual evidence suggests that Yeats probably did little more than select the nine plays.　　　[2] Pp. 2–3.

Kathleen and Various Legends and Lyrics (1892). It was republished in
Poems (1895); in *The Poetical Works of William B. Yeats* (1907); in *The
Collected Works in Verse and Prose*, Vol. III (1908); by itself titled *The
Countess Cathleen* (1912); in the Tauchnitz edition (1913); in *Selected
Poems* (1921); in *Plays and Controversies* (1923, 1924); with *The Land of
Heart's Desire* (1924, 1925); in *The Collected Plays of W. B. Yeats* (1934,
1935); and in *The Collected Plays of W. B. Yeats* (1952, 1953).

Yeats revised 'The Countess Cathleen' frequently. The revision for
the second printing, *Poems* (1895), was so drastic that intelligible collation was virtually impossible. I decided, therefore, to print the
original version (1892) complete on the verso pages and to print above
the line on the recto pages the basic text of 1952, with collations of
all other printings—that of 1895 to that of 1934—below the line. Even
so, the additions and deletions were so great that the collations frequently extend for several extra pages before they can be brought into
some harmony again with the basic text. Similarities between the
original version and the basic text I showed by bracketed line-numbers
in the verso margins; identities by unbracketed line-numbers.

Pp. 152–3 illustrate this set-up and arrangement of 'The Countess
Cathleen'. The first is a verso page and will face the second, a recto
page. In these pages the original version is closer to the basic text than
elsewhere, but even so there are no identities, although lines [831]–757
and [832]–758 are close.

Compounding the collation problem of 'The Countess Cathleen'
was the shift Yeats made from five scenes in the original printing
(1892) to four acts in the second printing (1895). He kept the four
acts until 1912, when he restored the five-scene arrangement that he
retained through the final version. Because of this shift from five scenes
to four acts and back again, I decided that collation would be more
understandable if I numbered the lines consecutively throughout the
play with no break between scenes or acts, but with scene- and act-
changes marked both above and below the line.

Yeats revised each of the printings from 1895 to 1908; he revised
rather extensively, besides restoring the five scenes, for the printings
of 1912: *The Countess Cathleen* (June), *The Poetical Works of William B.
Yeats*, Vol. II, Dramatic Poems (August), and *Poems* (September).
Yeats scholars and bibliographers have as a rule assumed that the
revision of 1912 was, except for quite minor changes, the final version.[1]
But examination of the Tauchnitz edition, published quite early in
1913,[2] proves the assumption wrong. Besides making this wrong

---

[1] For example, Allan Wade, in *A Bibliography of the Writings of W. B. Yeats*, 2nd ed., revd,
London, 1958, items 93–100.   [2] *Ibid.*, item 103.

assumption, Yeats scholars have overlooked Yeats's statement in the Preface to the Tauchnitz edition that '. . . the play ['The Countess Cathleen'], . . . differs from any published version, . . .'.[1] It is the Tauchnitz version of 1913 that is the earliest almost-final version of the play.

One of the main revisions for the Tauchnitz edition is in scene IV. As Yeats wrote this scene for the three 1912 printings, it went as follows:

Scene IV

Scene.—*A wood near the Castle, as in Scene II.*
The Spirits pass one by one carrying bags.

First Spirit. I'll never dance another step, not one.
Second Spirit. Are all the thousand years of dancing done?
Third Spirit. How can we dance after so great a sorrow?
Fourth Spirit. But how shall we remember it to-morrow?
Fifth Spirit. To think of all the things that we forget.
Sixth Spirit. That's why we groan and why our lids are wet.

The Spirits go out. A group of Peasants pass.

First Peasant. I have seen silver and copper, but not gold.
Second Peasant. It's yellow and it shines.
First Peasant. It's beautiful.
  The most beautiful thing under the sun,
  That's what I've heard.
Third Peasant. I have seen gold enough.
Fourth Peasant. I would not say that it's so beautiful.
First Peasant. But doesn't a gold piece glitter like the sun?
  That's what my father, who'd seen better days,
  Told me when I was but a little boy—
  So high—so high, it's shining like the sun,
  Round and shining, that is what he said.
Second Peasant. There's nothing in the world it cannot buy.
First Peasant. They've bags and bags of it.

They go out. The two Merchants follow silently.

When he revised the scene for the Tauchnitz edition he took out the six Spirits and moved Aleel's song beginning 'Impetuous heart, be still, be still', from Scene I (lines 122–127)—where it had been from the 1895 printing up to and including the three 1912 printings—to the end of this newest and practically final version of Scene IV.

Another striking alteration for the Tauchnitz version likewise concerned the Spirits, who, besides talking the foolishness noted above in the 1912 Scene IV, are present also in the 1912 Scene III talking equal nonsense until Yeats exorcized them for the Tauchnitz edition.

[1] P. [5]. The preface is dated October 1912.

All in all, the Tauchnitz edition contains the almost-final version of the entire play, and this version is reprinted first in the seventh English edition (1913) of *Poems* (1895),[1] then in the first (1916) so-called 'impression' of the 1912 *The Countess Cathleen*,[2] and thereafter.

I also used the verso–recto page arrangement in a number of other plays where it seemed the best way to show clearly how a play developed and where, as in 'The Countess Cathleen', it helped avoid excessive and confusing collation. The method seemed especially appropriate for those plays that have verse and prose versions: e.g. 'The Only Jealousy of Emer' (verse) and 'Fighting the Waves' (prose), 'The Hour-Glass' (verse and prose), 'The King of the Great Clock Tower' (verse-and-prose and verse). I followed the same arrangement, in part, for 'On Baile's Strand', where in the first three printings that portion of the text corresponding in general to lines 1–458 of the final version show differences so great that intelligible collation would again have been virtually impossible; I used it for 'The Resurrection' because of the marked differences between the first printing in *The Adelphi* and subsequent printings. In all cases I showed, as I had for 'The Countess Cathleen', similarities between the verso-page version and the basic text by bracketed line-numbers in the verso margins, and identities by unbracketed line-numbers.

For 'The Green Helmet', that also has verse and prose versions, I chose another arrangement. The first two printings were prose[3] and all others verse. The problem was different here in that the poetry versions were little more than a casting into verse of the prose versions. I decided that the play's development would be more obvious if I divided the page into three parts: the top part would have the lines of the basic text, the middle part the corresponding lines of the two prose texts with variations between them marked within these lines, and the bottom part the collations of the verse printings with the basic verse text. The bracketed line-numbers in the left-hand margin of the middle part of the page serve the same purpose as in the verso–recto arrangements.

Another editorial and bibliographical problem—one that is met constantly when studying editions of the plays, as well as of the poems—was Yeats's habit of revising for one edition and ignoring another though the printing dates might very nearly coincide.[4] This erratic

---

[1] Wade, *op. cit.*, item 100.

[2] *Ibid.*, item 93. It is no. 56a in the bibliography of this book. I was unable to find a copy until my MS. was well along. The same reason accounts for no. 10a and no. 28a.

[3] The prose versions are titled 'The Golden Helmet'. See Wade, *op. cit.*, items 74 and 78.

[4] I have written about this in relation to the poetry. See 'Some Textual Problems in Yeats', *Studies in Bibliography*, Vol. IX, Charlottesville, Va., 1957, pp. 51–67.

behaviour is noticeable especially in English vs. American editions. Two examples will show the confusion that results. The revision of 1912 of 'The Countess Cathleen' was, as I said, printed only three times when it was again and almost-finally revised for the Tauchnitz edition of 1913. But he continued using the revision of 1912 in the 1914, 1916, 1917, 1919, and 1921 reprintings of *The Poetical Works of William B. Yeats*, Vol. II, Dramatic Poems, published in New York. And to compound the confusion, he used in the 1921 American *Selected Poems* the 1913 Tauchnitz version of the play.[1] The bewildered student could well ask himself, if he were studying and comparing the play in the 1921 reprint of *The Poetical Works*, etc. (1912), and the 1921 *Selected Poems*, which version Yeats preferred.

My second example of 'another editorial–bibliographical problem' is 'Deirdre', whose bibliographical history presents several curiosities. Its initial printing was 1907; later in the same year it was published in America. Here again American reprints are ignored in revisions, for although the Stratford collected edition of 1908 was 'Deirdre's' next appearance in print, the revisions therein were not made for the 1909 and 1911 American reprints of the 1907 American edition.

Another curiosity about the American 'Deirdre' is that some of the stage directions are unique to the 1907 American edition and its reprints. One of the most striking of these is a lengthy insertion of directions after Deirdre and Naisi have entered the guest-house and the musicians have finished the song (line 148) that begins ' "Why is it," Queen Edain said', (line 125):

[*The sky outside is still bright so that the room is dim in the midst of a wood full of evening light, but gradually during what follows the light fades out of the sky; and except during a short time before the lighting of the torches, and at the end of all, the room is either dark amid light or light amid the darkness. The lighting and the character of the scenery, the straight trees, and the spaces of sky and mountain between them suggest isolation and silence.*

The musicians almost throughout remain near the brazier, but show the effect upon their minds of what is happening by their movements and the expression of their faces.]

It is almost as if Yeats didn't trust American companies to play 'Deirdre' without more explicit aid from him than he thought English companies needed.

A third curiosity about 'Deirdre' is the patchings that Yeats did from time to time and that he thrice printed by themselves. The first is in a note to the initial printing—London and Dublin, 1907—and

---

[1] This despite the fly-title on p. [49] of *Selected Poems* that reads 'The Countess Cathleen / (1893, revised 1911).'

consists of nine lines; the second, entitled 'A Different Version of Deirdre's Entrance', is in Appendix II of volume II of the Stratford edition of 1908 and consists of 56 lines; the third, called 'Alterations in Deirdre', printed in *Samhain* for November 1908 and as a separate 4-page leaflet shortly afterwards, consists of 127 lines. These I have collated with the basic text and printed complete in the notes to the play.

Finally, I had the problem of where to put Yeats's notes about the plays. I decided that rather than placing them all in an Appendix I would put the notes about a particular play at the end of that play and the general notes about the plays in an Appendix, cross-referencing all notes not only to each other but also to the Prefaces and Dedications that I placed in another Appendix. I have collated wherever possible.

So much for the major editorial and bibliographical problems I encountered. A last and general comment could be that the chief impressions one gets from a chronological study of Yeats's plays are the same impressions one gets from a similar study of the poetry: he was never content, he revised constantly, and he almost always improved.

LIST OF PLAYS

PLAYS NOT INCLUDED IN THE MAIN TEXT

   * Not in the basic text, *The Collected Plays of W. B. Yeats* (**97**), but included for purposes of comparison. See explanatory note at each play.

BIBLIOGRAPHY

THE Bibliography lists in chronological order the editions used in the collations.

Reprintings that did not involve revisions are grouped under one number (**12, 16, 29,** etc.); reprintings that involved revisions are given separate numbers and placed in their chronological order (**5, 6, 7, 18, 31, 49, 51, 61, 62, 66, 67, 72, 74, 78, 80** are reprintings involving revisions of *Poems*, 1895). There can of course be no proof that Yeats did not go over carefully, without making any changes, volumes that are listed merely as reprintings.

English and American editions of a particular volume that appeared about the same time and showed no textual variation save for misprints or seeming misprints were given a single number (**57, 69, 71,** etc.).

I discuss briefly in the introduction to the collations the question of the plays published after Yeats's death.

'Revd' and 'rptd' are abbreviations for 'revised' and 'reprinted'.

The letter v before a line number=variant.

1. *Mosada*. Dublin, 1886.
2. *The Wanderings of Oisin and Other Poems*. London, 1889. Reissued 1892. [Mosada, The Seeker, The Island of Statues, II, 3, Time and the Witch Vivien]
3. *The Countess Kathleen and Various Legends and Lyrics*. London, 1892; Boston and London, 1892.
4. *The Land of Heart's Desire*. London, 1894; Chicago, 1894.
5. *Poems*. London, 1895; London and Boston, 1895. [The Countess Cathleen, The Land of Heart's Desire]
6. *Poems* (1895). Revd and rptd London, 1899. [See 5]
7. *Poems* (1895). Revd and rptd London, 1901. [See 5]
8. *Cathleen Ni Hoolihan*. London, 1902.
9. *Where There is Nothing*. Dublin, 1902.
10. *Where There is Nothing*. New York, 1902.
10a. *Where There is Nothing*. New York, 1902. Large paper edition of 10.
11. *Where There is Nothing*. London, 1903; New York, 1903.
12. *The Land of Heart's Desire*. Portland, Maine, 1903. Rptd often to 1925. [For further bibliographical details see Allan Wade, *A Bibliography of the Writings of W. B. Yeats*. 2nd ed., revd, London, 1958, items 12, 13, 13A.]

13. *In the Seven Woods*. Dundrum, 1903. (Dun Emer press) [On Baile's Strand]

14. *In the Seven Woods*. New York and London, 1903. [See 13]

15. *The Hour-Glass*. London, 1903.

16. *The Hour-Glass and Other Plays*. New York and London, 1904. Rptd often to 1919. [See Wade, *op. cit.*, item 52] [The Hour-Glass, Cathleen ni Hoolihan, A Pot of Broth]

17. *The Hour-Glass, Cathleen Ni Houlihan, The Pot of Broth*. London, 1904. Rptd Dublin, 1905.

18. *Poems.* (1895). Revd and rptd London, 1904. [See 5]

19. *The King's Threshold*. New York, 1904.

20. *The King's Threshold: and On Baile's Strand*. London, 1904.
    The King's Threshold. Dublin, 1905.
    On Baile's Strand. Dublin, 1905.

21. *The Pot of Broth*. London, 1905.

22. *Cathleen Ni Houlihan*. London, 1906.

23. *Poems, 1899–1905*. London and Dublin, 1906. [On Baile's Strand, The King's Threshold]

24. *The Shadowy Waters* (Acting version). London, 1907.

25. *The Hour-Glass*. London, 1907. Rptd Stratford-upon-Avon, twice. [See Wade, *op. cit.*, item 67]

26. *On Baile's Strand*. London, 1907.

27. *Deirdre*. London and Dublin, 1907.

27a. Note on p. 48 of 27 has variant readings from Directions after line v149 to line v157.

28. *The Poetical Works of William B. Yeats*. Vol. II, Dramatical Poems. New York and London, 1907. Rptd 1909, 1911. [The Countess Cathleen, The Land of Heart's Desire, On Baile's Strand, The King's Threshold, Deirdre, Acting version of The Shadowy Waters]

28a. *The Unicorn from the Stars*. New York, 1908 (Jan. 15).

29. *The Unicorn from the Stars and Other Plays*. New York, 1908 (May 13). Rptd 1915. [The Unicorn from the Stars, Cathleen ni Houlihan, The Hour-Glass]

30. *The Golden Helmet*. New York, 1908.

31. *Poems.* (1895). Revd and rptd London, 1908. [See 5]

32. *The Collected Works in Verse and Prose of William Butler Yeats*. Vol. II. Stratford-on-Avon, 1908. [The King's Threshold, On Baile's Strand, Deirdre, Acting version of The Shadowy Waters]

32a. Appendix II of 32 has 'A Different Version of Deirdre's Entrance'; lines 149–v204 and 314–315b.

33. *The Collected Works*, etc. Vol. III. Stratford-on-Avon, 1908. [The

Countess Cathleen, The Land of Heart's Desire, The Unicorn from the Stars]

34. *The Collected Works*, etc. Vol. IV. 1908. [The Hour-Glass, Cathleen ni Houlihan, The Golden Helmet]

34a. *The Collected Works*, etc. Vol. VIII. [Prologue to The King's Threshold]

35. *Alterations in Deirdre*. London, 1908.

36. *Cathleen ni Houlihan*. London, 1909.

37. *The Land of Heart's Desire*. New York, 1909.

38. *The Green Helmet and Other Poems*. Dundrum, 1910. (Cuala press)

39. *The Green Helmet and Other Poems*. New York, 1911.

40. *Deirdre*. Stratford-upon-Avon, 1911.

41. *The Pot of Broth*. London, 1911.

42. *Cathleen ni Houlihan*. Stratford-upon-Avon, 1911.

43. *The Green Helmet*. Stratford-upon-Avon, 1911.

44. *The King's Threshold*. Stratford-upon-Avon, 1911.

45. *Plays for an Irish Theatre*. London and Stratford-upon-Avon, 1911. [Deirdre, The Green Helmet, On Baile's Strand, The King's Threshold, The Hour-Glass, Cathleen ni Houlihan, Acting version of The Shadowy Waters] Rptd 1913.

46. *The Countess Cathleen*. London, 1912 (June).

47. *The Land of Heart's Desire*. London, 1912. Rptd 1913, 1916, 1919, 1922 (2), 1923, 1924 (5), 1925.

48. *The Poetical Works of William B. Yeats*. Vol. II, Dramatic Poems. Revd and rptd New York and London, 1912 (August). Rptd 1914, 1916, 1917, 1919, 1921. [See 28]

49. *Poems* (1895). Revd and rptd London, 1912 (September). [See 5]

50. *The Green Helmet and Other Poems*. New York and London, 1912.

51. *Poems* (1895). Revd and rptd London, 1913. [See 5]

52. *A Selection from the Poetry of W. B. Yeats*. Leipzig (Tauchnitz), 1913 (January). Preface dated Oct. 1912. Rptd 1922. [The Countess Cathleen, On Baile's Strand, Deirdre]

53. *The Hour-Glass*. Dundrum, 1914. (Cuala press)

54. *Responsibilities: Poems and a Play*. Dundrum, 1914 (Cuala press)

55. *Deirdre*. Stratford-upon-Avon, 1914.

56. *The King's Threshold*. Stratford-upon-Avon, 1915.

56a. *The Countess Cathleen*. London, 1916. Rptd 1916, 1920, 1922, 1924.

57. *Responsibilities and Other Poems*. London, 1916; New York, 1916. Rptd London, 1917. [The Hour-Glass—1912]

58. *The Wild Swans at Coole.* Dundrum, 1917. (Cuala press) [At the Hawk's Well]

59. *The Well of Immortality* (At the Hawk's Well). New York (?), 1917 (?). [See Wade, *op. cit.*, item 119]

60. *Two Plays for Dancers.* Dundrum, 1919. (Cuala press) [The Dreaming of the Bones, The Only Jealousy of Emer]

61. *Poems* (1895). Revd and rptd London, 1919. [See 5]

62. *Poems* (1895). Revd and rptd London, 1920. [See 5]

63. *Selected Poems.* New York, 1921. [The Land of Heart's Desire, The Countess Cathleen, On Baile's Strand, Deirdre]

64. *Four Plays for Dancers.* London, 1921; New York, 1921. [At the Hawk's Well, The Only Jealousy of Emer, The Dreaming of the Bones, Calvary]

65. *Seven Poems and a Fragment.* Dundrum, 1922. (Cuala press) [A New End for The King's Threshold]

66. *Poems* (1895). Revd and rptd London, 1922 (1). [See 5]

67. *Poems* (1895). Revd and rptd London, 1922 (2). [See 5]

68.[1] *The Land of Heart's Desire.* Boston, 1922. Rptd Boston, 1925, 1928.

69. *Plays in Prose and Verse.* London, 1922; New York, 1924. Rptd London, 1922, 1926, 1931. [Cathleen ni Houlihan, The Pot of Broth, The Hour-Glass (prose), The King's Threshold, On Baile's Strand, Acting version of The Shadowy Waters, Deirdre, The Unicorn from the Stars, The Green Helmet, The Hour-Glass (verse), The Player Queen]

70. *The Player Queen.* London, 1922.

71. *Plays and Controversies.* London, 1923; New York, 1924. Rptd London, 1927. [The Countess Cathleen, The Land of Heart's Desire, At the Hawk's Well, The Only Jealousy of Emer, The Dreaming of the Bones, Calvary]

72. *Poems* (1895). Revd and rptd London, 1923. [See 5]

73. *The Countess Cathleen and The Land of Heart's Desire.* London, 1924. [See Wade, *op. cit.*, item 95]

74. *Poems* (1895). Revd and rptd London, 1924. [See 5]

75. *The Cat and the Moon and Certain Poems.* Dublin, 1924. (Cuala press)

76. *The Land of Heart's Desire and The Countess Cathleen.* London, 1925. Rptd London, 1929 (2). [See Wade, *op. cit.*, item 95]

77. *The Land of Heart's Desire.* San Francisco, 1926.

78. *Poems* (1895). Revd and rptd London, 1927.

---

[1] The dates of these printings are on the authority of a letter from the publisher, the Walter H. Baker Company of Boston, to the editor on 18 May 1961.

79. *Sophocles' King Oedipus*. London, 1928; New York, 1928.
80. *Poems* (1895). Revd and rptd London, 1929.
81. *Stories of Michael Robartes and his Friends*. Dublin, 1931 (Cuala press) [The Resurrection]
82. *The Words upon the Window Pane*. Dublin, 1934. (Cuala press)
83. *Wheels and Butterflies*. London, 1934; New York, 1935 [The Words upon the Window-pane, Fighting the Waves, The Resurrection, The Cat and the Moon]
84. *The Collected Plays of W. B. Yeats*. London, 1934; New York, 1935. [The Countess Cathleen, The Land of Heart's Desire, Cathleen ni Houlihan, The Pot of Broth, The King's Threshold, Acting version of the Shadowy Waters, Deirdre, At the Hawk's Well, The Green Helmet, On Baile's Strand, The Only Jealousy of Emer, The Hour-Glass (verse), The Unicorn from the Stars, The Player Queen, The Dreaming of the Bones, Calvary, The Cat and the Moon, Sophocles' King Oedipus, Sophocles' Oedipus at Colonus, The Resurrection, The Words upon the Window-Pane]
85. *The King of the Great Clock Tower*. Dublin, 1934. (Cuala press)
86. *The King of the Great Clock Tower*. New York, 1935.
87. *A Full Moon in March*. London, 1935. [A Full Moon in March, The King of the Great Clock Tower (verse)]
88. *The King's Threshold*. London, 1937.
89. *Nine One-Act Plays*. London, 1937. [The Land of Heart's Desire, Cathleen ni Houlihan, The Hour-Glass (prose), The Pot of Broth, On Baile's Strand, Deirdre, The Green Helmet, Acting version of The Shadowy Waters, The Words upon the Window-Pane]
90. *The Herne's Egg*. London, 1938.
91. *The Herne's Egg and Other Plays*. New York, 1938 [The Herne's Egg, A Full Moon in March, The King of the Great Clock Tower (verse)]
92. *Last Poems and Two Plays*. Dublin, 1939. (Cuala press) [The Death of Cuchulain, Purgatory]
93. *On the Boiler*. Dublin, 1939. (Cuala press) [Purgatory]
94. *Last Poems and Plays*. London, 1940; New York, 1940. Rptd New York, 1940. [Purgatory, The Death of Cuchulain]
95. *Mosada*. Dublin, 1943. (Cuala press)
96. *Diarmuid and Grania* by George Moore and W. B. Yeats. Dublin, 1951.
97. *The Collected Plays of W. B. Yeats*. London, 1952; New York, 1953. Rptd London, 1953. [See 84. In addition A Full Moon in March,

The King of the Great Clock Tower, The Herne's Egg, Purgatory, The Death of Cuchulain]

98. *The Variorum Edition of the Poems of W. B. Yeats.* New York, 1957. [The Island of Statues, Mosada, The Seeker, Time and the Witch Vivien]

THE COLLATIONS

THE basic text is **97E**, the English edition of *The Collected Plays* of 1952. Differences between **97** and **84** (*The Collected Plays* of 1934), as well as between **97** and the plays published after Yeats's death in January 1939, must be assessed by the individual reader.

Names of speakers are always italicized.

Directions after names of speakers are italicized and usually placed within square brackets with a period outside the closing bracket.

Lower case is used in stage directions and in definitions of the dramatis personae save in those instances where the use of upper case was judged to have significance.

Unless otherwise indicated the speakers in the textual variants are the same as those in the basic text. In the interest of clarity, however, the names of speakers are sometimes repeated in the variants.

The characters . . . [T] in the variants mean that the suspension points preceding the [T] are in the text(s) in question.

The notes at the end of each play are cross-referenced to each other and to the appendixes. The notes (including the material in the appendixes) are Yeats's explanations and comments on his work. They are collated wherever possible, the basis in each instance being that version of a note having the best framework for an easily understandable collation. A (————) sets off a version of a note so dissimilar to other versions that it would be confusing to collate it. A series of stars (* * *) sets off one complete note from another.

Where the English and American editions of a particular volume are listed under one number in the bibliography (**5, 57,** etc.) and a variant occurs in one only, the reference is **5E, 57E,** if in the English edition, and **5A, 57A,** if in the American edition.

Where a punctuation variant occurs within a line the words before and after the variant are given. If the punctuation variant is terminal, only the last word in the line is given.

Where the wording within a line changes, the words before and after the change are given.

Where the spelling, number, or hyphenation of a word varies, usually only the word itself is given.

If the only change in a line is a variant spelling, the line is, as a rule, not noted in the variants. If the textual variants include a word that has variant spellings, the spelling in the latest variant is used. Most variant spellings are listed in the notes.

THE COUNTESS CATHLEEN

The Countess Cathleen was the most complex of the plays to collate intelligibly, for Yeats changed it more than he did any of the others. In the first version, for instance, it had five scenes, in the next seven versions it had four acts, in the ninth version it became five scenes again—with an entirely new Scene IV—and remained so through the final version. The love scene between the Countess and Aleel at the beginning of Scene III was not inserted until the fourth printing.

To facilitate understanding of the play's growth I have printed the complete first version, the one most radically different from the final version, on the following verso pages. Collations of all other versions are on the recto pages. Similarities between the first and final versions are shown by bracketed line-numbers in the verso margins; identities by unbracketed line-numbers.

Line numbering is consecutive, with no break between scenes or acts.

THE COUNTESS KATHLEEN.

An Irish Drama

*

I Dedicate

this play

to

my friend,

Miss Maud Gonne,

at whose suggestion

it was

planned out and begun

some

three years ago.

*

"*The sorrowful are dumb for thee.*"

The Lament of Morian Shehone for Mary Bourke.

2

THE COUNTESS CATHLEEN

1892

'The sorrowful are dumb for thee'
Lament of Morian Shehone
for Miss Mary Bourke

TO

MAUD GONNE

Persons in the Play

Shemus Rua, *a peasant*   Aleel, *a Poet*
Mary, *his wife*   The Countess Cathleen
Teigue, *his son*   Oona, *her foster-mother*
Two Demons disguised as Merchants
Peasants, Servants, Angelical Beings.

The Scene is laid in Ireland and in old times

PRINTINGS   5, 6, 7, 18, 28, 31, 33, 46, 48, 49, 51, 52, 56a, 61, 62, 63, 66, 67, 71, 72, 73, 74, 76, 78, 80, 84, 97.

DATE   [lacking] 5-51, 61, 62, 66-80; (1892–1912) [*sic*] 52; (1893, revised 1911) [*sic*] 63.

EPIGRAPH   ... Morion ... 5-18, 31-62, 66-80; [lacking] 28, 63.

DEDICATION   To Miss Maud Gonne 5; [lacking] 28.

DRAMATIS PERSONAE   [Heading lacking] 5-31, 46-67, 72-76;
    ... *peasant* / Teig, *his son* / Aleel, *a young bard* / Maureen, *a gardener* / The Countess Cathleen / Oona, *her foster mother* (foster-mother 6, 7, 18, 31, 33) / Maire, *wife of* Shemus Rua / Two ... Merchants / Musicians / Peasants, servants, etc. / Angelical Beings, Spirits, and Faeries 5-18, 31, 33;
    Maire, *wife of* Shemus Rua / Teig, *his son* / Shemus Rua, *a peasant* / Musicians / Aleel, *a young bard* / The Countess ... Merchants / Maureen, *a gardener* / Peasants, Servants, etc. / Angelical Beings, Spirits, and Faeries 28;
    ... *Foster Mother* (foster-mother 48) / ... Beings, Spirits 46-49, 52;
    ... *Foster Mother* / ... 51, 56a-62, 66-80;
    Shemus Rua / Mary / Teig / Aleel / The ... / Oona / Two ... Beings, Spirits 63.

SETTING AND TIME.   ... *Ireland, and* ... 5-33, 48, 63.

Persons.

Shemus Rua, *Keeper of an hostelry known as "The Lady's Head."*

Teig, *His son, aged fourteen.*

Maurteen,[1] *A gardener.*

Michael,[1] *A servant.*

A Herdsman.

Kevin, *A young bard.*

Peasants, &c.

Two demons, disguised throughout as merchants.

The Countess Kathleen.

Oona, *Her foster-mother.*

Mary, *Wife of Shemus Rua.*

Peasant women, &c.

Angelical beings, spirits and fairies.

[1] These names are used only when Kathleen speaks to the 'Gardener' and the 'Servant' (see lines 185, p. 48 and 238, p. 56).

Scene 1

A room with lighted fire, and a door into the open air, through which one sees,
perhaps, the trees of a wood, and these trees should be painted in flat colour upon
a gold or diapered sky. The walls are of one colour. The scene should have the
effect of missal painting. Mary, a woman of forty years or so, is grinding a
quern.

1. *Mary.* What can have made the grey hen flutter so?
   [*Teigue, a boy of fourteen, is coming in with turf, which he lays*
   beside the hearth.

2. *Teigue.* They say that now the land is famine-struck
3.   The graves are walking.

   Mary.   What can the hen have heard?

4. *Teigue.* And that is not the worst; at Tubber-vanach

ACT OR SCENE NUMBER   Act 1 5-33; Scene 1 46-97.

STAGE DIRECTIONS   *The cabin of Shemus Rua. The door is in the centre of the wall*
at the back. The window is at the right side of it, and a little catholic (Catholic 6*)*
shrine hangs at the other. To the right is a pantry door, and to the left a dim fire.
A wood of oak, pine, hazel, and quicken is seen through the window half hidden in
vapour and twilight. Maire watches Teig, who fills a pot with water. He stops as
if to listen, and spills some of the water. 5, 6;
   The cottage of Shemus Rua. The door into the open air is at right side of room.
There is a window at one end of it, and a little Catholic shrine hangs at (one side of
the door, and a little shrine of the Virgin Mother at 28, 33*) the other. At the back*
is a door opening into a bedroom, and at the left side of the room a pantry door. A
wood of oak, pine (oak, beech, 28, 33*) hazel,* [from here, identical with 5, 6]
7-33;
   Scene.—(Scene. 48, 63) *A . . . .* 46-51, 61-74, 78; Scene.—*A . . . air at*
one side, and there may be a window at back through which one sees, the trees . . . .
52; Scene.—*A . . . wood and . . . .* 73, 76, 80.

1. *Maire.* You are all thumbs.
   Teig.   Hear how the dog bays, mother, 5-33.
   Directions after 1. [lacking] 5-33; [. . . *turf which* . . . .] 73, 76, 80.
2. And how the grey hen flutters in the coop. 5-33; . . . famine struck
   (struck, 48, 63) 46-80.
3. Strange things are going up and down the land, 5-33;
   . . . walking. *Mary.* There is something that the hen hears. (hears 73,
   76, 80) 46-80.
4. *Teig.* These famine times: by Tubber-vanach cross-roads 5-33.

The Scene is laid in Ireland in the Sixteenth Century.

SCENE I.

[*The Inn of Shemus Rua; a wood of oak, hazel and quicken
trees is seen through the window, half hidden in vapour
and twilight. The door is in the centre of the wall at
the back. The window is at the right side of it, and a
little catholic shrine hangs at the other. To the right
is a pantry door and to the left a dim fire of bogwood.
Mary watches Teig who fills a pot with water. He stops as
if to listen, and spills some of the water.*]

1. *Mary.* You are all thumbs.

　Teig.　　　　　　　　　　How yon dog bays,
[1]　　2.　And how the grey hen flutters in the coop.
[3]　　3.　Strange things are going up and down the land
[2, 4]　4.　These famine times. By Tubber-vanach cross roads,

5.   A woman met a man with ears spread out,
6.   And they moved up and down like a bat's wing.

7.   *Mary.* What can have kept your father all this while?

8.   *Teigue.* Two nights ago, at Carrick-orus churchyard,
9.   A herdsman met a man who had no mouth,
10.   Nor eyes, nor ears; his face a wall of flesh;
11.   He saw him plainly by the light of the moon.

12.   *Mary.* Look out, and tell me if your father's coming.

        [*Teigue goes to door.*

13.   *Teigue.* Mother!

      Mary.   What is it?

      Teigue.   In the bush beyond,
14.   There are two birds—if you can call them birds—
15.   I could not see them rightly for the leaves—
16.   But they've the shape and colour of horned owls,

---

6.   . . . like wings of bats. **5-33.**
7.   [lacking] **5-33.**
8.   *Maire.* Shemus stays late.
      Teig.   By Carrick-orus . . ., **5-33**; . . . ago at . . ., **48,
      63**; . . . night's . . ., **73, 76-80.**
10.   Nor ears, nor eyes: his . . .; **5-33**; . . . ears! his . . .; **71A, 73, 76-80.**
11.   . . . by the moon.
      Maire [*going over to the little shrine*]. White Virgin, (White Mary, **7-33**)
      5-33.
12.   *Maire.* Bring Shemus safe home from the hateful forest; **5-18, 31**;
      Bring Shemus home out of the wicked woods; **28, 33.**
      Directions after 12. [lacking] **5-33**; [. . . *to the door.*] **48, 63.**
12a. Save Shemus from the wolves; Shemus is reckless; (daring; **28, 33**)
13.   And save him from the demons of the woods,
14.   Who have crept out and pace upon the roads, (and wander on the
      roads, **28, 33**) **5-33.**
15.   Deluding dim-eyed souls now newly dead, **5-33**; . . . leaves. **46-80.**
16.   And those alive who have gone crazed with famine. **5-33**; . . . owls
      46, 49-62, 66-80.

V.E.P.Y.—B

5   5.   A woman met a man with ears spread out,
[6]   6.   And they moved up and down like wings of bats.

[7, 8]   7. *Mary.* Shemus stays late.

       Teig.   By Carrick-orus churchyard,
9   8.   A herdsman met with one who had no mouth,
[10]   9.   Nor ears, nor eyes—his face a wall of flesh.
[11]   10.   He saw him plainly by the moonlight.

      Mary [going over to the little shrine]. Virgin,
    11.   Bring Shemus safe home from the hateful forest;
    12.   Save Shemus from the wolves—Shemus is reckless;
    13.   And save him from the demons of the woods
    14.   Who have crept out and pace upon the roads
    15.   Deluding dim-eyed souls now newly dead,
    16.   And those alive who have gone crazed with famine.

17.   And I'm half certain they've a human face.

18. *Mary.* Mother of God, defend us!

    Teigue.   They're looking at me.

19.   What is the good of praying? father says.

20.   God and the Mother of God have dropped asleep.

21.   What do they care, he says, though the whole land

22.   Squeal like a rabbit under a weasel's tooth?

23. *Mary.* You'll bring misfortune with your blasphemies

24.   Upon your father, or yourself, or me.

25.   Would God that he were home—ah, there he is.

                                           [Shemus comes in.

26.   What was it kept you in the wood? You know

27.   I cannot get all sorts of accidents

28.   Out of my mind till you are home again.

29. *Shemus.* I'm in no mood to listen to your clatter.

30.   Although I tramped the woods for half a day,

31.   I've taken nothing, for the very rats,

32.   Badgers, and hedgehogs seem to have died of drought,

---

17.   Save him, White Virgin. (White Mary Virgin. **7-33**)
    Teig.   And but now

17a.   I thought I heard far-off tympans and harps.
                                    [Knocking at the door.] **5-33.**

18-24.   [lacking] **5-33.**

25.   *Maire.* Shemus has come.
    Teig.   May he bring better food **5-33**; I would to
God he . . . . **46-67, 72, 74.**

25a.   Than the lean crow he brought us yesterday. **5-33.**
    [Maire opens the door, and Shemus comes in with a dead wolf on his shoulder.] **5-33.**

26.   *Maire.* Shemus, you are late home: you have been lounging

26a.   And chattering with some one: you know well

27.   How the dreams trouble me, and how I pray,

28.   Yet you lie sweating on the hill from morn,

28a.   Or linger at the crossways with all comers, **5-33.**

28b.   Gilding your tongue with the calamitous times. **5-18, 31**; Telling
or gathering up calamity. **28, 33.**

29.   You'll (You would **7-33**) rail my head off. Here is a good dinner.
                                  [He throws the wolf on the table].

30.   A wolf is better than a carrion crow.

31.   I searched all day: the mice and rats and hedgehogs (hedge-hogs **28**)
5-33.

32.   Seemed to be dead, and I could hardly hear **5-33**; . . . hedgehogs,
seem . . ., **48-63.**

17.   Save him, dear Mary.
        [*A knock at the door. She kneels and looks through the
        keyhole.*]
                                        Who is knocking?

Shemus [*without*].   Shemus.

[34]   18. *Teig.* May he bring better food than yesterday;
        19.   No one dines merrily on a carrion crow.
                *Mary opens the door, and Shemus comes in with a dead wolf
                on his shoulder.*]

[26-28] 20. *Mary.* You are late home. You have been lounging
[26-28] 21.   And chattering with some one, idling somehow.
[26-28] 22.   You know dreams trouble me, and how I pray,
[26-28] 23.   Yet all day you lie sweating on the hill side,
[26-28] 24.   Or stand else in the gutter with all passers,
[26-28] 25.   Gilding your tongue with the calamitous times.

33.   And there was scarce a wind in the parched leaves.

34.   *Teigue.* Then you have brought no dinner.

    Shemus.   After that
35.   I sat among the beggars at the cross-roads,
36.   And held a hollow hand among the others.

37.   *Mary.* What, did you beg?

    Shemus.   I had no chance to beg,
38.   For when the beggars saw me they cried out
39.   They would not have another share their alms,
40.   And hunted me away with sticks and stones.

41.   *Teigue.* You said that you would bring us food or money.

42.   *Shemus.* What's in the house?

    Teigue.   A bit of mouldy bread.

43.   *Mary.* There's flour enough to make another loaf.

44.   *Teigue.* And when that's gone?

    Mary.   There is the hen in the coop.

---

  33.   A wing moving in all the famished woods, **5-33.**
33a.   Though the dead leaves and clauber of four forests
33b.   Cling to my footsole. I turned home but now,
33c.   And saw, sniffing the floor in a bare cow-house,
33d.   This young wolf here: the cross-bow brought him down.
33e.   *Maire.* Praised (Praise **7-33**) be the saints!
                                    [After a pause.]
                                Why did the house dog bay?
33f.   *Shemus.* He heard me coming and smelt food—what else? **5-33.**
34-41.   [lacking] **5-33.**
  37.   ['What,' lacking] **67.**
  41.   . . . money **56a-62, 66.**
  42.   *Teig.* We will not starve awhile.
    Shemus.   What food's (food is **7-33**) within? **5-33;**
  ['What's . . . house?' lacking] **67.**
  43.   *Teig.* There is a bag half full of meal, a pan **5-33.**
  44.   Half full of milk.
    Shemus.   And we have Maive the hen. (have one old hen. **28,
33**) **5-33;** . . . coop **56a-62, 66, 67, 72, 74, 78.**

[29]   26. *Shemus*. You'd rail my head off. There's good dinner here.
         [*Throwing the wolf on to the floor.*]

         27.   A lean wolf's more than a lean carrion crow.
[31-32] 28.   I searched all day: the mice, and rats, and hedgehogs
[32]   29.   Seem to be dead, and I could hardly hear
[33]   30.   A wing moving in all the famished woods,
[30]   31.   Though the dead leaves and clauber of four forests
[30]   32.   Cling to my foot-sole. I came home despairing,
         33.   And found sniffing the floor in a bare cow-house
         34.   This young wolf here. The cross-bow brought him down.

         35. *Mary*. Praised be the saints.

                                         [*After a pause.*]
                 Why did the house dog bay?

         36. *Shemus*. He heard me coming and smelt food—what else.

45. *Shemus.* My curse upon the beggars, my curse upon them!

46. *Teigue.* And the last penny gone.

Shemus.   When the hen's gone,
47. What can we do but live on sorrel and dock,
48. And dandelion, till our mouths are green?

49. *Mary.* God, that to this hour has found bit and sup,
50. Will cater for us still.

Shemus.   His kitchen's bare.
51. There were five doors that I looked through this day
52. And saw the dead and not a soul to wake them.

53. *Mary.* Maybe He'd have us die because He knows,
54. When the ear is stopped and when the eye is stopped,
55. That every wicked sight is hid from the eye,
56. And all fool talk from the ear!

            [*A stringed instrument without.*

Shemus.   Who's passing there?
57. And mocking us with music?

Teigue.   A young man plays it.

44a. *Teig.* The pinewood (bogwood **28, 33**) were less hard.
    Maire.   Before you came
44b. She made a great noise in the hencoop, Shemus.
44c. What fluttered in the window?
    Teig.   Two horned owls
44d. Have blinked and fluttered on the window sill
44e. From when the dog began to bay.
    Shemus.   Hush, hush, **5-33.**
    [*He fits an arrow to the crossbow, and goes towards the door. A sudden burst of music without.*] **5-33.**
45-57. [lacking] **5-33.**
  45. . . . them. **48, 63.**
  49. . . . hour's found . . ., **46-67, 72-80.**
  51. . . . day. **48, 63.**
  52. . . . them **73, 76-80.**
  56. . . . ear.
       Who's . . .?
    Directions in 56. [lacking] **46-80.**
  57. . . . music?
            [*A stringed instrument without.*]
    A . . . it, **46-80.**

[42] 37. What food's within?

    Mary.   A pan half full of milk,
[43] 38. Some oatmeal in a corner of the bag.

[44] 39. *Shemus.* And we have Madge, the hen.

    Teig.   Bog-wood were softer;
  40. She has grown sleepy with old age.

    Mary.   Before you came,
  41. She made a great noise in the hencoop, Shemus.

  42. *Shemus.* The dog scared her. Well we'll not starve at once.
    [*Hangs his crossbow up, and then catching sight of the shrine
    pauses.*]

  43. Red briony berries in a little jar,
  44. And ivy green as a drake's poll—no use.
  45. Why, dame, we'll all be dead soon; [*Pointing to the shrine*]
    she's asleep.

58.   There's an old woman and a lady with him.

59. *Shemus.* What is the trouble of the poor to her?
60.   Nothing at all or a harsh radishy sauce
61.   For the day's meat.

   Mary.   God's pity on the rich!
62.   Had we been through as many doors, and seen
63.   The dishes standing on the polished wood
64.   In the wax candle light, we'd be as hard,
65.   And there's the needle's eye at the end of all.

66. *Shemus.* My curse upon the rich!

   Teigue.   They're coming here.

67. *Shemus.* Then down upon that stool, down quick, I say,
68.   And call up a whey face and a whining voice,
69.   And let your head be bowed upon your knees.

---

58.   *Shemus.* They are off again: some lady or gentleman (again: ladies or
     gentlemen **28, 33**)
58a. Roves (Travel **28, 33**) in the woods with tympan and with harp.
58b. Teig, put the wolf upon the upper shelf (upon the biggest hook **28,
     33**) **5-33.**
59-66. [lacking] **5-33.**
 61. . . . rich. **46-80.**
 65. . . . all **72, 74.**
 66. . . . rich.
         They're . . . . **46-80.**
 67. And shut the door.
     [*Teig goes into the cupboard with the wolf: returns and fastens the door
     behind him.*]
         Sit on the creepy stool
 68. . . . a crying voice, **5-33.**
     Directions after 69.   [*He opens the door of the cabin.*] **5-33.**
69a. *Shemus.* Come in, kind gentles,—(gentles: **6-18, 31**) a full score of
     evenings **5-18, 31** ; Come in, your honours; a full score of evenings **28,
     33.**
69b. This threshold worn away by many a foot
69c. Has been passed only by the snails and birds
69d. And by our own poor hunger-shaken feet. **5-33.**
     [*The Countess Cathleen, Aleel (who carries a small square harp), Oona,
     and a little group of fantastically dressed musicians come in.*] **5, 6 ;** [*The*

[51]   46.   I passed by Margaret Nolan's: for nine days
[47]   47.   Her mouth was green from eating dock and nettles.
      48.   Now they have waked her.

         Mary.   I shall go the next.
      49.   Our parents' cabins bordered the same field.

[20]   50. *Shemus.* God and God's mother nod and sleep—at last
[19]   51.   They have grown weary of the prayers and candles,
[420] 52.   And Satan pours the famine from his bag,
[170] 53.   He does not nod, nor sleep, nor droop his eyelids;
      54.   I am half mindful to go pray to him
      55.   To cover all this table with red gold.
      56.   Teig, will you dare me to it?

         Teig.   Not I, father.

70. *Mary.* Had I but time to put the place to rights!

Cathleen, Oona, and Aleel enter

71. *Cathleen.* God save all here. There is a certain house,
72. An old grey castle with a kitchen garden,
73. A cider orchard and a plot for flowers,
74. Somewhere among these woods.

Mary.   We know it, lady.
75. A place that's set among impassable walls
76. As though world's trouble could not find it out.

77. *Cathleen.* It may be that we are that trouble, for we—
78. Although we've wandered in the wood this hour—
79. Have lost it too, yet I should know my way,
80. For I lived all my childhood in that house.

81. *Mary.* Then you are Countess Cathleen?

Cathleen.   And this woman,
82. Oona, my nurse, should have remembered it,
83. For we were happy for a long time there.

84. *Oona.* The paths are overgrown with thickets now,
85. Or else some change has come upon my sight.

86. *Cathleen.* And this young man, that should have known
        the woods—
87. Because we met him on their border but now,
88. Wandering and singing like a wave of the sea—
89. Is so wrapped up in dreams of terrors to come

Countess Cathleen, Aleel, who carries a small square harp, Oona, and a
little group of fantastically dressed musicians come in.] **7-33.**
70-105. [lacking] **5-33.**
70. . . . rights. **46-80.**
Directions after 70. [. . ., *Oona and* . . . .] **48, 63.**
72. . . . kitchen-garden, **52.**
73. . . . and plot . . ., **97A.**
74. . . ., Lady. **48, 63 ;** . . . woods
        We . . . . **73, 76, 80.**
84. . . . thicktes . . ., **51, 56a-62, 66, 67, 72, 74.**

[23]   57. *Mary.* O Shemus hush, maybe your mind might pray
          58.   Though your mouth prayed not. Think upon your soul.
[16, 134] 59.   What made that noise?

          Teig.   Two horned owls made it;
          60.   They have been blinking on the window-sill
          61.   Since father came. I had gone softly over
          62.   To lift the crossbow down and shoot at them,
          63.   When father's loud voice made them flutter off.
                  [*Shemus begins unfastening the feet of the wolf from a branch
                  to which they had been tied.*]

          64. *Mary.* That's quicken wood.

          Shemus.   Yes, wife. He swayed about
          65.   And so I tied him to a quicken branch,
          66.   And slung him from my shoulder.
                  [*He takes up the branch to throw it on the fire.*]

          Mary [*Taking it from him*].   Shemus! Shemus!

90.   That he can give no help.

Mary.   You have still some way,
91.   But I can put you on the trodden path
92.   Your servants take when they are marketing.
93.   But first sit down and rest yourself awhile,
94.   For my old fathers served your fathers, lady,
95.   Longer than books can tell—and it were strange
96.   If you and yours should not be welcome here.

97. *Cathleen.* And it were stranger still were I ungrateful
98.   For such kind welcome—but I must be gone,
99.   For the night's gathering in.

Shemus.   It is a long while
100.   Since I've set eyes on bread or on what buys it.

101. *Cathleen.* So you are starving even in this wood,
102.   Where I had thought I would find nothing changed.
103.   But that's a dream, for the old worm o' the world
104.   Can eat its way into what place it pleases.

                                    [*She gives money.*

105. *Teigue.* Beautiful lady, give me something too;
106.   I fell but now, being weak with hunger and thirst,
107.   And lay upon the threshold like a log.

108. *Cathleen.* I gave for all and that was all I had.
109.   But look, my purse is empty. I have passed
110.   By starving men and women all this day,
111.   And they have had the rest; but take the purse,
112.   The silver clasps on't may be worth a trifle.

---

94.   . . ., Lady, **48, 63.**
101.   . . . wood. **71A.**
102.   . . . changed **73, 76, 80**; . . . changed; **78.**
106.   *Cathleen.* Are you so hungry?
       Teig [*from beside the fire*]. Lady, I fell but now, (now **18-31**) **5-33**; . . .
       thirst. **56a-62, 66-80.**
107a. I have not tasted a crust for these four days.
       [*The Countess Cathleen empties her purse on to the table.*]
108.   Had I more money I would give it you, **5-33.**
109.   But we have passed by many cabins to-day, (to-day; **7-33**) **5-33**;
       Look, . . . **46-80.**
110-112. [lacking] **5-33.**
110.   But starving . . ., **97A.**

	67.	What, would you burn the blessed quicken wood?
	68.	A spell to ward off demons and ill fairies.
[134]	69.	You know not what the owls were that peered in,
[132]	70.	For evil wonders live in this old wood,
[132]	71.	And they can show in what shape please them best.
	72.	And we have had no milk to leave o' nights
	73.	To keep our own good people kind to us.
	74.	I fear the wood things, Shemus.

Shemus.   Famine fear

[173-184]	75.	Addles your mind. I'll chew the lean dog-wolf
[173-184]	76.	With no less mirth if, chaired beside the hearth,
[173-184]	77.	Rubbing its hands before the bogwood flame,
[173-184]	78.	Be Pooka, Sowlth, or demon of the pit.

[*A step outside.*]

[165]   79. *Mary* [*listening*]. Who knows what evil you have brought
          to us.

113.   And if you'll come to-morrow to my house
114.   You shall have twice the sum.

            [Aleel begins to play.

Shemus [*muttering*].   What, music, music!

115.   *Cathleen.* Ah, do not blame the finger on the string;
116.   The doctors bid me fly the unlucky times
117.   And find distraction for my thoughts, or else
118.   Pine to my grave.

Shemus.   I have said nothing, lady.

---

 113. And if you come . . . **5-33**; But if . . . **46-67, 72, 74.**
 114. . . . sum. I am the owner **5-33.**
114a. Of a long empty castle in these woods.
114b. *Maire.* Then you are Countess Cathleen: you and yours
114c. Are ever welcome under my poor roof. (poor thatch. **28, 33**)
114d. Will you sit down and warm you by the fire? (by the sods? **28, 33**)
114e. *Countess Cathleen.* (*Cathleen,* **28, 33**) We must find out this castle in
   the wood
114f. Before the chill o' the night.
       [*The musicians begin to tune their instruments.*]
       Do not blame me, (me **6**)
 115. Good woman, for the tympan and the harp:
 116. I was bid fly the terror of the times
 117. And wrap me round with music and sweet song
 118. Or else pine . . . grave. I have lost my way; **5-33.**
118a. And the bard Aleel, who should know these woods, **5, 6**;
   Aleel, the poet, who should know these woods, **7-33.**
118b. Because we met him on their border but now
118c. Wandering and singing like the foam of the sea,
118d. Is so wrapped up in dreams of terrors to come
118e. That he can give no help.
   Maire [*going to the door with her*].
       Beyond the hazel (You're almost there. **28, 33**) **5-33.**
118f. Is a green shadowed pathway, and it goes **5-18, 31**;
   There is a trodden way among the hazels **28, 33.**
118g. To your great castle in malevolent woods. **5-18, 31**;
   That brings your servants to their marketing. **28, 33.**
118h. *Aleel.* Shut to the door and shut the woods away, **5, 6**; When we are
   gone draw to the door and the bolt, **7-33.**
118i. For, till we lost them half-an-hour (half an hour **6-33**) ago,
118j. Two gray horned owls hooted above our heads
118k. Of terrors to come. Tympan and harp awake!
118l. For though the world drift from us like a sigh, **5-33.**

[165]   80.   I fear the wood things, Shemus.

> [*She hides the wolf in the pantry. A knock at the door. The shrine falls from the wall.*]

                                 Do not open.

> [*She points to the fallen shrine.*]

     81.   See! see!

Shemus.   I told you that the nail was loose.

> [*He opens the door. Two merchants stand without. They have bands of gold round their foreheads, and each carries a bag upon his shoulder.*]

     82.   *First Merchant.* This is an inn?

Shemus.   Aye, aye, "The Lady's Head,"

     83.   Called from the Countess Kathleen—her face, sir,

     84.   Is painted in four colours on the sign.

[194]   85.   *Second Merchant.* And have you food for two tired merchants, here?

119.   Why should the like of us complain?

Oona.   Have done.
120.   Sorrows that she's but read of in a book
121.   Weigh on her mind as if they had been her own.

[*Oona, Mary, and Cathleen go out. Aleel looks defiantly at Shemus.*]

122.   *Aleel* [*singing*]. Were I but crazy for love's sake
123.   I know who'd measure out his length,
124.   I know the heads that I should break,
125.   For crazy men have double strength.
126.   I know—all's out to leave or take,
127.   Who mocks at music mocks at love;
128.   Were I but crazy for love's sake,
129.   No need to pick and choose.

[*Snapping his fingers in Shemus' face.*]
                              Enough!

118m.   Music is master of all under the moon;
118n.   And play 'The Wind that blows by Cummen Strand.'
                                        [*Music.*] **5-33.**
  119.   Directions after 121. [lacking] **5-33.**
122-127.   [italicized] **5-33.**
  122.   *Aleel* [*Sings (Singing* **46-49**)] Impetuous heart, be still, be still;[1] (still:
          28, 33; still, **46-49**) **5-49**; . . . love . . . **71E.**
  123.   Your sorrowful love may (can **46-49**) never be told; **5-49.**
  124.   Cover it up with a lonely tune. **5-49**; . . . head . . . break **52.**
  125.   He who (that **46-49**) could bend all things to His will **5-49.**
  126.   Has covered the door of the infinite fold **5-49**; There! all's out now
          to . . ., **51-80.**
  127.   With the pale stars and the wandering moon. **5-49**; And who mocks
          music . . . love; (love. **52**) **51-80.**
          Directions after 127. [*While he is singing, he, Countess (singing the
          Countess* **7-33**) *Cathleen, Oona, and the musicians go out.*] **5-33**; [*He takes
          a step towards the door and then turns again.*] **46-49.**
128-145.   [lacking] **5, 6.**
  128.   Directions after 130. [lacking] **7-49.**
  128.   And when I'm (I am **52**) crazy . . . sake
  129.   I'll not go far to choose.
                              [*Snapping . . . .*]
                              Enough! (Enough **63**) **51-80.**

[1] Variant lines 122-127, **5-49**, reprinted in *Beltaine,* May 1899, and they are used below,
ll. 672-677.

[181]   86. *Shemus.* Sir, such rude victuals as the forest gives.
       87. Come in, kind sirs—for a full score of evenings
       88. This threshold, worn away by many feet,
       89. Has been passed only by the snails, and birds,
       90. And our own footfalls.

       Mary.   Sirs, do not come in,
       91. We have no food, none even for ourselves.

       92. *First Merchant.* A wolf lies on the third shelf in the cup-
           board.

                    [They enter.]

[213]   93. *Shemus.* Forgive her, gentles. She's not used to quality,
[215-217] 94. And is half mad with being much alone.
       95. How did you know I'd taken a young wolf?

130.   I know the heads that I should break.
            [*He takes a step towards the door and then turns again.*

131.   Shut to the door before the night has fallen,
132.   For who can say what walks, or in what shape
133.   Some devilish creature flies in the air; but now
134.   Two grey horned owls hooted above our heads.
            [*He goes out, his singing dies away. Mary comes in. Shemus has been counting the money.*

135.   *Shemus.* So that fool's gone.

        Teigue.   He's seen the horned owls too.
136.   There's no good luck in owls, but it may be
137.   That the ill luck's to fall upon his head.

138.   *Mary.* You never thanked her ladyship.

        Shemus.   Thank her
139.   For seven halfpence and a silver bit?

140.   *Teigue.* But for this empty purse?

        Shemus.   What's that for thanks,
141.   Or what's the double of it that she promised,
142.   With bread and flesh and every sort of food
143.   Up to a price no man has heard the like of
144.   And rising every day?

        Mary.   We have all she had;

---

130.   . . . heads (head **52**) . . . I shall break. **51-67, 72, 74.**
131.   *Aleel.* . . . door and shut the woods away, **7-33.**
132.   [lacking] **7-33**; . . . shape. **71A.**
133.   For, till they had vanished in the thick of the leaves, **7-33**;
        . . . air, but . . . **46-51, 56a-67, 72-80.**
134.   . . . grey-horned . . . . **46-80.**
        Directions after 134. [. . . *out.*] **7-33.**
135-145. [lacking] **7-33.**
135.   [lacking] **46-49, 63**; . . . too **52.**
137.   . . . upon their heads. **46-49, 63.**
138.   . . . her, **46-80.**
140.   . . . thanks **72-80.**
141.   . . . promised? **46-80.**
142.   . . . food,
143.   . . . of, **48, 63.**
144.   . . . day.
        We . . .; **46-80.**

96.   Fine wholesome food though somewhat strong i' the flavour.

[*The Second Merchant sits down by the fire and begins rubbing his hands. The First stands looking at the quicken bough on the chair.*]

[194] 97. *First Merchant.* I would rest here. The night is somewhat chilly,

[193] 98.   And my feet footsore going up and down

[193] 99.   From land to land and nation unto nation.

100.   The fire burns dimly; feed it with this bough.

[*Shemus throws the bough into the fire. The First Merchant sits down in the chair. The Merchants' chairs are on each side of the fire. The table is between them. Each lays his bag before him on the table. The night has closed in somewhat, and the main light comes from the fire.*]

145. She emptied out the purse before our eyes.

146. *Shemus* [*to Mary, who has gone to close the door*]. Leave that door
open.

    Mary.   When those that have read books,
147. And seen the seven wonders of the world,
148. Fear what's above or what's below the ground,
149. It's time that poverty should bolt the door.

150. *Shemus.* I'll have no bolts, for there is not a thing
151. That walks above the ground or under it
152. I had not rather welcome to this house
153. Than any more of mankind, rich or poor.

154. *Teigue.* So that they brought us money.

    Shemus.   I heard say
155. There's something that appears like a white bird,
156. A pigeon or a seagull or the like,
157. But if you hit it with a stone or a stick
158. It clangs as though it had been made of brass,
159. And that if you dig down where it was scratching
160. You'll find a crock of gold.

    Teigue.   But dream of gold
161. For three nights running, and there's always gold.

162. *Shemus.* You might be starved before you've dug it out.

163. *Teigue.* But maybe if you called, something would come.

---

146. *Maire* [*bolting the door*]. When wealthy and wise folk wander from
their peace
147. [lacking] **5-33.**
148. And fear wood things, poor folk may draw the bolt
149. And pray before the fire.
    [*Shemus counts out the money, and rings a piece upon the table.*]
    Shemus.   The Mother of God,
149a. Hushed by the waving of the immortal wings, **5-33.**
150-169. [lacking] **5-33.**
  158. . . . brass; **46-56a, 63.**
  163. . . . come, **46-80.**

101.   *Mary.* What have you in the bags?

Shemus.   Gentles, forgive.
102.   Women grow curious and feather-thoughted
103.   Through being in each others company
104.   More than is good for them.

First Merchant.   Our bags are full
[208] 105.   Of golden pieces to buy merchandize.
       [*They empty the bags on the table. It is covered with the gold
       pieces. They shine in the firelight. Mary goes to the door of
       the pantry, and watches the Merchants, muttering to herself.*]

106. *Teig.* These be great gentlemen.

First Merchant [*drawing a stone bottle from the depth of his bag*].
                  Come round the bogwood,
107.   And here is wine more fragrant than all roses.

164.   They have been seen of late.

Mary.   Is it call devils?
165.   Call devils from the wood, call them in here?

166. *Shemus.* So you'd stand up against me, and you'd say
167.   Who or what I am to welcome here.   [*He hits her.*
168.   That is to show who's master.

Teigue.   Call them in.

169. *Mary.* God help us all!

Shemus.   Pray, if you have a mind to.
170.   It's little that the sleepy ears above

---

170.   Has dropped in a doze and cannot hear the poor: **5-33.**
170a. I passed by Margaret Nolan's; for nine days
170b. Her mouth was green with dock and dandelion—(dandelion; **6-33**)
170c. And now they wake her.
       Maire.   I will go the next;
170d. Our parents' cabins bordered the same field.
170e. *Shemus.* God, and the Mother of God, have dropped asleep,
170f. For they are weary of the prayers and candles;
170g. But Satan pours the famine from his bag,
170h. And I am mindful to go pray to him
170i. To cover all this table with red gold.
170j. Teig, (Teig **6**) will you dare me to it?
       Teig.   Not I, father. (father **6, 7**)
170k. *Maire.* O Shemus, hush, (hush **6**) maybe your mind might pray
170l. In spite o' the mouth.
       Shemus.   Two crowns and twenty pennies. **5-33.**
170m. *Maire.* Is yonder quicken wood?
       Shemus [*picking the bough from the table*]. He swayed about,
170n. And so I tied him to a quicken bough **5-33.**
170o. And slung him from my shoulder.
       Maire [*taking the bough from him*]. Shemus! (Shemus **28**) Shemus!
170p. What, would you burn the blessed quicken wood?
170q. A spell to ward off demons and ill faeries.
170r. You know not what the owls were that peered (peeped **28, 33**) in,
170s. For evil wonders live in this old wood,
170t. And they can show in what shape please them best.
170u. And we have had no milk to leave o' (of **7-33**) nights
170v. To keep our own good people kind to us.
170w. And Aleel, who has talked with the great Sidhe, **5-33.**

108. *Second Merchant.* Wine that can hush asleep the petty war
109.   Of good and evil, and awake instead
110.   A scented flame flickering above that peace
111.   The bird of prey knows well in his deep heart.

112. *Shemus* [*bringing drinking cups*]. I do not understand you, but your
         wine
113.   Sets me athirst—its praise made your eyes lighten.
114.   May I, too, taste it?

     First Merchant.   Aye, come drink and drink,
115.   I bless all mortals who drink long and deep.
116.   My curse upon the salt-strewn road of monks.
     [*Teig and Shemus sit down at the table and drink.*]

117. *Teig.* You must have seen rare sights and done rare things.

171. Care for your words; but I'll call what I please.

172. *Teigue.* There is many a one, they say, had money from them.

173. *Shemus* [*at door*]. Whatever you are that walk the woods at night,
174. So be it that you have not shouldered up
175. Out of a grave—for I'll have nothing human—
176. And have free hands, a friendly trick of speech,
177. I welcome you. Come, sit beside the fire.
178. What matter if your head's below your arms
179. Or you've a horse's tail to whip your flank,
180. Feathers instead of hair, that's all but nothing.
181. Come, share what bread and meat is in the house,
182. And stretch your heels and warm them in the ashes.

170x. Is full of terrors to come.
        [*She lays the bough on a chair.*]
    Shemus.   I would eat my supper **5-33.**

171-176. [lacking] **5-33.**
  172. . . . them **52.**
  177. With no less mirth if chaired beside (if squatting by **28, 33**) the hearth **5-33.**
  178. Were pooka, sowlth, or demon of the pit **5-18, 31**; Were dulacaun, (dulacaun **33**) or demon of the pit **28, 33**; . . . arms, **48, 63.**
179-181. [lacking] **5-33.**
  180. . . . hair, that's but a straw, (straw. **48**; straw; **63**) **46-67, 72, 74**; . . . nothing, **71, 73, 76-80.**
  182. Rubbing its hands before the flame o' (of **7, 18, 31**) the pine. **5-18, 31**; Clawing its knees, its hoof among the . . . . **28, 33.**
    [*He rings another piece of money. A sound of footsteps outside the door.*] **5-33.**
182a. *Maire.* Who knows what evil you have brought to us?
182b. I fear the wood things, Shemus.
        [*A knock at the door.*]
        Do not open.
182c. *Shemus.* A crown and twenty pennies are not enough
182d. To stop the hole that lets the famine in.
        [*The little shrine falls.*] **5-33.**
182e. *Maire.* Look! look!
    Shemus [*kicking it to pieces*]. The Mother of God has dropped asleep, **5, 6**;
    Maire. Look! look!
    Shemus [*crushing it underfoot (under foot **28**)*]. The Mother of God has dropped asleep, **7-33.**
182f. And all her household things have gone to wrack. **5-33.**

[202]   118. *First Merchant.* What think you of the master whom we
serve?

119. *Shemus.* I have grown weary of all life, merchants,
120. Because I do not serve him.

         First Merchant.   More of this
[209-210]   121.   When we have eaten.

         Shemus.   Boil that dog-wolf, Mary.

122. *Mary [coming towards the fire].* The water will not boil
for you.

            [The First Merchant whispers to the water.]

         First Merchant.   It boils.

[212]   123. *Mary.* I will not cook for you.

         Shemus.   Mary's gone mad.

            [Teig and Shemus stand up and stagger about.]

124. *Shemus.* That wine's the suddenest wine man ever
tasted.

183.   And after that, let's share and share alike
184.   And curse all men and women. Come in, come in.
185.   What, is there no one there?   [*Turning from door.*
                                           And yet they say
186.   They are as common as the grass, and ride
187.   Even upon the book in the priest's hand.

[*Teigue lifts one arm slowly and points towards the door and begins
moving backward. Shemus turns, he also sees something and begins
moving backward. Mary does the same. A man dressed as an
Eastern merchant comes in carrying a small carpet. He unrolls it and
sits cross-legged at one end of it. Another man dressed in the same
way follows, and sits at the other end. This is done slowly and
deliberately. When they are seated they take money out of embroidered
purses at their girdles and begin arranging it on the carpet.*]

188. *Teigue.* You speak to them.

Shemus.   No, you.

Teigue.   'Twas you that called them.

189. *Shemus* [*coming nearer*]. I'd make so bold, if you would pardon it,
190.   To ask if there's a thing you'd have of us.
191.   Although we are but poor people, if there is,
192.   Why, if there is——

First Merchant.   We've travelled a long road,
193.   For we are merchants that must tramp the world,

182g. *Maire.* O Mary, Mother of God, be pitiful!
       [*Shemus opens the door. Two merchants stand without. They have bands
       of gold round their foreheads, and each carries a bag upon his shoulder.*]
       5-33.
182h. *First Merchant.* Have you food here?
       Shemus.   For those who can pay well. **5-33.**
183-192. [lacking] **5-33.**
       Directions after 187.   [. . . *toward* . . . *backwards. Shemus* . . . .] **46, 49,
       51, 56a-62, 66, 67, 71E, 72, 74**; [. . . *backwards. Shemus* . . . *in, carry-
       ing* . . . .] **48, 63**; [. . . *toward* . . . .] **52, 71A, 73, 76-80.**
  188. ['You speak to them.' lacking] **66.**
  193. *Second Merchant.* We are rich merchants seeking merchandise. **5-33.**

[218] 125. *Mary.* I will not cook for you. You are not human.

[219] 126.   Before you came two horned owls peered at us;

    127.   The dog bayed, and the tongue of Shemus maddened.

    128.   When you came in the Virgin's blessed shrine

    129.   Fell from its nail, and when you sat down here

    130.   You poured out wine as the wood sheogues do

    131.   When they'd entice a soul out of the world.

    132.   Why did you come to us? Was not death near?

[229] 133. *First Merchant.* We are two merchants.

    Mary.   If you be not demons

[231] 134.   Go and give alms among the starving poor,

[230] 135.   You seem more rich than any under the moon.

[232] 136. *First Merchant.* If we knew where to find deserving poor,

[233] 137.   We would give alms.

    Mary.   Then ask of Father John.

194.   And now we look for supper and a fire

195.   And a safe corner to count money in.

196. *Shemus.* I thought you were . . . but that's no matter now—

197.   There had been words between my wife and me

198.   Because I said I would be master here,

193a.   *Shemus.* Gentles, (Gentle **7**) come (comes **6, 7**) in.
        Maire.   Gentles, do not come in; (in: **6-18**) **5-18, 31** ;
        Shemus. Come in, your honours.
        Maire.   No, do not come in: **28, 33.**

193b.   We have no food, not even for ourselves.

193c.   *First Merchant.* There is a wolf on the third shelf (on the big hook **28, 33**) in the cupboard.
                        [*They enter.*] **5-33.**

193d.   Gentles, forgive: she is not used to quality, **5** ; Forgive her: she is not used to quality, **6-33.**

193e.   And is half mad (crazed **28, 33**) with being much alone.

193f.   How did you know I had taken a young wolf? **5-33.**

193g.   Fine wholesome food, though somewhat strong i' (in **7, 18, 31**) the flavour. **5-18, 31** ; Fine wholesome food, though maybe somewhat strong. **28, 33.**
        [*The Second Merchant sits down by the fire and begins rubbing his hands. The First Merchant stands looking at the quicken bough on the chair.*] **5-33.**

193h.   *First Merchant.* I would rest here: the night is somewhat chilly,

193i.   And my feet footsore going up and down

193j.   From land to land and nation unto nation:

193k.   The fire burns dimly; feed it with this bough. **5-33.**
        [*Shemus throws the bough into the fire. The First Merchant sits down on the chair. The Merchants' chairs are on each side of the fire. The table is between them. Each lays his bag before him on the table. The night has closed in somewhat, and the main light comes from the fire.*] **5-33.**

193l.   *Maire.* What have you in the bags?
        Shemus.   Gentles, forgive. (forgive, **6-18, 31**) **5-18, 31** ;
        Maire. What have you in the bags?
        Shemus.   Don't mind her, sir, (sir: **33**) **28, 33.**

193m.   *Shemus.* Women grow curious and feather-thoughted

193n.   Through being in each other's company

193o.   More than is good for them.
        First merchant.   Our bags are full

193p.   Of golden pieces to buy merchandise.
        [*They pour gold pieces on to the table out of their bags. It is covered with the gold pieces. They shine in the firelight. Maire goes to the door of the pantry, and watches the Merchants, muttering to herself.*] **5-33.**

[234]   138. *First Merchant.* We know the evils of mere charity,
[232]   139.   And would devise a more considered way.
[240]   140.   Let each man bring one piece of merchandize.

[242]   141. *Mary.* The starving have no piece of merchandize.

[243]   142. *First Merchant.* We do but ask what each man has.

           Mary.   Merchants,
[244]   143.   Their swine and cattle, fields and implements,
245   144.   Are sold and gone.

           First Merchant.   They have not sold all yet.

[246-248]   145. *Mary.* What have they?

           First Merchant.   They have still their souls.
           [*Mary shrieks. He beckons to Teig and Shemus.*]
           Come hither.
[263-266]   146.   See you these little golden heaps? Each one
[263-266]   147.   Is payment for a soul. From charity
[263-266]   148.   We give so great a price for those poor flames.

199. And ask in what I pleased or who I pleased,
200. And so . . . but that is nothing to the point,
201. Because it's certain that you are but merchants.

202. *First Merchant.* We travel for the Master of all merchants.

203. *Shemus.* Yet if you were that I had thought but now
204. I'd welcome you no less. Be what you please
205. And you'll have supper at the market rate.
206. That means that what was sold for but a penny

193q. *Teig.* These be great gentles. (These are great gentlemen. **28, 33**)
First Merchant [*taking a stone bottle out of his bag*].
Come about (to **28, 33**) the fire, **5-33.**

193r. And here is wine more fragrant than all roses. (all the roses. **7, 18,
31**) **5-18, 31**; Here is the headiest wine you ever tasted. **28, 33.**

193s. *Second Merchant.* Wine that can hush asleep the petty war
193t. Of good and evil, and awake instead
193u. A scented flame flickering above that peace **5-33.**
193v. The bird of prey knows well in his deep heart.
193w. *Shemus* [*bringing drinking cups (drinking-cups* **6-33**)]. I do not understand you, but your wine
193x. Sets me athirst—(athirst: **6-33**) its praise made your eyes lighten.
5-33.
193y. May I, too, taste it?
First Merchant.   Ay, come drink and drink, **5-18, 31**;
I am thirsting for it.
First Merchant.   Ay, come drink and drink, **28, 33.**
193z. I bless all mortals who drink long and deep.
193aa. My curse upon the salt-strewn road of monks.
[*Teig and Shemus sit down at the table and drink.*] **5-33.**
193bb. *Teig.* You must have seen rare sights and done rare things. (thing
6) **5-33.**
194-201. [lacking] **5-33.**
199. . . . pleased (pleased. **48, 63**) **46-80.**
200. . . . [T] But . . ., **48.**
202-207. [words of Shemus, 11. 203-207, printed as continuation of First
Merchant's words, 1. 202] **52.**
202. *First Merchant.* What think you of the master whom we serve?
5-33; . . . merchants **72, 74.**
202a. *Shemus.* I have grown weary of my days in the world **5-33.**
202b. Because I do not serve him.
First Merchant.   More of this
202c. When we have eaten, for we love right well
202d. A merry meal, a warm and leaping fire **5-33.**
203-209. [lacking] **5-33.**
205. . . . rate, **46-80.**

[263-266] 149. Say to all men we buy men's souls—away.

[*They do not stir.*]

[254] 150. This pile for you and this for you.

   Shemus. We go.

[*Teig and Shemus go out.*]

[272] 151. *Mary* [*kneeling*]. Destroyers of souls, may God destroy
    you quick.

[275] 152. *First Merchant*. No curses injure the immortal demons.

[273] 153. *Mary*. You shall at last dry like dry leaves, and hang
274 154. Nailed like dead vermin to the doors of God.

    155. *First Merchant*. Woman, you shall be ours. This famine
     shall not cease.

[281] 156. You shall eat grass, and dock, and dandelions,

[282] 157. And fail till this stone threshold seem a wall,

283 158. And when your hands can scarcely drag your body

207.   Is now worth fifty.

    First Merchant [*arranging money*]. Our Master bids us pay
208.   So good a price that all who deal with us
209.   Shall eat, drink, and be merry.

    Shemus [*to Mary*].   Bestir yourself,
210.   Go kill and draw the fowl, while Teigue and I
211.   Lay out the plates and make a better fire.

212.   *Mary.* I will not cook for you.

    Shemus.   Not cook! not cook!
213.   Do not be angry. She wants to pay me back
214.   Because I struck her in that argument.
215.   But she'll get sense again. Since the dearth came
216.   We rattle one on another as though we were
217.   Knives thrown into a basket to be cleaned.

218.   *Mary.* I will not cook for you, because I know
219.   In what unlucky shape you sat but now
220.   Outside this door.

    Teigue.   It's this, your honours:

---

207.   . . . fifty.
        [*Merchants begin putting money on carpet.*]
        Our . . . **46-67, 72-80.**
208.   . . . price, that . . . **46-80.**
210.   And easy hearts.
    Shemus.   Come, Maire, and cook the wolf. **5-33.**
210a.   *Maire* [*coming towards the fire*]. The water will not boil for you.
    [*The First Merchant whispers to the water.*]
    First Merchant.   It boils. **5, 6.**
211.   [lacking] **5-33.**
212.   *Maire.* . . . you.
    Shemus.   Maire is mad.
    [*Teig and Shemus stand up and stagger about.*]
212a.   *Shemus.* That wine's (wine is **7-33**) the suddenest wine man ever
    tasted. **5-33.**
213-217.   [lacking] **5-33.**
218.   *Maire.* . . . you: you are not human:
219.   Before you came two horned owls peered (looked **28, 33**) at us;
219a.   The dog bayed, and the tongue of Shemus maddened.
219b.   When you came in the Vigin's blessed shrine
219c.   Fell from its nail, and when you sat down here **5-33.**

[284] 159.   We shall be near you.

[To Second Merchant.]

Bring the food out.

[The Second Merchant brings the bag of meal from the pantry.]   Burn it.

[Mary faints.]

[284] 160.   Now she has swooned, our faces go unscratched;

[285] 161.   Bring me the grey hen too.

[The Second Merchant goes out through the door and returns with the hen strangled. He flings it on the floor. While he is away the First Merchant makes up the fire. The First Merchant then fetches the pan of milk from the pantry, and spills it on the ground. He returns, and brings out the wolf, and throws it down by the hen.]

These need much burning.

221.   Because of some wild words my father said
222.   She thinks you are not of those who cast a shadow.

223. *Shemus.* I said I'd make the devils of the wood
224.   Welcome, if they'd a mind to eat and drink;
225.   But it is certain that you are men like us.

226. *First Merchant.* It's strange that she should think we cast no
               shadow,
227.   For there is nothing on the ridge of the world
228.   That's more substantial than the merchants are
229.   That buy and sell you.

          Mary.   If you are not demons,
230.   And seeing what great wealth is spread out there,
231.   Give food or money to the starving poor.

232. *First Merchant.* If we knew how to find deserving poor
233.   We'd do our share.

          Mary.   But seek them patiently.

234. *First Merchant.* We know the evils of mere charity.

235. *Mary.* Those scruples may befit a common time.
236.   I had thought there was a pushing to and fro,
237.   At times like this, that overset the scale

219d.   You poured out wine as the wood sidheogs do
219e.   When they (they'd **28, 33**) entice a soul out of the world.
219f.   Why did you come to us? Was not death near? **5-33.**
220-228. [lacking] **5-33.**
 220.   . . . door.
               It is this way, your . . .: **63.**
 226.   . . . shadow **56a, 72, 74.**
 229.   *First Merchant.* We are two merchants.
          Maire.   If you be not demons (demons, **33**) **5-33.**
 230.   Go and give alms among the starving poor, (poor. **6, 7**)
 231.   You seem more rich than any under the moon.
 232.   . . . knew where to . . . poor,
 233.   We would give alms.
          Maire.   Then ask of Father John.
 234.   *First Merchant.* . . . charity, **5-33.**
235-238. [lacking] **5-33.**
 236.   . . . fro **48, 63.**

162.   This stool and this chair here will make good fuel.
         [*He begins breaking the chair.*]

End of Scene 1.

SCENE II.

[*A great hall in the castle of the Countess Kathleen. There is a large window of partly-coloured glass at the further end. The wall to the right juts out slightly, cutting off an angle of the room. A flight of stone steps leads up to a small arched door in the jutting wall. Through the door can be seen a little oratory. The hall is hung with tapestry representing the wars and loves and huntings of the Finian and Red-branch warriors. There are doors to the right and left. On the left side Oona sits as if asleep in a large oak chair. The Countess Kathleen stands looking through the window. She leaves it and goes over to Oona on tiptoe.*]

238.   And trampled measure down.

First Merchant.   **But if already**
239.   We'd thought of a more prudent way than that?

240.   *Second Merchant.* If each one brings a bit of merchandise,
241.   We'll give him such a price he never dreamt of.

242.   *Mary.* Where shall the starving come at merchandise?

243.   *First Merchant.* We will ask nothing but what all men have.

244.   *Mary.* Their swine and cattle, fields and implements
245.   Are sold and gone.

First Merchant.   **They have not sold all yet.**
246.   For there's a vaporous thing—that may be nothing,
247.   But that's the buyer's risk—a second self,
248.   They call immortal for a story's sake.

249.   *Shemus.* They come to buy our souls?

Teigue.   I'll barter mine.

---

239.   And would devise a more considered way. **5-18, 31 ;** And have been planning out a wiser way. **28, 33.**
240.   Let each man bring one piece of merchandise.
241.   [lacking] **5-33.**
242.   *Maire.* And have the starving any merchandise?
243.   *First Merchant.* We do but ask what each man has.
      Maire.   Merchants, (Merchants. **6**) **5-33.**
244.   . . . implements, **5-33, 48, 63.**
245.   . . . yet, **48, 63 ;** . . . yet **73, 76-80.**
246.   *Maire.* What have they?
      First Merchant.   They have still their souls.
              [*Maire shrieks. He beckons to Teig and Shemus.*]
                              Come hither. **5-33 ;**
    . . . vapourous . . ., **73, 76-80.**
246a.   See you these little golden heaps? Each one
246b.   Is payment for a soul. From charity
246c.   We give so great a price for those poor flames.
246d.   Say to all men we buy men's souls—away.
                          [*They do not stir.*] **5-33.**
247-253.   [lacking] **5-33.**
249.   You come . . . . **46, 49 ;** You come . . . mine; **48, 63 ;** . . . souls.
                             I'll . . . . **52.**

163. *Kathleen.* You were asleep.

Oona.   No, child, I was but thinking
164.   Why you have grown so sad.

Kathleen.   The famine frets me.

165. *Oona.* I have lived now near ninety winters, child,
166.   And I have known three things no doctor cures—
167.   Love, loneliness, and famine—nor found refuge
168.   Other than growing old and full of sleep.
169.   See you where Oisin and young Niam ride
170.   Wrapped in each other's arms, and where the Finians
171.   Follow their hounds along the fields of tapestry,
172.   How merry they lived once, yet men died then.
173.   I'll sing the ballad young bard Kevin sang
174.   By the great door, the light about his head,
175.   When he bid you cast off this cloud of care.

250.   Why should we starve for what may be but nothing?

251. *Mary.* Teigue and Shemus——

    Shemus.   What can it be but nothing?

252.   What has God poured out of His bag but famine?
253.   Satan gives money.

    Teigue.   Yet no thunder stirs.

254. *First Merchant.* There is a heap for each.

                          [*Shemus goes to take money.*
                          But, no, not yet,

255.   For there's a work I have to set you to.

256. *Shemus.* So, then, you're as deceitful as the rest,
257.   And all that talk of buying what's but a vapour
258.   Is fancy bread, I might have known as much,
259.   Because that's how the trick-o'-the-loop man talks.

260. *First Merchant.* That's for the work, each has its separate price;
261.   But neither price is paid till the work's done.

---

251.   . . . nothing, **48, 63**; . . . can be . . .? **71A.**
254.   *First Merchant.* This pile for you and this for you.
    Shemus.   We go.
                    [*Teig and Shemus go out.*] **5;**
    First Merchant. This pile for you and this for you.
                  [*Teig and Shemus take the money.*]
                    Cry out **6;**
    First Merchant. This pile is for you and this one here for you. (you, **28**) **7-33;**
    First Merchant. . . . But no, . . ., **46, 49-62, 66-80;**
    First Merchant. . . . each.
               [. . . *take the money.*]
                  But no, . . . yet. **48, 63.**
254a.   *Maire.* Shemus and Teig, Teig—
    Teig.   Out of the way.
    [*Shemus and Teig take the money.*] **7-33.**
255-   Directions after 271.   [lacking] **5.**
255-262. [lacking] **6-33.**
256.   So then you're . . ., **46-80.**
258.   . . . fancy bred. I . . ., **46;** . . . fancy-bread. I . . . much **48, 63.**

176. *Kathleen.* Sing how King Fergus in his brazen car
177. 　　　Drove with a troop of dancers through the woods.
　　　　　[She crouches down on the floor and lays her head upon Oona's
　　　　　knees.]

178. *Oona.* You always loved old things—loved best the tale,
179. 　　　Told many times. Dear, wherefore should you sadden
180. 　　　For wrongs you cannot hinder. The great God
181. 　　　Smiling condemns the lost. Be mirthful: He
182. 　　　Bids youth be merry and old age be wise.

183. *[A voice without.]* You may not see the Countess.

　　　[Another voice.]　　　　　　　　　　　I must see her.
　　　[Sound of a slight struggle. A servant enters from door to R.]

184. *Servant.* The gardener is resolved to speak with you.

262. *Teigue.* The same for me.

    Mary.   O God, why are You still?

263. *First Merchant.* You've but to cry aloud at every cross-road,
264.   At every house door, that we buy men's souls
265.   And give so good a price that all may live
266.   In mirth and comfort till the famine's done,
267.   Because we are Christian men.

    Shemus.   Come, let's away.

268. *Teigue.* I shall keep running till I've earned the price.

269. *Second Merchant* [*who has risen and gone towards fire*]. Stop; you must
    have proof behind the words,
270.   So here's your entertainment on the road.
                  [*He throws a bag of money on the ground.*
271.   Live as you please; our Master's generous.
    [*Teigue and Shemus have stopped. Teigue takes the money. They go
    out.*

272. *Mary.* Destroyers of souls, God will destroy you quickly.

---

262. .... Oh, God, ... you still? (still **49**) **46-80.**
263. *First Merchant.* In every cross-road, every market-place, **6**; Cry out
    at cross-roads and at chapel doors **7-33**; ... crossroad, **97A.**
264. And every lane, we ... souls for money, **6**; And market-places that
    ... souls, **7-33**; ... souls, **46-52, 63**; ... souls. **56a, 66, 67, 72-80.**
265. Giving so great a ... that men may ... **6-33.**
266. ... and ease until the famine ends.
                    [*Teig and Shemus go out.*] **6-33.**
267- Directions after 271. [lacking] **6-33.**
267. ... man.
        Come, ... **73, 76, 80.**
269. Stop, for we obey a generous Master, **46-49, 63**; ... words. **51, 56a-
    62, 66-80**; Stop. What could you do without a proof? **52.**
270. That would be served by comfortable men. **46-49, 63**; Here is your
    .... **52.**
    Directions after 270. [lacking] **46-49, 52, 63.**
271. And here's your entertainment on the road. **46-49, 63.**
    Directions after 271. [*He throws a bag of money on the ground. Teig and
    Shemus ....*] **52.**
272. *Maire* [*kneeling*]. Destroyers ... souls, may God destroy ... quickly!
    5-33.
272a. *First Merchant.* No curses injure the immortal demons. **5, 6**; No
    curse can overthrow the immortal demons. **7-33.**

185.   I cannot stay him.

    Kathleen.   You may come, Maurteen.
    [*The gardener, an old man, comes in from the R, and the
    servant goes out.*]

186.   *Gardener.* Forgive my clay-soiled coat—my muddy shoes.
[371]   187.   I bring ill words, your ladyship—too bad
[369]   188.   To send with any other.

    Kathleen.   These bad times
[372]   189.   Can any news be bad or any good?

[375]   190.   *Gardener.* A crowd of ugly lean-faced rogues last night
[375]   191.   —And may God curse them—climbed the garden wall.
       192.   There's scarce an apple now on twenty trees,
[378]   193.   And my asparagus and strawberry beds
       194.   Are trampled into clauber, and the boughs
       195.   Of beech and plum trees broken and torn down

273.   You shall at last dry like dry leaves and hang

274.   Nailed like dead vermin to the doors of God.

275.   *Second Merchant.* Curse to your fill, for saints will have their
        dreams.

276.   *First Merchant.* Though we're but vermin that our Master sent

277.   To overrun the world, he at the end

278.   Shall pull apart the pale ribs of the moon

279.   And quench the stars in the ancestral night.

280.   *Mary.* God is all-powerful.

        Second Merchant.   Pray, you shall need Him.

281.   You shall eat dock and grass, and dandelion,

282.   Till that low threshold there becomes a wall,

283.   And when your hands can scarcely drag your body

284.   We shall be near you.   [*Mary faints.*
        [*The First Merchant takes up the carpet, spreads it before the fire
        and stands in front of it warming his hands.*

        First Merchant.   Our faces go unscratched.

285.   Wring the neck o' that fowl, scatter the flour,

---

273.   *Maire. . . .* leaves, and . . . **5-33.**

275-279. [lacking] **5-33.**

280.   *First Merchant.* You (Woman, you 5) shall be ours. This famine shall
        not cease. **5-33;**
        . . . all powerful.

                        Pray, you (Pray, for you 52) . . . . **46, 49-62, 66-80.**

281.   *First Merchant. . . .* eat grass, and dock, and dandelion, **5-33;**
        Second Merchant. . . . dock, . . ., **48, 63.**

282.   And fail till this low threshold seems (seem **6-33**) a wall, **5-33.**

284.   . . . you.
        [*To Second Merchant.*] Bring the meal out.
                [*The Second Merchant brings the bag of meal from the pantry.*]
                        Burn it.   [*Maire faints.*] **5-33;**
        . . . unscratched, **46-72, 74.**

284a.   *First Merchant.* Now she has swooned, our faces go unscratched; **5-33.**

285.   Bring me the gray hen too.
        [*The Second Merchant goes out through the door and returns with the hen
        strangled. He flings it on the floor. While he is away the First Merchant
        makes up the fire. The First Merchant then fetches the pan of milk from*

196.   For some last fruit that hung there. My dog, too,
197.   My old blind Simon, he who had no tail,
198.   They murdered—God's red anger seize them.

199. *Kathleen.* I know how pears and all the tribe of apples
200.   Are daily in your love—how this ill chance
201.   Is sudden doomsday fallen on your year ;
202.   So do not say no matter. I but say
203.   I blame the famished season, and no more.
204.   Then be not troubled.

    Gardener.   Thanks, your ladyship.

205. *Kathleen.* What portents and what rumours of the dearth?

206. *Gardener.* The yellow vapour, in whose folds it came,
207.   That creeps along the hedges at nightfall,
208.   Makes my new shrubs and saplings poor and sickly.

286.   And look if there is bread upon the shelves.

287.   We'll turn the fowl upon the spit and roast it,

288.   And eat the supper we were bidden to,

289.   Now that the house is quiet, praise our Master,

290.   And stretch and warm our heels among the ashes.

Scene II

Front Scene.—*A wood with perhaps distant view of turreted house at one side, but all in flat colour, without light and shade and against a diapered or gold background.*

---

the pantry, and spills it on the ground. He returns, and brings out the wolf, and throws it down by the hen.]
      These need much burning. **5-33**;
      For she has fainted. Wring . . . fowl, **46-49, 63**; . . .
flour **51-62, 66-72, 74**; . . . fowl; scatter . . . flour **73, 76-80**.

285a.   *First Merchant.* This stool and this chair here will make good fuel.
      [*He begins breaking the chair.*] **5¹-33.**

285b.   *First Merchant.* My master will break up the sun and moon

285c.   And quench the stars in the ancestral night

285d.   And overturn the throne (thrones **7-33**) of God and the angels. **6-33.²**

286-290.   [lacking] **5-33.**

286.   Scatter the flour and search the shelves for bread. **46-49, 63.**

287.   . . . it **48, 63.**

288.   . . . to. **48**; . . . to **63.**

289.   . . . master, **46, 49, 52**; . . . quiet; praise . . . Master;
      63.

ACT OR SCENE NUMBER   Act II **5-33**; Scene II **46-97.**

STAGE DIRECTIONS   *A great hall in the castle of the Countess Cathleen. There is a large window at the farther end, through which the forest is visible. The wall to the right juts out slightly, cutting off an angle of the room. A flight of stone steps leads up to a small arched door in the jutting wall. Through the door can be seen a little oratory. The hall is hung with ancient tapestry, representing the loves and wars and huntings of the Fenian and Red Brand warriors. There (Red Branch heroes. There* **6-33**) *are doors to the right and left. On the left side Oona sits, as if asleep, beside a spinning wheel. (spinning-wheel.* **7-33**) *The Countess Cathleen stands farther*

---

¹ In **5**, Act I ends here.   ² In **6-33**, Act I ends here.

209.   I pray against it.
                    [*He goes towards the door, then pauses.*]
                    If her ladyship
210.   Would give me an old crossbow, I would watch
211.   Behind a bush and guard the pears o'nights
212.   And make a hole in somebody I know of.

213. *Kathleen.* They'll give you a long draught of ale below.
                    [*The gardener goes out.*]

214. *Oona.* What did he say; he stood on my deaf side?

215. *Kathleen.* His apples are stolen. Pruning time,
216.   The rounding and ripening of his pears and apples,
217.   For him's a long heart-moving history.

218. *Oona.* Now lay your head once more upon my knees.
219.   I'll sing how Fergus drove his brazen cars.
                    [*She chants with the thin voice of age.*]
220.   *Who will go drive with Fergus now,*

Countess Cathleen comes in leaning upon Aleel's arm.
Oona follows them.

291. *Cathleen* [*stopping*]. Surely this leafy corner, where one smells

---

back and more to the right, close to a group of the musicians (musicians, **28, 33**) *still
in their fantastic dresses, who are playing a merry tune.* **5-33**;
     Front Scene. *A* . . . . **48, 63**; . . . *views* . . . . **73, 76-80.**
     Directions before 291. [lacking] **5-33.**

291.   *Cathleen.* Be silent, I am tired of tympan and harp. (harp, **7-33**) **5-33.**
        [*The musicians go out. The Countess Cathleen goes over to Oona.*]
        5, 6.

291a.   And tired of music that but cries sleep, sleep, ('sleep, sleep,' **28, 33**)
        7-33.

291b.   Till joy and sorrow and hope and terror are gone.
        [*The Countess Cathleen goes over to Oona.*] **7-33.**

291c.   *Cathleen.* You were asleep. (asleep? **7-33**)
        Oona.   No, child, I was but thinking **5-33.**

291d.   Why you have grown so sad.
        Cathleen.   The famine frets me.

291e.   *Oona.* I have lived now near ninety winters, child,

291f.   And I have known three things no doctor (doctors **7**) cures—
        (cures, **6**)

291g.   Love, loneliness, and famine—(famine; **6-33**) nor found refuge

291h.   Other than growing old and full of sleep.

291i.   See you where Oisin and young Niamh ride (ride, **18, 31**)

291j.   Wrapped in each other's arms, and where the Fenians

291k.   Follow their hounds along the fields of tapestry;

291l.   How merry they lived once, yet men died then.

291m.   Sit down by me, and I will chaunt the song

291n.   About the Danaan nations in their raths

291o.   That Aleel sang for you by the great door

291p.   Before we lost him in the shadow of leaves. **5-33.**

291q.   *Cathleen.* No, sing the song he sang in the dim light,

291r.   When we first found him in the shadow of leaves,

291s.   About King Fergus in his brazen car

291t.   Driving with troops of dancers through the woods.
        [*She crouches down on the floor, and lays her head on Oona's knees.*]

291u.   *Oona.* Dear heart, make a soft cradle of old tales,

291v.   And songs, and music: wherefore should you sadden.

291w.   For wrongs you cannot hinder? the (The **6-33**) great God

291x.   Smiling condemns the lost: be mirthful: He

291y.   Bids youth (you **7-31**) be merry and old age be wise. **5-33.**

291z.   *Cathleen.* Tympan and harp awaken wandering dreams. **7-33.**

292-Directions before 364. [lacking] **5-33.**

221.   *And pierce the deep wood's woven shade,*
222.   *And dance upon the level shore?*
223.   *Young man, lift up your russet brow,*
224.   *And lift your tender eyelids, maid,*
225.   *And brood on hopes and fears no more.*
226.   You have dropped down again into your trouble.
227.   You do not hear me.

      Kathleen.   Ah, sing on, old Oona,
228.   I hear the horn of Fergus in my heart.

229. *Oona.* I do not know the meaning of the song.
230.   I am too old.

      Kathleen.   The horn is calling, calling.

231. *Oona.*
            And no more turn aside and brood
232.   *Upon Love's bitter mystery;*

292.   The wild bee's honey, has a story too?

293.   *Oona*. There is the house at last.

   Aleel.   A man, they say,

294.   Loved Maeve the Queen of all the invisible host,
295.   And died of his love nine centuries ago.
296.   And now, when the moon's riding at the full,
297.   She leaves her dancers lonely and lies there
298.   Upon that level place, and for three days
299.   Stretches and sighs and wets her long pale cheeks.

300.   *Cathleen*. So she loves truly.

   Aleel.   No, but wets her cheeks,
301.   Lady, because she has forgot his name.

302.   *Cathleen*. She'd sleep that trouble away—though it must be
303.   A heavy trouble to forget his name—
304.   If she had better sense.

   Oona.   Your own house, lady.

305.   *Aleel*. She sleeps high up on wintry Knocknarea
306.   In an old cairn of stones; while her poor women
307.   Must lie and jog in the wave if they would sleep—
308.   Being water-born—yet if she cry their names
309.   They run up on the land and dance in the moon
310.   Till they are giddy and would love as men do,
311.   And be as patient and as pitiful.
312.   But there is nothing that will stop in their heads,
313.   They've such poor memories, though they weep for it.
314.   O yes, they weep; that's when the moon is full.

---

292. . . . story, too? **63.**
294. . . . Maeve, the . . ., **48, 63.**
296. . . . now when . . ., **48, 63.**
299. . . . cheeks **74.**
301. ['Lady, beca' lacking] **67.**
304. . . ., Lady. **48, 63.**
305. . . . Knock-na-rea **46-80.**
308. . . . water born—. . . **46, 49-62, 66-80 ;** . . .—yet, if . . . names, **48, 63.**
310. . . . do. **72, 74.**
311. . . . pitiful, **48, 63.**
312. . . . heads **49, 51, 56a-62, 66-80.**
314. Oh, yes, ... **46-80.**

233.   *For Fergus rules the brazen cars,*
234.   *And rules the shadows of the wood,*
235.   *And the white breast of the dim sea*
236.   *And all dishevelled wandering stars.*

237. [*The servant's voice without.*] The Countess Kathleen must not be
     disturbed.

238. [*Another voice.*] Man, I must see her.

Kathleen.   Who now wants me, Michael?

239. *Servant* [*from the door.*] A herdsman and his history.

Kathleen.   He may come.
                        [*The herdsman enters from door to R.*]

240. *Herdsman.* Forgive this dusty gear. I have come far.
241.   My sheep were taken from the fold last night.
242.   You will be angry. I am not to blame.

315. *Cathleen.* Is it because they have short memories
316.   They live so long?

    Aleel.   What's memory but the ash
317.   That chokes our fires that have begun to sink?
318.   And they've a dizzy, everlasting fire.

319. *Oona.* There is your own house, lady.

    Cathleen.   Why, that's true,
320.   And we'd have passed it without noticing.

321. *Aleel.* A curse upon it for a meddlesome house!
322.   Had it but stayed away I would have known
323.   What Queen Maeve thinks on when the moon is pinched;
324.   And whether now—as in the old days—the dancers
325.   Set their brief love on men.

    Oona.   Rest on my arm.
326.   These are no thoughts for any Christian ear.

327. *Aleel.* I am younger, she would be too heavy for you.
    [*He begins taking his lute out of the bag. Cathleen, who has turned*
    towards Oona, turns back to him.
328.   This hollow box remembers every foot
329.   That danced upon the level grass of the world,
330.   And will tell secrets if I whisper to it.
            [*Sings*]
331.   Lift up the white knee;
332.   Hear what they sing,
333.   Those young dancers
334.   That in a ring
335.   Raved but now
336.   Of the hearts that broke
337.   Long, long ago
338.   For their sake.

---

317. . . . sink, **48, 63.**
319. . . ., Lady. . . ., **48, 63.**
    Directions after 327. [. . . *bag*, (*bag*; **49, 51, 61, 63, 71, 73, 76-80**)
    Cathleen, ...] **46-80.**
331. 'Lift . . . knee, **48, 63**; 'Lift . . . knee;' **52.**
332. That's what . . ., **46-49, 63.**
336. . . . that break **46-49, 63**; . . . that brake **51-62, 66, 67, 72, 74.**
337. . . . ago,
338. . . . sake.' **48, 63.**

243.   Go blame these robbing times.

Kathleen.   No blame's with you;
244.   I blame the famine.

Herdsman.   Kneeling, I give thanks.
245.   When gazing on your face the poorest, Lady,
246.   Forget their poverty; the rich their care.

247. *Kathleen.* What rumours and what portents of the famine?

248. *Herdsman.* As I came down the lane by Tubber-vanach
249.   A boy and man sat cross-legged on two stones.
250.   With moving hands and faces famine-thin,
251.   Gabbling to crowds of men and wives and boys
[407] 252.   Of how two merchants at "The Lady's Head"
[407] 253.   Buy souls for hell, giving a price so great
254.   That men may live through all the dearth in plenty.
255.   The vales are famine crazy—I'm right glad

339. *Oona.* New friends are sweet.

340. *Aleel.*   But the dance changes,
341.   Lift up the gown,
342.   All that sorrow
343.   Is trodden down.

344. *Oona.* The empty rattle-plate! Lean on this arm,
345.   That I can tell you is a christened arm,
346.   And not like some, if we are to judge by speech.
347.   But as you please. It is time I was forgot.
348.   Maybe it is not on this arm you slumbered
349.   When you were as helpless as a worm.

350. *Aleel.* Stay with me till we come to your own house.

351. *Cathleen* [*sitting down*]. When I am rested I will need no help.

352. *Aleel.* I thought to have kept her from remembering
353.   The evil of the times for full ten minutes;
354.   But now when seven are out you come between.

355. *Oona.* Talk on; what does it matter what you say,
356.   For you have not been christened?

     Aleel.   Old woman, old woman,
357.   You robbed her of three minutes' peace of mind,
358.   And though you live unto a hundred years,
359.   And wash the feet of beggars and give alms,
360.   And climb Cro-Patrick, you shall not be pardoned.

361. *Oona.* How does a man who never was baptized
362.   Know what Heaven pardons?

     Aleel.   You are a sinful woman.

---

340. 'But . . . changes. **46, 49, 51, 56a-62, 66, 67, 72-80** ; 'But . . ., **48, 63, 71,**
      84 ; . . . changes. **52.**
341. 'Lift . . ., **52.**
343. . . . down.' **46-84.**
351. . . . rested, I . . . . **48, 63.**
357. . . . minutes . . ., **46, 49-62, 66, 67, 72-76, 80.**
361. . . . baptized, **48, 63.**
362. . . . woman **46.**

256.   My home is on the mountain near to God.

[*He turns to go.*]

257. *Kathleen.* They'll give you ale and meat before you go.
258.   You must have risen at dawn to come so far.
259.   Keep your bare mountain—let the world drift by,
260.   The burden of its wrongs rests not on you.

261. *Herdsman.* I am content to serve your ladyship.

[*He goes.*]

262. *Oona.* What did he say; he stood on my deaf side?
263.   He seemed to give you word of woeful things.

264. *Kathleen.* O, I am sadder than an old air, Oona;
265.   My heart is longing for a deeper peace
266.   Than Fergus found amid his brazen cars:
267.   Would that like Adene my first forebear's daughter,
268.   Who followed once a twilight piercing tune,

363.   *Oona.* I care no more than if a pig had grunted.

Enter Cathleen's steward

364.   *Steward.* I am not to blame, for I had locked the gate.
365.   The forester's to blame. The men climbed in
366.   At the east corner where the elm-tree is.

367.   *Cathleen.* I do not understand you. Who has climbed?

368.   *Steward.* Then God be thanked, I am the first to tell you.
369.   I was afraid some other of the servants—
370.   Though I've been on the watch—had been the first,
371.   And mixed up truth and lies, your ladyship.

---

363.   . . . grunted **78.**
       Directions after 363. [lacking] **5-33.**
364.   *A voice [without].* You may not see the Countess.
       Another voice.   I must see her. **5-33;**
       . . . gate, **46-80.**
       Directions after 364. [*Sound of a slight (short **33**) struggle. A servant enters from door to R.*] **5-33.**
364a. *Servant.* The gardener is resolved to speak with you. I cannot stay him.
364b. *Cathleen.*   You may come in, (come, **7-33**) Maurteen. **5-33.**
       [*The gardener, an old man, comes in from the R., and the servant goes out.*] **5-33.**
364c. *Gardener.* Forgive my clay-soiled coat—my muddy shoes. **5-18, 31;**
       Forgive my working clothes and the dirt on me. **28, 33.**
364d. I bring ill words, your ladyship—(ladyship,—**33**) too bad
364e. To send with any other.
       Cathleen.   These bad times,
364f. Can any news be bad or any good?
365.   *Gardener.* A crowd of ugly lean-faced rogues last night (night; **6-31;**
       night—**33**) **5-33.**
366.   —And (And **6-33**) may God curse them!—(them! **6-31**) climbed the
       garden wall. **5-33;** . . . elm tree . . . . **48, 63.**
366a. There's (There is **7-33**) scarce an apple now on twenty trees,
366b. And my asparagus and strawberry beds
366c. Are trampled into clauber, and the boughs
366d. Of beech (peach **28, 33**) and plum-trees broken and torn down
       5-33.
367-377.   [lacking] **5-33.**
367.   . . . you, (you; **48, 63**) who . . .? **46-80.**
370.   . . . first **46, 52.**

269.   I could go down and dwell among the shee
270.   In their old ever-busy honeyed land.

271.   *Oona.* You should not say such things—they bring ill-luck.

272.   *Kathleen.* The image of young Adene on the arras,
273.   Walking along, one finger lifted up,
274.   And that wild song of the unending dance
275.   Of the dim Danaan nations in their raths,
276.   Young Kevin sang for me by the great door,
277.   Has filled me full of all these wicked words.

     [*The servant enters hastily, followed by three men. Two are peasants.*]

278.   *Servant.* The steward of the castle brings two men
279.   To talk with you.

     Steward.   And tell the strangest story

372. *Cathleen* [*rising*]. Has some misfortune happened?

  Steward.   Yes, indeed.

373. The forester that let the branches lie
374. Against the wall's to blame for everything,
375. For that is how the rogues got into the garden.

376. *Cathleen.* I thought to have escaped misfortune here.
377. Has any one been killed?

  Steward.   O no, not killed.
378. They have stolen half a cart-load of green cabbage.

---

374. . . . everything. **48, 63.**
377. . . . any one (anyone **52**) . . . killed?
          Oh, no, ... **46-80.**
378. *Gardener.* For some last fruit that hung there. My dog, too, **5-33;**
  . . . cabbage **73, 76, 80.**
378a. My old blind Simon, him who had no tail,
378b. They murdered—God's red anger seize them. (them! **28, 33**)
378c. *Cathleen.* I know how pears and all the tribe of apples
378d. Are daily in your love—how this ill chance
378e. Is sudden doomsday fallen on your year;
378f. So do not say no matter. I but say
378g. I blame the famished season, and no more. (and not you. **7-33**)
378h. Then be not troubled.
  Gardener.   Thanks, (I thank **7-33**) your ladyship.
378i. *Cathleen.* What portents (rumours **7-33**) and what rumours (portents
  7-33) of the famine?
378j. *Gardener.* The yellow vapour, in whose folds it came,
378k. That creeps along the hedges at nightfall, **5-33.**
378l. Makes my new shrubs and saplings poor and sickly. **5-18, 31 ;** Rots
  all the heart out of my cabbages. **28, 33.**
378m. I pray against it.
  [*He goes towards the door, then pauses.*]
         If her ladyship
378n. Sould give me an old crossbow, I would watch
378o. Behind a bush and guard the pears o' (of **7-33**) nights
378p. And make a hole in somebody I know of.
378q. *Cathleen.* They'll (They will **7-33**) give you a long draught of ale
  below.
  [*The gardener goes out.*] **5-33.**
378r. *Oona.* What did he say?—he stood on my deaf side.
378s. *Cathleen.* His apples are all stolen. Pruning time,
378t. And the slow ripening of his pears and apples,
378u. For him is a long, heart-moving history. **5-33.**

280.   Man's mouth has uttered.

      Kathleen.   More food gone;

[381]   281.   Yet learned theologians have laid down

[382-383] 282.   That he who has no food, offending no way,

[382-383] 283.   May take his meat and bread from too-full larders.

284.   *First Peasant.* We come to make amends for robbery.

285.   I stole five hundred apples from your trees,

286.   And laid them in a hole. And my friend here

287.   Last night stole two large mountain sheep of yours

288.   And hung them on a beam under his thatch.

289.   *Second Peasant.* His words are true.

      First Peasant.   Since then our luck has changed.

290.   As I came down the lane by Tubber-vanach

291.   I fell on Shemus Rua and his son,

[407]   292.   And they led me where two great gentlemen

378v.   *Oona.* Now lay your head once more upon my knees.

378w.   I'll (I will **7-33**) sing how Fergus drove his brazen cars.
       [She chaunts with the thin voice of age.]

378x.   *Who will go drive with Fergus now,*

378y.   *And pierce the deep wood's (woods' **33**) woven shade,*

378z.   *And dance upon the level shore?*

378aa.   *Young man, lift up your russet brow,*

378bb.   *And lift your tender eyelids, maid,*

378cc.   *And brood on hopes and fears no more.*

378dd.   You have dropped down again into your trouble.

378ee.   You do not hear me.
       Cathleen.   Ah, sing on, old Oona,

378ff.   I hear the horn of Fergus in my heart.

378gg.   *Oona.* I do not know the meaning of the song.

378hh.   I am too old.
       Cathleen.   The horn is calling, calling.

378ii.   *Oona. And no more turn aside and brood*

378jj.   *Upon Love's bitter mystery;*

378kk.   *For Fergus rules the brazen cars,*

378ll.   *And rules the shadows of the wood,*

378mm.   *And the white breast of the dim sea*

378nn.   *And all dishevelled wandering stars.*

378oo.   *The servant's voice [without].* The Countess Cathleen must not be disturbed.

378pp.   *Another voice.* Man, I must see her.
       Cathleen.   Who now wants me, Paudeen?

378qq.   *Servant [from the door].* A herdsman and his history.
       Cathleen.   He may come.
       [The herdsman enters from door to R.]

378rr.   *Herdsman.* Forgive this dusty (muddy **6**) gear: I have come far.

378ss.   My sheep were taken from the fold last night.

378tt.   You will be angry: I am not to blame.

378uu.   Go (But **6-33**) blame these robbing times.
       Cathleen.   No blame's with you.

378vv.   I blame the famine.
       Herdsman.   Kneeling, I give thanks.

378ww.   When gazing on your face, the poorest, Lady,

378xx.   Forget their poverty; (poverty, **7-33**) the rich their care.

378yy.   *Cathleen.* What rumours and what portents of the famine?

378zz.   *Herdsman.* As I came down the lane by Tubber-vanach

378aaa.   A boy and man sat cross-legged on two stones,

378bbb.   With moving hands and faces famine-thin,

378ccc.   Gabbling to crowds of men and wives and boys

378ddd.   Of how two merchants at a house in the woods

378eee.   Buy souls for hell, giving so great a price

378fff.   That men may live through all the dearth in plenty. **5-33.**

[407] 293.   Buy souls for money, and they bought my soul.
       294.   I told my friend here—my friend also trafficked.

295.   *Second Peasant.* His words are true.

       First Peasant.   Now people throng to sell,
296.   Noisy as seagulls tearing a dead fish.
297.   There soon will be no man or woman's soul
298.   Unbargained for in fivescore baronies.

299.   *Second Peasant.* His words are true.

       First Peasant.   When we had sold we talked,
300.   And having no more comfortable life
301.   Than this that makes us warm—our souls being
         bartered
[409] 302.   For all this money.

       Second Peasant.   And this money here.
       [*They bring handfuls of money from their pockets. Kathleen
       starts up.*]

379. *Cathleen.* But maybe they were starving.

Steward. That is certain.

380. To rob or starve, that was the choice they had.

381. *Cathleen.* A learned theologian has laid down

378ggg. The vales are famine crazy—(famine-crazy—**33**) I'm (I am **7-33**) right glad

378hhh. My home is on the mountain near to God.
   [*He turns to go.*]

378iii. *Cathleen.* They'll (They will **7-33**) give you ale and meat before you go.

378jjj. You must have risen at dawn to come so far.

378kkk. Keep your bare mountain—let the world drift by,

378lll. The burden of its wrongs rests not on you.

378mmm. *Herdsman.* I am content to serve your ladyship.
   [*He goes.*]

378nnn. *Oona.* What did he say?—he stood on my deaf side.

378ooo. He seemed to give you word of woful things. **5-33.**

378ppp. *Cathleen.* A story born out by (of **28, 33**) the dreaming eyes **7-33.**

378qqq. And crazy brain and credulous ears of famine. **7-33.**

378rrr. O, I am sadder than an old air, Oona, **5-33.**

378sss. My heart is longing for a deeper peace

378ttt. Than Fergus found amid his brazen cars:

378uuu. Would that like Edain (that, like Edain, **18, 31**) my first forebear's daughter (daughter, **33**)

378vvv. Who followed once a twilight (twilight's **7-33**) piercing tune,

378www. I could go down and dwell among the Sidhe

378xxx. In their old ever-busy honeyed land.

378yyy. *Oona.* You should not say such things—they bring ill-luck.

378zzz. *Cathleen.* The image of young Edain on the arras,

378aaaa. Walking along, one finger lifted up;

378bbbb. And that wild song of the unending dance

378cccc. Of the dim Danaan nations in their raths,

378dddd. Young Aleel sang for me by the great door,

378eee. Before we lost him in the shadow of leaves,

378ffff. Have filled me full of all these wicked words.
   [*The servant enters hastily, followed by three men. Two are peasants.*]

378gggg. *Servant.* The steward of the castle brings two men

378hhhh. To talk with you.
   Steward. And tell the strangest story

378iiii. The mouth of man has uttered.
   Cathleen. More food taken; **5-33.**

379-380. [lacking] **5-33.**

381. Yet learned theologians have laid . . . **5-33.**

303.   And fearing much to hang for robbery,

304.   We come to pay you for the sheep and fruit.

305.   How do you price them?

Kathleen.   Gather up your money.

306.   Think you that I would touch the demons' gold?

[412]   307.   Begone, give twice, thrice, twenty times their money,

[413]   308.   And buy again your souls. I will pay all.

[416]   309.   *First Peasant.* Nay, for we go now to be drunk and
            merry.

                                    [*They go.*]

[423-424]   310.   *Kathleen* [*to servant*]. Follow and bring them here again
                —beseech them.

                                    [*The servant goes.*]

[426]   311.   [*To Steward.*] Steward, you know the secrets of this
                house.

382.   That starving men may take what's necessary,
383.   And yet be sinless.

   Oona.   Sinless and a thief!
384.   There should be broken bottles on the wall.

385. *Cathleen.* And if it be a sin, while faith's unbroken
386.   God cannot help but pardon. There is no soul
387.   But it's unlike all others in the world,
388.   Nor one but lifts a strangeness to God's love

---

382.   That he who has no food, offending no way,
383.   May take his meat and bread from too-full larders. **5-33.**
383a. *First Peasant.* We come to make amends for robbery.
383b. I stole five hundred apples from your trees,
383c. And laid them in a hole; and my friend here
383d. Last night stole two large mountain sheep of yours
383e. And hung them on a beam under his thatch.
383f. *Second Peasant.* His words are true.
   First Peasant.   Since then our luck has changed.
383g. As I came down the lane by Tubber-vanach
383h. I fell on Shemus Rua and his son,
383i. And they led me where two great gentlemen
383j. Buy souls for money, and they bought my soul.
383k. I told my friend here—my friend also trafficked.
383l. *Second Peasant.* His words are true.
   First Peasant.   Now people throng to sell,
383m. Noisy as seagulls tearing a dead fish.
383n. There soon will be no man or woman's soul
383o. Unbargained for in fivescore baronies.
383p. *Second Peasant.* His words are true.
   First Peasant.   When we had sold we talked,
383q. And having no more comfortable life
383r. Than this that makes us warm—our souls being bartered
383s. For all this money. (money— **33**)
   Second Peasant.   And this money here; (here. **33**)
   [*They bring handfuls of money from their pockets. Cathleen starts up.*]
383t. And fearing much to hang for robbery,
383u. We come to pay you for the sheep and fruit. (fruit, **28**)
383v. How do you price them?
   Cathleen.   Gather up your money.
383w. Think you that I would touch the demons' gold? **5-33.**
384-411. [lacking] **5-33.**
   384.   . . . bottle . . . . **71A.**
   385.   . . . unbroken, **48, 63.**
   388.   . . . love, **48, 63.**

[427]   312.   How much have I in gold?

          Steward.   A hundred thousand.

428   313.   *Kathleen.* How much have I in castles?

          Steward.   As much more.

[429]   314.   *Kathleen.* How much have I in pastures?

          Steward.   As much more.

[430]   315.   *Kathleen.* How much have I in forests?

          Steward.   Fifty thousand.

[431]   316.   *Kathleen.* Keeping alone this house, sell all I have;
[433]   317.   Buy ships of grain and meal—long herds of cows,
[432]   318.   And hasten here once more. And while you're gone,
          319.   Bid some one give out gold to all who come.

[434]   320.   *Steward.* God's blessing light upon your ladyship;
[435]   321.   You will have saved the land.

                   Kathleen.   Make no delay,

389.   Till that's grown infinite, and therefore none
390.   Whose loss were less than irremediable
391.   Although it were the wickedest in the world.

Enter Teigue and Shemus

392.   *Steward.* What are you running for? Pull off your cap.
393.   Do you not see who's there?

  Shemus.   I cannot wait.
394.   I am running to the world with the best news
395.   That has been brought it for a thousand years.

396.   *Steward.* Then get your breath and speak.

  Shemus.   If you'd my news
397.   You'd run as fast and be as out of breath.

398.   *Teigue.* Such news, we shall be carried on men's shoulders.

399.   *Shemus.* There's something every man has carried with him
400.   And thought no more about than if it were
401.   A mouthful of the wind; and now it's grown
402.   A marketable thing!

  Teigue.   And yet it seemed
403.   As useless as the paring of one's nails.

404.   *Shemus.* What sets me laughing when I think of it,
405.   Is that a rogue who's lain in lousy straw,
406.   If he but sell it, may set up his coach.

407.   *Teigue.* [*laughing*]. There are two gentlemen who buy men's
    souls.

408.   *Cathleen.* O God!

  Teigue.   And maybe there's no soul at all.

---

392.   . . . cap, **46, 49-62, 66-80.**
398.   . . . shoulders **72, 74.**
399.   . . . him. **71A.**
404.   . . . it **48, 63.**
  V.E.P.Y.—D

409. *Steward.* They're drunk or mad.

Teigue.   Look at the price they give.
                                                    [*Showing money.*

410. *Shemus* [*tossing up money*]. 'Go cry it all about the world', they said.
411. " 'Money for souls, good money for a soul.' "

412. *Cathleen.* Give twice and thrice and twenty times their money,
413.   And get your souls again. I will pay all.

414. *Shemus.* Not we! not we! For souls—if there are souls—
415.   But keep the flesh out of its merriment.
416.   I shall be drunk and merry.

Teigue.   Come, let's away.   [*He goes.*

417. *Cathleen.* But there's a world to come.

Shemus.   And if there is,
418.   I'd rather trust myself into the hands
419.   That can pay money down than to the hands
420.   That have but shaken famine from the bag.
                                                    [*He goes out* R. *lilting*
421.   'There's money for a soul, sweet yellow money.
422.   There's money for men's souls, good money, money.'

---

411. 'Money . . . soul.' (soul' **73, 76, 80**) **46-80.**
412. *Cathleen.* Begone, give twice, thrice, twenty . . ., **5-33** ; . . . money.
        73, 76-80.
413. And buy again your souls. (buy your souls again. **7-33**)
        I . . . . **5-33.**
414. *First Peasant.* Nay, for we go now to be drunk and merry. [*They go.*]
        5, 6; *First Peasant.* We will not buy our souls again: a soul **7-33** ;
        Shemus. not we, not we. For . . .— **48, 63.**
415-422. [lacking] **5, 6.**
415.   . . . keeps . . . . **7-33.**
416. We shall be merry and drunk from moon till (to **33**) moon. **7-33** ;
        ['I' lacking] **49.**
416a. Keep from our way. Let no one stop our way. [*They go.*] **7-33.**
417-422. [lacking] **7-33.**
419.   . . . down, than . . . **48, 63.**
        Directions after 420. [. . . *out.* (*Lilting.*)] **52** ; [. . . *out but one hears*
        his voice lilting.] **63.**
421.   There's . . . . **63.**

332.   And whence came all the money?—my deaf side.

333.   Why, you are weeping—and such tears! Such tears!

334.   Look, child, how big they are.

                           Thy shadow falls

335.   O Weeping Willow of the World, O Eri,

336.   On this the loveliest daughter of thy race,

337.   Thy leaves blow round her.

                         I give God great thanks

338.   That I am old—lost in the sleep of age.

End of Scene II.

SCENE III.

[*The hall in the castle of the Countess Kathleen, as before. Midnight. The Two Merchants enter, cautiously, with empty bags over their shoulders.*]

339. *First Merchant.* And whence now, brother?

Second Merchant.   Tubber-vanach cross roads,

340.   Where I in image of a nine-monthed bonyeen

423. *Cathleen* [*to Aleel*]. Go call them here again, bring them by force,
424.   Beseech them, bribe, do anything you like;

            [*Aleel goes.*

425.   And you too follow, add your prayers to his.

       [*Oona, who has been praying, goes out.*

426.   Steward, you know the secrets of my house.
427.   How much have I?

    Steward.   A hundred kegs of gold.

428. *Cathleen.* How much have I in castles?

    Steward.   As much more.

429. *Cathleen.* How much have I in pasture?

    Steward.   As much more.

430. *Cathleen.* How much have I in forests?

    Steward.   As much more.

431. *Cathleen.* Keeping this house alone, sell all I have,
432.   Go barter where you please, but come again
433.   With herds of cattle and with ships of meal.

434. *Steward.* God's blessing light upon your ladyship.

---

423.   *Cathleen* [*to servant*]. Follow and bring them . . . again—beseech them.
    [*The servant goes.*] **5-33.**
424-425.   [lacking] **5-33.**
  424.   . . . like
  425.   . . . too, follow, ... **48, 63.**
  426.   *Cathleen* [*to Steward*]. Steward, . . . of this house.
  427.   . . . I in gold?
        A hundred thousand.
  429.   . . . pastures?
      As . . . . **5-33.**
  431.   Keeping alone this house, sell . . . have; **5, 6**; . . . have; **7-33**; . . .
    have. **71A.**
  432.   Buy ships of grain and meal—long herds of cows, **5, 6**;
    Go to some distant country and come again **7-33.**
  433.   And hasten here once more; and while you are gone, **5, 6**; With
    many herds of cows and ships of grain. **7-33.**
433a.   Bid some one give out gold to all who come. **5, 6.**
  434.   . . . ladyship; **5-33.**

341.   Sat down upon my haunches. Father John
342.   Came, sad and moody, murmuring many prayers.
343.   I seemed as though I came from his own sty.
344.   He saw the one brown ear—the breviary dropped—
345.   He ran—I ran—I ran into the quarry;
346.   He fell a score of yards. The man was dead.
347.   And then I thrust his soul into the bag,
348.   And hurried home. His right hand, on the way—
349.   The hand that blessed the poor and raised the host—
350.   Tore through the leather with sharp piety,
351.   And he escaped me.

First Merchant.   With this priest John dead,
352.   We shall be too much thronged with souls tomorrow.

353.   *Second Merchant.* My chosen venture was to kill this man,
354.   And yours to rob the Countess. You fare ill.

435.   You will have saved the land.

Cathleen.   Make no delay.   [*He goes* L.
                        Aleel and Oona return
436.   *Cathleen.* They have not come; speak quickly.

Aleel.   One drew his knife
437.   And said that he would kill the man or woman
438.   That stopped his way; and when I would have stopped him
439.   He made this stroke at me; but it is nothing.

440.   *Cathleen.* You shall be tended. From this day for ever
441.   I'll have no joy or sorrow of my own.

442.   *Oona.* Their eyes shone like the eyes of birds of prey.

---

435.   . . . delay, **5.**
        Directions at 435. [lacking] **5, 6**; [. . . *goes.*] **7-33, 63.**
435a.   And bid them house here all the old and ailing. [*He goes.*] **5, 6.**
        Directions before 436. [*Re-enter* (*Enter* **28, 33**) *servant.*] **5-33.**
436.   How did you thrive? Say quickly. You are pale? (pale. **6-33**) **5-33**;
        . . . knife, **48, 63**; . . . knife. **71A.**
437.   *Servant.* When I came near, the tallest of the rogues **5, 6.**
437-441. [lacking] **7-33.**
438.   Said he'd be no more stared at, and struck out. **5, 6**; . . . him, **48, 63.**
439.   [lacking] **5, 6**; . . . me, but . . . . **48, 63.**
440.   *Cathleen.* Will no one bring them to me?
        Servant.   No one dare. **5, 6.**
441.   [lacking] **5, 6.**
442.   *Servant.* Their eyes burn like . . . prey (prey. **31**; prey: **33**) **5-33.**
442a.   Now they are angry.
        Cathleen.   May God pity them! **5, 6**;
        I did not dare go near.
        Cathleen.   God pity them! **7-33.**[1]
442b.   *Servant.* I ran, for they have power not born of us. **5, 6.**
442c.   *Cathleen.* O leave me now, and let no voice be raised,
442d.   Or foot tread heavily, or stringed instrument
442e.   Make a kind music: for my peace is dead.
            [*The servant goes out, and Cathleen goes over to Oona and lays her head
            upon her knees.*]
442f.   *Oona.* What, child, dear, did they talk so much about, **5, 6.**

[1] Succeeding lines in **7-33** begin at 445.

355.   I found you sitting drowsed and motionless,

356.   Your chin bowed to your knees, while on all sides,

357.   Bat-like, from bough, and roof, and window ledge,

358.   Clung evil souls of men, and in the woods,

359.   Like streaming flames, floated upon the winds

360.   The elemental creatures.

First Merchant.   I fare ill!

361.   This holy Countess prayed so long and hard,

362.   That doors and windows barred with piety

363.   Defied me and my drudges out of Hell.

[536]   364.   But now she's fallen asleep over her prayers;

               [*He points to the oratory door. They peer through cautiously.*]

365.   She lies worn out upon the altar steps:

366.   A labourer, tired of ploughing His hard fields,

443. *Cathleen.* Come, follow me, for the earth burns my feet

444.　Till I have changed my house to such a refuge

445.　That the old and ailing, and all weak of heart,

446.　May escape from beak and claw; all, all, shall come

447.　Till the walls burst and the roof fall on us.

448.　From this day out I have nothing of my own.

　　　　　　　　　　　　　　　　　　　　　[She goes.

449. *Oona [taking Aleel by the arm and as she speaks bandaging his wound].*
　　　She has found something now to put her hand to,

450.　And you and I are of no more account

451.　Than flies upon a window-pane in the winter.

　　　　　　　　　　　　　　　　　　　　　[They go out.

442g.　And whence came all the money?—(money? **6**) my deaf side. **5, 6.**

442h.　Why, are you weeping—(weeping; **6**) and such tears! Such tears!

442i.　Look, child, how big they are. Your shadow falls,

442j.　O Weeping Willow of the World, O Erie,

442k.　On this the loveliest daughter of your race,

442l.　Your leaves blow round her. I give God great thanks

442m.　That I am old—(old, **6**) lost in the sleep of age. **5, 6.**[1]

443-451.　[lacking] **5, 6.**

443-444.　[lacking] **7-33.**

445.　*Cathleen.* Bring all the old . . . ailing to this house, **7-33.**

446.　[lacking] **7-33**; . . . come, **48, 63.**

447.　For I will have no sorrow of my own **7-33.**

448.　. . . day onward.

　　　　*[The servant goes out. Some of the musicians follow him, some linger
　　　　in the doorway. The Countess Cathleen kneels beside Oona.]*

　　　Cathleen. O, Mother, tell me (Can you tell me, mother, **28, 33**)
　　　7-33.

448a.　How I may mend the times, how staunch this wound

448b.　That bleeds in the earth, how overturn the famine,

448c.　How drive these demons to their darkness again. (again? **28, 33**)

448d.　*Oona.* The demons hold our hearts between their hands,

448e.　For the apple is in our blood, and though heart break

448f.　There is no medicine but Michael's trump.

448g.　Till it has ended parting and old age

448h.　And hail and rain and famine and foolish laughter;

448i.　The dead are happy, the dust is in their ears. **7-33.**[2]

449-451.　[lacking] **7-33.**

　　　Directions at 449.　[. . . *arm as . . . speaks, bandaging* . . . .] **73, 76-80.**

---

[1] Act II ends here in **5, 6.**　　　　[2] Act II ends here in **7-33.**

367.   And deafening His closed ears with cries on cries
368.   Hoping to draw His hands down from the stars
369.   To take the people from us.

Second Merchant.   We must hurry.

370.   We would half stifle if she woke and prayed.

[*They go out by the left-hand door, and enter again almost immediately, carrying full bags upon their shoulders.*]

371.   *First Merchant.* Brave thought, brave thought—a shining thought of mine!
372.   She now no more may bribe the poor—no more
373.   Cheat our great master of his merchandize,
374.   While our heels dangle at "The Lady's Head,"
375.   And grass grows on the threshold, and snails crawl
376.   Along the window-pane and the mud floor.

Scene III

Hall in the house of Countess Cathleen. At the left an oratory with steps leading up to it. At the right a tapestried wall, more or less repeating the form of the oratory, and a great chair with its back against the wall. In the centre are two or more arches through which one can see dimly the trees of the garden. Cathleen is kneeling in front of the altar in the oratory; there is a hanging lighted lamp over the altar. Aleel enters.

452. *Aleel.* I have come to bid you leave this castle and fly

---

ACT OR SCENE NUMBER [lacking] 5,[1] 6;[1] Act III 7-33; Scene III 46-97.

STAGE DIRECTIONS *The great hall . . . the castle of the Countess Cathleen. It is midnight, and there is no one in the hall. The two merchants enter, cautiously, with empty bags over their shoulders.* 5, 6;
    Hall of the Countess Cathleen as before. Servant enters and goes towards the oratory door. 7-33; Scene.—Hall . . . Left . . . Right . . . Centre . . . . 46, 49, 51, 56a-62, 66-72, 74; Scene. Hall . . . Left . . . Right . . . Centre . . . in the oratory. There . . . . 48, 63; Scene.—Hall . . . Left . . . Right . . . of the oratory. In the Centre . . . . 52; Scene.—Hall . . . Left . . . Right . . . Centre . . . trees in the . . . . 73, 76-80.

452-533. [lacking] 5, 6.

452. *Servant.* Here is yet another would see your ladyship. 7-33.

452a. *Cathleen* [*within*]. Who calls me?
    Servant.   There is a man would speak with you,

452b. And by his face he has some pressing news,

452c. Some moving tale.
    Cathleen [*coming to chapel door*]. I cannot rest or (to 18, 31) pray, 7-33.

452d. For all day long the messengers run hither

452e. On one another's heels, and every message

452f. More evil than the one that had gone before.

452g. Who is the messenger?
    Servant.   Aleel, the poet.

452h. *Cathleen.* There is no hour he is not welcome to me,

452i. Because I know of nothing but a harp string (harp-string 18, 31, 33)

452j. That can remember happiness. [*Servant goes out and Aleel comes in.*]
    And now

452k. I grow forgetful of evil for awhile. 7-33.

---

[1] Should be headed 'Act III.' 5, 6.

377.   Brother, where wander all these dwarfish folk,
378.   Hostile to men—the sheogues of the tides?

Second Merchant [*opening the great windows, and showing the tops of*
        the trees].
379.   There are none here. They tired and strayed from hence—
380.   Unwilling labourers.

First Merchant.   I will draw them in.
                            [*He cries through the window.*]
381.   Come hither, hither, hither, water folk:
382.   Come all you elemental populace;
383.   Leave lonely the long-hoarding surges: leave
384.   The cymbals of the waves to clash alone,
385.   And shaking the sea tangles from your hair,
386.   Gather about us.
                    [*After a pause.*]
                I can hear a sound

453.   Out of these woods.

      [Cathleen rises from the altar and comes into the hall.

  Cathleen.   What evil is there here

454.   That is not everywhere from this to the sea?

455. *Aleel.* They who have sent me walk invisible.

456. *Cathleen.* So it is true what I have heard men say,

457.   That you have seen and heard what others cannot.

458. *Aleel.* I was asleep in my bed, and while I slept

459.   My dream became a fire; and in the fire

460.   One walked and he had birds about his head.

461. *Cathleen.* I have heard that one of the old gods walked so.

462. *Aleel.* It may be that he is angelical;

463.   And, lady, he bids me call you from these woods.

464.   And you must bring but your old foster-mother,

465.   And some few serving-men, and live in the hills,

466.   Among the sounds of music and the light

467.   Of waters, till the evil days are done.

452l. I have come to bid you leave this castle, and fly **7-33.**
      Directions in 453. [lacking] **7-80.**

453. . . . here, **7-33, 48, 63** ; . . . here? **46, 52.**

456. Men say that the wise people of the raths **7-33.**

457. Have given you wisdom.
      Aleel.   I lay in the dusk

458. Upon the grassy margin of a lake

458a. Among the hills, where none of mortal creatures

459. But the swan comes—my sleep became a fire. **7-33.**

460. One walked in the fire with birds . . . . **7-33** ; . . . walked, and . . . .
      48, 63.

461. Ay, Aengus of the birds.
      Aleel.   He may be Aengus,

462. But it may be he bears an angelical name. **7-33.**

463. Lady, he bid . . . woods; **7-33** ; . . ., Lady, ... **48, 63.**

464. He bids you bring Oona, your foster-mother, **7-33.**

465. . . . serving-men and . . . hills **7-33** ; . . . serving men, . . ., **46-80.**

467. . . . waters till . . . are gone. [*He kneels.*] **7-33.**

387.   As from waves beating upon distant strands;
388.   And now the sheogues, like a surf of light,
389.   Pour eddying through the pathways of the oaks;
390.   And as they come, the sentient grass and leaves
391.   Bow towards them, and the tall, drouth-jaded oaks
392.   Fondle the murmur of their flying feet.

393.   *Second Merchant.* The green things love unknotted hearts and minds,
394.   And neither one with angels or with us,
395.   Nor risen in arms with evil or with good,
396.   In laughter roves, the litter of the waves.

    [*A crowd of faces fill up the darkness outside the window. A sheogue separates from the others, and standing in the window, speaks.*]

397.   *The Sheogue.* We come unwillingly, for she whose gold

468.   For here some terrible death is waiting you,
469.   Some unimagined evil, some great darkness
470.   That fable has not dreamt of, nor sun nor moon
471.   Scattered.

    Cathleen.   No, not angelical.

    Aleel.   This house
472.   You are to leave with some old trusty man,
473.   And bid him shelter all that starve or wander
474.   While there is food and house-room.

    Cathleen.   He bids me go
475.   Where none of mortal creatures but the swan
476.   Dabbles, and there you would pluck the harp, when the trees
477.   Had made a heavy shadow about our door,
478.   And talk among the rustling of the reeds,
479.   When night hunted the foolish sun away
480.   With stillness and pale tapers. No—no—no!
481.   I cannot. Although I weep, I do not weep
482.   Because that life would be most happy, and here
483.   I find no way, no end. Nor do I weep
484.   Because I had longed to look upon your face,
485.   But that a night of prayer has made me weary.

486.   *Aleel* [*prostrating himself before her*]. Let Him that made mankind,
       the angels and devils

---

468.   . . . you;
469.   Some unimaginable evil, . . . **7-33.**
471.   Scattered.
    Cathleen. And he had birds about his head?
472.   *Aleel.* Yes, yes, white birds. He bids you leave this house
472a.   With some old trusty serving-man, who will feed **7-33.**
473.   All that are starving and shelter all that wander **7-33;** . . . wander,
    48, 63.
474.   . . . house room. . . . **7-31, 46-80.**
476.   . . . harp when . . . **28, 33.**
478.   . . . reeds
479.   . . . away,
480.   . . . —no. **7-33.**
482.   . . . happy and . . . **71A.**
486.   *Aleel* [*throwing his arms about her feet*]. Let . . . **7-33;** . . . devils, **48, 63.**

398.   We must now carry to "The Lady's Head"
399.   Is dear to all our race. On the green plain
400.   Beside the sea a hundred shepherds live,
401.   To mind her sheep; and when the nightfall comes
402.   They leave a hundred pans of white ewes' milk
403.   Outside their doors, to feed us on our way
404.   From dancing with land sheogues in their raths,
405.   Driven homeward by the dawn.

First Merchant [*making a sign upon the air*]. Obey or suffer.

406.   *The Sheogue.* The sign of evil burns upon our hearts,
407.   And we obey.
     [*They crowd through the window, and take out of the bags a small
     bag each. They are less than the size of men and women, and are
     dressed in green jackets, with red caps, trimmed with shells.*]

First Merchant.   And now begone—begone!

                          [*They go.*]

487. And dearth and plenty, mend what He has made,
488. For when we labour in vain and eye still sees,
489. Heart breaks in vain.

Cathleen. How would that quiet end?

490. *Aleel.* How but in healing?

Cathleen. You have seen my tears,
491. And I can see your hand shake on the floor.

492. *Aleel* [*faltering*]. I thought but of healing. He was angelical.

493. *Cathleen* [*turning away from him*]. No, not angelical, but of the old
       gods,
494. Who wander about the world to waken the heart—
495. The passionate, proud heart—that all the angels,
496. Leaving nine heavens empty, would rock to sleep.
       [*She goes to the oratory door; Aleel holds his clasped hands towards
       her for a moment hesitatingly, and then lets them fall beside him.*

497. *Cathleen.* Do not hold out to me beseeching hands.
498. This heart shall never waken on earth. I have sworn,
499. By her whose heart the seven sorrows have pierced,
500. To pray before this altar until my heart
501. Has grown to Heaven like a tree, and there
502. Rustled its leaves, till Heaven has saved my people.

503. *Aleel.* [*who has risen*]. When one so great has spoken of love to one

---

487. And death and plenty (plenty, **31, 46, 48, 52, 63**) mend . . ., **7-48, 52,
       63.**
488. . . . sees **7-80.**
490. . . . tears. **7-33** ; . . . tears **46-80.**
492. [set as two short lines] **71A.**
494. . . . to awaken the . . . — **71A, 73, 76-80.**
495. . . . heart that . . . angels **7-33** ; . . . passionate proud . . ., **48, 63.**
496. . . . empty would . . . . **7-33.**
       Directions after 496. [. . . *the chapel door; . . . .*] **7-33** ; [. . . *to chapel
       door; (door.* **48, 63**) *Aleel . . . .*] **46-80.**
498. . . . sworn **7-33, 48, 63.**
499. . . . pierced **7-33.**
502. . . . leaves till . . . . **7-33.**

408. I bid them go for being garrulous
409. And flighty creatures—they had soon begun
410. To deafen us with their sea gossip. Now
411. We must go bring more money. Brother, brother,
412. I long to see my master's face again,
413. For I turn homesick.

Second Merchant.   I too tire of toil.
[*They go out, and return as before, with their bags full.*]

414. *Second Merchant* [*pointing to the oratory*]. How may we gain
   this woman for our lord?
415. This pearl, this turquoise fastened in his crown
416. Would make it shine like His we dare not name.
417. Now that the winds are heavy with our kind,
[539] 418. Might we not kill her, and bear off her spirit

504.   So little as I, though to deny him love,
505.   What can he but hold out beseeching hands,
506.   Then let them fall beside him, knowing how greatly
507.   They have overdared?
        [*He goes towards the door of the hall. The Countess Cathleen takes
        a few steps towards him.*

Cathleen.   If the old tales are true,
508.   Queens have wed shepherds and kings beggar-maids;
509.   God's procreant waters flowing about your mind
510.   Have made you more than kings or queens; and not you
511.   But I am the empty pitcher.

Aleel.   Being silent,
512.   I have said all, yet let me stay beside you.

513. *Cathleen.* No, no, not while my heart is shaken. No,
514.   But you shall hear wind cry and water cry,
515.   And curlew cry, and have the peace I longed for.

516. *Aleel.* Give me your hand to kiss.

Cathleen.   I kiss your forehead.

---

504.   . . . I, although to . . ., **7-33.**
505.   . . . hands **7-31.**
507.   . . . true
508.   . . . beggar maids; **7-31.**
510.   . . . you, **48, 63**; . . . kings and queens; . . . **73, 76-80.**
511.   . . . silent **73, 76-80.**
512.   . . . all—farewell, farewell; and yet no, **7-33**; . . . all; yet . . . . **48, 63.**
513-515.   [lacking] **7-33.**
513.   . . . . No. **71A.**
515.   . . . curlews . . . . **46-49, 63.**
516.   . . . kiss your brow, **7-33.**
516a.   But will not say farewell. I am often weary,
516b.   And I would hear the harp-string.
        Aleel.   I cannot stay,
516c.   For I would hide my sorrow among the hills—
516d.   Listen, listen (listen, **31, 33**) the hills are calling me.
                            [*They listen for a moment.*]
516e.   *Cathleen.* I hear the cry of curlew.
        Aleel.   Then I will out
516f.   Where I can hear wind cry and water cry
516g.   And curlew cry: how does the saying go
516h.   That calls them the three oldest cries in the world? **7-33.**

[540] 419.   Before the mob of angels were astir?
                 [*A number of little bags fall from his big leather one.*]

       420. *First Merchant.* Who tore the bag?

           Second Merchant.   The finger of priest John,
       421.   When he fled through the leather. I had thought
       422.   Because his was an old and little spirit
       423.   The tear would hardly matter.

           First Merchant.   This comes, brother,
       424.   Of stealing souls that are not rightly ours.
       425.   If we would win this turquoise for our lord,
       426.   It must go dropping down of its free will.   [*He listens.*]
       427.   The noise wakened the household. While you spoke
       428.   I heard chairs moved, and heard folk's shuffling feet.
[541] 429.   We still have time—they search the distant rooms.

517. And yet I send you from me. Do not speak;
518. There have been women that bid men to rob
519. Crowns from the Country-under-Wave or apples
520. Upon a dragon-guarded hill, and all
521. That they might sift the hearts and wills of men,
522. And trembled as they bid it, as I tremble
523. That lay a hard task on you, that you go,
524. And silently, and do not turn your head.
525. Good-bye; but do not turn your head and look;
526. Above all else, I would not have you look.

[Aleel goes.

527. I never spoke to him of his wounded hand,
528. And now he is gone. [*She looks out.*]
529. I cannot see him, for all is dark outside.
530. Would my imagination and my heart
531. Were as little shaken as this holy flame!

[*She goes slowly into the oratory. The distant sound of an alarm bell. The two Merchants enter hurriedly.*

516i. Farewell, farewell, I will go wander among them,
516j. Because there is no comfort under a roof-tree.

[*He goes out.*] **7-33.**

517-528. [lacking] **7-33.**
517. . . . speak. **48, 63.**
519. . . . Country-under-Wave, or . . . **48, 63.**
521. . . . sift men's hearts . . . wills, **46-80.**
524. . . . head; **46-80.**
525. Goodbye; . . .; **46, 49, 51, 56a-62, 66, 67, 72-80.**
527. . . . spoke about his . . ., **63.**
529. *Cathleen* [*looking through the door after him*]. I . . . him. He has come to the great door. **7-33.**
530. I must go pray. Would that my heart and mind **7-33.**
531. . . . this candle-light. **7-33**; . . . flame. **48, 63.**
Directions after 531. [. . . *goes into* (*goes slowly into* **46-49**) *the chapel. The two . . . enter.*] **7-49**; [. . . *into the chapel. The distant* . . . .] **51-80.**
531a. *Second Merchant.* Who was the man that came from the great door
531b. While we were still in the shadow?
First Merchant. Aleel, her lover.
531c. *Second Merchant.* It may be that he has turned her thought from us
531d. And we can gather our merchandise in peace.
531e. *First Merchant.* No, no, for she is kneeling.
Second Merchant. Shut the door.
531f. Are all our drudges here?
First Merchant [*closing the chapel door*]. I bid them follow.
531g. Can you not hear them breathing upon the stairs? **7-33.**

430.   Call hither now the sowlths and tevishies.

431.   *Second Merchant* [*going to the window*]. There are none here. They
             tired and strayed from hence—

432.   Unwilling labourers.

       First Merchant.   I will draw them in.
                                          [*He cries through the window.*]

433.   Come hither, you lost souls of men, who died
434.   In drunken sleep, and by each other's hands,
435.   When they had bartered you away to us
436.   At Shemus Rua's. Hither, tevishies,
437.   Who mourn among the scenery of your sins,
438.   Turning to animal and reptile forms
439.   —The visages of passions. Hither, sowlths;
440.   Leave marshes and the reed-encumbered pools,

532. *Second Merchant.* They are ringing the alarm, and in a moment
533.   They'll be upon us.

   First Merchant [*going to a door at the side*]. Here is the Treasury.
534.   You'd my commands to put them all to sleep.

531h.   I have sat this hour under the elder-tree. **7-33**
532-533.   [lacking] **7-49.**
  532.   . . . alarm and . . . **52.**
  533.   . . . Treasury, (treasury, **52**) **51-72, 74-80.**

  534.   *First Merchant.* And whence now, brother?
      Second Merchant.   Tubber-vanach crossroads, **5, 6.**
534a.[1]   Where I in image of a nine-monthed bonyeen
534b.   Sat down upon my haunches. Father John
534c.   Came, sad and moody, murmuring many prayers.
534d.   I seemed as though I came from his own sty.
534e.   He saw the one brown ear—the breviary dropped—
534f.   He ran—I ran—I ran into the quarry;
534g.   He fell a score of yards. The man was dead.
534h.   And then I thrust his soul into the bag,
534i.   And hurried home. His right hand, on the way—
534j.   The hand that blessed the poor and raised the host—
534k.   Tore through the leather with sharp piety,
534l.   And he escaped me.
      First Merchant. With this priest John dead, **5, 6.**
534m.   We shall be too much thronged with souls to-morrow.
534n.   *Second Merchant.* My chosen venture was to kill this man,
534o.   And yours to rob the Countess. You fare ill.
534p.   I found you sitting drowsed and motionless,
534q.   Your chin bowed to your knees, while on all sides,
534r.   Bat-like, from bough, and roof, and window ledge,
534s.   Clung evil souls of men, and in the woods,
534t.   Like streaming flames, floated upon the winds
534u.   The elemental creatures.
      First Merchant.   I fare ill!
534v.   This holy Countess prayed so long and hard,
534w.   That doors and windows barred with piety
534x.   Defied me and my drudges out of Hell.
534y.   But now she is fallen asleep over her prayers;
      [*He points to the oratory door. They peer through cautiously.*]
534z.   She lies worn out upon the altar steps:
534aa.   A labourer, tired of ploughing His hard fields, **5, 6.**

[1] The variants of 534 in **5, 6** are listed first; then the variants of 534 in **7-33**; finally the variants of 534 in **46-49.**

441. You shapeless fires, that once were souls of men,
442. And are a fading wretchedness.

Second Merchant.   They come not.

443. *First Merchant* [*making a sign upon the air*]. Come hither, sowlths and
      tevishies.

Second Merchant. I hear
444. A crying as of storm-distempered reeds.
445. And now the sowlths and tevishies rise up
446. Like steam out of the earth; the grass and leaves
447. Shiver and shrink away and sway about,
448. Blown by unnatural gusts of ice-cold air.

449. *First Merchant.* One are they with all forces of decay—
450. Ill longings, madness, lightning, hail and drouth.
      [*The darkness fills with vague forms, some animal shapes, some
      human, some mere nebulous lights.*]

534bb. And deafening His closed ears with cries on cries
534cc. Hoping to draw His hands down from the stars
534dd. To take the people from us.
        Second Merchant.   **We must hurry. 5, 6.**

534.   *Second Merchant.* I had bid you rob her treasury, and yet **7-33.**
534a.   I found you sitting drowsed and motionless,
534b.   Your chin bowed to your knees, while on all sides,
534c.   Bat-like from bough and roof and window-ledge,
534d.   Clung evil souls of men, and in the woods,
534e.   Like streaming flames (flames, **33**) floated upon the winds, (winds
        33)
534f.   The elemental creatures.
        First Merchant.   I have fared ill, (ill; **33**)
534g.   She prayed so hard I could not cross the threshold
534h.   Till this young man had turned her prayer to dreams.
534i.   You have had a man to kill, (kill: **33**) how have you fared?
534j.   *Second Merchant.* I lay in the image of a nine-monthed bonyeen,
534k.   By Tubber-vanach cross-roads: Father John
534l.   Came, sad and moody, murmuring many prayers;
534m.   I seemed as though I came from his own sty;
534n.   He saw the one brown ear; the breviary dropped;
534o.   He ran; I ran, I ran into the quarry, (quarry; **33**)
534p.   He fell a score of yards.
        First Merchant.   Now that he is dead
534q.   We shall be too much thronged with souls to-morrow.
534r.   Did his soul escape you?
        Second Merchant.   I thrust it in the bag.
534s.   But the hand that blessed the poor and raised the Host
534t.   Tore through the leather with sharp piety. **7-33.**

534.   *First Merchant.* Although I bid you rob her treasury, **46-49.**
534a.   I find you sitting drowsed and motionless,
534b.   And yet you understand that while it's full
534c.   She'll bid against us and so bribe the poor
534d.   That our great Master'll lack his merchandise.
534e.   You know that she has brought into this house
534f.   The old and ailing that are pinched the most
534g.   At such a time (time, **48**) and so should be bought cheap.
534h.   You've seen us sitting in the house in the wood,
534i.   While the snails crawled about the window-pane
534j.   And the mud floor, and not a soul to buy;
534k.   Not even the wandering fool's nor one of those
534l.   That when the world goes wrong must rave and talk,
534m.   Until they are as thin as a cat's ear.
534n.   But all that's nothing; you sit drowsing there.
534o.   With your back hooked, your chin upon your knees.
534p.   *Second Merchant.* How could I help it? For she prayed so hard **46-49.**

451.   Come you—and you—and you, and lift these bags.

452.   *A Tevish.* We are too violent—mere shapes of storms.

453.   *First Merchant.* Come you—and you—and you, and lift these bags.

454.   *A Sowlth.* We are too feeble, fading out of life.

455.   *First Merchant.* Come you, and you, who are the latest dead,
456.   And still wear human shape—the shape of power.
            [*The two robbing peasants of the last act come forward. Their faces
            have withered from much pain.*]
457.   Now, brawlers, lift the bags of gold.

        First Peasant.   Aye, aye!
458.   Unwillingly, unwillingly; for her,
459.   Whose gold we bear upon our shoulders thus,
460.   Has endless pity even for lost souls

535. *Second Merchant.* Some angel or else her prayers protected them.
[*Goes into the Treasury and returns with bags of treasure. First Merchant has been listening at the oratory door.*]

534q. I could not cross the threshold till her lover
534r. Had turned her thoughts to dream.
First Merchant. Well, well, to labour. **46-49.**

535. *Second Merchant.* We should half stifle if she woke and prayed. **5, 6;** *First Merchant.* Well, well, to labour—here is the treasury door. **7-33;** *First Merchant.* There is the treasury door and time runs on. **46-49.**

Directions after 535. [*They go out by the left-hand door, and enter again in a little while, carrying full bags upon their shoulders.*] **5-33.**

535a.[1] *First Merchant.* Brave thought, brave thought—a shining thought of mine!
535b. She now no more may bribe the poor—no more
535c. Cheat our great master of his merchandise,
535d. While our heels dangle at the house in the woods,
535e. And grass grows on the threshold, and snails crawl
535f. Along the window-pane and the mud floor.
535g. Brother, where wander all these dwarfish folk,
535h. Hostile to men, the sheogues (people **7-33**) of the tides? **5-33.**
535i. *Second Merchant* [*opening the great windows, and showing the tops of the trees*]. There are none here. They tired and strayed from hence; **5, 6;** *Second Merchant* [*going to the door*]. They are gone. They have already wandered away, **7-33.**
535j. Unwilling labourers.
First Merchant. I will draw them in. (will call them hither. **7-33**)
[*He cries through the* (*He opens the* **7-33**) *window.*] **5-33.**
535k. Come hither, hither, hither, water folk: (water-folk: **33**)
535l. Come (Come, **33**) all you elemental populace;
535m. Leave lonely the long-hoarding surges: leave
535n. The cymbals of the waves to clash alone,
535o. And, shaking the sea tangles (sea-tangles **33**) from your hair,
535p. Gather about us. [*After a pause.*] I can hear a sound
535q. As from waves beating upon distant strands; **5-33.**
535r. And now the sheogues, like a surf of light, **5, 6;** And the sea creatures, (sea-creatures, **33**) like a surf of light, **7-33.**
535s. Pour eddying through the pathways of the oaks; **5-33.**
535t. And as they come, the sentient grass and leaves
535u. Bow towards them, and the tall, drouth-jaded oaks
535v. Fondle the murmur of their flying feet.
535w. *Second Merchant.* The green things love unknotted hearts and minds; **5-33.**

---

[1] Variants of 535 in **5-33** and **46-49** are grouped and listed separately.

461.　In her good heart. At moments, now and then,
462.　When plunged in horror, brooding each alone,
463.　A memory of her face floats in on us.
464.　It brings more plumed miseries, half repose,
465.　And we wail one to other—we obey,
466.　For heaven's many-angled star reversed
467.　—Now sign of evil—burns into our hearts.

468. *First Merchant.* When these last bags lie at "The Lady's Head
469.　The burning shall give over—now begone.

　　　　　　[They go, and the forms and lights vanish also.]

470.　I bid them go, for they are lonely things,
471.　And when they see ought living love to sigh.
472.　*[Pointing to the oratory.]* Brother, I hear a sound in there—a
　　　　sound

535x.   And neither one with angels or with us,

535y.   Nor risen in arms with evil or (nor **7-33**) with good, **5-33.**

535z.   In laughter roves (rose **6**) the litter of the waves. [*A crowd of faces*
         *fill up the darkness outside the window. A sheogue (figure **7-33**) separates*
         *from the others, (others **7-33**) and speaks. (and standing in the window,*
         speaks. **5, 6**)] **5-33.**

535aa.   *The Sheogue. (Spirit.* **7-33**) We come unwillingly, for she whose
         gold **5-33.**

535bb.   We must now carry to the house in the woods (wood **28**)

535cc.   Is dear to all our race. On the green plain,

535dd.   Beside the sea, a hundred shepherds live

535ee.   To mind her sheep; and when the nightfall comes

535ff.   They leave a hundred pans of white ewes' milk

535gg.   Outside their doors, to feed us on our way (us when the dawn
         7-33) **5-33.**

535hh.   From dancing with land sheogues in their raths, **5, 6**; Has driven
         us out of Finbar's ancient house, **7-33.**

535ii.   And broken the long dance under the hill. **7-33.**

535jj.   Driven homeward by the dawn.
         First Merchant [*making a sign upon the air*]. Obey, or suffer. **5, 6**;
         First Merchant [*making a sign upon the air*]. Obey! I make a sign
         upon your hearts. **7-33.**

535kk.   *The Sheogue. (Spirit.* **7-33**) The sign of evil burns upon our hearts,
         5-33.

535ll.   And we obey.
         [*They crowd through the window, and take out of the bags a small*
         bag each. They are less than the size of men and women, and are
         dressed in green jackets, with red caps, trimmed with shells. (each.
         They are dressed in green robes and have ruddy hair. They are a little
         less than the size of men and women. **7-33**)]
         First Merchant.   And now begone—begone! [*They go.*] **5-33.**

535mm.   I bid them go, for, being garrulous

535nn.   And flighty creatures, they had soon begun

535oo.   To deafen us with their sea gossip. (sea-gossip. **33**) Now

535pp.   We must go bring more money. Brother, brother,

535qq.   I long to see my master's face again,

535rr.   For I turn homesick.
         Second Merchant.   I too tire of toil.
         [*They go out, and return as before, with their bags full.*] **5-33.**

         Directions after 535. [*Second Merchant goes out. First Merchant sits*
         cross-legged against a pillar, yawns and stretches.] **46-49.**

535a.   *First Merchant.* And so I must endure the weight of the world,
         (world. **48**) **46-49.**

535b.   Far from my Master and the revelry, **46-49.**

473.   That troubles me.

Second Merchant [going to the door of the oratory and peering through it].

Upon the altar steps

474.   The Countess tosses, murmuring in her sleep

[536]   475.   A broken paternoster.

[The First Merchant goes to the door and stands beside him.]

She's grown still.

[538]   476. *First Merchant.* A great plan floats into my mind—no wonder,

[544]   477.   For I come from the ninth and mightiest Hell,

[545]   478.   Where all are kings. I'll wake her from her sleep,

479.   And mix with all her thoughts, a thought to serve.

[He calls through the door.]

535c.	That's lasted since—shaped as a worm—he bore **46-49**.
535d.	The knowledgable pippin in his mouth
535e.	*To the first woman.* [*Second Merchant returns with bags.*] Where are those dancers gone?
535f.	They knew they were to carry it on their backs.
535g.	*Second Merchant.* I heard them breathing but a moment since,
535h.	But now they are gone, being unsteadfast things.
535i.	*First Merchant.* They knew their work. It seems that they imagine
535j.	We'd do such wrong to our great Master's name
535k.	As to bear burdens on our backs as men do.
535l.	I'll call them, and who'll dare to disobey?
535m.	Come, all you elemental populace (populace, **48**)
535n.	From Cruachan and Finbar's ancient house. (house, **48**)
535o.	Come, break up the long dance under the hill,
535p.	Or if you lie in the hollows of the sea,
535q.	Leave lonely the long hoarding surges, leave
535r.	The cymbals of the waves to clash alone,
535s.	And shaking the sea-tangles (sea tangles **48**) from your hair
535t.	Gather about us. [*The Spirits gather under the arches.*]
	Second Merchant. They come. Be still a while. [*Spirits dance and sing.*] **46-49**
535u.	*First Spirit* [*singing*]. Our hearts are sore, but we come **46-49**.
535v.	Because we have heard you call.
535w.	*Second Spirit.* Sorrow has made me dumb.
535x.	*First Spirit.* Her shepherds at nightfall
535y.	Lay many a plate and cup
535z.	Down by the trodden brink,
535aa.	That when the dance break up
535bb.	We may have meat and drink.
535cc.	Therefore our hearts are sore;
535dd.	And though we have heard and come (come, **48**)
535ee.	Our crying filled the shore.
535ff.	*Second Spirit.* Sorrow has made me dumb.
535gg.	*First Merchant.* What lies in the waves should be indifferent
535hh.	To good and evil, and yet it seems that these,
535ii.	Forgetful of their pure, impartial sea,
535jj.	Take sides with her.
	Second Merchant. Hush, hush, and still your feet.
535kk.	You are not now upon Maeve's dancing-floor.
535ll.	*A Spirit.* O, look what I have found, a string of pearls!
	[*They begin taking jewels out of bag.*] **46-49**.
535mm.	*Second Merchant.* You must not touch them, put them in the bag,
535nn.	And now take up the bags upon your backs
535oo.	And carry them to Shemus Rua's house
535pp.	On the wood's border.
	Spirits. No, no, no, no! (no. **48**) **46-49**.

[546] 480.   May we be well remembered in your prayers.
                   [*The Countess Kathleen wakes, and comes to the door of the
                   oratory. The Merchants descend into the room again. She
                   stands at the top of the stone steps.*]

[547] 481. *Kathleen.* What would you, sirs?

             First Merchant.   We are two merchant men,
[548] 482.   New come from foreign lands. We bring you news.
[551] 483.   Forgive our sudden entry—the great door
[551] 484.   Was open, we came in to seek a face.

[552] 485. *Kathleen.* The door stands always open to receive,
[553] 486.   With kindly welcome, starved and sickly folk,
[554] 487.   Or any who would fly the woeful times.
[555] 488.   Merchants, you bring me news.

             First Merchant.   We saw a man

536. *First Merchant.* She has fallen asleep.

> [*Second Merchant goes out through one of the arches at the back and stands listening. The bags are at his feet.*

Second Merchant.   We've all the treasure now,

537.   So let's away before they've tracked us out.

538. *First Merchant.* I have a plan to win her.

Second Merchant.   You have time enough

539.   If you would kill her and bear off her soul

540.   Before they are upon us with their prayers;

535qq.   *First Spirit.* No, no, let us away; **46-49.**
535rr.   From this we shall not come (come, **48**)
535ss.   Cry out to us who may.
535tt.   *Second Spirit.* Sorrow has made me dumb. [*They go.*]
535uu.   *Second Merchant.* They're gone, for little do they care for me,
535vv.   And if I called they would but turn and mock,
535ww.   But you they dare not disobey.
         First Merchant [*rising*].   These dancers
535xx.   Are always the most troublesome of spirits.
         [*He comes down the stage and stands facing the arches. He makes a gesture of command. The Spirits come back whimpering. They lift the bags and go out. Three speak as they are taking up the bags.*] **46-49.**
535yy.   *First Spirit.* From this day out we'll never dance again.
535zz.   *Second Spirit.* Never again.
         Third Spirit.   Sorrow has made me dumb. **46-49.**

536.   *Second Merchant* [*pointing to the oratory*]. How may we gain this woman for our lord? **5-33**; *Second Merchant* [*looking into chapel (into the chapel* **48**) *door*]. She has heard nothing; she . . . . **46-49**; . . . now. **52.**
         Directions after 536. [lacking] **5-49.**
536a.   This pearl, this turquoise fastened in his crown **5-33.**
536b.   Would make it shine like His we dare not name. **5-33**; Our Lord would be well pleased if we could win her. **46-49.**
536c.   Now that the winds are heavy with our kind, **5-49.**
537-538. [lacking] **5-49.**
538.   . . . enough, **52.**
539.   Might we not kill her, and . . . her spirit **5-49**; . . . soul, **52.**
540.   Before the mob of angels were astir? **5-49**; . . . their preyers; **52.**
         Directions after 540. [*A number of little bags fall from his big leather one.*] **5, 6**; [*A diadem and a heap of jewels fall from the bag.*] **7-33.**
540a.   *First Merchant.* Who tore the bag?
         Second Merchant.   The finger of priest (Priest **33**) John **5-33.**

[556]   489.   Heavy with sickness in the bog of Allan,
557   490.   Whom you had bid buy cattle. Near Fair Head
558   491.   We saw your grain ships lying all becalmed
[559]   492.   In the dark night, and not less still than they
560   493.   Burned all their mirrored lanthorns in the sea.

[561]   494.   *Kathleen.* My thanks to God, to Mary, and the angels,
[562]   495.   I still have bags of money, and can buy
[562]   496.   Meal from the merchants who have stored it up,
563   497.   To prosper on the hunger of the poor.
[564]   498.   You have been far, and know the signs of things:
[563]   499.   When will this yellow vapour no more hang
     500.   And creep about the fields, and this great heat
     501.   Vanish away—and grass show its green shoots?

[565-566]   502.   *First Merchant.* There is no sign of change—day copies
day,

541.   They search the Western Tower.

First Merchant.   That may not be.
542.   We cannot face the heavenly host in arms.
543.   Her soul must come to us of its own will;

540b.   When he fled through the leather. I had thought **5-33.**
540c.   Because his was an old and little spirit
540d.   The tear would hardly matter.
        First Merchant.   This comes, brother (brother, **6-33**)
540e.   Of stealing souls that are not rightly ours. **5-33.**
 541.   If we would win this turquoise for our lord, (lord **46-49**) **5-49** ; . . .
        western tower . . . . **52** ; . . . be; **63** ; . . . be **84.**
542.   [lacking] **5-49** ; . . . arms; **63.**
543.   It must go dropping down of its freewill. (free will; **46-49**) **5-49** ;[1]
        . . . will, **51-67, 72-80.**
        Directions after **543.** [*He listens.*] **5, 6.**
543a.   She will have heard the noise. She will stifle us **7-33.**
543b.   With holy names. [*He goes to the oratory door and opens it a little, and
        then closes it.*] No (No, **28, 33**) she has fallen asleep. **7-33.**
543c.   *First (Second* **7-33**) *Merchant.* The noise wakened the household.
        While you spoke **5-33.**
543d.   I heard chairs moved, and heard folk's (their **28**) shuffling feet.
        5-33.
543e.   And now they are coming hither.
        A Voice [*within*].   It was here. **7-33.**
543f.   *Another Voice.* No, further away.
        Another Voice. It was in the western tower (tower. **18-33**)
543g.   *Another Voice.* Come quickly; we will search the western tower. **7-33.**
543h.   *First Merchant.* We still have time—they search the distant rooms.
        5-33.
543i.   Call hither now the sowlths and tevishes. (the fading and the un-
        fading fires. **7-33**)
543j.   *Second Merchant* [*going to the window*]. There are none here. They
        tired and strayed from hence—**5-33.**
543k.   Unwilling labourers.
        First Merchant.   I will draw them in. [*He cries through the window.*]
543l.   Come hither, you lost souls of men, who died
543m.   In drunken sleep, and by each other's hands, (hands **7-33**)
543n.   When they had bartered you away to us (you—come hither all
        7-33) **5-33.**
543o.   At Shemus Rua's: hither, thivishes, **5, 6.**
543p.   Who mourn among the scenery of your sins, **5-33.**
543q.   Turning to animal and reptile forms, **5-33.**

[1] Succeeding lines in **46-49** begin at 543iii.

[567] 503. Green things are dead—the cattle too are dead,
504. Or dying—and on all the vapour hangs
505. And fattens with disease and glows with heat.
506. In you is all the hope of all the land.

568 507. *Kathleen.* And heard you of the demons who buy souls?

569 508. *First Merchant.* There are some men who hold they have
wolves' heads,
[570] 509. And say their limbs, dried by the infinite flame,
[571] 510. Have all the speed of storms ; others again
572 511. Say they are gross and little; while a few
573 512. Will have it they seem much as mortals are,
[574] 513. But tall and brown and travelled, like us, lady.
[575] 514. Yet all agree there's power in their looks
[576] 515. That makes men bow, and flings a casting net
577 516. About their souls, and that all men would go

543r.   The visages of passions: hither, sowlths; (passions; hither, hither—
        7-33) **5-33**.
543s.   Leave marshes and the reed-encumbered pools,
543t.   You shapeless fires, that were the souls of men,
543u.   And are a fading wretchedness.
        Second Merchant.   They come not.
543v.   *First Merchant* [*making a sign upon the air*]. Come hither, sowlths
        and thivishes (Come hither, hither, hither. **7-33**)
        Second Merchant.   I hear (I can hear **7-33**) **5-33**.
543w.   A crying as of storm-distempered reeds.
543x.   And now the sowlths and thivishes (the fading and the unfading
        fires **7-33**) rise up
543y.   Like steam out of the earth; the grass and leaves
543z.   Shiver and shrink away and sway about,
543aa. Blown by unnatural gusts of ice-cold air. **5-33**.
543bb. *First Merchant.* One are they with all forces of decay, **5, 6**; They
        are one with all the beings of decay, **7-33**.
543cc. Ill longings, madness, lightning, hail (hail, **6**) and drouth. [*The
        darkness fills with vague forms, some animal shapes, some human, some
        mere nebulous lights.*] **5, 6**; Ill longings, madness, lightning, famine,
        drouth. [*The whole stage is gradually filled with vague forms, some
        animal shapes, some human, some mere lights.*] **7-33**.
543dd. Come you—and you—and you, and lift these bags. **5-33**.
543ee. *A Thivish.* (*Spirit.* **7-33**) We are too violent: (violent; **7-33**) mere
        shapes of storm. **5-33**.
543ff. *First Merchant.* Come you—and you—and you, and lift these bags.
543gg. *A Sowlth.* (*Spirit.* **7-33**) We are too feeble, fading out of life.
543hh. *First Merchant.* Come you, and you, who are the latest dead,
543ii. And still wear human shape: the shape of power. **5-33**.
        [*The two robbing peasants of the last scene come forward. Their
        faces have withered from much pain.*]
543jj. Now, brawlers, lift the bags of gold.
        First Peasant.   Ay, Ay! (Yes, yes! **7-33**) **5-33**.
543kk. Unwillingly, unwillingly; for she,
543ll. Whose gold we bear upon our shoulders thus,
543mm. Has endless pity even for lost souls
543nn. In her good heart. At moments, now and then,
543oo. When plunged in horror, brooding each alone,
543pp. A memory of her face floats in on us.
543qq. It brings a crowned misery, half repose,
543rr. And we wail one to other; we obey,
543ss. For heaven's many-angled star reversed,
543tt. Now sign of evil, burns into our hearts. **5-33**.
543uu. *First Merchant.* When these last bags lie at the house in the woods
        5, 6; *First Merchant.* When these pale sapphires and these diadems
        7-33.

[578]   517.   And barter those poor flames—their spirits—only
579   518.   You bribe them with the safety of your gold.

[580]   519.   *Kathleen.* Praise be to God, to Mary, and the angels,
[580]   520.   That I am wealthy. Wherefore do they sell?
[588]   521.   Is the green grave so terrible?

                   First Merchant.   Some sell
[590]   522.   Because they will not see their children die,
591   523.   And some because their neighbours sold before,
592   524.   And some because there is a kind of joy
593   525.   In casting hope away, in losing joy,
594   526.   In ceasing all resistance, in at last
595   527.   Opening one's arms to the eternal flames,
[596]   528.   In casting all sails out upon the wind:
597   529.   To this—full of the gaiety of the lost—
598   530.   Would all folk hurry if your gold were gone.

544.   But being of the ninth and mightiest Hell,
545.   Where all are kings, I have a plan to win it.

543vv.   And these small bags of money are in our house, **7-33**.
543ww.   The burning shall give over; (over—**7-33**) now begone. **5-33**.
          [*They go, and the forms and lights vanish also.*] **5, 6.**
543xx.   *Second Merchant* [*lifting the diadem to put it upon his head*] No—no—
          no[1] **7-31**.
543yy.   I will carry the diadem.
          First Merchant.   No, brother, not yet. **7-31.**
543xx.[2]   *Second Merchant* [*lifting the diadem to put it upon his head*] No—no—
          no. I will carry the diadem. **33.**
543yy.   *First Merchant.* No, brother, not yet.[3] **33.**
543zz.   For none can carry her treasures wholly away
543aaa.   But spirits that are too light for good and evil,
543bbb.   Or, being evil, can remember good. **7-33.**
543ccc.   *First Merchant.* I bid them go, for they are lonely things, **5, 6**;
          Begone. I (Begone! [*The spirits vanish*]. I **33**) bad (bade **18-33**)
          them go, for they are lonely, **7-33.**
543ddd.   And when they see aught living love to sigh. **5-33.**
543eee.   [*Pointing to the oratory.*] Brother, I hear (heard **7-33**) a sound in
          there—a sound
543fff.   That troubles me.
          Second Merchant [*going to the door of the oratory and peering through it*].
                      Upon the altar steps
543ggg.   The Countess tosses, murmuring in her sleep **5-33.**
543hhh.   A broken paternoster. (*Paternoster.* **33**) [*The First Merchant goes to
          the door and stands beside him.*]
                      She's (She is **7-33**) grown still. (still, **7**) **5-33.**
543iii.   *First Merchant.* A great plan floats into my mind—no wonder, **5-33**;
          First Merchant. But I've a plan.
          Second Merchant.   To take her soul to-night? **46-49.**
    544. For I come from the . . ., **5-33**; *First Merchant.* Because I am of
          . . . hell **46-49**; . . . Hell **51, 56a-80**; . . . hell **52.**
    545. . . . kings. I'll (I will **7-33**) wake her from her sleep, **5-33**; Where
          are all kings, . . . plan. [*Voices.*]
          Second Merchant.   Too late; **46-49.**
545a.   And mix with all her thoughts, (thoughts **33**) a thought to serve.
          [*He calls through the door.*] **5-33**; For somebody is stirring in the
          house; the noise **46-49.**
545b.   That the sea creatures made as they came hither,
545c.   Their singing and their endless chattering, **46-49.**

---

[1] Short line in **7-31**.   [2] 543xx, 543yy repeated for clarity.   [3] Short line in **33**.

[599] 531. *Kathleen.* There is a something, merchant, in your voice
600 532.   That makes me fear. When you were telling how
[601] 533.   A man may lose his soul and lose his God,
[602] 534.   Your eyes lighted, and the strange weariness
[602] 535.   That hangs about you, vanished. When you told
[603] 536.   How my poor money serves the people—both—
[604] 537.   Merchants, forgive me—seemed to smile.

      First Merchant.   Man's sins
[604] 538.   Move us to laughter only, we have seen
      539.   So many lands and seen so many men.
[605] 540.   How strange that all these people should be swung
606 541.   As on a lady's shoe-string—under them
607 542.   The glowing leagues of never-ending flame.

[608] 543. *Kathleen.* There is a something in you that I fear—
[609] 544.   A something not of us. Were you not born

546.   Lady, we've news that's crying out for speech.
                    [*Cathleen wakes and comes to door of oratory.*

547.   *Cathleen.* Who calls?

       First Merchant.   Lady, we have brought news.

       Cathleen.   What are you?

548.   *First Merchant.* We are merchants, and we know the book of the
             world

549.   Because we have walked upon its leaves; and there

550.   Have read of late matters that much concern you;

551.   And noticing the castle door stand open,

545d. Has waked the house. I hear the chairs pushed back, **46-49.**
545e. And many shuffling feet. All the old men and women
545f. She's gathered in the house are coming hither.
545g. *A Voice* [*within*]. It was here.
       Another Voice.   No, farther away.
       Another Voice.   It was in the western tower.
545h. *Another Voice.* Come quickly, we will search the western tower.
545i. *First Merchant.* We still have time—they search the distant rooms.
545j. *Second Merchant.* Brother, I heard a sound in there—a sound
545k. That troubles me. [*Going to the door of the oratory and peering through it.*]
                    Upon the altar steps
545l. The Countess tosses, murmuring in her sleep
545m. A broken Paternoster. (paternoster. **48**)
       First Merchant.   Do not fear,
545n. For when she has awaked the prayer will cease.
545o. *Second Merchant.* What, would you wake her?
       First Merchant.   I will speak with her,
545p. And mix with all her thoughts a thought to serve.—**46-49.**
546.   *First Merchant.* May we be well remembered in your prayers! **5-33.**
       Directions after 546. [*The Countess Cathleen wakes, and . . . to the door
       . . . oratory. The Merchants descend into the room again. She stands at the
       top of the stone steps.*] **5-33**; [*. . . of the chapel.*] **46, 49, 52**; [*. . . to the
       door of the chapel.*] **48**; [*. . . of chapel.*] **51, 56a-80.**
547.   What would you, sirs?
                         We are two merchant men, **5-33**; . . . calls?
                              We . . .? **46-67, 72, 74.**
548.   New come from foreign lands. We bring you news. **5-33.**
549, 550.   [lacking] **5-33.**
551.   Forgive our sudden entry: the great door **5-33.**

552.   Came in to find an ear.

Cathleen.   The door stands open
553.   That no one who is famished or afraid
554.   Despair of help or of a welcome with it.
555.   But you have news, you say.

First Merchant.   We saw a man
556.   Heavy with sickness in the bog of Allen,
557.   Whom you had bid buy cattle. Near Fair Head
558.   We saw your grain ships lying all becalmed
559.   In the dark night; and not less still than they,
560.   Burned all their mirrored lanthorns in the sea.

561. *Cathleen.* Thanks be to God there's money in the house
562.   That can buy grain from those who have stored it up
563.   To prosper on the hunger of the poor.
564.   But you've been far and know the signs of things,
565.   When will this famine end?

First Merchant.   Day copies day,

---

552.   Was open, we came in to seek a face. **5-33**; . . . open, **46-80**; Come in . . . **97A.**
552a.   *Cathleen.* The door stands always open to receive, **5-33.**
553.   With kindly welcome, starved and sickly folk, **5-33**; . . . afraid, **46-80.**
554.   Or any who would fly the woful times. **5-33.**
555.   Merchants, you bring me news. (news? **33**)
                            We . . . **5-33;**
  . . . say. (say? **48, 63**)
                            We . . . man, **46-80.**
559.   . . . night, and . . . they **5-33.**
561.   My thanks to God, to Mary, (Mary **46-67, 72, 74**) and the angels, **5-67, 72, 74.**
561a.   I still have bags of money, and can buy **5-33**; That I have money in my treasury, **46-67, 72, 74.**
562.   Meal from the merchants who have stored it up, **5-33**; And can . . . **46-67, 72, 74.**
563.   . . . hungers . . . **28.**
564.   You have been far, and . . . signs (sign **28**) . . . things: **5-33.**
564a.   When will this yellow vapour no more hang **5-49, 63.**
564b.   And creep about the fields, and this great heat
564c.   Vanish away—(away, **46-49, 63**) and grass show its green shoots?
565.   *First Merchant.* There is no sign of change—day . . ., **5-49, 63.**

[618]   552. *Kathleen.* What would you?

         A Peasant.   As we nodded by the fire,
[617-618] 553.   Telling old shannachus we heard a noise
[619-620] 554.   Of falling money. We have searched in vain.

[620]   555. *Kathleen.* You are too timid. I heard naught at all.

         556. *An Old Man.* Aye, we are timid, for a rich man's word
         557.   Can shake our houses, and a moon of drouth
         558.   Shrivel our seedlings in the barren earth;
         559.   We are the slaves of wind, and hail, and flood;
         560.   Fear jogs our elbow in the market-place,
         561.   And nods beside us on the chimney-seat.
         562.   Ill-bodings are as native to our hearts
         563.   As are their spots unto the woodpeckers.

[621-622] 564. *Kathleen.* You need not shake with bodings in this
             house.

                              [*Oona enters from the door to L.*]

566.   And there's no sign of change, nor can it change,
567.   With the wheat withered and the cattle dead.

568.   *Cathleen.* And heard you of the demons who buy souls?

569.   *First Merchant.* There are some men who hold they have wolves'
        heads,
570.   And say their limbs—dried by the infinite flame—
571.   Have all the speed of storms; others, again,
572.   Say they are gross and little; while a few
573.   Will have it they seem much as mortals are,
574.   But tall and brown and travelled—like us, lady—
575.   Yet all agree a power is in their looks
576.   That makes men bow, and flings a casting-net
577.   About their souls, and that all men would go
578.   And barter those poor vapours, were it not
579.   You bribe them with the safety of your gold.

580.   *Cathleen.* Praise God that I am wealthy! Why do they sell?

581.   *First Merchant.* As we came in at the great door we saw

---

566.   [lacking] **5-49, 63** ; . . . change nor . . . change **52** ; . . . change **73, 76-80.**
567.   Green things are dead—the cattle too are dead, (dead—**46-49, 63**)
567a.   Or dying—and on all the vapour hangs (hangs, **46-49, 63**)
567b.   And fattens with disease and glows with heat.
567c.   In you is all the hope of all the land. **5-49, 63.**
569.   . . . wolves . . ., **18, 49, 78.**
570.   . . . limbs, dried . . . flame,
571.   . . .; others again **5-33.**
574.   . . . travelled, like . . ., lady. **5-33** ; . . . us—lady, (Lady, **48, 63**) **46-49, 52, 63.**
576.   . . . casting net **5-31.**
578.   . . . poor flames—their spirits—(spirit—**18, 31**) only **5-33.**
580.   Praise be to God, to Mary, and the angels, (angels **46-67, 72, 74**) **5-67, 72, 74** ; . . . wealthy. Why . . .? **71** ; [set as two short lines] **71A** ; . . . God, that . . .? **73, 76-80.**
580a.   That I am wealthy. (wealthy! **46, 49-62, 66, 67, 72, 74**) Wherefore do they sell? **5-67, 72, 74.**
581-587.   [lacking] **5.**
581.   The demons give a hundred crowns and more **6-33** ; . . . door, we . . . **48, 63** ; . . . doors . . . **73, 76-80.**

[623]   565. *Oona.* The treasure-room is broken in—mavrone—
                 mavrone

624   566. The door stands open, and the gold is gone.

                              [*The peasants raise a lamenting cry.*]

[625]   567. *Kathleen.* Be silent.   [*The cry ceases.*]
                              Saw you any one?

           Oona.   Mavrone,

[626]   568.   That my good mistress should lose all this money.

[627-628] 569. *Kathleen.* You three upon my right hand, ride and ride;
629   570.   I'll give a farm to him who finds the thieves.

                 [*A man with keys at his girdle has entered while she was
                 speaking.*

           571. *A Peasant.* The porter trembles.

           The Porter.   It is all no use;

630   572.   Demons were here. I sat beside the door
631   573.   In my stone nich, and two owls passed me by,

582. Your porter sleeping in his niche—a soul
583. Too little to be worth a hundred pence,
584. And yet they buy it for a hundred crowns.
585. But for a soul like yours, I heard them say,
586. They would give five hundred thousand crowns and more.

587. *Cathleen.* How can a heap of crowns pay for a soul?
588. Is the green grave so terrible a thing?

589. *First Merchant.* Some sell because the money gleams, and some
590. Because they are in terror of the grave,
591. And some because their neighbours sold before,
592. And some because there is a kind of joy
593. In casting hope away, in losing joy,
594. In ceasing all resistance, in at last
595. Opening one's arms to the eternal flames,
596. In casting all sails out upon the wind;
597. To this—full of the gaiety of the lost—
598. Would all folk hurry if your gold were gone.

599. *Cathleen.* There is a something, Merchant, in your voice
600. That makes me fear. When you were telling how
601. A man may lose his soul and lose his God
602. Your eyes were lighted up, and when you told
603. How my poor money serves the people, both—

---

582. For a poor soul like his who lies asleep
582a. By your great door under the porter's niche; **6-33.**
583. A little soul not worth a hundred pence. **6-33**; . . . pence **48, 63.**
584. [lacking] **6-33**; . . . yet they'd buy . . . crowns, **73, 76-80.**
585. But, for . . . , **6-33, 48, 63.**
586. They'd give . . . . **6, 52.**
588. . . . so terrible?
     First Merchant. Some sell
589. Because they will not see their children die, **5.**
590. [lacking] **5.**
596. . . . wind: **5-33.**
599. . . ., merchant, . . . **5-33**; . . . is something, . . . **48, 63.**
601. . . . God, **5-33, 48, 63.**
602. . . . eyes lighted, and the strange weariness
602a. That hangs about you vanished. When you told
603. . . . people—both—**5-33.**

632   574.   Whispering with human voices.

                An Old Man.   God forsakes us.

633   575.   *Kathleen.* Old man, old man, He never closed a door
[634]   576.   Unless one opened. I am desolate,
[635]   577.   For a most sad resolve wakes in my heart:
[636]   578.   But always I have faith. Old men and women
[636-637]   579.   Be silent; He does not forsake the world,
638   580.   But stands before it modelling in the clay
639   581.   And moulding there His image. Age by age
640   582.   The clay wars with His fingers and pleads hard
[641]   583.   For its old, heavy, dull, and shapeless ease;
[642]   584.   At times it crumbles—and a nation falls,
[643]   585.   Now moves awry—and demon hordes are born.
                                        [*The peasants cross themselves.*]
[644]   586.   But leave me now, for I am desolate,

604.   Merchants, forgive me—seemed to smile.

First Merchant.   I laugh
605.   To think that all these people should be swung
606.   As on a lady's shoe-string,—under them
607.   The glowing leagues of never-ending flame.

608. *Cathleen.* There is a something in you that I fear;
609.   A something not of us; were you not born
610.   In some most distant corner of the world?
         [*The Second Merchant, who has been listening at the door, comes
         forward, and as he comes a sound of voices and feet is heard.*

611. *Second Merchant.* Away now—they are in the passage—hurry,
612.   For they will know us, and freeze up our hearts
613.   With Ave Marys, and burn all our skin
614.   With holy water.

First Merchant.   Farewell; for we must ride
615.   Many a mile before the morning come;
616.   Our horses beat the ground impatiently.
         [*They go out. A number of Peasants enter by other door.*

617. *First Peasant.* Forgive us, lady, but we heard a noise.

---

  604.   Merchants, (Merchants 46, 49) forgive . . . smile.
                                     Man's sins **5-49, 63** ;
          Merchants forgive . . . **51, 56a-62, 66, 67, 71E, 72-80.**
  604a.   Move us to laughter only, (only; 46-49, 63) we have seen **5-49, 63.**
  604b.   So many lands and seen so many men. (men, 48, 63).
  605.   How strange that . . . **5-49, 63**
  606.   . . . shoe-string—under . . . **5-33.**
  607.   . . . flame! **33.**
  608.   . . . fear: **5-33** ; . . . fear **48, 63.**
  609.   . . . us. Were (us; but were 46-49) . . . **5-49.**
          Directions after 610. [. . . *door to the right, comes forward,* . . . *comes,*
          (*comes* 33) *a* . . . *heard through the door to his left.*] **5-33** ; [. . . *listening*
          beyond the arches, comes . . . .] **52.**
  611.   *Second Merchant* [*aside to First Merchant*]. Away . . ., **5-33** ; . . . .*the*
          garden—hurry **52.**
  614.   . . . . Farewell: we . . . **5-33.**
          Directions after 616. [. . . *out to R. A* . . . *enter at the same moment by*
          the opposite door.] **5-33** ; [. . . *out by a door at one side. A* . . . *enter.*] **52.**
  617.   [lacking] **5-33** ; . . ., Lady, ... **48, 63.**

645   587.   I hear a whisper from beyond the thunder.

[She steps down from the oratory door.]

646   588.   Yet stay an instant. When we meet again
647   589.   I may have grown forgetful. Oona, take
648   590.   These two—the larder and the dairy keys.

[To a peasant.]

649   591.   But take you this. It opens the small room
[650]   592.   Of herbs for medicine—of helebore,
[650]   593.   Of vervain, monkshood, plantain, and self-heal,
[651]   594.   And all the others; and the book of cures
[651]   595.   Is on the upper shelf. You understand
       596.   Because you doctored goats and cattle once.

[652]   597.   *The Peasant.* Why do you do this, lady—did you see
[653]   598.   Your coffin in a dream?

       Kathleen.   Ah, no, not that,

618. *Second Peasant.* We sat by the fireside telling vanities.

619. *First Peasant.* We heard a noise, but though we have searched the
house

620.   We have found nobody.

Cathleen.   You are too timid,

621.   For now you are safe from all the evil times,
622.   There is no evil that can find you here.

623. *Oona [entering hurriedly].* Ochone! The treasure-room is broken in.
624.   The door stands open, and the gold is gone.

[Peasants raise a lamentable cry.

625. *Cathleen.* Be silent. [*The cry ceases.*] Have you seen nobody?

Oona.   Ochone!

---

618.   *Cathleen.* What would you?
       A Peasant.   As we nodded by the fire, **5-33.**
619.   Telling old shannachus, (histories, **33**) we . . . noise **5-33** ; . . . house,
       48, 63.
620.   Of falling money. We have searched in vain. **5-33** ; . . . timid. **46-49,**
       52, 63.
621.   *Cathleen.* You are too timid. I heard naught at all. **5-33** ; . . . times.
       46-49, 52, 63.
621a. *The Old Peasant.* Ay, we are timid, for a rich man's word **5-33.**
621b. Can shake our houses, and a moon of drouth
621c. Shrivel our seedlings in the barren earth;
621d. We are the slaves of wind, and hail, and flood;
621e. Fear jogs our elbow in the market-place,
621f. And nods beside us on the chimney-seat.
621g. Ill-bodings are as native to (unto **7-33**) our hearts
621h. As are their spots unto the woodpeckers. **5-33.**
622.   *Cathleen.* You need not shake with bodings in this house. [*Oona enters
       from the door to L.*] **5-33.**
623.   *Oona.* The . . . in—mavrone—mavrone (mavrone; **6-33**) **5-33** ;
       Ochone! Ochone! The treasure room . . . in, (in. **51, 56a-62, 66-80**)
       46-80.
624.   . . . open and . . . . **33.**
       Directions after 624.   [*The peasants . . . a lamenting cry.*] **5-33** ; [. . . a
       cry.] **73, 76-80.**
625.   . . . ceases.] Saw you any one?
       Oona.   Mavrone, **5-33.**

[654] 599.　A sad resolve wakes in me. I have heard
655　600.　A sound of wailing in unnumbered hovels,
[656] 601.　And I must go down, down, I know not where.
[657] 602.　Pray for the poor folk who are crazed with famine;
[658] 603.　Pray, you good neighbours.

> [*The peasants all kneel. The Countess Kathleen ascends the steps to the door of the oratory, and turning round, stands there motionless for a little, and then cries in a loud voice.*]

Mary, queen of angels,

[659] 604.　And all you clouds on clouds of saints, farewell.

End of Scene III.

SCENE IV.

[*The Inn of Shemus Rua, as in Scene I. The Two Merchants are sitting, one at each end of the table, with rolls of parchment and many little heaps of gold before them.*]

626.   That my good mistress should lose all this money!

627. *Cathleen.* Let those among you not too old to ride
628.   Get horses and search all the country round.
629.   I'll give a farm to him who finds the thieves.
      [A man with keys at his girdle has come in while she speaks. There
      is a general murmur of 'The porter! the porter!'

630. *Porter.* Demons were here. I sat beside the door
631.   In my stone niche, and two owls passed me by,
632.   Whispering with human voices.

    Old Peasant.   God forsakes us.

633. *Cathleen.* Old man, old man, He never closed a door
634.   Unless one opened. I am desolate
635.   Because of a strange thought that's in my heart;
636.   But I have still my faith; therefore be silent;
637.   For surely He does not forsake the world,
638.   But stands before it modelling in the clay
639.   And moulding there His image. Age by age
640.   The clay wars with His fingers and pleads hard
641.   For its old, heavy, dull and shapeless ease;
642.   But sometimes—though His hand is on it still—

---

626. . . . money. **5-80.**
627. You three upon my right hand, ride and ride; **5-33**; . . . you—not
    . . . ride— **46-80.**
628. [lacking] **5-33**; . . . round, **46-80.**
629. I will give . . . . **7-33.**
    Directions after 629 [. . . *has entered while she was speaking.*] **5-33.**
629a. *A Peasant.* The porter trembles. (trembles **7, 28**)
    The Porter.   It is all no use; **5-33.**
632. . . . voices.
    The Old Peasant. God . . . . **5-33**; . . . voices.
                   Old Merchant. God. . . . **73, 76-80.**
634. . . . desolate. **5-80.**
635. For a most sad resolve wakes in . . . heart: **5-49, 63**; . . . heart: **51-62,**
    66, 67, 72, 74.
636. But always I have faith. Old men and women (women, **7-33**) **5-33.**
637. Be silent. He . . ., **5-33.**
639. . . . age, **48, 63.**
641. . . ., dull, and . . .; **5-33.**
642. At times it crumbles and a nation falls, **5-33.**

605. *First Merchant.* The woman may keep robbing us no
       more,

[681]   606.   For there are only mice now in her coffers.

[682-683] 607. *Second Merchant.* Last night, closed in the image of an
       owl,

684   608.   I hurried to the cliffs of Donegal,

[685-686] 609.   And saw, creeping on the uneasy surge,

[687]   610.   Those ships that bring the woman grain and meal;

[688]   611.   They are five days from us.

       First Merchant.   I hurried East,

[689]   612.   A gray owl flitting, flitting in the dew,

[690]   613.   And saw nine hundred oxen toil through Meath,

[691]   614.   Driven on by goads of iron. They, too, brother,

[691-692] 615.   Are full five days from us.

       Second Merchant.   Five days for traffic,
       [*While they have been speaking the peasants have come*

643.   It moves awry and demon hordes are born.

[Peasants cross themselves.

644.   Yet leave me now, for I am desolate.
645.   I hear a whisper from beyond the thunder.

[She comes from the oratory door.

646.   Yet stay an instant. When we meet again
647.   I may have grown forgetful. Oona, take
648.   These two—the larder and the dairy keys.

[To the Porter.]

649.   But take you this. It opens the small room
650.   Of herbs for medicine, every kind of herb.
651.   The book of cures is on the upper shelf.

652. *Porter.* Why do you do this, lady; did you see
653.   Your coffin in a dream?

    Cathleen.   Ah, no, not that.

654.   But I have come to a strange thought. I have heard
655.   A sound of wailing in unnumbered hovels,
656.   And I must go down, down—I know not where—
657.   Pray for all men and women mad from famine;
658.   Pray, you good neighbours.

[The Peasants all kneel. Countess Cathleen ascends the steps to the door of the oratory, and turning round stands there motionless for a little, and then cries in a loud voice:

                          Mary, Queen of angels,

---

643.   Now moves . . . . [*The peasants . . . .*] **5-33.**
644.   But leave . . . desolate, **5-33** ; . . . desolate, **46-80.**
    Directions after 645. [*She steps down from . . . .*] **5-33.**
    Directions after 648. [*To the Old Peasant.*] **5-33.**
650.   . . . medicine, of hellebore, (hellebore. **73, 76**) **5-67, 72-80.**
650a.   Of vervaine, monkshood, plantain, and self-heal, (self-heal **6-33** ;
    self-heal. **46-67, 72-80**) **5-67, 72-80.**
651.   And all the others; and the book . . . cures **5-33.**
651a.   Is on the upper shelf. You understand (understand, **6-33**) **5-33.**
651b.   Because you doctored goats and cattle once. **5-33.**
652.   *The Old Peasant.* Why . . ., lady—did . . . **5-33** ; . . ., Lady? Did . . .
    48, 63.
653.   . . . that, **5-33.**
654.   A sad resolve wakes in me. I have heard **5-49, 63.**
656.   . . ., down, I . . . where. **5-33.**
657.   . . . for the poor folk who are crazed with famine; **5-33.**
658.   . . ., queen . . ., **5-33** ; . . . angels **73, 76-80.**
    Directions in 658. [. . . *kneel. The Countess . . ., and, turning round,
    stands . . . voice.*] **5-33.**

in, led by Teig and Shemus, who take their stations, one on each side of the door, and keep them marshalled into rude order and encourage them from time to time with gestures and whispered words.]

[705] 616.   Here throng they; since the drouth they go in throngs,

[706] 617.   Like autumn leaves blown by the dreary winds

707   618.   Come, deal—come, deal.

First Merchant.   Who will come deal with us?

[708] 619.   *Shemus.* They're out of spirit, sir, with lack of food,

709   620.   Save four or five. Here, sir, is one of these;

710   621.   The others will gain courage in good time.

[711] 622.   *A Middle-Aged Man.* I come to deal if you give honest price.

[712] 623.   *First Merchant* [*reading in a parchment.*] John Maher, a man
            of substance, with dull mind,

---

659.   And all you clouds on clouds of saints, farewell!

Scene IV

Front Scene.—*A wood near the Castle, as in Scene II. A group of Peasants
pass.*

660. *First Peasant.* I have seen silver and copper, but not gold.

661. *Second Peasant.* It's yellow and it shines.

First Peasant.   It's beautiful.
662.   The most beautiful thing under the sun,
663.   That's what I've heard.

Third Peasant.   I have seen gold enough.

664. *Fourth Peasant.* I would not say that it's so beautiful.

665. *First Peasant.* But doesn't a gold piece glitter like the sun?
666.   That's what my father, who'd seen better days,
667.   Told me when I was but a little boy—
668.   So high—so high, it's shining like the sun,

Scene IV   [lacking] **5-33.**

STAGE DIRECTIONS   Scene.—(Scene. **48**) *A* . . . *II. The Spirits pass one by one
carrying bags.* **46-49**; Scene.—(Scene. **63**) *A* . . . . **51-67, 72-80.**

a.[1] *First Spirit.* I'll never dance another step, not one. **46-49.**

b. *Second Spirit.* Are all the thousand years of dancing done?

c. *Third Spirit.* How can we dance after so great a sorrow?

d. *Fourth Spirit.* But how shall we remember it to-morrow?

e. *Fifth Spirit.* To think of all the things that we forget.

f. *Sixth Spirit.* That's why we groan and why our lids are wet.
       [*The Spirits go out. A group of Peasants pass.*] **46-49.**

660. I . . . . **46-80.**

667. . . . boy **52.**

668. So high, so high—it's . . ., **48, 63**; And but so tall it's . . ., **52.**

[1] Lines a-f appear at the beginning of Scene IV in **46-49** only.

713   624.   And quiet senses and unventurous heart.

[714] 625.   The angels think him safe. Two hundred crowns,

[715] 626.   All for a soul, a little whiff of gas.

[716] 627.   *The Man.* I ask three hundred crowns. You have read there,

717   628.   That no mere lapse of days can make me yours.

[718] 629.   *First Merchant.* There's something more writ here—often at
               night

[719] 630.   He's wakeful from a dread of growing poor.

724   631.   There is this crack in you—two hundred crowns.

               [*The Man takes them and goes.*]

       632.   *Second Merchant.* Come, deal—one would half think you
               had no souls.

728   633.   If only for the credit of your parishes,

       634.   Come, deal, deal, deal, or will you always starve?

       635.   A woman lived here once, she would not deal—

669.   Round and shining, that is what he said.

670.   *Second Peasant.* There's nothing in the world it cannot buy.

671.   *First Peasant.* They've bags and bags of it.
          [*They go out. The two Merchants follow silently. Then Aleel
          passes over the stage singing.*

672.   *Aleel.*   Impetuous heart be still, be still,
673.   Your sorrowful love can never be told,
674.   Cover it up with a lovely tune.
675.   He who could bend all things to His will
676.   Has covered the door of the infinite fold
677.   With the pale stars and the wandering moon.

Scene V

*The house of Shemus Rua. There is an alcove at the back with curtains; in it a
bed, and on the bed is the body of Mary with candles round it. The two Merchants
while they speak put a large book upon a table, arrange money, and so on.*

678.   *First Merchant.* Thanks to that lie I told about her ships
679.   And that about the herdsman lying sick,

     Directions after 671.   [. . . *silently.*] **46-49.**
672-677.   [lacking] **46-49.**
672.   . . . heart, be . . ., **52, 71A** ; . . . still **73, 76-80.**
675.   . . . Will **97A.**
ACT OR SCENE NUMBER   Act III[1] **5, 6** ; Act IV **7-33** ; Scene V **46-97.**
STAGE DIRECTIONS   *The cabin of . . . Rua. The two Merchants are sitting,* (*sitting*
     7-28, 33) *one at each end of the table, with rolls of parchment and many little heaps
     of gold before them.* (*them. Through an open door, at the back, one sees into an inner
     room, in which there is a bed. On the bed is the body of Maire with candles about
     it.* **7-33**) **5-33** ; *Scene.—The* . . . . **46, 49-62, 66-80** ; *Scene. The* . . .
     Merchants, while . . . speak, put . . . . **48, 63.**
678.   The woman may keep robbing us no more, **5-33** ; . . . about the
     ships **73, 76-80.**
679-680.   [lacking] **5-33.**

          [1] Should be Act IV.

636.   She starved—she lies in there with red wallflowers,
637.   And candles stuck in bottles, round her head.

[729]   638.   *A Woman.* What price now will you give for mine?

         First Merchant.   Aye, aye,

[730]   639.   Soft, handsome, and still young—not much, I think.
                     [Reading in the parchment.]

[732]   640.   She has a little jar of new love-letters
[733]   641.   On a high shelf between the pepper-pot
[733-734] 642.   And wood-cased hour-glass.

         Woman.   Oh, the scandalous parchment!

[734, 735] 643.   *First Merchant [reading].* She hides them from her hus-
                  band, who buys horses,

[739]   644.   And is not much at home. You're almost safe.
[739-740] 645.   I give you fifty crowns.   *[She turns to go.]*
                        A hundred, then.
            [She takes them, and goes into the crowd.]

680.   We shall be too much thronged with souls to-morrow.

681. *Second Merchant*. What has she in her coffers now but mice?

682. *First Merchant*. When the night fell and I had shaped myself
683.   Into the image of the man-headed owl,
684.   I hurried to the cliffs of Donegal,
685.   And saw with all their canvas full of wind
686.   And rushing through the parti-coloured sea
687.   Those ships that bring the woman grain and meal.
688.   They're but three days from us.

　　　　Second Merchant.　　　　　　When the dew rose
689.   I hurried in like feathers to the east,
690.   And saw nine hundred oxen driven through Meath
691.   With goads of iron. They're but three days from us.

692. *First Merchant*. Three days for traffic.
　　　　　　　　　　[Peasants crowd in with Teigue and Shemus.

　　　Shemus.　　　　　　Come in, come in, you are welcome.

———————————————————————————————

680. . . . to-morrow **73, 76-80.**
681. *First Merchant*. For there are only mice now in her coffers. **5-33**; . . .
　　now, but . . .? **48, 63.**
682. *Second Merchant*. Last night, closed in the image of an owl, **5-33.**
683. [lacking] **5-33.**
685. . . . saw, creeping on the uneasy surge, **5-33.**
686. [lacking] **5-33.**
687. . . . meal; **5-33**; . . . women . . . . **73, 76-80.**
688. They are five days from us.
　　First Merchant.　　　　　I hurried East,
689. A gray owl flitting, flitting in the dew, **5-33.**
690. . . . oxen toil through Meath, (Meath **7-33**) **5-33**; . . . Meath, **48, 63.**
691. Driven on by goads . . . iron; they, too, brother, **5-33**; . . . us **73, 76,**
　　80.
692. Are full five days from us.
　　Second Merchant.　　　　　Five days for traffic.
　　　　[While they have been speaking the peasants have come in, led by Teig
　　　　and Shemus, who take their stations, one on each side of the door, and
　　　　keep them marshalled into rude order and encourage them from time to
　　　　time with gestures and whispered words.] **5-33.**

[743] 646.   Come—deal, deal, deal. 'Tis but for charity
[744] 647.   We buy such souls at all. A thousand sins
[745] 648.   Made them our master's long before we came.
       649.   Come, deal—come, deal. You seem resolved to starve
       650.   Until your bones show through your skin. Come, deal,
[698] 651.   Or live on nettles, grass, and dandelion.
       652.   Deal. Do you dream the famine shall go by?
       653.   The famine's hale and hearty—it is mine
       654.   And my great master's—it shall no wise cease
       655.   Until our purpose end. The yellow vapour
       656.   That brought it bears it over your dried fields
       657.   And fills with violent phantoms of the lost,
       658.   And grows more deadly as day copies day.
       659.   See how it dims the daylight. Is that peace

693.   That is my wife. She mocked at my great masters,
694.   And would not deal with them. Now there she is;
695.   She does not even know she was a fool,
696.   So great a fool she was.

    Teigue.   She would not eat
697.   One crumb of bread bought with our masters' money,
698.   But lived on nettles, dock, and dandelion.

699.   *Shemus.* There's nobody could put into her head
700.   That death is the worst thing can happen us,
701.   Though that sounds simple, for her tongue grew rank
702.   With all the lies that she had heard in chapel.
703.   Draw to the curtain. [*Teigue draws it.*] You'll not play the fool
704.   While these good gentlemen are there to save you.

705.   *Second Merchant.* Since the drought came they drift about in a
       throng,
706.   Like autumn leaves blown by the dreary winds.
707.   Come, deal—come, deal.

    First Merchant.   Who will come deal with us?

708.   *Shemus.* They are out of spirit, sir, with lack of food,
709.   Save four or five. Here, sir, is one of these;
710.   The others will gain courage in good time.

711.   *Middle-aged Man.* I come to deal—if you give honest price.

712.   *First Merchant* [*reading in a book*]. 'John Maher, a man of substance,
      with dull mind,

693-704.   [lacking] **5-33.**
697.   . . . master's . . ., **46-80.**
700.   . . . Death . . . us. (us; **63**) **46-51, 56a-72, 74** ; . . . Death . . ., **52, 73,**
   76-80.
704.   . . . are here to . . . . **63.**
705.   Here throng they; since the drouth they go in throngs, **5-33.**
707.   . . . us **56a, 72, 74.**
711.   *A Middle-Aged Man.* . . . deal if . . . .
712.   . . . *in a parchment*]. John . . ., **5-33.**

660.   Known to the birds of prey so dread a thing?
661.   They, and the souls obedient to our master,
662.   And those who live with that great other spirit
663.   Have gained an end, a peace, while you but toss
664.   And swing upon a moving balance beam.

Kevin [*a young man, who carries a harp with torn wires*].

[746] 665.   Here, take my soul, for I am tired of it;
[747] 666.   I do not ask a price.

First Merchant [*reading*]. A man of songs—
667.   Alone in the hushed passion of romance,
668.   His mind ran all on sheogues, and on tales
669.   Of Finian labours and the Red-branch kings,
670.   And he cared nothing for the life of man:
671.   But now all changes.

Kevin.   Aye, because her face,

713.   And quiet senses and unventurous heart.
714.   The angels think him safe.' Two hundred crowns,
715.   All for a soul, a little breath of wind.

716.   *Middle-aged Man.* I ask three hundred crowns. You have read there
717.   That no mere lapse of days can make me yours.

718.   *First Merchant.* There is something more writ here—'Often at night
719.   He is wakeful from a dread of growing poor,
720.   And thereon wonders if there's any man
721.   That he could rob in safety.'

    A Peasant.   Who'd have thought it?
722.   And I was once alone with him at midnight.

723.   *Another Peasant.* I will not trust my mother after this.

724.   *First Merchant.* There is this crack in you—two hundred crowns.

725.   *A Peasant.* That's plenty for a rogue.

    Another Peasant.   I'd give him nothing.

726.   *Shemus.* You'll get no more—so take what's offered you.
    [*A general murmur, during which the Middle-aged Man takes money, and slips into background, where he sinks on to a seat.*

727.   *First Merchant.* Has no one got a better soul than that?
728.   If only for the credit of your parishes,

---

713.   ... unventurous. **18, 31.**
714.   ... safe. Two . . ., **5-33.**
716.   *The Man.* I . . . there, (there **46-80**) **5-80.**
718.   There's (There is **7-33**) something . . . —often . . . **5-33**; . . . —
      'often . . . **46, 49, 52.**
719.   ... poor. **5-33.**
720-723. [lacking] **5-33.**
      Directions after 724. [*The Man takes them and goes.*] **5-33.**
725- Directions after 726. [lacking] **5-33.**
727.   *Second Merchant.* Come, deal—one would half think you had no souls. (souls **6**) **5-33.**
728.   If but for credit . . ., **63.**
728a. Come, deal, deal, deal, or will you always starve? **5-33.**
    V.E.P.Y.—F

752-753]   672.   The face of Countess Kathleen dwells with me.
753-754]   673.   The sadness of the world upon her brow—
            674.   The crying of these strings grew burdensome,
[755]   675.   Therefore I tore them—see—now take my soul.

756   676. *First Merchant.* We cannot take your soul, for it is hers.

757]   677. *Kevin.* Ah, take it—take it. It nowise can help her,
[758]   678.   And, therefore, do I tire of it.

            First Merchant.   No—no—
[759]   679.   We may not touch it.

            Kevin.   Is your power so small,
[760]   680.   Must I then bear it with me all my days?
[761]   681.   May scorn close deep about you.

            First Merchant.   Lead him hence;
762   682.   He troubles me.
                    [*Teig and Shemus lead the young man into the crowd.*]

            Second Merchant.   His gaze has filled me, brother,

729.   Traffic with us.

            A Woman.   What will you give for mine?

730.   *First Merchant* [*reading in book*]. 'Soft, handsome, and still young'—
            not much, I think.
731.   'It's certain that the man she's married to
732.   Knows nothing of what's hidden in the jar
733.   Between the hour-glass and the pepper-pot.'

734.   *The Woman.* The scandalous book!

        First Merchant.   'Nor how when he's away
735.   At the horse-fair the hand that wrote what's hid
736.   Will tap three times upon the window-pane.'

737.   *The Woman.* And if there is a letter, that is no reason
738.   Why I should have less money than the others.

739.   *First Merchant.* You're almost safe. I give you fifty crowns.
                                                    [*She turns to go.*

728b.   A woman lived here once, she would not deal—**5, 6**; Maire, the
        wife of Shemus, would not deal, **7-33**.
728c.   She starved—she lies in there with red wall-flowers,
728d.   And candles stuck in bottles, (bottles **33**) round her head. (bed.
        7-33)
729.   *A Woman.* What price, now, will you give for mine?
        First Merchant.   Ay, Ay, **5-33**.
730.   Soft, . . . young—not . . . . [*Reading in the parchment.*] **5-33**; . . .
        young—not . . . . **48, 63**.
731.   [lacking] **5, 6**; It's . . . **48, 63**.
732.   She has love letters in a little jar **5-33**.
733.   On a (the **18, 31, 33**) high shelf between the pepper-pot **5-33**; . . .
        pepper pot.' **97A**.
734.   And wood-cased hour glass. (hour-glass. **7-33**)
        The Woman.   O, the scandalous parchment! **5-33**;
        . . . book.
                'Nor . . . **46, 49-62, 66-80**.
735.   *First Merchant* [*reading*]. She hides them from her husband, who
        buys horses, **5-33**; . . . horse fair . . . **46-80**.
736-738.   [lacking] **5-33**.
736.   . . . window pane.' **48, 63**.
739.   And is not much at home. You are almost safe. **5-33**; . . . safe, I
        . . . . **46-80**.

763   683.   With shaking and a dreadful fear.

         First Merchant.   Lean forward

[764] 684.   And kiss my crown here where my master's lips

[765] 685.   Were pressed upon it when he sent us hither—

[766] 686.   You will have peace once more.

         [*The Second Merchant kisses the gold band that is about the head of the First Merchant.*]

         Shemus.   He is called Kevin,

[754] 687.   And has been crazy now these many days;

        688.   But has no harm in him: his fits soon pass,

        689.   And one can go and lead him like a child.

[770] 690.   *First Merchant.* Come, deal, deal, deal, deal, deal—are you dumb?

773   691.   *Shemus.* They say you beat the woman down too low.

740. A hundred, then.

    Shemus.   Woman, have sense—come, come.

741.   Is this a time to haggle at the price?

742.   There, take it up. There, take it up. That's right.

                                     [She takes them and goes into the crowd.

743. *First Merchant.* Come, deal, deal, deal. It is but for charity

744.   We buy such souls at all; a thousand sins

745.   Made them our Master's long before we came.

                                     Aleel enters

746. *Aleel.* Here, take my soul, for I am tired of it.

---

740.   I give you fifty crowns. [*She turns to go.*] A hundred, then. [*She takes them, and goes into the crowd.*] **5-33.**

741-.   Directions after 742.   [lacking] **5-33.**

742.   There, take it up. There, there. That's . . . . **46-80.**

743.   *First Merchant.* Come—deal, deal, deal; 'tis (it is **7, 28**) but . . . **5-7, 28** ; Come—deal, deal, deal; it is for . . . **18, 31, 33.**

745.   . . . master's . . . . **5-33.**

745a.   Come, deal—come, deal. You seem (seemed **28**) resolved to starve

745b.   Until your bones show through your skin. Come (Come, **6, 33**) deal,

745c.   Or live on nettles, grass, and dandelion.

745d.   Or do you dream the famine will go by?

745e.   The famine is hale and hearty; it is mine

745f.   And my great master's; it shall no wise (nowise **31**) cease

745g.   Until our purpose end: the yellow vapour

745h.   That brought it bears it over your dried fields

745i.   And fills with violent phantoms of the lost,

745j.   And grows more deadly as day copies day.

745k.   See how it dims the daylight. Is that peace

745l.   Known to the birds of prey so dread a thing?

745m.   They, and the souls obedient to our master,

745n.   And those who live with that great other spirit

745o.   Have gained an end, a peace, while you but toss

745p.   And swing upon a moving balance beam. **5-33.**

        Directions before 746. [. . . *enters*, (*enters*; **33**) *the wires of his harp are broken.*] **5-33.**

746.   . . . it; **5-33.**

[774]   692.   *First Merchant*. I offer this great price—a thousand pieces

[775]   693.   For an old woman who was ever ugly.

> [*An old woman comes forward, and he takes up a parchment, and reads.*]

[776]   694.   There is but little set down here against her;

[777]   695.   She stole fowl sometimes when the harvest failed.

[779]   696.   But always went to chapel twice a week,

[780]   697.   And paid her dues when prosperous. Take your money.

[781]   698.   *The Old Woman* [*curtseying*]. God bless you, sir.

> [*She screams.*]

O, sir, a pain went through me.

782   699.   *First Merchant*. That name is like a fire to all damned souls.

747.   I do not ask a price.

    Shemus.   Not ask a price?

748.   How can you sell your soul without a price?
749.   I would not listen to his broken wits.
750.   His love for Countess Cathleen has so crazed him
751.   He hardly understands what he is saying.

752.   *Aleel.* The trouble that has come on Countess Cathleen,
753.   The sorrow that is in her wasted face,
754.   The burden in her eyes, have broke my wits,
755.   And yet I know I'd have you take my soul.

756.   *First Merchant.* We cannot take your soul, for it is hers.

757.   *Aleel.* No, but you must. Seeing it cannot help her
758.   I have grown tired of it.

    First Merchant.   Begone from me,
759.   I may not touch it.

    Aleel.   Is your power so small?

---

747.   . . . price.
    First Merchant [*reading*]. A man of songs—(songs: **6-33**) **5-33.**
747a.   Alone in the hushed passion of romance,
747b.   His mind ran all on sidheoges, (sidheoges **33**) and on tales
747c.   Of Fenian labours and the Red Branch kings,
747d.   And he cared nothing for the life of man:
747e.   But now all changes.
    Aleel.   Ay, because her face, **5-33.**
748-751.   [lacking] **5-33.**
749.   . . . wits; **46-80.**
750.   . . . him, **48, 63.**
752.   The face of Countess Cathleen, dwells with me:
753.   The sadness of the world upon her brow:
754.   The crying of these strings grew burdensome,
755.   Therefore I tore them—see—(them; see; **6-33**) now take . . . . **5-33.**
757.   Ah, take it—(it; **6-33**) take it. It nowise can help her, (her **7, 28**)
    5-33; . . . her, **48, 63.**
758.   And, therefore, do I tire of it. **5-33.**
    First Merchant. No—no—(no; no; **6, 18, 31**; No; no **7, 28**; No; no.
    33) **5-33**; . . . me; **46**; . . . me! **48, 63.**
759.   We may . . . small, **5-33.**

700.   Begone [*she goes*]. See how the red gold pieces glitter.

[785] 701.   Deal. Do you fear because an old hag screamed?

702.   Are you all cowards?

A Peasant.   Nay, I am no coward.

703.   I will sell half my soul.

First Merchant.   How half your soul?

704.   *The Peasant.* Half of my chance of heaven.

First Merchant.   'Tis writ here

705.   This man in all things takes the moderate course,

706.   He sits on midmost of the balance beam,

707.   And no man has had good of him or evil.

708.   Begone, we will not buy you.

Second Merchant.   Deal, come deal.

[771] 709.   *First Merchant.* What, will you keep us from our ancient
               home,

760.   And must I bear it with me all my days?
761.   May you be scorned and mocked!

First Merchant.   Drag him away.
762.   He troubles me.

[*Teigue and Shemus lead Aleel into the crowd.*

Second Merchant.   His gaze has filled me, brother,
763.   With shaking and a dreadful fear.

First Merchant.   Lean forward
764.   And kiss the circlet where my Master's lips
765.   Were pressed upon it when he sent us hither;
766.   You shall have peace once more.

[*Second Merchant kisses the gold circlet that is about the head of the
First Merchant.*

                                    I, too, grow weary,
767.   But there is something moving in my heart
768.   Whereby I know that what we seek the most
769.   Is drawing near—our labour will soon end.
770.   Come, deal, deal, deal, deal, deal; are you all dumb?
771.   What, will you keep me from our ancient home,
772.   And from the eternal revelry?

Second Merchant.   Deal, deal.

773. *Shemus.* They say you beat the woman down too low.

---

760.   Must I then bear . . .? **5-33.**
761.   May scorn close deep about you!
                            Lead him hence; **5-33.**
        Directions in 762.   [. . . *lead the young man into* . . . .] **5.**
764.   . . . master's . . . **5-33.**
765.   . . . hither— (hither: **6-33**)
766.   You will have . . . more.
                    [*The Second . . . Merchant.*]
        Shemus.   He is called Aleel, **5-33.**
766a.   And has been crazy now these many days;
766b.   But has no harm in him: his fits soon pass,
766c.   And one can go and lead him like a child. **5-33.**
767-769.   [lacking] **5-33.**
770.   *First Merchant.* Come, (Come **6**) deal, . . ., deal— (deal; **6**) are . . .?
        5, 6 ; . . ., deal; you are all dumb? **28, 33** ; . . . dumb! **78.**
771-772.   [lacking] **5-33.**
771.   . . . home. **72, 74.**

[772] 710. And from the eternal revelry? Come, deal,
711. And we will hence to our great master. Deal,
712. Come, deal, deal.

The Peasants shout. The Countess comes! The Countess!

795 713. *Kathleen [entering].* And so you trade once more?

First Merchant. In spite of you.

796 714. What brings you here, saint with the sapphire eyes?

[797] 715. *Kathleen.* I have a soul to sell, but it is dear.

[798] 716. *First Merchant.* What matter, if the soul be precious!

Kathleen. Merchants,
[799] 717. These people starve, and therefore do they come
[800] 718. Thronging to you. I hear a cry come from them,
801 719. And it is in my ears by night and day,
[802] 720. And I would have five hundred thousand crowns,
[803] 721. That I feed may them till the dearth goes by;

774. *First Merchant.* I offer this great price: a thousand crowns
775. For an old woman who was always ugly.
      [An old Peasant Woman comes forward, and he takes up a book and reads:
776. There is but little set down here against her.
777. 'She has stolen eggs and fowl when times were bad,
778. But when the times grew better has confessed it;
779. She never missed her chapel of a Sunday
780. And when she could, paid dues.' Take up your money.

781. *Old Woman.* God bless you, sir. *[She screams.]* O, sir, a pain went
      through me!

782. *First Merchant.* That name is like a fire to all damned souls.
      [Murmur among the Peasants, who shrink back from her as she goes out.

Directions after 775. [. . . *up a parchment,* (*parchment* **6-33**) *and reads.*] **5-33.**
776. . . . her;
777. She stole fowl sometimes when the harvest failed, (failed **18**) **5-33.**
778. [lacking] **5-33.**
779. But always went to chapel twice a week, **5-33**; . . . Sunday, **48, 63.**
780. And paid her dues when prosperous. Take your money. **5-33.**
781. *The Old Peasant Woman* [*curtseying*]. God . . . me. **5-33**; . . . Oh, . . .! **46-80.**
      Directions after 782. [lacking] **5-33**; [. . . *out screaming.*] **73, 76-80.**
782a. *First Merchant.* Begone [*she goes*]. (Begone. [*She goes.*] **28, 33**) See how the red gold pieces glitter. **5-33.**
782b. Deal: do you fear because an old hag screamed?
782c. Are you all cowards?
      A Peasant.   Nay, I am no coward.
782d. I will sell half my soul.
      First Merchant.   How half your soul?
782e. *The Peasant.* Half of my (Half my **6-33**) chance of heaven.
      First Merchant.   'Tis (It is **7-33**) writ here
782f. This man in all things takes the moderate course,
782g. He sits on midmost of the balance beam,
782h. And no man has had good of him or evil.
782i. Begone, we will not buy you.
      Second Merchant.   Deal, come (come, **31, 33**) deal.
782j. *First Merchant.* What, will you keep us from our ancient home,
782k. And from the eternal revelry? Come, deal,
782l. And we will hence to our great master again.
782m. Come, deal, deal, deal.
      The Peasants shout, The Countess Cathleen comes! **5-33.**

[805]   722.   And all the wretched spirits you have bought

[805]   723.   For your gold crowns, released, and sent to God.

[807-808] 724.   The soul that I would sell is mine.

A Peasant.   **Do not—**

[809]   725.   Do not, dear lady, what do our souls matter?

[810]   726.   They are not dear to God as your soul is.

[811]   727.   O! what would heaven do without you, lady?

812   728.   *Another Peasant.* Look how their claws clutch in their
                leathern gloves.

[813]   729.   *First Merchant.* Five hundred thousand crowns—we give
                the price,

[814]   730.   The gold is here—the spirits, while you speak,

[815]   731.   Begin to labour upward, for your face

[816]   732.   Sheds a great light on them and fills their hearts

        733.   With those unveilings of the fickle light,

783. *A Peasant.* How she screamed out!

Second Peasant. And maybe we shall scream so.

784. *Third Peasant.* I tell you there is no such place as Hell.

785. *First Merchant.* Can such a trifle turn you from your profit?
786. Come, deal; come, deal.

Middle-aged Man. Master, I am afraid.

787. *First Merchant.* I bought your soul, and there's no sense in fear
788. Now the soul's gone.

Middle-aged Man. Give me my soul again.

789. *Woman* [*going on her knees and clinging to Merchant*]. And take this
money too, and give me mine.

790. *Second Merchant.* Bear bastards, drink or follow some wild fancy;
791. For cryings out and sighs are the soul's work,
792. And you have none. [*Throws the Woman off.*

Peasant. Come, let's away.

Another Peasant. Yes, yes.

793. *Another Peasant.* Come quickly; if that woman had not screamed
794. I would have lost my soul.

Another Peasant. Come, come away.
[*They turn to door, but are stopped by shouts of* 'Countess Cathleen! Countess Cathleen!'

783-Directions after 794. [lacking] **5-33.**
784. . . . hell. **46, 49-62, 66-80.**
786. . . . afraid **49.**
790. . . ., drink, or . . .; **48, 63.**
791. For sighs and cries are . . ., **46-80.**
793. . . . screamed, **48, 63.**

734.   Whereby our heavy labours have been marred

735.   Since first His spirit moved upon the deeps

736.   And stole them from us. Even before this day

737.   The souls were but half ours, for your bright eyes

738.   Had pierced them through and robbed them of content.

[817] 739.   But you must sign, for we do all in order,

[818] 740.   In buying such a soul—sign with this quill;

819 741.   It was a feather growing on the cock

[820] 742.   That crowed when Peter had denied his Master;

[821] 743.   'Tis a great honour thus to write with it.

[Kathleen leans forward to sign.]

Kevin [rushing forward and snatching the parchment from her].

744.   You shall yet know the love of some great chief,

[822] 745.   And children gathering round your knees. Leave you

[822] 746.   The peasants to the builder of the heavens.

795. *Cathleen* [*entering*]. And so you trade once more?

First Merchant.   In spite of you.

796.   What brings you here, saint with the sapphire eyes?

797. *Cathleen.* I come to barter a soul for a great price.

798. *Second Merchant.* What matter, if the soul be worth the price?

799. *Cathleen.* The people starve, therefore the people go

800.   Thronging to you. I hear a cry come from them

801.   And it is in my ears by night and day,

802.   And I would have five hundred thousand crowns

803.   That I may feed them till the dearth go by.

804. *First Merchant.* It may be the soul's worth it.

Cathleen.   There is more:

805.   The souls that you have bought must be set free.

806. *First Merchant.* We know of but one soul that's worth the price.

807. *Cathleen.* Being my own it seems a priceless thing.

808. *Second Merchant.* You offer us——

Cathleen.   I offer my own soul.

809. *A Peasant.* Do not, do not, for souls the like of ours

---

798.   . . . matter if . . .? **28, 33** ; . . . price. **48, 63.**
800.   . . . them, **5-33, 48, 63.**
801.   . . . day;
802.   . . . crowns,
803.   . . . by;
804.   [lacking] **5-33.**
805.   And have the wretched spirits you have bought
805a.   For your gold crowns, released, (crowns released **33**) and sent to
         God. (God **7, 28**) **5-33.**
806-807. [lacking] **5-33.**
807.   . . . own, it . . . . **48, 63, 78.**
808.   The soul that I would barter is my soul.
809.   Do not, do not,—(not; **6-33**) the souls of us poor folk **5-33.**

[823]   747. *Kathleen.* I have no thoughts. I hear a cry—a cry.

[824]   748. *Kevin [casting the parchment on the ground].* I had a vision
               under a green hedge,

825   749. A hedge of hips and haws—men yet shall hear

[826-827] 750. Archangels rolling over the high mountains

[826-827] 751. Old Satan's empty skull.

         First Merchant.   Take him away
         *[Teig and Shemus lead him away. Kathleen picks up the
         parchment and signs, and then turns towards the peasants.]*

[828]   752. *Kathleen.* Take up the money, and now come with me.

829   753. When we are far from this polluted place

[830]   754. I will give each one of you what he needs.
         *[She goes out, the peasants crowding round her and
         kissing her dress. The Two Merchants are left alone.]*

810.   Are not precious to God as your soul is.

811.   O, what would Heaven do without you, lady?

812.   *Another Peasant.* Look how their claws clutch in their leathern
         gloves.

813.   *First Merchant.* Five hundred thousand crowns; we give the price.

814.   The gold is here; the souls even while you speak

815.   Have slipped out of our bond, because your face

816.   Has shed a light on them and filled their hearts.

817.   But you must sign, for we omit no form

818.   In buying a soul like yours.

         Second Merchant.   Sign with this quill.

819.   It was a feather growing on the cock

820.   That crowed when Peter dared deny his Master,

821.   And all who use it have great honour in Hell.

                              [Cathleen leans forward to sign.

822.   *Aleel [rushing forward and snatching the pen from her].*
         Leave all things to the Builder of the Heavens.

---

811.   O! what . . . heaven (Heaven **46-72, 74, 84**) . . .? **5-84.**
813.   . . . crowns—we . . . price, **5** ; . . . price, **6-33.**
814.   . . . here—(here; **6-33** spirits,) the while . . . speak, **5-33** ; . . . souls,
         even . . . speak, **48, 63.**
815.   Begin to labour upward, for your . . . **5-33.**
816.   Sheds a great light . . . fills their hearts **5-33** ; . . . hearts; **78.**
816a.   With those (whose **7-31**) unveilings of the fickle light,
816b.   Whereby our heavy labours have been marred
816c.   Since first His spirit moved upon the deeps
816d.   And stole them from us; even before this day
816e.   The souls were but half ours, for your bright eyes
816f.   Had pierced them through and robbed them of content. **5-33.**
818.   . . . yours; sign . . . quill; **5-33**; [set as short line: In . . . yours.] **63.**
819.   *First Merchant.* It . . . **5-33** ; [set as long line: Sign . . . cock] **63.**
821.   . . . hell. (Hell. **18, 31, 33.**) **5-33.**
                              [*Cathleen* . . . .] **5-33.**
821a.   *Aleel [rushing forward and snatching the parchment from her].* You shall
         yet know the love of some great chief, **5, 6.**
821b.   And children gathering round your knees. Leave you **5, 6.**
822.   The peasants to . . . builder . . . heavens. **5, 6** ; *Aleel* [. . . *the parchment
         from* . . .]. . . . builder . . . heavens. **7-49, 63** ; . . . builder . . . heavens.
         51-62, 66-80.

[769]   755. *First Merchant.* Now are our days of heavy labour done.

             756. *Second Merchant.* We have a precious jewel for Satan's
                   crown.

[831]   757. *First Merchant.* We must away, and wait until she dies,
[832]   758.   Sitting above her tower as twin grey owls,
[833]   759.   Watching as many years as may be, guarding
[834]   760.   Our precious jewel—waiting to seize her soul.

[835-836]   761. *Second Merchant.* And we shall not wait long. I saw a look
[836]   762.   That seemed the dimness of the tomb in her,
[837]   763.   And she walks slowly, as with leaden slippers,
             764.   And has her eyes fixed often on the ground,
             765.   As though she saw the worms a-beckoning.

[840]   766. *First Merchant.* Away! Now leap we feathered on the air.
                                                          [*They rush out.*]

                              End of Scene IV.

823. *Cathleen.* I have no thoughts; I hear a cry—a cry.

824. *Aleel [casting the pen on the ground].* I have seen a vision under a
     green hedge,
825. A hedge of hips and haws—men yet shall hear
826. The archangel rolling Satan's empty skull
827. Over the mountain-tops.

First Merchant. Take him away.
[*Teigue and Shemus drag him roughly away so that he falls upon the
floor among the Peasants. Cathleen picks up parchment and signs,
then turns towards the Peasants.*

828. *Cathleen.* Take up the money, and now come with me;
829. When we are far from this polluted place
830. I will give everybody money enough.
     [*She goes out, the Peasants crowding round her and kissing her dress.
     Aleel and the two Merchants are left alone.*

831. *Second Merchant.* We must away and wait until she dies,
832. Sitting above her tower as two grey owls,
833. Waiting as many years as may be, guarding
834. Our precious jewel; waiting to seize her soul.

835. *First Merchant.* We need but hover over her head in the air,

---

823.   . . . thoughts: I . . . . **5-33.**
        Directions at 824. [. . . *the parchment on* . . . .] **5-49, 63.**
824.   I had a vision . . ., **5-33.**
826.   . . . Archangels . . . **46-80.**
827.   . . . mountain tops. . . . **48, 63.**
        Directions after 827. [. . . *up the parchment . . . signs, and then* . . . .]
        5-33 ; [. . . *up the pen and* . . . .] **52.**
828.   . . . money; and . . . me. **5-33.**
        Directions after 830. [. . . *around* . . . .] **71A.**
830a.   *Second Merchant.* Now are our days of heavy labour done, (done. **6-
        33**)
830b.   *First Merchant.* We have a precious jewel for Satan's crown.
831.   *Second Merchant.* . . . away, and . . ., **5-33.**
832.   . . . as twin gray . . ., **5.**
833.   Watching as . . . **5-33.**
835.   . . . air **49** ; ['We need' lacking] **67.**

SCENE V.

[*The room in the castle of Countess Kathleen, as in Scenes II and III. Dawn breaks faintly through the large window. A number of peasants enter hastily, half dressed, as though aroused suddenly from sleep. Oona is among them.*]

767. *First Peasant.* There's nothing here.

    Second Peasant.   It could not be far off,
768.   A screeching noise—I heard it plain. Neal heard it.

769. *Neal* [*an old peasant*]. I sleep alone in the room under this.
770.   Last night was cold and windy, I had stuffed
771.   My muffler underneath the door, and pushed
772.   My great cloak up the chimney, yet the wind
773.   Sang through the keyhole.

    First Peasant.   But the noise—

    Neal.   The noise—

836. For she has only minutes. When she signed
837. Her heart began to break. Hush, hush, I hear
838. The brazen door of Hell move on its hinges,
839. And the eternal revelry float hither
840. To hearten us.

Second Merchant. Leap feathered on the air
841. And meet them with her soul caught in your claws.
   [*They rush out. Aleel crawls into the middle of the room. The twilight has fallen and gradually darkens as the scene goes on. There is a distant muttering of thunder and a sound of rising storm.*

842. *Aleel.* The brazen door stands wide, and Balor comes
843. Borne in his heavy car, and demons have lifted
844. The age-weary eyelids from the eyes that of old
845. Turned gods to stone; Barach, the traitor, comes
846. And the lascivious race, Cailitin,
847. That cast a Druid weakness and decay
848. Over Sualtim's and old Dectora's child;
849. And that great king Hell first took hold upon
850. When he killed Naoise and broke Deirdre's heart;
851. And all their heads are twisted to one side,
852. For when they lived they warred on beauty and peace
853. With obstinate, crafty, sidelong bitterness.
   Oona enters.

---

836. . . . minutes: when she came **5-33.**
836a. I saw the dimness of the tomb in her,
836b. And marked her walking as with leaden shoes
836c. And looking on the ground as though the worms
836d. Were calling her, and when she wrote her name
837. . . . . Hush! Hush! I . . . **5-33.**
838. . . . hell . . ., **5** ; . . . hinges. **56a, 72, 74.**
838, 839. [printed as one line] **71.**
840. . . . . Leap, feathered, on . . . **5-33.**
845. . . .; Barach the traitor comes; **5-33** ; . . . comes; **46, 48, 52, 63.**
847. . . . druid . . . **33-80.**
850. . . . heart, **5-31, 46, 48, 52, 63** ; . . . heart **49, 51, 56a-62, 66-80.**
   Directions after 853. [. . . *enters, but remains standing by the door. Aleel half rises, leaning upon one arm and one knee.*] **5-33** ; [*He moves about as though the air was* (*air above him was* **51, 56a-62, 66, 67, 72, 74**) *full*

774. I'm coming to the noise. I lay awake
775. Thinking I should catch cold and surely die,
776. And wondering if I could close up the keyhole
777. With an old piece of cloth shaped like a tongue
778. That hangs over a tear here in my coat,
779. When right above there came a screech of birds,
780. A sound of voices and a noise of blows,
781. It surely came from here, and yet all's empty.

782. *Third Peasant.* And I am sure the noise was further off.

783. *First Peasant.* We will go search the northern tower.

   [*They all go except Oona and a Young Peasant.*]

   Young Peasant [*going close up to Oona*].   Oona,
784. I peered out through the window in the passage,
785. And saw bard Kevin wandering in the wood;
786. Sometimes he laid his head upon the ground.

854.   Crouch down, old heron, out of the blind storm.

855.   *Oona.* Where is the Countess Cathleen? All this day
856.   Her eyes were full of tears, and when for a moment
857.   Her hand was laid upon my hand it trembled,
858.   And now I do not know where she is gone.

859.   *Aleel.* Cathleen has chosen other friends than us,
860.   And they are rising through the hollow world.
861.   Demons are out, old heron.

Oona.   God guard her soul!

862.   *Aleel.* She's bartered it away this very hour,
863.   As though we two were never in the world.

                                        [*He points downward.*

864.   First, Orchil, her pale, beautiful head alive,
865.   Her body shadowy as vapour drifting
866.   Under the dawn, for she who awoke desire
867.   Has but a heart of blood when others die;
868.   About her is a vapoury multitude
869.   Of women alluring devils with soft laughter;
870.   Behind her a host heat of the blood made sin,
871.   But all the little pink-white nails have grown

---

of spirits. Oona . . . .] **46-51, 56a, 62, 66, 67, 72, 74** ; [*He crouches down
as though spirits were whirling in the air above him. Oona . . . .*] **52** ;
[*lacking*] **73, 76-80.**

854.   *Aleel.* Crouch . . . . **5-31.**
856.   She has been pale and weakly: when her hand
857.   Touched mine over the spindle her hand trembled,
858.   . . . she has gone. **5-33.**
859.   . . . us. **48, 63.**
860.   [lacking] **48, 63.**
         Directions after 860.   [*He points downward.*] **5-33.**
861-Directions after 863.   [lacking] **5-33.**
861.   . . . soul. **46-80.**
         Directions after 863.   [lacking] **46, 48, 63.**
863a.   And they are rising through the hollow world.
                        [*He points downward. (downwards.* **48, 63**)] **46, 48, 63.**
864.   . . . pale beautiful . . ., **5-33** ; . . . head **56a** (1924), **61, 62, 66, 67, 72,
         74.**
868.   . . . her in a . . . **97A.**
869.   . . . women, alluring . . .; **33** ; . . . laughter **48, 63.**
870.   . . . heat o' the . . . sin **5, 6.**
871.   . . . pink white . . . **71A.**

787. They say he hears the sheogues down below
[754] 788. Nailing four boards.

Oona. For love has made him crazy,
789. And loneliness and famine dwell with him.

790. *Young Peasant.* Then, is not love a thing of bitterness?

946 791. *Oona.* The years like great black oxen tread the world,
[947] 792. And God, the herdsman, goads them on behind,
[948] 793. When one has lain long under their hard hoofs,
[948] 794. One falls forgetting.

Young Peasant. I have not known love,
795. I am too young; I will go ask old Neal. [*He goes.*]

796. *Oona* [*alone*]. They wake one up with some mad cry of thieves
797. Or fire, because they dream—now all folk dream
[855] 798. From being so long hungry. [*She listens.*]
My dear mistress

872.   To be great talons.
              [*He seizes Oona and drags her into the middle of the room and points*
              downward with vehement gestures. The wind roars.
                          They begin a song
873.   And there is still some music on their tongues.

874.   *Oona* [*casting herself face downwards on the floor*]. O Maker of all,
              protect her from the demons,
875.   And if a soul must needs be lost, take mine.
              [*Aleel kneels beside her, but does not seem to hear her words. The*
              Peasants return. They carry the Countess Cathleen and lay her upon
              the ground before Oona and Aleel. She lies there as if dead.

876.   *Oona.* O that so many pitchers of rough clay
877.   Should prosper and the porcelain break in two!
                          [*She kisses the hands of Cathleen.*

878.   *A Peasant.* We were under the tree where the path turns,
879.   When she grew pale as death and fainted away.
880.   And while we bore her hither cloudy gusts
881.   Blackened the world and shook us on our feet.
882.   Draw the great bolt, for no man has beheld
883.   So black, bitter, blinding, and sudden a storm.
                          [*One who is near the door draws the bolt.*

884.   *Cathleen.* O, hold me, and hold me tightly, for the storm

---

Directions in 872.   [. . . *downwards* . . . .] **5-33.**
872.   . . . song, **48, 63.**
874.   . . . maker of the world, protect . . ., **5, 6** ; . . . maker . . ., **7-33** ;
              [. . . *downwards* (*downward* **48, 63, 71A**) . . . .] O, Maker . . ., **46-80.**
875.   . . . need . . . . **5-18, 31, 46-51, 56a-80.**
              Directions after 875.   [. . . *words; he is gazing down as if through the*
              earth. The peasants . . . .] **5-33.**
876.   O, that . . . **46-80.**
877.   . . . two. **5-31.**
              Directions after 877.   [. . . *of the Countess Cathleen.*] **5-33.**
878.   . . . turns
879.   . . . away, **5-33.**
880.   . . . hither, cloudy . . . **5-33, 48, 63.**
881.   . . . feet: **5-33** ; . . . feet; **46-80.**
883a. *Oona.* Hush, hush, she has awakened from her swoon. **5-33.**
884.   O hold . . . **5-33.**

[855] 799.   Must have dropped off to sleep. All night

800.   She has been pacing in the chapel there.

    [She goes over to the oratory steps and finds them covered with feathers.]

801.   I know what clamour frighted them—some bird,

802.   Some hawk or kestrel, chased its prey to this;

803.   These are owls feathers. I will go and see

804.   What window has swung open over-night.

    [She goes into the oratory and returns hastily, leaving the door open. A bright light streams through the open door.]

805.   My hour has come, oh blessed queen of heaven,

806.   I am to die, for I have seen a vision.

807.   O, they are coming, they are coming, coming.

    [A row of spirits carrying the lifeless body of the

885.   Is dragging me away.
        [*Oona takes her in her arms. A woman begins to wail.*

Peasants.   Hush!

Other Peasants.   Hush!

Peasant Women.   Hush!

Other Peasant Women.   Hush!

886. *Cathleen* [*half rising*]. Lay all the bags of money in a heap,
887.   And when I am gone, old Oona, share them out
888.   To every man and woman: judge, and give
889.   According to their needs.

A Peasant Woman.   And will she give
890.   Enough to keep my children through the dearth?

891. *Another Peasant Woman.* O Queen of Heaven, and all you blessed
      saints,

---

885.   . . . *wail.*]
    A Peasant.   Hush.
    Another Peasant.   Hush.
    A Peasant Woman.   Hush.
    Another Peasant Woman.   Hush. **5-33;**
    Peasant. (*Peasants.* **71**) Hush!
    Peasants.   Hush!
    Peasant Women.   Hush!
    Other Peasant Women.   Hush! (Hush **51, 56a-62,**
    66, 67, 72, 74) **46-80.**
886.   . . . money at my feet, **5-33.**
    [*They lay the bags at her feet.*] **5-33.**
887.   And send and bring old Neal when I am dead,
888.   And bid him hear each man and judge and give:
888a. He doctors you with herbs, and can best say
889.   Who has the less and who the greater need.
890.   *A Peasant Woman* [*at the back of the crowd*]. And will he give enough
    out of the bags
890a. To keep my children till the dearth go by? **5-33.**
891.   . . . Heaven and . . . saints, (Saints, **33**) **5-33;** O, Queen . . ., **46-72,**
    74; O, Queen . . . saints. **73, 76-80.**

Countess Kathleen descend slowly from the oratory. Oona has crouched down upon the floor. The spirits lay the body upon the ground with the head upon the knees of Oona. While descending from the oratory they sing.]

Song.

808.	*All the heavy days are over;*
809.	*Leave the body's coloured pride*
810.	*Underneath the grass and clover*
811.	*With the feet laid side by side.*
812.	*One with her are mirth and duty,*
813.	*Bear the gold embroidered dress—*
814.	*For she needs not her sad beauty—*
815.	*To the scented oaken press.*

892.   Let us and ours be lost so she be shriven.

893.   *Cathleen.* Bend down your faces, Oona and Aleel;
894.   I gaze upon them as the swallow gazes
895.   Upon the nest under the eave, before
896.   She wander the loud waters. Do not weep
897.   Too great a while, for there is many a candle
898.   On the High Altar though one fall. Aleel,
899.   Who sang about the dancers of the woods
900.   That know not the hard burden of the world,
901.   Having but breath in their kind bodies, farewell!
902.   And farewell, Oona, you who played with me,
903.   And bore me in your arms about the house
904.   When I was but a child and therefore happy,
905.   Therefore happy, even like those that dance.
906.   The storm is in my hair and I must go.   [*She dies.*

907.   *Oona.* Bring me the looking-glass.
         [*A woman brings it to her out of the inner room. Oona holds it over
         the lips of Cathleen. All is silent for a moment. And then she speaks
         in a half scream;*

                         O, she is dead!

908.   *A Peasant.* She was the great white lily of the world.

---

892.   . . . lost, so . . . . **5-33, 48, 63.**
893.   . . . Aleel: **5-33.**
896.   He . . . waters: do . . . **5-33.**
897.   . . . awhile, . . . **52.**
898.   . . . high altar . . . . Aleel, (Aleel 6) **5-33**; . . . Altar, though . . ., **48, 63.**
899.   . . . about the people of the raths, **5-33**; . . . woods, **46, 49-62, 66-80.**
902.   . . . farewell (farewell, **7-33**) Oona, who spun flax with me **5-33.**
903-904. [lacking] **5-33.**
905.   Soft as their sleep when every dance is done: **5-33.**
906.   . . . hair, and . . . . **48, 63.**
907.   . . . looking-glass.
         [. . . *holds the glass over* . . . *of the Countess Cathleen* . . . *moment. And*
         (*moment; and* 33) *then* . . . *scream.*]
                         O, . . . dead. (dead, **7**; dead! **33**) **5-33.**
         Directions in 907.   [. . . *scream:*] **46, 49-62, 66-80**; [. . . *room, Oona* . . .
         scream.] **48, 63.**
908.   *A Peasant Woman.* She. . . . **5-33.**

816.   *Hers the kiss of mother Mary,*
817.   *The long hair is on her face,*
818.   *Still she goes with footsteps wary,*
819.   *Full of earth's old timid grace.*

820.   *She goes down the floor of heaven,*
821.   *Shining bright as a new lance,*
822.   *And her guides are angels seven,*
823.   *While young stars about her dance.*

824. *Oona.* Who are you, sirs.

   First Spirit.   We are angelical.
[941] 825.   She gave away her soul for others—God,
[942] 826.   Who sees the motive and the deed regards not,
827.   Bade us go down and save her from the demons,
[943] 828.   Who do not know the deed can never bind.

909. *Another Peasant.* She was more beautiful than the pale stars.

910. *An Old Peasant Woman.* The little plant I loved is broken in two.
   [Aleel takes looking-glass from Oona and flings it upon the floor so that it is broken in many pieces.

911. *Aleel.* I shatter you in fragments, for the face
912.   That brimmed you up with beauty is no more:
913.   And die, dull heart, for she whose mournful words
914.   Made you a living spirit has passed away
915.   And left you but a ball of passionate dust.
916.   And you, proud earth and plumy sea, fade out!
917.   For you may hear no more her faltering feet,
918.   But are left lonely amid the clamorous war
919.   Of angels upon devils.
   [He stands up; almost every one is kneeling, but it has grown so dark that only confused forms can be seen.
                  And I who weep
920.   Call curses on you, Time and Fate and Change,
921.   And have no excellent hope but the great hour
922.   When you shall plunge headlong through bottomless space.
   [A flash of lightning followed immediately by thunder.

923. *A Peasant Woman.* Pull him upon his knees before his curses
924.   Have plucked thunder and lightning on our heads.

925. *Aleel.* Angels and devils clash in the middle air,
926.   And brazen swords clang upon brazen helms.
   [A flash of lightning followed immediately by thunder.
927.   Yonder a bright spear, cast out of a sling,
928.   Has torn through Balor's eye, and the dark clans
929.   Fly screaming as they fled Moytura of old.
   [Everything is lost in darkness.

---

909. *Another Peasant Woman.* She . . . stars. (stars **6**) **5-33;**
    A Peasant. She . . . . **46-80.**
910. . . . love . . . . **46, 49-62, 66-80.**
    Directions after 910. [. . . *takes the looking-glass* . . . .] **5-33.**
915. . . . dust: (dust; **6-33**; dust, **48, 63**) **5-33, 48, 63.**
916. . . . out, **5-33.**
917. . . . feet **5-31.**
    Directions in 919. [. . . *everyone* . . . .] **33, 52.**
    Directions after 922, 926. [. . . *followed by immediate thunder.*] **5, 6;**
    [. . . *lightning, followed* . . . .] **78.**
926. . . . helms: **5-33.**

	829.	We came and waited; some score minutes since,
	830.	As mortals measure time, her body died,
	831.	For her heart broke. The demons, as two owls,
	832.	Came sweeping hither, murmuring against God.
[925]	833.	We drove them hence; and half our company
[937]	834.	Bore the bright spirit to the floors of peace,
	835.	And half now give the body to your care.
	836.	Let it have noble burial; build a high
	837.	And ample tomb, for she who died and lives
	838.	Was noble in her life and in her beauty;
	839.	And when men gaze upon the flying dawn,
	840.	We bid them dream of her.

[*While he is speaking the other spirits ascend the steps and pass
        into the oratory. Last of all he,*

930. *An Old Man.* The Almighty wrath at our great weakness and sin
931.   Has blotted out the world and we must die.
>   [*The darkness is broken by a visionary light. The Peasants seem to
>   be kneeling upon the rocky slope of a mountain, and vapour full of
>   storm and ever-changing light is sweeping above them and behind
>   them. Half in the light, half in the shadow, stand armed angels.
>   Their armour is old and worn, and their drawn swords dim and
>   dinted.[1] They stand as if upon the air in formation of battle and look
>   downward with stern faces. The Peasants cast themselves on the
>   ground.*

932. *Aleel.* Look no more on the half-closed gates of Hell,
933.   But speak to me, whose mind is smitten of God,
934.   That it may be no more with mortal things,
935.   And tell of her who lies there.
>   [*He seizes one of the angels.*
>   Till you speak
936.   You shall not drift into eternity.

937. *The Angel.* The light beats down; the gates of pearl are wide;
938.   And she is passing to the floor of peace,
939.   And Mary of the seven times wounded heart
940.   Has kissed her lips, and the long blessed hair
941.   Has fallen on her face; The Light of Lights
942.   Looks always on the motive, not the deed,
943.   The Shadow of Shadows on the deed alone.
>   [*Aleel releases the Angel and kneels.*

---

930.   . . . Almighty, wrath . . . **33.**
        Directions after 931.   [. . . *ever-changing* (*everchanging* **5, 6**; *ever changing*
        28) . . . *angels. Their* (*angels; their* **48, 63**) . . . *battle* (*battle,* **5**) *and* . . .
        downward (*downwards* **5**) . . . .] **5, 6, 28, 48, 63.**
932.   . . . *half closed* . . ., **48, 63.**
933.   . . . God **5-18, 31.**
934.   . . . things; **5-33.**
935.   . . . lies here.
                        [*He* . . . .] . . . . **5-33;** . . . speak, **48, 63.**
937.   . . . down: the . . . wide, **5-33;** . . . wide. **46, 49-56a, 67, 72, 74;** . . .
        wide, **48, 63;** . . . wide **61, 62, 66, 71, 73, 76-80.**

[1] See note, p. 178.

too, ascends the steps and stands in the doorway for a moment,
gazing at Oona.]

                      You shall soon follow:

841.   Farewell! the red rose by the seat of God,
842.   Which is among the angelic multitude
843.   What she, whose body lies here, was to men,
844.   Is brightening in my face, I bear no more
845.   The heavy burden of your mortal days.
      [*He enters the oratory, and the bright light fades away. Oona*
      for a time remains silent.]

[907] 846. *Oona* [*with a sudden shriek*]. The Countess Kathleen is dead.
                      [*The peasants come running in.*]
                          Look, she is dead.
      [*She raises one of the arms and lets it fall again.*]

[908] 847. *First Peasant* [*wringing his hands*]. O, she was the white lily
      of the world.

848. *Second Peasant.* Ah, never shall another be so good.

[909] 849. *Third Peasant.* She was more beautiful than the great stars.

850. *Oona.* Be silent. Do you dare to keen her? Dare
851.   To set your grief by mine? Stoop—lift her up;
852.   Now carry her and lay her on her bed,
[945] 853. When I have keened I will go be with her,
[945] 854. I will go die, for I have seen a vision.
                    [*They go out carrying the body.*]

             THE END

944. *Oona.* Tell them who walk upon the floor of peace
945. That I would die and go to her I love;
946. The years like great black oxen tread the world,
947. And God the herdsman goads them on behind,
948. And I am broken by their passing feet.

[*A sound of far-off horns seems to come from the heart of the light. The vision melts away, and the forms of the kneeling Peasants appear faintly in the darkness.*]

THE END

947. ... behind **49, 51, 56a-62, 66-80.**
Directions after 948. [... *Light.* . . . .] **46-80.**

The Countess Cathleen.—I found the story of the Countess Cathleen in what professed to be a collection of Irish folklore in an Irish newspaper some years ago. I wrote to the compiler, asking about its source, but got no answer, but have since heard that it was translated from *Les Matinées de Timothé Trimm* a good many years ago, and has been drifting about the Irish press ever since. Léo Lespès gives it as an Irish story, and though the editor of *Folklore* has kindly advertised for information, the only Christian variant I know of is a Donegal tale, given by Mr. Larminie in his *West Irish Folk Tales and Romances,* of a woman who goes to hell for ten years to save her husband, and stays there another ten, having been granted permission to carry away as many souls as could cling to her skirt. Léo Lespès may have added a few details, but I have no doubt of the essential antiquity of what seems to me the most impressive form of one of the supreme parables of the world. The parable came to the Greeks in the sacrifice of Alcestis, but her sacrifice was less overwhelming, less apparently irremediable. Léo Lespès tells the story as follows:—

Ce que je vais vous dire est un récit du carême irlandais. Le boiteux, l'aveugle, le paralytique des rues de Dublin ou de Limerick, vous le diraient mieux que moi, cher lecteur, si vous alliez le leur demander, un sixpence d'argent à la main.—Il n'est pas une jeune fille catholique à laquelle on ne l'ait appris pendant les jours de préparation à la communion sainte, pas un berger des bords de la Blackwater qui ne le puisse redire à la veillée.

Il y a bien longtemps qu'il apparut tout-à-coup dans la vieille Irlande deux marchands inconnus dont personne n'avait ouï parler, et qui parlaient néanmoins avec la plus grande perfection la langue du pays. Leurs cheveux étaient noirs et ferrés avec de l'or et leurs robes d'une grande magnificence.

Tous deux semblaient avoir le même âge; ils paraissaient être des hommes de cinquante ans, car leur barbe grisonnait un peu.

Or, à cette époque, comme aujourd'hui, l'Irlande était pauvre, car le soleil avait été rare, et des récoltes presque nulles. Les indigents ne savaient à quel saint se vouer, et la misère devenait de plus en plus terrible.

Dans l'hôtellerie où descendirent les marchands fastueux on chercha á pénétrer leurs desseins: mais ce fut en vain, ils demeurèrent silencieux et discrets.

Et pendant qu'ils demeurèrent dans l'hôtellerie, ils ne cessèrent de compter et de recompter des sacs de pièces d'or, dont la vive clarté s'apercevait à travers les vitres du logis.

Gentlemen, leur dit l'hôtesse un jour, d'où vient que vous êtes si opulents, et que, venus pour secourir la misère publique, vous ne fassiez pas de bonnes œuvres?

—Belle hôtesse, répondit l'un d'eux, nous n'avons pas voulu aller au-devant d'infortunes honorables, dans la crainte d'être trompés par des misères fictives: que la douleur frappe à la porte, nous ouvrirons.

Le lendemain, quand on sut qu'il existait deux opulents étrangers prêts à prodiguer l'or, la foule assiégea leur logis; mais les figures des gens qui en sortaient étaient bien diverses. Les uns avaient la fierté dans le regard, les autres portaient la honte au front. Les deux trafiquants achetaient des âmes pour le démon. L'âme d'un vieillard valait vingt pièces d'or, pas un penny de plus; car Satan avait eu le temps d'y former hypothèque. L'âme d'une épouse en valait cinquante quand elle était jolie, ou cent quand elle était laide. L'âme d'une jeune fille se payait des prix fous: les fleurs les plus belles et les plus pures sont les plus chères.

Pendant ce temps, il existait dans la ville un ange de beauté, la comtesse Ketty O'Connor. Elle était l'idole du peuple, et la providence des indigents. Dès qu'elle eut appris que des mécréants profitaient de la misère publique pour dérober des cœurs à Dieu, elle fit appeler son majordome.

—Master Patrick, lui dit elle, combien ai-je de pièces d'or dans mon coffre?

—Cent mille.

—Combien de bijoux?

—Pour autant d'argent.

—Combien de châteaux, de bois et de terres?

—Pour le double de ces sommes.

—Eh bien! Patrick, vendez tout ce qui n'est pas or et apportez-m'en le montant. Je ne veux garder à moi que ce castel et le champ qui l'entoure.

Deux jours après, les ordres de la pieuse Ketty étaient exécutés et le trésor était distribué aux pauvres au fur et à mesure de leurs besoins.

Ceci ne faisait pas le compte, dit la tradition, des commis-voyageurs du malin esprit, qui ne trouvaient plus d'âme à acheter.

Aidés par un valet infâme, ils pénétrèrent dans la retraite de la noble dame et lui dérobèrent le reste de son trésor . . . en vain lutta-t-elle de toutes ses forces pour sauver le contenu de son coffre, les larrons diaboliques furent les plus forts. Si Ketty avait eu les moyens de faire un signe de croix, ajoute la légende irlandaise, elle les eût mis en fuite, mais ses mains étaient captives—Le larcin fut effectué. Alors les pauvres sollicitèrent en vain près de Ketty dépouillée, elle ne pouvait plus secourir leur misère;—Elle les abandonnait à la tentation. Pourtant il n'y avait plus que huit jours à passer pour que les grains et les fourrages arrivassent en abondance des pays d'Orient. Mais, huit jours, c'était un siècle: huit jours nécessitaient une somme immense pour subvenir aux exigences de la disette, et les pauvres allaient ou expirer dans les angoisses de la faim, ou, reniant les saintes maximes de l'Évangile, vendre à vil prix leur âme, le plus beau présent de la munificence du Seigneur tout puissant.

Et Ketty n'avait plus une obole, car elle avait abandonné son château aux malheureux.

Elle passa douze heures dans les larmes et le deuil, arrachant ses cheveux couleur de soleil et meurtrissant son sein couleur du lis: puis elle se leva résolue, animée par un vif sentiment de désespoir.

Elle se rendit chez les marchands d'âmes.

—Que voulez-vous? dirent ils.

—Vous achetez des âmes?

—Oui, un peu malgré vous, n'est-ce pas, sainte aux yeux de saphir?

—Aujourd'hui je viens vous proposer un marché, reprit-elle.

—Lequel?

—J'ai une âme à vendre; mais elle est chère.

—Qu'importe si elle est précieuse? l'âme, comme le diamant, s'apprécie à sa blancheur.

—C'est la mienne, dit Ketty.

Les deux envoyés de Satan tressaillirent. Leurs griffes s'allongèrent sous leurs gants de cuir; leurs yeux gris étincelèrent:—l'âme, pure, immaculée, virginale de Ketty!... c'était une acquisition inappréciable.

—Gentille dame, combien voulez-vous?

—Cent cinquante mille écus d'or.

—C'est fait, dirent les marchands: et ils tendirent à Ketty un parchemin cacheté de noir, qu'elle signa en frissonnant.

La somme lui fut comptée.

Dès qu'elle fut rentrée, elle dit au majordome:

—Tenez, distribuez ceci. Avec la somme que je vous donne les pauvres attendront la huitaine nécessaire et pas une de leurs âmes ne sera livrée au démon.

Puis elle s'enferma et recommanda qu'on ne vint pas la déranger.

Trois jours se passèrent; elle n'appela pas; elle ne sortit pas.

Quand on ouvrit sa porte, on la trouva raide et froide: elle était morte de douleur.

Mais la vente de cette âme si adorable dans sa charité fut déclarée nulle par le Seigneur: car elle avait sauvé ses concitoyens de la morte éternelle.

Après la huitaine, des vaisseaux nombreux amenèrent à l'Irlande affamée d'immenses provisions de grains.

La famine n'était plus possible. Quant aux marchands, ils disparurent de leur hôtellerie, sans qu'on sût jamais ce qu'ils étaient devenus.

Toutefois, les pêcheurs de la Blackwater prétendent qu'ils sont enchaînés dans une prison souterraine par ordre de Lucifer jusqu'au moment où ils pourront livrer l'âme de Ketty qui leur a échappé. Je vous dis la légende telle que je la sais.

—Mais les pauvres l'ont raconté d'âge en âge et les enfants de Cork et de Dublin chantent encore la ballade dont voici les derniers couplets:—

> Pour sauver les pauvres qu'elle aime
> Ketty donna
> Son esprit, sa croyance même:
> Satan paya
> Cette âme au dévoûment sublime,
> En écus d'or,
> Disons pour racheter son crime,
> *Confiteor.*

Mais l'ange qui se fit coupable
　　Par charité
Au séjour d'amour ineffable
　　Est remonté.
Satan vaincu n'eut pas de prise
　　Sur ce cœur d'or;
Chantons sous la nef de l'église,
　　Confiteor.

N'est-ce pas que ce récit, né de l'imagination des poètes catholiques de la verte Érin, est un véritable récit de carême?

'The Countess Cathleen' was acted in Dublin in 1899, with Mr. Marcus St. John and Mr. Trevor Lowe as the First and Second Demons, Mr. Valentine Grace as Shemus Rua, Master Charles Sefton as Teig, Madame San Carola as Mary, Miss Florence Farr as Aleel, Miss Anna Mather as Oona, Mr. Charles Holmes as the Herdsman, Mr. Jack Wilcox as the Gardener, Mr. Walford as a Peasant, Miss Dorothy Paget as a Spirit, Miss M. Kelly as a Peasant Woman, Mr. T. E. Wilkinson as a Servant, and Miss May Whitty as The Countess Cathleen. Some of the characters so represented have dropped out of the play during revision. The players had to face a very vehement opposition stirred up by a politician and a newspaper, the one accusing me in a pamphlet, the other in long articles day after day, of blasphemy because of the language of the demons or of Shemus Rua, and because I made a woman sell her soul and yet escape damnation, and of a lack of patriotism because I made Irish men and women, who, it seems, never did such a thing, sell theirs. The politician or the newspaper persuaded some forty Catholic students to sign a protest against the play, and a Cardinal, who avowed that he had not read it, to make another, and both politician and newspaper made such obvious appeals to the audience to break the peace, that a score or so of police were sent to the theatre to see that they did not. I had, however, no reason to regret the result, for the stalls, containing almost all that was distinguished in Dublin, and a gallery of artisans alike insisted on the freedom of literature.

After the performance in 1899 I added the love scene between Aleel and the Countess, and in this new form the play was revived in New York by Miss Wycherley, as well as being played a good deal in England and America by amateurs. Now at last I have made a complete revision to make it suitable for performance at the Abbey Theatre. The first two scenes are almost wholly new, and throughout the play I have added or left out such passages as a stage experience of some years showed me encumbered the action; the play in its first form having been written before I knew anything of the theatre. I have left the old end, however, in the version printed in the body of this book, because the change for dramatic purposes has been made for no better reason than that audiences—even at the Abbey Theatre—are almost ignorant of Irish mythology—or because a shallow stage made the elaborate vision of armed angels upon a mountainside impossible. The new end is particularly suited to the Abbey stage, where the stage platform can be brought out in front of the proscenium and have a flight of steps at one side up which the Angel comes, crossing towards the back of the stage at the opposite side. The principal lighting is from two arc lights in the balcony which throw their lights into the faces of the players, making footlights unnecessary. The room at Shemus Rua's house is suggested by a great grey curtain—a colour which becomes full of rich tints under the stream of light from the arcs. The short front scene before the last is just long enough when played with incidental music to allow the scene set behind it to be changed. The play when played without interval in this way lasts a little over an hour.

The play was performed at the Abbey Theatre for the first time on December 14, 1911, Miss Maire O'Neill taking the part of the Countess, and the last scene from the going out of the Merchants was as follows:—

> [*Merchants rush out. Aleel crawls into the*
> *middle of the room; the twilight has fallen*
> *and gradually darkens as the scene goes on.*]
>
> *Aleel.* They're rising up—they're rising through the earth,
> Fat Asmodel and giddy Belial,
> And all the fiends. Now they leap in the air.
> But why does Hell's gate creak so? Round and round,
> Hither and hither, to and fro they're running.
>
> [*He moves about as though the air was full of*
> *spirits. Oona enters.*]
> Crouch down, old heron, out of the blind storm.
>
> *Oona.* Where is the Countess Cathleen? All this day
> Her eyes were full of tears, and when for a moment
> Her hand was laid upon my hand, it trembled.
> And now I do not know where she is gone.
>
> *Aleel.* Cathleen has chosen other friends than us,
> And they are rising through the hollow world.
> Demons are out, old heron.
>
> *Oona.*   God guard her soul.
>
> *Aleel.* She's bartered it away this very hour,
> As though we two were never in the world.
>
> [*He kneels beside her, but does not seem to hear her words. The Peasants*
> *return. They carry the Countess Cathleen and lay her upon the ground before*
> *Oona and Aleel. She lies there as if dead.*]
> *Oona.* O, that so many pitchers of rough clay
> Should prosper and the porcelain break in two!
>
>   [*She kisses the hands of Cathleen.*]
> *A Peasant.* We were under the tree where the path turns
> When she grew pale as death and fainted away.
>
> *Cathleen.* O, hold me, and hold me tightly, for the storm
> Is dragging me away.

[*Oona takes her in her arms. A Woman begins to wail.*]

Peasants.   Hush!

Peasants.   Hush!

Peasant Women.   Hush!

Other Peasant Women.   Hush!

Cathleen [*half rising*]. Lay all the bags of money in a heap,
 And when I am gone, old Oona, share them out
 To every man and woman: judge, and give
 According to their needs.

A Peasant Woman.   And will she give
 Enough to keep my children through the dearth?

Another Peasant Woman. O, Queen of Heaven,
  and all you blessed saints,
 Let us and ours be lost, so she be shriven.

Cathleen. Bend down your faces, Oona and Aleel;
 I gaze upon them as the swallow gazes
 Upon the nest under the eave, before
 She wander the loud waters. Do not weep
 Too great a while, for there is many a candle
 On the High Altar though one fall. Aleel,
 Who sang about the dancers of the woods,
 That know not the hard burden of the world,
 Having but breath in their kind bodies, farewell!
 And farewell, Oona, you who played with me
 And bore me in your arms about the house
 When I was but a child—and therefore happy,
 Therefore happy even like those that dance.
 The storm is in my hair and I must go.

             [*She dies.*

Oona. Bring me the looking-glass.

 [*A Woman brings it to her out of inner room. Oona holds glass over the lips
 of Cathleen. All is silent for a moment, then she speaks in a half-scream.*]
       O, she is dead!

A Peasant. She was the great white lily of the world.

A Peasant. She was more beautiful than the pale stars.

An Old Peasant Woman. The little plant I loved is broken in two.

 [*Aleel takes looking-glass from Oona and flings it upon floor, so that it is
 broken in many pieces.*]

Aleel. I shatter you in fragments, for the face
 That brimmed you up with beauty is no more;
 And die, dull heart, for you that were a mirror
 Are but a ball of passionate dust again!
 And level earth and plumy sea, rise up!
 And haughty sky, fall down!

A Peasant Woman.   Pull him upon his knees,
 His curses will pluck lightning on our heads.

Aleel. Angels and devils clash in the middle air,
And brazen swords clang upon brazen helms.
Look, look, a spear has gone through Belial's eye!
[*A winged Angel, carrying a torch and a sword, enters from the R. with eyes fixed upon some distant thing. The Angel is about to pass out to the L., when Aleel speaks. The Angel stops a moment and turns.*]
Look no more on the half-closed gates of Hell,
But speak to me whose mind is smitten of God,
That it may be no more with mortal things:
And tell of her who lies there.
[*The Angel turns again and is about to go, but is seized by Aleel.*]
                                        Till you speak
You shall not drift into eternity.
The Angel. The light beats down; the gates of pearl are wide.
And she is passing to the floor of peace,
And Mary of the seven times wounded heart
Has kissed her lips, and the long blessed hair
Has fallen on her face; the Light of Lights
Looks always on the motive, not the deed,
The Shadow of Shadows on the deed alone.
                        [*Aleel releases the Angel and kneels.*]
Oona. Tell them to walk upon the floor of peace,
That I would die and go to her I love;
The years like great black oxen tread the world,
And God the herdsman goads them on behind,
And I am broken by their passing feet.   **78, 80.**

The Countess Cathleen.—I found . . . Whitty as *The Countess Kathleen.* They had to face . . . light from the arcs. The two or more arches in the third scene permit the use of a gauze. The short front scene . . . .
                                46, 49, 51, 56a-62, 66-76.

The Countess Cathleen was acted in Dublin . . . Whitty as the Countess Cathleen. They had to face . . . light from the arcs. The two or more arches in the third scene permit the use of a gauze. The short front scene . . . as follows:—
            . . . ,
    . . . her I love,
    . . . .
                                52, 63.

I found . . . récit de carême?
'The Countess Cathleen' was first acted in Dublin on May 8th, 1899, at the Ancient Concert Rooms, with Mr. Marcus . . . Whitty as The Countess Kathleen. They had to face . . . America by amateurs; now . . . light from the arcs. The two or more arches in the third scene permit the use of a gauze. The short front scene . . . as follows:—

. . .

   O, Queen of Heaven, and all you blessed saints

. . .

   . . . her I love,

. . .   **Appendix II, 48.**

The Countess Cathleen.—I found . . . un sixpence d'argent . . . la comtesse
Ketty O'Donnor. Elle était . . . freedom of literature, and I myself have the
pleasure of recording strange events.

   The play has since been revived in New York by Miss Wycherley, but I
did not see her performance.   **33.**

The Countess Cathleen.—I found . . . un sixpence d'argent . . . la comtesse
Ketty O'Donnor. Elle était . . . freedom of literature, and I myself have the
pleasure of recording strange events.   **7, 18, 31.**

[headed Appendix II / The Dates and Places of Performance of the Plays]
  'The Countess Cathleen' was first acted in Dublin on May 8, 1899, at
the Ancient Concert Rooms, with Mr. Marcus . . . Whitty as the Countess
Cathleen.

   They had to face . . . newspaper; the . . . articles, day . . . blasphemy,
because . . . Demons in the first act, and because . . . women, who it . . . thing,
sell theirs. I could but answer that I knew many that sold their souls daily
and for a lesser price, but the controversy grew very fierce, and the politician
and the newspaper made such . . . peace that something over a score of
police were sent into the theatre to keep order. However, the stalls containing . . . artisans, alike insisted upon the freedom of literature. The
greatest difficulty before the creator of a living Irish drama has been, and
to some extent still is, the extreme sensitiveness of a nation, which has come
to look upon Irish literature not as a free play of the mind over the surface
and in the depths of life, but as a defence delivered before a prejudiced jury,
who have heard a very confident advocate on the other side.

   'The Countess Cathleen' was revived in New York about a year ago (I
have not the exact date by me) by Miss Wycherley, and will probably be
played next autumn, a good deal altered for technical reasons, at the
Abbey Theatre.   **28.**

The Countess Cathleen.—I included the legend on which this poem is founded
in *Fairy and Folk Tales of the Irish Peasantry,* under the belief that it was
indigenous Irish folklore: I have since heard that it is of recent introduction.
The editor of *Folklore* kindly printed an advertisement asking for information
as to variants, origin, &c., but without any result. The only story at all like
it that I know of is a story in Mr. Larminie's *West Irish Folk Tales* of a mother
who went to hell for seven years to redeem the soul of her son, and stayed
another seven years to redeem other souls.   **6.**

The Countess Cathleen.—The writer included the legend on which this poem
is founded in his *Fairy and Folk Tales of the Irish Peasantry,* under the belief

that it was indigenous Irish folklore: he has since heard that it is of recent introduction. The editor of *Folklore* has kindly printed an advertisement asking for information as to variants, origin, etc.   5.

The Countess Cathleen. The play is founded on a West of Ireland folk tale.   3.

*   *   *

Note for directions after 931.—When I was in my twenties I saw a drawing or etching by some French artist of an angel standing against a midnight sky. The angel was old, wingless, and armed like a knight, as impossibly tall as one of those figures at Chartres Cathedral, and its face was worn by time and by innumerable battles. I showed my father the drawing but he thought nothing of it because it was out of proportion, and I did not then know that an artist may exaggerate as he will for the sake of expression. Generally a judgment from my father would put me off anything, but this time that image remained and I imitated it in the old angels at the (angels at the **E**) end of *The Countess Cathleen.*

Pages From a Diary Written in Nineteen Hundred and Thirty. Dublin, The Cuala Press, 1944, pp. 19, 20. Reprinted in *Explorations.* London, 1962; New York, 1962, pp. 305-306.

*   *   *

Variant Spellings

Adene 3-18, 31 ; *Edain* 28, 33.

Allan 5-33 ; *Allen* 46-97.

aught 5, 6, 33 ; *ought* 3, 7-31.

Ave Maries 3-6 ; *Ave Marys* 7-97.

ay 3 ; *aye* 5-33.

bad 7 ; *bade* 18-33.

baptised 51 ; *baptized* 46-49, 52-97.

Cathleen 5-97 ; *Kathleen* 3.

chant 3 ; *chaunt* 5-33.

Croaghpatrick 46-80 ; *Cro-Patrick* 84, 97.

Dectera 5-18, 31, 46-80 ; *Dectora* 28, 33, 84, 97.

Edain (see *Adene*).

Eri 3, 5 ; *Erie* 6.

faery 5-33 ; *fairy* 3.

Fenian 5-33 ; *Finian* 3.

forbear 5-7, 28 ; *forebear* 3, 18, 31, 33.

gray, grey 3 ; *gray* 5-33 ; *grey* 46-97.

helebore 3 ; *hellebore* 5-97.

knowledgable **46, 49**; *knowledgeable* **48.**
Maire **5-33**; *Mary* **3, 46-97**; *Maries* **3-6**; *Marys* **7-97.**
merchandise **5-97**; *merchandize* **3.**
Naisi **5-80**; *Naoisi* **84, 97.**
Niam **3, 6-18, 31**; *Neave* **5**; *Niamh* **28, 33.**
nich **3**; *niche* **5-97.**
O **5-33, 84, 97**; *O, Oh* **3, 46-80.**
Oisin **3, 6-33**; *Usheen* **5.**
Orchil **5-33, 84, 97**; *Orchill* **46-80.**
shee **3-18, 31**; *sidhe* **28, 33.**
sheogue **3, 5-18, 31**; *sidheoge* **28, 33.**
stanch **7-31**; *staunch* **33.**
sty **5, 6, 33**; *stye* **3, 7-31.**
Sualtam **5-33**; *Sualtem* **46-80**; *Sualtim* **84, 97.**
Teig **3-80**; *Teigue* **84, 97.**
tevish, tevishes **3**; *thivish, thivishes, thivishies* **5**; *thivish, thivishes* **6.**
woeful **3**; *woful* **5-33.**

* * *

[See also the notes on *The Land of Heart's Desire*, p. 211; *The Legendary and Mythological Foundation of the Plays and Poems*, p. 1282; *Glossary*, p. 1284; and *Prefaces to 3, 5-80, 28, 48, 52, 69, 71, 84*, pp. 1288, 1293, 1303, 1306, 1307, 1309.]

THE LAND OF HEART'S DESIRE

1894

'O Rose, thou art sick'
William Blake

TO

FLORENCE FARR

Persons in the Play

Maurteen Bruin	Mary Bruin
Bridget Bruin	Father Hart
Shawn Bruin	A Faery Child

The Scene is laid in the Barony of Kilmacowen, in the
County of Sligo, and at a remote time

A room with a hearth on the floor in the middle of a deep alcove to the right. There are benches in the alcove and a table; and a crucifix on the wall. The alcove is full of a glow of light from the fire. There is an open door facing the audience to the left, and to the left of this a bench. Through the door one can see the forest. It is night, but the moon or a late sunset glimmers through the trees and carries the eye far off into a vague, mysterious world. Maurteen Bruin, Shawn Bruin, and Bridget Bruin sit in the alcove at the table or about the fire.

PRINTINGS 4, 5, 6, 7, 12, 18, 28, 31, 33, 37, 47, 48, 49, 51, 61, 62, 63, 66, 67, 68, 71, 72, 73, 74, 76, 77, 78, 80, 84, 89, 97.

DATE [lacking] 4-62, 66-80; (1894, revised 1911) 63.

DEDICATION [lacking] 4, 37, 68, 77; To Miss Florence . . . 5.

EPIGRAPH [lacking] 4, 37, 63, 68, 77.

DRAMATIS PERSONAE[1] [Heading lacking] 5-7, 18-31, 47-67, 72-76; Persons 4-37; Dramatis Personae 12; Characters 68; Persons of the . . . 71, 78, 80.

    Maurteen Bruin / Shawn Bruin / Father Hart / Bridget Bruin [lacking 5] / Maire Bruin / A . . . 4-37, 77;

[1] In 4-37, the full names of the characters are generally used; in 68 they are often abbreviated, e.g. to Maur., Bridg., Father, and Child.

They are dressed in the costume of some remote time, and near them sits an old priest, Father Hart. He may be dressed as a friar. There is food and drink upon the table. Mary Bruin stands by the door reading a book. If she looks up she can see through the door into the wood.

1. *Bridget.* Because I bid her clean the pots for supper
2.   She took that old book down out of the thatch;
3.   She has been doubled over it ever since.
4.   We should be deafened by her groans and moans

Maurteen Bruin, *a peasant* / Shawn Bruin, *his son* / Father Hart, *a priest* / Bridget Bruin, *Maurteen's wife* / Maire Bruin, *their daughter-in-law* / A Child **68.**

PLACE AND TIME. . . . *Kilmacowen in . . . Sligo, and the time is the end of Eighteenth (of the Eighteenth* **5, 77**) *Century. The characters are supposed to speak in Gaelic.* **4, 5, 37, 77**; *The scene . . . Sligo, and the characters are supposed to speak in Gaelic. They wear the costume of a century ago.* **6-33**; [lacking] **68**; *The Scene . . . time.* **73, 76, 78, 80.**

Note.—The passages enclosed in square brackets are those left out when the play is performed at the Abbey Theatre, Dublin. **73, 76, 78, 80.**[1]

STAGE DIRECTIONS. *The kitchen of Maurteen Bruin's house. An open grate with a turf fire is at the left side of the room, with a table in front of it. There is a door leading to the open air at the back, and another door a little to its left, leading into (to* **68**) *an inner room. There is a window, a settle, (settle* **68**) *and a large dresser on the right side of the room, and a great bowl of primroses on the sill of the window. Maurteen Bruin, Father Hart, and Bridget Bruin are sitting at the table. Shawn (Shaun* **6, 7**) *Bruin is setting the table for supper. Maire Bruin sits on the settle reading a yellow manuscript.* **4-37, 68, 77**; Scene.—(Scene. **48, 63**) *A . . . Right. . . . Left, ...* **47-67, 71-76, 78, 80.**

1. . . . I bade her go and feed the calves, **4-37, 68, 77**; . . . supper. **48**; . . . supper, **63.**
2. . . . thatch **4-37, 68, 73, 76, 77**; . . . thatch, **48, 63.**
3. And has . . . it all day. **4-37, 68, 77.**
4. We would be . . . **4-37, 68, 77**; . . . moans, **48, 63.**

[1] Cf. note 1, p. 182; and note, p. 212.

5.   Had she to work as some do, Father Hart;
6.   Get up at dawn like me and mend and scour
7.   Or ride abroad in the boisterous night like you,
8.   The pyx and blessed bread under your arm.

9. *Shawn.* Mother, you are too cross.

Bridget.   You've married her,
10.   And fear to vex her and so take her part.

11. *Maurteen [to Father Hart].* It is but right that youth should side with
        youth;
12.   She quarrels with my wife a bit at times,
13.   And is too deep just now in the old book!
14.   But do not blame her greatly; (she will grow
15.   As quiet as a puff-ball in a tree
16.   When but the moons of marriage dawn and die
17.   For half a score of times.)[1]

Father Hart.   Their hearts are wild,
18.   As be the hearts of birds, till children come.

19. *Bridget.* She would not mind the kettle, milk the cow,
20.   Or even lay the knives and spread the cloth.

21. *Shawn.* Mother, if only——

Maurteen.   Shawn, this is half empty;

---

5. . . . Hart, **4-37, 48, 63, 68, 77.**
6. . . . me, and . . . scour; **4-37, 68, 77**; . . . scour; **47-49, 63.**
9. You . . . cross.
                    The young side with the young. (young **6**) **4-37, 68, 77.**
10-11. [lacking] **4-37, 68, 77.**
10. . . . her, and . . . . **48.**
13. . . . book; **4, 37, 77**; . . . book, **33.**
14. . . . greatly: (she . . . **97A.**
17. . . . wild **4-37, 68, 77.**
17, Note 1. [lacking] **4-68, 72, 74, 77**; [For a similar note in **73, 76, 78, 80**
        see p. 181].
19. . . . the griddle, milk . . ., **4-37, 68, 77.**
21-22. [lacking] **4-37, 68, 77.**

[1] Amateurs perform this more often than any other play of mine, and I urge them to omit
all lines that I have enclosed in heavy round brackets ( ).—W.B.Y. **84, 89, 97.**

22.   Go, bring up the best bottle that we have.

23. *Father Hart.* I never saw her read a book before,
24.   What can it be?

      Maurteen [to Shawn]. What are you waiting for?
25.   You must not shake it when you draw the cork;
26.   It's precious wine, so take your time about it.

                                        [Shawn goes.

27. *[To Father Hart.]* (There was a Spaniard wrecked at Ocris Head,
28.   When I was young, and I have still some bottles.)
29.   He cannot bear to hear her blamed; the book
30.   Has lain up in the thatch these fifty years;
31.   My father told me my grandfather wrote it,
32.   And killed a heifer for the binding of it—
33.   (But supper's spread, and we can talk and eat.)
34.   It was little good he got out of the book,
35.   Because it filled his house with rambling fiddlers,
36.   And rambling ballad-makers and the like.
37.   (The griddle-bread is there in front of you.)
38.   Colleen, what is the wonder in that book,
39.   That you must leave the bread to cool? Had I
40.   Or had my father read or written books

---

23. . . . before: **4, 37, 77** ; . . . *before;* **5-33, 68** ; . . . *never* . . ., **71A, 73, 76, 78, 80.**
24. What may it . . .?
    Maurteen.   I do not rightly know: (know; **7-33, 68**) **4-37, 68, 77.**
25-29. [lacking] **4-37, 68, 77.**
26. . . . take you time . . . . **71A.**
    Directions at 27. *[To Priest.]* **47-76, 78-89.**
30. It has been in the thatch for fifty years. **4-37, 68, 77** ; . . . *years,* **48, 63.**
32. Killed a red heifer and bound it with the hide. **4-37, 68, 77.**
33. But draw your chair this way—supper is spread; (spread. **33**) **4-37, 68, 77** ; . . . *eat* **49-62, 66, 67** ; . . . *eat]* **71-76, 78-89.**
34. And little . . ., **4-37, 68, 77.**
35. . . . with roaming bards,
36. And roaming ballad-makers . . . *like,*
36a. And wasted all his goods.—Here is the wine; (wine: **5-33, 68**)
37. The griddle bread's beside you, Father Hart.
38. . . ., what have you got there in the book
39. . . . I, **4-37, 68, 77.**
40. . . . father, read . . . **4-37, 68, 77** ; . . . *books,* **48, 63.**

41.   There were no stocking stuffed with yellow guineas
42.   To come when I am dead to Shawn and you.

43. *Father Hart.* You should not fill your head with foolish dreams.
44.   What are you reading?

     Mary.   How a Princess Edain,
45.   A daughter of a King of Ireland, heard
46.   A voice singing on a May Eve like this,
47.   And followed, half awake and half asleep,
48.   Until she came into the Land of Faery,
49.   Where nobody gets old and godly and grave,
50.   Where nobody gets old and crafty and wise,
51.   Where nobody gets old and bitter of tongue.
52.   And she is still there, busied with a dance
53.   Deep in the dewy shadow of a wood,
54.   (Or where stars walk upon a mountain-top.)

55. *Maurteen.* Persuade the colleen to put down the book;
56.   My grandfather would mutter just such things,
57.   And he was no judge of a dog or a horse,
58.   And any idle boy could blarney him;
59.   Just speak your mind.

    Father Hart.   Put it away, my colleen;
60.   (God spreads the heavens above us like great wings
61.   And gives a little round of deeds and days,
62.   And then come the wrecked angels and set snares,
63.   And bait them with light hopes and heavy dreams,
64.   Until the heart is puffed with pride and goes

---

41. . . . stocking full of silver and gold **4-37, 68, 77**; There was no . . . **47, 48, 63.**
42. . . . come, when . . . dead, to . . . . **4-37, 68, 77.**
46. . . . eve . . ., **4.**
47. . . . followed half . . ., **47, 51-62, 66-76, 78, 80.**
48. . . . land . . . faery, **4-37, 68, 77.**
51. . . . tongue; **4-37, 68, 77.**
52. . . . dance, **4-37, 48, 63 ,68, 77.**
54. . . . mountain top. **4, 5, 37, 77.**
55. . . . put by the book: **4-37, 68, 77.**
57. . . . or horse, **4-37, 68, 77.**
58. . . . him. **4, 37, 77**; . . . him: **5-33, 68.**
59. . . . colleen.
60. . . . wings, **4-37, 48, 63, 68, 77.**
64. . . . goes, **4-37, 68, 77.**

65.   Half shuddering and half joyous from God's peace;)
66.   For it was some wrecked angel, blind with tears,
67.   Who flattered Edain's heart with merry words.
68.   My colleen, I have seen some other girls
69.   Restless and ill at ease, but years went by
70.   And they grew like their neighbours and were glad
71.   In minding children, working at the churn,
72.   And gossiping of weddings and of wakes;
73.   (For life moves out of a red flare of dreams
74.   Into a common light of common hours,
75.   Until old age bring the red flare again.)

76.   *Maurteen.* That's true—but she's too young to know it's true.

77.   *Bridget.* She's old enough to know that it is wrong
78.   To mope and idle.

        Maurteen.   I've little blame for her;
79.   She's dull when my big son is in the fields,
80.   And that and maybe this good woman's tongue
81.   Have driven her to hide among her dreams
82.   Like children from the dark under the bedclothes.

83. *Bridget.* She'd never do a turn if I were silent.

84. *Maurteen.* And maybe it is natural upon May Eve
85.   To dream of the Good People. But tell me, girl,
86.   If you've the branch of blessed quicken wood

---

    65.   . . . joyous, from . . .; **4, 5, 37, 77**; . . . joyous, from . . . peace: **6-33,
           68**; . . . peace], **73, 76, 78, 80.**
    66.   And it . . ., blind from tears, **4-37, 68, 77**; And it . . ., **47-67, 72, 74.**
    75.   . . . brings . . . . **68.**
76-77.   [lacking] **4-37, 68, 77.**
    78.   *Shawn.* Yet do not blame her greatly, Father Hart,
    79.   For she is dull while I am in . . .,
    80.   And mother's tongue were harder still to bear,
    81.   But for her fancies: this is May Eve (Eve, **37, 77**) too, **4-37, 68, 77.**
82-84.   [lacking] **4-37, 68, 77.**
    82.   . . . bed-clothes. **47, 49-67, 72-76, 78, 80.**
    85.   When the good people post about the world, **4-37, 68, 77**; . . . good
           people. . . ., **47-67, 71-76, 78, 80.**
   85a.   And surely one may think of them to-night.
    86.   Maire, have you the primroses to fling **4-37, 68, 77.**

87.   That women hang upon the post of the door
88.   That they may send good luck into the house?
89.   Remember they may steal new-married brides
90.   After the fall of twilight on May Eve,
91.   Or what old women mutter at the fire
92.   Is but a pack of lies.

    Father Hart.   It may be truth.
93.   We do not know the limit of those powers
94.   God has permitted to the evil spirits
95.   For some mysterious end. You have done right [*to Mary*];
96.   It's well to keep old innocent customs up.
    [*Mary Bruin has taken a bough of quicken wood from a seat and hung*
    it on a nail in the door-post. A girl child strangely dressed, perhaps in
    faery green, comes out of the wood and takes it away.

97.   *Mary.* I had no sooner hung it on the nail

---

87.   Before the door to make a golden path
88.   For them to bring good . . . house. (house? **7-37, 68, 77**) **4-37, 68, 77.**
89.   Remember, they . . . **4-33, 68**; Remember, they . . . new married . . .
    37, 77.
90.   Upon May Eve.
    Maire Bruin [*going over to the window and taking the flowers from the bowl*].
    Here are the primroses. [*She goes to the door and strews the primroses*
    outside.] **4, 37, 77**; . . . Eve. [*Maire Bruin goes over to the window and takes*
    flowers from the bowl and strews them outside the door.] **5-33, 68.**
91-94.   [lacking] **4-37, 68, 77.**
95.   *Father Hart.* You do well, daughter, because God permits **4-37, 68,**
    77; . . . *Mary*]. **48, 63.**
96.   Great power to the good people on May Eve. **4-37, 68, 77.**
    Directions after 96.   [lacking] **4-37, 68, 77.**
96a.   *Maurteen Bruin.* (*Shawn Bruin.* **6-33, 68**) They can work all their will
    with primroses—(primroses; **6-33, 68**)
96b.   Change them to golden money, or little flames
96c.   To burn up those who do them any wrong. **4-37, 68, 77.**
97.   . . . sooner flung them by the door **4, 5, 37, 77**; *Maire Bruin* [*in a*
    dreamy voice]. I . . . sooner flung them by the door **6-33, 68.**
97a.   Than (Then **12** (1903)) the wind cried and hurried them away.
    (away; **6-33, 68**) **4-37, 68, 77.**
97b.   *Bridget Bruin.* May God have mercy on us!
    Maire Bruin.   The good people **4, 5, 37, 77.**

98.   Before a child ran up out of the wind;

99.   She has caught it in her hand and fondled it.

100.   (Her face is pale as water before dawn.)

101.   *Father Hart.* Whose child can this be?

   Maurteen.   No one's child at all.

102.   She often dreams that some one has gone by,

103.   When there was nothing but a puff of wind.

104.   *Mary.* They have taken away the blessed quicken wood,

105.   They will not bring good luck into the house;

106.   Yet I am glad that I was courteous to them,

107.   For are not they, likewise, children of God?

108.   *Father Hart.* Colleen, they are the children of the Fiend,

109.   And they have power until the end of time,

110.   When God shall fight with them a great pitched battle

111.   And hack them into pieces.

   Mary.   He will smile,

112.   Father, perhaps, and open His great door.

113.   *Father Hart.* Did but the lawless angels see that door

---

98-104.   [lacking] **4, 5, 37, 77.**

  98.   And then a child came running in the wind **6-33, 68.**

  99.   And caught them in . . . hands . . . fondled them: **6-33, 68** ; . . . it;
      47-67, 71-76, 78-89.

  99a.   Her dress was green: (green; **6**) her hair was of red gold;

  100.   . . . face was pale . . . . **6-33, 68.**

  102.   . . . by **6-31, 68** ; . . . someone . . . by **33.**

  104.   [lacking] **6-33, 68.**

  105.   Will not be lucky to the house this year, **4, 5, 37, 77** ; . . . house, **6-33,
      68.**

  105a.   For they have blown the primroses away; **6-33, 68.**

  106.   But I . . ., **4, 5, 37, 77.**

  108.   No, child; they . . . fiend, **4, 5, 37, 77** ; . . . fiend, **6-31, 47-67, 71-76,
      78, 80** ; . . . of the field, **68.**

  109.   . . . Time, **4-80.**

  112.   . . . . his . . . door, **4-6, 68** ; . . . door, **7-37, 77.**

  112a.   And call the pretty and kind into his (His **7-37, 77**) home. (house.
      6-33, 68) **4-37, 68, 77.**

  113.   . . . door, **4-37, 48, 63, 68, 77.**

114.   They would fall, slain by everlasting peace;
115.   And when such angels knock upon our doors,
116.   Who goes with them must drive through the same storm.
         [*An arm comes round the door-post and knocks and beckons. It is clearly seen in the silvery light. Mary Bruin goes to door and stands in it for a moment. Maurteen Bruin is busy filling Father Hart's plate. Bridget Bruin stirs the fire.*

117.   *Mary* [*coming to table*]. There's somebody out there that beckoned me
118.   And raised her hand as though it held a cup,
119.   And she was drinking from it, so it may be
120.   That she is thirsty.
         [*She takes milk from the table and carries it to the door.*

         Father Hart.   That will be the child
121.   That you would have it was no child at all.

122.   *Bridget.* (And maybe, Father, what he said was true;
123.   For there is not another night in the year
124.   So wicked as to-night.

         Maurteen.   Nothing can harm us
125.   While the good Father's underneath our roof.

126.   *Mary.* A little queer old woman dressed in green.

127.   *Bridget.* The Good People beg for milk and fire

---

114.   . . . peace **48, 63.**
115.   . . . doors **4-37, 68, 77.**
116.   . . . storm **18.**
         Directions after 116. [*A knock at the door. Maire Bruin opens it and then goes to the dresser and fills a porringer with milk and hands it through the door and takes it back empty and closes the door.*] **4-37, 68, 77**; [*A thin old arm . . . .*] **47-67, 72-76, 78, 80**; [. . . *comes around the . . . .*] **71A.**
117-125. [lacking] **4-37, 68, 77.**
117.   . . . beckons me **73, 76, 78, 80.**
126.   . . . woman cloaked in green,
126a.   Who came to beg a porringer of milk. **4-37, 68, 77.**
127.   . . . good people go asking milk . . . **4-37, 68, 77**; . . . good people . . . **47, 49-62, 66, 67, 71-76, 78, 80**; . . . good people . . . fire, **48, 63.**

128.   Upon May Eve—woe to the house that gives,
129.   For they have power upon it for a year.

130.   *Maurteen.* Hush, woman, hush!

    Bridget.   She's given milk away.
131.   I knew she would bring evil on the house.

132.   *Maurteen.* Who was it?

    Mary.   Both the tongue and face were strange.

133.   *Maurteen.* Some strangers came last week to Clover Hill;
134.   She must be one of them.)

    Bridget.   I am afraid.

135.   *Father Hart.* The Cross will keep all evil from the house
136.   While it hangs there.

    Maurteen.   Come, sit beside me, colleen,
137.   And put away your dreams of discontent,
138.   For I would have you light up my last days,
139.   Like the good glow of the turf; and when I die
140.   You'll be the wealthiest hereabout, for, colleen,
141.   I have a stocking full of yellow guineas
142.   Hidden away where nobody can find it.

---

128.   ... Eve—Woe (Eve.—Woe **7, 33**) on the ... gives, (gives 5) **4-37, 68, 77.**

129a. I knew you would bring evil on the house. **4-37, 68, 77.**

130-131. [lacking] **4-37, 68, 77.**

  132. ... was she?

           Both .... **4-37, 68, 77.**

134a. *Maurteen.* The priest will keep all harm out of the house.

  135. ... Cross (cross **5-33, 68**) ... all harm out of the ... **4-37, 68, 77.**

  136. ..., colleen **5.**

  138. ... days

  139. Like a bright torch of pine, and ...

  140. I will make you the ... hereabout; (hereabout: **5-33, 68**)

  141. For hid away where nobody can find

  142. I have a stocking full of silver and gold. **4-37, 68, 77.**

143. *Bridget.* You are the fool of every pretty face,
144.   And I must spare and pinch that my son's wife
145.   May have all kinds of ribbons for her head.

146. *Maurteen.* Do not be cross; she is a right good girl!
147.   (The butter is by your elbow, Father Hart.
148.   My colleen, have not Fate and Time and Change
149.   Done well for me and for old Bridget there?)
150.   We have a hundred acres of good land,
151.   And sit beside each other at the fire.
152.   I have this reverend Father for my friend,
153.   I look upon your face and my son's face—
154.   We've put his plate by yours—and here he comes,
155.   And brings with him the only thing we have lacked,
156.   Abundance of good wine. [*Shawn comes in.*] Stir up the fire,
157.   And put new turf upon it till it blaze;
158.   To watch the turf-smoke coiling from the fire,
159.   And feel content and wisdom in your heart,
160.   This is the best of life; (when we are young
161.   We long to tread a way none trod before,
162.   But find the excellent old way through love,
163.   And through the care of children, to the hour
164.   For bidding Fate and Time and Change good-bye.)
          [*Mary stands for a moment in the door (and then takes a sod of turf
          from the fire and goes out through the door. Shawn follows her and
          meets her coming in.*)

---

144. . . . must pinch and pare that . . . **4-37, 68, 77.**
147. The butter's by . . . . **4-6, 37, 77** ; . . . Hart, **48, 63.**
151. . . . fire, **4-37, 68, 77.**
152. The wise priest of our parish to our right,
153. And you and our dear son to left of us.
154-155. [lacking] **4-37, 68, 77.**
156. To sit beside the board and drink good wine **4-37, 68, 77.**
157. [lacking] **4-37, 68, 77** ; . . . blaze. **48, 63.**
158. And watch . . . turf smoke . . . fire **4-37, 68, 77.**
162. . . . love
163. . . . children to . . . **4-37, 68, 77.**
164. . . . goodbye. **6-18, 31, 47, 49-62, 66, 67, 72-76, 78, 80.**
          Directions after 164. [*A knock at the door. Maire Bruin opens it and
          then . . . turf out of the hearth in the tongs and passes it through the door and
          closes the door and remains standing by it.*] **4-37, 68, 77** ; [*Mary takes*

165. *Shawn.* What is it draws you to the chill o' the wood?
166.   There is a light among the stems of the trees
167.   That makes one shiver.

      Mary.   A little queer old man
168.   Made me a sign to show he wanted fire
169.   To light his pipe.

      Bridget.   You've given milk and fire
170.   Upon the unluckiest night of the year and brought,
171.   For all you know, evil upon the house.
172.   Before you married you were idle and fine
173.   And went about with ribbons on your head;
174.   And now—no, Father, I will speak my mind—
175.   She is not a fitting wife for any man——

176. *Shawn.* Be quiet, mother!

      Maurteen.   You are much too cross.

177. *Mary.* What do I care if I have given this house,
178.   Where I must hear all day a bitter tongue,
179.   Into the power of faeries!

      Bridget.   You know well
180.   How calling the Good People by that name,
181.   Or talking of them over-much at all,

....] 47-67, 72, 74; [. . . *door, and takes (and then takes* **71**) ....] **71,**
73, 76, 78, 80; ['acting' brackets lacking] **71, 73, 76, 78, 80.**
165-166. [lacking] **4-37, 68, 77.**
167. *Maire Bruin.* A little . . . man in a green coat, **4-37, 68, 77.**
167-169. [Mary's speech, 'A . . . pipe.' enclosed in 'acting' brackets] **71, 73,**
      76, 78, 80.
168. Who asked a burning sod to light his pipe. **4-37, 68, 77.**
169. *Bridget Bruin.* You have now given . . . fire (fire, **5-33, 68**) and brought
      (brought, **5-37, 68, 77**) **4-37, 68, 77;** . . . fire, **48, 63.**
170. [lacking] **4-37, 68, 77;** . . . year, and . . ., **48, 63.**
172. . . . fine, **4-37, 48, 63, 68, 77.**
174. [lacking] **4-37, 68, 77;** . . . mind **47, 49;** . . . mind, **48, 63.**
175. And now you are a good-for-nothing wife. **4-37, 68, 77.**
176. . . . cross! **4-37, 68, 77** [second hemistich printed as new line] ; . . .,
      Mother! . . . . **47-67, 72-76, 78, 80.**
180. . . . good people . . . name **4-37, 68, 77;** . . . good people . . ., **47-67,**
      71-76, 78, 80.
181. . . . over much . . . all **4-31, 37, 68, 77;** . . . all **33;** . . . over much . . .,
      47, 49-62, 66, 67, 71-76, 78, 80; . . . overmuch . . ., **48, 63.**

182.   May bring all kinds of evil on the house.

183. *Mary.* Come, faeries, take me out of this dull house!
184.   Let me have all the freedom I have lost;
185.   Work when I will and idle when I will!
186.   Faeries, come take me out of this dull world,
187.   For I would ride with you upon the wind,
188.   (Run on the top of the dishevelled tide,)
189.   And dance upon the mountains like a flame.

190. *Father Hart.* You cannot know the meaning of your words.

191. *Mary.* Father, I am right weary of four tongues:
192.   A tongue that is too crafty and too wise,
193.   A tongue that is too godly and too grave,
194.   A tongue that is more bitter than the tide,
195.   And a kind tongue too full of drowsy love,
196.   Of drowsy love and my captivity.

                    [*Shawn Bruin leads her to a seat at the left of the door.*

197. *Shawn.* Do not blame me; I often lie awake
198.   Thinking that all things trouble your bright head.
199.   How beautiful it is—your broad pale forehead
200.   Under a cloudy blossoming of hair!
201.   Sit down beside me here—these are too old,
202.   And have forgotten they were ever young.

203. *Mary.* O, you are the great door-post of this house,
204.   And I the branch of blessed quicken wood,

---

184. . . . lost— **4, 37, 77.**
186. . . ., come, take . . ., **33.**
187. . . . wind. **47-67, 71E, 72-76, 78, 80.**
189. . . . flame! **4-37, 68, 77.**
190. . . . words! **4, 37, 77**; . . . words **5.**
        Directions after 196. [. . . *Bruin comes over to her and leads her to the
        settle.*] **4-37, 68, 77.**
197. . . . me: I . . . **4-31, 37, 68, 77.**
198. . . . head—
199. . . . is—such broad pale brows **4-37, 68, 77.**
203. O you . . ., **68.**
204. . . . I (I, **5-33, 68**) the red nasturtium (nasturtium, **5-33, 68**) climbing
        up. **4-37, 68, 77.**
        Directions after 204. [*She takes Shawn's hand* (hand, **5-33, 68**) *but looks
        shyly at the priest and lets it go.*] **4-37, 68, 77.**

205.   And if I could I'd hang upon the post
206.   Till I had brought good luck into the house.

    [*She would put her arms about him, but looks shyly at the priest and lets her arms fall.*

207.   *Father Hart.* My daughter, take his hand—by love alone
208.   God binds us to Himself and to the hearth,
209.   That shuts us from the waste beyond His peace,
210.   From maddening freedom and bewildering light.

211.   *Shawn.* Would that the world were mine to give it you,
212.   And not its quiet hearths alone, but even
213.   All that bewilderment of light and freedom,
214.   If you would have it.

    Mary.   I would take the world
215.   And break it into pieces in my hands
216.   To see you smile watching it crumble away.

217.   *Shawn.* Then I would mould a world of fire and dew,
218.   With no one bitter, grave or over-wise,
219.   And nothing marred or old to do you wrong,
220.   And crowd the enraptured quiet of the sky
221.   With candles burning to your lonely face.

222.   *Mary.* Your looks are all the candles that I need.

205-directions after 206.   [lacking] **4-37, 68, 77.**
205.   . . . post, **47-67, 71-76, 78, 80.**
207.   Good daughter, . . . **4-37, 68, 77** ; . . . hand; by . . . **48, 63.**
208.   . . . hearth **4-37, 68, 77.**
209.   And shuts . . ., **4-37, 77** ; . . . peace **47, 48, 63** ; And shuts . . . his . . ., **68.**
211.   . . . you
212.   With every quiet hearth and barren waste, **4-37, 68, 77.**
213.   The maddening freedom of its woods and tides, **4-37, 68, 77** ; . . . freedom. **47-49, 63.**
214.   And the bewildering lights (light **5-33, 68**) upon its hills.
215.   Then I would take and break it in my hands **4-37, 68, 77.**
217.   . . . dew **4-37, 47** (1912), **68, 77.**
218.   . . ., grave, or over wise, **4-31, 37, 63, 68, 77** ; . . ., grave, or . . ., **33** ; . . . over wise, **47-62, 66, 67, 71-76, 78, 80.**
219.   . . . wrong. **4-31, 37, 68, 77** ; . . . wrong; **33.**

223. *Shawn.* Once a fly dancing in a beam of the sun,
224.   Or the light wind blowing out of the dawn,
225.   Could fill your heart with dreams none other knew,
226.   But now the indissoluble sacrament
227.   Has mixed your heart that was most proud and cold
228.   With my warm heart for ever; the sun and moon
229.   Must fade and heaven be rolled up like a scroll,
230.   But your white spirit still walk by my spirit.

                                   [*A Voice singing in the wood.*

231. *Maurteen.* There's some one singing. Why, it's but a child.
232.   It sang, 'The lonely of heart is withered away.'
233.   A strange song for a child, but she sings sweetly.
234.   Listen, listen!   [*Goes to door.*

    Mary.   O, cling close to me,
235.   Because I have said wicked things to-night.

236. *The Voice.* The wind blows out of the gates of the day,
237.   The wind blows over the lonely of heart,
238.   And the lonely of heart is withered away.
239.   While the faeries dance in a place apart,
240.   Shaking their milk-white feet in a ring,

---

223.   . . . beam o' the . . ., **4-6, 37, 77**; . . . sun **68**.
228.   . . . ever; (forever; **37, 68, 77**) and sun . . . **4-37, 68, 77.**
229.   . . . scroll; **4-80.**
230.   . . . walks . . . . **71A, 73, 76, 78, 80.**
        Directions after 230. [lacking] **4, 37, 77**; [. . . *Voice sings in the distance.*] **5-33, 68.**
230a.   For not a power in earth and heaven and hell **4, 37, 77.**
230b.   Can break this bond binding heart unto heart.
        Directions after 230b. [*A Voice sings in the distance.*] **4, 37, 77.**
231-233. [lacking] **4-37, 68, 77.**
233.   . . . sweetly, **63.**
234.   *Maire Bruin.* Did you hear something call? O, (O **68**) guard me close, **4-37, 68, 77**; . . . , Listen! . . . . **47, 49.**
235.   . . . to-night; **6-33, 68.**
235a.   And seen a pale-faced child with red-gold hair,
235b.   And longed to dance upon the winds with her. **6-33, 68.**
236-247. [italicized] **5-33.**
236.   *A Voice* [*close to the door*]. The . . . , **4-37, 68, 77.**
237.   . . . heart **4-12, 28, 37, 68, 77.**
238.   . . . away, **4-37, 68, 77**; . . . away **73, 76, 78, 80.**

241.   Tossing their milk-white arms in the air;
242.   For they hear the wind laugh and murmur and sing
243.   Of a land where even the old are fair,
244.   And even the wise are merry of tongue;
245.   But I heard a reed of Coolaney say,
246.   'When the wind has laughed and murmured and sung
247.   The lonely of heart is withered away!'

248. *Maurteen.* Being happy, I would have all others happy,
249.   So I will bring her in out of the cold.

                                   [*He brings in the Faery Child.*

250. *The Child.* (I tire of winds and waters and pale lights.

251. *Maurteen.* And that's no wonder, for when night has fallen)
252.   The wood's a cold and a bewildering place,
253.   But you are welcome here.

     The Child.   I am welcome here.

---

241. . . . air: **18, 31.**
242. . . . laugh, and . . . **4-37, 68, 77.**
246. . . . sung, **4-37, 77.**
247. The ('The **5, 6**) . . . heart must wither . . . !' **4-6, 37, 77**; 'The . . . !'
      7, 18, 31.
248. I am right happy, and would make all else
248a. Be happy too. I hear a child outside,
249. And will go bring . . . . **4-37, 68, 77.**
      Directions after 249. [*He opens the door. A child dressed in a green jacket
      with* (and **5**) *a red cap comes into the house.*] **4, 5, 37, 77**; [*He opens the door.
      A child dressed in pale green and with red gold* (red-gold **7-33, 68**) *hair
      comes into the house.*] **6-33, 68.**
250. . . . lights! **4-37, 68, 77**; ['acting' bracket at beginning of line
      lacking] **73, 76, 78, 80.**
251. [lacking] **4-37, 68, 77.**
252. *Maurteen.* You are most welcome. It is cold out there; **4-37, 68, 77**;
      . . . place; **48, 63.**
253. Who'd think to face such cold on a May Eve. (Eve? **6, 28, 33, 37,
      77**) **4-6, 28, 33, 37, 77**; Who would think to face such cold on a
      May Eve? **7-18, 31, 68.**

254.   (But when I tire of this warm little house)
255.   There is one here that must away, away.

256.   *Maurteen.* O, listen to her dreamy and strange talk.
257.   Are you not cold?

         The Child.   I will crouch down beside you,
258.   For I have run a long, long way this night.

259.   *Bridget.* You have a comely shape.

         Maurteen.   Your hair is wet.

260.   *Bridget.* I'll warm your chilly feet.

         Maurteen.   You have come indeed
261.   A long, long way—for I have never seen
262.   Your pretty face—and must be tired and hungry.
263.   Here is some bread and wine.

         The Child.   The wine is bitter.

---

254.   *The Child.* And when . . . house, (house **7-33, 68**) **4-37, 68, 77**; For
        when . . . house (house, **48, 63**) **47-67, 71-76, 78, 80**.
255.   . . . here who must . . . , away, **4-37, 68, 77**; But there . . . . **71**.
255a.   To where the woods, the stars, and (And **37, 77**) the white streams
255b.   Are holding a continual festival. **4-37, 68, 77**.
256.   O listen . . . . **4E, 5-37, 68, 77**; O listen . . . talk **4A**.
257.   Come to the fire.
                         I'll (I will **7-33, 68**) sit upon your knee, **4-37, 68,**
        77; . . . you. **78**.
258.   . . . run from where the winds are born,
258a.   And long to rest my feet a little while.
        [*She sits upon his knee.*]
259.   How pretty you are!
                         Your . . . wet with dew! **4-37, 68, 77**.
260.   I'll chafe your poor chilled feet. You must have come **4, 37, 77**;
        I'll (I will **6-33, 68**) warm . . . feet.
        [*She takes the child's feet in her hands.*]
                                     You must have come **5-33, 68**.
261.   . . . way, for . . . **4-37, 68, 77**.
262.   . . . face, and . . . hungry; **4-37, 68, 77**; . . . hungry, **47-67, 71-76, 78,**
        80.
263.   . . . wine.
                 They are both nasty. **4-6, 37, 77**.

264.   Old mother, have you no sweet food for me?

265.   *Bridget.* I have some honey.   [*She goes into the next room.*

        Maurteen.   You have coaxing ways.
266.   The mother was quite cross before you came.
            [*Bridgit returns with the honey and fills a porringer with milk.*

267.   *Bridget.* She is the child of gentle people; look
268.   At her white hands and at her pretty dress.
269.   I've brought you some new milk, but wait a while
270.   And I will put it to the fire to warm,
271.   For things well fitted for poor folk like us
272.   Would never please a high-born child like you.

273.   *The Child.* From dawn, when you must blow the fire ablaze,
274.   You work your fingers to the bone, old mother.
275.   The young may lie in bed and dream and hope,
276.   But you must work your fingers to the bone
277.   Because your heart is old.

        Bridget.   The young are idle.

278.   *The Child.* Your memories have made you wise, old father;

---

264.   . . . you nothing nice for me. (me? **5, 6, 37, 77**) **4-6, 37, 77.**
265.   . . . honey! [*She . . . .*]
                            You are a dear child; **4-37, 68, 77**; . . . ways,
        47, 49-67, 71-76, 78, 80; . . . honey [*she . . .*].
                            You . . . ways, **48.**
        Directions after 266. [. . . *honey,* (*honey;* **12** (1903)) *and goes to the*
        dresser and fills . . . .] **4-37, 68, 77**; [. . . *fills porringer . . . .*] **47, 49.**
269.   . . . awhile, (a while, **37, 77**) **4-6, 37, 77**; I have brought . . . awhile,
        (awhile **31**; a while, **68**) **7-33, 68.**
270.   . . . it by the . . . , **4-37, 68, 77.**
273.   Old mother, my old mother, the green dawn
273a.   Brightens above while you blow up the fire;
274.   And evening finds you spreading the white cloth. **4-37, 68, 77.**
276.   . . . you work on because your heart is old.
277.   *Bridget.* The young are idle.
        The Child.   Old father, you are wise, (wise **5-12, 28,**
        68)
277a.   And all the years have gathered in your heart **4-37, 68, 77.**
278.   To whisper of the wonders that are gone. **4-37, 68, 77**; . . . father,
        48, 63.

279.   The young must sigh through many a dream and hope,
280.   But you are wise because your heart is old.

[Bridget gives her more bread and honey.

281. *Maurteen.* O, who would think to find so young a girl
282.   Loving old age and wisdom?

The Child.   No more, mother.

283. *Maurteen.* What a small bite! The milk is ready now.

[Hands it to her.

284.   What a small sip!

The Child.   Put on my shoes, old mother.
285.   For I would like to dance now I have eaten.
286.   The reeds are dancing by Coolaney lake,
287.   And I would like to dance until the reeds
288.   And the white waves have danced themselves asleep.

*[Bridget puts on the shoes, and the Child is about to dance, but
suddenly sees the crucifix and shrieks and covers her eyes.*

289.   What is that ugly thing on the black cross?

290. *Father Hart.* You cannot know how naughty your words are!

Directions after 280.   [lacking] **4-37, 68, 77.**
281.   . . . a child **4-37, 77**; O who . . . a child **68.**
282.   . . . wisdom. (wisdom? **6-33, 68**)
        [*Bridget gives her more bread and honey.*]
                                No . . . . **4-37, 68, 77.**
283.   . . . now; **4-37, 68, 77**; . . . now [*hands* . . .]. **48.**
        Directions after 283.   [lacking] **4-37, 68, 77.**
284.   . . . mother, **4-37, 68, 73, 76-80**;
        . . . sip.
                Put . . . . **48, 63**; . . . mother **51-62, 66, 67, 72, 74.**
285.   . . . have dined. **4-6, 37, 77**; Now I would . . . eaten, **47, 49-62, 66, 67, 72, 74**; Now I would . . . dance, now . . . . **48, 63**; . . . eaten, **71.**
287a.   And the loud wind, the white wave on the shore, **4, 37, 77.**
288.   And all the stars have . . . themselves to sleep. **4, 37, 77**; . . . themselves to sleep. **5-33, 68.**
        Directions after 288.   [*Bridget having put on her shoes, she gets off the
        old man's knees and is* . . . .] **4-37, 68, 77.**
290.   . . . are: **78.**

291.   That is our Blessed Lord.

        The Child.   Hide it away!

292.   *Bridget.* I have begun to be afraid again.

293.   *The Child.* Hide it away!

        Maurteen.   That would be wickedness!

294.   *Bridget.* That would be sacrilege!

        The Child.   The tortured thing!
295.   Hide it away!

        Maurteen.   Her parents are to blame.

296.   *Father Hart.* That is the image of the Son of God.

297.   *The Child* [*caressing him*]. Hide it away, hide it away!

        Maurteen.   No, no.

298.   *Father Hart.* Because you are so young and like a bird,

299.   That must take fright at every stir of the leaves,

300.   I will go take it down.

        The Child.   Hide it away!

---

291.   . . . Our (our **7-28, 33, 68**) . . . Lord!

                            Hide . . . ! **4-28, 33, 37, 68, 77**;

        . . . blessed Lord!

                        Hide . . . ! **31** ; . . . away. **48, 63**.

292.   . . . afraid (afraid, **5-33, 68**) again! **4-37, 68, 77**.

293.   [Hemistichs misplaced as follows]

        The Child.   Hide it away! (away. **63**)

        Maurteen. That would be wickedness! **47-67, 72-76, 78, 80**.

295.   . . . away.

                    Her . . . . **4, 37, 77**.

        Directions after 296. [*The Child puts her arm round his neck lovingly and*

        (*neck and* **5-33, 68**) *kisses him.*] **4-37, 68, 77**.

297.   *The Child.* Hide . . . away! Hide . . . away!

                                    No! no! **4-37, 68, 77**;

        [second hemistich printed as new line] **63**.

298.   . . . and little a child **4-37, 68, 77**.

299.   [lacking] **4-37, 68, 77** ; . . . leaves. **51, 71, 72, 74**.

300.   . . . away, **4-37, 68, 77**.

        V.E.P.Y.—H

301.   And cover it out of sight and out of mind!
        [*Father Hart takes crucifix from wall and carries it towards inner
        room.*

302.   *Father Hart.* Since you have come into this barony,
303.   I will instruct you in our blessed Faith;
304.   And being so keen-witted you'll soon learn.
                                                    [*To the others.*]
305.   We must be tender to all budding things.
306.   Our Maker let no thought of Calvary
307.   Trouble the morning stars in their first song.
                                        [*Puts crucifix in inner room.*

308.   *The Child.* Here is level ground for dancing; I will dance.
                                [*Sings*]
309.   The wind blows out of the gates of the day,
310.   The wind blows over the lonely of heart,
311.   And the lonely of heart is withered away.
                                                    [*She dances.*

312.   *Mary* [*to Shawn*]. Just now when she came near I thought I heard

---

301.   . . . mind. **4-37, 68, 77.**
        Directions after 301. [put after name of speaker in line 302] **4, 37,**
        [**77**; . . . *takes it down and . . . towards* (*toward* **68**) *the inner* . . . .] **5-33, 68.**
302.   *Father Hart* [*takes it down and carries it towards the inner room.*]
        Since . . . barony **4, 37, 77;** . . . barony **5-31, 68.**
303.   . . . faith: **4-37, 68, 77;** . . . faith; **47-67, 71-76, 78, 80.**
304.   Being a clever child (child, **33**) you will soon **4-37, 68, 77;**
        . . . keen witted . . . . **47, 49-62, 66, 67, 71, 72, 74;** . . . so keen of wit
        you'll . . . . **73, 76, 78, 80.**
305.   . . . tender with all . . . things, (things. **6-33, 68**) **4-37, 68, 77;** . . .
        things, **47-67, 71-74, 76, 78, 80.**
        Directions after 307. [*Puts the crucifix in the inner* . . . .] **4-37, 68, 77.**
308.   O, what a nice, smooth floor to dance upon! **4-6, 37, 77;** . . . dancing.
        I . . . . **7-33, 68.**
        Directions before 309. [lacking] **4-37, 68, 77.**
309.   . . . wind is blowing on the waving reeds, (reeds **5**) **4-37, 68, 77;** 'The
        . . ., **47-67, 72-76, 78, 80.**
310.   . . . wind is blowing on the heart of man.
        Directions after 310. [*She dances, swaying about like the reeds.*] **4-37,**
        68, 77.
311 and directions. [lacking] **4-37, 68, 77.**
311.   . . . away.' **47-67, 72-76, 78, 80.**

313.   Other small steps beating upon the floor,
314.   And a faint music blowing in the wind,
315.   Invisible pipes giving her feet the tune.

316. *Shawn.* I heard no steps but hers.

    Mary.   I hear them now.
317.   The unholy powers are dancing in the house.

318. *Maurteen.* Come over here, and if you promise me
319.   Not to talk wickedly of holy things
320.   I will give you something.

    The Child.   Bring it me, old father.

321. *Maurteen.* Here are some ribbons that I bought in the town
322.   For my son's wife—but she will let me give them
323.   To tie up that wild hair the winds have tumbled.

324. *The Child.* Come, tell me, do you love me?

    Maurteen.   Yes, I love you.

325. *The Child.* Ah, but you love this fireside. Do you love me?

---

314.   . . . wind— **4, 37, 77.**
315.   . . . the time. **4-37, 68, 77.**
316.   . . . step . . . hers.
          Look to the bolt! **4-37, 68, 77**; . . . now, **47-67, 71-76, 78, 80.**
317.   Because the . . . are abroad. **4-37, 68, 77.**
318.   *Maurteen* [*to the Child*]. Come . . . **4-37, 68, 77**; . . . me, **48, 63**; . . . promise **72, 74.**
319.   . . . things, **48, 63.**
320.   I'll give . . . father! **4-6, 37, 77**; . . . father! **7-33, 68.**
    Directions after 320. [*Maurteen goes into the next room.*] **4-37, 68, 77.**
320a. *Father Hart.* I will have queen cakes when you come to me!
    Directions after 320a. [*Maurteen returns and lays a piece of money on the table. The Child makes a gesture of refusal.*]
321.   It will buy lots of toys; see how it glitters! **4-37, 68, 77.**
322-323. [lacking] **4-37, 68, 77.**
324.   . . . me?
        I . . . you!
325.   Ah! (Ah, **33**) but . . . fireside!
    Father Hart.   I love you (you. **5-37, 68, 77**) **4-37, 68, 77.**

326. *Father Hart.* When the Almighty puts so great a share
327.   Of His own ageless youth into a creature,
328.   To look is but to love.

    The Child.   But you love Him?

329. *Bridget.* She is blaspheming.

    The Child.   And do you love me too?

330. *Mary.* I do not know.

    The Child.   You love that young man there,
331.   Yet I could make you ride upon the winds,
332.   (Run on the top of the dishevelled tide,)
333.   And dance upon the mountains like a flame.

334. *Mary.* O Queen of Angels and kind saints defend us!
335.   Some dreadful thing will happen. A while ago
336.   She took away the blessed quicken wood.

337. *Father Hart.* You fear because of her unmeasured prattle;

326-327.   [lacking] **4-37, 68, 77.**
   328.   *The Child.* But you love Him (him **68**) above. (above **7**)
          Bridget.   She is blaspheming (blaspheming. **5-37, 68, 77**)
          4-37, 68, 77.
   329.   *The Child [to Maire].* And do you likewise love me?
          Maire.   I don't know (know. **5, 37, 77**) **4, 5, 37, 77**;
          The Child [to Maire]. And do you love me?
          Maire.   I—I do not know. **6-33, 68.**
   330.   *The Child.* You . . . that great tall fellow over there: **4-37, 68, 77.**
   333.   . . . flame! **4-37, 68, 77.**
   334.   Queen of the Angels . . . Saints (Saints, **7-33, 68**) . . . ! **4-37, 68, 77**;
          Queen . . . ! **47-67, 71-76, 78-89.**
   335.   . . . dreadful fate has fallen: before she came **4, 37, 77**; . . . dreadful
          fate has fallen: a . . . **5-33, 68.**
   336.   The wind cried out and took the primroses, **4-37, 68, 77.**
   336a.   And I gave milk and fire, and when she came **4, 5, 37, 77**; And she
          ran by me laughing in the wind, **6-33, 68.**
   336b.   She made you hide the blessed crucifix; **4, 5, 37, 77**; And I gave
          milk and fire, and she came in **6-33, 68.**
   336c.   She wears, too, the green jacket and red cap **4, 5, 37, 77**; And made
          you hide the blessed crucifix. **6-33, 68.**
   336d.   Of the unholy creatures of the Raths. **4, 5, 37, 77.**
   337.   . . . her wild, pretty prattle; **4-37, 68, 77.**

338.   She knows no better. Child, how old are you?

339.   *The Child.* When winter sleep is abroad my hair grows thin,
340.   My feet unsteady. When the leaves awaken
341.   My mother carries me in her golden arms.
342.   I'll soon put on my womanhood and marry
343.   The spirits of wood and water, but who can tell
344.   When I was born for the first time? I think
345.   I am much older than the eagle-cock
346.   (That blinks and blinks on Ballygawley Hill,)
347.   And he is the oldest thing under the moon.

348.   *Father Hart.* O, she is of the faery people.

The Child.   One called.

349.   I sent my messengers for milk and fire;
350.   She called again and after that I came.
        [*All except Shawn and Mary Bruin gather behind the priest for protection.*

---

338.   . . . better.
        [*To the Child.*] Child, . . . ? **4-37, 68, 77.**
339.   My own dear people live a long, long time, **4-6, 37, 77**; . . . grows
        then, **48**; . . . sleep's abroad . . . , **73, 76, 78, 80.**
340.   So I am young; but measure by your years **4-6, 37, 77.**
341-344. [lacking] **4-6, 37, 77.**
341.   . . . arms; **47-67, 71-76, 78, 80.**
342.   I will . . . **7, 18, 31, 68.**
345.   And I am older . . . eagle cock **4-6, 37, 77**; . . . eagle cock **7-33, 47-76,
        78, 80.**
346.   Who blinks . . . Ballydawley . . . , **4, 37, 77**; Who blinks . . . , **5, 6.**
347.   And he's the . . . . **4, 37, 77.**
347a.   At times I merely care to dance and dance—(dance, **5, 6**)
347b.   At times grow wiser than the eagle cock. **4-6, 37, 77.**
348.   What are you?
                                I am of the faery people. **4-6, 37, 77;**
        She is . . . people.
                                I am Brig's daughter. **7-33, 68;**
        O she . . . .
                        . . . called, **47-67, 71-76, 78, 80.**
349.   . . . fire, **4-67, 71-80**; . . . fire. **68.**
350.   And then I heard one call to me and came. **4-37, 68, 77**; . . . again,
        and . . . . **48, 63.**
        Directions after 350.   [*They all except Maire Bruin gather about the . . .
        protection. Maire Bruin stays on the settle as if in a trance (settle in a stupor*

351. *Shawn* [*rising*]. Though you have made all these obedient,
352.   You have not charmed my sight and won from me
353.   A wish or gift to make you powerful;
354.   I'll turn you from the house.

     Father Hart.   No, I will face her.

355. *The Child.* Because you took away the crucifix
356.   I am so mighty that there's none can pass,
357.   Unless I will it, where my feet have danced
358.   Or where I've whirled my finger-tips.

                     [*Shawn tries to approach her and cannot.*

     Maurteen.   Look, look!
359.   There something stops him—look how he moves his hands
360.   As though he rubbed them on a wall of glass!

361. *Father Hart.* I will confront this mighty spirit alone;
362.   Put fear away; the Father is with us,
363.   (The Holy Martyrs and the Innocents,
364.   The adoring Magi in their coats of mail,)
365.   And He who died and rose on the third day,

     5-33, 68) *of* terror. *The Child takes primroses from the great bowl and begins to strew them between herself and the priest and about Maire Bruin. During the following dialogue Shawn Bruin goes more than once to the brink of the primroses, but shrinks back to the others timidly.*] **4-37, 68, 77.**

351-360. [lacking] **4-37, 68, 77.**
  352. . . . sight, and . . . **48, 63.**
  356. . . . pass **48, 63.**
  358. . . . finger-tops. . . . ! **47, 49-62, 66, 67, 71-76, 78, 80** ; . . . finger
        tops. . . . ! **48, 63.**
  360. . . . glass. **48, 63.**
  361. . . . alone. **4-37, 68, 77.**
        Directions after 361.   [*They cling to him and hold him back.*] **4-37, 68, 77.**
 361a. *The Child* [*while she strews the primroses*]. No one whose heart is heavy
        with human tears
 361b. Can cross these little cressets of the wood. **4-37, 68, 77.**
  362. *Father Hart.* Be not afraid, the . . . , **4-80.**
 362a. And all the nine angelic hierarchies, **4-37, 68, 77.**
  363. . . . martyrs . . . , **73, 76, 78, 80.**
  365. . . . day **47.**

366.   (And all the nine angelic hierarchies.)
         [*The Child kneels upon the settle beside Mary and puts her arms
         about her.*

367.   Cry, daughter, to the Angels and the Saints.

368. *The Child.* You shall go with me, newly-married bride,
369.   And gaze upon a merrier multitude.
370.   (White-armed Nuala, Aengus of the Birds,
371.   Fiachra of the hurtling foam, and him
372.   Who is the ruler of the Western Host,
373.   Finvara, and their Land of Heart's Desire,)
374.   Where beauty has no ebb, decay no flood,
375.   But joy is wisdom, time an endless song.
376.   I kiss you and the world begins to fade.

377. *Shawn.* Awake out of that trance—and cover up
378.   Your eyes and ears.

         Father Hart.   She must both look and listen,
379.   For only the soul's choice can save her now.
380.   Come over to me, daughter; stand beside me;
381.   Think of this house and of your duties in it.

382. *The Child.* Stay and come with me, newly-married bride,

---

366. And Mary (Maire 6) with her seven times wounded heart.
      Directions after 366.   [*The Child ceases strewing the primroses, and kneels
      . . . about her neck.*] **4-37, 68, 77.**
367. Cry daughter to . . . . **4** ; . . . , daughter to . . . . **68.**
368. . . . , newly married . . . , **28.**
369. . . . multitude : **4, 5, 37, 77** ; . . . multitude; **6-33, 68.**
370. . . . Nuala and Ardroe the Wise, **4-6, 37, 77** ; . . . Nuala and Aengus
      . . . birds, **7-33, 68.**
371. And Feacra . . . **12-33, 68.**
372. . . . western host, (host. **28**) **4-37, 68, 77.**
373. Finvarra and . . . , **48, 63.**
375. . . . , Time . . . . **4-80.**
377-380. [lacking] **4-37, 68, 77.**
378. . . . listen **73, 76, 78, 80.**
381. *Father Hart.* Daughter, I call you unto home and love! **4-37, 68, 77.**
382. Stay, and . . . , **4-18, 31-37, 68, 77** ; Stay, and . . . newly married . . . ,
      28.

383.	For if you hear him you grow like the rest;
384.	Bear children, cook, and bend above the churn,
385.	And wrangle over butter, fowl, and eggs,
386.	Until at last, grown old and bitter of tongue,
387.	You're crouching there and shivering at the grave.

388. *Father Hart.* Daughter, I point you out the way to Heaven.

389.	*The Child.* But I can lead you, newly-married bride,
390.	Where nobody gets old and crafty and wise,
391.	Where nobody gets old and godly and grave,
392.	Where nobody gets old and bitter of tongue,
393.	And where kind tongues bring no captivity;
394.	For we are but obedient to the thoughts
395.	That drift into the mind at a wink of the eye.

396.	*Father Hart.* By the dear Name of the One crucified,
397.	I bid you, Mary Bruin, come to me.

398. *The Child.* I keep you in the name of your own heart.

---

383. For, if . . . him, you . . . rest: **4-37, 68, 77** ; . . . rest, **48, 63.**
384. . . . , cook, be mindful of the . . . , **4-37, 68, 77.**
386. And sit at last there, old . . . bitter of tongue, (bitter tongue **7-18, 31, 68**)
387. Watching the white stars war upon your hopes. **4-37, 68, 77.**
388. . . . heaven! **4, 5, 37, 77** ; . . . heaven (heaven. **12-33, 68**) **6-33, 68.**
389. . . . , newly married . . . , **28.**
393. . . . captivity,
394. . . . are only true to the far lights (lights, **18, 31**)
395. We follow singing, over valley and hill. **4-37, 68, 77.**
396. . . . name . . . one . . . , **4-31, 37, 68** ; . . . name . . . , **33, 77.**
398. . . . heart! **4-37, 68, 77.**
Directions after 398. [*She leaves the settle, and stooping takes up a mass of primroses and kisses them.*] **4-37, 68, 77.**
398a. *The Child.* We have great power to-night, dear golden folk (folk, **5-37, 68, 77**)
398b. For he took down and hid the crucifix.
398c. And my invisible brethren fill the house;
398d. I hear their footsteps going up and down.
398e. O, (O **68**) they shall soon rule all the hearts of men
398f. And own all lands; last night they merrily danced
398g. About his chapel belfry! [*To Maire.*] Come away,
398h. I hear my brethren bidding us away! **4-37, 68, 77.**

399.   *Father Hart.* It is because I put away the crucifix
400.   That I am nothing, and my power is nothing.
401.   I'll bring it here again.

       Maurteen [*clinging to him*]. No.

       Bridget.   Do not leave us.

402.   *Father Hart.* O, let me go before it is too late;
403.   It is my sin alone that brought it all.

                                   [*Singing outside.*

404.   *The Child.* I hear them sing, 'Come, newly-married bride,
405.   Come to the woods and waters and pale lights.'

406.   *Mary.* I will go with you.

       Father Hart.   She is lost, alas!

407.   *The Child* [*standing by the door*]. But clinging mortal hope must fall
           from you,

399-400.   [lacking] **4-37, 68, 77.**
399.   Because I . . .
400.   I am but nothing, ... **63, 73, 76, 78, 80.**
401.   *Father Hart.* I will go fetch the crucifix again. **4-37, 68, 77.**
       Directions after 401. [*They hang about him in terror and prevent him
       from moving.*] **4-37, 68, 77.**
401a. *Bridget.* The enchanted flowers will kill us if you go.
401b. *Maurteen.* They turn the flowers to little twisted flames.
401c. *Shawn.* The little twisted flames burn up the heart. **4-37, 68, 77.**
402-403.   [lacking] **4-37, 68, 77.**
404.   . . . them call us (us, **37, 77**) newly-married bride. **4, 37, 77** ; . . .
       them crying, 'Newly-married ('Newly married **28, 68**) . . . , **5-33, 68.**
405.   [lacking] **4, 37, 77** ; 'Come . . . lights.' (lights. **7, 18**) **5-7, 18, 31** ;
       Come, to . . . , **47-67, 71-76, 78, 80.**
406a. *The Child* [*standing by the door*]. Then, follow (follow: **5-7, 28, 33**) but
       the heavy body of clay, (clay **5-7, 28, 33**) **4-7, 28, 33, 37, 77.**
407.   And clinging [changed to 'But clinging' by errata slip in **7**] . . .
       you; (you **5-7, 28** ; you, **33**) **4-7, 28, 33, 37, 77** ; . . . you **12, 18, 68.**

408.   For we who ride the winds, run on the waves,

409.   And dance upon the mountains are more light

410.   Than dewdrops on the banner of the dawn.

411.   *Mary.* O, take me with you.

    Shawn.   Beloved, I will keep you.

412.   I've more than words, I have these arms to hold you,

413.   Nor all the faery host, do what they please,

414.   Shall ever make me loose you from these arms.

415.   *Mary.* Dear face! Dear voice!

    The Child.   Come, newly-married bride.

416.   *Mary.* I always loved her world—and yet—and yet——

417.   *The Child.* White bird, white bird, come with me, little bird.

---

408.   . . . waves **12** (1909, 1910).
409.   . . . mountains, are . . . **4-37, 48, 63, 68, 77.**
410.   . . . banners . . . . **4-37, 68, 77;** . . . dew-drops . . . . **48, 63.**
411.   Then take my soul. [changed to 'O take me with you' by errata slip in **7**]
    [*Shawn Bruin goes over to her.*]
    Beloved, do not leave me! **4-7, 28, 33, 37, 77;** O (O, **18, 31**) take . . . you. (you! **18, 31**)
    [*Shawn Bruin goes over to her.*]
    Beloved, do not leave me! **12, 18, 31, 68.**
412.   What will my life be if you go with her? **4, 37, 77;** [lacking] **5-33, 68.**
413.   Remember when I met you by the well **4-37, 68, 77.**
414.   And took your hand in mine and spoke of love. **4-37, 68, 77;** . . . loosen . . . . **47-62, 66, 67, 71, 72, 74;** Can ever loosen you out of these . . . . **63.**
415.   . . . bride! **4-18, 31-37, 68, 77;** . . . , newly married bride! **28.**
416.   . . . yet **4, 37, 77.**
    Directions after 416.   [*Sinks into his arms.*] **5-33, 68.**
416a.   *Maire.* I think that I would stay if I could stay. **4, 37, 77.**
    Directions after 416a.   [*Sinks into his arms.*] **4, 37, 77.**
417.   *The Child* [*from the door*]. White . . . bird! (bird **6**; bird. **7-33, 68**) **4-37, 68, 77.**

418. *Mary.* She calls me!

    The Child.   Come, come with me, little bird.

                 [Distant dancing figures appear in the wood.

419. *Mary.* I can hear songs and dancing.

    Shawn.   Stay with me.

420. *Mary.* I think that I would stay—and yet—and yet——

421. *The Child.* Come, little bird with crest of gold.

    Mary [very softly].   And yet——

422. *The Child.* Come, little bird with silver feet!

              [Mary Bruin dies, and the Child goes.

    Shawn.   She is dead!

423. *Bridget.* Come from that image; body and soul are gone.

---

418. . . . calls my soul! [changed to 'She calls to me' by errata slip in **7**]
               Come with . . . bird! **4-7, 28, 33, 37, 77**;
 . . . calls to me!
               Come with . . . bird! **12, 18, 31, 68**;
 . . . me! Come with **47-62, 66, 67, 71-76, 78, 80**;
She is calling me!
               Come with . . . . **63**.
    Directions after 418.   [lacking] **4-37, 68, 77**.
419. . . . dancing!
            Stay . . . me! (me. **68**) **4-37, 68, 77**.
420. Dear, I would stay—and yet and yet——
    The Child.   White bird! **4, 37, 77**.
421. . . . gold!
        And . . .—**4-37, 68, 77**; . . . bird, with . . .—**47-67, 71-76, 78, 80**.
    Directions in 422.   [lacking] **4, 37, 77**.
422. . . . feet!
    Shawn. Dead, dead! **4, 37, 77**;
 . . . feet! [*Maire dies.*]
    Shawn. Dead, dead! **5, 6**.
423-425. [lacking] **4-6, 37, 77**.
423. . . . image there: she is far away. (away: **33**) [changed to 'Come from that image: body and soul are gone' by errata slip in **7**] **7, 28, 33**;
 . . . image: body . . . gone. (gone, **18, 31, 68**) **12, 18, 31, 68**; . . . gone **47**; . . . gone; **48, 63**.

424.   You have thrown your arms about a drift of leaves,
425.   Or bole of an ash-tree changed into her image.

426. *Father Hart.* Thus do the spirits of evil snatch their prey
427.   Almost out of the very hand of God;
428.   And day by day their power is more and more,
429.   And men and women leave old paths, for pride
430.   Comes knocking with thin knuckles on the heart.
         [*Outside there are dancing figures, and it may be a white bird, and*
         many voices singing:
431.   The wind blows out of the gates of the day,
432.   The wind blows over the lonely of heart,
433.   And the lonely of heart is withered away;
434.   (While the faeries dance in a place apart,
435.   Shaking their milk-white feet in a ring,
436.   Tossing their milk-white arms in the air;
437.   For they hear the wind laugh and murmur and sing
438.   Of a land where even the old are fair,
439.   And even the wise are merry of tongue;
440.   But I heard a reed of Coolaney say—
441.   'When the wind has laughed and murmured and sung,
442.   The lonely of heart is withered away.')

                              THE END

_____

424.   . . . leaves **7-33, 68.**
425.   . . . ash tree . . . . **48, 63.**
426.   . . . the evil spirits snatch . . . **4-6, 37, 77** ; . . . prey, **47-67, 71- 76, 78, 80.**
        Directions before 431. [*A Voice sings outside—*] **4, 5, 37, 77** ; [. . . figures and . . .:] **97A.**
        Speaker and directions at 431. *A Voice* [*singing outside*]. **6-33, 68.**
431-442. [italicized] **5-33.**
431.   'The . . . , **47-67, 72-76, 78, 80.**
432.   . . . heart **68.**
433.   . . . away, **4, 5, 18, 31, 37, 68, 77** ; . . . away **6-12, 28, 33.**
437.   . . . laugh, and . . . **18, 31, 33, 68, 97A.**
440.   . . . say, **4-37, 68, 77.**
441.   . . . sung **68.**
442.   . . . heart must wither . . . .' **4-6, 37, 77** ; 'The . . . .' **18, 31** ; . . . away.' " **47-67, 72-76, 78, 80** ; . . . away!' **68.**
        Directions after 442. [*The song is taken up by many voices, who sing*
        loudly, as if in triumph. Some of the voices seem to come from within the house.]
        4-37, 68, 77.

NOTES

First Performed at the Avenue Theatre
March 29, 1894.

Maurteen Bruin .	.	Mr. James Welch
Shawn Bruin .	.	Mr. A. E. W. Mason
Father Hart (*The Priest*		Mr. G. R. Foss
of Kilmacowen)		
Bridget Bruin (*Maurteen*		Miss Charlotte Morland
Bruin's Wife)		
Maire Bruin (*Shawn*	.	Miss Winifred Fraser
Bruin's Wife)		
A Faery Child .	.	Miss Dorothy Paget

4.

The Land of Heart's Desire.—This little play was produced at the Avenue Theatre in the spring of 1894, with the   cast:—Maurteen Bruin, Mr. . . . Welch; Shawn Bruin, Mr. . . . Mason; Father Hart, Mr. . . . Foss; Bridget Bruin, Miss . . . Moreland; Maire Bruin, Miss . . . Fraser; A . . . Child, Miss . . . Paget. (Paget. It ran for a little over six weeks. **7, 12**) Glossary, **5-7**; [no heading] **12.**

The Land of Heart's Desire.—This [follows the version in **5-7** to 'weeks.', with two new sentences added:] It was revived in America in 1901, when it was taken on tour by Mrs. Lemoyne. It was again played, under the auspices of the Irish Literary Society of New York, in 1903, and has lately been played in San Francisco. **18, 31, 33.**

'The Land of Heart's Desire' was first played at the Avenue Theatre, London, in the spring of 1894, with Mr. James Welch as Maurteen Bruin; Mr. A. E. W. Mason, Shawn Bruin; Father Hart, Mr. G. R. Foss; Bridget Bruin, Miss Charlotte Morland; Maire Bruin, Miss Winifred Fraser; A Faery Child, Dorothy Paget. It ran for about six weeks, and Mrs. LeMoyne and Miss Wycherley have toured with it in the United States, Mrs. LeMoyne playing it with Browning's 'In a Balcony' and Miss Wycherley with my 'Hour Glass' and 'Cathleen ni Houlihan.'

'The Dates and Places of Performance of the Plays.' Appendix II, **28.**

This little play [follows the version in **18, 31, 33** to 'Lemoyne.', with the following added:] It has been played two or three times professionally since then in America and a great many times in England and America by amateurs. Till lately it was not part of the repertory of the Abbey Theatre, for I had grown to dislike it without knowing what I disliked in it. This winter, however, I have made many revisions and now it plays well enough to give me pleasure. It is printed in this book in the new form, which was acted for the first time on February 22, 1912, at the Abbey Theatre, Dublin.

At the Abbey Theatre, where the platform of the stage comes out in front of the curtain, the curtain falls before the priest's last words. He remains outside the curtain and the words are spoken to the audience like an epilogue.

Abbey Theatre, Dublin.   W. B. YEATS.

March, 1912. Note, **47**; Appendix II, **48**; Glossary and Notes, **49-67, 72, 74**; Note, **73, 76**.

'The Land of Heart's Desire'. This little play [follows the version in **47** to 'epilogue.', with the following added:] w.b.y., 1912.

When revived last spring the passages between brackets were left out.— w.b.y., 1923.   Note, **71**.

The Land of Heart's Desire.—This little play [follows the version in **18, 31, 33** to 'Lemoyne.', with the following added:] It has since then been played several times professionally in America and England and a great many times in England and America by amateurs.   Notes, **78, 80**.

*   *   *

Preface to 'The Land of Heart's Desire' in **71**.

This play contains more of my first experiments in blank verse than any other in my books, for *The Countess Cathleen*, though published before it, was all rewritten for later editions. Many passages that pleased me when I wrote them, and some that please me still, are mere ornament without dramatic value. A revival of the play but a few days ago at the Abbey Theatre enabled me to leave out these and other passages and to test the play without them. I think that it gained greatly, became indeed for the first time tolerable drama; certainly for the first time for many years gave its author pleasure. Amateurs perform it more often than any other play of mine, and I urge them to omit all lines that I have enclosed in brackets. It should sound simple and natural if played with the text I recommend, and it may be that it would read better too, being a more perfect action, but I hesitate to leave out altogether what many people like, what, it may be, I can no longer judge. Somebody, Dr. Todhunter, the dramatic poet, I think, had said in my hearing that dramatic poetry must be oratorical, and I think that I wrote partly to prove that false; but every now and then I lose courage, as it seems, and remembering that I had some reputation as a lyric poet wrote for the reader of lyrics. When I saw it played with all needless and all mere lyrical passages cut away, I recalled the kind of pleasure that I had sought to create, and at last listened with the hope that this pleasure had reached those about me. Mr. Lennox Robinson, the producer, had kept all the players except the fairy child as still and statuesque as possible, so that the blank verse where there is so little animation seemed their natural utterance.

                                                                   W. B. YEATS.
March 10.

*   *   *

Variant spellings

Ballygawley 5-33, 47-67, 71-76, 78-97; *Ballygawly* 68; *Ballydawley* 4, 37, 77.
Edain 33, 84-97; *Edane* 28, 47-67, 71-76, 78, 80; *Edene* 4, 5, 37, 77; *Adene* 6-18, 31, 68.
Feacra 4-89; *Fiachra* 97.
Finvara 97; *Finvaragh* 84, 89; *Finvarra* 4-80.
Maire 4-37, 68, 77; *Mary* 47-67, 71-76, 78-97.
Shaun, Shawn 6, 7; *Shawm* 4, 5, 12-97.

* * *

[See also the notes on *Cathleen ni Houlihan*, p. 232; *The Legendary and Mythological Foundation of the Plays and Poems*, p. 1282; *Glossary*, p. 1284; *and Prefaces to 5-80, 28, 48, 69, 71*, pp. 1288, 1293, 1306, 1307.]

CATHLEEN NI HOULIHAN

1902

Persons in the Play

Peter Gillane

Michael Gillane, *his son, going to be married*

Patrick Gillane, *a lad of twelve, Michael's brother*

Bridget Gillane, *Peter's wife*

Delia Cahel, *engaged to Michael*

The Poor Old Woman

Neighbours

Interior of a cottage close to Killala, in 1798. Bridget is standing at a table undoing a parcel. Peter is sitting at one side of the fire, Patrick at the other.

1. *Peter.* What is that sound I hear?

2. *Patrick.* I don't hear anything. [*He listens.*] I hear it
3.   now. It's like cheering. [*He goes to the window and looks*

PRINTINGS[1]   *Samhain*, October 1902; **8, 16, 17, 22, 29, 34, 36, 42, 45, 69, 84, 89, 97.**

DATE   [lacking] **S-22, 34-69.**

EPIGRAPH   " Young she is, and fair she is, and would be
           crowned a queen,
       Were the King's son at home here with
           Kathaleen-Ny-Houlahan!" **8.**

DEDICATION   To the Memory of William Rooney **8.**

DRAMATIS PERSONAE   / [heading lacking] / Peter ... **S, 17, 22, 42** ; Dramatis Personae / Peter ... **8** ; Persons / Peter ... **16** ; Characters / Peter ... **29.**

STAGE DIRECTIONS   Scene.—*Interior* .... **S** ; Scene *Interior* .... **8** ; Scene: *Interior* .... **16, 22, 29, 42-69** ; Scene: *Interior* ... 1798, *Bridget* .... **17.**

NAME OF SPEAKER   ['The Poor Old Woman' for 'Old Woman' throughout] **16.**

TEXT   Title ... Hoolihan **S, 8, 16.**

1. ... is the sound ... ? **97A.**

[1] I have not collated the version of the lyrics (lines 182-185, 190-197, 288-293, 313-316) that Yeats quoted in his letter to *The United Irishman*, 5 May 1902, because I did not feel that they represented anything but a casual version. *The United Irishman* letter is reprinted in full on pp. 234-5.

4. *out.*] I wonder what they are cheering about. I don't
5. see anybody.

6. *Peter.* It might be a hurling.

7. *Patrick.* There's no hurling to-day. It must be down in
8. the town the cheering is.

9. *Bridget.* I suppose the boys must be having some sport
10. of their own. Come over here, Peter, and look at
11. Michael's wedding clothes.

12. *Peter* [*shifts his chair to table*]. Those are grand clothes,
13. indeed.

14. *Bridget.* You hadn't clothes like that when you married
15. me, and no coat to put on of a Sunday more than
16. any other day.

17. *Peter.* That is true, indeed. We never thought a son of
18. our own would be wearing a suit of that sort for his
19. wedding, or have so good a place to bring a wife to.

20. *Patrick* [*who is still at the window*]. There's an old woman
21. coming down the road. I don't know is it here she is
22. coming.

23. *Bridget.* It will be a neighbour coming to hear about
24. Michael's wedding. Can you see who it is?

25. *Patrick.* I think it is a stranger, but she's not coming to

---

6. . . . hurling match. **S-29.**
7. . . . today. . . . **8.**
10. . . . own. **S;** . . ., Peter and . . . **8.**
11-19. [lacking] **S.**
11. . . . wedding-clothes. **17-69.**
12. . . . clothes **8.**
15. . . . put on on a Sunday any more . . . **8;** . . . Sunday any more . . .
    17-29.
17. . . . true indeed. . . . **8.**
18. . . . sort on his **8;** . . . sort at his **16.**
19. wedding or . . . bring his wife . . . . **8.**
20 *Patrick.* There is an . . . **S;** . . . *window*]. There is an . . . **16.**
21. . . . here she's **S, 16;** . . . know, is . . . here she's **17-29.**
22. coming? **8, 17-69.**
25. . . . stranger, and she's . . . **S, 16.**

26.   the house. She's turned into the gap that goes down
27.   where Maurteen and his sons are shearing sheep. [*He*
28.   *turns towards Bridget.*] Do you remember what Winny
29.   of the Cross-Roads was saying the other night about
30.   the strange woman that goes through the country
31.   whatever time there's war or trouble coming?

32.   *Bridget.* Don't be bothering us about Winny's talk, but
33.   go and open the door for your brother. I hear him
34.   coming up the path.

35.   *Peter.* I hope he has brought Delia's fortune with him
36.   safe, for fear the people might go back on the bargain
37.   and I after making it. Trouble enough I had making it.
                [*Patrick opens the door and Michael comes in.*

38.   *Bridget.* What kept you, Michal? We were looking
39.   out for you this long time.

40.   *Michael.* I went round by the priest's house to bid him
41.   be ready to marry us to-morrow.

42.   *Bridget.* Did he say anything?

---

26.   . . . house. She has not turned up the path. She's . . . **S, 16** ; . . . down
      to **8.**
27.   . . . Murteen . . . shearing their sheep. . . . **8.**
28.   . . . *towards them.*] Do . . . Winnie **S, 16** ; . . . *towards them.*] Do . . . **8.**
29.   . . . Cross Roads . . . **S-89.**
31.   the time . . . ? **S, 16.**
32.   . . . talk but **8** ; . . . Winnie's talk but **16.**
34a. *Bridget.* Come over here, Peter, and look at Michael's wedding
34b. clothes. [*Peter shifts his chair to table.*] Those are grand clothes, indeed.
34c. *Bridget.* You hadn't clothes like that when you married me, and no
34d. coat to put on of a Sunday more than any other day.
34e. *Peter.* That is true, indeed. We never thought a son of our own
34f. would be wearing a suit of that sort at his wedding, or have so
34g. good a place to bring a wife to.
34h. *Patrick* [*who is still at the window*]. Here is Michael coming back,
34i. father. **S.**
36.   . . . fear her people . . . back of the bargain, **S, 16** ; . . . fear her people
      . . . **8, 17-45.**
37.   . . . had in making . . . . **8.**
      Directions after 37.   [. . . *door, and* . . . .] **S, 16.**

43. *Michael.* He said it was a very nice match, and that he
44.   was never better pleased to marry any two in his
45.   parish than myself and Delia Cahel.

46. *Peter.* Have you got the fortune, Michael?

47. *Michael.* Here it is.
    [*Michael puts bag on table and goes over and leans against chimney-jamb. Bridget, who has been all this time examining the clothes, pulling the seams and trying the lining of the pockets, etc., puts the clothes on the dresser.*

    Peter [*getting up and taking the bag in his hand and turning*
48.   *out the money*]. Yes, I made the bargain well for you,
49.   Michael. Old John Cahel would sooner have kept a
50.   share of this a while longer. 'Let me keep the half of
51.   it until the first boy is born,' says he. 'You will not,'
52.   says I. 'Whether there is or is not a boy, the whole
53.   hundred pounds must be in Michael's hands before
54.   he brings your daughter to the house.' The wife
55.   spoke to him then, and he gave in at the end.

56. *Bridget.* You seem well pleased to be handling the
57.   money, Peter.

58. *Peter.* Indeed, I wish I had had the luck to get a hundred
59.   pounds, or twenty pounds itself, with the wife I
60.   married.

61. *Bridget.* Well, if I didn't bring much I didn't get much.
62.   What had you the day I married you but a flock of

Directions after 47. [*He puts . . . on the table . . . chimney jamb. Bridget who . . . .*] **S**; [*he puts . . . chimney jamb.*] / *Bridget.* [*who . . . been examining . . . pockets and the like, puts . . . .*] **8**; [*He puts . . . on the table . . . chimney jamb. . . . seams, and . . . .*] **16**; [*He puts . . . .*] **17**; [*He puts . . . against the chimney-jamb. . . . .*] **22, 29.**
48. *. . . money,*] Yes, . . . you **8**; . . . , I make the *. . .*, **22.**
50. *. . . awhile . . .* **29.**
51. it till the *. . . ,*' **S-29.**
52. *. . . I 'Whether . . .* **S.**
54. *. . . daughter in the . . .* **8, 17-29.**
58. Indeed I *. . .* **8**; *. . .* wish I'd had the *. . .* **S, 16.**
61. *. . . much, I . . . .* **16.**

63. hens and you feeding them, and a few lambs and you
64. driving them to the market at Ballina? [*She is vexed and*
65. *bangs a jug on the dresser.*] If I brought no fortune I
66. worked it out in my bones, laying down the baby,
67. Michael that is standing there now, on a stook of
68. straw, while I dug the potatoes, and never asking big
69. dresses or anything but to be working.

70. *Peter.* That is true, indeed.   [*He pats her arm.*

71. *Bridget.* Leave me alone now till I ready the house for
72. the woman that is to come into it.

73. *Peter.* You are the best woman in Ireland, but money
74. is good, too. [*He begins handling the money again and sits*
75. *down.*] I never thought to see so much money within
76. my four walls. We can do great things now we have it.
77. We can take the ten acres of land we have the chance
78. of since Jamsie Dempsey died, and stock it. We will
79. go to the fair at Ballina to buy the stock. Did Delia
80. ask any of the money for her own use, Michael?

81. *Michael.* She did not, indeed. She did not seem to take
82. much notice of it, or to look at it at all.

83. *Bridget.* That's no wonder. Why would she look at it
84. when she had yourself to look at, a fine, strong young
85. man? It is proud she must be to get you; a good

---

64. . . . Ballina. [*She . . . vexed, and* **S**; . . . Ballina [*she . . .* **8**; . . . *vexed, and*
    16; . . . Ballina. [*She . . .* **17-69.**
65. . . . *dresser*] if . . . **8**; . . . fortune, I **29.**
66. . . . baby— **S, 16.**
67. Michael, that . . . **S**; Michael, that . . . now—on . . . **16.**
68. . . . potatoes and . . . **8.**
69. . . . anything, but . . . . **S.**
70. . . . true indeed. **8.**
74. . . . good too. [. . . *again, and* . . .
75. . . . money between **8.**
77. . . . have a chance **S-45.**
78. . . . died and . . . **8.**
79. . . . fair of Ballina . . . **S-45.**
81. . . . not indeed. . . .
82. . . . it or . . . . **8.**
84. . . . at—a fine strong . . . **S, 16**; . . . fine strong . . . **8.**
85. man; it . . . good, **S**; man, it . . . **8, 17, 22**; man. It . . . you—a good,
    16; . . . you, a . . . **29**; . . . ? it . . . **34-45.**

86. steady boy that will make use of the money, and not
87. be running through it or spending it on drink like
88. another.

89. *Peter.* It's likely Michael himself was not thinking
90.   much of the fortune either, but of what sort the girl
91.   was to look at.

92. *Michael [coming over towards the table].* Well, you would
93.   like a nice comely girl to be beside you, and to go
94.   walking with you. The fortune only lasts for a while,
95.   but the woman will be there always.

96. *Patrick [turning round from the window].* They are cheer-
97.   ing again down in the town. Maybe they are landing
98.   horses from Enniscrone. They do be cheering when
99.   the horses take the water well.

100. *Michael.* There are no horses in it. Where would they
101.   be going and no fair at hand? Go down to the town,
102.   Patrick, and see what is going on.

Patrick [opens the door to go out, but stops for a moment on
103.   *the threshold].* Will Delia remember, do you think, to
104.   bring the greyhound pup she promised me when she
105.   would be coming to the house?

106. *Michael.* She will surely.

                  [Patrick goes out, leaving the door open.

107. *Peter.* It will be Patrick's turn next to be looking for

---

86. . . . boy, that . . . , and will not **S, 16 ;** . . . money and . . . **8.**
87. . . . it, or . . . drink, like **S, 16.**
    Directions in 92. [. . . *toward* . . . .] **16.**
93. . . . you and . . .
94. . . . while **8.**
95. . . . always. [*Cheers.*] **29.**
97. . . . . May be . . . **8, 17, 22.**
101. . . . town
102. Patrick and . . . .
    Directions at 103. [. . . *out but* . . . .]
103. . . . remember do . . . think to **8.**
106. . . . will, surely. **S, 16.**
    Directions after 106. [. . . *out.*] **8;** [. . . *out leaving* . . . .] **17, 22.**

108.   a fortune, but he won't find it so easy to get it and
109.   he with no place of his own.

110.   *Bridget.* I do be thinking sometimes, now things are
111.   going so well with us, and the Cahels such a good
112.   back to us in the district, and Delia's own uncle a
113.   priest, we might be put in the way of making Patrick
114.   a priest some day, and he so good at his books.

115.   *Peter.* Time enough, time enough. You have always
116.   your head full of plans, Bridget.

117.   *Bridget.* We will be well able to give him learning, and
118.   not to send him tramping the country like a poor
119.   scholar that lives on charity.

120.   *Michael.* They're not done cheering yet.
        [*He goes over to the door and stands there for a moment, putting up
        his hand to shade his eyes.*

121.   *Bridget.* Do you see anything?

122.   *Michael.* I see an old woman coming up the path.

123.   *Bridget.* Who is it, I wonder? It must be the strange
124.   woman Patrick saw a while ago.

125.   *Michael.* I don't think it's one of the neighbours any-
126.   way, but she has her cloak over her face.

---

108.   . . . it, and **S, 16** ; . . . fortune: but . . . **8.**
113.   . . . Patrick himself **S, 16** ; . . . put into the . . . **8.**
114.   . . . someday, ... **8.**
115.   . . . enough; you . . . **S, 16, 29** ; . . . enough, you . . . **8, 17, 22, 34-69.**
116.   . . . plans. **S, 16.**
118.   . . . him trampling the . . .
119.   . . . charity. [*Cheers.*] **29.**
120.   . . . yet **S.**
        Directions after 120. [. . . *the window and . . . moment putting* . . . .] **8** ;
        [. . . *moment putting* . . . .] **17, 22.**
123.   . . . wonder? **S, 16** ; . . . it I wonder. It . . . **8** ; . . . wonder. It . . .
        17-29.
124.   [lacking] **S, 16** ; woman Peter (Patrick **29**) saw awhile . . . . **8, 29.**
125.   . . . its . . . neighbours, **S** ; . . . neighbours, **16.**
126.   but . . . .
126a.   *Bridget.* Maybe its (it's **16**) the same woman Patrick saw a while
        ago. **S, 16.**

127. *Bridget.* It might be some poor woman heard we were
128.   making ready for the wedding and came to look for
129.   her share.

130. *Peter.* I may as well put the money out of sight. There
131.   is no use leaving it out for every stranger to look at.
      [*He goes over to a large box in the corner, opens it and puts the bag
      in and fumbles at the lock.*

132. *Michael.* There she is, father! [*An Old Woman passes the
133.   window slowly. She looks at Michael as she passes.*] I'd
134.   sooner a stranger not to come to the house the night
135.   before my wedding.

136. *Bridget.* Open the door, Michael; don't keep the poor
137.   woman waiting.
      [*The Old Woman comes in. Michael stands aside to make way for
      her.*

138. *Old Woman.* God save all here!

139. *Peter.* God save you kindly!

140. *Old Woman.*[1] You have good shelter here.

141. *Peter.* You are welcome to whatever shelter we have.

142. *Bridget.* Sit down there by the fire and welcome.

143. *Old Woman* [*warming her hands*]. There is a hard wind
144.   outside.

---

128.   . . . wedding, and . . . **S, 16.**
130.   . . . . There's
131.   no . . . . **S, 16.**
       Directions after 131. [. . . *box by the wall, opens* . . . *in, and fumbles with
       the* . . . .] **S, 16**; [. . . *box in the wall, opens* . . . .] **8**; [. . . *it, and* . . . .]
       29.
       Directions in 133. [. . . *slowly, she* . . . .] **8, 17, 22, 34-69**; [. . . *slowly;
       she* . . . .] **29.**
135.   before the wedding. **S, 16.**
136.   . . . , Michael, don't . . . **S**; . . . door Michael, don't . . . **8.**
       Directions after 137. [. . . *in, Michael* . . . .] **S, 8**; [. . . *in; Michael*
       . . . .] **16.**
139.   . . . kindly. **S, 16.**
143.   There's a . . . **S, 16.**

[1] From here on *Old Woman* is *O.W.* in **S.**

[*Michael watches her curiously from the door. Peter comes over to the table.*

145. *Peter.* Have you travelled far to-day?

146. *Old Woman.* I have travelled far, very far; there are few
147.　have travelled so far as myself, and there's many a
148.　one that doesn't make me welcome. There was one
149.　that had strong sons I thought were friends of mine,
150.　but they were shearing their sheep, and they wouldn't
151.　listen to me.

152. *Peter.* It's a pity indeed for any person to have no place
153.　of their own.

154. *Old Woman.* That's true for you indeed, and it's long
155.　I'm on the roads since I first went wandering.

156. *Bridget.* It is a wonder you are not worn out with so
157.　much wandering.

158. *Old Woman.* Sometimes my feet are tired and my hands
159.　are quiet, but there is no quiet in my heart. When
160.　the people see me quiet, they think old age has come
161.　on me and that all the stir has gone out of me. But
162.　when the trouble is on me I must be talking to my
163.　friends.

164. *Bridget.* What was it put you wandering?

165. *Old Woman.* Too many strangers in the house.

146.　. . . far, there . . . **8, 17, 22.**
147.　. . . myself. **S, 16** ; . . . myself. and . . . **8.**
148-151.　[lacking] **S, 16.**
149.　. . . sons that I . . . mine
150.　. . . sheep and . . . **8.**
152.　It is a pity, indeed, for . . . **S, 16.**
154.　That is true . . . you, indeed, and it is long **S** ; . . . indeed and . . . **8** ;
　　That is true . . . , and it is long **16.**
155.　I am on . . . road . . . wandering. It is seldom I have any rest. **S, 16.**
160.　. . . quiet they . . . **S, 8.**
161.　on me, and . . . of me.
162-163.　[lacking]
164.　. . . you astray? **S, 16.**

166. *Bridget.* Indeed you look as if you'd had your share of
167.   trouble.

168. *Old Woman.* I have had trouble indeed.

169. *Bridget.* What was it put the trouble on you?

170. *Old Woman.* My land that was taken from me.

171. *Peter.* Was it much land they took from you?

172. *Old Woman.* My four beautiful green fields.

173. *Peter [aside to Bridget].* Do you think could she be the
174.   widow Casey that was put out of her holding at Kil-
175.   glass a while ago?

176. *Bridget.* She is not. I saw the widow Casey one time at
177.   the market in Ballina, a stout fresh woman.

178. *Peter [to Old Woman].* Did you hear a noise of cheering,
179.   and you coming up the hill?

180. *Old Woman.* I thought I heard the noise I used to hear
181.   when my friends came to visit me.

                                [She begins singing half to herself.
182.   I will go cry with the woman,
183.   For yellow-haired Donough is dead,
184.   With a hempen rope for a neckcloth,
185.   And a white cloth on his head,—

186. *Michael [coming from the door].* What is it that you are

---

166.   . . . if you had had . . . **S, 16.**
174.   Widow . . . **S, 16.**
175.   glas . . . ? **S, 16 ;** . . . awhile . . . ? **29.**
176.   . . . Widow . . .
177.   . . . stout, fresh . . . . **S, 16.**
178.   . . . cheering **8.**
181.   . . . me **8.**
182-185.   [printed both with and without music] **17.**
182.   . . . woman **8.**
183.   . . . dead ; **S, 16 ;** . . . yellow haired . . . dead ; **8.**
184.   . . . neckcloth
185.   . . . head. **S-16.**
186.   . . . is that . . . **S-36.**

187.   singing, ma'am?

188.   *Old Woman.* Singing I am about a man I knew one time,
189.   yellow-haired Donough that was hanged in Galway.
                          [*She goes on singing, much louder.*
190.   I am come to cry with you, woman,
191.   My hair is unwound and unbound;
192.   I remember him ploughing his field,
193.   Turning up the red side of the ground,
194.   And building his barn on the hill
195.   With the good mortared stone;
196.   O! we'd have pulled down the gallows
197.   Had it happened in Enniscrone!

198.   *Michael.* What was it brought him to his death?

199.   *Old Woman.* He died for love of me: many a man has
200.   died for love of me.

201.   *Peter [aside to Bridget].* Her trouble has put her wits
202.   astray.

203.   *Michael.* Is it long since that song was made? Is it long
204.   since he got his death?

205.   *Old Woman.* Not long, not long. But there were others
206.   that died for love of me a long time ago.

207.   *Michael.* Were they neighbours of your own, ma'am?

208.   *Old Woman.* Come here beside me and I'll tell you
209.   about them. [*Michael sits down beside her on the hearth.*] There
210.   was a red man of the O'Donnells from the north,

---

187.   singing ma'am? **8, 17.**
189.   . . . Donough, that . . . . **S, 16, 22, 29**; yellow haired . . . . **8.**
         Directions after 189.   [. . . *singing much* . . . .] **S, 16, 36**; [lacking] **8.**
190.   . . . you woman, **8.**
193.   . . . ground. **S-16.**
         [between 193 and 194 a break] **S-36.**
196.   Oh! . . . **42-69.**
199.   . . . me; many . . . **S-16.**
207.   . . . own ma'am? **8, 17, 22.**
         Directions in 209.   [. . . *her at the* . . . .] **S-69.**
210.   . . . O'Donells . . . North, **S, 16.**

211. and a man of the O'Sullivans from the south, and
212. there was one Brian that lost his life at Clontarf by
213. the sea, and there were a great many in the west,
214. some that died hundreds of years ago, and there are
215. some that will die to-morrow.

216. *Michael.* Is it in the west that men will die to-morrow?

217. *Old Woman.* Come nearer, nearer to me.

218. *Bridget.* Is she right, do you think? Or is she a woman
219. from beyond the world?

220. *Peter.* She doesn't know well what she's talking about,
221. with the want and the trouble she has gone through.

222. *Bridget.* The poor thing, we should treat her well.

223. *Peter.* Give her a drink of milk and a bit of the oaten
224. cake.

225. *Bridget.* Maybe we should give her something along
226. with that, to bring her on her way. A few pence or a
227. shilling itself, and we with so much money in the
228. house.

229. *Peter.* Indeed I'd not begrudge it to her if we had it to
230. spare, but if we go running through what we have,
231. we'll soon have to break the hundred pounds, and
232. that would be a pity.

233. *Bridget.* Shame on you, Peter. Give her the shilling and

---

211. . . . South, . . .
212. . . . Clontarf, by
213. . . . West, **S, 16.**
215. . . . tomorrow. **8.**
216. . . . West . . . ? **S, 16 ;** . . . tomorrow. **8.**
218. . . . ? or . . . **S, 16 ;** . . . right do . . . **8.**
219. from the North? **S, 16 ;** from the north? **8, 17, 22.**
223. . . . milk, and . . . **S.**
226. . . . that to . . . way; a (way—a **16**) . . . pence, or . . . **S, 16 ;** . . . pence, or . . . **8, 17-29.**
229. Indeed, I'd . . . **S, 16.**
230. spare; but . . . **16.**
233. . . . you Peter. . . . **8 ;** . . . shilling, and **22, 29.**

234.   your blessing with it, or our own luck will go from
235.   us.   [*Peter goes to the box and takes out a shilling.*

236. *Bridget* [*to the Old Woman*]. Will you have a drink of
237.   milk, ma'am?

238. *Old Woman.* It is not food or drink that I want.

239. *Peter* [*offering the shilling*]. Here is something for you.

240. *Old Woman.* This is not what I want. It is not silver I
241.   want.

242. *Peter.* What is it you would be asking for?

243. *Old Woman.* If any one would give me help he must
244.   give me himself, he must give me all.
             [*Peter goes over to the table staring at the shilling in his hand in a
             bewildered way, and stands whispering to Bridget.*

245. *Michael.* Have you no one to care you in your age,
246.   ma'am?

247. *Old Woman.* I have not. With all the lovers that brought
248.   me their love I never set out the bed for any.

249. *Michael.* Are you lonely going the roads, ma'am?

250. *Old Woman.* I have my thoughts and I have my hopes.

251. *Michael.* What hopes have you to hold to?

252. *Old Woman.* The hope of getting my beautiful fields
253.   back again; the hope of putting the strangers out of
254.   my house.

---

237. milk? **S-29.**
240. That is not what . . . **S-29.**
243. . . . anyone . . . **S-17, 29-45, 89.**
244. . . . all **8.**
         Directions after 244. [. . . *way and* . . . .] **S**; [. . . *table, staring* . . . *way
         and* . . . .] **16**; [. . . *table, staring* . . . .] **29.**
245. . . . no man of your own, (own **8**) **S-22.**
248. . . . love, I . . . . **S-45.**
249. . . . roads ma'am? **8.**

255. *Michael.* What way will you do that, ma'am?

256. *Old Woman.* I have good friends that will help me.
257.   They are gathering to help me now. I am not afraid.
258.   If they are put down to-day they will get the upper
259.   hand to-morrow. [*She gets up.*] I must be going to
260.   meet my friends. They are coming to help me and I
261.   must be there to welcome them. I must call the
262.   neighbours together to welcome them.

263. *Michael.* I will go with you.

264. *Bridget.* It is not her friends you have to go and wel-
265.   come, Michael; it is the girl coming into the house
266.   you have to welcome. You have plenty to do; it is
267.   food and drink you have to bring to the house. The
268.   woman that is coming home is not coming with
269.   empty hands; you would not have an empty house
270.   before her. [*To the Old Woman.*] Maybe you don't
271.   know, ma'am, that my son is going to be married
272.   to-morrow.

273. *Old Woman.* It is not a man going to his marriage that
274.   I look to for help.

275. *Peter* [*to Bridget*]. Who is she, do you think, at all?

276. *Bridget.* You did not tell us your name yet, ma'am.

277. *Old Woman.* Some call me the Poor Old Woman, and
278.   there are some that call me Cathleen, the daughter of

---

255. . . . that ma'am **8.**
258. . . . to-day, they . . . **S, 16, 29.**
260. . . . me, and . . . **S, 16, 22, 29.**
261. . . . call
262. neighbours . . . . **8.**
265. come Michael; . . . **8.**
266. . . . do, it . . . **8, 17-69.**
268. . . . that is coming is not . . . **S, 16.**
269. . . . hands, you . . . **8.**
271. know ma'am that . . . **8.**
275. . . . she do . . . think at . . . ?
276. . . . yet ma'am.
277. . . . 'Poor . . . Woman,' . . . **8.**
278. . . . Cathleen ny Hoolihan. **S;** . . . Cathleen the . . . **8, 16.**

279.   Houlihan.

280. *Peter.* I think I knew some one of that name, once.
281.   Who was it, I wonder? It must have been some one
282.   I knew when I was a boy. No, no; I remember, I
283.   heard it in a song.

284. *Old Woman* [*who is standing in the doorway*]. They are
285.   wondering that there were songs made for me; there
286.   have been many songs made for me. I heard one on the
287.   wind this morning.

                              [*Sings*]
288.   Do not make a great keening
289.   When the graves have been dug to-morrow.
290.   Do not call the white-scarfed riders
291.   To the burying that shall be to-morrow.

292.   Do not spread food to call strangers
293.   To the wakes that shall be to-morrow;
294.   Do not give money for prayers
295.   For the dead that shall die to-morrow. . . .

296.   They will have no need of prayers, they will have no
297.   need of prayers.

298. *Michael.* I do not know what that song means, but tell
299.   me something I can do for you.

300. *Peter.* Come over to me, Michael.

---

279. [lacking] **S.**
280. . . . name once. **S, 16**; . . . someone . . . name once. **8, 17-34**; . . .
      someone . . . . **36-45.**
281. . . . someone **S, 17, 29-45**; . . . it I . . . someone **8.**
282. . . . . No, no, I remember I **S-16**; . . . . No, no, I . . . **17-29.**
      Directions before 288. [*She sings.*] **S-29.**
288-289. [printed both with and without music] **17.**
289. . . . to-morrow; **S**; . . . tomorrow. **8.**
290. . . . white scarfed . . .
291. . . . tomorrow. **8.**
      [between 291 and 292 no break] **8-17, 34-45, 69A, 97A.**
293. . . . tomorrow. **8**; . . . to-morrow. **16.**
295. . . . tomorrow. **8**; . . . to-morrow. **16.**
      [between 295 and 296 no break] **S, 16.**
296. they . . . **17-69.**
298. . . . means; but . . . **S, 16.**

301. *Michael*. Hush, father, listen to her.

302. *Old Woman*. It is a hard service they take that help me.
303.   Many that are red-cheeked now will be pale-cheeked;
304.   many that have been free to walk the hills and the
305.   bogs and the rushes will be sent to walk hard streets
306.   in far countries; many a good plan will be broken;
307.   many that have gathered money will not stay to
308.   spend it; many a child will be born and there will be
309.   no father at its christening to give it a name. They
310.   that have red cheeks will have pale cheeks for my
311.   sake, and for all that, they will think they are well
312.   paid.   [*She goes out; her voice is heard outside singing.*
313.   They shall be remembered for ever,
314.   They shall be alive for ever,
315.   They shall be speaking for ever,
316.   The people shall hear them for ever.

317. *Bridget* [*to Peter*]. Look at him, Peter; he has the look
318.   of a man that has got the touch. [*Raising her voice.*]
319.   Look here, Michael, at the wedding clothes. Such
320.   grand clothes as these are! You have a right to fit
321.   them on now; it would be a pity to-morrow if they
322.   did not fit. The boys would be laughing at you. Take
323.   them, Michael, and go into the room and fit them on.
                        [*She puts them on his arm.*

---

301.   Hush (Hush, **16**) father; listen . . . . **S, 16.**
303.   . . . red cheeked . . . pale cheeked; **8.**
305.   . . . rushes, will . . . **17, 22, 34-69.**
308.   . . . born, and . . . **22, 29.**
310.   that had red . . . **S-34.**
311.   sake; and . . . that they . . . **S, 16**; sake; and . . . **8, 17-34.**
        Directions in 312.   [. . . *out. Her* . . . .] **S, 16**; [. . . *out, her* . . . .] **8-22.**
313, 314, 315. . . . ever; **S** ; . . . ever **16.**
313-314.   [printed both with and without music] **17.**
317.   . . . him Peter; . . . **8.**
319.   . . . wedding clothes [*taking clothes from dresser*]. **S, 16** ; . . . clothes. **8** ;
        . . . wedding-clothes. Such **17-29.**
320.   You . . . **S-16** ; . . . are. You . . . **17-29.**
321.   . . . now, it . . . tomorrow . . . **8** ; . . . now. It . . . **16** ; . . . now, it . . .
        17, 22, 34-69.
322.   . . . fit; the . . . **S, 16.**
323.   them Michael and . . . . **8.**

324. *Michael*. What wedding are you talking of ? What clothes
325.   will I be wearing to-morrow?

326. *Bridget*. These are the clothes you are going to wear
327.   when you marry Delia Cahel to-morrow.

328. *Michael*. I had forgotten that.
          [*He looks at the clothes and turns towards the inner room, but stops
          at the sound of cheering outside.*

329. *Peter*. There is the shouting come to our own door.
330.   What is it has happened?
          [*Neighbours come crowding in, Patrick and Delia with them.*

331. *Patrick*. There are ships in the Bay; the French are land-
332.   ing at Killala!
          [*Peter takes his pipe from his mouth and his hat off, and stands up.
          The clothes slip from Michael's arm.*

333. *Delia*. Michael! [*He takes no notice.*] Michael! [*He turns
334.   towards her.*] Why do you look at me like a stranger?
          [*She drops his arm. Bridget goes over towards her.*

335. *Patrick*. The boys are all hurrying down the hillside to
336.   join the French.

337. *Delia*. Michael won't be going to join the French.

338. *Bridget* [*to Peter*]. Tell him not to go, Peter.

339. *Peter*. It's no use. He doesn't hear a word we're saying.

---

327. . . . tomorrow. **8.**
          Directions after 328. [. . . *room but* . . . .] **8**; [. . . *toward* . . . .] **16.**
          Directions after 330. [*Patrick and Delia come in.*] **29.**
331. . . . bay; . . . **S, 16.**
332. . . . Killala. **S-16.**
          Directions after 332. [. . . *off and* . . . .] **S-16.**
334. . . . stranger. **36.**
          Directions after 334. [. . . *toward* . . . .] **16.**
335. . . . hillsides . . . **S-45.**
336. meet the . . . . **S-16.**
338-339. [lacking] **8.**

340. *Bridget.* Try and coax him over to the fire.

341. *Delia.* Michael, Michael! You won't leave me! You
342. won't join the French, and we going to be married!

> [*She puts her arms about him, he turns towards her as if about to yield.*

> ### Old Woman's voice outside.

343.   They shall be speaking for ever,
344.   The people shall hear them for ever.

> [*Michael breaks away from Delia, stands for a second at the door, then rushes out, following the Old Woman's voice. Bridget takes Delia, who is crying silently, into her arms.*

345. *Peter* [*to Patrick, laying a hand on his arm*]. Did you see
346.   an old woman going down the path?

347. *Patrick.* I did not, but I saw a young girl, and she had
348.   the walk of a queen.

THE END

---

340. Try, Delia, and . . . . **S, 16.**
341. . . . , Michael, you . . . **S, 16**; Michael! Michael! . . . **8, 22, 29.**
342. . . . French and . . . married to-morrow! **S, 16.**
      Directions after 342. [. . . *him. He turns to her* . . . .] **S** ; [. . . *him. He turns to her* . . . .] **16** ; [. . . *him; he* . . . *yield. Old woman's voice outside.*] **29.**
      Directions before 343. . . . *outside:* **S** ; . . . *outside—***16.**
343. . . . be remembered for ever; (ever **16**) **S, 16.**
      Directions after 344. [. . . *from Delia and goes towards neighbours at the door.*] **S, 17, 22** ; [. . . *from her and goes out.*] **8** ; [. . . *from Delia and goes out.*] **16, 29.**
344a. *Michael.*—Come, we have no time to lose; we must follow her. [*Michael and the neighbours go out.*] **S, 17, 22.**
345. *Peter* [*laying his hand on Patrick's arm*].—Did . . . **S** ; *Bridget.* [*To Patrick.*] Did . . . **8** ; *Bridget* [*laying her hand on Patrick's arm*]. Did . . . **16.**
347. . . . not; but . . . **S** ; . . . girl and . . . **8, 16.**

NOTES

MY DEAR LADY GREGORY, I dedicate to you two volumes of plays that are in part your own.

When I was a boy I used to wander about at Rosses Point and Ballisodare listening to old songs and stories. I wrote down what I heard and made poems out of the stories or put them into the little chapters of the first edition of 'The Celtic Twilight,' and that is how I began to write in the Irish way.

Then I went to London to make my living, and though I spent a part of every year in Ireland and tried to keep the old life in my memory by reading every country tale I could find in books or old newspapers, I began to forget the true countenance of country life. The old tales were still alive for me indeed, but with a new, strange, half unreal life, as if in a wizard's glass, until at last, when I had finished 'The Secret Rose,' and was half-way through 'The Wind Among the Reeds,' a wise woman in her trance told me that my inspiration was from the moon, and that I should always live close to water, for my work was getting too full of those little jewelled thoughts that come from the sun and have no nation. I had no need to turn to my books of astrology to know that the common people are under the moon, or to Porphyry to remember the image-making power of the waters. Nor did I doubt the entire truth of what she said to me, for my head was full of fables that I had no longer the knowledge and emotion to write. Then you brought me with you to see your friends in the cottages, and to talk to old wise men on Slieve Echtge, and we gathered together, or you gathered for me, a great number of stories and traditional beliefs. You taught me to understand again, and much more perfectly than before, the true countenance of country life.

One night I had a dream almost as distinct as a vision, of a cottage where there was well-being and firelight and talk of a marriage, and into the midst of that cottage there came an old woman in a long cloak. She was Ireland herself, that Cathleen ni Houlihan for whom so many songs have been sung and about whom so many stories have been told and for whose sake so many have gone to their death. I thought if I could write this out as a little play I could make others see my dream as I had seen it, but I could not get down out of that high window of dramatic verse, and in spite of all you had done for me I had not the country speech. One has to live among the people, like you, of whom an old man said in my hearing, 'She has been a serving-maid among us,' before one can think the thoughts of the people and speak with their tongue. We turned my dream into the little play, 'Cathleen ni Hoolihan,' and when we gave it to the little theatre in Dublin and found that the working people liked it, you helped me to put my other dramatic fables into speech. Some of these have already been acted, but some may not be acted for a long time, but all seem to me, though they were but a part of a summer's work, to have more of that countenance of country life than anything I have done since I was a boy.

Feb. 1903.   W. B. YEATS.

Dedication of volumes one and two of Plays for an Irish Theatre.   **II.**

'Cathleen Ni Houlihan,' first performance, Dublin, October, 1902.

[On 'Contents,' page] **16.**

I cannot give the full cast of 'Cathleen ni Houlihan,' which was first played at St. Teresa's Hall, on April 3, 1902, for I have been searching the cupboard of the Abbey Theatre, where we keep old Playbills, and can find no record of it, nor did the newspapers of the time mention more than the principals. Mr. W. G. Fay played the old countryman, and Miss Quinn his wife, while Miss Maud Gonne was Cathleen ni Houlihan, and very magnificently she played. The Play has been constantly revived, and has, I imagine, been played more often than any other, except perhaps Lady Gregory's 'Spreading the News,' at the Abbey Theatre, Dublin. Notes, **29.**

My dear Lady Gregory,—

When I was a boy [follows the version in **11** with the exceptions noted] . . . *The Celtic Twilight*, and . . . , half-unreal . . . *The Secret Rose*, . . . *The Wind Among the Reeds*, . . . Houlihan . . . , *Cathleen ni Houlihan*, . . . working-people . . . boy.

Feb. 1903. W. B. Yeats.

This play was first played on April 2, 1902, in St. Teresa's Hall, Dublin, with the following cast:—Cathleen, Miss Maude Gonne; Delia Cahel, Miss Maire nic Sheublagh; Bridget Gillan, Miss M. T. Quinn; Patrick Gillan, Mr. C. Caufield; Michael Gillan, Mr. T. Dudley Digges; Peter Gillan, Mr. W. G. Fay.

Miss Maud Gonne played very finely, and her great height made Cathleen seem a divine being fallen into our mortal infirmity. Since then the part has been twice played in America by women who insisted on keeping their young faces, and one of these when she came to the door dropped her cloak, as I have been told, and showed a white satin dress embroidered with shamrocks. Upon another,—or was it the same occasion?—the player of Bridget wore a very becoming dress of the time of Louis the Fourteenth. The most beautiful woman of her time, when she played my Cathleen, 'made up' centuries old, and never should the part be played but with a like sincerity. This was the first play of our Irish School of folk-drama, and in it that way of quiet movement and careful speech which has given our players some little fame first showed itself, arising partly out of deliberate opinion and partly out of the ignorance of the players. Does art owe most to ignorance or to knowledge? Certainly it comes to its deathbed full of knowledge. I cannot imagine this play, or any folk-play of our school, acted by players with no knowledge of the peasant, and of the awkwardness and stillness of bodies that have followed the plough, or too lacking in humility to copy these things without convention or caricature.

The lines beginning 'Do not make a great keening' and 'They shall be remembered for ever' are said or sung to an air heard by one of the players in a dream. This music is with the other music at the end of the third volume.

Appendix II, *Cathleen ni Houlihan.* **34.**

My dear Lady Gregory,—
When I was a boy [follows the version in 34 to 'players in a dream.']

Notes, 45.

My dear Lady Gregory—When I was a boy [follows the version in 45 with the date '1907' added after the word 'dream'].   Notes, 69.

* * *

The little song in 'Cathleen ni Houlihan' beginning, 'I will come and cry with you, woman,' is sung by our players to an old Irish air, and the lines beginning, 'Do not make a great keening' and 'They shall be remembered for ever' to an air heard in a dream by one of the players.

Note on the Music. 17.

* * *

Wade, *op. cit.*, item no. 40, says that 'The lyrics [in Cathleen ni Houlihan] had previously appeared in *The United Irishman*, May 5, 1902.' The complete article in which the lyrics appeared reads as follows:

MR. YEATS' NEW PLAY.

Mr. Yeats, who returned to Dublin a few days ago to attend the final rehearsals of his new play, in answer to some questions we submitted to him has kindly sent us the following reply:—

My subject is Ireland and its struggle for independence. The scene is laid in the West of Ireland at the time of the French landing. I have described a household preparing for the wedding of the son of the house. Everyone expects some good thing from the wedding. The bridegroom is thinking of his bride, the father of the fortune which will make them all more prosperous, and the mother of a plan of turning this prosperity to account by making her youngest son a priest, and the youngest son of a greyhound pup the bride promised to give him when she marries. Into this household comes Kathleen Ni Houlihan herself, and the bridegroom leaves his bride, and all the hopes come to nothing. It is the perpetual struggle of the cause of Ireland and every other ideal cause against private hopes and dreams, against all that we mean when we say the world. I have put into the mouth of Kathleen Ni Houlihan verses about those who have died or are about to die for her, and these verses are the key of the rest. She sings of one yellow-haired Donough in stanzas that were suggested to me by some old Gaelic folk-song:

I will go cry with the woman,
For yellow-haired Donough is dead,
With a hempen-rope for a neck-cloth,
And a white cloth on his head.

I am come to cry with you woman,
 My hair is unbound and unwound;
I remember him ploughing his field,
 Turning up the red side of the ground.

And building his barn on the hill,
 With the good-mortared stone;
Oh, we'd have pulled down the gallows,
 Had it happened at Enniscrone.

And just before she goes out she sings:

Do not make a great keening
 When the graves have been dug to-morrow;
Do not call the white-scarfed riders
 To the buryings that shall be to-morrow;
Do not spread the food to call strangers,
 To the wakes that shall be to-morrow,

And after a few words of dialogue she goes out crying:

They shall be remembered for ever;
They shall be alive for ever;
They shall be speaking for ever,
The people shall hear them for ever.

I have written the whole play in the English of the West of Ireland, the English of people who think in Irish. My play, 'The Land of Heart's Desire,' was, in a sense, the call of the heart, the heart seeking its own dream; this play is the call of country, and I have a plan of following it up with a little play about the call of religion, and printing the three plays together some day.

The United Irishman, May 5, 1902.

* * *

Variant spellings

Cathleen ny Houlihan S.
Hoolihan 8, 16; *Houlihan* 17-97.
Kilglas S, 16; *Kilglass* 8, 17-97.
Maurteen S, 16, 84-97; *Murteen* 8, 17-69.
O'Donell S, 16, 42-89; *O'Donnell* 8, 17-36, 97.
Winnie S, 16; *Winny* 8, 17-97.

* * *

[See also the notes on *The Land of Heart's Desire* p. 211; *The Pot of Broth* p. 254; and *Prefaces to 29, 93,* pp. 1295, 1312.]

THE POT OF BROTH

1904

Persons in the Play

John Coneely, *an elderly man*
Sibby Coneely, *a young or middle-aged woman*
A Tramp

A cottage kitchen. Fire on the hearth; table with cabbage, onions, a plate of meal, etc. Half-open door. A Tramp enters, looks about.

1. *Tramp.* What sort are the people of this house, I
2. wonder? Was it a good place for me to come to look
3. for my dinner, I wonder? What's in that big pot?
4. [*Lifts cover.*] Nothing at all! What's in the little pot?
5. [*Lifts cover.*] Nothing at all! What's in that bottle, I
6. wonder? [*Takes it up excitedly and tastes.*] Milk! milk
7. in a bottle! I wonder they wouldn't afford a tin can
8. to milk the cow into! Not much chance for a poor
9. man to make a living here. What's in that chest?
10. [*Kneels and tries to lift cover.*] Locked! [*Smells at the key-*
11. *hole.*] There's a good smell—there must be a still not
12. far off.

PRINTINGS   *The Gael*, September 1903; **16, 17, 21, 41, 69, 84, 89, 97.**

DATE   September, 1903. **G**; [lacking] **16-41.**

DRAMATIS PERSONAE   Persons / A Beggarman / John Coneely / Sibby Coneely **G, 16**; [no heading] John Coneely / Sibby Coneely / A Tramp **17-41.**

STAGE DIRECTIONS   Scene Description. (Scene: **16**) *A . . . hearth. Table . . . cabbages,* (*cabbage,* **16**) *a plate . . . . Half open* (*Half-open* **16**) *door.* **G, 16**; Scene: *A . . . .* **17-69.**

NAMES OF SPEAKERS   ['Beggar' for 'Tramp' throughout except where 'Beggarman' is noted] **G, 16.**

TEXT   Title A Pot . . . **G, 16.**

1. *Beggarman* (*Beggar* **16**) [*enters, looks about*]. What . . . **G, 16.**
   Directions in 6. [. . . *and smells.*] **G, 16.**
8. . . . into! **16.**
9. What's . . . ? **G, 16.**
11. . . . smell there—there must . . . **G-41.**

[*Gets up and sits on chest. A noise heard outside, shouts, footsteps, and loud frightened cackling.*

13. *Tramp.* What in the earthly world is going on outside?
14. Any one would think it was the Fiannta-h-Eireann
15. at their hunting!

16. *Sibby's voice.* Stop the gap, let you stop the gap, John.
17. Stop that old schemer of a hen flying up on the
18. thatch like as if she was an eagle!

19. *John's voice.* What can I do, Sibby? I all to had my hand
20. upon her when she flew away!

21. *Sibby's voice.* She's out into the garden! Follow after
22. her! She has the wide world before her now.

23. *Tramp.* Sibby he called her. I wonder is it Sibby
24. Coneely's house I am in? If that's so it's a bad
25. chance I have of going out heavier than I came in. I
26. often heard of her, a regular slave-driver that would
27. starve the rats. A niggard with her eyes on kippeens,
28. that would skin a flea for its hide! It was the bad
29. luck of the world brought me here, and not a house
30. or a village between this and Tubber. And it isn't
31. much I have left to bring me on there. [*Begins empty-
32. ing out his pockets on the chest.*] There's my pipe and not
33. a grain to fill it with! There's my handkerchief I got

Directions after 12.   [. . . *footsteps, and a loud* (*loud,* **17-41**) *frightened*
. . . .] **G-41.**
14. Anyone . . . Fiannta Eireann **G, 16;** Anyone . . . **17, 41.**
16. . . . , John! **G-41.**
18. . . . eagle. **21.**
20. on her . . . ! **G-41.**
22. . . . now! **G, 16, 41.**
23. 'Sibby,' he . . . **16.**
24. . . . in! If . . . **G, 17-69;** . . . in! If . . . so, it's . . . **16.**
25. . . . in! I **G, 16.**
26. . . . regular old slave driver (slave-driver **16, 21**) . . . **G-41;** . . . slave
driver . . . **69.**
27. . . . rats! (rats **17-41**) An old niggard . . . , **G-41.**
32. . . . pipe, and . . . **16-41.**
33. . . . handkerchief that I . . . **G-41.**

34. at the coronation dinner! There's my knife and no-
35. thing left of it but the handle. [*Shakes his pocket out.*]
36. And there's a crust of the last dinner I got, and the
37. last I'm likely to get till to-morrow. That's all I have
38. in the world unless the stone I picked up to pelt at
39. that yelping dog a while ago. [*Takes stone out of pocket*
40. *and tosses it up and down.*] In the time long ago I usen't
41. to have much trouble to find a dinner, getting over
42. the old women and getting round the young ones! I
43. remember the time I met the old minister on the
44. path and sold him his own flock of turkeys. My wits
45. used to fill my stomach then, but I'm afraid they're
46. going from me now with all the hardship I went
47. through.   [*Cackling heard again and cries.*

48. *Sibby's voice.* Catch her, she's round the bush! Put your
49. hands in the nettles, don't be daunted!
                                    [*A choked cackle and prolonged screech.*

50. *Tramp.* There's a dinner for somebody anyway. That
51. it may be for myself! How will I come round her, I
52. wonder? There is no more pity in her heart than
53. there's a soul in a dog. If all the saints were standing
54. barefoot before her she'd bid them to call another
55. day. It's myself I have to trust to now, and my share
56. of talk. [*Looks at the stone.*] I know what I'll do, I know
57. what the tinker did with a stone, and I'm as good a

---

34. . . . Coronation dinner. There's . . . knife (knife, **16**) and . . . **G, 16**;
     . . . knife, and . . . **21**.
     Directions in 35. [*Shakes the pocket* . . . .]
36. . . . there's the crumb of . . . **G-41**.
38. . . . world, unless . . . to peg at
39. . . . awhile (a while **16**) . . . . [. . . *of other pocket* **G-41**.
40. . . . usedn't **17-41**.
41. . . . trouble to get a . . . **G, 16**.
     Directions in 47. [. . . *again, and* . . . .] **G, 16**.
49. hand . . . ! **G, 16**.
50. . . . somebody, anyway! (any way! **17-41**) . . . **G-41**.
51. . . . her I **G**; . . . myself. How . . . **17, 21**; . . . be myself! . . . **69A**.
54. there barefoot (barefoot, **16**) she'd . . . **G-41**.
55. . . . trust now, . . . **G, 16**.
56. . . . do; I . . . **16**.
57. what a friend of mine did one time with . . . **G, 16**; what Charlie
     Ward did one time with . . . **17-41**.

58. man as he is anyway. [*He jumps up and waves the stone*
59. *over his head.*] Now, Sibby! If I don't do it one way I'll
60. do it another. My wits against the world!

61.   There's broth in the pot for you, old man,
62.   There's broth in the pot for you, old man,
63.   There's cabbage for me
64.   And broth for you,
65.   And beef for Jack the journeyman.

66.   I wish you were dead, my gay old man,
67.   I wish you were dead, my gay old man,
68.   I wish you were dead
69.   And a stone at your head,
70.   So as I'd marry poor Jack the journeyman.

71. *John's voice* [*outside*]. Bring it in, bring it in, Sibby.
72. You'll be late with the priest's dinner.

73. *Sibby's voice.* Can't you wait a minute till I'll draw it?

Enter John

74. *John.* I didn't know there was any one in the house.

75. *Tramp.* It's only this minute I came in, tired with the
76. length of the road I am, and fasting since morning.

77. *John* [*begins groping among the pots and pans*]. I'll see can
78. I find anything here for you . . . I don't see much . . .
79. Maybe there's something in the chest.

---

58. . . . is, anyway. . . . **G, 16**; . . . any way. . . . **17-41.**
59. . . . . Now Sibby! . . . **G**; . . . way, I'll **16.**
60. . . . world! [*Sings*] **G-41.**
61-65. [printed both with and without music] **17.**
63. . . . me, **17-41.**
68. . . . dead, **G, 16, 41.**
70. And I'd . . . .
    Directions before 71. [*Voices outside.*]
71. *John's Voice.* Bring . . . . **G, 16.**
73. . . . till I draw . . . ? **G-41.**
74. . . . anyone . . . . **G-17, 41.**
75. . . . in; tired . . . **16.**
79. maybe . . . . **17-69.**

*[He takes key from a hiding-place at back of hearth, opens chest, takes
out bottle, takes out a ham-bone and is cutting a bit from it when
Sibby enters, carrying chicken by the neck. John drops the ham-bone on a
bench.*

80. *Sibby.* Hurry now, John, after all the time you have
81.   wasted. Why didn't you steal up on the old hen that
82.   time she was scratching in the dust?

83. *John.* Sure I thought one of the chickens would be the
84.   tenderest.

85. *Sibby.* Cock you up with tenderness! All the expense
86.   I'm put to! My grand hen I've been feeding these
87.   five years! Wouldn't that have been enough to part
88.   with? Indeed I wouldn't have thought of parting with
89.   her itself, but she had got tired of laying since Easter.

90. *John.* Well, I thought we ought to give his Reverence
91.   something that would have a little good in it.

92. *Sibby.* What does the age of it matter? A hen's a hen
93.   when it's on the table. [*Sitting down to pluck chicken.*]
94.   Why couldn't the Kernans have given the priest his
95.   dinner the way they always do? What did it matter
96.   their mother's brother to have died? It is an excuse
97.   they had made up to put the expense of the dinner
98.   on me.

Directions after 79. [. . . *hiding place* (*hiding-place* **16**) *at the back of the
hearth,* . . . *out ham bone* . . . , *carrying hen by the neck.*] **G, 16** ; [. . . *hiding
place* (*hiding-place* **17, 21**) . . . *ham bone* . . . *ham bone* . . . .] **17-41** ; [. . .
ham bone . . . *ham bone* . . . .] **69.**
80. Hurry, now, . . . **G, 16.**
83. Sure, I . . . **G-41.**
84. tenderest— **17-41.**
85. . . . tenderness (tenderness, **16-41**) indeed! All . . . **G-41.**
86. . . . hen I have been . . . **G, 16.**
88. with! (with? **16**) Indeed, I . . . **G-41.**
89. her at all, but . . . . **G, 16** ; . . . itself but . . . . **17-69.**
    Directions after 89. [*At sound of her voice John has dropped ham bone on a
    bench.*] **G, 16.**
90. . . . reverence **G-41.**
    Directions in 93. [*She sits down on a bench to pluck the chicken.*] **69A.**
95. dinner, the . . . **G, 16.**

99. *John.* Well, I hope you have a good bit of bacon to put
100.   in the pot along with the chicken.

101. *Sibby.* Let me alone. The taste of meat on the knife is
102.   all that high-up people like the clergy care for, nice
103.   genteel people, no way greedy like potato-diggers or
104.   harvest men.

105. *John.* Well, I never saw the man, gentle or simple,
106.   wouldn't be glad of his fill of bacon and he hungry.

107. *Sibby.* Let me alone, I'll show the Kernans what I can
108.   do. I have what is better than bacon, a nice bit of
109.   a ham I am keeping in the chest this good while,
110.   thinking we might want it for company. [*She catches*
111.   *sight of Tramp and calls out.*] Who is there? A beggar-
112.   man, is it? Then you may quit this house if you please.
113.   We have nothing for you. [*She gets up and opens the*
      door.]

114. *Tramp* [*comes forward*]. It is a mistake you are making,
115.   ma'am, it is not asking anything I am. It is giving I
116.   am more used to. I was never in a house yet but there
117.   would be a welcome for me in it again.

118. *Sibby.* Well, you have the appearance of a beggar, and
119.   if it isn't begging you are, what way do you make
120.   your living?

121. *Tramp.* If I was a beggar, ma'am, it is to common
122.   people I would be going and not to a nice grand

---

101. . . . alone, the . . . **G, 16.**
103. . . . potato diggers . . . **G, 17, 41, 69 ;** . . . greedy, like . . . potato diggers . . . **16.**
105. . . . man gentle . . . simple **G, 16.**
106. . . . bacon, and . . . . **17-41.**
108. . . . have what's better . . . **G-41.**
111. . . . beggar **17, 21, 69 ;** . . . . out]. *Sibby.* Who . . . beggar **41.**
112. . . . please, **G ;** . . . house, if . . . please; **16 ;** man is . . . please, **17-41 ;** man is . . . . **69.**
113. we . . . . [. . . *opens door*]. **G-41.**
115. ma'am; it . . . **G, 16.**
119. . . . are what . . . **69.**
122. . . . going, and . . . **21.**

123.   woman like yourself, that is only used to be talking
124.   with high-up noble people.

125.   *Sibby.* Well, what is it you are asking? If it's a bit to
126.   eat you want, I can't give it to you, for I have com-
127.   pany coming that will clear all before them.

128.   *Tramp.* Is it me ask anything to eat? [*Holds up stone.*] I
129.   have here what is better than beef and mutton, and
130.   currant cakes and sacks of flour.

131.   *Sibby.* What is it at all?

132.   *Tramp* [*mysteriously*]. Those that gave it to me wouldn't
133.   like me to tell that.

134.   *Sibby* [*to John*]. Do you think is he a man that has
135.   friends among the Sidhe?

136.   *John.* Your mind is always running on the Sidhe since
137.   the time they made John Molloy find buried gold on
138.   the bridge of Limerick. I see nothing in it but a
139.   stone.

140.   *Tramp.* What can you see in it, you that never saw
141.   what it can do?

142.   *John.* What is it it can do?

143.   *Tramp.* It can do many things, and what it's going to
144.   do now is to make me a drop of broth for my dinner.

145.   *Sibby.* I'd like to have a stone that could make broth.

146.   *Tramp.* No one in the world but myself has one, ma'am,
147.   and no other stone in the world has the same power,
148.   for it has enchantment on it. All I'll ask of you now,
149.   ma'am, is the loan of a pot with a drop of boiling

---

125.   . . . ? If it is a . . . **41**.
126.   . . . want I . . . **G**.
128.   . . . me to ask . . . **G-41**.
129.   . . . here what's better . . . mutton and **G, 16 ;** . . . here what's better
        . . . **17-41**.
130.   . . . cakes, and . . . **17-41**.
131.   . . . it all? **G, 16**.

150.   water in it.

151. *Sibby.* You're welcome to that much. John, fill the
152.   small pot with water. [*John fills the pot from a kettle.*

153. *Tramp.* [*putting in stone*]. There now, that's all I have to
154.   do but to put it on the fire to boil, and it's a grand
155.   pot of broth will be before me then.

156. *Sibby.* And is that all you have to put in it?

157. *Tramp.* Nothing at all but that—only, maybe, a bit
158.   of an herb for fear the enchantment might slip away
159.   from it. You wouldn't have a bit of Slanlus in the
160.   house, ma'am, that was cut with a black-handled
161.   knife?

162. *Sibby.* No, indeed, I have none of that in the house.

163. *Tramp.* Or a bit of the Fearavan that was picked when
164.   the wind was from the north?

165. *Sibby.* No, indeed, I'm sorry there's none.

166. *Tramp.* Or a sprig of the Athair-talav, the father of
167.   herbs?

168. *John.* There's plenty of it by the hedge. I'll go out and
169.   get it for you.

170. *Tramp.* O, don't mind taking so much trouble; those
171.   leaves beside me will do well enough. [*He takes a
          couple of good handfuls of the cabbage and onions and puts
          them in.*]

---

151. . . . much, John. fill . . . **G.**
152. . . . water. [. . . *pot.*] And I'll bring out the hen and draw it. [*She goes
          out.*] **G, 16.**
157. . . . that,—only maybe (only, maybe, **21**) a . . . **G-41.**
158. of herb (herb, **16**) for . . . **G, 16.**
159. . . . of the Slán-lus . . . **G-41.**
160. house ma'am, . . . **17, 41.**
162. No indeed, ... **17.**
170. Oh, . . . **G, 16, 69.**

172. *Sibby.* But where at all did you get the stone?

173. *Tramp.* Well, this is how it happened. I was out one
174.   time, and a grand greyhound with me, and it fol-
175.   lowed a hare, and I went after it. And I came up at
176.   last to the edge of a gravel pit where there were a
177.   few withered furze bushes, and there was my fine
178.   hound sitting up, and it shivering, and a little old
179.   man sitting before it, and he taking off a hareskin
180.   coat. [*Looking round at the ham-bone.*] Give me the loan
181.   of a kippeen to stir the pot with. . . . [*He takes the
        ham-bone and puts it into the pot.*]

182. *John.* Oh! the ham-bone!

183. *Tramp.* I didn't say a ham-bone, I said a hareskin coat.

184. *Sibby.* Hold your tongue, John, if it's deaf you are
185.   getting.

186. *Tramp* [*stirring the pot with the ham-bone*]. Well, as I was
187.   telling you, he was sitting up, and one time I thought
188.   he was as small as a nut, and the next minute I
189.   thought his head to be in the stars. Frightened I was.

190. *Sibby.* No wonder, no wonder at all in that.

191. *Tramp.* He took the little stone then—that stone I have
192.   with me—out of the side pocket of his coat, and he
193.   showed it to me. 'Call off your dog', says he, 'and
194.   I'll give you that stone, and if ever you want a good

---

172.   . . . where did . . . stone, at all? **G-41.**
173.   Well, it is how . . . happened: (happened. **21**) I . . . **17-69.**
176.   . . . pit, where . . . **21.**
177.   . . . furzy . . . **97A.**
179.   . . . before him, and . . . hare-skin (hareskin **69E**) **G-69.**
        Directions in 180. [. . . *ham bone.*] **G-69.**
        Directions at 181. [*ham bone . . . .*] **G-69.**
182.   . . . ! The ham bone! **G, 16**; . . . ham bone! **17-69.**
183.   . . . ham bone, . . . hare-skin . . . . **G-69.**
184.   . . . deaf you're **G-41.**
        Directions in 186. [. . . *with the same ham bone.*] **G, 16**; [. . . *ham bone.*]
        17-69.
193.   . . . me, 'Call . . . **17.**

195.   drop of broth or a bit of stirabout, or a drop of poteen
196.   itself, all you have to do is to put it down in a pot
197.   with a drop of water and stir it awhile, and you'll
198.   have the thing you were wanting ready before you.'

199. *Sibby.* Poteen! Would it make that?

200. *Tramp.* It would, ma'am; and wine, the same as the
201.   Clare Militia uses.

202. *Sibby.* Let me see what does it look like now. [*Is bend-ing forward.*]

203. *Tramp.* Don't look at it for your life, ma'am. It might
204.   bring bad luck on any one that would look at it, and
205.   it boiling. I must put a cover on the pot, or I must
206.   colour the water some way. Give me a handful of
207.   that meal.
     [*Sibby holds out a plate of meal and he puts in a handful or two.*

208. *John.* Well, he is a gifted man!

209. *Sibby.* It would be a great comfort to have a stone like
210.   that. [*She has finished plucking the chicken which lies in her lap.*]

211. *Tramp.* And there's another thing it does, ma'am, since
212.   it came into Catholic hands. If you put it into a pot
213.   of a Friday with a bit of the whitest meat in Ireland
214.   in it, it would turn it as black as black.

215. *Sibby.* That is no less than a miracle. I must tell Father
216.   John about that.

---

195.   ... broth, or ... **G-41.**
197.   ... a while, ... **16.**
198.   ... you. **G.**
204.   ... anyone that might look ... **G, 16**; ... anyone ... **17, 41.**
207.   ... meal? **41.**
208.   Well, he's a ... ! **G-41.**
     Directions in 210.   [... *the hen which* ....] **G, 16.**
211.   ... does ma'am since **17, 41.**
215.   ... miracle; I ...
216.   Jones about .... **G, 16.**

217. *Tramp.* But to put a bit of meat with it any other day
218. of the week, it would do it no harm at all, but good.
219. Look here now, ma'am, I'll put that nice little hen
220. you have in your lap in the pot for a minute till
221. you'll see. [*Takes it and puts it in.*]

222. *John* [*sarcastically*]. It's a good job this is not a Friday!

223. *Sibby.* Keep yourself quiet, John, and don't be inter-
224. rupting the talk or you'll get a knock on the head
225. like the King of Lochlann's grandmother.

226. *John.* Go on, go on, I'll say no more.

227. *Tramp.* If I'm passing this way some time of a Friday,
228. I'll bring a nice bit of mutton, or the breast of a
229. turkey, and you'll see how it will be no better in
230. two minutes than a fistful of bog mould.

231. *Sibby* [*getting up*]. Let me take the chicken out now.

232. *Tramp.* Stop till I'll help you, ma'am, you might scald
233. your hand. I'll show it to you in a minute as white
234. as your own skin, where the lily and the rose are
235. fighting for mastery. Did you ever hear what the boys
236. in your own parish were singing after you being
237. married from them—such of them that had any voice
238. at all and not choked with crying, or senseless with
239. the drop of drink they took to comfort them and to
240. keep their wits from going, with the loss of you?

[*Sibby sits down again complacently.*

241. *Sibby.* Did they do that indeed?

---

218. . . . week it . . . all but . . . . **G** ; . . . week it . . . . **41**.
219. . . . here, now, . . . little chicken **G, 16**.
221. you see. . . . . **G-41**.
222. . . . Friday? **41**.
224. . . . talk, or . . . **16**.
225. . . . grandmother! **17-41**.
227. . . . Friday **17-41**.
232. . . . till I help . . . , ma'am, (ma'am; **16**) you . . . **G-41**.
237. . . . them?—such . . . **G, 16**.
240. . . . going with . . . you. **G, 16** ; . . . you. **69E**.
241. . . . that, indeed? **G, 16**.

242. *Tramp*. They did, ma'am, this is what they used to be
243.   singing:

244.   Philomel, I've listened oft
245.   To thy lay, near weeping willow—

246.   No, that's not it—it's a queer thing the memory is—

247.   'Twas at the dance at Dermody's that first I
248.   caught a sight of her.

249.   No, that's not it either—ah, now I have it.

250.   My Paistin Finn is my sole desire,
251.   And I am shrunken to skin and bone.

252. *Sibby*. Why would they call me Paistin?

253. *Tramp*. And why wouldn't they? Would you wish them
254.   to put your right name in a song, and your man ready
255.   to knock the brains of any man will as much as look
256.   your side of the road?

257. *Sibby*. Well, maybe so.

258. *Tramp*. I was standing by the man that made the song,
259.   and he writing it with an old bit of a carpenter's
260.   pencil, and the tears running down—

261.   My Paistin Finn is my sole desire,

---

242.   . . . , ma'am. This . . . **16**.
243.   singing. [*Sings*.] **G, 16 ; . . .**: [*Sings*.] **17-41**.
244.   The spouse of Naoise, Erin's woe,
245.   Helen and Venus long ago, (ago **17, 21**)
245a.   Their charms would fade, their fame would flee,
245b.   Beside mo gradh, mo stor, mo chree,
225c.   My Sibby (Sibby, **17-41**) O! **G-41**.
246-266.   [lacking] **G-41**.
247.   . . . Dermody's, that . . . **69**.
250.   My pretty Paistin is my heart's desire,
251.   Yet I am (Yet am I **84, 89**) . . . . **69-89**.
261.   My pretty Paistin is my heart's desire, **69-89**.

262.   And I am shrunken to skin and bone,
263.   For all my heart has had for its hire
264.   Is what I can whistle alone and alone.
265.   *Oro, oro!*
266.   *To-morrow night I will break down the door.*

[*Sibby takes a fork and rises to take out the chicken. Tramp puts his hand to stop her and goes on:*

267.   What is the good of a man and he
268.   Alone and alone with a speckled shin?
269.   I would that I drank with my love on my knee,
270.   Between two barrels at the inn.
271.   *Oro, oro!*
272.   *To-morrow night I will break down the door.*

[*Sibby half rises again. Tramp puts his hand upon her hand.*

273. *Tramp.* Wait now till you hear the end [*sings*]:

---

262.   Yet I am (Yet am I **69E, 84, 89**) shrunken . . . bone (bone, **84, 89**)
     69-89.
263.   . . . my toil has . . . **69, 84**; . . . all that my . . . **89.**
264.   Is drinking her health when lone, alone— **69, 84.**
265-266. [lacking] **69, 84.**
265.   *Aro, Aro.*
266.   *Tomorrow* . . . . **89.**
     Directions before 267. [. . . *the hen. Beggar puts* (*puts up* **16**) *his* . . . *on.*]
     G, 16; [. . . *chicken,* (*chicken;* **41**) *Tramp* . . . *on.*] **17-41.**
267.   Her eyes are gray like morning dew, **G-41**; Oh I would think that I
     had my fee, **69.**
268.   Her curling hair falls to her shoe, **G-41**; Though I am shrunken to
     bone and skin, **69**; Drinking alone with . . . ? **84.**
269.   The swan is blacker than (than— **17-41**) [*looks round for a simile, then
     at his hand*] my nail, **G-41**; Could I but drink, my love . . . knee **69**;
     O could I drink, my love . . . , **84.**
270.   Beside my queen, my Granuaile,
271.   My Sibby (Sibby, **17-41**) O! **G-41.**
271-272. [lacking] **69, 84.**
271.   *Aro, Aro.* **89.**
272.   [lacking] **G-41**; *Tomorrow* . . . . **89.**
     Directions before 273. [. . . *again,* (*again.* **16**; *again;* **41**) *Beggarman*
     (*Tramp* **17-41**) *puts up his hand.*] **G-41.**
273.   Wait till . . . hear to the end. [*Sings.*] **G-21.**

274.   Alone and alone nine nights I lay
275.   Between two bushes under the rain;
276.   I thought to have whistled her down that way,
277.   I whistled and whistled and whistled in vain.
278.   *Oro, oro!*
279.   *Tomorrow night I will break down the door.*

[*He repeats the verse, Sibby singing too and beating time with fork.*]

280. *Sibby* [*to John*]. I always knew I was too good for you!
    [*She goes on humming.*]

281. *John.* Well, he has the poor woman bewitched.

282. *Sibby* [*suddenly coming to her wits*]. Did you take the
283.   chicken out yet?

Tramp [*taking it out and giving it a good squeeze into the pot*].
284.   I did, ma'am. Look at it there.

                [*He takes it and lays it on table.*]

---

274. The King of France would give his throne **G-41**; Nine nights I lay in (lay and in **84**) longing sore **69, 84.**
275. To share her pillow (*what's the rhyme at all*), **G, 16**;
To share her pillow (what's the rhyme at all?) **17-41.**
276. So would I myself.... [T] **G-41**; Thinking to meet my love once more **69**; I had thought to have called her out to the door, **84.**
Directions after 276.   [*Sibby begins to keep time with fork.*] **G-41.**
277. The Spanish fleet is on the sea **G-41**; I cried and whistled but vain, all vain. **69**; But there I lay and I whistled in .... **84.**
278. To carry away mo gradh, (grah, **G**) mo chree! (mo stor! **17-41**) **G-41**; *Aro, Aro.* **89.**
278-279.   [lacking] **69, 84.**
279. My Sibby (Sibby, **17-41**) O! **G-41**; *To-morrow* .... **97A.**
Directions after 279.   [lacking] **G-41.**
280. *Sibby.* [*stands up with the fork in her hand and sings to herself*] The ('The **16**) Spanish fleet is on the sea,' etc. [*To John*] I always ... ! **G, 16**;
Sibby. [*Stands up with the fork in her hand and sings to herself* 'The Spanish fleet is on the sea,' etc.—*To John.*] I always ... ! **17-41.**
281. ... the old woman bewitched! (bewitched. **17-41**) **G-41.**
284. ..., ma'am; (ma'am, **17-41**) look .... **G-41.**
Directions after 284.   [*She takes ... on (on the **41**) table.* **G-41**; [... *lays on* ....] **69.**

285. *John.* How is the broth getting on?

286. *Tramp* [*tasting it with a spoon*]. It's grand. It's always
287.   grand.

288. *Sibby.* Give me a taste of it.

Tramp [*takes the pot off and slips the ham-bone behind him*].
289.   Give me some vessel till I'll give this sky-woman a
290.   taste of it.
          [*John gives him an egg-cup which he fills and gives to Sibby. John
          gives him a mug, and he fills this for himself, pouring it back and
          forward from the mug to a bowl that is on the table, and drinking
          gulps now and again. Sibby blows at hers and smells it.*

291. *Sibby.* There's a good smell on it anyway. [*Tasting.*] It's
292.   lovely. O, I'd give the world and all to have the
293.   stone that made that!

294. *Tramp.* The world and all wouldn't buy it, ma'am. If
295.   I was inclined to sell it the Lord Lieutenant would
296.   have given me Dublin Castle and all that's in it long
297.   ago.

298. *Sibby.* O, couldn't we coax it out of you any way at all?

299. *Tramp* [*drinking more soup*]. The whole world wouldn't
300.   coax it out of me except maybe for one thing . . .
301.   [*looks depressed*]. Now I think of it, there's only one
302.   reason I might think of parting with it at all.

---

286. . . . grand; it's . . . **G-41.**
      Directions before 289. [. . . *off* (*off*, **17-41**) *and . . . ham bone . . . .*]
      G-69.
289. . . . till I give this shy woman . . . **G, 16 ;** . . . till I give . . . **17-41.**
      Directions after 290. [. . . *egg cup, which . . . from it to . . . table* (*table*,
      16) *and . . . .*] **G, 16 ;** . . . *egg-cup, which . . . him a mug,* (*mug* **21**) *and
      . . . .*] **17-41.**
291. . . . it, anyway. . . . **G, 16.**
292. lovely! Oh, . . . **17-41.**
294. The riches of the world wouldn't . . . **G-41.**
295. . . . it, the . . . **16, 21.**
298. Oh! couldn't . . . ? **G-41 ;** Oh, . . . ? **69.**
300. coax me out of it, except . . . thing. **G, 16 ;** . . . me, except . . . **17-41.**
301. . . . it there's . . . **69.**
302. . . . parting it . . . . **G, 17-69.**

303. *Sibby* [*eagerly*]. What reason is that?

304. *Tramp.* It's a misfortune that overtakes me, ma'am,
305.   every time I make an attempt to keep a pot of my
306.   own to boil it in, and I don't like to be always under
307.   a compliment to the neighbours, asking the loan of
308.   one. But whatever way it is, I never can keep a pot
309.   with me. I had a right to ask one of the little man
310.   that gave me the stone. The last one I bought got the
311.   bottom burned out of it one night I was giving a
312.   hand to a friend that keeps a still, and the one before
313.   that I hid under a bush one time I was going into
314.   Ennis for the night, and some boys in the town
315.   dreamed about it and went looking for treasure
316.   in it, and they found nothing but eggshells, but
317.   they brought it away for all that. And another
318.   one . . .

319. *Sibby.* Give me the loan of the stone itself, and I'll
320.   engage I'll keep a pot for it. . . . Wait now till I'll
321.   make some offer to you. . . .

322. *Tramp* [*aside*]. I'd best not be stopping to bargain, the
323.   priest might be coming in on me. [*Gets up.*] Well,
324.   ma'am, I'm sorry I can't oblige you. [*Goes to door,*
325.   *shades his eyes and looks out, turns suddenly.*] I have
326.   no time to lose, ma'am, I'm off. [*Comes to table*
327.   *and takes his hat.*] Well, ma'am, what offer will you
328.   make?

---

307. . . . neighbours asking . . . **G, 16.**
312. . . . still; and . . . **16.**
314. . . . boys of the . . . **G-41.**
316. . . . it and . . . **G.**
317. . . . that, and . . .
318. one. **G, 16.**
319. . . . itself and . . . **G, 16**; Give the loan . . . **17-41.**
320. . . . . wait . . . till I **G** ; . . . till I **16-41.**
321. . . . you. **G-41.**
322. . . . bargain; the **G, 16.**
323. . . . coming on . . . , **G-41.**
    Directions in 325. . . . *out; turns* . . . .] **17-41.**
326. . . . , ma'am; I'm . . . **16.**
    Directions in 327. . . . *takes up his* . . . .] **G-41.**

329. *John*. You might as well leave it for a day on trial first.

330. *Tramp* [*to John*]. I think it likely I'll not be passing this
331. way again. [*To Sibby*.] Well, now, ma'am, as you were
332. so kind, and for the sake of the good treatment you
333. gave me, I'll ask nothing at all for it. Here it is for
334. you and welcome, and that you may live long to use
335. it! But I'll just take a little bit in my bag that'll do
336. for my supper, for fear I mightn't be in Tubber before
337. night. [*He takes up the chicken.*] And you won't be-
338. grudge me a drop of whiskey when you can make plenty
339. for yourself from this out. [*Takes the Bottle.*]

340. *John*. You deserve it, you deserve it indeed. You are a
341. very gifted man. Don't forget the kippeen!

342. *Tramp*. It's here! [*Slaps his pocket and exit. John follows
      him.*]

343. *Sibby* [*looking at the stone in her hand*]. Broth of the best,
344. stirabout, poteen, wine itself, he said! And the people
345. that will be coming to see the miracle! I'll be as rich
346. as Biddy Early before I die!   [*John comes back.*

347. *Sibby*. Where were you, John?

348. *John*. I just went out to shake him by the hand. He's

---

329. . . . trial, first. **G, 16.**
331. . . . . Well now, . . . **21, 41.**
332. . . . kind as for . . . **G, 16.**
333. . . . me I'll . . . nothing for it at all. Here . . . **G, 16 ;** . . . nothing for
      it at all. Here . . . **17-41 ;** . . . me I'll . . . **69.**
334. . . . welcome, that . . . **G, 16.**
335. it. But . . . **17-41.**
336. . . . supper to-night, for fear . . . **G, 16.**
      Directions in 337. [*Takes . . . .*] **G, 16.**
338. . . . me the drop . . . **G, 16.**
340. . . . it, indeed. . . . **G-41.**
      Directions at 341. . . . kippeen! [*Beggarman takes the ham bone also and
      exit. John follows him.*] **G, 16.**
342 and Directions. [lacking] **G, 16.**
342. . . . here. [*Slaps . . . .*] **41.**
343. . . . best— **G, 16.**
344. stirabout—poteen—wine . . . **G, 16 ;** . . . ! and . . . **17-41.**
346. . . . die! [*John enters.*] **G, 16.**
347. [speaker lacking] **G, 16.**

349.   a very gifted man.

350.   *Sibby.* He is so indeed.

351.   *John.* And the priest's at the top of the boreen coming
352.   for his dinner. Maybe you'd best put the stone in
353.   the pot again.

THE END

350.   . . . so, indeed. **G, 16, 21.**

NOTES

'A Pot of Broth,' first performance, Dublin, October, 1902.

[On 'Contents' page] **16.**

The words and the air of 'There's Broth in the Pot' were taken down from an old woman known as Cracked Mary, who wanders about the plain of Aidhne, and who sometimes sees unearthly riders on white horses coming through stony fields to her hovel door in the night time. **17.**

I did not include this play in Mr. Bullen's collected edition of my work as it seemed too slight a thing to perpetuate, but I found a little time ago that my own theatre had put it into rehearsal without asking my leave; and that some American had written for rights in it, and another American produced it without rights. I have therefore retouched it a little, and changed a song that I had always hated, and once more admit it to my canon. If it has a lasting interest, it is that it was the first comedy in dialect, of our movement, and gave Mr. William Fay his first opportunity as a comedian. I have no record of the cast on its first production in, I think, 1902, for that was before the Abbey Theatre and its records; except that Mr. William Fay was Tramp, and played it not only with great humour but with great delicacy and charm. In some country village an audience of farmers once received it in stony silence, and at the fall of the curtain a farmer stood up and said nobody there had ever seen a play. Then Mr. William Fay explained what a play was, and the farmer asked that it might be performed again, and at the second performance there was much laughter and cheers. I hardly know how much of the play is my work, for Lady Gregory helped me as she has helped in every play of mine where there is dialect, and sometimes where there is not. In those first years of the Theatre we all helped one another with plots, ideas, and dialogue, but certainly I was the most indebted as I had no mastery of speech that purported to be of real life. This play may be more Lady Gregory's than mine, for I remember once urging her to include it in her own work, and her refusing to do so. The dialect, unlike that of *Cathleen ni Houlihan*, which was written about the same date, has not, I think, the right temper, being gay, mercurial, and suggestive of rapid speech. Probably we were still under the influence of the Irish novelists, who never escaped, even when they had grown up amid country speech, from the dialect of Dublin. The dialect of *Cathleen ni Houlihan* is, I think, true in temper but it has no richness, no abundance. The first use of Irish dialect, rich, abundant, and correct, for the purposes of creative art was in J. M. Synge's *Riders to the Sea*, and Lady Gregory's *Spreading the News*. Notes, **69.**

* * *

Variant spellings

Ahartalav **G, 16**; *Athair-talav* **17-97.**
color **G**; *colour* **16-97.**
Faravan **G, 16**; *Fearaván* **17, 21, 41**; *Fearavan* **69-97.**
Fiannta Eireann **G, 16**; *Fiannta-h-Eireann* **17-97.**
Slan-lus **G, 16**; *Slán-lus* **17-41**; *Slanlus* **69-97.**

* * *

[See also *Preface to 29*, p. 1295.]

THE KING'S THRESHOLD

1904

IN MEMORY OF

FRANK FAY

AND HIS BEAUTIFUL SPEAKING IN THE

CHARACTER OF SEANCHAN

Persons in the Play

King Guaire	The Lord High Chamberlain
Seanchan (*pronounced* Shanahan)	A Soldier
His Pupils	A Monk
The Mayor of Kinvara	Court Ladies
Two Cripples	Two Princesses
Brian, *an old servant*	Fedelm

PRINTINGS   *The United Irishman*, 9 September 1903 (Prologue[1] only); **19, 20, 23, 28, 32, 34a** (Prologue only), **44, 45, 48, 56, 65** (lines 841-904), **69, 84, 88, 97.**

TITLE   . . . Threshold / A Play in Verse **19.**

DATE   [lacking] **19-69, 88.**

DEDICATION   [lacking] **19, 20, 44, 56, 88**; To Frank Fay / Because of his . . . **23, 32, 45, 69**; To Frank Fay / *Because of his . . . speaking and acting in the part of* . . . . **28, 48.**

DRAMATIS PERSONAE   Cast of Characters / Seanchan, *Chief Poet of Ireland.* / King Guaire. / The Chamberlain of King Guaire. / *A Soldier.* / *A Monk.* / The Mayor of Kinvara. / *A Cripple.* / *Another Cripple.* / Cian, Brian, *Servants of Seanchan.* / Senias, Arias, *Pupils of Seanchan.* / Princess Buan. / Princess Finnhua, *her Sister.* / Fedelm, *Seanchan's Sweetheart.* / Aileen, / Essa, *Ladies of the Court.* / *Pupils.* / *Courtiers.* **19;**
    List of Characters / King Guaire. / The Chamberlain of King Guaire. / A Soldier. / A Monk. / The Mayor of Kinvara. / A Cripple. / Another Cripple. / Aileen, / Essa, Ladies of the Court. / Princess Buan. / Princess Finnhua, her Sister. / Fedelm, Seanchan's Sweetheart. / Cian, / Brian, Servants of Seanchan. / Senias, / Arias, Pupils of Seanchan. / Seanchan (pronounced Shanahan), Chief Poet of Ireland. / Pupils, Courtiers. **20;**

[1] For Prologue see p. 313.

Steps before the Palace of King Guaire at Gort. A table or litter in front of steps at one side, with food on it, and a bench. Seanchan lying on steps. Pupils before steps. King on the upper step before a curtained door.

1. *King.* I welcome you that have the mastery
2.   Of the two kinds of Music: the one kind
3.   Being like a woman, the other like a man.
4.   Both you that understand stringed instruments,
5.   And how to mingle words and notes together
6.   So artfully that all the Art's but Speech
7.   Delighted with its own music; and you that carry
8.   The twisted horn, and understand the notes
9.   That lacking words escape Time's chariot;
10.   For the high angels that drive the horse of Time—
11.   The golden one by day, by night the silver—

Persons / King Guaire / Seanchan's Pupils / The Mayor of Kinvara / Two Cripples / Seanchan (*pronounced Shanahan*) / The Lord Chamberlain / A Monk / Two Court Ladies / A Soldier / Two ... **28, 48.**

STAGE DIRECTIONS   Scene: *Steps ... table in ... steps to right with ... it. Seanchan ... steps to left. Pupils ... on top of steps at centre.* **19, 20**; *Steps* (Scene. *Steps* **23, 45** (1913)) ... *table in ... bench by table. Seanchan ....* **23, 32, 45, 56**; Scene. *Steps ... palace ... table in ... side with ... it. Seanchan ....* **28, 48**; Scene: *Steps ....* **69, 88.**

TEXT

2.   ... music; the ...
3.   ... man; **19, 20.**
6.   ... artfully, that ... art's (art is **20**) but speech **19, 20**; ... artfully, that ... **23-69, 88.**
8.   The long twisted horn (horn, **23-69, 88**) and understand
9.   The heady notes that (that, **23-69, 88**) being without words (words, **23-69, 88**)
9a.   Can hurry beyond time (Time **23-69, 88**) and fate (Fate **23-69, 88**) and change: (change; **20**; Change. **23-69, 88**) **19-69, 88.**
10.   Even the high ... time, 19; ... time, **20.**
11.   ... silver, **19, 20.**

12.   Are not more welcome to one that loves the world
13.   For some fair woman's sake.

                                                    I have called you hither
14.   To save the life of your great master, Seanchan,
15.   For all day long it has flamed up or flickered
16.   To the fast-cooling hearth.

         Oldest Pupil.   When did he sicken?
17.   Is it a fever that is wasting him?

18. *King.* No fever or sickness. He has chosen death:
19.   Refusing to eat or drink, that he may bring
20.   Disgrace upon me; for there is a custom,
21.   An old and foolish custom, that if a man
22.   Be wronged, or think that he is wronged, and starve
23.   Upon another's threshold till he die,
24.   The common people, for all time to come,
25.   Will raise a heavy cry against that threshold,
26.   Even though it be the King's.

         Oldest Pupil.   My head whirls round;

---

16.   . . . hearth.
         Senias.   When . . . ? **19, 20** ; . . . fast cooling . . . ? **23-69, 88.**
18.   He did not sicken, but three days ago
19.   He said he would not eat, and lay down there
19a. And has not eaten since. Till yesterday
19b. I thought that hunger and weakness had been enough,
19c. But finding them too trifling and too light
19d. To hold his mouth from biting at the grave
19e. I called you hither, and have called others yet.
19f. The girl he is to wed at harvest-time,
19g. That should be of all living the most dear,
19h. Is coming from the South, and had I known
19i. Of any other neighbours or good friends
19j. That might persuade him, I had brought them hither,
19k. Even though I'd to ransack the world for them.
19l. *Senias.* What was it put him to this work, High King? **19, 20.**
20-35. [lacking] **19, 20.**

27.   I do not know what I am to think or say.
28.   I owe you all obedience, and yet
29.   How can I give it, when the man I have loved
30.   More than all others, thinks that he is wronged
31.   So bitterly that he will starve and die
32.   Rather than bear it? Is there any man
33.   Will throw his life away for a light issue?

34.   *King.* It is but fitting that you take his side
35.   Until you understand how light an issue
36.   Has put us by the ears. Three days ago
37.   I yielded to the outcry of my courtiers—
38.   Bishops, Soldiers, and Makers of the Law—
39.   Who long had thought it against their dignity
40.   For a mere man of words to sit amongst them
41.   At the great council of the State and share
42.   In their authority. I bade him go,
43.   Though at the first with kind and courteous words,
44.   But when he pleaded for the poets' right,
45.   Established at the establishment of the world,

---

29.   . . . it when . . . **28, 48** ; . . . loved, **44, 45, 56.**
30.   . . . others thinks . . . **28, 48.**
31.   . . . bitterly, that . . . **23-69, 88.**
32.   . . . it. Is . . . **23.**
35.   Till you have heard how light the issue is **28, 48.**
36.   You will call it no great matter. Three . . . **19, 20** ; That has put . . . **28, 48.**
37.   . . . courtiers,
38.   . . . , soldiers, . . . makers . . . law, **19, 20.**
40.   . . . among . . . **19, 20.**
41.   At my own table; and when the meal was spread **19, 20** ; At my own table. When the meal was spread, (spread **44, 45, 56**) **23-56** ; . . . state . . . **69, 88.**
42.   I ordered Seanchan to good company, **19, 20** ; I ordered Seanchan to a lower table; **23-56.**
43.   But to a lower table; and when he pleaded **19, 20** ; [lacking] **23-56.**
44.   The poet's right, established when the world **19, 20** ; And when . . . , **23-56.**
45.   Was first established, I said that I was King **19, 20.**

46.   I said that I was King, and that all rights
47.   Had their original fountain in some king,
48.   And that it was the men who ruled the world,
49.   And not the men who sang to it, who should sit
50.   Where there was the most honour. My courtiers—
51.   Bishops, Soldiers, and Makers of the Law—
52.   Shouted approval; and amid that noise
53.   Seanchan went out, and from that hour to this,
54.   Although there is good food and drink beside him,
55.   Has eaten nothing.

    Oldest Pupil.   I can breathe again.
56.   You have taken a great burden from my mind,
57.   For that old custom's not worth dying for.

58. *King.* Persuade him to eat or drink. Till yesterday
59.   I thought that hunger and weakness had been enough;
60.   But finding them too trifling and too light
61.   To hold his mouth from biting at the grave,
62.   I called you hither, and all my hope's in you,
63.   And certain of his neighbours and good friends
64.   That I have sent for. While he is lying there,
65.   Perishing there, my good name in the world

---

46.   And made and unmade rights at my own pleasure. **19, 20.**
47.   [lacking] **19, 20** ; . . . King, **28, 48.**
50.   . . . courtiers,
51.   . . . , soldiers, . . . makers . . . law
52.   . . . approval, and amid the shout (amidst that noise **20**) **19, 20.**
53.   Seanchan rose up and gathering up his cloak **19** ; . . . hour, **23, 28, 48** ; . . . this **44, 45, 56, 69, 88.**
53a.   Hurried out of the hall and from that hour **19.**
54.   Altho' . . . , **28, 48.**
55.   . . . nothing. If a man is wronged, **19, 20** ; . . . nothing.
                              I breathe . . . . **28, 48.**
56.   [lacking] **19, 20** ; . . . mind **69, 88.**
57.   [lacking] **19, 20** ; . . . custom is not . . . . **28, 48.**
58.   Or thinks that he is wronged, and will lie down **19, 20** ; . . . . . 'Till . . . **28, 48.**
59.   Upon another's threshold until he dies,
60.   The common people for all time to come
61.   Will raise a heavy cry against that threshold,
62.   Even though it is the King's. He lies there now
63.   Perishing; he is calling against my majesty, **19, 20.**
64.   That old custom that has no meaning in it, **19, 20** ; . . . there **23-69, 88.**
65.   And as he perishes, my name . . . **19, 20** ; Perishing, my . . . **23-69, 88.**

66.   Is perishing also. I cannot give way,
67.   Because I am King; because, if I give way,
68.   My nobles would call me a weakling, and, it may be,
69.   The very throne be shaken.

    Oldest Pupil.   I will persuade him.
70.   Your words had been enough persuasion, King;
71.   But being lost in sleep or reverie,
72.   He cannot hear them.

    King.   Make him eat or drink.
73.   Nor is it all because of my good name
74.   I'd have him do it, for he is a man
75.   That might well hit the fancy of a king,
76.   Banished out of his country, or a woman's
77.   Or any other's that can judge a man
78.   For what he is. But I that sit a throne,
79.   And take my measure from the needs of the State,
80.   Call his wild thought that overruns the measure,
81.   Making words more than deeds, and his proud will
82.   That would unsettle all, most mischievous,

---

66.   ... way **19, 20**.
67.   ... King, because if ... way **19, 20**; ...; King. Because if ... gave ..., **23-56**; ...; because if ... gave ..., **69, 88**.
68.   ..., and it ... be **19, 20**; ... Nobles ..., and it ... be **23-69, 88**; ... Nobles ..., **84**.
69.   ... shaken; but should you
69a.   That are his friends speak to him and persuade him
69b.   To turn his mouth from the ill-savouring grave
69c.   And eat good food, he shall not lack my favour; **19, 20**.
69d.   For I will give him grass and tillage lands, **19**; For I will give plough-land and grazing-land, **20**.
69e.   Or all but anything he has set his heart on. **19, 20**.
70-72. [lacking] **19, 20**.
73.   It is not all ...
74.   I would have (I'd have **20**) him live, for I have found him a ... **19, 20**.
75.   ... king **19, 20, 28, 48**.
76.   ... woman's, **19-32, 48**.
78.   ... is; but ..., **19**.
79.   ... state,
80.   ... over-runs ..., **19, 20**.
81.   ... will, **28, 48**.
82.   ... all most ..., **69A**.

83.   And he himself a most mischievous man.

[He turns to go, and then returns again.

84.   Promise a house with grass and tillage land,
85.   An annual payment, jewels and silken wear,
86.   Or anything but that old right of the poets.

[He goes into palace.

87.   *Oldest Pupil.* The King did wrong to abrogate our right;
88.   But Seanchan, who talks of dying for it,
89.   Talks foolishly. Look at us, Seanchan;
90.   Waken out of your dream and look at us,
91.   Who have ridden under the moon and all the day,
92.   Until the moon has all but come again,
93.   That we might be beside you.

> *Seanchan [half turning round, leaning on his elbow, and*
> *speaking as if in a dream].* I was but now

94.   In Almhuin, in a great high-raftered house,
95.   With Finn and Osgar. Odours of roast flesh
96.   Rose around me, and I saw the roasting spits;
97.   And then the dream was broken, and I saw

Directions after 83.   [lacking] **19, 20** ; [*The King has gone up the steps;*
he . . . .] **28, 48.**

83a.   *Senias.* King, whether you did right or wrong in this
83b.   Let the King say, for all that I need say
83c.   Is that there's nothing that cries out for death
83d.   In the withholding of that ancient right,
83e.   And that I will persuade him. Your own words
83f.   Had been enough persuasion were it not
83g.   That he is lost in dreams that hunger makes,
83h.   And therefore heedless, or lost in heedless sleep.
84.   *King.* I leave him to your love, that it may promise **19, 20.**
85.   Plough-lands and grass-lands, jewels . . . , **19, 20** ; . . . silken ware,
23-69, 88.
Directions after 86.   [. . . *goes out. The Pupils, who have been standing*
perfectly quiet, all turn towards Seanchan, and move a step nearer.] **19, 20.**
87.   *Senias.* The . . . right, **19, 20.**
89.   . . . , Seanchan, **19, 20.**
91.   Who had ridden . . . , **89A.**
Directions in 93.   [*Seanchan turns half round leaning* . . . , *and speaks as*
. . . .] **19, 20** ; [. . . , *and speaks as* . . . .] **23.**
94.   At Almhuin, . . . , **19, 20.**
96.   . . me and . . . spits, **19, 20** ; . . . roasting-spits; **23-32, 48.**

98.   Grania dividing salmon by a stream.

99.   *Oldest Pupil.* Hunger has made you dream of roasting
        flesh;

100.   And though I all but weep to think of it,

101.   The hunger of the crane, that starves himself

102.   At the full moon because he is afraid

103.   Of his own shadow and the glittering water,

104.   Seems to me little more fantastical

105.   Than this of yours.

       Seanchan.   Why, that's the very truth.

106.   It is as though the moon changed everything—

107.   Myself and all that I can hear and see;

108.   For when the heavy body has grown weak,

109.   There's nothing that can tether the wild mind

110.   That, being moonstruck and fantastical,

111.   Goes where it fancies. I have even thought

112.   I knew your voice and face, but now the words

113.   Are so unlikely that I needs must ask

114.   Who is it that bids me put my hunger by.

115.   *Oldest Pupil.* I am your oldest pupil, Seanchan;

116.   The one that has been with you many years—

117.   So many that you said at Candlemas

---

98.   . . . a pool, **19, 20**; . . . stream; **23, 28, 48.**

98a.   And then I was awakened by your voice. **19-28, 48.**

99.   *Senias.* It is your hunger that makes you . . . of flesh

100.   Roasting, and for your hunger I could weep;

101.   And yet the hunger . . . crane that starves

102.   Because the moonlight glittering on the pool

103.   And flinging a pale shadow has made it shy, **19, 20.**

105.   Than this that's blown into so great a trouble.

105a. *Seanchan* [*Who has turned away again*]. There is much truth in that,
       for all things alter (change **20**) **19, 20.**

106.   At times (times, **20**) as if the moonlight altered them, **19, 20**; . . .
       every thing— **23, 28, 48.**

107.   And my mind alters as if it were the crane's;

108.   . . . weak **19, 20.**

110.   That being . . . fantastical **19, 20.**

111.   . . . . I had even . . . **19-44, 45** (1911), **48, 56.**

114.   . . . by?

115.   *Senias.* I . . .;

116.   . . . years, **19, 20.**

117.   . . . many, that . . . **23-69, 88.**

    V.E.P.Y.—K

118.   I had almost done with school, and all but knew
119.   Every thing that's known of poetry.

120.   *Seanchan*. My oldest pupil? No, that cannot be,
121.   For it is some one of the courtly crowds
122.   That have been round about me from sunrise,
123.   And I am tricked by dreams; but I'll refute them.
124.   At Candlemas I bid that pupil tell me
125.   Why poetry is honoured, wishing to know
126.   If he had any weighty argument
127.   For distant countries and strange, churlish kings.
128.   What did he answer?

Oldest Pupil.   I said the poets hung
129.   Images of the life that was in Eden
130.   About the child-bed of the world, that it,
131.   Looking upon those images, might bear
132.   Triumphant children. But why must I stand here,
133.   Repeating an old lesson, while you starve?

134.   *Seanchan*. Tell on, for I begin to know the voice.
135.   What evil thing will come upon the world
136.   If the Arts perish?

Oldest Pupil.   If the Arts should perish,

---

118.   That I . . . , and knew
119.   All but all that poets understand. **19-69, 88.**
120.   . . . pupil. No, . . . be;
121.   . . . someone . . .
122.   . . . sunrise
123.   . . . dreams, but . . . .
124.   I asked the pupil that I loved the best,
125.   At Candlemas, why . . . honoured,
126.   Wishing to know how he'd defend our craft **19, 20.**
127.   In distant lands among strange churlish Kings. **19, 20 ;** . . . Kings. **28, 48.**
128.   And he'd an answer.
        Senias.   I . . . **19, 20.**
130.   . . . childbed . . . , **19, 20.**
132.   . . . children; but . . . here
133.   . . . lesson while . . . ?
134.   . . . voice; **19, 20.**
136.   . . . arts . . . ?
        Senias.   . . . arts . . . perish **19, 20 ;** . . . the Art should . . . , **84.**

137.   The world that lacked them would be like a woman
138.   That, looking on the cloven lips of a hare,
139.   Brings forth a hare-lipped child.

Seanchan.   But that's not all:
140.   For when I asked you how a man should guard
141.   Those images, you had an answer also,
142.   If you're the man that you have claimed to be,
143.   Comparing them to venerable things
144.   God gave to men before He gave them wheat.

145.   *Oldest Pupil.* I answered—and the word was half your
             own—
146.   That he should guard them as the Men of Dea
147.   Guard their four treasures, as the Grail King guards
148.   His holy cup, or the pale, righteous horse
149.   The jewel that is underneath his horn,
150.   Pouring out life for it as one pours out
151.   Sweet heady wine. . . . But now I understand;
152.   You would refute me out of my own mouth;
153.   And yet a place at council, near the King,
154.   Is nothing of great moment, Seanchan.
155.   How does so light a thing touch poetry?
             [*Seanchan is now sitting up. He still looks dreamily in front of him.*

156.   *Seanchan.* At Candlemas you called this poetry
157.   One of the fragile, mighty things of God,
158.   That die at an insult.

         Oldest Pupil [to other Pupils]. Give me some true answer,

---

137.   . . . woman, **23-69, 88.**
138.   That looking . . . hare **19, 20**; That looking . . . , **23-69, 88.**
139.   . . . all. **19, 20.**
141.   . . . images you . . . , **19, 20.**
144.   . . . he . . . . **19-69, 88.**
145.   *Senias.* . . . answered, and . . . own, **19, 20.**
146.   . . . them, as . . . Men (men **20**) . . . **19, 20**; . . . men . . . **28, 48.**
148.   . . . pale righteous . . . **19, 20.**
150.   . . . it, as . . .
151.   . . . wine—but . . . understand **19, 20.**
152.   . . . mouth, **19.**
153.   . . . at table near . . . King **19, 20**; . . . at table, near . . . , **23-56.**
157.   . . . fragile mighty . . . God
158.   . . . insult.
         Senias. [*to* . . . .] . . . answer, (answer. **20**) **19, 20.**

159.   Upon that day he spoke about the Court
160.   And called it the first comely child of the world,
161.   And said that all that was insulted there
162.   The world insulted, for the Courtly life
163.   Is the world's model. How shall I answer him?
164.   Can you not give me some true argument?
165.   I will not tempt him with a lying one.

166. *Youngest Pupil.* O, tell him that the lovers of his music
167.   Have need of him.

     Seanchan.   But I am labouring
168.   For some that shall be born in the nick o' time,
169.   And find sweet nurture, that they may have voices,
170.   Even in anger, like the strings of harps;
171.   And how could they be born to majesty
172.   If I had never made the golden cradle?

173. *Youngest Pupil [throwing himself at Seanchan's feet].* Why
     did you take me from my father's fields?
174.   If you would leave me now, what shall I love?
175.   Where shall I go? What shall I set my hand to?
176.   And why have you put music in my ears,
177.   If you would send me to the clattering houses?
178.   I will throw down the trumpet and the harp,
179.   For how could I sing verses or make music
180.   With none to praise me, and a broken heart?

181. *Seanchan.* What was it that the poets promised you,
182.   If it was not their sorrow? Do not speak.
183.   Have I not opened school on these bare steps,
184.   And are you not the youngest of my scholars?
185.   And I would have all know that when all falls

---

159. For on that day we spoke . . . court (Court, **23-56**) **19-56.**
160. [lacking] **19-56.**
162. . . . courtly life, **19, 20** ; . . . life, **23-56.**
162a. Being the first comely child of the world, **19-56.**
166-172. [lacking] **19, 20.**
  166. Oh, . . . **44, 45** (1911), **56.**
  168. . . . time **28, 48.**
  173. *Arias. [throwing* . . . ? **19, 20.**
  175. . . . go, what . . . ?
  176. . . . ears **19, 20.**
  180. . . . me and . . . ?
  181. . . . you **19, 20.**
  184. . . . are not you the . . . ? **19-69, 88.**

186. In ruin, poetry calls out in joy,
187. Being the scattering hand, the bursting pod,
188. The victim's joy among the holy flame,
189. God's laughter at the shattering of the world.
190. And now that joy laughs out, and weeps and
      burns
191. On these bare steps.

Youngest Pupil.   O master, do not die!

192. *Oldest Pupil.* Trouble him with no useless argument.
193. Be silent! There is nothing we can do
194. Except find out the King and kneel to him,
195. And beg our ancient right. For here are some
196. To say whatever we could say and more,
197. And fare as badly. Come, boy, that is no use.
                 [Raises Youngest Pupil.
198. If it seem well that we beseech the King,
199. Lay down your harps and trumpets on the stones
200. In silence, and come with me silently.
201. Come with slow footfalls, and bow all your heads,

---

189. . . . world,
190. . . . out and . . .
191. . . . steps.
    Arias.   O Master, . . . die. **19, 20.**
    Directions after 191. [*Three men come in. Cian and Brian, old men carrying basket with food, and Mayor of Kinvara. They stand at the side listening.*] **19, 20.**
192. *Senias.* Trouble . . . .
193. . . . silent; there . . .
194. . . . him **19, 20.**
195. . . . right. These three have come **19, 20;** . . . right.
       For . . . **23-69, 88.**
197. . . . , boy, that's no use; **19, 20.**
    Directions after 197. [*He lifts the Boy up.*] **19, 20** ; [*Raises Young Pupil.*] **23.**
200. . . . silence and . . . .
201. . . . footfalls and . . . , **19, 20.**

202.   For a bowed head becomes a mourner best.

> [*They lay harps and trumpets down one by one, and then go out very solemnly and slowly, following one another. Enter Mayor, two Cripples, and Brian, an old servant. The Mayor, who has been heard, before he came upon the stage, muttering 'Chief Poet', 'Ireland', etc., crosses in front of Seanchan to the other side of the steps. Brian takes food out of basket. The Cripples are watching the basket. The Mayor has an Ogham stick in his hand.*]

Directions after 202.   [. . . *lay the harps* . . . *one and* . . . *one another.*] **19, 20**; [. . . *basket. The Cripples are interested in the basket. The Mayor has* . . . .] **23**; [. . . , *two Cripples, and an old* . . . *Mayor, who has an ogham stick in his hand, crosses. Brian takes* . . . *are interested in the basket.*] **28, 48.**

202a. *Cian.* Show him the food (Let's show the food **20**) that's in the basket.
    Mayor [*who carries an Ogham stick*].   No, **19, 20**.
202b. I must get through my speech or I'll forget it;
202c. Besides, there is no reason why he'd eat
202d. Till he has heard my reasons.
    Cian.   It were better
202e. To show what we have brought him in the basket,
202f. For we have nothing that he has not liked
202g. From boyhood.
    Brian.   For we have not brought kings' food
202h. That's cooked for everybody and for nobody. (and nobody. **20**)
202i. *Mayor.* You are not showing right respect to me,
202j. Or to the people of Kinvara, when you wish
202k. That something else should come before my message.
202l. *Seanchan.* What brings you here? I never sent for you.
202m. *Cian.* He must be famishing, he looks so pale.
202n. We had better get the food out first. I tell you,
202o. That we have brought the things he likes the best.
202p. *Mayor.* No, no; I lost a word at every cross road
202q. And maybe if I do not speak it now
202r. I'll have forgot it.
    Cian.   Well, out with it quickly.
202s. *Seanchan.* Why, what's this foolery?
    Mayor.   No foolery;
202t. A message from the richest, best born townsman
202u. Of your own town, and from your aged father.
202v. *Cian.* Run through it while I am getting out the food. **19, 20.**

203.[1] *Mayor [as he crosses].* 'Chief poet, Ireland, townsman,
204.   grazing land', those are the words I have to keep in
205.   mind, 'Chief poet, Ireland, townsman, grazing land'.
206.   I have got them all right now, they are all here cut
207.   upon the Ogham stick, 'Chief poet, Ireland, towns-
208.   man, grazing land', and that's the right order. [*He
          keeps muttering over his speech during what follows.*]

209. *First Cripple.* It would serve the King right if Seanchan
210.   drove away his luck. What's there about a king that's
211.   in the world from birth to burial like another man,
212.   that he should change old customs that were in it
213.   as long as the world has been a world?

214. *Second Cripple.* If I were the King I wouldn't meddle
215.   with him; there is something queer about a man that

02w. *Mayor.* How was I to begin? What was the word **19, 20.**
202x. That was to keep it in my memory?
202y. Wait, I have notched it on this Ogham stick.
202z. 'Chief Poet,' 'Ireland,' 'Townsman'; that is it. **19, 20.**
203-240. [lacking] **19, 20.**
   203. . . . Poet,' 'Ireland,' 'Townsman,' 'grazing ('Grazing **32-45, 56, 69,
         88**) land.' /
   204. Those . . . in mind— /
   205. 'Chief Poet,' 'Ireland,' 'Townsman,' 'grazing ('Grazing **32-45, 56,
         69, 88**) land.' /
   206. . . . have the words. They . . . all upon the ogham. (Ogham. **32-45,
         56, 69, 88**) / **23-69, 88.**
   07. 'Chief Poet,' 'Ireland,' 'Townsman,' 'grazing ('Grazing **32-45, 56,
         69, 88**) land.' / 23, **32-45, 56, 69, 88 ;** [lacking] **28, 48.**
         Directions at 208. [lacking] **28, 48.**
   208. But what's their order? [. . . .]
         First Cripple.   The King were rightly served /
   209. If Seanchan drove his good luck away. /
   210. What's . . . king, that's in the world /
   211. From . . . burial, (burial **32-45, 56, 69, 88**) like . . . man, /
   212. That . . . customs, that . . . it /
   213. As . . . as ever the . . . ? /
   214. . . . were king I would not meddle with him, /
   215. For there . . . a poet. / **23-69, 88.**

[1] Lines 203-349 are in prose in **84, 97,** in verse in **19-69, 88.** Line-ends of **19-69, 88,** are shown by slant lines.

216.   makes rhymes. I knew a man that would be making
217.   rhymes year in year out under a thorn at the crossing
218.   of three roads, and he was no sooner dead than every
219.   thorn-tree from Inchy to Kiltartan withered, and he
220.   a ragged man like ourselves.

221.   *First Cripple.* Those that make rhymes have a power
222.   from beyond the world.

223.   *Mayor.* I am getting ready.

224.   *First Cripple.* Was it he that told you about the blessed
225.   well? And the little holy fish?

226.   *Mayor.* Hush! Hush!

227.   *Second Cripple.* It was he surely.

228.   *First Cripple.* And it rising up out of the blessed well
229.   to cure the crippled.

230.   *Second Cripple.* Rising up every seventh year.

231.   *Mayor.* I'm half ready now.

232.   *Brian.* There's not a mischief I begrudge the King, if
233.   it were any other man but my master—

---

216.   I knew of one that . . . making rhyme /
217.   Under . . . thorn at crossing of three roads. /
217a.   He was as ragged as ourselves, and yet /
218.   He was . . . every thorn tree /
219.   From . . . withered away. /
220.   *First Cripple.* The King is but a fool!
        Mayor.   I (Hush! I **23**) am getting ready. (ready, **44, 56**) /
221.   *First Cripple.* A poet has power from beyond the world, /
222.   That he may set our thoughts upon old times, /
223-224.   [lacking]
225.   And lucky queens and little . . . fish /
226-227.   [lacking]
228.   That rise up every seventh year—
        Mayor.   Hush! hush! /
229.   *First Cripple.* To . . . crippled.
        Mayor.   I am half ready now. /
230-231.   [lacking]
232.   *Brian.* . . . mischief I'd begrudge the King /
233.   If it . . . other—
        Mayor.   Hush! I am ready. / **23-69, 88.**

234. *Mayor.* Hush, I am ready.

235. *Brian.* That died to bring it upon him. There, I have

236.   set out the food, and if my master won't eat it, I'll

237.   home and get provision for his wake, for that's no

238.   great way off.

239. *Mayor.* It's my turn.

240. *Brian.* Have your say, but don't be long about it.

241. *Mayor* [*going close to Seanchan*]. Chief poet of Ireland, I

242.   am the Mayor of your own town, Kinvara. I am

243.   come to tell you that the news of this great trouble

244.   between you and the King of Gort has plunged us

245.   into sorrow, part for you our honoured townsman,

246.   and part for our good town. [*Begins to hesitate, scratch-*

247.   *ing his head.*] But what comes after that? Something

248.   about the King.

249. *Brian.* Get on, the food is all set out, and maybe when

250.   you are done he'll eat a bit.

---

234. [lacking] **23-69, 88.**

235. *Brian.* That . . . to get it. I have brought out the food, /

236. And . . . master will not eat of it, /

237. I'll home . . . wake, /

238. For that's no great . . . off. Well, have your say, / **23-69, 88.**

239. [lacking] **23-69, 88.**

240. But . . . it.
    Mayor [*goes* (*going* **28, 48**) *close to Seanchan*]. Chief poet of Ireland, /
    23-69, 88.

241. *Mayor.* Chief . . . Ireland, when we heard that trouble / **19, 20**;
    [lacking] **23-69, 88.**

242-243. [lacking] **19, 20.**

242. I am the . . . town Kinvara, /

243. And I am come . . . news / **23-69, 88.**

244. Had come between you and the king of Ireland / **19, 20**; Of this great
    trouble with the King of Gort / **23-69, 88.**

245. It (Has **23-69, 88**) plunged us in deep sorrow, (sorrow— **23-69, 88**)
    part for you, / **19-69, 88.**

246. Our honoured townsman, part . . . town. / **19-69, 88.**
    Directions at 246. [lacking] **19, 20**; [. . . *hesitate; scratching his head.*]
    23-69, 88.

247-255. [lacking] **19, 20.**

247. But . . . comes now? Something about the King. / **23-69, 88.**

248. [lacking] **23-69, 88.**

249. *Brian.* Get on! get on! The food . . . out. / **23, 32-45, 56, 69, 88**; Get
    on! get on! The . . . is ready now. / **28, 48.**

250. [lacking] **23-69, 88.**

251. *Mayor.* Don't hurry me.

252. *First Cripple.* Give me a taste of it, he'll not begrudge it.

253. *Second Cripple.* Let them that have their limbs starve if
254.   they like, we have to keep in mind the stomach God
255.   has left to us.

256. *Mayor.* Hush! I have it. The King was said to be most
257.   friendly, and we had good reason for thinking that
258.   he was about to give us those grazing lands we so
259.   much need, being so pinched that our mowers mow
260.   with knives between the stones. We asked nothing
261.   but what was reasonable. We ask you for the sake
262.   of the town to do what the King wants and then
263.   maybe he'll do what we want; we ask nothing but
264.   what's reasonable.

265. *Seanchan.* Reason, O reason in plenty. Yet you have
266.   yellowy white hair and not too many teeth. How
267.   comes it that you have been so long in the world and

---

251.   . . . me.
    First Cripple.   Give us a taste of it. /
252.   He'll . . . it.
    Second Cripple.   Let them that have their limbs /
253.   [lacking]
254.   Starve if they will. We . . . mind /
255.   The stomach God has left to us. (left us. **32-45, 56, 69, 88**)
    Mayor.   Hush! I have it! / **23-69, 88.**
256.   The . . . most friendly to us, / **19-69, 88.**
257.   And we had reasons, (have reason, **23-69, 88**) as you'll recollect, /
258.   For thinking that he . . . give /
258a.   Those grazing lands inland we so much need, / **19-69, 88.**
259.   Being pinched between the water and the rocks. (stones. **23-69, 88**) /
    19-69, 88.
260.   But now his friendliness being ill repaid / **19, 20**; Our mowers mow
    with . . . stones; / **23-69, 88.**
260a.   Will be turned from us and our town get nothing. / **19, 20.**
260b.   But there was something else—I'll find the word / **19, 20.**
260c.   That was to keep it in my memory. / **19, 20.**
261-74. [lacking] **19, 20.**
261.   The sea washes the meadows. You know well / **23-69, 88.**
262-263. [lacking]
264.   We have asked nothing but what's . . . . /
265.   *Seanchan.* Reason in plenty. Yellowy white hair, /
266.   A hollow face, and . . . teeth. /
267.   How comes it he has been . . world / **23-69, 88.**

268.   not found reason out? [*While saying this he has turned*
        half round; he hardly looks at the Mayor.]

269. *Brian* [*trying to pull the Mayor away*]. What's the good in
270.   saying all that, haven't they been reasoning with him
271.   all day long? No wonder he is tired of it. I have set
272.   the food before him ready.

273. *Mayor* [*shoving Brian away*]. Don't hurry me. It's small
274.   respect you are showing to the town. Get further off.
275.   [*To Seanchan.*] We would not have you think, weighty
276.   as these considerations are, that they have been as
277.   weighty in our minds as our desire that one we take
278.   so much pride in, a man that is an honour to our
279.   town, should live and prosper. Therefore we be-
280.   seech you to give way in what is after all a matter of
281.   no importance, a matter of mere sentiment, that we
282.   may always keep our pride in you. [*He finishes this
        speech with a pompous air, motions to Brian to bring the
        food, and sits on seat.*]

---

268. And not . . . Reason out?
              [. . . *this* (*this*, **28, 48**) . . . *round. He* . . . .]

    Brian [. . . *pull Mayor* . . . .] What good is there /
269. In telling him what he has heard all day! / **23-69, 88.**
270-272. [lacking] **23-69, 88.**
273. I will set food before him.
    Mayor [. . . .]   . . . me! /
274. It's small respect you're showing . . . town! / **23-69, 88.**
275. 'Pride'—that's the word,—we . . . think, / **19, 20**; Get farther off!
    [*To* . . . .] . . . think, / **23-69, 88.**
276. Weighty as . . . are, / **19-69, 88.**
276a. That they have been as weighty in our minds /
277. As . . . take much pride in, /
278. A man that's been an . . . our town, /
279. Should . . . prosper, (prosper; **23-69, 88**) therefore we beseech you /
280. To . . . in a matter of no moment, /
281. A . . . sentiment, a trifle, / (sentiment—a trifle— / **23-69, 88**)
282. That we may . . . you. / **19-69, 88.**
    Directions at 282. [lacking] **19, 20**; [. . . *food to Seanchan, and* . . . .]
    23-69, 88.
282a. *Seanchan.* Their pride, their pride, what do they know of pride? /
282b. My pupils do not know it, for they beg /
282c. From the King's favour what is theirs by right, /
282d. And how can men, that God has made so weak /
282e. They need a rich man's favour every day, / **19, 20.**

283. *Brian.* Master, eat this, it's not king's food that's
284. cooked for everybody and nobody. Here's barley-
285. bread out of your father's oven and dulse from Duras.
286. Here is the dulse, your honour, it is wholesome, it
287. has the good taste of the sea. [*Takes dulse in one hand
      and bread in the other and presses them into Seanchan's
      hands. Seanchan shows by his movements his different feeling
      to Brian.*]

288. *First Cripple.* He has taken it and there will be nothing
289. left.

290. *Second Cripple.* He wanted his own sort. What's honey
291. to a cat, corn to a dog, or a green apple to a ghost in
292. a churchyard?

293. *Seanchan* [*pressing food back into Brian's hands*]. Eat it your-
294. self, old man, you have come a long journey and, it
295. may be, ate nothing on the road.

282f. Know anything of pride?
       Cian [*to Mayor.*]   You have spoken it wrongly. /
282g. You have forgotten something out of it about the cattle dying. / **19,
       20.**
283-84. [lacking] **19, 20.**
  283. *Brian.* Master, master, (Master, **45** (1913), **69, 88**) . . . this! It's . . .
         food, /
  284. That's cooked . . . nobody. / **23-69, 88.**
285-87. [lacking] **19, 20.**
  285. Here's barley bread (barley-bread **32-45, 56, 69, 88**) . . . oven, /
  286. And dulse from Duras. Here . . . honour; /
  287. It's wholesome, and has . . . sea. / **23-69, 88.**
         Directions at 287.   [. . . *in other* . . . *movement* . . . .] **23-69, 88** ; [. . .
         hand. . . . .] **97A.**
288-92. [lacking] **19, 20.**
  288. . . . it, (it **56**) and there'll . . . left! /
  289. [lacking]
  290. *Second Cripple.* Nothing at all; (all, **44, 45, 56, 69, 88**) he . . . sort. /
  291. What's honey to . . . dog, /
  292. Or a green apple to a ghost in a churchyard? / **23-69, 88.**
293-322. [lacking] **19, 20.**
  293. *Seanchan* [. . . .] . . . yourself, for you have come a journey, / **23-69,
         88.**
  294. [lacking] **23-69, 88.**
  295. And it may be have eaten nothing on the way. / **23, 28, 48** ;
         And it may be eat (ate **69**) nothing on the way. / **32-45, 56, 69, 88.**

296. *Brian.* How could I eat it and your honour starving? It
297.   is your father that sends it. He cried because the
298.   stiffness that is in his bones prevented him coming,
299.   and he bade me tell you that he is old and has need
300.   of you, that the people will be pointing at him, that
301.   he will not be able to lift up his head if you turn
302.   the King's favour away, that he cared you well and
303.   you in your young age, and that it's right you should
304.   care him now.

305. *Seanchan.* What did my mother say?

306. *Brian.* Your mother gave no message, for when they
307.   told her that you had it in mind to starve or get
308.   again the ancient right of the poets, she said, 'No
309.   message will do any good. We cannot change him,'
310.   and she went indoors, lay down upon the bed and
311.   turned her face out of the light. [*A pause.*] Here's
312.   pigeons' eggs from Duras, and these were laid by

---

296. *Brian.* . . . it, and . . . starving! /
297. It is . . . father sends it, and he cried /
298. Because the stiffness . . . bones
299. Prevented him from coming, and bid (bade **69**) me . . . you /
299a. That he is old, that he has need of you,
300. And that . . . him, /
301. And he not able . . . head, /
301a. If you should turn the King's favour away; /
302. And he adds to it, that . . . well, /
303. And you . . . right /
304. That you should care . . . now.
      Seanchan [*who is now interested.*] And is that all? /
305. What . . . say? (say! **45, 69**)
      Brian.   She gave no message; / **23-69, 88.**
306. [lacking] **23-69, 88.**
307. For when they told her you had . . . starve, / **23, 32-45, 56, 69, 88**;
      For when they told her you were resolved to starve, / **28, 48.**
308. Or get again . . . poets, /
309. She said: 'No message can do . . . good. /
309a. He will not send the answer that you want. /
310. We cannot change him.' And . . . indoors, /
311. Lay down upon the bed, and turned . . . face /
311a. Out of the light. And thereupon your father /
311b. Said: 'Tell him that his mother sends no message, /
311c. Albeit broken down and miserable.' /
                                   [*A pause.*] **23-69, 88.**
312. Here is (Here's **32-45, 56**) a pigeon's egg . . . these others / **23-56**;
      Here's pigeon's eggs . . . these others / **69, 88.**

313.   your own hens.

314.   *Seanchan.* She sent no message. Our mothers know us,
315.   they knew us before birth, and that is why they know
316.   us even better than sweethearts upon whose breasts
317.   we have lain. Tell them that my mother was in the
318.   right, go tell them that, go tell them that she knew me.

319.   *Mayor.* What is he saying? I never understood a poet's
320.   talk more than the baa of a sheep. [*Comes over from*
321.   *seat. Seanchan turns away.*] You have not heard, it may
322.   be, having been so much away, how many cattle died
323.   last winter from lacking grass, how much sickness
324.   there was because the poor had nothing but salt fish
325.   to live on through the winter.

---

313.   Were laid by your . . . hens.
        Seanchan.   She has sent no message. /
314.   Our . . . us; they know us to the bone. /
315.   They knew . . . why /
316.   They know us . . . than the sweethearts /
317.   Upon whose breasts we . . . lain.
                                Go quickly! Go /
317a.   And tell them that my mother was (is **69, 88**) in the right. /
317b.   There is no answer. Go and tell them that. /
318.   Go tell them that she . . . me.
        Mayor.   What is he saying? /
319.   I . . . poet's talk /
320.   More . . . sheep!
        [*Comes over from seat. Seanchan turns away.*]
                                You have not heard, / **23-69, 88.**
321.   [lacking] **23-69, 88.**
322.   *Mayor.* Maybe you do not know, being much away, / **19, 20**; It
        may be, . . . away, / **23-69, 88.**
322a.   How many of our (the **23-69, 88**) cattle died last winter /
323.   From . . . grass, and that there was much sickness / **19-69, 88.**
324.   Because the poor had (have **23-69, 88**) nothing . . . fish / **19-69, 88.**
325.   To live upon. The people all came out / **19, 20**;
        To . . . winter?
        Brian.   Get away, / **23-69, 88.**
325a.   And stood about the doors as I went by. /
325b.   *Seanchan.* What would you have of me? /
325c.   For there are men that shall be born at last /
325d.   And find sweet nurture that they may have voices /
325e.   Even in anger like the strings of harps. /
325f.   Yet how could they be born to majesty /
325g.   If I had never made the golden cradle? /
325h.   *Mayor.* What is it? 'Father'—'Mother'; that is it; / **19, 20.**

325i.	Your father sends this message.
	Cian. He is listening. /
325j.	*Mayor.* He says that he is old and that he needs you, /
325k.	And that the people will be pointing at him /
325l.	And he not able to lift up his head /
325m.	If you should turn the King's favour away. /
325n.	And he adds to it, that he cared you well, /
325o.	And you in your young age, and that it's right /
325p.	That you should care him now.
	Cian. And when he spoke /
325q.	He cried because the stiffness of his bones /
325r.	Prevented him from coming.
	Mayor. But your mother /
325s.	Has sent no message, for when they had told her /
325t.	The way it is between you and the King /
325u.	She said, 'No message can do any good, /
325v.	He will not send the answer that you want; /
325w.	We cannot change him,' and she went indoors (indoors, 20) /
325x.	Lay down upon her bed and turned her face /
325y.	Out of the light. And thereupon your father /
325z.	Said, 'Tell him how she is, and that she sends /
325aa.	No message,' I have nothing more to say. /
325bb.	Cian and Brian, you can set out the food. /

[*He sits down on steps. Seanchan is silent.*]

325cc.	*Mayor.* I have a horse waiting outside the town /
325dd.	To bring me home, and all the neighbours wait /
325ee.	Your answer. What answer am I to bring? /
325ff.	*Seanchan.* Give them my answer—no, I have no answer: /
325gg.	My mother knew it.
	Mayor. Maybe you have forgotten /
325hh.	That all our fields are so heaped up with stones /
325ii.	That the goats famish, and the mowers mow /
325jj.	With knives, and that the King half promised us— /
	Seanchan. Thrust that old cloak of yours into your mouth /
325kk.	Till it's done gabbling.
	Mayor. But—
	Cian. You have said enough; /
325ll.	I knew that you would never speak it right. /
325mm.	*Seanchan.* Our mothers know us, they know us to the bone, /
325nn.	They knew us before birth, and that is why /
325oo.	They know us even better than the sweethearts /
325pp.	Upon whose breasts we have lain.
	Brian. We have brought your honour /
325qq.	The food that you have always liked the best, /
325rr.	Young pigeons from Kinvara, and watercress /
325ss.	Out of the stream that's by the blessed well, /
325tt.	And dulse from Duras. Here is the dulse, your honour, / **19, 20.**

326. *Brian.* Get away and leave the place to me, for your
327.   sack's empty.

328. *Mayor.* Is it get away? Is that the way I'm to be spoken

---

325uu.   It is wholesome, and has the good taste of the sea. /
325vv.   *Seanchan.* O Brian, you would spread the table for me /
325ww.   As you would spread it when I was in my childhood; /
325xx.   But all that's finished.
         Mayor.   I knew he would not care /
325yy.   For country things now that he's grown accustomed /
325zz.   To the King's dishes. I told Brian too /
325aaa. He'd have his pains for nothing, But he's old, (old. **20**) /
         [*Goes over to table at right. While he is speaking Cian and Brian
         are in vain offering Seanchan food.*]
325bbb. And what dishes! Venison from Slieve Echtge /
325ccc. Fattened with poor men's crops. Flesh (crops; flesh **20**) of wild
         pig; /
325ddd. Not fat nor lean, but streaky and right well cured; /
325eee. Bread that's the whitest I have ever (whitest that I've ever **20**)
         seen. / **19, 20.**
325fff. *Cian.* You're in the right, he will not eat for us. /
                                        [*Pouring wine into cup.*] **19**;
         You're in the right, you're in the right, he will not eat. /
                                        [*Pouring wine into cup.*] **20.**
325ggg. *Mayor.* Bring him this (some **20**) wine, it will give him strength
         to eat. /
                  [*Brian brings wine over towards Seanchan.*] **19, 20.**
325hhh. No wonder if the King is proud and merry, /
325iii. And keeps all day in the saddle, when he's such wine (saddle,
         when even I **20**) / **19, 20.**
325jjj. I am half drunken with the odour of it, / **19**; Am well-nigh
         drunken with the odour of it, / **20.**
325kkk. O (And **20**) if I dared—I dare not.
         Cian.   Drink it, sir. /
325lll. *Brian.* Drink a few drops.
         Seanchan.   Drink it yourself, old man. /
325mmm. For you have come a journey, and I daresay /
325nnn. You did not eat or drink upon the road. /
325ooo. *Cian.* How can I drink it when your honour's thirsty? / **19, 20.**
326-First Directions after 418. [lacking] **19, 20.**
   326. And . . . me! It's my turn now, /
   327. For your sack's empty!
         Mayor.   Is . . . get away! ('get away'! **32-45, 56, 69, 88**) /
   328. Is that . . . to! / **23-69, 88.**

329. to? Am I not the Mayor? Am I not in authority? Am
330. I not in the King's place? Answer me that.

331. *Brian.* Then show the people what a king is like; root
332. up old customs, old habits, old rights.

333. *Mayor.* Holy Saint Colman!

334. *First Cripple.* That's what the King does, and that's
335. what you'd like to do.

336. *Second Cripple.* Foul the holy well.

337. *First Cripple.* Roast the lucky fish.

338. *Second Cripple.* Put it into your own stomach, and it
339. meant to cure cripples.

340. *Mayor.* How dare you take his name into your mouth,
341. how dare you lift up your voice against the King?

342. *Brian.* How dare you praise him? I will have nobody

---

329. Am . . . not Mayor? Amn't I authority? /
330. Amn't I in . . . that! /
331. . . . like : /
332. Pull down old merings and root custom up, /
332a. Whitewash the dung-hills, (dunghills, **32-45, 56, 69, 88**) fatten hogs and geese, /
332b. Hang your gold chain about an ass's neck, /
332c. And burn the blessed thorn trees out of the fields, /
333. And drive what's comely away!
　　Mayor.　　　　　Holy . . . Coleman! /
334. *First Cripple.* Fine talk! fine talk! What else does the King do? / **23-69, 88.**
334a. He fattens hogs and drives the poet away! / **23-56;** He fattens hogs and hunts the wise man out. / **69, 88.**
334b. *Second Cripple.* He starves the song-maker!
　　First Cripple.　　　　　He fattens geese! / **23-56;**
　　Second Cripple. He fattens geese.
　　First Cripple.　　　　　And drives away the swan. / **69, 88.**
335-339. [lacking] **23-69, 88.**
340. *Mayor.* . . . mouth! /
341. How . . . lift your . . . King! /
342. What would we be without him?
　　Brian.　　　　　Why do you . . . him? / **23-69, 88.**

343.   praise him or any other king that robs my master.

344. *Mayor.* And hadn't he the right to? And hadn't he the
345.   right to strike your master's head off, being the
346.   King? Or your head, or my head! I say, Long live
347.   the King! because he didn't take our heads from us.
348.   Call out long life for him.

349. *Brian.* Is it cry out for him?
         [*The five following speeches should be spoken in a
         rhythmical chant, or should rise into song.*]
350.   There's nobody'll call out for him,
351.   But smiths will turn their anvils,
352.   The millers turn their wheels,
353.   The farmers turn their churns,
354.   The witches turn their thumbs,
355.   Till he be broken and splintered into pieces.

356. *Mayor.* He might, if he'd a mind to it,
357.   Be digging out our tongues,
358.   Or dragging out our hair,
359.   Or bleaching us like calves,
360.   Or weaning us like lambs,
361.   But for the kindness and the softness that is in
            him.

362. *First Cripple.* The curse of the poor be upon him,
363.   The curse of the widows upon him,

342a. I will have nobody speak well of him, /
343.   Or . . . . /
344.   And had he not the . . . to? and the right /
345.   To . . . master's (Master's **69A**) . . . the King, (King! **69A**) /
346.   Or yours or mine? I say, 'Long live the King ! (King!' **28, 48**) /
347.   Because he does not take . . . us.' (us. **28, 48**) /
348.   Call out (out, **32-45, 56, 69, 88**) 'Long life to him!'
          Brian.   Call out for him! /
             [*Speaking at same time with Mayor.*] **23-69, 88.**
349 and Directions after 349. [lacking] **23-69, 88.**
350.   . . . nobody'll (nobody will **28, 48**) call . . . ,
351.   But the smiths (But smiths **32-45, 56, 69, 88**) . . . , **23-69, 88.**
355.   'Till (Till **28, 45-56, 69, 88**) . . . .
356.   *Mayor* [*at same time with Brian*]. He . . . , **23-69, 88.**
          Directions after 361. [*They gasp for breath.*] **23-69, 88.**
361a. *First Cripple.* I'll curse him till I drop!
          [*Speaking at same time as Second Cripple and Mayor and Brian, who
          have begun again.*] **23-69, 88.**

364. The curse of the children upon him,
365. The curse of the bishops upon him,
366. Until he be as rotten as an old mushroom!

367. *Second Cripple.* The curse of wrinkles be upon him!
368. Wrinkles where his eyes are,
369. Wrinkles where his nose is,
370. Wrinkles where his mouth is,
371. And a little old devil looking out of every wrinkle!

372. *Brian.* And nobody will sing for him,
373. And nobody will hunt for him,
374. And nobody will fish for him,
375. And nobody will pray for him,
376. But ever and always curse him and abuse him.

377. *Mayor.* I say, Long live the King.

[*Brian seizes the Mayor.*

378.[1] Help! Help!

379. *Brian.* That's how I shout for the King.

380. *Mayor.* Help! Help! Am I not in the King's place, am
381. I not in authority?

---

367. *Second Cripple* [*speaking at same time as First Cripple and Mayor and Brian.*] The . . . ! **23-69, 88.**
372. *Brian* [*speaking at same time with Mayor and Cripples*]. And . . . , **23, 32-45, 56, 69, 88**; Nobody'll call for him, **28, 48.**
372a. And nobody will sing for him, **28, 48.**
376a. *Mayor* [*speaking at same time with Cripples (Cripple* **28, 48**) *and Brian*]. What good is in a poet? (poet, **28, 48**)
376b. Has he money in a stocking,
376c. Or cider in the cellar,
376d. Or flitches in the chimney,
376e. Or anything anywhere but his own idleness?

[*Brian seizes Mayor.*] **23-69, 88.**

377 and Directions. [lacking] **23-69, 88.**
378. *Mayor.* Help! help! Am I not in authority? **23-69, 88**; [speaker's name omitted] **45, 69, 88.**
379. *Brian.* That's how I'll shout . . . King!
380. *Mayor,* Help! help! Am . . . place?
381. [lacking] **23-69, 88.**

[1] Lines 378 and 379 may be intended as one line of verse. *Ed.*

382. *Brian.* So you are—so you are. That's why I've got a
383.   hold of you.

384. *First Cripple.* We're teaching the King to be kind to
385.   the poor.

386. *Mayor.* Help! Help! Wait till we're in Kinvara!

      First Cripple [*beating the Mayor on the legs with his crutch*].
387.   I'll beat the royalty out of his legs.
388.   [*The Chamberlain comes down steps shouting*, 'Silence!
389. silence! silence!'

390. *Chamberlain.* How dare you make this uproar at the
           doors,
391. Deafening the very greatest in the land,
392. As if the farmyards and the rookeries
393. Had all been emptied!

      First Cripple.   It is the Chamberlain.

                                          [*Cripples go out.*

394. *Chamberlain.* Pick up the litter there, and get you gone!
395.   Be quick about it! Have you no respect
396.   For this worn stair, this all but sacred door,
397.   Where suppliants and tributary kings
398.   Have passed, and the world's glory knelt in silence?
399.   Have you no reverence for what all other men
400.   Hold honourable?

      Brian.   If I might speak my mind,
401. I'd say the King would have his luck again
402. If he would let my master have his rights.

403. *Chamberlain.* Pick up your litter! Take your noise away!
404.   Make haste, and get the clapper from the bell!

382-383. [lacking] **23-69, 88.**
  384. *Brian.* I'll teach him to be . . . poor!
  385. [lacking]
  386. *Mayor.* Help ! help! . . . till we are in . . . !
  387. *First Cripple* [*beating Mayor . . . with crutch*]. I'll shake the . . . legs!
  387a. *Second Cripple* [*burying his nails in Mayor's face*]. I'll scrumble the
           ermine out of his skin! **23-69, 88.**
  388-389. *Enter Chamberlain* [*Comes . . . steps, shouting . . .!*'] **28, 48.**
    400. . . . I speak . . . , **28, 48.**

405. *Brian* [*putting last of food into basket*]. What do the great
    and powerful care for rights
406.   That have no armies?
                    [*Chamberlain begins shoving them out with his staff.*

Mayor.   My lord, I am not to blame.
407.   I'm the King's man, and they attacked me for it.
408. *Brian.* We have our prayers, our curses and our prayers,
409.   And we can give a great name or a bad one.
    [*Mayor is shoving Brian out before him with one hand. He keeps
    his face to Chamberlain, and keeps bowing. The Chamberlain
    shoves him with his staff.*

410. *Mayor.* We could not make the poet eat, my lord.
                    [*Chamberlain shoves him with his staff.*

411.   Much honoured [*is shoved again*]—honoured to speak
    with you, my lord;
412.   But I'll go find the girl that he's to marry.
413.   She's coming, but I'll hurry her, my lord.
414.   Between ourselves, my lord [*is shoved again*], she is a
    great coaxer.
415.   Much honoured, my lord. O, she's the girl to do it;
416.   For when the intellect is out, my lord,
417.   Nobody but a woman's any good.
                    [*Is shoved again.*

418.   Much honoured, my lord [*is shoved again*], much
    honoured, much honoured!
                    [*Is shoved out, shoving Brian out before him.*]
                    [*All through this scene, from the outset of the quarrel, Seanchan has*

---

406.   . . . armies!
        [*Chamberlain* . . . . **23-69, 88.**
    Directions after 410. [*. . . with staff.*] **23-32, 48.**
412-415. [lacking] **28, 48.**
415.   . . . . Oh, . . .; **44, 45, 56, 69, 88.**
416.   But when . . . , **28, 48.**
    Directions after 417. [*Same business for Chamberlain.*] **28, 48.**
418.   . . . lord, much honoured, much honoured! [*Exit R. with Brian.*] **28,
    48.**
    2nd Directions after 418. [*He offers cup again. The King's Household
    comes in. Chamberlain with long staff, a Soldier, a Monk, two Ladies, followed
    by Cripples who beg from the ladies, who keep close together at right, talking
    to each other at intervals. Soldier goes over to Mayor, and talks to him.*] **19, 20 ;**
    [*. . . side, Court Ladies seen . . . .*] **28, 48 ;** [*. . . Soldier, and . . . .*] **45**
    (1913).

kept his face turned away, or hidden in his cloak. While the Chamber-
lain has been speaking, the Soldier and the Monk have come out of
the palace. The Monk stands on top of steps at one side, Soldier a
little down steps at the other side. Court Ladies are seen at opening
in the palace curtain behind Soldier. Chamberlain is in the centre.

419. *Chamberlain* [*to Seanchan*]. Well, you must be contented,
      for your work
420.   Has roused the common sort against the King,
421.   And stolen his authority. The State
422.   Is like some orderly and reverend house
423.   Wherein, the master being dead of a sudden,
424.   The servants quarrel where they have a mind to,
425.   And pilfer here and there.
                  [*Pause, finding that Seanchan does not answer.*
                      How many days
426.   Will you keep up this quarrel with the King,
427.   And the King's nobles, and myself, and all,
428.   Who'd gladly be your friends, if you would let them?
                      [*Going near to Monk.*
429.   If you would try, you might persuade him, father.

---

419.   *Chamberlain.* Well, have you it in imagination still
420.   To overthrow the dignity of the King, **19, 20.**
421-424. [lacking] **19, 20.**
422.   . . . house, **23, 32-45, 56, 69, 88 ;** . . . some ancient, orderly, and . . .
       house, **28, 48.**
423.   Wherein the master, (master **28, 48**) being . . . , **23-69, 88.**
425.   Or is the game finished? [*A pause.*]
                      How . . . **19, 20.**
427.   With the . . . nobles and myself and all
428.   . . . friends if . . . ? **19, 20.**
     Directions after 428. [lacking] **19, 20.**
428a.   *Soldier* [*who has been speaking to Mayor and Servants.*] Was it you that
      sent his servants and the Mayor
428b.   Of his own town to wheedle him into life?
428c.   *Chamberlain.* It was the King himself.
     Soldier.   Was it worth our while
428d.   To have got rid of him from the King's table
428e.   If he is to be humoured and made much of?
428f.   *Chamberlain.* It seems that he has not eaten yet, although
428g.   He's had another dozen hours of hunger. **19, 20.**
429-440. [lacking] **19, 20.**

430.   I cannot make him answer me, and yet,
431.   If fitting hands would offer him the food,
432.   He might accept it.

     Monk.   Certainly I will not.

433.   I've made too many homilies, wherein
434.   The wanton imagination of the poets
435.   Has been condemned, to be his flatterer.
436.   If pride and disobedience are unpunished
437.   Who will obey?

     Chamberlain [*going to other side towards Soldier*]. If you
         would speak to him,
438.   You might not find persuasion difficult,
439.   With all the devils of hunger helping you.

440.   *Soldier.* I will not interfere, and if he starve
441.   For being obstinate and stiff in the neck,
442.   'Tis but good riddance.

     Chamberlain.   One of us must do it.
443.   It might be, if you'd reason with him, ladies,
444.   He would eat something, for I have a notion
445.   That if he brought misfortune on the King,
446.   Or the King's house, we'd be as little thought of
447.   As summer linen when the winter's come.

448.   *First Girl.* But it would be the greater compliment

---

430. . . . yet **23-69, 88.**
436. . . . unpunished, **23, 28, 48.**
440. . . . interfere, for if . . . **23, 28, 48.**
441. *Soldier.* If he's so proud and obstinate a neck
441a. I'd let him starve.
     Monk.   Persuade him to eat, my lord.
441b. His death would make a scandal, and stir up
442. The common people.
     Chamberlain.   And I have a fancy **19, 20.**
443-444. [lacking] **19, 20.**
445. . . . if it brought . . . , **19, 20.**
448. *Aileen.* [*To Cian*]. You've had no luck, old man.
     Cian.   We have not, lady.
448a. *Aileen.* Maybe he's out of humour with your ways,
448b. Having grown used to sprightlier service.
     Cian.   Maybe.
448c. But the King's messengers have gone for one **19, 20.**

449.   If Peter'd do it.

Second Girl.   Reason with him, Peter.
450.   Persuade him to eat; he's such a bag of bones!

451.   *Soldier.* I'll never trust a woman's word again!
452.   There's nobody that was so loud against him
453.   When he was at the council; now the wind's changed,
454.   And you that could not bear his speech or his silence
455.   Would have him there in his old place again;
456.   I do believe you would, but I won't help you.

457.   *Second Girl.* Why will you be so hard upon us, Peter?
458.   You know we have turned the common sort against
         us,
459.   And he looks miserable.

First Girl.   We cannot dance,
460.   Because no harper will pluck a string for us.

461.   *Second Girl.* I cannot sleep with thinking of his face.

462.   *First Girl.* And I love dancing more than anything.

463.   *Second Girl.* Do not be hard on us; but yesterday
464.   A woman in the road threw stones at me.
465.   You would not have me stoned?

First Girl.   May I not dance?

466.   *Soldier.* I will do nothing. You have put him out,
467.   And now that he is out—well, leave him out.

448d.   That will persuade him. [*To Brian.*] Come, let us go, (go; **20**)
448e.   For she might lose her way in this fine place.
448f.   Come, we have been too long upon the tree,
                        [*Plucking sleeve of Mayor.*] **19, 20.**
448g.   And there are little golden pippins here.
448h.   *Soldier.* Give me the dish, I'll hand it him myself.
448i.   *Aileen.* I wonder if she is pretty.
                        [*Mayor and Servants have gone out.*] **19, 20.**
449-1st hemistich **469.** [lacking] **19, 20.**
   453.   . . . the table; now . . . ,
   454.   . . . silence, **23-69, 88.**
   458.   . . . us. **44, 45, 56, 69, 88.**

468. *First Girl.* Do it for my sake, Peter.

> *Second Girl.*   And for mine.
> [*Each girl as she speaks takes Peter's hand with her right hand, stroking down his arm with her left. While Second Girl is stroking his arm, First Girl leaves go and gives him the dish.*

469. *Soldier.* Well, well; but not your way.   [*To Seanchan.*]
>   Here's meat for you.

470.   It has been carried from too good a table
471.   For men like you, and I am offering it
472.   Because these women have made a fool of me.
>   [*A pause.*

473.   You mean to starve? You will have none of it?
474.   I'll leave it there, where you can sniff the savour.
475.   Snuff it, old hedgehog, and unroll yourself!
476.   But if I were the King, I'd make you do it
477.   With wisps of lighted straw.

> *Seanchan.*   You have rightly named me.

478.   I lie rolled up under the ragged thorns
479.   That are upon the edge of those great waters
480.   Where all things vanish away, and I have heard
481.   Murmurs that are the ending of all sound.
482.   I am out of life; I am rolled up, and yet,
483.   Hedgehog although I am, I'll not unroll
484.   For you, King's dog! Go to the King, your master.
485.   Crouch down and wag your tail, for it may be
486.   He has nothing now against you, and I think
487.   The stripes of your last beating are all healed.
>   [*The Soldier has drawn his sword.*

Directions after 468. [... *Peter's hand with one hand, stroking ... with the other. While ... Girl lets go ....*] **28, 48.**

2nd hemistich 469. *Soldier.*   Eat this, old hedgehog. **19, 20.**

470-474. [lacking] **19, 20.**

475. Sniff up the savour and ... yourself.

476. ... King I'd ...

477. ... me, **19, 20.**

482. ... life, I ..., **19, 20.**

484. ... dog. Go ... master, **19, 20** ; ..., king's ... king, ... **23.**

Directions after 486. [*The soldier has drawn his sword.*] **28, 48.**

Directions after 487. [lacking] **19, 20, 28, 48.**

488. *Chamberlain [striking up sword].* Put up your sword, sir;
          put it up, I say!
489.   The common sort would tear you into pieces
490.   If you but touched him.

          Soldier.   If he's to be flattered,
491.   Petted, cajoled, and dandled into humour,
492.   We might as well have left him at the table.
                              [Goes to one side sheathing sword.

493. *Seanchan.* You must needs keep your patience yet awhile,
494.   For I have some few mouthfuls of sweet air
495.   To swallow before I have grown to be as civil
496.   As any other dust.

          Chamberlain.   You wrong us, Seanchan.
497.   There is none here but holds you in respect;
498.   And if you'd only eat out of this dish,
499.   The King would show how much he honours you.
                                   [Bowing and smiling.
500.   Who could imagine you'd so take to heart

---

488. *Chamberlain.* Don't answer, you were never to his mind.
489. And now you have angered him to no good purpose.
489a. But put the dish down and I will speak to him. **19, 20.**
490-Directions after 492. [lacking] **19, 20.**
          Directions after 492. [. . . *side, sheathing* . . . .] **28, 48.**
493. . . . need . . . , **23-69, 88.**
496. . . . , Seanchan,
497. . . . respect,
498. . . . if you would only . . . dish **19, 20.**
          Directions after 499. [lacking] **19, 20.**
499a. *Aileen. [giving Cripple money.]* You are always discontended. Look
          at this cripple,
499b. He has had to cover up his eyes with rags
499c. Because they are too weak to look at the sun,
499d. And has a crooked body, and yet he is cheerful.
499e. Stand there where he can see you. **19, 20.**
          [Cripple goes over and stands in front of Seanchan, bowing and smiling.]
          19, 20.
          Chamberlain.   We have come to you
499f. Because we wish you a long, prosperous life; **19, 20.**
500. . . . you'd take . . . **28, 48.**

501.   Being driven from the council? I am certain
502.   That you, if you will only think it over,
503.   Will understand that it is men of law,
504.   Leaders of the King's armies, and the like,
505.   That should sit there.

    Seanchan.   Somebody has deceived you,
506.   Or maybe it was your own eyes that lied,
507.   In making it appear that I was driven
508.   From the great council. You have driven away
509.   The images of them that weave a dance
510.   By the four rivers in the mountain garden.

511.   *Chamberlain.* You mean we have driven poetry away.
512.   But that's not altogether true, for I,
513.   As you should know, have written poetry.
514.   And often when the table has been cleared,
515.   And candles lighted, the King calls for me,
516.   And I repeat it him. My poetry
517.   Is not to be compared with yours; but still,
518.   Where I am honoured, poetry, in some measure,
519.   Is honoured too.

    Seanchan.   Well, if you are a poet,

---

  501.   Being put from the high table.
           Seanchan.   It was not I **19, 20 ;**
           Being put from the high table? I . . . **23-56.**
  501a.   That you have driven away from the high table,
  501b.   But the images of them that weave a dance,
  501c.   By the four rivers in the mountain garden.
  501d.   *Monk.* He means we have driven poetry away. **19, 20.**
  502.   [lacking] **19, 20.**
  503.   *Chamberlain.* It is the men who are learned in the laws, **19, 20.**
  504.   Or have led the King's armies that should sit **19, 20 ;** . . . king's . . . , **23.**
  505.   At the King's table. Nor has poetry **19, 20.**
506-511.   [lacking] **19, 20.**
  508.   . . . the King's table. You . . . **23-56.**
  512.   Been altogether driven away, for . . . ,
  513.   . . . poetry,
  514.   . . . cleared
  515.   . . . me **19, 20.**
  517.   . . . yours, but still **19, 20.**
  518.   . . . , poetry is honoured (honoured— **23, 32-45, 56, 69, 88**) **19-69, 88.**
  519.   In some measure.
                If . . . , **19-69, 88.**

520.   Cry out that the King's money would not buy,
521.   Nor the high circle consecrate his head,
522.   If poets had never christened gold, and even
523.   The moon's poor daughter, that most whey-faced
            metal,
524.   Precious; cry out that not a man alive
525.   Would ride among the arrows with high heart,
526.   Or scatter with an open hand, had not
527.   Our heady craft commended wasteful virtues.
528.   And when that story's finished, shake your coat
529.   Where little jewels gleam on it, and say,
530.   A herdsman, sitting where the pigs had trampled,
531.   Made up a song about enchanted kings,
532.   Who were so finely dressed one fancied them
533.   All fiery, and women by the churn
534.   And children by the hearth caught up the song
535.   And murmured it, until the tailors heard it.

536. *Chamberlain*. If you would but eat something, you'd
            find out
537.   That you have had these thoughts from lack of food,
538.   For hunger makes us feverish.

        Seanchan.   Cry aloud
539.   That when we are driven out we come again
540.   Like a great wind that runs out of the waste
541.   To blow the tables flat; and thereupon

---

523.   ... metal **19.**
524.   Precious; and cry ... that none alive **19-69, 88.**
525.   ... heart **19, 20.**
529.   Where the little ... say
530.   ... herdsman sitting ... trampled **19, 20.**
532.   ... dressed, one ... **23-69, 88.**
535.   ... it until .... **19, 20.**
535a.   *Monk*. How proud these poets are. (are! **20**) It was full time
535b.   To break their pride.
        Seanchan.   And I would have you say
536-538. [lacking] **19, 20.**
536.   ... something you'd ... **23-69, 88.**
537.   ... food **28, 48.**
538.   ... aloud, **23, 32-45, 56, 69, 88.**
541.   ... flat.
        Chamberlain.   If you'd eat something
541a.   You'd find you have these thoughts because you are hungry.
541b.   *Seanchan*. And when you have told them all these things, lie down
        19, 20.

542.   Lie down upon the threshold till the King
543.   Restore to us the ancient right of the poets.

544. *Monk.* You cannot shake him. I will to the King,
545.   And offer him consolation in his trouble,
546.   For that man there has set his teeth to die.
547.   He is a man that hates obedience,
548.   Discipline, and orderliness of life;
549.   I cannot mourn him.

    First Girl.   'Twas you that stirred it up.
550.   You stirred it up that you might spoil our dancing.
551.   Why shouldn't we have dancing? We're not in Lent.
552.   Yet nobody will pipe or play to us;
553.   And they will never do it if he die.
554.   And that is why you are going.

    Monk.   What folly's this?

555. *First Girl.* Well, if you did not do it, speak to him—
556.   Use your authority; make him obey you.
557.   What harm is there in dancing?

    Monk.   Hush! begone!
558.   Go to the fields and watch the hurley players,
559.   Or any other place you have a mind to.
560.   This is not woman's work.

    First Girl.   Come! let's away!
561.   We can do nothing here.

    Monk.   The pride of the poets!
562.   Dancing, hurling, the country full of noise,

---

 542. On this bare threshold and starve until the . . . **19, 20.**
543a. *Aileen.* Let's come away. There's no use talking to him,
543b. For he's resolved to die, and that's no loss:
543c. We will go watch the hurley.
     Monk.   You should obey
543d. The King's commandment and not question it,
543e. For it is God himself who has made him king.
543f. *Essa.* Let's hear his answer to the monk.
     Seanchan.   Stoop down, **19, 20.**
544-568. [lacking] **19, 20.**
 547. And being one that . . . ,
 548. . . . life, **23-69, 88.**

563.   And King and Church neglected. Seanchan,
564.   I'll take my leave, for you are perishing
565.   Like all that let the wanton imagination
566.   Carry them where it will, and it's not likely
567.   I'll look upon your living face again.

568.   *Seanchan.* Come nearer, nearer!

Monk.   Have you some last wish?

569.   *Seanchan.* Stoop down, for I would whisper it in your ear.
570.   Has that wild God of yours, that was so wild
571.   When you'd but lately taken the King's pay,
572.   Grown any tamer? He gave you all much trouble.

573.   *Monk.* Let go my habit!

Seanchan.   Have you persuaded him
574.   To chirp between two dishes when the King
575.   Sits down to table?

Monk.   Let go my habit, sir!

                              [*Crosses to centre of stage.*

576.   *Seanchan.* And maybe he has learned to sing quite softly
577.   Because loud singing would disturb the King,
578.   Who is sitting drowsily among his friends

---

563.   . . . king . . . church . . . , **23.**
569.   For there is something I would say to you. **19, 20.**
570.   . . . yours that . . . **19, 20 ;** . . . your's, . . . **44, 45, 56.**
572.   . . . trouble
572a.   Being so unruly and inconsiderate.
573.   *Aileen.* What does he mean?
        Monk.   Let go my habit, Seanchan.
573a.   *Seanchan.* Or it may be you have persuaded him **19, 20.**
574.   . . . dishes, when . . . **28, 48.**
575.   . . . table.
        Monk.   Let . . . , sir. **19, 20.**
        Directions after 575.   [lacking] **19, 20.**
575a.   I will not listen to this blasphemous wretch. **19 ;** What do I care
        about your insolent dreams. **20.**
576.   . . . learnt . . . **19-32, 48.**
577.   . . . King **19, 20.**

579.   After the table has been cleared. Not yet!

      [*Seanchan has been dragged some feet clinging to the Monk's habit.*

580.   You did not think that hands so full of hunger

581.   Could hold you tightly. They are not civil yet.

582.   I'd know if you have taught him to eat bread

583.   From the King's hand, and perch upon his finger.

584.   I think he perches on the King's strong hand,

585.   But it may be that he is still too wild.

586.   You must not weary in your work; a king

587.   Is often weary, and he needs a God

588.   To be a comfort to him.

      [*The Monk plucks his habit away and goes into palace. Seanchan holds up his hand as if a bird perched upon it. He pretends to stroke the bird.*

                          A little God,

589.   With comfortable feathers, and bright eyes.

590.   *First Girl.* There will be no more dancing in our time.

591.   For nobody will play the harp or the fiddle.

592.   Let us away, for we cannot amend it,

593.   And watch the hurley.

Second Girl.   Hush! he is looking at us.

594.   *Seanchan.* Yes, yes, go to the hurley, go to the hurley,

---

579.   . . . cleared—

      Monk.   **Let go.**

           [. . . *feet, clinging* . . . .]

580.   *Seanchan.* Not yet; you did not think that hungry hands

581.   Could be so strong. They . . . yet— **19, 20.**

584.   . . . hand. **23-88.**

586.   . . . King

587.   . . . weary and . . .

588.   . . . him.

      [. . . *away. Seanchan* . . . .]

                     . . . god,

589.   With soft well-coloured feathers, ... **19, 20.**

590-591. [lacking] **19, 20.**

590.   . . . time, **23-69, 88.**

592.   *Aileen.* We have listened long enough.

      Essa.   **Let us away,**

593.   Where we can watch the young men at the hurley. **19, 20.**

594.   . . . , yes, go the . . . , **45** (1911).

595.   Go to the hurley! Gather up your skirts—
596.   Run quickly! You can remember many love songs;
597.   I know it by the light that's in your eyes—
598.   But you'll forget them. You're fair to look upon.
599.   Your feet delight in dancing, and your mouths
600.   In the slow smiling that awakens love.
601.   The mothers that have borne you mated rightly.
602.   They'd little ears as thirsty as your ears
603.   For many love songs. Go to the young men.
604.   Are not the ruddy flesh and the thin flanks
605.   And the broad shoulders worthy of desire?
606.   Go from me! Here is nothing for your eyes.
607.   But it is I that am singing you away—
608.   Singing you to the young men.

> [*The two young Princesses come out of palace. While he has been speaking the Girls have shrunk back holding each other's hands.*

First Girl.   Be quiet!
609.   Look who it is has come out of the house.
610.   Princesses, we are for the hurling field.
611.   Will you go there?

First Princess.   We will go with you, Aileen.

---

595.   ... hurley, gather ... skirts,
596.   ... quickly. You ...;
597.   ... eyes, **19, 20.**
598.   ... them.   You are fair to look on, **19** ; ... look on, **20.**
601.   ... rightly, **19-28, 48.**
602.   For they had little ... thirsty as are yours **19, 20** ; For they had little ... **23, 28, 48.**
603.   ... love-songs. ... men: **19, 20.**
606.   ... me. Here ... eyes,
607.   ... away, **19, 20.**
608.   ... men.
> [... *Princesses Buan and Finnhua come in. While ... speaking Aileen and Essa have ... back, (back* **20**) *holding* ....]
Aileen.   ... quiet; **19, 20** ;
... the two young men ... ! **44, 56.**
Directions in 608. [... *he had been speaking (speaking,* **28, 48**) *the* ....] **23, 28, 48.**
609.   ... is that has .... **19, 20** ; ... who is it has .... **28, 48.**
611.   ... you come too?
Princess Buan.   We ..., Aileen, **19, 20** ;
... you come too?
First Princess.   We .... **23, 28, 48.**

612.   But we must have some words with Seanchan,
613.   For we have come to make him eat and drink.

614.   *Chamberlain.* I will hold out the dish and cup for him
615.   While you are speaking to him of his folly,
616.   If you desire it, Princess.   [*He has taken dish and cup.*

    First Princess.   No, Finula
617.   Will carry him the dish and I the cup.
618.   We'll offer them ourselves.   [*They take cup and dish.*

    First Girl.   They are so gracious;
619.   The dear little Princesses are so gracious.
      [*Princess holds out her hand for Seanchan to kiss it. He does not
      move.*
620.   Although she is holding out her hand to him,
621.   He will not kiss it.

    First Princess.   My father bids us say
622.   That, though he cannot have you at his table,
623.   You may ask any other thing you like
624.   And he will give it you. We carry you
625.   With our own hands a dish and cup of wine.

626.   *First Girl.* O, look! he has taken it! He has taken it!

---

616.   . . . . [. . . *taken up dish* . . . .]
    Princess Buan.   I'll have the (Give me the **20**) cup. **19,
    20.**
617.   And put the dish into Finnhua's hands. **19**; My sister there will
    carry the dish of meat: **20.**
618.   . . . ourselves.
    Aileen.   They . . . gracious, **19, 20.**
    Directions in 618.   [lacking] **19, 20**; [. . . *take the cup* . . . .] **28, 48.**
619.   . . . princesses . . . gracious.
      [*Princess Buan holds . . . it; he* . . . .]
620.   . . . him
621.   . . . it.
    Princess Buan.   My . . .
622.   That though . . . , **19, 20.**
625.   A dish and a cup of wine, with our own hands,
625a.   To show in what great honour you are held.
625b.   Will you not drink a little? Does he not show
625c.   Every befitting honour to the poets? **19, 20.**
626.   *Aileen.* O look, he . . . it, he . . . ! **19, 20**; Oh, . . . ! **44, 45, 56, 69, 88.**

V.E.P.Y.—L

627.   The dear Princesses! I have always said
628.   That nobody could refuse them anything.
         *[Seanchan takes the cup in one hand. In the other he holds for a
         moment the hand of the Princess.*

629. *Seanchan.* O, long, soft fingers and pale finger-tips,
630.   Well worthy to be laid in a king's hand!
631.   O, you have fair white hands, for it is certain
632.   There is uncommon whiteness in these hands.
633.   But there is something comes into my mind,
634.   Princess. A little while before your birth,
635.   I saw your mother sitting by the road
636.   In a high chair; and when a leper passed,
637.   She pointed him the way into the town.
638.   He lifted up his hand and blessed her hand—
639.   I saw it with my own eyes. Hold out your hands;
640.   I will find out if they are contaminated,
641.   For it has come into my thoughts that maybe
642.   The King has sent me food and drink by hands
643.   That are contaminated. I would see all your hands.
644.   You've eyes of dancers; but hold out your hands,
645.   For it may be there are none sound among you.
                    [The Princesses have shrunk back in terror.

---

627. . . . princesses, I . . . **19, 20.**
      Directions after 628.   [. . . *hand, in* . . . .] **19, 20.**
629. O long soft . . . finger-tips **19, 20;** O long, . . . , **23-32, 48;** Oh long,
      . . . , **44, 45, 56, 69, 88.**
630. . . . hand; **19, 20.**
631. O you . . . **19, 20;** Oh, . . . **44, 45, 56, 69, 88.**
634. . . . birth **19, 20.**
636. . . . chair, and . . . passed
637. . . . town,
638. And he lifted his . . . hand;
639. . . . hands, **19, 20.**
640. . . . contaminated; **19, 20;** . . . contaminated. **23, 28, 48.**
641. . . . may be **19, 20.**
643. . . . hands,
644. . . . dancers, but . . . ,
645. . . . you—
                    [*The* . . . .] **19, 20.**

646. *First Princess.* He has called us lepers.

[*Soldier draws sword.*

Chamberlain.   He's out of his mind,

647.   And does not know the meaning of what he said.

648. *Seanchan* [*standing up*]. There's no sound hand among
          you—no sound hand.

649.   Away with you! away with all of you!

650.   You are all lepers! There is leprosy

651.   Among the plates and dishes that you have carried.

652.   And wherefore have you brought me leper's wine?

[*He flings the contents of the cup in their faces.*

653.   There, there! I have given it to you again. And now

654.   Begone, or I will give my curse to you.

655.   You have the leper's blessing, but you think

656.   Maybe the bread will something lack in savour

657.   Unless you mix my curse into the dough.

[*They go out hurriedly in all directions. Seanchan is staggering in
          the middle of the stage.*

658.   Where did I say the leprosy had come from?

659.   I said it came out of a leper's hand,

Enter Cripples

660.   And that he walked the highway. But that's folly,

661.   For he was walking up there in the sky.

---

646. *Princess Buan.* He . . . lepers.
Chamberlain.   He's . . . ,
Directions in 646. [lacking] **19, 20.**

648.   . . . *up*.] There are no . . . hands . . . you. No (you—no **28, 48**) . . .
hands. **19, 20, 28, 48.**

649.   . . . you, away . . . you,

650.   . . . lepers. There . . . **19, 20.**

651.   . . . have brought me. **20.**

652.   I would know why you have brought . . . ?

[. . . *flings the wine in* . . . .]

653.   . . ., there, I . . . again, and . . .

654.   Begone or . . . . **19, 20.**
Directions after 657. [. . . *out to L., all except the Cripples. Seanchan*
. . . .] **19, 20** ; [. . . *out to R., all. Seanchan* . . . .] **28, 48.**

658.   . . . leprosy came from? **19, 20, 28, 48.**

659.   . . . hand
Directions after 659. [lacking]

660.   . . . highway; but . . . ,

661.   . . . sky **19, 20.**

662.   And there he is even now, with his white hand
663.   Thrust out of the blue air, and blessing them
664.   With leprosy.

       First Cripple.   He's pointing at the moon
665.   That's coming out up yonder, and he calls it
666.   Leprous, because the daylight whitens it.

667. *Seanchan.* He's holding up his hand above them all—
668.   King, noblemen, princesses—blessing all.
669.   Who could imagine he'd have so much patience?

670. *First Cripple* [*clutching the other Cripple*]. Come out of this!

       Second Cripple [*pointing to food*]. If you don't need it, sir,
671.   May we not carry some of it away?
            [*They cross towards food and pass in front of Seanchan.*

672. *Seanchan.* Who's speaking? Who are you?

       First Cripple.   Come out of this!

673. *Second Cripple.* Have pity on us, that must beg our
        bread
674.   From table to table throughout the entire world,
675.   And yet be hungry.

       Seanchan.   But why were you born crooked?

---

662.   . . . now with . . .
663.   . . . air and . . . **19, 20.**
664.   . . . leprosy.
       A Cripple. (*Cripple.* **28, 48**) He's . . . **19, 20, 28, 48.**
667.   . . . all, **19** ; . . . all **20.**
668.   . . . , Noblemen, Princesses, blessing . . . . **19, 20.**
669.   . . . patience. **20.**
670.   *First Cripple.* Come . . . this.
                 [*Clutching other Cripple.*]
       Second Cripple.   If . . . , **19, 20** ;
       Cripple [. . . *the Cripple next him*]. Come . . . !
       Other Cripple [. . . .]   If . . . , **28, 48.**
       Directions after 671.   [*He points to food.*] **19, 20** ; [lacking] **28, 48.**
672.   . . . this. **19, 20** ; *Cripple.* . . . . . **28, 48.**
673.   *Other Cripple.* . . . **28, 48.**
674.   . . . world **19, 20.**
675.   . . . hungry.
       Seanchan [*intensely, to them*]. But . . . ? **28, 48.**

676.   What bad poet did your mothers listen to

677.   That you were born so crooked?

    First Cripple.   Come away!

678.   Maybe he's cursed the food, and it might kill us.

679.   *Second Cripple.* Yes, better come away.   [*They go out.*

    Seanchan [*staggering and speaking wearily*].

                                          He has great strength

680.   And great patience to hold his right hand there,

681.   Uplifted, and not wavering about.

682.   He is much stronger than I am, much stronger.

                   [*Sinks down on steps. Mayor and Fedelm have entered.*

683.   *Mayor.* He is delirious now.

    Fedelm.   Before I speak

684.   Of food or drink I'll take him out of this.

685.   For while he is on this threshold and can hear,

686.   It may be, the voices that made mock of him,

687.   He would not listen.

    Mayor.   No, speak to him at once.

---

676.   . . . Mothers . . . **19, 20.**
677.   . . . away. **19, 20**;
         . . . crooked?
         Cripple.   Come . . . ! **23-69, 88.**
678.   . . . food and . . . . **19, 20.**
679.   *Other Cripple.* Yes, ...
         Seanchan [*staggering, and . . .*]. He . . . **23-69, 88.**
680.   . . . there **19, 20.**
681.   Uplifted and . . . about; (about. **23, 28, 48**) **19-23, 28, 48.**
         Directions after 682.   [*He sinks . . . steps.*]
             [*Enter from R. Fedelm, Cian and Brian.*] **19, 20**; [. . . *steps. Enter
             Mayor . . . Fedelm.*] **23-56.**
682a.   *Cian* (*Brian.* **20**) There he is lying. Go over to him now
683.   And bid him eat.
         Fedelm.   I'll get him out of this **19, 20**;
         Fedelm [*her finger on her lips*]. Say nothing! I will get him out of this
         23-56.
684.   Before I have said a word of food and drink; **19-56.**
687.   . . . listen.
         Cian. (*Brian.* **20**) That is a good plan. **19, 20**;
         . . . listen. I'd be alone with him. **23-56.**

688.   Press food upon him while delirious
689.   And he may eat not knowing what he does.

                                        [*Mayor goes out.*

690. *Fedelm.* Seanchan! Seanchan!

                              [*He remains looking into the sky.*
                         Can you not hear me, Seanchan?

691.   It is myself.

              [*He looks at her, dreamily at first, then takes her hand.*

     Seanchan.   Is this your hand, Fedelm?
692.   I have been looking at another hand
693.   That is up yonder.

     Fedelm.   I have come for you.

694. *Seanchan.* Fedelm, I did not know that you were here.

695. *Fedelm.* And can you not remember that I promised
696.   That I would come and take you home with me
697.   When I'd the harvest in? And now I've come,
698.   And you must come away, and come on the instant.

699. *Seanchan.* Yes, I will come. But is the harvest in?
700.   This air has got a summer taste in it.

701. *Fedelm.* But is not the wild middle of the summer

Directions after 687. [*Mayor goes out. Fedelm goes to Seanchan and
kneels before him.*] **23-56.**
687a.   But there is little time, for he is weakening. **19, 20.**
687b.   Fedelm [*crying*]. I cannot think of any other plan
687c.   Although it breaks my heart.
        Brian. (*Cian.* **20**)   Let's leave them now,
687d.   For she will press the honey from her bag
687e.   When we are gone.
        Cian. (*Brian.* **20**)   It will be hard to move him
687f.   If hunger and thirst have got into his bones.
            [*They go out, (out* **20**) *leaving Fedelm and Seanchan alone. Fedelm
            runs over to Seanchan and kneels down before him.*] **19, 20.**
688-Directions after 689. [lacking] **19-56.**
690.   . . . not see me, . . . ?
691.   . . . myself.
            [*Seanchan looks . . . her dreamily . . . .*]
                                            . . . ? **19, 20.**
697.   . . . ? and . . . , **19, 20.**
699.   . . . come; but . . . ? **19, 20.**

702. A better time to marry? Come with me now!

703. *Seanchan* [*seizing her by both wrists*]. Who taught you that?
        For it's a certainty,
704. Although I never knew it till last night,
705. That marriage, because it is the height of life,
706. Can only be accomplished to the full
707. In the high days of the year. I lay awake:
708. There had come a frenzy into the light of the stars,
709. And they were coming nearer, and I knew
710. All in a minute they were about to marry
711. Clods out upon the ploughlands, to beget
712. A mightier race than any that has been.
713. But some that are within there made a noise,
714. And frighted them away.

Fedelm.   Come with me now!
715. We have far to go, and daylight's running out.

716. *Seanchan.* The stars had come so near me that I caught
717. Their singing. It was praise of that great race
718. That would be haughty, mirthful, and white-bodied,
719. With a high head, and open hand, and how,
720. Laughing, it would take the mastery of the world.

721. *Fedelm.* But you will tell me all about their songs
722. When we're at home. You have need of rest and care,
723. And I can give them you when we're at home.
724. And therefore let us hurry, and get us home.

---

702. . . . now. **19, 20.**
703. . . . that, for . . . , **19, 20.**
707. . . . awake,
708. . . . stars
709. . . . nearer and . . . **19, 20.**
711. . . . plough-lands, . . .
712. . . . been;
713. . . . noise
714. . . . now; **19, 20.**
717. . . . singing; it . . . **19, 20.**
718. . . . white-bodied **19, 20** ; . . . whitebodied, **23.**
719. . . . how **19, 20.**
723. . . . home,
724. . . . hurry and . . . . **19, 20.**

725.   *Seanchan.* It's certain that there is some trouble here,
726.   Although it's gone out of my memory.
727.   And I would get away from it. Give me your help.

> [*Trying to rise.*

728.   But why are not my pupils here to help me?
729.   Go, call my pupils, for I need their help.

730.   *Fedelm.* Come with me now, and I will send for them,
731.   For I have a great room that's full of beds
732.   I can make ready; and there is a smooth lawn
733.   Where they can play at hurley and sing poems
734.   Under an apple-tree.

    Seanchan.   I know that place:
735.   An apple-tree, and a smooth level lawn
736.   Where the young men can sway their hurley sticks.

> [*Sings*]

737.   The four rivers that run there,
738.   Through well-mown level ground,
739.   Have come out of a blessed well
740.   That is all bound and wound
741.   By the great roots of an apple
742.   And all the fowls of the air
743.   Have gathered in the wide branches
744.   And keep singing there.

> [*Fedelm, troubled, has covered her eyes with her hands.*

745.   *Fedelm.* No, there are not four rivers, and those rhymes
746.   Praise Adam's paradise.

    Seanchan.   I can remember now,
747.   It's out of a poem I made long ago

---

725.   *Seanchan.* That's true; and there's some trouble here, although
726.   I cannot now remember what it is, **19, 20**.
    Directions after 727.   [lacking] **19, 20.**
732.   ... ready, and ... **19, 20**; ... lawn, **28, 48.**
734.   ... place, **19, 20**; ... apple tree. ...: **23, 28, 48.**
735.   ... apple-tree (apple tree **20**) ... lawn, **19, 20**; ... apple tree, ...
    23, 28, 48.
741.   ... apple, **19-69, 88.**
742.   ... all fowls ... **19, 20**; ... fowl ... **23-69, 88.**
745.   ... rivers and ... **28, 48.**
746.   ... Paradise.
        ... now. **19, 20.**

748. About the Garden in the East of the World,
749. And how spirits in the images of birds
750. Crowd in the branches of old Adam's crab-tree.
751. They come before me now, and dig in the fruit
752. With so much gluttony, and are so drunk
753. With that harsh wholesome savour, that their
feathers
754. Are clinging one to another with the juice.
755. But you would lead me to some friendly place,
756. And I would go there quickly.

Fedelm [helping him to rise]. Come with me.
   [He walks slowly, supported by her, till he comes to table.

757. Seanchan. But why am I so weak? Have I been ill?
758. Sweetheart, why is it that I am so weak?

           [Sinks on to seat.

759. Fedelm [goes to table]. I'll dip this piece of bread into the
wine,
760. For that will make you stronger for the journey.

761. Seanchan. Yes, give me bread and wine; that's what I
want,
762. For it is hunger that is gnawing me.
   [He takes bread from Fedelm, hesitates, and then thrusts it back into
   her hand.
763. But no; I must not eat it.

Fedelm.   Eat, Seanchan,
764. For if you do not eat it you will die.

---

748. . . . garden . . . east . . . world, **19, 20, 28, 48.**
750. . . . crab-tree;
751. . . . now and . . . **19, 20.**
753. . . . harsh, wholesome savour that . . . **19, 20.**
755. . . . would take me . . . ,
756. . . . quickly.
 Fedelm. Come with me.
  [She helps him to rise. He walks . . . her, (her **20**) till . . . to the table at
  R.] **19, 20.**
 Directions after 758. [He sinks . . . to the seat.] **19, 20.**
 Directions in 759. [lacking] **19, 20.**
761. . . . wine, that's . . . , **19, 20.**
763. . . . no, I . . . , **19, 20**; But, no; . . . , Seanchan. **23-69, 88**; But, no;
. . . , **84.**
764. . . . it, you . . . . **28, 48.**

765. *Seanchan.* Why did you give me food? Why did you
        come?

766.   For had I not enough to fight against
767.   Without your coming?

    Fedelm.   Eat this little crust,
768.   Seanchan, if you have any love for me.

769. *Seanchan.* I must not eat it—but that's beyond your wit.
770.   Child! child! I must not eat it, though I die.

771. *Fedelm [passionately].* You do not know what love is; for
        if you loved,
772.   You would put every other thought away.
773.   But you have never loved me.

    Seanchan [seizing her by wrist]. You, a child,
774.   Who have but seen a man out of the window,
775.   Tell me that I know nothing about love,
776.   And that I do not love you? Did I not say
777.   There was a frenzy in the light of the stars
778.   All through the livelong night, and that the night
779.   Was full of marriages? But that fight's over
780.   And all that's done with, and I have to die.

781. *Fedelm [throwing her arms about him].* I will not be put
        from you, although I think
782.   I had not grudged it you if some great lady,
783.   If the King's daughter, had set out your bed.
784.   I will not give you up to death; no, no!
785.   And are not these white arms and this soft neck

---

769. . . . it: but . . . wit;
770. Child, child, I . . . it though . . . .
771. *Fedelm.* You . . . is, for . . . loved **19, 20.**
772. . . . away **20.**
773. . . . .
    Seanchan [. . . by the wrist]. . . . child (child. **20**) **19, 20.**
    Directions in 773. [. . . *by the wrist*] **28, 48.**
774. Who had but . . . , **97A.**
776. . . . you. Did . . . **19, 20** ; . . . you! Did . . . **23-32, 48.**
779. . . . over. **19, 20** ; . . . over, **23-56.**
784. . . . , no, **19, 20.**

786.   Better than the brown earth?

Seanchan [*struggling to disengage himself*]. Begone from me!
787.   There's treachery in those arms and in that voice.
788.   They're all against me. Why do you linger there?
789.   How long must I endure the sight of you?

790. *Fedelm.* O, Seanchan! Seanchan!

Seanchan [*rising*].   Go where you will,
791.   So it be out of sight and out of mind.
792.   I cast you from me like an old torn cap,
793.   A broken shoe, a glove without a finger,
794.   A crooked penny; whatever is most worthless.

795. *Fedelm* [*bursts into tears*]. O, do not drive me from you!

Seanchan [*takes her in his arms*]. What did I say,
796.   My dove of the woods? I was about to curse you.
797.   It was a frenzy. I'll unsay it all.
798.   But you must go away.

Fedelm.   Let me be near you.
799.   I will obey like any married wife.
800.   Let me but lie before your feet.

Seanchan.   Come nearer. [*Kisses her.*
801.   If I had eaten when you bid me, sweetheart,
802.   The kiss of multitudes in times to come

---

786.   . . . earth?
    Seanchan. I swear an oath
786a. Upon the holy tree that I'll not eat
786b. Until the King restore the right of the poets.
786c. O Sun and Moon, and all things that have strength,
786d. Become my strength that I may put a curse
786e. On all things that would have me break this oath.
      [*Fedelm has sunk down in the ground while he says this, and crouches
      at his feet.*] **19, 20.**
787-797. [lacking] **19, 20.**
 795. Oh, . . . ! **44, 45, 56, 69, 88.**
 798. *Fedelm.* Seanchan, do not curse me; from this out **19, 20.**
     Directions after 800. [*He kisses . . . .*] **19, 20.**

803.   Had been the poorer.

            [*Enter King from palace, followed by the two Princesses.*

         King [*to Fedelm*].   Has he eaten yet?

804.   *Fedelm.* No, King, and will not till you have restored
805.   The right of the poets.

         King [*coming down and standing before Seanchan*]. Seanchan,
            you have refused
806.   Everybody I have sent, and now
807.   I come to you myself.

         Fedelm.   Come nearer, King.
808.   He is now so weak he cannot hear your voice.

809.   *King.* Seanchan, put away your pride as I
810.   Have put my pride away. I had your love
811.   Not a great while ago, and now you have planned
812.   To put a voice by every cottage fire,
813.   And in the night when no one sees who cries,
814.   To cry against me till my throne has crumbled.
815.   And yet if I give way I must offend
816.   My courtiers and nobles till they, too,
817.   Strike at the crown. What would you have of me?

818.   *Seanchan.* When did the poets promise safety, King?

819.   *King.* Seanchan, I bring you bread in my own hands,
820.   And bid you eat because of all these reasons,

---

803.   . . . poorer.
       King. [*entering from house*]. Has . . . ? **19, 20.**
       Directions in 803.   [. . . *King from house.*] **28, 48.**
806.   Everybody that I . . . **19-56.**
807.   . . . myself, (myself; **23-56**) and I have come **19-56**; . . . , King, **69,**
       88.
808.   [lacking]
809.   To bid you put your pride as far away
810.   As I have . . . my pride. I . . . **19-56.**
812.   To waken a cry by . . . fire **19**; . . . fire **20.**
813.   . . . cries **19, 20.**
816.   . . . they too **19, 20**; . . . and my nobles . . . , **28, 48.**
820.   . . . eat it because . . . , **19, 20.**

821.   And for this further reason, that I love you.

> [*Seanchan pushes bread away, with Fedelm's hand.*

822.   You have refused, Seanchan?

Seanchan.   We have refused it.

823.   *King.* I have been patient, though I am a king,
824.   And have the means to force you. But that's ended,
825.   And I am but a king, and you a subject.
826.   Nobles and courtiers, bring the poets hither;

> *Enter Court Ladies, Monk, Soldiers, Chamberlain, and*
> *Courtiers with Pupils, who have halters round their necks.*

827.   For you can have your way. I that was man,
828.   With a man's heart, am now all king again.
829.   Speak to your master; beg your lives of him;
830.   Show him the halter that is round your necks.
831.   If his heart's set upon it, he may die;
832.   But you shall all die with him.   [*Goes up steps.*

> Beg your lives!

---

821.   . . . reason that . . . .
         Directions after 821.   [. . . *away with* . . . .] **19, 20.**
822.   . . . refused it, Seanchan. (Seanchan? **23-56**)
         Seanchan.   . . . . **19-56.**
823.   . . . patient though . . . ,
824.   . . . you—but . . . ,
825.   . . . king and . . . .
         [*He goes up steps.*] **19, 20.**
826.   . . . hither **19, 20**; . . . hither. **28, 48.**
         Directions after 826.   [lacking] **19, 20**; [. . . , *Soldier*, ...] **23, 32,**
         44, 45, 56; [*Enter Courtiers with* . . . .] **28, 48.**
827.   . . . way: I . . . man **19, 20.**
828.   . . . heart am . . . again, **19, 20**; . . . again, **23-69.**
828a.   Remembering that the seed I come of, although (though **23-56**)
828b.   A hundred kings have sown it and resown it,
828c.   Has neither trembled nor shrunk backward yet
828d.   Because of the hard business of a king, **19-56.**
         Directions after 828d.   [*Princesses, Ladies, and Courtiers have come in*
         with Pupils, who have halters round their necks.] **19, 20.**
829.   . . . master, beg your life of him, **19, 20**; . . . your life of . . . ; **23-88.**
830.   . . . halters that are round . . . necks;
831.   . . . . it he . . . die,
823.   . . . him; beg . . . lives; **19, 20.**

833.   Begin, for you have little time to lose.
834.   Begin it, you that are the oldest pupil.

835.   *Oldest Pupil.* Die, Seanchan, and proclaim the right of
       the poets.

836.   *King.* Silence! you are as crazy as your master.
837.   But that young boy, that seems the youngest of you,
838.   I'd have him speak. Kneel down before him, boy;
839.   Hold up your hands to him that you may pluck
840.   That milky-coloured neck out of the noose.

841.   *Youngest Pupil.* Die, Seanchan, and proclaim the right
      of the poets.

---

833.   . . . lose;
834.   . . . it you . . . . **19, 20.**
835.   *Senias [going up to Seanchan].* Die, ... **19, 20 ;** . . . poets, **97A.**
836.   Silence, you . . . . **19, 20.**
837.   . . . boy that . . . , **19, 20 ;** . . . you **45** (1913), **69.**
838.   . . . , boy, **19, 20.**
839.   . . . that he may . . . **19, 20 ;** . . . him, that . . . **23-32, 45** (1911), **48,**
      56.
840.   . . . milky coloured . . . . **19, 20, 28, 48.**
841.   *Arias.* Die, . . . poets.
      [*All the Pupils turn towards the King, holding out the ends of their*
      halters.] **19, 20 ;**
      Youngest Pupil [*going to Seanchan*]. Die, ... **28, 48 ;** Die Seanchan
      and . . . . **65.**
841a.   *Senias.* (*Oldest Pupil.* **23-56**) Gather the halters up into your hands
841b.   And lead (drive **23-56**) us where you will, for in all things (things,
      23-56)
841c.   But in our art (Art, **23-56**) we are obedient. **19-56.**
      Directions after 841c. [*The King comes slowly down the steps.*] **19, 20 ;**
      [*They hold the ends of the halter (halters* **45** (1913)) *towards the King.*
      The King comes slowly down steps.] **23, 32-45, 56 ;** [*The King comes*
      slowly down steps.] **28, 48.**
841d.   *King* [*kneeling down before Seanchan*]. Kneel (*King.* Kneel **23-56**) down,
      kneel down, (down; **23-56**) he has the greater power. **19-56.**
841e.   There is no power but has its root in his—
841f.   I understand it now. There is no power
841g.   But his that can withhold the crown or give it,
841h.   Or make it reverent (reverend **32-45, 56**) in the eyes of men,
841i.   And therefore I have laid it in his hands, **23-56.**

842. *Seanchan.* Come nearer me that I may know how face
843.   Differs from face and touch you with my hands.
844.   O more than kin, O more than children could be,
845.   For children are but born out of our blood
846.   And share our frailty. O my chicks, my chicks!
847.   That I have nourished underneath my wings
848.   And fed upon my soul.

                              [*He rises and walks down steps.*
                    I need no help.
849.   He needs no help that joy has lifted up
850.   Like some miraculous beast out of Ezekiel.
851.   The man that dies has the chief part in the story,
852.   And I will mock and mock that image yonder,
853.   That evil picture in the sky—no, no!
854.   I have all my strength again, I will outface it.
855.   O, look upon the moon that's standing there
856.   In the blue daylight—take note of the complexion,
857.   Because it is the white of leprosy
858.   And the contagion that afflicts mankind
859.   Falls from the moon. When I and these are dead
860.   We should be carried to some windy hill
861.   To lie there with uncovered face awhile
862.   That mankind and that leper there may know

841j. *King.* I give my crown to you.
        [*All kneel except Seanchan, Fedelm and Pupils. Seanchan rises slowly,
        supported by one of the Pupils and by Fedelm.*]
        Seanchan.   O crown, O crown, **19, 20**;
        King. And I will do his will.
        [*He has put (He puts* **28, 48***) the crown into Seanchan's hands.*]
        Seanchan [*who has been assisted to rise by his pupils*].
                O (O, **44, 45, 56**) crown! O (O, **44, 45, 56**) crown! **23-56**.
841k. It is but right if (right the **23-56**) hands that made the crown
841l. In the old time should give it when they will. (it where they please.
        23-56) **19-56**.
        Directions after 841l. [*He places the crown on the King's head.*] **23,
        32-45, 56**; [lacking] **19, 20, 28, 48**.
842-893. [lacking] **19-56**.
   842. . . . me, that . . .
   843. . . . face, and . . . . **65**.
   846. . . . chicks, **65**.
        Directions in 848. [*He stands up and begins to walk . . . .*] **65**.
   852. . . . will mock and mock and mock that . . . yonder
   853. . . . , no— **65**.
   855. O look . . . **65, 69, 88**.
   856. . . . daylight—notice her complexion **65**; . . . complexion **69, 88**.

863.   Dead faces laugh.   *[He falls and then half rises.*
            King! King! Dead faces laugh.

                                    [He dies.

864.   *Oldest Pupil.* King, he is dead; some strange triumphant
            thought
865.   So filled his heart with joy that it has burst,
866.   Being grown too mighty for our frailty,
867.   And we who gaze grow like him and abhor
868.   The moments that come between us and that death
869.   You promised us.

        King.   Take up his body.
870.   Go where you please and lay it where you please,
871.   So that I cannot see his face or any
872.   That cried him towards his death.

        Youngest Pupil.   Dead faces laugh!
873.   The ancient right is gone, the new remains,
874.   And that is death.

                    [They go towards the King holding out their halters.
                    We are impatient men,
875.   So gather up the halters in your hands.

876.   *King.* Drive them away.
            *[He goes into the palace. The Soldiers block the way before the
            Pupils.*

        Soldier.   Here is no place for you,
877.   For he and his pretensions now are finished.
878.   Begone before the men-at-arms are bidden
879.   To beat you from the door.

        Oldest Pupil.   Take up his body
880.   And cry that, driven from the populous door,

---

863.   . . . .
                King, king, dead . . . .
864.   King, king, he . . .
865.   . . . burst **65.**
873.   . . . remains **65, 69, 88.**
        Directions in 874. [. . . *king* . . . .] **65.**
876.   . . . you. **69.**
878.   . . . men at arms . . .
879.   To hurl you . . . **65.**
880.   . . . that driven . . . door **65, 69, 88.**

881.   He seeks high waters and the mountain birds
882.   To claim a portion of their solitude.
        [*They make a litter with cloak and staffs or use one discovered,
        heaped with food, at the opening of the play.*

883.   *Youngest Pupil.* And cry that when they took his ancient
            right
884.   They took all common sleep; therefore he claims
885.   The mountain for his mattress and his pillow.

886.   *Oldest Pupil.* And there he can sleep on, not noticing,
887.   Although the world be changed from worse to worse,
888.   Amid the changeless clamour of the curlew.
        [*They raise the litter on their shoulders and move a few steps.*

889.   *Youngest Pupil* [*motioning to them to stop*]. Yet make
            triumphant music; sing aloud,
890.   For coming times will bless what he has blessed
891.   And curse what he has cursed.

        Oldest Pupil.   No, no, be still,
892.   Or pluck a solemn music from the strings.
893.   You wrong his greatness speaking so of triumph.

894.   *Youngest Pupil.* O silver trumpets, be you lifted up
895.   And cry to the great race that is to come.
896.   Long-throated swans upon the waves of time,
897.   Sing loudly, for beyond the wall of the world

Directions after 882.   [. . . *staffs and lay Seanchan on it.*] **65.**
886.   . . . noticing **65.**
887.   . . . changed for worse . . . , **84.**
889.   . . . aloud **65, 69, 88.**
891.   . . . still; **65.**
892.   . . . strings **69E, 88.**
894.   *Seanchan.* O . . . trumpets, (trumpets **20**) . . . **19, 20**; O (O, **44, 45, 56**)
        . . . trumpets! Be . . . up, **23-56.**
        Directions after 894.   [*He lays the crown on the King's head.*] **19, 20.**
896.   . . . swans among the . . . time **19, 20**; . . . swans, amid the . . . Time,
        23-56; . . . time **65.**
897.   . . . loudly for . . . **69, 88.**

898.   That race may hear our music and awake.

Oldest Pupil [motioning the musicians to lower their trumpets].

899.   Not what it leaves behind it in the light
900.   But what it carries with it to the dark
901.   Exalts the soul; nor song nor trumpet-blast
902.   Can call up races from the worsening world
903.   To mend the wrong and mar the solitude
904.   Of the great shade we follow to the tomb.

[Fedelm and the Pupils go out carrying the litter. Some play a mournful music.

THE END

---

898.   It waits and it may hear and come to us. **19, 20**; It waits, and it may hear and come to us! (us. **32, 44, 45, 56**) **23-56.**
         Directions after 898.   [*Some of the Pupils blow a blast upon their horns.*]
         19, 20; [*The pupils blow a trumpet blast.*] **23, 32, 44, 45, 56**; [*A trumpet blast.*] **28, 48.**
         Speaker and Directions before 899-End.   [lacking] **19-56.**
901.   . . . trumpet blast **69, 88.**

NOTES

A PROLOGUE

An old man with a red dressing-gown, red slippers and red nightcap, holding a brass candlestick with a guttering candle in it, comes on, in front of curtain.

Old Man—'I've got to speak the prologue. [*He shuffles on a few steps.*] My nephew, that's one of the players, came to me and I in my bed, and my prayers said, and the candle put out, and he told me there were so many characters in this new play, that all the company were in it, whether they had been long or short at the business, and that there wasn't one left to speak the prologue. Wait a bit, there's a draught here. [*He pulls the curtain closer together.*] That's better. And that's why I'm here, and maybe I'm a fool for my pains.

'And my nephew said, there are a good many plays to be played for you, some to-night and some on other nights through the winter, and the most of them are simple enough, and tell out their story to the end. But as to the big play you are to see to-night, my nephew taught me to say what the poet had taught him to say about it. [*Puts down candlestick and puts right finger on left thumb.*] First, he who told the story of Seanchan on King Guaire's threshold long ago in the old books told it wrongly, for he was a friend of the king, or maybe afraid of the king, and so put the king in the right. But he that tells the story now, being a poet, has put the poet in the right.

'And then [*touches other finger*] I am to say: Some think it would be a finer tale if Seanchan had died at the end of it, and the king had the guilt at his door, for that might have served the poet's cause better in the end. But that is not true, for if he that is in the story but a shadow and an image of poetry had not risen up from the death that threatened him, the ending would not have been true and joyful enough to be put into the voices of players and proclaimed in the mouths of trumpets, and poetry would have been badly served. [*He takes up the candlestick again.*]

'And as to what happened Seanchan after, my nephew told me he didn't know, and the poet didn't know, and it's likely there's nobody that knows. But my nephew thinks he never sat down at the king's table again, after the way he had been treated, but that he went to some quiet green place in the hills with Fedelm, his sweetheart, where the poor people made much of him because he was wise, and where he made songs and poems, and it's likely enough he made some of the old songs and the old poems the poor people on the hillsides are saying and singing to-day. [*A trumpet-blast.*]

'Well, it's time for me to be going. That trumpet means that the curtain is going to rise, and after a while the stage there will be filled up with great ladies and great gentlemen, and poets, and a king with a crown on him, and all of them as high up in themselves with the pride of their youth and their strength and their fine clothes as if there was no such thing in the world as cold in the shoulders, and speckled shins, and the pains in the bones and the stiffness in the joints that make an old man that has the whole load of the world on him ready for his bed.

'And it would be better for me, that nephew of mine to be thinking less of his play-acting, and to have remembered to boil down the knapweed with a bit of threepenny sugar, for me to be wetting my throat with now and again through the night, and drinking a sup to ease the pains in my bones.'

I have made this prologue for a book of plays which I have written for the Irish National Theatre Society. The first play in the volume will be 'On the King's Threshold,' which is to be performed for the first time in the Molesworth Hall, on the 24th, 25th and 26th of this month. This and a volume of prose plays to be published at the same time will contain practically all my one-act plays. I have as far as possible taken the usual steps to retain the acting rights, but in some cases will be ready to give leave to societies of amateurs to perform them in country places, after consultation with Mr. Fay.   W. B. YEATS.

The United Irishman, September 9, 1903.

A Prologue

An Old Man . . . Man. I've . . . nephew, who is one . . . me, and . . . pains.

And . . . right.

And . . . *again.*]

And . . . *trumpet-blast.*]

Well, . . . bed. [*He turns to go out but turns back again.*]

And . . . bones. [*He goes out.*]

[Text italics; directions after opening, roman *Ed.*]   **19.**

A Prologue[1] (Prologue[1] **44, 45, 56**)

An Old Man . . . on from side of stage and goes in front of the dull green curtain . . . . Man. I've . . . nephew, who is one of the play actors, came to me, and . . . I'm (I am **34a-45, 56**) . . . pains.

And . . . *again.*]

And . . . right.

And . . . *trumpet-blast.*]

Well, . . . bed. [*He begins to shuffle away, and then stops.*]

And . . . bones. [*He goes out at side of stage.*]

[1] Written for the first production of 'The King's Threshold' in Dublin, but not used, as, owing to the smallness of the company, nobody could be spared to speak it. (it.—W.B.Y., 1904. **34a-45, 56**) 20, **34a-45, 56**.

* * *

Both these plays have been written for Mr. Fay's 'Irish National Theatre.' 'The King's Threshold' was played in October, 1903, and 'On Baile's Strand' will be played in February or March, 1904. Both are founded on Old Irish Prose Romances, but I have borrowed some ideas for the arrange-

ment of my subject in 'The King's Threshold' from 'Sancan the Bard,' a
play published by Mr. Edwin Ellis some ten years ago.   w.b.y.

Note, 20L.[1]

'The King's Threshold' was first played 7 October, 1903, in the Molesworth Hall by the Irish National Theatre Society, and with the following
cast: Seanchan, F. Fay; King Guaire, P. Kelly; the Lord High Chamberlain, Shamus O'Sullivan; Soldier, W. Conroy; Monk, S. Sheridan-Neill;
Mayor, W. Fay; a Cripple, P. Columb; a Court Lady, Honor Saville;
another Court Lady, Dora Melville; a Princess, Sara Allgood; another
Princess, Dora Gunning; Fedelm, Maire MacShiubhlaigh; a Servant, P.
MacShiubhlaigh; another Servant, P. Josephs; a Pupil, G. Roberts;
another Pupil, Cartia McChormac.

It has been revised a good many times since then, and although the play
has not been changed in the radical structure, the parts of the Mayor,
Servant, and Cripples are altogether new, and the rest is altered here and
there. It was written when our Society was having a hard fight for the
recognition of pure art in a community of which one half was buried in the
practical affairs of life, and the other half in politics and a propagandist
patriotism. I took the plot of it from a Middle Irish story about the demands
of the poets at the court of King Guaire, but twisted it about and revised
its moral that the poet might have the best of it. One of my fellow-playwrights
is going, I have hope, to take the other side and make a play that can be
played after it, as in Greece the farce followed the tragedy.   Notes, 23.

'The King's Threshold' . . . played October 7, 1903, . . . Cripple, P.
Colomb; a Court Lady, Honour Lavelle; another . . . , Maire NicShiubh-
laigh; a . . . , Cartia MacChormac.

It . . . life and . . . patriotism.   Notes, 28, 48.

'The King's Threshold' . . . cast: Seanchan . . Frank Fay / King Guaire
. . P. Kelly / Lord High Chamberlain . . Seumus O'Sullivan / Soldier . .
William Conroy / Monk . . S. Sheridan-Neill / Mayor . . William Fay / A
Cripple . . Patrick Colum / A Court Lady . . Honor Lavelle / Another Court
Lady . . Dora Melville / A Princess . . Sara Algood / Another Princess . .
Dora Gunning / Fedelm . . Maire ni Shiubhlaigh / A Servant . . P. Mac-
Shiubhlaigh / Another Servant . . P. Josephs / A Pupil . . G. Roberts /
Another Pupil . . Cartia MacCormac

It has been revised . . . patriotism.

Appendix IV. The Dates and Places of Performance of Plays, 32 ; Notes,
45.

'The King's Threshold' was first played [follows the version in 32, 45 with
the date '1911,' and two new paragraphs added after the word 'patriotism.']

When I wrote this play neither suffragette nor patriot had adopted the
hunger strike, nor had the hunger strike been used anywhere, so far as I
know, as a political weapon.

---

[1] The London printing.

I have given the play the tragic end I would have given it at the first, had not a friend advised me to 'write comedy and have a few happy moments in the theatre.' My friend meant that tragic emotion, depending as it does upon gradually deepening reverie, is so fragile, that it is shattered by a wrong movement or cadence, or even by a light in the wrong place.— 1922.   Notes, 69.

Upon the revival of this play at the Abbey Theatre a few weeks ago it was played with this new end. There were a few other changes. I had originally intended to end the play tragically and would have done so but for a friend who used to say 'O do write comedy & have a few happy moments in the Theatre.' My unhappy moments were because a tragic effect is very fragile and a wrong intonation, or even a wrong light or costume will spoil it all. However the play remained always of the nature of tragedy and so subject to vicissitude.

Note on the new end to 'The King's Threshold.'   65.

* * *

Variant spellings

Almhuim **19** ; *Almhuin* **20-97.**
Finnhua **19, 20** ; *Finula* **23-97.**

* * *

[See also the notes on *On Baile's Strand*, p. 526, *The Legendary and Mythological Foundation of the Plays and Poems*, p. 1282, *The Legendary and Mythological Foundation of the Plays*, p. 1283; *Glossary*, p. 1284; and *Prefaces to 23, 69*, pp. 1293, 1306.]

THE SHADOWY WATERS

(Acting Version)

1911

Persons in the Play

Forgael   Sailors

Aibric   Dectora

A mast and a great sail, a large tiller, a poop rising several feet above the stage, and from the overhanging stern a lanthorn hangs. The sea or sky is represented by a semicircular cloth of which nothing can be seen except a dark abyss. The persons move but little. Some sailors are discovered crouching by the sail. Forgael is asleep and Aibric standing by the tiller on the raised poop.

PRINTINGS   **24, 28** (Appendix III), **32** (Appendix I), **45** (Appendix), **48** (Appendix III), **69, 84, 89, 97**.

DATE   1906. **24**; [lacking] **28-69**.

DRAMATIS PERSONAE   [no heading] **24, 32**; [lacking] **28, 45, 48**.

STAGE DIRECTIONS   Scene. *The deck of an ancient ship. At the right of the stage is the mast, with a large square sail hiding a deal of the sky and sea on that side. The tiller is at the left of the stage; it is a long oar coming through an opening in the bulwark. The deck rises into a high poop behind the tiller, and the stern of the ship curves overhead. There is a stringed instrument upon the poop. All the woodwork is of dark green; and the sail is dark green, with a blue pattern upon it, having a little copper colour here and there. The sky and sea are dark blue. All the persons of the play are dressed in various tints of green and blue, the men with helmets and swords of copper, the woman with copper ornaments upon her dress. When the play opens there are four persons upon the deck. Aibric stands by the tiller. Forgael sleeps upon the raised portion of the deck. Two sailors are watching him.* **24**;

The scene is the same as in the text[1] *except that the sail is dull copper colour. The poop rises several . . . stern hangs a lanthorn with a greenish light. The sea . . .*

---

[1] 'The text' referred to is the text of the narrative poem 'The Shadowy Waters' that is in the main body of **32**.

1. *First Sailor*. It is long enough, and too long, Forgael
2.   has been bringing us through the waste places of the
3.   great sea.

4. *Second Sailor*. We did not meet with a ship to make a
5.   prey of these eight weeks, or any shore or island to
6.   plunder or to harry. It is a hard thing, age to be
7.   coming on me, and I not to get the chance of doing
8.   a robbery that would enable me to live quiet and
9.   honest to the end of my lifetime.

10. *First Sailor*. We are out since the new moon. What
11.   is worse again, it is the way we are in a ship, the
12.   barrels empty and my throat shrivelled with drought,
13.   and nothing to quench it but water only.

14. *Forgael* [*in his sleep*]. Yes; there, there; that hair that is
15.   the colour of burning.

16. *First Sailor*. Listen to him now, calling out in his sleep.

17. *Forgael* [*in his sleep*]. That pale forehead, that hair the
18.   colour of burning.

19. *First Sailor*. Some crazy dream he is in, and believe me
20.   it is no crazier than the thought he has waking. He
21.   is not the first that has had the wits drawn out from
22.   him through shadows and fantasies.

23. *Second Sailor*. That is what ails him. I have been thinking
24.   it this good while.

25. *First Sailor*. Do you remember that galley we sank at
26.   the time of the full moon?

---

abyss, for the stage is lighted by arclights (arc-lights **32, 45**) *so placed upon a bridge over the proscenium as to throw a perpendicular light upon the stage. The light is dim, and there are deep shadows which waver as if with the passage of clouds over the moon. The persons are dressed in blue and green, and move . . . .* **28-48**; *. . . lanthorn hanging. The . . . .* **69-89**.

TEXT   Title . . . Waters / Acting Version, / As first played at the Abbey Theatre, December 8th, 1906. **24**; Acting Version of (of / **45**) The Shadowy / Waters (Shadowy Waters **45**) **28, 45, 48**; . . . Waters / Acting Version **69**.

27. *Second Sailor.* I do. We were becalmed the same night,
28.   and he sat up there playing that old harp of his until
29.   the moon had set.

30. *First Sailor.* I was sleeping up there by the bulwark,
31.   and when I woke in the sound of the harp a change
32.   came over my eyes, and I could see very strange
33.   things. The dead were floating upon the sea yet, and
34.   it seemed as if the life that went out of every one
35.   of them had turned to the shape of a man-headed
36.   bird—grey they were, and they rose up of a sudden
37.   and called out with voices like our own, and flew
38.   away singing to the west. Words like this they were
39.   singing: 'Happiness beyond measure, happiness
40.   where the sun dies'.

41. *Second Sailor.* I understand well what they are doing.
42.   My mother used to be talking of birds of the sort.
43.   They are sent by the lasting watchers to lead men
44.   away from this world and its women to some place
45.   of shining women that cast no shadow, having lived
46.   before the making of the earth. But I have no mind
47.   to go following him to that place.

48. *First Sailor.* Let us creep up to him and kill him in his
49.   sleep.

50. *Second Sailor.* I would have made an end of him long
51.   ago, but that I was in dread of his harp. It is said
52.   that when he plays upon it he has power over all the
53.   listeners, with or without the body, seen or unseen,
54.   and any man that listens grows to be as mad as
55.   himself.

56. *First Sailor.* What way can he play it, being in his sleep?

57. *Second Sailor.* But who would be our captain then to
58.   make out a course from the Bear and the Polestar,
59.   and to bring us back home?

60. *First Sailor.* I have that thought out. We must have
61.   Aibric with us. He knows the constellations as well

---

44. . . . its woemen to . . . **24.**
57. . . . Captain . . .
58. . . . Pole-star, **24, 28, 48.**

62. as Forgael. He is a good hand with the sword. Join
63. with us; be our captain, Aibric. We are agreed to
64. put an end to Forgael, before he wakes. There is no
65. man but will be glad of it when it is done. Join with
66. us, and you will have the captain's share and profit.

67. *Aibric.* Silence! for you have taken Forgael's pay.

68. *First Sailor.* Little pay we have had this twelvemonth.
69. We would never have turned against him if he had
70. brought us, as he promised, into seas that would be
71. thick with ships. That was the bargain. What is the
72. use of knocking about and fighting as we do unless
73. we get the chance to drink more wine and kiss more
74. women than lasting peaceable men through their long
75. lifetime? You will be as good a leader as ever he was
76. himself, if you will but join us.

77. *Aibric.* And do you think that I will join myself
78. To men like you, and murder him who has been
79. My master from my earliest childhood up?
80. No! nor to a world of men like you
81. When Forgael's in the other scale. Come! come!
82. I'll answer to more purpose when you have drawn
83. That sword out of its scabbard.

  First Sailor.   You have awaked him.
84. We had best go, for we have missed this chance.

                [*Sailors go out.*

85. *Forgael.* Have the birds passed us? I could hear your
    voice,

86. But there were others.
  Aibric.   I have seen nothing pass.

---

63. . . . Captain, . . . **24, 28, 48.**
64. . . . Forgael before . . . **24.**
66. . . . Captain's . . . . **24, 28, 48.**
77. . . . myself. **69A.**
79. . . . up. **24.**
  2nd hemistich 83, and 84. [Printed as prose] **24-69.**
  Directions after 84. [lacking] **24-32, 48.**
85. . . . voice. **24-69.**
86. [set as two lines ending others. / pass.] **28, 48.**

87. *Forgael.* You are certain of it? I never wake from sleep
88.   But that I am afraid they may have passed;
89.   For they're my only pilots. I have not seen them
90.   For many days, and yet there must be many
91.   Dying at every moment in the world.

92. *Aibric.* They have all but driven you crazy, and already
93.   The sailors have been plotting for your death;
94.   Whatever has been cried into your ears
95.   Has lured you on to death.

   Forgael.   No; but they promised—

96. *Aibric.* I know their promises. You have told me all.
97.   They are to bring you to unheard-of passion,
98.   To some strange love the world knows nothing of,
99.   Some Ever-living woman as you think,
100.   One that can cast no shadow, being unearthly.
101.   But that's all folly. Turn the ship about,
102.   Sail home again, be some fair woman's friend;
103.   Be satisfied to live like other men,
104.   And drive impossible dreams away. The world
105.   Has beautiful women to please every man.

106. *Forgael.* But he that gets their love after the fashion
107.   Loves in brief longing and deceiving hope
108.   And bodily tenderness, and finds that even
109.   The bed of love, that in the imagination
110.   Had seemed to be the giver of all peace,
111.   Is no more than a wine-cup in the tasting,
112.   And as soon finished.

   Aibric.   All that ever loved
113.   Have loved that way—there is no other way.

---

87. . . . it. I . . .
88. . . . passed. **24, 28, 48.**
93. . . . death, **24-45** ; . . . death **48.**
94. And all the birds have cried . . . ears, (ears **32, 45**) **24-48** ; . . . cried
     unto your . . . **69A.**
97. . . . unheard of . . . ,
98. . . . of. **24, 28, 48.**
99. . . . ever-living . . . , **24, 32, 45** ; . . . ever-living . . . think. **28, 48.**
100. . . . shadows, ... **24.**
111. . . . wine cup . . . , **24-32, 48.**

114. *Forgael.* Yet never have two lovers kissed but they
115.   Believed there was some other near at hand,
116.   And almost wept because they could not find it.

117. *Aibric.* When they have twenty years; in middle life
118.   They take a kiss for what a kiss is worth,
119.   And let the dream go by.

        Forgael.   It's not a dream,
120.   But the reality that makes our passion
121.   As a lamp shadow—no—no lamp, the sun.
122.   What the world's million lips are thirsting for
123.   Must be substantial somewhere.

        Aibric.   I have heard the Druids
124.   Mutter such things as they awake from trance.
125.   It may be that the dead have lit upon it,
126.   Or those that never lived; no mortal can.

127. *Forgael.* I only of all living men shall find it.

---

122.   ... for, 24-69.
125.   ... the ever-living know it— 24.
126.   No mortal can.
        Forgael.   It may be that you have hit it, 24; ... lived, no
       .... 28, 48.
126a. And there's no fountain of reality
126b. But trance alone, that we should be at peace
126c. Could we but give us wholly to the dreams,
126d. And get into their world that to the sense
126e. Is shadow, and not linger wretchedly
126f. Among substantial things; for it is dreams
126g. That lift us to the flowing, changing world
126h. That the heart longs for. What is love itself,
126l. Even though it be the lightest of light love,
126j. But dreams that hurry from beyond the world
126k. To make low laughter more than meat and drink,
126l. Though it but set us sighing—Aibric, Aibric
126m. Could we but mix ourselves into a dream,
126n. Not in its image on the mirror.
        Aibric.   While
126o. We're in the body that's impossible.
126p. None but the dead or those that never lived
126q. Can know that ecstacy. At the dream's end
126r. The dreamer wakes to know that he is wretched. 24.

128. *Aibric*. Then seek it in the habitable world,
129.   Or leap into that sea and end a journey
130.   That has no other end.

    Forgael.   I cannot answer.
131.   I can see nothing plain; all's mystery.
132.   Yet sometimes there's a torch inside my head
133.   That makes all clear, but when the light is gone
134.   I have but images, analogies,
135.   The mystic bread, the sacramental wine,
136.   The red rose where the two shafts of the cross,
137.   Body and soul, waking and sleep, death, life,
138.   Whatever meaning ancient allegorists
139.   Have settled on, are mixed into one joy.
140.   For what's the rose but that? miraculous cries,
141.   Old stories about mystic marriages,
142.   Impossible truths? But when the torch is lit
143.   All that is impossible is certain,
144.   I plunge in the abyss.   *[Sailors come in.*

145. *First Sailor*. Look there! there in the mist! A ship of
        spices!

146. *Second Sailor*. We would not have noticed her but for
147.   the sweet smell through the air. Ambergris and
148.   sandalwood, and all the herbs the witches bring from
149.   the sunrise.

150. *First Sailor*. No; but opoponax and cinnamon.

151. *Forgael* [*taking the tiller from Aibric*]. The Ever-living have
152.   kept my bargain; they have paid you on the nail.

153. *Aibric*. Take up that rope to make her fast while we
154.   are plundering her.

---

130. [set as two lines ending end. / answer.] **24, 28, 48.**
132. Yet, sometimes . . . **24-69.**
140. . . . that; miraculous . . . , **24, 28, 48.**
142. . . . truths. But . . . **24, 28, 48.**
145. . . . there! There . . . spices. **24-32, 48 ;** . . . spcies. **45, 69.**
150. . . . opoponax . . . . **69A.**
151. . . . ever-living . . . **24-48.**
152. . . . bargain for me, and paid . . . . **24, 28, 48.**

155. *First Sailor.* There is a king on her deck and a queen.
156. Where there is one woman it is certain there will be
157. others.

158. *Aibric.* Speak lower or they'll hear.

159. *First Sailor.* They cannot hear; they are too much taken
160. up with one another. Look! he has stooped down
161. and kissed her on the lips.

162. *Second Sailor.* When she finds out we have as good men
163. aboard she may not be too sorry in the end.

164. *First Sailor.* She will be as dangerous as a wild cat.
165. These queens think more of the riches and the great
166. name they get by marriage than of a ready hand and
167. a strong body.

168. *Second Sailor.* There is nobody is natural but a robber.
169. That is the reason the whole world goes tottering
170. about upon its bandy legs.

171. *Aibric.* Run upon them now, and overpower the crew
172. while yet asleep.
    [*Sailors and Aibric go out. The clashing of swords and confused voices are heard from the other ship, which cannot be seen because of the sail.*

173. *Forgael* [*who has remained at the tiller*]. There! there! They
       come! Gull, gannet, or diver,
174. But with a man's head, or a fair woman's.
175. They hover over the masthead awhile
176. To wait their friends, but when their friends have
       come
177. They'll fly upon that secret way of theirs,
178. One—and one—a couple—five together.

---

155. . . . deck, and . . . . **24-32, 48.**
171. Run at them . . . **24, 28, 48.**
       Directions after 172. [. . . *swords is heard* . . . .] **24.**
173. *Forgael.* [*Who* . . .]. There! There! They . . . , **24, 28, 48.**
177. . . . their's, **24.**
178a. And I will hear them talking in a minute.
178b. Yes! voices; but I do not catch the words. **24.**

179.   And now they all wheel suddenly and fly
180.   To the other side, and higher in the air,
181.   They've gone up thither, friend's run up by
            friend;
182.   They've gone to their beloved ones in the air,
183.   In the waste of the high air, that they may wander
184.   Among the windy meadows of the dawn.
185.   But why are they still waiting? Why are they
186.   Circling and circling over the masthead?
187.   Ah! now they all look down—they'll speak of me
188.   What the Ever-living put into their minds,
189.   And of that shadowless unearthly woman
190.   At the world's end. I hear the message now,
191.   But it's all mystery. There's one that cries,
192.   'From love and hate'. Before the sentence ends
193.   Another breaks upon it with a cry,
194.   'From love and death and out of sleep and waking'.
195.   And with the cry another cry is mixed,
196.   'What can we do, being shadows?' All mystery,
197.   And I am drunken with a dizzy light.
198.   But why do they still hover overhead?
199.   Why are you circling there? Why do you linger?
200.   Why do you not run to your desire,
201.   Now that you have happy winged bodies?
202.   Being too busy in the air, and the high air,
203.   They cannot hear my voice. But why that circling?
                    [*The Sailors have returned. Dectora is with them.*
204.   [*Turning and seeing her.*] Why are you standing with
            your eyes upon me?

180a.   And now a laggard with a woman's head **24.**
181.   Comes crying, "I have run upon the sword, **24**; . . . friend. **28, 48.**
182.   I have fled to my beloved in . . . , **24**; . . . beloved in . . . , **28, 48.**
183.   . . . , that we may . . .
184.   . . . dawn." **24.**
188.   . . . ever-living . . . , **24-48.**
190.   . . . now. **24-69.**
196.   . . . do being . . . mystery. **24**; . . . do being . . . , **28, 48.**
200.   . . . desire?
201.   . . . bodies. **24-32, 48.**
        Directions after 203. [*. . . them. She is dressed in pale green, with copper
        ornaments on her dress, and has a copper crown upon her head. Her hair is
        dull red.*] **24-48.**
204.   *Forgael* [*Turning* (*turning* **32**) . . . ? **24-32, 45** (1911), **48.**

205.   You are not the world's core. O no, no, no!
206.   That cannot be the meaning of the birds.
207.   You are not its core. My teeth are in the world,
208.   But have not bitten yet.

Dectora.   I am a queen,
209.   And ask for satisfaction upon these
210.   Who have slain my husband and laid hands upon me.

211. *Forgael.* I'd set my hopes on one that had no shadow:—
212.   Where do you come from? who brought you to this
            place?
213.   Why do you cast a shadow? Answer me that.

214. *Dectora.* Would that the storm that overthrew my ships,
215.   And drowned the treasures of nine conquered nations,
216.   And blew me hither to my lasting sorrow,
217.   Had drowned me also. But, being yet alive,
218.   I ask a fitting punishment for all
219.   That raised their hands against him.

Forgael.   There are some
220.   That weigh and measure all in these waste seas—
221.   They that have all the wisdom that's in life,
222.   And all that prophesying images
223.   Made of dim gold rave out in secret tombs;
224.   They have it that the plans of kings and queens
225.   Are dust on the moth's wing; that nothing matters
226.   But laughter and tears—laughter, laughter and tears—
227.   That every man should carry his own soul
228.   Upon his shoulders.

Dectora.   You've nothing but wild words,
229.   And I would know if you would give me vengeance.

---

205.   . . . . Oh . . . ! **45, 69.**
        Directions after 210. [*Breaking loose from the Sailors who are holding her*]. **24.**
211.   Let go my hands.
        Forgael.   Why do you cast a shadow? **24** ; . . . shadow,— **28, 32, 48.**
212.   . . . ? Who . . . ?
213.   They would not send me one that casts a shadow. **24.**
214.   Would that storm . . . , **69A.**
226.   . . . , laughter, and tears **24-32, 48.**

230. *Forgael.* When she finds out that I'll not let her go—
231.   When she knows that.

   Dectora.   What is that you are muttering?
232.   That you'll not let me go? I am a queen.

233. *Forgael.* Although you are more beautiful than any,
234.   I almost long that it were possible,
235.   But if I were to put you on that ship,
236.   With sailors that were sworn to do your will,
237.   And you had spread a sail for home, a wind
238.   Would rise of a sudden, or a wave so huge
239.   It had washed among the stars and put them out,
240.   And beat the bulwark of your ship on mine,
241.   Until you stood before me on the deck—
242.   As now.

   Dectora. Has wandering in these desolate seas
243.   And listening to the cry of wind and wave
244.   Driven you mad?

   Forgael.   But, queen, I am not mad.

245. *Dectora.* And yet you say the water and the wind
246.   Would rise against me.

   Forgael.   No, I am not mad—
247.   If it be not that hearing messages
248.   From lasting watchers that outlive the moon
249.   At the most quiet midnight is to be stricken.

250. *Dectora.* And did those watchers bid you take me
       captive?

251. *Forgael.* Both you and I are taken in the net.
252.   It was their hands that plucked the winds awake

---

230. ... that I will not . . .— **24, 28, 48.**
231. ... muttering— **24-48.**
238. ... huge, **24-69.**
242. ... now.
   Dectora. Does wandering . . . **24-69.**
244. Bring madness?
   Forgael.   Queen, I . . . . **24-69.**
248. ... moon, **24, 28, 48.**

253. And blew you hither; and their mouths have
   promised
254. I shall have love in their immortal fashion.
255. They gave me that old harp of the nine spells
256. That is more mighty than the sun and moon,
257. Or than the shivering casting-net of the stars,
258. That none might take you from me.

  Dectora [*first trembling back from the mast where the harp is,*
    and then laughing].   For a moment
259. Your raving of a message and a harp
260. More mighty than the stars half troubled me.
261. But all that's raving. Who is there can compel
262. The daughter and granddaughter of a king
263. To be his bedfellow?

  Forgael.   Until your lips
264. Have called me their beloved, I'll not kiss them.

265. *Dectora*. My husband and my king died at my feet,
266. And yet you talk of love.

  Forgael.   The movement of time
267. Is shaken in these seas, and what one does
268. One moment has no might upon the moment
269. That follows after.

  Dectora.   I understand you now.
270. You have a Druid craft of wicked music,
271. Wrung from the cold women of the sea—
272. A magic that can call a demon up,
273. Until my body give you kiss for kiss.

274. *Forgael*. Your soul shall give the kiss.

  Dectora.   I am not afraid
275. While there's a rope to run into a noose
276. Or wave to drown. But I have done with words,
277. And I would have you look into my face

---

262. . . . grand-daughter . . . kings **24, 28, 48** ; . . . grand-daughter . . .
   32 ; . . . grandaughter . . . **45.**
270. . . . wicked sound. **24-69.**
272. . . . up. **24, 28, 48.**
274. . . . afraid, **24-69.**

278.   And know that it is fearless.

          Forgael.   Do what you will,
279.   For neither I nor you can break a mesh
280.   Of the great golden net that is about us.

281. *Dectora.* There's nothing in the world that's worth a
            fear.
          [She passes Forgael and stands for a moment looking into his face.
282.   I have good reason for that thought.
                        [She runs suddenly on to the raised part of the poop.
                                                And now
283.   I can put fear away as a queen should.
                        [She mounts on the bulwark, and turns towards Forgael.
284.   Fool, fool! Although you have looked into my face
285.   You did not see my purpose. I shall have gone
286.   Before a hand can touch me.

          Forgael [folding his arms].   My hands are still;
287.   The Ever-living hold us. Do what you will,
288.   You cannot leap out of the golden net.

289. *First Sailor.* There is no need for you to drown. Give
290.   us our pardon and we will bring you home on your
291.   own ship, and make an end of this man that is leading
292.   us to death.

293. *Dectora.* I promise it.

          Aibric.   I stand upon his side.
294.   I'd strike a blow for him to give him time
295.   To cast his dreams away.

296. *First Sailor.* He has put a sudden darkness over the
297.   moon.

298. *Dectora.* Nine swords with handles of rhinoceros horn

---

278.   ... that is it fearless. ... , **28.**
        Directions after 283.   [... *bulwark and* ....] **24-32, 48.**
287.   ... ever-living ... , **24-48.**
293.   [set as two lines ending it. / side.] **24, 28, 48 ; ....**
                                        I am on his .... **24-45, 69.**
294.   ... time. **69A.**

299.   To him that strikes him first!

300. *First Sailor.* I will strike him first. No! for that music
301.   of his might put a beast's head upon my shoulders,
302.   or it may be two heads and they devouring one
303.   another.

304. *Dectora.* I'll give a golden galley full of fruit
305.   That has the heady flavour of new wine
306.   To him that wounds him to the death.

307. *First Sailor.* I'll strike at him. His spells, when he dies,
308.   will die with him and vanish away.

309. *Second Sailor.* I'll strike at him.

    The Others.   And I! And I! And I!
                                 [Forgael plays upon the harp.

310. *First Sailor [falling into a dream].* It is what they are
311.   saying, there is some person dead in the other ship;
312.   we have to go and wake him. They did not say what
313.   way he came to his end, but it was sudden.

314. *Second Sailor.* You are right, you are right. We have to
315.   go to that wake.

316. *Dectora.* He has flung a Druid spell upon the air,
317.   And set you dreaming.

---

   299.   . . . first. **24-32, 48.**
   300.   . . . . No! he has
   301.   brought down fire out of the moon; he is holding it
301a.   between us.
301b.   *Second Sailor.* Fire from the moon. If that strikes
301c.   into us it will burn out the strength and the marrow
301d.   from our bones. **24.**
302-303. [lacking] **24.**
   307.   *Second Sailor.* I'll . . . spells **24, 28, 48.**
   309.   . . . him whatever fire from **24**; [set as two lines ending him. /
            I!] **28-69**; I will . . . ! **48.**
309a.   the moon he is holding up to save him.
309b.   *The Others.* And I! And I! And I! **24.**
          Directions after 309. [lacking] **24, 28, 48.**
   311.   saying. There . . .;
   312.   We . . . **24.**

318. *Second Sailor.* What way can we raise a keen, not know-
319.   ing what name to call him by?

320. *First Sailor.* Come on to his ship. His name will come
321.   to mind in a moment. All I know is he died a
322.   thousand years ago, and was never yet waked.

323. *Second Sailor.* How can we wake him having no ale?

324. *First Sailor.* I saw a skin of ale aboard her—a pigskin
325.   of brown ale.

326. *Third Sailor.* Come to the ale, a pigskin of brown ale,
327.   a goatskin of yellow!

328. *First Sailor* [*singing*]. Brown ale and yellow; yellow and
329.   brown ale; a goatskin of yellow!

330. *All* [*singing*]. Brown ale and yellow; yellow and brown
331.   ale!   [*Sailors go out.*

332. *Dectora.* Protect me now, gods that my people swear by!
        [*Aibric has risen from the ground where he had fallen. He has begun
        looking for his sword as if in a dream.*

333. *Aibric.* Where is my sword that fell out of my hand
334.   When I first heard the news? Ah, there it is!
        [*He goes dreamily towards the sword, but Dectora runs at it and
        takes it up before he can reach it.*

335. [*Sleepily.*] Queen, give it me.

     Dectora.   No, I have need of it.

336. *Aibric.* Why do you need a sword? But you may keep it.
337.   Now that he's dead I have no need of it,
338.   For everything is gone.

     A Sailor [*calling from the other ship*]. Come hither, Aibric,
339.   And tell me who it is that we are waking.

---

324.   . . . pig-skin . . . . **69**.
327.   . . . yellow. **24-32, 48**.
329.   . . . yellow. **24-32, 48**.
332.   . . . , gods, that . . . by. (by! **32, 45, 69**) **24-69**.
335.   *Aibric* [*sleepily.*] . . . it, **24** ; *Aibric* [*sleepily.*] . . . . **28-48**.
336.   . . . it, **24-84**.

340. *Aibric* [*half to Dectora, half to himself*]. What name had
         that dead king? Arthur of Britain?

341.   No, no—not Arthur. I remember now.

342.   It was golden-armed Iollan, and he died

343.   Broken-hearted, having lost his queen

344.   Through wicked spells. That is not all the tale,

345.   For he was killed. O! O! O! O! O! O!

346.   For golden-armed Iollan has been killed.

         [*He goes out. While he has been speaking, and through part of what
         follows, one hears the singing of the Sailors from the other ship.
         Dectora stands with the sword lifted in front of Forgael. He changes
         the tune.*

347. *Dectora.* I will end all your magic on the instant.

         [*Her voice becomes dreamy, and she lowers the sword slowly, and
         finally lets it fall. She spreads out her hair. She takes off her crown
         and lays it upon the deck.*

348.   The sword is to lie beside him in the grave.

349.   It was in all his battles. I will spread my hair,

350.   And wring my hands, and wail him bitterly,

351.   For I have heard that he was proud and laughing,

352.   Blue-eyed, and a quick runner on bare feet,

353.   And that he died a thousand years ago.

354.   O! O! O! O!

                   [*Forgael changes the tune*]
                   But no, that is not it.

355.   I knew him well, and while I heard him laughing

356.   They killed him at my feet. O! O! O! O!

357.   For golden-armed Iollan that I loved.

358.   But what is it that made me say I loved him?

359.   It was that harper put it in my thoughts,

360.   But it is true. Why did they run upon him,

361.   And beat the golden helmet with their swords?

362. *Forgael.* Do you not know me, lady? I am he

363.   That you are weeping for.

---

343. Brokenhearted, . . . **24-48, 69E.**
         Directions after 346. [. . . *follows* (*follows,* **28, 48**) *one* . . . *Forgael.*]
         24, 28, 48.

354. O! O! O! [*Forgael* . . .]
                           But . . . . **24-69.**

358. . . . made him say . . . ? **97A.**

Dectora.   No, for he is dead.

364. O! O! O! O! for golden-armed Iollan.

365. *Forgael.* It was so given out, but I will prove
366. That the grave-diggers in a dreamy frenzy
367. Have buried nothing but my golden arms.
368. Listen to that low-laughing string of the moon
369. And you will recollect my face and voice,
370. For you have listened to me playing it
371. These thousand years.
      [*He starts up, listening to the birds. The harp slips from his hands, and remains leaning against the bulwarks behind him.*
                              What are the birds at there?
372. Why are they all a-flutter of a sudden?
373. What are you calling out above the mast?
374. If railing and reproach and mockery
375. Because I have awakened her to love
376. By magic strings, I'll make this answer to it:
377. Being driven on by voices and by dreams
378. That were clear messages from the Ever-living,
379. I have done right. What could I but obey?
380. And yet you make a clamour of reproach.

381. *Dectora* [*laughing*]. Why, it's a wonder out of reckoning
382. That I should keen him from the full of the moon
383. To the horn, and he be hale and hearty.

384. *Forgael.* How have I wronged her now that she is merry?
385. But no, no, no! your cry is not against me.
386. You know the councils of the Ever-living,
387. And all the tossing of your wings is joy,
388. And all that murmuring's but a marriage song;
389. But if it be reproach, I answer this:
390. There is not one among you that made love
391. By any other means. You call it passion,
392. Consideration, generosity;
393. But it was all deceit, and flattery

---

364. O! O! O! for .... **24-69.**
      Directions in 371. [... *him. The light goes out of it*]. **24, 28, 48.**
376. My magic ...: **24, 28, 48.**
378. ... ever-living, **24-48.**
386. ... ever-living, **24-48.**

394.   To win a woman in her own despite,
395.   For love is war, and there is hatred in it;
396.   And if you say that she came willingly—

397. *Dectora.* Why do you turn away and hide your face
398.   That I would look upon for ever?

Forgael.   My grief!

399. *Dectora.* Have I not loved you for a thousand years?

400. *Forgael.* I never have been golden-armed Iollan.

401. *Dectora.* I do not understand. I know your face
402.   Better than my own hands.

Forgael.   I have deceived you
403.   Out of all reckoning.

Dectora.   Is it not true
404.   That you were born a thousand years ago,
405.   In islands where the children of Aengus wind
406.   In happy dances under a windy moon,
407.   And that you'll bring me there?

Forgael.   I have deceived you;
408.   I have deceived you utterly.

Dectora.   How can that be?
409.   Is it that though your eyes are full of love
410.   Some other woman has a claim on you,
411.   And I've but half?

Forgael.   O no!

Dectora.   And if there is,
412.   If there be half a hundred more, what matter?
413.   I'll never give another thought to it;
414.   No, no, nor half a thought; but do not speak.
415.   Women are hard and proud and stubborn-hearted,
416.   Their heads being turned with praise and flattery;
417.   And that is why their lovers are afraid

---

397. . . . face,
398. . . . grief. **24-69.**
407. . . . me to her?
      Forgael.   I . . .; **24.**
411. . . . ?
      Forgael. Oh, no! . . . , **24-69.**

418.   To tell them a plain story.

Forgael.   That's not the story;
419.   But I have done so great a wrong against you,
420.   There is no measure that it would not burst.
421.   I will confess it all.

Dectora.   What do I care,
422.   Now that my body has begun to dream,
423.   And you have grown to be a burning coal
424.   In the imagination and intellect?
425.   If something that's most fabulous were true—
426.   If you had taken me by magic spells,
427.   And killed a lover or husband at my feet—
428.   I would not let you speak, for I would know
429.   That it was yesterday and not to-day
430.   I loved him; I would cover up my ears,
431.   As I am doing now. [*A pause.*] Why do you weep?

432.   *Forgael.* I weep because I've nothing for your eyes
433.   But desolate waters and a battered ship.

434.   *Dectora.* O, why do you not lift your eyes to mine?

435.   *Forgael.* I weep—I weep because bare night's above,
436.   And not a roof of ivory and gold.

437.   *Dectora.* I would grow jealous of the ivory roof,
438.   And strike the golden pillars with my hands.
439.   I would that there was nothing in the world
440.   But my beloved—that night and day had perished,
441.   And all that is and all that is to be,
442.   And all that is not the meeting of our lips.

443.   *Forgael.* Why do you turn your eyes upon bare night?
444.   Am I to fear the waves, or is the moon
445.   My enemy?

Dectora.   I looked upon the moon,
446.   Longing to knead and pull it into shape
447.   That I might lay it on your head as a crown.

---

423.   . . . burning sod **24.**
434.   Oh, . . . ? **45, 69.**
442.   All that . . . . . **24-48.**
443.   I too, I too. Why do you look away? **24.**

448.   But now it is your thoughts that wander away,
449.   For you are looking at the sea. Do you not know
450.   How great a wrong it is to let one's thought
451.   Wander a moment when one is in love?
        [*He has moved away. She follows him. He is looking out over the sea, shading his eyes.*

452.   Why are you looking at the sea?

Forgael.   Look there!
453.   There where the cloud creeps up upon the moon.

454.   *Dectora.* What is there but a troop of ash-grey birds
455.   That fly into the west?
        [*The scene darkens, but there is a ray of light upon the figures.*

Forgael.   But listen, listen!

456.   *Dectora.* What is there but the crying of the birds?

457.   *Forgael.* If you'll but listen closely to that crying
458.   You'll hear them calling out to one another
459.   With human voices.

Dectora.   Clouds have hid the moon.
460.   The birds cry out, what can I do but tremble?

461.   *Forgael.* They have been circling over our heads in the air,
462.   But now that they have taken to the road
463.   We have to follow, for they are our pilots;
464.   They're crying out. Can you not hear their cry?—
465.   'There is a country at the end of the world
466.   Where no child's born but to outlive the moon.'
        [*The Sailors come in with Aibric. They carry torches.*

467.   *Aibric.* We have lit upon a treasure that's so great

---

453.   [lacking] **24.**
        Directions in 455.   [lacking] **24.**
459.   . . . voices.
        Dectora.   O, I can hear them now
460.   What are they? Unto what country do they fly? **24.**
463.   . . . pilots, **97A.**
464.   . . . cry— **24-32, 48.**
        Directions after 466.   [. . . *Aibric. They are in great excitement*]. **24.**

468. Imagination cannot reckon it.
469. The hold is full—boxes of precious spice,
470. Ivory images with amethyst eyes,
471. Dragons with eyes of ruby. The whole ship
472. Flashes as if it were a net of herrings.
473. Let us return to our own country, Forgael,
474. And spend it there. Have you not found this queen?
475. What more have you to look for on the seas?

476. *Forgael.* I cannot—I am going on to the end.
477. As for this woman, I think she is coming with me.

478. *Aibric.* Speak to him, lady, and bid him turn the ship.
479. He knows that he is taking you to death;
480. He cannot contradict me.

   Dectora.   **Is that true?**

481. *Forgael.* I do not know for certain.

   Dectora.   **Carry me**
482. To some sure country, some familiar place.
483. Have we not everything that life can give
484. In having one another?

   Forgael.   **How could I rest**
485. If I refused the messengers and pilots
486. With all those sights and all that crying out?

---

481. . . . certain, but I know
481a. That I have the best of pilots.
   Aibric.   **Shadows, illusions,**
481b. That the shape-changers, the ever-laughing ones,
481c. The immortal mockers have cast into his mind,
481d. Or called before his eyes.
   Dectora.   **O carry me 24.**
486a. *Dectora.* But I will cover up your eyes and ears,
486b. That you may never hear the cry of the birds,
486c. Or look upon them.
   Forgael.   **Were they but lowlier**
486d. I'd do your will, but they are too high—too high.
486e. *Dectora.* Being too high, their heady prophecies
486f. But harry us with hopes that come to nothing,
486g. Because we are not proud, imperishable,
486h. Alone and winged.
   Forgael.   **Our love shall be like theirs**
486i. When we have put their changeless image on. **24.**

487. *Dectora*. I am a woman, I die at every breath.

488. *Aibric [to the Sailors]*. To the other ship, for there's no
               help in words.

489. And I will follow you and cut the rope

490. When I have said farewell to this man here,

491. For neither I nor any living man

492. Will look upon his face again.
            [*Sailors go out, leaving one torch perhaps in a torch-holder on the
            bulwark.*

            Forgael [to Dectora].   Go with him,

493. For he will shelter you and bring you home.

494. *Aibric [taking Forgael's hand]*. I'll do it for his sake.

      Dectora.   No. Take this sword

495. And cut the rope, for I go on with Forgael.

496. *Aibric*. Farewell! Farewell!
                              [*He goes out. The light grows stronger.*

      Dectora.   The sword is in the rope—

497. The rope's in two—it falls into the sea,

498. It whirls into the foam. O ancient worm,

499. Dragon that loved the world and held us to it,

500. You are broken, you are broken. The world drifts
               away,

501. And I am left alone with my beloved,

502. Who cannot put me from his sight for ever.

503. We are alone for ever, and I laugh,

504. Forgael, because you cannot put me from you.

505. The mist has covered the heavens, and you and I

506. Shall be alone for ever. We two—this crown—

507. I half remember. It has been in my dreams.

508. Bend lower, O king, that I may crown you with it.

509. O flower of the branch, O bird among the leaves,

510. O silver fish that my two hands have taken

487a. *Aibric*. Let the birds scatter for the tree is broken **24**.
  488. And there's . . . words. [*To the Sailors*]. To the other ship, **24**; . . .
         words, **28, 32, 48**.
         Directions in 492. [. . . *out*]. **24**.
  494. [set as two lines ending sake. / sword] **28, 48**.
         Directions in 496. [. . . *out*]. **24, 28, 48**.
  496. [set as two lines ending Farewell! / rope—] **28, 48**.

511. Out of the running stream, O morning star,
512. Trembling in the blue heavens like a white fawn
513. Upon the misty border of the wood,
514. Bend lower, that I may cover you with my hair,
515. For we will gaze upon this world no longer.

[The harp begins to burn as with fire.

516. *Forgael [gathering Dectora's hair about him].* Beloved, hav-
      ing dragged the net about us,
517. And knitted mesh to mesh, we grow immortal;
518. And that old harp awakens of itself
519. To cry aloud to the grey birds, and dreams,
520. That have had dreams for father, live in us.

THE END

Directions after 515. [*The scene darkens, and the harp once more begins
      . . . .*] 24.
520. . . . fathers, ... **24, 28, 48.**

NOTES

[These notes refer to both the narrative poem and the play. They cannot be completely disentangled. *Ed.*]

I began 'The Shadowy Waters' when I was a boy, and when I published a version of it six or seven years ago, the plot had been so often re-arranged and was so overgrown with symbolical ideas that the poem was obscure and vague. It found its way on to the stage more or less by accident, for our people had taken it as an exercise on the speaking of verse, and it pleased a few friends, though it must have bewildered and bored the greater portion of the audience. The present version is practically a new poem, and is, I believe, sufficiently simple, appealing to no knowledge more esoteric than is necessary for the understanding of any of the more characteristic love poems of Shelley or of Petrarch. If the audience will understand it as a fairy-tale, and not look too anxiously for a meaning, all will be well.

Once upon a time, when herons built their nests in old men's beards, Forgael, a Sea-King of ancient Ireland, was promised by certain human-headed birds love of a supernatural intensity and happiness. These birds were the souls of the dead, and he followed them over seas towards the sunset, where their final rest is. By means of a magic harp, he could call them about him when he would and listen to their speech. His friend Aibric, and the sailors of his ship, thought him mad, or that this mysterious happiness could come after death only, and that he and they were being lured to destruction. Presently they captured a ship, and found a beautiful woman upon it, and Forgael subdued her and his own rebellious sailors by the sound of his harp. The sailors fled upon the other ship, and Forgael and the woman drifted on alone following the birds, awaiting death and what comes after, or some mysterious transformation of the flesh, an embodiment of every lover's dream.

The scenery and the lighting have been arranged by Mr. Robert Gregory.

The Arrow. No. 2, Nov. 24, 1906   W.B.Y.

* * *

The Shadowy Waters. The first version of 'The Shadowy Waters' was first performed on 14 January, 1904, in the Molesworth Hall, Dublin, by the Irish National Theatre Society, and with the following players in the principal parts: Forgael, F. Fay; Aibric, Shamus O'Sullivan; Dectora, Maire MacShiubhlaigh. Its production was an accident, for in the first instance I had given it to the company that they might have something for practice in the speaking of my sort of blank verse till I had a better play finished. It played badly enough, but a little better than I had feared; and as I had been in America, when it was first played, I got it played again privately, and gave it to Miss Farr for a theosophical convention, that I might discover how to set it to rights as a stage play. I hope I have set it to rights now, and that if it finds an audience familiar with the longing of a lover for impossible things, and longings that are like his, it will hold the attention and have some pleasure in it for the players. I have not yet seen this new version played, but have rehearsed it, and Mr. Robert Gregory has designed the boat and sail. The colours of all will be as at the first performance, dark blue and dark green, but for Dectora a lighter green against the darker tints in sky and boat, with some glimmer of copper here and there, and the lighting a not very bright moonlight. The effect of this monotony of colour was to my eyes beautiful, and made the players seem like people in a dream. I have described these colours a little in the stage directions, not because I think of them as a necessary part of the play, but because it is necessary for some remote and decorative picture of the action, to float up into the mind's eye of the reader, who must imagine some sort of a stage scenery. When we began to get together the properties in this new version, the stage carpenter found it very difficult to make the crescent-shaped harp that was to burn with fire; and besides, no matter how well he made the frame, there was no way of making the strings take fire. I had, therefore, to give up the harp for a sort of psaltery, a little like the psaltery Miss Farr speaks to, where the strings could be slits covered with glass or gelatine on the surface of a shallow and perhaps semi-transparent box; and besides, it amused one to picture, in the centre of a myth, the instrument of our new art. This necessitated changing the lines where the word 'harp' occurred as follows:—

Instead of the lines

> 'Were't not
> That there is magic in that harp of his,'

read

> 'Were't not
> That there is magic, or a Druid life
> Hidden in that stringed instrument of his.'

And instead of the lines from

> 'He has caught the crescent moon,'

down to

> 'If we strike,'

read

> 'He has called a creeping fire out of the moon
> And carries it between us.
>
> *Second Sailor.*   A moony fire
> Is crawling in the flame that it may leap
> Into our bones and burn them to the marrow.'

And instead of the line

> 'It was that harper put it in my thoughts,'

read

> 'It was that plucker of the strings that made me.'

And in the last speech, instead of the line
                'And that old harp awakens of itself,'
read
                'And now the strings awaken of themselves.'

There is no reason for objecting to a mechanical effect when it represents some material thing, becomes a symbol, a player, as it were. One permits it in obedience to the same impulse that has made religious men decorate with jewels and embroidery the robes of priests and hierophants, even until the robe, stiffened and weighted, seems more important than the man who carries it. He has become a symbol, and his robe has become a symbol of something incapable of direct expression, something that is superhuman. If the harp cannot suggest some power that no actor could represent by sheer acting, for the more acting the more human life, the enchanting of so many people by it will seem impossible. Perhaps very wonderful music might do that if the audience were musicians, but lacking the music and that audience it is better to appeal to the eye. The play will, I hope, be acted as on its first production, with a quiet gravity and a kind of rhythmic movement, and a very scrupulous cherishing of the music of the verse. The 'O O O' of the lamentation will be sung as Miss Farr sings the 'Ochones' in her recitation of 'The Lament of Emer.'   **23.**

The first version . . . January 14th, 1904, . . . , Dublin, with the . . . : Forgael . . Frank Fay / Aibric . . Seumas O'Sullivan / Dectora . . Maire ni Shiubhlaigh

Its production . . . might have some practice . . . verse until I . . . enough from the point of view of any ordinary playgoer, but pleased many of my friends; and as I had . . . America when it was played, . . . Theosophical Convention, . . . how to make a better play of it. I then completely rewrote it in the form it has in the text of this book, but this version had once again to be condensed and altered for its production in Dublin, 1906. Mr. Sinclair took the part of Aibric, and Miss Darragh that of Dectora, while Mr. Frank Fay was Forgael as before. It owed a considerable portion of what success it met with both in its new and old form to a successful colour scheme and to dreamy movements and intonations on the part of the players. The scenery for its performance in 1906 was designed by Mr. Robert Gregory.
                                    Appendix IV, **32.**

The . . . Waters. The . . . on January 14, 1904, with the . . . parts:—Forgael, F. J. Fay; Aibric, Seumas O'Sullivan; Dectora, Maire . . . .

Its production [follows the version in **32** except that 'was played' is 'was produced'].   Notes, **45.**

The first version . . . January 14, 1904, . . . , Dublin, with the following . . . parts: Forgael, F. Fay; Aibric, Seumas O'Sullivan; Dectora, Maire Nic Shiubhlaigh. Its . . . might have some practice . . . America when . . . privately and . . . convention that . . . set it aright as a play. I then completely rewrote it in the form that it has in the text of this book, but this version had once againt to be condensed and altered for its production in Dublin on November 28, 1906. Mr. Sinclair then took the part of Aibric and Miss Darragh that of Dectora, while Mr. F. Fay was Forgael, as before. The scenery was designed by Mr. Robert Gregory.   Appendix II, **28, 48.**

This version of the longer play which is in *Later Poems* was first played in Dublin at the Abbey Theatre in 1906. Mr. Sinclair took the part of Aibric, Mr. Frank Fay that of Forgael, while Miss Darragh played that of Dectora. The scenery with its decorated boat and sail in green and gold and copper was designed by Mr. Robert Gregory.   Notes, **69.**

*   *   *

Variant spellings

grandaughter **45;** *grand-daughter* **24-32, 48;** *granddaughter* **69-97.**
opopanax **69A;** *opoponax* **24-48, 69E, 84-97.**

*   *   *

[See also the notes on *The Legendary and Mythological Foundation of the Plays and Poems*, p. 1282, *The Legendary and Mythological Foundation of the Plays*, p. 1283; and *Preface to 23*, p. 1283.]

DEIRDRE
1907

TO

MRS. PATRICK CAMPBELL

WHO IN THE GENEROSITY OF HER GENIUS HAS PLAYED MY

DEIRDRE IN DUBLIN AND LONDON WITH THE ABBEY COMPANY,

AS WELL AS WITH HER OWN PEOPLE, AND

IN MEMORY OF

ROBERT GREGORY

WHO DESIGNED THE BEAUTIFUL SCENE SHE PLAYED IT IN.

Persons in the Play

Musicians

Fergus, *an old man*

Naoise (*pronounced* Neesh-e), *a young king*

Deirdre, *his queen*

A Dark-faced Messenger

Conchubar (*pronounced* Conohar), *the old King of Uladh, who is still strong and vigorous*

A Dark-faced Executioner

PRINTINGS   **27, 27a** (v149-v157), **28, 32, 32a** (11. 149-v165, v173-v204, 314-315b); *Samhain*, November 1908 (11. 149-v165, v173-v204, 289-309a, 319-v325, v328-v329, 333-v335, 340-v351, v353-357, v359-371f); **35** (as S plus 1. 504), **40, 45, 48, 52, 55, 63, 69, 84, 89, 97.**

DATE   [lacking] **27-32, 45, 48, 63, 69**; 1906. **52.**

DEDICATION   To Robert Gregory / Who invented for this Play beautiful / Costumes and a beautiful Scene **27, 32**; [lacking] **28, 40, 48, 52-63**; . . . people, and / To Robert . . . . **45, 69.**

DRAMATIS PERSONAE   Persons / and Players at the first performance on November 24, 1906, / at the Abbey Theatre, Dublin: / Musicians Miss Sara Allgood / Miss Maire O'Neill / Miss Brigit O'Dempsey [these three names bracketed as the Musicians] / Fergus, . . . man Arthur Sinclair / Naisi, a . . . king F. J. Fay / Deirdre, . . . queen Miss Darragh / A . . . Messenger U. Wright / Conchubar (pronounced Conochar), . . . vigorous J. M. Kerrigan / Dark-faced Executioner A. Power / On a revival of this play in the spring of 1907, Miss Mona / Limerick took the part of Deirdre. **27**;

Persons / Musicians / Fergus (*an old man*) / Dark-faced Men (*from oversea*) / Naisi (*a young king*) / Deirdre (*a young queen*) / Conchubar (*an old king but still strong and vigorous. He is the high king of Uladh. His name is*

344

A Guest-house in a wood. It is a rough house of timber; through the doors and some of the windows one can see the great spaces of the wood, the sky dimming, night closing in. But a window to the left shows the thick leaves of a coppice; the landscape suggests silence and loneliness. There is a door to right and left, and through the side windows one can see anybody who approaches either door, a moment before he enters. In the centre, a part of the house is curtained off; the curtains are drawn. There are unlighted torches in brackets on the walls. There is, at one side, a small table with a chess-board and chessmen upon it. At the other side of the room there is a brazier with a fire; two women, with musical instruments beside them, crouch about the brazier: they are comely women of about forty. Another woman, who carries a stringed instrument, enters hurriedly; she speaks, at first standing in the doorway.

1. *First Musician.* I have a story right, my wanderers,
2.   That has so mixed with fable in our songs
3.   That all seemed fabulous. We are come, by chance,
4.   Into King Conchubar's country, and this house
5.   Is an old guest-house built for travellers
6.   From the seashore to Conchubar's royal house,

---

pronounced Conohar) **28**;
   . . . Naisi, *a* . . . Conchubar, *the* . . . *vigorous* / Dark-faced . . . **32**;
   [no heading] **40, 48-55**;
   . . . Naisi, (Naoise, **89**) *a* . . . (*pronounced* Conochar), *the* . . . *vigorous* / Dark-faced (A Dark-faced **84, 89**) . . . **40-48, 55, 69-89**;
   . . . Naisi, *a* . . . *queen* / Conchubar (*pronounced* Conochar) *the* . . . *vigorous* / Men with dark faces **52**;
   [lacking] **63**.

STAGE DIRECTIONS   Scene: *A* . . . *upon it, and a wine flagon and a loaf of bread. At the* . . . . **27**; Scene. *A guesthouse* . . . *timber and through* . . . *doors and windows* . . . *see the boughs and leaves. There is* . . . *left and in the centre a* . . . *off. The* . . . *drawn. There is at* . . . *side a* . . . *it and a wine flagon and loaf of bread. The light is darkening towards evening. There are unlighted torches in brackets on the walls. At the other* . . . *fire. Two* . . . *brazier. They* . . . *hurriedly. She speaks at* . . . . **28**; . . . *upon it, and a wine flagon and loaf of bread. At the* . . . . **32**; Scene: (Scene. **63**) *A* . . . . **40, 45, 52-69**; Scene. *A* . . . *the brazier; they* . . . . **48**.

TEXT

2. . . . songs, **27, 32-69**.
3. . . . come by chance **28**.
5. . . . guesthouse . . .
6. . . . house **28**.

7.   And there are certain hills among these woods
8.   And there Queen Deirdre grew.

Second Musician.   That famous queen
9.   Who has been wandering with her lover Naoise
10. Somewhere beyond the edges of the world?

11. *First Musician* [*going nearer to the brazier*]. Some dozen
            years ago, King Conchubar found
12. A house upon a hillside in this wood,
13. And there a child with an old witch to nurse her,
14. And nobody to say if she were human,
15. Or of the gods, or anything at all
16. Of who she was or why she was hidden there,
17. But that she'd too much beauty for good luck.
18. He went up thither daily, till at last
19. She put on womanhood, and he lost peace,
20. And Deirdre's tale began. The King was old.
21. A month or so before the marriage-day,
22. A young man, in the laughing scorn of his youth,
23. Naoise, the son of Usna, climbed up there,
24. And having wooed, or, as some say, been wooed,
25. Carried her off.

Second Musician   The tale were well enough
26. Had it a finish.

First Musician.   Hush! I have more to tell;

---

7.   . . . woods, **27-63.**
8.   . . . queen, **28.**
9.   . . . lover, Naisi, **27, 32 ;** . . . Naisi, **40-89.**
10.   And none to friend but lovers and wild hearts? **27-69.**
11.   . . . ago King . . . **28.**
13.   . . . a comely child . . . witch
14.   To nurse her, and there's nobody can say
14a. If she were human, (human **28**) or of those begot
14b. By an invisible king of the air in a storm
15.   On a king's daughter, or anything . . . **27-69.**
16.   . . . there **27, 32-69.**
18.   . . . daily till . . .
19.   . . . womanhood and . . . ,
20.   . . . king . . . old; **28.**
21.   . . . marriage day, (day **28**) **27-69.**
23.   . . . Son . . . ,
24.   . . . , or as . . . say been . . . , **28.**
26.   . . . tell. **28.**

27.   But gather close about that I may whisper
28.   The secrets of a king.

Second Musician.   There's none to hear!

29. *First Musician.* I have been to Conchubar's house and
           followed up
30.   A crowd of servants going out and in
31.   With loads upon their heads: embroideries
32.   To hang upon the walls, or new-mown rushes
33.   To strew upon the floors, and came at length
34.   To a great room.

Second Musician.   Be silent; there are steps!

*Enter Fergus, an old man, who moves about from door to
window excitedly through what follows.*

35. *Fergus.* I thought to find a message from the King.
36.   You are musicians by these instruments,
37.   And if as seems—for you are comely women—
38.   You can praise love, you'll have the best of luck,
39.   For there'll be two, before the night is in,
40.   That bargained for their love, and paid for it
41.   All that men value. You have but the time
42.   To weigh a happy music with a sad,
43.   To find what is most pleasing to a lover,
44.   Before the son of Usna and his queen

---

27.   ... close that ... whisper it: (it. **28**) **27-69**.
27a.   I speak of terrible, mysterious ends— (ends, **28**) **27-55, 69**; I carry
         terrible, mysterious news— **63**.
28.   ... hear. **28**.
29.   ... house, and ... **27, 32**.
31.   ... heads, embroideries
32.   ... walls or ... **28**.
34.   ... silent, there ... ! **28**.
35.   [lacking] **27-32**; ... king. **40-69**.
36.   ... musicians, by ... ,
37.   ... seems, for ... women, **28**.
39.   ... two before ... in
40.   ... love and ... **28**.
42.   ... sad; **27, 40-69**; ... with the sad; **32**.
44.   ... Son ... **28**.

45.   Have passed this threshold.

First Musician.   Deirdre and her man!

46. *Fergus.* I was to have found a message in this house,
47.   And ran to meet it. Is there no messenger
48.   From Conchubar to Fergus, son of Rogh?

49. *First Musician.* Are Deirdre and her lover tired of life?

50. *Fergus.* You are not of this country, or you'd know
51.   That they are in my charge and all forgiven.

52. *First Musician.* We have no country but the roads of the
          world.

53. *Fergus.* Then you should know that all things change
          in the world,
54.   And hatred turns to love and love to hate,
55.   And even kings forgive.

First Musician.   An old man's love
56.   Who casts no second line is hard to cure;
57.   His jealousy is like his love.

Fergus.   And that's but true.
58.   You have learned something in your wanderings.
59.   He was so hard to cure that the whole court,
60.   But I alone, thought it impossible;
61.   Yet after I had urged it at all seasons,
62.   I had my way, and all's forgiven now;
63.   And you shall speak the welcome and the joy
64.   That I lack tongue for.

First Musician.   Yet old men are jealous.

---

45. . . . man. **28.**
46. I thought to find a message from the king, **27-32.**
48. . . . , Son . . . ? **28.**
48a. I was to have found a message in this house. **27-32.**
50. . . . country or . . . **28.**
51. . . . charge, and . . . . **27-32.**
53. . . . world **28.**
56. . . . line, is . . .; **27, 32-69.**
59. . . . cure, that . . . , **27, 32-69.**
61. . . . seasons
62. . . . way and . . .; **28.**

65. *Fergus* [*going to door*]. I am Conchubar's near friend, and
       that weighed somewhat,
66.   And it was policy to pardon them.
67.   The need of some young, famous, popular man
68.   To lead the troops, the murmur of the crowd,
69.   And his own natural impulse, urged him to it.
70.   They have been wandering half a dozen years.

71. *First Musician.* And yet old men are jealous.

    Fergus [*coming from door*].   Sing the more sweetly
72.   Because, though age is arid as a bone,
73.   This man has flowered. I've need of music, too;
74.   If this grey head would suffer no reproach,
75.   I'd dance and sing—
        [*Dark-faced men with strange, barbaric dress and arms begin to pass by
        the doors and windows. They pass one by one and in silence.*
               and dance till the hour ran out,
76.   Because I have accomplished this good deed.

77. *First Musician.* Look there—there at the window, those
       dark men,
78.   With murderous and outlandish-looking arms—
79.   They've been about the house all day.

    Fergus [*looking after them*].   What are you?
80.   Where do you come from, who is it sent you here?

---

65. . . . friend and . . . , **28.**
67. . . . young famous popular . . . **28.**
69. . . . impulse urged . . . . **28.**
70. . . . half-a-dozen . . . . **27, 32-69**; They had been . . . . **28.**
72. Because though . . . bone
73. . . . music too. **28.**
    Directions in 75. [lacking] **27-32.**
75. . . . run out **28.**
77. . . . there, there, at . . . window; those . . . ,
78. . . . arms, **28.**
79. . . . day.
    [*Dark faced men with strange barbaric dress and arms pass by the doors
    and windows. They pass one by one and in silence.*]
    What . . . ? **27-32.**

81. *First Musician.* They will not answer you.

Fergus.   They do not hear.

82. *First Musician.* Forgive my open speech, but to these
        eyes
83.   That have seen many lands they are such men
84.   As kings will gather for a murderous task
85.   That neither bribes, commands, nor promises
86.   Can bring their people to.

Fergus.   And that is why
87.   You harped upon an old man's jealousy.
88.   A trifle sets you quaking. Conchubar's fame
89.   Brings merchandise on every wind that blows.
90.   They may have brought him Libyan dragon-skin,
91.   Or the ivory of the fierce unicorn.

92. *First Musician.* If these be merchants, I have seen the
        goods
93.   They have brought to Conchubar, and understood
94.   His murderous purpose.

Fergus.   Murderous, you say?
95.   Why, what new gossip of the roads is this?
96.   But I'll not hear.

First Musician.   It may be life or death.
97.   There is a room in Conchubar's house, and there——

98. *Fergus.* Be silent, or I'll drive you from the door.
99.   There's many a one that would do more than that,
100.   And make it prison, or death, or banishment

---

83.   . . . lands, they . . . **27, 32-69.**
84.   . . . task, **27-69.**
90.   . . . dragon skin **28.**
93.   . . . Conchubar and . . . **28.**
94.   . . . purpose. (purpose **52**)
              Murderous you say. (Murderous, . . . ? **52**) **28, 52.**
95.   Why what . . . ? **28.**
96.   . . . hear.
              I may . . . . **63.**
97.   . . . house and . . . ——
98.   . . . silent or . . . . **28.**
100. . . . it life or death in very truth **28.**

101.   To slander the High King.

[Suddenly restraining himself and speaking gently.
                        He is my friend;
102.   I have his oath, and I am well content.
103.   I have known his mind as if it were my own
104.   These many years, and there is none alive
105.   Shall buzz against him, and I there to stop it.
106.   I know myself, and him, and your wild thought
107.   Fed on extravagant poetry, and lit
108.   By such a dazzle of old fabulous tales
109.   That common things are lost, and all that's strange
110.   Is true because 'twere pity if it were not.

[Going to the door again.
111.   Quick! quick! your instruments! they are coming now.
112.   I hear the hoofs a-clatter. Begin that song!
113.   But what is it to be? I'd have them hear
114.   A music foaming up out of the house
115.   Like wine out of a cup. Come now, a verse
116.   Of some old time not worth remembering,
117.   And all the lovelier because a bubble.
118.   Begin, begin, of some old king and queen,
119.   Of Lugaidh Redstripe or another; no, not him,
120.   He and his lady perished wretchedly.

First Musician [*singing*]
121.   'Why is it', Queen Edain said,
122.   'If I do but climb the stair . . .

123.   *Fergus.* Ah! that is better. . . . They are alighted now.

---

101.   . . . high . . .; **27, 40-63, 69E** ; . . . high king [*suddenly* . . .].
                                                . . . friend. **28.**
102.   . . . oath and . . . . **28.**
105.   . . . him; and . . . . **28.**
111.   Quick, quick! . . . instruments; they . . . now, **28.**
112.   . . . song; **27, 32, 40, 45** (1911), **48-69** ; . . . song. **28** ; . . . the roofs
        a-clatter . . . song; **45** (1913).
116.   . . . remembering **28.**
        Name of singer before 121.   *Musician* **27, 28.**
121, 122, 125, 132, 134, 140.   [quotation marks lacking] **28.**
121.   . . . it Queen . . . said **28.**
122.   . . . stair? **28** ; . . . stair . . . .' **32** ; . . . stair' . . . **48, 63.**
123.   . . . better . . . . [T] they . . . . **28.**

124.   Shake all your cockscombs, children; these are lovers.

                                                    [*Fergus goes out.*

                        First Musician
125.   'Why is it', Queen Edain said,
126.   'If I do but climb the stair
127.   To the tower overhead,
128.   When the winds are calling there,
129.   Or the gannets calling out
130.   In waste places of the sky,
131.   There's so much to think about
132.   That I cry, that I cry?'

                        Second Musician
133.   But her goodman answered her:
134.   'Love would be a thing of naught
135.   Had not all his limbs a stir
136.   Born out of immoderate thought;
137.   Were he anything by half,
138.   Were his measure running dry.
139.   Lovers, if they may not laugh,
140.   Have to cry, have to cry.'

[*Deirdre, Naoise, and Fergus have been seen for a moment through
the windows, but now they have entered.*

                    The Three Musicians [*together*]
141.   But is Edain worth a song

---

124.   . . . , children, these . . . lovers!
125.   . . . said: **28.**
127.   . . . overhead
128.   . . . there **28.**
129.   . . . out, **27, 32, 40-69.**
131.   . . . about, **27, 32, 40-69.**
136.   . . . thought. **27, 28.**
138.   . . . dry, **27, 28.**
Directions after 140.   [. . . *Fergus, who have been seen approaching the door, come
        in.*] **28**; [. . . *entered. Naisi*[1] *lays down shield and spear and helmet, as if
        weary. He goes to the door opposite to the door he entered by. He looks out on
        to the road that leads to Conchubar's house. If he is anxious, he would not have
        Fergus or Deirdre notice it. Presently he comes from the door, and goes to the
        table where the chessboard is.*] **27a, 32.**

[1] **27a** begins with 'Naisi', then jumps to v149-v157. It is included in the collations. See
also p. 390.

142.   Now the hunt begins anew?
143.   Praise the beautiful and strong;
144.   Praise the redness of the yew;
145.   Praise the blossoming apple-stem.
146.   But our silence had been wise.
147.   What is all our praise to them
148.   That have one another's eyes?

149. *Deirdre.* Silence your music, though I thank you for it;
150.   But the wind's blown upon my hair, and I
151.   Must set the jewels on my neck and head
152.   For one that's coming.

      Naoise.   Your colour has all gone

---

142. . . . anew.
143. . . . strong.
144. . . . Yew.
145. . . . apple stem.
      Directions after 145. [*They turn away, seeing that Deirdre and Naisi are too full of thought to listen.*] **28.**
147. . . . them, **27-32, 40, 45, 52, 55, 69.**
148. . . . eyes; **40**; . . . eyes. **45** (1911).
      Directions after 148. [*The sky outside is still bright so that the room is dim in the midst of a wood full of evening light, but gradually during what follows the light fades out of the sky; and except during a short time before the lighting of the torches, and at the end of all, the room is either dark amid light or light amid the darkness. The lighting and the character of the scenery, the straight trees, and the spaces of sky and mountain between them suggest isolation and silence.*
      The musicians almost throughout remain near the brazier, but show the effect upon their minds of what is happening by their movements and the expression of their faces.] **28**;
      [*Deirdre, Naisi and Fergus enter. Deirdre is carrying a little embroidered bag. She goes over towards the women.*] **32a.**[1]
149. *Fergus.* You are welcome, lady.
      Deirdre.   Conchubar has not come.
150. Were the peace honest, (honest **28**) he'd have come himself **27-32.**
151. To prove it so.
      Fergus.   He is no more in love. **27, 28**;
      To prove it so.
      Fergus.   Being no more in love, (love **27a**) **27a, 32.**
152-155. [lacking] **27, 28.**
152. He stays in his own house, arranging where **27a, 32.**

---

[1] **32a** comprises these directions, lines 149-v165, v173-v204, 314-315b. S and **35** comprise lines 149-v165, v173-v204, 289-309a, 319-371f, 504 (**35** only). They are included in the collations. See also pp. 391-4.

153.   As 'twere with fear, and there's no cause for that.

154. *Deirdre.* These women have the raddle that they use
155.   To make them brave and confident, although
156.   Dread, toil, or cold may chill the blood o' their
          cheeks.
157.   You'll help me, women. It is my husband's will
158.   I show my trust in one that may be here
159.   Before the mind can call the colour up.
160.   My husband took these rubies from a king
161.   Of Surracha that was so murderous
162.   He seemed all glittering dragon. Now wearing them
163.   Myself wars on myself, for I myself—
164.   That do my husband's will, yet fear to do it—
165.   Grow dragonish to myself.

> [*The women have gathered about her. Naoise has stood looking at
> her, but Fergus brings him to the chess-table.*

Naoise.   No messenger!

---

153. The curlew and the plover go, and where
154. The speckled heath-cock in a golden dish.
155. *Deirdre.* But there's no messenger.
       Fergus.   He'll come himself **27a, 32.**
156. He will have come before the night is in; (in, **28**) **27, 28**; When all's
       in readiness and the night (and night **27a**) closed in; **27a, 32**; . . . ,
       toil or . . . . **32a, S.**
157. But till that hour,[1] (hour **28**) these birds out of the waste **27-32.**
158. Shall put his heart and mind (mine **28**) into the music. **27-32**; . . .
       one, that . . . **S-69.**
159. There's many a day that I have almost wept
160. To think that one so delicately made **27-32.**
161. Might never know the sweet and natural life **27-32**; . . . murderous,
       S; . . . murderous. **35.**
162. Of women born to that magnificence, (magnificence **28**) **27-32.**
163. Quiet and music, courtesy and peace. **27-32**; . . . I, myself— **S, 35.**
164. *Deirdre.* I have found life obscure and violent, (violent **28**) **27-32.**
       Directions in 165. [lacking] **27-32**; [. . . *chesstable.* (*chess table.* **63,**
       69)] **40-48, 55-69.**
165. And think it ever so; but none the less **27-32.**
       Second hemistich 165–first hemistich 172. [lacking] **40-63.**

---

[1] **27a** ends here.

166.   It's strange that there is none to welcome us.

167. *Fergus.* King Conchubar has sent no messenger
168.   That he may come himself.

    Naoise.   And being himself,
169.   Being High King, he cannot break his faith.
170.   I have his word and I must take that word,
171.   Or prove myself unworthy of my nurture
172.   Under a great man's roof.

    Fergus.   We'll play at chess
173.   Till the King comes. It is but natural
174.   That she should doubt him, for her house has been
175.   The hole of the badger and the den of the fox.

176. *Naoise.* If I had not King Conchubar's word I'd think
177.   That chess-board ominous.

    Fergus.   How can a board
178.   That has been lying there these many years
179.   Be lucky or unlucky?

    Naoise.   It is the board

---

166. I thank you for your kindness, (kindness **28**) and thank these
167. That put it into music.
    Fergus.   Your house has been
168-174. [lacking] **27-32.**
  173. ... king come. ... **32a, S ;** ... king ... **35-84.**
  174. ... should fear him, ... **32a-63.**
  175. ... badger or the ... fox; (fox, **28**)
175a. But all that's finished, (finished **28**) and your days will pass **27-32.**
175b. From this day out where life is smooth on the tongue, **27, 32 ;** In some elaborate leisured court, where all **28.**
175c. Because the grapes were trodden long ago. **27, 32 ;** The wine of life was trodden long ago. **28.**
  176. If I was childish, (were childish **28, 32a-63**) and had faith in omens, (omens **32a**) **27-69.**
176a. I'd rather not have lit on that old chessboard (chess-board **28, 52**)
  177. At my home-coming. (home coming. **28 ;** homecoming. **32a**)
                      There's a tale about it– (it: **28 ;** it,– **32a**)
  178. It has ... years— (years, **28 ;** years,– **32a**)
  179. Some wild old sorrowful tale.
                  It ... **27-69.**

180.   Where Lugaidh Redstripe and that wife of his,
181.   Who had a seamew's body half the year,
182.   Played at the chess upon the night they died.

183. *Fergus.* I can remember now, a tale of treachery,
184.   A broken promise and a journey's end—
185.   But it were best forgot.

> [*Deirdre has been standing with the women about her. They have been helping her to put on her jewels and to put the pigment on her cheeks and arrange her hair. She has gradually grown attentive to what Fergus is saying.*]

  Naoise.   If the tale's true,
186.   When it was plain that they had been betrayed,
187.   They moved the men and waited for the end
188.   As it were bedtime, and had so quiet minds
189.   They hardly winked their eyes when the sword
              flashed.

190. *Fergus.* She never could have played so, being a woman,
191.   If she had not the cold sea's blood in her.

192. *Dierdre.* The gods turn clouds and casual accidents

---

181.   ... sea-mew's ..., **28**; ... year **32a**; ... a seaman's body ... **48**;
        ... a sea-bird's body ..., **63**.
183.   ... now a ..., **27-32**; ... now: a ..., **32a**.
184.   ... end; (end, **28**) **27-32**; ... end. **32a**; ... end **S**; ...
        promise, and ...— **35**.
        Directions in 185. [lacking] **27-32**.
185.   ... tale is true, **27-32**; ... true,— **32a**; ... true **S**.
187.   ... men, and ... end, **27, 32**.
188.   ... bed time and ... **28**.
191.   ... cold sea-mew's blood .... **28**.
192.   I have heard that th'ever-living warn mankind **27, 32**; I have heard
        the ever-living warn mankind (mankind, **28**; man-kind **40, 45**
        (1911)) **28, 32a-63**; I have heard the Ever-living warn mankind **69**.
192a.   By changing clouds, (clouds **32a-63**) and casual accidents, (accidents
        32a, S, 69) **27-69**.

193.   Into omens.

    Naoise.   It would but ill become us,
194.   Now that King Conchubar has pledged his word,
195.   Should we be startled by a cloud or a shadow.

196. *Deirdre.* There's none to welcome us.

    Naoise.   Being his guest,
197.   Words that would wrong him can but wrong ourselves.

198. *Deirdre.* An empty house upon the journey's end!
199.   Is that the way a king that means no mischief

---

193.   Or what seem so.
    Fergus.   If there had been ill luck **27-32**;
    Or what seem so. Stood th'ever-living there, **32a-35**;
    Or what seem so.
              It . . . , **40-69.**
193a.   In lighting on this chessboard (chess-board **28**) of a sudden, **27-32**;
    Old Lir (Lir, **35**) and Aengus from his glassy tower, **32a-35.**
193b.   This flagon that stood on it when we came **27-32**; And (Or **35**)
    that hill-haunting Bodb (Bodb, **35**) to warn us hence,— (hence, **S,**
    35) **32a-35.**
193c.   Has made all right again, for it should mean **27-32**; Our honour
    is so knitted up with staying, **32a-35.**
193d.   All wrongs forgiven, hospitality **27-32.**
193e.   For bitter memory, peace after war, (war; **28**)
193f.   While that loaf there should add prosperity.
193g.   Deirdre will see the world, as it were, new-made, (new made **28**)
193h.   If she'll but eat and drink.
    Naisi.   The flagon's dry, **27-32.**
193i.   Full of old cobwebs, and the bread is mouldy, (mouldy– **28**)
193j.   Left by some traveller gone upon his way
193k.   These many weeks.
    Deirdre.   No one to welcome us, (us **28**) **27-32.**
194-197. [lacking] **27-32.**
194.   King Conchubar's word and Fergus' word being pledged, **32a-35.**
195.   [lacking]
196.   I'd brave them out and stay.
    Deirdre.   No welcomer,
197.   [lacking] **32a-35.**
198.   And a bare house . . . end. (end! **32a-35**) **27-35.**
199.   . . . the welcome that a king spreads out **27-32**; . . . no wrong
    32a-35.

200.   Honours a guest?

Fergus.   He is but making ready
201.   A welcome in his house, arranging where
202.   The moorhen and the mallard go, and where
203.   The speckled heathcock on a golden dish.

204.   *Deirdre.* Had he no messenger?

Naoise.   Such words and fears
205.   Wrong this old man who's pledged his word to us.
206.   We must not speak or think as women do,
207.   That when the house is all abed sit up
208.   Marking among the ashes with a stick
209.   Till they are terrified.—Being what we are
210.   We must meet all things with an equal mind.
211.   [*To Fergus.*] Come, let us look if there's a messenger
212.   From Conchubar. We cannot see from this
213.   Because we are blinded by the leaves and twigs,

---

200.   For those that he would honour?
       Naisi.   Hush! no more. **27, 32**;
       For those that he would honour?
       Fergus.   He makes ready **28.**
201-204.   [lacking] **27, 32.**
202.   The peacock and the plover go, . . . **28.**
203.   . . . heath-cock in a . . . . **28, 32a.**
204.   Has he . . . Messenger?– (messenger? **28, 35**; messenger— **32a**[1])
                            Be silent, Deirdre, (Deirdre. **28**) **28, S, 35.**
205.   You are King Conchubar's guest, being in his house. **27-32**;
       You are King Conchubar's guest, etc. (guest (& c.) **35**) **S, 35**[2].
206.   You speak as . . . do that sit alone, (alone **40-63**) **27-63.**
207.   [lacking] **27-63**; . . . a-bed . . . **69-89.**
208.   Marking the . . . stick till they **27-32.**
209.   Are in a dreamy terror. Being a queen, **27-32**; . . . terrified.—You
       are a queen: **40-63.**
210.   You should have too calm thought to start at shadows. **27-69.**
211.   *Fergus.* Come, . . . **27-32.**
212.   From Conchubar's house. A little way without **27, 32**; From Con-
       chubar's house. The trees are not so close **28.**
213.   One sees the road for half a mile or so, **27, 32**; Upon that side, and
       one can see the path, **28.**

       [1] Except for lines 314-315b, **32a** ends here.
       [2] S and **35** stop here; they begin again at 289.

214.   But it may be the wood will thin again.
215.   It is but kind that when the lips we love
216.   Speak words that are unfitting for kings' ears
217.   Our ears be deaf.

    Fergus.   But now I had to threaten
218.   These wanderers because they would have weighed
219.   Some crazy fantasy of their own brain
220.   Or gossip of the road with Conchubar's word.
221.   If I had thought so little of mankind
222.   I never could have moved him to this pardon.
223.   I have believed the best of every man,
224.   And find that to believe it is enough
225.   To make a bad man show him at his best,
226.   Or even a good man swing his lantern higher.

    [*Naoise and Fergus go out. The last words are spoken as they go*
    through the door. One can see them through part of what follows,
    either through door or window. They move about, talking or looking
    along the road towards Conchubar's house.

227.   *First Musician.* If anything lies heavy on your heart,
228.   Speak freely of it, knowing it is certain
229.   That you will never see my face again.

230.   *Deirdre.* You've been in love?

    First Musician.   If you would speak of love

---

214.   Where the trees thin or thicken.
    Naisi.   When those we love **27, 32**; Now
here, now there, as the trees thin or thicken **28**.
215.   [lacking] **27, 32**; For half a mile or so.
    Naisi.   When those we love **28**.
216.   . . . words unfitting to the ear of kings, **27-32**.
217.   Kind ears are deaf.
               Before you came **27, 32**;
Kind ears are deaf.
               Not half an hour ago **28**.
218.   I had to threaten these that would . . . **27-32**.
221.   . . . mankind, **28, 48, 63**.
225.   . . . best **28**.
    Directions after 226. [. . . *about talking, or* . . . .] **48, 63**.
230.   . . . love, **27-89, 97A**.

V.E.P.Y.—N

231.   Speak freely. There is nothing in the world
232.   That has been friendly to us but the kisses
233.   That were upon our lips, and when we are old
234.   Their memory will be all the life we have.

235.   *Deirdre.* There was a man that loved me. He was old;
236.   I could not love him. Now I can but fear.
237.   He has made promises, and brought me home;
238.   But though I turn it over in my thoughts,
239.   I cannot tell if they are sound and wholesome,
240.   Or hackles on the hook.

     First Musician.   I have heard he loved you
241.   As some old miser loves the dragon-stone
242.   He hides among the cobwebs near the roof.

243.   *Deirdre.* You mean that when a man who has loved like
         that
244.   Is after crossed, love drowns in its own flood,
245.   And that love drowned and floating is but hate;
246.   And that a king who hates sleeps ill at night
247.   Till he has killed; and that, though the day laughs,
248.   We shall be dead at cock-crow.

     First Musician.   You've not my thought.
249.   When I lost one I loved distractedly,
250.   I blamed my crafty rival and not him,

---

231.   ... freely; there ... **28.**
233.   ... old, **28.**
235.   ... old. **28**; ... me.
                      He ...; **48, 63.**
236.   ... fear **27**; ... him, now ... . **28.**
237.   ... home. **27**; ... home, **28.**
238.   ... thoughts
239.   ... wholesome **28.**
240.   ... you, **27-69.**
241.   ... dragon stone **28.**
244.   ... flood **28**; ... drowns, in ... , **48, 63.**
245.   ... hate. **27-32.**
246.   ... hates, sleeps ... night, **27-69.**
247.   ... killed, and ... , **27, 32**; ... laugh, **28.**
248.   ... cockcrow. (cock-crow. **40-69**)
         You have not ... . **27-69.**

251. And fancied, till my passion had run out,
252. That could I carry him away with me,
253. And tell him all my love, I'd keep him yet.

254. *Deirdre.* Ah! now I catch your meaning, that this king
255.   Will murder Naoise, and keep me alive.

256. *First Musician.* 'Tis you that put that meaning upon
        words
257.   Spoken at random.

    Deirdre.   Wanderers like you,
258. Who have their wit alone to keep their lives,
259. Speak nothing that is bitter to the ear
260. At random; if they hint at it at all
261. Their eyes and ears have gathered it so lately
262. That it is crying out in them for speech.

263. *First Musician.* We have little that is certain.

    Deirdre.   Certain or not,
264. Speak it out quickly, I beseech you to it;
265. I never have met any of your kind
266. But that I gave them money, food, and fire.

267. *First Musician.* There are strange, miracle-working,
        wicked stones,
268. Men tear out of the heart and the hot brain
269. Of Libyan dragons.

    Deirdre.   The hot Istian stone,
270. And the cold stone of Fanes, that have power
271. To stir even those at enmity to love.

---

251. ... fancied till ... out **28**; ... fancied till ... , **40-63.**
252. ... me **28.**
260. ... random. If ... hint of it ... all, **28.**
263. ... not. **63.**
264. ... it. **28.**
265. ... kind, **27, 32-69.**
266. ... , food and .... **40-63.**
267. ... , miracle working, ... stones **28.**
270. ... Fanes that ... **28.**

272. *First Musician.* They have so great an influence, if but
          sewn
273.   In the embroideries that curtain in
274.   The bridal bed.

    Deirdre.   O Mover of the stars
275.   That made this delicate house of ivory,
276.   And made my soul its mistress, keep it safe!

277. *First Musician.* I have seen a bridal bed, so curtained in,
278.   So decked for miracle in Conchubar's house,
279.   And learned that a bride's coming.

    Deirdre.   And I the bride?
280.   Here is worse treachery than the seamew suffered,
281.   For she but died and mixed into the dust
282.   Of her dear comrade, but I am to live
283.   And lie in the one bed with him I hate.
284.   Where is Naoise? I was not alone like this
285.   When Conchubar first chose me for his wife;
286.   I cried in sleeping or waking and he came,
287.   But now there is worse need.

    Naoise [entering with Fergus].   Why have you called?
288.   I was but standing there, without the door.

---

272.   ... influence if . . . **28.**
274.   ... stars,
275.   ... ivory **28.**
276.   ... safe. **27-32.**
277.   ... bed so . . . ,
278.   ... miracle, in . . . ,
279.   ... bride is . . . ?
280.   ... sea-mew . . . , **28.**
282.   ... comrade; but . . . **28.**
285.   ... wife, **27, 40, 45** (1911), **52, 55** ; . . wife. **28.**
288a. *Deirdre [going to the other door].* The horses are still saddled, (saddled; **28**) follow me,
288b. And hurry to our ships, and get us gone.
288c. *Naisi [stopping her (her, **28**) and partly speaking to her, partly to Fergus].* There's naught (nought **28**) to fear; the king's forgiven all.
288d.[1] She has the heart of a wild bird that fears
288e.[1] The net of the fowler or the wicker cage, **27-32.**

          [1] See 302-303.

289.   *Deirdre.* I have heard terrible mysterious things,[1]
290.   Magical horrors and the spells of wizards.

291.   *Fergus.* Why, that's no wonder. You have been listening
292.   To singers of the roads that gather up
293.   The stories of the world.

       Deirdre.   But I have one
294.   To make the stories of the world but nothing.

295.   *Naoise.* Be silent if it is against the King
296.   Whose guest you are.

       Fergus.   No, let her speak it out.
297.   I know the High King's heart as it were my own,
298.   And can refute a slander, but already
299.   I have warned these women that it may be death.

300.   *Naoise.* I will not weigh the gossip of the roads

288f.   And has been ever so. Although it's hard (hard, **28**)
288g.   It is but needful that I stand against you,
288h.   And if I did not (not, **28**) you'd despise me for it,
288i.   As women do the husbands that they lead (lead, **28**)
288j.   Whether for good or evil.
        Deirdre.   I have heard **27-32.**
289.   Monstrous, terrible, mysterious things, (things— **28**) **27-32 ;** . . .
        things. **S.**
291.   . . . wonder, you've been . . . **27, 32 ;** . . . wonder; you . . . **28 ;** Why
        that's . . . **S.**
293.   The tales of the whole world, and when they weary (weary, **28**)
293a.   Imagine new, or lies about the living,
293b.   Because their brains are ever upon fire.
294.   *Deirdre.* Is then the king that sends no messenger, (messenger **28**)
        27-32.
295.   And leaves an empty house before a guest, (guest **28**) **27-32 ;** . . .
        king **S-69.**
295a.   So clear in all he does that no dim word **27-32.**
296.   Can light us to a doubt?
        Fergus.   However dim (dim, **28, 32**) **27-32 ;** . . .
        out **S ;** . . . out, **35-69.**
297.   Speak it, for I have known King Conchubar **27-32 ;** . . . own **S.**
298.   Better than my own heart, and I can quench
299.   Whatever words have made you doubt him.
        Naisi.   No,
300.   I cannot weigh . . . **27-32.**

[1] S and **35** start again here.

301.   With the King's word. I ask your pardon for her:
302.   She has the heart of the wild birds that fear
303.   The net of the fowler or the wicker cage.

304.   *Deirdre.* Am I to see the fowler and the cage
305.   And speak no word at all?

     Naoise.   You would have known,
306.   Had they not bred you in that mountainous place,
307.   That when we give a word and take a word
308.   Sorrow is put away, past wrong forgotten.

309.   *Deirdre.* Though death may come of it?

     Naoise.   Though death may come.

310.   *Deirdre.* When first we came into this empty house

---

301.   With a king's word, and were the end but death, (death **28**) **27-32**;
    . . . king's word, I . . . her, **S** ; . . . king's . . .: **35, 45** (1913), **55, 69** ;
    . . . king's . . . ask you pardon . . .: **40, 45** (1911), **48, 52, 63**.
302.   I may not doubt him.
    Deirdre.   Naisi, I must speak.
303.   *Fergus.* Let us begone, this (begone. This **28**) house is no fit place,
    27-32.
304.   Being full of doubt—Deirdre is right.
       [*To Deirdre, who has gone towards the door she had entered by.*]
                       No, no, **27, 32** ;
    Being full of doubt, Deirdre is right. [*To Deirdre*] No, no, **28**.
305.   Not by that door that opens on the path **27-32** ;
    . . . all.
          You . . . known **S**.
306.   That runs to the seashore, but this that leads **27-32** ; . . . place **S**.
307.   To Conchubar's house. We'll wait no messenger, **27-32** ; . . . word,
    S, 35.
308.   But go to his well-lighted house, (house **28**) and there (there, **28**)
    27-32.
309.   Where the rich world runs up into a wick **27-32** ;
    . . . it.
          Though . . . . **S**.
309a. *Fergus.* To those that slander kings.
    Deirdre.   Then I will say **S-63**
310-318. [lacking] **S-63**.
310.   And that burns steadily, because no wind **27-32**.

311.   You had foreknowledge of our death, and even
312.   When speaking of the paleness of my cheek
313.   Your own cheek blanched.

    Naoise.   Listen to this old man.
314.   He can remember all the promises
315.   We trusted to.

    Deirdre.   You speak from the lips out,
316.   And I am pleading for your life and mine.

317.   *Naoise.* Listen to this old man, for many think
318.   He has a golden tongue.

    Deirdre.   Then I will say
319.   What it were best to carry to the grave.
320.   Look at my face where the leaf raddled it
321.   And at these rubies on my hair and breast.
322.   It was for him, to stir him to desire,
323.   I put on beauty; yes, for Conchubar.

324.   *Naoise.* What frenzy put these words into your mouth?

325.   *Deirdre.* No frenzy, for what need is there for frenzy
326.   To change what shifts with every change of the wind,
327.   Or else there is no truth in men's old sayings?

---

311.   Can blow upon it, bring all doubts to an end.
312.   The table has been spread by this, the court
313.   Has ridden from all sides to welcome you
314.   To safety and to peace. **27-32.**
    Deirdre.   Safety and peace! **27-32a[1].**
315.   I had them when a child, but never since. **27-32** ; I had them when
     a child, but from that hour **32a** ; . . . out **69.**
315a.   I have found life obscure and violent,
315b.   And think that I shall find it so for ever. **32a.**
316-348.   [lacking] **27-32.**
319.   . . . grave, **S.**
320a.   And at these harmless though unlidded eyes
321.   About my . . . breast. It was for him,
322.   To wake his love, to stir . . . desire (desire, **35**) **S, 35.**
323.   . . . beauty, yes for . . . . **S.**
325.   No frenzy (frenzy, **35**) but a sudden change that turned **S, 35.**
326-327.   [lacking] **S, 35.**

---

           [1] Lines **314-315b** are the remainder of **32a.**

328.   Was I not born a woman?

Naoise.   You're mocking me.

329. *Deirdre.* And is there mockery in this face and eyes,
330.   Or in this body, in these limbs that brought
331.   So many mischiefs? Look at me and say
332.   If that that shakes my limbs be mockery.

333. *Naoise.* What woman is there that a man can trust
334.   But at the moment when he kisses her
335.   At the first midnight?

Deirdre.   Were it not most strange
336.   That woman should put evil in men's hearts
337.   And lack it in themselves? And yet I think
338.   That being half good I might change round again
339.   Were we aboard our ship and on the sea.

340. *Naoise.* We'll to the horses and take ship again.

341. *Fergus.* Fool, she but seeks to rouse your jealousy
342.   With crafty words.

Deirdre.   Were we not born to wander?
343.   These jewels have been reaped by the innocent
              sword
344.   Upon a mountain, and a mountain bred me;
345.   But who can tell what change can come to love
346.   Among the valleys? I speak no falsehood now.
347.   Away to windy summits, and there mock

---

328.   Old hate to love. You are mocking me (me. **35**)
329.   . . . in my face . . . eyes? **S, 35.**
330-332. [lacking] **S, 35.**
335.   . . . midnight. (midnight ? **35**) Come, for I command it (it: **35**) **S, 35.**
336-339. [lacking] **S, 35.**
337.   . . . themselves?
              Naisi.   Come, I command it:
338-339. [lacking] **40-63.**
340.   . . . again **40, 45, 69E.**
342.   . . . words.
                     Where . . . ? **63.**
346.   . . . valleys. I . . . . **S.**
347.   We'll to the windy summits (summits, **35**) and . . . **S, 35.**

348.   The night-jar and the valley-keeping bird!

349. *Fergus.* Men blamed you that you stirred a quarrel up
350.   That has brought death to many. I have made peace,
351.   Poured water on the fire, but if you fly
352.   King Conchubar may think that he is mocked
353.   And the house blaze again: and in what quarter,
354.   If Conchubar were the treacherous man you think,
355.   Would you find safety now that you have come
356.   Into the very middle of his power,
357.   Under his very eyes?

       Deirdre.   Under his eyes
358.   And in the very middle of his power!
359.   Then there is but one way to make all safe:
360.   I'll spoil this beauty that brought misery
361.   And houseless wandering on the man I loved.
362.   These wanderers will show me how to do it;
363.   To clip this hair to baldness, blacken my skin
364.   With walnut juice, and tear my face with briars.

---

348. . . . bird, **S** ; . . . bird. **35.**
349. . . . blame . . . you have stirred . . . **27-32.**
350. . . . have poured **27-63** ; . . . peace; **69E.**
351. Water upon the . . . **27, 32-63** ; Water upon the fire; but . . . **28** ; . . . fire; but . . . **69A.**
352. [lacking] **27-63.**
353. A second time (time, **28, S-63**) the house is in a blaze (blaze, **S-63**) **27-63** ; . . . again; and . . . , **69.**
354. And all the screaming household can (will **S-63**) but blame
355. The savage heart of beauty for it all; **27-63.**
356. And Naisi that but helped to tar the wisp **27-S** ; And Naisi, that has helped to tar the wisp, (whisp, **52**) **35-63.**
357. Be but a (Shall be a **S-63**) hunted outlaw all his days. (days **28**) **27-63** ; . . . eyes.
       Under . . . **69.**
358. [lacking] **27-63** ; . . . power. **69.**
359. I will be blamed no more! (more; **28**) there's but one way, (way. **28, 32**) **27-32** ; I will be blamed no more. There's but one way. (way: **35-63**) **S-63** ; . . . safe, **69-89.**
360. . . . misery, **27, S.**
361. . . . loved, **27-32** ; . . . loved **S.**
361a. And so buy peace between him and the king. **27-32.**
362. . . . it, **27-32** ; . . . it **S.**
363. . . . clip my hair . . . **27-32.**
364. with . . . juice and . . . briars, **S.**

365.   O that the creatures of the woods had torn
366.   My body with their claws!

Fergus.   What, wilder yet!

367.   *Deirdre [to Naoise].* Whatever were to happen to my
              face
368.   I'd be myself, and there's not any way
369.   But this to bring all trouble to an end.

370.   *Naoise.* Leave the gods' handiwork unblotched, and
              wait
371.   For their decision, our decision is past.
                    [*A Dark-faced Messenger comes to the threshold.*

---

365.   Oh! that wild creatures . . . **27-32**; Oh, that . . . **S-69.**
366.   This body . . . claws.
         Naisi.   What is your meaning? **27-32**;
         . . . claws.
         Fergus.   What, . . . ! **S.**
366a.   *Naisi.* What are you saying? That he loves you still? **27-32.**
367.   *Deirdre.* Whatever (What ever **28**) . . . to this face, (face **28**)
368.   . . . myself; and . . .
369.   . . . this way to bring trouble . . . . **27-32.**
370.   Answer me—does King Conchubar still love— (love, **28**) **27-32**;
         What have you told to put such frenzy in her? **S-63.**
370a.   *Fergus.* Yes, speak it out.
         Naisi.   I give you my protection (protection, **35-
         45, 52**; protection; **48, 63**)
370b.   Are you afraid to speak? Does the king love her? **S-63.**
371.   Does he still covet you?
         Deirdre.   Tell out the plot, **27-32**;
         Will no one answer?
         Deirdre.   Tell out all the plot (plot, **35-63**) **S-63**; . . .
         their decession, our decession is . . . . **69.**
371a.   The plan, (spells, **S**) the network, all the treachery, (treachery; **35-
         63**) **27-63.**
371b.   And (Tell **S-63**) of the bridal chamber and the bed, **27-63.**
371c.   The magical stones, the wizard's handiwork. **27-63.**
371d.   *Naisi.* Ah, (Ah! **35-63**) now I understand why it is you fear **S-63.**
371e.   *Naisi.* Take care of Deirdre, (Deirdre **28**) if I die in this, **27-32**; To
         waken death with words. Take care of Deirdre (Deirdre: **35-63**)
         S-63.
371f.   For she must never fall into his hands, **27-32**; She must not fall
         alive into his hands. (hands, **40-63**) **S-63.**[1]

[1] S and 35 end here except for line 504.

372. *Fergus.* Peace, peace; the messenger is at the door;
373.   He stands upon the threshold; he stands there;
374.   He stands, King Conchubar's purpose on his lips.

375. *Messenger.* Supper is on the table. Conchubar
376.   Is waiting for his guests.

Fergus.   All's well again!
377.   All's well! All's well! You cried your doubts so loud
378.   That I had almost doubted.

Naoise.   We doubted him,
379.   And he the while but busy in his house
380.   For the more welcome.

Deirdre.   The message is not finished.

371g.   Whatever the cost.
            Deirdre.   Where would you go to, Naisi? **27-63.**
371h.   *Naisi.* I go to drag the truth from Conchubar,
371i.   Before his people, in the face of his army,
371j.   And if it be as black as you have made it,
371k.   To kill him there.
            Deirdre.   You never would return; **27-63.**
371l.   I'll never look upon your face again.
371m.   Oh, keep him, Fergus; (Fergus, **28**) do not let him go,
371n.   But hold him from it. You are both wise and kind.
371o.   *Naisi.* When you were all but Conchubar's wife, I took you; (you. **28**)
371p.   He tried to kill me, and he would have done it
371q.   If I had been so near as I am now.
371r.   And now that you are mine, he has planned to take you.
            Directions after 371r. [*Dark-faced messenger comes into the house,* (*house* **48, 63**) *unnoticed.*] **27, 32-63**; [*Dark-faced messenger comes into the house.*] **28.**
371s.   Should I be less than Conchubar, being a man? **27-63.**
372-374. [lacking] **27-63.**
375.   . . . table, (table; **32**) Conchubar **27, 32-63**; The supper is spread out and Conchubar **28.**
376.   . . . well, again! **27, 32, 40, 45** (1911), **48-63**; . . . again, **28.**
377.   All's well! all's . . . loud, **27, 32**; All's well, all's well, you . . . **28**; All's well! all's . . . **40-63.**
378.   . . . doubted.
            I would have killed him, **27-63.**
379.   . . . house, **28.**

381. *Fergus.* Come quickly, Conchubar will laugh, that I——
382.   Although I held out boldly in my speech—
383.   That I, even I——

    Deirdre.   Wait, wait! He is not done.

384. *Messenger.* Deirdre and Fergus, son of Rogh, are
        summoned;
385.   But not the traitor that bore off the Queen.
386.   It is enough that the King pardon her,
387.   And call her to his table and his bed.

388. *Naoise.* So, then, it's treachery.

    Fergus.   I'll not believe it.

389. *Naoise.* Lead on and I will follow at your heels
390.   That I may challenge him before his court
391.   To match me there, or match me in some place
392.   Where none can come between us but our swords,
393.   For I have found no truth on any tongue
394.   That's not of iron.

    Messenger.   I am Conchubar's man,

---

381. . . . quickly, Conchubar . . . laugh that I,
382. . . . speech,
383. . . . —
       Wait, wait he . . . . **28.**
383a. *Fergus.* That am so great a friend, (friend **28**) have doubted him.
    27-32.
384. Deirdre, and . . . , son (Son **28**) . . . summoned; (summoned, **28**)
    27-32; Deirdre, and Fergus son . . .; **48, 63.**
385. . . . queen.
386. . . . king . . . , **27-63.**
388. So then, ... **27, 40-69**; So then it's . . . . **28.**
389-390. [lacking]
391. Tell Conchubar to meet me in . . . place (place, **28**) **27-63.**
392. . . . us, but . . . swords. **27**; Where we can settle all with the grey
    edge. **28**; . . . swords. **32.**
393. [lacking] **27-32.**
394. *Messenger.* I have done my message; I am . . . man; (man, **28**) **27-
    32**; . . . man; **40-63.**

395. I am content to serve an iron tongue:
396. That Tongue commands that Fergus, son of Rogh,
397. And Deirdre come this night into his house,
398. And none but they.   *[He goes, followed by Naoise.*

Fergus.   Some rogue, some enemy,
399. Has bribed him to embroil us with the King;
400. I know that he has lied because I know
401. King Conchubar's mind as if it were my own,
402. But I'll find out the truth.

        [He is about to follow Naoise, but Deirdre stops him.

Deirdre.   No, no, old man.
403. You thought the best, and the worst came of it;
404. We listened to the counsel of the wise,
405. And so turned fools. But ride and bring your friends.
406. Go, and go quickly. Conchubar has not seen me;
407. It may be that his passion is asleep,
408. And that we may escape.

Fergus.   But I'll go first,
409. And follow up that Libyan heel, and send

---

395. I take no message from a traitor's lips. [*He goes.*] **27-32**; I take no message but he bids me do it. [*He goes.*] **40-63**.
396-397. [lacking] **27-63**.
397. . . . house **69**.
398. *Naisi.* No, but you must; (must, **28**) and I will have you swear **27-32**; *Naisi.* I bid you. I will have you swear to take it. [*He follows Messenger out.*] **40-63**.
Directions in 398. [. . . *goes followed* . . . .] **69**.
399. *Naisi.* To carry it unbroken. [*He follows Messenger out.*]
Fergus.   He has been suborned. (It is but lies. **28**) **27-32**; *Fergus.* Some enemy has paid him well for this. **40-63**; . . . king; **69**.
400. [lacking]
401. I know King . . . mind (mind, **28**) as it . . . own;
402. I'll learn the truth from him.
        [*He . . . him.*]
        No, . . . man, (man; **28**) **27-63**.
403. . . . best and . . . it,
404. . . . wise **28**.
406. . . . me.
407. . . . asleep **28**.
409. . . . heel and . . . **28**.

410.   Such words to Conchubar that he may know
411.   At how great peril he lays hands upon you.

Naoise enters

412. *Naoise.* The Libyan, knowing that a servant's life
413.   Is safe from hands like mine, but turned and mocked.

414. *Fergus.* I'll call my friends, and call the reaping-hooks,
415.   And carry you in safety to the ships.
416.   My name has still some power. I will protect,
417.   Or, if that is impossible, revenge.

[Goes out by other door.

Naoise [who is calm, like a man who has passed beyond life].
418.   The crib has fallen and the birds are in it;
419.   There is not one of the great oaks about us
420.   But shades a hundred men.

Deirdre.   Let's out and die,
421.   Or break away, if the chance favour us.

422. *Naoise.* They would but drag you from me, stained
              with blood.
423.   Their barbarous weapons would but mar that beauty,
424.   And I would have you die as a queen should—
425.   In a death-chamber. You are in my charge.
426.   We will wait here, and when they come upon us,
427.   I'll hold them from the doors, and when that's over,
428.   Give you a cleanly death with this grey edge.

---

410. . . . Conchubar, that . . . **27-63.**
412. . . . a messenger **28.**
413. . . . mocked **84.**
414. . . . reaping hooks **28** ; . . . reaping-hooks. **89.**
417. Or if . . . . **28.**
     Directions before 418. [. . . *calm like* . . . .] **48, 63.**
418. . . . it. **28.**
420. . . . die
421. . . . away if . . . . **28.**
424. . . . die, as . . . should, **28.**
425. . . . death chamber. . . . . **27-69.**
426. . . . here and . . . , **28.**

429. *Deirdre*. I will stay here; but you go out and fight.

430.   Our way of life has brought no friends to us,

431.   And if we do not buy them leaving it,

432.   We shall be ever friendless.

    Naoise.   What do they say?

433.   That Lugaidh Redstripe and that wife of his

434.   Sat at this chess-board, waiting for their end.

435.   They knew that there was nothing that could save
         them,

436.   And so played chess as they had any night

437.   For years, and waited for the stroke of sword.

438.   I never heard a death so out of reach

439.   Of common hearts, a high and comely end.

440.   What need have I, that gave up all for love,

441.   To die like an old king out of a fable,

442.   Fighting and passionate? What need is there

443.   For all that ostentation at my setting?

444.   I have loved truly and betrayed no man.

445.   I need no lightning at the end, no beating

446.   In a vain fury at the cage's door.

447.   [*To Musicians*.] Had you been here when that man
         and his queen

448.   Played at so high a game, could you have found

449.   An ancient poem for the praise of it?

450.   It should have set out plainly that those two,

451.   Because no man and woman have loved better,

452.   Might sit on there contentedly, and weigh

453.   The joy comes after. I have heard the seamew

454.   Sat there, with all the colour in her cheeks,

455.   As though she'd say: 'There's nothing happening

---

429. . . . here, but . . . . **28**.

431. . . . them, leaving . . . , **28**.

433. . . . and his sweetheart sat **28**.

434. . . . chessboard, ... **27, 32-48, 55-69** ; Before this chessboard, ... **28**.

435. . . . them

436. . . . chess, as . . . **28**.

437. . . . sword, **48, 63**.

439. . . . end: **27, 32**.

442. . . . passionate! What . . .

443. . . . setting!

444. . . . man; **28**.

453. . . . sea-mew **28**.

456.   But that a king and queen are playing chess.'

457.   *Deirdre.* He's in the right, though I have not been born
458.   Of the cold, haughty waves, my veins being hot,
459.   And though I have loved better than that queen,
460.   I'll have as quiet fingers on the board.
461.   O, singing women, set it down in a book,
462.   That love is all we need, even though it is
463.   But the last drops we gather up like this;
464.   And though the drops are all we have known of life,
465.   For we have been most friendless—praise us for it,
466.   And praise the double sunset, for naught's lacking
467.   But a good end to the long, cloudy day.

468.   *Naoise.* Light torches there and drive the shadows out,
469.   For day's grey end comes up.
        [*A Musician lights a torch in the fire and then crosses before the
        chess-players, and slowly lights the torches in the sconces. The light is
        almost gone from the wood, but there is a clear evening light in the
        sky, increasing the sense of solitude and loneliness.*

        Deirdre.   Make no sad music.
470.   What is it but a king and queen at chess?
471.   They need a music that can mix itself
472.   Into imagination, but not break
473.   The steady thinking that the hard game needs.

---

457.   . . . right, but I . . . **28.**
458.   . . . waves. My veins are hot. **27, 32**; Out of the cold sea. My veins
        are fiery— **28**; . . . hot. **40-63**; . . . cold, heighty waves, . . . , **97A.**
459.   But though . . . , **27, 32**; Though I love better than that sea-born
        queen, **28.**
461.   Oh, . . . book **27-40, 45** (1911), **48-63.**
463.   . . . this, **27, 28.**
464.   . . . life— **28**; . . . life,— **48, 63.**
465.   . . . it **27, 32-45, 52, 55, 69**; . . . friendless,—praise . . . it (it. **63**) **48,
        63.**
466.   . . . lacking, **27, 32-69.**
468.   . . . out **28**; . . . out. **40-84.**
469.   . . . day's red end . . . . **27, 32**; . . . day's red end . . . up.
                                    [Directions lacking]
                                            Make . . . . **28.**

[*During the chess, the Musicians sing this song*]

474.	Love is an immoderate thing
475.	And can never be content
476.	Till it dip an ageing wing
477.	Where some laughing element
478.	Leaps and Time's old lanthorn dims.
479.	What's the merit in love-play,
480.	In the tumult of the limbs
481.	That dies out before 'tis day,
482.	Heart on heart, or mouth on mouth,
483.	All that mingling of our breath,
484.	When love-longing is but drouth
485.	For the things come after death?

[*During the last verses Deirdre rises from the board and kneels at Naoise's feet.*

486. *Deirdre.* I cannot go on playing like that woman
487.   That had but the cold blood of the sea in her veins.

488. *Naoise.* It is your move. Take up your man again.

489. *Deirdre.* Do you remember that first night in the woods
490.   We lay all night on leaves, and looking up,
491.   When the first grey of the dawn awoke the birds,
492.   Saw leaves above us? You thought that I still slept,
493.   And bending down to kiss me on the eyes,
494.   Found they were open. Bend and kiss me now,

Directions before 474. [*The Three Musicians.*] **28.**
475. . . . content, **27-69.**
476. . . . wing, **27, 32-69.**
478. Leaps, and . . . . **28 ;** . . . dims, **45** (1913).
479. . . . love play,
480. . . . limbs,
481. . . . day: **28.**
482. . . . mouth **27.**
483. . . . breath **28.**
484. . . . love longing . . . drought **27, 28 ;** . . . love longing . . . **40-69.**
Directions after 485. [. . . *Deirdre puts down the chessmen and goes round and kneels* . . . .] **28.**
489. . . . woods? **28.**
492. . . . us. You . . . , **27-32.**

495.   For it may be the last before our death.
496.   And when that's over, we'll be different;
497.   Imperishable things, a cloud or a fire.
498.   And I know nothing but this body, nothing
499.   But that old vehement, bewildering kiss.

                              [*Conchubar comes to the door.*

500.   *First Musician.* Children, beware!

        Naoise [*laughing*].   He has taken up my challenge;
501.   Whether I am a ghost or living man
502.   When day has broken, I'll forget the rest,
503.   And say that there is kingly stuff in him.
            [*Turns to fetch spear and shield, and then sees that Conchubar has
            gone.*

504.   *First Musician.* He came to spy upon you, not to fight.[1]

505.   *Naoise.* A prudent hunter, therefore, but no king.
506.   He'd find if what has fallen in the pit
507.   Were worth the hunting, but has come too near,
508.   And I turn hunter. You're not man, but beast.
509.   Go scurry in the bushes, now, beast, beast,
510.   For now it's topsy-turvy, I upon you.

                              [*He rushes out after Conchubar.*

511.   *Deirdre.* You have a knife there, thrust into your
            girdle.
512.   I'd have you give it me.

        First Musician.   No, but I dare not.

---

496.   . . . different,
497·   . . . things,—a . . . fire,— **28**.
        Speaker at 500, 512, 513, 516, 521, 524, 536. ['Musician' for 'First
        Musician'] **27-69**.
500.   . . . challenge. **28**.
        Directions after 503. [. . . *shield, and sees that* . . . .] **55**.
504.[1] *Deirdre.* He . . . upon us, not . . . . **27-32**.
507.   . . . hunting but . . . near; **28**.
510.   . . . topsy-turvey. (-turvy. **69-89**) I . . . . **40-89**.
        Directions after 510. [. . . *Conchubar. The house is now dark but for the
        light of the torches and a faint evening light in the sky.*] **28**.
511.   . . . girdle; **28** ; . . . there thrust . . . . **32**.

                      [1] The final alteration in **35**.

513. *Deirdre.* No, but you must.

First Musician. If harm should come to you,
514. They'd know I gave it.

Deirdre [snatching knife]. There is no mark on this
515. To make it different from any other
516. Out of a common forge.

[*Goes to the door and looks out.*

First Musician. You have taken it,
517. I did not give it you; but there are times
518. When such a thing is all the friend one has.

519. *Deirdre.* The leaves hide all, and there's no way to find
520. What path to follow. Why is there no sound?

[*She goes from door to window.*

521. *First Musician.* Where would you go?

Deirdre. To strike a blow for Naoise,
522. If Conchubar call the Libyans to his aid.
523. But why is there no clash? They have met by this!

524. *First Musician.* Listen. I am called wise. If Conchubar win,
525. You have a woman's wile that can do much,
526. Even with men in pride of victory.
527. He is in love and old. What were one knife
528. Among a hundred?

Deirdre [going towards them]. Women, if I die,
529. If Naoise die this night, how will you praise?
530. What words seek out? for that will stand to you;
531. For being but dead we shall have many friends.
532. All through your wanderings, the doors of kings
533. Shall be thrown wider open, the poor man's hearth
534. Heaped with new turf, because you are wearing this

[*Gives Musician a bracelet.*

535. To show that you have Deirdre's story right.

---

521. . . . Naisi **28**.
522. . . . calls . . . . **48, 63**.
524. . . . called far-seeing. If . . . , **27, 32**; Listen, I . . . called far seeing.
If . . . , **28**.
525. . . . much **28**.
Directions after 534. [*Gives bracelet.*] **28**.

536. *First Musician.* Have you not been paid servants in love's
          house
537.   To sweep the ashes out and keep the doors?
538.   And though you have suffered all for mere love's
          sake
539.   You'd live your lives again.

Deirdre.   Even this last hour.
          Conchubar enters with dark-faced men

540. *Conchubar.* One woman and two men; that is the
          quarrel
541.   That knows no mending. Bring in the man she chose
542.   Because of his beauty and the strength of his youth.
                    [*The dark-faced men drag in Naoise entangled in a net.*

543. *Naoise.* I have been taken like a bird or a fish.

544. *Conchubar.* He cried 'Beast, beast!' and in a blind-
          beast rage
545.   He ran at me and fell into the nets,
546.   But we were careful for your sake, and took him
547.   With all the comeliness that woke desire
548.   Unbroken in him. I being old and lenient,
549.   I would not hurt a hair upon his head.

550. *Deirdre.* What do you say? Have you forgiven him?

551. *Naoise.* He is but mocking us. What's left to say
552.   Now that the seven years' hunt is at an end?

553. *Deirdre.* He never doubted you until I made him,
554.   And therefore all the blame for what he says

---

538. . . . sake, **48.**
540. . . . is a quarrel **27, 32-63** ; . . . men, that is a quarrel **28.**
541. . . . . Bring the . . . **27-32.**
          Directions after 542. [*Naisi is dragged in in a net.*] **28.**
544. . . . cried Beast, beast, and . . . **27** ; . . . cried beast, beast, and . . .
          blind beast . . . **28.**
545. . . . nets.
546. . . . sake and . . . **28.**
548. . . . lenient— **27, 32-63** ; . . . him, for being . . . lenient **28** ; . . . lenient
          69.

555.   Should fall on me.

Conchubar.   But his young blood is hot,

556.   And if we're of one mind, he shall go free,
557.   And I ask nothing for it, or, if something,
558.   Nothing I could not take. There is no king
559.   In the wide world that, being so greatly wronged,
560.   Could copy me, and give all vengeance up,
561.   Although her marriage-day had all but come,
562.   You carried her away; but I'll show mercy.
563.   Because you had the insolent strength of youth
564.   You carried her away; but I've had time
565.   To think it out through all these seven years.
566.   I will show mercy.

Naoise.   You have many words.

567. *Conchubar.* I will not make a bargain; I but ask
568.   What is already mine.

              [*Deirdre moves slowly towards Conchubar while he is speaking, her eyes fixed upon him.*

                                You may go free

569.   If Deirdre will but walk into my house
570.   Before the people's eyes, that they may know,
571.   When I have put the crown upon her head,
572.   I have not taken her by force and guile.
573.   The doors are open, and the floors are strewed
574.   And in the bridal chamber curtains sewn
575.   With all enchantments that give happiness
576.   By races that are germane to the sun,
577.   And nearest him, and have no blood in their veins—

---

557. . . . , or if . . . , **28.**
560. . . . me and . . . .
561. . . . marriage day . . . , **28.**
563. . . . youth, **28.**
565. . . . years; **28.**
567. . . . bargain, I . . . **28.**
      Directions in 568. [lacking] **27-32.**
570. . . . know
571. . . . head **27-69.**
573. . . . strewed, **27-63.**
575. . . . happiness, **27-69.**
576. . . . are neighbours to . . . , **27** ; . . . that being neighbours of the . . . , **28.**
577. And kindred to him, . . . – **27** ; And of his kindred have . . . veins,– **28.**

578.   For when they're wounded the wound drips with
        wine—
579.   Nor speech but singing. At the bridal door
580.   Two fair king's daughters carry in their hands
581.   The crown and robe.

Deirdre.   O no! Not that, not that!
582.   Ask any other thing but that one thing.
583.   Leave me with Naoise. We will go away
584.   Into some country at the ends of the earth.
585.   We'll trouble you no more; and there is no one
586.   That will not praise you if you pardon us.
587.   'He is good, he is good', they'll say to one another;
588.   'There's nobody like him, for he forgave
589.   Deirdre and Naoise.'

Conchubar.   Do you think that I
590.   Shall let you go again, after seven years
591.   Of longing and of planning here and there,
592.   And trafficking with merchants for the stones
593.   That make all sure, and watching my own face
594.   That none might read it?

Deirdre [*to Naoise*].   It's better to go with him.
595.   Why should you die when one can bear it all?
596.   My life is over; it's better to obey.
597.   Why should you die? I will not live long, Naoise.
598.   I'd not have you believe I'd long stay living;
599.   O no, no, no! You will go far away.
600.   You will forget me. Speak, speak, Naoise, speak,
601.   And say that it is better that I go.
602.   I will not ask it. Do not speak a word,
603.   For I will take it all upon myself.

---

578.   . . . wounded, the . . . wine,– **28**.
579.   . . . door. **45** (1913).
581.   . . . . Oh, no! . . . that. (that, **48, 63**) **27, 32-69** ; . . . . Oh, no. Not . . .
      that. **28**.
582.   . . . thing than that . . . . **28** ; . . . thing, **97A**.
583.   . . . away. **28, 45** (1913), **69**.
585.   . . . more. You will be praised
586.   By everybody if . . . . **27-32**.
587.   . . . another, **28**.
591.   . . . longing, and . . . , **97A**.
598.   . . . living. **28**.
599.   Oh . . . . **27, 32-69** ; Oh, no, no, no. You . . . . **28**.

604.   Conchubar, I will go.

Naoise.   And do you think
605.   That, were I given life at such a price,
606.   I would not cast it from me? O my eagle!
607.   Why do you beat vain wings upon the rock
608.   When hollow night's above?

Deirdre.   It's better, Naoise.
609.   It may be hard for you, but you'll forget.
610.   For what am I, to be remembered always?
611.   And there are other women. There was one,
612.   The daughter of the King of Leodas;
613.   I could not sleep because of her. Speak to him;
614.   Tell it out plain, and make him understand.
615.   And if it be he thinks I shall stay living,
616.   Say that I will not.

Naoise.   Would I had lost life
617.   Among those Scottish kings that sought it of me
618.   Because you were my wife, or that the worst
619.   Had taken you before this bargaining!
620.   O eagle! If you were to do this thing,
621.   And buy my life of Conchubar with your body,
622.   Love's law being broken, I would stand alone
623.   Upon the eternal summits, and call out,
624.   And you could never come there, being banished.

625.   *Deirdre [kneeling to Conchubar].* I would obey, but cannot.
             Pardon us.
626.   I know that you are good. I have heard you praised

---

605.   That were . . . price **28.**
606.   . . . ? O, my . . . ! **27, 32-63** ; . . . eagle **28.**
610.   . . . I to . . . always, **28.**
612.   . . . king . . . Leodas,
613.   . . . him,
614.   . . . plain and . . . understand, **28.**
617.   . . . me, **27-69.**
619.   . . . bargaining.
        Directions after 619. [*He rises to his knees, struggling to free himself from the net, but sinks back.*] **28.**
620.   . . . ! if . . . , **27, 32** ; . . . eagle, if . . . , **28.**
623.   . . . out **28.**
625.   . . . obey but . . . . **28.**

627.   For giving gifts; and you will pardon us,
628.   Although I cannot go into your house.
629.   It was my fault. I only should be punished.

> *[Unseen by Deirdre, Naoise is gagged.*

630.   The very moment these eyes fell on him,
631.   I told him; I held out my hands to him;
632.   How could he refuse? At first he would not—
633.   I am not lying—he remembered you.
634.   What do I say? My hands?—No, no, my lips—
635.   For I had pressed my lips upon his lips—
636.   I swear it is not false—my breast to his;

> *[Conchubar motions; Naoise, unseen by Deirdre, is taken behind
> the curtain.*

637.   Until I woke the passion that's in all,
638.   And how could he resist? I had my beauty.
639.   You may have need of him, a brave, strong man,
640.   Who is not foolish at the council-board,
641.   Nor does he quarrel by the candle-light
642.   And give hard blows to dogs. A cup of wine
643.   Moves him to mirth, not madness.

> *[She stands up.*
>
> What am I saying?

644.   You may have need of him, for you have none
645.   Who is so good a sword, or so well loved
646.   Among the common people. You may need him,
647.   And what king knows when the hour of need may
            come?

---

627.   ... gifts. And ... , **28.**
        Directions after 629. [lacking] **28.**
631.   ... him, I ... him.
632.   And how ... not.—
633.   ... lying.—He ....
634.   ... hands, no, no, my lips,
635.   ... lips, **28.**
636.   ... false. My ... his **28** ; ... his: **69A.**
        Directions after 636. [*Conchubar makes a sign, and Naisi, ...*] **28** ;
        [...; *Naisi unseen ....*] **40, 45, 52, 55.**
640.   ... council board, (board 56) **27-63.**
641.   ... candlelight, **28** ; ... candle light **45** (1913).
643.   [set as two lines ending madness. / saying?] **28.**
644.   .. him for ...
645.   ... sword or ...
646.   .. him. **28.**

648.   You dream that you have men enough. You laugh.

649.   Yes; you are laughing to yourself. You say,

650.   'I am Conchubar—I have no need of him.'

651.   You will cry out for him some day and say,

652.   'If Naoise were but living'—[*she misses Naoise*].
            Where is he?

653.   Where have you sent him? Where is the son of
            Usna?

654.   Where is he, O, where is he?
            [*She staggers over to the Musicians. The Executioner has come out
            with a sword on which there is blood; Conchubar points to it. The
            Musicians give a wail.*

655.   *Conchubar.* The traitor who has carried off my wife

656.   No longer lives. Come to my house now, Deirdre,

657.   For he that called himself your husband's dead.

658.   *Deirdre.* O, do not touch me. Let me go to him.

                                                                [*Pause.*

659.   King Conchubar is right. My husband's dead.

660.   A single woman is of no account,

661.   Lacking array of servants, linen cupboards,

662.   The bacon hanging—and King Conchubar's house

663.   All ready, too—I'll to King Conchubar's house.

664.   It is but wisdom to do willingly

665.   What has to be.

        Conchubar.   But why are you so calm?

666.   I thought that you would curse me and cry out,

667.   And fall upon the ground and tear your hair.

---

648.   . . . laugh; **28.**
649.   Yes, you . . . , **28.**
650.   I . . . him. **27**; I . . . Conchubar; I . . . him. **28.**
652.   If . . . living— . . . ? **27, 28.**
653.   . . . him, where . . . Usnach?
654.   . . . , oh, . . . ? **28.**
        Directions after 654. [. . . *with sword* . . . .] **27, 32-69**; [. . . *a drawn
        sword . . . blood. Conchubar* . . . .] **28.**
655.   . . . who had carried . . . **28.**
658.   Oh, . . . him— **28.**
661.   . . . cupboards. **28.**
663.   . . . ready too— . . . . **28.**

668.   *Deirdre* [*laughing*]. You know too much of women to
          think so;
669.   Though, if I were less worthy of desire,
670.   I would pretend as much; but, being myself,
671.   It is enough that you were master here.
672.   Although we are so delicately made,
673.   There's something brutal in us, and we are won
674.   By those who can shed blood. It was some woman
675.   That taught you how to woo: but do not touch me:
676.   I shall do all you bid me, but not yet,
677.   Because I have to do what's customary.
678.   We lay the dead out, folding up the hands,
679.   Closing the eyes, and stretching out the feet,
680.   And push a pillow underneath the head,
681.   Till all's in order; and all this I'll do
682.   For Naoise, son of Usna.

       Conchubar.   It is not fitting.
683.   You are not now a wanderer, but a queen,
684.   And there are plenty that can do these things.

685.   *Deirdre* [*motioning Conchubar away*]. No, no. Not yet. I
          cannot be your queen
686.   Till the past's finished, and its debts are paid.
687.   When a man dies, and there are debts unpaid,
688.   He wanders by the debtor's bed and cries,
689.   'There's so much owing.'

       Conchubar.   You are deceiving me.
690.   You long to look upon his face again.
691.   Why should I give you now to a dead man

---

668.   . . . so, **28.**
669.   Though if . . . ,
670.   . . . much. But, . . . , **28.**
675.   . . . me, **27, 32** ; . . . woo; but . . . me, **28.**
676.   For I'll go with you and do all your will **27-32** ; . . . yet **40-69.**
677.   When I have done whatever's customary. **27-32.**
679.   . . . eyes and . . . , **28.**
681.   . . . order, and . . . **28.**
683.   . . . wanderer but . . . , **28.**
       Directions in 685.   [lacking] **28.**
685.   . . . queen, **40-69** ; . . . yet. cannot . . . **89.**
687.   . . . dies and . . . , **27-32.**
689.   There's . . . owing. . . . . **27-32.**

692.   That took you from a living?

[*He makes a step towards her.*]

Deirdre.   In good time.

693.   You'll stir me to more passion than he could,
694.   And yet, if you are wise, you'll grant me this:
695.   That I go look upon him that was once
696.   So strong and comely and held his head so high
697.   That women envied me. For I will see him
698.   All blood-bedabbled and his beauty gone.
699.   It's better, when you're beside me in your strength,
700.   That the mind's eye should call up the soiled body,
701.   And not the shape I loved. Look at him, women.
702.   He heard me pleading to be given up,
703.   Although my lover was still living, and yet
704.   He doubts my purpose. I will have you tell him
705.   How changeable all women are; how soon
706.   Even the best of lovers is forgot
707.   When his day's finished.

Conchubar.   No; but I will trust

708.   The strength that you have praised, and not your
            purpose.

709.   *Deirdre* [*almost with a caress*]. It is so small a gift and you
            will grant it
710.   Because it is the first that I have asked.

---

692.   [set as two lines ending living? / time] **28** ; . . . time **28.**
694.   . . . this, **28.**
697.   . . . me; for . . . **28.**
699.   . . . better when beside . . . strength **28** ; . . . better when . . . , **55.**
700.   . . . body **28.**
702.   . . . up **28.**
704.   . . . him, **55.**
705.   . . . are. How . . . **27-40, 45** (1911), **48-69.**
706.   . . . forgot, **27, 32-69.**
707.   . . . .
            No, but . . . **28.**
708.   . . . strength you have spoken of, (of **28**) and . . . . **27-32.**
709.   I'll have this gift[1] **27, 28** ; I'll have this gift—the first that I have
            asked. **32** ; . . . gift, and . . . **48, 63.**
710.   [lacking] **32.**

[1] Short line.

711.　He has refused. There is no sap in him;
712.　Nothing but empty veins. I thought as much.
713.　He has refused me the first thing I have asked—
714.　Me, me, his wife. I understand him now;
715.　I know the sort of life I'll have with him;
716.　But he must drag me to his house by force.
717.　If he refuses [*she laughs*], he shall be mocked of all.
718.　They'll say to one another, 'Look at him
719.　That is so jealous that he lured a man
720.　From over sea, and murdered him, and yet
721.　He trembled at the thought of a dead face!'

　　　　　　　　　　　[*She has her hand upon the curtain.*

722.　*Conchubar.* How do I know that you have not some
　　　　　knife,
723.　And go to die upon his body?

　　Deirdre.　　　　　　　　　　Have me searched,
724.　If you would make so little of your queen.
725.　It may be that I have a knife hid here
726.　Under my dress. Bid one of these dark slaves
727.　To search me for it.　　　　　　　　　　[*Pause.*

　　Conchubar.　　　　　Go to your farewells, Queen.

728.　*Deirdre.* Now strike the wire, and sing to it a while,
729.　Knowing that all is happy, and that you know
730.　Within what bride-bed I shall lie this night,

711.　. . . him, **27-32.**
713.　. . . I ask,
714.　. . . now,
715.　. . . him, **28.**
717.　. . . refuse . . . . **27-63.**
718.　. . . him, **28.**
720.　. . . oversea, . . .
721.　. . . face.' **28.**
　　　Directions after 721.　[. . . *upon curtain.*] **27-84.**
722.　. . . knife
723.　. . . searched **28.**
727.　. . . , queen. **27-69.**
　　　Direction in 727.　[lacking] **28.**
728.　. . . wire (wire, **32**) and . . . awhile, **28, 32** ; . . . awhile, **52** ; . . . wire
　　　and . . . , **69A.**
729.　. . . happy and . . . **28.**
730.　. . . night **48, 63.**

731. And by what man, and lie close up to him,
732. For the bed's narrow, and there outsleep the cock-
       crow.   [*She goes behind the curtain.*

733. *First Musician.* They are gone, they are gone. The proud
       may lie by the proud.

734. *Second Musician.* Though we were bidden to sing, cry
       nothing loud.

735. *First Musician.* They are gone, they are gone.

     Second Musician.   Whispering were enough.

736. *First Musician.* Into the secret wilderness of their love.

737. *Second Musician.* A high, grey cairn. What more is to
       be said?

738. *First Musician.* Eagles have gone into their cloudy bed.
       [*Shouting outside. Fergus enters. Many men with scythes and sickles
       and torches gather about the doors. The house is lit with the glare of
       their torches.*

739. *Fergus.* Where's Naoise, son of Usna, and his queen?
740. I and a thousand reaping-hooks and scythes
741. Demand him of you.

     Conchubar.   You have come too late.
742. I have accomplished all. Deirdre is mine;
743. She is my queen, and no man now can rob me.
744. I had to climb the topmost bough, and pull
745. This apple among the winds. Open the curtain

---

731. . . . him **69.**
732. . . . narrow; and . . . . **28.**
737. . . . , gray cairn, what . . . ? **28.**
     Directions after 738. [. . . *enters.*] **28.**
740. . . . reaping hooks . . . **28.**
742. . . . mine, **28.**
743. . . . man can . . . . **97A.**
744. . . . bough and . . . **27-32.**
745. . . . curtain, **27, 32-63, 69E ;** . . . curtain. **69A.**

746.   That Fergus learn my triumph from her lips.

[*The curtain is drawn back. The Musicians begin to keen with low voices.*

747.   No, no; I'll not believe it. She is not dead—
748.   She cannot have escaped a second time!

749.   *Fergus.* King, she is dead; but lay no hand upon her.
750.   What's this but empty cage and tangled wire,
751.   Now the bird's gone? But I'll not have you touch it.

752.   *Conchubar.* You are all traitors, all against me—all.
753.   And she has deceived me for a second time;
754.   And every common man can keep his wife,
755.   But not the King.

[*Loud shouting outside*: 'Death to Conchubar!' 'Where is Naoise?' etc. *The dark-faced men gather round Conchubar and draw their swords; but he motions them away.*

I have no need of weapons,
756.   There's not a traitor that dare stop my way.
757.   Howl, if you will; but I, being King, did right
758.   In choosing her most fitting to be Queen,
759.   And letting no boy lover take the sway.

THE END

Directions after 746.   [. . . *back.*] **28.**
747.   No, no. I'll . . . dead.
748.   . . . time. **28.**
750.   . . . wire **28.**
751.   . . . ? but . . . . **27, 32-63** ; . . . gone; but . . . . **28.**
752.   . . . me, all; **28.**
753.   . . . time. **27, 32-63.**
754.   . . . man may keep . . . , **27-32.**
Directions in 755.   [. . . . *The* (*The* **52**) *dark-skinned men* . . . .] **27, 32-45, 52-69.**
755.   . . . king.
[*One can see through doors and windows men, who carry scythes and sickles, and many torches. The wood is lighted with the torches which shine into the house. The crowd shouts:* 'Death . . . Conchubar,' 'Where . . . Naisi?' . . . dark-skinned men . . . .]
. . . weapons. **28** ; . . . weapons. **52.**
756.   [lacking] **28.**
757.   . . . king, . . . **27, 32-63** ; Howl if . . . will but . . . king, . . . **28** ; . . . ; but, I being king, . . . **69.**
758.   . . . queen, **27, 32-69** ; . . . queen **28.**
759.   . . . lover come between. **28.**

NOTES

[Many of the changes that Yeats made in 'Deirdre' were published initially in the notes to **27** (**27a**), **32** (**32a**), in *Samhain* (**S**) for November 1908, and in the four-page pamphlet *Alterations in Deirdre* (**35**). They are collated in the body of the text; they are also transcribed complete in these notes: **32a, S,** and **35** are collated.]

The legend on which 'Deirdre' is founded is, perhaps, the most famous of all Irish legends. The best version is that in Lady Gregory's 'Cuchulain of Muirthemne,' and is made up out of more than a dozen old texts. All these texts differ more or less, sometimes in essential things, and in arranging the story for the bounds of a one-act play, I have had to leave out many details, even some important persons, that are in all the old versions. I have selected certain things which seem to be characteristic of the tale as well as in themselves dramatic, and I have separated these from much that needed an epic form or a more elaborate treatment. Deirdre was the Irish Helen, and Naisi her Paris, and Concobar her Menelaus, and the events took place, according to the conventional chronology of the Bards, about the time of the birth of Christ. Concobar was High King of Ulster, and Naisi King of one of the sub-kingdoms, and the scene of the play is laid in a guest-house among woods in the neighbourhood of Armagh, where Concobar had his palace.

Fergus, who in the old poems is a mixture of chivalry and folly, had been High King before Concobar, but had been tricked into abdicating in his favour. I have made no use of this abdication in my play, except that it helps to justify the popular influence I have attributed to him. I have introduced three wandering musicians, who are not in the legend, and Mr. Arthur Darlay has written the music of their songs. The scenery has been designed by Mr. Robert Gregory.   W. B. Y.

The Arrow, 24 November 1906.

*   *   *

'Deirdre' was first played at the Abbey Theatre, Dublin, on November 27, 1906, with Miss Darragh as Deirdre; Mr. Frank Fay as Naisi; Mr. Sinclair as Fergus; Mr. Kerrigan as Conchobar; and Miss Sara Allgood, Miss M'Neill, and Miss O'Dempsey as the Musicians. The scenery was by Mr. Robert Gregory.   Appendix II, **28**.

... Deirdre, Mr. ... Naisi, Mr. ... Fergus, Mr. ... Conchubar, and ... Algood, Miss McNeill, ... Gregory.   Appendix IV, **32**.

Deirdre was ... Theatre, Dublin, on November 24, 1906, with the following cast:—

Musicians	{	Miss Sara Allgood Miss Maire O'Neill Miss Brigit O'Dempsey
Fergus, *an old man*		Arthur Sinclair
Naisi, *a young king*		F. J. Fay
Deirdre, *his Queen*		Miss Darragh
A Dark-faced Messenger		U. Wright
Conchubar		J. M. Kerrigan
Dark-faced Executioner		A. Power

Since then the principal part has been taken by Miss Mona Limerick, Miss Sara Allgood and Miss Maire (and Maire **52, 63**) O'Neill; and by Mrs. Patrick Campbell who played it in Dublin and London with the Abbey Company in 1907 and 1908, (1908 **52, 63**) as well as playing it with a company of her own in London in the Autumn of 1907.

Notes, 45, 52, 63.

'Deirdre' was . . . November 27, 1906, with . . . Gregory.

Since then the principal part has been taken by Miss Mona Limerick, Miss Sara Allgood, and Miss Maire O'Neill, and by Mrs. Patrick Campbell, who played it in Dublin and London with the Abbey Company in 1907 and 1908, as well as playing it with a company of her own in London in the autumn of 1907.

Abbey Theatre, Dublin, March, 1912.   **W. B. YEATS**

Appendix II, 48.

This play was first played [follows the version in **52, 63** with these changes:] . . . November 26, 1906, . . . Bridget . . . Fergus . . Arthur Sinclair / Naisi . . . F. J. Fay / Deirdre . . Miss Darragh / Messenger . . U. Wright / Conchubar . . J. M. Kerrigan / Executioner . . A. Power

Since . . . Allgood, and Miss Maire O'Neill, and . . . Campbell, who . . . 1908, as . . . autumn of 1907. I have revised it a good deal of recent years, especially this last year.—1922.   Notes, **69**.

*   *   *

While correcting the proof, I noticed that a passage which I had cut out, because it overweighted what should have been a swift movement in the middle of the play, was necessary to prepare for the words of the messenger. It should come after the entrance of DEIRDRE and NAISI (pp. 10-11)[1] where the movement is slow. Their first lines should read as follows:—

> [*NAISI lays down shield and spear and helmet, as if weary. He goes to the door opposite to the door he entered by. He looks out on to the road that leads to Conchubar's house. If he is anxious, he would not have Fergus or Deirdre notice it. Presently he comes from the door, and goes to the table where the chessboard is.*

[1] At directions after line 140.

v 149.   *Fergus*. You are welcome, lady.
              Deirdre.   Conchubar has not come.
,, 150.   Were the peace honest, he'd have come himself
,, 151.   To prove it so.
              Fergus.   Being no more in love
,, 152.   He stays in his own house, arranging where
,, 153.   The curlew and the plover go, and where
,, 154.   The speckled heath-cock in a golden dish.
,, 155.   *Deirdre*. But there's no messenger.
              Fergus.   He'll come himself
,, 156.   When all's in readiness and night closed in,
,, 157.   But till that hour, &c.   Note, **27 (27a)**.

After the first performance of this play in the autumn of 1906, I rewrote the play up to the opening of the scene where Naisi and Deirdre play chess. The new version was played in the spring of 1907, and after that I rewrote from the entrance of Deirdre to her questioning the musicians, but felt, though despairing of setting it right, that it was still mere bones, mere dramatic logic. The principal difficulty with the form of dramatic structure I have adopted is that, unlike the loose Elizabethan form, it continually forces one by its rigour of logic away from one's capacities, experiences, and desires, until, if one have not patience to wait for the mood, or to rewrite again and again till it comes, there is rhetoric and logic and dry circumstance where there should be life. After the version printed in the text of this book had gone to press, Mrs. Patrick Campbell came to our Abbey Theatre and, liking what she saw there, offered to come and play Deirdre among us next November, and this so stirred my imagination that the scene came right in a moment. It needs some changes in the stage directions at the beginning of the play. There is no longer need for loaf and flagon, but the women at the braziers should when the curtain rises be arraying themselves—the one holding a mirror for the other perhaps. The play then goes on unchanged till the entrance of Deirdre, when the following scene is substituted for that on pages 139-140.[1] (Bodb is pronounced Bove.)

> *Deirdre, Naisi and Fergus enter. Deirdre is carrying a little embroidered bag.*
> *She goes over towards the women.*

149.   *Deirdre*. Silence your music, though I thank you for it;
150.   But the wind's blown upon my hair, and I
151.   Must set the jewels on my neck and head
152.   For one that's coming.
           Naisi.   Your colour has all gone
153.   As 'twere with fear, and there's no cause for that.
154.   *Deirdre*. These women have the raddle that they use
155.   To make them brave and confident, although

156.   Dread, toil or cold may chill the blood o' their cheeks.
157.   You'll help me, women. It is my husband's will
158.   I show my trust in one that may be here
159.   Before the mind can call the colour up.
160.   My husband took these rubies from a king
161.   Of Surracha that was so murderous
162.   He seemed all glittering dragon. Now wearing them
163.   Myself wars on myself, for I myself—
164.   That do my husband's will, yet fear to do it—
vı65.   Grow dragonish to myself.

[*The Women have gathered about her. Naisi has stood looking at her, but Fergus leads him to the chess-table.*

Fergus.   We'll play at chess
vı73.   Till the king come. It is but natural
vı74.   That she should fear him, for her house has been
175.   The hole of the badger and the den of the fox.
vı76.   *Naisi.* If I were childish and had faith in omens
176a.   I'd rather not have lit on that old chessboard
vı77.   At my homecoming.
Fergus.   There's a tale about it,—
178.   It has been lying there these many years,—
vı79.   Some wild old sorrowful tale.
Naisi.   It is the board
180.   Where Lugaidh Redstripe and that wife of his
181.   Who had a seamew's body half the year
182.   Played at the chess upon the night they died.
vı83.   *Fergus.* I can remember now: a tale of treachery,
184.   A broken promise and a journey's end.
vı85.   But it were best forgot.

[*Deirdre has been standing with the women about her. They have been helping her to put on her jewels and to put the pigment on her cheeks and arrange her hair. She has gradually grown attentive to what Fergus is saying.*

Naisi.   If the tale's true,—
186.   When it was plain that they had been betrayed,
187.   They moved the men and waited for the end
188.   As it were bedtime, and had so quiet minds
189.   They hardly winked their eyes when the sword flashed.
190.   *Fergus.* She never could have played so, being a woman,
191.   If she had not the cold sea's blood in her.
vı92.   *Deirdre.* I have heard the ever-living warn mankind
192a.   By changing clouds and casual accidents
vı93.   Or what seem so.
Naisi.   Stood th' ever-living there,
193a.   Old Lir and Aengus from his glassy tower,
193b.   And that hill-haunting Bodb to warn us hence,—
193c.   Our honour is so knitted up with staying,

v194. King Conchubar's word and Fergus' word being pledged,
v196. I'd brave them out and stay.
　　　Deirdre.　　　　　　　　　　No welcomer,
v198. And a bare house upon the journey's end!
v199. Is that the way a king that means no wrong
200. Honours a guest?
　　Fergus.　　　　　　　　He is but making ready
201. A welcome in his house, arranging where
202. The moorhen and the mallard go, and where
203. The speckled heath-cock, in a golden dish.
v204. *Deirdre.* Has he no messenger—
　　　　　　　　　　　[Etc., etc.]

The play then goes on unchanged, except that on page 151, instead of
the short speech of Deirdre, beginning 'Safety and peace,' one should read
v314.　　　　　　　　　　　　'Safety and peace!
v315. I had them when a child, but from that hour
315a. I have found life obscure and violent,
315b. And think that I shall find it so for ever.'
　　　　'A Different Version of Deirdre's Entrance.' Appendix II. **32**
　　　　(32a).

————

There are two passages in this play as published which I always knew to
be mere logic, mere bones, and yet (yet, **35**) after many attempts (attempts,
35) I thought it impossible to alter them. When, however, Mrs. Campbell
offered to play the part (part, **35**) my imagination began to work again. I
think they are now as they should be.

Instead of the lines from the end of the musician's (musicians' **35**) song
[line 148] to 'Haste no more' ('Hush! no more' **35**) [variant of line 200]
insert the following:—

[S and **35** are collated below with **32a**]
156. . . . , toil or . . . . **35.**
158. . . . one, that . . . **S, 35.**
161. . . . murderous, **S** ; . . . murderous. **35.**
　　　Directions in 165. [. . . *Fergus brings him* . . . .] **S, 35.**
173. . . . comes . . . . **35.**
v176. . . . omens,
177. . . . home-coming.
　　　　　　　　　There's . . . it—
178. . . . years— **S, 35.**
180. . . . his,
181. . . . year, **S, 35.**
v183. . . . now, a . . . , **S, 35.**
184. . . . promise, and . . . end **S** ; . . . end— **35.**
v185. . . . true **S** ; . . . true, **35.**
192a. . . . accidents, **35.**
193a. . . . Lir, and . . . , **35.**

193b.   . . . hence, **S** ; . . . Bodb, to . . . hence, **35.**

203.   . . . heathcock **S, 35.**

v204.   . . . Messenger?— **S** ; . . . messenger? **35.** [End of collation with **32a**] *Naisi.* Be silent, Deirdre, **S, 35.**

205.   You are King Conchubar's guest, etc. (guest (&c.) **35**) **S, 35.**
         Instead of the lines from 'The horses are still saddled' etc. [line 288a] to 'For she must never fall into his hands' [line 371f] insert the following:—

289.   *Deirdre.* I have heard terrible mysterious things. (things, **35**)

290.   Magical horrors and the spells of wizards.

291.   *Fergus.* Why (Why, **35**) that's no wonder. You have been listening

292.   To singers of the roads that gather up

293.   The stories of the world.
         Deirdre.   But I have one

294.   To make the stories of the world but nothing.

v295.   *Naisi.* Be silent if it is against the king

v296.   Whose guest you are.
         Fergus.   No, let her speak it out (out, **35**)

297.   I know the High King's heart as it were my own (own, **35**)

298.   And can refute a slander, but already

299.   I have warned these women that it may be death.

300.   *Naisi.* I will not weigh the gossip of the roads

v301.   With the king's word, (word. **35**) I ask your pardon for her, (her: **35**)

302.   She has the heart of the wild birds that fear

303.   The net of the fowler or the wicker cage.

304.   *Deirdre.* Am I to see the fowler and the cage

v305.   And speak no word at all. (all? **35**)
         Naisi. You would have known (known, **35**)

306.   Had they not bred you in that mountainous place (place, **35**)

v307.   That when we give a word and take a word,

308.   Sorrow is put away, past wrong forgotten.

309.   *Deirdre.* Though death may come of it. (it? **35**)
         Naisi.   Though death may come.

309a.   *Fergus.* To those that slander kings.
         Deirdre.   Then I will say

319.   What it were best to carry to the grave, (grave. **35**)

320.   Look at my face where the leaf raddled it

320a.   And at these harmless though unlidded eyes

v321.   About my hair and breast. It was for him,

v322.   To wake his love, to stir him to desire (desire, **35**)

v323.   I put on beauty, yes (beauty; yes, **35**) for Conchubar.

324.   *Naisi.* What frenzy put these words into your mouth?

v325.   *Deirdre.* No frenzy (frenzy, **35**) but a sudden change that turned

v328.   Old hate to love.
         Naisi.   You are mocking me (me. **35**) **S, 35.**

v329.   *Deirdre*. And is there mockery in my face and eyes?
333.   *Naisi*. What woman is there that a man can trust
334.   But at the moment when he kisses her
v335.   At the first midnight. (midnight? **35**) Come, for I command it
              (it: **35**)
340.   We'll to the horses and take ship again.
341.   *Fergus*. Fool, she but seeks to rouse your jealousy
342.   With crafty words.
         Deirdre.   Were we not born to wander?
343.   These jewels have been reaped by the innocent sword
344.   Upon a mountain, and a mountain bred me;
345.   But who can tell what change can come to love
346.   Among the valleys. (valleys? **35**) I speak no falsehood now.
v347.   We'll to the windy summits (summits, **35**) and there mock
v348.   The night-jar and the valley-keeping bird (bird. **35**)
349.   *Fergus*. Men blamed you that you stirred a quarrel up
v350.   That has brought death to many. I have poured
v351.   Water upon the fire, but if you fly
v353.   A second time, the house is in a blaze,
v354.   And all the screaming household will but blame
v355.   The savage heart of beauty for it all;
v356.   And Naisi (Naisi, **35**) that but (has **35**) helped to tar the wisp
              (wisp, **35**)
v357.   Shall be a hunted outlaw all his days.
v359.   *Deirdre*. I will be blamed no more. There's but one way. (way: **35**)
360.   I'll spoil this beauty that brought misery, (misery **35**)
361.   And houseless wandering on the man I loved (loved. **35**)
362.   These wanderers will show me how to do it (it; **35**)
363.   To clip this hair to baldness, blacken my skin
364.   with (With **35**) walnut juice (juice, **35**) and tear my face with
              briars, (briars. **35**)
v365.   Oh, that the creatures of the woods had torn
366.   My body with their claws. (claws! **35**)
         Fergus.   What, wilder yet!
367.   *Deirdre* [*to Naisi*]. Whatever were to happen to my face
368.   I'd be myself, and there's not any way
369.   But this to bring all trouble to an end.
v370.   *Naisi*. What have you told to put such frenzy in her?
370a.   *Fergus*. Yes, speak it out.
         Naisi.   I give you my protection (protection, **35**)
370b.   Are you afraid to speak? Does the king love her?
v371.   Will no one answer?
         Deirdre.   Tell out all the plot (plot, **35**)
371a.   The spells, (plan, **35**) the network, all the treachery, (treachery;
              35)
371b.   Tell of the bridal chamber and the bed, **S. 35**.

371c.   The magical stones, the wizard's handiwork.

371d.   *Naisi.* Ah, (Ah! **35**) now I understand why it is you fear

371e.   To waken death with words. Take care of Deirdre (Deirdre: **35**)

371f.   She must not fall alive into his hands. **S, 35.**

On page 32 the sentence, 'He came to spy upon us, not to fight,' [line 504] should read, 'He came to spy upon you, not to fight' and it should be given to the musician.

Alterations in 'Deirdre.' *Samhain*, November 1908 (**S**) ; **35.**

Deirdre, like the other plays in this book, has been altered many times after performance, till at last I had come to think I had put all my knowledge into it and could not, apart from the always incalculable pleasure good playing brings, look for greater pleasure than it had already given me. But now because of Mr. Craig's scene which is fitted to so many moods and actions, and makes possible natural and expressive light and shade, I have begun to alter it again and to find in this a new excitement. Sooner or later it will be tried at the Abbey Theatre with what is, I believe, a new stage effect. The barbarous dark-faced men, who have not hitherto been all I imagined (perhaps because our stage is shallow), will not show themselves directly to the eyes when they pass the door, nor will the dark-faced messenger when he comes and says that supper's ready, nor it may be Conchubar when he comes to spy and not to fight. I will see passing shadows and standing shadows only. Perhaps the light that casts them may grow blood-red as the sun sets, but of that I am not sure. I have tried these shadows upon the stage and thought them impressive, but as I have not tried them before an audience I leave the old directions for the present. Should these shadows become a permanent part of the representation I will have to abandon the windows and doors through which one sees at present a wood and evening sky. But, perhaps, shadows of leaves seen on the wall beside the door under a shifting light will accompany the Musician's long opening speech.

Should these effects become permanent, some slight changes in the text will be necessary. I record them here partly for my own use and that of my players. On page 20, after 'Should I be less than Conchubar, being a man' [line 371s] I will insert these two speeches—

> '*Deirdre.* There, there upon the wall.
> *Naisi.*   Could he find none
> But a dark skin and Libyan axe to face me?'

And on page 23 after 'and drive the shadows out' [line 468] instead of 'For day's grey end comes up.—Make no sad music' [line 469] read—

> '*First Musician.* The sconces are all empty.
> *Deirdre.*   If the sun
> Now that he fades must need call shadows up,
> Call them with sound but sound it airily.'[1]

---

[1] There is no record of these changes' being used.

and then go on 'What is it but a king and queen at chess?' [line 470] as before.

If the play be played in this way the dark men when they enter with the king bring torches, but I may let the king enter as at present when he comes to spy, the shadow of fear become a substance at last, for the passing of the second musician across the stage holding her torch has dramatic value.

Notes 45.

* * *

. . . . I am haunted by certain moments: . . . ; Mrs. Patrick Campbell in my 'Deirdre,' passionate and solitary; . . . .

From 'Preliminaries,' IV, 93.

* * *

Variant spellings

briar 27, 32-97; *brier* 28.
cockcombs 28; *cockscombs* 27, 32-97.
gray 28; *grey* 27, 32-97.
Istain 27, 32-97; *Istian* 28.
Lugaid 84, 89; *Lugaidh* 27-69, 97.
Naisi 27-69; *Naoise* 84-97.
naught 27-32, 45 (1911), 48-63, 84-97; *nought* 28 (both spellings), 45 (1913), 69.
phantasy 27-89; *fantasy* 97.
Rogh 27-63, 97; *Roigh* 69-89.
topsy-turvey 27, 45-63; *topsy-turvy* 28, 32, 69-97.
Ulad 84, 89; *Uladh* 27-55, 69, 97.
Usna 27, 32-97; *Usnach* 27 (both spellings), 28, 32 (both spellings).

* * *

[See also the notes on *The Only Jealousy of Emer*, p. 566, *The King of the Great Clock Tower*, p. 1008, *The Legendary and Mythological Foundation of the Plays*, p. 1283; *Glossary*, p. 1284; and *Prefaces to 45, 69*, pp. 1296, 1306.]

AT THE HAWK'S WELL

1917

Persons in the Play

Three Musicians (*their faces made up to resemble masks*)
The Guardian of the Well (*with face made up to resemble a mask*)
An Old Man (*wearing a mask*)
A Young Man (*wearing a mask*)

Time—*The Irish Heroic Age*

The stage is any bare space before a wall against which stands a patterned screen. A drum and a gong and a zither have been laid close to the screen before the play begins. If necessary, they can be carried in, after the audience is seated, by the First Musician, who also can attend to the lights if there is any special lighting. We had two lanterns upon posts—designed by Mr. Dulac—at the outer corners of the stage, but they did not give enough light, and we found it better to play by the light of a large chandelier. Indeed, I think, so far as my present experience goes, that the most effective lighting is the lighting we are most accustomed to in

---

PRINTINGS[1] *Harper's Bazaar*,[2] March 1917; *To-day* (London), June 1917; **58, 64, 71, 84, 97.**

DATE [lacking] **HB-71.**

DRAMATIS PERSONAE ... Well (*face* ... **HB**; [lacking] **T, 58**; Persons of the ... **64, 71.**

TIME The Time— ... **HB, 64, 71**; [lacking] **T, 58.**

STAGE DIRECTIONS ... *in after* ... *seated by* .... *Indeed I* ... *strangers* ... *two musicians* ... *cloth singing* ... : **HB**; *Scene: The* ... *space in a room against a wall. Against the wall are placed before the play begins, a drum, cymbals, and a stringed instrument. The three Musicians enter slowly. One carries a black cloth. He stands in the middle of the space. The others stand one on either side and slowly unfold the cloth till a part of the stage is hidden. As they unfold it they move backward and outward so that the cloth makes an angle, with one Musician at the apex. Hid by the cloth a girl enters and crouches on the ground. The Musicians sing while the cloth is being unfolded. (unfolded and folded up again.* **T**) **T, 58**; .... *Indeed* (*Indeed,* **71**) *I* ... *two musicians* ... *so:* **64, 71.**

[1] The pamphlet *The Well of Immortality* (v. Wade, *op. cit.*, item 119) is not included in the printings since it is obvious that Yeats could have had no hand in it.
[2] In **HB** the dialogue is in italics, the stage directions in roman.

our rooms. These masked players seem stranger when there is no mechnaical means of separating them from us. The First Musician carries with him a folded black cloth and goes to the centre of the stage towards the front and stands motionless, the folded cloth hanging from between his hands. The two other Musicians enter and, after standing a moment at either side of the stage, go towards him and slowly unfold the cloth, singing as they do so:

1.	I call to the eye of the mind
2.	A well long choked up and dry
3.	And boughs long stripped by the wind,
4.	And I call to the mind's eye
5.	Pallor of an ivory face,
6.	Its lofty dissolute air,
7.	A man climbing up to a place
8.	The salt sea wind has swept bare.

As they unfold the cloth, they go backward a little so that the stretched cloth and the wall make a triangle with the First Musician at the apex supporting the centre of the cloth. On the black cloth is a gold pattern suggesting a hawk. The Second and Third Musicians now slowly fold up the cloth again, pacing with a rhythmic movement of the arms towards the First Musician and singing:

9.	What were his life soon done!
10.	Would he lose by that or win?
11.	A mother that saw her son
12.	Doubled over a speckled shin,
13.	Cross-grained with ninety years,
14.	Would cry, 'How little worth
15.	Were all my hopes and fears
16.	And the hard pain of his birth!'

TEXT   Title . . . Well / *or Waters of Immortality* / By William Butler Yeats / With Edmund Dulac's Costume Designs **HB ;** . . . Well: A Play **T, 58.**

2. . . . dry, **T, 58.**
5. . . . face **HB.**
   Directions after 8.   [lacking] **T ;** [*They fold up the cloth singing*] **58.**
9. I have dreamed of a life soon done,
10. Will he . . . ? **HB-58.**
12. . . . shin
13. . . . years
14. . . . cry 'how . . . **HB.**

The words 'a speckled shin' are familiar to readers of Irish legendary stories in descriptions of old men bent double over the fire. While the cloth has been spread out, the Guardian of the Well has entered and is now crouching upon the ground. She is entirely covered by a black cloak; beside her lies a square blue cloth to represent a well. The three Musicians have taken their places against the wall beside their instruments of music; they will accompany the movements of the players with gong or drum or zither.

First Musician [*singing*].

17.   The boughs of the hazel shake,
18.   The sun goes down in the west.

Second Musician [*singing*].

19.   The heart would be always awake,
20.   The heart would turn to its rest.
                [*They now go to one side of the stage rolling up the cloth.*

21. *First Musician* [*speaking*]. Night falls;
22.   The mountain-side grows dark;
23.   The withered leaves of the hazel
24.   Half choke the dry bed of the well;
25.   The guardian of the well is sitting
26.   Upon the old grey stone at its side,
27.   Worn out from raking its dry bed,

Directions after 16.   [. . . *cloak. The three Musicians* . . . .] **HB, 64, 71** ; [*The Musicians sit down near the wall*] **T, 58.**
17.   . . . shake;
18.   . . . West. **T, 58.**
19.   . . . awake **HB** ; . . . awake: **T** ; . . . awake; **58.**
Directions after 20.   [. . . *cloth. A Girl has taken her place by a square blue cloth representing a well. She is motionless.*] **HB, 64, 71** ; [lacking] **T, 58.**
Directions in 21.   [lacking] **T, 58.**
21.   . . . falls **HB.**
22.   . . . dark **HB** ; . . . dark, **T, 58.**
24.   Half-choke . . . well (well; **64, 71**) **HB, 64, 71** ; . . . well. **T, 58.**
26.   . . . side
27.   . . . bed **HB.**

28.   Worn out from gathering up the leaves.
29.   Her heavy eyes
30.   Know nothing, or but look upon stone.
31.   The wind that blows out of the sea
32.   Turns over the heaped-up leaves at her side;
33.   They rustle and diminish.

34. *Second Musician.* I am afraid of this place.

Both Musicians [singing].

35.   'Why should I sleep?' the heart cries,
36.   'For the wind, the salt wind, the sea wind,
37.   Is beating a cloud through the skies;
38.   I would wander always like the wind.'

An Old Man enters through the audience

39. *First Musician [speaking].* That old man climbs up hither,
40.   Who has been watching by his well
41.   These fifty years.
42.   He is all doubled up with age;
43.   The old thorn-trees are doubled so
44.   Among the rocks where he is climbing.
       [*The Old Man stands for a moment motionless by the side of the
       stage with bowed head. He lifts his head at the sound of a drum-tap.
       He goes towards the front of the stage moving to the taps of the drum.
       He crouches and moves his hands as if making a fire. His movements,
       like those of the other persons in the play, suggest a marionette.*

---

30.   . . . stone **HB.**
32.   . . . side. **HB.**
       Speakers at 35.   *Musicians.* **T, 58.**
35.   . . . sleep,' the . . . , **HB, 64, 71E**; . . . cries **58**; . . . cries. **71A.**
36.   . . . wind **HB-64.**
37.   . . . skies. **T, 58.**
       Directions after 38.   [lacking] **T, 58.**
39.   . . . hither
40.   . . . by this well **HB-58.**
42.   . . . age **HB.**
       Directions after 44.   [. . . *drum tap.* . . . .] **HB, 64, 71**; [*An Old Man
       enters through the audience from the other side. He crouches down a little way
       from the well, moving his hands as if he were making a fire. He has, however,
       nothing in his hands. (hands. His movements keep time to strokes upon the drum.*
       58)] **T, 58**; [. . . *drum-top.* . . . .] **97A.**

45. *First Musician* [*speaking*]. He has made a little heap of
    leaves;
46.   He lays the dry sticks on the leaves
47.   And, shivering with cold, he has taken up
48.   The fire-stick and socket from its hole.
49.   He whirls it round to get a flame;
50.   And now the dry sticks take the fire,
51.   And now the fire leaps up and shines
52.   Upon the hazels and the empty well.

    Musicians [*singing*].
53.   'O wind, O salt wind, O sea wind!'
54.   Cries the heart, 'it is time to sleep;
55.   Why wander and nothing to find?
56.   Better grow old and sleep.'

57. *Old Man* [*speaking*]. Why don't you speak to me? Why
    don't you say:
58.   'Are you not weary gathering those sticks?
59.   Are not your fingers cold?' You have not one word,
60.   While yesterday you spoke three times. You said:
61.   'The well is full of hazel leaves.' You said:
62.   'The wind is from the west.' And after that:
63.   'If there is rain it's likely there'll be mud.'
64.   To-day you are as stupid as a fish,
65.   No, worse, worse, being less lively and as dumb.

                      [*He goes nearer.*
66.   Your eyes are dazed and heavy. If the Sidhe
67.   Must have a guardian to clean out the well

Speaker and directions in 45.   [lacking] **58.**
45. . . . leaves **HB.**
47. And shivering . . . cold he . . . **HB.**
49. . . . flame **HB.**
50. . . . fire **HB, 64, 71.**
51. . . . shines. **HB.**
53. . . . wind,' **T, 58.**
54. . . . sleep **HB ;** . . . sleep. **T, 58.**
55. . . . find **HB.**
57. . . . say, **HB, T, 71A ;** . . . me? why . . . say, **58 ;** . . . say **64, 71E.**
59. . . . word **HB.**
60. . . . times, you . . . : **HB ;** . . . said, **T, 58.**
61. . . . hazel-leaves.' . . . said, **T, 58.**
62. . . . that, **HB ;** . . . West.' . . . that, **T, 58.**
64. . . . fish; **T, 58.**

68. And drive the cattle off, they might choose somebody
69. That can be pleasant and companionable
70. Once in the day. Why do you stare like that?
71. You had that glassy look about the eyes
72. Last time it happened. Do you know anything?
73. It is enough to drive an old man crazy
74. To look all day upon these broken rocks,
75. And ragged thorns, and that one stupid face,
76. And speak and get no answer.

Young Man [*who has entered through the audience during the last speech*]. Then speak to me,
77. For youth is not more patient than old age;
78. And though I have trod the rocks for half a day
79. I cannot find what I am looking for.

Old Man. Who speaks?
80. Who comes so suddenly into this place
81. Where nothing thrives? If I may judge by the gold
82. On head and feet and glittering in your coat,
83. You are not of those who hate the living world.

84. *Young Man.* I am named Cuchulain, I am Sualtim's son.

85. *Old Man.* I have never heard that name.

Young Man. It is not unknown.
86. I have an ancient house beyond the sea.

87. *Old Man.* What mischief brings you hither?—you are like those
88. Who are crazy for the shedding of men's blood,

---

74. . . . rocks
75. . . . thorns and . . . , **HB-58.**
76. . . . me **HB.**
77. . . . age **HB;** . . . age, **T;** . . . age. **58.**
78. And I . . .
79. Nor found what . . . ? **HB-58.**
84. . . . Cuchulain. I . . . Sualtam's . . . . **T, 58, 71.**
85. . . . name.
86. *Cuchulain.* (*Young Man.* **T**) It is not unknown. I have an ancient house beyond the sea. **HB, T.**
87. . . . hither, you . . . **HB, 64;** . . . hither? You . . . **T, 58;** . . . hither—you **71, 84.**
88. . . . man's . . . , **T, 58.**

89.   And for the love of women.

Young Man.   A rumour has led me,
90.   A story told over the wine towards dawn.
91.   I rose from table, found a boat, spread sail,
92.   And with a lucky wind under the sail
93.   Crossed waves that have seemed charmed, and found
           this shore.

94. *Old Man.* There is no house to sack among these hills
95.   Nor beautiful woman to be carried off.

96. *Young Man.* You should be native here, for that rough
           tongue
97.   Matches the barbarous spot. You can, it may be,
98.   Lead me to what I seek, a well wherein
99.   Three hazels drop their nuts and withered leaves,
100.   And where a solitary girl keeps watch
101.   Among grey boulders. He who drinks, they say,
102.   Of that miraculous water lives for ever.

103. *Old Man.* And are there not before your eyes at the
           instant
104.   Grey boulders and a solitary girl
105.   And three stripped hazels?

Young Man.   But there is no well.

106. *Old Man.* Can you see nothing yonder?

Young Man.   I but see

---

89.   . . . women?
                    A . . . , **HB, T, 64-84.**
       [between 90 and 91 a break] **58.**
91.   . . . sail **HB, 64, 71.**
92.   . . . sail, **T, 58.**
93.   . . . charmed and . . . . **HB, T ;** . . . charmed.
       Old Man.   There is no house **58.**
94.   To sack . . . hills, champion to conquer **58.**
95.   Nor a fair woman . . . . **HB, T.**
96.   . . . here for . . .
97.   . . . spot, you . . . , **HB.**
98.   . . . seek—a . . . **T, 58.**
99.   . . . leaves **HB.**
102.   . . . forever. **HB.**

107.   A hollow among stones half-full of leaves.

108. *Old Man.* And do you think so great a gift is found
109.   By no more toil than spreading out a sail,
110.   And climbing a steep hill? O, folly of youth,
111.   Why should that hollow place fill up for you,
112.   That will not fill for me? I have lain in wait
113.   For more than fifty years, to find it empty,
114.   Or but to find the stupid wind of the sea
115.   Drive round the perishable leaves.

     Young Man.   So it seems
116.   There is some moment when the water fills it.

117. *Old Man.* A secret moment that the holy shades
118.   That dance upon the desolate mountain know,
119.   And not a living man, and when it comes
120.   The water has scarce plashed before it is gone.

121. *Young Man.* I will stand here and wait. Why should the luck
122.   Of Sualtim's son desert him now? For never
123.   Have I had long to wait for anything.

124. *Old Man.* No! Go from this accursed place! This place
125.   Belongs to me, that girl there, and those others,
126.   Deceivers of men.

     Young Man.   And who are you who rail
127.   Upon those dancers that all others bless?

128. *Old Man.* One whom the dancers cheat. I came like you
129.   When young in body and in mind, and blown
130.   By what had seemed to me a lucky sail.

---

111. . . . you?
112. Are you a better man than I (I, **T, 58**) who have . . . **HB-58.**
113. . . . years to . . . , **HB-71.**
115. . . . leaves?
             So . . . **HB-58.**
122. . . . Sualtam's . . . ? for . . . **T, 58.**
124. . . . place, this . . . **HB, 64, 71 ;** . . . place: this . . . **T, 58.**
125. . . . there and . . . , **HB-71.**
128. . . . came, like you, **T, 58.**

131.   The well was dry, I sat upon its edge,
132.   I waited the miraculous flood, I waited
133.   While the years passed and withered me away.
134.   I have snared the birds for food and eaten grass
135.   And drunk the rain, and neither in dark nor shine
136.   Wandered too far away to have heard the plash,
137.   And yet the dancers have deceived me. Thrice
138.   I have awakened from a sudden sleep
139.   To find the stones were wet.

Young Man.   My luck is strong,
140.   It will not leave me waiting, nor will they
141.   That dance among the stones put me asleep;
142.   If I grow drowsy I can pierce my foot.

143.   *Old Man.* No, do not pierce it, for the foot is tender,
144.   It feels pain much. But find your sail again
145.   And leave the well to me, for it belongs
146.   To all that's old and withered.

Young Man.   No, I stay.
        [*The Guardian of the Well gives the cry of the hawk.*
147.   There is that bird again.

Old Man.   There is no bird.

148.   *Young Man.* It sounded like the sudden cry of a hawk,
149.   But there's no wing in sight. As I came hither
150.   A great grey hawk swept down out of the sky,
151.   And though I have good hawks, the best in the world
152.   I had fancied, I have not seen its like. It flew
153.   As though it would have torn me with its beak,
154.   Or blinded me, smiting with that great wing.

---

131.   ... dry; I ... edge. **T, 58.**
132.   ... flood; I ... **58.**
134.   ... grass,
135.   ... rain and ... **T, 58.**
139.   ... strong; **T, 58.**
141.   ... asleep, **HB, T ;** ... asleep. **58.**
143.   ... it for ... , **HB.**
        Directions after 146. [*The Girl gives ....*] **HB-71.**
151.   ... hawks,—the ...
152.   ... fancied,—I ... **58.**
153.   ... beak **HB-58.**
154.   ... me smiting .... **HB ;** ... blinded smiting me with .... **T, 58.**

155.   I had to draw my sword to drive it off,
156.   And after that it flew from rock to rock.
157.   I pelted it with stones, a good half-hour,
158.   And just before I had turned the big rock there
159.   And seen this place, it seemed to vanish away.
160.   Could I but find a means to bring it down
161.   I'd hood it.

Old Man.   The Woman of the Sidhe herself,

162.   The mountain witch, the unappeasable shadow.
163.   She is always flitting upon this mountain-side,
164.   To allure or to destroy. When she has shown
165.   Herself to the fierce women of the hills
166.   Under that shape they offer sacrifice
167.   And arm for battle. There falls a curse
168.   On all who have gazed in her unmoistened eyes;
169.   So get you gone while you have that proud step
170.   And confident voice, for not a man alive
171.   Has so much luck that he can play with it.
172.   Those that have long to live should fear her most,
173.   The old are cursed already. That curse may be
174.   Never to win a woman's love and keep it;
175.   Or always to mix hatred in the love;
176.   Or it may be that she will kill your children,
177.   That you will find them, their throats torn and
        bloody,

---

157.   ... half hour, **HB** ; ... stones a ... , **T, 58.**
158.   ... there, **T, 58.**
161.   ... woman ... , **HB-71.**
162.   ... shadow, **HB, 58.**
162a. In one or another shape, now hawk or wolf,
162b. Or panic-stricken deer, as the mood takes her, **T.**
163.   ... mountain side **58.**
164.   ... destroy. Go from this place
165.   Before a beak or claw is in your flesh, **T.**
166-170.   [lacking] **T.**
166.   ... shape, they ...
167.   ... battle; and there ... **58.**
168.   ... eyes **HB** ; ... have looked on that unmoistened eye; **58.**
170.   ... voice—for there's no man ... **58.**
171.   Before she has put a lifelong curse upon you. **T** ; ... it— **58.**
171a. Before she has put a lifelong curse upon you. **58.**
174.   ... it **HB** ; ... it, **T, 58.**
175.   ... love, **HB.**
176.   ... children— **T, 58.**

178.   Or you will be so maddened that you kill them
179.   With your own hand.

Young Man.   Have you been set down there
180.   To threaten all who come, and scare them off?
181.   You seem as dried up as the leaves and sticks,
182.   As though you had no part in life.

[The Guardian of the Well gives hawk cry again.
               That cry!

183.   There is that cry again. That woman made it,
184.   But why does she cry out as the hawk cries?

185. *Old Man.* It was her mouth, and yet not she, that cried.
186.   It was that shadow cried behind her mouth;
187.   And now I know why she has been so stupid
188.   All the day through, and had such heavy eyes.
189.   Look at her shivering now, the terrible life
190.   Is slipping through her veins. She is possessed.
191.   Who knows whom she will murder or betray
192.   Before she awakes in ignorance of it all,
193.   And gathers up the leaves? But they'll be wet;
194.   The water will have come and gone again;
195.   That shivering is the sign. O, get you gone,
196.   At any moment now I shall hear it bubble.
197.   If you are good you will leave it. I am old,
198.   And if I do not drink it now, will never;
199.   I have been watching all my life and maybe
200.   Only a little cupful will bubble up.

---

178.   . . . you will kill . . . **HB-58.**
180.   . . . come and . . . ? **T, 58.**
       Directions in 182. [*Girl gives* . . . .] **HB-71.**
186.   . . . mouth, **HB-58.**
188.   . . . through and . . . .
189.   . . . now; the . . . **T, 58.**
191.   . . . or deceive **HB-58.**
192.   . . . all **T, 58.**
193.   . . . leaves! (leaves? **T, 58**) But they will be wet, **HB-58** ; . . . leaves!
       But . . . ; **64, 71.**
194.   . . . again, **HB.**
195.   . . . . Oh, . . . gone! **T, 58.**
196.   . . . bubble, **HB** ; . . . bubble; **T.**
197.   . . . old, **HB.**
198.   . . . now will . . . ; **HB-58.**

201. *Young Man.* I'll take it in my hands. We shall both
    drink,
202. And even if there are but a few drops,
203. Share them.

    Old Man.   But swear that I may drink the first;
204. The young are greedy, and if you drink the first
205. You'll drink it all. Ah, you have looked at her;
206. She has felt your gaze and turned her eyes on us;
207. I cannot bear her eyes, they are not of this world,
208. Nor moist, nor faltering; they are no girl's eyes.
    [*He covers his head. The Guardian of the Well throws off her cloak
    and rises. Her dress under the cloak suggests a hawk.*

209. *Young Man.* Why do you fix those eyes of a hawk upon
    me?
210. I am not afraid of you, bird, woman, or witch.
    [*He goes to the side of the well, which the Guardian of the Well has
    left.*
211. Do what you will, I shall not leave this place
212. Till I have grown immortal like yourself.
    [*He has sat down; the Guardian of the Well has begun to dance,
    moving like a hawk. The Old Man sleeps. The dance goes on for
    some time.*

    First Musician [*singing or half-singing*].
213.   O God, protect me

---

201. ... drink **HB.**
202. ... drops **HB-58.**
203. ... first, **HB**; ... first. **58.**
204. ... greedy and ... **HB.**
205. ... her **HB**; ... all. Why did you look at her? **T, 58.**
206. ... us. **T.**
207. ... eyes, that are ... of the world, **T, 58.**
208. ... moist nor .... **HB-58.**
    Directions after 208. [... *head.*] **T, 58.**
209. ... you gaze upon me with the eyes ... hawk? **HB-71.**
    Directions after 210. [... *well which the Girl has ....*] **T**; [... *to the
place upon the stage the girl has ....*] **58.**
    Directions after 212. [... *down, the* (*down. The* **T, 58**) *Girl has ...
for two* (*for some two* **T, 58**) *minutes.*] **HB-58**; [... *down, the Girl has
....*] **64, 71.**
    Directions before 213. [... *half-singing the first three lines, then speaking*]
HB; [lacking] **T, 58.**
213. ... God protect ... **HB-64, 71E.**

214.   From a horrible deathless body
215.   Sliding through the veins of a sudden.
                    [*The dance goes on for some time. The Young Man rises slowly.*

216. *First Musician* [*speaking*]. The madness has laid hold upon
            him now,
217.   For he grows pale and staggers to his feet.
                                        [*The dance goes on.*

218. *Young Man.* Run where you will,
219.   Grey bird, you shall be perched upon my wrist.
220.   Some were called queens and yet have been perched
            there.   [*The dance goes on.*

221. *First Musician* [*speaking*]. I have heard water plash; it
            comes, it comes;
222.   Look where it glitters. He has heard the plash;
223.   Look, he has turned his head.
                    [*The Guardian of the Well has gone out. The Young Man drops his
                    spear as if in a dream and goes out.*

Musicians [*singing*].
224.   He has lost what may not be found
225.   Till men heap his burial-mound
226.   And all the history ends.

Directions after 215.   [. . . *some two minutes. The* . . . .] **HB**; [. . . *some
two minutes. Cuchulain rises* . . . .] **T, 58**.
Directions in 216.   [lacking] **HB, T**; Speaker and directions in 216.
[lacking] **58**.
219.   . . . wrist, **HB, 64, 71**; . . . wrist; **T, 58**.
Directions after 220.   [. . . *on for some two* (*two more* **T, 58**) *minutes.*]
HB-58.
221.   *Musicians.* I . . . plash [*The Hawk goes out*] it . . . comes, **HB**; *Musicians.*
I . . . plash (splash. **58**) [*The Hawk goes out.*] It . . . comes, **T, 58**; . . .
plash! it . . . ; **71A**.
222.   It glitters among the stones (stones, **T, 58**) and he . . . plash. **HB-58**;
It glitters among the stones and he . . . ; **64, 71**.
223.   . . . head! **T, 58**.
Directions after 223.   [*The Young Man drops* (*Cuchulain drops* **T**) *his
spear as if in a dream and goes out as if in a dream.*] **HB, T**; [*Cuchulain
drops his spear as if in a dream and goes out as if in a dream. The Musicians
sing.*] **58**; [*The Hawk has* . . . .] **64, 71**.
225.   . . . burial mound **HB, T, 64, 71**; . . . men have heaped his mound **58**.

227.   He might have lived at his ease,
228.   An old dog's head on his knees,
229.   Among his children and friends.

[*The Old Man creeps up to the well.*

230. *Old Man.* The accursed shadows have deluded me,
231.   The stones are dark and yet the well is empty;
232.   The water flowed and emptied while I slept.
233.   You have deluded me my whole life through,
234.   Accursed dancers, you have stolen my life.
235.   That there should be such evil in a shadow!

236. *Young Man* [*entering*]. She has fled from me and hidden
          in the rocks.

237. *Old Man.* She has but led you from the fountain. Look!
238.   Though stones and leaves are dark where it has flowed,
239.   There's not a drop to drink.

[*The Musicians cry* 'Aoife!' 'Aoife!' *and strike gong.*

Young Man.   What are those cries?
240.   What is that sound that runs along the hill?
241.   Who are they that beat a sword upon a shield?

242. *Old Man.* She has roused up the fierce women of the
          hills,
243.   Aoife, and all her troop, to take your life,
244.   And never till you are lying in the earth

---

227. . . . ease
228. . . . knees **HB.**
       Directions after 229. [. . . *to where the well is supposed to be.*] **58.**
230. . . . me **HB** ; . . . me; **T, 58.**
231. . . . empty **HB.**
232. . . . slept; **HB, 64, 71.**
233. . . . through. **HB-71.**
234. . . . life **HB.**
235. . . . shadow. **HB-64.**
238. The stones . . . , **HB-58.**
239. Yet there is not . . . ? **HB-71.**
       Directions in 239. [. . . *cry out and* . . . .] **HB** ; [. . . *cry out, and clash a cymbal.* (*clash their cymbals.* **58**)] **T, 58.**
244. . . . earth, **HB.**

245.   Can you know rest.

Young Man.   The clash of arms again!

246.   *Old Man.* O, do not go! The mountain is accursed;
247.   Stay with me, I have nothing more to lose,
248.   I do not now decieve you.

Young Man.   I will face them.
        [*He goes out, no longer as if in a dream, but shouldering his spear
        and calling:*

249.   He comes! Cuchulain, son of Sualtim, comes!
        [*The Musicians stand up; one goes to centre with folded cloth. The
        others unfold it. While they do so they sing. During the singing, and
        while hidden by the cloth, the Old Man goes out. When the play is
        performed with Mr. Dulac's music, the Musicians do not rise or
        unfold the cloth till after they have sung the words* 'a bitter life'.

                [*Songs for the unfolding and folding of the cloth*]

250.   Come to me, human faces,
251.   Familiar memories;
252.   I have found hateful eyes
253.   Among the desolate places,
254.   Unfaltering, unmoistened eyes.

---

246.   Oh, . . . accursed, **HB**; Oh, . . . go. The . . . accursed, **T, 58**; Oh,
        . . . ; **64, 71.**
247.   . . . me I . . . , **HB**; . . . me. I . . . lose. **T, 58.**
        Directions after 248. [. . . *out no . . . calling (calling.* **T**)] **HB, T**;
        [. . . *out not in . . . calling.*] **58**; [. . . *out no . . . calling (calling:* **71**)] **64,**
        71.
        Directions after 249. [*The Chorus stands up, one . . . Centre . . . out.*]
        HB; [*The Chorus stands up. One . . . cloth; the . . . singing the Old Man
        . . . out, taking the well with him. They then fold up the cloth again, singing.*]
        T; [*The Chorus stands up. One . . . cloth; the . . . it singing. During . . .
        singing the Old . . . out.*] **58**; [. . . *up, one . . . .*'] **64.**
        Directions before 250. [lacking] **HB-58.**
250.   . . . me human . . . ,
251.   . . . memories, **HB.**

255.	Folly alone I cherish,
256.	I choose it for my share;
257.	Being but a mouthful of air,
258.	I am content to perish;
259.	I am but a mouthful of sweet air.
260.	O lamentable shadows,
261.	Obscurity of strife!
262.	I choose a pleasant life
263.	Among indolent meadows;
264.	Wisdom must live a bitter life.

[They then fold up the cloth, singing.

265.	'The man that I praise',
266.	Cries out the empty well,
267.	'Lives all his days
268.	Where a hand on the bell
269.	Can call the milch cows
270.	To the comfortable door of his house.
271.	Who but an idiot would praise
272.	Dry stones in a well?'
273.	'The man that I praise',
274.	Cries out the leafless tree,
275.	'Has married and stays
276.	By an old hearth, and he

---

256. . . . share, **HB, 64**; . . . share. **T, 58.**
258. . . . perish, **HB, 64.**
[between 259 and 260 no break] **HB.**
261. . . . strife, **HB-71.**
262. . . . life, **HB, 64, 71.**
263. . . . meadows, **HB.**
Directions after 264. [. . . *cloth* (*cloth,* **64**) *again singing.*] **HB, 64**; [*lacking*] **T**; [*The Musicians fold . . . cloth again singing.*] **58.**
Directions before 265-280. [lacking] **T.**
265. '. . . Man . . .' **58.**
269. . . . milch-cows **58.**
[between 272 and 273 no break] **HB.**
273. '. . . Man . . . ,' **58.**
276. . . . hearth and . . . **HB.**

277.   On naught has set store
278.   But children and dogs on the floor.
279.   Who but an idiot would praise
280.   A withered tree?'   [*They go out.*

THE END

Directions after 280.   [lacking] 58.

NOTES

A couple of years ago I was sitting in my stall at the Court Theatre in London watching one of my own plays, 'The King's Threshold'. In front of me were three people, seemingly a husband, a wife and a woman friend. The husband was bored; he yawned and stretched himself and shifted in his seat, and I watched him with distress. I was inclined to be angry, but reminded myself that music where there are no satisfying audible words bores me as much, for I have no ear or only a primitive one. Presently, when the little princesses came upon the stage in their red clothes, the woman friend, who had seemed also a little bored, said: 'They do things very well,' and became attentive. The distinguished painter who had designed the clothes at any rate could interest her. The wife who had sat motionless from the first said when the curtain had fallen and the applause—was it politeness or enthusiasm?—had come to an end, 'I would not have missed it for the world'. She was perhaps a reader of my poetry who had persuaded the others to come, and she had found a pleasure the book could not give her in the combination of words and speech. Yet when I think of my play, I do not call her to the mind's eye, or even her friend who found the long red gloves of the little princesses amusing, but always that bored man; the worst of it is that I could not pay my players or the seamstress or the owner of the stage, unless I could draw to my plays those who prefer light amusement or have no ear for verse, and fortunately they are all very polite.

Being sensitive, or not knowing how to escape the chance of sitting behind the wrong people, I have begun to shrink from sending my muses where they are but half-welcomed; and even in Dublin, where the pit has an ear for verse, I have no longer the appetite to carry me through the daily rehearsals. Yet I need a theatre; I believe myself to be a dramatist; I desire to show events and not merely tell of them; and two of my best friends were won for me by my plays, and I seem to myself most alive at the moment when a room full of people share the one lofty emotion. My blunder has been that I did not discover in my youth that my theatre must be the ancient theatre that can be made by unrolling a carpet or marking out a place with a stick, or setting a screen against the wall. Certainly those who care for my kind of poetry must be numerous enough, if I can bring them together to pay half a dozen players who can bring all their properties in a cab and perform in their leisure moments.

I have found my first model—and in literature if we would not be parvenus we must have a model—in the 'Noh' stage of aristocratic Japan. I have described in the introduction to Mr. Pound's 'Certain Noble Plays of Japan' (Cuala Press, Dundrum, Ireland) what has seemed to me important on that most subtle stage. I do not think of my discovery as mere economy, for it has been a great gain to get rid of scenery, to substitute for a crude landscape painted upon canvas three performers who, sitting before the wall or a patterned screen, describe landscape or event, and accompany movement with drum and gong, or deepen the emotion of the words with zither or flute. Painted scenery, after all, is unnecessary to my friends and to myself, for our imagination kept living by the arts can imagine a mountain covered with thorn-trees in a drawing-room without any great trouble, and we have many quarrels with even good scene-painting.

Then too the masks forced upon us by the absence of any special lighting, or by the nearness of the audience who surround the players upon three sides, do not seem to us eccentric. We are accustomed to faces of bronze and of marble, and what could be more suitable than that Cuchulain, let us say, a half-supernatural legendary person, should show to us a face, not made before the looking-glass by some leading player—there too we have many quarrels—but moulded by some distinguished artist? We are a learned people, and we remember how the Roman theatre, when it became more intellectual, abandoned 'make-up' and used the mask instead, and that the most famous artists of Japan modelled masks that are still in use after hundreds of years. It would be a stirring adventure for a poet and an artist working together to create once more heroic or grotesque types that, keeping always an appropriate distance from life, would seem images of those profound emotions that exist only in solitude and in silence. Nor has any one told me after a performance that they have missed a changing facial expression, for the mask seems to change with the light that falls upon it, and besides in poetical and tragic art, as every 'producer' knows, expression is mainly in those movements that are of the entire body.

'At the Hawk's Well' was performed for the first time in April, 1916, in a friend's drawing-room, and only those who cared for poetry were invited. It was played upon the floor, and the players came in by the same door as the audience, and the audience and the players and I myself were pleased. A few days later it was revived in Lady Islington's big drawing-room at Chesterfield Gardens for the benefit of a war charity. The cast was as follows: the Young Man, Mr. Henry Ainley; the Old Man, Mr. Adam Wade; the Guardian of the Well, Mr. Itow; and the three musicians, Mr. Dulac, Mrs. Mann and Mr. Foulds. The music was by Mrs. Mann and Mr. Foulds. And round the platform upon three sides were three hundred fashionable people including Queen Alexandra, and once more my muses were but half welcome. I remember, however, with a little pleasure that we found a newspaper photographer planting his camera in a dressing-room and explained to him that as fifty people could pay our expenses, we did not invite the press and that flashlight photographs were not desirable for their own sake. He was incredulous and persistent—a whole page somewhere or other was at our disposal—and it was nearly ten minutes before we could persuade him to go away. What a relief after directing a theatre for so many years—for I am one of the two directors of the Abbey Theatre in Dublin—to think no more of pictures unless Mr. Dulac or some other distinguished man has made them, nor of all those paragraphs written by young men, perhaps themselves intelligent, who must applaud the common taste or starve!

Perhaps I shall turn to something else now that our Japanese dancer, Mr. Itow, whose minute intensity of movement in the dance of the hawk so well suited our small room and private art, has been hired by a New York theatre, or perhaps I shall find another dancer. I am certain, however, that whether I grow tired or not—and one does grow tired of always quarrying the stone for one's statue—I have found out the only way the subtler forms of literature can find dramatic expression. Shakespeare's art was public, now resounding and declamatory, now lyrical and subtle, but always public, because poetry was a part of the general life of a people who had been trained by the Church to listen to difficult words and who sang, instead of the songs of the music-halls, many songs that are still beautiful. A man who had sung 'Barbara Allan' in his own house would not, as I have heard the gallery of the Lyceum Theatre, receive the love speeches of Juliet with an ironical chirruping. We must recognize the change as the painters did when, finding no longer palaces and churches to decorate, they made framed pictures to hang upon a wall. Whatever we lose in mass and in power we should recover in elegance and in subtlety. Our lyrical and our narrative poetry alike have used their freedom and have approached nearer, as Pater said all the arts would if they were able, to 'the condition of music'; and if our modern poetical drama has failed, it is mainly because, always dominated by the example of Shakespeare, it would restore an irrevocable past.

Preface, *Harper's Bazar*, March 1917. [This version was reprinted, with the exception of the cast of characters and with minor punctuational changes, in *Theatre Arts Magazine*, January 1919, under the title 'Instead of a Theatre'; and about half of it—to the phrase 'in their leisure moments'—in *Theatre Arts Monthly*, April 1939, under the title 'Yeats on his own Work.']

A couple . . . husband and wife . . . seat as I . . . music, where . . . words, bores . . . ear, or . . . a very primitive one. Presently, when . . . said, 'They . . . rate was able to interest . . . wife, who . . . first, said . . . poetry, who . . . pleasure in . . . speech—a pleasure the book did not give her. Yet . . . play I . . . man. And the worst . . . players, or . . . seamstress, or . . . owner of the building, unless . . . amusement, or who have verse and literature, and fortunately . . . polite. [No paragraph] Being . . . escape the . . . half welcome, and . . . has a liking for poetry, I have . . . theatre. I . . . plays, and . . . roomful . . . carpet, or . . . together, to . . . moments.

I have . . . Japan' (Cuala Press) what had seemed . . . economy. It has been . . . scenery and substitute . . . who, sitting against a screen covered with some one unchangeable pattern, or against the wall of a room, describe . . . scenery, after all, is . . . imagination, kept . . . arts, can . . . scene-painting. [No paragraph] Then, too, the . . . lighting and by . . . audience, who . . . face not . . .—there, too, we . . . modelled . . . besides, the poetical . . . producer knows, is mainly in . . . body.

*At . . . Well** [*This play will be published in the next number of *To-day*.] . . . April 1916 in . . . for literature were . . . drawing-room in Chesterfield . . . charity.† [†The cast was as follows:—The Young Man, Mr. Henry

Ainley; The Old Man, Mr. Allan Wade; The Guardian of the Well, Mr.
Ito. The Three Musicians were Mr. Dulac, Mrs. Mann, and Mr. Foulds;
and the music was by Mrs. Mann and Mr. Foulds.] There was a platform
jutting out from a wall, and some three hundred . . . people, including . . .
Alexandra, were round the platform on three sides, and once . . . pleasure,
that . . . expenses we . . . Press, and . . . persistent, and it was nearly . . .
relief, after . . . theatre so many . . . pictures, unless Dulac . . . them, and not
at all of those paragraphs which are written by . . . starve.

Perhaps . . . dancer Ito, whose . . . Hawk . . . public—now . . . public;
because . . . of his people, who . . . church . . . words and sang, instead . . .
love-speeches . . . change, as . . . we lost in mass . . . music,' and . . . failed
it . . . past.

                    'Instead of a Theatre', *To-day* (London), May, 1917.

A couple . . . husband and wife . . . seat and . . . music, where . . . words,
bores . . . ear, or . . . a very primitive . . . . Presently, when . . . , said, 'They
. . . rate was able to . . . wife, who . . . first, said . . . poetry, who . . . speech—
a pleasure the book did not give her. Yet . . . play I . . . man. And . . .
players, or . . . seamstress, or . . . the building, unless . . . amusement, or
. . . ear for rhythmical speech, but fortunately . . . polite. Being sensitive,
and not . . . pit has a liking for poetry, I have . . . theatre. I believe . . . them;
two . . . plays; and . . . myself more alive . . . roomful of people have the
one . . . ancient theatre made by unrolling a carpet, or . . . against a wall
. . . together, to . . . moments. I have . . . Japan' (Cuala Press) what had
seemed . . . that subtle . . . economy. It . . . scenery and substitute . . . who,
sitting against a screen covered with some one unchangeable pattern, or
against the wall of a room, describe . . . drum or cymbal, . . . zither and
flute. . . . scenery, after all, is . . . imagination, kept . . . arts, can . . . thorn-
trees, in . . . even the best scene-painting. Then, too, the . . . lighting and by
. . . audience, who . . . face not . . .—there, too, we . . . Theatre, when . . .
modelled . . . artist, working together, to . . . besides, expression in . . .
producer knows, is mainly . . . .

'At . . . April 1916 in . . . cared for literature were . . . Gardens, for . . .
Ito. The Three Musicians were Mr. Dulac, Mrs. Mann, and Mr. Foulds;
and the music . . . Foulds. There was a platform jutting out from a wall, and
some three hundred . . . people, including . . . Alexandra, were round the
platform on three sides, and once . . . pleasure, that . . . expenses we . . .
Press, and . . . flash-light . . . persistent, and it . . . before Dulac persuaded
him . . . relief, after . . . pictures, unless Dulac or . . . them, and not all of
those paragraphs which are written . . . starve.

Perhaps . . . dancer Ito, . . . Hawk . . . public; now . . . public; because
. . . of his people, who . . . church . . . words, and sang, instead . . . Allen'
. . . love-speeches . . . wall.

Whatever . . . failed it . . . past. December 1916
                              A Note on 'At the Hawk's Well.'   **58.**

A couple . . . wife, and . . . music, where . . . words, bores . . . primitive ear. Presently . . . wife, who . . . first, said . . . pleasure, the . . . her, in . . . players, or the seamstress, or . . . polite.

Being . . . together, to . . . half-a-dozen . . . *Japan* (now included in my *Cutting of an Agate*) what . . . moments.

I . . . scene-painting.

Then . . . modelled . . . artist, working together, to . . . body.

'At . . . charity. And round the platform . . . people, including . . . Alexandria, and . . . press, and . . . starve!

Perhaps . . . words, and . . . past.

Note on the first performance of 'At the Hawk's Well.' **64, 69.**

A couple . . . wife, and . . . words, bores . . . primitive ear. Presently . . . well, and . . . wife, who . . . pleasure, the . . . her, in . . . players or seamstress or . . . polite.

Being . . . half-a-dozen . . . moments.

I . . . described in *Certain* . . . *Japan* what has . . . scene-painting.

Then . . . modelled . . . together, to . . . that he has missed . . . besides, in . . . body.

'At the . . . war charity. And round . . . people, and . . . dressing-room, and . . . press, and . . . starve!

Perhaps . . . words, and . . . past.

W.B.Y., 1916.

Note on the first performance of 'At the Hawk's Well.' **71.**

* * *

Variant Spellings

Aoife **T, 58, 84, 97**; *Eofe* **HB, 64, 71**.
Sualtam **HB-71**; *Sualtim* **84, 97**.

* * *

[See also the notes on *The Only Jealousy of Emer*, p. 566; *The Resurrection*, pp. 932; *Glossary*, p. 1284; and *Prefaces to 64, 69*, pp. 1304, 1306.]

THE GREEN HELMET

An Heroic Farce

1910

Persons in the Play

Laegaire (*pronounced* Leary)
Conall
Cuchulain (*pronounced* Cuhoolin)
Red Man, *a Spirit*
Emer

Laegaire's Wife
Conall's Wife
Laeg, *Cuchulain's chariot-driver*
Stable Boys and Scullions
Black Men, etc.

PRINTINGS   30¹, 34¹, 38, 39 ; *The Forum*, September 1911; **43, 45, 50, 69, 84, 89, 97.**

TITLE   The Golden Helmet **30, 34** ; . . . Helmet: / An . . . **45.**

SUBTITLE   [lacking] **30, 34, F.**

DATE   [lacking] **30-69.**

DRAMATIS PERSONAE   . . . Play / Cuchulain / Leagerie / Conal / Emer, *Cuchulain's wife* / Leagerie's . . . / Conal's . . . *chariot-driver* / Red Man / Horseboys and Scullions / Three Black Men **30, 34;**
   The Persons of the . . . / Laegaire / Conall / Cuchulain / Red . . . *Spirit* / Emer / Conall's Wife / Laegaire's Wife / Laeg, . . . chariot-driver / Horse Boys **38-F;**
   [heading lacking] Laegaire / Conall / Cuchulain / Emer / Horse Boys and Scullions / Laegaire's Wife / Laeg, . . . *chariot-driver* / Red Man, *A Spirit* / Black **43;**
   . . . Play / Laegaire / Conall / Cuchulain / Red . . . Laegaire's Wife / Laeg, . . . *chariot-driver* / Horse Boys. . . . **45, 69;**
   The Persons of the . . . / Laegaire / Conall / Cuchulain / Emer / . . . *chariot-driver* / Red Man, *A Spirit* / Horse Boys . . . . **50;** . . . Play / Laegaire / Conall / Cuchulain / Red . . . . **84, 89.**

¹ The text in **30** and **34** is in prose. Beginning on p. 422 the text of **30** is reprinted in full in the centre section of the page, with variants from **34** noted in the body of the text of **30**. Similarities between the prose and poetry versions are shown by the bracketed line-numbers in the left-hand margin.

A house made of logs. There are two windows at the back and a door which cuts off one of the corners of the room. Through the door one can see low rocks which make the ground outside higher than it is within, and beyond the rocks a misty moon-lit sea. Through the windows one can see nothing but the sea. There is a great chair at the opposite side to the door, and in front of it a table with cups and a flagon of ale. Here and there are stools.

At the Abbey Theatre the house is orange-red and the chairs and tables and flagons black, with a slight purple tinge which is not clearly distinguishable from the black. The rocks are black with a few green touches. The sea is green and luminous, and all the characters except the Red Man and the Black Men are dressed in various shades of green, one or two with touches of purple which look nearly black. The Black Men all wear dark purple and have eared caps, and at the end their eyes should look green from the reflected light of the sea. The Red Man is altogether in red. He is very tall, and his height increased by horns on the Green Helmet. The effect is intentionally violent and startling.

STAGE DIRECTIONS   *A . . . see rocks, which . . . outside the door higher . . . within, and the sea. Through . . . sea. There are three great chairs at . . . door, with a table before them. There are cups . . . ale on the table. At . . . orange red, and . . . chairs, tables . . . are black, with . . . characters, except . . . Men (Men,* **34**) *. . . various tints of . . . looks . . . Black Men are in dark purple and the Red Man is altogether dressed in . . . tall and . . . height is increased . . . on the Golden Helmet. The Helmet has in reality more dark green than gold about it. The Black Men have cats' heads painted on their black cloth caps. The effect . . . .* **30, 34**;

Scene: *A . . . the door, one . . . misty (misty,* **F**) *moon-lit . . . can see (sea* **39**) *nothing . . . orange red . . . luminous and . . . height increased (height is increased* **F**) *. . . .* **38-F**;

Scene: *A . . . orange red . . . .* **43-69**; *. . . orange red . . . .* **84, 89**.

1.   *Laegaire.* What is that? I had thought that I saw, though but in the
       wink of an eye,

2.   A cat-headed man out of Connacht go pacing and spitting by;

3.   But that could not be.

     Conall. You have dreamed it—there's nothing out there.

4.   I killed them all before daybreak—I hoked them out of their
       lair;

5.   I cut off a hundred heads with a single stroke of my sword,

6.   And then I danced on their graves and carried away their hoard.

7.   *Laegaire.* Does anything stir on the sea?

     Conall.   Not even a fish or a gull:

8.   I can see for a mile or two, now that the moon's at the full.

                                     [A distant shout.

9.   *Laegaire.* Ah—there—there is some one who calls us.

     Conall.   But from the landward side,

10. And we have nothing to fear that has not come up from the
       tide;

11. The rocks and the bushes cover whoever made that noise,

[2, 3, 7] *Conal.* Not a sail, not a wave, and if the sea were not purring
[7, 8]   a little like a cat, not a sound. There is no danger yet. I
[8]   can see a long way for the moonlight is on the sea. *[A horn sounds.*
[9]   *Leagerie.* Ah, there is something.
[9, 10]   *Conal.* It must be from the land, and it is from the sea that
[10, 12]   danger comes. We need not be afraid of anything that comes
[12, 11]   from the land. *[Looking out of door.]* I cannot see anybody,
[11]   the rocks and the trees hide a great part of the pathway
[11]   upon that side. **30, 34.**

TEXT

1. . . . eye? **38, 39.**
3. . . . there **38, 39, 43, 45, 69E, 84, 89.**
4. . . . out their . . .; **45** (1913).
7. . . . gull, **38, 39;** . . . gull. **F.**
9. . . . someone . . . , **43-50.**

12.   But the land will do us no harm.

    Laegaire.   It was like Cuchulain's voice.

13.   *Conall.* But that's an impossible thing.

    Laegaire.   An impossible thing indeed.

14.   *Conall.* For he will never come home, he has all that he could need
15.   In that high windy Scotland—good luck in all that he does.
16.   Here neighbour wars on neighbour, and why there is no man
           knows,
17.   And if a man is lucky all wish his luck away,
18.   And take his good name from him between a day and a day.

19.   *Laegaire.* I would he'd come for all that, and make his young wife
           know
20.   That though she may be his wife, she has no right to go
21.   Before your wife and my wife, as she would have done last night

---

[12]   *Leagerie* [*sitting at table*]. It sounded like Cuchulain's horn,
[13]   but that's not possible.
[13, 14] *Conal.* Yes, that's impossible. He will never come home from
[14, 15]   Scotland. He has all he wants there. Luck in all he does.
[15]   Victory and wealth and happiness flowing in on him, while
[16, 18]   here at home all goes to rack, and a man's good name drifts
[18]   away between night and morning.
[19]   *Leagerie.* I wish he would come home for all that, and put quiet
[19, 20]   and respect for those that are more than she is into that young
[20]   wife of his. Only this very night your wife and my wife had to
[20, 21]   forbid her to go into the dining-hall before them. **30, 34.**

---

12.   . . . harm,
           It . . . . **38, 39.**
14.   . . . he never will come . . . **38-F.**
15.   . . . does, **38, 39.**
16.   . . . neighbour and . . . knows **38, 39** ; . . . neighbor . . . neighbor and
       . . . , **F** ; . . . neighbour and . . . , **43-69.**
21.   . . . have gone last . . . **38-50.**

V.E.P.Y.—P

22.   Had they not caught at her dress, and pulled her as was right;
23.   And she makes light of us though our wives do all that they can.
24.   She spreads her tail like a peacock and praises none but her man.

25.   *Conall.* A man in a long green cloak that covers him up to the chin
26.   Comes down through the rocks and hazels.

          Laegaire.   Cry out that he cannot come in.

27.   *Conall.* He must look for his dinner elsewhere, for no one alive shall
             stop
28.   Where a shame must alight on us two before the dawn is up.

29.   *Laegaire.* No man on the ridge of the world must ever know that but
             us two.

30.   *Conall* [*outside door*]. Go away, go away, go away.

          Young Man [*outside door*]. I will go when the night is through

---

[21]   She is young, and she is Cuchulain's wife, and so she must
[24]   spread her tail like a peacock.
[25]   *Conal* [*at door*]. I can see the horn-blower now, a young man
[25]   wrapped in a cloak.
[26]   *Leagerie.* Do not let him come in. Tell him to go elsewhere for
[27]   shelter. This is no place to seek shelter in.
[27]   *Conal.* That is right. I will tell him to go away, for nobody
[28]   must know the disgrace that is to fall upon Ireland this night.
[29]   *Leagerie.* Nobody of living men but us two must ever know that.
[30]   *Conal* [*outside door*]. Go away, go away!
          [*A young man covered by a long cloak is standing upon the rocks outside
          the door. (outside door.* **34**)] **30, 34.**

---

23.   . . . all they . . . . **69A.**
26.   . . . hazels,
          Laegaire. Cry . . . . **38-F.**
          Directions in **30.**   [*Outside the door.*] . . . .
          [*Outside the door.*] . . . **F.**

31.   And I have eaten and slept and drunk to my heart's delight.

32.   *Conall.* A law has been made that none shall sleep in this house
      to-night.

33.   *Young Man.* Who made that law?

      Conall.   We made it, and who has so good a right?

34.   Who else has to keep the house from the Shape-Changers till
      day?

35.   *Young Man.* Then I will unmake the law, so get you out of the way.
                          [*He pushes past Conall and goes into house.*

36.   *Conall.* I thought no living man could have pushed me from the
      door,

37.   Nor could any living man do it but for the dip in the floor;

38.   And had I been rightly ready there's no man living could do it,

39.   Dip or no dip.

      Laegaire.   Go out—if you have your wits, go out,

---

[31]   *Young Man.* I am a traveller, and I am looking for sleep and food.
[32]   *Conal.* A law has been made that nobody is to come into this
[32]   house to-night.
[33]   *Young Man.* Who made that law?
[33]   *Conal.* We two made it, and who has so good a right? for we have
[34]   to guard this house and to keep it from robbery, and from
[34]   burning, (burning 34) and from enchantment.
[35]   *Young Man.* Then I will unmake the law. Out of my way!
           [*He struggles with Conal and shoves past into the house.*]
[36]   *Conal.* I thought no living man but Leagerie could have stood
[37]   against me; and Leagerie himself could not have shoved past me.
[37, 38]   What is more, no living man could if I were not taken by
           surprise. How could I expect to find so great a strength?
[39, 40] *Leagerie.* Go out of this: there is another house a **30, 34**.

---

33.   . . . right **38, 39**; . . . right, **F.**
      Directions after 35. [. . . *into the house.*] **F.**
36.   . . . thought that no . . . door **38-45** (1911); . . . door **45** (1913), **69**; . . .
      thought that no . . . , **50.**

40.   A stone's throw further on you will find a big house where
41.   Our wives will give you supper, and you'll sleep sounder there,
42.   For it's a luckier house.

    Young Man.   I'll eat and sleep where I will.

43. *Laegaire.* Go out or I will make you.

    Young Man [*forcing up Laegaire's arm, passing him and putting his shield
on the wall over the chair*]. Not till I have drunk my fill,

44.   But may some dog defend me, for a cat of wonder's up.
45.   Laegaire and Conall are here, the flagon full to the top,
46.   And the cups—

    Laegaire.   It is Cuchulain.

    Cuchlain.   The cups are dry as a bone.
                                        [*He sits on chair and drinks.*

47. *Conall.* Go into Scotland again, or where you will, but begone

---

48.   From this unlucky country that was made when the Devil spat.

49. *Cuchulain.* If I lived here a hundred years, could a worse thing come than that

50.   Laegaire and Conall should know me and bid me begone to my face?

51. *Conall.* We bid you begone from a house that has fallen on shame and disgrace.

52. *Cuchulain.* I am losing patience, Conall—I find you stuffed with pride,

53.   The flagon full to the brim, the front door standing wide;

54.   You'd put me off with words, but the whole thing's plain enough,

55.   You are waiting for some message to bring you to war or love

56.   In that old secret country beyond the wool-white waves,

57.   Or it may be down beneath them in foam-bewildered caves

58.   Where nine forsaken sea-queens fling shuttles to and fro;

59.   But beyond them, or beneath them, whether you will or no,

---

        what is going to happen.

[49]   *Cuchulain.* What more is there that can happen so strange as that

[50]   I should come home after years and that you should bid me

[50]   begone?

[51]   *Conal.* I tell you that this is no fit house to welcome you, for

[51]   it is a disgraced house.

[54, 55] *Cuchulain.* What is it you are hinting at? You were sitting there

[53]   with ale beside you and the door open, and quarrelsome

[55]   thoughts. You are waiting for something or someone. It is for

[55-58] some messenger who is to bring you some spoil, or to some

[55-58] adventure that you will keep for yourselves. **30, 34.**

---

48. . . . devil . . . . **38-69.**

49. . . . that, **38, 39.**

57. . . . caves, **39.**

58. . . . sea queens . . . ; **38-69.**

60.   I am going too.

Laegaire.   Better tell it all out to the end;
61.   He was born to luck in the cradle, his good luck may amend
62.   The bad luck we were born to.

Conall.   I'll lay the whole thing bare.
63.   You saw the luck that he had when he pushed in past me there.
64.   Does anything stir on the sea?

Laegaire.   Not even a fish or a gull.

65. *Conall.* You were gone but a little while. We were there and the
         ale-cup full.
66.   We were half drunk and merry, and midnight on the stroke,
67.   When a wide, high man came in with a red foxy cloak,
68.   With half-shut foxy eyes and a great laughing mouth,
69.   And he said, when we bid him drink, that he had so great a
         drouth
70.   He could drink the sea.

Cuchulain.   I thought he had come for one of you

[60, 61] *Leagerie.* Better tell him, for he has such luck that it may be
[61]   his luck will amend ours.
[62, 63] *Conal.* Yes, I had better tell him, for even now at this very
[63, 37]   door we saw what luck he had. He had the slope of the ground
[37, 64]   to help him. Is the sea quiet?
[64]   *Leagerie* [*looks out of window*]. There is nothing stirring.
[65]   *Conal.* Cuchulain, a little after you went out of this country
[65, 66]   we were sitting here drinking. We were merry. It was late,
[66, 67]   close on to midnight, when a strange-looking man with red hair
[67]   and a great sword in his hand came in through that door. He
[69]   asked for ale and we gave it to him, for we were **30, 34.**

---

65.   We were gone . . . . **39.**
66.   . . . stroke **38-69.**
67.   . . . wide high . . . , **38-F.**
68.   . . . half shut . . . , **38, 39.**
69.   . . . said when . . . **38-69.**
70.   . . . come from one . . . **50.**

71.   Out of some Connacht rath, and would lap up milk and mew;
72.   But if he so loved water I have the tale awry.

73. *Conall.* You would not be so merry if he were standing by,
74.   For when we had sung or danced as he were our next of kin
75.   He promised to show us a game, the best that ever had been;
76.   And when we had asked what game, he answered,
       'Why, whip off my head!
77.   Then one of you two stoop down, and I'll whip off his', he said.
78.   'A head for a head', he said, 'that is the game that I play'.

79. *Cuchulain.* How could he whip off a head when his own had been
       whipped away?

80. *Conall.* We told him it over and over, and that ale had fuddled his
       wit,
81.   But he stood and laughed at us there, as though his sides would
       split,
82.   Till I could stand it no longer, and whipped off his head at a
       blow,

---

          tired of drinking with one another. He became merry, and for
[74]   every joke we made he made a better, and presently we all
[74, 75]   three got up and danced, and then we sang, and then he said he
[75, 76]   would show us a new game. He said he would stoop down and that
[76, 77]   one of us was to cut off his head, and afterwards one of us,
[77]   or whoever has (had **34**) a mind for the game, was to stoop down
[78]   and have his head whipped off. 'You take off my head,' said
[78]   he, 'and then I take off his head, and that will be a bargain
[78]   and a debt between us. A head for a head, that is the game,'
[80]   said he. We laughed at him and told him he was drunk, for how
[79]   could he whip off a head when his own had been whipped off?
[81, 82]   Then he began abusing us and calling us names, so I ran **30, 34.**

---

71.   ... Connaught ... mew. **38-F.**
76.   ..., 'why (Why **F**) whip ... head, **38-F.**
77.   ... you stoop .... **39.**
81.   ... split **38, 39, 43, 45.**

83.   Being mad that he did not answer, and more at his laughing so,

84.   And there on the ground where it fell it went on laughing at me.

85. *Laegaire.* Till he took it up in his hands—

      Conall.   And splashed himself into the sea.

86. *Cuchulain.* I have imagined as good when I've been as deep in the
      cup.

87. *Laegaire.* You never did.

    Cuchulain.   And believed it.

    Conall.   Cuchulain, when will you stop

88.   Boasting of your great deeds and weighing yourself with us two,

89.   And crying out to the world, whatever we say or do,

90.   That you've said or done a better?—Nor is it a drunkard's tale,

91.   Though we said to ourselves at first that it all came out of the
      ale,

[82, 84]   at him and cut his head off, and the head went on laughing
[84, 85]   where it lay, and presently he caught it up in his hands and
[85]   ran out and plunged into the sea.
[86]   *Cuchulain* [*laughs*]. I have imagined as good, when I had as much
[86]   ale, and believed it too.
[87]   *Leagerie* [*at table*]. I tell you, Cuchulain, you never did. You
[87]   never imagined a story like this.
[87, 88]   *Conal.* Why must you be always putting yourself up against
[88, 90]   Leagerie and myself? and what is more, it was no imagination
[90, 91]   at all. We said to yourselves that all came out of the **30, 34.**

---

85.   . . . hands.
     Conall.   And . . . .
86.   . . . when I have been . . . . **38-F.**
88.   . . . deeds, and . . . , **38-45** (**1911**).
89.   . . . world whatever . . . , **38-69.**
90.   That you have said . . . better—nor (better?—nor **39**) . . . tale? (tale.
     39) **38, 39** ; That you have said . . . , **F.**
91.   . . . of ale, **38-F.**

92.   And thinking that if we told it we should be a laughing-stock
93.   Swore we should keep it secret.

Laegaire.   But twelve months upon the clock—

94. *Conall.* A twelvemonth from the first time—

Laegaire.   And the jug full up to the brim:
95.   For we had been put from our drinking by the very thought of
       him—

96. *Conall.* We stood as we're standing now—

Laegaire.   The horns were as empty—

Conall.   When
97.   He ran up out of the sea with his head on his shoulders again.

---

[92]   flagon, and we laughed, and we said we will tell nobody about
]93]   it. We made an oath to tell nobody. But twelve months **after**
[93, 94] when we were sitting by this table, the flagon between us—
[94]   *Leagerie.* But full up to the brim. (brim— **34**)
[95]   *Conal.* The thought of that story had put us from our drinking.
[95]   (drinking— **34**)
[96]   *Leagerie.* We were telling it over to one another. (another— **34**)
[97]   *Conal.* Suddenly that man came in with his head on his shoulders
[97, 98] again, and the big sword in his hand. He asked for **30, 34.**

---

92.   . . . laughing stock **38-45** (1911); . . . laughing-stock, **50.**
93.   . . . clock. **38, 39, 43-69.**
94.   . . . twelve month . . . time. (time— **F**)
      Laegaire. And . . . brim. (brim, **F**) **38-F**;
      . . . twelve month (twelvemonth **50, 69A**) . . . time.
      Laegaire. And . . . : **43-69.**
95.   . . . him. **38, 39, 43-69.**
96.   . . . now.
      Laegaire. The . . . empty.
      Conall.   When **38, 39, 43-69.**

98.   *Cuchulain*. Why, this is a tale worth telling.

    Conall.   And he called for his debt and his right,

99.   And said that the land was disgraced because of us two from
        that night

100.   If we did not pay him his debt.

    Laegaire.   What is there to be said

101.   When a man with a right to get it has come to ask for your
        head?

102.   *Conall*. If you had been sitting there you had been silent like us.

103.   *Laegaire*. He said that in twelve months more he would come
        again to this house

104.   And ask his debt again. Twelve months are up to-day.

105.   *Conall*. He would have followed after if we had run away.

106.   *Laegaire*. Will he tell every mother's son that we have broken our
        word?

107.   *Cuchulain*. Whether he does or does not, we'll drive him out with
        the sword,

---

[98]   payment of his debt, and because neither I nor Leagerie would
           let him
           cut off our heads he began abusing us and making little of

[99]   us, and saying that we were a disgrace, and that all Ireland

[99]   was disgraced because of us. We had not a word to say.

[102]   *Leagerie*. If you had been here you would have been as silent as

[102]   we were.

[103]   *Conal*. At last he said he would come again in twelve months and

[104]   give us one more chance to keep our word and pay our debt.

[106]   After that he went down into the sea again. Will he tell the

[106]   whole world of the disgrace that has come upon us, do you
           think?

[107]   *Cuchulain*. Whether he does or does not, we will stand there in

[107]   the door with our swords out and drive him down to the sea
           again. **30, 34.**

---

98.   . . . right **38, 39 ;** . . . telling—
    Conall.   And . . . right **F.**

99.   . . . disgraced, because . . . night, **38-F.**

104.   . . . today. **39.**

107.   . . . not we'll . . . , **38-50.**

108.   And take his life in the bargain if he but dare to scoff.

109. *Conall.* How can you fight with a head that laughs when you've
            whipped it off?

110. *Laegaire.* Or a man that can pick it up and carry it out in his hand?

111. *Conall.* He is coming now, there's a splash and a rumble along the
            strand

112.   As when he came last.

    Cuchulain.   Come, and put all your backs to the door.
    [*A tall red-headed, red-cloaked man stands upon the threshold against
    the misty green of the sea; the ground, higher without than within the
    house, makes him seem taller even than he is. He leans upon a great
    two-handed sword.*]

113. *Laegaire.* It is too late to shut it, for there he stands once more

---

[109] *Conal.* What is the use of fighting with a man whose head laughs
[109]   when it has been cut off?
    Leagerie. We might run away, but he would follow us everywhere.
[111] *Conal.* He is coming; the sea is beginning to splash and rumble
[112]   as it did before he came the last time.
[112] *Cuchulain.* Let us shut the door and put our backs against it.
[113] *Leagerie.* It is too late. Look, there he is at the door. He is
[113]   standing on the threshold.
        [*A man dressed in red, with a great sword and red, (red* **34**) *ragged hair,
        and having a Golden Helmet on his head, is standing on the threshold.*]
        30, 34.

---

112.   . . . put your . . . . **39.**
    Directions after 112.   [. . . *red-headed red-cloaked* . . . *sea, the ground
    higher* . . . *two-handled sword.*] **38, 39**; [. . . *tall, red-headed,* . . . *two-
    handled sword.*] **F**; [. . . *tall, red-headed,* . . . .] **43-69.**

114.   And laughs like the sea.

          Cuchulain.   Old herring—You whip off heads! Why, then,
115.   Whip off your own, for it seems you can clap it on again.
116.   Or else go down in the sea, go down in the sea, I say,
117.   Find that old juggler Manannan and whip his head away;
118.   Or the Red Man of the Boyne, for they are of your own sort,
119.   Or if the waves have vexed you and you would find a sport
120.   Of a more Irish fashion, go fight without a rest
121.   A caterwauling phantom among the winds of the West.
122.   But what are you waiting for? Into the water, I say!
123.   If there's no sword can harm you, I've an older trick to play,
124.   An old five-fingered trick to tumble you out of the place;
125.   I am Sualtim's son, Cuchulain—What, do you laugh in my
              face?

[114, 116] *Cuchulain.* Go back into the sea, old red head! If you will take
[114]   off heads, take off the head of the sea turtle of Muirthemne,
[117]   or of the pig of Connaught that has a moon in his belly, or of
[117, 118]   that old juggler Manannan, son of the sea, or of the red man
[118, 121]   of the Boyne, or of the King of the Cats, for they are of your
[122]   own sort, and it may be they understand your ways. Go, I say,
[123]   for when a man's head is off it does not grow again. What are
[123]   you standing there for? Go down, I say. If I cannot harm you
[123, 124]   with the sword I will put you down into the sea with my hands.
[125]   Do you laugh at me, old red head? Go down before I lay my
[124]   hands upon you. **30, 34.**

---

114.   . . . heads? Why then **38-F** ; . . . , then **43-69.**
116.   . . . sea I . . . , **38-F.**
118.   . . . Boynes' for . . . , **38, 39** ; . . . Boynes, . . . , **F** ; . . . Boyne for . . . ,
          43, 45.
121.   . . . west. **38-70.**
122.   . . . for, into . . . water I say? (say! **F**) **38-F** ; . . . ? into . . . water I
          . . . ! **43, 45, 69** ; . . . ? into . . . ! **50.**
125.   . . . son Cuchulain—what, . . . ? **38-69.**

126. *Red Man.* So you too think me in earnest in wagering poll for poll!

127.   A drinking joke and a gibe and a juggler's feat, that is all,

128.   To make the time go quickly—for I am the drinker's friend,

129.   The kindest of all Shape-Changers from here to the world's end,

130.   The best of all tipsy companions. And now I bring you a gift:

131.   I will lay it there on the ground for the best of you all to lift

                        [He lays his Helmet on the ground.

132.   And wear upon his own head, and choose for yourselves the
     best.

133.   O, Laegaire and Conall are brave, but they were afraid of my
     jest.

134.   Well, maybe I jest too grimly when the ale is in the cup.

135.   There, I'm forgiven now—

              [Then in a more solemn voice as he goes out.
                  Let the bravest take it up.
        [Conall takes up Helmet and gazes at it with delight.

---

[126]   *Red Man.* So you also believe I was in earnest when I asked for
[126, 127] a man's head? It was but a drinker's joke, an old juggling
[128]   feat, to pass the time. I am the best of all drinkers and tipsy
[129]   companions, the kindest there is among the Shape-changers of
[129, 130] the world. Look, I have brought this Golden Helmet as a gift.
[131]   It is for you or for Leagerie or for Conal, for the best man,
[131, 132] and the bravest fighting-man amongst you, and you yourselves
[132, 133] shall choose the man. Leagerie is brave, and Conal is brave.
[133]   They risk their lives in battle, but they were not brave
[133]   enough for my jokes and my juggling. [*He lays the Golden
[134]   Helmet on the ground.*] Have I been too grim a joker? Well,
[135]   I am forgiven now, for there is the Helmet, and let the
[135]   strongest take it. [*He goes out.*] 30, 34.

---

126.   ... earnest is wagering ... poll, 38 ; ... poll, 39 ; ... you, too, think
     ... poll, F.

127.   ... feat that ... , 38, 39.

129.   ... end. 38, 39.

130.   ... companions, and ... gift, 38-F.

131.   ... lift, 38-69.

133.   O! Laegaire .... 38-50 ; Oh, ... 69.
     Directions after 135.   [... *up the Helmet* ....] F.

     Laegaire [singing, with a swaggering stride].

136.	Laegaire is best;
137.	Between water and hill,
138.	He fought in the West
139.	With cat-heads, until
140.	At the break of day
141.	All fell by his sword,
142.	And he carried away
143.	Their hidden hoard.

                                [He seizes the Helmet.

144. *Conall.* Laegaire, that Helmet is mine, for what did you find in the
      bag
145.   But the straw and the broken delf and the bits of dirty rag
146.   You'd taken for good money?

    Cuchulain.   No, no, but give it me.
                                    [He takes Helmet.

147. *Conall.* The Helmet's mine or Laegaire's—you're the youngest of
      us three.

---

[144] *Conal [taking Helmet].* It is my right. I am a year older than
    Leagerie, and I have fought in more battles.
    Leagerie [strutting about the stage, sings].

[136]	Leagerie of the Battles
[141]	Has put to the sword
[139]	The cat-headed men
[142]	And carried away
[143]	Their hidden gold.

                        [He snatches Helmet at the last word.
[144] *Conal.* Give it back to me, I say. What was the treasure but
[145]   withered leaves when you got to your own door?
[146] *Cuchulain [Taking the Helmet from Leagerie].* Give it to me, I
[146]   say.
[147] *Conal.* You are too young, Cuchulain. What deeds have you to be
[147]   set beside our deeds? **30, 34.**

138.	. . . west
139.	. . . cat heads, . . . **38-69.**
144.	*Conall.* Give it me, for . . . **38-69.**
	Directions after 146. [. . . *takes the Helmet.*] **F.**
147.	. . . Laegaire's—you are the . . . . **38-F.**

148. *Cuchulain* [*filling Helmet with ale*]. I did not take it to keep it—the
      Red Man gave it for one,
149.   But I shall give it to all—to all of us three or to none;
150.   That is as you look upon it—we will pass it to and fro,
151.   And time and time about, drink out of it and so
152.   Stroke into peace this cat that has come to take our lives.
153.   Now it is purring again, and now I drink to your wives,
154.   And I drink to Emer, my wife.

                      [*A great noise without and shouting.*
              Why, what in God's name is that noise?

155. *Conall.* What else but the charioteers and the kitchen and stable
      boys
156.   Shouting against each other, and the worst of all is your own,
157.   That chariot-driver, Laeg, and they'll keep it up till the dawn,
158.   And there's not a man in the house that will close his eyes
      to-night,

[148, 149] *Cuchulain.* I have not taken it for myself. It will belong to us
[149]   all equally. [*He goes to table and begins filling Helmet with*
[150, 151]   *ale.*] We will pass it round and drink out of it turn about and
[152]   no one will be able to claim that it belongs to him more than
[153]   another. I drink to your wife, Conal, and to your wife,
[153, 154]   Leagerie, and I drink to Emer my own wife. [*Shouting and*
[154]   *blowing of horns in the distance.*] What is that noise?
[155]   *Conal.* It is the horseboys and the huntboys and the scullions
[156]   quarrelling. I know the sound, for I have heard it often of
[156, 157]   late. It is a good thing that you are home, Cuchulain, for it
[157]   is your own horseboy and chariot-driver, Laeg, that is the
[157, 161]   worst of all, and now you will keep him quiet. They take **30, 34.**

Directions at 148. [*filling the Helmet* ....] **F.**
148. .... —The ...., **39.**
153. ... again and ..., **38-F.**
154. .... Why what...? **38, 39, 43, 45, 69E;** ... wife
                         [*A* ....]
                         Why what...? **F.**
155. ... Charioteers .... **38, 39.**
156. ... own **38, 39, 43, 45.**

159.   Or be able to keep them from it, or know what set them to
        fight.   [*A noise of horns without.*

160.   There, do you hear them now? Such hatred has each for each

161.   They have taken the hunting-horns to drown one another's
        speech

162.   For fear the truth may prevail.—Here's your good health and
        long life

163.   And, though she be quarrelsome, good health to Emer, your
        wife.

        [*The Charioteers, Stable Boys, and Scullions come running in. They
        carry great horns and other instruments, ladles, and the like.*

164.   *Laeg.* I am Laeg, Cuchulain's driver, and my master's cock of the
        yard.

165.   *Another Charioteer.* Conall would scatter his feathers.
                                            [*Confused murmurs.*

        Laegaire [*to Cuchulain*]. No use, they won't hear a word.

---

[161]   down the great hunting-horns when they cannot drown one
[160, 161]   another's voices by shouting. There—there—do you hear them
[160, 162]   now? [*Shouting so as to be heard above the noise.*] I drink to
[162, 163]   your good health, Cuchulain, and to your young wife, though it
[163]   were well if she did not quarrel with my wife.
             [*Many men, among whom is Laeg, chariot-driver of Cuchulain, come
             in with great horns of many fantastic shapes.*]
[164]   *Laeg.* I am Cuchulain's chariot-driver, and I say that my master
[164]   is the best.
[166]   *Another.* He is not, but Leagerie is.
[165]   *Another.* No, but Conal is. **30, 34.**

---

160.   There do . . . ? such . . . each (each, **F**) **38-F** ; . . . ? such . . . **43-69.**
161.   . . . hunting horns . . . **38-F** ; . . . hunting horns . . . one other's
        speech **43-69.**
162.   . . . prevail—here's . . . life (life, **F**) **38-F** ; . . . life, **50.**
163.   And though . . . quarrelsome good . . . . **38, 39.**
        Directions after 163. [. . . , *Stable Boys* (*Boys,* **45** (1913), **69**) *and
        Kitchen Boys come* . . . *horns, ladles* (*ladles,* **45** (1913), **69**) *and* . . . .] **38-69.**
165.   *Another. Conall* . . . . **38-69.**

166. *Conall.* They'll keep it up till the dawn.

    Another Charioteer.   It is Laegaire that is the best,
167.   For he fought with cats in Connacht while Conall took his rest
168.   And drained his ale-pot.

    Another.   Laegaire—what does a man of his sort
169.   Care for the like of us? He did it for his own sport.

170. *Another.* It was all mere luck at the best.

    Another.   But Conall, I say—

    Another.   Let me speak.

171. *Laeg.* You'd be dumb if the cock of the yard would but open his
    beak.

172. *Another.* Before your cock was born, my master was in the fight.

173. *Laeg.* Go home and praise your grand-dad. They took to the
    horns for spite,
174.   For I said that no cock of your sort had been born since the
    fight began.

175. *Another.* Conall has got it, the best man has got it, and I am his
    man.

---

[171] *Laeg.* Make them listen to me, Cuchulain.
[172] *Another.* No, but listen to me.
[174] *Laeg.* When I said Cuchulain should have the Helmet, they blew
[173]   the horns.
[175] *Another.* Conal has it. The best man has it. **30, 34.**

---

166. . . . dawn.
    Another.   It . . . best (best, **F-84**) **38-84.**
168. . . . ale pot. . . . **38-69.**
169. . . . ? he . . . . **38, 39.**
170. . . . say.
    Another. Let . . . . **38-F.**

176. *Cuchulain.* Who was it started this quarrel?

    A Stable Boy.   It was Laeg.

    Another.   It was Laeg done it all.

177. *Laeg.* A high, wide, foxy man came where we sat in the hall,
178.   Getting our supper ready, with a great voice like the wind,
179.   And cried that there was a helmet, or something of the kind,
180.   That was for the foremost man upon the ridge of the earth.
181.   So I cried your name through the hall,
       [*The others cry out and blow horns, partly drowning the rest of his speech.*

                             but they denied its worth,
182.   Preferring Laegaire or Conall, and they cried to drown my voice;

---

[176]   *Cuchulain.* Silence, all of you. What is all this uproar, Laeg,
[176]   and who began it?
       [*The Scullions and the Horseboys point at Laeg and cry, 'He began it.' They keep up an all but continual murmur through what follows.*]
[177]   *Laeg.* A man with a red beard came where we were sitting, and as
[178]   he passed me he cried out that they were taking a golden
[179]   helmet or some such thing from you and denying you the
[180, 181]   championship of Ireland. I stood up on that and I cried out
[181]   that you were the best of the men of Ireland. But the others
[182, 183]   cried for Leagerie or Conal, and because I have a big **30, 34.**

---

176.   Who started . . . .
177.   . . . high wide foxy . . . hall, (hall **39**) **38-F.**
179.   . . . helmet or . . . kind **38, 39** ; . . . cried out that . . . Helmet or . . . kind **F.**
181.   . . . hall (hall. **F**)
       [. . . *horns partly* . . . .]
           But . . . worth **38, 39** ; . . . hall. (hall **43, 45, 69**)
            [*The* . . . ,
           But (but **43, 45, 69**) . . . , **F-45, 69.**
182.   . . . Conall and . . . ; **38-F.**

183. But I have so strong a throat that I drowned all their noise
184. Till they took to the hunting-horns and blew them into my face,
185. And as neither side would give in—we would settle it in this place.
186. Let the Helmet be taken from Conall.

A Stable Boy. No, Conall is the best man here.

187. *Another.* Give it to Laegaire that made the murderous cats pay dear.

188. *Cuchulain.* It has been given to none: that our rivalry might cease,
189. We have turned that murderous cat into a cup of peace.
190. I drank the first; and then Conall; give it to Laegaire now

    [*Conall gives Helmet to Laegaire.*

191. That it may purr in his hand and all of our servants know
192. That, since the ale went in, its claws went out of sight.

[183, 184] voice they got down the horns to drown my voice, and as
[185] neither I nor they would keep silent we have come here to
[185, 186] settle it. I demand that the Helmet be taken from Conal and be
[186] given to you.
    [*The Horseboys and the Scullions shout (shout,* 34) '*No, no; give it to Leagerie,*' '*The best man has it,* (*it,*' 34) *etc.*]
[188] *Cuchulain.* It has not been given to Conal or to anyone. I have
[189, 190] made it into a drinking-cup that it may belong to all. I
[190] drank and then Conal drank. Give it to Leagerie, Conal, that
[190, 191] he may drink. That will make them see that it belongs to all
[191] of us, 30, 34.

---

184. . . . hunting horns . . . , 38-69.
188. . . . none—that . . . , 38-F.
189. . . . peace, 38-45, 69.
190. . . . now. 45 (1913), 69; . . . now, 50.
    Directions after 190. [. . . *gives horn to* . . . .] 38-F.
192. That since . . . in its . . . . 38-F; That since . . . . 43-69.

193. *A Servant.* That's well—I will stop my shouting.

      Another.   Cuchulain is in the right;
194. I am tired of this big horn that has made me hoarse as a rook.

195. *Laegaire.* Cuchulain, you drank the first.

      Another.   By drinking the first he took
196. The whole of the honours himself.

      Laegaire.   Cuchulain, you drank the first.

197. *Another.* If Laegaire drink from it now, he claims to be last and
      worst.

198. *Another.* Cuchulain and Conall have drunk.

      Another.   He is lost if he taste a drop

199. *Laegaire* [*laying Helmet on table*]. Did you claim to be better than us
      by drinking first from the cup?

200. *Cuchulain* [*his words are partly drowned by the murmurs of the crowd
      though he speaks very loud*]. That juggler from the sea, that old
      red herring it is

---

[193]   *A Scullion or Horseboy.* Cuchulain is right.
[193, 194] *Another.* Cuchulain is right, and I am tired of blowing on the
[194]   big horn.
[195]   *Laeg.* Cuchulain, you drank first.
[196]   *Another.* He gives it to Leagerie now, but he has taken the
[196]   honour of it for himself. Did you hear him say he drank the
[197]   first? He claimed to be the best by drinking first.
           Another. Did Cuchulain drink the first?
[196]   *Laeg* [*triumphantly*]. You drank the first, Cuchulain.
[199]   *Conal.* Did you claim to be better than us by drinking first?
              [*Leagerie and Conal draw their swords.*]
[200]   *Cuchulain.* Is it that old dried herring, that old red **30, 34.**

---

195. *Laeg.* Cuchulain, ... drink (drank **F-69**) ... **38-69.**
196. ... himself-
      Laeg. Cuchulain, ... **38-69.**
197. ... now he .... **38, 39, 43-69;** ... drinks ... now he .... **F.**
      Directions in 199. [*laying horn on table. (on the table.* **F**)] **38-F.**
200. ... old herring ... **39.**

201.   Who has set us all by the ears—he brought the Helmet for this,
202.   And because we would not quarrel he ran elsewhere to shout
203.   That Conall and Laegaire wronged me, till all had fallen out.
           [*The murmur grows less so that his words are heard.*

204.   Who knows where he is now or whom he is spurring to fight?
205.   So get you gone, and whatever may cry aloud in the night,
206.   Or show itself in the air, be silent until morn.

207. *A Servant.* Cuchulain is in the right—I am tired of this big horn.

208. *Cuchulain.* Go!
           [*The Servants turn towards the door but stop on hearing the voices of
           women outside.*

Laegaire's Wife [*without*]. Mine is the better to look at.

Conall's Wife [*without*].   But mine is better born.

---

[201]	juggler who has made us quarrel for his own comfort? [*The*
[201]	*Horseboys and the Scullions murmur excitedly.*] He gave the
[201, 202]	Helmet to set us by the ears, and because we would not quarrel
[202-204]	over it, he goes to Laeg and tells him that I am wronged. Who
[204]	knows where he is now, or who he is stirring up to make
[204-206]	mischief between us? Go back to your work and do not stir
[205, 206]	from it whatever noise comes to you or whatever shape shows
[206]	itself.
[207]	*A Scullion.* Cuchulain is right. I am tired of blowing on the
[207]	big horn.
[208]	*Cuchulain.* Go in silence.
	[*The Scullions and Horseboys turn towards the door, but stand still
	on hearing the voice of Leagerie's Wife outside the door.*]
[208]	*Leagerie's Wife.* My man is the best. I will go in the first. I
	will go in the first. **30, 34.**

---

201.   . . . this. **F.**
204.   . . . or who he . . . fight? (fight. **45** (1913), **69E**) **38, 39, 43-69.**
208.   Go. [*The* . . . . **38, 39**; Go. [*The* . . . *toward* . . . . **F.**
           Directions in 208.   [. . . *toward* . . . .] **50.**

209. *Emer* [*without*]. My man is the pithier man.

    Cuchulain.   Old hurricane, well done!

210.   You've set our wives to the game that they may egg us on;

211.   We are to kill each other that you may sport with us.

212.   Ah, now they've begun to wrestle as to who'll be first in the
        house.

                    [*The women come to the door struggling.*

213. *Emer.* No, I have the right of place, for I married the better man.

214. *Conall's Wife* [*pulling Emer back*]. My nails in your neck and
        shoulder.

    Laegaire's Wife.   And go before me if you can.

---

[209] *Emer.* My man is the best, and I will go in first.
[208] *Conal's Wife.* No, for my man is the best, and it is I that
[208]   should go first.
       [*Leagerie's Wife and Conal's Wife struggle in the doorway.*]
          Leagerie's Wife sings.
          My man is the best.
          What other has fought
          The cat-headed men
          That mew in the sea
          And carried away
          Their long-hidden gold?
          They struck with their claws
          And bit with their teeth,
          But Leagerie my husband
          Put all to the sword.
Conal's Wife [*Putting her hand over the other's mouth and getting in front of
    her.*]
          My husband has fought
          With strong men in armour.
          Had he a quarrel **30, 34.**

---

209.   ... done **38, 39**; ... done, **F.**
212.   ..., now, they've ... first at the .... **38-69.**
213.   ... place for .... **38-69;** ... of the place, ... **97A.**
215.   ... west. ... **69A.**
    Directions in 215. [... *keep out the others, who* ....] **F.**

215.   My husband fought in the West.

Conall's Wife [*kneeling in the door so as to keep the others out who pull at her*]. But what did he fight with there
216.   But sidelong and spitting and helpless shadows of the dim air?
217.   And what did he carry away but straw and broken delf?

218.   *Laegaire's Wife.* Your own man made up that tale trembling alone
          by himself,
219.   Drowning his terror.

Emer [*forcing herself in front*]. I am Emer, it is I go first through the
          door.
220.   No one shall walk before me, or praise any man before
221.   My man has been praised.

Cuchulain [*putting his spear across the door so as to close it*].
                    Come, put an end to their quarrelling:
222.   One is as fair as the other, each one the wife of a king.

	With cats, it is certain
	He'd war with none
	But the stout and heavy
	With good claws on them.
[215]	What glory in warring
[216]	With hollow shadows
[216]	That helplessly mew?

Emer. [*Thrusting herself between them and forcing both of them
[219]   back with her hands.*] I am Emer, wife of Cuchulain, and no
[220]   one shall go in front of me, or sing in front of me, or praise
[220, 221]   any that I have not a mind to hear praised.
                    [*Cuchulain puts his spear across the door.*] **30, 34.**

---

218.   . . . himself **38, 39.**
          Directions in 219.   [. . . *herself to the front.*] **F.**
221.   . . . praised.
          Cuchulain. [*spreading his arms across . . .*]
                    . . . quarrelling (quarrelling; F) **38-F.**
          Directions in 221.   [*spreading his arms across . . . .*] **43-50.**
222.   . . . other and each . . . . **38-F ;** . . . other, and each **43, 45** (1911),
          50.

223.   Break down the painted walls, break them down, down to the
       floor!

224.   Our wives shall come in together, each one at her own door.
       *[Laegaire and Conall begin to break down the walls. Their wives go
       each to the hole her husband is making. Emer stands at the door and
       sings. Some of those who carry musical instruments may play an
       accompaniment.*

       Emer.

225.   Nothing that he has done;
226.   His mind that is fire,
227.   His body that is sun,
228.   Have set my head higher
229.   Than all the world's wives.
230.   Himself on the wind
231.   Is the gift that he gives,
232.   Therefore women-kind,

---

[224] *Cuchulain.* All of our three wives shall come in together, and
[224]   by three doors equal in height and breadth and in honour.
[223]   Break down the bottoms of the windows.
          *[While Conal and Leagerie are breaking down the bottoms of the windows
          each of their wives goes to the window where her husband is. While the
          windows are being broken down Emer sings.*
                              My man is the best.
                              And Conal's wife
                              And the wife of Leagerie
                              Know that they lie
                              When they praise their own
                              Out of envy of me.
                              My man is the best,
[231]   First for his own sake, **30, 34.**

---

223.   . . . painted boards between the sill and the floor
224.   That they come . . .
       Directions after 224. [. . . *break out the bottoms of the windows,*
       (*windows* ; **F**) *then their* . . . *go to the windows, each to the window where her
       husband is. Emer* . . . *sings while the boards are being broken out.*] **38–70.**
225.   . . . done, **38–F, 50.**
228.   . . . higher, **38, 39.**
232.   . . . women kind, **38–45** ; . . . womenkind, **50.**

233.	When their eyes have met mine,
234.	Grow cold and grow hot,
235.	Troubled as with wine
236.	By a secret thought,
237.	Preyed upon, fed upon
238.	By jealousy and desire,
239.	For I am moon to that sun,
240.	I am steel to that fire.

[*Holes have been broken in the walls. Cuchulain takes his spear from the door, and the three women come in at the same moment.*

241. *Emer.*   Cuchulain, put off this sloth and awake:
242.   I will sing till I've stiffened your lip against every knave that would take
243.   A share of your honour.

Laegaire's Wife. You lie, for your man would take from my man.

[233-238]	Being the bravest
[233-238]	And handsomest man
[233-238]	And the most beloved
[233-238]	By the women of Ireland
[238]	That envy me,
	And then for his wife's sake
	Because I'm the youngest
	And handsomest queen.

[*When the windows have been made into doors, Cuchulain takes his spear from the door where Emer is, and all three come in at the same moment.*]

[241]	*Emer.* I am come to praise you and to put courage into you,
[242]	Cuchulain, as a wife should, that they may not take the
[243]	championship of the men of Ireland from you.
[243]	*Leagerie's Wife.* You lie, Emer, for it is Cuchulain and Conal
[243]	who are taking the championship from my husband.
[244]	*Conal's Wife.* Cuchulain has taken it. **30, 34.**

---

234. . . . hot **38-45, 69.**
238. . . . desire. **50.**
240. . . . fire, **50.**
Directions after 240. [*The windows are now broken down to floor.* (*to the floor.* **F**) *Cuchulain . . . .*]
241. [short line, unless combined with line 240]
241. . . . awake, **38, 39 ;** . . . off your sloth . . . awake, **F.**
243. . . . of our honor . . . . **38-F.**

244. *Conall's Wife* [*to Laegaire's Wife*]. You say that, you double-face, and your own husband began.

245. *Cuchulain* [*taking up Helmet from table*]. Townland may rail at townland till all have gone to wrack,

246. 　The very straws may wrangle till they've thrown down the stack;

247. 　The very door-posts bicker till they've pulled in the door,

248. 　The very ale-jars jostle till the ale is on the floor,

249. 　But this shall help no further.

　　　　　　　　　　　　　　　[*He throws Helmet into the sea.*

　　Laegaire's Wife.　　　　　　It was not for your head,

250. 　And so you would let none wear it, but fling it away instead.

251. *Conall's Wife.* But you shall answer for it, for you've robbed my man by this.

252. *Conall.* You have robbed us both, Cuchulain.

　　Laegaire.　　　　　　　　The greatest wrong there is

---

[245] *Cuchulain.* Townland against townland, barony against barony,
[245] 　kingdom against kingdom, province against province, and if
[247] 　there be but two doorposts to a door the one fighting against
[247] 　the other. [*He takes up the Helmet which Leagerie had laid
　　　　down up* (*upon* **34**) *the table when he went to break out the
[249] 　bottom of the window.*] This Helmet will bring no more wars
[249] 　into Ireland. [*He throws it into the sea.*]
[249] *Leagerie's Wife.* You have done that to rob my husband.
[250] *Conal's Wife.* You could not keep it for yourself, and so you
[250] 　threw it away that nobody else might have it.
[252] *Conal.* You should not have done that, Cuchulain.
[252] *Leagerie.* You have done us a great wrong. **30, 34**.

244. 　. . . double face, ... F.
　　　Directions at 245. [. . . *up the Helmet from the table.*] F.
245. 　Town land . . . town land . . . , **38-69**.
246. 　. . . stack. **38, 39** ; . . . stack, F.
248. 　. . . ale jars . . . , **38-F**.
249. 　. . . head **38, 39**.
　　　Directions in 249. [. . . *throws the Helmet* . . . .] F.
250. 　. . . it but . . . . **38-45, 69**.

253.   On the wide ridge of the world has been done to us two this
         day.

254. *Emer* [*drawing her dagger.*] Who is for Cuchulain?

Cuchulain.   Silence!

Emer.   Who is for Cuchulain, I say?
         [*She sings the same words as before, flourishing her dagger about.
         While she is singing, Conall's Wife and Laegaire's Wife draw their
         daggers and run at her, but Cuchulain forces them back. Laegaire and
         Conall draw their swords to strike Cuchulain.*

Laegaire's Wife [*crying out so as to be heard through Emer's singing*].
255.   Deafen her singing with horns!

Conall's Wife.   Cry aloud! blow horns! make a noise!

256. *Laegaire's Wife.* Blow horns, clap hands, or shout, so that you
         smother her voice!

---

[254]   *Emer.* Who is for Cuchulain?
[254]   *Cuchulain.* Let no one stir.
[254]   *Emer.* Who is for Cuchulain, I say?
         [*She draws her dagger from about her belt and sings the same words
         as before, flourishing it about. While she has been singing, Conal's
         Wife and Leagerie's Wife have drawn their daggers and run at her
         to kill her, but Cuchulain has forced them back. Conal and Leagerie
         have drawn their swords to strike Cuchulain.*]
[255, 256] *Conal's Wife* [*While Emer is still singing*]. Silence her voice,
[255, 256]   silence her voice, blow the horns, make a noise! **30, 34.**

---

254. . . . ? Silence.
             Who . . . ? **38-45, 69-89.**
255. . . . horns.
             Cry . . . !
256. . . . voice. **38-F.**

[*The Stable Boys and Scullions blow their horns or fight among themselves. There is a deafening noise and a confused fight. Suddenly three black hands come through the windows and put out the torches. It is now pitch-dark, but for a faint light outside the house which merely shows that there are moving forms, but not who or what they are, and in the darkness one can hear low terrified voices.*

257. *A Voice.* Coal-black, and headed like cats, they came up over the strand.

258. *Another Voice.* And I saw one stretch to a torch and cover it with his hand.

259. *Another Voice.* Another sooty fellow has plucked the moon from the air.

[*The Scullions and Horseboys blow their horns or fight among themselves. There is a deafening noise and a confused fight. Sudden (Suddenly **34**) three black hands upon black arms and holding (hands holding **34**) extinguishers come through the window and extinguish the torches. It is now pitch dark but for a very faint light outside the house which merely shows that there are moving forms, but not who or what they are, and in the darkness one can hear low terrified voices.*]

[258] *First Voice.* Did you see them putting out the torches?

[257] *Another Voice.* They came up out of the sea, three black men.

[257] *Another Voice.* They have heads of cats upon them.

[257] *Another Voice.* They came up mewing out of the sea.

[259] *Another Voice.* How dark it is! one of them has put his hand

[259]   over the moon. **30, 34.**

Directions after 256. [*The horse boys . . . fight. Suddenly, three . . . pitch dark, ...*] **38-F** ; [*The horse boys . . . pitch dark, ...*] **43-69.**

257. Coal black, . . . cats. They . . . . **38-F.**

[*A light gradually comes into the house from the sea, on which the moon begins to show once more. There is no light within the house, and the great beams of the walls are dark and full of shadows, and the persons of the play dark too against the light. The Red Man is seen standing in the midst of the house. The black cat-headed men crouch and stand about the door. One carries the Helmet, one the great sword.*]

260. *Red Man.* I demand the debt that's owing. Let some man kneel down there
261.   That I may cut his head off, or all shall go to wrack.

262. *Cuchulain.* He played and paid with his head, and it's right that we pay him back,
263.   And give him more than he gave, for he comes in here as a guest:
264.   So I will give him my head.   [*Emer begins to keen.*
    Little wife, little wife, be at rest.
265.   Alive I have been far off in all lands under the sun,
266.   And been no faithful man; but when my story is done

[*A light gradually comes into the windows as if shining from the sea. The Red Man is seen standing in the midst of the house.*]

[260]   *Red Man.* I demand the debt that is owing. I demand that some
[260, 261]   man shall stoop down that I may cut his head off as my head
[261]   was cut off. If my debt is not paid, no peace shall come to
[261]   Ireland, and Ireland shall lie weak before her enemies. But if
  my debt is paid there shall be peace.
  Cuchulain. The quarrels of Ireland shall end. What is one man's
[264]   life? I will pay the debt with my own head. [*Emer wails.*] Do
[264]   not cry out, Emer, for if I were not myself, if I were not
[265]   Cuchulain, one of those that God has made reckless, the women
[266]   of Ireland had not loved me, and you had not held your head
  so high. **30, 34.**

Directions after 259. [. . . *gradually coming into* . . . .] **38, 39**; [. . . *dark, too, against* . . . .] **F.**
261. . . . off or . . . . **38-F.**
262. . . . head and . . . , **38-69.**
263. . . . guest, **38-F.**
265. . . . under sun, **38-43, 50, 69.**
266. . . . man, but . . . **38-F.**

267.   My fame shall spring up and laugh, and set you high above all.

268.   *Emer* [*putting her arms about him*]. It is you, not your fame that I
        love.

        Cuchulain [*tries to put her from him*]. You are young, you are wise,
            you can call
269.   Some kinder and comelier man that will sit at home in the
            house.

270.   *Emer*. Live and be faithless still.

        Cuchulain [*throwing her from him*]. Would you stay the great
            barnacle-goose
271.   When its eyes are turned to the sea and its beak to the salt of
            the air?

272.   *Emer* [*lifting her dagger to stab herself*]. I, too, on the grey wing's
            path!

        Cuchulain [*seizing dagger*]. Do you dare, do you dare, do you dare?
273.   Bear children and sweep the house.
                        [*Forcing his way through the servants who gather round.*
                            Wail, but keep from the road.
                        [*He kneels before Red Man. There is a pause.*

        [*He stoops, bending his head. Three Black Men come to the door.
        Two hold torches, and one stooping between them holds up the
        Golden Helmet. The Red Man gives one of the Black Men his*
[274]   *sword and takes the Helmet.*] What do you wait for, old man?
[274] Come, raise up your sword! **30, 34.**

---

268.   . . . you not . . . . **38, 39**; [. . . *arm* . . . .] . . . fame, that . . . . **F**; . . .
        fame, that . . . . **50.**
270.   Live, and . . . **38-F.**
272.   . . . gray winds path.
        Cuchulain. [*seizing* . . . dare. **38, 39**;
        . . . gray wind's path.
        Cuchulain. [*seizing the dagger*]. . . . dare! **F**;
        . . . path.
        Cuchulain. [*seizing* . . . ? **45-69.**
273.   . . . road **38, 39.**
        Directions after 273.   [. . . *before the Red* . . . .] **F.**

274.   Quick to your work, old Radish, you will fade when the cocks
        have crowed.
        [*A black cat-headed man holds out the Helmet. The Red Man takes
        it.*

275.   *Red Man.* I have not come for your hurt, I'm the Rector of this
        land,
276.   And with my spitting cat-heads, my frenzied moon-bred band,
277.   Age after age I sift it, and choose for its championship
278.   The man who hits my fancy.
        [*He places the Helmet on Cuchulain's head.*
                                            And I choose the laughing lip
279.   That shall not turn from laughing, whatever rise or fall;
280.   The heart that grows no bitterer although betrayed by all;
281.   The hand that loves to scatter; the life like a gambler's throw;
282.   And these things I make prosper, till a day come that I know,
283.   When heart and mind shall darken that the weak may end the
        strong,
284.   And the long-remembering harpers have matter for their song.

                            THE END

---

[275]   *Red Man.* I will not harm you, Cuchulain. I am the guardian of
[275, 277] this land, and age after age I come up out of the sea to try
[277, 278] the men of Ireland. I give you the championship because you
[278, 279] are without fear, and you shall win many battles with laughing
[279, 280] lips and endure wounding and betrayal without bitterness of
[280]   heart; and when men gaze upon you, their hearts shall grow
[282]   greater and their minds clear; until the day come when I
[283, 284] darken your mind, that there may be an end to the story, and
[284]   a song on the harp-string. **30, 34.**

---

274.   . . . work old . . . . **38, 39.**
275.   . . . hurt, I am the . . . ,
276.   . . . spitting-cat heads, . . . , **38-F.**
279.   . . . laughing whatever . . . fall, **38, 39, 43-69;** . . . laughing whatever
        may rise . . . fall, **F;** . . . fall, **85.**
280.   . . . all,
281.   . . . scatter, the . . . ; **38-F.**
282.   . . . comes . . . , **F.**
284.   . . . long remembering . . . . **38-43, 50.**

NOTES

The Golden Helmet was produced at the Abbey Theatre on March 19, 1908, with the following cast:—Cuchulain, J. M. Kerrigan; Conal, Arthur Sinclair; Leagerie, Fred. O'Donovan; Laeg, Sydney Morgan; Emer, Sara Allgood; Conal's Wife, Maire O'Neill; Leagerie's Wife, Eileen O'Doherty; Red Man, Ambrose Power; Horseboys, Scullions, and Black Men, S. Hamilton, T. J. Fox, U. Wright, D. Robertson, T. O'Neill, I. A. O'Rourke, P. Kearney.

In performance we left the black hands to the imagination, and probably when there is so much noise and movement on the stage they would always fail to produce any effect. Our stage is too small to try the experiment, for they would be hidden by the figures of the players. We staged the play with a very pronounced colour-scheme, and I have noticed that the more obviously decorative is the scene and costuming of any play, the more it is lifted out of time and place, and the nearer to faeryland do we carry it. One gets also much more effect out of concerted movements—above all, if there are many players—when all the clothes are the same colour. No breadth of treatment gives monotony when there is movement and change of lighting. It concentrates attention on every new effect and makes every change of outline or of light and shadow surprising and delightful. Because of this one can use contrasts of colour, between clothes and background or in the background itself, the complementary colours for instance, which would be too obvious to keep the attention in a painting. One wishes to make the movement of the action as important as possible, and the simplicity which gives depth of colour does this, just as, for precisely similar reasons, the lack of colour in a statue fixes the attention upon the form.

The play is founded upon an old Irish story, *The Feast of Bricriu*, given in *Cuchulain of Muirthemne*, and is meant as an introduction to *On Baile's Strand*.

Appendix III, **34.**

A prose version of this play called *The Golden Helmet* was produced at the Abbey Theatre on March 19, 1908, and the present version on February 10, 1910, when Mr. Kerrigan took the part of Cuchulain and Mr. Sinclair and Mr. O'Donovan those of Conall and Laegaire respectively. Miss Allgood, Miss O'Neill and Miss Magee were the three queens.

In performance . . . form.

Notes, **45.**

A prose version [follows the version in **45** to 'form.' with '**1911**' added].

Notes, **69.**

*   *   *

Variant spellings

comlier **38, 39**; *comelier* **30, 34, 43-97.**
Conal **30, 34**; *Conall* **38-97.**

Connacht **F, 84-97**; *Connaught* **38, 39, 43-69.**
gray **39, F**; *grey* **30-38, 43-97.**
honor **F**; *honour* **30-39, 43-97.**
Laegaire **38-97**; *Leagerie* **30, 34.**
neighbor **F**; *neighbour* **30-39, 43-97.**

* * *

[See also the notes on *The Only Jealousy of Emer*, p. 566; *The Legendary and Mythological Foundation of the Plays*, p. 1283; *Glossary*, p. 1284; and *Prefaces to 64, 69*, pp.1304, 1306.]

ON BAILE'S STRAND

Note: Reproduced below and on succeeding verso pages are lines 1-313 of the texts of **13, 14, 20,** corresponding in general to lines 1-458 of the final text in **97E.** The differences are so great that intelligible collation was impossible. The few similarities are shown by bracketed line-numbers in the verso margins. The basic verso text and line-lengths are from **13:** variants in **14, 20** are marked; otherwise **13, 14, 20** are identical. Complete collation begins at line 459.

PRINTINGS **13, 14, 20.**

DATE [lacking]

DEDICATION [lacking]

DRAMATIS PERSONAE The Persons of the Play **13, 14;** [heading lacking] **20.** Cuchullain, the King of Muirthemne / Concobar, the High King of Ullad / Daire, a King / Fintain, a blind man / Barach, a fool / a Young Man / Young Kings and old (Old **14, 20**) Kings

STAGE DIRECTIONS Scene: *A great hall by the sea close to Dundalgan. There are two great chairs on either side of the hall, each raised a little from the ground, and on the back of the one chair is carved and painted a woman with a fish's tail, and on the back of the other a hound. There are smaller chairs and benches riased in tiers round the walls. There is a great ale vat at one side near a small door, and a large door at the back through which one can see the sea. Barach, a tall thin man with long ragged hair, dressed in skins, comes in at the side door. He is leading Fintain, a fat blind man, who is somewhat older.*

TEXT Title On Baile's Strand, (Strand: **14**) A Play **13, 14.**

1. *Barach.* I will shut the door, for this wind out of the sea gets
2.   into my bones, and if I leave but an inch for the wind
3.   there is one like a flake of sea-frost that might come
4.   into the house.

5. *Fintain.* What is his name, fool?

ON BAILE'S STRAND

1904

TO

WILLIAM FAY

BECAUSE OF THE BEAUTIFUL FANTASY OF HIS

PLAYING IN THE CHARACTER OF THE FOOL

Persons in the Play

A Fool

A Blind Man

Cuchulain, *King of Muirthemne*

Conchubar, *High King of Uladh*

A Young Man, son of *Cuchulain*

Kings and Singing Women

PRINTINGS   13, 14, 20 [for the first part of these three printings see opposite page]; 23, 26, 28, 32, 45, 48, 52, 63, 69, 84, 89, 97.

DATE   [lacking] 23-48, 69.

DEDICATION   ... phantasy ... 23, 32-45; [lacking] 26, 52, 63; ... phantasy ... the part of ... 28, 48.

DRAMATIS PERSONAE   Persons of the ... Ulad ... 23;
   Cuchulain, *the King of Muirthemne* / Conchubar, (Conchubar, (*pronounced Conochar*) 52) *the High* ... Ulad / Daire,[1] *a King* / Fintain,[2] *a blind man* / Barach,[3] *a fool* / A Young Man / Young Kings and old Kings 26, 52;
   Persons / A ... Conchubar, *High King of Ulster* / A ... Man / Kings and Women 28, 48;
   [lacking] 63;
   ... Ulad ... 32, 84, 89.

[1] Called 'A King' in the text of 26 and 52.
[2] Called 'Blind Man' in the text of 26 and 52.
[3] Called 'Fool' in the text of 26 and 52.

6. *Barach.* It's a woman from among the Riders of the Sidhe.

7.   It's Boann herself from the river. She has left the

[24-25]   8.   Dagda's bed, and gone through the salt of the sea and

9.   up here to the strand of Baile, and all for love of me.

10.   Let her keep her husband's bed, for she'll have none

11.   of me. Nobody knows how lecherous these goddes-

12.   ses are. I see her in every kind of shape but oftener

13.   than not she's in the wind and cries 'give a kiss and

14.   put your arms about me.' But no (no, **14, 20**) she'll have no more

15.   of me. Yesterday when I put out my lips to kiss her,

16.   there was nothing there but the wind. She's bad, Fin-

17.   tain. O, she's bad. I had better shut the big door too.

     [*He is going towards the big door but turns hearing Fintain's voice.*]

[13]   18. *Fintain.* [*Who has been feeling about with his stick.*] What's

19.   this and this?

20. *Barach.* They are chairs.

21. *Fintain.* And this?

22. *Barach.* Why, that's a bench.

23. *Fintain.* And this?

24. *Barach.* A big chair.

[36]   25. *Fintain.* [*Feeling the back of the chair.*] There is a sea-woman

A great hall at Dundealgan, not 'Cuchulain's great ancient house' but an assembly-house nearer to the sea. A big door at the back, and through the door misty light as of sea-mist. There are many chairs and one long bench. One of these chairs, which is towards the front of the stage, is bigger than the others. Somewhere at the back there is a table with flagons of ale upon it and drinking-horns. There is a small door at one side of the hall. A Fool and Blind Man, both ragged, and their features made grotesque and extravagant by masks, come in through the door at the back. The Blind Man leans upon a staff.

1. *Fool.* What a clever man you are though you are blind!
2. There's nobody with two eyes in his head that is as
3. clever as you are. Who but you could have thought
4. that the henwife sleeps every day a little at noon? I
5. would never be able to steal anything if you didn't
6. tell me where to look for it. And what a good cook
7. you are! You take the fowl out of my hands after I
8. have stolen it and plucked it, and you put it into
9. the big pot at the fire there, and I can go out and run
10. races with the witches at the edge of the waves and
11. get an appetite, and when I've got it, there's the hen

STAGE DIRECTIONS   Scene. *A . . . Dundealgan; not . . . house,' but . . . assembly house . . . sea mist . . . chairs on either side raised one above another, (above the other,* **23***) tier above tier. One of these chairs, which is turned towards (is towards* **23***) . . . others. An elaborate cloak lies on a chair at the other side. Somewhere . . . drinking horns. . . . Blind Man come . . . back. They wear patched and ragged clothes. (clothes, and the Blind Man leans upon a staff.* **23, 26***)* **23, 26, 52**; Scene. *A . . . assembly house . . . sea mist. . . . drinking horns. . . . ragged, come . . . .* **28, 48, 63**; *A* (Scene: *A* **45** (1913)) *. . . assembly house . . . sea mist. . . . ragged, come . . . .* **32, 45**; Scene: *A . . . assembly house . . . sea mist . . . .* **69**; *. . . assembly house . . . .* **84, 89** ; *. . . door the misty . . . .* **97A.**

TEXT

1. . . . are, though . . . ! **23, 26, 52.**
4. . . . noon! I **23, 26, 52** ; . . . hen wife . . . **28, 48, 63.**
7. . . . hands, after . . . **23.**
8. . . . stolen it, and you pluck it, and put it . . . **23, 26, 52.**
11. . . . appetite; and . . . **23, 26, 52.**

26.　　carved upon it.

27. *Barach.* And there is another big chair on the other side of
28.　　the hall.

29. *Fintain.* Lead me to it. [*He mutters while the fool is leading*
30.　　*him.*] That is what the High King Concobar has

[40-41]　31.　　on his shield. The High King will be coming. They
32.　　have brought out his chair. [*He begins feeling the*
33.　　*back of the other chair.*] And there is a dog's head
34.　　on this. They have brought out our master's chair.
35.　　Now I know what the horse-boys were talking
36.　　about. We must not stay here. The Kings are going
37.　　to meet here. Now that Concobar and our master,
38.　　that is his chief man, have put down all the enemies
39.　　of Ullad, they are going to build up Emain again.
40.　　They are going to talk over their plans for building
41.　　it. Were you ever in Concobar's town before it was
42.　　burnt? O, he is a great King, for though Emain was
43.　　burnt down, every war had made him richer. He has
44.　　gold and silver dishes, and chessboards and candle-
45.　　sticks made of precious stones. Fool, have they taken
46.　　the top from the ale vat?

47. *Barach.* They have.

48. *Fintain.* Then bring me a horn of ale quickly, for the Kings
49.　　will be here in a minute. Now I can listen. Tell me
50.　　what you saw this morning?

12.   waiting inside for me, done to the turn.

13. *Blind Man* [*who is feeling about with his stick*]. Done to the
14.   turn.

15. *Fool* [*putting his arm round Blind Man's neck*]. Come now,
16.   I'll have a leg and you'll have a leg, and we'll draw
17.   lots for the wish-bone. I'll be praising you, I'll be
18.   praising you while we're eating it, for your good
19.   plans and for your good cooking. There's nobody in
20.   the world like you, Blind Man. Come, come. Wait a
21.   minute. I shouldn't have closed the door. There are
22.   some that look for me, and I wouldn't like them not
23.   to find me. Don't tell it to anybody, Blind Man.
24.   There are some that follow me. Boann herself out
25.   of the river and Fand out of the deep sea. Witches
26.   they are, and they come by in the wind, and they
27.   cry, 'Give a kiss, Fool, give a kiss', that's what they
28.   cry. That's wide enough. All the witches can come
29.   in now. I wouldn't have them beat at the door and
30.   say, 'Where is the Fool? Why has he put a lock on
31.   the door?' Maybe they'll hear the bubbling of the
32.   pot and come in and sit on the ground. But we won't
33.   give them any of the fowl. Let them go back to the
34.   sea, let them go back to the sea.

---

12.   . . . me done . . . turn! **23, 26, 52.**
       Directions in 13.   [. . . *his hands.*] **52.**
17.   . . . you—I'll . . . **23, 26, 52**; . . . wishbone . . . **63**; . . . wish-bone,
       I'll . . . **45, 69.**
18.   . . . it—for . . . **23, 26, 52**; . . . you, while . . . **28-48, 63.**
20.   . . . , come—wait . . .
21.   minute—I . . . **23, 26, 52.**
22.   . . . wouldn't let them **26, 52.**
23.   find . . . any body, ... **26**; find . . . . **52.**
24.   . . . me: Boann . . . **23, 26, 52.**
25.   . . . sea—witches **23**; . . . river, and . . . sea—witches **26, 52.**
26.   . . . wind and . . .
27.   . . . kiss!' That's . . .
28.   . . . enough; all . . . **23, 26, 52.**
30.   say: 'Where . . . **28-48, 69**; say: 'Where's the . . . **63.**
31.   . . . of a
32.   . . . ground—but . . .
33.   . . . fowl—let . . . **23, 26, 52.**

51. *Barach.* About the young man and the fighting?

52. *Fintain.* Yes.

[65ff.] 53. *Barach.* And after that we can go and eat the fowl, for I am
       54.   hungry.

[69]   55. *Fintain.* Time enough, time enough. You're in as great a hur-
       56.   ry as when you brought me to Aine's Seat, where
       57.   the mad dogs gather when the moon's at the full.
       58.   Go on with your story.

[76ff.] 59. *Barach.* I was creeping under a ditch, with the fowl in my
       60.   leather bag, keeping to the shore where the farmer
       61.   could not see me, when I came upon a ship drawn
       62.   up upon the sands, a great red ship with a woman's
       63.   head upon it.

[97-98] 64. *Fintain.* A ship out of Aoife's country. They have all a wo-
       65.   man's head on the bow.

[97]   66. *Barach.* There was a young man with a pale face and red
       67.   hair standing beside it. Some of our people came
       68.   up whose turn it was to guard the shore. I heard them
       69.   ask the young man his name. He said he was under
       70.   bonds not to tell it. Then words came between them,
       71.   and they fought, and the young man killed half of them,
[85-92] 72.   and the others ran away, (away. **14, 20**)

35. *Blind Man* [*feeling legs of big chair with his hands*]. Ah!
36.   [*Then, in a louder voice as he feels the back of it.*] Ah—
37.   ah—

38. *Fool.* Why do you say 'Ah-ah'?

39. *Blind Man.* I know the big chair. It is to-day the High
40.   King Conchubar is coming. They have brought out
41.   his chair. He is going to be Cuchulain's master in
42.   earnest from this day out. It is that he's coming for.

43. *Fool.* He must be a great man to be Cuchulain's
44.   master.

45. *Blind Man.* So he is. He is a great man. He is over all
46.   the rest of the kings of Ireland.

47. *Fool.* Cuchulain's master! I thought Cuchulain could
48.   do anything he liked.

49. *Blind Man.* So he did, so he did. But he ran too wild,
50.   and Conchubar is coming to-day to put an oath
51.   upon him that will stop his rambling and make him
52.   as biddable as a house-dog and keep him always at
53.   his hand. He will sit in this chair and put the oath
54.   upon him.

55. *Fool.* How will he do that?

56. *Blind Man.* You have no wits to understand such
57.   things. [*The Blind Man has got into the chair.*] He will
58.   sit up in this chair and he'll say: 'Take the oath,

Directions in 35. [. . . *of chair* . . . .] **26, 52.**
35.   . . . . Ha! **28, 48, 63.**
Directions in 36. [*Then in* . . . .] **23, 26, 52.**
36.   . . . .] Ah! **28, 48, 63.**
37.   ah! **26, 28, 48-63.**
38.   . . . 'ah-ah' **23, 26, 52**; . . . say A-h! **28, 48, 63.**
40.   King is . . . **28, 48, 63.**
49.   . . . did; but . . . , **23, 26, 52.**
52.   . . . house dog . . . **23-28, 48, 63.**
Directions after 54.   [*He sits in chair.*] **23, 26, 52.**
Directions in 57.   [lacking]
58.   . . . chair, and . . . say, 'Take . . . , **23, 26, 52.**

73. *Fintain.* It matters nothing to us, but he has come at last.

74. *Barach.* Who has come?

[95-96; 123]　75. *Fintain.* I know who that young man is. There is not
　　　　　　　another
76. like him in the world. I saw him when I had my eye-
77. sight.

78. *Barach.* You saw him?

[135]　79. *Fintain.* I used to be in Aoife's country when I had my eye-
80. sight.

[137-138]　81. *Barach.* That was before you went on shipboard and were
82. blinded for putting a curse on the wind?

[140-141]　83. *Fintain.* Queen Aoife had a son that was red haired and
　　　　　　　pale
84. faced like herself, and everyone said that he would
85. kill Cuchullain some day, but I would not have that
86. spoken of.

[177]　87. *Barach.* Nobody could do that. Who was his father?

88. *Fintain.* Nobody but Aoife knew that, not even he himself.

89. *Barach.* Not even he himself. (himself! **14, 20**) Was Aoife
　　　　　　　a goddess and lech-
90. erous?

91. *Fintain.* I overheard her telling that she never had but one
[131-132]　92. lover, and that he was the only man who overcame
93. her in battle. There were some who thought him one
94. of the Riders of the Sidhe, because the child was

59.   Cuchulain. I bid you take the oath. Do as I tell you.
60.   What are your wits compared with mine, and what
61.   are your riches compared with mine? And what sons
62.   have you to pay your debts and to put a stone over
63.   you when you die? Take the oath, I tell you. Take
64.   a strong oath.'

65.   *Fool* [*crumpling himself up and whining*]. I will not. I'll
66.   take no oath. I want my dinner.

67.   *Blind Man*. Hush, hush! It is not done yet.

68.   *Fool*. You said it was done to a turn.

69.   *Blind Man*. Did I, now? Well, it might be done, and
70.   not done. The wings might be white, but the legs
71.   might be red. The flesh might stick hard to the
72.   bones and not come away in the teeth. But, believe
73.   me, Fool, it will be well done before you put your
74.   teeth in it.

75.   *Fool*. My teeth are growing long with the hunger.

76.   *Blind Man*. I'll tell you a story—the kings have story-
77.   tellers while they are waiting for their dinner—I
78.   will tell you a story with a fight in it, a story with a
79.   champion in it, and a ship and a queen's son that
80.   has his mind set on killing somebody that you and
81.   I know.

82.   *Fool*. Who is that? Who is he coming to kill?

---

59.   Cuchulain; I . . . .
60.   . . . mine! And . . . **23, 26, 52**.
63.   . . . tell you; take **23, 26, 52**.
65.   . . . not—I'll
66.   . . . oath—I . . . . **23, 26, 52**.
67.   Hush! hush! . . . . **23, 52**.
69.   . . . , now! Well, . . . done and **23, 26, 52** ; . . . I now? . . . **28, 48, 63**.
71.   . . . red; the . . .
72.   . . . teeth . . . [T] but believe **23, 26, 52**.
76.   . . . story. The . . . story (story- **52**)
77.   . . . dinner. I **23, 26, 52**.
79.   . , , , and ship and queen, a son . . . **28, 48**.

95.   great of limb and strong beyond others. The child
96.   was begotten over the mountains; but come nearer
97.   and I will tell you something.

98.   *Barach.* You have thought something?

99.   *Fintain.* When I hear the young girls talking about the col-
100.   our of Cuchullain's eyes, and how they have seven col-
101.   ours, I have thought about it. That young man has
102.   Aoife's face and hair, but he has Cuchullain's eyes.

103.   *Barach.* How can he have Cuchullain's eyes?

[135]   104.   *Fintain.* He is Cuchullain's son.

105.   *Barach.* And his mother has sent him hither to fight his
106.   father.

107.   *Fintain.* It is all quite plain. Cuchullain went into Aoife's
108.   country when he was a young man that he might
109.   learn skill in arms, and there he became Aoife's
110.   lover.

111.   *Barach.* And now she hates him because he went away, and
112.   has sent the son to kill the father. I knew she was a
113.   goddess.

114.   *Fintain.* And she never told him who his father was, that he
115.   might do it. I have thought it all out, fool, (fool. **14, 20**)
        I know a
116.   great many things because I listen when nobody is

83. *Blind Man.* Wait, now, till you hear. When you were
84.   stealing the fowl, I was lying in a hole in the sand,
85.   and I heard three men coming with a shuffling sort
86.   of noise. They were wounded and groaning.

87. *Fool.* Go on. Tell me about the fight.

88. *Blind Man.* There had been a fight, a great fight, a
89.   tremendous great fight. A young man had landed on
90.   the shore, the guardians of the shore had asked his
91.   name, and he had refused to tell it, and he had killed
92.   one, and others had run away.

93. *Fool.* That's enough. Come on now to the fowl. I wish
94.   it was bigger. I wish it was as big as a goose.

95. *Blind Man.* Hush! I haven't told you all. I know who
96.   that young man is. I heard the men who were run-
97.   ning away say he had red hair, that he had come
98.   from Aoife's country, that he was coming to kill
99.   Cuchulain.

100. *Fool.* Nobody can do that.

                        [To a tune]
101.   Cuchulain has killed kings,
102.   Kings and sons of kings,
103.   Dragons out of the water,
104.   And witches out of the air,
105.   Banachas and Bonachas and people of the woods.

106. *Blind Man.* Hush! hush!

---

83. Wait now till . . . 28, 48, 63.
84. . . . fowl I . . . , 23, 26, 52.
87. . . . on, tell . . . . 23, 26, 52.
91. name and . . .
92. one and . . . .
93. . . . on, now, to . . . 23, 26, 52.
94. . . . goose . . . [T] 28, 48, 63.
97. . . . he come (came 26, 52) 23, 26, 52.
100. Nobody could do . . . . 23, 26, 52.
      Directions before 101.   [lacking] 28, 48, 63; [Singing.] 52.

117.   noticing and I keep my wits awake. What ails you
118.   now?

119. *Barach.* I have remembered that I am hungry.

120. *Fintain.* Well, forget it again, and I will tell you about Aoife's
121.   country. It is full of wonders. There are a great many
122.   Queens there who can change themselves into wol-
123.   ves and into swine and into white hares, and when
124.   they are in their own shapes they are stronger than
125.   almost any man; and there are young men there who
126.   have cat's eyes and if a bird chirrup or a mouse squeak
127.   they cannot keep them shut (shut, **20**) even though it is bed-
128.   time and they sleepy; and listen, for this is a great
129.   wonder, a very great wonder, (wonder: **20**) there is a long
      narrow
130.   bridge, and when anybody goes to cross it, that the
131.   Queens do not like, it flies up as this bench would if
132.   you were to sit on the end of it. Everybody who goes
133.   there to learn skill in arms has to cross it. It was in
134.   that country too that Cuchullain got his spear made
135.   out of dragon bones. There were two dragons fight-
136.   ing in the foam of the sea, and their grandam was the
137.   moon, and six (nine **20**) Queens came along the shore.

138. *Barach.* I won't listen to your story.

139. *Fintain.* It is a very wonderful story. Wait till you hear what
140.   the six (nine **20**) Queens did. Their right hands were all made

Fool [*still singing*].

107.   Witches that steal the milk,
108.   Fomor that steal the children,
109.   Hags that have heads like hares,
110.   Hares that have claws like witches,
111.   All riding a-cock-horse

[*Spoken*]

112.   Out of the very bottom of the bitter black North.

113. *Blind Man.* Hush, I say!

114. *Fool.* Does Cuchulain know that he is coming to kill
115.   him?

116. *Blind Man.* How would he know that with his head in
117.   the clouds? He doesn't care for common fighting.
118.   Why would he put himself out, and nobody in it
119.   but that young man? Now if it were a white fawn
120.   that might turn into a queen before morning—

121. *Fool.* Come to the fowl. I wish it was as big as a pig; a
122.   fowl with goose grease and pig's crackling.

123. *Blind Man.* No hurry, no hurry. I know whose son it is.
124.   I wouldn't tell anybody else, but I will tell you,—a
125.   secret is better to you than your dinner. You like
126.   being told secrets.

127. *Fool.* Tell me the secret.

128. *Blind Man.* That young man is Aoife's son. I am sure
129.   it is Aoife's son, it flows in upon me that it is Aoife's

---

Directions before 107.   [lacking] **28, 48, 63.**
111.   . . . a cock-horse **23, 26, 45, 52, 69**; . . . a cock horse **28, 48, 63**;
    . . . a-cockhorse **32.**
Directions before 112.   [lacking] **28, 48, 63.**
112.   . . . north. **28-48, 63, 69.**
119.   but a young . . . **28, 48, 63**; . . . ? Now, if . . . **23, 26, 32, 52.**
120.   . . . morning. **23**; . . . morning . . . [T] **28, 48, 63.**
121.   . . . pig. A **23, 26, 52**; . . . fowl . . . [T] I . . . pig . . . [T] a **28, 48, 63.**
122.   . . . goose-grease . . . . **23, 26, 52.**
124.   . . . you. A **23, 26, 52.**
128.   . . . son . . . [T] I . . . **23, 26, 52.**
129.   . . . son; (son, **28, 48, 63**) it is borne in . . . **23-28, 48-63.**

141.   of silver.

142. *Barach.* No, I will have my dinner first. You have eaten the
143.   fowl I left in front of the fire. The last time you sent
144.   me to steal something you made me forget all about
145.   it till you had eaten it up.

146. *Fintain.* No, there is plenty for us both.

147. *Barach.* Come with me where it is.

      Fintain. [*Who is being led towards the door at the back by*
148.   *Barach.*] O, it is all right, it is in a safe place.

149. *Barach.* It is a fine fowl. It was the biggest in the yard.

150. *Fintain.* It had a good smell, but I hope that the wild dogs
[144] 151.   have not smelt it. [*Voices are heard outside the door*
152.   *at the side.*] Here is our master. Let us stay and talk
153.   with him. Perhaps Cuchullain will give you a new
154.   cap with a feather. He told me that he would give
155.   you a new cap with a feather, a feather with an eye
156.   that looks at you, a peacock's feather.

157. *Barach.* No, no (no. **14, 20**) [*He begins pulling Fintain towards*
      the door.]

158. *Fintain.* If you do not get it now, you may never get it, for
159.   the young man may kill him.

130.   son. You have often heard me talking of Aoife, the
131.   great woman-fighter Cuchulain got the mastery over
132.   in the North?

133. *Fool.* I know, I know. She is one of those cross queens
134.   that live in hungry Scotland.

135. *Blind Man.* I am sure it is her son. I was in Aoife's
136.   country for a long time.

137. *Fool.* That was before you were blinded for putting a
138.   curse upon the wind.

139. *Blind Man.* There was a boy in her house that had her
140.   own red colour on him, and everybody said he was
141.   to be brought up to kill Cuchulain, that she hated
142.   Cuchulain. She used to put a helmet on a pillar-
143.   stone and call it Cuchulain and set him casting at it.
144.   There is a step outside—Cuchulain's step.

                 [*Cuchulain passes by in the mist outside the big door.*

145. *Fool.* Where is Cuchulain going?

146. *Blind Man.* He is going to meet Conchubar that has
147.   bidden him to take the oath.

148. *Fool.* Ah, an oath, Blind Man. How can I remember so
149.   many things at once? Who is going to take an oath?

150. *Blind Man.* Cuchulain is going to take an oath to Con-
151.   chubar who is High King.

152. *Fool.* What a mix-up you make of everything, Blind
153.   Man! You were telling me one story, and now you

---

131.   . . . woman fighter . . . **23, 26, 52.**
132.   . . . north. **28, 48, 63 ;** . . . north? **32, 45, 69.**
134.   . . . lives . . . . **28, 48, 63.**
140.   . . . him and . . . **28-48, 63, 69.**
142.   . . . pillar
143.   . . . at it. . . . [T] **23, 26, 52.**
146.   . . . Conchubar, that . . . **23, 26, 52.**
148.   Ah! an . . . Man. . . . [T] How . . . **23, 26, 52.**
151.   chubar, who . . . . **23, 26, 52.**
153.   Man. You . . . **28, 32, 48, 63.**

160. *Barach.* No, no (no, **14, 20**) I am hungry. What a head you
    have, blind

[3-4] 161.   man. (man! **20**) Who but you would have remembered
    that

162.   the hen-wife slept for a little at noon every day. (day! **20**)

Fintain. [*Who is being led along very slowly and unwillingly.*]

163.   Yes (Yes, **14, 20**) I have a good head. The fowl should be
    done

164.   just right, but one never knows when a wild dog may

165.   come out of the woods. [*They go out through the big door at
    the back. As they go out Cuchullain and certain young Kings
    come in at the side door. Cuchullain (Cuchullain,* **20**) *though
    still young (young,* **20**) *is a good deal older than the others.
    They are all very gaily dressed, and have their hair fastened
    with balls of gold. The young men crowd around Cuchullain
    with wondering attention.*]

166. *First Young King.* You have hurled that stone beyond our
    utmost mark

167.   Time after time, but yet you are not weary.

168. *Second Young King.* He has slept on the bare ground of
    Fuad's Hill

169.   This week past, waiting for the bulls and the deer.

170. *Cuchullain.* Well, why should I be weary?

First Young King.   **It is certain**

154. are telling me another story . . . . How can I get the
155. hang of it at the end if you mix everything at the
156. beginning? Wait till I settle it out. There now, there's
157. Cuchulain [*he points to one foot*], and there is the young
158. man [*he points to the other foot*] that is coming to kill
159. him, and Cuchulain doesn't know. But where's Con-
160. chubar? [*Takes bag from side.*] That's Conchubar with
161. all his riches—Cuchulain, young man, Conchubar.—
162. And where's Aoife? [*Throws up cap.*] There is Aoife,
163. high up on the mountains in high hungry Scotland.
164. Maybe it is not true after all. Maybe it was your
165. own making up. It's many a time you cheated me
166. before with your lies. Come to the cooking-pot, my
167. stomach is pinched and rusty. Would you have it to
168. be creaking like a gate?

169. *Blind Man.* I tell you it's true. And more than that is
170. true. If you listen to what I say, you'll forget your
171. stomach.

172. *Fool.* I won't.

173. *Blind Man.* Listen. I know who the young man's father
174. is, but I won't say. I would be afraid to say. Ah,
175. Fool, you would forget everything if you could know
176. who the young man's father is.

---

154. . . . story. How . . . I understand
155. things, when they begin to happen, if . . . mix up everything . . .
156. beginning?—Wait . . . out. [*Takes off shoes.*] There . . .
    Directions in 157. [lacking]
    Directions in 158. [lacking] **23, 26, 52.**
159. . . . know, but . . . **28, 48, 63.**
161. . . . riches.—Cuchulain—Conchubar—the Young Man.— **23, 26, 52;**
    . . . , Conchobar— **28, 32, 48, 63.**
164. [*Begins putting on shoes.*] Maybe it's not true, (true **26, 52**) after . . . **23,
    26, 52.**
166. . . . cooking pot, . . . **28, 48, 63.**
167. . . . it
168. be . . . ? **23, 26, 52.**
170. . . . say you'll . . . **23, 26, 52.**
171. stomach . . . [T] **28, 48, 63.**
172. . . . won't! **23, 26, 52.**
173. *Blind Man.* I know . . . **28, 48, 63.**
174. . . . say; I . . . say. . . . [T] Ah, **23, 26, 52.**
176. . . . is! **23, 26, 52.**

171.   His father was the god who wheels the sun,
172.   And not king Sualtam.

     Third Young King. [*To a young King who is beside him.*] He came in the dawn,

173.   And folded Dectara in a sudden fire.

174. *Fourth Young King.* And yet the mother's half might well grow weary,
175.   And it new come from labours over sea.

176. *Third Young King.* He has been on islands walled about with silver,
177.   And fought with giants.
     [*They gather about the ale vat and begin to drink.*]

     Cuchullain.   Who was it that went out?

178. *Third Young King.* As we came in?

     Cuchullain.   Yes.

     Third Young King.   Barach and blind Fintain.

179. *Cuchullain.* They always flock together; the blind man
180.   Has need of the fool's eyesight and strong body,
181.   While the poor fool has need of the other's wit,

177. *Fool*. Who is it? Tell me now quick, or I'll shake you.

178.   Come, out with it, or I'll shake you.

                                             [*A murmur of voices in the distance.*

179. *Blind Man*. Wait, wait. There's somebody coming. . . .

180.   It is Cuchulain is coming. He's coming back with

181.   the High King. Go and ask Cuchulain. He'll tell

182.   you. It's little you'll care about the cooking-pot

183.   when you have asked Cuchulain that . . .

                              [*Blind Man goes out by side door.*

184. *Fool*. I'll ask him. Cuchulain will know. He was in

185.   Aoife's country. [*Goes up stage.*] I'll ask him. [*Turns*

186.   *and goes down stage.*] But, no, I won't ask him, I would

187.   be afraid. [*Going up again.*] Yes, I will ask him. What

188.   harm in asking? The Blind Man said I was to ask

189.   him. [*Going down.*] No, no. I'll not ask him. He

190.   might kill me. I have but killed hens and geese and

191.   pigs. He has killed kings. [*Goes up again almost to big*

192.   *door.*] Who says I'm afraid? I'm not afraid. I'm no

193.   coward. I'll ask him. No, no, Cuchulain, I'm not

194.   going to ask you.

195.   He has killed kings,

196.   Kings and the sons of kings,

---

177. . . . now, quick, ...

178. . . . you! **23, 26, 52.**

    Directions after 178. [lacking] **28, 48, 63.**

179. . . . , wait; there's . . . **23** ; . . . , wait, there's . . . **26, 52** ; . . . coming. **28, 48, 63** ; . . . . There's something coming . . . . **97A.**

182. . . . cooking pot **28, 48, 63.**

183. . . . that. **23, 26, 52.**

    Directions after 183. [lacking] **28, 48, 63** ; [. . . *side-door.*] **52.**

185. . . . country. [*Going towards door at back.*] I'll . . . **23, 26, 52.**

186. . . . *goes to door at side.*] But no, . . . him. I . . . **23, 26, 52** ; . . . , no. I . . . **28, 32, 48, 63.**

187. . . . *up towards door at* (*door and* **26, 52**) *back again.*] . . . him.—What

188. . . . asking?—The blind man . . .

189. him.—[*Going to door at side again.*] . . . , no; I'll . . . him.—He

190. . . . me.—I . . .

191, 192. . . . *to door at back.*] Who . . . not afraid; I'm . . .

193. . . . him.—No, . . .

194. . . . you. [*Running to door at side.*] **23, 26, 52.**

196. Kings and sons . . . , **63, 69A.**

182.   And night and day is up to his ears in mischief
183.   That the blind man imagines. There's no hen-yard
184.   But clucks and cackles when he passes by
185.   As if he'd been a fox. If I'd that ball
186.   That's in your hair and the big stone again,
187.   I'd keep them tossing, though the one is heavy
188.   And the other light in the hand. A trick I learnt
189.   When I was learning arms in Aoife's country.

190. *First Young King.* What kind of woman was that Aoife?

Cuchullain.   Comely.

191. *First Young King.* But I have heard that she was never married,
192.   And yet that's natural, for I have never known
193.   A fighting woman, but made her favours cheap,
194.   Or mocked at love till she grew sandy dry.

195. *Cuchullain.* What manner of woman do you like the best?
196.   A gentle or a fierce. (fierce? **20**)

197.   Dragons out of the water,
198.   And witches out of the air,
199.   Banachas and Bonachas and people of the woods.

*[Fool goes out by side door, the last words being heard outside.
Cuchulain and Conchubar enter through the big door at the back.
While they are still outside, Cuchulain's voice is heard raised in
anger. He is a dark man, something over forty years of age. Conchubar is much older and carries a long staff, elaborately carved or
with an elaborate gold handle.*

200. *Cuchulain.* Because I have killed men without your bidding
201.   And have rewarded others at my own pleasure,
202.   Because of half a score of trifling things,
203.   You'd lay this oath upon me, and now—and now
204.   You add another pebble to the heap,
205.   And I must be your man, well-nigh your bondsman,
206.   Because a youngster out of Aoife's country
207.   Has found the shore ill-guarded.

       Conchubar.   He came to land
208.   While you were somewhere out of sight and hearing,
209.   Hunting or dancing with your wild companions.

210. *Cuchulain.* He can be driven out. I'll not be bound.
211.   I'll dance or hunt, or quarrel or make love,

---

199.   Bocanachs . . . Bananachs . . . wood. **26, 52.**
        Directions after 199. [*He runs out, the last . . . still outside Cuchulain's
        . . . older, though not feeble-looking.*] **23, 26, 52**; [*Fool goes out side . . .
        carved, or . . . .*] **28, 48**; [*. . . carved, or . . . .*] **32**; [*Fool goes out side . . .
        at back. . . . carved, or . . . .*] **63.**
200.   . . . bidding, **23, 26, 52**; . . . bidding; **69.**
202.   . . . things **28-48, 63, 69.**
203.   You lay . . . me; and . . . **23, 26, 52**; . . . now and . . . **28, 48, 63.**
204.   . . . heap. **28-48, 63.**
205.   . . . , wellnigh . . . , **23, 26, 52.**
206.   . . . country. **45.**
207.   . . . ill guarded. . . . **23-28, 48, 52, 63.**
208.   . . . hearing; **23, 26, 52.**
211.   . . . love; **63.**

First Young King.   A gentle (gentle, **20**) surely.

	197.	*Cuchullain.* I think that a fierce woman's better, a woman
	198.	That breaks away when you have thought her won,
	199.	For I'd be fed and hungry at one time.
[332]	200.	I think that all deep passion is but a kiss
[333]	201.	In the mid battle, and a difficult peace
[334]	202.	'Twixt oil and water, candles and dark night,
[335]	203.	Hill-side and hollow, the hot-footed sun,
[336]	204.	And the cold sliding slippery-footed moon,
[337]	205.	A brief forgiveness between opposites
[338]	206.	That have been hatreds for three times the age
[339]	207.	Of his (this **20**) long 'stablished ground. Here's Concobar;
	208.	So I'll be done, but keep beside me still,
	209.	For while he talks of hammered bronze and asks
	210.	What wood is best for building, we can talk
	211.	Of a fierce woman.

212. Wherever and whenever I've a mind to.
213. If time had not put water in your blood,
214. You never would have thought it.

Conchubar.   I would leave
215. A strong and settled country to my children.

216. *Cuchulain.* And I must be obedient in all things;
217. Give up my will to yours; go where you please;
218. Come when you call; sit at the council-board
219. Among the unshapely bodies of old men;
220. I whose mere name has kept this country safe,
221. I that in early days have driven out
222. Maeve of Cruachan and the northern pirates,
223. The hundred kings of Sorcha, and the kings
224. Out of the Garden in the East of the World.
225. Must I, that held you on the throne when all
226. Had pulled you from it, swear obedience
227. As if I were some cattle-raising king?
228. Are my shins speckled with the heat of the fire,
229. Or have my hands no skill but to make figures
230. Upon the ashes with a stick? Am I
231. So slack and idle that I need a whip
232. Before I serve you?

Conchubar.   No, no whip, Cuchulain,
233. But every day my children come and say:
234. 'This man is growing harder to endure.
235. How can we be at safety with this man
236. That nobody can buy or bid or bind?

---

212. Wherever or whenever . . . .
213. . . . blood **23, 26, 52.**
216. . . . things: **23.**
217. . . . yours, go . . . please,
218. Come where you will, sit . . . **23, 26, 52.**
219. . . . men! **23, 26, 52;** . . . men. **28, 32, 48, 63.**
220. I, whose . . . ,
221. I, that . . . **23, 26, 52.**
223. . . . Sorcha and . . . **23, 26, 52.**
224. . . . World! **23, 26, 52;** . . . garden . . . east . . . world. **28, 48, 63.**
225. . . . I that . . . throne, when . . . **23, 26, 52.**
232. . . . , Cuchulain. **23, 26, 52.**
233. . . . say
234. This . . . . **28, 48, 63.**
235. . . . man, **23, 26, 52.**

[*Concobar, a man much older than Cuchullain, has come in through the great door at the back. He has many kings about him. One of these kings, Daire, a stout old man, is somewhat drunk.*]

Concobar. [*To one of those about him.*] Has the ship gone yet?

212.   We have need of more bronze workers and that ship
213.   I sent to Africa for gold is late.[1]

214.   *Cuchullain.* I knew their talk.

Concobar. [*Seeing Cuchullain.*] You are before us (us, **14, 20**) King.

215.   *Cuchullain.* So much the better, for I welcome you
216.   Into my Muirthemne.

Concobar.   But who are these?
217.   The odour from their garments when they stir
218.   Is like a wind out of an apple garden.

[348-349] 219. *Cuchullain.* My swordsmen and harp players and fine dancers,
220.   My bosom friends.

Concobar.   I should have thought, Cuchullain,

---

[1] In **14** this speech of Concobar's is written as prose.

237.   We shall be at his mercy when you are gone;
238.   He burns the earth as if he were a fire,
239.   And time can never touch him.'

Cuchulain.   And so the tale
240.   Grows finer yet; and I am to obey
241.   Whatever child you set upon the throne,
242.   As if it were yourself!

Conchubar.   Most certainly.
243.   I am High King, my son shall be High King;
244.   And you for all the wildness of your blood,
245.   And though your father came out of the sun,
246.   Are but a little king and weigh but light
247.   In anything that touches government,
248.   If put into the balance with my children.

249. *Cuchulain.* It's well that we should speak our minds out plainly,
250.   For when we die we shall be spoken of
251.   In many countries. We in our young days
252.   Have seen the heavens like a burning cloud
253.   Brooding upon the world, and being more
254.   Than men can be now that cloud's lifted up,
255.   We should be the more truthful. Conchubar,
256.   I do not like your children—they have no pith,
257.   No marrow in their bones, and will lie soft
258.   Where you and I lie hard.

Conchubar.   You rail at them

---

237.   . . . gone.
238.   . . . if it were . . . , **23, 26, 52.**
239.   . . . him.
       Cuchulain. And . . . **28, 48, 63.**
240.   . . . yet, and . . .
241.   . . . throne **23, 26, 52.**
242.   . . . yourself.
       Conchobar. Most . . . .
243.   . . . King. **28, 48, 63.**
244.   . . . you, for . . . , **23, 26, 52.**
246.   . . . king, and . . . **23, 26, 52.**
254.   . . . be, now . . . ,
255.   . . . truthful, Conchubar.
256.   . . . children. They . . . , **23, 26, 52.**
257.   . . . marrow, in . . . **28, 48, 63.**

221.   My graver company would better match
222.   Your greatness and your years; but I waste breath
223.   In harping on that tale.

Cuchullain.   You do, great King.
224.   Because their youth is the kind wandering wave
225.   That carries me about the world; and if it sank,
226.   My sword would lose its lightness.

Concobar.   Yet, Cuchullain,
227.   Emain should be the foremost town of the world.

228. *Cuchullain.* It is the foremost town.

Concobar.   No, no, it's not.
229.   Nothing but men can make towns great, and he,
230.   The one over-topping man that's in the world,
231.   Keeps far away.

Daire.   He will not hear you, King,
232.   And we old men had best keep company
233.   With one another. I'll fill the horn for you.

Concobar. I will not drink, old fool. You have drunk a horn
235.   At every door we came to.

Daire.   You'd better drink,

259.   Because you have no children of your own.

260. *Cuchulain*. I think myself most lucky that I leave
261.   No pallid ghost or mockery of a man
262.   To drift and mutter in the corridors
263.   Where I have laughed and sung.

    Conchubar.   That is not true,
264.   For all your boasting of the truth between us;
265.   For there is no man having house and lands,
266.   That have been in the one family, called
267.   By that one family's name for centuries,
268.   But is made miserable if he know
269.   They are to pass into a stranger's keeping,
270.   As yours will pass.

    Cuchulain.   The most of men feel that,
271.   But you and I leave names upon the harp.

272. *Conchubar*. You play with arguments as lawyers do,
273.   And put no heart in them. I know your thoughts,
274.   For we have slept under the one cloak and drunk
275.   From the one wine-cup. I know you to the bone,
276.   I have heard you cry, aye, in your very sleep,
277.   'I have no son', and with such bitterness
278.   That I have gone upon my knees and prayed
279.   That it might be amended.

    Cuchulain.   For you thought
280.   That I should be as biddable as others
281.   Had I their reason for it; but that's not true;
282.   For I would need a weightier argument

---

262.   . . . corridors, **28-48, 63, 69**.
263.   . . . true **28, 48, 63**.
264.   . . . us, **23, 26, 52** ; . . . us. **28, 48, 63**.
265.   For (For, **28, 48, 63**) there is none that having . . . , **23-28, 48-63**.
266.   . . . family, **23, 26, 52** ; . . . family **28-48, 63, 69**.
267.   And called by the one name . . . , **23-69**.
270.   . . . that; **23, 26, 52**.
275.   . . . wine cup. . . . bone. **23-48, 63, 69** ; . . . bone. **52**.
276.   . . . cry—aye, . . . sleep— **23, 26, 52** ; . . . , aye in . . . , **28-48, 63, 69**.
277.   . . . son!' and . . . **23, 26, 52**.
281.   . . . true, **23, 26, 32, 52** ; . . . it, but . . . true, **28, 48, 63**.

236.   For old men light upon their youth again
237.   In the brown ale. When I have drunk enough,
238.   I am like Cuchullain as one pea another,
239.   And live like a bird's flight from tree to tree.

240. *Concobar.* We'll to our chairs for we have much to talk of,
241.   And we have Ullad and Muirthemne, and here
242.   Is Conall Muirthemne in the nick of time.

    [*He goes to the back of stage to welcome a company of Kings who come in through the great door. The other Kings gradually get into their places. Cuchullain sits in his great chair with certain of the young men standing around him. Others of the young men, however, remain with Daire at the ale vat. Daire holds out the horn of ale to one or two of the older Kings as they pass him going to their places. They pass him by, most of them silently refusing,* (refusing. **14, 20**)]

243.   *Daire.* Will you not drink?

283. Than one that marred me in the copying,
284. As I have that clean hawk out of the air
285. That, as men say, begot this body of mine
286. Upon a mortal woman.

 Conchubar.   Now as ever
287. You mock at every reasonable hope,
288. And would have nothing, or impossible things.
289. What eye has ever looked upon the child
290. Would satisfy a mind like that?

 Cuchulain.   I would leave
291. My house and name to none that would not face
292. Even myself in battle.

 Conchubar.   Being swift of foot,
293. And making light of every common chance,
294. You should have overtaken on the hills
295. Some daughter of the air, or on the shore
296. A daughter of the Country-under-Wave.

297. *Cuchulain.* I am not blasphemous.

 Conchubar.   Yet you despise
298. Our queens, and would not call a child your own,
299. If one of them had borne him.

 Cuchulain.   I have not said it.

200. *Conchubar.* Ah! I remember I have heard you boast,
301. When the ale was in your blood, that there was one
302. In Scotland, where you had learnt the trade of war,
303. That had a stone-pale cheek and red-brown hair;

---

284. . . . air,
285. That as . . . say begot . . . **23, 26, 52.**
287. . . . every measurable hope,
288. . . . nothing or . . . . **23, 26, 52.**
290. . . . that!
 Cuchulain. I . . . **23.**
292. . . . foot **28, 48, 63.**
296. . . . country-under-wave. **28, 48, 63.**
298. . . . own **23, 26, 52.**
300. Ah, I . . . , **23, 26, 52.**
302. . . . learned . . . , **23, 26, 52.**
303. . . . hair, **23, 26, 52**; . . . hair. **28, 32, 48, 63.**

     An Old King.   Not till the council's over.

244. *A Young King.* But I'll drink, Daire.

     Another Young King.   Fill me a horn too, Daire.

245. *Another Young King.* If I'd drunk half that you have drunk to-day
       (to-day, **14, 20**)
246.   I'd be upon all fours.

     Daire.   That would be natural
247.   When Mother Earth had given you this good milk
248.   From her great breasts.

     Cuchullain. [*To one of the young Kings beside him.*]
                       One is content awhile
249.   With a soft warm woman who folds up our lives
250.   In silky network. Then, one knows not why,
251.   But one's away after a flinty heart.

252. *The Young King.* How long can the net keep us?

     Cuchullain.   All our lives

304.   And that although you had loved other women,
305.   You'd sooner that fierce woman of the camp
306.   Bore you a son than any queen among them.

307. *Cuchulain.* You call her a 'fierce woman of the camp',
308.   For, having lived among the spinning-wheels,
309.   You'd have no woman near that would not say,
310.   'Ah! how wise!' 'What will you have for supper?'
311.   'What shall I wear that I may please you, sir?'
312.   And keep that humming through the day and night
313.   For ever. A fierce woman of the camp!
314.   But I am getting angry about nothing.
315.   You have never seen her. Ah! Conchubar, had you seen her
316.   With that high, laughing, turbulent head of hers
317.   Thrown backward, and the bowstring at her ear,
318.   Or sitting at the fire with those grave eyes
319.   Full of good counsel as it were with wine,
320.   Or when love ran through all the lineaments
321.   Of her wild body—although she had no child,
322.   None other had all beauty, queen or lover,
323.   Or was so fitted to give birth to kings.

324. *Conchubar.* There's nothing I can say but drifts you farther
325.   From the one weighty matter. That very woman—
326.   For I know well that you are praising Aoife—
327.   Now hates you and will leave no subtlety
328.   Unknotted that might run into a noose

---

304.   . . . you have loved . . . , **97A.**
307.   . . . fierce . . . camp; **23, 26, 52.**
308.   But having . . . , **23, 26, 52**; For having . . . spinning wheels, **28, 48,
       63**; For having . . . , **32, 45, 69, 84.**
310.   'Ah, how . . . ?' **23, 26, 52.**
313.   Forever. . . . camp!—**23, 26, 52**; . . . ever—a . . . camp—**28, 48, 63**;
       Forever. . . . ! **32, 45.**
315.   . . . . Ah, Conchubar, . . . her, **23, 26, 52**; . . . her, ah! Conchobar,
       . . . **28, 48, 63.**
317.   . . . bow-string . . . , **23, 26, 32, 45** (1911), **52**; . . . backward and . . .
       bow-string . . . , **28, 48, 63.**
322.   . . . queen, and lover, **28, 48, 63**; . . . , queen, or . . . , **32, 45, 69.**
324.   . . . say that drifts . . . **97A.**
325.   . . . matter—that . . . — **28, 48, 63.**
327.   . . . you, and . . . subtilty **23, 26, 52.**
       V.E.P.Y.—R

253.   If there are children, and a dozen moons
254.   If there are none, because a growing child
255.   Has so much need of watching it can make
256.   A passion that's as changeable as the sea
257.   Change till it holds the wide earth to its heart.
258.   At least I have heard a father say it, but I
259.   Being childless do not know it. Come nearer yet;
260.   Though he is ringing that old silver rod
261.   We'll have our own talk out. They cannot hear us.

[*Concobar who is now seated in his great chair, opposite Cuchullain,
beats upon the pillar of the house that is nearest to him with a rod of
silver, till the Kings have become silent. Cuchullain alone continues to
talk in a low voice to those about him, but not so loud as to disturb
the silence. Concobar rises and speaks standing.*]

329.   About your throat, no army in idleness
330.   That might bring ruin on this land you serve.

331.   *Cuchulain.* No wonder in that, no wonder at all in that.
332.   I never have known love but as a kiss
333.   In the mid-battle, and a difficult truce
334.   Of oil and water, candles and dark night,
335.   Hillside and hollow, the hot-footed sun
336.   And the cold, sliding, slippery-footed moon—
337.   A brief forgiveness between opposites
338.   That have been hatreds for three times the age
339.   Of this long-'stablished ground.

         Conchubar.   Listen to me.
340.   Aoife makes war on us, and every day
341.   Our enemies grow greater and beat the walls
342.   More bitterly, and you within the walls
343.   Are every day more turbulent; and yet,
344.   When I would speak about these things, your fancy
345.   Runs as it were a swallow on the wind.
         [*Outside the door in the blue light of the sea-mist are many old and
         young Kings; amongst them are three Women, two of whom carry a
         bowl of fire. The third, in what follows, puts from time to time
         fragrant herbs into the fire so that it flickers up into brighter flame.*
346.   Look at the door and what men gather there—
347.   Old counsellors that steer the land with me,
348.   And younger kings, the dancers and harp-players

---

329.   ... throat—no ... **28, 48, 63.**
331.   ... that—no .... **23, 26, 52.**
333.   ... mid battle, ... **28, 48, 63.**
335.   ... sun, **23-69.**
336.   ... cold sliding, ... — **23, 26, 52** ; ... moon, **28, 48, 63.**
339.   ... me: **23, 26, 52** ; ... long 'stablished .... **28, 48, 63.**
343.   ... yet **23, 26, 52** ; ... turbulent, and ..., **28, 48, 63.**
344.   ..., your mind **23-28, 48-63.**
         Directions after 345.   [lacking: see below, l. 355] **23, 26, 52** ; [...
         sea mist ... *Kings, amongst* ... *bowl full of* ....] **28, 48, 63** ; [... *sea
         mist* ... *bowl full of* ....] **32, 45** ; [... *sea mist* ....] **69.**
346.   ... door, and ... — **23, 26, 52** ; ... there, **28, 48, 63.**
347.   ... me **23, 26, 52.**
348.   ... harp players **28, 48, 63.**

262. *Concobar.* I have called you hither (hither, **14, 20**) Kings of Ullad,
       and Kings
263.   Of Muirthemne and Connall Muirthemne,
264.   And tributary Kings, for now there is peace—
265.   It's time to build up Emain that was burned
266.   At the outsetting of these wars; for we,
267.   Being the foremost men, should have high chairs
268.   And be much stared at and wondered at, and speak
269.   Out of more laughing overflowing hearts
270.   Than common men. It is the art of kings
271.   To make what's noble nobler in men's eyes
272.   By wide uplifted roofs, where beaten gold,
273.   That's ruddy with desire, marries pale silver
274.   Among the shadowing beams; and many a time
275.   I would have called you hither to this work,
276.   But always, when I'd all but summoned you,

349. That follow in your tumults, and all these
350. Are held there by the one anxiety.
351. Will you be bound into obedience
352. And so make this land safe for them and theirs?
353. You are but half a king and I but half;
354. I need your might of hand and burning heart,
355. And you my wisdom.

Cuchulain [*going near to door*]. Nestlings of a high nest,
356. Hawks that have followed me into the air
357. And looked upon the sun, we'll out of this
358. And sail upon the wind once more. This king
359. Would have me take an oath to do his will,
360. And having listened to his tune from morning,
361. I will no more of it. Run to the stable
362. And set the horses to the chariot-pole,
363. And send a messenger to the harp-players.
364. We'll find a level place among the woods,
365. And dance awhile.

A Young King.   Cuchulain, take the oath.
366. There is none here that would not have you take it.

367. *Cuchulain.* You'd have me take it? Are you of one mind?

---

351. ... obedience, **23, 26, 52.**
352. ... safe from them . . . ? **69.**
353. ... king, and . . . half. **23, 26, 52**; . . . half! **69A.**
    Directions after first hemistich in 355. [*Outside the door in the blue light of the sea mist are many old and young kings; amongst them are three women, two of whom carry a bowl full of fire. The third woman puts from time to time fragrant herbs into the fire so that it flickers up into brighter flame.*] **23, 26, 52.**
    Directions after speaker in 355. [. . . *to the door.*] **23, 26, 52.**
356. ... me in the . . . **45** (1913).
359. ... will **28, 48, 63.**
362. ... chariot pole,
363. ... harp players. **28, 48, 63.**
364. ... woods **23, 26, 52.**

277.   Some war or some rebellion would break out.

278. *Daire.* Where's Maine Morgor and old Usnach's children,
279.   And that high-headed even-walking queen, (Queen, **14, 20**)
280.   And many near as great that got their death
281.   Because you hated peace. (peace? **20**) I can remember
282.   The people crying out when Deirdre passed
283.   And Maine Morgor had a cold grey eye.
284.   Well (Well, **14, 20**) well, I'll throw this heel-tap on the ground,
285.   For it may be they are thirsty.

    A King. ·   Be silent (silent, **14, 20**) fool.

286. *Another King.* Be silent (silent, **14, 20**) Daire.

    Concobar.   Let him speak his mind.
287.   I have no need to be afraid of ghosts,
288.   For I have made but necessary wars.
289.   I warred to strengthen Emain, or because

368. *The Kings.* All, all, all, all!

   A Young King.   Do what the High King bids you.

369. *Conchubar.* There is not one but dreads this turbulence
370.   Now that they're settled men.

   Cuchulain.   Are you so changed,
371.   Or have I grown more dangerous of late?
372.   But that's not it. I understand it all.
373.   It's you that have changed. You've wives and children now,
374.   And for that reason cannot follow one
375.   That lives like a bird's flight from tree to tree.—
376.   It's time the years put water in my blood
377.   And drowned the wildness of it, for all's changed,
378.   But that unchanged.—I'll take what oath you will:
379.   The moon, the sun, the water, light, or air,
380.   I do not care how binding.

   Conchubar.   On this fire
381.   That has been lighted from your hearth and mine;
382.   The older men shall be my witnesses,
383.   The younger, yours. The holders of the fire
384.   Shall purify the thresholds of the house
385.   With waving fire, and shut the outer door,
386.   According to the custom; and sing rhyme
387.   That has come down from the old law-makers
388.   To blow the witches out. Considering

---

368. . . . !
   A King. Do . . . . **23, 26, 52**; . . . all.
                Do . . . . **28, 48, 63.**
369. . . . turbulence,
370. . . . that they are settled . . . , **23, 26, 52.**
375. . . . tree— **26, 52**; . . . tree to tree . . . [T] **28, 48, 63.**
378. . . . unchanged . . . [T] I'll . . . will, **28, 48, 63.**
379. . . . , light or . . . , **69A.**
380. . . . binding.
   Conchubar. [*who has seated himself in his great chair*].
             On . . . **23, 26, 52.**
381. . . . mine, **23, 26, 52**; . . . mine. **28, 48, 63.**
383. . . . younger yours. . . . **23, 26, 52.**
385. . . . door **28, 48, 63.**
386. . . . to old custom, and . . . **23, 26, 52**; . . . rhymes **28, 48, 63.**
387. That have come . . . **28, 48, 63.**

290.   When wars are out they marry and beget
291.   And have their generations like mankind
292.   And there's no help for it; but I'm well content
293.   That they have ended and left the town so great,
294.   That its mere name shall be in times to come
295.   Like a great ale vat where the men of the world
296.   Shall drink no common ale but the hard will,
[452]   297.   The unquenchable hope, the friendliness of the sword.

> [*He takes thin boards on which plans have been carved by those about him.*]

298.   Give me the building plans, and have you written
299.   That we—Cuchullain is looking in his shield;
300.   It may be the pale riders of the wind
301.   Throw pictures on it, or that Mananan,
302.   His father's friend and sometime fosterer,
303.   Foreknower of all things, has cast a vision,

389. That the wild will of man could be oath-bound,
390. But that a woman's could not, they bid us sing
391. Against the will of woman at its wildest
392. In the Shape-Changers that run upon the wind.

[*Conchubar has gone on to his throne.*

The Women. [*They sing in a very low voice after the first few words so that the others all but drown their words.*

393. May this fire have driven out
394. The Shape-Changers that can put
395. Ruin on a great king's house
396. Until all be ruinous.
397. Names whereby a man has known
398. The threshold and the hearthstone,
399. Gather on the wind and drive
400. The women none can kiss and thrive,
401. For they are but whirling wind,
402. Out of memory and mind.
403. They would make a prince decay
404. With light images of clay
405. Planted in the running wave;
406. Or, for many shapes they have,
407. They would change them into hounds
408. Until he had died of his wounds,
409. Though the change were but a whim;
410. Or they'd hurl a spell at him,
411. That he follow with desire
412. Bodies that can never tire
413. Or grow kind, for they anoint

---

389.   ... could by oath be bound, **23, 26**.
392.   ... shape-changers .... **23, 26, 32, 45, 52, 69E**; ... shape changers .... **28, 48, 63**; ... shape-changers ... runs .... **69A**.
       Directions after 392. [lacking] **23, 26, 52**.
       Directions before 393. [*The song of the Women.*] **23, 26, 52**; [... *drowned* ....] **28, 48, 63**; [... *others will all* ....] **97A**.
394.   ... shape-changers ... **23, 26, 32, 45, 52, 69**; ... shape changers ... **28, 48, 63**.
400.   Women ..., **23, 26, 52**; ... women, none ..., **28-48, 63, 69**.
404.   ... clay, **28-48, 63, 69**.
405.   ... wave, **28, 48, 63**.
407.   ... hounds, **28, 32, 48, 63**.
410.   ... him **28, 48, 63**.
412.   ... tire; **28, 48**; ... tire, **32, 45, 69**.

304.   Out of the cold dark of the rich sea,

305.   Foretelling Emain's greatness. **13-20.**

Cuchullain.   No, great king (King, **14, 20**)

306.   I looked on this out of mere idleness, **13-20.**

307.   Imagining a woman that I loved. [*The sound of a trumpet without.*] **13, 14;** Imagining a far off country and one **20.**

307a.   That held it with a sword, although a woman. **20.**

307b.   *Concobar.* A woman needs but laugh, or a friend sigh, **20.**

307c.   And you're afar off sounding through the world. **20.**

307d.   While I plan Emain's greatness. [*The sound of a trumpet without.*] Open the doors! **20.**

[454]   308.   Open the door (door, **14**) for that is a herald's trumpet. **13, 14;** I hear a herald's trumpet, and await, **20.**

308a.   It may be, the heavy fleeces of the sea. **20.**

308b.   And golden and silver apples or ancient crowns **20.**

414.   All their bodies, joint by joint,
415.   With a miracle-working juice
416.   That is made out of the grease
417.   Of the ungoverned unicorn.
418.   But the man is thrice forlorn,
419.   Emptied, ruined, wracked, and lost,
420.   That they follow, for at most
421.   They will give him kiss for kiss
422.   While they murmur, 'After this
423.   Hatred may be sweet to the taste'.
424.   Those wild hands that have embraced
425.   All his body can but shove
426.   At the burning wheel of love
427.   Till the side of hate comes up.
428.   Therefore in this ancient cup
429.   May the sword-blades drink their fill
430.   Of the home-brew there, until
431.   They will have for masters none
432.   But the threshold and hearthstone.

433. *Cuchulain* [*speaking, while they are singing*]. I'll take and keep this
       oath, and from this day
434.   I shall be what you please, my chicks, my nestlings.
435.   Yet I had thought you were of those that praised
436.   Whatever life could make the pulse run quickly,

---

414. . . . bodies joint . . . joint **23, 26, 52.**
417. . . . unicorn; **23, 26, 52.**
418. . . . is twice forlorn, **28, 48, 63.**
421. . . . kiss; **28-48, 63, 69.**
422. . . . murmur 'After . . . **26, 52.**
423. . . . taste'; **23, 26, 52.**
426. . . . love, **28-48, 63, 69.**
427. . . . up; **28, 48, 63.**
428. Therefore, in . . . **26, 52.**
429. . . . sword blades . . . **28, 48, 63.**
430. . . . homebrew . . . **28-48, 63, 69.**
431. . . . master . . . **23, 26, 52.**
     Directions after 432. [*After 'Memory and Mind' their words die away to a murmur, but are loud again at 'Therefore in.' The others do not speak when these words are loud.*]
     Directions in 433. [*Speaking while . . . .*]
434. . . . please, my nestlings. **23, 26, 52.**
435. . . . you one of . . . **23, 26.**

308c.   Long hidden in the well at the World's End, **20**.

308d.   Or glittering garments of the salmon, tributes **20**.

308e.   From the Great Plain, or the high people of Sorcha, **20**.

308f.   Or the walled garden in the east of the world. **20**.

     [*The great door at the back is flung open; a young man
(Young Man, **20**) who is fully armed and carries a shield
with a woman's head painted on it, stands upon the
threshold. Behind him are trumpeters. He walks into the
centre of the hall, the trumpeting ceases.*] **13-20**.

309.   What is your message?

[457]   *Young Man.*   I am of Aoife's army. **13-20**.

310. *First King.* Queen Aoife and her army have fallen upon us. **13-20**.

311. *Second King.* Out swords! Out swords!

     Third King.   They are about the house. **13-20**.

437.   Even though it were brief, and that you held
438.   That a free gift was better than a forced.—
439.   But that's all over.—I will keep it, too;
440.   I never gave a gift and took it again.
441.   If the wild horse should break the chariot-pole,
442.   It would be punished. Should that be in the oath?
         [*Two of the Women, still singing, crouch in front of him holding the
         bowl over their heads. He spreads his hands over the flame.*
443.   I swear to be obedient in all things
444.   To Conchubar, and to uphold his children.

445. *Conchubar.* We are one being, as these flames are one:
446.   I give my wisdom, and I take your strength.
447.   Now thrust the swords into the flame, and pray
448.   That they may serve the threshold and the hearthstone
449.   With faithful service.
         [*The Kings kneel in a semicircle before the two Women and Cuchu-
         lain, who thrusts his sword into the flame. They all put the points of
         their swords into the flame. The third Woman is at the back near the
         big door.*

Cuchulain.   O pure, glittering ones
450.   That should be more than wife or friend or mistress,
451.   Give us the enduring will, the unquenchable hope,
452.   The friendliness of the sword!—
         [*The song grows louder, and the last words ring out clearly. There is
         a loud knocking at the door, and a cry of* 'Open! open!'

453. *Conchubar.* Some king that has been loitering on the way.
454.   Open the door, for I would have all know

---

437.   . . . it was brief, . . . **28, 48, 64** ; . . . , and though you . . . **23, 26.**
438.   . . . forced; **23, 26, 52** ; . . . forced— **28, 48, 63.**
439.   . . . , too. **23, 26, 32, 52** ; . . . over—I . . . , too. **28, 48, 63** ; . . . , too,
       45, 69.
441.   . . . chariot-pole
442.   . . . oath?— **23, 26, 52.**
445.   . . . one. **23, 26, 52.**
447.   . . . swords in the . . . **23, 26, 52.**
       Directions in 449.   [*. . . sword in the . . . swords in the . . . .*]
449.   . . . pure glittering ones, **23, 26, 52.**
450.   . . . mistress **45.**
       Directions after 452.   [*. . . a low knocking . . .* 'Open, open.'] **28, 48, 63.**

455.   That the oath's finished and Cuchulain bound,
456.   And that the swords are drinking up the flame.
        [*The door is opened by the third Woman, and a Young Man with a
        drawn sword enters.*

457.   *Young Man.* I am of Aoife's country.
        [*The Kings rush towards him. Cuchulain throws himself between.*

Cuchulain.   Put up your swords.
458.   He is but one. Aoife is far away.

---

455.   . . . finished, and . . . bound **23, 26, 52.**
457.   . . . Aoife's army.
        [*The* **23, 26, 32, 45, 52;**
        . . . Aoife's army.
        [*The* . . . . *Cuchulain thrusts his sword between.*]
        Put . . . swords, **28, 48, 63.**

459. *Young Man.* I have come alone into the midst of you
460.   To weigh this sword against Cuchulain's sword.

461. *Conchubar.* And are you noble? for if of common seed,
462.   You cannot weigh your sword against his sword
463.   But in mixed battle.

     Young Man.   I am under bonds
464.   To tell my name to no man; but it's noble.

465. *Conchubar.* But I would know your name and not your bonds.
466.   You cannot speak in the Assembly House,
467.   If you are not noble.

     First Old King.   Answer the High King!

468. *Young Man.* I will give no other proof than the hawk gives
469.   That it's no sparrow!
                    [*He is silent for a moment, then speaks to all.*
                    Yet look upon me, kings.
470.   I, too, am of that ancient seed, and carry

459.[1] . . . alone in the . . . **14, 20.**
460.   . . . weight . . . . **63.**
       Directions after 460. [*There is a murmur amongst the kings.* (*Kings.* **14,
       20**)] **13-20.**
461.   . . . seed **13-26, 52.**
462.   Yon cannot . . . **45** (1913).
464.   . . . man, but . . . . **13-20.**
465.   . . . bonds **13** ; . . . name, and . . . . **23, 26, 52.**
466.   . . . House **13-26, 52.**
467.   . . . noble.
       A King. . . . King. **13-20** ; . . . .
                              First King. . . . ! **23, 26, 52.**
468.   . . . Man. [*Drawing his sword*] I . . . **13-20** ; . . . gives— **23-69.**
469.   . . . sparrow.
          [. . . *silent a moment* (*moment,* **20**) *then* . . . .]
                  . . . , kings; (*Kings;* **14, 20**) **13-20** ;
       . . . , Kings. **97A.**
       Directions in 469. [. . . *moment then* . . . .] **28, 48, 63.**
470.   I too am . . . seed and . . . **13-20** ; I too am . . . **23, 26, 52.**

   [1] From here on, 'Fintain' for 'Blind Man' and 'Barach' for 'Fool.' **13-20.**

471.   The signs about this body and in these bones.

472.   *Cuchulain.* To have shown the hawk's grey feather is enough,
473.   And you speak highly, too. Give me that helmet.
474.   I'd thought they had grown weary sending champions.
475.   That sword and belt will do. This fighting's welcome.
476.   The High King there has promised me his wisdom;
477.   But the hawk's sleepy till its well-beloved
478.   Cries out amid the acorns, or it has seen
479.   Its enemy like a speck upon the sun.
480.   What's wisdom to the hawk, when that clear eye
481.   Is burning nearer up in the high air?

   *[Looks hard at Young Man; then comes down steps and grasps
   Young Man by shoulder.*

---

472.   . . . enough **13, 14.**
473.   . . . highly too.
   *[Cuchullain comes down from his great chair. He remains standing on
   the steps of the chair. The young (Young **20**) kings (Kings **14, 20**)
   gather about him and begin to arm him.]*
                    Give . . . helmet! **13-20**;
   . . . helmet! **23, 26, 52.**
474.   . . . champions **23.**
475.   That coat will do. I'd half forgotten, boy, **13, 14**; That leathern
   coat will do. The High King there **20.**
476.   How all those great kings came into the mouse-trap **13, 14**; Being
   old in wisdom can think of times to come, **20.**
477.   That had been baited with Maeve's pretty daughter.
478.   How Findabair, that blue-eyed Findabair—
479.   But the tale is worthy of a winter's night. **13, 14.**
480-481.   [lacking] **13, 14.**
480.   What's Emain to . . . hawk when . . . **20.**
481.   . . . air! **20-26, 52.**
481a.   That buckle should be tighter. Give me your shield. **13-20.**
481b.   There is good level ground at Baile's Yew-tree (Yew-tree, **20**)
481c.   Some dozen yards from here, and it's but truth
481d.   That I am sad to-day and this fight welcome. **13-20.**
   Directions before 482. *[He looks . . . at the young man, (Young Man,
   14, 20) and then steps down on to the (on the **20**) floor of the Assembly House.
   He grasps the young man (Young Man **14, 20**) by the shoulder.]* **13-20**;
   [. . . grasps the Young . . . by his shoulder.] **23, 26, 52.**

482.   Hither into the light.
    [*To Conchubar.*]   The very tint
483.   Of her that I was speaking of but now.
484.   Not a pin's difference.
    [*To Young Man.*]   You are from the North,
485.   Where there are many that have that tint of hair—
486.   Red-brown, the light red-brown. Come nearer, boy,
487.   For I would have another look at you.
488.   There's more likeness—a pale, a stone-pale cheek.
489.   What brought you, boy? Have you no fear of death?

490.   *Young Man.* Whether I live or die is in the gods' hands.

491.   *Cuchulain.* That is all words, all words; a young man's talk.
492.   I am their plough, their harrow, their very strength;
493.   For he that's in the sun begot this body
494.   Upon a mortal woman, and I have heard tell
495.   It seemed as if he had outrun the moon
496.   That he must follow always through waste heaven,
497.   He loved so happily. He'll be but slow
498.   To break a tree that was so sweetly planted.

---

482.   . . . light.
    [*Turning to one of the young kings. (Kings.* **14**; *Young Kings.* **20**)]
        That's the very (The very **20**) . . . **13-20**;
    . . . light!
    [*To* . . . **23, 26, 52.**
483.   . . . now: **13-20**; . . . now **63**.
484.   . . .
    [*To the young man. (Young Man.* **14, 20**)]
    . . . North (North, **20**) **13-20**;
    . . . North **28-52, 63, 69.**
485.   . . . hair **13, 14**; . . . hair, **20**.
486.   Red brown, . . . red brown. . . . , boy! **13, 14**; . . . , boy! **20**.
488.   . . . likeness, a . . . stone pale . . . . **13-20.**
489.   . . . you boy? . . . ? **13**; . . . death! **26, 52.**
490.   . . . Gods' . . . . **13-28, 48, 52, 63.**
491.   . . . all words, . . . words, a . . . talk; **13-20**; . . . all words, . . . words,
    a . . . . **28, 48, 63.**
492.   . . . strength, **13-20.**
495.   . . . moon, **13-26, 52**; . . . moon; **28-48, 69.**
496.   . . . must always follow through . . . , **13-20, 28, 48, 63.**

499.   Let's see that arm. I'll see it if I choose.

500.   That arm had a good father and a good mother,

501.   But it is not like this.

Young Man.   You are mocking me;

502.   You think I am not worthy to be fought.

503.   But I'll not wrangle but with this talkative knife.

504.   *Cuchulain.* Put up your sword; I am not mocking you.

505.   I'd have you for my friend, but if it's not

506.   Because you have a hot heart and a cold eye,

507.   I cannot tell the reason.

[*To Conchubar.*]   He has got her fierceness,

508.   And nobody is as fierce as those pale women.

509.   But I will keep him with me, Conchubar,

510.   That he may set my memory upon her

511.   When the day's fading.—You will stop with us,

512.   And we will hunt the deer and the wild bulls;

513.   And, when we have grown weary, light our fires

514.   Between the wood and water, or on some mountain

---

499.   . . . arm; I'll . . . I like. **13-20** ; . . . arm! I'll . . . I like. **23, 26, 52** ; . . . I like. **28, 48, 63.**

500.   . . . mother **13, 14.**

501.   . . . me. **13-20** ; . . . me! **23, 26, 52.**

502.   . . . fought, **13-20.**

504.   . . . sword, I . . . you **13** ; . . . sword, I . . . . **14, 20.**

505.   . . . friend; but . . . **23, 26, 52.**

506.   . . . eye **13-20.**

507.   . . . reason. You've got . . . fierceness (fierceness, **14, 20**) **13-20** ; . . . fierceness. **28, 48, 63.**
Directions before 509. [*To the young kings.* (*Kings.* **14**; *Young Kings.* **20**)] **13-20.**

509.   We'll keep him here in Muirthemne awhile. **13-20** ; And I . . . , **23, 26, 52.**

510.   *A Young King.* You are the leader of our pack and therefore **13-20** ; . . . upon it **23, 26, 52.**

511.   May cry what you will.
Cuchullain.   You'll stop . . . us **13-20** ; . . . fading.
You . . . , **23, 26, 52** ; . . . fading—you . . . , **28, 48, 63.**

512.   . . . bulls **13, 14** ; . . . bulls, **20** ; . . . we shall hunt . . . ; **52.**

514.   In sandy places where the wool-white foam **13-20** ; . . . water or . . . **28, 48, 63.**

515.   Where the Shape-Changers of the morning come.
516.   The High King there would make a mock of me
517.   Because I did not take a wife among them.
518.   Why do you hang your head? It's a good life:
519.   The head grows prouder in the light of the dawn,
520.   And friendship thickens in the murmuring dark
521.   Where the spare hazels meet the wool-white foam.
522.   But I can see there's no more need for words
523.   And that you'll be my friend from this day out.

524.   *Conchubar.* He has come hither not in his own name
525.   But in Queen Aoife's, and has challenged us
526.   In challenging the foremost man of us all.

---

515.   Is murmuring and breaking, and it maybe (may be **14, 20**) **13-20**;
        . . . shape-changers . . . . **23, 26, 32, 45, 52, 69**; . . . shape changers
        . . . . **28, 48, 63.**
516.   That long-haired women will come out of the dunes
517.   To dance in the yellow fire-light; (fire-light. **14-20**) You hang your
        head (head, **14, 20**) **13-20.**
518.   Young man, as if it was not a good life; **13-20**; . . . life. **23, 26, 52**;
        . . . head—it's . . . : **28, 48, 63.**
519.   And yet what's better than to hurl the spear, **13-20.**
519a.   And hear the long-remembering harp, and dance; (dance? **20**) **13-20.**
520.   Friendship grows quicker in . . . dark; **13-20**; . . . dark, **23, 26, 52.**
521.   [lacking] **13-20.**
522.   . . . words, **23, 26, 52.**
523.   . . . friend now.
        First Old King. Concobar (Concobar, **14, 20**)
523a.   Forbid their friendship (friendship, **14, 20**) for it will get twisted
523b.   To a reproach against us.
        Concobar.   Until now
523c.   I'd never need to cry Cuchullain on
523d.   And would not now.
        First Old King.   They'll say his manhood's quenched. **13-20**;
        [set as two lines] **14.**
524-533. [lacking] **13-20.**
524.   . . . hither, not . . . name, **23, 26, 52.**
525.   . . . Aoife's name; and . . . **23, 26, 52**; . . . challenged you **28, 48, 63.**
526.   Because you are the . . . all— **28, 48, 63.**

527. *Cuchulain.* Well, well, what matter?

      Conchubar.   You think it does not matter,
528.   And that a fancy lighter than the air,
529.   A whim of the moment, has more matter in it.
530.   For, having none that shall reign after you,
531.   You cannot think as I do, who would leave
532.   A throne too high for insult.

      Cuchulain.   Let your children
533.   Re-mortar their inheritance, as we have,
534.   And put more muscle on.—I'll give you gifts,
535.   But I'd have something too—that arm-ring, boy.
536.   We'll have this quarrel out when you are older.

537. *Young Man.* There is no man I'd sooner have my friend
538.   Than you, whose name has gone about the world
539.   As if it had been the wind; but Aoife'd say

---

527. . . . matter!
            You . . . , **23, 26, 52** ; . . . matter; **28-48, 63, 69.**
529. . . . moment has . . . it, **23, 26, 52** ; . . . moment has . . . . **28-48, 63, 69.**
530. For having . . . , **23-89.**
531. . . . think, as . . . **23, 26, 52.**
533. . . . inheritance as . . . , **23, 26, 52.**
534. I'll give . . . gifts, but I'll have something too (too, **14, 20**) **13-20** ; . . . on. I'll . . . , **23, 26, 52** ; . . . on —I will give . . . , **28, 48, 63.**
535. An arm-ring or the like, and if you will **13-20** ; But I'll have . . . arm ring, ... **28, 48** ; But I'll have something, too— . . . arm ring, ... **63.**
536. We'll fight it out . . . older, boy. **13-20** ; . . . have the quarrel . . . . **28, 48, 63.**
536a. *An Old King.* Aoife will make some story out of this.
536b. *Cuchullain.* Well, well (well, **14, 20**) what matter, I'll have that arm-ring, boy. **13-20.**
538. . . . you whose . . . **13-20.**
539. . . . wind, but . . . **13-20, 28, 48, 63.**

540.   I had turned coward.

      Cuchulain.   I will give you gifts
541.   That Aoife'll know, and all her people know,
542.   To have come from me.   *[Showing cloak.*
                    My father gave me this.
543.   He came to try me, rising up at dawn
544.   Out of the cold dark of the rich sea.
545.   He challenged me to battle, but before
546.   My sword had touched his sword, told me his name,
547.   Gave me this cloak, and vanished. It was woven
548.   By women of the Country-under-Wave
549.   Out of the fleeces of the sea. O! tell her
550.   I was afraid, or tell her what you will.
551.   No; tell her that I heard a raven croak
552.   On the north side of the house, and was afraid.

553. *Conchubar.* Some witch of the air has troubled Cuchulain's mind.

554. *Cuchulain.* No witchcraft. His head is like a woman's head
555.   I had a fancy for.

      Conchubar.   A witch of the air
556.   Can make a leaf confound us with memories.

---

540. . . . coward.
               I'll give . . . **13-20** ; . . . gifts, **26, 52.**
541. . . . know and . . . know
542. To have been my gifts. Mananan (Mananan, **20**) son of the sea (sea, **20**) **13-20.**
     Directions in 542. [. . . *cloak, (cloak* **52**) *which is on a chair.*] **23, 26, 52.**
542. [set as two lines] **28, 48.**
543-546. [lacking] **13-20.**
547. . . . this heavy purple (heavy embroidered **20**) cloak. Nine Queens
548. Of the Land-under-Wave had woven it **13-20.**
551. No! tell . . .
552. . . . house and . . . .
553. *An Old King.* Some . . . .
554. . . . witchcraft, his . . .
555. . . . for.
     Second Old King. A . . . **13-20.**

557. They run upon the wind and hurl the spells
558. That make us nothing, out of the invisible wind.
559. They have gone to school to learn the trick of it.

560. *Cuchulain.* No, no—there's nothing out of common here;
561. The winds are innocent.—That arm-ring, boy.

562. *A King.* If I've your leave I'll take this challenge up.

563. *Another King.* No, give it me, High King, for this wild Aoife
564. Has carried off my slaves.

Another King.　　　　　　　　　　No, give it me,
565. For she has harried me in house and herd.

566. *Another King.* I claim this fight.

Other Kings [together].　　　　　And I! And I! And I!

567. *Cuchulain.* Back! back! Put up your swords! Put up your swords!

557, 558, 560. [lacking] **13-20.**
557. They ride upon . . . **23, 26, 52.**
560. . . . , no, there's . . . ; **23, 26, 52** ; . . . here. **28, 48, 63.**
561. But there's no trick in this. That . . . . **13-20** ; . . . innocent. That . . . ,
　　　boy! **23, 26, 52** ; . . . innocent—that arm ring, ... **28, 48, 63.**
562. *Third Old King.* He shall not go unfought, I'll fight with him. **13-20** ;
　　　. . . leave, I'll . . . . **23-28, 48, 52, 63.**
563. *Fourth Old King.* No! I will fight with him.
　　　First Old King.　　　　　　　　　　I claim the fight, **13-20** ;
　　　. . . , for that wild . . . **23, 26, 52.**
564. For when we sent an army to her land— **13-20** ; . . . it to me, **28,**
　　　48, 63.
564a. *Second Old King.* I claim the fight, for one of Aoife's galleys
565. Stole my great cauldron and a herd of pigs. **13-20.**
566. *Third Old King.* No, no (no, **14, 20**) I claim it, for at Lammas' time—
　　　13-20 ; . . . .
　　　　　　　　　And I! and I! and I! **23, 26, 52** ;
　　　. . . claim the fight.
　　　　　　　　　And . . . I. (I! **63**) **28, 48, 63.**
567. . . . ! Back! Put . . . ! **13-20** ; . . . ! Put . . . ! put . . . ! **23, 26, 52** ;
　　　. . . swords. **28, 48, 63.**

568.   There's none alive that shall accept a challenge
569.   I have refused. Laegaire, put up your sword!

570.   *Young Men.* No, let them come. If they've a mind for it,
571.   I'll try it out with any two together.

572.   *Cuchulain.* That's spoken as I'd have spoken it at your age.
573.   But you are in my house. Whatever man
574.   Would fight with you shall fight it out with me.
575.   They're dumb, they're dumb. How many of you would meet
                                                          [*Draws sword.*
576.   This mutterer, this old whistler, this sand-piper,
577.   This edge that's greyer than the tide, this mouse
578.   That's gnawing at the timbers of the world,
579.   This, this—Boy, I would meet them all in arms
580.   If I'd a son like you. He would avenge me
581.   When I have withstood for the last time the men
582.   Whose fathers, brothers, sons, and friends I have killed
583.   Upholding Conchubar, when the four provinces
584.   Have gathered with the ravens over them.
585.   But I'd need no avenger. You and I
586.   Would scatter them like water from a dish.

587.   *Young Man.* We'll stand by one another from this out.
588.   Here is the ring.

        Cuchulain.   No, turn and turn about.

---

569.   ... sword. **13-20, 28, 48, 63** ; .... Laegaire put ... ! **26, 52.**
570.   No (No, **14, 20**) let ... come, let any three together. **13-20** ; ... come!
        If ... , **23, 26, 52.**
571.   If they've a mind to, I'll try it out with four. **13-20.**
572.   ... I'd spoken ... age, **13-20** ; ... have spoken at .... **52, 69A.**
575.   ... dumb. They're dumb. .... **13-20** ; ... , dumb! How ... **23** ; ... ,
        dumb? How ... **26, 52.**
        Directions at 575. [*Drawing his sword.*] **13-20.**
579.   ... —Boy I ... **13** ; ... , this—? Boy, ... **23, 26, 52.**
583.   Upholding Ullad; when ... **13-20.**
587.   ... out **13.**
588.   ... about **13, 14** ; ... about, **20.**

589.   But my turn's first because I am the older.

                                        [*Spreading out cloak.*

590.   Nine queens out of the Country-under-Wave
591.   Have woven it with the fleeces of the sea
592.   And they were long embroidering at it.—Boy,
593.   If I had fought my father, he'd have killed me,
594.   As certainly as if I had a son
595.   And fought with him, I should be deadly to him;
596.   For the old fiery fountains are far off
597.   And every day there is less heat o' the blood.

598.   *Conchubar* [*in a loud voice*]. No more of this. I will not have this
              friendship.
599.   Cuchulain is my man, and I forbid it.
600.   He shall not go unfought, for I myself—

601.   *Cuchulain.* I will not have it.

         Conchubar.   You lay commands on me?

---

589.   ... turn is first, because .... **13-20**; ... first, because .... **23, 26, 52**.
         Directions after 589.   [lacking] **13-20**; [*Taking up cloak.*] **28, 48, 63**.
590.   Cloidna embroidered these bird wings, but Fand **13-20**; ... Country-
         under-wave **45**.
591.   Made all these little golden eyes with the hairs **13-20**; ... sea, **23, 26,
         52**.
592.   That she had stolen out of Aengus' beard, **13-20**; ... it. Boy, **23, 26,
         52**; ... it—Boy, **28, 48, 63**.
593.   And therefore none that has this cloak about him **13-20**; ... me **23,
         26, 52**; ... me. **28, 48, 63**.
594.   Is crossed in love. The heavy inlaid brooch **13-20**; ... son, **23, 26,
         52**.
595.   That Buan hammered has a merit too. **13-20**.
              [*He begins spreading the cloak out on a bench* (bench, **14, 20**) *showing
              it to the Young Man. Suddenly Concobar beats with his silver rod on a
              pillar beside his chair. All turn towards him.*] **13-20**;
         ... him I ... him, **23**; ... him, **26, 52**; ... him. **28, 48, 63**.
596, 597.   [lacking] **13-20**.
596.   ... off, **23, 26, 52**.
598.   ... of that, I ... friendship (friendship. **14, 20**) **13-20**; .... of that; I
         .... **23, 26, 52**.
599.   ... man and ... it;
600.   ... unfought for ... —
601.   [lacking] **13-20**.

602. *Cuchulain* [*seizing Conchubar*]. You shall not stir, High King. I'll hold you there.

603. *Conchubar*. Witchcraft has maddened you.

  The Kings [*shouting*].   Yes, witchcraft! witchcraft!

604. *First Old King*. Some witch has worked upon your mind, Cuchulain.

605. The head of that young man seemed like a woman's

606. You'd had a fancy for. Then of a sudden

607. You laid your hands on the High King himself!

608. *Cuchulain*. And laid my hands on the High King himself?

609. *Conchubar*. Some witch is floating in the air above us.

610. *Cuchulain*. Yes, witchcraft! witchcraft! Witches of the air!

---

602. ... stir (stir, **14, 20**) High King, I'll .... **13-20** ; ... King; I'll .... **23, 26, 52.**

603. ..., witchcraft, witchcraft. **13-20** ; ..., witchcraft, witchcraft! **28, 48, 63.**

604. [lacking] **13-20** ; *First King.* .... **23, 26, 52.**

605. *A King.* You saw another's head upon his shoulders **13-20.**

606. All of a sudden, a woman's head (head, **14, 20**) Cuchullain, **13-20** ; You had ... **23, 26, 52.**

607. Then raised your hand against the King of Ullad. **13-20** ; ... himself. **23, 26, 52.**
  Directions after 607. [*He has taken his hands from the High King. He stands as if he were dazed.*] **23, 26, 52.**

608. *Cuchullain.* [*Letting Concobar go, and looking wildly about him.*] Yes, yes, all of a sudden, all of a sudden. **13-20** ; ... himself. **23, 26, 52** ; ... himself! **28, 48, 63.**

608a. *Daire.* Why (Why, **14, 20**) there's no witchcraft in it, I myself

608b. Have made a hundred of these sudden friendships

608c. And fought it out next day. But that was folly (folly, **14, 20**)

608d. For now that I am old I know it is best

608e. To live in comfort.
  A King.   Pull the fool away. (away! **20**)

608f. *Daire.* I'll throw a heel-tip to the one that dies. **13-20.**

610. ..., witchcraft, witchcraft and the power of witchcraft.
    [*To the Young Man.*] **13-20** ;
  ..., witchcraft, witchcraft. Witches ... air. **23-28, 48-63** ; ..., witchcraft, witchcraft! ... ! **32, 45, 69.**

611.   [*To Young Man.*] Why did you? Who was it set you to this
        work?
612.   Out, out! I say, for now it's sword on sword!

613.   *Young Man.* But . . . but I did not.

        Cuchulain.   Out, I say, out, out!
        [*Young Man goes out followed by Cuchulain. The Kings follow them
        out with confused cries, and words one can hardly hear because of the
        noise. Some cry, 'Quicker, quicker!' 'Why are you so long at
        the door?' 'We'll be too late!' 'Have they begun to fight?'
        'Can you see if they are fighting?' and so on. Their voices drown
        each other. The three Women are left alone.*

610a.   Which of the shape changers put you to it? **28, 48, 63.**
  611. Why . . . you do it? Was it Calatin's daughters? **13-20.**
  612. Out, out (out, **14, 20**) I . . . sword. **13-20**; Out! out, I say! for . . . !
        23, 26, 52.
  613. But, but, I . . . ! **13-20**; . . . say! out! out! **23, 26, 52**; [set as two
        lines.] **20, 28, 48, 63.**
        Directions after 613. [lacking] **13-20**; [. . . ? 'We'll (We'll **26**) . . .
        fight?' *and so on; and one, it may be,* 'I saw him fight with Ferdia!'
        Their . . . .] **23, 26, 32, 45, 52**; [. . . *out, followed* . . . *Kings follow.*] **28,
        48, 63.**
613a.   Sword upon sword; (sword. **14, 20**)
        [*He goes towards the door at back* (back, **14, 20**) *followed by Young
        Man. He turns on the threshold and cries out, looking at the Young Man.*]
                                    That hair my hands were drowned in!
        [*He goes out* (out, **14, 20**) *followed by Young Man. The other Kings
        begin to follow them out.*] **13-20**;
        Kings.   Hurry, hurry! We'll be too late. **28, 48, 63.**
613b.   *A King.* I saw him fight with Ferdiad.
        Second King.   We'll be too late (late, **20**) **13-20**;
        Go quicker through the door! Quicker, quicker! [*Making a confused
        noise. The three Women are left alone. One is standing by the door. Two
        remain at one side, holding bowl.*] **28, 48, 63.**
613c.   They're such a long time getting through the door.
613d.   *Third King.* Run quicker, quicker.
        Daire.   I was at the Smith's
613e.   When he that was the boy Setanta then—
                                    [*Sound of fighting outside.*] **13-20.**

614. *First Woman.* I have seen, I have seen!

Second Woman.   What do you cry aloud?

615. *First Woman.* The Ever-living have shown me what's to come.

616. *Third Woman.* How? Where?

First Woman.   In the ashes of the bowl.

617. *Second Woman.* While you were holding it between your hands?

618. *Third Woman.* Speak quickly!

First Woman.   I have seen Cuchulain's roof-tree
619.   Leap into fire, and the walls split and blacken.

620. *Second Woman.* Cuchulain has gone out to die.

Third Woman.   O! O!

621. *Second Woman.* Who could have thought that one so great as he
622.   Should meet his end at this unnoted sword!

623. *First Woman.* Life drifts between a fool and a blind man
624.   To the end, and nobody can know his end.

625. *Second Woman.* Come, look upon the quenching of this greatness.
              [*The other two go to the door, but they stop for a moment upon the
              threshold and wail.*

613f.   *Third King.* He will have killed him. They have begun the fight!
              [*They all go out, leaving the house silent and empty. There is a pause
              during which one hears the clashing of the swords. Barach and Fintain
              come in from side door. Barach is dragging Fintain.*] **13-20.**
614-Directions before 628.   [lacking] **13-20.**
614.   . . . seen.
              What . . . ? **23, 26, 52.**
614, 616, 618, 620.   [each line set as two lines] **28, 48, 63.**
615.   . . . ever-living . . . . **23-69.**
618.   . . . !
              I saw Cuchulain's . . . **23, 26, 52;** . . . quickly.
                                                        I . . . **28, 48, 63.**
622.   . . . sword? **28, 48, 63.**
623.   . . . Fool . . . Blind Man **23, 26, 52.**

626. *First Woman.* No crying out, for there'll be need of cries
627.   And rending of the hair when it's all finished.

    [*The Women go out. There is the sound of clashing swords from time to time during what follows.*

    Enter the Fool, dragging the Blind Man.

628. *Fool.* You have eaten it, you have eaten it! You have
629.   left me nothing but the bones.

    [*He throws Blind Man down by big chair.*

630. *Blind Man.* O, that I should have to endure such a
631.   plague! O, I ache all over! O, I am pulled to pieces!
632.   This is the way you pay me all the good I have done
633.   you.

634. *Fool.* You have eaten it! You have told me lies. I might
635.   have known you had eaten it when I saw your slow,
636.   sleepy walk. Lie there till the kings come. O, I will
637.   tell Conchubar and Cuchulain and all the kings
638.   about you!

639. *Blind Man.* What would have happened to you but for

---

626.   . . . out, no need of crying out **63**.
627.   And knocking at the breast when . . . . **23-52**; Nor beating upon breast when . . . . **63**.
    Directions after 627. [*. . . is a sound . . . .*] **23, 26, 32, 52, 63**.
    Directions before 628. [*. . . Fool dragging . . . .*] **23-69**.
628.   . . . it, you . . . it, you . . . **13-20** ; . . . it, you . . . it. You . . . **28, 48, 63**.
629.   . . . bones! **23, 26, 52**.
    Directions after 629. [lacking] **13-20**.
630.   O that . . . **28, 48, 63**.
631.   plague. O, . . . over. O, . . . pulled in pieces. **13-20** ; . . . ! O I . . . ! O I . . . ! **28, 48, 63**.
633.   you! **13-26, 32, 52**.
634.   . . . it, you . . . lies about a **13-20** ; . . . it. You . . . lies. You said **28, 48, 63**.
635.   wild dog. Nobody has seen a wild dog about the place **13-20** ; it was done to a turn. You had eaten it all the time. **28, 48, 63**.
636.   this twelve month. Lie . . . kings. (Kings **14, 20**) . . . ! **13-20**.
636-638.   [lacking] **28, 48, 63**.
637.   . . . Kings **14, 20**.

640.   me, and you without your wits? If I did not take care
641.   of you, what would you do for food and warmth?

642. *Fool.* You take care of me? You stay safe, and send me
643.   into every kind of danger. You sent me down the cliff
644.   for gulls' eggs while you warmed your blind eyes in
645.   the sun; and then you ate all that were good for food.
646.   You left me the eggs that were neither egg nor bird.

> [*Blind Man tries to rise; Fool makes him lie down again.*]

647.   Keep quiet now, till I shut the door. There is some
648.   noise outside—a high vexing noise, so that I can't be
649.   listening to myself. [*Shuts the big door.*] Why can't
650.   they be quiet? Why can't they be quiet? [*Blind Man*
651.   *tries to get away.*] Ah! you would get away, would you?
652.   [*Follows Blind Man and brings him back.*] Lie there! lie
653.   there! No, you won't get away! Lie there till the
654.   kings come. I'll tell them all about you. I will tell

---

640.   . . . wits. If . . . **13, 14.**
641.   . . . you what . . . warmth! **13, 14** ; . . . you what . . . ? **20** ; . . . warmth!
        69.
642.   . . . safe and . . . **13-20** ; . . . me! You . . . **23, 26, 32, 45, 52** ; . . . me!
        You . . . safe and . . . **28, 48, 63.**
644.   . . . gull's . . . **13-20, 23, 26** ; . . . eggs, while . . . **28, 48, 63.**
645.   . . . sun. And . . . . **13-20.**
        Directions after 646.   [*The blind man tries . . . rise. Barach makes . . . .*]
        13-20 ; [*. . . rise. Fool . . . .*] **28, 48, 63.**
647.   . . . now till . . . **13-20** ; . . . now till . . . door. [*Goes up.*] There . . . **28,**
        48, 63.
648.   . . . outside. There are swords crossing; a high . . . noise so . . . **13-20** ;
        outside, a high, vexing . . . **28, 48, 63.**
649.   . . . myself. [*He goes to the big door at the back and shuts it.*] Why . . . **13-20** ;
        . . . [*Shuts door.*] . . . **28, 48, 63.**
650-652. . . . quiet, why . . . quiet. (quiet! **20**) Ah, you would get away
        (away, **14, 20**) would you? [*He follows the blind man who has been crawling
        along the wall and makes him lie down close to the king's (King's **14, 20**)
        chair.*] Lie there, lie **13-20.**
650.   . . . quiet! why . . . quiet! [*Blind . . .* **23, 26, 32, 45, 52, 69** ;
        . . . quiet, why . . . **28, 48, 63** ; . . . ? why . . . **84, 89.**
651.   . . . you! **23, 26, 32, 45, 52, 69** ; . . . *away.*] Oh! you . . . ? **97A.**
652.   . . . there, lie **28, 48, 63.**
653.   there. No (No, **14, 20**) you . . . away. Lie . . . **13-20** ; there. [*Throws
        him down. Blind Man again attempts to go.*] No, . . . away. Lie . . . **28, 48,**
        63.
654.   kings (Kings **14, 20**) come, I'll . . . . I shall tell **13-20.**

655. it all. How you sit warming yourself, when you have
656. made me light a fire of sticks, while I sit blowing it
657. with my mouth. Do you not always make me take
658. the windy side of the bush when it blows, and the
659. rainy side when it rains?

660. *Blind Man.* O, good Fool! listen to me. Think of the
661. care I have taken of you. I have brought you to many
662. a warm hearth, where there was a good welcome for
663. you, but you would not stay there; you were always
664. wandering about.

665. *Fool.* The last time you brought me in, it was not I
666. who wandered away, but you that got put out be-
667. cause you took the crubeen out of the pot when
668. nobody was looking. Keep quiet, now!

669. *Cuchulain [rushing in].* Witchcraft! There is no witch-
670. craft on the earth, or among the witches of the air,
671. that these hands cannot break.

672. *Fool.* Listen to me, Cuchulain. I left him turning the
673. fowl at the fire. He ate it all, though I had stolen it.
674. He left me nothing but the feathers.

675. *Cuchulain.* Fill me a horn of ale!

---

658. . . . blows and . . . **13-20.**
659. . . . rains. **69E.**
660. O good fool (fool, **14, 20**) listen . . . **13-20**; Oh, . . . Fool, listen . . .
   28, 48, 63; Oh, . . . **32, 45, 69.**
663. . . . there, you . . . **13-20.**
665. . . . in it . . . **23, 26, 32, 45, 52, 69.**
667. . . . pot, when **13-20.**
668. you thought nobody . . . quiet now, keep **13-20**; . . . quiet now. **28,
   48, 63.**
668a. quiet till I shut the door. Here is Cuchulain, now
668b. you will be beaten. I am going to tell him everything. **13-20.**
669. *Cuchullain. [Comes in and says to the fool.]* Give me
670. that horn.
   [*The fool give him a horn which Cuchullain fills with ale and drinks.*
   13-20.
671. [lacking] **13-20.**
672. *Fintain.* Do not listen to him, listen to me. **13-20.**
673-674. [lacking] **13-20.**
675. *Cuchullain.* What are you wrangling over? **13-20**; . . . ale. **28, 48, 63.**

676. *Blind Man.* I gave him what he likes best. You do not
677.   know how vain this Fool is. He likes nothing so
678.   well as a feather.

679. *Fool.* He left me nothing but the bones and feathers.
680.   Nothing but the feathers, though I had stolen it.

681. *Cuchulain.* Give me that horn. Quarrels here, too!
682.   [*Drinks.*] What is there between you two that is
683.   worth a quarrel? Out with it!

684. *Blind Man.* Where would he be but for me? I must be
685.   always thinking—thinking to get food for the two
686.   of us, and when we've got it, if the moon is at the
687.   full or the tide on the turn, he'll leave the rabbit in
688.   the snare till it is full of maggots, or let the trout
689.   slip back through his hands into the stream.
         [*The Fool has begun singing while the Blind Man is speaking.*

---

676. *Barach.* He is fat and good for nothing. He has left **13-20.**
677. me the bones and the feathers. **13-20** ; . . . fool . . . **28-52, 63.**
678. *Cuchullain.* What feathers? **13-20.**
     Directions at 678. . . . feather. [*Cuchulain goes up to big door and looks
     out while Blind Man speaks.*] **28, 48, 63.**
679. *Barach.* I left him turning a fowl at the fire. He ate
680. it all. He left me nothing but the bones and feathers.
681. *Fintain.* Do not believe him. You do not know how vain **13-20** ; . . .
     horn! Quarrels . . . ! **23, 26, 32, 45, 52** ; *Cuchulain.* [*turning.*] Fill me
     . . . horn. [*Fool brings horn.*] Quarrels here (here, **63**) too. **28, 48, 63.**
682. this fool is. I gave him the feathers, because I **13-20** ; [*Drinks and
     hands horn to Fool.*] What . . . **28, 48, 63.**
683. thought he would like nothing so well.
     [*Barach is sitting on a bench playing with a heap of feathers (feathers,
     20) which he has taken out of the breast of his coat.*] **13-20** ; . . . it. **28,
     48, 63.**
683a. *Barach.* [*Singing.*] When you were an acorn on the tree top— **13-20.**
685. . . . thinking, thinking . . .
686. . . . moon's at . . . **13-20.**
688. its snare . . .
689. slip through . . . hands back into the water. **13-20.**
     Directions after 689. [lacking] **13-20** ; [*Fool . . . while Blind . . . .*]
     28, 48, 63.

Fool [*singing*].

690.   When you were an acorn on the tree-top,
691.   Then was I an eagle-cock;
692.   Now that you are a withered old block,
693.   Still am I an eagle-cock.

694. *Blind Man.* Listen to him, now. That's the sort of talk
695.   I have to put up with day out, day in.

> [*The Fool is putting the feathers into his hair. Cuhulain takes a handful of feathers out of a heap the Fool has on the bench beside him, and out of the Fool's hair, and begins to wipe the blood from his sword with them.*]

696. *Fool.* He has taken my feathers to wipe his sword. It is
697.   blood that he is wiping from his sword.

Cuchulain [*goes up to door at back and throws away feathers*].

698.   They are standing about his body. They will not
699.   awaken him, for all his witchcraft.

700. *Blind Man.* It is that young champion that he has killed.
701.   He that came out of Aoife's country.

Name of singer before 690. [lacking]
Directions before 690. [*Sings.*] **23, 26, 52.**
Directions before 690. [lacking] **28, 48, 63.**

690. . . . tree top, **13-23.**
691. . . . eagle cock; **13-69.**
693. . . . eagle cock! **13-20** ; . . . eagle cock. **23-69.**
694. . . . him now! That's . . . **13-20** ; . . . him now. . . . **23-28, 48, 52, 63.**
695. . . . with (with, **20**) day out day . . . . **13-20.**
Directions after 695. [. . . *out of the heap and out of the fool's hair* (*hair,* **20**) *and* . . . .] **13-20** ; [. . . *putting the feathers of the hen into* . . . *feathers and begins* . . . .] **28, 48, 63.**
697. . . . sword!
697a. *Fintain.* Whose blood? Whose blood? **13-20.**
Directions before 698-699. [lacking] **13-20.**
Directions before 698. [*Cuchulain goes* . . . *to big door and throws feathers away.*] **28, 48, 63.**
699. . . . him for . . . . **52, 63.**
700. *Cuchullain.* That young champion's.
701. *Fintain.* . . . country? **13-20.**
701a. *Cuchullain.* The Kings are standing round his body.
701b. *Fintain.* Did he fight long? **13-20.**

702. *Cuchulain.* He thought to have saved himself with
703.   witchcraft.

704. *Fool.* That Blind Man there said he would kill you. He
705.   came from Aoife's country to kill you. That Blind
706.   Man said they had taught him every kind of weapon
707.   that he might do it. But I always knew that you
708.   would kill him.

709. *Cuchulain [to the Blind Man].* You knew him, then?

710. *Blind Man.* I saw him, when I had my eyes, in Aoife's
711.   country.

712. *Cuchulain.* You were in Aoife's country?

713. *Blind Man.* I knew him and his mother there.

714. *Cuchulain.* He was about to speak of her when he died.

715. *Blind Man.* He was a queen's son.

716. *Cuchulain.* What queen? what queen? [*Seizes Blind Man,*
717.   *who is now sitting upon the bench.*] Was it Scathach?
718.   There were many queens. All the rulers there were
719.   queens.

720. *Blind Man.* No, not Scathach.

721. *Cuchulain.* It was Uathach, then? Speak! speak!

722. *Blind Man.* I cannot speak; you are clutching me too

---

704. . . . blind man . . .
705. . . . blind
706. man . . . **13-26, 32, 45, 52, 69.**
709. . . . him then? **13**; *Cuchulain.* You . . . him then? **28, 48, 63.**
710. . . . him when . . . **13-20**; . . . him when . . . eyes in . . . **28, 48, 63.**
715. . . . Queen's . . . . **13-20.**
716. . . . Queen? . . . Queen? [*He seizes the blind man.*] **13-20**; *Cuchulain*
[*rushing at and seizing Blind Man*]. What queen, what queen? **28, 48,**
63.
717. Was it Scathach? **13-20, 28, 48, 63.**
718. . . . Queens. . . . **13, 14;** . . . Queens. . . . rulers were **20.**
719. Queens. **13-20.**
721. . . . Uathach (Uathach, **20**) then. Speak, speak! **13-20.**
722. . . . speak, you . . . **13-20;** . . . speak. You . . . **28, 48, 63.**

723.   tightly. [*Cuchulain lets him go.*] I cannot remember
724.   who it was. I am not certain. It was some queen.

725.   *Fool.* He said a while ago that the young man was
726.   Aoife's son.

727.   *Cuchulain.* She? No, no! She had no son when I was
728.   there.

729.   *Fool.* That Blind Man there said that she owned him
730.   for her son.

731.   *Cuchulain.* I had rather he had been some other woman's
732.   son. What father had he? A soldier out of Alba? She
733.   was an amorous woman—a proud, pale, amorous
734.   woman.

735.   *Blind Man.* None knew whose son he was.

736.   *Cuchulain.* None knew! Did you know, old listener at
737.   doors?

738.   *Blind Man.* No, no; I knew nothing.

739.   *Fool.* He said a while ago that he heard Aoife boast
740.   that she'd never but the one lover, and he the only
741.   man that had overcome her in battle.   [*Pause.*

742.   *Blind Man.* Somebody is trembling, Fool! The bench
743.   is shaking. Why are you trembling? Is Cuchulain
744.   going to hurt us? It was not I who told you,
745.   Cuchulain.

---

724. . . . Queen. **13-20.**
725. . . . a little while . . . **28, 48, 63** ; . . . awhile . . . **52.**
727. . . . ? No, no, she . . . **13-20** ; She! No, no. She . . . **28, 48, 63.**
729. . . . blind man . . . **13-69.**
733. . . . woman, a proud (proud, **20**) pale amorous **13-20** ; . . . woman,—a
    . . . **28, 48, 63.**
736. . . . knew? Did . . . ? **13-20.**
738. . . . , no, I . . . . **13-20** ; . . . , no. I . . . . **28, 48, 63.**
739. . . . awhile . . . **28-63.**
    Directions in 741. [*A pause.*] **13-20, 28, 48, 63.**
742. Somebody is trembling. Why are you trembling, fool? The . . . **13-20** ;
    . . . , Fool. The . . . **28, 48, 63.**
743. . . . shaking, why . . . **13-20.**

746. *Fool.* It is Cuchulain who is trembling. It is Cuchulain
747.   who is shaking the bench.

748. *Blind Man.* It is his own son he has slain.

749. *Cuchulain.* 'Twas they that did it, the pale windy people.
750.   Where? where? where? My sword against the thunder!
751.   But no, for they have always been my friends;
752.   And though they love to blow a smoking coal
753.   Till it's all flame, the wars they blow aflame
754.   Are full of glory, and heart-uplifting pride,
755.   And not like this. The wars they love awaken
756.   Old fingers and the sleepy strings of harps.
757.   Who did it then? Are you afraid? Speak out!
758.   For I have put you under my protection,
759.   And will reward you well. Dubthach the Chafer?
760.   He'd an old grudge. No, for he is with Maeve.
761.   Laegaire did it! Why do you not speak?
762.   What is this house? [*Pause.*] Now I remember all.
         [*Comes before Conchubar's chair, and strikes out with his sword, as if
         Conchubar was sitting upon it.*
763.   'Twas you who did it—you who sat up there

---

746. . . . trembling. He is shaking **13-20** ; . . . trembling. It is he **28, 48, 63**.
747. the bench with his knees. **13-20.**
748. *Cuchulain.* He was my son, and I have killed my son. [*A pause.*] **13-20** ;
     . . . son that he has killed. **28, 48, 63.**
749. . . . people, **13-20** ; . . . pale, windy . . . . **23, 28-48, 63.**
750. Where, where, where? . . . thunder. **13-20** ; . . . thunder, **28, 48, 63.**
754. . . . heart uplifting . . . , **13-20** ; . . . glory and . . . , **28, 48, 63** ; . . .
     heart up-lifting . . . , **45** (1913).
755. . . . this; the . . . **13-20.**
757. . . . afraid; speak out, **13-20** ; . . . it, then? . . . ! **23, 28, 32, 48, 63** ;
     . . . it, then? . . . ? speak out? **26, 52.**
758. . . . protection **13-20** ; . . . protection. **69A.**
759. . . . Chafer.
760. He had an . . . **13-20, 28, 48, 63.**
761. . . . it. Why . . . ? **13-20** ; 'Twas Laegaire . . . ? **52.**
     Directions in 762. [*A pause.*] **13-20.**
     Directions after 762. [lacking] **13-20** ; [. . . *sword as* . . . .] **23** ;
     [. . . *chair and* . . . *sword.*] **28, 48, 63.**
762a. *Fintain.* He will kill us. O, I am afraid! **13-20.**
763. *Cuchullain.* [*Who is before Concobar's chair.*] 'Twas . . . it, you . . . **13-20** ;
     . . . there, **28, 48, 63.**

764.   With your old rod of kingship, like a magpie
765.   Nursing a stolen spoon. No, not a magpie,
766.   A maggot that is eating up the earth!
767.   Yes, but a magpie, for he's flown away.
768.   Where did he fly to?

Blind Man.   He is outside the door.

769. *Cuchulain.* Outside the door?

Blind Man.   Between the door and the sea.

770. *Cuchulain.* Conchubar, Conchubar! the sword into your heart!
        [*He rushes out. Pause. Fool creeps up to the big door and looks after
        him.*

771. *Fool.* He is going up to King Conchubar. They are all
772.   about the young man. No, no, he is standing still.
773.   There is a great wave going to break, and he is look-
774.   ing at it. Ah! now he is running down to the sea,
775.   but he is holding up his sword as if he were going
776.   into a fight. [*Pause.*] Well struck! well struck!

---

764.   With that old branch of silver, like . . . **13-20** ; . . . magpie, **28, 48, 63**.
765.   . . . spoon. Magpie, Magpie, **13-20** ; . . . magpie. **28, 48, 63**.
766.   . . . earth; **13**.
        Directions after 766.   [*Begins hacking at the chair with his sword.*] **13-20.**
767.   No, but . . . magpie for . . . . **13, 14** ; No, but . . . . **20.**
768, 769.   [set as four lines] **32, 45, 52.**
769.   . . . door?
        Fintain. He is under Baile's yew-tree. **13-20** ; [set as two lines] **20, 28,
        32, 48, 63.**
770.   . . . , Concobar, the . . . heart. **13-20** ; . . . heart. **28, 48, 63** ; . . .
        heart? **52, 69.**
        Directions after 770.   [*He goes out. A pause. The fool goes to the great
        door at back and looks out after . . . .*] **13-20** ; [*. . . to big . . . .*] **28, 48, 63.**
771.   . . . Concobar; they . . . **13-20.**
772.   under the tree. No, ... **13-20** ; . . . . No, no. He . . . . **28, 48, 63.**
773.   . . . break and . . . **13-20.**
776.   . . . fight. [*A pause.*] . . . struck, well . . . ! **13-20.**

777.   *Blind Man.* What is he doing now?

778.   *Fool.* O! he is fighting the waves!

779.   *Blind Man.* He sees King Conchubar's crown on every
780.   one of them.

781.   *Fool.* There, he has struck at a big one! He has struck
782.   the crown off it; he has made the foam fly. There
783.   again, another big one!

784.   *Blind Man.* Where are the kings? What are the kings
785.   doing?

786.   *Fool.* They are shouting and running down to the
787.   shore, and the people are running out of the houses.
788.   They are all running.

789.   *Blind Man.* You say they are running out of the houses?
790.   There will be nobody left in the houses. Listen, Fool!

791.   *Fool.* There, he is down! He is up again. He is going
792.   out in the deep water. There is a big wave. It has
793.   gone over him. I cannot see him now. He has killed
794.   kings and giants, but the waves have mastered him,
795.   the waves have mastered him!

---

777.   . . . now! **26, 52.**

778.   . . . waves. **13, 14, 23, 26, 52**; Oh! . . . waves. **20**; Oh! . . . ! **28, 45-63, 69.**

781.   . . . one. He . . . **13-20.**

782.   . . . it, he . . . **13-20**; . . . it. He . . . **28, 48, 63.**

783.   again another . . . one. [*Shouting without.*] **13-20.**

784.   . . . Kings? What . . . Kings **14, 20**; . . . kings! What . . . **26, 52.**

787.   . . . houses,

788.   they . . . . **13-20.**

789.   . . . houses, **13-20**; . . . houses. **28, 48, 63.**

790.   there . . . , fool. **13-20**; . . . , Fool. **28, 48, 63.**

791.   . . . again! He . . . **13-20**; . . . down. He . . . again He . . . **28, 48**; . . . down. He . . . **63.**

792.   out into the . . . water. **13-20**; out into the . . . **23, 28, 32, 48, 63**; going into the . . . **26, 52.**

793-795.   [lacking] **13-20.**

795.   . . . him. **28, 48, 63.**

796. *Blind Man.* Come here, Fool!

797. *Fool.* The waves have mastered him.

798. *Blind Man.* Come here!

799. *Fool.* The waves have mastered him.

800. *Blind Man.* Come here, I say.

  Fool [*coming towards him, but looking backwards towards the
801. door*]. What is it?

802. *Blind Man.* There will be nobody in the houses. Come
803. this way; come quickly! The ovens will be full. We
804. will put our hands into the ovens.   [*They go out.*

THE END

Both these plays have been ....
The King's Threshold was played in October, 1903, and *On Baile's
Strand* will be played in February or March ....
Old Irish Prose Romances, but I have borrowed some ideas for the arrange-
ment of my subject in 'The .... than the romance in a
play published by Mr. Edwin Ellis some ten years ago. ... W. B. Y. Note, to

The first version of *On Baile's Strand* was ....
the Abbey Theatre, Dublin, by the Irish National ....
with the following cast: Cuchulain, Frank Fay; Conchubar, George
Roberts; ......

Blind Man, ...
.... Cuchulain. The old ....
ing: R. Nash, N. Power, U. Wright, E. Keogan, Emma Vernon, Doreen
....
cycle.

796. ... fool; come here, I say.
797-800. [lacking] **13-20.**
797. ... him!
798-799. [lacking] **28, 48, 63.**
800. ... say! **23, 26, 52.**
          Directions at 801. [... *him but* ....] **13-20**; [... *backward* .....] **23,
          26, 52.**
803. ... way, come quickly; the ... full (full; **14, 20**) we **13-20**; ... quickly.
          The ... **28, 48, 63.**

Both these plays have been written for Mr. Fay's 'Irish National Theatre.' 'The King's Threshold' was played in October, 1903, and 'On Baile's Strand' will be played in February or March, 1904. Both are founded on Old Irish Prose Romances, but I have borrowed some ideas for the arrangement of my subject in 'The King's Threshold' from 'Sancan the Bard,' a play published by Mr. Edwin Ellis some ten years ago.   w.b.y. Note, **20**.

———

The first version of this play was performed on 27 December, 1904, at the Abbey Theatre, Dublin, by the Irish National Theatre Society, and with the following cast: Cuchulain, Frank Fay; Conchubar, George Roberts; Daire (an old King, not now in the play), G. Macdonald; the Blind Man, Shamus O'Sullivan; the Fool, William Fay; the Young Man, P. MacShiubhlaigh. The old and young Kings were played by the following: R. Nash, N. Power, U. Wright, E. Kegan, Emma Vernon, Doreen Gunning, Sara Allgood.

It was revived by the National Theatre Society, Ltd., in a somewhat altered version at Oxford, Cambridge, and London a few months later. I then entirely rewrote it up to the entrance of the Young Man, and changed it a good deal from that on to the end, and this new version was played at the Abbey Theatre in April, 1906. It is now as right as I can make it with my present experience, but it must always be a little over-complicated when played by itself. It is one of a cycle of plays dealing with Cuchulain, with his friends and enemies. One of these plays will have Aoife as its central character, and the principal motive of another will be the power of the witches over Cuchulain's life. The present play is a kind of cross-road where too many interests meet and jostle for the hearer to take them in at a first hearing unless he listen carefully, or know something of the story of the other plays of the cycle. Mr. Herbert Hughes has written the music for the Fool's song in the opening dialogue, and another friend a little tune for the three women. These songs, like all other songs in our plays, are sung so as to preserve as far as possible the intonation and speed of ordinary passionate speech, for nothing can justify the degradation of an element of life even in the service of an art. Very little of the words of the song of the three women can be heard, for they must be for the most part a mere murmur under the voices of the men. It seemed right to take some trouble over them, just as it is right to finish off the statue where it is turned to the wall, and besides there is always the reader and one's own pleasure.   Notes, **23**.

———

'On Baile's Strand' was first played, but in a version considerably different from the present, on December 27, 1904, at the Abbey Theatre, Dublin, and with the following cast: . . . Fay; Conchobar, . . . king, . . . , Seumas . . . kings . . . Vernon, Dora Gunning, . . . cross-road, where . . . of the cycle.   Appendix II, **28**

On Baile's Strand was first played, in a version considerably different from the present, on December 27th, 1904, at the opening of the Abbey Theatre Dublin, and with the following cast:

Cuchulain . . Frank (F. J. **52-69**) Fay / Conchubar . . George Roberts / Daire (*an old King* (*king* **52, 63**) *not now in the play*) . . G. MacDonald / The Blind Man . . Seumas O'Sullivan / The Fool . . William Fay / The Young Man . . P. MacShiubhlaigh.

The old . . . kings . . . Keegan, . . . Vernon, Dora (Vernon, Miss Garvey, Dora **45, 52, 63**) Gunning, Sara (Sarah **52, 63**) Allgood. It was necessary to put women into men's parts owing to the smallness of our company at that time. (time. It were indefensible could we have helped it. **52, 63**)

The play was revived . . . Abbey Theatre for the first time in April, 1906. (1906.—Collected Works, 1907. **69**)

Appendix IV, 32 ; Notes, 45, 52, 63, 69.

'On Baile's Strand' was first played [follows the version in **28** except that the sentence 'The old and young kings . . . Allgood.' is omitted].

Appendix II, 48.

*   *   *

. . . . I am haunted by certain moments: . . . ; William Fay at the end of 'On Baile's Strand'; . . . .

From 'Preliminaries,' IV, 93.

*   *   *

Variant spellings

Banachas **28, 32-48, 63-97** ; *Bananachs* **23, 26, 52.**
Bocanachs **23, 26, 52** ; *Bonachas* **28, 32-48, 63-97**; *Bonochas* **45** (1913), **69E.**
Conchobar **28, 48, 63** ; *Conchubar* **23, 26, 32, 45, 52, 69-97** ; *Concobar* **13-20.**
Cuchulain **23-97** ; *Cuchullain* **13-20.**
gray **20** ; *grey* **13, 14, 23-97.**
phantasy **23, 28-48** ; *fantasy* **69-97.**
subtlety **52, 84-97** ; *subtilty* **23-48, 63, 69.**
Ulad **23, 26, 32, 84, 89** ; *Uladh* **45, 52, 69, 97** ; *Ullad* **13-20.**

*   *   *

[See also the notes on *The King's Threshold*, p. 313, *The Only Jealousy of Emer*, p. 566, *The Hour-Glass* (in prose), p. 640, *The Resurrection*, p. 932, *The Legendary and Mythological Foundation of the Plays*, p. 1283, *Glossary*, p. 1284; and *Prefaces to 23, 45, 64, 69, 75*, pp. 1293, 1296, 1304, 1306, 1307.]

FIGHTING THE WAVES

First performed at the Abbey Theatre
on 13th August 1929

TO

HILDO VAN KROP

WHO MADE THE MASKS

PERSONS IN THE PLAY

Three Musicians
Cuchulain
The Ghost of Cuchulain
Emer
Eithne Inguba
The Figure of Cuchulain
The Woman of the Sidhe

NOTE: *Fighting the Waves*, a prose rewriting of *The Only Jealousy of Emer*, was printed in **83**. The text below and on succeeding verso pages is from the English edition of **83**. The collation of *The Only Jealousy of Emer* is on the recto pages. Similarities between the two versions are shown by bracketed line-numbers in the margin; identities by un-bracketed line-numbers. Line lengths are the same as those in **83E**.

THE ONLY JEALOUSY OF EMER

1919

Persons in the Play

Three Musicians (*their faces made up to resemble masks*)
The Ghost of Cuchulain (*wearing a mask*)
The Figure of Cuchulain (*wearing a mask*)
Emer
Eithne Inguba } (*masked, or their faces made up to resemble masks*)
Woman of the Sidhe (*wearing a mask*)

*Enter Musicians, who are dressed and made up as in 'At the Hawk's Well'.
They have the same musical instruments, which can either be already upon the
stage or be brought in by the First Musician before he stands in the centre with
the cloth between his hands, or by a player when the cloth has been unfolded. The
stage as before can be against the wall of any room, and the same black cloth can
be used as in 'At the Hawk's Well'.*

[*Song for the folding and unfolding of the cloth*]

First Musician.

1.   A woman's beauty is like a white
2.   Frail bird, like a white sea-bird alone
3.   At daybreak after stormy night
4.   Between two furrows upon the ploughed land:

PRINTINGS   *Poetry* (Chicago), January 1919; **60, 64, 71, 84, 97.**

DATE   [lacking] **P-71.**

DRAMATIS PERSONAE   [lacking] **P, 60**; Persons Of The . . . **64, 71.**

STAGE DIRECTIONS   . . . *Musicians, with musical instruments. The First Musician
pauses at the centre and stands with a cloth . . . hands. The stage can . . . room.*
P ; . . . *dressed as in the earlier play. They . . . when the cloth is unfolded. . . .
room.* **60 ;** . . . *when the cloth is unfolded. The . . . , and the black cloth is used
. . . .'* **64.**

TEXT
Directions before 1.   *First Musician* [*during the unfolding and folding of the
cloth*]. **P, 60.**

Prologue

*Musicians and speaker off stage. There is a curtain with
a wave pattern. A man wearing the Cuchulain mask
enters from one side with sword and shield. He dances
a dance which represents a man fighting the waves. The
waves may be represented by other dancers: in his frenzy
he supposes the waves to be his enemies: gradually he
sinks down as if overcome, then fixes his eyes with a
cataleptic stare upon some imaginary distant object. The
stage becomes dark, and when the light returns it is empty.
The Musicians enter. Two stand one on either side of the
curtain, singing.*

First Musician.

1	1.	A woman's beauty is like a white
2	2.	Frail bird, like a white sea-bird alone
3	3.	At daybreak after stormy night
4	4.	Between two furrows upon the ploughed land:
[5]	5.	A sudden storm and it was thrown
6	6.	Between dark furrows upon the ploughed land.
7	7.	How many centuries spent

5.	A sudden storm, and it was thrown
6.	Between dark furrows upon the ploughed land.
7.	How many centuries spent
8.	The sedentary soul
9.	In toils of measurement
10.	Beyond eagle or mole,
11.	Beyond hearing or seeing,
12.	Or Archimedes' guess,
13.	To raise into being
14.	That loveliness?
15.	A strange, unserviceable thing,
16.	A fragile, exquisite, pale shell,
17.	That the vast troubled waters bring
18.	To the loud sands before day has broken.
19.	The storm arose and suddenly fell
20.	Amid the dark before day had broken.
21.	What death? what discipline?
22.	What bonds no man could unbind,
23.	Being imagined within
24.	The labyrinth of the mind,
25.	What pursuing or fleeing,
26.	What wounds, what bloody press,
27.	Dragged into being
28.	This loveliness?

[*When the cloth is folded again the Musicians take their place against the wall. The folding of the cloth shows on one side of the stage the curtained bed or litter on which lies a man in his grave-clothes. He wears an heroic mask. Another man with exactly similar clothes and mask crouches near the front. Emer is sitting beside the bed.*]

29. *First Musician* [*speaking*]. I call before the eyes a roof

---

5. . . . storm and . . . **P-71.**
12. . . . Archimedes . . . , **P-71.**
15. . . . strange unserviceable . . . , **P-71.**
22. . . . unbind **P-71.**
24. . . . mind?
25. . . . fleeing? **P, 60.**
26. . . . press? **P, 60**; . . . press **64, 71.**
28. . . . loveliness. **P, 60.**
Directions after 28. [. . . . *Another man in the same clothes* . . . .] **P**; [. . . *against wall.* . . . *bed.*] **60.**

30. With cross-beams darkened by smoke;
31. A fisher's net hangs from a beam,
32. A long oar lies against the wall.
33. I call up a poor fisher's house;
34. A man lies dead or swooning,
35. That amorous man,
36. That amorous, violent man, renowned Cuchulain,
37. Queen Emer at his side.
38. At her own bidding all the rest have gone;
39. But now one comes on hesitating feet,
40. Young Eithne Inguba, Cuchulain's mistress.
41. She stands a moment in the open door.
42. Beyond the open door the bitter sea,
43. The shining, bitter sea, is crying out,
44. [*singing*] White shell, white wing!
45. I will not choose for my friend
46. A frail, unserviceable thing
47. That drifts and dreams, and but knows
48. That waters are without end
49. And that wind blows.

50. *Emer* [*speaking*]. Come hither, come sit down beside the bed;
51. You need not be afraid, for I myself
52. Sent for you, Eithne Inguba.

Eithne Inguba.   No, Madam,
53. I have too deeply wronged you to sit there.

54. *Emer.* Of all the people in the world we two,
55. And we alone, may watch together here,
56. Because we have loved him best.

Eithne Inguba.   And is he dead?

---

30. . . . smoke. **P, 60.**
33. . . . house. **P, 60.**
34. . . . swooning— **P.**
36. . . . Cuchulain— **P.**
38. . . . gone. **P, 60.**
41. . . . door, **60-71.**
43. . . . sea is . . . , **P, 60.**
44. . . . wing, **P** ; . . . wing **60.**
46. . . . frail unserviceable . . . **P-71.**
50. . . . bed **P, 60.**

24 24. The labyrinth of the mind,
25 25. What pursuing or fleeing,
[26] 26. What wounds, what bloody press
27 27. Dragged into being
28 28. This loveliness?

[*When the curtain is drawn the Musicians take their place against the wall. One sees a bed with curtains: the man lying on the bed is Cuchulain; the part is taken, however, by a different actor, who has a mask similar to that of the dancer— the Cuchulain mask. Emer stands beside the bed. The Ghost of Cuchulain crouches near the foot of the bed.*]

[29] 29. *First Musician [speaking]*. I call before your eyes
[30] 30. some poor fisherman's house dark with smoke,
[31-32] 31. nets hanging from the rafters, here and there an

57. *Emer.* Although they have dressed him out in his grave-clothes
58.   And stretched his limbs, Cuchulain is not dead;
59.   The very heavens when that day's at hand,
60.   So that his death may not lack ceremony,
61.   Will throw out fires, and the earth grow red with blood.
62.   There shall not be a scullion but foreknows it
63.   Like the world's end.

    Eithne Inguba.   How did he come to this?

64. *Emer.* Towards noon in the assembly of the kings
65.   He met with one who seemed a while most dear.
66.   The kings stood round; some quarrel was blown up;
67.   He drove him out and killed him on the shore
68.   At Baile's tree, and he who was so killed
69.   Was his own son begot on some wild woman
70.   When he was young, or so I have heard it said;
71.   And thereupon, knowing what man he had killed,
72.   And being mad with sorrow, he ran out;
73.   And after, to his middle in the foam,
74.   With shield before him and with sword in hand,
75.   He fought the deathless sea. The kings looked on
76.   And not a king dared stretch an arm, or even
77.   Dared call his name, but all stood wondering
78.   In that dumb stupor like cattle in a gale,
79.   Until at last, as though he had fixed his eyes
80.   On a new enemy, he waded out
81.   Until the water had swept over him;
82.   But the waves washed his senseless image up
83.   And laid it at this door.

    Eithne Inguba.   How pale he looks!

---

58. . . . dead. **P.**
66. . . . around; . . . ; **71.**
68. . . . tree. And . . . **P.**
69. . . . begot of some . . . **71A.**
70. . . . said. **P.**
73. . . . after to . . . , **P** ; . . . after to . . . foam **60** ; . . . foam **64, 71.**
78. . . . gale; **P.**
81. . . . him. **P.**

[32-34]   32.   oar perhaps, and in the midst upon a bed a man

[34-35]   33.   dead or swooning. It is that famous man Cuchulain,

[35-36]   34.   the best man with every sort of weapon, the best

[36-37]   35.   man to gain the love of a woman; his wife Queen

[37-38]   36.   Emer is at his side; there is no one with her, for

[38-39]   37.   she has sent everyone away, but yonder at the door

[39]   38.   someone stands and hesitates, wishes to come into

[39-40]   39.   the room and is afraid to do so; it is young Eithne

[40]   40.   Inguba, Cuchulain's mistress. Beyond her, through

[41-43]   41.   the open door, the stormy sea. Beyond the foot

42.   of the bed, dressed in grave-clothes, the ghost of

43.   Cuchulain is kneeling.

First Musician [*singing*]

44   44.   White shell, white wing!

45   45.   I will not choose for my friend

46   46.   A frail, unserviceable thing

84. *Emer.* He is not dead.

    Eithne Inguba.   You have not kissed his lips
85.   Nor laid his head upon your breast.

    Emer.   It may be
86.   An image has been put into his place,
87.   A sea-borne log bewitched into his likeness,
88.   Or some stark horseman grown too old to ride
89.   Among the troops of Manannan, Son of the Sea,
90.   Now that his joints are stiff.

    Eithne Inguba.   Cry out his name.
91.   All that are taken from our sight, they say,
92.   Loiter amid the scenery of their lives
93.   For certain hours or days, and should he hear
94.   He might, being angry, drive the changeling out.

95. *Emer.* It is hard to make them hear amid their darkness,
96.   And it is long since I could call him home;
97.   I am but his wife, but if you cry aloud
98.   With the sweet voice that is so dear to him
99.   He cannot help but listen.

    Eithne Inguba.   He loves me best,
100.   Being his newest love, but in the end
101.   Will love the woman best who loved him first
102.   And loved him through the years when love seemed lost.

103. *Emer.* I have that hope, the hope that some day somewhere
104.   We'll sit together at the hearth again.

105. *Eithne Inguba.* Women like me, the violent hour passed over,

---

86.   . . . place. **97A.**
87.   . . . sea-born . . . , **P, 60.**
93.   . . . days; and . . . **P.**
94.   . . . angry drive . . . . **60.**
99.   . . . best **P.**
103.   . . . day and somewhere **P, 60.**
105.   . . . me when the . . . hour is over **P, 60.**

47	47.	That drifts and dreams, and but knows
48	48.	That waters are without end
49	49.	And that wind blows.

| [50] | 50. | *Emer.* Come hither, come sit beside the bed; do |
| [51-52] | 51. | not be afraid, it was I that sent for you. |

| [52-53] | 52. | *Eithne Inguba.* No, madam, I have wronged |
| [53] | 53. | you too deeply to sit there. |

[54]	54.	*Emer.* We two alone of all the people in the
[55-56]	55.	world have the right to watch together here, because
[56]	56.	we have loved him best.

| [56] | 57. | *Eithne Inguba* [*coming nearer*]. Is he dead? |

| | 58. | *Emer.* The fishermen think him dead, it was |
| [57] | 59. | they that put the grave-clothes upon him. |

| | 60. | *Eithne Inguba* [*feeling the body*]. He is cold. |

106.   Are flung into some corner like old nut-shells.
107.   Cuchulain, listen.

Emer.   No, not yet, for first
108.   I'll cover up his face to hide the sea;
109.   And throw new logs upon the hearth and stir
110.   The half-burnt logs until they break in flame.
111.   Old Manannan's unbridled horses come
112.   Out of the sea, and on their backs his horsemen;
113.   But all the enchantments of the dreaming foam
114.   Dread the hearth-fire.

> [*She pulls the curtains of the bed so as to hide the sick man's face,
> that the actor may change his mask unseen. She goes to one side of the
> platform and moves her hand as though putting logs on a fire and
> stirring it into a blaze. While she makes these movements the
> Musicians play, marking the movements with drum and flute
> perhaps.*
>
> *Having finished she stands beside the imaginary fire at a distance
> from Cuchulain and Eithne Inguba.*

Call on Cuchulain now.

115.   *Eithne Inguba.* Can you not hear my voice?

Emer.   Bend over him;
116.   Call out dear secrets till you have touched his heart,
117.   If he lies there; and if he is not there,
118.   Till you have made him jealous.

Eithne Inguba.   Cuchulain, listen.

---

106.   . . . nut shells. **60** ; . . . nutshells. **71.**
107.   . . . yet—for . . . **P** ; . . . yet for . . . **60.**
109.   . . . hearth, and . . . **P.**
110.   . . . half burnt . . . . **P, 60.**
112.   . . . sea and . . . horsemen **60.**
114.   . . . hearth fire.
        [. . . *of platform* . . . *finished, she* (*finished she* **60**) . . . .]
        Call . . . . **P, 60.**
        Directions in 114.   [. . . *of platform* . . . .] **71.**
115.   . . . him. **P** ; . . . voice.
        Bend . . . him. **60.**
116.   . . . heart
117.   . . . not there **P-71.**

61.   There is no breath upon his lips.

62. *Emer.* Those who win the terrible friendship of
63.   the gods sometimes lie a long time as if dead.

64. *Eithne Inguba.* I have heard of such things;
[63]   65.   the very heart stops and yet they live after. What
[63]   66.   happened?

[65, 67]   67. *Emer.* He fought and killed an unknown man,
[68-69]   68.   and found after that it was his own son that he had
[68]   69.   killed.

70. *Eithne Inguba.* A son of yours and his?

71. *Emer.* So that is your first thought! His son
72.   and mine. [*She laughs.*] Did you think that he
73.   belonged to you and me alone? He loved women
74.   before he heard our names, and he will love women
[68]   75.   after he has forgotten us both. The man he killed

119.   *Emer.* Those words sound timidly; to be afraid
120.   Because his wife is but three paces off,
121.   When there is so great need, were but to prove
122.   The man that chose you made but a poor choice:
123.   We're but two women struggling with the sea.

124.   *Eithne Inguba.* O my beloved, pardon me, that I
125.   Have been ashamed. I thrust my shame away.
126.   I have never sent a message or called out,
127.   Scarce had a longing for your company
128.   But you have known and come; and if indeed
129.   You are lying there, stretch out your arms and speak;
130.   Open your mouth and speak, for to this hour
131.   My company has made you talkative.
132.   What ails your tongue, or what has closed your ears?
133.   Our passion had not chilled when we were parted
134.   On the pale shore under the breaking dawn.
135.   He cannot speak: or else his ears are closed
136.   And no sound reaches him.

     Emer.   Then kiss that image;
137.   The pressure of your mouth upon his mouth
138.   May reach him where he is.

     Eithne Inguba [*starting back*].   It is no man.
139.   I felt some evil thing that dried my heart
140.   When my lips touched it.

     Emer.   No, his body stirs;
141.   The pressure of your mouth has called him home;

---

119.   You speak too timidly; . . . **P, 6o.**
120.   . . . off **6o.**
121.   . . . great a need, . . . **P, 64, 71** ; . . . great a need were . . . **6o.**
122.   . . . choice. **P, 6o.**
124.   . . . beloved pardon . . . **6o.**
125.   . . . ashamed and you in so great need. **P-71.**
127.   . . . company,
128.   . . . come. And . . . **P.**
129.   . . . there stretch . . . ; **P, 6o.**
130.   . . . speak for . . . **6o.**
132.   Why do you mope, and what . . . ears. (ears? **P**) **P, 6o,**
135.   He will not hear me: or his . . . **P, 6o,**
136.   . . . image: **P** ; . . . , image **6o,**

[69-70]   76.   was the son of some woman he loved long ago, and

77.   I think he loved her better than he has loved you

78.   or me.

79. *Eithne Inguba.* That is natural, he must have

80.   been young in those days and loved as you and I love.

81. *Emer.* I think he loved her as no man ever loved,

[71]   82.   for when he heard the name of the man he had killed,

[72]   83.   and the name of that man's mother, he went out of

[72-74]   84.   his senses utterly. He ran into the sea, and with shield

[74-75]   85.   before him and sword in hand he fought the deathless

[75]   86.   sea. Of all the many men who had stood there to look

[76-77]   87.   at the fight not one dared stop him or even call his

[77]   88.   name; they stood in a kind of stupor, collected

[78-79]   89.   together in a bunch like cattle in a storm, until,

[79-80]   90.   fixing his eyes as it seemed upon some new enemy,

[80-81]   91.   he waded out further still and the waves swept

[81]   92.   over him.

93. *Eithne Inguba.* He is dead indeed, and he has

94.   been drowned in the sea.

[84]   95.   *Emer.* He is not dead.

[84]   96.   *Eithne Inguba.* He is dead, and you have not

[84-85]   97.   kissed his lips nor laid your head upon his breast.

[85-86]   98.   *Emer.* That is some changeling they have put

[86-87]   99.   there, some image of somebody or something be-

[87]   100.   witched in his likeness, a sea-washed log, it may

[88]   101.   be, or some old spirit. I would throw it into the

102.   fire, but I dare not. They have Cuchulain for a

103.   hostage.

142.   He has thrown the changeling out.

Eithne Inguba [*going further off*].   Look at that arm;
143.   That arm is withered to the very socket.

144.   *Emer* [*going up to the bed*]. What do you come for; and from where?

Figure of Cuchulain.   I have come
145.   From Manannan's court upon a bridleless horse.

146.   *Emer.* What one among the Sidhe has dared to lie
147.   Upon Cuchulain's bed and take his image?

148.   *Figure of Cuchulain.* I am named Bricriu—not the man—that
          Bricriu,
149.   Maker of discord among gods and men,
150.   Called Bricriu of the Sidhe.

Emer.   Come for what purpose?

Figure of Cuchulain [*sitting up, parting curtain and showing its distorted
151.   face, as Eithne Inguba goes out*]. I show my face, and everything
          he loves
152.   Must fly away.

Emer.   You people of the wind
153.   Are full of lying speech and mockery:
154.   I have not fled your face.

Figure of Cuchulain.   You are not loved.

155.   *Emer.* And therefore have no dread to meet your eyes
156.   And to demand him of you.

Figure of Cuchulain.   For that I have come.
157.   You have but to pay the price and he is free.

---

142.   . . . arm— **P** ; . . . arm **60**.
144.   . . . for, and . . . **P** ; . . . for and . . . **60**.
        Directions before 151. [. . . *up and showing . . . face, while Eithne* (*face.
        Eithne* **60**) . . . . **P, 60** ; [. . . *up parting* . . . .] **64-84** ; [. . . *as Inguba*
        . . . .] **97A**.
151.   . . . face and . . . **P-71**.
153.   . . . mockery. **P, 60**.

[94] 104. *Eithne Inguba.* I have heard of such changelings.

    105. *Emer.* Before you came I called his name again
    106. and again. I told him that Queen Maeve and all
    107. her Connacht men are marching north and east,
    108. and that there is none but he to make a stand
[97] 109. against them, but he would not hear me. I am
[97] 110. but his wife, and a man grows tired of a wife. But
[97-98] 111. if you call upon him with that sweet voice, that
[98-99] 112. voice that is so dear to him, he cannot help but
[99] 113. listen.

[100] 114. *Eithne Inguba.* I am but his newest love, and
[100-101] 115. in the end he will turn to the woman who has
[101-102] 116. loved him longest, who has kept the house for him
[102] 117. no matter where he strayed or to whom.

[103] 118. *Emer.* I have indeed that hope, the hope that
[104] 119. some day he and I will sit together at the fire as
[104] 120. when we were first married.

[105] 121. *Eithne Inguba.* Women like me awake a violent
[105-106] 122. love for a while, and when the time is over are
[106-107] 123. flung into some corner like an old eggshell. Cuchu-
[107] 124. lain, listen!

[107] 125. *Emer.* No, not yet; for first I must cover up
[108-109] 126. his face, I must hide him from the sea. I must
[109-110] 127. throw new logs upon the fire and stir the half-
[110, 113] 128. burnt logs into a flame. The sea is full of enchant-
[113] 129. ment, whatever lies on that bed is from the sea,
[113-114] 130. but all enchantments dread the hearth-fire.

158. *Emer.* Do the Sidhe bargain?

    Figure of Cuchulain.   When they would free a captive
159.   They take in ransom a less valued thing.
160.   The fisher, when some knowledgeable man
161.   Restores to him his wife, or son, or daughter,
162.   Knows he must lose a boat or net, or it may be
163.   The cow that gives his children milk; and some
164.   Have offered their own lives. I do not ask
165.   Your life, or any valuable thing;
166.   You spoke but now of the mere chance that some day
167.   You'd be the apple of his eye again
168.   When old and ailing, but renounce that chance
169.   And he shall live again.

    Emer.   I do not question
170.   But you have brought ill-luck on all he loves;
171.   And now, because I am thrown beyond your power
172.   Unless your words are lies, you come to bargain.

173. *Figure of Cuchulain.* You loved your mastery, when but newly
        married,
174.   And I love mine for all my withered arm;
175.   You have but to put yourself into that power
176.   And he shall live again.

    Emer.   No, never, never.

177. *Figure of Cuchulain.* You dare not be accursed, yet he has dared.

178. *Emer.* I have but two joyous thoughts, two things I prize,

---

158.   . . . they set free . . . **P, 60.**
160.   . . . fisher when . . . **60-71.**
165.   . . . thing. **P.**
167.   You'd sit together by the hearth again: (again; **60**)
168.   Renounce that chance, that miserable hour, **P, 60.**
170.   . . . ill luck . . . ; **P, 64, 71** ; . . . ill luck . . . loves **60.**
173.   . . . your power when . . . married, (married **60**)
174.   . . . mine although I am old and withered. (withered; **60**) **P, 60.**
176.   . . . , never, never! **P.**
177.   . . . accursed yet . . . . **60.**
178.   . . . prize— **P** ; . . . prize. **97A.**

[*She pulls the curtains of the bed so as to hide the sick man's face, that the actor may change his mask unseen. She goes to one side of the stage and moves her hand as though putting logs on a fire and stirring it into a blaze. While she makes these movements the Musicians play, marking the movements with drum and flute perhaps. Having finished she stands beside the imaginary fire at a distance from Cuchulain and Eithne Inguba.*]

[114] 131. Call on Cuchulain now.

[115] 132. *Eithne Inguba.* Can you hear my voice, Cuchu-
133. lain?

[115-116] 134. *Emer.* Bend over whatever thing lies there, call
[116-117] 135. out dear secrets and speak to it as though it were
[117] 136. his very self.

[118] 137. *Eithne Inguba.* Cuchulain, listen!

[119] 138. *Emer.* Those are timid words. To be afraid
[120-121] 139. because his wife is standing by when there is so
[121] 140. great need but proves that he chose badly. Re-
[123] 141. member who you are and who he is, that we are
[123] 142. two women struggling with the sea.

[124] 143. *Eithne Inguba.* O my beloved! Pardon me,
[125] 144. pardon me that I could be ashamed when you were
[126] 145. in such need. Never did I send a message, never
[126-127] 146. did I call your name, scarce had I a longing for your
[127-128] 147. company but that you have known and come.
[130] 148. Remember that never up to this hour have you

179.   A hope, a memory, and now you claim that hope.

180. *Figure of Cuchulain.* He'll never sit beside you at the hearth
181.   Or make old bones, but die of wounds and toil
182.   On some far shore or mountain, a strange woman
183.   Beside his mattress.

   Emer.   You ask for my one hope
184.   That you may bring your curse on all about him.

185. *Figure of Cuchulain.* You've watched his loves and you have not
    been jealous,
186.   Knowing that he would tire, but do those tire
187.   That love the Sidhe? Come closer to the bed
188.   That I may touch your eyes and give them sight.
  [*He touches her eyes with his left hand, the right being withered.*

189. *Emer* [*seeing the crouching Ghost of Cuchulain*]. My husband is there.

   Figure of Cuchulain.   I have dissolved the dark
190.   That hid him from your eyes, but not that other
191.   That's hidden you from his.

   Emer.   O husband, husband!

192. *Figure of Cuchulain.* He cannot hear—being shut off, a phantom

---

179.   . . . memory; and . . . . **P.**
185.   . . . jealous **P-71.**
187.   . . . Sidhe?
  Emer. What dancer of the Sidhe, (Sidhe **60**)
187a.   What creature of the reeling moon has pursued him? **P-71.**
188.   *Figure of Cuchulain.* I have but to touch . . . sight;
188a.   But stand at my left side.
  [*He touches her eyes with his left hand, the right being withered.*]
  Emer.   My husband there.
189.   *Figure of Cuchulain.* But out of reach—I . . . dark. (dark **60, 64**) **P-71.**
190.   . . . eyes but . . . **60.**
191.   . . . his.
    Husband, husband!
192.   Be silent, he is but a phantom now, (now **60-71**) **P-71.**

[131]   149.   been silent when I would have you speak, remember
[131]   150.   that I have always made you talkative. If you are
             151.   not lying there, if that is some stranger or someone
             152.   or something bewitched into your likeness, drive
             153.   it away, remember that for someone to take your
[128]   154.   likeness from you is a great insult. If you are
[129-130]   155.   lying there, stretch out your arms and speak, open
[130, 135]   156.   your mouth and speak. [*She turns to Emer.*] He
[135]   157.   does not hear me, no sound reaches him, or it
[135-136]   158.   reaches him and he cannot speak.

[136]   159.   *Emer.* Then kiss that image; these things are a
[137]   160.   great mystery, and maybe his mouth will feel the
[137]   161.   pressure of your mouth upon that image. Is it not
             162.   so that we approach the gods?

[138]   163.   *Eithne Inguba* [*starting back*]. I felt it was some
[139]   164.   evil, devilish thing!

[140-141]   165.   *Emer.* No, his body stirs, the pressure of your
[141-142]   166.   mouth has called him. He has thrown the change-
[142]   167.   ling out.

[142]   168.   *Eithne Inguba* [*going further off*]. Look at that
[142-143]   169.   hand! That hand is withered to the bone.

[144]   170.   *Emer* [*going up to the bed*]. What are you, what
[144]   171.   do you come for, and from where?

[144]   172.   *Figure of Cuchulain.* I am one of the spirits
[145]   173.   from the sea.

[146-147]   174.   *Emer.* What spirit from the sea dares lie upon
[147]   175.   Cuchulain's bed and take his image?

193. That can neither touch, nor hear, nor see;
194. The longing and the cries have drawn him hither.
195. He heard no sound, heard no articulate sound;
196. They could but banish rest, and make him dream,
197. And in that dream, as do all dreaming shades
198. Before they are accustomed to their freedom,
199. He has taken his familiar form; and yet
200. He crouches there not knowing where he is
201. Or at whose side he is crouched.

[*A Woman of the Sidhe has entered and stands a little inside the door.*

Emer.   Who is this woman?

202. *Figure of Cuchulain.* She has hurried from the Country-under-Wave
203. And dreamed herself into that shape that he
204. May glitter in her basket; for the Sidhe
205. Are dexterous fishers and they fish for men
206. With dreams upon the hook.

Emer.   And so that woman
207. Has hid herself in this disguise and made
208. Herself into a lie.

Figure of Cuchulain.   A dream is body;
209. The dead move ever towards a dreamless youth
210. And when they dream no more return no more;
211. And those more holy shades that never lived
212. But visit you in dreams.

Emer.   I know her sort.
213. They find our men asleep, weary with war,
214. Lap them in cloudy hair or kiss their lips;
215. Our men awake in ignorance of it all,

---

193. And he can . . . see. (see; **60-71**) **P-71**.
199. . . . form, and . . . **P, 60.**
      Directions in 201. [. . . *entered, and* . . . .] **P.**
202. . . . Country-Under-Wave, (Wave **60-71**) **P-71**.
205. Are fishers also and . . . **P, 60.**
214. Or weary with the chase, and (chase and **60**) kiss . . . lips
214a. And drop their hair upon them. From (them, from **60**; them; from
      64, 71) that hour **71**.
215. . . . men, who yet knew nothing of . . . , **P-71** ; . . . all **84.**

[148]　　176. *Figure of Cuchulain.* I am called Bricriu, I am
[149]　　177.　　the maker of discord.

[150]　　178. *Emer.* Come for what purpose?

　　　　　　　　　　　　　　　　　　　　　　　[Exit Eithne Inguba.

[151]　　179. *Figure of Cuchulain.* I show my face and every-
[151-152]　180.　　thing he loves must fly.

[154]　　181. *Emer.* I have not fled your face.

[154]　　182. *Figure of Cuchulain.* You are not loved.

[155]　　183. *Emer.* And therefore have no dread to meet your
[155-156]　184.　　eyes and to demand my husband.

[194]　　185. *Figure of Cuchulain.* He is here, your lamenta-
[194]　　186.　　tions and that woman's lamentations have brought
[196]　　187.　　him in a sort of dream, but you can never win him
[187-188]　188.　　without my help. Come to my left hand and I
[188]　　189.　　will touch your eyes and give you sight.

[191]　　190. *Emer [seeing the Ghost of Cuchulain].* Husband!
[191]　　191.　　Husband!

[189-199]　192. *Figure of Cuchulain.* He seems near, and yet
[192-193]　193.　　is as much out of reach as though there were a
[189-190]　194.　　world between. I have made him visible to you.
[190-191]　195.　　I cannot make you visible to him.

　　　　　196. *Emer.* Cuchulain! Cuchulain!

[192-193]　197. *Figure of Cuchulain.* Be silent, woman! He
[193, 157]　198.　　can neither see nor hear. But I can give him to you
[157]　　199.　　at a price. *[Clashing of cymbals, etc.]* Listen to that.
　　　　　200.　　Listen to the horses of the sea trampling! Fand,
　　　　　201.　　daughter of Manannan, has come. She is reining

216.   But when we take them in our arms at night
217.   We cannot break their solitude.

                                        [*She draws a knife from her girdle.*

      Figure of Cuchulain.   No knife
218.   Can wound that body of air. Be silent; listen;
219.   I have not given you eyes and ears for nothing.

              [*The Woman of the Sidhe moves round the crouching Ghost of
              Cuchulain at front of stage in a dance that grows gradually quicker,
              as he slowly awakes. At moments she may drop her hair upon his
              head, but she does not kiss him. She is accompanied by string and
              flute and drum. Her mask and clothes must suggest gold or bronze or
              brass or silver, so that she seems more an idol than a human being.
              This suggestion may be repeated in her movements. Her hair, too,
              must keep the metallic suggestion.*

220.   *Ghost of Cuchulain.* Who is it stands before me there
221.   Shedding such light from limb and hair
222.   As when the moon, complete at last
223.   With every labouring crescent past,
224.   And lonely with extreme delight,
225.   Flings out upon the fifteenth night?

226.   *Woman of the Sidhe.* Because I long I am not complete.
227.   What pulled your hands about your feet,
228.   Pulled down your head upon your knees,

---

216.   Are lonely, and when at fall of night we press
217.   Their hearts upon our hearts their hearts are cold.
              [*She draws a knife from her girdle.*]
218.   And so you think to wound her with a knife.
218a. She has an airy body. Look and listen— (listen; **60-71**) **P-71**.
       Directions after 219.   [. . . *hair too must* . . . .] **P** ; [. . . *head but* . . .
       silver so . . . *hair too,* . . . .] **60** ; [. . . *head but* . . . .] **64, 71**.
220.   . . . there, **P**.
222.   . . . moon complete . . . **60**.
227.   . . . feet **60-71**.
228.   And your head down upon . . . , **P-71**.
       V.E.P.Y.—T

202.   in her chariot, that is why the horses trample so.
203.   She is come to take Cuchulain from you, to take
[289]   204.   him away for ever, but I am her enemy, and I can
[289]   205.   show you how to thwart her.

206.   *Emer.* Fand, daughter of Manannan!

207.   *Figure of Cuchulain.* While he is still here you
[157]   208.   can keep him if you pay the price. Once back in
[186]   209.   Manannan's house he is lost to you for ever. Those
[186-187]   210.   who love the daughters of the sea do not grow weary,
211.   nor do the daughters of the sea release their lovers.

212.   *Emer.* There is no price I will not pay.

[166]   213.   *Figure of Cuchulain.* You spoke but now of a
[166-167]   214.   hope that some day his love may return to you, that
[180]   215.   some day you may sit by the fire as when first married.

216.   *Emer.* That is the one hope I have, the one thing
217.   that keeps me alive.

[168-169]   218.   *Figure of Cuchulain.* Renounce it, and he shall
[169]   219.   live again.

[176]   220.   *Emer.* Never, never!

221.   *Figure of Cuchulain.* What else have you to
222.   offer?

223.   *Emer.* Why should the gods demand such a
224.   sacrifice?

225.   *Figure of Cuchulain.* The gods must serve
226.   those who living become like the dead.

229.   And hid your face?

Ghost of Cuchulain.   Old memories:
230.   A woman in her happy youth
231.   Before her man had broken troth,
232.   Dead men and women. Memories
233.   Have pulled my head upon my knees.

234.   *Woman of the Sidhe.* Could you that have loved many a woman
235.   That did not reach beyond the human,
236.   Lacking a day to be complete,
237.   Love one that, though her heart can beat,
238.   Lacks it but by an hour or so?

239.   *Ghost of Cuchulain.* I know you now, for long ago
240.   I met you on a cloudy hill
241.   Beside old thorn-trees and a well.
242.   A woman danced and a hawk flew,
243.   I held out arms and hands; but you,
244.   That now seem friendly, fled away,
245.   Half woman and half bird of prey.

246.   *Woman of the Sidhe.* Hold out your arms and hands again;
247.   You were not so dumbfounded when
248.   I was that bird of prey, and yet

229a.   A dying boy, with handsome face
229b.   Upturned upon a beaten place;
229c.   A sacred yew-tree on a strand;
229d.   A woman that held in steady hand (hand, **64, 71**)
230.   In all the happiness of her youth **P-71.**
231a.   A burning wisp to light the door;
231b.   And many a round or crescent more; **P-71.**
237.   . . . that though . . . , **60-71.**
238.   . . . so. **60.**
239.   . . . now for . . . **60.**
240.   . . . on the mountain side, (mountain-side, **71A**)
241.   Beside a well that seemed long dry,
242.   Beside old thorns where the hawk flew. **P-71.**
243.   . . . hands, but (hands but **60**) . . . , **P, 60.**
244.   . . . away **P-71.**
246.   . . . again. **P ;** . . . again **60.**
248.   . . . prey and . . . **60.**

227. *Emer.* I will get him in despite of all the gods,
228.   but I will not renounce his love.
   [*Fand, the Woman of the Sidhe, enters. Emer draws a*
   dagger and moves as if to strike her.

[217-218] 229. *Figure of Cuchulain* [*laughing*]. You think to
[217-218] 230.   wound her with a knife! She has an airy body, an
231.   invulnerable body. Remember that though your
232.   lamentations have dragged him hither, once he has
233.   left this shore, once he has passed the bitter sea,
234.   once he lands in Manannan's house, he will be as
235.   the gods who remember nothing.
   [*The Woman of Sidhe, Fand, moves round the*
   crouching Ghost of Cuchulain at front of stage
   in a dance that grows gradually quicker as he
   awakes. At moments she may drop her hair upon
   his head, but she does not kiss him. She is
   accompanied by string and flute and drum. Her
   mask and clothes must suggest gold or bronze or
   brass and silver, so that she seems more an idol
   than a human being. This suggestion may be
   repeated in her movements. Her hair, too, must
   keep the metallic suggestion. The object of the
   dance is that having awakened Cuchulain he will
   follow Fand out; probably he will seek a kiss
   and the kiss will be withheld.

[286] 236. *Figure of Cuchulain.* Cry out that you renounce
[287] 237.   his love, cry that you renounce his love for ever.
   [*Fand and Cuchulain go out.*

[288] 238. *Emer.* No, no, never will I give that cry.

249.   I am all woman now.

Ghost of Cuchulain.   I am not
250.   The young and passionate man I was,
251.   And though that brilliant light surpass
252.   All crescent forms, my memories
253.   Weigh down my hands, abash my eyes.

254. *Woman of the Sidhe.* Then kiss my mouth. Though memory
255.   Be beauty's bitterest enemy
256.   I have no dread, for at my kiss
257.   Memory on the moment vanishes:
258.   Nothing but beauty can remain.

259. *Ghost of Cuchulain.* And shall I never know again
260.   Intricacies of blind remorse?

261. *Woman of the Sidhe.* Time shall seem to stay his course;
262.   When your mouth and my mouth meet
263.   All my round shall be complete
264.   Imagining all its circles run;
265.   And there shall be oblivion
266.   Even to quench Cuchulain's drouth,
267.   Even to still that heart.

Ghost of Cuchulain.   Your mouth!
        [*They are about to kiss, he turns away.*
268.   O Emer, Emer!

Woman of the Sidhe. So then it is she
269.   Made you impure with memory.

270. *Ghost of Cuchulain.* O Emer, Emer, there we stand;
271.   Side by side and hand in hand

---

250.   . . . was **60, 71A.**
256.   . . . dread for . . . **60.**
257.   . . . vanishes; **97A.**
261.   . . . course,
262.   For when . . . **P, 60.**
267.   . . . mouth.
        [*They* . . . . **P-71.**
268.   . . . , Emer.
        So . . . **60-71.**
270.   Still in that dream I see you stand,
271.   A burning wisp in your right hand, **P-71.**

[288-289]   239. *Figure of Cuchulain.* Fool, fool! I am Fand's
[289]   240.   enemy. I come to tell you how to thwart her and
[290-291]   241.   you do nothing. There is yet time. Listen to the
[291]   242.   horses of the chariot, they are trampling the shore.
[292]   243.   They are wild and trampling. She has mounted
[293]   244.   into her chariot. Cuchulain is not yet beside her.
[295]   245.   Will you leave him to such as she? Renounce his
[295]   246.   love, and all her power over him comes to an end.

[297]   247. *Emer.* I renounce Cuchulain's love. I renounce
[297]   248.   it for ever.
              [*Figure of Cuchulain falls back upon the bed,
              drawing or partly drawing its curtain that he
              may change his mask.
              Eithne Inguba enters.*

272.   Tread the threshold of the house
273.   As when our parents married us.

274. *Woman of the Sidhe.* Being among the dead you love her
275.   That valued every slut above her
276.   While you still lived.

> *Ghost of Cuchulain*   O my lost Emer!

277. *Woman of the Sidhe.* And there is not a loose-tongued schemer
278.   But could draw you, if not dead,
279.   From her table and her bed.
280.   But what could make you fit to wive
281.   With flesh and blood, being born to live
282.   Where no one speaks of broken troth,
283.   For all have washed out of their eyes
284.   Wind-blown dirt of their memories
285.   To improve their sight?

> *Ghost of Cuchulain.*   Your mouth, your mouth!
> [*She goes out followed by Ghost of Cuchulain.*

286. *Figure of Cuchulain.* Cry out that you renounce his love; make
     haste
287.   And cry that you renounce his love for ever.

288. *Emer.* No, never will I give that cry.

> *Figure of Cuchulain.*   Fool, fool!

---

272.   To wait my coming to the house— (house, **60-71**) **P-71.**
274.   . . . her, **P.**
276.   . . . Emer. **60-71.**
277.   . . . loose tongued . . . **60.**
278.   . . . you if . . . , **P. 60.**
280.   How could you be fit . . . **P, 60.**
282.   . . . troth— **P** ; . . . troth **60.**
284.   Wind blown . . . **60.**
285.   . . . mouth, your mouth.
          [*Their lips approach but* (*approach, but* **71**) *Cuchulain turns away as
          Emer speaks.*] **P-71.**
286-287. [lacking] **P-71.**
288.   *Emer.* If he may live I am content, **P. 60** ; If but the dead will set
          him free **64, 71.**
288a.   Content that he shall turn on me— (me, **60**) **P, 60** ; That I may
          speak with him at whiles **64, 71.**

249. *Eithne Inguba.* Cuchulain, Cuchulain! Re-

250. member our last meeting. We lay all night among

251. the sand-hills; dawn came; we heard the crying

[298] 252. of the birds upon the shore. Come to me, beloved.

[299-300] 253. [*The curtain of the bed moves.*] Look, look! He has

[300] 254. come back, he is there in the bed, he has his own

[301] 255. rightful form again. It is I who have won him.

[302] 256. It is my love that has brought him back to life!
       [*The figure in the bed pulls back the curtain. He
       wears the mask of Cuchulain.*

[302] 257. *Emer.* Cuchulain wakes!

[303] 258. *Cuchulain.* Your arms, your arms! O Eithne In-

[304] 259. guba, I have been in some strange place and am
       afraid.

288b. If but the dead will set him free **P, 60 ;** By the hearth-stone, I am content— **64, 71.**

288c. That I may speak with him at whiles— (whiles, **60**) **P, 60 ;** Content that he shall turn on me **64, 71.**

288d. Eyes that the cold moon or the harsh sea (moon, or the vague sea, **64, 71**)

288e. Or what I know not's made indifferent.

288f. *Ghost of Cuchulain.* What a wise silence has fallen in this dark!

288g. I know you now in all your ignorance

288h. Of all whereby a lover's quiet is rent.

288i. What dread so great as that he should forget

288j. The least chance sight or sound, or scratch or mark

288k. On an old door, or frail bird heard and seen

288l. In the incredible clear light love cast

288m. All round about her some forlorn lost day?

288n. That face, though fine enough, is a fool's face

288o. And there's a folly in the deathless Sidhe

288p. Beyond man's reach.
     Woman of the Sidhe.   I told you to forget

288q. After my fashion; you would have none of it;

288r. So now you may forget in a man's fashion.

288s. There's an unbridled horse at the sea's edge. (edge; **64, 71**)

288t. Mount—it (Mount; it **60-71**) will carry you in an eye's wink

288u. To where the King of Country-Under-wave, (-Wave, **60-71**)

288v. Old Mananan, nods above the board and moves

288w. His chessmen in a dream. Demand your life, (life **60-71**)

288x. And come again on the unbridled horse.

288y. *Ghost of Cuchulain.* Forgive me those rough words. How could you know

288z. That man is held to those whom he has loved

288aa. By pain they gave, or pain that he has given— (given, **60-71**)

288bb. Intricacies of pain.
     Woman of the Sidhe. I am ashamed

288cc. That being of the deathless shades I chose

288dd. A man so knotted to impurity.
       [*The Ghost of Cuchulain goes out.*]

288ee. *Woman of the Sidhe* [*to figure of Cuchulain*]. To you that have no living light, but dropped

288ff. From a last leprous crescent of the moon (moon, **60-71**)

288gg. I owe it all.
     Figure of Cuchulain. Because you have failed

288hh. I must forego your thanks, I that took pity

288ii. Upon your love and carried our your plan

288jj. To tangle all his life and make it nothing

288kk. That he might turn to you.
     Woman of the Sidhe.   Was it from pity

288ll. You taught the woman to prevail against me? **P-71.**

Epilogue

*[The Musicians, singing as follows, draw the wave-curtain
until it masks the bed, Cuchulain, Eithne Inguba, and Emer.*

First Musician

305	260.	Why does your heart beat thus?
306	261.	Plain to be understood,
307	262.	I have met in a man's house
308	263.	A statue of solitude,
[309]	264.	Moving there and walking,
310	265.	Its strange heart beating fast
[311]	266.	For all our talking;
312	267.	O still that heart at last.
313	268.	O bitter reward
314	269.	Of many a tragic tomb!
315	270.	And we though astonished are dumb
[316]	271.	And give but a sigh and a word,
317	272.	A passing word.
318	273.	Although the door be shut
319	274.	And all seem well enough,
320	275.	Although wide world hold not
321	276.	A man but will give you his love
322	277.	The moment he has looked at you,

289.   I am Fand's enemy come to thwart her will,

290.   And you stand gaping there. There is still time.

291.   Hear how the horses trample on the shore,

292.   Hear how they trample! She has mounted up.

293.   Cuchulain's not beside her in the chariot.

294.   There is still a moment left; cry out, cry out!

295.   Renounce him, and her power is at an end.

296.   Cuchulain's foot is on the chariot-step.

297.   Cry———

Emer.   I renounce Cuchulain's love for ever.
> [*The Figure of Cuchulain sinks back upon the bed, half-drawing the curtain. Eithne Inguba comes in and kneels by bed.*

298. *Eithne Inguba.* Come to me, my beloved, it is I.

299.   I, Eithne Inguba. Look! He is there.

300.   He has come back and moved upon the bed.

301.   And it is I that won him from the sea,

288mm. *Figure of Cuchulain.* You know my nature—by what name I am called.

288nn. *Woman of the Sidhe.* Was it from pity that you hid the truth

288oo. That men are bound to women by the wrongs

288pp. They do or suffer?
        Figure of Cuchulain. You know what being I am.

288qq. *Woman of the Sidhe.* I have been mocked and disobeyed—your power

288rr. Was more to you than my good-will, and now

288ss. I'll have you learn what my ill-will can do: (do; **60-71**)

288tt. I lay you under bonds upon the instant

288uu. To stand before our (your **64, 71**) King and face the charge

288vv. And take the punishment.
        Figure of Cuchulain.   I'll stand there first, (first. **60**)

288ww. And tell my story first; and (first, and **60-71**) Mananan

288xx. Knows that his own harsh sea made my heart cold. (cold **71A**)

288yy. *Woman of the Sidhe.* My horse is there and shall outrun your horse.
        [*The Figure of Cuchulain falls back, the Woman of the Sidhe goes out. Drum taps, music resembling horse hoofs.*] **P-71.**

289-Directions after 298. [lacking] **P-71.**

298. *Eithne Inguba [entering quickly].* I heard the beat of hoofs, but saw no horse; (horse, **60-71**)

299. And then came other hoofs, and (hoofs and **60**) after that

300. I heard low angry cries, and (cries and **60-71**) thereupon **P-71.**

301. [lacking] **P-71.**

323	278.	He that has loved the best
324	279.	May turn from a statue
325	280.	His too human breast.
326	281.	O bitter reward
327	282.	Of many a tragic tomb!
328	283.	And we though astonished are dumb
[329]	284.	And give but a sigh and a word,
330	285.	A passing word.
331	286.	What makes your heart so beat?
332	287.	Is there no man at your side?
333	288.	When beauty is complete
334	289.	Your own thought will have died
335	290.	And danger not be diminished;
336	291.	Dimmed at three-quarter light,
337	292.	When moon's round is finished
338	293.	The stars are out of sight.
339	294.	O bitter reward
340	295.	Of many a tragic tomb!
341	296.	And we though astonished are dumb
[342]	297.	And give but a sigh and a word,
343	298.	A passing word.

302.   That brought him back to life.

Emer.   Cuchulain wakes.
       [*The figure turns round. It once more wears the heroic mask.*

303.   *Cuchulain.* Your arms, your arms! O Eithne Inguba,
304.   I have been in some strange place and am afraid.
           [*The First Musician comes to the front of stage, the others from each
           side, and unfold the cloth singing.*

           [*Song for the unfolding and folding of the cloth*]

       The Musicians.
305.   Why does your heart beat thus?
306.   Plain to be understood,
307.   I have met in a man's house
308.   A statue of solitude,
309.   Moving there and walking;
310.   Its strange heart beating fast
311.   For all our talking.
312.   O still that heart at last.

313.   O bitter reward
314.   Of many a tragic tomb!
315.   And we though astonished are dumb
316.   Or give but a sigh and a word,
317.   A passing word.

318.   Although the door be shut
319.   And all seem well enough,
320.   Although wide world hold not
321.   A man but will give you his love
322.   The moment he has looked at you,
323.   He that has loved the best

---

302.   I ceased to be afraid.
       Emer.   Cuchulain . . . . **P-71.**
303.   Eithne Inguba, take (Inguba take **60**) me in your arms— (arms, **60**)
       P, 60 ; . . . , your arms. O . . . , **64, 71.**
       Directions after 304.   [. . . *side. They unfold . . . cloth, singing.*] **P** ;
       [. . . *side and* . . . . .] **60-71.**
305.   What makes her heart . . . thus, **P, 60.**
306.   . . . understood? **P** ; . . . understood **60-71.**
312.   Oh, still . . . last! **P.**
313.   . . . reward! **P, 60.**
316.   And give . . . word, (word **60**) **P-71.**

[*The Musicians return to their places, Fand, the Woman of
of the Sidhe, enters and dances a dance which expresses her
despair for the loss of Cuchulain. As before there may be
other dancers who represent the waves. It is called, in order to
balance the first dance, 'Fand mourns among the waves.' It is
essentially a dance which symbolises, like water in the fortune-
telling books, bitterness. As she takes her final pose of despair
the Curtain falls.*

THE END

324.	May turn from a statue
325.	His too human breast.
326.	O bitter reward
327.	Of many a tragic tomb!
328.	And we though astonished are dumb
329.	Or give but a sigh and a word,
330.	A passing word.
331.	What makes your heart so beat?
332.	What man is at your side?
333.	When beauty is complete
334.	Your own thought will have died
335.	And danger not be diminished;
336.	Dimmed at three-quarter light,
337.	When moon's round is finished
338.	The stars are out of sight.
339.	O bitter reward
340.	Of many a tragic tomb!
341.	And we though astonished are dumb
342.	Or give but a sigh and a word,
343.	A passing word.

[When the cloth is folded again the stage is bare.

THE END

326.	. . . reward! **P, 60.**
329.	. . . word **60.**
332.	Some one should stay at her side. **P, 60**; Is there no man at . . .? **64, 71.**
334.	Her own . . . **P, 60.**
336.	. . . three quarter light **60**; . . . light **64, 71.**
339.	. . . reward! **P, 60.**
342.	. . . word **60.**

NOTES

While writing these plays, intended for some fifty people in a drawing-room or a studio, I have so rejoiced in my freedom from the stupidity of an ordinary audience that I have filled 'The Only Jealousy of Emer' with those little known convictions about the nature and history of a woman's beauty, which Robartes found in the *Speculum* of Gyraldus and in Arabia Deserta among the Judwalis. The soul through each cycle of its development is held to incarnate through twenty-eight typical incarnations, corresponding to the phases of the moon, the light part of the moon's disc symbolizing the subjective and the dark part of the objective nature, the wholly dark moon (called Phase 1) and the wholly light (called Phase 15) symbolizing complete objectivity and complete subjectivity respectively. In a poem called, 'The Phases of the Moon' in *The Wild Swans at Coole* I have described certain aspects of this symbolism which, however, may take 100 pages or more of my edition of the Robartes papers, for, as expounded by him, it purports to be a complete classification and analysis of every possible type of human intellect, Phase 1 and Phase 15 symbolizing, however, two incarnations not visible to human eyes nor having human characteristics. The invisible fifteenth incarnation is that of the greatest possible bodily beauty, and the fourteenth and sixteenth those of the greatest beauty visible to human eyes. Much that Robartes has written might be a commentary on Castiglione's saying that the physical beauty of woman is the spoil or monument of the victory of the soul, for physical beauty, only possible to subjective natures, is described as the result of emotional toil in past lives. Objective natures are declared to be always ugly, hence the disagreeable appearance of politicians, reformers, philanthropists, and men of science. A saint or sage before his final deliverance has one incarnation as a woman of supreme beauty.

In writing these little plays I knew that I was creating something which could only fully succeed in a civilization very unlike ours. I think they should be written for some country where all classes share in a half-mythological, half-philosophical folk-belief which the writer and his small audience lift into a new subtlety. All my life I have longed for such a country, and always found it quite impossible to write without having as much belief in its real existence as a child has in that of the wooden birds, beasts, and persons of his toy Noah's Ark. I have now found all the mythology and philosophy I need in the papers of my old friend and rival, Robartes.

Note on 'The Only Jealousy of Emer', **64**.

While writing . . . *The Only Jealousy of Emer* with convictions . . . symbolising . . . symbolising . . . symbolism, which needs, however, 100 pages or more for its exposition, for it purports . . . , symbolising, . . . Robartes has found might . . . beauty.

In . . . civilisation . . . philosophy I need.
Note on 'The Only Jealousy of Emer', 71.

* * *

I

I wrote *The Only Jealousy of Emer* for performance in a private house or studio, considering it, for reasons which I have explained, unsuited to a public stage. Then somebody put it on a public stage in Holland and Hildo van Krop made his powerful masks. Because the dramatist who can collaborate with a great sculptor is lucky, I rewrote the play not only to fit it for such a stage but to free it from abstraction and confusion. I have retold the story in prose which I have tried to make very simple, and left imaginative suggestion to dancers, singers, musicians. I have left the words of the opening and closing lyrics unchanged, for sung to modern music in the modern way they suggest strange patterns to the ear without obtruding upon it their difficult, irrelevant words. The masks get much of their power from enclosing the whole head; this makes the head out of proportion to the body, and I found some difference of opinion as to whether this was a disadvantage or not in an art so distant from reality; that it was not a disadvantage in the case of the Woman of the Sidhe all were agreed. She was a strange, noble, unforgettable figure.

I do not say that it is always necessary when one writes for a general audience to make the words of the dialogue so simple and so matter-of-fact; but it is necessary where the appeal is mainly to the eye and to the ear through songs and music. *Fighting the Waves* is in itself nothing, a mere occasion for sculptor and dancer, for the exciting dramatic music of George Antheil.

II

'It is that famous man Cuchulain. . . .' In the eighties of the last century Standish O'Grady, his mind full of Homer, retold the story of Cuchulain that he might bring back an heroic ideal. His work, which founded modern Irish literature, was hasty and ill-constructed, his style marred by imitation of Carlyle; twenty years later Lady Gregory translated the whole body of Irish heroic legend into the dialect of the cottages in those great books *Cuchulain of Muirthemne* and *Gods and Fighting Men*, her eye too upon life. In later years she often quoted the saying of Aristotle: 'To think like a wise man, but express oneself like the common people,' and always her wise man was heroic man. Synge wrote his *Deirdre of the Sorrows* in peasant dialect, but died before he had put the final touches to anything but the last act, the most poignant and noble in Irish drama. I wrote in blank verse, which I tried to bring as close to common speech as the subject permitted, a number of connected plays—*Deirdre, At the Hawk's Well, The Green Helmet, On Baile's*

Strand, The Only Jealousy of Emer. I would have attempted the Battle of the Ford and the Death of Cuchulain, had not the mood of Ireland changed.

III

When Parnell was dragged down, his shattered party gave itself up to nine years' vituperation, and Irish imagination fled the sordid scene. A. E.'s *Homeward Songs by the Way*; Padraic Colum's little songs of peasant life; my own early poems; Lady Gregory's comedies, where, though the dramatic tension is always sufficient, the worst people are no wickeder than children; Synge's *Well of the Saints* and *Playboy of the Western World*, where the worst people are the best company, were as typical of that time as Lady Gregory's translations. Repelled by what had seemed the sole reality, we had turned to romantic dreaming, to the nobility of tradition.

About 1909 the first of the satirists appeared, 'The Cork Realists,' we called them, men that had come to maturity amidst spite and bitterness. Instead of turning their backs upon the actual Ireland of their day, they attacked everything that had made it possible, and in Ireland and among the Irish in England made more friends than enemies by their attacks. James Joyce, the son of a small Parnellite organiser, had begun to write, but remained unpublished.

> An age is the reversal of an age;
> When strangers murdered Emmet, Fitzgerald, Tone,
> We lived like men that watch a painted stage.
> What matter for the scene, the scene once gone!
> It had not touched our lives; but popular rage,
> *Hysterica passio*, dragged this quarry down.
> None shared our guilt; nor did we play a part
> Upon a painted stage when we devoured his heart.

But even if there had been no such cause of bitterness, of self-contempt, we could not, considering that every man everywhere is more of his time than of his nation, have long kept the attention of our small public, no, not with the whole support, and that we never had, of the Garrets and Cellars. Only a change in European thought could have made that possible. When Stendhal described a masterpiece as a 'mirror dawdling down a lane' he expressed the mechanical philosophy of the French eighteenth century. Gradually literature conformed to his ideal; Balzac became old-fashioned; romanticism grew theatrical in its strain to hold the public; till, by the end of the nineteenth century, the principal characters in the most famous books were the passive analysts of events, or had been brutalised into the likeness of mechanical objects. But Europe is changing its philosophy. Some four years ago the Russian Government silenced the mechanists because social dialectic is impossible if matter is trundled about by some limited force. Certain typical books—*Ulysses*, Mrs. Virginia Woolf's *Waves*, Mr. Ezra

Pound's *Draft of XXX Cantos*—suggest a philosophy like that of the *Samkara* school of ancient India, mental and physical objects alike material, a deluge of experience breaking over us and within us, melting limits whether of line or tint; man no hard bright mirror dawdling by the dry sticks of a hedge, but a swimmer, or rather the waves themselves. In this new literature announced with much else by Balzac in *Le Chef-d'œuvre inconnu,* as in that which it superseded, man in himself is nothing.

IV

I once heard Sir William Crookes tell half a dozen people that he had seen a flower carried in broad daylight slowly across the room by what seemed an invisible hand. His chemical research led to the discovery of radiant matter, but the science that shapes opinion has ignored his other research that seems to those who study it the slow preparation for the greatest, perhaps the most dangerous, revolution in thought Europe has seen since the Renaissance, a revolution that may, perhaps, establish the scientific complement of certain philosophies that in all ancient countries sustained heroic art. We may meet again, not the old simple celebration of life tuned to the highest pitch, neither Homer nor the Greek dramatists, something more deliberate than that, more systematised, more external, more self-conscious, as must be at a second coming, Plato's Republic, not the Siege of Troy.

I shall remind the Garrets and Cellars of certain signs, that they may, as a Chinese philosopher has advised, shape things at their beginning, when it is easy, not at the end, when it is difficult. I first name Mr. Sacheverell Sitwell's lovely 'Pastoral'; point out that he has celebrated those Minoan shepherds, those tamers of the wild bulls, their waists enclosed from childhood in wide belts of bronze, that they might attain wasp-like elegance; that he prefers them to the natural easy Sicilian shepherds, preferring as it were cowboys to those that 'watched their flocks by night'; then Dr. Gogarty's praise of 'the Submarine Men trained through a lifetime'; and remind them of their own satisfaction in that praise. Then they might, after considering the demand of the black, brown, green, and blue shirts, 'Power to the most disciplined,' ask themselves whether D'Annunzio and his terrible drill at Fiume may not prove as symbolic as Shelley, whose art and life became so completely identified with romantic contemplation that young men in their late teens, when I was at that age, identified him with poetry itself.

Here in Ireland we have come to think of self-sacrifice, when worthy of public honour, as the act of some man at the moment when he is least himself, most completely the crowd. The heroic act, as it descends through tradition, is an act done because a man is himself, because, being himself, he can ask nothing of other men but room amid remembered tragedies; a sacrifice of himself to himself, almost, so little may he bargain, of the moment to the moment. I think of some Elizabethan play where, when mutineers threaten to hang the ship's captain, he replies: 'What has that to do with me?' So lonely is that ancient act, so great the pathos of its joy, that I have never been able to read without tears a passage in *Sigurd the Volsung* describing how the new-born child lay in the bed and looked 'straight on the sun'; how the serving-women washed him, bore him back to his mother, wife of the dead Sigmund; how 'they shrank in their rejoicing before the eyes of the child'; 'the best sprung from the best'; how though 'the spring morn smiled . . . the hour seemed awful to them.'

> But Hiordis looked on the Volsung,
> on her grief and her fond desire.
> And the hope of her heart was quickened,
> and her heart was a living fire;
> And she said: 'Now one of the earthly
> on the eyes of my child hath gazed
> Nor shrunk before their glory,
> nor stayed her love amazed:
> I behold thee as Sigmund beholdeth,—
> and I was the home of thine heart—
> Woe's me for the day when thou wert not,
> and the hour when we shall part!'

How could one fail to be moved in the presence of the central mystery of the faith of poets, painters, and athletes? I am carried forty years back and hear a famous old athlete wind up a speech to country lads—'The holy people have above them the communion of saints; we the communion of the *Tuatha de Danaan of Erin.*'

Science has driven out the legends, stories, superstitions that protected the immature and the ignorant with symbol, and now that the flower has crossed our rooms, science must take their place and demonstrate as philosophy has in all ages, the States are justified, not by multiplying or, as it would seem, comforting those that are inherently miserable, but because sustained by those for whom the hour seems 'awful', and by those born out of themselves, the best born of the best.

Since my twentieth year, these thoughts have been in my mind, and now that I am old I sing them to the Garrets and the Cellars:

> Move upon Newton's town,
> The town of Hobbes and of Locke,
> Pine, spruce, come down
> Cliff, ravine, rock:
> What can disturb the corn?
> What makes it shudder and bend?
> The rose brings her thorn,
> The Absolute walks behind.

V

Yet it may be that our science, our modern philosophy, keep a subconscious knowledge that their raft, roped together at the end of the seventeenth century, must, if they so much as glance at that slow-moving flower, part and abandon us to the storm, or it may be, as Professor Richet suggests at the end of his long survey of psychical research from the first experiments of Sir William Crookes to the present moment, that all it can do is, after a steady scrutiny, to prove the poverty of the human intellect, that we are lost amid alien intellects, near but incomprehensible, more incomprehensible than the most distant stars. We may, whether it scrutinise or not, lacking its convenient happy explanations, plunge as Rome did in the fourth century according to some philosopher of that day into 'a fabulous, formless darkness.'

> Should H. G. Wells afflict you
> Put whitewash in a pail;
> Paint: 'Science—opium of the suburbs'
> On some waste wall.

VI

'First I must cover up his face, I must hide him from the sea.' I am deeply grateful for a mask with the silver glitter of a fish, for a dance with an eddy like that of water, for music that suggested, not the vagueness, but the rhythm of the sea. A Dublin journalist showed his scorn for 'the new paganism' by writing: 'Mr. Yeats' play is not really original, for something of the kind doubtless existed in Ancient Babylon,' but a German psycho-analyst has traced the 'mother complex' back to our mother the sea—after all Babylon was a modern inland city—to the loneliness of the first crab or crayfish that climbed ashore and turned lizard; while Gemistus Plethon not only substituted the sea for Adam and Eve, but, according to a friend learned in the Renaissance, made it symbolise the garden's ground or first original, 'that concrete universal which all philosophy is seeking'.

VII

'Everything he loves must fly,' everything he desires; Emer too must renounce desire, but there is another love, that which is like the man-at-arms in the Anglo-Saxon poem, 'doom eager.' Young, we discover an opposite through our love; old, we discover our love through some opposite neither hate nor despair can destroy, because it is another self, a self that we have fled in vain.

'Fighting the Waves,' Introduction, **83**.

I

I wrote . . . Hildo Krop . . . re-wrote . . . re-told . . . head, this . . . body
and . . . woman from the Sidhe . . . figure.
I do not . . . matter of fact; but . . . Antheil.

II

I have written a series of plays upon certain events of the Irish heroic age,
set out in their chronological order. In 'Deirdre' the hero Naoise, who holds
what the translators call the 'championship of the Red Branch,' dies, making
way for his successor in the championship, Cuchullain, to whom I have
given four plays: 'The Hawk's Well,' 'The Green Helmet,' 'On Baile's
Strand' and the present play, or my verse play on the same theme 'The
Only Jealousy of Emer'. If the first phase of our dramatic movement had
lasted I would have dramatised other episodes from his life. Lady Gregory,
John Synge and I, Standish O'Grady before us, James Stephens after us,
planned a literature, comic or tragic, founded upon the inventions and
habits of Gaelic-speaking Ireland. O'Grady started us off by re-creating
Cuchullain in the image of Achilles, and when Lady Gregory wrote her
'Folk History Plays' and I my plays in verse, we thought them like Greek
plays; the simple fable, the logically constructed plot, the chorus of the
people, their words full of vague suggestion, a preoccupation with what is
unchanging and therefore without topical or practical interest. We have
been succeeded by a school of satire that has for its subject the actual life
of the village and the slum, and more recently by what may grow into a
school of psychological drama; but we might, if the Irish Government at
the establishment of the Free State had done something no revolution of
strong farmers, clerks and lawyers would permit, have founded a school
that could have substituted, as only a literature without satirical or realistic
prepossessions could, positive desires for the negative passion of a national
movement beaten down into party politics, compelled for a century to
attack everything, to suspect everybody. Only a Caesar could do what I
want, but now that the Cellars and Garrets have taken to some kind of half
pious communism they may produce one. I write for Caesar's eyes.

III

Some of us were discussing the definition of a gentleman when Lionel
Johnson closed the discussion with these words: 'A gentleman is a man who
knows Greek,' and somebody in Lady Gregory's 'Jackdaw' boasts that he
once slept 'in the one bed with two boys that were learning Greek.' The
pressure of other subjects has decided that one of the classical languages
must go, and every man not a pedant or a man stupefied by the memory
that Latin was once the Volapuk or Esperanto of Europe, knows that it

should be Latin. Latin literature had great style and an air of authority but it lacked always fundamental thought. Our eighteenth century and our seventeenth towards its end, drank it dry, and though our heads ache, men of letters feel that at last they can approach Greece without Roman pre-possessions. Roman civilization was the hardening and objectifying, or the decadence, of that Greek civilization which yet survived in Byzantium, half ruined for a millennium, and had stretched back, as we know and our fathers did not, for a millennium. I would have Caesar compel a boy to begin Greek with his school life, when well grounded to learn Irish by the 'direct method,' school and university to teach him the two languages, the two literatures, in association. Let him translate Greek into Irish and learn that our chariot fighting Red Branch resembled the chariot-fighting Greeks and Trojans; that D'Arbois de Joubainville spent his life in the study of Irish for no other reason; that the sacred grove where Oedipus was carried off by the gods differed in nothing from the groves where, according to Connaught tales, men, women and children are carried off; that Greek literature was founded on a folk belief differing but little from that of Ireland; that Roman, like English literature, was founded upon the written word; that our 'saints and scholars' belong to a Europe where Byzantium reigned, a Europe where the great houses of Rome like so many great houses in Dublin to-day had sunk into slum tenements; that the Book of Kells mixed the grotesque heads of northern Europe with the Byzantine vine formalised and generalised; that our stone crosses got a part of their design from the Painters' Books of Mount Athos; that in general character the patterns upon the croziers and missal boxes in our National Museum are Byzantine Greek. And this new and powerful instrument of nationality will meet no opposition from fathers of families for it supersedes no commercial language. Preserve Gaelic where it is already spoken with some device of scholarship or bounties—see that there are teachers for all that would learn and you can eject those reporters in Dáil and Senate who are manufacturing a new language. Then let Caesar talk to the Curator of the Museum; first doubling the Museum's inadequate grant. We know nothing of the past if we do not know where men lived, what they handled and wore. Every farmer knows some field where there is a rath or 'forth' and that the ancient inhabitants of the country lived there. The Museum should contain a life-size restoration of the house they lived in, with such furniture as they used, and life-sized figures dressed as they were dressed. It does not matter if the restoration be but guess work, criticism and amendation can come later. Because in most districts there is some old castle where the farmer climbed as a boy, let there be a second room to show how such castles were adorned and furnished in the thirteen or fourteenth century, and then a third room, a typical drawingroom, diningroom or library of the last quarter of our Eighteenth century with examples of the arts and crafts of an epoch when our civilization seemed about to climax. Then let the authorities enquire what old sights and ruins in the neighbourhood of Dublin picnic parties most frequent—The Seven Churches, Mellifont, Tara perhaps—and put somewhere near those

laboring **P** ; *labouring* **60-97.**
Mananan **P-71** ; *Manannan* **84, 97.**

* * *

[See also the notes on *The King of the Great Clock Tower*, p. 1008; *Glossary*, p. 1284; and *Prefaces to 60, 64, Preface in 71 to 'Four Plays for Dancers,'* 69, 83, 84, pp. 1304, 1306, 1308, 1309.]

THE HOUR-GLASS

A Morality

(Prose Version)[1]

1903

Persons in the Play

A Wise Man	A Fool
Some Pupils	An Angel
The Wise Man's Wife and Two Children	

A large room with a door at the back and another at the side opening to an inner room. A desk and a chair in the middle. An hour-glass on a bracket near the door. A creepy stool near it. Some benches. An astronomical globe perhaps. Perhaps a large ancient map of the world on the wall or some musical instruments. Floor may be strewed with rushes. A Wise Man sitting at his desk.

PRINTINGS   *The North American Review*, September 1903; **15, 16, 17, 25, 29, 34, 45, 69, 89.**

DATE   [at bottom of page] Copyright, 1903, by W. B. Yeats. All rights reserved. **NAR, 15**; [lacking] **16-69.**

DRAMATIS PERSONAE   Characters (Dramatis Personae **NAR-16**) / A . . . Man. Some Pupils. / A Fool. An . . . **NAR-16, 29**; [no heading] . . . Man. Some Pupils. / A Fool. An . . . **17, 25.**

STAGE DIRECTIONS   *SCENE.* (Scene: **17, 25, 45**) *A . . . globe. A blackboard. A large . . . wall. Some . . . . Floor strewed . . . .* **NAR, 15, 17, 25, 45**;
  Scene: *A . . . benches. The wise man . . . .* **16**;
  A (Scene: *A* **29**) *. . . side* (*side,* **34**) *or else a curtained place where the persons* (*where persons* **34**) *can enter by parting the curtains. A desk . . . chair at one side. An hour-glass on a stand* (*a bracket or stand* **34**) *near the door. A creepy . . . benches. A Wise . . . .* **29, 34**;
  Scene: *A . . . .* **69.**

TEXT   Title The Hour-Glass: / A . . . **17-69.**

---

[1] The prose version, not included in **84** and **97**, is collated on the verso pages. The basic text and line-lengths are from **89**. The verse version is collated on the recto pages. Similarities are shown by bracketed line-numbers in the margin; identities by unbracketed line-numbers.

THE HOUR-GLASS

1914

Persons in the Play

A Wise Man   Teigue, *a Fool*
Bridget, *his wife*   Angel
          Children and Pupils

The stage is brought out into the orchestra so as to leave a wide space in front of the stage curtain. Pupils come in and stand before the stage curtain, which is still closed. One Pupil carries a book.

PRINTINGS *The Mask*, Florence, April 1913; **53, 54, 57, 69, 84, 97.**

DATE [lacking] **M-54, 69**; 1912 **57.**

PREFACE A Preface to the New Version.

I took the plot of 'The Hour Glass' from an Irish Folk Tale but tried to put my own philosophy into the words. An action on the stage, however, is so much stronger than a word that when the Wise Man abused himself before the Fool I was always ashamed. My own meanings had vanished and I saw before me a cowardly person who seemed to cry out 'the wisdom of this world is foolishness' and to understand the words not as may a scholar and a gentleman but as do ignorant preachers.

I began a revision of the words from the moment when the play converted a music hall singer and sent him to mass and to confession; but no revision of words could change the effect of the Wise Man down on his knees before the Fool; so last year I changed action and all.

I made a new play of it and when I had finished discovered how I might have taken the offence out of the old by a change of action so slight that a reader would hardly have noticed it. I shall let 'our second company' go on playing the old version thus amended in Irish provincial towns but think the new one better for myself and my friends.

W. B. Yeats   M.

DRAMATIS PERSONAE [lacking] **M**[1]; The Persons of the Play / Wise . . . **53-57**; . . . Play / Wise . . . **69.**

STAGE DIRECTIONS. Scene: *The Wise Man's house. An Hour-glass on a stand and / a big chair with a great book on a desk before it. / (Enter Pupils)* **M**; *Pupils . . . curtain which . . . .* **53, 54**; *Pupils . . . .* **57**; *When played at the Abbey Theatre the stage . . . .* **69.**

---

[1] In *The Mask* the pupils, as speakers, are designated 1st, 2nd, 3rd, 4th, 5th pupil.

　　　　　1. *Wise Man* [*turning over the pages of a book*]. Where is that
　　　　　2. 　　passage I am to explain to my pupils to-day? Here it
[63, 64]　3. 　　is, and the book says that it was written by a beggar
[46, 65]　4. 　　on the walls of Babylon: 'There are two living coun-
[46-47]　5. 　　tries, the one visible and the one invisible; and when
[48]　　6. 　　it is winter with us it is summer in that country, and
[48]　　7. 　　when the November winds are up among us it is
[49]　　8. 　　lambing-time there.' I wish that my pupils had asked
[50]　　9. 　　me to explain any other passage. [*The Fool comes in and
　　　　　　　　　stands at the door holding out his hat. He has a pair of shears
[53]　　10. 　*in the other hand.*] It sounds to me like foolishness; and
　　　　　11. 　　yet that cannot be, for the writer of this book, where
　　　　　12. 　　I have found so much knowledge, would not have set
　　　　　13. 　　it by itself on this page, and surrounded it with so
　　　　　14. 　　many images and so many deep colours and so much
　　　　　15. 　　fine gilding, if it had been foolishness.

20　　　　16. *Fool.* Give me a penny.

　　　　　17. *Wise Man* [*turns to another page*]. Here he has written:
[81-83]　18. 　　'The learned in old times forgot the visible country.'
　　　　　19. 　　That I understand, but I have taught my learners

6.　... country; and **16.**
9.　... passage, for this is a hard passage. [*The* ... **NAR-17.**
　　Directions after 9.　[... *door, holding* ....] **16.**

1. *First Pupil.* He said we might choose the subject for
2. the lesson.

3. *Second Pupil.* There is none of us wise enough to do
4. that.

5. *Third Pupil.* It would need a great deal of wisdom to
6. know what it is we want to know.

7. *Fourth Pupil.* I will question him.

8. *Fifth Pupil.* You?

9. *Fourth Pupil.* Last night I dreamt that some one came
10. and told me to question him. I was to say to him,
11. 'You were wrong to say there is no God and no
12. soul—maybe, if there is not much of either, there
13. is yet some tatters, some tag on the wind—so to
14. speak—some rag upon a bush, some bob-tail of a
15. god'. I will argue with him—nonsense though it be
16. —according to my dream, and you will see how
17. well I can argue, and what thoughts I have.

18. *First Pupil.* I'd soon as listen to dried peas in a bladder
19. as listen to your thoughts.

Teigue the Fool comes in.

20. *Fool.* Give me a penny.

21. *Second Pupil.* Let us choose a subject by chance. Here

TEXT Title. . . . Hour Glass **M** ; . . . Hour-Glass / New Version **53-57** ; . . . Hour-Glass / (In Verse) **69.**

6. . . . what we . . . . **M.**
9. . . . someone . . . **M-54.**
11. 'you . . . **M-54.**
12. soul . . . [T] maybe, . . .
13. . . . wind, some
14. rag . . . [T] so to speake of divinity, some bob-tail . . . **M.**
15. . . . him, . . . [T] nonsense . . . **M** ; . . . him, —nonsense . . . **53-57.**
16. . . . [T] according . . . **M.**
18. . . . bladder, **M-69.**
Directions after **19.** [*Fool* . . . .] **M-69.**

	20.	better.
118	21.	*Fool.* Won't you give me a penny?
[119-121]	22.	*Wise Man.* What do you want? The words of the wise
[119-121]	23.	Saracen will not teach you much.
[122]	24.	*Fool.* Such a great wise teacher as you are will not refuse
[122-123]	25.	a penny to a Fool.
[125]	26.	*Wise Man.* What do you know about wisdom?
[126]	27.	*Fool.* O, I know! I know what I have seen.
[127]	28.	*Wise Man.* What is it you have seen?
[129]	29.	*Fool.* When I went by Kilcluan, where the bells used to
[130]	30.	be ringing at the break of every day, I could hear

---

25.   . . . fool. **34.**
29.   . . . Kilcluan where . . . **NAR-69.**

22. is his big book. Let us turn over the pages slowly.
23. Let one of us put down his finger without looking.
24. The passage his finger lights on will be the subject
25. for the lesson.

26. *Fool*. Give me a penny.

27. *Third Pupil* [*taking up book*]. How heavy it is!

28. *Fourth Pupil*. Spread it on Teigue's back, and then we
29. can all stand round and see the choice.

30. *Second Pupil*. Make him spread out his arms.

31. *Fourth Pupil*. Down on your knees. Hunch up your
32. back. Spread your arms out now, and look like a
33. golden eagle in a church. Keep still, keep still.

34. *Fool*. Give me a penny.

35. *Third Pupil*. Is that the right cry for an eagle-cock?

36. *Second Pupil*. I'll turn the pages—you close your eyes
37. and put your finger down.

38. *Third Pupil*. That's it, and then he cannot blame us for
39. the choice.

40. *First Pupil*. There, I have chosen. Fool, keep still—
41. and if what's wise is strange and sounds like non-
42. sense, we've made a good choice.

43. *Fifth Pupil*. The Master has come.

---

22. . . . slowly,
23. let . . . looking,
24. the . . . **M.**
27. . . . is. **M-84.**
33. . . . still, Keep still. **53, 54, 57E.**
35. . . . eagle cock? **M-69.**
36. . . . pages . . . [T] you . . . **M.**
40. . . . choosen. . . . still . . . [T] **M.**
43. Here is the master coming. **M.**

[131]   31.   nothing but the people snoring in their houses. When
[132]   32.   I went by Tubber-vanach, where the young men used
[133]   33.   to be climbing the hill to the blessed well, they were
[134]   34.   sitting at the cross-roads playing cards. When I went
[135]   35.   by Carrigoras, where the friars used to be fasting and
[136]   36.   serving the poor, I saw them drinking wine and obey-
[137]   37.   ing their wives. And when I asked what misfortune
[138]   38.   had brought all these changes, they said it was no
[139]   39.   misfortune, but it was the wisdom they had learned
[140]   40.   from your teaching.

[143]   41.   *Wise Man.* Run round to the kitchen, and my wife will
[143-144] 42.   give you something to eat.

[145]   43.   *Fool.* That is foolish advice for a wise man to give.

146   44.   *Wise Man.* Why, Fool?

[147]   45.   *Fool.* What is eaten is gone. I want pennies for my bag.
[148]   46.   I must buy bacon in the shops, and nuts in the
[149]   47.   market, and strong drink for the time when the sun
[150]   48.   is weak. And I want snares to catch the rabbits and
[150-151] 49.   squirrels and the hares, and a pot to cook them

---

32.   . . . Tubbervanach (Tubbervanach, **34**) where . . . **NAR-69.**
34.   . . . crossroads . . . **NAR, 15.**
35.   . . . Carrigoras where . . . **NAR-16.**

44. *Fool.* Will anybody give a penny to a fool?
   [*One of the Pupils draws back the stage curtains showing the Master sitting at his desk. There is an hour-glass upon his desk or in a bracket on the wall. One Pupil puts the books before him.*

45. *First Pupil.* We have chosen the passage for the lesson,
46. Master. 'There are two living countries, one visible
47. and one invisible, and when it is summer there, it
48. is winter here, and when it is November with us,
49. it is lambing-time there.'

50. *Wise Man.* That passage, that passage! What mischief
51. has there been since yesterday?

52. *First Pupil.* None, Master.

53. *Wise Man.* Oh yes, there has; some craziness has fallen
54. from the wind, or risen from the graves of old men,
55. and made you choose that subject.—Diem noctemque
56. contendo, sed quos elegi, quos amavi, in tirocinium
57. vel hi labuntur.

58. *Fourth Pupil.* I knew that it was folly, but they would
59. have it.

60. *Third Pupil.* Had we not better say we picked it by
61. chance?

62. *Second Pupil.* No; he would say we were children still.

63. *First Pupil.* I have found a sentence under that one that
64. says—as though to show it had a hidden meaning—
65. a beggar wrote it upon the walls of Babylon.

Directions after 44. [*Wise Man comes in.*] **M**; [... *curtain ... sitting at his desk. One pupil ... book ....*] **53, 54**; [... *curtain ... book ....*] **57**; [... *book ....*] **69.**
50. ... passage; what ... **M**; ... ! what ... **53-69.**
53. Oh, yes, ... **M-54.**
55. ... subject. [*He goes to desk.*] **M**; ... subject. **53-57.**
56-57. [lacking] **M-57.**
62. No, he .... **M-54.**
63. ... one, that
64. says ... [T] as ... meaning ... [T] **M.**
V.E.   —U

[151]   50.   in.

[152-153]   51.   *Wise Men.* Go away. I have other things to think of
[152-153]   52.   now than giving you pennies.

154   53.   *Fool.* Give me a penny and I will bring you luck. The
[155]   54.   fishermen give me leave to sleep among the nets in
[156]   55.   their lofts in the winter-time because they say I bring
[156-157]   56.   them luck; and in the summer-time the wild creatures
[157-158]   57.   let me sleep near their nests and their holes. It is
[158-159]   58.   lucky even to look at me or to touch me, but it is
[159-160]   59.   much more lucky to give me a penny. [*Holds out his*
[160]   60.   *hand.*] If I wasn't lucky, I'd starve.

[161]   61.   *Wise Man.* What have you got the shears for?

---

53.   . . . luck. Bresal the
54.   Fisherman lets me sleep . . .
55.   his loft . . . because he says . . .
56.   him luck; . . . **NAR-45.**

66. *Wise Man.* Then find some beggar and ask him what it
67.   means, for I will have nothing to do with it.

68. *Fourth Pupil.* Come, Teigue, what is the old book's
69.   meaning when it says that there are sheep that drop
70.   their lambs in November?

71. *Fool.* To be sure—everybody knows, everybody in the
72.   world knows, when it is spring with us, the trees
73.   are withering there, when it is summer with us, the
74.   snow is falling there, and have I not myself heard
75.   the lambs that are there all bleating on a cold
76.   November day—to be sure, does not everybody with
77.   an intellect know that? And maybe when it's night
78.   with us, it is day with them, for many a time I have
79.   seen the roads lighted before me.

80. *Wise Man.* The beggar who wrote that on Babylon wall
81.   meant that there is a spiritual kingdom that cannot
82.   be seen or known till the faculties, whereby we
83.   master the kingdom of this world, wither away like
84.   green things in winter. A monkish thought, the most
85.   mischievous thought that ever passed out of a man's
86.   mouth.—Virgas ut partus educant colligunt aves,
87.   mens hominis nugas.

88. *First Pupil.* If he meant all that, I will take an oath
89.   that he was spindle-shanked, and cross-eyed, and had
90.   a lousy itching shoulder, and that his heart was
91.   crosser than his eyes, and that he wrote it out of
92.   malice.

93. *Second Pupil.* Let's come away and find a better subject.

94. *Fourth Pupil.* And maybe now you'll let me choose.

---

71.   . . . sure . . . [T] everybody . . . **M.**
72.   . . . Spring . . . **M-69.**
73.   . . . Summer . . . **54-69.**
76.   . . . day . . . [T] to . . . **M.**
77.   . . . that; and . . . **M-69.**
80.   . . . beggar, who . . . wall, **69.**
82.   . . . faculties whereby . . .
83.   . . . world wither away, like **M-57.**
86.   mouth. **M-57.**
87.   [lacking] **M-57.**

162	62.	*Fool.* I won't tell you. If I told you, you would drive
163	63.	them away.
[164-165]	64.	*Wise Man.* Whom would I drive away?
166	65.	*Fool.* I won't tell you.
167	66.	*Wise Man.* Not if I give you a penny?
168	67.	*Fool.* No.
169	68.	*Wise Man.* Not if I give you two pennies?
170	69.	*Fool.* You will be very lucky if you give me two
171	70.	pennies, but I won't tell you!
172	71.	*Wise Man.* Three pennies?
[173]	72.	*Fool.* Four, and I will tell you!
[174]	73.	*Wise Man.* Very well, four. But I will not call you
[174-175]	74.	Teigue the Fool any longer.

70. ... you. NAR-17.

95. *First Pupil.* Come.

96. *Wise Man.* Were it but true, 'twould alter everything
97.   Until the stream of the world had changed its course,
98.   And that and all our thoughts had run
99.   Into some cloudy thunderous spring
100.   They dream to be its source—
101.   Aye, to some frenzy of the mind;
102.   And all that we have done would be undone,
103.   Our speculation but as the wind.   *[A pause.*
104.   I have dreamed it twice.

105. *First Pupil.* Something has troubled him.

                                        [Pupils go out.

106. *Wise Man.* Twice have I dreamed it in a morning dream,
107.   Now nothing serves my pupils but to come
108.   With a like thought. Reason is growing dim;
109.   A moment more and Frenzy will beat his drum
110.   And laugh aloud and scream;
111.   And I must dance in the dream.
112.   No, no, but it is like a hawk, a hawk of the air,
113.   It has swooped down—and this swoop makes the third—
114.   And what can I, but tremble like a bird?

115. *Fool.* Give me a penny.

116. *Wise Man.* That I should dream it twice, and after that,
117.   that they should pick it out!

---

96. ... true t'would ... everything. **M** ; ... true t'would ('twould
    54-69) ... **53-69.**
98. ... all out thoughts ...
99. ... spring.
100. ... source ... [T]
101. ... mind,
102. Till all that we have done's, undone **M.**
103. Our speculative wind, **M** ; ... speculation as .... **53, 54.**
    Directions in **103.** [lacking] **M.**
108. ... dim. **M-54.**
110. ... scream.
111. ... dream, **M-54.**
113. ... down ... [T] and ... third ... [T] **M.**
117. That ... out. **M** ; ... out. **53-69.**

[176]　75.　*Fool.* Let me come close to you where nobody will hear

[177]　76.　　me. But first you must promise you will not drive

178　77.　　them away. [*Wise Man nods.*] Every day men go out

179　78.　　dressed in black and spread great black nets over the

180　79.　　hills, great black nets.

[181]　80.　*Wise Man.* Why do they do that?

[182-183]　81.　*Fool.* That they may catch the feet of the angels. But

[183-184]　82.　　every morning, just before the dawn, I go out and cut

[184-185]　83.　　the nets with my shears, and the angels fly away.

[186-187]　84.　*Wise Man.* Ah, now I know that you are Teigue the

[187-188]　85.　　Fool. You have told me that I am wise, and I have

[188]　86.　　never seen an angel.

189　87.　*Fool.* I have seen plenty of angels.

88.　*Wise Man.* Do you bring luck to the angels too?

118. *Fool.* Won't you give me a penny?

119. *Wise Man.* What do you want? What can it matter to
120. you whether the words I am reading are wisdom or
121. sheer folly?

122. *Fool.* Such a great, wise teacher will not refuse a penny
123. to a fool.

124. *Wise Man.* Seeing that everybody is a fool when he is
125. asleep and dreaming, why do you call me wise?

126. *Fool.* O, I know,—I know, I know what I have seen.

127. *Wise Man.* Well, to see rightly is the whole of wisdom,
128. whatever dream be with us.

129. *Fool.* When I went by Kilcluan, where the bells used
130. to be ringing at the break of every day, I could hear
131. nothing but the people snoring in their houses.
132. When I went by Tubber-vanach, where the young
133. men used to be climbing the hill to the blessed well,
134. they were sitting at the cross-roads playing cards.
135. When I went by Carrick-orus, where the friars used
136. to be fasting and serving the poor, I saw them
137. drinking wine and obeying their wives. And when
138. I asked what misfortune had brought all these
139. changes, they said it was no misfortune, but that it
140. was the wisdom they had learned from your teaching.

141. *Wise Man.* And you too have called me wise—you
142. would be paid for that good opinion doubtless.—
143. Run to the kitchen; my wife will give you food and
144. drink.

145. *Fool.* That's foolish advice for a wise man to give.

---

120. ... reading, are ... **M-54.**
122. ... great wise ... **M-54.**
126. O, I know, ... [T] I .... **M.**
132. ... Tubbervanach, ... **M-69.**
134. ... crossroads .... **M.**
141. ... wise ... [T] you **M.**
142. ... doubtless .... [T] **M** ; ... doubtless— **53-69.**
143. ... kitchen, my ... **M-69.**
145. ... give, **53.**

[191]   89. *Fool.* O, no, no! No one could do that. But they are
[191-192] 90.   always there if one looks about one; they are like the
[192]   91.   blades of grass.

           92. *Wise Man.* When do you see them?

[196, 198] 93. *Fool.* When one gets quiet, then something wakes up
[198-199] 94.   inside one, something happy and quiet like the stars
           95.   —not like the seven that move, but like the fixed
           96.   stars.

           97. *Wise Man.* And what happens then?

[199-200] 98. *Fool.* Then all in a minute one smells summer flowers,
[200-201] 99.   and tall people go by, happy and laughing, and their
           100.   clothes are the colour of burning sods.

           101. *Wise Man.* Is it long since you have seen them, Teigue
           102.   the fool?

---

93. . . . quiet; then . . . **NAR-16.**
96. stars. [*He points upward.*] **NAR-45.**

146. *Wise Man.* Why, Fool?

147. *Fool.* What is eaten is gone—I want pennies for my
148.   bag. I must buy bacon in the shops, and nuts in the
149.   market, and strong drink for the time the sun is
150.   weak, and snares to catch the rabbits and the hares,
151.   and a big pot to cook them in.

152. *Wise Man.* I have more to think about than giving
153.   pennies to your like, so run away.

154. *Fool.* Give me a penny and I will bring you luck. The
155.   fishermen let me sleep among their nets in the loft
156.   because I bring them luck; and in the summer-time,
157.   the wild creatures let me sleep near their nests and
158.   their holes. It is lucky even to look at me, but it is
159.   much more lucky to give me a penny. If I was not
160.   lucky I would starve.

161. *Wise Man.* What are the shears for?

162. *Fool.* I won't tell you. If I told you, you would drive
163.   them away.

164. *Wise Man.* Drive them away! Whom would I drive
165.   away?

166. *Fool.* I won't tell you.

167. *Wise Man.* Not if I give you a penny?

168. *Fool.* No.

169. *Wise Man.* Not if I give you two pennies?

170. *Fool.* You will be very lucky if you give me two
171.   pennies, but I won't tell you.

172. *Wise Man.* Three pennies?

---

147.   . . . gone . . . [T] I . . . **M.**
150.   . . . rabbits, and . . . , **M-54.**
156.   . . . luck, and . . . summer time, **M-54;** . . . summer time, **57, 69.**
164.   , , , away, who would . . . **M-54;** . . . away! Who would . . . **57, 69.**

[207]   103. *Fool.* Not long, glory be to God! I saw one coming
[208-209]   104.   behind me just now. It was not laughing, but it had
             105.   clothes the colour of burning sods, and there was
             106.   something shining about its head.

[215]   107. *Wise Man.* Well, there are your four pennies. You, a
             108.   Fool, say 'Glory be to God', but before I came the
             109.   wise men said it. Run away now. I must ring the
             110.   bell for my scholars.

             111. *Fool.* Four pennies! That means a great deal of luck.
             112.   Great teacher, I have brought you plenty of luck!
                                            [*He goes out shaking the bag.*

             113. *Wise Man.* Though they call him Teigue the Fool, he is
             114.   not more foolish than everybody used to be, with
             115.   their dreams and their preachings and their three
             116.   worlds; but I have overthrown their three worlds

---

108.   fool, . . . 'glory . . . **NAR, 15, 17-29**; fool, . . . **16, 34-69.**
109.   . . . said it.
110.   [lacking] **29, 34.**

173. *Fool.* Four, and I will tell you.

174. *Wise Man.* Very well—four, but from this out I will
175.   not call you Teigue the Fool.

176. *Fool.* Let me come close to you, where nobody will
177.   hear me; but first you must promise not to drive
178.   them away. [*Wise Man nods.*] Every day men go out
179.   dressed in black and spread great black nets over the
180.   hills, great black nets.

181. *Wise Man.* A strange place that to fish in.

182. *Fool.* They spread them out on the hills that they may
183.   catch the feet of the angels; but every morning, just
184.   before the dawn, I go out and cut the nets with the
185.   shears and the angels fly away.

186. *Wise Man* [*speaking with excitement*]. Ah, now I know that
187.   you are Teigue the Fool. You say that I am wise,
188.   and yet I say there are no angels.

189. *Fool.* I have seen plenty of angels.

190. *Wise Man.* No, no, you have not.

191. *Fool.* They are plenty if you but look about you. They
192.   are like the blades of grass.

193. *Wise Man.* They are plenty as the blades of grass—I
194.   heard that phrase when I was but a child and was
195.   told folly.

196. *Fool.* When one gets quiet. When one is so quiet that
197.   there is not a thought in one's head maybe, there
198.   is something that wakes up inside one, something

---

174. . . . well . . . [T] four, . . . **M.**
175. . . . you, Teigue . . . . **M-54.**
177. . . . me, but . . . **M-54.**
183. . . . morning just **M-69.**
    Directions in 186. [*With some excitement*]. **M.**
187. . . . Fool, You . . . , **53, 54,**
188. . . . say, there **M-69,**
191. . . . you, they **M.**
193. . . . grass . . . [T] I **M,**

117.   with the seven sciences. [*He touches the books with his*
118.   *hands.*] With Philosophy that was made from the
119.   lonely star, I have taught them to forget Theology;
120.   with Architecture, I have hidden the ramparts of
121.   their cloudy Heaven; with Music, the fierce planets'
122.   daughter whose hair is always on fire, and with
123.   Grammar that is the moon's daughter, I have shut
124.   their ears to the imaginary harpings and speech of
125.   the angels; and I have made formations of battle with
126.   Arithmetic that have put the hosts of Heaven to the
127.   rout. But, Rhetoric and Dialectic, that have been
128.   born out of the light star and out of the amorous
129.   star, you have been my spearman and my catapult!
130.   O! my swift horsemen! O! my keen darting argu-
131.   ments, it is because of you that I have overthrown
132.   the hosts of foolishness! [*An Angel, in a dress the colour of embers,*
        and carrying a blossoming apple bough in her hand and a gilded halo
        about her head, stands upon the threshold.]

Directions in 117-118. [lacking] **34.**

118.   . . . made for the **NAR-25, 45.**
121.   . . . heaven; . . . **NAR-69.**
126.   . . . heaven . . . **NAR-69.**
130.   Oh! . . . horseman. Oh! . . . . **15.**
        Directions at 132. [*colour . . . in his hand . . . about his head,* . . . .]
        NAR, 16; [. . . *apple-bough* . . . .] **34.**

199. happy and quiet, and then all in a minute one can
200. smell summer flowers, and tall people go by, happy
201. and laughing, but they will not let us look at their
202. faces. O no, it is not right that we should look at
203. their faces.

204. *Wise Man.* You have fallen asleep upon a hill; yet even
205. those that used to dream of angels dream now of
206. other things.

207. *Fool.* I saw one but a moment ago—that is because I
208. am lucky. It was coming behind me, but it was not
209. laughing.

210. *Wise Man.* There's nothing but what men can see when
211. they are awake. Nothing, nothing.

212. *Fool.* I knew you would drive them away.

213. *Wise Man.* Pardon me, Fool,
214. I had forgotten whom I spoke to.
215. Well, there are your four pennies—Fool you are called,
216. And all day long they cry, 'Come hither, Fool'.

> [*The Fool goes close to him.*

217. Or else it's, 'Fool, be gone'.

> [*The Fool goes further off.*

218. Or, 'Fool, stand there'.

> [*The Fool straightens himself up.*

---

202. .... Oh, no, ... **M-54.**
204. ... hill, yet, even **M-69.**
207. ... ago ... [T] that ... **M.**
212. [set as second hemistich of line of verse] **M.**
214. ... forgotten who I .... **M-57.**
215. ... pennies ... [T] Fool, you ... called **M** ; ... —Fool, you ...
      called **53, 54.**
216. ..., 'come ... , Fool. (Fool.' **53, 54**) **M-54.**
      Directions after 216. [*Fool ....*] **M.**
217. ... gone' **M-54.**
      Directions after 217. [*Fool ....*] **M.**
218. ... there' **M-54.**
      Directions after 218. [*Fool ... himself.*] **M.**

[223]   133.   Before I came, men's minds were stuffed with folly
              134.   about a Heaven where birds sang the hours, and
                      about
[227-228]   135.   angels that came and stood upon men's thresholds.
              136.   But I have locked the visions into Heaven and
                      turned
              137.   the key upon them. Well, I must consider this
                      passage
              138.   about the two countries. My mother used to say
              139.   something of the kind. She would say that when
              140.   our bodies sleep our souls awake, and that whatever
              141.   withers here ripens yonder, and that harvests are
              142.   snatched from us that they may feed invisible people.
              143.   But the meaning of the book may be different, for
              144.   only fools and women have thoughts like that; their
              145.   thoughts were never written upon the walls of Baby-
[239]   146.   lon. [*He sees the Angel.*] What are you? Who are you?
[240]   147.   I think I saw some that were like you in my dreams
[241]   148.   when I was a child—that bright thing, that dress
[243]   149.   that is the colour of embers! But I have done with

---

134.   . . . heaven . . . **NAR-69.**
136.   . . . heaven . . . **NAR-69.**
143.   . . . book must be . . . **NAR-17.**
146.   lon. I must ring the bell for my pupils. [*He* . . . ? **29, 34.**

219.   Or, 'Fool, go sit in the corner'.

> [*The Fool sits in the corner.*
>
> And all the while

220.   What were they all but fools before I came?
221.   What are they now but mirrors that seem men
222.   Because of my image? Fool, hold up your head.

> [*The Fool does so.*

223.   What foolish stories they have told of the ghosts
224.   That fumbled with the clothes upon the bed,
225.   Or creaked and shuffled in the corridor,
226.   Or else, if they were pious bred,
227.   Of angels from the skies,
228.   That coming through the door,
229.   Or, it may be, standing there,
230.   Would solidly out-stare
231.   The steadiest eyes with their unnatural eyes,
232.   Aye, on a man's own floor.

> [*An Angel has come in. It may be played by a man if a man can be
> found with the right voice, and in that case 'she' should be changed to
> 'he' throughout, and may wear a little golden domino and a halo made
> of metal. Or the whole face may be a beautiful mask, in which case
> the sentence in lines 17[1] and 18[1] on page 306[1] should not be spoken.*

---

219.   . . . corner'
        [*Fool . . . in corner.*]
        And . . . **M** ; . . . , 'Fool go . . . corner'
        [*The . . . .*]
        And . . . **53, 54.**
220.   . . . came. **M-54.**
221.   . . . now, but . . . men. (men, **53-57**) **M-57** ; . . . now, but . . . **69.**
222.   . . . image. Fool, ... **M-54** ; . . . ? Fool. hold . . . . **57A.**
        Directions after 222.   [*Fool . . . .*] **M-84.**
228.   That came through a man's door, **M.**
229.   . . . maybe, . . . , **M-54, 57E.**
230.   . . . out stare **M-57.**
232.   Aye, even on his own . . . . **M.**
        Directions after 232.   [*Angel has come in.*] **M** ; [. . . *in. It should be . . .
        voice, and may . . . golden mask and . . . metal.*] **53, 54** ; [. . . *in. It should be
        . . . voice, and may . . . case the last sentence on page 136 should . . . .*] **57** ;
        [. . . *lines 14 and 15 on page 339 should . . . .*] **69E** ; [. . . *lines 17 and 18
        on page 306 should . . . .*] **84** ; [. . . *lines 21 and 22 on page 200 should
        . . . .*] **97A.**

[1] In this edition, lines 202 and 203 on page 595.

[243]   150.   dreams, I have done with dreams.

[244]   151. *Angel.* I am the Angel of the Most High God.

             152. *Wise Man.* Why have you come to me?

[245]   153. *Angel.* I have brought you a message.

[246]   154. *Wise Man.* What message have you got for me?

[247]   155. *Angel.* You will die within the hour. You will die when
[247-248]   156.   the last grains have fallen in this glass. [*She turns the
                         hour-glass.*]

[249-250]   157. *Wise Man.* My time to die has not come. I have my
[248-249]   158.   pupils. I have a young wife and children that I cannot
[249-250]   159.   leave. Why must I die?

[251]   160. *Angel.* You must die because no souls have passed over
[252]   161.   the threshold of Heaven since you came into this
[253]   162.   country. The threshold is grassy, and the gates are
[253-254]   163.   rusty, and the angels that keep watch there are

---

        Directions in 156. [*He turns* . . . **NAR-16.**
161.   . . . heaven . . . **16.**

233. Yet it is strange, the strangest thing I have known,
234. That I should still be haunted by the notion
235. That there's a crisis of the spirit wherein
236. We get new sight, and that they know some trick
237. To turn our thoughts for their own needs to frenzy.
238. Why do you put your finger to your lip,
239. And creep away?   *[The Fool goes out.*
   [Wise Man sees Angel.] What are you? Who are you?
240. I think I saw some like you in my dreams,
241. When but a child. That thing about your head,—
242. That brightness in your hair—that flowery branch;
243. But I have done with dreams, I have done with dreams.

244. *Angel.* I am the crafty one that you have called.

245. *Wise Man.* How that I called?

   Angel.   I am the messenger.

246. *Wise Man.* What message could you bring to one like me?

247. *Angel [turning the hour-glass].* That you will die when the last grain of sand
248. Has fallen through this glass.

   Wise Man.   I have a wife,
249. Children and pupils that I cannot leave:
250. Why must I die, my time is far away?

251. *Angel.* You have to die because no soul has passed

---

235. . . . the soul wherein
236. . . . , and how if when it comes **M.**
237. They have some craft to turn it into frenzy. **M;** . . . own ends to frenzy, (frenzy. **57, 69) 53-69.**
238. . . . lips, **M.**
   Directions in 239. *[Fool . . . .]* **M-84.**
241. . . . head, **M.**
242. . . . hair . . . [T] that . . . branch . . . [T] **M;** . . . branch **53, 54.**
243. . . . dreams . . . [T] I . . . . **M.**
   Directions in 247. [lacking] **M-54.**
248. . . . wife. **57A.**
249. . . . leave, **M-54.**
251. You are to . . . **M.**

[254]   164.   lonely.

[255]   165.   *Wise Man.* Where will death bring me to?

[258]   166.   *Angel.* The doors of Heaven will not open to you, for
[257]   167.   you have denied the existence of Heaven; and the
[256-257] 168.   doors of Purgatory will not open to you, for you have
[256]   169.   denied the existence of Purgatory.

[259]   170.   *Wise Man.* But I have also denied the existence of
[259]   171.   Hell!

[260]   172.   *Angel.* Hell is the place of those who deny.

[265]   173.   *Wise Man* [*kneels*]. I have, indeed, denied everything,
[265-266] 174.   and have taught others to deny. I have believed in

---

166.   . . . heaven . . .
167.   . . . heaven; . . .
168.   . . . purgatory . . .
169.   . . . purgatory. **16.**
171.   hell! **16.**
173.   . . . everything **NAR, 15, 17;** . . . have indeed denied everything **16.**

252. The heavenly threshold since you have opened school,
253. But grass grows there, and rust upon the hinge;
254. And they are lonely that must keep the watch.

255. *Wise Man.* And whither shall I go when I am dead?

256. *Angel.* You have denied there is a Purgatory,
257. Therefore that gate is closed; you have denied
258. There is a Heaven, and so that gate is closed.

259. *Wise Man.* Where then? For I have said there is no Hell.

260. *Angel.* Hell is the place of those who have denied;
261. They find there what they planted and what dug,
262. A Lake of Spaces, and a Wood of Nothing,
263. And wander there and drift, and never cease
264. Wailing for substance.

Wise Man.   Pardon me, blessed Angel,
265. I have denied and taught the like to others.
266. But how could I believe before my sight
267. Had come to me?

Angel.   It is too late for pardon.

268. *Wise Man.* Had I but met your gaze as now I meet it—
269. But how can you that live but where we go
270. In the uncertainty of dizzy dreams
271. Know why we doubt? Parting, sickness, and death,
272. The rotting of the grass, tempest, and drouth,

---

256. ... denied the purgatorial fire **M** ; ... purgatory, **53-69.**
258. That there's a heaven, and that . . . . **M** ; ... heaven, ... **53-69.**
259. ... then? I have denied there is a hell **M** ; ... hell. **53-69.**
260. ... denied, **M.**
262. ... lake ... spaces, ... wood ... nothing,
263. ... drift and ... cease, **M.**
266. Believing nothing but what sense has taught,
267. And the mind's abstract.
                       It . . . . **M.**
268. ... but seen your face as ... I see it, **M-54** ; ... I met it— **57.**
269. ... you ... [T] that ... go,
270. ... dreams ... [T] **M.**
271. ... doubt. Parting, disease and . . . , **M** ; . . . doubt. Parting, sickness
and . . . , **53, 54** ; . . . , sickness and . . . , **57.**
272. . . . , tempest and . . . , **M-57.**

	175.	nothing but what my senses told me. But, O!
[264]	176.	beautiful angel, forgive me, forgive me!
[267]	177.	*Angel.* You should have asked forgiveness long ago.
[268]	178.	*Wise Man.* Had I seen your face as I see it now, O!
	179.	beautiful angel, I would have believed, I would have
[269]	180.	asked forgiveness. Maybe you do not know how easy
[271]	181.	it is to doubt. Storm, death, the grass rotting, many
[272-273]	182.	sicknesses, those are the messengers that came to me.
[274]	183.	O! why are you silent? You carry the pardon of the
[275, 277]	184.	Most High; give it to me! I would kiss your hands if
[276, 277]	185.	I were not afraid—no, no, the hem of your dress!
	186.	*Angel.* You let go undying hands too long ago to take
	187.	hold of them now.
[285]	188.	*Wise Man.* You cannot understand. You live in a

---

175. . . . , oh! **NAR-69.**

176. . . . Angel, . . . ! **NAR-34.**

178. . . . , oh! **16-69.**

179. . . . Angel, . . . **NAR-17.**

188. . . . in that **NAR-29.**

188a. country people only see in their dreams. You live in a **NAR-17.**

273. These are the messengers that came to me.
274. Why are you silent? You carry in your hands
275. God's pardon, and you will not give it me.
276. Why are you silent? Were I not afraid,
277. I'd kiss your hands—no, no, the hem of your dress.

278. *Angel*. Only when all the world has testified,
279. May soul confound it, crying out in joy,
280. And laughing on its lonely precipice.
281. What's dearth and death and sickness to the soul
282. That knows no virtue but itself? Nor could it,
283. So trembling with delight and mother-naked,
284. Live unabashed if the arguing world stood by.

285. *Wise Man*. It is as hard for you to understand
286. Why we have doubted as it is for us
287. To banish doubt.—What folly have I said?
288. There can be nothing that you do not know.
289. Give me a year—a month—a week—a day,
290. I would undo what I have done—an hour—
291. Give me until the sand has run in the glass.

292. *Angel*. Though you may not undo what you have done,
293. I have this power—if you but find one soul,
294. Before the sands have fallen, that still believes,
295. One fish to lie and spawn among the stones
296. Till the great Fisher's net is full again,

---

274. . . . hands, **M.**
275. . . . me, **M-54.**
277. . . . hands, no, ... **M-54.**
279. . . . joy.
280. [lacking] **M.**
281. . . . soul,
282. . . . itself, nor . . . , **M-54.**
283. . . . mother naked, **M.**
285. . . . is so hard . . . **M.**
286. . . . doubted, as . . . **M-69.**
287. To put our doubts away . . . [T] what have . . . said, **M** ; . . . doubt—
   what . . . ? **53-69.**
288. . . . know, **M-54** ; . . . know: **57, 69.**
289. . . . year . . . [T] a month . . . [T] a week . . . [T] a . . . ,
290. . . . done . . . [T] an hour . . . [T] **M.**
293. . . . power . . . [T] if . . . , **M.**
294. That still believes that it shall never cease, **M-54.**
296. . . . fisher's . . . , **M-69.**

[285]	189.	country that we can only dream about. Maybe it is
[286]	190.	as hard for you to understand why we disbelieve as
[287]	191.	it is for us to believe. O! what have I said? You
[288-289]	192.	know everything! Give me time to undo what I have
[289]	193.	done. Give me a year—a month—a day—an hour!
[290-291]	194.	Give me to this hour's end, that I may undo what I
[290]	195.	have done!

[292]	196.	*Angel.* You cannot undo what you have done. Yet I
[293]	197.	have this power with my message. If you can find one
[294]	198.	that believes before the hour's end, you shall come to
[297]	199.	Heaven after the years of Purgatory. For, from one
	200.	fiery seed, watched over by those that sent me, the
	201.	harvest can come again to heap the golden threshing-
[308-309]	202.	floor. But now farewell, for I am weary with the

---

189. country people only see in their dreams. Maybe . . . **29.**
191. . . . . Oh! . . . said! You **NAR-69,**
199. heaven . . . purgatory. . . . . **16.**
201. . . . threshing **NAR, 17-29, 45, 69,**
202. . . . weary of the **NAR-34.**

297. You may, the purgatorial fire being passed,
298. Spring to your peace.

Pupils sing in the distance.

299.   Who stole your wits away
300.   And where are they gone?

301. *Wise Man.*   My pupils come.
302. Before you have begun to climb the sky
303. I shall have found that soul. They say they doubt,
304. But what their mothers dinned into their ears
305. Cannot have been so lightly rooted up;
306. Besides, I can disprove what I once proved—
307. And yet give me some thought, some argument,
308. More mighty than my own.

Angel.   Farewell—farewell,
309. For I am weary of the weight of time.

[*Angel goes out. Wise Man makes a step to follow and pauses. Some of his Pupils come in at the other side of the stage.*

310. *First Pupil.* Master, Master, you must choose the subject.
[*Enter other Pupils with Fool, about whom they dance; all the Pupils may have little cushions on which presently they seat themselves.*

311. *Second Pupil.* Here is a subject—Where have the Fool's wits gone?
[*singing.*

---

299. 'Who . . .
300. . . . gone?' **M-57.**
301. . . . come, **M-57, 69E.**
303. . . . found belief . . . [T] they . . . , **M.**
305. Has not been broken down . . . [T] I have long thought it, **M ;** . . .
      up, **53, 54.**
306. . . . proved, **M.**
308. . . . .
      Farewell . . . [T] farewell, **M.**
      Directions after 309. [. . . *out, Wise . . . Step . . . pauses. Pupils . . . at
      other side.*] **M.**
310. Master, master, you . . . . **53-69.**
      Directions after 310. [. . . *dance.*] **M.**
311. . . . subject . . . [T] where . . . ? **M ;** . . . subject—where . . . ? **53-69.**

[309]   203.   weight of time.

204.   *Wise Man.* Blessed be the Father, blessed be the Son,
205.   blessed be the Spirit, blessed be the Messenger They
206.   have sent!

207.   *Angel* [*at the door, and pointing at the hour-glass*]. In a little
208.   while the uppermost glass will be empty.

                                              [*Goes out.*

209.   *Wise Man.* Everything will be well with me. I will call
210.   my pupils; they only say they doubt. [*Pulls the bell.*]
211.   They will be here in a moment. I hear their feet out-
212.   side on the path. They want to please me; they pre-
213.   tend that they disbelieve. Belief is too old to be
214.   overcome all in a minute. Besides I can prove what
215.   I once disproved. [*Another pull at the bell.*] They are
216.   coming now. I will go to my desk. I will speak

Directions in 207.   [. . . *door and* . . . .] **NAR-34.**
211.   . . . moment.
212.   They want . . . **29, 34.**
214.   . . . . Besides, I . . . **16, 29, 34.**

312.	Who dragged your wits away
313.	Where no one knows?
314.	Or have they run off
315.	On their own pair of shoes?

316. *Fool.* Give me a penny.

317. *First Pupil.* The Master will find your wits.

318. *Second Pupil.* And when they are found, you must not
319.   beg for pennies.

320. *Third Pupil.* They are hidden somewhere in the badger's hole,
321.   But you must carry an old candle-end
322.   If you would find them.

323. *Fourth Pupil.* They are up above the clouds.

324. *Fool.* Give me a penny, give me a penny.

First Pupil [*singing*].

325.	I'll find your wits again.
326.	Come, for I saw them roll
327.	To where old badger mumbles
328.	In the black hole.

Second Pupil [*singing*].

329.	No, but an angel stole them
330.	The night that you were born,
331.	And now they are but a rag
332.	On the moon's horn.

333. *Wise Man.* Be silent.

---

312.   'Who ... **M-57.**
315.   ... pairs ... shoes?' **M** ; ... shoes?' **53-57.**
317.   ... wits, **53-57.**
321.   ... candle end, (end **57, 69**) **M-69.**
324.   ... penny, ... penny, Teigue. **M.**
325.   'I'll ... again, **M-57** ; ... again, **69E.**
326.   ... roll, **M-69.**
328.   ... hole.' **53-57.**
329.   'No, ... **M-57.**
331.   ... rag, **M-69.**
332.   ... horn.' **53-57.**

217.   quietly, as if nothing had happened.

>   [*He stands at the desk with a fixed look in his eyes.*
>
>   *Enter Pupils and the Fool*

218.   *Fool.* Leave me alone. Leave me alone. Who is that
219.   pulling at my bag? King's son, do not pull at my
220.   bag.

221.   *A Young Man.* Did your friends the angels give you that
222.   bag? Why don't they fill your bag for you?

Directions after 217.   [. . . *eyes. The voices of the pupils are heard outside singing (heard singing* **34**) *these words.*] **29, 34.**
217a.   I was going the road one day, (day— **34**)
217b.   O the brown and the yellow beer, (beer— **34**)
217c.   And I met with a man that was no right man (man: **34**)
217d.   O my dear, O my dear. (dear! **34**) **29, 34.**
     Directions after 217d.   [*The sound grows louder as they come nearer, but ceases on the threshold.*] **29.**

334. *First Pupil.* Can you not see that he is troubled?

[*All the Pupils are seated.*]

335. *Wise Man.* Nullum esse deum dixi, nullam dei matrem:
336.   mentitus vero: nam recte intelligenti sunt et
337.   deus et dei mater.

338. *First Pupil.* Argumentis igitur proba; nam argumenta
339.   poscit qui rationis est particeps.

340. *Wise Man.* Pro certo habeo e vobis unum quidem in
341.   fide perstitisse, unum altius quam me vidisse.

342. *Second Pupil.* You answer for us.

    Third Pupil [*in a whisper to First Pupil*]. Be careful what you say;
343.   If he persuades you to an argument,
344.   He will but turn us all to mockery.

345. *First Pupil.* We had no minds until you made them for us.

    Directions after 334.   [lacking] **M.**
334a. *Wise Man.* What do you think of when alone at night?
334b. Do not the things your mothers spoke about (about, **57**)
334c. Before they took the candle from the bedside,
334d. Rush up into the mind and master it,
334e. Till you believe in them against your will? **M-57.**
335-341. [lacking] **M-57.**
  342. *2nd Pupil* [*to 1st pupil*]. You . . . .
    3rd Pupil [*in a whisper*].

                           Be . . . say. **M ;**
    Second Pupil [*to first pupil*]. You . . . .
    Third Pupil [*in . . . .*]   . . . say (say; **57**) **53-57 ;**
    Third Pupil. You answer . . . us.

    Third Pupil [*in . . . .*] Be . . . . say; **69.**

  343. . . . argument **M-54.**
  344. He will make a mock of you and us. **M.**
  345. *1st Pupil.* You have made our minds, **M ;** . . . us; **53-57.**
345a. Our bodies only, (only **53-57**) were our mother's (mothers' **57A**) work.
345b. *Wise Man.* You answer with incredible things. It is certain
345c. That there is one, . . . [T] though (one,— though **53-57**) it may be but one . . . [T] (one— **53-57**)
345d. Believes in God and in some heaven and hell. (hell— **53-57**) **M-57.**

[316]   223. *Fool.* Give me pennies! Give me some pennies!

224. *A Young Man.* What do you want pennies for? That
225.   great bag at your waist is heavy.

[148]   226. *Fool.* I want to buy bacon in the shops, and nuts in the
[149]   227.   market, and strong drink for the time when the sun
[150]   228.   is weak, and snares to catch rabbits and the squirrels
[151]   229.   that steal the nuts, and hares, and a great pot to cook
[151]   230.   them in.

231. *A Young Man.* Why don't your friends tell you where
232.   buried treasures are?

233. *Another.* Why don't they make you dream about
234.   treasures? If one dreams three times there is always
235.   treasure.

---

224.   Let go his cloak, it is coming to pieces. **NAR-16**; . . . for, that **17**,
        25, 45, 69; . . . for?—that **29**; . . . ? that **34**.
224a.   What do you want pennies for, with that **NAR-16**.
225.   . . . waist? **NAR-16**; . . . heavy? **17, 25, 45, 69**.
231-235.   [All these lines spoken by *A Young Man*.] **29, 34**.
234.   . . . times, there . . . **16**.

346. *Wise Man.* Quae destruxi necesse est omnia reaedificem.

347. *First Pupil.* Haec rationibus nondum natis opinabamur:
348.   nunc vero adolevimus: exuimus incunabula.

349. *Wise Man.* You are afraid to tell me what you think
350.   Because I am hot and angry when I am crossed.
351.   I do not blame you for it; but have no fear,
352.   For if there's one that sat on smiling there
353.   As though my arguments were sweet as milk,
354.   Yet found them bitter, I will thank him for it,
355.   If he but speak his mind.

    First Pupil.   There is no one, Master.
356.   There is not one but found them sweet as milk.

357. *Wise Man.* The things that have been told us in our childhood
358.   Are not so fragile.

    Second Pupil.   We are not children now.

359. *First Pupil.* Non iam pueri sumus; corpus tantummodo
360.   ex matre fictum est.

361. *Second Pupil.* Docuisti; et nobis persuadetur.

362. *Wise Man.* Mendaciis vos imbui, mentisque simulacris.

345e. In all those things we put into our prayers.
345f. *First Pupil.* We thought those things before our minds were
       born (born, **53-57**).
345g. But that was long ago . . . [T] we (ago—we **53-57**) are not children.
       M-57.
346-348. [lacking] **M-57.**
 348. . . . Vero . . . . **69.**
 350. . . . crossed, **M-54.**
 351. . . . it, but . . . fear, (fear **53, 54**) **M-54**; . . . fear **69.**
 352. . . . if there is one . . . smilling . . . **M**; . . . there, **53-69.**
 353. . . . milk **M-69.**
 355. . . . one Master, **M**; . . . , Master, **53-69.**
 358. . . . are no longer children. **M-57.**
359-360. [lacking] **M-57.**
 361. *Third Pupil.* We all believe in you and in what you have taught.
       M-57.
362-363. [lacking] **M-57.**
 362. Mendacia vobis imbui . . . simulacra. **69, 84.**

[324]   236. *Fool* [*holding out his hat*]. Give me pennies! Give me
[324]   237.   pennies!
         [*They throw pennies into his hat. He is standing close to the
         door, that he may hold out his hat to each newcomer.*
         238. *A Young Man.* Master, will you have Teigue the Fool
         239.   for a scholar?
         240. *Another Young Man.* Teigue, will you give us your
         241.   pennies if we teach you lessons? No, he goes to
         242.   school for nothing on the mountains. Tell us what
         243.   you learn on the mountains, Teigue?
[333]   244. *Wise Man.* Be silent all! [*He has been standing silent, looking
         245.   away.*] Stand still in your places, for there is some-
         246.   thing I would have you tell me.
         [*A moment's pause. They all stand round in their places.
         Teigue still stands at the door.*

243. ..., Teigue. **29.**
244. ... all. [*He* ... **NAR-16.**

363. *Second Pupil.* Nulli non persuasisti.

364. *Other Pupils* [*speaking together*]. Nulli, nulli, nulli.

365. *Wise Man.* I have deceived you—where shall I go for words?—
366.   I have no thoughts—my mind has been swept bare.
367.   The messengers that stand in the fiery cloud
368.   Fling themselves out, if we but dare to question,
369.   And after that the Babylonian moon
370.   Blots all away.

    First Pupil [*to other Pupils*]. I take his words to mean
371.   That visionaries and martyrs, when they are raised
372.   Above translunary things, and there enlightened,
373.   As the contention is, may lose the light,
374.   And flounder in their speech when the eyes open.

375. *Second Pupil.* How well he imitates their trick of speech.

376. *Third Pupil.* Their air of mystery.

    Fourth Pupil.   Their empty gaze
377.   As though they'd looked upon some wingéd thing,
378.   And would not condescend to mankind after.

379. *First Pupil.* Master, we all have learnt that truth is learnt
380.   When the intellect's deliberate and cold,
381.   As it were a polished mirror that reflects
382.   An unchanged world; not when the steel dissolves

---

364. *Other Pupils.* All, all, all, all, in you, nothing but you. **M-57.**
365. . . . you . . . [T] where . . . words, **M** ; . . . words—**53-69.**
366. . . . have not thoughts . . . [T] my . . . . **M.**
367. . . . cloud, **M-69.**
369. . . . that, the . . . moon, (moon **53-69**) **M-69.**
371. . . . visionaries, and martyrs when . . . **M-69.**
373. . . . light.
374. And blunder in . . . . **M.**
376. . . . mystery,
          Their . . . gaze, **M** ; . . . gaze, **53-57** ; . . . gaze. **69.**
377. . . . winged . . . , **M-69.**
379. . . . , we have all learnt . . . **53.**
382. . . . world; and not . . . steel melts, **M-57.**

247. *Wise Man.* Is there any one amongst you who believes
248.   in God? In Heaven? Or in Purgatory? Or in Hell?

249. *All the Young Men.* No one, Master! No one!

250. *Wise Man.* I knew you would all say that; but do not
[351] 251.   be afraid. I will not be angry. Tell me the truth. Do
252.   you not believe?

[345] 253. *A Young Man.* We once did, but you have taught us to
254.   know better.

255. *Wise Man.* O! teaching, teaching does not go very deep!
256.   The heart remains unchanged under it all. You have
[349] 257.   the faith that you always had, and you are afraid to
[349] 258.   tell me.

259. *A Young Man.* No, no, Master!

---

247. . . . anyone . . . **16, 29.**
248. . . . heaven? . . . purgatory? . . . hell? **16.**
255. Oh, teaching! teaching . . . ! **29.**
256. . . . . You believe **NAR-25.**
257. just as you always did, and . . . **NAR-25 ;** . . . you have always . . . **29.**
259. . . . , Master. **16.**

383.   Bubbling and hissing, till there's naught but fume.

384. *Wise Man.* When it is melted, when it all fumes up,
385.   They walk as when beside those three in the furnace
386.   The form of the fourth.

         First Pupil.   Master, there's none among us
387.   That has not heard your mockery of these,
388.   Or thoughts like these, and we have not forgot.

389. *Wise Man.* Something incredible has happened—some one has
             come
390.   Suddenly like a grey hawk out of the air,
391.   And all that I declared untrue is true.

392. *First Pupil* [*to other Pupils*]. You'd think, the way he says it, that
             he felt it.
393.   There's not a mummer to compare with him.
394.   He's something like a man.

395. *Second Pupil.* Argumentum, domine, profer.

396. *Wise Man.* What proof have I to give, but that an angel
397.   An instant ago was standing on that spot?

                                        [*The Pupils rise.*

398. *Third Pupil.* You dreamed it.

      Wise Man.   I was awake as I am now.

399. *First Pupil* [*to the others*]. I may be dreaming now for all I know.
400.   He wants to show we have no certain proof

---

385.   . . . walk, as . . . **M-69.**
389.   . . . happened . . . [T] someone . . . come, **M ;** . . . —someone . . .
         come, **53, 54.**
392.   . . . think the . . . felt it, (it. **54, 57, 69E**) **M-57, 69E.**
393.   . . . him, **M.**
394.   . . . man.
         Second Pupil. Give us some proof. **M-57.**
395.   [lacking] **M-57.**
397.   . . . spot. **M-69.**
         Directions after 397.   [lacking] **M.**
398.   . . . it, Master.
                        I . . . . **M-54.**

[354-355] 260. *Wise Man.* If you tell me that you have not changed, I
[354-355] 261.   shall be glad and not angry.

262. *A Young Man* [*to his Neighbour*]. He wants somebody to
263.   dispute with.

264. *His Neighbour.* I knew that from the beginning.

265. *A Young Man.* That is not the subject for to-day; you
266.   were going to talk about the words the beggar wrote
267.   upon the walls of Babylon.

268. *Wise Man.* If there is one amongst you that has not
269.   changed, he will be my best friend. Surely there is
[357-358] 270.   one amongst you. [*They are all silent.*] Surely what you
[357-358] 271.   learned at your mothers' knees has not been so soon

---

260.   . . . that you believe I **NAR-25** ; . . . changed I **34-69.**
268.   . . . that believes,
269.   he . . . **NAR-34.**
271.   . . . mother's . . . **NAR-69.**

401.   Of anything in the world.

Second Pupil.   There is this proof
402.   That shows we are awake—we have all one world
403.   While every dreamer has a world of his own,
404.   And sees what no one else can.

Third Pupil.   Teigue sees angels.
405.   So when the Master says he has seen an angel,
406.   He may have seen one.

First Pupil.   Both may still be dreamers,
407.   Unless it's proved the angels were alike.

408. *Second Pupil.* What sort are the angels, Teigue?

Third Pupil.   That will prove nothing,
409.   Unless we are sure prolonged obedience
410.   Has made one angel like another angel
411.   As they were eggs.

First Pupil.   The Master's silent now:
412.   For he has found that to dispute with us—
413.   Seeing that he has taught us what we know—
414.   Is but to reason with himself. Let us away,
415.   And find if there is one believer left.

416. *Wise Man.* Yes, Yes. Find me but one that still can say:
417.   Credo in patrem et filium et spiritum sanctum.

418. *Third Pupil.* He'll mock and maul him.

Fourth Pupil.   From the first I knew

---

401. . . . proof, **M-54.**
402. . . . awake . . . [T] we . . . **M.**
406. . . . dreamers. **M-54** ; . . . dreamers; **57-84.**
408. . . . nothing. **M-54.**
409. For all we know, prolonged . . . **M** ; . . . sure, prolonged . . . **53, 54.**
410. . . . angel, **M-54.**
412. . . . us . . . [T]
413. . . . know . . . [T] **M.**
416. . . . , yes. . . . still believes **M-57** ; . . . , yes. . . . : **69A.**
417. The things that we were told when we were children. **M-57.**
418. Our Master'll mock . . . .
                    . . . first **M.**

272.   forgotten.

273. *A Young Man.* Master, till you came, no teacher in this
274.   land was able to get rid of foolishness and ignorance.
275.   But every one has listened to you, every one has
276.   learned the truth. You have had your last disputa-
277.   tion.

278. *Another.* What a fool you made of that monk in the
279.   market-place! He had not a word to say.

280. *Wise Man* [*comes from his desk and stands among them in the
         middle of the room*]. Pupils, dear friends, I have
281.   deceived you all this time. It was I myself who was
282.   ignorant. There is a God. There is a Heaven. There is
283.   fire that passes and there is fire that lasts for ever.
         [*Teigue, through all this, is sitting on a stool by the door,
         reckoning on his fingers what he will buy with his money.*

284. *A Young Man* [*to another*]. He will not be satisfied till we
285.   dispute with him. [*To the Wise Man*] Prove it, Master.
286.   Have you seen them?

287. *Wise Man* [*in a low, solemn voice*]. Just now, before you
[389] 288.   came in, some one came to the door, and when I
[397] 289.   looked up I saw an angel standing there.

[398] 290. *A Young Man.* You were in a dream. Anybody can see
291.   an angel in his dreams.

[398] 292. *Wise Man.* O, my God! It was not a dream! I was
[398] 293.   awake, waking as I am now. I tell you I was awake
294.   as I am now.

[399] 295. *A Young Man.* Some dream when they are awake, but
296.   they are the crazy, and who would believe what they
297.   say? Forgive me, Master, but that is what you taught
298.   me to say. That is what you said to the monk when he
299.   spoke of the visions of the saints and the martyrs.

---

282.   . . . heaven. . . . **16.**
283.   . . . forever. **NAR, 15, 69A** ; . . . passes, and . . . . **16, 34.**
288.   . . . , someone . . . **17-45.**
292.   Oh, . . . dream. I . . . **16.**
296.   . . . crazy and . . . **NAR, 15.**

419. He wanted somebody to argue with. [*They go.*

420. *Wise Man.* I have no reason left. All dark, all dark!
      [*Pupils return laughing. They push forward Fourth Pupil.*

421. *First Pupil.* Here, Master, is the very man you want.
422. He said, when we were studying the book,
423. That maybe after all the monks were right,
424. And you mistaken, and if we but gave him time,
425. He'd prove that it was so.

Fourth Pupil.   I never said it.

426. *Wise Man.* Dear friend, dear friend, do you believe in God?

427. *Fourth Pupil.* Master, they have invented this to mock me.

428. *Wise Man.* You are afraid of me.

Fourth Pupil.   They know well, Master,
429. That all I said was but to make them argue.
430. They've pushed me in to make a mock of me,
431. Because they knew I could take either side
432. And beat them at it.

Wise Man.   If you can say the creed
433. With but a grain, a mustard-grain of faith,
434. You are my soul's one friend.   [*Pupils laugh.*
                                 Mistress or wife
435. Can give us but our good or evil luck
436. Amid the howling world, but you shall give
437. Eternity, and those sweet-throated things

---

419. I knew he'd have us find some disputant. **M.**
420. . . . left, all . . . dark. **M-54.**
423. . . . right. **M.**
426. . . . Friend, . . . Friend, . . . ? **M.**
428. . . . , Master. **M.**
431. . . . side, **M ;** . . . they know I . . . **97A.**
432. . . . you believe in God, **M-57.**
433. [lacking] **M-57 ;** . . . mustard grain . . . , **69.**
434. . . . wife,
435. . . . luck, **M.**
437. Eternity . . . [T] and . . . sweet throated . . . **M.**

300. *Another Young Man.* You see how well we remember
301. your teaching.

[448, 440] 302. *Wise Man.* Out, out from my sight! I want somebody
[441] 303. who has not changed. That is the grain the angel
304. spoke of—I must find it before I die. I tell you I
[446] 305. must find it. The sands are falling there and you
[447-448] 306. answer me with arguments. Out with you, out of
[448] 307. my sight!   [*The Young Men laugh.*

308. *A Young Man.* How well he plays at faith! He is like
309. the monk when he had nothing more to say.

[447] 310. *Wise Man.* Out, out, this is no time for laughter! Out
311. with you, though you are a king's son!
                                    [*They begin to hurry out.*

312. *A Young Man.* Come, come; he wants us to find some
[419] 313. one who will dispute with him.   [*All go out.*

[449] 314. *Wise Man* [*alone; he goes to the door at the side*]. I will call
[449, 453] 315. my wife. She will believe; women always believe.
[452] 316. [*He opens the door and calls.*] Bridget! Bridget! [*Bridget
comes in wearing her apron, her sleeves turned up from her
[444] 317. floury arms.*] Bridget, tell me the truth; do not say
[456, 457] 318. what you think will please me. Do you sometimes
[457, 458] 319. say your prayers?

[459] 320. *Bridget.* Prayers! No, you taught me to leave them off
[460] 321. long ago. At first I was sorry, but I am glad now, for
[461] 322. I am sleepy in the evenings.

---

302. . . . want some one (someone **29, 34**) **NAR-34.**
303. with belief. I must find that grain . . . Angel
304. . . . of before . . .
305. . . . it, and you **NAR-34.**
306. . . . you, or I
307. will beat you with my stick! [*The* . . . .] **NAR-25.**
310. . . . , out, or I will lay this stick about your shoulders! Out **NAR-25;**
      Out, out! This . . . **34.**
311. . . . King's . . . ! **NAR-16.**
312. . . . someone
313. who . . . . **29-45.**
      Directions in 314. [*Alone. He* . . . .] **16.**
321. . . . now for **NAR, 15, 17, 25, 34-69.**
322. . . . evening. **29.**

438.   That drift above the moon.

          [Pupils look at one another and are silent.

Second Pupil.   How strange he is!

439. *Wise Man.* The angel that stood there upon that spot
440.   Said that my soul was lost unless I found
441.   One that had faith.

    Fourth Pupil.   Cease mocking at me, Master,
442.   For I am certain that there is no God
443.   Nor immortality, and they that said it
444.   Made a fantastic tale from a starved dream
445.   To plague our hearts. Will that content you, Master?

446. *Wise Man.* The giddy glass is emptier every moment,
447.   And you stand there, debating, laughing and wrangling.
448.   Out of my sight! Out of my sight, I say.

                        [He drives them out.

449.   I'll call my wife, for what can women do,
450.   That carry us in the darkness of their bodies,
451.   But mock the reason that lets nothing grow
452.   Unless it grow in light? Bridget, Bridget!
453.   A woman never gives up all her faith,

---

438.   . . . moon. [*Pupils are* . . . .]

                  . . . is. **M** ; . . . moon. [*The pupils* . . . .]

                              . . . is. **53-69.**

    Directions in 438.   [*The pupils* . . . .] **84.**

439.   . . . spot, **M-69.**
440.   . . . found, . . . [T] **M** ; . . . found, **53, 54** ; . . . found out **57.**
440a.   Before the sands in the hour-glass had run out . . . [T] **M** ;
       Before the sands in the Hour-glass had run out, **53, 54.**
441.   . . . that believed.

                   Cease . . . , Master. (Master, **54, 57**) **M-57.**

442.   I am so certain . . . God,
443.   I'll curse him if you will, and after curse
444.   The soul that has been made after his image . . . [T] **M.**
445.   If but their lies were true. Will that convince you **M** ; . . . your
       master? **53, 54.**
445a.   That I have set my heart on what you teach? **M.**
452.   . . . light. Bridget, Bridget, (Bridget. **53-69**) **M-69.**
453.   [lacking] **M** ; . . . never ceases to believe. (believe, **57**) **53-57.**

[462]   323. *Wise Man.* But do you not believe in God?

[463-464]   324. *Bridget.* O, a good wife only believes what her husband
[463-464]   325. tells her!

[465-466]   326. *Wise Man.* But sometimes when you are alone, when I
[465-466]   327. am in the school and the children asleep, do you not
[467-468]   328. think about the saints, about the things you used to
[468]   329. believe in? What do you think of when you are
             330. alone?

[469]   331. *Bridget* [*considering*]. I think about nothing. Sometimes
[469-470]   332. I wonder if the linen is bleaching white, or I go out
[470-471]   333. to see if the crows are picking up the chickens' food.

[472]   334. *Wise Man.* O, what can I do! Is there nobody who
[475]   335. believes he can never die? I must go and find some-
             336. body! [*He goes towards the door, but stops with his eyes*
[477]   337. *fixed on the hour-glass.*] I cannot go out; I cannot leave
[478]   338. that. Go and call my pupils again. I will make them
[480]   339. understand. I will say to them that only amid spiritual
[479]   340. terror or only when all that laid hold on life is shaken
[480-481]   341. can we see truth. There is something in Plato, but
[487]   342. —No, do not call them. They would answer as I have
[487]   343. bid.

488   344. *Bridget.* You want somebody to get up an argument
489   345. with.

[490]   346. *Wise Man.* O, look out of the door and tell me if there

---

326. . . . sometimes, when . . . **29.**
332. . . . the pig is fattening well, or . . . **NAR-16.**
333. . . . chicken's . . . . **NAR, 15.**
335. believes? I . . . **NAR-25.**
      Directions in 336. [. . . *toward . . . door but* . . . .] **16.**
338. that! **NAR-17**; that. **25**; that; go . . . again—I . . . **29** ; . . . . . Go, and
      . . . **34.**
339-343. [lacking] **NAR-25.**
339. understand—I . . . **29.**
340. terror, or . . . **29, 34.**
341. . . . truth—but **29.**
342. no, . . . them, they . . . **29**; —no, . . . **34.**

454.   Say what we will. Bridget, come quickly, Bridget.

        [Bridget comes in wearing her apron. Her sleeves are turned up from
          her arms, which are covered with flour.]

455.   Wife, what do you believe in? Tell me the truth,
456.   And not—as is the habit with you all—
457.   Something you think will please me. Do you pray?
458.   Sometimes when you're alone in the house, do you pray?

459. *Bridget.* Prayers—no, you taught me to leave them off
460.   long ago. At first I was sorry, but I am glad now,
461.   for I am sleepy in the evenings.

462. *Wise Man.* Do you believe in God?

463. *Bridget.* O, a good wife only believes in what her
464.   husband tells her.

465. *Wise Man.* But sometimes, when the children are asleep
466.   And I am in the school, do you not think
467.   About the martyrs and the saints and the angels,
468.   And all the things that you believed in once?

469. *Bridget.* I think about nothing. Sometimes I wonder if
470.   the linen is bleaching white, or I go out to see if the
471.   crows are picking up the chickens' food.

472. *Wise Man.* My God,—my God! I will go out myself.
473.   My pupils said that they would find a man

---

454. . . . will . . . [T] Bridget, ... **M ;** . . . will—Bridget, ... **53, 54.**
    Directions after 454. [. . . *sleeves turned . . . her floury arms.*] **M-54 ;**
    [. . . *sleeves turned . . . arms which . . . .*] **57 ;** [. . . *arms which . . . .*] **69.**
455. . . . ? Tell the . . . ,
456. . . . not . . . [T] as . . . all . . . [T] **M.**
457. . . . pray **M-54.**
459. Prayers . . . [T] no, . . . **M.**
460. . . . now **84.**
465. . . . asleep, **M.**
467. . . . Martyrs . . . saints and angels, **M ;** . . . Martyrs . . . , **53-57.**
469. . . . nothing . . . [T] sometimes . . . **M ;** . . . nothing—sometimes . . .
    53-69.
471. . . . chicken's . . . . **53-57.**
472. . . . God . . . [T] my . . . . **M.**
473. . . . said they . . . **97A.**

[490-491] 347.   is anybody there in the street. I cannot leave this
[491-492] 348.   glass; somebody might shake it! Then the sand
[493]   349.   would fall more quickly.

[494]   350.   *Bridget.* I don't understand what you are saying.
[495]   351.   [*Looks out.*] There is a great crowd of people talking
[495]   352.   to your pupils.

[496]   353.   *Wise Man.* O, run out, Bridget, and see if they have
[497-498] 354.   found somebody that, all the time I was teaching,
[497-498] 355.   understood nothing or did not listen!

[499]   356.   *Bridget* [*wiping her arms in her apron and pulling down her*
                        sleeves]. It's a hard thing to be married to a man of
[500]   357.   learning that must be always having arguments.
           358.   [*Goes out and shouts through the kitchen door.*] Don't be
           359.   meddling with the bread, children, while I'm out.

           360.   *Wise Man* [*kneels down*]. '*Confiteor Deo Omnipotenti, beatae*
           361.   *Mariae—salvum—salvum . . .*' I have forgotten it all.
           362.   It is thirty years since I have said a prayer. I must
           363.   pray in the common tongue, like the clown begging
           364.   in the market, like Teigue the Fool! [*He prays.*] Help
           365.   me, Father, Son and Spirit!
                   [*Bridget enters, followed by the Fool, who is holding out*
                   his hat to her.]

505   366.   *Fool.* Give me something; give me a penny to buy
[506]   367.   bacon in the shops, and nuts in the market, and
[507]   368.   strong drink for the time when the sun grows weak.

---

347.   . . . street! I . . . **29.**
354.   . . . that believes! **NAR-25 ;** . . . that all . . . time while I . . . teaching
        29 ; . . . that all . . . teaching **34.**
355.   [lacking] **NAR-25 ;** . . . listen. **29.**
356.   . . . .] It is a . . . **69A.**
360.   [. . . *down*]. '*Salvum me fac, Deus*— **NAR-25 ;** . . . *omnipotente* (*Omni-*
        potenti **34**) *beatae,* **29, 34.**
361.   *salvum—salvum* . . . .' [T] I . . . **NAR-25 ;**
        Mariae . . . . [T] I . . . . **29, 34.**
363.   . . . like a clown . . . **NAR-69.**
365.   . . . , Son, and . . . ! **16, 29, 34.**
368.   . . . sun is weak. **29.**

474. Whose faith I never shook—they may have found him.
475. Therefore I will go out—but if I go,
476. The glass will let the sands run out unseen.
477. I cannot go—I cannot leave the glass.
478. Go call my pupils—I can explain all now.
479. Only when all our hold on life is troubled,
480. Only in spiritual terror can the Truth
481. Come through the broken mind—as the pease burst
482. Out of a broken pease-cod.

[*He clutches Bridget as she is going.*
Say to them

483. That Nature would lack all in her most need,
484. Could not the soul find truth as in a flash,
485. Upon the battle-field, or in the midst
486. Of overwhelming waves, and say to them—
487. But no, they would but answer as I bid.

488. *Bridget.* You want somebody to get up an argument
489. with.

490. *Wise Man.* Look out and see if there is any one
491. There in the street—I cannot leave the glass,
492. For somebody might shake it, and the sand
493. If it were shaken might run down on the instant.

494. *Bridget.* I don't understand a word you are saying.
495. There's a crowd of people talking to your pupils.

496. *Wise Man.* Go out and find if they have found a man
497. Who did not understand me when I taught,
498. Or did not listen.

---

474. That had the old belief . . . [T] they (belief—they **53, 54**) . . . . **M-54.**
475. . . . out . . . [T] but . . . go **M** ; . . . go **53, 54.**
477. . . . go . . . . [T] I . . . . **M.**
478. . . . pupils . . . [T] I . . . now, **M** ; . . . now, **53-69.**
479. . . . is shaken, **M-54.**
481. . . . mind . . . [T] as . . . **M.**
482. . . . them, **M-69.**
483. . . . nature . . . , **M-54.**
485. . . . battle field or . . .
486. . . . them . . . [T] **M.**
490. . . . anyone **M-54.**
491. . . . street . . . [T] I . . . , **M.**

[508]   369. *Bridget.* I have no pennies. [*To the Wise Man.*] Your
[508-509]   370.   pupils cannot find anybody to argue with you.
[509-510]   371.   There is nobody in the whole country who has
[510]   372.   enough belief to fill a pipe since you put down the
[511-512]   373.   monk. Can't you be quiet now and not always
[512-513]   374.   wanting to have arguments? It must be terrible to
[513]   375.   have a mind like that.

[514]   376. *Wise Man.* I am lost! I am lost!

[515]   377. *Bridget.* Leave me alone now; I have to make the bread
516   378.   for you and the children.

             379. *Wise Man.* Out of this, woman, out of this, I say!
             380.   [*Bridget goes through the kitchen door.*] Will nobody find
             381.   a way to help me! But she spoke of my children. I
             382.   had forgotten them. They will not have changed. It
             383.   is only those who have reason that doubt; the young
[517]   384.   are full of faith. Bridget, Bridget, send my children
             385.   to me.

[518]   386. *Bridget* [*inside*]. Your father wants you; run to him
             387.   now.
                    [*The two Children come in. They stand together a little way
                    from the threshold of the kitchen door, looking timidly at
                    their father.*]

[519-520]   388. *Wise Man.* Children, what do you believe? Is there a
[520]   389.   Heaven? Is there a Hell? Is there a Purgatory?

[526]   390. *First Child.* We haven't forgotten, father.

[526]   391. *The Other Child.* O no, father. [*They both speak together as
[527-528]   392.   if in school.*] There is nothing we cannot see; there is
[528]   393.   nothing we cannot touch.

---

371.   . . . who had **NAR-16.**
372.   . . . pipe with since . . . **NAR-45.**
373.   . . . always be **NAR-17.**
382.   . . . will believe. It **NAR-34.**
385.   . . . me! **NAR-16.**
389.   heaven? . . . hell? . . . purgatory? **16.**
391.   Oh, no, . . . *together, as* **29.**
392.   . . . .] There is no Heaven; (heaven; **16**) there is no Hell; (hell; **16**)
       there is
393.   . . . cannot see. **NAR-16.**

499. *Bridget.* It is a hard thing to be married to a man of
500.   learning that must always be having arguments.

[*She goes out.*

501. *Wise Man.* Strange that I should be blind to the great secret,
502.   And that so simple a man might write it out
503.   Upon a blade of grass with the juice of a berry,
504.   And laugh and cry, because it was so simple.

Enter Bridget followed by the Fool.

505. *Fool.* Give me something; give me a penny to buy
506.   bacon in the shops and nuts in the market, and
507.   strong drink for the time when the sun is weak.

508. *Bridget.* I have no pennies. [*To Wise Man.*] Your pupils
508.   cannot find anybody to argue with you. There's
510.   nobody in the whole country with religion enough
511.   for a lover's oath. Can't you be quiet now, and not
512.   always wanting to have arguments? It must be
513.   terrible to have a mind like that.

514. *Wise Man.* Then I am lost indeed.

515. *Bridget.* Leave me alone now, I have to make the bread
516.   for you and the children.

[*She goes into kitchen. The Fool follows her.*

517. *Wise Man.* Children, children!

518. *Bridget.* Your father wants you, run to him.

[*Children run in.*

Directions after 500.   [lacking] **M-54.**
500a. Children, don't be meddling with the bread while I am out.   [*She goes out.*] **M-54.**
503.   . . . grass or bit of rush **M-54, 57A** ; . . . berry; **57E, 69.**
503a. With naught but berry juice, and laugh to himself **M-54, 57A.**
504.   Writing it out, because . . . . **M-54, 57A.**
Directions after 504.   [*Enter Fool and Bridget.*] **M.**
510.   . . . with belief enough **M-57.**
512.   . . . arguments. It . . . **M-54, 57E, 69.**
Directions after 516.   [. . . *kitchen.*] **M-69.**

[529]   394. *First Child.* Foolish people used to think that there
[530]   395. was, but you are very learned and you have taught
[530]   396. us better.

[531]   397. *Wise Man.* You are just as bad as the others, just as bad
         398. as the others! Do not run away! Come back to me!
         399. [*The Children begin to cry and run away.*] Why are you
         400. afraid? I will teach you better—no, I will never teach
[531]   401. you again. Go to your mother! no, she will not be
         402. able to teach them . . . Help them, O God! . . . The
[533]   403. grains are going very quickly. There is very little sand
[533]   404. in the uppermost glass. Somebody will come for me
[534]   405. in a moment; perhaps he is at the door now! All
         406. creatures that have reason doubt. O that the grass
         407. and plants could speak! Somebody has said that
[535-536]   408. they would wither if they doubted. O, speak to me,
[537]   409. O grass-blades! O fingers of God's certainty, speak
         410. to me! You are millions and you will not speak. I
         411. dare not know the moment the messenger will come
         412. for me. I will cover the glass. [*He covers it with a cloth.*
               Sees the Fool, who is sitting by the door playing with some
               flowers which he has stuck in his hat. He has begun to blow
[551]   413. *a dandelion head.*] What are you doing?

[552]   414. *Fool.* Wait a moment. [*He blows.*] Four, five, six.

553   415. *Wise Man.* What are you doing that for?

---

395. were, but . . . **NAR-16.**
398. . . . others! Out of the room with you, out of the room! **NAR-25** ; . . . away; come . . . me. **29** ; . . . away, come . . . ! **34.**
399. . . . *away.*] Go away, go
400. away! I will teach you . . . **NAR-25.**
401. . . . mother; (mother— **16**) no, . . . **NAR-16.**
402. . . . God! [*Alone.*] The **NAR, 16** ; . . . them . . . [T] help . . . God! [*Alone.*] The **15.**
407. and the planets could . . **:** **NAR-16.**
408. . . . . O speak . . . , **NAR-34** ; . . . . Oh speak . . . , **45, 69.**
409. . . . grass blades! **NAR-69.**
410. . . . me. You . . . **NAR-16.**
     Directions at 412. [. . . *it and brings it to the desk, and the Fool is* . . . *door fiddling with* . . . .] **NAR-16** ; [. . . *it and brings it to the desk. Sees* . . . *dandelion head.* (*dandelion-head.* **34**) **17-34** ; [. . . *dandelion-head.*] **45, 69.**

519. *Wise Man.* Come to me, children. Do not be afraid.

520.   I want to know if you believe in Heaven,

521.   God or the soul—no, do not tell me yet;

522.   You need not be afraid I shall be angry;

523.   Say what you please—so that it is your thought—

524.   I wanted you to know before you spoke

525.   That I shall not be angry.

526. *First Child.* We have not forgotten, father.

Second Child.   O no, father.

527. *Both Children* [*as if repeating a lesson*]. There is nothing

528.   we cannot see, nothing we cannot touch.

529. *First Child.* Foolish people used to say that there was,

530.   but you have taught us better.

531. *Wise Man.* Go to your mother, go—yet do not go.

532.   What can she say? If I am dumb you are lost;

533.   And yet, because the sands are running out,

534.   I have but a moment to show it all in. Children,

535.   The sap would die out of the blades of grass

536.   Had they a doubt. They understand it all,

537.   Being the fingers of God's certainty,

538.   Yet can but make their sign into the air;

539.   But could they find their tongues they'd show it all;

540.   But what am I to say that am but one,

---

521. . . . soul . . . [T] no, . . . yet, **M** ; . . . yet, **53, 54**.

522. . . . angry, **M-69**.

523. . . . please . . . [T] so . . . thought . . . [T] **M**.

524. . . . spoke, **M-69**.

525. . . . angry, **M**.

526. . . . , Father.

                Oh, (Oh 57) . . . , Father. **M-57**.

531. . . . , go . . . [T] yet . . . go **M** ; . . . go **53, 54**.

532. For she can teach you nothing. If . . . dumb **M-54**.

532a. You shall be lost among the woods of nothing, **M** ; I will have drowned you in the Lake of Spaces **53, 54**.

533. And I (I, **53, 54**) because . . . out (out, **53, 54**) **M-54**.

534. Have . . . . Children **M** ; Have . . . . , **53, 54**.

538. . . . air.

539. . . . tongues . . . [T] they'd (tongues—they'd **53, 54**) . . . all **M-54**.

[554-555]   416. *Fool.* I am blowing at the dandelion to find out what
[554-555]   417.   time it is.

[556-557]   418. *Wise Man.* You have heard everything! That is why you
[557]   419.   want to find out what hour it is! You are waiting to
[559]   420.   see them coming through the door to carry me away.
[560-561]   421.   [*Fool goes on blowing.*] I will not have you sitting there.
[560-561]   422.   I will have no one here when they come. [*He seizes the
                    Fool by the shoulders, and begins to force him out through
            423.   the door, then suddenly changes his mind.*] No, I have
            424.   something to ask you. [*He drags him back into the
[564]   425.   room.*] Is there a Heaven? Is there a Hell? Is there a
[564]   426.   Purgatory?

565   427. *Fool.* So you ask me now. I thought when you were
[566]   428.   asking your pupils, I said to myself, if he would ask
[566]   429.   Teigue the Fool, Teigue could tell him all about it,
            430.   for Teigue has learned all about it when he has been
            431.   cutting the nets.

[569]   432. *Wise Man.* Tell me quickly!

[570]   433. *Fool.* I said, Teigue knows everything. Not even the
[571-572]   434.   cats or the hares that milk the cows have Teigue's
[572-573]   435.   wisdom. But Teigue will not speak; he says nothing.

[574]   436. *Wise Man.* Tell me, tell me! For under the cover the
[575]   437.   grains are falling, and when they are all fallen I shall
[576]   438.   die; and my soul will be lost if I have not found
            439.   somebody that knows and believes! Speak, speak!

[577]   440. *Fool* [*looking wise*]. I will not speak! I will not tell you
[577-578]   441.   what is in my mind, and I won't tell you what is in
[578-579]   442.   my bag. You might steal away my thoughts. I met a
[579-580]   443.   bodach on the road yesterday, and he said, 'Teigue,

---

421.   . . . *blowing.*] Out through the door with you! **NAR-34.**
424.   . . . you? [*He* . . . **15.**
425.   . . . heaven? . . . hell? . . .
426.   purgatory? **16.**
427.   . . . now. When . . . **34.**
432.   Tell me; tell me! **NAR-34.**
433.   owls and the hares . . . **NAR-16.**
437.   . . . falling and . . . **NAR, 15.**
439.   . . . that believes! . . . !
440.   . . . *wise.*] No, no, I won't tell . . . **NAR-34.**

541.   When they are millions and they will not speak?—

                                           [Children have run out.

542.   But they are gone; what made them run away?

                   The Fool comes in with a dandelion.

543.   Look at me, tell me if my face is changed,
544.   Is there a notch of the Fiend's nail upon it
545.   Already? Is it terrible to sight
546.   Because the moment's near?   *[Going to glass*

                       I dare not look,

547.   I dare not know the moment when they come.
548.   No, no, I dare not. *[Covers glass.]* Will there be a footfall,
549.   Or will there be a sort of rending sound,
550.   Or else a cracking, as though an iron claw
551.   Had gripped the threshold-stone?

                    [The Fool has begun to blow the dandelion.
                       What are you doing?

552. *Fool.* Wait a minute—four—five—six—

553. *Wise Man.* What are you doing that for?

554. *Fool.* I am blowing the dandelion to find out what hour
555.   it is.

556. *Wise Man.* You have heard everything and that is why
557.   You'd find what hour it is—you'd find that out
558.   That you may look upon a fleet of devils
559.   Dragging my soul away. You shall not stop,
560.   I will have no one here when they come in,

---

541.   . . . speak. **M-54**; . . . speak— **57, 69.**
544.   . . . fiend's . . . **M-69.**
545.   . . . sight? **M-57.**
546.   . . . near. [*Going.* . . . .]
           I . . . , **M-57.**
547.   . . . come
548. To carry me away. [*Covers* . . . footfall
549.   . . . of tearing sound, **M-54.**
551.   . . . threshold stone. (stone? **53-69**)
            [*Fool* . . . .]
            What . . . ? **M-69.**
552.   . . . minute . . . [T] four . . . [T] five . . . [T] six . . . [T] **M.**
556.   . . . everything, and . . . **M-69.**
557.   . . . is . . . [T] you'd . . . out, **M**; . . . out, **53-69.**

[580-581] 444.   tell me how many pennies are in your bag; I will
[581-582] 445.   wager three pennies that there are not twenty pennies
[583]   446.   in your bag; let me put in my hand and count them.'
[583-584] 447.   But I pulled the strings tighter, like this; and when
[584-585] 448.   I go to sleep every night I hide the bag where no one
[585]   449.   knows.

450. *Wise Man* [*goes towards the hour-glass as if to uncover it*].
     No,

451. no, I have not the courage. [*He kneels.*] Have pity
     upon

452. me, Fool, and tell me!

453. *Fool.* Ah, now that is different. I am not afraid of you

454. now. What is that I am to tell you? But I must come

455. near; somebody in there might hear what the angel

456. said.

457. *Wise Man.* But speak and I am saved. What did the

---

444.   . . . bag. I . . . **NAR-16.**
       Directions in 450.   [. . . *toward* . . . .] **16.**
451.   . . . courage! [*He* . . . **NAR-16.**
453.   Ah! Now, that . . .
454.   now. But . . . **NAR-45.**
455.   near you; somebody . . . Angel **NAR-16**; nearer to you; somebody
       . . . Angel (angel 45) **17-45**; near, somebody . . . **69.**
457.   *Wise Man.* Oh, what did the Angel (angel **45**) tell you?
457a. *Fool.* Once I was alone on the hills, and an angel (Angel **16**) came
       by and he
457b. said, 'Teigue the Fool, do not forget the Three Fires; the (Fires:
       the **16**) Fire that pun-
457c. ishes, the Fire that purifies, and the Fire wherein the soul rejoices
       forever!' (for ever!' **16, 29, 45** (1913)) **NAR-45.**
457d. *Wise Man.* He believes! I am saved! Help me. (me! **45**) The sand
       has run out. **NAR-25, 45**; He believes! I am saved! The sand has
       run out . . . . [T] **29, 34.**
457e. I am dying . . . . [T] [*Fool helps him to his chair.*] I am going from the
       NAR-25, 45; [*Fool helps him to his chair.*] I am going from the **29, 34.**
457f. country of the seven wandering stars, and I am going to the country
       of **NAR-45.**
457g. the fixed stars! Ring the bell. [*Fool rings the bell.*] Are they coming?
       NAR-25; the fixed stars! . . . [T] **29**; the fixed stars! **34, 45.**
457h. Ah! now I hear their feet. . . . [T] I will speak to them. I understand
       it all **NAR-25**; I understand it all **29-45.**

561.   I will have no one sitting there—no one!

562.   And yet—and yet—there is something strange about you.

563.   I half remember something. What is it?

564.   Do you believe in God and in the soul?

565.   *Fool.* So you ask me now. I thought when you were

566.   asking your pupils, 'Will he ask Teigue the Fool?

567.   Yes, he will, he will; no, he will not—yes, he will'.

568.   But Teigue will say nothing. Teigue will say nothing.

569.   *Wise Man.* Tell me quickly.

570.   *Fool.* I said, 'Teigue knows everything, not even the

571.   green-eyed cats and the hares that milk the cows

572.   have Teigue's wisdom'; but Teigue will not speak,

573.   he says nothing.

574.   *Wise Man.* Speak, speak, for underneath the cover there

575.   The sand is running from the upper glass,

576.   And when the last grain's through, I shall be lost.

577.   *Fool.* I will not speak. I will not tell you what is in my

578.   mind. I will not tell you what is in my bag. You

579.   might steal away my thoughts. I met a bodach on

580.   the road yesterday, and he said, 'Teigue, tell me how

581.   many pennies are in your bag; I will wager three

582.   pennies that there are not twenty pennies in your

583.   bag; let me put in my hand and count them'. But

584.   I gripped the bag the tighter, and when I go to sleep

585.   at night I hide the bag where nobody knows.

---

561.   . . . there . . . [T] no one . . . [T] **M** ; . . . —no one— **53-69.**

562.   . . . yet . . . [T] and yet . . . [T] there . . . . **M** ; . . . you **53** ; . . . you, **54.**

563.   Are you the one I seek? Do you believe

564.   In God and the soul, in the undying stuff

564a.   That all things have been made of from the first? **M-54.**

566.   . . . , 'will . . . ask, Teigue . . . Fool. **M-54.**

567.   . . . will, no, . . . not . . . [T] yes he . . . .' **M** ; . . . will, no, . . . —yes he . . . .' **53, 54.**

572.   . . . wisdom' but, Teigue . . . , **M-54.**

576.   . . . lost

576a.   Unless I have lit upon unshaken faith

576b.   Somewhere in somebody. **M-54.**

584.   . . . tighter and . . . **M-54, 97A.**

585.   . . . night, I . . . . **M-54.**

[593]	459.	*Fool.* O no, no, no. How could poor Teigue see angels?
[593-594]	460.	O, Teigue tells one tale here, another tale there,
[594-596]	461.	and everybody gives him pennies. If Teigue had not
[595-596]	462.	his tales he would starve.

458. angel say to you?

[*He backs away and goes out.*

[597-598]	463.	*Wise Man.* My last hope is gone and now that it is too
[598]	464.	late I can see it all. Those words about winter and
	465.	summer, about our November being the lambing-
[599]	466.	time in that other country—all, all is plain now. We
[599-600]	467.	sink in on God, we find Him in becoming nothing
[599-600]	468.	—we perish into reality. [*The Fool comes back.*
[601]	469.	*Fool.* There was one there—there by the threshold stone,
[602]	470.	writing there; and she said, 'Go in, Teigue, and tell
[603-604]	471.	him everything that he asks you. He will give you a
[604]	472.	penny if you tell him.'
[599-600]	473.	*Wise Man.* We perish into reality—strange that I never

---

457i. now. One sinks in on God; we do not see the truth; God sees the truth in **NAR-45.**

457j. us. I cannot speak, I am too weak. Tell them, Fool, that when the life **NAR-25 ;** us. Ring the bell. [*Fool rings the bell.*] Are they coming? Tell them, Fool, that when the life **29 ;** us. Ring the bell. They are coming. Tell them, Fool, that when the life **34, 45.**

457k. and the mind are broken (broken, **16**) the truth comes through them like peas through **NAR-45.**

457l. a broken peascod. But no, I will pray—Yet (yet **16**) I cannot pray. Pray, Fool, **NAR-25 ;** a broken peascod. Pray, Fool, **29-45.**

457m. that they may be given a sign and save their souls alive. Your prayers are **NAR-25 ;** that they may be given a sign and carry their souls alive out of the dying world. Your prayers are **29-45.**

457n. better than mine. **NAR-45.**
  [*Fool bows his head. Wise Man's head sinks on his arm on the books. Pupils enter.*] **NAR-25, 45 ;** [*Fool bows his head. Wise Man's head sinks on his arm on the books. Pupils are heard singing as before, but now they come right into the room before (right on to the stage before **34**) they cease their song.*] **29, 34.**

458-491. [lacking] **NAR-45.**
460. O Teigue . . . , **69.**
465. . . . lambing **69.**
467. . . . him . . . **69.**

586. *Wise Man.* There's but one pinch of sand, and I am lost
587.   If you are not he I seek.

588. *Fool.* O, what a lot the Fool knows, but he says
589.   nothing.

590. *Wise Man.* Yes, I remember now. You spoke of angels.
591.   You said but now that you had seen an angel.
592.   You are the one I seek, and I am saved.

593. *Fool.* O no. How could poor Teigue see angels? O,
594.   Teigue tells one tale here, another there, and every-
595.   body gives him pennies. If Teigue had not his tales
596.   he would starve.   [*He breaks away and goes out.*

597. *Wise Man.* The last hope is gone,
598.   And now that it's too late I see it all:
599.   We perish into God and sink away
600.   Into reality—the rest's a dream.

The Fool comes back.

---

586.   . . . sand . . . [T] and . . . **M.**
590.   *Wise Man* [*seizing him*]. I kneel to you . . . [T] you (you—you **53, 54**)
      are the man I have sought. (Sought **53, 54**) **M-54.**
591.   [lacking] **M-54** ; . . . you have seen . . . . **97A.**
592.   You alone can save me. **M-54.**
593.   No, no, what should poor Teigue know, Teigue **M-54.**
594.   that is out in all weathers, Teigue that sleeps in the **M-54.**
595.   fishers' loft, poor Teigue the Fool. **M-54** ; . . . give . . . **97A.**
      Directions after 595.   [*He breaks away and goes out.*] **M-54.**
596 and Directions.   [lacking] **M-54.**
597.   . . . gone. **M.**
598.   . . . all, **M-69.**
600.   . . . reality . . . [T] the . . . . **M.**
      Directions after 600.   [lacking] **M.**
600a.   *Fool* [*coming back on tip-toe and peering under cover of Hour-glass and*
      singing in a low voice].
      'I hear the wind a-blow,
600b.   And the grass a-grow
600c.   And all that I know, I know,' **M.**

[598]   474.   saw it until now.

475.   *Fool*. Will you give me a penny if I tell you?

476.   *Wise Man*. O no, do not tell me anything. I am content
477.   to know that God's will prevails whatever that be.

[606-607]   478.   *Fool*. Waiting till the moment had come—that is what
[607-608]   479.   the one out there was saying, but I might tell you
[608]   480.   what you asked. That is what he was saying.

[609-610]   481.   *Wise Man*. Be silent. May God's will prevail though
[610]   482.   that be my damnation! What was I born for but that
[615-616]   483.   I might cry that His will be fulfilled upon the
[617]   484.   instant, though that be my damnation? I am dying.
485.   The sand has run out. Ring the bell, ring for my
486.   pupils. [*Fool rings.*] For I am going from the country
487.   of the seven wandering stars, and am going to the
488.   country of the fixed stars. [*Voices of Pupils singing.*]
489.   They are coming. I must make all plain to them,
490.   that they may wish His will be fulfilled though that
491.   be our damnation. There is no other truth.   [*Dies.*

Pupils enter

492.   *Young Man*. Look at the Fool turned bell-ringer.

493.   *Another*. What have you called us in for, Teigue?

494.   *Fool*. There was something he wanted to say, but you
[625]   495.   must wake him, he has fallen asleep.

496.   *Young Man*. No wonder he has dreams. He is so fast

---

482.   . . . damnation. What . . . **69.**
484.   . . . damnation. I . . . . **69.**
492.   *A Young* . . . bell-ringer!
493.   . . . , Teigue? What are you going to
493a. tell us? **NAR-45.**
494-495. [lacking] **NAR-45.**
496.   *Another*. No . . . has had dreams! See, he is fast **NAR-45.**

601. *Fool*. There was one there—there by the threshold,
602.   waiting there; and he said, 'Go in, Teigue, and tell
603.   him everything that he asks you. He will give you
604.   a penny if you tell him.'

605. *Wise Man*. I know enough, that know God's will prevails.

606. *Fool*. Waiting till the moment had come—That is
607.   what the one out there was saying, but I might tell
608.   you what you asked. That is what he was saying.

609. *Wise Man*. Be silent. May God's will prevail on the instant,
610.   Although His will be my eternal pain.
611.   I have no question:
612.   It is enough, I know what fixed the station
613.   Of star and cloud.
614.   And knowing all, I cry
615.   That whatso God has willed
616.   On the instant be fulfilled,
617.   Though that be my damnation.
618.   The stream of the world has changed its course,
619.   And with the stream my thoughts have run
620.   Into some cloudy thunderous spring
621.   That is its mountain source—
622.   Aye, to some frenzy of the mind,
623.   For all that we have done's undone,
624.   Our speculation but as the wind.

[He dies.

625. *Fool*. Wise Man—Wise Man, wake up and I will tell

601-611. [lacking] **M.**
601. ... threshold stone, **53-69.**
602. ... there and said, 'go in Teigue, ... **53, 54.**
612. *Wise Man*. I know ... **M.**
614. ... cry, **M-54.**
615. ... what so ... willed, **M-54**; ... what so ... **57, 69.**
618. ... course **M-54.**
619. ... run, **M.**
621. ... source, **M.**
623. ... all we ... undone.
624. ... speculation wind. **M.**
625. ... man ... [T] Wise man, ... **M**; ... man— ... man, ... **53-69.**

[625]   497.   asleep that I cannot wake him. O, he is dead. . . .

Pupils gather round

[631]   498.   *Fool.* Look, look, what has come from his mouth . . . a
[631]   499.   little winged thing . . . a little shining thing . . . it
    500.   has gone to the door. . . . O, look, there in the
    501.   door. . . . [*The Angel appears at the door, she opens her hands*
    502.   *and closes them again.*] The Angel has taken it in her
    503.   hands.

    504.   *A Young Man.* What are you pointing at?

    505.   *Fool.* The Angel has taken it in her hands. She will open
[637]   506.   her hands in the Garden of Paradise.

    507.   *Young Man.* There is nobody there—there is nobody in
    508.   the door.

THE END

---

497.   asleep now. [*Goes over and touches him. (touches the Wise Man.* **16**)] Oh,
. . . dead! **NAR-34**; asleep now. [*Goes over and touches him.*] He is so
fast asleep I cannot wake him. Oh, he . . . dead! **45.**

497a.   *Fool. Do not stir! He asked for a sign that you might be saved.* [*All*
NAR-45.

498.   *are silent for a moment*] . . . [T] Look at the butterfly! **NAR, 15**; *are*
silent for a moment] Look what . . . **16-45.**

499.   *A Young Man.* It is his soul! [*They all kneel. The butterfly goes up. The*
Fool points upward] **NAR, 15**; . . . thing. It **16**; . . . thing . . . . [T]
It **17-45.**

500-508.   [lacking] **NAR, 15.**

500.   . . . gone to the **16**; is gone . . . door. **17-45**; . . . . O look, . . . **69.**

501.   door. [*The . . . appears in the doorway, stretches out her . . .*

502.   *and . . . .*] The Angel (angel **45**) has . . .

503.   hands . . . [T] she (She **17-45**) will open her hands **16-45.**

504-505.   [lacking] **16-45.**

506.   in . . . Paradise. [*They all kneel.*] **16-45.**

507-508.   [lacking] **16-45.**

626. you everything for a penny. It is I, poor Teigue the
627. Fool. Why don't you wake up, and say, 'There is a
628. penny for you, Teigue'? No, no, you will say nothing.
629. You and I, we are the two fools, we know every-
630. thing, but we will not speak.

Angel enters holding a casket.

631. O, look what has come from his mouth! O, look
632. what has come from his mouth—the white butterfly!
633. He is dead, and I have taken his soul in my hands;
634. but I know why you open the lid of that golden box.
635. I must give it to you. There then [*he puts butterfly in*
636. *casket*], he has gone through his pains, and you will
637. open the lid in the Garden of Paradise. [*He closes*
638. *curtain and remains outside it.*] He is gone, he is gone,
639. he is gone, but come in, everybody in the world,
640. and look at me.
641.   I hear the wind a-blow,
642.   I hear the grass a-grow,
643.   And all that I know, I know.
644. But I will not speak, I will run away.   [*He goes out.*

THE END

626a. Fool that you were looking for. I am the man you were to
626b. find before the sand ran out . . . [T] the man who believes in
627. God. Why . . . up and . . . **M.**
628. . . . , Teigue.' No, . . . **M-54.**
632. . . . his hands . . . [T] the . . . butterfly. **M** ; . . . butterfly. **53, 54.**
633. . . . dead and . . . ; **M-54.**
635. . . . then, [*he* . . .
636. *casket*] He (he **54, 57**) . . . **M-57.**
638. *curtain*] He . . ., **M.**
639. . . . in everybody . . . world **M-54, 57E, 69.**
641. 'I . . . a-blow **M** ; 'I . . . a blow **53-57** ; . . . a blow, **69.**
642. . . . a grow, **53-69.**
643. . . . know.' **M-57.**

NOTES

The Hour-Glass (in prose)

'The Hour-Glass,' first performance, Dublin, March, 1903.

[on 'Contents' page] **16.**

The 'Hour-Glass' was first played at the Molesworth Hall, Dublin, on March 14, 1903, with the following cast:—The Wise Man . . J. W. Digges / Bridget, his wife . . Maire T. Quinn / Her children . . Eithne and Padragan ni Shiubhleigh / Her pupils . . P. I. Kelly / Seumas O'Sullivan / P. Colum / P. MacShiubhlaigh / The Angel . . Maire ni Shiubhlaigh / The Fool . . F. J. Fay.

The Play has been revived many times since then as a part of the repertoire at the Abbey Theatre, Dublin.

Note, **29.**

This play is founded upon the following story, recorded by Lady Wilde in *Ancient Legends of Ireland*, 1887, vol. i., pp. 60-67:—

THE PRIEST'S SOUL.

In former days there were great schools in Ireland where every sort of learning was taught to the people, and even the poorest had more knowledge at that time than many a gentleman has now. But as to the priests, their learning was above all, so that the fame of Ireland went over the whole world, and many kings from foreign lands used to send their sons all the way to Ireland to be brought up in the Irish schools.

Now, at this time there was a little boy learning at one of them who was a wonder to every one for his cleverness. His parents were only labouring people, and of course very poor; but young as he was, and poor as he was, no king's or lord's son could come up to him in learning. Even the masters were put to shame; for when they were trying to teach him he would tell them something they had never heard of before, and show them their ignorance. One of his great triumphs was in argument, and he would go on till he proved to you that black was white, and then when you gave in, for no one could beat him in talk, he would turn round and show you that white was black, or may be that there was no colour at all in the world. When he grew up his poor father and mother were so proud of him that they resolved to make him a priest, which they did at last, though they nearly starved themselves to get the money. Well, such another learned man was not in Ireland, and he was as great in argument as ever, so that no one could stand before him. Even the Bishops tried to talk to him, but he showed them at once they knew nothing at all.

Now, there were no schoolmasters in those times, but it was the priests taught the people; and as this man was the cleverest in Ireland all the foreign kings sent their sons to him as long as he had houseroom to give them. So he grew very proud, and began to forget how low he had been, and, worst of all, even to forget God, who had made him what he was. And the pride of arguing got hold of him, so that from one thing to another he went on to prove that there was no Purgatory, and then no Hell, and then no Heaven, and then no God; and at last that men had no souls, but were no more than a dog or a cow, and when they died there was an end of them. 'Who ever saw a soul?' he would say. 'If you can show me one, I will believe.' No one could make any answer to this; and at last they all came to believe that as there was no other world, every one might do what they liked in this, the priest setting the example, for he took a beautiful young girl to wife. But as no priest or bishop in the whole land could be got to marry them, he was obliged to read the service over for himself. It was a great scandal, yet no one dared to say a word, for all the kings' sons were on his side, and would have slaughtered any one who tried to prevent his wicked goings-on. Poor boys! they all believed in him, and thought every word he said was the truth. In this way his notions began to spread about, and the whole world was going to the bad, when one night an angel came down from Heaven, and told the priest he had but twenty-four hours to live. He began to tremble, and asked for a little more time.

But the angel was stiff, and told him that could not be.

'What do you want time for, you sinner?' he asked.

'Oh, sir, have pity on my poor soul!' urged the priest.

'Oh, ho! You have a soul, then?' said the angel. 'Pray how did you find that out?'

'It has been fluttering in me ever since you appeared,' answered the priest. 'What a fool I was not to think of it before!'

'A fool, indeed,' said the angel. 'What good was all your learning, when it could not tell you that you had a soul?'

'Ah, my lord,' said the priest, 'if I am to die, tell me how soon I may be in heaven.'

'Never,' replied the angel. 'You denied there was a Heaven.'

'Then, my lord, may I go to Purgatory?'

'You denied Purgatory also; you must go straight to Hell,' said the angel.

'But, my lord, I denied Hell also,' answered the priest, 'so you can't send me there either.'

The angel was a little puzzled.

'Well,' said he, 'I'll tell you what I can do for you. You may either live now on earth for a hundred years enjoying every pleasure, and then be cast into Hell for ever; or you may die in twenty-four hours in the most horrible torments, and pass through Purgatory, there to remain till the Day of Judgment, if only you can find some one person that believes, and through his belief mercy will be vouchsafed to you and your soul will be saved.'

The priest did not take five minutes to make up his mind.

'I will have death in the twenty-four hours,' he said, 'so that my soul may be saved at last.'

On this the angel gave him directions as to what he was to do, and left him.

Then, immediately, the priest entered the large room where all his scholars and the kings' sons were seated, and called out to them—

'Now, tell me the truth, and let none fear to contradict me. Tell me what is your belief. Have men souls?'

'Master,' they answered, 'once we believed that men had souls; but, thanks to your teaching, we believe so no longer. There is no Hell, and no Heaven, and no God. This is our belief, for it is thus you taught us.'

Then the priest grew pale with fear, and cried out: 'Listen! I taught you a lie. There is a God, and man has an immortal soul. I believe now all I denied before.'

But the shouts of laughter that rose up drowned the priest's voice, for they thought he was only trying them for argument.

'Prove it, master,' they cried, 'prove it! Who has ever seen God? Who has ever seen the soul?'

And the room was stirred with their laughter.

The priest stood up to answer them, but no word could he utter; all his eloquence, all his powers of argument, had gone from him, and he could do nothing but wring his hands and cry out—

'There is a God! there is a God! Lord, have mercy on my soul!'

And they all began to mock him, and repeat his own words that he had taught them—

'Show him to us; show us your God.'

And he fled from them groaning with agony, for he saw that none believed, and how then could his soul be saved?

But he thought next of his wife.

'She will believe,' he said to himself. 'Women never give up God.'

And he went to her; but she told him that she believed only what he taught her, and that a good wife should believe in her husband first, and before and above all things in heaven or earth.

Then despair came on him, and he rushed from the house and began to ask every one he met if they believed. But the same answer came from one and all: 'We believe only what you have taught us,' for his doctrines had spread far and wide through the county.

Then he grew half mad with fear, for the hours were passing. And he flung himself down on the ground in a lonesome spot, and wept and groaned in terror, for the time was coming fast when he must die.

Just then a little child came by.

'God save you kindly,' said the child to him.

The priest started up.

'Child, do you believe in God?' he asked.

'I have come from a far country to learn about Him,' said the child.

'Will your honour direct me to the best school that they have in these parts?'

'The best school and the best teacher is close by,' said the priest, and he named himself.

'Oh, not to that man,' answered the child, 'for I am told he denies God and Heaven and Hell, and even that man has a soul, because we can't see it; but I would soon put him down.'

The priest looked at him earnestly. 'How?' he inquired.

'Why,' said the child, 'I would ask him if he believed he had life to show me his life.'

'But he could not do that, my child,' said the priest. 'Life cannot be seen; we have it, but it is invisible.'

'Then, if we have life, though we cannot see it, we may also have a soul, though it is invisible,' answered the child.

When the priest heard him speak these words he fell down on his knees before him, weeping for joy, for now he knew his soul was safe; he had met at last one that believed. And he told the child his whole story: all his wickedness, and pride, and blasphemy against the great God; and how the angel had come to him and told him of the only way in which he could be saved, through the faith and prayers of some one that believed.

'Now, then,' he said to the child, 'take this penknife and strike it into my breast, and go on stabbing the flesh until you see the paleness of death on my face. Then watch—for a living thing will soar up from my body as I die, and you will then know that my soul has ascended to the presence of God. And when you see this thing, make haste and run to my school and call on all my scholars to come and see that the soul of their master has left the body, and that all he taught them was a lie, for that there is a God who punishes sin, and a Heaven and a Hell, and that man has an immortal soul, destined for eternal happiness or misery.'

'I will pray,' said the child, 'to have courage to do this work.'

And he kneeled down and prayed. Then when he rose up he took the penknife and struck it into the priest's heart, and struck and struck again till all the flesh was lacerated; but still the priest lived, though the agony was horrible, for he could not die until the twenty-four hours had expired. At last the agony seemed to cease, and the stillness of death settled on his face. Then the child, who was watching, saw a beautiful living creature, with four snow-white wings, mount from the dead man's body into the air and go fluttering round his head.

So he ran to bring the scholars; and when they saw it they all knew it was the soul of their master, and they watched with wonder and awe until it passed from sight into the clouds.

And this was the first butterfly that was ever seen in Ireland; and now all men know that the butterflies are the souls of the dead waiting for the moment when they may enter Purgatory, and so pass through torture to purification and peace.

But the schools of Ireland were quite deserted after that time, for people said, What is the use of going so far to learn when the wisest man in all

Ireland did not know if he had a soul till he was near losing it; and was only saved at last through the simple belief of a little child?

The Hour-Glass was first played in The Molesworth Hall, Dublin, with the following cast:—Wise Man, Mr. T. Dudley Digges; His Wife, Miss M. T. Quinn; The Fool, Mr. F. J. Fay; Pupils, P. J. Kelly, P. Columb, C. Caufield.

We always play it in front of an olive-green curtain, and dress the Wise Man and his Pupils in various shades of purple. Because in all these decorative schemes one needs, as I think, a third colour subordinate to the other two, we have partly dressed the Fool in red-brown, which is repeated in the furniture. There is some green in his dress and in that of the Wife of the Wise Man who is dressed mainly in purple.

One sometimes has need of more lines of the little song, and I have put into English rhyme three of the many verses of a Gaelic ballad:

> I was going the road one day
>   (O the brown and the yellow beer!)
> And I met with a man that was no right man
>   (O my dear, my dear).
>
> 'Give me your wife,' said he,
>   (O the brown and the yellow beer!)
> 'Till the sun goes down and an hour of the clock'
>   (O my dear, my dear).
>
> 'Good-bye, good-bye, my husband,'
>   (O the brown and the yellow beer!)
> 'For a year and a day by the clock of the sun'
>   (O my dear, my dear).

34.

The Hour-Glass was first played in the Molesworth Hall, Dublin, on March 14, 1903, with the following cast:—Wise Man, Mr. T. Dudley Digges; His Wife, Miss M. T. Quinn; The Fool, Mr. F. J. Fay; Pupils, Messrs. P. J. Kelly, P. Colum, C. C. Caufield. It has since become a regular part of the répertoire of the Abbey Company.

Up to the present year we always played it in front of an olive-green curtain, and dressed the Wise Man and his Pupils in various shades of purple (with a little green here and there); and because in all these decorative schemes, which are based on colour, one needs, I think, a third colour subordinate to the other two, we dressed the Fool in red-brown, and put touches of red-brown in the Wife's dress and painted the chair and desk the same colour. Last winter, however, we revived the play with costumes taken chiefly from designs by Mr. Gordon Craig, and with the screens he has shown us how to make and use, arranged as in the drawing in this book, and with effects that depend but little on colour, and greatly upon delicate changes of tone. The Fool was dressed as in Mr. Craig's drawing, but he advised us against using the mask till he was able to see to the making of it himself. The same Fool and mask, the Fat Fool of folklore who is 'as wide and wild as a hill' and not the Thin Fool of modern romance, may go with a masked Blind Man into *On Baile's Strand*.   Notes 45.

The Hour-Glass was first played in the Molesworth Hall, Dublin, on March 14, 1903, with the following cast:—Wise Man, Mr. T. Dudley Digges; His Wife, Miss M. T. Quinn; The Fool, Mr. F. J. Fay; Pupils, Messrs. P. J. Kelly, P. Colum, C. C. Caufield. It has since become a regular part of the repertoire of the Abbey Company, and has of recent years been played before screens designed by Mr. Gordon Craig, scene and costume being copied as far as possible from the designs by Mr. Craig in my *Plays for an Irish Theatre* (1911) and from sketches sent me at the time. The early version of the Play, which was only too effective, converting a music-hall singer and sending him to Mass for six weeks, made me ashamed, but I did not know till very lately how to remedy it. I had made my Wise Man humble himself to the Fool and receive salvation as a reward, but now I have given it a new end which is closer to my own thought as well as more effective theatrically. The Fool too, when it is now played at the Abbey Theatre, wears a mask designed by Mr. Gordon Craig which makes him seem less a human being than a principle of the mind.

One sometimes has need of a few words for the Pupils to sing at their first or second entrance, and I have put into English rhyme three of the many verses of a Gaelic Ballad.

> I was going the road one day
>   (O the brown and the yellow beer),
> And I met with a man that was no right man
>   (O my dear, O my dear).
>
> 'Give me your wife,' said he
>   (O the brown and the yellow beer),
> 'Till the sun goes down and an hour of the clock'
>   (O my dear, O my dear).
>
> 'Good-bye, good-bye, my husband
>   (O the brown and the yellow beer),
> 'For a year and a day by the clock of the sun'
>   (O my dear, O my dear).

                                                              1907–1922.
                                                              Notes, 69.

*   *   *

The Hour-Glass (verse)

I took the plot of 'The Hour Glass' from an Irish Folk Tale but tried to put my own philosophy into the words. An action on the stage, however, is so much stronger than a word that when the Wise Man abused himself before the Fool I was always ashamed. My own meanings had vanished and I saw before me a cowardly person who seemed to cry out 'the wisdom of this world is foolishness' and to understand the words not as may a scholar and a gentleman but as do ignorant preachers.

I began a revision of the words from the moment when the play converted a music hall singer and sent him to mass and to confession; but no revision of words could change the effect of the Wise Man down on his knees before the Fool; so last year I changed action and all.

I made a new play of it and when I had finished discovered how I might have taken the offence out of the old by a change of action so slight that a reader would hardly have noticed it. I shall let 'our second company' go on playing the old version thus amended in Irish provincial towns but think the new one better for myself and my friends.

w. b. yeats A Preface to the New Version, **M.**
[Rptd. here from p. 577, above, for comparison.]

A friend suggested to me the subject of this play, an Irish folk tale from Lady Wilde's 'Ancient Legends.' I have for years struggled with something which is charming in the naive legend but a platitude on the stage. I did not discover till a year ago that if the wise man humbled himself to the fool and received salvation as his reward, so much more powerful are pictures than words, no explanatory dialogue could set the matter right. I was faintly pleased when I converted a music-hall singer and kept him going to Mass for six weeks, so little responsibility does one feel for that mythological world, but I was always ashamed when I saw any friend of my own in the theatre. Now I have made my philosopher accept God's will, whatever it is, and find his courage again, and helped by the elaboration of verse, have so changed the fable that it is not false to my own thoughts of the world.

Notes, 54.

A friend . . . folk-tale . . . feel for those to whom one has never been introduced; but I was . . . world. Notes, 57.

First performed at the Abbey Theatre, Dublin, on November 21, 1912, with Mr. Nugent Monck in the principal part.

Since then I have changed it a good deal, and got Mr. Alan Porter to put into mediaeval Latin certain passages, as I found that in performance verbal repetitions which did not get on the nerves in the prose version, did so when all the first half of the play was in verse. We listen more intently to verse than to prose, and therefore notice verbal repetition more quickly. Nothing said in Latin, necessary to the understanding of the play, cannot be inferred from who speaks and who is spoken to.—1922. Notes, **69.**

* * *

Variant spellings

color **NAR, 15**; *colour* **16-89.**
Carrick-orus **84, 97**; *Carrigoras* **M-69.**
O, Oh **NAR-97.**
Teig **34**; *Teigue* **NAR-29, 45-97.**

*   *   *

[See also the notes on *The Land of Heart's Desire*, p. 211; *The Legendary and Mythological Foundation of the Plays*, p. 1283; and *Prefaces to 29, 45, 69, 84*, pp. 1295, 1296, 1306, 1309.]

THE UNICORN FROM THE STARS

1908

Persons in the Play

Father John

Thomas Hearne, *a coachbuilder*

Andrew Hearne, *his brother*

Martin Hearne, *his nephew*

Johnny Bocach⎱

Paudeen ⎰
⎱ beggars
Biddy Lally ⎰

Nanny

Period: early nineteenth century

Act I

Interior of a coachbuilder's workshop. Parts of a gilded coach, among them an ornament representing a lion and unicorn. Thomas working at a wheel. Father John coming from door of inner room.

1. *Father John.* I have prayed over Martin. I have prayed
2.   a long time, but there is no move in him yet.

3. *Thomas.* You are giving yourself too much trouble,
4.   Father. It's as good for you to leave him alone till
5.   the doctor's bottle will come. If there is any cure at
6.   all for what is on him, it is likely the doctor will
7.   have it.

8. *Father John.* I think it is not doctor's medicine will

PRINTINGS   **28a, 29, 33, 69, 84, 97.**

DATE   [lacking] **28a-69.**

DRAMATIS PERSONAE   Characters / Father ... / ... *coach builder* / ... Bacach / ... **28a, 29**[1]; ... Bacach / ... **33, 69.**

PERIOD   [lacking] **28a-69.**

STAGE DIRECTIONS   Scene: *Interior ... coach builder's ... coach. Thomas ....* **28a**; Scene: *Interior ... coach builder's ... representing the lion and the unicorn. ....* **29.**

     [1] In **28a** and **29** Johnny Bacach is usually Johnny B.

9.   help him in this case.

10.   *Thomas.* It will, it will. The doctor has his business
11.   learned well. If Andrew had gone to him the time I
12.   bade him and had not turned again to bring yourself
13.   to the house, it is likely Martin would be walking at
14.   this time. I am loth to trouble you, Father, when the
15.   business is not of your own sort. Any doctor at all
16.   should be able and well able to cure the falling
17.   sickness.

18.   *Father John.* It is not any common sickness that is on
19.   him now.

20.   *Thomas.* I thought at the first it was gone to sleep he
21.   was. But when shaking him and roaring at him
22.   failed to rouse him, I knew well it was the falling
23.   sickness. Believe me, the doctor will reach it with
24.   his drugs.

25.   *Father John.* Nothing but prayer can reach a soul that is
26.   so far beyond the world as his soul is at this moment.

27.   *Thomas.* You are not saying that the life is gone out
28.   of him!

29.   *Father John.* No, no, his life is in no danger. But where
30.   he himself, the spirit, the soul, is gone, I cannot say.
31.   It has gone beyond our imaginings. He is fallen into
32.   a trance.

33.   *Thomas.* He used to be queer as a child, going asleep
34.   in the fields, and coming back with talk of white
35.   horses he saw, and bright people like angels or what-
36.   ever they were. But I mended that. I taught him to
37.   recognise stones beyond angels with a few strokes of
38.   a rod. I would never give in to visions or to trances.

39.   *Father John.* We who hold the Faith have no right to

TEXT
12.   ... him, and ... **28a, 29.**
16.   ... able, and ... able, to ... **28a, 29.**
20.   ... gone asleep he **28a, 29.**
34.   ... fields and ... **28a, 29.**
39.   ... faith ... **28a-69.**

40. speak against trance or vision. Saint Elizabeth had
41. them, Saint Benedict, Saint Anthony, Saint Colum-
42. cille. Saint Catherine of Siena often lay a long time
43. as if dead.

44. *Thomas.* That might be so in the olden time, but
45. those things are gone out of the world now. Those
46. that do their work fair and honest have no occasion
47. to let the mind go rambling. What would send my
48. nephew, Martin Hearne, into a trance, supposing
49. trances to be in it, and he rubbing the gold on the
50. lion and unicorn that he had taken in hand to make
51. a good job of for the top of the coach?

52. *Father John* [*taking up ornament*]. It is likely it was that
53. sent him off. The flashing of light upon it would be
54. enough to throw one that had a disposition to it
55. into a trance. There was a very saintly man, though
56. he was not of our Church, he wrote a great book called
57. *Mysterium Magnum*, was seven days in a trance. Truth,
58. or whatever truth he found, fell upon him like a
59. bursting shower, and he a poor tradesman at his work.
60. It was a ray of sunlight on a pewter vessel that was
61. the beginning of all. [*Goes to the door and looks in.*]
62. There is no stir in him yet. It is either the best thing
63. or the worst thing can happen to any one, that is
64. happening to him now.

65. *Thomas.* And what in the living world can happen to
66. a man that is asleep on his bed?

67. *Father John.* There are some would answer you that it
68. is to those who are awake that nothing happens, and
69. it is they that know nothing. He is gone where all

---

40. . . . vision. St. Elizabeth . . . **28a** ; . . . vision. St. Teresa had **29** ; . . .
vision, Saint . . . **84.**
41. them, St. Benedict, St. Anthony, St. Colum-
42. cille. St. Catherine . . . **28a, 29.**
51. . . . coach. **28a.**
Directions in 52. [*taking it up*]. **28a, 29.**
56. . . . church, . . . **28a, 29, 69** ; . . . church; he . . . **33.**
57. 'Mysterium Magnum,' . . . , **28a, 29** ; . . . *Magnum* was . . . , **33.**
Directions in 61. [. . . *door of inner room.*] **29.**
63. . . . anyone that . . . **28a, 29** ; . . . anyone, . . . **33.**
66. . . . bed. **69.**

70.   have gone for supreme truth.

71.   *Thomas* [*sitting down again and taking up tools*]. Well,
72.   maybe so. But work must go on and coachbuilding
73.   must go on, and they will not go on the time there is
74.   too much attention given to dreams. A dream is a
75.   sort of a shadow, no profit in it to any one at all. A
76.   coach, now, is a real thing and a thing that will last
77.   for generations and be made use of to the last, and
78.   maybe turn to be a hen-roost at its latter end.

79.   *Father John*. I think Andrew told me it was a dream of
80.   Martin's that led to the making of that coach.

81.   *Thomas*. Well, I believe he saw gold in some dream,
82.   and it led him to want to make some golden thing,
83.   and coaches being the handiest, nothing would do
84.   him till he put the most of his fortune into the
85.   making of this golden coach. It turned out better
86.   than I thought, for some of the lawyers came looking
87.   at it at Assize time, and through them it was heard
88.   of at Dublin Castle . . . and who now has it ordered
89.   but the Lord Lieutenant! [*Father John nods*.] Ready
90.   it must be and sent off it must be by the end of the
91.   month. It is likely King George will be visiting
92.   Dublin, and it is he himself will be sitting in it yet.

93.   *Father John*. Martin has been working hard at it, I
94.   know.

95.   *Thomas*. You never saw a man work the way he did,
96.   day and night, near ever since the time six months ago
97.   he first came home from France.

98.   *Father John*. I never thought he would be so good at a
99.   trade. I thought his mind was only set on books.

100.   *Thomas*. He should be thankful to myself for that.

---

72.   . . . coach building **28a, 29.**
75.   . . . anyone . . . **28a-33.**
76.   coach now is . . . **28a, 29.**
77.   . . . of the . . . **29.**
82.   . . . some gold thing, **97A.**
87.   . . . assize . . . **28a, 29.**
96.   . . . time, six . . . ago, **28a, 29.**

101.   Any person I will take in hand, I make a clean job
102.   of them the same as I would make of any other thing
103.   in my yard—coach, half-coach, hackney-coach, ass-
104.   car, common-car, post-chaise, calash, chariot on
105.   two wheels, on four wheels. Each one has the shape
106.   Thomas Hearne put on it, and it in his hands; and
107.   what I can do with wood and iron, why would I not
108.   be able to do it with flesh and blood, and it in a way
109.   my own?

110.   *Father John.* Indeed, I know you did your best for
111.   Martin.

112.   *Thomas.* Every best. Checked him, taught him the
113.   trade, sent him to the monastery in France for to
114.   learn the language and to see the wide world; but
115.   who should know that if you did not know it,
116.   Father John, and I doing it according to your own
117.   advice?

118.   *Father John.* I thought his nature needed spiritual
119.   guidance and teaching, the best that could be found.

120.   *Thomas.* I thought myself it was best for him to be
121.   away for a while. There are too many wild lads
122.   about this place. He to have stopped here, he might
123.   have taken some fancies, and got into some trouble,
124.   going against the Government maybe the same as
125.   Johnny Gibbons that is at this time an outlaw,
126.   having a price upon his head.

127.   *Father John.* That is so. That imagination of his might
128.   have taken fire here at home. It was better putting
129.   him with the Brothers, to turn it to imaginings of

---

101.   . . . hand I . . . **28a, 29.**
103.   . . . , half coach, . . . , ass **28a** ; . . . yard, coach, half coach, . . . , ass
          29.
104.   . . . , common car, . . . **28a, 29.**
110.   Indeed I . . . **28a, 29.**
114.   . . . world, but **28a.**
117.   advice. **28a.**
123.   . . . fancies and . . . , **28a, 29.**
124.   . . . maybe, the . . . **28a** ; . . . Government, maybe, the . . . **29.**
125.   . . . outlaw **28a, 29.**

130.   Heaven.

131.   *Thomas.* Well, I will soon have a good hardy trades-
132.   man made of him now that will live quiet and rear
133.   a family, and be maybe appointed coachbuilder to
134.   the Royal Family at the last.

135.   *Father John* [*at window*]. I see your brother Andrew com-
136.   ing back from the doctor; he is stopping to talk
137.   with a troop of beggars that are sitting by the side
138.   of the road.

139.   *Thomas.* There, now, is another that I have shaped.
140.   Andrew used to be a bit wild in his talk and in his
141.   ways, wanting to go rambling, not content to settle
142.   in the place where he was reared. But I kept a guard
143.   over him; I watched the time poverty gave him a
144.   nip, and then I settled him into the business. He
145.   never was so good a worker as Martin, he is too fond
146.   of wasting his time talking vanities. But he is
147.   middling handy, and he is always steady and civil
148.   to customers. I have no complaint worth while to be
149.   making this last twenty years against Andrew.

Andrew comes in

150.   *Andrew.* Beggars there outside going the road to the
151.   Kinvara Fair. They were saying there is news that
152.   Johnny Gibbons is coming back from France on the
153.   quiet; the King's soldiers are watching the ports for
154.   him.

155.   *Thomas.* Let you keep now, Andrew, to the business
156.   you have in hand. Will the doctor be coming him-

---

130.   heaven. **28a-69.**
133.   . . . and maybe . . . coach builder . . . **28a ;** . . . and maybe be appointed
        coach builder . . . **29.**
134.   . . . royal family . . . . **28a, 29.**
139.   There now is . . . . **28a, 29.**
145.   . . . Martin; he . . . **29.**
147.   middlinghandy, . . . **69E.**
150.   . . . there are outside . . . **29.**
151.   Kinevara fair. . . . **28a ;** . . . fair. . . . **29.**
153.   quiet, the king's . . . **28a ;** quiet. The king's . . . **29 ;** . . . king's . . . **33, 69.**

157. self or did he send a bottle that will cure Martin?

158. *Andrew.* The doctor can't come, for he's down with
159. the lumbago in the back. He questioned me as to
160. what ailed Martin, and he got a book to go looking
161. for a cure, and he began telling me things out of it,
162. but I said I could not be carrying things of that sort
163. in my head. He gave me the book then, and he has
164. marks put in it for the places where the cures are.
165. . . . Wait now. . . . [*Reads*] 'Compound medicines
166. are usually taken inwardly, or outwardly applied; in-
167. wardly taken, they should be either liquid or solid;
168. outwardly, they should be fomentations or sponges
169. wet in some decoctions.'

170. *Thomas.* He had a right to have written it out himself
171. upon a paper. Where is the use of all that?

172. *Andrew.* I think I moved the mark maybe. . . . Here,
173. now, is the part he was reading to me himself. . . .
174. 'The remedies for diseases belonging to the skins
175. next the brain, headache, vertigo, cramp, convul-
176. sions, palsy, incubus, apoplexy, falling sickness.'

177. *Thomas.* It is what I bid you to tell him, that it was the
178. falling sickness.

179. *Andrew* [*dropping book*]. O, my dear, look at all the
180. marks gone out of it! Wait, now, I partly remember
181. what he said . . . a blister he spoke of . . . or to be
182. smelling hartshorn . . . or the sneezing powder

---

157. self, or . . . ?
158. . . . he is down . . .
159. lumbago . . . **28a, 29.**
165. . . . wait . . . **28a-69.**
166. . . . applied. In-
167. . . . taken they . . . ;
168. outwardly they . . . **28a, 29.**
172. . . . here **28a, 29** ; . . . here, **33, 69.**
173. now is . . .
174. 'the . . .
175. . . . brain: headache, . . . **28a, 29.**
177. . . . him that . . . **28a, 33, 69** ; . . . him—that . . . **29.**
179. O my . . .
180. . . . it. Wait now, . . . **28a, 29.**

183.   ... or if all fails, to try letting the blood.

184. *Father John.* All this has nothing to do with the real
185.   case. It is all waste of time.

186. *Andrew.* That is what I was thinking myself, Father.
187.   Sure it was I was the first to call out to you when I
188.   saw you coming down from the hillside, and to
189.   bring you in to see what could you do. I would have
190.   more trust in your means than in any doctor's learn-
191.   ing. And in case you might fail to cure him, I have a
192.   cure myself I heard from my grandmother—God rest
193.   her soul!—and she told me she never knew it to fail.
194.   A person to have the falling sickness, to cut the top
195.   of his nails and a small share of the hair of his head,
196.   and to put it down on the floor, and to take a harry-
197.   pin and drive it down with that into the floor and
198.   to leave it there. 'That is the cure will never fail',
199.   she said, 'to rise up any person at all having the
200.   falling sickness.'

201. *Father John* [*hand on ear*]. I will go back to the hillside,
202.   I will go back to the hillside; but no, no, I must
203.   do what I can. I will go again, I will wrestle, I will
204.   strive my best to call him back with prayer.

                                        [*Goes in and shuts door.*

205. *Andrew.* It is queer Father John is sometimes, and very
206.   queer. There are times when you would say that he
207.   believes in nothing at all.

208. *Thomas.* If you wanted a priest, why did you not get
209.   our own parish priest that is a sensible man, and a
210.   man that you would know what his thoughts are?

---

188.   ... hillside and ... **29** ; ... hill-side, ... **33-84.**
192.   ... grandmother ... [T] God ...
193.   ... soul ... [T] and .... **28a, 29.**
196.   ... floor and ... **28a, 29.**
        Directions in 201.   [*hands ... ears*]. **29.**
201.   ... hill-side, **33-84** ; ... hillside. **97A.**
202.   ... hillside, but ... **28a, 29** ; ... hill-side; ... **33-84.**
203.   ... can, I ... **28a, 29.**
        Directions after 204.   [*Goes into room and ....*] **29.**
210.   , , , are. **28a.**

211. You know well the Bishop should have something
212. against Father John to have left him through the
213. years in that poor mountainy place, minding the
214. few unfortunate people that were left out of the last
215. famine. A man of his learning to be going in rags the
216. way he is, there must be some good cause for that.

217. *Andrew.* I had all that in mind and I bringing him.
218. But I thought he would have done more for Martin
219. than what he is doing. To read a Mass over him I
220. thought he would, and to be convulsed in the reading
221. it, and some strange thing to have gone out with a
222. great noise through the doorway.

223. *Thomas.* It would give no good name to the place such
224. a thing to be happening in it. It is well enough for
225. labouring-men and for half-acre men. It would be
226. no credit at all such a thing to be heard of in this
227. house, that is for coachbuilding the capital of the
228. county.

229. *Andrew.* If it is from the Devil this sickness comes, it
230. would be best to put it out whatever way it would
231. be put out. But there might no bad thing be on the
232. lad at all. It is likely he was with wild companions
233. abroad, and that knocking about might have shaken
234. his health. I was that way myself one time.

235. *Thomas.* Father John said that it was some sort of a
236. vision or a trance, but I would give no heed to what
237. he would say. It is his trade to see more than other
238. people would see, the same as I myself might be
239. seeing a split in a leather car-hood that no other
240. person would find out at all.

241. *Andrew.* If it is the falling sickness is on him, I have

---

211. ... bishop ... **33, 69.**
225. labouring men ... **28a, 29.**
227. house that ... coach building ... **28a ;** ... coach building ... **29.**
229. ... devil ... **28a-69.**
234. ... time. ... [T] **28a, 29.**
236. ... or trance, ... **97A.**
239. ... car hood ... **28a-69.**

242. no objection to that—a plain straight sickness that
243. was cast as a punishment on the unbelieving Jews.
244. It is a thing that might attack one of a family, and
245. one of another family, and not to come upon their
246. kindred at all. A person to have it, all you have to do
247. is not to go between him and the wind, or fire, or
248. water. But I am in dread trance is a thing might run
249. through the house the same as the cholera morbus.

250. *Thomas.* In my belief there is no such thing as a trance.
251. Letting on people do be to make the world wonder
252. the time they think well to rise up. To keep them
253. to their work is best, and not to pay much attention
254. to them at all.

255. *Andrew.* I would not like trances to be coming on my-
256. self. I leave it in my will if I die without cause, a
257. holly-stake to be run through my heart the way I will
258. lie easy after burial, and not turn my face down-
259. wards in my coffin. I tell you I leave it on you in my
260. will.

261. *Thomas.* Leave thinking of your own comforts, Andrew,
262. and give your mind to the business. Did the smith
263. put the irons yet on to the shafts of this coach?

264. *Andrew.* I will go see did he.

265. *Thomas.* Do so, and see did he make a good job of it.
266. Let the shafts be sound and solid if they are to be
267. studded with gold.

268. *Andrew.* They are, and the steps along with them—

---

242. . . . that . . . [T] a plain, straight . . . **28a, 29 ;** . . . plain, straight . . .
 33.
244. . . . family and
245. . . . family and . . . **28a, 29.**
247. . . . wind or fire or **28a, 29.**
248. . . . . But, I . . . dread, trance . . . **28a.**
249. . . . house, the . . . . **28a, 29.**
263. . . . onto . . . ? **28a ;** . . . on the . . . ? **97A.**
264. I'll go . . . . **28a, 29.**
266. . . . *are* . . . **28a, 29.**
268. . . . them . . . [T] **28a, 29.**

269.　　glass sides for the people to be looking in at the
270.　　grandeur of the satin within—the lion and the uni-
271.　　corn crowning all. It was a great thought Martin had
272.　　the time he thought of making this coach!

273. *Thomas.* It is best for me to go see the smith myself
274.　　and leave it to no other one. You can be attending
275.　　to that ass-car out in the yard wants a new tyre on
276.　　the wheel—out in the rear of the yard it is. [*They go
277.　　to door.*] To pay attention to every small thing, and to
278.　　fill up every minute of time shaping whatever you
279.　　have to do, that is the way to build up a business.

　　　　　　　　　　　　　　　　　　　　　　　　[*They go out.*

280. *Father John* [*bringing in Martin*]. They are gone out now
281.　　—the air is fresher here in the workshop—you can
282.　　sit here for a while. You are now fully awake, you
283.　　have been in some sort of a trance or a sleep.

284. *Martin.* Who was it that pulled at me? Who brought
285.　　me back?

286. *Father John.* It is I, Father John, did it. I prayed a long
287.　　time over you and brought you back.

288. *Martin.* You, Father John, to be so unkind! O leave
289.　　me, leave me alone!

290. *Father John.* You are in your dream still.

291. *Martin.* It was no dream, it was real. Do you not smell
292.　　the broken fruit—the grapes? The room is full of
293.　　the smell.

270.　. . . within . . . [T] the . . .
271.　. . . all . . . [T] it . . . **28a, 29.**
273.　. . . myself . . . [T] **28a, 29.**
275.　. . . ass car . . . tyre in **28a, 29 ;** . . . tyre in **33.**
276.　. . . wheel . . . [T] out . . . **28a, 29.**
278.　. . . time, shaping . . . **28a, 29.**
281.　. . . [T] the air . . . workshop . . . [T] you . . . **28a, 29.**
282.　. . . awake; you **29.**
291.　. . . real . . . [T] do . . . **28a, 29.**
292.　. . . fruit . . . [T] the grapes . . . [T] the room . . . **28a, 29 ;** . . . grapes?
　　　the . . . **33, 69.**

294. *Father John.* Tell me what you have seen, where you
295.   have been.

296. *Martin.* There were horses—white horses rushing by,
297.   with white shining riders—there was a horse with-
298.   out a rider, and some one caught me up and put me
299.   upon him and we rode away, with the wind, like the
300.   wind—

301. *Father John.* That is a common imagining. I know many
302.   poor persons have seen that.

303. *Martin.* We went on, on, on. We came to a sweet-
304.   smelling garden with a gate to it, and there were
305.   wheatfields in full ear around, and there were vine-
306.   yards like I saw in France, and the grapes in bunches.
307.   I thought it to be one of the townlands of Heaven.
308.   Then I saw the horses we were on had changed to
309.   unicorns, and they began trampling the grapes and
310.   breaking them. I tried to stop them, but I could not.

311. *Father John.* That is strange, that is strange. What is it
312.   that brings to mind? I heard it in some place, *mono-*
313.   *ceros de astris*, the unicorn from the stars.

314. *Martin.* They tore down the wheat and trampled it on
315.   stones, and then they tore down what were left of the

---

294. . . . seen where . . . **28a, 29.**
295. . . . been? **33, 69.**
296. . . . horses . . . [T] white . . . ,
297. . . . white, shining riders . . . [T] there . . . **28a, 29.**
298. . . . someone . . . **28a-33.**
299. . . . him, and . . .
300. wind . . . [T] **28a, 29.**
303. . . . on, on, on . . . [T] we . . .
304. . . . it . . . [T] and . . .
305. wheat-fields . . . around . . . [T] and . . .
306. . . . bunches . . . [T] **28a, 29.**
307. . . . heaven. **28a-69.**
309. . . . began tramping the . . . **84.**
310. . . . them . . . [T] I . . . . **28a, 29 ;** . . . them but . . . . **33, 69.**
312. . . . mind . . . [T] I . . . , *mono-* (*Mono-* **29**) **28a, 29.**
313. *coros di astris*, ... **28a ;** *coros di Astris*, . . . Unicorn . . . Stars. **29.**
315. . . . of **28a, 33, 69.**

316.   grapes and crushed and bruised and trampled them.
317.   I smelt the wine, it was flowing on every side—then
318.   everything grew vague. I cannot remember clearly,
319.   everything was silent; the trampling now stopped,
320.   we were all waiting for some command. O! was it
321.   given? I was trying to hear it; there was some one
322.   dragging, dragging me away from that. I am sure
323.   there was a command given, and there was a great
324.   burst of laughter. What was it? What was the com-
325.   mand? Everything seemed to tremble round me.

326. *Father John.* Did you awake then?

327.   *Martin.* I do not think I did, it all changed—it was
328.   terrible, wonderful! I saw the unicorns trampling,
329.   trampling, but not in the wine-troughs. O, I forget!
330.   Why did you waken me?

331. *Father John.* I did not touch you. Who knows what
332.   hands pulled you away? I prayed, that was all I did.
333.   I prayed very hard that you might awake. If I had
334.   not, you might have died. I wonder what it all meant?
335.   The unicorns—what did the French monk tell me?
336.   —strength they meant, virginal strength, a rushing,
337.   lasting, tireless strength.

---

316.   ... them ... [T]
317.   ... side ... [T] then
318.   ... vague ... [T] I ... clearly ... [T]
319.   ... silent ... [T] the ... stopped ... [T] **28a, 29.**
321.   given! I ... it ... [T] there ... **28a, 29**; given! I ... someone **33, 69.**
322.   ... that ... [T] I ...
323.   ... given ... [T] and ... **28a, 29.**
325.   ... around .... **28a, 29.**
327.   ... did ... [T] it ... changed ... [T] it ... **28a, 29.**
328.   ..., wonderful. I ..., **28a, 29, 69A.**
329.   trampling ... [T] but ... wine troughs ... [T] Oh, I ... ! **28a, 29**; ... wine troughs. Oh, ... ! **33, 69.**
332.   ... prayed; that .... **29.**
334.   ... meant.
335.   ... unicorns ... [T] what ... me ... [T]
336.   strength ... meant ... [T] virginal ..., **28a, 29.**

338. *Martin.* They were strong. O, they made a great noise
339. with their trampling.

340. *Father John.* And the grapes, what did they mean? It
341. puts me in mind of the psalm, *Et calix meus inebrians*
342. *quam praeclarus est.* It was a strange vision, a very
343. strange vision, a very strange vision.

344. *Martin.* How can I get back to that place?

345. *Father John.* You must not go back, you must not think
346. of doing that. That life of vision, of contemplation,
347. is a terrible life, for it has far more temptation in it
348. than the common life. Perhaps it would have been
349. best for you to stay under rules in the monastery.

350. *Martin.* I could not see anything so clearly there. It is
351. back here in my own place the visions come, in the
352. place where shining people used to laugh around me,
353. and I a little lad in a bib.

354. *Father John.* You cannot know but it was from the
355. Prince of this world the vision came. How can one
356. ever know unless one follows the discipline of the
357. Church? Some spiritual director, some wise learned
358. man, that is what you want. I do not know enough.
359. What am I but a poor banished priest, with my
360. learning forgotten, my books never handled and
361. spotted with the damp!

362. *Martin.* I will go out into the fields where you cannot
363. come to me to awake me. I will see that townland

338. ... strong ... [T] Oh, ... **28a, 29.**
339. ... trampling!
340. ... grapes ... [T] what ... mean (mean? **29**) ... [T] It
341. ... psalm ... [T] *Et* ... **28a, 29.**
346. ... that, that ... , **28a ;** ... that; that ... , **29.**
347. ... more of temptation ... **28a-69.**
352. ... me **28a, 29.**
357. church? ... wise, learned **28a, 29.**
358. man that .... **69E.**
359. ... priest with ...
360. ... forgotten ... [T] my ... handled, and
361. ... damp? **28a, 29.**
363. ... awake me ... [T] I ... **28a, 29.**

364. again; I will hear that command. I cannot wait, I
365. must know what happened, I must bring that com-
366. mand to mind again.

Father John [putting himself between Martin and the door].
367. You must have patience as the Saints had it. You
368. are taking your own way. If there is a command
369. from God for you, you must wait His good time to
370. receive it.

371. *Martin.* Must I live here forty years, fifty years . . . to
372. grow as old as my uncles, seeing nothing but com-
373. mon things, doing work . . . some foolish work?

374. *Father John.* Here they are coming; it is time for me
375. to go. I must think and I must pray. My mind is
376. troubled about you. [*To Thomas as he and Andrew come*
377. *in.*] Here he is; be very kind to him, for he has
378. still the weakness of a little child.   [*Goes out.*

379. *Thomas.* Are you well of the fit, lad?

380. *Martin.* It was no fit. I was away—for a while—no,
381. you will not believe me if I tell you.

382. *Andrew.* I would believe it, Martin, I used to have very
383. long sleeps myself and very queer dreams.

384. *Thomas.* You had, till I cured you, taking you in hand
385. and binding you to the hours of the clock. The cure
386. that will cure yourself, Martin, and will waken you,
387. is to put the whole of your mind on to your golden
388. coach; to take it in hand and to finish it out of face.

389. *Martin.* Not just now. I want to think—to try and

---

364. again . . . [T] I . . . 28a, 29 ; . . . wait. I 97A.
365. . . . happened. I . . . 97A.
367. . . . saints . . . 28a-84.
374. . . . coming. It . . . 28a, 29.
377. . . . him for . . . 28a, 33, 69.
380. . . . away . . . [T] for . . . while . . . [T] no, 28a, 29 ; . . . awhile—no,
         33, 69.
387. . . . onto . . . 28a.
388. coach, to . . . hand, and . . . .
389. . . . think . . . [T] to . . . 28a, 29.

390. remember what I saw, something that I heard, that
391. I was told to do.

392. *Thomas.* No, but put it out of your mind. There is no
393. man doing business that can keep two things in his
394. head. A Sunday or a holy-day, now, you might go
395. see a good hurling or a thing of the kind, but to be
396. spreading out your mind on anything outside of the
397. workshop on common days, all coachbuilding would
398. come to an end.

399. *Martin.* I don't think it is building I want to do. I
400. don't think that is what was in the command.

401. *Thomas.* It is too late to be saying that, the time you
402. have put the most of your fortune in the business.
403. Set yourself now to finish your job, and when it is
404. ended maybe I won't begrudge you going with the
405. coach as far as Dublin.

406. *Andrew.* That is it, that will satisfy him. I had a great
407. desire myself, and I young, to go travelling the roads
408. as far as Dublin. The roads are the great things,
409. they never come to an end. They are the same as the
410. serpent having his tail swallowed in his own mouth.

411. *Martin.* It was not wandering I was called to. What
412. was it? What was it?

413. *Thomas.* What you are called to, and what every one
414. having no great estate is called to, is to work. Sure
415. the world itself could not go on without work.

416. *Martin.* I wonder if that is the great thing, to make
417. the world go on? No, I don't think that is the great

---

394. . . . Holyday now you . . . **28a, 29.**
397. . . . coach building (coach-building **33**) . . . **28a-33.**
401. . . . that the . . . **28a, 29.**
404. ended, maybe . . . **28a, 29.**
406. . . . it; that . . . **28a, 29.**
407. . . . traveling . . . **97A.**
408. . . . things; **28a, 29.**
412. . . . ? what . . . ? **33.**
413. . . . everyone **28a-33.**
417. . . . on. No, . . . **28a, 29.**

418.   thing—what does the Munster poet call it?—'this
419.   crowded slippery coach-loving world'. I don't think
420.   I was told to work for that.

421.   *Andrew.* I often thought that myself. It is a pity the
422.   stock of the Hearnes to be asked to do any work
423.   at all.

424.   *Thomas.* Rouse yourself, Martin, and don't be talking
425.   the way a fool talks. You started making that golden
426.   coach, and you were set upon it, and you had me
427.   tormented about it. You have yourself wore out
428.   working at it, and planning it, and thinking of it,
429.   and at the end of the race, when you have the
430.   winning-post in sight, and horses hired for to bring
431.   it to Dublin Castle, you go falling into sleeps and
432.   blathering about dreams, and we run to a great
433.   danger of letting the profit and the sale go by. Sit
434.   down on the bench now, and lay your hands to
435.   the work.

436.   *Martin* [*sitting down*]. I will try. I wonder why I ever
437.   wanted to make it; it was no good dream set me
438.   doing that. [*He takes up wheel.*] What is there in a
439.   wooden wheel to take pleasure in it? Gilding it out-
440.   side makes it no different.

441.   *Thomas.* That is right, now. You had some good plan
442.   for making the axle run smooth.

       Martin [*letting wheel fall and putting his hands to his head*].
443.   It is no use. [*Angrily.*] Why did you send the priest
444.   to awake me? My soul is my own and my mind is
445.   my own. I will send them to where I like. You have
446.   no authority over my thoughts.

447.   *Thomas.* That is no way to be speaking to me. I am
448.   head of this business. Nephew or no nephew, I will

---

418.   thing . . . [T] what . . . it . . . [T] 'this **28a, 29.**
424.   . . . yourself Martin, . . . **69A.**
428.   . . . at it and . . . it and . . . , **28a, 29.**
430.   winning post . . . **28a, 29.**
437.   . . . it, it . . . **28a.**
441.   . . . right now. . . . **28a, 29.**
448.   . . . . Nephew, or . . . **33, 69.**

449.   have no one come cold or unwilling to the work.

450.   *Martin.* I had better go; I am of no use to you. I am
451.   going—I must be alone—I will forget if I am not
452.   alone. Give me what is left of my money and I will
453.   go out of this.

     Thomas [*opening a press and taking out a bag and throwing*
454.   *it to him*]. There is what is left of your money! The
455.   rest of it you have spent on the coach. If you want
456.   to go, go, and I will not have to be annoyed with you
457.   from this out.

458.   *Andrew.* Come now with me, Thomas. The boy is
459.   foolish, but it will soon pass over. He has not my
460.   sense to be giving attention to what you will say.
461.   Come along now, leave him for a while; leave him
462.   to me, I say, it is I will get inside his mind.
     [*He leads Thomas out. Martin bangs door angrily after them and sits
     down, taking up lion and unicorn.*

463.   *Martin.* I think it was some shining thing I saw. What
464.   was it?

465.   *Andrew* [*opening door and putting in his head*]. Listen to
466.   me, Martin.

467.   *Martin.* Go away, no more talking; leave me alone.

468.   *Andrew.* O, but wait. I understand you. Thomas doesn't
469.   understand your thoughts, but I understand them.
470.   Wasn't I telling you I was just like you once?

471.   *Martin.* Like me? Did you ever see the other things,
472.   the things beyond?

---

450. . . . go. I . . .
451. going . . . [T] I . . . alone . . . [T] I . . .
452. . . . money, and . . . **28a, 29.**
461. . . . now; leave . . . **28a, 29 ;** . . . awhile; . . . **33, 69.**
462. . . . say; it . . . . **28a, 29 ;** . . . me I . . . . **33, 69.**
     Directions after 462. [. . . . *Martin, when they have gone, sits* . . . .] **29.**
463. . . . saw . . . [T] What **28a, 29.**
467. . . . away—no . . . talking—leave . . . . **28a, 29.**
468. *Andrew* [*coming in*]. Oh, . . . **29.**
471. . . . me, did . . . , **28a.**

473.   *Andrew*. I did. It is not the four walls of the house
474.   keep me content. Thomas doesn't know. O no, he
475.   doesn't know.

476.   *Martin*. No, he has no vision.

477.   *Andrew*. He has not, nor any sort of a heart for a frolic.

478.   *Martin*. He has never heard the laughter and the music
479.   beyond.

480.   *Andrew*. He has not, nor the music of my own little
481.   flute. I have it hidden in the thatch outside.

482.   *Martin*. Does the body slip from you as it does from
483.   me? They have not shut your window into eternity?

484.   *Andrew*. Thomas never shut a window I could not get
485.   through. I knew you were one of my own sort.
486.   When I am sluggish in the morning, Thomas says,
487.   'Poor Andrew is getting old'. That is all he knows.
488.   The way to keep young is to do the things youngsters
489.   do. Twenty years I have been slipping away, and he
490.   never found me out yet!

491.   *Martin*. That is what they call ecstasy, but there is no
492.   word that can tell out very plain what it means.
493.   That freeing of the mind from its thoughts; when
494.   we put those wonders into words, those words seem
495.   as little like them as blackberries are like the moon
496.   and sun.

497.   *Andrew*. I found that myself the time they knew me
498.   to be wild, and used to be asking me to say what
499.   pleasure did I find in cards, and women, and drink.

---

474.   ... know, oh, no, ... **28a, 29** ; .... Oh, no, ... **33** ; ... Oh ... **69**.
477.   ... for frolic. **28a, 29** ; ... not, not any .... **97A**.
481.   ... the hole by the door. [*Takes it out*]. **28a**.
486.   ... sluggish, in ... morning Thomas ... , **28a** ; ... morning Thomas ... , **29**.
493.   ... thoughts. Those **28a, 29** ; ... thoughts, those **33**.
494.   wonders we know; when we put them into words, the words ... **28a, 29** ; wonders we know when we put them into words; the words ... **33, 69**.

500. *Martin.* You might help me to remember that vision
501.   I had this morning, to understand it. The memory
502.   of it has slipped from me. Wait, it is coming back,
503.   little by little. I know that I saw the unicorns
504.   trampling, and then a figure, a many-changing figure,
505.   holding some bright thing. I knew something was
506.   going to happen or to be said, something that would
507.   make my whole life strong and beautiful like the rush-
508.   ing of the unicorns, and then, and then—

509. *Johnny Bocach's voice* [*at window*]. A poor person I am,
510.   without food, without a way, without portion, with-
511.   out costs, without a person or a stranger, without
512.   means, without hope, without health, without
513.   warmth—

514. *Andrew* [*looking towards window*]. It is that troop of
515.   beggars. Bringing their tricks and their thieveries
516.   they are to the Kinvara Fair.

517. *Martin* [*impatiently*]. There is no quiet—come to the
518.   other room. I am trying to remember.
             [*They go to door of inner room, but Andrew stops him.*]

519. *Andrew.* They are a bad-looking fleet. I have a mind
520.   to drive them away, giving them a charity.

521. *Martin.* Drive them away or come away from their
522.   voices.

523. *Another Voice.* I put under the power of my prayer
524.   All that will give me help.

---

502. . . . . Wait; it . . . , **28a, 29.**
506. . . . said,—something . . . **28a ;** . . . said, . . . [T] something . . . **29.**
508. . . . , and then, and then . . . [T] **28a, 29.**
509. *Johnny Bacach* [*at* . . .]. A . . . , **28a.**
513. warmth . . . [T] **28a, 29.**
515. beggars, bringing . . . **28a ;** beggars; bringing . . . **29.**
516. . . . Kinevara fair. **28a ;** . . . fair. **29.**
517. . . . quiet . . . [T] come . . .
518. . . . remember . . . [T] **28a, 29.**
520. . . . away . . . [T] giving . . . . **28a.**
523. . . . prayer, **28a, 29.**
524. . . . help **28a ;** . . . help, **29.**

525.	Rafael keep him Wednesday,
526.	Sachiel feed him Thursday,
527.	Hamiel provide him Friday,
528.	Cassiel increase him Saturday.

529. Sure giving to us is giving to the Lord and laying up
530. a store in the treasury of Heaven.

531. *Andrew*. Whisht! He is entering by the window!

                                            [Johnny climbs up.

532. *Johnny*. That I may never sin, but the place is empty.

533. *Paudeen [outside]*. Go in and see what can you make a
534. grab at.

535. *Johnny [getting in]*. That every blessing I gave may be
536. turned to a curse on them that left the place so bare!
537. *[He turns things over.]* I might chance something in this
538. chest if it was open.

                               [Andrew begins creeping towards him.

539. *Nanny [outside]*. Hurry on, now, you limping crabfish,
540. you! We can't be stopping here while you'll boil
541. stirabout!

     Johnny [seizing bag of money and holding it up high in both
542.   *hands]*. Look at this, now, look!

                               [Andrew comes behind, seizes his arm.

---

525. . . . Wednesday;
526. . . . Thursday;
527. . . . Friday; **28a, 29.**
[between 528 and 529 no break] **28a-69, 97A.**
530. . . . heaven. **28a-69.**
531. . . . is coming in by . . . ! **29**; Whisht? He . . . ! **97A.**
Directions after 531. [*Johnny B. climbs in.*] **28a, 29.**
532. . . . empty! **29.**
Directions in 533. [lacking] **28a-69.**
538. press if . . . open . . . . [T] **28a**; . . . open . . . . [T] **29.**
539. . . . on now, . . . , **28a, 29**; . . . crabfish **33, 69.**
Directions before 542. [. . . *up in* . . . .]
542. . . . this now, . . . ! **28a, 29.**
Directions after 542. [*Andrew seizes* . . . .] **28a**; [. . . *behind and seizes*
. . . .] **29.**

543. *Johnny* [*letting bag fall with a crash*]. Destruction on us all!

Martin [*running forward, seizes him. Heads at the window*
544.   *disappear*]. That is it! O, I remember. That is what
545.   happened. That is the command. Who was it sent you
546.   here with that command?

547. *Johnny.* It was misery sent me in, and starvation and
548.   the hard ways of the world.

549. *Nanny* [*outside*]. It was that, my poor child, and my one
550.   son only. Show mercy to him now and he after leav-
551.   ing gaol this morning.

552. *Martin* [*to Andrew*]. I was trying to remember it—when
553.   he spoke that word it all came back to me. I saw a
554.   bright many-changing figure; it was holding up a
555.   shining vessel [*holds up arms*]; then the vessel fell
556.   and was broken with a great crash; then I saw the
557.   unicorns trampling it. They were breaking the world
558.   to pieces—when I saw the cracks coming I shouted for
559.   joy! And I heard the command, 'Destroy, destroy,
560.   destruction is the life-giver! destroy!'

561. *Andrew.* What will we do with him? He was thinking
562.   to rob you of your gold.

563. *Martin.* How could I forget it or mistake it? It has all
564.   come upon me now; the reasons of it all, like a flood,
565.   like a flooded river.

Directions in 543. [*letting it fall* . . . .] **28a.**
Directions before 544. [. . . . *Heads disappear.*] **28a-69.**
544. . . . ! Oh, . . . remember! That . . .
545. happened! That . . . command! Who . . . **28a, 29.**
547. . . . in and . . . **28a, 29 ;** . . . starvation, and **33.**
550. . . . now, and . . . **28a, 29.**
552. . . . it . . . [T] when **28a, 29.**
554. bright, many-changing figure . . . [T] it . . .
555. . . . vessel . . . [T] [*holds . . . arms*] then . . .
556. . . . crash . . . [T] then . . . **28a, 29.**
558. . . . pieces . . . [T] when . . . coming, I . . . **28a, 29.**
559. . . . , destroy; **28a, 29 ;** . . . command 'Destroy, . . . **33.**
560. . . . life-giver; destroy.' **28a, 29.**
564. . . . now . . . [T] the . . . , **28a, 29.**

566. *Johnny* [*weeping*]. It was the hunger brought me in and
567. the drouth.

568. *Martin.* Were you given any other message? Did you
569. see the unicorns?

570. *Johnny.* I saw nothing and heard nothing; near dead I am
571. with the fright I got and with the hardship of the
572. gaol.

573. *Martin.* To destroy, to overthrow all that comes be-
574. tween us and God, between us and that shining
575. country. To break the wall, Andrew, to break the
576. thing—whatever it is that comes between; but where
577. to begin—?

578. *Andrew.* What is it you are talking about?

579. *Martin.* It may be that this man is the beginning. He
580. has been sent—the poor, they have nothing, and so
581. they can see Heaven as we cannot. He and his com-
582. rades will understand me. But how to give all men
583. high hearts that they may all understand?

584. *Johnny.* It's the juice of the grey barley will do that.

585. *Andrew.* To rise everybody's heart, is it? Is it that was
586. your meaning all the time? If you will take the blame
587. of it all, I'll do what you want. Give me the bag of
588. money then. [*He takes it up.*] O, I've a heart like
589. your own. I'll lift the world, too. The people will be

---

573. . . . destroy . . . [T] to . . . **28a, 29.**
575. . . ., Andrew, to [Blank space] **28a** ; . . ., Andrew, the **29.**
576. thing, whatever . . . between, but . . . **28a, 29** ; . . . between, but . . .
      33, 69.
577. . . . begin . . . . [T] **28a** ; . . . begin? . . . [T] **29** ; . . . begin— **33, 69.**
580. . . . sent . . . [T] the . . . **28a, 29.**
581. . . . heaven . . . **28a-69.**
582. . . . . But now to . . .
583. . . . understand. **28a, 29.**
586. . . . meaning [Blank space] If . . . **28a** ; . . . meaning? . . . [T] If . . .
      29.
588. money, then. [. . . *up.*] Oh, . . . **29.**
589. . . . own! I'll . . . world too! The . . . **28a, 29.**

590. running from all parts. O, it will be a great day in
591. this district.

592. *Johnny.* Will I go with you?

593. *Martin.* No, you must stay here; we have things to do
594. and to plan.

595. *Johnny.* Destroyed we all are with the hunger and the
596. drouth.

597. *Martin.* Go, then, get food and drink, whatever is
598. wanted to give you strength and courage. Gather
599. your people together here, bring them all in. We
600. have a great thing to do, I have to begin—I want to
601. tell it to the whole world. Bring them in, bring
602. them in, I will make the house ready.

> [*He stands looking up as if in ecstasy; Andrew and Johnny Bocach go out.*

597. Go then, . . .
598. . . . courage; gather
599. . . . here; bring . . . **28a, 29.**
600. . . . do. I . . . to commence . . . [T] I . . . **28a ;** . . . do. I . . . begin
    . . . [T] I . . . **29 ;** . . . do. I . . . **33, 69.**
    Directions after 602. [lacking] **28a, 29.**

Act II

*The same workshop. Martin seen arranging mugs and bread, etc., on a table.
Father John comes in, knocking at open door as he comes; his mind intensely
absorbed.*

1. *Martin.* Come in, come in, I have got the house ready.
2. Here is bread and meat—everybody is welcome.

[*Hearing no answer, turns round.*

3. *Father John.* Martin, I have come back. There is some-
4. thing I want to say to you.

5. *Martin.* You are welcome, there are others coming.
6. They are not of your sort, but all are welcome.

7. *Father John.* I have remembered suddenly something
8. that I read when I was in the seminary.

9. *Martin.* You seem very tired.

10. *Father John* [*sitting down*]. I had almost got back to my
11. own place when I thought of it. I have run part of
12. the way. It is very important; it is about the trance
13. that you have been in. When one is inspired from
14. above, either in trance or in contemplation, one re-
15. members afterwards all that one has seen and read.
16. I think there must be something about it in Saint
17. Thomas. I know that I have read a long passage about
18. it years ago. But, Martin, there is another kind of
19. inspiration, or rather an obsession or possession. A
20. diabolical power comes into one's body, or over-
21. shadows it. Those whose bodies are taken hold of in
22. this way, jugglers, and witches, and the like, can

STAGE DIRECTIONS   Scene: *Martin . . . he comes. His . . . .* **28a** ; Scene: . . .
workshop a few minutes later. Martin . . . door as he comes. **29.**

2.   . . . meat . . . [T] everybody . . . . **28a, 29.**
3.   . . . back . . . [T] There . . . **28a, 29.**
5.   . . . welcome; there . . . coming . . . . [T] **28a, 29.**
12.   . . . important. It . . . **28a, 29.**
16.   . . . St. **28a-69.**
20.   . . . body or . . . **28a, 29.**
21.   . . . it; those . . . **28a.**
22.   . . . , jugglers and witches and . . . **28a, 29.**

23.   often tell what is happening in distant places, or
24.   what is going to happen, but when they come out of
25.   that state they remember nothing. I think you said—

26. *Martin.* That I could not remember.

27. *Father John.* You remembered something, but not all.
28.   Nature is a great sleep; there are dangerous and evil
29.   spirits in her dreams, but God is above Nature. She
30.   is a darkness, but He makes everything clear; He is
31.   light.

32. *Martin.* All is clear now. I remember all, or all that
33.   matters to me. A poor man brought me a word, and
34.   I know what I have to do.

35. *Father John.* Ah, I understand, words were put into his
36.   mouth. I have read of such things. God sometimes
37.   uses some common man as His messenger.

38. *Martin.* You may have passed the man who brought it
39.   on the road. He left me but now.

40. *Father John.* Very likely, very likely, that is the way
41.   it happened. Some plain, unnoticed man has some-
42.   times been sent with a command.

43. *Martin.* I saw the unicorns trampling in my dream.
44.   They were breaking the world. I am to destroy; de-
45.   struction was the word the messenger spoke.

46. *Father John.* To destroy?

47. *Martin.* To bring again the old disturbed exalted life,
48.   the old splendour.

49. *Father John.* You are not the first that dream has come

---

23. . . . places or **69A.**
25. . . . state, they . . . **28a, 29.**
30. . . . clear—He . . . **28a, 29.**
35. . . . understand, and words . . . **28a ;** . . . understand; words . . . **29.**
37. . . . his . . . . **33, 69.**
44. . . . destroy, that **28a, 29 ;** . . . destroy, de- **33, 69.**
45. is the word . . . . **28a, 29.**

50. to. [*Gets up, and walks up and down.*] It has been
51. wandering here and there, calling now to this man,
52. now to that other. It is a terrible dream.

53. *Martin.* Father John, you have had the same thought.

54. *Father John.* Men were holy then, there were saints
55. everywhere. There was reverence; but now it is all
56. work, business, how to live a long time. Ah, if one
57. could change it all in a minute, even by war and vio-
58. lence! There is a cell where Saint Ciaran used to pray;
59. if one could bring that time again!

60. *Martin.* Do not deceive me. You have had the com-
61. mand.

62. *Father John.* Why are you questioning me? You are
63. asking me things that I have told to no one but my
64. confessor.

65. *Martin.* We must gather the crowds together, you and I.

66. *Father John.* I have dreamed your dream, it was long
67. ago. I had your vision.

68. *Martin.* And what happened?

69. *Father John* [*harshly*]. It was stopped; that was an end.
70. I was sent to the lonely parish where I am, where
71. there was no one I could lead astray. They have left
72. me there. We must have patience; the world was
73. destroyed by water, it has yet to be consumed by fire.

74. *Martin.* Why should we be patient? To live seventy
75. years, and others to come after us and live seventy

Directions in 50. [*Gets up and . . . .*] **28a, 29.**
54. . . . then; there . . . **28a, 29.**
55. . . . reverence, but . . . **28a ;** everywhere, there . . . reverence, but . . .
 29.
58. lence. . . . [T] There . . . St. . . . pray,
59. . . . again. **28a, 29.**
66. . . . dream; it . . . **28a, 29.**
69. . . . stopped. That . . . . **28a, 29.**
75. . . . after is and . . . **28a.**

76. years, it may be; and so from age to age, and all the
77. while the old splendour dying more and more.
   [*A noise of shouting. Andrew, who has been standing at the door, comes in.*

78. *Andrew.* Martin says truth, and he says it well. Planing
79. the side of a cart or a shaft, is that life? It is not.
80. Sitting at a desk writing letters to the man that
81. wants a coach, or to the man that won't pay for the
82. one he has got, is that life, I ask you? Thomas argu-
83. ing at you and putting you down—'Andrew, dear
84. Andrew, did you put the tyre on that wheel yet?'
85. Is that life? No, it is not. I ask you all, what do you
86. remember when you are dead? It's the sweet cup in
87. the corner of the widow's drinking-house that you
88. remember. Ha, ha, listen to that shouting! That is
89. what the lads in the village will remember to the
90. last day they live.

91. *Martin.* Why are they shouting? What have you told
92. them?

93. *Andrew.* Never you mind; you left that to me. You
94. bade me to lift their hearts and I did lift them.
95. There is not one among them but will have his head
96. like a blazing tar-barrel before morning. What did
97. your friend the beggar say? The juice of the grey
98. barley, he said.

99. *Father John.* You accursed villain! You have made them
100. drunk!

101. *Andrew.* Not at all, but lifting them to the stars. That

---

76. years it . . . be, and . . . **28a, 29**; years it . . . **33, 69**.
   Directions after 77. [. . . *door for a moment, comes* . . . .] **29**.
81. . . . coach or . . . men . . . **28a**; . . . coach or . . . **29**.
83. . . . down, 'Andrew, . . . **28a, 29**.
84. Andrew, have you . . . ?' **28a**.
85. . . . all what . . . **28a, 29**; . . . life? Not, it . . . **33**.
87. . . . drinking house . . . **28a, 29**.
90. . . . live! **28a, 29**.
93. . . . mind. You . . .
94. . . . hearts, and . . . . **28a, 29**.
96. . . . tar barrel . . .
97. . . . friend, the beggar, say? . . . . **28a, 29**.

102. is what Martin bade me to do, and there is no one
103. can say I did not do it.

> [*A shout at door, and Beggars push in a barrel. They cry, 'Hi! for the noble master!' and point at Andrew.*

104. *Johnny.* It's not him, it's that one!

> [*Points at Martin.*

105. *Father John.* Are you bringing this devil's work in at
106. the very door? Go out of this, I say! get out! Take
107. these others with you!

108. *Martin.* No, no; I asked them in, they must not be
109. turned out. They are my guests.

110. *Father John.* Drive them out of your uncle's house!

111. *Martin.* Come, Father, it is better for you to go. Go
112. back to your own place. I have taken the command.
113. It is better perhaps for you that you did not take it.

> [*Father John and Martin go out.*

114. *Biddy.* It is well for that old lad he didn't come be-
115. tween ourselves and our luck. Himself to be after his
116. meal, and ourselves staggering with the hunger! It
117. would be right to have flayed him and to have made
118. bags of his skin.

119. *Nanny.* What a hurry you are in to get your enough!
120. Look at the grease on your frock yet, with the dint
121. of the dabs you put in your pocket! Doing cures and
122. foretellings, is it? You starved pot-picker, you!

. Directions after 103. [. . . *door and . . . barrel.* 'All hi! for . . . master!'
   Point . . . . **28a** ; [. . . *door and . . . . They all cry,* '. . . . **29.**
106. . . . ! Get . . . **28a, 29.**
108. . . . , no, I . . . in; they . . . **28a, 29.**
113. . . . better, perhaps, for . . . . **28a, 29.**
   Directions after 113. [*They go . . . .*] **28a** ; [*Martin and Father John go
   . . . .*] **29.**
115. . . . luck. It **28a, 29.**
116. [lacking] **28a, 29** ; . . . with hunger! . . . **69A.**
120. . . . yet with . . . **28a, 29.**
122. . . . pot picker, . . . ! **28a, 29** ; foretellings is . . . ! **33, 69, 84.**

123. *Biddy.* That you may be put up to-morrow to take the
124.   place of that decent son of yours that had the yard
125.   of the gaol wore with walking it till this morning!

126. *Nanny.* If he had, he had a mother to come to, and he
127.   would know her when he did see her; and that is
128.   what no son of your own could do and he to meet
129.   you at the foot of the gallows.

130. *Johnny.* If I did know you, I knew too much of you
131.   since the first beginning of my life! What reward
132.   did I ever get travelling with you? What store did
133.   you give me of cattle or of goods? What provision
134.   did I get from you by day or by night but your own
135.   bad character to be joined on to my own, and I
136.   following at your heels, and your bags tied round
137.   about me!

138. *Nanny.* Disgrace and torment on you! Whatever you
139.   got from me, it was more than any reward or any bit
140.   I ever got from the father you had, or any honour-
141.   able thing at all, but only the hurt and the harm of
142.   the world and its shame!

143. *Johnny.* What would he give you, and you going with
144.   him without leave! Crooked and foolish you were
145.   always, and you begging by the side of the ditch.

146. *Nanny.* Begging or sharing, the curse of my heart upon
147.   you! It's better off I was before ever I met with you
148.   to my cost! What was on me at all that I did not cut
149.   a scourge in the wood to put manners and decency
150.   on you the time you were not hardened as you are!

151. *Johnny.* Leave talking to me of your rods and your
152.   scourges! All you taught me was robbery, and it is

---

127. . . . her, and . . .
128. . . . do, and . . .
129. . . . gallows! **28a, 29.**
130. . . . I didk now you, . . . **28a.**
134. . . . night? But . . .
135. . . . onto . . . **28a.**
137. . . . me? **29.**
144. . . . leave? Crooked . . . **28a, 29.**
147. . . . you, **28a, 29.**

153.   on yourself and not on myself the scourges will be
154.   laid at the day of the recognition of tricks.

155.   *Paudeen.* 'Faith, the pair of you together is better than
156.   Hector fighting before Troy!

157.   *Nanny.* Ah, let you be quiet. It is not fighting we are
158.   craving, but the easing of the hunger that is on us
159.   and of the passion of sleep. Lend me a graineen of
160.   tobacco now till I'll kindle my pipe—a blast of it
161.   will take the weight of the road off my heart.

                           [*Andrew gives her some. Nanny grabs at it.*

162.   *Biddy.* No, but it's to myself you should give it. I that
163.   never smoked a pipe this forty year without saying
164.   the tobacco prayer. Let that one say did ever she do
165.   that much.

166.   *Nanny.* That the pain of your front tooth may be in
167.   your back tooth, you to be grabbing my share!

                                        [*They snap at tobacco.*

168.   *Andrew.* Pup, pup, pup! Don't be snapping and quarrel-
169.   ling now, and you so well treated in this house. It is
170.   strollers like yourselves should be for frolic and for
171.   fun. Have you ne'er a good song to sing, a song that
172.   will rise all our hearts?

173.   *Paudeen.* Johnny Bocach is a good singer, it is what he
174.   used to be doing in the fairs, if the oakum of the
175.   gaol did not give him a hoarseness within the throat.

176.   *Andrew.* Give it out so, a good song, a song will put
177.   courage and spirit into any man at all.

---

155.   Faith, . . . **28a, 29**.
160.   tobacco till . . . **28a, 29**.
       Directions after 161.   [. . . *grabs it.*] **97A**.
164.   . . . say, did . . . **28a, 29**.
165.   . . . much? **28a, 29**.
168.   . . . , pup. Don't . . . **28a, 29**.
173.   . ⸴ . singer; it . . . **28a, 29**.
175.   . . . hoarseness in the . . . .
176.   . . . song; a song . . . **28a, 29**.

Johnny [*singing*].

178.   'O come all ye airy bachelors,
179.   A warning take by me,
180.   A sergeant caught me fowling,
181.   And he fired his gun so free.

182.   His comrades came to his relief,
183.   And I was soon trepanned,
184.   And bound up like a woodcock
185.   That had fallen into their hands.

186.   The judge said transportation,
187.   The ship was on the strand;
188.   They have yoked me to the traces
189.   For to plough Van Diemen's land!'

190. *Andrew*. That's no good of a song but a melancholy
191. sort of a song. I'd as lief be listening to a saw going
192. through timber. Wait, now, till you will hear myself
193. giving out a tune on the flute.   [*Goes out for it.*

194. *Johnny*. It is what I am thinking, there must be a great
195. dearth and a great scarcity of good comrades in this
196. place, a man like that youngster, having means in
197. his hand, to be bringing ourselves and our rags into
198. the house.

199. *Paudeen*. You think yourself very wise, Johnny Bocach.
200. Can you tell me, now, who that man is?

---

178. Come, all . . . , **28a, 29, 33**; O come, all . . . , **69, 84.**
179. . . . me: **28a, 29.**
181. And fired . . . . **28a-69.**
183. . . . trepanned;
184. And, bound . . . woodcock, **28a, 29.**
185. Had fallen . . . . **28a-69.**
186. . . . transportation; **28a, 29.**
189. . . . Dieman's land! **28a, 29**; . . . Dieman's (Diemen's **69A**) Land! **33, 69**; . . . Land! **84.**
190. . . . song, but . . . **28a, 29.**
     Directions after 193. [*Goes fumbling for* . . . .] **28a.**
194. . . . thinking there . . . **28a-69.**
196. . . . youngster having a nice way of living **28a**; . . . youngster having . . . **29.**
197. to be . . . **28a**; . . . hand to . . . **29.**
200. . . . me now who . . . ? **28a, 29.**
     V.E.P.Y.—Z

201. *Johnny*. Some decent lad, I suppose, with a good way
202.   of living and a mind to send up his name upon the
203.   roads.

204. *Paudeen*. You that have been gaoled this eight months
205.   know little of this countryside. It isn't a limping
206.   stroller like yourself the Boys would let come among
207.   them. But I know. I went to the drill a few nights
208.   and I skinning kids for the mountainy men. In a
209.   quarry beyond the drill is—they have their plans
210.   made—it's the Square House of the Brownes is to be
211.   made an attack on and plundered. Do you know,
212.   now, who is the leader they are waiting for?

213. *Johnny*. How would I know that?

     Paudeen [*singing*].
214.   'O, Johnny Gibbons, my five hundred healths to you!
215.   It's long you are away from us over the sea!'

216. *Johnny* [*standing up excitedly*]. Sure, that man could not
217.   be Johnny Gibbons that is outlawed!

218. *Paudeen*. I asked news of him from the old lad, and I
219.   bringing in the drink along with him. 'Don't be
220.   asking questions', says he; 'take the treat he gives
221.   you', says he. 'If a lad that has a high heart has a
222.   mind to rouse the neighbours', says he, 'and to
223.   stretch out his hand to all that pass the road, it is in

---

205. . . . countryside. . . . [T] It . . .
206. . . . boys . . .
207. . . . nights, **28a, 29.**
209. . . . is . . . [T] they . . . **28a, 29.**
210. made . . . . [T] It's . . . square house . . . Browns . . . **28a, 29 ;** . . .
      square house . . . **33, 69.**
211. . . . know
212. now who . . . ? **28a, 29.**
214. Oh, . . . you. **28a-69 ;** O, . . . ! **84.**
215. It is long . . . sea! **28a-69 ;** . . . sea! **84.**
216. Sure that . . . **28a-84.**
217. . . . John . . . outlawed. **28a, 29.**
218. . . . lad [*points at Andrew*], and . . . **28a ;** . . . lad [*points after Andrew*],
      and . . . **29.**
221. . . . that had a . . . **28a, 29.**

224. France he learned it', says he, 'the place he is but lately
225. come from, and where the wine does be standing open
226. in tubs. Take your treat when you get it', says he,
227. 'and make no delay or all might be discovered and
228. put an end to.'

229. *Johnny.* He came over the sea from France! It is Johnny
230. Gibbons, surely, but it seems to me they were calling
231. him by some other name.

232. *Paudeen.* A man on his keeping might go by a hundred
233. names. Would he be telling it out to us that he
234. never saw before, and we with that clutch of chatter-
235. ing women along with us? Here he is coming now.
236. Wait till you see is he the lad I think him to be.

237. *Martin* [*coming in*]. I will make my banner, I will paint
238. the unicorn on it. Give me that bit of canvas, there
239. is paint over here. We will get no help from the
240. settled men—we will call to the lawbreakers, the
241. tinkers, the sievemakers, the sheepstealers.

[*He begins to make banner.*

242. *Biddy.* That sounds to be a queer name of an army.
243. Ribbons I can understand, Whiteboys, Rightboys,
244. Threshers, and Peep o' Days, but Unicorns I never
245. heard of before.

246. *Johnny.* It is not a queer name but a very good name.
247. [*Takes up lion and unicorn.*] It is often you saw that
248. before you in the dock. There is the unicorn with the
249. one horn, and what is it he is going against? The lion

---

227. . . . delay, or . . . 28a, 29.
229. . . . came o'er the . . . 28a.
230. Gibbons surely, . . . 28a, 29.
236. . . . is the lad . . . . 28a.
237. . . . banner; I . . .
238. . . . Unicorn . . . canvas; there 28a, 29.
241. tinkers—the sievemakers—the . . . . 28a, 29.
243. . . . understand, Rightboys, 28a.
244. . . . Peep-o'-day, . . . 28a, 29 ; . . . Peep o' Day, . . . 33-84.
246. . . name, but . . . . 29.
   Directions in 247. [. . . *Lion* . . . *Unicorn*.] 28a, 29.
248. . . . Unicorn . . . 28a, 29.
249. . . . what it is he . . . Lion 28a ; . . . Lion 29 ; . . . what it is he . . . 33, 69.

250.   of course. When he has the lion destroyed, the
251.   crown must fall and be shivered. Can't you see it is
252.   the League of the Unicorns is the league that will
253.   fight and destroy the power of England and King
254.   George?

255.   *Paudeen.* It is with that banner we will march and the
256.   lads in the quarry with us, it is they will have the
257.   welcome before him! It won't be long till we'll be
258.   attacking the Square House! Arms there are in it,
259.   riches that would smother the world, rooms full of
260.   guineas, we will put wax on our shoes walking them;
261.   the horses themselves shod with no less than silver!

262.   *Martin* [*holding up banner*]. There it is ready! We are
263.   very few now, but the army of the Unicorns will be
264.   a great army! [*To Johnny.*] Why have you brought
265.   me the message? Can you remember any more? Has
266.   anything more come to you? You have been drinking,
267.   the clouds upon your mind have been destroyed.
268.   . . . Can you see anything or hear anything that is
269.   beyond the world?

270.   *Johnny.* I can not. I don't know what do you want me
271.   to tell you at all.

272.   *Martin.* I want to begin the destruction, but I don't
273.   know where to begin. . . . You do not hear any other
274.   voice?

---

250.   . . . Lion . . . 28a, 29.
251.   Crown . . . 28a ; Crown . . . see? It . . . 29.
252.   . . . Unicorns, is . . . 28a.
254.   George. 29.
256.   . . . us; it . . . 28a, 29.
258.   . . . it;
259.   . . . world; rooms 28a, 29.
260.   guineas—we . . . ; 28a, 29 ; guineas we . . . ; 33.
        Directions in 262.   [lacking] 28a ; [. . . *up the banner.*] 29.
266.   . . . drinking; 28a ; . . . you? Who told you to come 29.
267.   to me? Who gave you the message? 29.
270.   I cannot. . . . 28a, 29.
271.   . . . all? 33.
273.   . . . begin . . . [T] you . . . 28a-69.

275. *Johnny.* I do not. I have nothing at all to do with Free-
276.   masons or witchcraft.

277. *Paudeen.* It is Biddy Lally has to do with witchcraft.
278.   It is often she threw the cups and gave out prophecies
279.   the same as Columcille.

280. *Martin.* You are one of the knowledgeable women.
281.   You can tell where it is best to begin, and what will
282.   happen in the end.

283. *Biddy.* I will foretell nothing at all. I rose out of it
284.   this good while, with the stiffness and the swelling
285.   it brought upon my joints.

286. *Martin.* If you have foreknowledge you have no right
287.   to keep silent. If you do not help me I may go to
288.   work in the wrong way. I know I have to destroy,
289.   but when I ask myself what I am to begin with, I
290.   am full of uncertainty.

291. *Paudeen.* Here now are the cups handy and the leavings
292.   in them.

293. *Biddy* [*taking cups and pouring one from another*]. Throw
294.   a bit of white money into the four corners of the
295.   house.

296. *Martin.* There! [*Throwing it.*]

297. *Biddy.* There can be nothing told without silver. It is
298.   not myself will have the profit of it. Along with
299.   that I will be forced to throw out gold.

300. *Martin.* There is a guinea for you. Tell me what comes
301.   before your eyes.

302. *Biddy.* What is it you are wanting to have news of?

303. *Martin.* Of what I have to go out against at the begin-

---

275. . . . free- **28a, 29.**
281. . . . tell me where . . . **28a-69 ;** . . . is to . . . **97A.**
286. . . . foreknowledge, you . . .
287. . . . me, I . . . **28a, 29.**

304.   ning . . . There is so much . . . the whole world, it
305.   may be.

306.   *Biddy* [*throwing from one cup to another and looking*]. You
307.   have no care for yourself. You have been across the
308.   sea, you are not long back. You are coming within
309.   the best day of your life.

310.   *Martin*. What is it? What is it I have to do?

311.   *Biddy*. I see a great smoke, I see burning . . . There is
312.   a great smoke overhead.

313.   *Martin*. That means we have to burn away a great deal
314.   that men have piled up upon the earth. We must
315.   bring men once more to the wildness of the clean
316.   green earth.

317.   *Biddy*. Herbs for my healing, the big herb and the little
318.   herb, it is true enough they get their great strength
319.   out of the earth.

320.   *Johnny*. Who was it the green sod of Ireland belonged
321.   to in the olden times? Wasn't it to the ancient race
322.   it belonged? And who has possession of it now but
323.   the race that came robbing over the sea? The mean-
324.   ing of that is to destroy the big houses and the towns,
325.   and the fields to be given back to the ancient race.

326.   *Martin*. That is it. You don't put it as I do, but what
327.   matter? Battle is all.

328.   *Paudeen*. Columcille said, the four corners to be burned,
329.   and then the middle of the field to be burned. I tell
330.   you it was Columcille's prophecy said that.

331.   *Biddy*. Iron handcuffs I see and a rope and a gallows,
332.   and it maybe is not for yourself I see it, but for some
333.   I have acquaintance with a good way back.

---

304.   ning . . . [T] there . . . world it **28a, 33, 69** ; . . . there . . . **29**.
308.   sea ; you . . . **28a, 29**.
311.   . . . burning . . . [T] there . . . **28a-69**.
318.   herb ; it . . . **28a, 29**.
328.   . . . said the . . . , **28a, 29**.

334. *Martin.* That means the Law. We must destroy the Law.
335.   That was the first sin, the first mouthful of the apple.

336. *Johnny.* So it was, so it was. The Law is the worst loss.
337.   The ancient Law was for the benefit of all. It is the
338.   Law of the English is the only sin.

339. *Martin.* When there were no laws men warred on one
340.   another and man to man, not with machines made
341.   in towns as they do now, and they grew hard and
342.   strong in body. They were altogether alive like Him
343.   that made them in His image, like people in that un-
344.   fallen country. But presently they thought it better
345.   to be safe, as if safety mattered or anything but the
346.   exaltation of the heart, and to have eyes that danger
347.   had made grave and piercing. We must overthrow
348.   the laws and banish them.

349. *Johnny.* It is what I say, to put out the laws is to put
350.   out the whole nation of the English. Laws for them-
351.   selves they made for their own profit, and left us
352.   nothing at all, no more than a dog or a sow.

353. *Biddy.* An old priest I see, and I would not say is he the
354.   one was here or another. Vexed and troubled he is,
355.   kneeling fretting and ever-fretting in some lone-
356.   some ruined place.

357. *Martin.* I thought it would come to that. Yes, the

---

334. ... law. ... law. **28a-69.**
336. .... law ....
337. ... law ...
338. law .... **28a-84.**
339. ... were laws ... **28a.**
340. ... with one machine against
341. another as ... **29.**
342. ... him
343. ... his ... **33, 69.**
345. ... anything, but ... **28a;** ... mattered, or ... **29.**
346. ... heart and ... **28a, 29.**
348. ... them! **29.**
351. ... profit and ... **28a, 29;** ... they make for ... **97A.**
355. ... , kneeling, fretting, and ever fretting, in ... **28a;** ... fretting,
     and ever fretting, in ... **29.**
356. some, ruined .... **28a, 29.**

358. Church too—that is to be destroyed. Once men
359. fought with their desires and their fears, with all that
360. they call their sins, unhelped, and their souls be-
361. came hard and strong. When we have brought back
362. the clean earth and destroyed the Law and the Church,
363. all life will become like a flame of fire, like a burn-
364. ing eye . . . O, how to find words for it all . . . all
365. that is not life will pass away.

366. *Johnny.* It is Luther's Church he means, and the hump-
367. backed discourse of Seaghan Calvin's Bible. So we
368. will break it, and make an end of it.

369. *Martin.* We will go out against the world and break it
370. and unmake it. [*Rising.*] We are the army of the Uni-
371. corn from the Stars! We will trample it to pieces.—
372. We will consume the world, we will burn it away
373. —Father John said the world has yet to be con-
374. sumed by fire. Bring me fire.

375. *Andrew* [*to Beggars*]. Here is Thomas. Hide—let you hide.
      [*All except Martin hurry into next room.*

Thomas comes in

376. *Thomas.* Come with me, Martin. There is terrible work
377. going on in the town! There is mischief gone abroad.
378. Very strange things are happening!

379. *Martin.* What are you talking of? What has happened?

---

358. church too . . . [T] that . . . **28a, 29**.
362. . . . law . . . church, **28a, 29** ; . . . law . . . Church **33, 69**.
365. . . . away! **28a, 29**.
368. . . . it and . . . . **28a, 29**.
      Directions in 369. *Martin* [*rising*]. **29**.
      Directions in 370. [lacking] **28a, 29**.
371. . . . pieces.
372. . . . away.
373. Father . . . **28a, 29**.
374. . . . me fire. Give me the lamp! **28a**.
      Directions after 374. [*Thomas comes in.*] **28a**.
375. [lacking] **28a** ; . . . Thomas coming! **29**.
      Directions after 375 and before 376. [lacking] **28a**.
377. . . . abroad! **28a, 29**.

380. *Thomas.* Come along, I say, it must be put a stop to.
381.   We must call to every decent man. It is as if the
382.   Devil himself had gone through the town on a blast
383.   and set every drinking-house open!

384. *Martin.* I wonder how that has happened. Can it have
385.   anything to do with Andrew's plan?

386. *Thomas.* Are you giving no heed to what I'm saying?
387.   There is not a man, I tell you, in the parish and
388.   beyond the parish but has left the work he was doing
389.   whether in the field or in the mill.

390. *Martin.* Then all work has come to an end? Perhaps
391.   that was a good thought of Andrew's.

392. *Thomas.* There is not a man has come to sensible years
393.   that is not drunk or drinking! My own labourers
394.   and my own serving-men are sitting on counters and
395.   on barrels! I give you my word, the smell of the
396.   spirits and the porter, and the shouting and the cheer-
397.   ing within, made the hair to rise up on my scalp.

398. *Martin.* And yet there is not one of them that does not
399.   feel that he could bridle the four winds.

400. *Thomas* [*sitting down in despair*]. You are drunk too. I
401.   never thought you had a fancy for it.

402. *Martin.* It is hard for you to understand. You have
403.   worked all your life. You have said to yourself every
404.   morning, 'What is to be done to-day?' and when you

---

380. . . . say; it . . . to!
381. . . . man! . . . [T] It . . . **28a, 29.**
382. devil . . . **28a-69.**
383. . . . drinking house . . . ! **28a, 29.**
387. . . . parish, and **28a, 29.**
388. . . . parish, but . . . work they were doing, **28a** ; . . . parish, but . . . doing, **29.**
394. . . . serving-man . . .
395. . . . word the . . . **28a, 29.**
396. . . . porter and . . . **28a-69.**
397. . . . within made . . . . **28a, 29.**
398. And there is not yet one . . . **28a** ; And there . . . **29.**
400. . . . drunk, too. . . . **29.**

405.   were tired out you have thought of the next day's
406.   work. If you gave yourself an hour's idleness, it was
407.   but that you might work the better. Yet it is only
408.   when one has put work away that one begins to live.

409.   *Thomas.* It is those French wines that did it.

410.   *Martin.* I have been beyond the earth. In Paradise, in
411.   that happy townland, I have seen the shining people.
412.   They were all doing one thing or another, but not
413.   one of them was at work. All that they did was but
414.   the overflowing of their idleness, and their days
415.   were a dance bred of the secret frenzy of their hearts,
416.   or a battle where the sword made a sound that was
417.   like laughter.

418.   *Thomas.* You went away sober from out of my hands;
419.   they had a right to have minded you better.

420.   *Martin.* No man can be alive, and what is Paradise
421.   but fulness of life, if whatever he sets his hand to in
422.   the daylight cannot carry him from exaltation to
423.   exaltation, and if he does not rise into the frenzy
424.   of contemplation in the night silence. Events that
425.   are not begotten in joy are misbegotten and darken
426.   the world, and nothing is begotten in joy if the joy
427.   of a thousand years has not been crushed into a
428.   moment.

429.   *Thomas.* And I offered to let you go to Dublin in the
430.   coach!

431.   *Martin* [*giving banner to Paudeen*]. Give me the lamp.
432.   The lamp has not yet been lighted, and the world is
433.   to be consumed!   [*Goes into inner room.*

434.   *Thomas* [*seeing Andrew*]. Is it here you are, Andrew? What

---

405.   are tired . . . **28a-69.**
410.   . . . paradise, . . . **28a ;** . . . earth, in paradise, . . . **29.**
411.   . . . townland. I . . . **29.**
420.   . . . alive; and . . . paradise **28a ;** . . . paradise **29-69.**
424.   . . . silence? Events . . . **28a ;** . . . night of silence. . . . **69A.**
        Directions after 430.   [*Andrew and the beggars have returned cautiously.*]
        29.
432.   . . . lighted and . . . **33, 69.**

435. are these beggars doing? Was this door thrown open
436. too? Why did you not keep order? I will go for the
437. constables to help us!

438. *Andrew.* You will not find them to help you. They
439. were scattering themselves through the drinking-
440. houses of the town, and why wouldn't they?

441. *Thomas.* Are you drunk too? You are worse than
442. Martin. You are a disgrace!

443. *Andrew.* Disgrace yourself! Coming here to be making
444. an attack on me and badgering me and disparaging
445. me! And what about yourself that turned me to be a
446. hypocrite?

447. *Thomas.* What are you saying?

448. *Andrew.* You did, I tell you! Weren't you always at
449. me to be regular and to be working and to be going
450. through the day and the night without company and
451. to be thinking of nothing but the trade? What did
452. I want with a trade? I got a sight of the faery gold
453. one time in the mountains. I would have found it
454. again and brought riches from it but for you keeping
455. me so close to the work.

456. *Thomas.* O, of all the ungrateful creatures! You know
457. well that I cherished you, leading you to live a
458. decent, respectable life.

459. *Andrew.* You never had respect for the ancient ways.
460. It is after the mother you take it, that was too soft
461. and too lumpish, having too much of the English in

---

435. . . . open, **28a** ; . . . are the beggars . . . open, **29.**
436. too? . . . [T] Why . . . **28a, 29** ; . . . order. I . . . **69A.**
439. . . . drinking
440. . . . town; and . . . ?
441. . . . drunk, too? . . .
442. . . . disgrace. **28a, 29.**
445. me. And . . . **28a, 29.**
448. . . . you. Weren't . . . **28a, 29.**
452. . . . fairy . . . **28a-69.**
460. . . . it that . . . **28a.**

462.   her blood. Martin is a Hearne like myself. It is he
463.   has the generous heart! It is not Martin would make
464.   a hypocrite of me and force me to do night-walking
465.   secretly, watching to be back by the setting of the
466.   seven stars!   [*He begins to play his flute.*

467.   *Thomas.* I will turn you out of this, yourself and this
468.   filthy troop! I will have them lodged in gaol.

469.   *Johnny.* Filthy troop, is it? Mind yourself! The change
470.   is coming. The pikes will be up and the traders will
471.   go down.

                              All seize Thomas and sing

472.   'O, the lion shall lose his strength,
473.   And the bracket-thistle pine,
474.   And the harp shall sound sweet, sweet at length,
475.   Between the eight and nine!'

476.   *Thomas.* Let me out of this, you villains!

477.   *Nanny.* We'll make a sieve of holes of you, you old
478.   bag of treachery!

479.   *Biddy.* How well you threatened us with gaol, you
480.   skim of a weasel's milk!

481.   *Johnny.* You heap of sicknesses! You blinking hang-
482.   man! That you may never die till you'll get a blue
483.   hag for a wife!   [*Martin comes back with lighted lamp.*

484.   *Martin.* Let him go.   [*They let Thomas go, and fall back.*]

---

464.   . . . night walking **28a, 29.**
470.   . . . coming! The . . . **28a, 29.**
471.   . . . down! **28a-69.**
        Directions after 471. [. . . *seize him and* . . . .] **28a, 29.**
472.   When the Lion will (shall **29**) lose . . . , **28a-69**; O, . . . , **84.**
473.   . . . braket thistle begin to pine,— **28a, 29**; . . . braket-thistle begin
        to pine, **33, 69.**
474.   The harp . . . length (length, **33, 69**) **28a-69.**
475.   . . . and the nine! **28a-69**; . . . nine! **84.**
479.   . . . gaol! You . . . ! **28a, 29.**
483.   . . . wife. [*Martin* . . . .] **97A.**
        Directions in 483. [. . . *with candle.*] **28a.**
        Directions in 484. [. . . *go and* . . . .] **28a, 29.**

485. Spread out the banner. The moment has come to
486. begin the war.

487. *Johnny.* Up with the Unicorn and destroy the Lion!
488. Success to Johnny Gibbons and all good men!

489. *Martin.* Heap all those things together there. Heap
490. those pieces of the coach one upon another. Put that
491. straw under them. It is with this flame I will begin
492. the work of destruction. All nature destroys and
493. laughs.

494. *Thomas.* Destroy your own golden coach!

495. *Martin* [*kneeling before Thomas*]. I am sorry to go a way
496. that you do not like and to do a thing that will vex
497. you. I have been a great trouble to you since I was
498. a child in the house, and I am a great trouble to you
499. yet. It is not my fault. I have been chosen for what
500. I have to do. [*Stands up.*] I have to free myself first
501. and those that are near me. The love of God is a
502. very terrible thing! [*Thomas tries to stop him, but is
     prevented by Beggars. Martin takes a wisp of straw and
503. lights it.*] We will destroy all that can perish! It is
504. only the soul that can suffer no injury. The soul of
505. man is of the imperishable substance of the stars!
                    [*He throws wisp into heap—it blazes up.*

Directions in 495.   [*kneeling*]. **28a, 29.**
496.   . . . like, and . . . **28a, 29.**
        Directions after 502.   [. . . *by tinkers. Martin* . . . .] **28a, 29.**
        Directions after 505.   [*lacking*] **28a** ; [. . . *throws his wisp into the heap.
        It* . . . .] **29.**

Act III

*Before dawn. A wild rocky place. Nanny and Biddy Lally squatting by a fire.
Rich stuffs, etc., strewn about. Paudeen watching by Martin, who is lying as if
dead, a sack over him.*

1. *Nanny* [*to Paudeen*]. Well, you are great heroes and
2. great warriors and great lads altogether, to have put
3. down the Brownes the way you did, yourselves and
4. the Whiteboys of the quarry. To have ransacked the
5. house and have plundered it! Look at the silks and
6. the satins and the grandeurs I brought away! Look
7. at that now! [*Holds up a velvet cloak.*] It's a good little
8. jacket for myself will come out of it. It's the singers
9. will be stopping their songs and the jobbers turning
10. from their cattle in the fairs to be taking a view of
11. the laces of it and the buttons! It's my far-off
12. cousins will be drawing from far and near!

13. *Biddy.* There was not so much gold in it all as what
14. they were saying there was. Or maybe that fleet of
15. Whiteboys had the place ransacked before we our-
16. selves came in. Bad cess to them that put it in my
17. mind to go gather up the full of my bag of horse-
18. shoes out of the forge. Silver they were saying they
19. were, pure white silver; and what are they in the end
20. but only hardened iron! A bad end to them! [*Flings*
21. *away horseshoes.*] The time I will go robbing big
22. houses again it will not be in the light of the full
23. moon I will go doing it, that does be causing every
24. common thing to shine out as if for a deceit and a
25. mockery. It's not shining at all they are at this time,
26. but duck-yellow and dark.

27. *Nanny.* To leave the big house blazing after us, it was
28. that crowned all! Two houses to be burned to ashes

STAGE DIRECTIONS Scene: *A wild, rocky . . . squatting. Stuffs, etc., ...
Paudeen sitting, watching . . . lying, as . . . . 28a ; Scene: Before dawn a few
hours later. A wild, rocky . . . by fire . . . . Paudeen sitting, watching . . . lying,
as . . . . 29.*
2. *. . . altogether to . . .*
20. *. . . them. [Flings* 28a.
26. *. . . duck yellow . . . . 28a-69.*

29. in the one night. It is likely the servant-girls were
30. rising from the feathers and the cocks crowing from
31. the rafters for seven miles around, taking the flames
32. to be the whitening of the dawn.

33. *Biddy.* It is the lad is stretched beyond you have to be
34. thankful to for that. There was never seen a leader
35. was his equal for spirit and for daring. Making a
36. great scatter of the guards the way he did. Running
37. up roofs and ladders, the fire in his hand, till you'd
38. think he would be apt to strike his head against
39. the stars.

40. *Nanny.* I partly guessed death was near him, and the
41. queer shining look he had in his two eyes, and he
42. throwing sparks east and west through the beams. I
43. wonder now was it some inward wound he got, or
44. did some hardy lad of the Brownes give him a tip on
45. the skull unknownst in the fight? It was I myself
46. found him, and the troop of the Whiteboys gone,
47. and he lying by the side of a wall as weak as if he
48. had knocked a mountain. I failed to waken him
49. trying him with the sharpness of my nails, and his
50. head fell back when I moved it, and I knew him to
51. to be spent and gone.

52. *Biddy.* It's a pity you not to have left him where he
53. was lying and said no word at all to Paudeen or to
54. that son you have, that kept us back from following
55. on, bringing him here to this shelter on sacks and
56. upon poles.

57. *Nanny.* What way could I help letting a screech out of
58. myself, and the life but just gone out of him in the
59. darkness, and not a living Christian by his side but
60. myself and the great God?

---

30. ... feathers, and ... **28a, 29.**
34. thankful for ... seen the like of a ... **28a.**
35. for spirit ... daring! Making ... **28a ;** ... daring! Making ... **29.**
36. ... did! Running **28a, 29.**
41. ... eyes. And ... **28a.**
48. ... him, **28a, 29.**
53. ... lying, and ... **28a, 29.**
58. myself and ... **28a, 29.**

61. *Biddy*. It's on ourselves the vengeance of the red
62.   soldiers will fall, they to find us sitting here the same
63.   as hares in a tuft. It would be best for us follow after
64.   the rest of the army of the Whiteboys.

65. *Nanny*. Whisht! I tell you. The lads are cracked about
66.   him. To get but the wind of the word of leaving
67.   him, it's little but they'd knock the head off the
68.   two of us. Whisht!

Enter Johnny Bocach with candles

69. *Johnny* [*standing over Martin*]. Wouldn't you say now
70.   there was some malice or some venom in the air,
71.   that is striking down one after another the whole
72.   of the heroes of the Gael?

73. *Paudeen*. It makes a person be thinking of the four last
74.   ends, death and judgment, Heaven and Hell. Indeed
75.   and indeed my heart lies with him. It is well I
76.   knew what man he was under his byname and his
77.   disguise.

[*Sings*]

78.   'O, Johnny Gibbons, it's you were the prop to us.
79.   You to have left us, we are foals astray!'

80. *Johnny*. It is lost we are now and broken to the end of
81.   our days. There is no satisfaction at all but to be
82.   destroying the English, and where now will we get
83.   so good a leader again? Lay him out fair and straight
84.   upon a stone, till I will let loose the secret of my

---

65. Whist, I . . . **28a** ; Whist, I . . . you! The . . . **29**.
70. . . . air **28a**.
71. . . . after the other the . . . **28a, 29**.
74. . . . , heaven . . . hell. . . . **28a-69**.
76. . . . by-name . . . **28a, 29**.
78. Oh, . . . us! **28a, 29** ; O . . . . **33-84**.
79. . . . us (us, **33, 69**) we are put astray! **28a-69** ; . . . us, we're foals put
    astray! **84**.
82. . . . English; and . . . **28a, 29**.

85. heart keening him!
   [Sets out candles on a rock, propping them up with stones.]

86. *Nanny.* Is it mould candles you have brought to set
87. around him, Johnny Bocach? It is great riches you
88. should have in your pocket to be going to those
89. lengths and not to be content with dips.

90. *Johnny.* It is lengths I will not be going to the time
91. the life will be gone out of your own body. It is not
92. your corpse I will be wishful to hold in honour the
93. way I hold this corpse in honour.

94. *Nanny.* That's the way always, there will be grief and
95. quietness in the house if it is a young person has
96. died, but funning and springing and tricking one
97. another if it is an old person's corpse is in it. There
98. is no compassion at all for the old.

99. *Paudeen.* It is he would have got leave for the Gael to
100. be as high as the Gall. Believe me, he was in
101. prophecies. Let you not be comparing yourself with
102. the like of him.

103. *Nanny.* Why wouldn't I be comparing myself? Look at
104. all that was against me in the world. Would you be
105. matching me against a man of his sort, that had the
106. people shouting him and that had nothing to do but
107. to die and to go to Heaven?

108. *Johnny.* The day you go to Heaven that you may never
109. come back alive out of it! But it is not yourself will
110. ever hear the saints hammering at their musics! It is
111. you will be moving through the ages, chains upon
112. you, and you in the form of a dog or a monster. I tell

Directions after 85. [. . . *candles in holders.*] **28a** ; [. . . *a rack, propping
them up with . . . .*] **29.**
94. . . . always: there . . . **28a, 29.**
104. . . . world; would . . .
105. . . . sort that . . .
106. . . . shouting for him . . . **28a, 29.**
107. . . . heaven?
108. . . . heaven . . . **28a-69.**
111. . . . ages chains . . .
112. . . . monster! I . . . **28a, 29.**

113.   you that one will go through Purgatory as quick as
114.   lightning through a thorn-bush.

115.   *Nanny.* That's the way, that's the way.
                            [*Croons*]
116.   Three that are watching my time to run,
117.   The worm, the Devil, and my son,
118.   To see a loop around their neck,
119.   It's that would make my heart to lep!

120.   *Johnny.* Five white candles. I wouldn't begrudge them
121.   to him indeed. If he had held out and held up, it is
122.   my belief he would have freed Ireland!

123.   *Puadeen.* Wait till the full light of the day and you'll
124.   see the burying he'll have. It is not in this place we
125.   will be waking him. I'll make a call to the two
126.   hundred Ribbons he was to lead on to the attack on
127.   the barracks at Aughanish. They will bring him
128.   marching to his grave upon the hill. He had surely
129.   some gift from the other world, I wouldn't say but
130.   he had power from the other side.

131.   *Andrew* [*coming in very shaky*]. Well, it was a great night
132.   he gave to the village, and it is long till it will be
133.   forgotten. I tell you the whole of the neighbours are
134.   up against him. There is no one at all this morning
135.   to set the mills going. There was no bread baked in
136.   the night-time, the horses are not fed in the stalls,
137.   the cows are not milked in the sheds. I met no man

---

113.   . . . purgatory . . . **28a**; you, that . . . purgatory . . . **29.**
114.   . . . thorn bush. **28a, 29.**
115.   . . . way, **28a**; . . . way: **29.**
        [between 115 and 116 no break] **28a, 29.**
        Directions before 116.   [lacking] **28a, 29.**
116.   . . . mytime to run— **28a**; . . . run **29.**
117.   . . . devil, . . . son. (son, **33, 69**)
118.   . . . neck **28a-69.**
119.   . . . leap! **29.**
121.   . . . him, indeed. . . . **28a, 29**; . . . up it . . . **33, 69.**
129.   . . . world. I . . . **28a.**
        Directions in 131.   [. . . *in, very* . . . .] **29.**
136.   . . . night-time; the . . . stalls; **28a, 29.**

138. able to make a curse this night but he put it on my
139. head and on the head of the boy that is lying there
140. before us. . . . Is there no sign of life in him at all?

141. *Johnny.* What way would there be a sign of life and the
142. life gone out of him this three hours or more?

143. *Andrew.* He was lying in his sleep for a while yesterday,
144. and he wakened again after another while.

145. *Nanny.* He will not waken, I tell you. I held his hand
146. in my own and it getting cold as if you were pouring
147. on it the coldest cold water, and no running in his
148. blood. He is gone, sure enough, and the life is gone
149. out of him.

150. *Andrew.* Maybe so, maybe so. It seems to me yesterday
151. his cheeks were bloomy all the while, and now he is
152. as pale as wood ashes. Sure, we all must come to it at
153. the last. Well, my white-headed darling, it is you
154. were the bush among us all, and you to be cut down
155. in your prime. Gentle and simple, every one liked
156. you. It is no narrow heart you had, it is you were for
157. spending and not for getting. It is you made a good
158. wake for yourself, scattering your estate in one night
159. only in beer and in wine for the whole province;
160. and that you may be sitting in the middle of Paradise
161. and in the chair of the Graces!

162. *Johnny.* Amen to that. It's pity I didn't think the time
163. I sent for yourself to send the little lad of a mes-
164. senger looking for a priest to overtake him. It might
165. be in the end the Almighty is the best man for us all!

166. *Andrew.* Sure, I sent him on myself to bid the priest to

---

138. . . . my own **28a, 29.**
145. . . . waken. I . . . you I . . . **28a, 29.**
148. . . . gone sure . . . **28a, 29, 84;** . . . gone sure enough and . . . **33, 69.**
152. . . . wood-ashes. Sure we . . . **28a, 29;** . . . . Sure we . . . **33-84.**
155. . . . , everyone . . . **28a-33.**
156. . . . had; it . . . **28a, 29.**
160. . . . paradise
161. . . . graces! **28a, 29.**
166. Sure I . . . **28a-84.**

167.   come. Living or dead I would wish to do all that is
168.   rightful for the last and the best of my own race and
169.   generation.

170.   *Biddy* [*jumping up*]. Is it the priest you are bringing in
171.   among us? Where is the sense in that? Aren't we
172.   robbed enough up to this with the expense of the
173.   candles and the like?

174.   *Johnny*. If it is that poor starved priest he called to that
175.   came talking in secret signs to the man that is gone,
176.   it is likely he will ask nothing for what he has to do.
177.   There is many a priest is a Whiteboy in his heart.

178.   *Nanny*. I tell you, if you brought him tied in a bag he
179.   would not say an Our Father for you, without you
180.   having a half-crown at the top of your fingers.

181.   *Biddy*. There is no priest is any good at all but a spoiled
182.   priest. A one that would take a drop of drink, it is
183.   he would have courage to face the hosts of trouble.
184.   Rout them out he would, the same as a shoal of fish
185.   from out the weeds. It's best not to vex a priest, or
186.   to run against them at all.

187.   *Nanny*. It's yourself humbled yourself well to one the
188.   time you were sick in the gaol and had like to die,
189.   and he bade you to give over the throwing of the cups.

190.   *Biddy*. Ah, plaster of Paris I gave him. I took to it
191.   again and I free upon the roads.

192.   *Nanny*. Much good you are doing with it to yourself
193.   or any other one. Aren't you after telling that corpse
194.   no later than yesterday that he was coming within
195.   the best day of his life?

196.   *Johnny*. Whisht, let ye. Here is the priest coming.

---

167. . . . dead, I . . . **28a, 29.**
174. . . . poor, starved . . . **28a, 29.**
177. . . . Whiteboy to the heart. **28a.**
178-186. [lacking] **28a.**
180. . . . half crown . . . . **29.**
182. priest; a . . . **29.**
196. Whist, . . . ye! Here . . . . **29.**

Father John comes in

197. **Father John.** It is surely not true that he is dead?

198. **Johnny.** The spirit went from him about the middle
199. hour of the night. We brought him here to this
200. sheltered place. We were loth to leave him without
201. friends.

202. **Father John.** Where is he?

203. **Johnny** [*taking up sacks*]. Lying there stiff and stark. He
204. has a very quiet look as if there was no sin at all or
205. no great trouble upon his mind.

206. **Father John** [*kneels and touches him*]. He is not dead.

207. **Biddy** [*pointing to Nanny*]. He is dead. If it was letting
208. on he was, he would not have let that one rob him
209. and search him the way she did.

210. **Father John.** It has the appearance of death, but it is
211. not death. He is in a trance.

212. **Paudeen.** Is it Heaven and Hell he is walking at this
213. time to be bringing back newses of the sinners in
214. pain?

215. **Biddy.** I was thinking myself it might be away he was,
216. riding on white horses with the riders of the forths.

217. **Johnny.** He will have great wonders to tell out, the time
218. he will rise up from the ground. It is a pity he not
219. to waken at this time and to lead us on to overcome
220. the troop of the English. Sure, those that are in a
221. trance get strength that they can walk on water.

---

203. . . . there, stiff . . .
204. . . . look, as . . . **28a, 29.**
205. no trouble . . . . **28a.**
208. . . . let them rob . . . **28a.**
212. . . . heaven . . . hell . . . **28a, 29.**
215. . . . might away . . . , **28a-69.**
217. . . . out the . . . **28a-69.**
220. . . . . Sure those . . . **28a-84.**
221. . . . strength, that . . . . **33, 69.**

222. *Andrew*. It was Father John wakened him yesterday the
223.   time he was lying in the same way. Wasn't I telling
224.   you it was for that I called to him?

225. *Biddy*. Waken him now till they'll see did I tell any
226.   lie in my foretelling. I knew well by the signs, he was
227.   coming within the best day of his life.

228. *Paudeen*. And not dead at all! We'll be marching to
229.   attack Dublin itself within a week. The horn will
230.   blow for him, and all good men will gather to him.
231.   Hurry on, Father, and waken him.

232. *Father John*. I will not waken him. I will not bring him
233.   back from where he is.

234. *Johnny*. And how long will it be before he will waken
235.   of himself?

236. *Father John*. Maybe to-day, maybe to-morrow, it is hard
237.   to be certain.

238. *Biddy*. If it is *away* he is, he might be away seven years.
239.   To be lying like a stump of a tree and using no food
240.   and the world not able to knock a word out of him,
241.   I know the signs of it well.

242. *Johnny*. We cannot be waiting and watching through
243.   seven years. If the business he has started is to be
244.   done we have to go on here and now. The time there
245.   is any delay, that is the time the Government will
246.   get information. Waken him now, Father, and you'll
247.   get the blessing of the generations.

248. *Father John*. I will not bring him back. God will bring
249.   him back in His own good time. For all I know he
250.   may be seeing the hidden things of God.

251. *Johnny*. He might slip away in his dream. It is best to
252.   raise him up now.

---

226.   ... signs he ... **28a, 29.**
236.   ... to-morrow; it ... **28a, 29.**
238.   ... is away .... **28a ;** ... is he .... **33, 69.**
244.   done, we ... **28a, 29.**
249.   ... his ... **33, 69.**

253. *Andrew.* Waken him, Father John, I thought he was
254.   surely dead this time, and what way could I go face
255.   Thomas through all that is left of my lifetime, after
256.   me standing up to face him the way I did? And if I
257.   do take a little drop of an odd night, sure, I'd be
258.   very lonesome if I did not take it. All the world
259.   knows it's not for love of what I drink, but for love
260.   of the people that do be with me! Waken him,
261.   Father, or maybe I would waken him myself.

                                                           [*Shakes him.*

262. *Father John.* Lift your hand from touching him. Leave
263.   him to himself and to the power of God.

264. *Johnny.* If you will not bring him back why wouldn't
265.   we ourselves do it? Go on now, it is best for you to
266.   do it yourself.

267. *Father John.* I woke him yesterday. He was angry with
268.   me, he could not get to the heart of the command.

269. *Johnny.* If he did not, he got a command from myself
270.   that satisfied him, and a message.

271. *Father John.* He did—he took it from you—and how
272.   do I know what devil's message it may have been
273.   that brought him into that devil's work, destruction
274.   and drunkenness and burnings? That was not a message
275.   from Heaven! It was I awoke him, it was I kept him
276.   from hearing what was maybe a divine message, a
277.   voice of truth, and he heard you speak and he be-
278.   lieved the message was brought by you. You have
279.   made use of your deceit and his mistaking—you have
280.   left him without house or means to support him,

---

253. . . . John. I . . . **28a-69.**
254. . . . time; and . . .
255. . . . lifetime after **28a, 29.**
257. . . . , sure I'd . . . **28a-84.**
264. . . . back, why . . . **28a, 29.**
268. me; he . . . . **28a, 29.**
271. . . . did . . . [T] he . . . you . . . [T] and . . . **28a, 29.**
274. . . . burnings! That . . . **28a-69.**
275. . . . heaven! . . . him; it . . . **28a, 29;** . . . heaven! . . . **33, 69.**
277. . . . truth; and . . . speak, and . . . **28a, 29.**
279. . . . mistaking . . . [T] you . . . **28a, 29.**

281.   you are striving to destroy and to drag him to entire
282.   ruin. I will not help you, I would rather see him die
283.   in his trance and go into God's hands than awake
284.   him and see him go into Hell's mouth with vaga-
285.   bonds and outcasts like you!

286.   *Johnny* [*turning to Biddy*]. You should have knowledge,
287.   Biddy Lally, of the means to bring back a man that
288.   is away.

289.   *Biddy.* The power of the earth will do it through its
290.   herbs, and the power of the air will do it kindling
291.   fire into flame.

292.   *Johnny.* Rise up and make no delay. Stretch out and
293.   gather a handful of an herb that will bring him back
294.   from whatever place he is in.

295.   *Biddy.* Where is the use of herbs, and his teeth clenched
296.   the way he could not use them?

297.   *Johnny.* Take fire so, in the Devil's name, and put it to
298.   the soles of his feet.   [*Takes a lighted sod from fire.*

299.   *Father John.* Let him alone, I say!

                                           [*Dashes away the sod.*

300.   *Johnny.* I will not leave him alone! I will not give in to
301.   leave him swooning there and the country waiting
302.   for him to awake!

303.   *Father John.* I tell you I awoke him! I sent him into
304.   thieves' company! I will not have him wakened again
305.   and evil things, it may be, waiting to take hold of
306.   him! Back from him, back, I say! Will you dare to
307.   lay a hand on me! You cannot do it! You cannot

---

284.   . . . hell's . . . **28a-69.**
295.   . . . herbs and . . . **28a, 29.**
297.   . . . so in . . . devil's name and . . . **28a, 29 ;** . . . so in . . . devil's . . .
        33, 69.
        Directions after 298.   [lacking] **28a ;** [*Takes lighted . . . .*] **29.**
305.   . . . things it . . . be waiting . . . **28a ;** . . . things it maybe waiting
        . . . **33, 69.**
306.   . . . say? Will . . . **28a.**
307.   . . . me! You . . . **28a, 33, 69.**

308.   touch him against my will!

309.   *Biddy*. Mind yourself, do not be bringing us under the
310.   curse of the Church.

> *[Johnny steps back. Martin moves.*

311.   *Father John*. It is God has him in His care. It is He is
312.   awaking him. [*Martin has risen to his elbow.*] Do not
313.   touch him, do not speak to him, he may be hearing
314.   great secrets.

315.   *Martin*. That music, I must go nearer—sweet mar-
316.   vellous music—louder than the trampling of the uni-
317.   corns; far louder, though the mountain is shaking
318.   with their feet—high joyous music.

319.   *Father John*. Hush, he is listening to the music of
320.   Heaven!

321.   *Martin*. Take me to you, musicians, wherever you are!
322.   I will go nearer to you; I hear you better now, more
323.   and more joyful; that is strange, it is strange.

324.   *Father John*. He is getting some secret.

325.   *Martin*. It is the music of Paradise, that is certain,
326.   somebody said that. It is certainly the music of
327.   Paradise. Ah, now I hear, now I understand. It is
328.   made of the continual clashing of swords!

329.   *Johnny*. That is the best music. We will clash them
330.   sure enough. We will clash our swords and our pikes
331.   on the bayonets of the red soldiers. It is well you
332.   rose up from the dead to lead us! Come on, now,

---

309.   . . . yourself, (yourself; **29**) don't be . . .
310.   . . . church.
        Directions after 310. [*Johnny falls back*. . . . .] **28a, 29.**
315.   . . . nearer . . . [T] sweet, mar-
316.   . . . music . . . [T] louder . . .
317.   corns . . . [T] far . . .
318.   feet . . . [T] high, joyous . . . . **28a, 29.**
320.   heaven. **28a, 29.**
325.   . . . paradise, . . . , **28a, 29.**
327.   paradise. . . . **28a, 29.**
332.   . . . on now, **28a, 29.**

333.   come on!

334.   *Martin.* Who are you? Ah, I remember—where are you
335.   asking me to come to?

336.   *Paudeen.* To come on, to be sure, to the attack on the
337.   barracks at Aughanish. To carry on the work you
338.   took in hand last night.

339.   *Martin.* What work did I take in hand last night? O
340.   yes, I remember—some big house—we burned it
341.   down—but I had not understood the vision when I
342.   did that. I had not heard the command right. That
343.   was not the work I was sent to do.

344.   *Paudeen.* Rise up now and bid us what to do. Your
345.   great name itself will clear the road before you. It is
346.   you yourself will have freed all Ireland before the
347.   stooks will be in stacks!

348.   *Martin.* Listen, I will explain—I have misled you. It
349.   is only now I have the whole vision plain. As I lay
350.   there I saw through everything, I know all. It was
351.   but a frenzy, that going out to burn and to destroy.
352.   What have I to do with the foreign army? What I have
353.   to pierce is the wild heart of time. My business is
354.   not reformation but revelation.

355.   *Johnny.* If you are going to turn back now from leading
356.   us, you are no better than any other traitor that ever
357.   gave up the work he took in hand. Let you come
358.   and face now the two hundred men you brought out
359.   daring the power of the Law last night, and give
360.   them your reason for failing them.

361.   *Martin.* I was mistaken when I set out to destroy

---

334.   . . . remember. . . . [T] Where . . . **28a, 29.**
339.   . . . ? Oh, **28a-69.**
340.   . . . remember . . . [T] some . . . house . . . [T] we . . .
341.   down . . . [T] But . . . **28a, 29.**
347.   stocks will . . . ! **28a.**
348.   . . . explain . . . [T] I . . . **28a, 29.**
351.   . . . frenzy that . . . . **28a, 33, 69.**
358.   . . . out, **28a, 29.**
359.   . . . law . . . **28a-84.**

362. Church and Law. The battle we have to fight is
363. fought out in our own mind. There is a fiery
364. moment, perhaps once in a lifetime, and in that
365. moment we see the only thing that matters. It is
366. in that moment the great battles are lost and won,
367. for in that moment we are a part of the host of
368. Heaven.

369. *Paudeen.* Have you betrayed us to the naked hangman
370. with your promises and with your drink? If you
371. brought us out here to fail us and to ridicule us, it
372. is the last day you will live!

373. *Johnny.* The curse of my heart on you! It would be
374. right to send you to your own place on the flagstone
375. of the traitors in Hell. When once I have made an
376. end of you I will be as well satisfied to be going to
377. my death for it as if I was going home!

378. *Martin.* Father John, Father John, can you not hear?
379. Can you not see? Are you blind? Are you deaf?

380. *Father John.* What is it? What is it?

381. *Martin.* There on the mountain, a thousand white uni-
382. corns trampling; a thousand riders with their swords
383. drawn—the swords clashing! O, the sound of the
384. swords, the sound of the clashing of the swords!
     [*He goes slowly off stage. Johnny takes up a stone to throw at him.*

385. *Father John* [*seizing his arm*]. Stop—do you not see he is
386. beyond the world?

387. *Biddy.* Keep your hand off him, Johnny Bocach. If he

---

362. church . . . law. . . . **28a, 29.**
363. . . . minds. . . . **29.**
364. . . . , perhaps, once . . . **28a.**
368. heaven. **28a-69.**
370. . . . promise . . . **97A.**
375. . . . hell. . . . **28a-69.**
376. . . . you, I . . . **28a, 29.**
377. . . . it, as . . . ! **28a.**
383. drawn . . . [T] the . . . ! Oh, . . . **28a, 29.**
385. Stop . . . [T] do . . . **28a, 29.**

388.   is gone wild and cracked, that's natural. Those that
389.   have been wakened from a trance on a sudden are
390.   apt to go bad and light in the head.

391. *Paudeen.* If it is madness is on him, it is not he him-
392.   self should pay the penalty.

393. *Biddy.* To prey on the mind it does, and rises into the
394.   head. There are some would go over any height and
395.   would have great power in their madness. It is
396.   maybe to some secret cleft he is going, to get know-
397.   ledge of the great cure for all things, or of the Plough
398.   that was hidden in the old times, the Golden Plough.

399. *Paudeen.* It seemed as if he was talking through honey.
400.   He had the look of one that had seen great wonders.
401.   It is maybe among the old heroes of Ireland he went,
402.   raising armies for our help.

403. *Father John.* God take him in His care and keep him
404.   from lying spirits and from all delusions!

405. *Johnny.* We have got candles here, Father. We had
406.   them to put around his body. Maybe they would
407.   keep away the evil things of the air.

408. *Paudeen.* Light them so, and he will say out a Mass for
409.   him the same as in a lime-washed church.

                                    [*They light the candles.*
                        Thomas comes in

410. *Thomas.* Where is he? I am come to warn him. The de-
411.   struction he did in the night-time has been heard of.
412.   The soldiers are out after him, and the constables—
413.   there are two of the constables not far off—there are

---

396.   . . . going to . . . **28a, 29.**
401.   . . . went **28a-84.**
403.   . . . his . . . **33.**
404.   . . . delusions. **28a, 29.**
        Directions after 409. [. . . *candles on the rock. Thomas* . . . .] **29.**
412.   . . . him and . . . constables . . . [T] **28a, 29 ;** . . . him and . . . — **33, 69.**
413.   . . . off . . . [T] there . . . **28a, 29.**

414. others on every side—they heard he was here in the
415. mountain—where is he?

416. *Father John.* He has gone up the path.

417. *Thomas.* Hurry after him! Tell him to hide himself—
418. this attack he had a hand in is a hanging crime. Tell
419. him to hide himself, to come to me when all is quiet
420. —bad as his doings are, he is my own brother's son;
421. I will get him on to a ship that will be going to
422. France.

423. *Father John.* That will be best; send him back to the
424. Brothers and to the wise Bishops. They can unravel
425. this tangle, I cannot. I cannot be sure of the truth.

426. *Thomas.* Here are the constables; he will see them and
427. get away. Say no word. The Lord be praised that he
428. is out of sight.

Constables come in

429. *Constable.* The man we are looking for, where is he?
430. He was seen coming here along with you. You have
431. to give him up into the power of the Law.

432. *Johnny.* We will not give him up. Go back out of this
433. or you will be sorry.

434. *Paudeen.* We are not in dread of you or the like of you.

---

414. . . . side . . . [T] they . . .
415. mountain . . . [T] where . . . ? **28a, 29.**
417. . . . himself . . . [T] **28a, 29**; Hurray after . . . — **97A.**
418. . . . hand, (hand **29**) in . . . crime. . . . [T] Tell **28a, 29.**
420. . . . [T] bad . . . are he . . . own mother's son, **28a**; . . . [T] bad . . . ;
   29.
421. . . . him onto a . . . **28a.**
423. . . . best, send . . . **33, 69.**
424. . . . Bishops They . . . **28a.**
425. . . . cannot; I . . . . **28a**; . . . tangle. I cannot; I . . . . **29.**
426. . . . constables, he . . . **33, 69.**
427. . . . away. . . . [T] Say . . . word. . . . [T] The . . . **28a, 29.**
431. . . . law. **28a-69.**
432. . . . up! Go . . . **28a, 29.**

435. *Biddy.* Throw them down over the rocks!

436. *Nanny.* Give them to the picking of the crows!

437. *All.* Down with the Law!

438. *Father John.* Hush! He is coming back. [*To Constables.*]
439.   Stop, stop—leave him to himself. He is not trying
440.   to escape, he is coming towards you.

441. *Paudeen.* There is a sort of brightness about him. I
442.   misjudged him calling him a traitor. It is not to this
443.   world he belongs at all. He is over on the other side.

Martin [*standing beside the rock where the lighted candles are*].
444.   *Et calix meus inebrians quam praeclarus est!*

445. *Father John.* I must know what he has to say. It is not
446.   from himself he is speaking.

447. *Martin.* Father John, Heaven is not what we have be-
448.   lieved it to be. It is not quiet, it is not singing and
449.   making music, and all strife at an end. I have seen it,
450.   I have been there. The lover still loves, but with a
451.   greater passion, and the rider still rides, but the
452.   horse goes like the wind and leaps the ridges, and
453.   the battle goes on always, always. That is the joy of
454.   Heaven, continual battle. I thought the battle was
455.   here, and that the joy was to be found here on earth,
456.   that all one had to do was to bring again the old

---

437. . . . law! **28a-69.**
439. . . . , stop . . . [T] leave . . .
440. . . . escape; he . . . . . **28a, 29.**
      Directions before 444. [lacking] **28a**; [*Martin has come in. He stands higher than the others upon some rocks.*] **29.**
444. . . . *inebrians me quam* . . . ! **28a.**
447. . . . , heaven . . .
448. . . . quiet; it . . .
449. . . . music and . . . , **28a, 29.**
450. . . . loves but . . . **33, 69.**
451. . . . passion; and . . . **28a, 29**; . . . rides but . . . **33, 69.**
452. . . . ridges; and **28a, 29.**
454. heaven, . . . **28a, 29.**
456. . . . old, **28a, 29.**

457. wild earth of the stories—but no, it is not here; we
458. shall not come to that joy, that battle, till we have
459. put out the senses, everything that can be seen and
460. handled, as I put out this candle. [*He puts out candle.*]
461. We must put out the whole world as I put out this
462. candle [*puts out another candle*]. We must put out the
463. light of the stars and the light of the sun and the
464. light of the moon [*puts out the rest of the candles*], till
465. we have brought everything to nothing once again.
466. I saw in a broken vision, but now all is clear to me.
467. Where there is nothing, where there is nothing—
468. there is God!

469. *Constable.* Now we will take him!

470. *Johnny.* We will never give him up to the Law!

471. *Paudeen.* Make your escape! We will not let you be
472. followed.

> [*They struggle with Constables; the women help them; all disappear struggling. There is a shot. Martin stumbles and falls. Beggars come back wtih a shout.*]

473. *Johnny.* We have done for them; they will not meddle
474. with you again.

475. *Paudeen.* O, he is down!

476. *Father John.* He is shot through the breast. O, who has

---

457. . . . stories, but . . . **28a, 29.**
   Directions in 460. [lacking]
460. handled as . . . . **28a.**
   Directions in 462. [lacking] **28a.**
462. candle; we . . . **28a** ; candle [*he puts out candle*]; we . . . **29.**
   Directions in 464. [lacking] **28a** ; [*he puts out the remaining candles and comes down to where the others are*] **29.**
467. . . . nothing . . . [T] **28a, 29.**
470. . . . law! **28a-69.**
   Directions after 472. [. . . *Constables, the* . . . *them, all* . . . . *Martin falls dead. Beggars* . . . .] **28a** ; [. . . *disappear, struggling.* . . . *Martin falls dead. Beggars* . . . .] **29.**
473. . . . them, they . . . **33, 69.**
476. . . . the heart. Oh, . . . **28a** ; . . . breast, O, . . . **97A.**

477.   dared meddle with a soul that was in the tumults
478.   on the threshold of sanctity?

479. *Johnny.* It was that gun went off and I striking it from
480.   the constable's hand.

481. *Martin* [*looking at his hand, on which there is blood*]. Ah,
482.   that is blood! I fell among the rocks. It is a hard
483.   climb. It is a long climb to the vineyards of Eden.
484.   Help me up. I must go on. The Mountain of
485.   Abiegnos is very high—but the vineyards—the vine-
486.   yards!

        [*He falls back dead. The men uncover their heads.*

487. *Paudeen* [*to Biddy*]. It was you misled him with your
488.   foretelling that he was coming within the best day
489.   of his life.

490. *Johnny.* Madness on him or no madness, I will not
491.   leave that body to the Law to be buried with a dog's
492.   burial or brought away and maybe hanged upon a
493.   tree. Lift him on the sacks, bring him away to the
494.   quarry; it is there on the hillside the boys will give
495.   him a great burying, coming on horses and bearing
496.   white rods in their hands.

        [*Nanny lays the velvet cloak over him. They lift him and carry the
        body away singing:*

497.   'Our hope and our darling, our heart dies with you,
498.   You to have failed us, we are foals astray!'

499. *Father John.* He is gone and we can never know where

---

485. Abeignos . . . vineyards . . . [T] the vine- **28a** ; . . . high . . . [T] but
      . . . vineyards . . . [T] the . . . **29.**
486. yards. **28a.**
      Directions after 486.   [. . . *back, dead.* . . . .] **29.**
491. . . . law . . . **28a-69.**
492. . . . maybe hanging upon . . . **97A.**
493. . . . sacks; bring . . . **28a, 29.**
      Directions after 496.   [*They . . . away, singing.*] **28a, 29.**
497. Our . . . you. (you, **33-84**).
498. . . . astray! **28a-84.**
499. . . . gone, and . . . **28a, 29.**

500.   that vision came from. I cannot know—the wise
501.   Bishops would have known.

502.   *Thomas* [*taking up banner*]. To be shaping a lad through
503.   his lifetime, and he to go his own way at the last,
504.   and a queer way. It is very queer the world itself is,
505.   whatever shape was put upon it at the first.

506.   *Andrew*. To be too headstrong and too open, that is
507.   the beginning of trouble. To keep to yourself the
508.   thing that you know, and to do in quiet the thing
509.   you want to do. There would be no disturbance at
510.   all in the world, all people to bear that in mind!

THE END

---

500. . . . know; the . . . **28a, 29.**
505. . . . first! **28a, 29.**
509. . . . do, there . . . **28a, 29.**

V.E.P.Y.—2A

NOTES

'The Unicorn from the Stars' was first played at the Abbey Theatre on November 23, 1907, with the following cast:—Father John . . Ernest Vaughan / Thomas Hearne . . Arthur Sinclair / Andrew Hearne . . J. A. O'Rourke / Martin Hearne . . F. J. Fay / Johnny Bacach . . W. G. Fay / Paudeen . . J. M. Kerrigan / Biddy Lally . . Maire O'Neill / Nanny . . Bridget O'Dempsey.   Notes, **29.**

Some years ago I wrote in a fortnight with the help of Lady Gregory and another friend a five act tragedy called *Where there is Nothing*.[1] I wrote at such speed that I might save from a plagiarist a subject that seemed worth the keeping till greater knowledge of the stage made an adequate treatment possible. I knew that my first version was hurried and oratorical, with events cast into the plot because they seemed lively or amusing in themselves, and not because they grew out of the characters and the plot; and I came to dislike a central character so arid and so dominating. We cannot sympathize with a man who sets his anger at once lightly and confidently to overthrow the order of the world; but our hearts can go out to him, as I think, if he speak with some humility, so far as his daily self carries him, out of a cloudy light of vision. Whether he understand or know, it may be that the voices of Angels and Archangels have spoken in the cloud and whatever wildness come upon his life, feet of theirs may well have trod the clusters. I began with this new thought to dictate the play to Lady Gregory, but since I had last worked with her, her knowledge of the stage and her mastery of dialogue had so increased that my imagination could not go neck to neck with hers. I found myself, too, with an old difficulty, that my words flow freely alone when my people speak in verse, or in words that are like those we put into verse; and so after an attempt to work alone I gave my scheme to her. The result is a play almost wholly hers in handiwork, which I can yet read, as I have just done after the stories of *The Secret Rose*, and recognize thoughts, a point of view, an artistic aim which seem a part of my world. Her greatest difficulty was that I had given her for chief character a man so plunged in trance that he could not be otherwise than all but still and silent, though perhaps with the stillness and the silence of a lamp; and the movement of the play as a whole, if we were to listen to hear him, had to be without hurry or violence. The strange characters, her handiwork, on whom he sheds his light, delight me. She has enabled me to carry out an old thought for which my own knowledge is insufficient and to commingle the ancient phantasies of poetry with the rough, vivid, ever-contemporaneous tumult of the roadside; to create for a moment a form that otherwise I could but dream of, though I do that always, an art that prophesies though with worn and failing voice of the day when Quixote and Sancho Panza long estranged may once again go out gaily into the bleak air. Ever since I began

[1] See pp. 1064-1165.

712

to write I have awaited with impatience a linking, all Europe over, of the hereditary knowledge of the country-side, now becoming known to us through the work of wanderers and men of learning, with our old lyricism so full of ancient frenzies and hereditary wisdom, a yoking of antiquities, a Marriage of Heaven and Hell.

The Unicorn from the Stars was first played at the Abbey Theatre on November 23rd, 1907, with the following cast:—Father John, Ernest Vaughan; Thomas Hearne, a coachbuilder, Arthur Sinclair; Andrew Hearne, brother of Thomas, J. A. O'Rourke; Martin Hearne, nephew of Thomas, F. J. Fay; Johnny Bacach, a beggar, W. G. Fay; Paudeen, J. M. Kerrigan; Biddy Lally, Maire O'Neill; Nanny, Brigit O'Dempsey.

March, 1908. w. b. yeats. Notes, **33.**

I wrote in 1902, with the help of Lady Gregory and another friend, a play called *Where There Is* (*there is* **69E**) *Nothing*, but had to write at great speed to meet a sudden emergency. Five acts had to be finished in, I think, a fortnight, instead of the five years that would have been somewhat nearer my natural pace. It became hateful to me because, in desperation, I had caught up from a near table a pamphlet of Tolstoy's on the Sermon on the Mount, and made out of it a satirical scene that became the pivot of the play. The scene seemed amusing on the stage, but its crude speculative commonplaces filled me with shame and I withdrew the play from circulation. That I might free myself from what seemed a contamination, I asked Lady Gregory to help me turn my old plot into *The Unicorn from the Stars*. I began to dictate, but since I had last worked with her, her mastery of the stage and her knowledge of dialect had so increased that my imagination could not go neck to neck with hers. I found myself, too, stopped by an old difficulty, that my words never flow freely but when people speak in verse; and so after an attempt to work alone I gave up my scheme to her. The result is a play almost wholly hers in handiwork, which is so much mine in thought that she does not wish to include it in her own works. I can indeed read it after the stories of *The Secret Rose* and recognize thoughts, points of view, and artistic aims which seem a part of my world. Her greatest difficulty was that I had given her in my re-shaping of the plot—swept as I hoped of dogmatism and rhetorical arrogance—for chief character, a man so plunged in trance that he could not be otherwise than all but still and silent, though perhaps with the stillness and silence of a lamp; and the movement of the play as a whole, if we were to listen, if we were to understand what he said, had to be without hurry or violence. The strange characters, her handiwork, on whom he sheds his light, delight me. She has enabled me to carry out an old thought for which my own knowledge is insufficient, and to commingle the ancient phantasies of poetry with the rough, vivid, ever-contemporaneous tumult of the roadside; to share in the creation of a form that otherwise I could but dream of, though I do that always, an art that murmured, though with worn and failing voice, of the day when Quixote and Sancho Panza, long estranged, may once again go out gaily into the bleak air. Ever since I began to write I have awaited with impatience a linking all Europe over of the hereditary knowledge of the countryside, now becoming known to us through the work of wanderers and men of learning, with our old lyricism so full of ancient frenzies and hereditary wisdom; a yoking of antiquities; a Marriage of Heaven and Hell.

The Unicorn from (and 69E) the Stars was first [follows from here the version in **29**, except that in **69E** 'Nanny' is 'Nancy']   Notes, **69**.

* * *

Variant spellings

Abeignos **28a**; *Abiegnos* **29-97**.
Bacach **28a-69**; *Bocach* **84, 97**.
bracket **84, 97**; *braket* **28a-69**.
Brownes **33-97**; *Browns* **28a, 29**.
hally-stake **69A**; *holly stake* **28a, 29**; *holly-stake* **33, 69E, 84, 97**.
Holyday **28a, 29**; *holy-day* **33-97**.
Kinevara **28a**; *Kinvara* **29-97**.
monoceros de astris **33-97**; *Monocoros di astris (Astris* **29) 28a, 29**.
O, Oh **28a-69**; *O* **84, 97**.
Van Dieman **28a-33, 69E**; *Van Diemen* **69A, 84, 97**.
Whisht **33-97**; *Whist* **28a, 29**.

* * *

[See also the notes on *The Resurrection*, p. 932; and *Prefaces to 29, 69, 84*, pp. 1295, 1306, 1309.]

THE PLAYER QUEEN

1922

Persons in the Play

Decima	The Stage Manager
Septimus	The Tapster
Nona	An Old Beggar
The Queen	Old Men, Old Women, Citizens,
The Prime Minister	Countrymen, Players, etc.
The Bishop	

Scene I: *An open space at the meeting of three streets*

Scene II: *The Throne-Room*

Scene I

An open space at the meeting of three streets. One can see for some way down one of these streets, and at some little distance it turns, showing a bare piece of wall lighted by a hanging lamp. Against this lighted wall are silhouetted the heads and shoulders of two Old Men. They are leaning from the upper windows, one on either side of the street. They wear grotesque masks. A little to one side of the stage is a great stone for mounting a horse from. The houses have knockers.

1. *First Old Man.* Can you see the Queen's castle? You
2.   have better sight than I.

3. *Second Old Man.* I can just see it rising over the tops of
4.   the houses yonder on its great rocky hill.

5. *First Old Man.* Is the dawn breaking? Is it touching the
6.   tower?

Printings   *The Dial*, November 1922; **69, 70, 84, 97.**

Date   [lacking] **D-70.**

Dramatis Personae   Cast of Characters / Decima / . . . , Players, et cetera. **D.**

Scene Description   [lacking] **D**; . . . / The Throne Room. **69, 70.**

Stage Directions   Scene I.: . . . *streets and* . . . . **D-70.**

Text

1.   . . . Castle? . . . **D.**

7.   *Second Old Man.* It is beginning to break upon the
8.   tower, but these narrow streets will be dark for a long
9.   while. [*A pause.*] Do you hear anything? You have
10.   better hearing than I.

11.   *First Old Man.* No, all is quiet.

12.   *Second Old Man.* At least fifty passed by an hour since,
13.   a crowd of fifty men walking rapidly.

14.   *First Old Man.* Last night was very quiet, not a sound,
15.   not a breath.

16.   *Second Old Man.* And not a thing to be seen till the
17.   Tapster's old dog came down the street upon this
18.   very hour from Cooper Malachi's ash-pit.

19.   *First Old Man.* Hush, I hear feet, many feet. Perhaps
20.   they are coming this way. [*Pause.*] No, they are
21.   going the other way, they are gone now.

22.   *Second Old Man.* The young are at some mischief,—the
23.   young and the middle-aged.

24.   *First Old Man.* Why can't they stay in their beds, and
25.   they can sleep too—seven hours, eight hours? I mind
26.   the time when I could sleep ten hours. They will
27.   know the value of sleep when they are near upon
28.   ninety years.

29.   *Second Old Man.* They will never live so long. They
30.   have not the health and strength that we had. They
31.   wear themselves out. They are always in a passion
32.   about something or other.

33.   *First Old Man.* Hush! I hear a step now, and it is com-
34.   ing this way. We had best pull in our heads. The
35.   world has grown very wicked and there is no knowing
36.   what they might do to us or say to us.

37.   *Second Old Man.* Yes, better shut the windows and

---

17.   tapster's . . . **D-70.**
22.   . . . mischief, the **D.**
25.   . . . hours. I . . . **D-70.**
36.   . . . us, or . . . . **D.**

38.   pretend to be asleep.

[They pull in their heads. One hears a knocker being struck in the distance, then a pause, and a knocker is struck close at hand. Another pause, and Septimus, a handsome man of thirty-five, staggers on to the stage. He is very drunk.

39. *Septimus.* An uncharitable place, an unchristian place.

40. *[He begins banging at a knocker.]* Open there, open there.

41. I want to come in and sleep.

[A Third Old Man puts his head from an upper window.

42. *Third Old Man.* Who are you? What do you want?

43. *Septimus.* I am Septimus. I have a bad wife. I want to

44.   come in and sleep.

45. *Third Old Man.* You are drunk.

46. *Septimus.* Drunk! So would you be if you had as bad a

47.   wife.

48. *Third Old Man.* Go away.   *[He shuts the window.*

49. *Septimus.* Is there not one Christian in this town? *[He*

      begins hammering the knocker of First Old Man, but there

50. *is no answer.]* No one there? All dead or drunk maybe

51. —bad wives! There must be one Christian man.

[He hammers a knocker at the other side of the stage. An Old Woman puts her head out of the window above.

52. *Old Woman [in a shrill voice].* Who's there? What do

53.   you want? Has something happened?

54. *Septimus.* Yes, that's it. Something has happened. My

55.   wife has hid herself, has run away, or has drowned

56.   herself.

Directions after 38. [. . . *pause and* . . . *pause and Septimus a* . . . *thirty-five staggers* . . . .] **D** ; [. . . *pause and* . . . *pause and* . . . .] **69, 70.**

39. . . . unChristian . . . . **69E, 70.**

49. . . . town. [*He* **69E, 70.**

    Directions at 49. [. . . *of the First* . . . .] **D-70.**

51. . . . wives. There . . . . **D-70.**

53. . . . want. Has . . . ? **69E, 70.**

57. *Old Woman.* What do I care about your wife? You are
58.　drunk.

59. *Septimus.* Not care about my wife! But I tell you that
60.　my wife has to play by order of the Prime Minister
61.　before all the people in the great hall of the Castle
62.　precisely at noon, and she cannot be found.

63. *Old Woman.* Go away, go away! I tell you, go away.
　　　　　　　　　　　　　　　[She shuts the window.

64. *Septimus.* Treat Septimus, who has played before Kubla
65.　Khan, like this! Septimus, dramatist and poet! [*The
　　Old Woman opens the window again and empties a jug of
66.　water over him.*] Water! drenched to the skin—must
67.　sleep in the street. [*Lies down.*] Bad wife—others have
68.　had bad wives, but others were not left to lie down
69.　in the open street under the stars, drenched with cold
70.　water, a whole jug of cold water, shivering in the
71.　pale light of the dawn, to be run over, to be trampled
72.　upon, to be eaten by dogs, and all because their wives
73.　have hidden themselves.

　　　Enter two Men a little older than Septimus.
　　　They stand still and gaze into the sky

74. *First Man.* Ah, my friend, the little fair-haired one is
75.　a minx.

76. *Second Man.* Never trust fair hair—I will have nothing
77.　but brown hair.

78. *First Man.* They have kept us too long—brown or fair.

79. *Second Man.* What are you staring at?

80. *First Man.* At the first streak of the dawn on the Castle
81.　tower.

82. *Second Man.* I would not have my wife find out for the
83.　world.

57.　... wife! You ... **D-70.**
62.　... noon and .... **D-70.**
65.　... this. Septimus, ... **D-70.**
74.　Ah my ... **D,**

84. *Septimus* [*sitting up*]. Carry me, support me, drag me,
85.   roll me, pull me, or sidle me along, but bring me
86.   where I may sleep in comfort. Bring me to a stable—
87.   my Saviour was content with a stable.

88. *First Man.* Who are you? I don't know your face.

89. *Septimus.* I am Septimus, a player, a playwright, and
90.   the most famous poet in the world.

91. *Second Man.* That name, sir, is unknown to me.

92. *Septimus.* Unknown?

93. *Second Man.* But my name will not be unknown to you.
94.   I am called Peter of the Purple Pelican, after the
95.   best known of my poems, and my friend is called
96.   Happy Tom. He also is a poet.

97. *Septimus.* Bad, popular poets.

98. *Second Man.* You would be a popular poet if you could.

99. *Septimus.* Bad, popular poets.

100. *First Man.* Lie where you are if you can't be civil.

101. *Septimus.* What do I care for any one now except Venus
102.   and Adonis and the other planets of heaven?

103. *Second Man.* You can enjoy their company by yourself.
                                    [*The two Men go out.*

104. *Septimus.* Robbed, so to speak; naked, so to speak—
105.   bleeding, so to speak—and they pass by on the other
106.   side of the street.
       [*A crowd of Citizens and Countrymen enter. At first only a few, and
       then more and more till the stage is filled by an excited crowd.*

---

85.   . . . me or . . . **D.**
89.   . . . playwright and **69, 70.**
95.   best-known . . . **D.**
102. . . . heaven! **D-70.**
103, . . . company for yourself. **97A.**
       Directions after 106. [. . . *few and* . . . .] **D.**

107. *First Citizen.* There is a man lying here.

108. *Second Citizen.* Roll him over.

109. *First Citizen.* He is one of those players who are housed
110.   at the Castle. They arrived yesterday.

111. *Second Citizen.* Drunk, I suppose. He'll be killed or
112.   maimed by the first milk-cart.

113. *Third Citizen.* Better roll him into the corner. If we
114.   are in for a bloody day's business, there is no need
115.   for him to be killed—an unnecessary death might
116.   bring a curse upon us.

117. *First Citizen.* Give me a hand here.

                                   [*They begin rolling Septimus.*

118. *Septimus* [*muttering*]. Not allowed to sleep! Rolled off
119.   the street! Shoved into a stony place! Unchristian
120.   town!
          [*He is left lying at the foot of the wall to one side of the stage.*

121. *Third Citizen.* Are we all friends here, are we all agreed?

122. *First Citizen.* These men are from the country. They
123.   came in last night. They know little of the business.
124.   They won't be against the people, but they want to
125.   know more.

126. *First Countryman.* Yes, that is it. We are with the
127.   people, but we want to know more.

128. *Second Countryman.* We want to know all, but we are
129.   with the people.
          [*Other voices take up the words,* 'We want to know all, but we
          are with the people', etc. *There is a murmur of voices together.*

130. *Third Citizen.* Have you ever seen the Queen, country-
131.   man?

_____

Directions after 210.   [*Septimus is* . . . .] **D.**
Directions after 129.   [. . . *words:* 'We . . . people' et cetera. . . . .] **D.**

132. *First Countryman.* No.

133. *Third Citizen.* Our Queen is a witch, a bad evil-living
134.   witch, and we will have her no longer for Queen.

135. *Third Countryman.* I would be slow to believe her father's
136.   daughter a witch.

137. *Third Citizen.* Have you ever seen the Queen, country-
138.   man?

139. *Third Countryman.* No.

140. *Third Citizen.* Nor has any one else. Not a man here
141.   has set eyes on her. For seven years she has been shut
142.   up in that great black house on the great rocky hill.
143.   From the day her father died she has been there with
144.   the doors shut on her, but we know now why she
145.   has hidden herself. She has no good companions in
146.   the dark night.

147. *Third Countryman.* In my district they say that she is a
148.   holy woman and prays for us all.

149. *Third Citizen.* That story has been spread about by the
150.   Prime Minister. He has spies everywhere spreading
151.   stories. He is a crafty man.

152. *First Countryman.* It is true, they always deceive us
153.   country people. We are not educated like the people
154.   of the town.

155. *A Big Countryman.* The Bible says, Suffer not a witch
156.   to live. Last Candlemas twelvemonth I strangled a
157.   witch with my own hands.

158. *Third Citizen.* When she is dead we will make the
159.   Prime Minister King.

160. *Second Citizen.* No, no, he is not a king's son.

161. *Second Countryman.* I'd send a bellman through the
162.   world. There are many kings in Arabia, they say.

---

153.   countrypeople. . . . **69, 70.**
155.   , , , , suffer . . . **D.**

163. *Third Countryman.* The people must be talking. If you
164. and I were to hide ourselves, or to be someway hard
165. to understand, maybe they would put some bad
166. name on us. I am not against the people, but I want
167. testimony.

168. *Third Citizen.* Come, Tapster, stand up there on the
169. stone and tell what you know.
                    [*The Tapster climbs up on the mounting-stone.*

170. *Tapster.* I live in the quarter where her Castle is.
171. The garden of my house and the gardens of all the
172. houses in my row run right up to the rocky hill that
173. has her Castle on the top. There is a lad in my
174. quarter that has a goat in his garden.

175. *First Citizen.* That's Strolling Michael—I know him.

176. *Tapster.* That goat is always going astray. Strolling
177. Michael got out of his bed early one morning to go
178. snaring birds, and nowhere could he see that goat.
179. So he began climbing up the rock, and up and up he
180. went, till he was close under the wall, and there he
181. found the goat and it shaking and sweating as though
182. something had scared it. Presently he heard a thing
183. neigh like a horse, and after that a something like a
184. white horse ran by, but it was no horse, but a uni-
185. corn. He had his pistol, for he had thought to bring
186. down a rabbit, and seeing it rushing at him as he
187. imagined, he fired at the unicorn. It vanished all in a
188. moment, but there was blood on a great stone.

189. *Third Citizen.* Seeing what company she keeps in the
190. small hours, what wonder that she never sets foot
191. out of doors!

192. *Third Countryman.* I wouldn't believe all that night
193. rambler says—boys are liars. All that we have against
194. her for certain is that she won't put her foot out of
195. doors. I knew a man once that when he was five-and-
196. twenty refused to get out of his bed. He wasn't ill
197. —no, not he, but he said life was a vale of tears, and

---

175. . . . strolling . . . . **69, 70.**
191. . . . doors. **D, 69E, 70 ;** . . . doors? **69A.**
195. . . . five and **D-70.**

198. for forty and four years till they carried him out to
199. the churchyard he never left that bed. All tried him
200. —parson tried him, priest tried him, doctor tried
201. him, and all he'd say was, 'Life is a vale of tears'.
202. It's too snug he was in his bed, and believe me, that
203. ever since she has had no father to rout her out of a
204. morning she has been in her bed, and small blame
205. to her maybe.

206. *The Big Countryman.* But that's the very sort that are
207. witches. They know where to find their own friends
208. in the lonely hours of the night. There was a witch
209. in my own district that I strangled last Candlemas
210. twelvemonth. She had an imp in the shape of a red
211. cat, that sucked three drops of blood from her poll
212. every night a little before the cock crew. It's with
213. their blood they feed them; until they have been fed
214. with the blood they are images and shadows; but
215. when they have it drunk they can be for a while
216. stronger than you or me.

217. *Third Countryman.* The man I knew was no witch, he
218. was no way active. 'Life is a vale of tears,' he said.
219. Parson tried him, doctor tried him, priest tried him
220. —but that was all he'd say.

221. *First Citizen.* We'd have no man go beyond evidence
222. and reason, but hear the Tapster out, and when you
223. have you'll say that we cannot leave her alive this
224. day—no, not for one day longer.

225. *Tapster.* It's not a story that I like to be telling, but
226. you are all married men. Another night that boy
227. climbed up after his goat, and it was an hour earlier
228. by his clock and no light in the sky, and when he
229. came to the Castle wall he clambered along the wall
230. among the rocks and bushes till he saw a light from
231. a little window over his head. It was an old wall full
232. of holes, where mortar had fallen out, and he climbed
233. up, putting his toes into the holes, till he could look

---

203. . . . has no . . . **69A.**
204. . . . bed and . . . **D.**
211. cat that . . . **D.**
227. . . . goat and . . . **D-70.**
233. up putting . . . **D.**

234.   in through the window; and when he looked in,
235.   what did he see but the Queen!

236. *First Countryman.* And did he say what she was like?

237. *Tapster.* He saw more than that. He saw her coupling
238.   with a great white unicorn.

>   [*Murmurs among the crowd.*

239. *Second Countryman.* I will not have the son of the uni-
240.   corn to reign over us, although you will tell me he
241.   would be no more than half a unicorn.

242. *First Countryman.* I'll not go against the people, but
243.   I'd let her live if the Prime Minister promised to
244.   rout her out of bed in the morning and to set a guard
245.   to drive off the unicorn.

246. *The Big Countryman.* I have strangled an old witch with
247.   these two hands, and to-day I will strangle a young
248.   witch.

     Septimus [*who has slowly got up and climbed up on to the
249.   mounting-stone which the Tapster has left*]. Did I hear
250.   somebody say that the Unicorn is not chaste? It is a
251.   most noble beast, a most religious beast. It has a
252.   milk-white skin and a milk-white horn, and milk-
253.   white hooves, but a mild blue eye, and it dances in
254.   the sun. I will have no one speak against it, not while
255.   I am still upon the earth. It is written in 'The Great
256.   Beastery of Paris' that it is chaste, that it is the
257.   most chaste of all the beasts in the world.

258. *The Big Countryman.* Pull him out of that, he's drunk.

259. *Septimus.* Yes, I am drunk, I am very drunk, but that
260.   is no reason why I should permit any one to speak
261.   against the Unicorn.

---

235. ... Queen. **D, 69E, 70** ; ... Queen? **69A.**
247. ... to-day, I ... **97A.**
250. ... unicorn ... **D-70.**
252. ... skin and milk-white ... **97A.**
255. ... the great
256. beastery ... Paris that ... **D.**
261. ... unicorn. **D-70.**

262. *Second Citizen.* Let's hear him out. We can do nothing
263.   till the sun's up.

264. *Septimus.* Nobody shall speak against the Unicorn. No,
265.   my friends and poets, nobody. I will hunt it if you
266.   will, though it is a dangerous and cross-grained beast.
267.   Much virtue has made it cross-grained. I will go with
268.   you to the high tablelands of Africa where it lives,
269.   and we will there shoot it through the head, but I
270.   will not speak against its character, and if any man
271.   declares it is not chaste I will fight him, for I affirm
272.   that its chastity is equal to its beauty.

273. *The Big Countryman.* He is most monstrously drunk.

274. *Septimus.* No longer drunk, but inspired.

275. *Second Citizen.* Go on, go on, we'll never hear the like
276.   again.

277. *The Big Countryman.* Come away. I've enough of this—
278.   we have work to do.

279. *Septimus.* Go away, did you say, and my breast-feathers
280.   thrust out and my white wings buoyed up with
281.   divinity? Ah! but I can see it now—you are bent
282.   upon going to some lonely place where uninterrupted
283.   you can speak against the character of the Unicorn,
284.   but you shall not, I tell you that you shall not. [*He
       comes down off the stone and squares up at the crowd which*
285.   *tries to pass him.*] In the midst of this uncharitable
286.   town I will protect that noble, milk-white, flighty
287.   beast.

288. *The Big Countryman.* Let me pass.

289. *Septimus.* No, I will not let you pass.

290. *First Countryman.* Leave him alone.

---

264. . . . unicorn. . . . , **D-70.**
268. . . . table-lands . . . , **D.**
274. . . . drunk but . . . . **69, 70.**
279. . . . breast feathers **D-70.**
283. . . . unicorn, **D-70.**
      Directions at 284.   [*Septimus comes* . . . .] **D.**

291. *Second Countryman.* No violence—it might bring ill-
292.   luck upon us.

> [*They try to hold back the Big Countryman.*

293. *Septimus.* I will oppose your passing to the death. For
294.   I will not have it said that there is a smirch, or a
295.   blot, upon the most milky whiteness of an heroic
296.   brute that bathes by the sound of tabors at the rising
297.   of the sun and the rising of the moon, and the rising
298.   of the Great Bear, and above all, it shall not be said,
299.   whispered, or in any wise published abroad by you
300.   that stand there, so to speak, between two washings;
301.   for you were doubtless washed when you were born,
302.   and, it may be, shall be washed again after you are
303.   dead.   [*The Big Countryman knocks him down.*

304. *First Citizen.* You have killed him.

305. *The Big Countryman.* Maybe I have, maybe I have not—
306.   let him lie there. A witch I strangled last Candlemas
307.   twelvemonth, a witch I will strangle to-day. What
308.   do I care for the likes of him?

309. *Third Citizen.* Come round to the east quarter of the
310.   town. The basket-makers and the sieve-makers will
311.   be out by this.

312. *Fourth Citizen.* It is a short march from there to the
313.   Castle gate.

> [*They go up one of the side streets, but return quickly in confusion
> and fear.*

314. *First Citizen.* Are you sure that you saw him?

315. *Second Citizen.* Who could mistake that horrible old
316.   man?

317. *Third Citizen.* I was standing by him when the ghost
318.   spoke out of him seven years ago.

---

294.   . . . smirch or . . .
295.   blot upon . . . **D.**
297.   . . . moon and . . . **D.**
302.   and it . . . **D.**
317.   . . . ghosts **D.**

319. *First Countryman.* I never saw him before. He has never
320.   been in my district. I don't rightly know what sort
321.   he is, but I have heard of him, many a time I have
322.   heard of him.

323. *First Citizen.* His eyes become glassy, and that is the
324.   trance growing upon him, and when he is in the
325.   trance his soul slips away and a ghost takes its place
326.   and speaks out of him—a strange ghost.

327. *Third Citizen.* I was standing by him the last time.
328.   'Get me straw,' said that old man, 'my back itches.'
329.   Then all of a sudden he lay down, with his eyes wide
330.   open and glassy, and he brayed like a donkey. At
331.   that moment the King died and the King's daughter
332.   was Queen.

333. *First Countryman.* They say it is the donkey that carried
334.   Christ into Jerusalem, and that is why it knows its
335.   rightful sovereign. He goes begging about the coun-
336.   try and there is no man dare refuse him what he asks.

337. *The Big Countryman.* Then it is certain nobody will take
338.   my hand off her throat. I will make my grip tighter.
339.   He will be lying down on the straw and he will bray,
340.   and when he brays she will be dead.

341. *First Countryman.* Look! There he is coming over the
342.   top of the hill, and the mad look upon him.

343. *Second Countryman.* I wouldn't face him for the world
344.   this night. Come round to the market-place, we'll
345.   be less afraid in a big place.

346. *The Big Countryman.* I'm not afraid, but I'll go with
347.   you till I get my hand on her throat.
          [*They all go out but Septimus. Presently Septimus sits up; his head
          is bleeding. He rubs with his fingers his broken head and looks at the
          blood on his fingers.*

348. *Septimus.* Unchristian town! First I am, so to speak,
349.   thrown out into the street, and then I am all but
350.   murdered; and I drunk, and therefore in need of

---

334.   . . . Jerusalem and . . . **D-70.**
       Directions after 347.   [. . . *up, his . . . rubs his fingers on his* . . . . **D.**

351.   protection. All creatures are in need of protection at
352.   some time or other. Even my wife was once a frail
353.   child in need of milk, of smiles, of love, as if in the
354.   midst of a flood, in danger of drowning, so to speak.
          [*An Old Beggar with long matted hair and beard and in ragged
          clothes comes in.*

355.   *The Old Beggar.* I want straw.

356.   *Septimus.* Happy Tom and Peter of the Purple Pelican
357.   have done it all. They are bad, popular poets, and
358.   being jealous of my fame, they have stirred up the
359.   people. [*He catches sight of the Old Beggar.*] There is a
360.   certain medicine which is made by distilling cam-
361.   phor, Peruvian bark, spurge and mandrake, and mix-
362.   ing all with twelve ounces of dissolved pearls and
363.   four ounces of the oil of gold; and this medicine is
364.   infallible to stop the flow of blood. Have you any of
365.   it, old man?

366.   *The Old Beggar.* I want straw.

367.   *Septimus.* I can see that you have not got it, but no
368.   matter, we shall be friends.

369.   *The Old Beggar.* I want straw to lie down on.

370.   *Septimus.* It is no doubt better that I should bleed to
371.   death. For that way, my friend, I shall disgrace
372.   Happy Tom and Peter of the Purple Pelican, but it
373.   is necessary that I shall die somewhere where my last
374.   words can be taken down. I am therefore in need of
375.   your support.
          [*Having got up he now staggers over to the Old Beggar and leans
          upon him.*

376.   *The Old Beggar.* Don't you know who I am—aren't you
377.   afraid? When something comes inside me, my back
378.   itches. Then I must lie down and roll, and then I
379.   bray and the crown changes.

---

361.   . . . , peruvian . . . **69, 70.**
        Directions after 375.   [*. . . old man and . . . .*] **D-70.**
376.   . . . am, aren't . . . **D.**

380. *Septimus.* Ah! you are inspired. Then we are indeed
381.   brothers. Come, I will rest upon your shoulder and
382.   we will mount the hill side by side. I will sleep in
383.   the Castle of the Queen.

384. *The Old Beggar.* You will give me straw to lie upon?

385. *Septimus.* Asphodels! Yet, indeed, the asphodel is a
386.   flower much overrated by the classic authors. Still if
387.   a man has a preference, I say, for the asphodel——
       [They go out and one hears the voice of Septimus murmuring in the
       distance about asphodels.
       [The First Old Man opens his window and taps with his crutch at
       the opposite window. The Second Old Man opens his window.

388. *First Old Man.* It is all right now. They are all gone.
389.   We can have our talk out.

390. *Second Old Man.* The whole Castle is lit by the dawn
391.   now, and it will begin to grow brighter in the street.

392. *First Old Man.* It's time for the Tapster's old dog to
393.   come down the street.

394. *Second Old Man.* Yesterday he had a bone in his mouth.

---

385. . . . ! Yet indeed the . . . **D.**
386. . . . . Still, if **D-70.**
387. . . . preference, a preference, I say for . . . — **D ;** . . . say for . . . —
    69, 70.
391. . . . will soon begin . . . . **D-70.**

Scene II

*The Throne-Room in the Castle. Between pillars are gilded openwork doors,
except at one side, where there is a large window. The morning light is slanting
through the window, making dark shadows among the pillars. As the scene goes
on, the light, at first feeble, becomes strong and suffused, and the shadows disappear. Through the openwork doors one can see down long passages, and one of
these passages plainly leads into the open air. One can see daylight at the end of it.
There is a throne in the centre of the room and a flight of steps that leads to it.*

*The Prime Minister, an elderly man with an impatient manner and voice, is
talking to a group of Players, among whom is Nona, a fair, comely, comfortable-
looking young woman of perhaps thirty-five; she seems to take the lead.*

1. *Prime Minister.* I will not be trifled with. I chose the
2. play myself; I chose 'The Tragical History of Noah's
3. Deluge' because when Noah beats his wife to make
4. her go into the Ark everybody understands, every-
5. body is pleased, everybody recognises the mulish
6. obstinacy of their own wives, sweethearts, sisters.
7. And now, when it is of the greatest importance to
8. the State that everybody should be pleased, the play
9. cannot be given. The leading lady is lost, you say,
10. and there is some unintelligible reason why nobody
11. can take her place; but I know what you are all
12. driving at—you object to the play I have chosen.
13. You want some dull, poetical thing, full of long
14. speeches. I will have that play and no other. The
15. rehearsal must begin at once and the performance
16. take place at noon punctually.

17. *Nona.* We have searched all night, sir, and we cannot
18. find her anywhere. She was heard to say that she

STAGE DIRECTIONS . . . *throne-room* . . . *open-work* . . . *window making shadows*
. . . *light at* . . . *feeble becomes* . . . *open-work* . . . . **D** ;
   Scene II.: (Scene II: **69A**) . . . *throne-room* . . . *players*, ... **69, 70.**

TEXT

2. . . . chose the tragical history . . .
3. deluge because . . . **D.**

19. would drown rather than play a woman older than
20. thirty. Seeing that Noah's wife is a very old woman,
21. we are afraid that she has drowned herself indeed.

[*Decima, a very pretty woman, puts her head out from under the throne where she has been lying hidden.*

22. *Prime Minister.* Nonsense! It is all a conspiracy. Your
23. manager should be here. He is responsible. You can
24. tell him when he does come that if the play is not
25. performed, I will clap him into gaol for a year and
26. pitch the rest of you over the border.

27. *Nona.* O, sir, he couldn't help it. She does whatever
28. she likes.

29. *Prime Minister.* Does whatever she likes—I know her
30. sort; would pull the world to pieces to spite her
31. husband or her lover. I know her—a bladder full of
32. dried peas for a brain, a brazen, bragging baggage.
33. Of course he couldn't help it, but what do I care?
34. [*Decima pulls in her head.*] To gaol he goes—somebody
35. has got to go to gaol. Go and cry her name every-
36. where. Away with you! Let me hear you cry it out.
37. Call the baggage. Louder. Louder. [*The Players go out*
38. *crying, 'Where are you, Decima?'*] O, Adam! why did
39. you fall asleep in the garden? You might have known
40. that, while you were lying there helpless, the Old
41. Man in the Sky would play some prank upon you.

[*The Queen, who is young, with an ascetic timid face, enters in a badly fitting state dress.*

42. Ah!

43. *Queen.* I will show myself to the angry people as you
44. have bidden me. I am almost certain that I am ready
45. for martyrdom. I have prayed all night. Yes, I am
46. almost certain.

---

33. . . . care. **D, 69E, 70.**
38. . . . you Decima?'] Oh, . . . **D.**
40. that while . . . **D-70.**
Directions after 41. [. . . *badly-fitting* . . . .] **69, 70.**

47. *Prime Minister.* Ah!

48. *Queen.* I have now attained to the age of my patroness,
49.   Holy Saint Octema, when she was martyred at Antioch.
50.   You will remember that her unicorn was so pleased
51.   at the spectacle of her austerity that he caracoled in
52.   his excitement. Thereupon she dropped out of the
53.   saddle and was trampled to death under the feet of
54.   the mob. Indeed, but for the unicorn, the mob would
55.   have killed her long before.

56. *Prime Minister.* No, you will not be martyred. I have a
57.   plan to settle that. I will stop their anger with a
58.   word. Who made that dress?

59. *Queen.* It was my mother's dress. She wore it at her
60.   coronation. I would not have a new one made. I do
61.   not deserve new clothes. I am always committing sin.

62. *Prime Minister.* Is there sin in an egg that has never
63.   been hatched, that has never been warmed, in a
64.   chalk egg?

65. *Queen.* I wish I could resemble Holy Saint Octema in
66.   everything.

67. *Prime Minister.* What a dress! It is too late now. No-
68.   thing can be done. It may appear right to those on
69.   the edge of the crowd. The others must be con-
70.   quered by charm, dignity, royal manner. As for the
71.   dress, I must think of some excuse, some explana-
72.   tion. Remember that they have never seen your face,
73.   and you will put them in a bad humour if you hang
74.   your head in that dumbfounded way.

75. *Queen.* I wish I could return to my prayers.

76. *Prime Minister.* Walk! Permit me to see your Majesty
77.   walk. No, no, no. Be more majestic. Ah! If you had

---

49. . . . Octema when . . . . **D.**
54. . . . mob. But indeed for . . . **D,**
61. . . . clothes, I . . . . **D.**
76. . . . Your . . . **D.**

78. known the queens I have known—they had a way
79. with them. Morals of a dragoon, but a way, a way!
80. Put on a kind of eagle look, a vulture look.

81. *Queen*. There are cobble-stones—if I might go barefoot
82. it would be a blessed penance. It was especially the
83. bleeding feet of Saint Octema that gave pleasure to
84. the unicorn.

85. *Prime Minister*. Sleep of Adam! Barefoot—barefoot, did
86. you say? [*A pause.*] There is not time to take off your
87. shoes and stockings. If you were to look out of the
88. window there, you would see the crowd becoming
89. wickeder every minute. Come! [*He gives his arm to
       the Queen.*]

90. *Queen*. You have a plan to stop their anger so that I
91. shall not be martyred?

92. *Prime Minister*. My plan will be disclosed before the
93. face of the people and there alone.   [*They go out.
       [Nona comes in with a bottle of wine and a boiled lobster and lays
       them on the middle of the floor. She puts her finger on her lip and
       stands in the doorway towards the back of the stage.*

     Decima [comes cautiously out of her hiding-place singing].
94.   'He went away', my mother sang,
95.   'When I was brought to bed.'
96.   And all the while her needle pulled
97.   The gold and silver thread.

98.   She pulled the thread and bit the thread
99.   And made a golden gown,
100.   She wept because she had dreamt that I
101.   Was born to wear a crown.

---

78.   . . . Queens . . .
79.   . . . a way, a way.
79a.   Give the people some plain image or they will invent one, **D-70**.
85.   . . .—barefoot did **D**.
       Directions before 94.   [. . . *hiding place* . . . .] **D-70**.

[*She is just reaching her hand for the lobster when Nona comes
forward holding out towards her the dress and mask of Noah's wife
which she has been carrying over her left arm.*

102. *Nona.* Thank God you are found! [*Getting between her
103. and the lobster.*] No, not until you have put on this
104. dress and mask. I have caught you now, and you are
105. not going to hide again.

106. *Decima.* Very well, when I have had my breakfast.

107. *Nona.* Not a mouthful till you are dressed ready for
108. the rehearsal.

109. *Decima.* Do you know what song I was singing just
110. now?

111. *Nona.* It is that song you're always singing. Septimus
112. made it up.

113. *Decima.* It is the song of the mad singing daughter of
114. a harlot. The only song she had. Her father was a
115. drunken sailor waiting for the full tide, and yet she
116. thought her mother had foretold that she would
117. marry a prince and become a great queen. [*Singing.*]
118.   'When she was got', my mother sang,
119.   'I heard a seamew cry,
120.   I saw a flake of yellow foam
121.   That dropped upon my thigh.'

122.   How therefore could she help but braid
123.   The gold upon my hair,
124.   And dream that I should carry
125.   The golden top of care?
126. The moment ago as I lay here I thought I could play

Directions between 101 and 102.   [. . . *she had been* . . . .] **D-70.**
102. . . . found. [*Getting* . . . **D.**
104. . . . now and . . . **D-70.**
115. . . . tide and . . . **D.**
119. . . . sea-mew . . . , **D.**
125. . . . care. **D-70.**

127.   a queen's part, a great queen's part; the only part
128.   in the world I can play is a great queen's part.

129.   *Nona.* You play a queen's part? You that were born
130.   in a ditch between two towns and wrapped in a sheet
131.   that was stolen from a hedge.

132.   *Decima.* The Queen cannot play at all, but I could play
133.   so well. I could bow with my whole body down to
134.   my ankles and could be stern when hard looks were
135.   in season. O, I would know how to put all summer
136.   in a look and after that all winter in a voice.

137.   *Nona.* Low comedy is what you are fit for.

138.   *Decima.* I understood all this in a wink of the eye, and
139.   then just when I am saying to myself that I was
140.   born to sit up there with soldiers and courtiers, you
141.   come shaking in front of me that mask and that
142.   dress. I am not to eat my breakfast unless I play an
143.   old peaky-chinned, drop-nosed harridan that a foul
144.   husband beats with a stick because she won't clamber
145.   among the other brutes into his cattle-boat. [*She
       makes a dart at the lobster.*]

146.   *Nona.* No, no, not a drop, not a mouthful till you have
147.   put these on. Remember that if there is no play
148.   Septimus must go to prison.

149.   *Decima.* Would they give him dry bread to eat?

150.   *Nona.* They would.

151.   *Decima.* And water to drink and nothing in the water?

152.   *Nona.* They would.

153.   *Decima.* And a straw bed?

154.   *Nona.* They would, and only a little straw maybe.

---

127.   . . . Queen's . . . Queen's . . .
128.   . . . Queen's . . . .
129.   . . . Queen's . . . **D-70.**
145.   . . . cattle boat. . . . **69, 70.**

155. *Decima.* And iron chains that clanked.

156. *Nona.* They would.

157. *Decima.* And keep him there for a whole week?

158. *Nona.* A month maybe.

159. *Decima.* And he would say to the turnkey, 'I am here
160.   because of my beautiful cruel wife, my beautiful
161.   flighty wife'?

162. *Nona.* He might not, he'd be sober.

163. *Decima.* But he'd think it, and every time he was hungry,
164.   every time he was thirsty, every time he felt the
165.   hardness of the stone floor, every time he heard the
166.   chains clank, he would think it, and every time he
167.   thought it I would become more beautiful in his
168.   eyes.

169. *Nona.* No, he would hate you.

170. *Decima.* Little do you know what the love of man is.
171.   If that Holy Image of the church where you put all
172.   those candles at Easter was pleasant and affable, why
173.   did you come home with the skin worn off your
174.   two knees?

175. *Nona* [*in tears*]. I understand—you cruel, bad woman!
176.   —you won't play the part at all, and all that Septimus
177.   may go to prison, and he a great genius that can't
178.   take care of himself.
      [*Seeing Nona distracted with tears Decima makes a dart and almost
      gets the lobster.*

---

155.   ... clanked? **D.**
161.   ... wife.' **D-70.**
163.   ... it and ... , **69, 70.**
171.   ... Church ... **D-84.**
175.   ... cruel (cruel, **70**) bad woman—
176.   you ... **D-70.**
177.   ... prison and ... **D.**
      Directions after 178. [... *tears, Decima* ....] **D.**

179. *Nona.* No, no! Not a mouthful, not a drop. I will break
180.   the bottle if you go near it. There is not another
181.   woman in the world would treat a man like that, and
182.   you were sworn to him in church—yes, you were,
183.   there is no good denying it. [*Decima makes another dart,
         but Nona, who is still in tears, puts the lobster in her
184.   pocket.*] Leave the food alone; not one mouthful will
185.   you get. I have never sworn to a man in church, but
186.   if I did swear, I would not treat him like a tinker's
187.   donkey—before God I would not—I was properly
188.   brought up; my mother always told me it was no
189.   light thing to take a man in church.

190. *Decima.* You are in love with my husband.

191. *Nona.* Because I don't want to see him gaoled you say
192.   I am in love with him. Only a woman with no heart
193.   would think one can't be sorry for a man without
194.   being in love with him—a woman who has never
195.   been sorry for anybody! But I won't have him gaoled;
196.   if you won't play the part I'll play it myself.

197. *Decima.* When I married him, I made him swear never
198.   to play with anybody but me, and well you know it.

199. *Nona.* Only this once, and in a part nobody can do
200.   anything with.

201. *Decima.* That is the way it begins, and all the time you
202.   would be saying things the audience couldn't hear.

---

181.   . . . that and **D-70.**
182.   . . . Church— . . . , **D-84.**
184.   . . . alone, not . . . **D.**
185.   . . . Church, . . .
186.   . . . swear I . . . **D-70.**
188.   . . . up, my . . . **D.**
189.   . . . Church. **D-70.**
194.   . . . him. A . . . **D-70.**
195.   . . . anybody, but . . . jailed, **D-70.**
196.   . . . part, I'll . . . . **D.**
199.   . . . once and . . . **69, 70.**
201.   . . . begins and . . . **D-70.**

203. *Nona.* Septimus will break his oath, and I have learnt
204.   the part. Every line of it.

205. *Decima.* Septimus would not break his oath for any-
206.   body in the world.

207. *Nona.* There is one person in the world for whom he
208.   will break his oath.

209. *Decima.* What have you in your head now?

210. *Nona.* He will break it for me.

211. *Decima.* You are crazy.

212. *Nona.* Maybe I have my secrets.

213. *Decima.* What are you keeping back? Have you been
214.   sitting in corners with Septimus? giving him sym-
215.   pathy because of the bad wife he has, and all the
216.   while he has sat there to have the pleasure of talking
217.   about me?

218. *Nona.* You think that you have his every thought be-
219.   cause you are a devil.

220. *Decima.* Because I am a devil I have his every thought.
221.   You know how his own song runs. The man speaks
222.   first—[*singing*]
223.   Put off that mask of burning gold
224.   With emerald eyes,

---

203. . . . oath and . . . **D-70.**
204. . . . part . . . [T] every . . . . **D.**
214. . . . Septimus, giving . . . **D.**
215. . . . has and . . . **D-70.**
222. first [*singing*]:
223. 'Put . . .
224. . . . eyes.'

225.   and then the woman answers—
226.   O no, my dear, you make so bold
227.   To find if hearts be wild and wise
228.   And yet not cold.

229. *Nona.* His every thought—that is a lie. He forgets
230.   all about you the moment you're out of his sight.

231. *Decima.* Then look what I carry under my bodice. This
232.   is a poem praising me, all my beauties one after the
233.   other—eyes, hair, complexion, shape, disposition,
234.   mind—everything. And there are a great many verses
235.   to it. And here is a little one he gave me yesterday
236.   morning. I had turned him out of bed and he had to
237.   lie alone by himself.

238. *Nona.* Alone by himself!

239. *Decima.* And as he lay there alone, unable to sleep, he
240.   made it up, wishing that he were blind so as not to
241.   be troubled by looking at my beauty. Hear how it
242.   goes! [*sings again*]

243.   O would that I were an old beggar
244.   Without a friend on this earth
245.   But a thieving rascally cur,
246.   A beggar blind from his birth;
247.   Or anything else but a man
248.   Lying a lone on a bed
249.   Remembering a woman's beauty,
250.   Alone with a crazy head.

251. *Nona.* Alone in his bed indeed. I know that long poem,
252.   that one with all the verses; I know it to my hurt,

---

225. and the . . . answers: **D.**
226. 'Oh . . . **D-70.**
228. . . . cold.' **D.**
232. . . . after
233. another—eyes, . . ., **D.**
245. . . . cur **D.**

253. though I haven't read a word of it. Four lines in
254. every verse, four beats in every line, and fourteen
255. verses—my curse upon it!

256. *Decima* [*taking out a manuscript from her bodice*]. Yes, four-
257. teen verses. There are numbers to them.

258. *Nona.* You have another there—ten verses all in fours
259. and threes.

260. *Decima* [*looking at another manuscript*]. Yes, the verses
261. are in fours and threes. But how do you know all
262. this? I carry them here. They are a secret between
263. him and me, and nobody can see them till they have
264. lain a long while upon my heart.

265. *Nona.* They have lain upon your heart, but they were
266. made upon my shoulder. Ay, and down along my
267. spine in the small hours of the morning; so many
268. beats a line, and for every beat a tap of the fingers.

269. *Decima.* My God!

270. *Nona.* That one with the fourteen verses kept me from
271. my sleep two hours, and when the lines were finished
272. he lay upon his back another hour waving one arm
273. in the air, making up the music. I liked him well
274. enough to seem to be asleep through it all, and many
275. another poem too—but when he made up that short
276. one you sang he was so pleased that he muttered the
277. words all about his lying alone in his bed thinking of
278. you, and that made me mad. So I said to him, 'Am
279. I not beautiful? Turn round and look.' O, I cut it
280. short, for even I can please a man when there is but
281. one candle. [*She takes a pair of scissors that are hanging round
     her neck and begins snipping at the dress for Noah's
282. wife.*] And now you know why I can play the part
283. in spite of you and not be driven out. Work upon
284. Septimus if you have a mind for it. Little need I
285. care. I will clip this a trifle and re-stitch it again—
286. I have a needle and thread ready.

---

278. . . . him, am **D.**
279. . . . look. Oh, . . . **D.**
285. . . . will slip this . . . restitch . . . — **D.**

[The Stage Manager comes in ringing a bell. He is followed by various players all dressed up in the likeness of various beasts.

287. *Stage Manager.* Put on that mask—get into your clothes.
288.   Why are you standing there as if in a trance?

289. *Nona.* Decima and I have talked the matter over and
290.   we have settled that I am to play the part.

291. *Stage Manager.* Do as you please. Thank God it's a part
292.   that anybody can play. All you have got to do is to
293.   copy an old woman's squeaky voice. We are all here
294.   now but Septimus, and we cannot wait for him. I
295.   will read the part of Noah. He will be here before
296.   we are finished, I daresay. We will suppose that the
297.   audience is upon this side, and that the Ark is over
298.   there with a gangway for the beasts to climb. All
299.   you beasts are to crowd up on the prompt side. Lay
300.   down Noah's hat and cloak there till Septimus
301.   comes. As the first scene is between Noah and the
302.   beasts, you can go on with your sewing.

303. *Decima.* No, I must first be heard. My husband has
304.   been spending his nights with Nona, and that is why
305.   she sits clipping and stitching with that vainglorious
306.   air.

307. *Nona.* She made him miserable, she knows every trick
308.   of breaking a man's heart—he came to me with his
309.   troubles—I seemed to be a comfort to him, and now
310.   —why should I deny it?—he is my lover.

311. *Decima.* I will take the vainglory out of her. I have
312.   been a plague to him. O, I have been a badger and a
313.   weasel and a hedgehog and pole-cat, and all because
314.   I was dead sick of him. And, thank God!, she has got

Directions after 286. [. . . *in likeness* . . . .] **69, 70.**
294. . . . Septimus and . . . **D.**
296. . . . dare say. . . . **D** ; . . . finished I . . . **69, 70.**
302. beasts you . . . .
303. . . . must be . . . **D.**
313. . . . polecat, . . . **D.**
314. . . . God! she . . . **D-70.**

315.   him and I am free. I threw away a part and I threw
316.   away a man—she has picked both up.

317.   *Stage Manager.* It seems to me that it all concerns you
318.   two. It's your business and not ours. I don't see why
319.   we should delay the rehearsal.

320.   *Decima.* I will have no rehearsal yet. I'm too happy
321.   now that I am free. I must find somebody who will
322.   dance with me for a while. Come, we must have
323.   music. [*She picks up a lute which has been laid down*
324.   *amongst some properties.*] You can't all be claws and
325.   hoofs.

326.   *Stage Manager.* We've only an hour and the whole play
327.   to go through.

328.   *Nona.* O, she has taken my scissors, she is only pre-
329.   tending not to care. Look at her! She is mad! Take
330.   them away from her! Hold her hand! She is going to
331.   kill me or to kill herself. [*To Stage Manager.*] Why
332.   don't you interfere? My God! She is going to kill me.

333.   *Decima.* Here, Peter.
       [*She begins cutting through the breast-feathers of the Swan.*

334.   *Nona.* She is doing it all to stop the rehearsal, out of
335.   vengeance; and you stand there and do nothing.

336.   *Stage Manager.* If you have taken her husband, why
337.   didn't you keep the news till the play was over? She
338.   is going to make them all mad now, I can see that
339.   much in her eyes.

340.   *Decima.* Now that I have thrown Septimus into her lap,
341.   I will choose a new man, Shall it be you, Turkey-

---

322.   . . . . Come we . . . **69, 70.**
329.   . . . ! she . . . **D.**
332.   . . . ! she . . . . **D.**
333.   . . . , Peter. Play the lute. **D-70.**
       Directions after 333.   [. . . *breast feathers* . . . .] **69-70.**
338.   . . . now. I . . . **D-70.**
341.   . . . man. Shall . . . — **D-70, 97A.**

342.   cock? or you, Bullhead?

343.   *Stage Manager.* There is nothing to be done. It is all
344.   your fault. If Septimus can't manage his wife, it's
345.   certain that I can't.   [*He sits down helplessly.*

346.   *Decima.* Dance, Bullhead, dance—no—no—stop. I will
347.   not have you for my man, slow on the feet and heavy
348.   of build, and that means jealousy, and there is a sort
349.   of melancholy in your voice. What a folly that I
350.   should find love nothing, and yet through sympathy
351.   with that voice should stretch and yawn as if I loved!
352.   Dance, Turkey-cock, dance—no, stop. I cannot have
353.   you, for my man must be lively on his feet and
354.   have a quick eye. I will not have that round eye

---

342.   . . . , Bull-head? **D.**
345a.   *First Player* [*who is in the fore* (*four* **69, 70**) *legs of the Bull*]. Come
345b.   live with me and be my love.
346.   . . . , Bull-head, (Bullhead, **69, 70**) dance. [*The Bull dances.*]
347.   You're too slow on your feet.
347a.   *First Player.* Although I am slow I am twice as good as any other, for
347b.   I am double, (double— **69, 70**) one in the fore legs (forelegs **69, 70**)
       and one behind.
348.   *Decima.* You are heavy of build and . . . jealousy (jealousy, **69, 70**)
       and . . .
349.   . . . voice, (voice; **69, 70**) and what . . . folly (folly, **69, 70**) now that
       I have found out
350.   [lacking]
351.   love (love, **69, 70**) to stretch . . . loved.
351a.   *Second Player* [*who is in the form of a Turkey-cock*]. Come live with me
351b.   and be my love, for as everybody can see from my ruff and my red
351c.   wattle and my way of strutting and my chuckling speech, I have
351d.   a cheerful appetite.
352.   *Decima.* Dance, dance. [*The Turkey-cock dances.*] Ah, Turkey-cock, you
353.   are lively on your feet and I would find it hard to hide if
353a.   you followed. Would you expect me to be faithful?
353b.   *Second Player.* No, neither I nor you. I have a score of wives.
353c.   *Nona.* You are a disgrace.
353d.   *Second Player.* Be content now that you have a man of your own.
354.   *Decima.* You are quick of mind, Turkey-cock, (Turkey-cock. **69, 70**)
354a.   I see that by your bright eyes, but I want to let **D-70.**

355.   fixed upon me now that I have sent my mind asleep.
356.   Yet what do I care who it is, so that I choose and get
357.   done with it? Dance, all dance, and I will choose the
358.   best dancer among you. Quick, quick, begin to
359.   dance.   [*All dance round Decima.*

Decima [*singing*].

360.   Shall I fancy beast or fowl?
361.   Queen Pasiphae chose a bull,
362.   While a passion for a swan
363.   Made Queen Leda stretch and yawn,
364.   Wherefore spin ye, whirl ye, dance ye,
365.   Till Queen Decima's found her fancy.

Chorus

366.   Wherefore spin ye, whirl ye, dance ye,
367.   Till Queen Decima's found her fancy.

Decima.

368.   Spring and straddle, stride and strut,
369.   Shall I chose a bird or brute?
370.   Name the feather or the fur
371.   For my single comforter?

Chorus

372.   Wherefore spin ye, whirl ye, dance ye,
373.   Till Queen Decima's found her fancy.

Decima.

374.   None has found, that found out love,
375.   Single bird or brute enough;
376.   Any bird or brute may rest
377.   An empty head upon my breast.

---

355.   my mind go asleep.
356.   [lacking]
357.   All dance, all, all, and . . . choose
358.   the best dancer amongst you.
358a. *First Player.* No, let us toss for it. I understand that better.
359.   *Decima.* Quick, quick, begin to dance.
360.   . . . fowl, **D-70.**
369.   . . . choose . . . ? **D-70.**
371.   . . . comforter. **D.**

Chorus

378.   Wherefore spin ye, whirl ye, dance ye,
379.   Till Queen Decima's found her fancy.

380. *Stage Manager.* Stop, stop, here is Septimus.

Septimus [the blood still upon his face, and but little soberer].
381.   Gather about me, for I announce the end of the
382.   Christian Era, the coming of a New Dispensation,
383.   that of the New Adam, that of the Unicorn; but
384.   alas, he is chaste, he hesitates, he hesitates.

385. *Stage Manager.* This is not a time for making up
386.   speeches for your new play.

387. *Septimus.* His unborn children are but images; we
388.   merely play with images.

389. *Stage Manager.* Let us get on with the rehearsal.

390. *Septimus.* No; let us prepare to die. The mob is climb-
391.   ing up the hill with pitchforks to stick into our vitals
392.   and burning wisps to set the roof on fire.

393. *First Player [who has gone to the window].* My God, it's
394.   true. There is a great crowd at the bottom of the hill.

395. *Second Player.* But why should they attack us?

---

381.   [. . . *blood upon his face still, but . . . soberer*]. Prepare to die. **D**; [. . .
        face and . . .]. Gather . . . **69, 70.**
381a.   Consider whether you will speak as Cato, as Demosthenes, as Cicero
381b.   triumphing over death in sonorous eloquence, or like Petronius
381c.   Arbiter telling witty, scandalous tales.
382-384. [lacking]
  385.   Come, Septimus, this . . .
  386.   . . . for the new play. Let us get on with the rehearsal.
387-389. [lacking]
  390.   Look at my wounds and know that the . . . **D.**
395a.   *Septimus.* Happy Tom and Peter of the Purple Pelican have
395b.   stirred up the mob. **D.**

396. *Septimus.* Because we are the servants of the Unicorn.

397. *Third Player [at window].* My God, they have dung-
398. forks and scythes set on poles and they are coming
399. this way.   [*Many Players gather round the window.*

400. *Septimus [who has found the bottle and is drinking].* Some
401. will die like Cato, some like Cicero, some like Demos-
402. thenes, triumphing over death in sonorous eloquence,
403. or, like Petronius Arbiter, will tell witty, scandalous
404. tales; but I will speak, no, I will sing, as if the mob
405. did not exist. I will rail upon the Unicorn for his
406. chastity. I will bid him trample mankind to death and
407. beget a new race. I will even put my railing into
408. rhyme, and all shall run sweetly, sweetly, for, even
409. if they blow up the floor with gunpowder, they are
410. merely the mob.
411.   Upon the round blue eye I rail,
412.   Damnation on the milk-white horn.
413. A telling sound, a sound to linger in the ear—hale,
414. tale, bale, gale—my God, I am even too sober to
415. find a rhyme! [*He drinks and then picks up a lute*]—a
416. tune that my murderers may remember my last
417. words and croon them to their grandchildren.
                  [*For the next few speeches he is busy making his tune.*

418. *First Player.* The players of this town are jealous. Have
419. we not been chosen before them all, because we are
420. the most famous players in the world? It is they who
421. have stirred up the mob.

---

396. [lacking] **D.**
400. . . . *drinking*]. I will die railing
401-404. [lacking]
405. upon the unicorn because he will
406. not trample . . . death, and upon some women
407. beget . . . race, but I will rail sweetly. We must not allow
408. our murderers to discompose us. For after all even
409. . . . gunpowder they . . .
410. . . . mob. I will even put my railing into rhyme. **D.**
415. . . . rhyme.—[*he* . . . *lute*] a **D** ; . . . rhyme. [*He* . . . **69, 70.**
416. . . . that even my . . . **D.**
       Directions after 417. [. . . *speeches Septimus is* . . . .] **D.**

422. *Second Player*. It is of me they are jealous. They know
423.   what happened at Xanadu. At the end of that old
424.   play 'The Fall of Troy' Kubla Kahn sent for me and
425.   said that he would give his kingdom for such a voice,
426.   and for such a presence. I stood before him dressed
427.   as Agamemnon just as when in a great scene at the
428.   end I had reproached Helen for all the misery she
429.   had wrought.

430. *First Player*. My God, listen to him! Is it not always
431.   the comedian who draws the crowd? Am I dreaming,
432.   or was it not I who was called six times before the
433.   curtain? Answer me that—

434. *Second Player*. What if you were called six dozen times?
435.   The players of this town are not jealous because of
436.   the crowd's applause. They have that themselves.
437.   The unendurable thought, the thought that wrenches
438.   their hearts, the thought that puts murder into their
439.   minds is that I alone, alone of all the world's players,
440.   have looked as an equal into the eyes of Kubla Khan.

441. *Stage Manager*. Stop quarrelling with one another and

---

422.   *Third Player*. When we played at Kzanadu, my performance was
422a.   so incomparable that the men who pulled the strings
422b.   of the puppet-show left all the puppets lying on
422c.   their backs and came to have a look at me.
423.   *Fourth Player*. Listen to him! His performance indeed! I ask
423a.   you all to speak the truth. If you are honest men
423b.   you will say that it was my performance that
424.   drew the town. Why, Kubla Kahn himself gave me
425.   the name of the 'Talking Nightingale.' (Talking Nightingale. **69,
     70**)
426-429. [lacking]
430.   *Fifth Player*. My . . .
431.   . . . the people? Am . . . ,
432.   and was . . .
433.   . . . that.
434-441. [lacking] **D-70**.

442.   listen to what is happening out there. There is a
443.   man making a speech, and the crowd is getting
444.   angrier and angrier, and which of you they are
445.   jealous of I don't know, but they are all coming this
446.   way and maybe they will burn the place down as if
447.   it were Troy, and if you will do what I say you will
448.   get out of this.

449. *First Player.* Must we go dressed like this?

450. *Second Player.* There is not time to change, and besides,
451.   should the hill be surrounded, we can gather in
452.   some cleft of the rocks where we can be seen only
453.   from a distance. They will suppose we are a drove of
454.   cattle or a flock of birds.

> [*All go out except Septimus, Decima, and Nona. Nona is making
> a bundle of Noah's hat and cloak and other properties. Decima is
> watching Septimus.*

455. *Septimus* [*while the Players are going out*]. Leave me to die
456.   alone? I do not blame you. There is courage in red
457.   wine, in white wine, in beer, even in thin beer sold
458.   by a blear-eyed potboy in a bankrupt tavern, but
459.   there is none in the human heart. When my master

---

442.   *Sixth Player* [*at window*]. There is somebody making a speech.
443.   I cannot see who it is.
444-445.   [lacking]
446.   *Second Player.* Depend upon it, he is telling them to put
447.   burning wisps upon dung-forks and put them
447a.   into the rafters. That is what they did in the old
447b.   play of the Burning of Troy. Depend upon it, they
448.   will burn the whole house.
448a.   *Fifth Player* [*coming from window*]. I will stay here no longer. (longer.
     [*Exit.*] **D**)
448b.   *Other Players.* Nor I, nor I. (I. [*Exit.*] **69, 70**) **D-70.**
450.   . . . is no time . . . besides **D, 69E, 70** ; . . . is no time . . . , **69A.**
458.   . . . pot-boy . . . **D.**
459.   . . . heart. Oh, I will journey
459a.   to a cavern in Africa and sing into the ear of the
459b.   unicorn epithalamiums until, unable to endure
459c.   any longer his desirous heart, he becomes the new Adam. **D.**

460. the Unicorn bathes by the light of the Great Bear,
461. and to the sound of tabors, even the sweet river-
462. water makes him drunk; but it is cold, it is cold,
463. alas! it is cold.

464. *Nona.* I'll pile these upon your back. I shall carry the
465. rest myself and so we shall save all.

[*She begins tying a great bundle of properties on Sepitmus' back.*

466. *Septimus.* You are right. I accept the reproach. It is
467. necessary that we who are the last artists—all the rest
468. have gone over to the mob—shall save the images
469. and implements of our art. We must carry into
470. safety the cloak of Noah, the high-crowned hat of
471. Noah, and the mask of the sister of Noah. She was
472. drowned because she thought her brother was telling
473. lies; certainly we must save her rosy cheeks and rosy
474. mouth, that drowned, wicked mouth.

475. *Nona.* Thank God you can still stand upright on your
476. legs.

477. *Septimus.* Tie all upon my back and I will tell you the
478. great secret that came to me at the second mouthful
479. of the bottle. Man is nothing till he is united to an
480. image. Now the Unicorn is both an image and beast;
481. that is why he alone can be the new Adam. When
482. we have put all in safety we will go to the high
483. tablelands of Africa and find where the Unicorn is
484. stabled and sing a marriage song. I will stand before
485. the terrible blue eye.

486. *Nona.* There, now, I have tied them on.

460-463. [lacking] **D.**
471. . . . , and the golden face of the Almighty, and the horns of Satan.
472-474. [lacking] **D-70.**
480. . . . unicorn . . . beast, **D.**
483. table-lands . . . Africa to find . . . unicorn . . .
484. stabled. I will . . . **D.**
486. There now I . . . . **D-70.**

[She begins making another bundle for herself, but forgets the mask of the sister of Noah. It lies near the throne.

487. *Septimus.* You will make Ionian music—music with its
488. eyes upon that voluptuous Asia—the Dorian scale
489. would but confirm him in his chastity. One Dorian
490. note might undo us, and above all we must be careful
491. not to speak of Delphi. The oracle is chaste.

492. *Nona.* Come, let us go.

493. *Septimus.* If we cannot fill him with desire he will de-
494. serve death. Even unicorns can be killed. What they
495. dread most in the world is a blow from a knife that
496. has been dipped in the blood of a serpent that died
497. gazing upon an emerald.
     [Nona and Septimus are about to go out, Nona leading Septimus.

498. *Decima.* Stand back, do not dare to move a step.

499. *Septimus.* Beautiful as the Unicorn, but fierce.

500. *Decima.* I have locked the gates that we may have a
501. talk.   *[Nona lets the hat of Noah fall in her alarm.*

502. *Septimus.* That is well, very well. You would talk with
503. me because to-day I am extraordinarily wise.

504. *Decima.* I will not unlock the gate till I have a promise
505. that you will drive her from the company.

506. *Nona.* Do not listen to her; take the key from her.

507. *Septimus.* If I were not her husband I would take the
508. key, but because I am her husband she is terrible.
509. The Unicorn will be terrible when it loves.

510. *Nona.* You are afraid.

Directions after 486.   [. . . *herself.*] **D-70**; [. . . *Throne.*] **84.**
490.   . . . us and . . . **D.**
499.   . . . unicorn, ... **D**; . . . unicorn but . . . . **69, 70.**
506.   . . . her, take . . . . **D.**
509.   . . . unicorn . . . . **D.**

511. *Septimus.* Could not you yourself take it? She does not
512.   love you, therefore she will not be terrible.

513. *Nona.* If you are a man at all you will take it.

514. *Septimus.* I am more than a man, I am extraordinarily
515.   wise. I will take the key.

516. *Decima.* If you come a step nearer I will shove the key
517.   through the grating of the door.

518. *Nona* [*pulling him back*]. Don't go near her; if she shoves
519.   it through the door we shall not be able to escape.
520.   The crowd will find us and murder us.

521. *Decima.* I will unlock this gate when you have taken an
522.   oath to drive her from the company, an oath never
523.   to speak with her or look at her again, a terrible oath.

524. *Septimus.* You are jealous; it is very wrong to be jealous.
525.   An ordinary man would be lost—even I am not yet
526.   wise enough. [*Drinks again.*] Now all is plain.

527. *Decima.* You have been unfaithful to me.

528. *Septimus.* I am only unfaithful when I am sober. Never
529.   trust a sober man. All the world over they are un-
530.   faithful. Never trust a man who has not bathed by
531.   the light of the Great Bear. I warn you against all
532.   sober men from the bottom of my heart. I am extra-
533.   ordinarily wise.

534. *Nona.* Promise, if it is only an oath she wants. Take
535.   whatever oath she bids you. If you delay we shall all
536.   be murdered.

537. *Septimus.* I can see your meaning. You would explain
538.   to me that an oath can be broken, more especially
539.   an oath under compulsion, but no, I say to you, no,
540.   I say to you, certainly not. Am I a rascally sober man,

---

511. . . . not yourself . . . **69A.**
518. . . . her, if . . . **D.**
530. faithful.
531. I warn . . . **D.**

541.   such a man as I have warned you against? Shall I be
542.   forsworn before the very eyes of Delphi, so to speak,
543.   before the very eyes of that cold, rocky oracle? What
544.   I promise I perform, therefore, my little darling, I
545.   will not promise anything at all.

546. *Decima.* Then we shall wait here. They will come in
547.   through this door, they will carry dung-forks with
548.   burning wisps. They will put the burning wisps into
549.   the roof and we shall be burnt.

550. *Septimus.* I shall die railing upon that beast. The
551.   Christian era has come to an end, but because of the
552.   machinations of Delphi he will not become the new
553.   Adam.

554. *Decima.* I shall be avenged. She starved me, but I shall
555.   have killed her.

556. *Nona* [*who has crept behind Decima and snatched the key*]. I
557.   have it, I have it!

        [*Decima tries to take the key again, but Septimus holds her.*

558. *Septimus.* Because I am an unforsworn man I am strong:
559.   a violent virginal creature, that is how it is put in
560.   'The Great Beastery of Paris'.

561. *Decima.* Go, then, I shall stay here and die.

562. *Nona.* Let us go. A half hour since she offered herself
563.   to every man in the company.

---

542.   foresworn . . . Delphi so . . . , **D.**
543.   . . . cold rocky . . . **D.**
544.   . . . darlings, . . . **97A.**
547.   there and there, they . . . **D-70.**
550.   . . . beast because
551.   owing to a pedantic scruple or some congenital chill of the blood or
        because . . . **D.**
        Directions after 557. [. . . *again but* . . . .] **69, 70.**
558.   . . . strong. **D.**
559-560. [lacking] **D.**
561.   Go then. I . . . . **D ;** . . . , then. I . . . . **69, 70.**
562.   . . . since, she . . . **D.**

564. *Decima.* If you would be faithful to me, Septimus, I
565. would not let a man of them touch me.

566. *Septimus.* Flighty, but beautiful.

567. *Nona.* She is a bad woman. [*Nona runs out.*

568. *Septimus.* A beautiful, bad, flighty woman I will follow,
569. but follow slowly. I will take with me this noble
570. hat. [*He picks up Noah's hat with difficulty.*] No, it may
571. lie there, what have I to do with that drowned,
572. wicked mouth—beautiful, drowned, flighty mouth?
573. I will have nothing to do with it, but I will save the
574. noble, high-crowned hat of Noah. I will carry it thus
575. with dignity. I will go slowly that they may see I
576. am not afraid. [*Singing.*
577. Upon the round blue eye I rail,
578. Damnation on the milk-white horn.
579. But not one word of Delphi. I am extraordinarily
580. wise. [*He goes.*

581. *Decima.* Betrayed, betrayed, and for a nobody. For a
582. woman that a man can shake and twist like so much
583. tallow. A woman that till now never looked higher
584. than a prompter or a property man. [*The Old Beggar*
585. *comes in.*] Have you come to kill me, old man?

586. *Old Beggar.* I am looking for straw. I must soon lie
587. down and roll, and where will I get straw to roll on?
588. I went round to the kitchen, and 'Go away', they
589. said. They made the sign of the cross as if it were a
590. devil that puts me rolling.

591. *Decima.* When will the mob come to kill me?

---

568. . . . woman. I . . . , **D.**
570. . . . *difficulty.*] I will
571-572. [lacking]
573. save . . . **D-70.**
577. . . . rail **D-70.**
578. . . . horn **D.**
Directions in 580. [*Septimus goes.*] **D.**
588. . . . kitchen and . . . **D** ; . . . kitchen and . . . away' they **69, 70.**

592.   *Old Beggar.* Kill you? It is not you they are going to
593.   kill. It's the itching in my back that drags them
594.   hither, for when I bray like a donkey, the crown
595.   changes.

596.   *Decima.* The crown? So it is the Queen they are going
597.   to kill.

598.   *Old Beggar.* But, my dear, she can't die till I roll and
599.   bray, and I will whisper to you what it is that rolls. It
600.   is the donkey that carried Christ into Jerusalem, and
601.   that is why he is so proud; and that is why he knows
602.   the hour when there is to be a new King or a new
603.   Queen.

604.   *Decima.* Are you weary of the world, old man?

605.   *Old Beggar.* Yes, yes, because when I roll and bray I am
606.   asleep. I know nothing about it, and that is a great
607.   pity. I remember nothing but the itching in my back.
608.   But I must stop talking and find some straw.

609.   *Decima* [*picking up the scissors*]. Old man, I am going to
610.   drive this into my heart.

611.   *Old Beggar.* No, no; don't do that. You don't know
612.   what you will be put to when you are dead, into
613.   whose gullet you will be put to sing or to bray. You
614.   have a look of a foretelling sort. Who knows but you
615.   might be put to foretell the death of kings; and bear
616.   in mind I will have no rivals, I could not endure a
617.   rival.

618.   *Decima.* I have been betrayed by a man, I have been
619.   made a mockery of. Do those who are dead, old man,
620.   make love and do they find good lovers?

621.   *Old Beggar.* I will whisper you another secret. People
622.   talk, but I have never known of anything to come
623.   from there but an old jackass. Maybe there is no-
624.   thing else. Who knows but he has the whole place to
625.   himself? But there, my back is beginning to itch, and

---

611.   . . . , no, don't . . . **D.**
620.   . . . love, and . . . ? **69A.**
625.   himself. But . . . **D-70.**

626. I have not yet found any straw.
　　 [*He goes out. Decima leans the scissors upon the arm of the throne
　　 and is about to press herself upon them when the Queen enters.*

627. Queen [*stopping her*]. No, no—that would be a great sin.

628. *Decima.* Your Majesty!

629. *Queen.* I thought I would like to die a martyr, but that
630. 　　 would be different, that would be to die for God's
631. 　　 glory. The Holy Saint Octema was a martyr.

632. *Decima.* I am very unhappy.

633. *Queen.* I, too, am very unhappy. When I saw the great
634. 　　 angry crowd and knew that they wished to kill me,
635. 　　 though I had wanted to be a martyr, I was afraid
636. 　　 and ran away.

637. *Decima.* I would not have run away, O no; but it is
638. 　　 hard to drive a knife into one's own flesh.

639. *Queen.* In a moment they will have come and they will
640. 　　 beat in the door, and how shall I escape them?

641. *Decima.* If they could mistake me for you, you would
642. 　　 escape.

643. *Queen.* I could not let another die instead of me. That
644. 　　 would be very wrong.

645. *Decima.* O, your Majesty, I shall die whatever you
646. 　　 do, and if only I could wear that gold brocade and
647. 　　 those gold slippers for one moment, it would not be
648. 　　 so hard to die.

649. *Queen.* They say that those who die to save a rightful
650. 　　 sovereign show great virtue.

---

627. . . . , no,—that . . . . **69, 70.**
637. . . . away. Oh no, but . . . **D-70.**
646. do and . . . **D.**
650. Sovereign . . . . **D.**

651. *Decima.* Quick! the dress.

652. *Queen.* If you killed yourself your soul would be lost,
653.   and now you will be sure of Heaven.

654. *Decima.* Quick, I hear them coming.

> [*Decima puts on the Queen's robe of state and her slippers. Underneath her robe of state the Queen wears some kind of nun-like dress. The following speech is spoken by the Queen while she is helping Decima to fasten the dress and the slippers.*

655. *Queen.* Was it love? [*Decima nods.*] O, that is a great
656.   sin. I have never known love. Of all things, that is
657.   what I have had most fear of. Saint Octema shut
658.   herself up in a tower on a mountain because she was
659.   loved by a beautiful prince. I was afraid it would
660.   come in at the eye and seize upon me in a moment.
661.   I am not naturally good, and they say people will
662.   do anything for love, there is so much sweetness in
663.   it. Even Saint Octema was afraid of it. But you will
664.   escape all that and go up to God as a pure virgin.
665.   [*The change is now complete.*] Good-bye, I know how I
666.   can slip away. There is a convent that will take me
667.   in. It is not a tower, it is only a convent, but I have
668.   long wanted to go there to lose my name and dis-
669.   appear. Sit down upon the throne and turn your face
670.   away. If you do not turn your face away, you will be
671.   afraid.   [*The Queen goes out.*

> [*Decima is seated upon the throne. A great crowd gathers outside the gates. A Bishop enters.*

672. *Bishop.* Your loyal people, your Majesty, offer you their
673.   homage. I bow before you in their name. Your royal
674.   will has spoken by the mouth of the Prime Minister
675.   —has filled them with gratitude. All misunderstand-
676.   ings are at an end, all has been settled by your con-
677.   descension in bestowing your royal hand upon the
678.   Prime Minister. [*To crowd.*] Her Majesty, who has
679.   hitherto shut herself away from all men's eyes that
680.   she might pray for this kingdom undisturbed, will

---

653. . . . heaven. **D-70.**
670. . . . away you . . . **D.**
672. . . . , Your . . . **D.**
680. . . . Kingdom . . . **D.**

681.   henceforth show herself to her people. [*To Player*
682.   *Queen.*] So beautiful a Queen need never fear the
683.   disobedience of her people [*shouts from crowd of*
        'Never'].

684. *Prime Minister* [*entering hurriedly*]. I will explain all,
685.   your Majesty—there was nothing else to be done
686.   —this Bishop has been summoned to unite us [*seeing*
687.   *the Queen*]; but, sleep of Adam!—this—who is this?

688. *Decima.* Your emotion is too great for words. Do not
689.   try to speak.

690. *Prime Minister.* This—this . . . !

691. *Decima* [*standing up*]. I am Queen. I know what it is to
692.   be Queen. If I were to say to you I had an enemy you
693.   would kill him—you would tear him in pieces, would
694.   you not? [*Shouts:* 'We would kill him', 'We would
695.   tear him in pieces', *etc.*] But I do not bid you kill
696.   any one—I bid you obey my husband when I have
697.   raised him to the throne. He is not of royal blood,
698.   but I choose to raise him to the throne. That is my
699.   will. Show me that you will obey him so long as I
700.   bid you to obey.   [*Great cheering.*
        [*Septimus, who has been standing among the crowd, comes forward
        and takes the Prime Minister by the sleeve. Various persons kiss the
        hand of the supposed Queen.*

---

682.   . . . queen . . . **69, 70.**
683.   . . . people. [*Shouts* . . . 'Never!'] **D** ; . . . '*never.*'] **69E, 70** ; . . . people.
       [*Shouts from the crowd* . . . .'] **69A.**
685.   . . . done. **D.**
686.   This . . . us. [*Seeing* **D** ; —This . . . **69, 70.**
687.   . . . *Queen*] But sleep . . . Adam—this— . . . ?
688.   . . . words, do . . . **D.**
690.   This—this— **D** ; This—this! **69, 70.**
691.   . . . queen. . . .
692.   . . . queen. . . . **69, 70.**
693.   . . . pieces. **D-70.**
694.   [*Shouts* 'We . . . him.' 'We . . . **D** ; [*Shouts* '*we would kill him,*' '*we would*
       69, 70.
695.   . . . pieces' et cetera.] But . . . **D** ; *tear him in pieces,*' *etc.*] . . . **69E, 70** ;
       tear him in pieces,' *etc.*] But . . . you to kill **69A.**
       Directions after 700.   [*Septimus who . . . crowd comes* . . . .] **D.**

701. *Septimus.* My lord, that is not the Queen; that is my
702.   bad wife.   [*Decima looks at them.*

703. *Prime Minister.* Did you see that? Did you see the devil
704.   in her eye? They are mad after her pretty face, and
705.   she knows it. They would not believe a word I say;
706.   there is nothing to be done till they cool.

707. *Decima.* Are all here my faithful servants?

708. *Bishop.* All, your Majesty.

709. *Decima.* All?

710. *Prime Minister* [*bowing low*]. All, your Majesty.

      Decima [*singing*].

711.   She pulled the thread, and bit the thread
712.   And made a golden gown.

713.   Hand me that plate. While I am eating I will have a
714.   good look at my new man.
                 [*The plate and a bottle of wine are handed to her. The bray of a
                 donkey is heard and the Old Beggar is dragged in.*

715. *Bishop.* At last we have found this impostor out. He
716.   has been accepted by the whole nation as if he were
717.   the Voice of God. As if the crown could not be
718.   settled firmly on any head without his help. It's plain
719.   that he has been in league with the conspirators, and
720.   believed that your Majesty had been killed. He is

---

701.   . . . Lord, . . . Queen, that . . . **D** ; . . . Lord, . . . queen; . . . **69, 70.**
704.   . . . eye. They . . . face (face, **69**) and **D-70** ; . . . eye. They . . . **84.**
705.   . . . say, **D.**
708.   . . . , Your . . . . **D.**
710.   . . . , Your . . . . **D.**
712.   . . . made the golden . . . . **D.**
713.   . . . plate of lobster and that bottle of wine. While . . . **D-70.**
       Directions after 714.   [. . . *and bottle* . . . *in amid the hoots of the mob.*]
       D ; [. . . *and bottle* . . . .] **69, 70.**
718.   . . . help. [*Shouts from the mob of* 'imposter,' ('*Imposter,*' **69A**) 'rogue,'
       (*Rogue,* **69A**) *etc.*]. It's . . . **69, 70.**
720.   . . . Your . . . **D.**

721.   keeping it up still. Look at his glassy eye. But his
722.   madman airs won't help him now.

723.   *Prime Minister.* Carry him to prison, we will hang him
724.   in the morning. [*Shaking Septimus.*] Do you under-
725.   stand that there has been a miracle, that God or the
726.   Fiend has spoken, and that the crown is on her head
727.   for good, that fate has brayed on that man's lips?
728.   [*Aloud.*] We will hang him in the morning.

729.   *Septimus.* She is my wife.

730.   *Prime Minister.* The crown has changed and there is no
731.   help for it. Sleep of Adam, I must have that woman
732.   for wife. The Oracle has settled that.

733.   *Septimus.* She is my wife, she is my bad, flighty wife.

734.   *Prime Minister.* Seize this man. He has been whispering
735.   slanders against Her Majesty. Cast him beyond the
736.   borders of the kingdom, and his players after him.

737.   *Decima.* He must not return upon pain of death. He
738.   has wronged me, and I will never look upon his face
739.   again.

---

723.   [lacking] **D-70.**
724.   *Prime Minister* [*shaking . . .* **D-70.**
726.   . . . Crown . . . **D.**
727.   . . . lips. **D, 69E, 70.**
730.   . . . Crown . . . **D.**
732.   . . . that. [*Takes Septimus away to prison.*] **D** ; . . . that. [*Take him away to prison.*] **69, 70.**
735.   . . . her . . . **69, 70.**
736.   . . . Kingdom (kingdom **69, 70**) and find the **D-70.**
736a.   company of players he belongs to. They also are banished and must not
736b.   return on pain of death. Now, my Lord Bishop, I am ready.
736c.   *Decima* [*singing*]. She wept because she had dreamt that I
736d.   Was born to wear a crown.
736e.   [*She flings the lobster's claw at the Prime Minister.*] Come—crack that claw. **D-70.** [1]

---

[1] **D.70** the play ends here.

740.   *Prime Minister.* Away with him.

741.   *Decima.* My good name is dearer than my life, but I
742.   will see the players before they go.

743.   *Prime Minister.* Sleep of Adam! What has she got into
744.   her head? Fetch the players.

745.   *Decima* [*picking up the mask of the sister of Noah*]. My loyal
746.   subjects must forgive me if I hide my face—it is not
747.   yet used to the light of day, it is a modest face. I
748.   will be much happier if His Holiness will help
749.   me to tie the mask.

750.   *Prime Minister.* The players come.
                    Enter Players, who all bow to the new Queen

751.   *Decima.* They had some play they were to perform, but
752.   I will make them dance instead, and after that they
753.   must be richly rewarded.

754.   *Prime Minister.* It shall be as you will.

755.   *Decima.* You are banished and must not return upon
756.   pain of death, and yet not one of you shall be poorer
757.   because banished. That I promise. But you have lost
758.   one thing that I will not restore. A woman player
759.   has left you. Do not mourn her. She was a bad, head-
760.   strong, cruel woman, and seeks destruction some-
761.   where and with some man she knows nothing of;
762.   such a woman they tell me that this mask would
763.   well become, this foolish, smiling face! Come, dance.
              [*They dance, and at certain moments she cries* 'Good-bye, good-
              bye' *or else* 'Farewell'. *And she throws them money.*]

THE END

NOTES

I began in, I think, 1907, a verse tragedy, but at that time the thought I have set forth in *Per Amica Silentia Lunae* was coming into my head, and I found examples of it everywhere. I wasted the best working months of several years in an attempt to write a poetical play where every character became an example of the finding or not finding of what I have called the Antithetical Self; and because passion and not thought makes tragedy, what I made had neither simplicity nor life. I knew precisely what was wrong and yet could neither escape from thought nor give up my play. At last it came into my head all of a sudden that I could get rid of the play if I turned it into a farce; and never did I do anything so easily, for I think that I wrote the present play in about a month; and when it was performed at the Stage Society in 1919 I forgot that it was my own work, so completely that I discovered from the surprise of a neighbour, that, indignant with a house that seemed cold to my second act (since much reformed), I was applauding. If it could only have come into my head three years earlier. Since then the play has been revived twice at the Abbey Theatre.

It is the only play of mine which has not its scene laid in Ireland. While at work at the Abbey Theatre I had made many experiments with Mr. Gordon Craig's screens (see The Tragic Theatre in *The Cutting of an Agate*), and both the tragedy I first planned, and the farce I wrote, were intended to be played in front of those screens. My *dramatis personae* have no nationality because Mr. Craig's screens, where every line must suggest some mathematical proportion, where all is phantastic, incredible, and luminous, have no nationality.—1922.   Notes, **69**; Note, **70**.

*   *   *

Variant spellings

foresworn **D-70**; *forsworn* **84, 97.**
gaol **97**; *jail* **D-84.**
Kzanadu **D-70**; *Xanadu* **84, 97.**
O **84, 97**; *Oh* **D-70.**

*   *   *

[See also the notes on *The Resurrection*, p. 932; and *Preface to 69*, p. 1306.]

THE DREAMING OF THE BONES

1919

Persons in the Play

Three Musicians (*their faces made up to resemble masks*)
A Young Man
A Stranger (*wearing a mask*)
A Young Girl (*wearing a mask*)

Time—1916

The stage is any bare place in a room close to the wall. A screen, with a pattern of mountain and sky, can stand against the wall, or a curtain with a like pattern hang upon it, but the pattern must only symbolise or suggest. One Musician enters and then two others; the first stands singing, as in preceding plays, while the others take their places. Then all three sit down against the wall by their instruments, which are already there—a drum, a zither, and a flute. Or they unfold a cloth as in 'At the Hawk's Well', while the instruments are carried in.

[Song for the folding and unfolding of the cloth]

First Musician [or all three Musicians, singing].

1.	Why does my heart beat so?
2.	Did not a shadow pass?
3.	It passed but a moment ago.

PRINTINGS *The Little Review*, January 1919; **60, 64, 71, 84, 97.**

DATE [at bottom of page] Copyright 1918 by W. B. Yeats **LR**; [lacking] **60-71.**

DRAMATIS PERSONAE [lacking] **LR, 60**; Persons of the . . . **64, 71.**

TIME [lacking] **LR, 60.**

STAGE DIRECTIONS . . . *screen with* . . . *sky can* . . . *wall* (*wall,* **60**) *or* . . . *symbolize* . . . *others;* (*others,* **60**) *the* . . . *singing while* . . . *in 'The* . . . . **LR, 60.**

Directions for cloth [lacking] **LR, 60.**

TEXT
  Speaker before 1. *First Musician | (or all the musicians (all three musicians,* **60**)) *singing* **LR, 60.**

4.	Who can have trod in the grass?
5.	What rogue is night-wandering?
6.	Have not old writers said
7.	That dizzy dreams can spring
8.	From the dry bones of the dead?
9.	And many a night it seems
10.	That all the valley fills
11.	With those fantastic dreams.
12.	They overflow the hills,
13.	So passionate is a shade,
14.	Like wine that fills to the top
15.	A grey-green cup of jade,
16.	Or maybe an agate cup.

[*The three Musicians are now seated by the drum, flute, and zither at the back of the stage. The First Musician speaks.*]

17.	The hour before dawn and the moon covered up;
18.	The little village of Abbey is covered up;
19.	The little narrow trodden way that runs
20.	From the white road to the Abbey of Corcomroe
21.	Is covered up; and all about the hills
22.	Are like a circle of agate or of jade.
23.	Somewhere among great rocks on the scarce grass
24.	Birds cry, they cry their loneliness.
25.	Even the sunlight can be lonely here,
26.	Even hot noon is lonely. I hear a footfall—
27.	A young man with a lantern comes this way.
28.	He seems an Aran fisher, for he wears
29.	The flannel bawneen and the cow-hide shoe.
30.	He stumbles wearily, and stumbling prays.

[*A Young Man enters, praying in Irish.*]

| 31. | Once more the birds cry in their loneliness, |

---

11. . . . dreams, **LR.**
14. . . . fill . . . **LR.**
Directions between 16 and 17. [lacking] **LR, 60.**
[between 16 and 17 no break] **60.**
17. (*speaking*) The . . . up. **LR, 60.**
22. . . . Jade. **LR ;** . . . Agate . . . Jade. **60-71.**
24. . . . cry; they . . . .
25. . . . here. **LR.**
Directions between 30 and 31. . . . *Irish* / CHORUS **LR.**

32.   But now they wheel about our heads; and now
33.   They have dropped on the grey stone to the northeast.
       [*A Stranger and a Young Girl, in the costume of a past time, come in.*
       They wear heroic masks.

34. *Young Man* [*raising his lantern*]. Who is there? I cannot see what you
       are like.
35.   Come to the light.

       Stranger.   But what have you to fear?

36. *Young Man.* And why have you come creeping through the dark?
                                   [*The Girl blows out lantern.*
37.   The wind has blown my lantern out. Where are you?
38.   I saw a pair of heads against the sky
39.   And lost them after; but you are in the right,
40.   I should not be afraid in County Clare;
41.   And should be, or should not be, have no choice,
42.   I have to put myself into your hands,
43.   Now that my candle's out.

       Stranger.   You have fought in Dublin?

44. *Young Man.* I was in the Post Office, and if taken
45.   I shall be put against a wall and shot.

46. *Stranger.* You know some place of refuge, have some plan
47.   Or friend who will come to meet you?

       Young Man.   I am to lie
48.   At daybreak on the mountain and keep watch
49.   Until an Aran coracle puts in

Directions between 33 and 34.   *A Young Man and a Young . . . time come*
. . . . **LR**; [*A man and a girl both in* . . . .] **60**; [*A man and a girl,* . . . .]
64, 71.
Directions at 34.   [*in bawneen, raising* . . . .] **LR**.
34.   . . . like, Come **LR**; . . . like **60, 64, 71E**.
35.   to . . . ? **LR**.
36.   . . . dark. **60, 64**.
39.   . . . after. But . . . , **LR**; . . . after, but . . . right **60**.
41.   And 'should be' or 'should not be' have . . . choice; **LR**; . . . be or
    . . . be have . . . , **60**; . . . be have . . . , **65, 71**.

50. At Muckanish or at the rocky shore
51. Under Finvara, but would break my neck
52. If I went stumbling there alone in the dark.

53. *Stranger.* We know the pathways that the sheep tread out,
54. And all the hiding-places of the hills,
55. And that they had better hiding-places once.

56. *Young Man.* You'd say they had better before English robbers
57. Cut down the trees or set them upon fire
58. For fear their owners might find shelter there.
59. What is that sound?

    Stranger.   An old horse gone astray.
60. He has been wandering on the road all night.

61. *Young Man.* I took him for a man and horse. Police
62. Are out upon the roads. In the late Rising
63. I think there was no man of us but hated
64. To fire at soldiers who but did their duty
65. And were not of our race, but when a man
66. Is born in Ireland and of Irish stock,
67. When he takes part against us—

    Stranger.   I will put you safe,
68. No living man shall set his eyes upon you;
69. I will not answer for the dead.

    Young Man.   The dead?

70. *Stranger.* For certain days the stones where you must lie
71. Have in the hour before the break of day
72. Been haunted.

    Young Man.   But I was not born at midnight.

---

59. ... astray **60.**
66. ... stock **LR, 60.**
67. ... safe. **LR.**
68. ... you. **LR, 60.**
72. ... haunted.
    Young Man. I .... **LR.**

73. *Stranger*. Many a man that was born in the full daylight
74.   Can see them plain, will pass them on the high-road
75.   Or in the crowded market-place of the town,
76.   And never know that they have passed.

     Young Man.   My Grandam
77.   Would have it they did penance everywhere;
78.   Some lived through their old lives again.

     Stranger.   In a dream;
79.   And some for an old scruple must hang spitted
80.   Upon the swaying tops of lofty trees;
81.   Some are consumed in fire, some withered up
82.   By hail and sleet out of the wintry North,
83.   And some but live through their old lives again.

84. *Young Man*. Well, let them dream into what shape they please
85.   And fill waste mountains with the invisible tumult
86.   Of the fantastic conscience. I have no dread;
87.   They cannot put me into gaol or shoot me;
88.   And seeing that their blood has returned to fields
89.   That have grown red from drinking blood like mine,
90.   They would not if they could betray.

     Stranger.   This pathway
91.   Runs to the ruined Abbey of Corcomroe;
92.   The Abbey passed, we are soon among the stone
93.   And shall be at the ridge before the cocks
94.   Of Aughanish or Bailevelehan
95.   Or grey Aughtmana shake their wings and cry.
                              [*They go round the stage once.*

---

73. . . . man born . . . **LR, 60.**
77. . . . everywhere
78. Or lived . . . . **LR, 60.**
81. . . . fires, . . . **LR.**
86. . . . dread. **LR.**
87. . . . jail . . . me, (me; **71E**) **LR-71.**
88. And, seeing . . . **LR** ; . . . fields, **64E, 71.**
89. . . . mine **60** ; They have . . . , **84.**
90. . . . betray. **LR.**
91. *Stranger*. Runs . . . Corcomroe—this pathway; **LR.**

96. *First Musician* [*speaking*]. They've passed the shallow well and the
flat stone

97. Fouled by the drinking cattle, the narrow lane

98. Where mourners for five centuries have carried

99. Noble or peasant to his burial;

100. An owl is crying out above their heads.

[*Singing*]

101. Why should the heart take fright?

102. What sets it beating so?

103. The bitter sweetness of the night

104. Has made it but a lonely thing.

105. Red bird of March, begin to crow!

106. Up with the neck and clap the wing,

107. Red cock, and crow!

[*They go round the stage once. The First Musician speaks.*]

108. And now they have climbed through the long grassy field

109. And passed the ragged thorn-trees and the gap

110. In the ancient hedge; and the tomb-nested owl

111. At the foot's level beats with a vague wing.

[*Singing*]

112. My head is in a cloud;

113. I'd let the whole world go;

114. My rascal heart is proud

115. Remembering and remembering.

---

99. . . . burial. **LR, 60.**
   [between 100 and 101 no break] **60.**
101. (*singing*) Why . . . fright **60.**
102. . . . so?— **LR.**
105. . . . crow, **LR-71.**
107. . . . crow. **LR-71.**
   Directions before 108. [. . . *go once round . . . stage.*] **LR**; [. . . *go once round . . . stage. The* . . . . **60.**
108. (*speaking*) And . . . **LR.**
109. . . . thorn trees . . . **LR-71.**
   [between 111 and 112 no break] **60.**
113. . . . go. **60.**
114. . . . proud, **LR.**

116.   Red bird of March, begin to crow!
117.   Up with the neck and clap the wing,
118.   Red cock, and crow!

[*They go round the stage once. The First Musician speaks.*

119.   They are among the stones above the ash,
120.   Above the briar and thorn and the scarce grass;
121.   Hidden amid the shadow far below them
122.   The cat-headed bird is crying out.

[*Singing*]

123.   The dreaming bones cry out
124.   Because the night winds blow
125.   And heaven's a cloudy blot.
126.   Calamity can have its fling.
127.   Red bird of March, begin to crow!
128.   Up with the neck and clap the wing,
129.   Red cock, and crow!

130.   *Stranger.* We're almost at the summit and can rest.
131.   The road is a faint shadow there; and there
132.   The Abbey lies amid its broken tombs.
133.   In the old days we should have heard a bell
134.   Calling the monks before day broke to pray;
135.   And when the day had broken on the ridge,

---

116.   . . . crow, **LR-71.**
117.   . . . wing **60.**
118.   . . . crow. **LR, 64, 71** ; . . . cock and crow. **60.**
       Directions before 119.   [. . . *once.*] [*speaking*] **LR** ; [. . . *stage. The*
       . . . .] **60.**
119.   . . . ash **60-71.**
120.   . . . grass.
121.   . . . them, **LR.**
       [between 122 and 123 no break] **60.**
125.   . . . blot; **LR-64.**
127.   . . . crow, **LR, 71** ; . . . March begin . . . crow, **60, 64.**
128.   . . . wing **60.**
129.   . . . crow. **LR, 64, 71** ; . . . cock and crow. **60.**
131.   . . . there, and . . . **LR.**
132.   . . . abbey . . . . **LR, 60.**
134.   . . . to prayer, **LR.**
135.   . . . day has broken . . . , **LR-71.**

136. The crowing of its cocks.

Young Man. Is there no house
137. Famous for sanctity or architectural beauty
138. In Clare or Kerry, or in all wide Connacht,
139. The enemy has not unroofed?

Stranger. Close to the altar
140. Broken by wind and frost and worn by time
141. Donough O'Brien has a tomb, a name in Latin.
142. He wore fine clothes and knew the secrets of women,
143. But he rebelled against the King of Thomond
144. And died in his youth.

Young Man. And why should he rebel?
145. The King of Thomond was his rightful master.
146. It was men like Donough who made Ireland weak—
147. My curse on all that troop, and when I die
148. I'll leave my body, if I have any choice,
149. Far from his ivy-tod and his owl. Have those
150. Who, if your tale is true, work out a penance
151. Upon the mountain-top where I am to hide,
152. Come from the Abbey graveyard?

Young Girl. They have not that luck,
153. But are more lonely; those that are buried there
154. Warred in the heat of the blood; if they were rebels
155. Some momentary impulse made them rebels,
156. Or the commandment of some petty king
157. Who hated Thomond. Being but common sinners,
158. No callers-in of the alien from oversea,

---

138. . . . Connaught **LR** ; . . . Connacht **60, 64.**
142. . . . women **60.**
143. . . . king . . . **LR.**
148. . . . choice **64A.**
149. . . . ivy tod . . . **LR** ; . . . ivy tod . . . owl ; have . . . **60-71.**
152. . . . graveyard?
      The Girl. They . . . , **LR, 60.**
153. . . . lonely, those . . . there, **LR, 60** ; . . . there, **64, 71.**
155. . . . rebels **LR-64.**
157. . . . Thomond ; being . . . , **LR.**
158. . . . callers in . . . aliens . . . , **LR** ; . . . callers in . . . oversea **60** ; . . .
      callers in . . . , **64, 71.**

159.   They and their enemies of Thomond's party
160.   Mix in a brief dream-battle above their bones;
161.   Or make one drove; or drift in amity;
162.   Or in the hurry of the heavenly round
163.   Forget their earthly names. These are alone,
164.   Being accursed.

Young Man.   But if what seems is true
165.   And there are more upon the other side
166.   Than on this side of death, many a ghost
167.   Must meet them face to face and pass the word
168.   Even upon this grey and desolate hill.

169.   *Young Girl.* Until this hour no ghost or living man
170.   Has spoken, though seven centuries have run
171.   Since they, weary of life and of men's eyes,
172.   Flung down their bones in some forgotten place,
173.   Being accursed.

Young Man.   I have heard that there are souls
174.   Who, having sinned after a monstrous fashion,
175.   Take on them, being dead, a monstrous image
176.   To drive the living, should they meet its face,
177.   Crazy, and be a terror to the dead.

Young Girl.   But these
178.   Were comely even in their middle life
179.   And carry, now that they are dead, the image
180.   Of their first youth, for it was in that youth
181.   Their sin began.

Young Man.   I have heard of angry ghosts
182.   Who wander in a wilful solitude.

---

160.   . . . dream battle . . . bones (bones, **60**) **LR, 60 ;** . . . dream battle
        . . . ; **64, 71.**
161.   . . . drove and drift in amity, **LR ;** . . . drove or . . . amity, **60.**
163.   . . . names; these . . . alone **60 ;** . . . alone **64, 71.**
164.   . . . accursed.
        And if . . . **LR, 60.**
170.   . . . spoken though . . . **60-71.**
172.   . . . place **60-71.**
174.   . . . fashion **60.**
176.   . . . face. **LR.**
178.   . . . life, **LR.**

183. *Young Girl*. These have no thought but love; nor any joy
184.　　　But that upon the instant when their penance
185.　　　Draws to its height, and when two hearts are wrung
186.　　　Nearest to breaking, if hearts of shadows break,
187.　　　His eyes can mix with hers; nor any pang
188.　　　That is so bitter as that double glance,
189.　　　Being accursed.

　　　Young Man.　　　But what is this strange penance—
190.　　　That when their eyes have met can wring them most?

191. *Young Girl*. Though eyes can meet, their lips can never meet.

192. *Young Man*. And yet it seems they wander side by side.
193.　　　But doubtless you would say that when lips meet
194.　　　And have not living nerves, it is no meeting.

196. *Young Girl*. Although they have no blood, or living nerves,
196.　　　Who once lay warm and live the live-long night
197.　　　In one another's arms, and know their part
198.　　　In life, being now but of the people of dreams,
199.　　　Is a dream's part; although they are but shadows,
200.　　　Hovering between a thorn-tree and a stone,
201.　　　Who have heaped up night on wingéd night; although
202.　　　No shade however harried and consumed
203.　　　Would change his own calamity for theirs,
204.　　　Their manner of life were blessed could their lips

183.　*The Girl*. . . . love, nor joy **LR**; *The Girl*. . . . ; nor joy **60**; . . . ; nor
　　　joy **64, 71**.
185.　. . . height and . . . **LR-71**.
187.　. . . hers, nor . . . **LR**.
189.　. . . penance
190.　. . . ring . . . ? **LR**.
191.　*The Girl*. . . . meet (meet, **60**) their . . . . **LR, 60**.
195.　*The Girl*. . . . blood or . . . nerves **LR, 60**.
197.　. . . arms; and . . . **LR**.
199.　. . . shadows **LR, 60**.
200.　. . . thorn tree . . . stone **LR, 60**; . . . thorn tree . . . , **64, 71**.
201.　. . . winged . . . **LR-71**.

205. A moment meet; but when he has bent his head
206. Close to her head, or hand would slip in hand,
207. The memory of their crime flows up between
208. And drives them apart.

Young Man.   The memory of a crime—
209. He took her from a husband's house, it may be,
210. But does the penance for a passionate sin
211. Last for so many centuries?

Young Girl.   No, no;
212. The man she chose, the man she was chosen by,
213. Cared little and cares little from whose house
214. They fled towards dawn amid the flights of arrows,
215. Or that it was a husband's and a king's;
216. And how, if that were all, could she lack friends,
217. On crowded roads or on the unpeopled hill?
218. Helen herself had opened wide the door
219. Where night by night she dreams herself awake
220. And gathers to her breast a dreaming man.

221. *Young Man.* What crime can stay so in the memory?
222. What crime can keep apart the lips of lovers
223. Wandering and alone?

Young Girl.   Her king and lover
224. Was overthrown in battle by her husband,
225. And for her sake and for his own, being blind
226. And bitter and bitterly in love, he brought
227. A foreign army from across the sea.

228. *Young Man.* You speak of Diarmuid and Dervorgilla

---

206. . . . head or . . . hand **LR, 60.**
209. . . . house it . . . , **LR-71.**
211. . . . centuries?
       The Girl. No, no, **LR, 60.**
212. . . . by **60-71.**
214. . . . arrows **60.**
215. . . . was husband's . . . ; **97A.**
216. . . . how if . . . all could . . . friends **LR, 60.**
223. . . . alone?
       The Girl. Her . . . **LR, 60.**
224. . . . husband **60, 64.**
228. . . . Dermot and of Dervorgilla **LR-71.**

229.   Who brought the Norman in?

Young Girl.   Yes, yes, I spoke
230.   Of that most miserable, most accursed pair
231.   Who sold their country into slavery; and yet
232.   They were not wholly miserable and accursed
233.   If somebody of their race at last would say,
234.   'I have forgiven them'.

Young Man.   O, never, never
235.   Shall Diarmuid and Dervorgilla be forgiven.

236. *Young Girl.* If some one of their race forgave at last
237.   Lip would be pressed on lip.

Young Man.   O, never, never
238.   Shall Diarmuid and Dervorgilla be forgiven.
239.   You have told your story well, so well indeed
240.   I could not help but fall into the mood
241.   And for a while believe that it was true,
242.   Or half believe; but better push on now.
243.   The horizon to the east is growing bright.
                    [*They go round stage once. The Musicians play.*
244.   So here we're on the summit. I can see
245.   The Aran Islands, Connemara Hills,
246.   And Galway in the breaking light; there too
247.   The enemy has toppled roof and gable,

---

229.   . . . in?
         The Girl. Yes, yes, (yes **60**) I . . . **LR, 60.**
231.   . . . slavery, and . . . **LR-71.**
232.   . . . accursed, **LR.**
233.   . . . say **LR**; . . . say: **60-71.**
235.   Will Dermot . . . . **LR, 60.**
236.   *The Girl.* If someone . . . **LR, 60.**
238.   Will Dermot . . . forgiven (forgiven. **60**) **LR, 60.**
241.   . . . true **LR-71.**
242.   . . . believe, but . . . . **LR, 60.**
243.   . . . East . . . . **LR-84.**
         Directions between 243 and 244.   [*They go once round stage*] **LR, 60.**
246.   The Galway . . . **97A.**
247.   . . . toppled wall and roof **LR, 60**; . . . gable; **64, 71.**

248. And torn the panelling from ancient rooms;
249. What generations of old men had known
250. Like their own hands, and children wondered at,
251. Has boiled a trooper's porridge. That town had lain,
252. But for the pair that you would have me pardon,
253. Amid its gables and its battlements
254. Like any old admired Italian town;
255. For though we have neither coal, nor iron ore,
256. To make us wealthy and corrupt the air,
257. Our country, if that crime were uncommitted,
258. Had been most beautiful. Why do you dance?
259. Why do you gaze, and with so passionate eyes,
260. One on the other; and then turn away,
261. Covering your eyes, and weave it in a dance?
262. Who are you? what are you? you are not natural.

263. *Young Girl.* Seven hundred years our lips have never met.

264. *Young Man.* Why do you look so strangely at one another,
265.   So strangely and so sweetly?

      Young Girl.   Seven hundred years.

266. *Young Man.* So strangely and so sweetly. All the ruin,
267.   All, all their handiwork is blown away
268.   As though the mountain air had blown it away

---

248. . . . torn from ancient walls to boil his pot
249. The oaken panelling that had been dear
250. To generations of children and old men.
251. But for that pair for whom you would have my pardon
252. It might be now like Bayeux or like Caen **LR, 6o.**
253. [lacking] **LR.**
254. Or little Italian town amid its wall; (walls **6o**)
255. . . . coal nor . . . ore
256. . . . us rich and cover heaven with smoke, (smoke **6o**) **LR, 6o.**
257. . . . uncommitted **6o.**
259. . . . gaze and . . . eyes **6o.**
260. . . . other and . . . , **LR** ; . . . other and . . . away **6o.**
261. . . . eyes and weaving it . . . ? **LR** ; . . . eyes and . . . dance, **6o.**
262. . . . ? What . . . ? You . . . . **LR.**
263. *The Girl.* Seven . . . . **LR, 6o.**
265. . . . sweetly?
      The Girl.   Seven . . . . **LR, 6o.**

269. Because their eyes have met. They cannot hear,
270. Being folded up and hidden in their dance.
271. The dance is changing now. They have dropped their eyes,
272. They have covered up their eyes as though their hearts
273. Had suddenly been broken—never, never
274. Shall Diarmuid and Dervorgilla be forgiven.
275. They have drifted in the dance from rock to rock.
276. They have raised their hands as though to snatch the sleep
277. That lingers always in the abyss of the sky
278. Though they can never reach it. A cloud floats up
279. And covers all the mountain-head in a moment;
280. And now it lifts and they are swept away.

[The Stranger and the Young Girl go out.

281. I had almost yielded and forgiven it all—
282. Terrible the temptation and the place!

[The Musicians begin unfolding and folding a black cloth. The First Musician comes forward to the front of the stage, at the centre. He holds the cloth before him. The other two come one on either side and unfold it. They afterwards fold it up in the same way. While it is unfolded, the Young Man leaves the stage.

[Songs for the unfolding and folding of the cloth]

The Musicians [*singing*].

I

283.   At the grey round of the hill
284.   Music of a lost kingdom

---

273. . . .—Never, . . . **LR.**
275. . . . rock,
276. . . . their heads as . . .
277. . . . sky, **LR.**
279. . . . mountain head . . . moment. **LR, 60;** . . . mountain head . . . ;
     64, 71.
     Directions between 280 and 281.   [lacking] **LR, 60.**
282. This is indeed a place of terrible temptation. **LR-71.**
     Directions between 282 and 283.   [. . . *stage.*] *The Musician* (*singing*)
     LR; [. . . *stage.*] *The Musicians* **60.**
283. (*singing*) At . . . **60.**

285.	Runs, runs and is suddenly still.
286.	The winds out of Clare-Galway
287.	Carry it: suddenly it is still.
288.	I have heard in the night air
289.	A wandering airy music;
290.	And moidered in that snare
291.	A man is lost of a sudden,
292.	In that sweet wandering snare.
293.	What finger first began
294.	Music of a lost kingdom?
295.	They dream that laughed in the sun.
296.	Dry bones that dream are bitter,
297.	They dream and darken our sun.
298.	Those crazy fingers play
299.	A wandering airy music;
300.	Our luck is withered away,
301.	And wheat in the wheat-ear withered,
302.	And the wind blows it away.

II

303.	My heart ran wild when it heard
304.	The curlew cry before dawn
305.	And the eddying cat-headed bird;
306.	But now the night is gone.
307.	I have heard from far below
308.	The strong March birds a-crow.
309.	Stretch neck and clap the wing,
310.	Red cocks, and crow!

THE END

291.	... sudden **LR**.
294.	... kingdom **LR** ; ... kingdom. **60**.
296.	... bitter. **LR**.
308.	... a-crow, **LR-71**.
310.	... crow. **LR-71**.

NOTES

Dervorgilla's few lines can be given, if need be, to Dermot, and Dervorgilla's part taken by a dancer who has the training of a dancer alone; nor need that masked dancer be a woman.

The conception of the play is derived from the world-wide belief that the dead dream back, for a certain time, through the more personal thoughts and deeds of life. The wicked, according to Cornelius Agrippa, dream themselves to be consumed by flames and persecuted by demons; and there is precisely the same thought in a Japanese 'Noh' play, where a spirit, advised by a Buddhist priest she has met upon the road, seeks to escape from the flames by ceasing to believe in the dream. The lovers in my play have lost themselves in a different but still self-created winding of the labyrinth of conscience. The Judwalis distinguish between the Shade which dreams back through events in the order of their intensity, becoming happier as the more painful and, therefore, more intense wear themselves away, and the Spiritual Being, which lives back through events in the order of their occurrence, this living back being an exploration of their moral and intellectual origin.

All solar natures, to use the Arabian terms, during life move towards a more objective form of experience, the lunar towards a more subjective. After death a lunar man, reversing the intellectual order, grows always closer to objective experience, which in the spiritual world is wisdom, while a solar man mounts gradually to the most extreme subjective experience possible to him. In the spiritual world subjectivity is innocence, and innocence, in life an accident of nature, is now the highest achievement of the intellect. I have already put the thought in verse.

> He grows younger every second[1]
> That were all his birthdays reckoned
> Much too solemn seemed;
> Because of what he had dreamed,
> Or the ambitions that he served,
> Much too solemn and reserved.
> Jaunting, journeying
> To his own dayspring,
> He unpacks the loaded pern
> Of all 'twas pain or joy to learn,
> Of all that he had made.
> The outrageous war shall fade;
> At some old winding whitethorn root
> He'll practise on the shepherd's flute,
> Or on the close-cropped grass
> Court his shepherd lass,
> Or run where lads reform our daytime

[1] From Yeats's poem 'Shepherd and Goatherd.'

> Till that is their long shouting playtime;
> Knowledge he shall unwind
> Through victories of the mind,
> Till, clambering at the cradle side,
> He dreams himself his mother's pride,
> All knowledge lost in trance
> Of sweeter ignorance.

The Shade is said to fade out at last, but the Spiritual Being does not fade, passing on to other states of existence after it has attained a spiritual state, of which the surroundings and aptitudes of early life are a correspondence. When, as in my poem, I speak of events while describing the ascent of the Spiritual Being, I but use them as correspondence or symbol. Robartes writes to John Aherne, under the date of May 1917, a curious letter on this subject: 'There is an analogy between the dreaming back of the Body of Passion' (I have used instead of this term the more usual term Shade), 'and our ordinary dreams—and between the life of Spirit and Celestial Body taken together' (I have substituted for both terms the less technical, though, I fear, vague term Spiritual Being), 'and those coherent thoughts of dreamless sleep, which, as I know on my personal knowledge, coincide with dreams. These dreams are at one time their symbols, and at another live with an independent life. I have several times been present while my friend, an Arab doctor in Bagdad, carried on long conversations with a sleeping man. I do not say a hypnotized man, or even a somnambulist, for the sleep seemed natural sleep produced by fatigue, though sometimes with a curious suddenness. The sleeper would discuss the most profound truths and yet while doing so make, now and again, some movement that suggested dreaming, although the part that spoke remained entirely unconscious of the dream. On waking he would often describe a long dream, sometimes a symbolic reflection of the conversation, but more often produced by some external stimulus—a fall in temperature in the rooms, or some condition of body perhaps. Now and again these dreams would interrupt the conversation, as when he dreamed he had feathers in his mouth and began to blow. Seeing, therefore, that I have observed a separation between two parts of the nature during life, I find no difficulty in believing in a more complete separation, affirmed by my teachers, and supported by so much tradition, when the body is no longer there to hold the two parts together.'

I wrote my play before the Robartes papers came into my hands, and in making the penance of Dermot and Dervorgilla last so many centuries I have done something for which I had no warrant in these papers, but warrant there certainly is in the folk-lore of all countries. At certain moments the Spiritual Being, or rather that part of it which Robartes calls 'the Spirit,' is said to enter into the Shade, and during those moments it can converse with living men, though but within the narrow limits of its dream.

Note on 'The Dreaming of the Bones.' **64.**

Dervorgilla's . . . Robartes writes to John Aherne, under . . . sleeping man, and I have myself joined in those conversations. I do not say . . . hypnotised . . . together?

I wrote . . . hands, even before I myself had received much of their thought from a different source, and in making the penance . . . these papers or from that source, but warrant . . . folklore . . . dream.   Note, **71**.

* * *

Variant spellings

Augenish **LR** ; *Aughanish* **60-97**.
Aughmans **LR** ; *Aughtmana* **60-97**.
Bailevelehan **64-97** ; *Bailevlehan* **60** ; *Balyvelehan* **LR**.
Connacht **60-71, 97** ; *Connaught* **LR, 84**.
Connemara **60-97** ; *Connemare* **LR**.
coracle **60-97** ; *corricle* **LR**.
Dermot **LR-84** ; *Diarmuid* **97**.
Donnogh **LR** ; *Donogh* **60-84** ; *Donough* **97**.
Finvara **97** ; *Finvaragh* **84** ; *Finvarra* **LR-71**.
gaol **97** ; *jail* **LR-84**.
O **84, 97** ; *Oh* **LR-71**.
symbolise **71-97** ; *symbolize* **LR-74**.

* * *

[See also *Prefaces to 60, 64, 69, Preface in 71 to 'Four Plays for Dancers'*, pp. 1305, 1306.]

CALVARY

1920

Persons in the Play

Three Musicians (*their faces made up to resemble masks*)
Christ (*wearing a mask*)
Lazarus (*wearing a mask*)
Judas (*wearing a mask*)
Three Roman Soldiers (*their faces masked or made up to resemble masks*)

At the beginning of the play the First Musician comes to the front of the bare place, round three sides of which the audience are seated, with a folded cloth hanging from his joined hands. Two other Musicians come, as in the preceding play, one from either side, and unfold the cloth so that it shuts out the stage, and then fold it again, singing and moving rhythmically. They do the same at the end of the play, which enables the players to leave the stage unseen.

[Song for the folding and unfolding of the cloth]

First Musician.

1.   Motionless under the moon-beam,
2.   Up to his feathers in the stream;
3.   Although fish leap, the white heron
4.   Shivers in a dumbfounded dream.

Second Musician.

5.   God has not died for the white heron.

Third Musician.

6.   Although half famished he'll not dare

PRINTINGS 64, 71, 84, 97.
DATE [lacking] 64, 71.
DRAMATIS PERSONAE Persons of the . . . 64, 71.
STAGE DIRECTIONS . . . *preceding plays, one* . . . . 64-84.
TEXT
    Directions before 1. [. . . *and the unfolding* . . .] 64, 71.
    2. . . . stream, 64.

7.   Dip or do anything but stare

8.   Upon the glittering image of a heron,

9.   That now is lost and now is there.

Second Musician.

10.   God has not died for the white heron.

First Musician.

11.   But that the full is shortly gone

12.   And after that is crescent moon,

13.   It's certain that the moon-crazed heron

14.   Would be but fishes' diet soon.

Second Musician.

15.   God has not died for the white heron.

[*The three Musicians are now seated by the drum, flute, and zither at the back of stage.*

16. *First Musician.* The road to Calvary, and I beside it

17.   Upon an ancient stone. Good Friday's come,

18.   The day whereon Christ dreams His passion through.

19.   He climbs up hither but as a dreamer climbs.

20.   The cross that but exists because He dreams it

21.   Shortens His breath and wears away His strength.

22.   And now He stands amid a mocking crowd,

23.   Heavily breathing.

[*A player with the mask of Christ and carrying a cross has entered and now stands leaning upon the cross.*

Those that are behind

24.   Climb on the shoulders of the men in front

25.   To shout their mockery: 'Work a miracle',

26.   Cries one, 'and save yourself'; another cries,

27.   'Call on your father now before your bones

28.   Have been picked bare by the great desert birds';

29.   Another cries, 'Call out with a loud voice

30.   And tell him that his son is cast away

31.   Amid the mockery of his enemies'.

[*Singing*]

32.   O, but the mockers' cry

33.   Makes my heart afraid,

34.   As though a flute of bone

---

26.   . . . one, and 'Save . . . , **64, 71**.

29.   . . . cries: 'Call . . . **64**.

35.   Taken from a heron's thigh,
36.   A heron crazed by the moon,
37.   Were cleverly, softly played.

[Speaking]

38. Who is this from whom the crowd has shrunk,
39. As though he had some look that terrified?
40. He has a deathly face, and yet he moves
41. Like a young foal that sees the hunt go by
42. And races in the field.

[A player with the mask of Lazarus has entered.

Lazarus.   He raised me up.
43. I am the man that died and was raised up;
44. I am called Lazarus.

Christ.   Seeing that you died,
45. Lay in the tomb four days and were raised up,
46. You will not mock at me.

Lazarus.   For four whole days
47. I had been dead and I was lying still
48. In an old comfortable mountain cavern
49. When you came climbing there with a great crowd
50. And dragged me to the light.

Christ.   I called your name:
51. 'Lazarus, come out', I said, and you came out
52. Bound up in cloths, your face bound in a cloth.

53. *Lazarus.* You took my death, give me your death instead.

54. *Christ.* I gave you life.

Lazarus.   But death is what I ask.
55. Alive I never could escape your love,
56. And when I sickened towards my death I thought,
57. 'I'll to the desert, or chuckle in a corner,
58. Mere ghost, a solitary thing.' I died
59. And saw no more until I saw you stand

---

50.   . . . name, **64, 71E**; . . . name. **71A.**
56.   . . . thought
57.   I'll . . . corner
58.   . . . thing. I . . . **64, 71.**

60.   In the opening of the tomb; 'Come out!' you called;
61.   You dragged me to the light as boys drag out
62.   A rabbit when they have dug its hole away;
63.   And now with all the shouting at your heels
64.   You travel towards the death I am denied.
65.   And that is why I have hurried to this road
66.   And claimed your death.

Christian.   But I have conquered death,
67.   And all the dead shall be raised up again.

68. *Lazarus.* Then what I heard is true. I thought to die
69.   When my allotted years ran out again;
70.   And that, being gone, you could not hinder it;
71.   But now you will blind with light the solitude
72.   That death has made; you will disturb that corner
73.   Where I had thought I might lie safe for ever.

74. *Christ.* I do my Father's will.

Lazarus.   And not your own;
75.   And I was free four days, four days being dead.
76.   Climb up to Calvary, but turn your eyes
77.   From Lazarus that cannot find a tomb
78.   Although he search all height and depth: make way,
79.   Make way for Lazarus that must go search
80.   Among the desert places where there is nothing
81.   But howling wind and solitary birds.   [*He goes out.*

82. *First Musician.* The crowd shrinks backward from the face that
         seems
83.   Death-stricken and death-hungry still; and now
84.   Martha, and those three Marys, and the rest
85.   That live but in His love are gathered round Him.
86.   He holds His right arm out, and on His arm
87.   Their lips are pressed and their tears fall; and now
88.   They cast them on the ground before His dirty
89.   Blood-dabbled feet and clean them with their hair.

---

65.   . . . road;
66.   And that is why I claim . . . death.
                              I . . . death **64, 71.**
70.   . . . , being done, you . . . ; **97A.**
76.   . . . Calvary but . . . **64.**
83.   Death stricken . . . death hungry . . . **64, 71,**

[*Sings*]

90.   Take but His love away,
91.   Their love becomes a feather
92.   Of eagle, swan or gull,
93.   Or a drowned heron's feather
94.   Tossed hither and thither
95.   Upon the bitter spray
96.   And the moon at the full.

97. *Christ.* I felt their hair upon my feet a moment
98.   And then they fled away—why have they fled?
99.   Why has the street grown empty of a sudden
100.   As though all fled in terror?

         Judas [*who has just entered*]. I am Judas
101.   That sold you for the thirty pieces of silver.
102. *Christ.* You were beside me every day, and saw
103.   The dead raised up and blind men given their sight,
104.   And all that I have said and taught you have known,
105.   Yet doubt that I am God.

         Judas.   I have not doubted;
106.   I knew it from the first moment that I saw you;
107.   I had no need of miracles to prove it.

108. *Christ.* And yet you have betrayed me.

         Judas.   I have betrayed you
109.   Because you seemed all-powerful.

         Christ.   My Father
110.   Even now, if I were but to whisper it,
111.   Would break the world in His miraculous fury
112.   To set me free.

         Judas.   And is there not one man
113.   In the wide world that is not in your power?

114. *Christ.* My Father put all men into my hands.

115. *Judas.* That was the very thought that drove me wild.

---

90.   . . . away **64, 71.**
100. . . . fled from it in . . . **64, 71.**
115. . . . wild, **64, 71.**

116.   I could not bear to think you had but to whistle
117.   And I must do; but after that I thought,
118.   'Whatever man betrays Him will be free';
119.   And life grew bearable again. And now
120.   Is there a secret left I do not know,
121.   Knowing that if a man betrays a God
122.   He is the stronger of the two?

Christil.   **But if**

123.   'Twere the commandment of that God Himself,
124.   That God were still the stronger.

Judas.   When I planned it

125.   There was no live thing near me but a heron
126.   So full of itself that it seemed terrified.

127.   *Christ.* But my betrayal was decreed that hour
128.   When the foundations of the world were laid.

129.   *Judas.* It was decreed that somebody betray you—
130.   I'd thought of that—but not that I should do it,
131.   I the man Judas, born on such a day,
132.   In such a village, such and such his parents;
133.   Nor that I'd go with my old coat upon me
134.   To the High Priest, and chuckle to myself
135.   As people chuckle when alone, and do it
136.   For thirty pieces and no more, no less,
137.   And neither with a nod nor a sent message,
138.   But with a kiss upon your cheek. I did it,
139.   I, Judas, and no other man, and now
140.   You cannot even save me.

Christ.   Begone from me.
              [*Three Roman Soldiers have entered.*

141.   *First Roman Soldier.* He has been chosen to hold up the cross.

---

117.   . . . thought
118.   Whatever . . . free; **64, 71.**
122.   . . . two.
                 But . . .
123.   . . . Himself
124.   . . . stronger?
             When . . . **64, 71.**
135.   . . . , and that I'd do . . . **64, 71.**
137.   . . . nod, a look, nor . . . , **64, 71.**

[*During what follows, Judas holds up the cross while Christ stands with His arms stretched out upon it.*

142. *Second Roman Soldier.* We'll keep the rest away; they are too
         persistent;
143.   They are always wanting something.

       Third Roman Soldier.   Die in peace.
144.   There's no one here but Judas and ourselves.

145. *Christ.* And who are you that ask your God for nothing?

146. *Third Roman Soldier.* We are the gamblers, and when you are dead
147.   We'll settle who is to have that cloak of yours
148.   By throwing dice.

       Second Roman Soldier. Our dice were carved
149.   Out of an old sheep's thigh at Ephesus.

150. *First Roman Soldier.* Although but one of us can win the cloak
151.   That will not make us quarrel; what does it matter?
152.   One day one loses and the next day wins.

153. *Second Roman Soldier.* Whatever happens is the best, we say,
154.   So that it's unexpected.

       Third Roman Soldier.   Had you sent
155.   A crier through the world you had not found
156.   More comfortable companions for a death-bed
157.   Than three old gamblers that have asked for nothing.

158. *First Roman Soldier.* They say you're good and that you made the
         world,
159.   But it's no matter.

       Second Roman Soldier. Come now; let us dance
160.   The dance of the dice-throwers, for it may be
161.   He cannot live much longer and has not seen it.

---

153. . . . best we say **64, 71.**
156. . . . deathbed **64-84.**
159. . . . . Come; now let . . . **64, 71.**

162. *Third Roman Soldier.* If he were but the God of dice he'd know it,
163.   But he is not that God.

    First Roman Soldier.   One thing is plain,
164.   To know that he has nothing that we need
165.   Must be a comfort to him.

    Second Roman Soldier.   In the dance
166.   We quarrel for a while, but settle it
167.   By throwing dice, and after that, being friends,
168.   Join hand to hand and wheel about the cross.

                                            [They dance.

169. *Christ.* My Father, why hast Thou forsaken Me?

          [Song for the folding and unfolding of the cloth]
First Musician.
170.   Lonely the sea-bird lies at her rest,
171.   Blown like a dawn-blenched parcel of spray
172.   Upon the wind, or follows her prey
173.   Under a great wave's hollowing crest.

Second Musician.
174.   God has not appeared to the birds.

Third Musician.
175.   The ger-eagle has chosen his part
176.   In blue deep of the upper air
177.   Where one-eyed day can meet his stare;
178.   He is content with his savage heart.

Second Muiscian.
179.   God has not appeared to the birds.

---

165. . . . him.
        Begin the dance. **64.**
    [They dance round the cross, moving as if throwing dice.] **64.**
166-168 and directions.   [lacking] **64.**
169. . . . Me. **64E, 71.**
    Directions before 170.   *[Song of the . . .]* **64, 71.**
170. . . . rest **71.**

First Musician.

180.   But where have last year's cygnets gone?
181.   The lake is empty; why do they fling
182.   White wing out beside white wing?
183.   What can a swan need but a swan?

Second Musician.

184.   God has not appeared to the birds.

THE END

NOTES

I have written the little songs of the chorus to please myself, confident that singer and composer, when the time came for performance, would certainly make it impossible for the audience to know what the words were. I used to think that singers should sing a recipe for a good dish, or a list of local trains, or something else they want to get by heart, but I have changed my mind and now I prefer to give him some mystery or secret. A reader can always solve the mystery and learn the secret by turning to a note, which need not be as long as those Dante put to several of the odes in the *Convito*. I use birds as symbols of subjective life, and my reason for this, and for certain other things, cannot be explained fully till I have published some part at any rate of those papers of Michael Robartes, over which I have now spent several years. The following passage in a letter written by Robartes to Aherne in the spring of 1917 must suffice. 'At present I rather pride myself on believing all the superstitions of the Judwalis, or rather in believing that there is not one amongst them that may not be true, but at first my West European mind rebelled. Once in the early morning, when I was living in a horse-hair tent among other similar tents, a young Arab woke me and told me to come with him if I would see a great wonder. He brought me to a level place in the sand, just outside the tent of a certain Arab, who had arrived the night before and had, as I knew, a reputation as a wonder-worker, and showed me certain marks on the sand. I said they were the marks of a jackal, but he would not have this. When he had passed by a little after sunrise there was not a mark, and a few minutes later the marks were there. No beast could have come and gone unseen. When I asked his explanation he said they were made by the wonder-worker's "Daimon" or "Angel." "What," I said, "has it a beast's form?" "He goes much about the world," he said; "he has been in Persia and Afghanistan, and as far west as Tripoli. He is interested in things, in places, he likes to be with many people, and that is why his Daimon has the form of a beast, but your Daimon would have a bird's shape because you are a solitary man." Later on, when I mastered their philosophy, I came to learn that the boy had but classified the wonder-worker and myself according to their division of all mankind into those who are dominated by objects and those who are dominated by the self or *Zat*, or, as we would say, into objective and subjective natures. Certain birds, especially as I see things, such lonely birds as the heron, hawk, eagle, and swan, are the natural symbols of subjectivity, especially when floating upon the wind alone or alighting upon some pool or river, while the beasts that run upon the ground, especially those that run in packs, are the natural symbols of objective man. Objective men, however personally alone, are never alone in their thought, which is always developed in agreement or in conflict with the thought of others and always seeks the welfare of some cause or institution, while subjective men are the more lonely the more they are true to type, seeking always that which is unique or personal.'

I have used my bird-symbolism in these songs to increase the objective loneliness of Christ by contrasting it with a loneliness, opposite in kind, that unlike His can be, whether joyous or sorrowful, sufficient to itself. I have surrounded Him with the images of those He cannot save, not only with the birds, who have served neither God nor Caesar, and await for none or for a different saviour, but with Lazarus and Judas and the Roman soldiers for whom He has died in vain. 'Christ,' writes Robartes, 'only pitied those whose suffering is rooted in death, in poverty, or in sickness, or in sin, in some shape of the common lot, and he came especially to the poor who are most subject to exterior vicissitude.' I have therefore repesented in Lazarus and Judas types of that intellectual despair that lay beyond His sympathy, while in the Roman soldiers I suggest a form of objectivity that lay beyond His help. Robartes said in one of the conversations recorded by Aherne: 'I heard much of *Three Songs of Joy,* written by a certain old Arab, which owing to the circumstances of their origin were considered as proofs of great sanctity. He held the faith of Kusta ben Luki, but did not live with any of the two or three wandering companies of Judwalis. He lived in the town of Hâyel as servant to a rich Arab merchant. He himself had been a rich merchant of Aneyza and had been several times to India. On his return from one of these journeys he had found his house in possession of an enemy and was himself driven from Aneyza by the Wahâbies on some charge, I think of impiety, and it was then he made his first song of joy. A few years later his wife and child were murdered by robbers in the desert, and after certain weeks, during which it was thought that he must die of grief, his face cleared and his step grew firm and he made his second song. He gave away all his goods and became a servant in Hâyel, and a year or two later, believing that his death was near, he made his third song of joy. He lived, however, for several months, and when I met him had the use of all his faculties. I asked him about the "Three Songs", for I knew that even on his deathbed, as became the votary of a small contentious sect, he would delight in exposition. I said, (though I knew from his songs themselves, that this was not his thought, but I wanted his explanation in his own words): "You have rejoiced that the Will of God should be done even though you and yours must suffer." He answered with some emotion: "Oh, no, Kusta ben Luki has taught us to divide all things into Chance and Choice; one can think about the world and about man, or anything else until all has vanished but these two things, for they are indeed the first cause of the animate and inanimate world. They exist in God, for if they did not He would not have freedom, He would be bound by His own Choice. In God alone, indeed, can they be united, yet each be perfect and without limit or hindrance. If I should throw from the dice-box there would be but six possible sides on each of the dice, but when God throws He uses dice that have all numbers and sides. Some worship His Choice; that is easy; to know that He has willed for some unknown purpose all that happens is pleasant; but I have spent my life in worshipping His Chance, and that moment when I understand the immensity of His Chance is the moment when I am nearest

Him. Because it is very difficult and because I have put my understanding into three songs I am famous among my people.'',

Note on 'Calvary,' 64, 71.

*   *   *

Variant spelling

geer-eagle **64-84**; *ger-eagle* **97**.
O **84, 97**; *Oh* **64, 71**.

*   *   *

[See also *Prefaces to 64, 69*, pp. 1304, 1306; *Preface in 71 to 'Four Plays for Dancers'*, p. 1304; *Preface to 84*, p. 1309.]

THE CAT AND THE MOON
1926

TO

JOHN MASEFIELD

Persons in the Play

A Blind Beggar
A Lame Beggar
Three Musicians

SCENE.—*The scene is any bare place before a wall against which stands a patterned screen, or hangs a patterned curtain suggesting Saint Colman's Well. Three Musicians are sitting close to the wall, with zither, drum, and flute. Their faces are made up to resemble masks.*

First Musician [*singing*].

1.   The cat went here and there
2.   And the moon spun round like a top,

PRINTINGS   *The Criterion,* July 1924; *The Dial,* July 1924; **75, 83, 84, 97.**

DATE   [lacking] **C, D, 83**; 1917 [after line 301] **75.**

DEDICATION   [lacking] **C, D, 75**[1]; . . . Masefield / *who made me a ship* **83.**

DRAMATIS PERSONAE   [lacking] **C-75**; Three Musicians / The Blind Beggar / The Lame Beggar **83.**

STAGE DIRECTIONS   Scene (Scene: **D**) / *The . . . suggesting St.* (*St* **D**) *Colman's* . . . . **C, D**; Scene: *The . . . suggesting St. Colman's . . . , drum and* . . . . **75**; . . . , *drum and* . . . . **84.**

TEXT   Title . . . Moon / *A Play for Dancers* **C, D.**
  Title and Date of First Performance . . . Moon / *First performed at the Abbey Theatre / on 9th May* 1926 **83.**

1. . . . Cat . . . **C, D.**

[1] The complete volume is dedicated to Lady Gregory. See *Preface to 75,* p. 1307.

3.   And the nearest kin of the moon,

4.   The creeping cat, looked up.

5.   Black Minnaloushe stared at the moon,

6.   For, wander and wail as he would,

7.   The pure cold light in the sky

8.   Troubled his animal blood.

[Two beggars enter—a blind man with a lame man on his back. They wear grotesque masks. The Blind Beggar is counting the paces.

9. *Blind Beggar.* One thousand and six, one thousand and

10. seven, one thousand and nine. Look well now, for

11. we should be in sight of the holy well of Saint

12. Colman. The beggar at the cross-roads said it was

13. one thousand paces from where he stood and a few

14. paces over. Look well now, can you see the big ash-

15. tree that's above it?

16. *Lame Beggar* [*getting down*]. No, not yet.

17. *Blind Beggar.* Then we must have taken a wrong turn;

18. flighty you always were, and maybe before the day

19. is over you will have me drowned in Kiltartan River

20. or maybe in the sea itself.

21. *Lame Beggar.* I have brought you the right way, but

22. you are a lazy man, Blind Man, and you make very

23. short strides.

24. *Blind Beggar.* It's great daring you have, and how could

25. I make a long stride and you on my back from the

26. peep o' day?

27. *Lame Beggar.* And maybe the beggar of the cross-roads

---

3. ... moon **C, 75.**
4. ... cat looked .... **C-75.**
6. For wander ... would (would, **83**) **C-83.**
10. ... now for **D, 75.**
11. ... of St. (St **C, D**) **C-75.**
12. ... cross-road ... **C, D ;** ... cross road ... **75.**
14. ... now; can ... ash **C ;** ... ash **D, 75.**
17. ... turn, **75.**
18. ... maybe, before ... **C.**
19. ... over, you ... **C-75, 84.**
24. *Blind Man.* It's ... **75.**

28.   was only making it up when he said a thousand
29.   paces and a few paces more. You and I, being beggars,
30.   know the way of beggars, and maybe he never paced
31.   it at all, being a lazy man.

32. *Blind Beggar.* Get up. It's too much talk you have.

33. *Lame Beggar* [*getting up*]. But as I was saying, he being a
34.   lazy man—O, O, O, stop pinching the calf of my
35.   leg and I'll not say another word till I'm spoken to.
        [*They go round the stage once, moving to drum-taps, and as they move
        the following song is sung.*

    First Musician [*singing*].
36.   Minnaloushe runs in the grass
37.   Lifting his delicate feet.
38.   Do you dance, Minnaloushe, do you dance?
39.   When two close kindred meet
40.   What better than call a dance?
41.   Maybe the moon may learn,
42.   Tired of that courtly fashion,
43.   A new dance turn.

44. *Blind Beggar.* Do you see the big ash-tree?

45. *Lame Beggar.* I do then, and the wall under it, and the
46.   flat stone, and the things upon the stone; and here
47.   is a good dry place to kneel in.

48. *Blind Beggar.* You may get down so. [*Lame Beggar gets
49.   down.*] I begin to have it in my mind that I am a
50.   great fool, and it was you who egged me on with
51.   your flighty talk.

---

32.   ... up—it's .... C; ... up.—It's .... D, 75.
33.   But, as ... C.
34.   ...—oh, oh, oh, ... C-75.
        Directions after 35. [... *drum taps*, ...] C-75.
        Directions before 36, after speaker. [lacking] C.
        Speaker and Directions before 36. [lacking] D.
40.   ... dance, C-75.
43.   And new ....
44.   ... ash tree? C-75.
45.   ... the well under ... C.
50.   ... fool and ... 75.

52. *Lame Beggar.* How should you be a great fool to ask the
53.   saint to give you back your two eyes?

54. *Blind Beggar.* There is many gives money to a blind
55.   man and would give nothing but a curse to a whole
56.   man, and if it was not for one thing—but no matter
57.   anyway.

58. *Lame Beggar.* If I speak out all that's in my mind you
59.   won't take a blow at me at all?

60. *Blind Beggar.* I will not this time.

61. *Lame Beggar.* Then I'll tell you why you are not a great
62.   fool. When you go out to pick up a chicken, or
63.   maybe a stray goose on the road, or a cabbage from
64.   a neighbour's garden, I have to go riding on your
65.   back; and if I want a goose, or a chicken, or a
66.   cabbage, I must have your two legs under me.

67. *Blind Beggar.* That's true now, and if we were whole
68.   men and went different ways, there'd be as much
69.   again between us.

70. *Lame Beggar.* And your own goods keep going from
71.   you because you are blind.

72. *Blind Beggar.* Rogues and thieves ye all are, but there
73.   are some I may have my eyes on yet.

74. *Lame Beggar.* Because there's no one to see a man slip-
75.   ping in at the door, or throwing a leg over the wall
76.   of a yard, you are a bitter temptation to many a
77.   poor man, and I say it's not right, it's not right at
78.   all. There are poor men that because you are blind
79.   will be delayed in Purgatory.

---

55. man that would . . . **D.**
56. . . . thing, but . . . **D, 75.**
57. any way. **C-75.**
59. wont . . . ?
60. *Blind Man.* I . . . . **C, 75.**
67. . . . now; and . . . **D ;** . . . now and . . . **75.**
70. . . . going out from **C.**
74. Because's there's . . . **C.**
77. . . . man, & I . . . **75.**

80. *Blind Beggar.* Though you are a rogue, Lame Man,
81.   maybe you are in the right.

82. *Lame Beggar.* And maybe we'll see the blessed saint this
83.   day, for there's an odd one sees him, and maybe that
84.   will be a grander thing than having my two legs,
85.   though legs are a grand thing.

86. *Blind Beggar.* You're getting flighty again, Lame Man;
87.   what could be better for you than to have your two
88.   legs?

89. *Lame Beggar.* Do you think now will the saint put an
90.   ear on him at all, and we without an Ave or a Pater-
91.   noster to put before the prayer or after the prayer?

92. *Blind Beggar.* Wise though you are and flighty though
93.   you are, and you throwing eyes to the right of you
94.   and eyes to the left of you, there's many a thing you
95.   don't know about the heart of man.

96. *Lame Beggar.* But it stands to reason that he'd be put
97.   out and he maybe with a great liking for the Latin.

98. *Blind Beggar.* I have it in mind that the saint will be
99.   better pleased at us not knowing a prayer at all, and
100.   that we had best say what we want in plain language.
101.   What pleasure can he have in all that holy company
102.   kneeling at his well on holidays and Sundays, and
103.   they as innocent maybe as himself?

104. *Lame Beggar.* That's a strange thing to say, and do you
105.   say it as I or another might say it, or as a blind man?

106. *Blind Beggar.* I say it as a blind man, I say it because
107.   since I went blind in the tenth year of my age, I have
108.   been hearing and remembering the knowledges of
109.   the world.

110. *Lame Beggar.* And you who are a blind man say that

---

86.   . . . Man, **D, 75.**
89.   . . . now the saint will put . . . **C, D.**
92.   . . . are, and . . . **C**; *Blind Man.* Wise . . . **75.**
99.   . . . us nor knowing . . . **C.**
110.   . . . you that are . . . **C, D.**

111. a saint, and he living in a pure well of water, would
112. soonest be talking with a sinful man.

113. *Blind Beggar*. Do you mind what the beggar told you
114. about the holy man in the big house at Laban?

115. *Lame Beggar*. Nothing stays in my head, Blind Man.

116. *Blind Beggar*. What does he do but go knocking about
117. the roads with an old lecher from the county of
118. Mayo, and he a woman-hater from the day of his
119. birth! And what do they talk of by candle-light and
120. by daylight? The old lecher does be telling over all
121. the sins he committed, or maybe never committed
122. at all, and the man of Laban does be trying to head
123. him off and quiet him down that he may quit
124. telling them.

125. *Lame Beggar*. Maybe it is converting him he is.

126. *Blind Beggar*. If you were a blind man you wouldn't
127. say a foolish thing the like of that. He wouldn't
128. have him different, no, not if he was to get all Ire-
129. land. If he was different, what would they find to
130. talk about, will you answer me that now?

131. *Lame Beggar*. We have great wisdom between us, that's
132. certain.

133. *Blind Beggar*. Now the Church says that it is a good

112a. *Blind Beggar*. You have no sense in you, no real sense at all.
113. Did you ever know a holy man but had a wicked man for his
114. comrade and his heart's darling? There is not a more holy man
115. in the barony than the man who has the big house at Laban, and
116. he goes knocking about the roads day and night with that old
117. letcher from the county of Mayo, (Mayo **75**) and he a woman-
      hater (woman hater **75**) from the
118. day of his birth. And well you know that all (know and all **D**; know
      & all **75**) the neighbours **C-75**.
119. know what they talk of by daylight and candlelight. **C-75**; birth.
      And . . . **83**.
120. The . . . lecher (letcher **75**) . . . **C-75**.
128. . . . different no, . . . **75**.
130. . . . about? Will . . . ? **C**.
133. . . . church . . . **C-75**.

134.   thought, and a sweet thought, and a comfortable
135.   thought, that every man may have a saint to look
136.   after him, and I, being blind, give it out to all the
137.   world that the bigger the sinner the better pleased
138.   is the saint. I am sure and certain that Saint Colman
139.   would not have us two different from what we are.

140. *Lame Beggar.* I'll not give in to that, for, as I was saying,
141.   he has a great liking maybe for the Latin.

142. *Blind Beggar.* Is it contradicting me you are? Are you
143.   in reach of my arm? [*swinging stick*].

144. *Lame Beggar.* I'm not, Blind Man, you couldn't touch
145.   me at all; but as I was saying—

146. *First Musician* [*speaking*]. Will you be cured or will you
147.   be blessed?

148. *Lame Beggar.* Lord save us, that is the saint's voice and
149.   we not on our knees.   [*They kneel.*

150. *Blind Beggar.* Is he standing before us, Lame Man?

151. *Lame Beggar.* I cannot see him at all. It is in the ash-tree
152.   he is, or up in the air.

153. *First Musician.* Will you be cured or will you be
154.   blessed?

155. *Lame Beggar.* There he is again.

156. *Blind Beggar.* I'll be cured of my blindness.

157. *First Musician.* I am a saint and lonely. Will you be-
158.   come blessed and stay blind and we will be together
159.   always?

---

138.   . . . that St. (St **D**) Colman **C-75.**
140.   . . . , for as . . . , **D** ; . . . into . . . , for as . . . , **75.**
142.   . . . ? are . . . **75.**
144.   . . . , blind man, . . . **75.**
145.   . . . ; but, as . . .— **C.**
148.   . . . voice, and **C.**
151.   . . . ash tree **D** ; *Lame Man.* . . . , ash tree **75.**
158.   . . . blind, and . . . **C.**

160. *Blind Beggar.* No, no, your Reverence, if I have to
161.   choose, I'll have the sight of my two eyes, for those
162.   that have their sight are always stealing my things
163.   and telling me lies, and some maybe that are near
164.   me. So don't take it bad of me, Holy Man, that I
165.   ask the sight of my two eyes.

166. *Lame Beggar.* No one robs him and no one tells him
167.   lies; it's all in his head, it is. He's had his tongue on
168.   me all day because he thinks I stole a sheep of his.

169. *Blind Beggar.* It was the feel of his sheepskin coat put
170.   it into my head, but my sheep was black, they say,
171.   and he tells me, Holy Man, that his sheepskin is of
172.   the most lovely white wool so that it is a joy to be
173.   looking at it.

174. *First Musician.* Lame Man, will you be cured or will
175.   you be blessed?

176. *Lame Beggar.* What would it be like to be blessed?

177. *First Musician.* You would be of the kin of the blessed
178.   saints and of the martyrs.

179. *Lame Beggar.* Is it true now that they have a book and
180.   that they write the names of the blessed in that
181.   book?

182. *First Musician.* Many a time I have seen the book, and
183.   your name would be in it.

184. *Lame Beggar.* It would be a grand thing to have two legs
185.   under me, but I have it in my mind that it would be
186.   a grander thing to have my name in that book.

---

160. . . . , no your . . .
161. . . . eyes for . . . **75.**
164. me, so . . . **C, D.**
166. . . . him, and . . . **C, D.**
167. . . . head it . . . **C, D**; lies, it's . . . **75, 84.**
170. . . . black they . . . , **C**; . . . head but . . . black they . . . , **75.**
172. . . . wool, so . . . **C.**
182. . . . time have I seen that book, . . . **C, D**; . . . book and **75.**
184. . . . have my two . . . **C, D**; *Lame Man.* It . . . **75.**
185. . . . me but . . . **75.**

187. *First Musician.* It would be a grander thing.

188. *Lame Beggar.* I will stay lame, Holy Man, and I will be
189.   blessed.

190. *First Musician.* In the name of the Father, the Son and
191.   the Holy Spirit I give this Blind Man sight and I
192.   make this Lame Man blessed.

193. *Blind Beggar.* I see it all now, the blue sky and the big
194.   ash-tree and the well and the flat stone,—all as I
195.   have heard the people say—and the things the pray-
196.   ing people put on the stone, the beads and the
197.   candles and the leaves torn out of prayer-books, and
198.   the hairpins and the buttons. It is a great sight and
199.   a blessed sight, but I don't see yourself, Holy Man
200.   —is it up in the big tree you are?

201. *Lame Beggar.* Why, there he is in front of you and he
202.   laughing out of his wrinkled face.

203. *Blind Beggar.* Where, where?

204. *Lame Beggar.* Why, there, between you and the ash-tree.

205. *Blind Beggar.* There's nobody there—you're at your lies
206.   again.

207. *Lame Beggar.* I am blessed, and that is why I can see the
208.   holy saint.

209. *Blind Beggar.* But if I don't see the saint, there's some-
210.   thing else I can see.

---

190. . . . Son, and **C, D, 83.**
191. . . . blind man . . .
192. . . . lame man . . . . **C, D.**
193. *Blind Man.* I . . . sky, (sky **75**) and . . . **C, 75**; I . . . sky, and . . . **D.**
194. ash tree . . . stone—all . . . **C**; ash tree, and . . . well, and . . . stone—
      all . . . **D**; ash tree . . . **75.**
197. . . . prayer-books and **C**; . . . prayer books and **D.**
200. —Is . . . ? **C, D.**
201. Why there . . . you, and . . . **C**; Why there . . . **D, 75.**
204. Why there, ... **C**; Why there, . . . ash tree. **D, 75.**
209. . . . see that saint, . . . **C, D.**

211. *Lame Beggar.* The blue sky and green leaves are a great
212.   sight, and a strange sight to one that has been long
213.   blind.

214. *Blind Beggar.* There is a stranger sight than that, and
215.   that is the skin of my own black sheep on your back.

216. *Lame Beggar.* Haven't I been telling you from the peep
217.   o' day that my sheepskin is that white it would
218.   dazzle you?

219. *Blind Beggar.* Are you so swept with the words that
220.   you've never thought that when I had my own two
221.   eyes, I'd see what colour was on it?

222. *Lame Beggar* [*very dejected*]. I never thought of that.

223. *Blind Beggar.* Are you that flighty?

224. *Lame Beggar.* I am that flighty. [*Cheering up.*] But am I
225.   not blessed, and it's a sin to speak against the
226.   blessed?

227. *Blind Beggar.* Well, I'll speak against the blessed, and
228.   I'll tell you something more that I'll do. All the
229.   while you were telling me how, if I had my two
230.   eyes, I could pick up a chicken here and a goose
231.   there, while my neighbours were in bed, do you
232.   know what I was thinking?

233. *Lame Beggar.* Some wicked blind man's thought.

234. *Blind Beggar.* It was, and it's not gone from me yet. I
235.   was saying to myself, I have a long arm and a strong
236.   arm and a very weighty arm, and when I get my own
237.   two eyes I shall know where to hit.

---

211. . . . and the green . . . **C, D.**
218. . . . you. **75.**
220. . . . that, when . . . **C.**
221. . . . colour it was . . . ? **C** ; . . . it. **75.**
225. . . . blessed? and . . . **C.**
226. blessed. **C-83.**
228. I tell . . . **C** ; I tell . . . more, that . . . **D.**
235. . . . myself (myself: **D**) I . . . **C-83.**
237. . . . I know . . . . **C-75.**

238. *Lame Beggar.* Don't lay a hand on me. Forty years we've
239.   been knocking about the roads together, and I
240.   wouldn't have you bring your soul into mortal peril.

241. *Blind Beggar.* I have been saying to myself, I shall know
242.   where to hit and how to hit and who to hit.

243. *Lame Beggar.* Do you not know that I am blessed?
244.   Would you be as bad as Caesar and as Herod and
245.   Nero and the other wicked emperors of antiquity?

246. *Blind Beggar.* Where'll I hit him, for the love of God,
247.   where'll I hit him?
              [*Blind Beggar beats Lame Beggar. The beating takes the form of a
              dance and is accompanied on drum and flute. The Blind Beggar goes
              out.*

248. *Lame Beggar.* That is a soul lost, Holy Man.

249. *First Musician.* Maybe so.

250. *Lame Beggar.* I'd better be going, Holy Man, for he'll
251.   rouse the whole country against me.

252. *First Musician.* He'll do that.

253. *Lame Beggar.* And I have it in my mind not to even
254.   myself again with the martyrs, and the holy con-
255.   fessors, till I am more used to being blessed.

256. *First Musician.* Bend down your back.

257. *Lame Beggar.* What for, Holy Man?

258. *First Musician.* That I may get up on it.

---

241.   ... , I know **C** ; ... myself: I know **D** ; ... myself I know **75** ; ...
          myself I ... **83.**
242.   ... hit, and who .... **C.**
243.   ... blessed. **75.**
244.   ... Caesar, and ... Herod, and **C.**
245.   Nero, and ... ? **C** ; ... Antiquity? **D.**
          Directions after 247. [... *beggar ... lame beggar. ... on flute and drum.
          The blind beggar ....*] **C** ; [... *dance, and ... on flute and drum. The
          ....*] **D.**
248.   There is .... **D.**

259. *Lame Beggar*. But my lame legs would never bear the
260. weight of you.

261. *First Musician*. I'm up now.

262. *Lame Beggar*. I don't feel you at all.

263. *First Musician*. I don't weigh more than a grasshopper.

264. *Lame Beggar*. You do not.

265. *First Musician*. Are you happy?

266. *Lame Beggar*. I would be if I was right sure I was
267. blessed.

268. *First Musician*. Haven't you got me for a friend?

269. *Lame Beggar*. I have so.

270. *First Musician*. Then you're blessed.

271. *Lame Beggar*. Will you see that they put my name in
272. the book?

273. *First Musician*. I will then.

274. *Lame Beggar*. Let us be going, Holy Man.

275. *First Musician*. But you must bless the road.

276. *Lame Beggar*. I haven't the right words.

277. *First Musician*. What do you want words for? Bow to
278. what is before you, bow to what is behind you, bow
279. to what is to the left of you, bow to what is to the
280. right of you.   [*The Lame Beggar begins to bow.*

281. *First Musician*. That's no good.

282. *Lame Beggar*. No good, Holy Man?

283. *First Musician*. No good at all. You must dance.

Directions after 274. [*They go out to drum and flute as before.*] **C-75.**
275-Directions after 289. [lacking] **C-75.**

284. *Lame Beggar.* But how can I dance? Ain't I a lame man?

285. *First Musician.* Aren't you blessed?

286. *Lame Beggar.* Maybe so.

287. *First Musician.* Aren't you a miracle?

288. *Lame Beggar.* I am, Holy Man.

289. *First Musician.* Then dance, and that'll be a miracle.

> [*The Lame Beggar begins to dance, at first clumsily, moving about with his stick, then he throws away the stick and dances more and more quickly. Whenever he strikes the ground strongly with his lame foot the cymbals clash. He goes out dancing, after which follows the First Musician's song.*

First Musician [*singing*].

290.   Minnaloushe creeps through the grass
291.   From moonlit place to place.
292.   The sacred moon overhead
293.   Has taken a new phase.
294.   Does Minnaloushe know that his pupils
295.   Will pass from change to change,
296.   And that from round to crescent,
297.   From crescent to round they range?
298.   Minnaloushe creeps through the grass
299.   Alone, important and wise,
300.   And lifts to the changing moon
301.   His changing eyes.

THE END

Directions after 289.   [. . . *quickly. Perhaps whenever* . . . .] **84.**
291.   . . . moonlight . . . place, (place **75**) **C-75** ; . . . moonlight . . . . **84.**
296.   . . . crescent **C, D.**
299.   .. . , important, and . . . , **C.**

NOTES

I wrote this play with the intention of including it in 'Four Plays for Dancers', but did not do so as it was in a different mood. I published the musicians' song however in 'The Wild Swans at Coole'. I have amused myself by imagining incidents and metaphors that are related to certain beliefs of mine as are the patterns upon a Persian carpet to some ancient faith or philosophy. It has pleased me to think that the half of me that feels can sometimes forget all that belongs to the more intellectual half but a few images. The night's dream takes up and plays in the same forgetful fashion with our waking thoughts. Minnaloushe and the Moon were perhaps—it all grows faint to me—an exposition of man's relation to what I called the Antithetical Tincture, and when the Saint mounts upon the back of the Lame Beggar he personifies a certain great spiritual event which may take place when Primary Tincture, as I have called it, supersedes Antithetical— 'The burning bow . . . . . . is drawn between deformity of body and mind.' I have altogether forgotten whether other parts of the fable have, as is very likely, a precise meaning, and that is natural, for I generally forget in contemplating my copy of an old Persian carpet that its winding and wandering vine had once that philosophical meaning, which has made it very interesting to Josef Stryzgowski and was part of the religion of Zoroaster. The Well itself is within a couple of miles of my Galway house, Thoor Ballylee, and is sacred to St. Colman, and began a few years ago to work miracles again, rejuvenated by a Gaelic League procession in its honour. There is some story, which I have half forgotten, of a lame man and a blind man's arrival at it, though not of their quarrel there. I intended my play to be what the Japanese call a 'Kiogen,' and to come as a relaxation of attention between, let us say 'The Hawk's Well' and 'The Dreaming of the Bones,' & as the Musicians would be already in their places, I have not written any verses to be sung at the unfolding and the folding of a cloth. It is all the slighter because probably unfinished, and must remain unfinished until it has been performed and I know how the Lame Man is to move. Is he to remain, after he comes from the other's back, upon one knee, or crouching till he can pick up, as I have no doubt he does, the Blind Man's stick? Or is he but to walk stiffly, or limp as if a leg were paralysed? Whatever his movements are they must be artificial and formal, like the movement upon a puppet stage, or in a dance, & I may have to give him more words here and there to explain these movements. But it may never be played, never seem worth the trouble of making those two masks, or of writing the music and so I let it go as it is.   Notes, 75.

* * *

I

These plays, which substitute speech and music for painted scenery, should suit Cellars and Garrets, though I do not recommend *The Resurrection* to the more pious Communist or Republican cellars; it may not be as orthodox as I think; I recommend *The Cat and the Moon*, for no audience could discover its dark, mythical secrets. Myth is not, as Vico perhaps thought, a rudimentary form superseded by reflection. Belief is the spring of all action; we assent to the conclusions of reflection but believe what myth presents; belief is love, and the concrete alone is loved; nor is it true that myth has no purpose but to bring round some discovery of a principle or a fact. The saint may touch through myth the utmost reach of human faculty and pass not to reflection but to unity with the source of his being.

The Japanese labour leader and Christian saint Kagawa,[1] perhaps influenced by Vico though his millennium-haunted mind breaks Vico's circle, speaks of that early phase of every civilisation where a man must follow his father's occupation, where everything is prescribed, as buried under dream and myth. It was because the Irish country people kept something of that early period (had they not lived in Asia until the battle of the Boyne?) that I wrote my *Celtic Twilight*, that Lady Gregory wrote her much richer *Poets and Dreamers*, that she wrote and I annotated those *Visions and Beliefs* in whose collection I had some share. Though Lady Gregory's work is careful and accurate we had little scientific curiosity, but sought wisdom, peace, and a communion with the people. Perhaps a similar emotion made my brother paint country fairs and little streets and the remembered faces of pilots seen at Rosses in his childhood, and Synge create *The Well of the Saints*. I feel at the entrance of the saint in the last act of the play what Lady Gregory must have felt when at the sight of an old man in a wood she said to me, 'That man may have the wisdom of the ages.' Dr. Hyde and his League were different; they sought the peasant, and it is the peasant perhaps who prevails wherever Gaelic is taught, but we sought the peasant's imagination which presses beyond himself as if to the next age. 'Twenty years have I spent upon the battlefields of the world,' said the pensioner in my brother's picture. The choral song, a life lived in common, a futile battle, then thought for its own sake, the last island, Vico's circle and mine, and then the circle joined.

> Decline of day,
> A leaf drifts down;
> O dark leaf clay
> On Nineveh's crown!

II

A couple of miles as the crow flies from my Galway house is a blessed well. Some thirty years ago the Gaelic League organised some kind of procession or 'pattern' there, somebody else put a roof over it, somebody else was cured of a lame leg or a blind eye or the falling sickness. There are many offerings at the well-side left by sufferers; I seem to remember bits of cloth

---

[1] 'What is so wonderful about our Saviour,' he writes, 'is that though He lived surrounded by women there was never any scandal.'

torn perhaps from a dress, hairpins, and little pious pictures. The tradition is that centuries ago a blind man and a lame man dreamed that somewhere in Ireland a well would cure them and set out to find it, the lame man on the blind man's back. I wanted to give the Gaelic League, or some like body, a model for little plays, commemorations of known places and events, and wanted some light entertainment to join a couple of dance plays or *The Resurrection* and a dance play, and chose for theme the lame man, the blind man, and the well. It seemed that I could be true to the associations of such places if I kept in mind, while only putting the vaguest suggestion of it into the play, that the blind man was the body, the lame man was the soul. When I had finished I found them in some medieval Irish sermon as a simile of soul and body, and then that they had some like meaning in a Buddhist Sutra. But as the populace might well alter out of all recognition, deprive of all apparent meaning, some philosophical thought or verse, I wrote a little poem where a cat is disturbed by the moon, and in the changing pupils of its eyes seems to repeat the movement of the moon's changes, and allowed myself as I wrote to think of the cat as the normal man and of the moon as the opposite he seeks perpetually, or as having any meaning I have conferred upon the moon elsewhere. Doubtless, too, when the lame man takes the saint upon his back, the normal man has become one with that opposite, but I had to bear in mind that I was among dreams and proverbs, that though I might discover what had been and might be again an abstract idea, no abstract idea must be present. The spectator should come away thinking the meaning as much his own manufacture as that of the blind man and the lame man had seemed mine. Perhaps some early Christian— Bardaisan had speculations about the sun and moon nobody seems to have investigated—thought as I do, saw in the changes of the moon all the cycles: the soul realising its separate being in the full moon, then, as the moon seems to approach the sun and dwindle away, all but realising its absorption in God, only to whirl away once more: the mind of a man, separating itself from the common matrix, through childish imaginations, through struggle— Vico's heroic age—to roundness, completeness, and then externalising, intellectualising, systematising, until at last it lies dead, a spider smothered in its own web: the choice offered by the sages, either with the soul from the myth to union with the source of all, the breaking of the circle, or from the myth to reflection and the circle renewed for better or worse. For better or worse according to one's life, but never progress as we understand it, never the straight line, always a necessity to break away and destroy, or to sink in and forget.

[See also *Picture 65*, *71*, *83*, pp. *1305*, *1308*.]

III

When Lady Gregory's *Visions and Beliefs* had all been collected I began, that I might write my notes, to study spiritualism, of which I had hitherto known nothing. I went from medium to medium, choosing by preference mediums in poor districts where the questioners were small shopkeepers,

workmen, and workmen's wives, and found there almost all that Lady
Gregory had recorded, though without some of its beauty. It seemed at first
that all was taken literally, but I soon found that the medium and some of
the questioners knew that something from beyond time was expressing
itself in whatever crude symbols they could best understand. I remembered
a Sligo visionary who could neither read nor write and said her fairies were
big or little according to something in her mind. I began taking notes,
piecing together a philosophy resembling that of the villages and of certain
passages in the *Spiritual Diary* and *Heaven and Hell* of Swedenborg, and to
study natures that seemed upon the edge of the myth-haunted semi-somnam-
bulism of Kagawa's first period. Perhaps now that the abstract intellect has
split the mind into categories, the body into cubes, we may be about to
turn back towards the unconscious, the whole, the miraculous; according
to a Chinese sage darkness begins at midday. Perhaps in my search, as in
that first search with Lady Gregory among the cottages, I but showed a
first effect of that slight darkening.

IV

'The holy man in the big house,' on page 148, and his friend from Mayo
were meant for Edward Martyn and George Moore, both of whom were
living when the play was written. I think the audience understood the
reference, but when the play is performed where the reference is not understood it might be best to cut out all from 'Do you mind what the beggar
told you' down to 'will you answer me that now?' and put into the Blind
Beggar's mouth instead the words 'He would soonest.'

'The Cat and the Moon,' Introduction, **83.**

*   *   *

Variant spelling

lecher **C, D, 83-97**; *letcher* **75.**

*   *   *

[See also *Preface to 75, 83*, pp. 1307, 1308.]

SOPHOCLES' KING OEDIPUS

A Version for the Modern Stage

1928

Persons in the Play

Oedipus, *King of Thebes*	Tiresias, *a seer*
Jocasta, *wife of Oedipus*	A Priest
Antigone, *daughter of Oedipus*	Messengers
Ismene, *daughter of Oedipus*	A Herdsman
Creon, *brother-in-law of Oedipus*	Chorus

SCENE

The Palace of King Oedipus at Thebes

1. *Oedipus.* Children, descendants of old Cadmus, why do
2. you come before me, why do you carry the branches
3. of suppliants, while the city smokes with incense
4. and murmurs with prayer and lamentation? I would
5. not learn from any mouth but yours, old man, there-
6. fore I question you myself. Do you know of any-
7. thing that I can do and have not done? How can I,

PRINTINGS **79, 84, 97.**

DATE [lacking] **79.**

DRAMATIS PERSONAE The Cast of First Production of King / Oedipus, Abbey Theatre, Dublin, Tuesday, / December 7, 1926. / Oedipus F. J. McCormick / Jocasta Eileen Crowe / Creon Barry Fitzgerald / Priest Eric Gorman / Tiresias Michael J. Dolan / Boy D. Breen / First Messenger Arthur Shields / Herdsman Gabriel J. Fallon / Second Messenger P. J. Carolan / Nurse May Craig / Children Raymond and Edna Fardy / Servants Tony Quinn, Michael Scott, / C. Haughton / Leader of the Chorus J. Stevenson / Chorus Peter Nolan, Walter Dillon, / T. Moran, M. Finn, / D. Williams / **79** ;
... *brother-in-law of Oedipus* / Theseus, *King of Athens* / Tiresias, ... **84.**

STAGE DIRECTIONS Scene: *Outside the* ... *Oedipus* **79**; [lacking] **84.**

PRODUCTION NOTE *Produced by* Lennox Robinson **79.**

8.   being the man I am, being King Oedipus, do other
9.   than all I know? I were indeed hard of heart did I
10.   not pity such suppliants.

11. *Priest.* Oedipus, King of my country, we who stand
12.   before your door are of all ages, some too young to
13.   have walked so many miles, some—priests of Zeus
14.   such as I—too old. Among us stand the pick of the
15.   young men, and behind in the market-places the
16.   people throng, carrying suppliant branches. We all
17.   stand here because the city stumbles towards death,
18.   hardly able to raise up its head. A blight has fallen
19.   upon the fruitful blossoms of the land, a blight
20.   upon flock and field and upon the bed of marriage—
21.   plague ravages the city. Oedipus, King, not God but
22.   foremost of living men, seeing that when you first
23.   came to this town of Thebes you freed us from that
24.   harsh singer, the riddling Sphinx, we beseech you,
25.   all we suppliants, to find some help; whether you
26.   find it by your power as a man, or because, being
27.   near the Gods, a God has whispered you. Uplift our
28.   State; think upon your fame; your coming brought
29.   us luck, be lucky to us still; remember that it is
30.   better to rule over men than over a waste place,
31.   since neither walled town nor ship is anything if it
32.   be empty and no man within it.

33. *Oedipus.* My unhappy children! I know well what need
34.   has brought you, what suffering you endure; yet,
35.   sufferers though you be, there is not a single one
36.   whose suffering is as mine—each mourns himself,
37.   but my soul mourns the city, myself, and you. It is

TEXT

11-17. . . . country, you can see our ages who are before your door; some
        it may be too young for such a journey, and some too old, Priests of
        Zeus such as I, and these chosen young men; while the rest of the
        people crowd the market-places with their suppliant branches, for the
        city stumbles . . . , **79.**
21.   . . . god . . . **79.**
24.   . . . sphinx, . . . ,
25.   . . . help. Whether . . . **79.**
27.   . . . gods, . . . god . . . **79.**
29.   . . . still, remember . . . **79.**
34.   . . . endure, yet **79.**

38. not therefore as if you came to arouse a sleeping
39. man. No! Be certain that I have wept many tears and
40. searched hither and thither for some remedy. I have
41. already done the only thing that came into my head
42. for all my search. I have sent the son of Menoeceus,
43. Creon, my own wife's brother, to the Pythian House
44. of Phoebus, to hear if deed or word of mine may yet
45. deliver this town. I am troubled, for he is a long
46. time away—a longer time than should be—but when
47. he comes I shall not be an honest man unless I do
48. whatever the God commands.

49. *Priest.* You have spoken at the right time. They have
50. just signalled to us that Creon has arrived.

51. *Oedipus.* O King Apollo, may he bring brighter fortune,
52. for his face is shining!

53. *Priest.* He brings good news, for he is crowned with
54. bay.

55. *Oedipus.* We shall know soon. Brother-in-law, Menoe-
56. ceus' son, what news from the God?

57. *Creon.* Good news; for pain turns to pleasure when we
58. have set the crooked straight.

59. *Oedipus.* But what is the oracle?—so far the news is
60. neither good nor bad.

61. *Creon.* If you would hear it with all these about you,
62. I am ready to speak. Or do we go within?

63. *Oedipus.* Speak before all. The sorrow I endure is less
64. for my own life than these.

65. *Creon.* Then, with your leave, I speak. Our lord
66. Phoebus bids us drive out a defiling thing that has
67. been cherished in this land.

41. ... in to ... **79.**
48. ... god .... **79.**
52. ... shining. **79.**
56. ... god? **79.**
59. ... oracle—so ... **79E.**

68. *Oedipus*. By what purification?

69. *Creon*. King Laius was our King before you came to
70.   pilot us.

71. *Oedipus*. I know—but not of my own knowledge, for I
72.   never saw him.

73. *Creon*. He was killed; and the God now bids us re-
74.   venge it on his murderers, whoever they be.

75. *Oedipus*. Where shall we come upon their track after
76.   all these years? Did he meet his death in house or
77.   field, at home or in some foreign land?

78. *Creon*. In a foreign land: he was journeying to Delphi.

79. *Oedipus*. Did no fellow-traveller see the deed? Was
80.   there none there who could be questioned?

81. *Creon*. All perished but one man who fled in terror
82.   and could tell for certain but one thing of all he had
83.   seen.

84. *Oedipus*. One thing might be a clue to many things.

85. *Creon*. He said that they were fallen upon by a great
86.   troop of robbers.

87. *Oedipus*. What robbers would be so daring unless bribed
88.   from here?

89. *Creon*. Such things were indeed guessed at, but Laius
90.   once dead no avenger arose. We were amid our
91.   troubles.

92. *Oedipus*. But when royalty had fallen what troubles
93.   could have hindered search?

94. *Creon*. The riddling Sphinx put those dark things out
95.   of our thoughts—we thought of what had come to
96.   our own doors.

---

69. . . . our king . . . **79**.
73. . . . god . . . **79**.
94. . . . sphinx . . . **79**.

97. *Oedipus.* But I will start afresh and make the dark things
98. plain. In doing right by Laius I protect myself, for
99. whoever slew Laius might turn a hand against me.
100. Come, my children, rise up from the altar steps; lift
101. up these suppliant boughs and let all the children
102. of Cadmus be called hither that I may search out
103. everything and find for all happiness or misery as
104. God wills.

105. *Priest.* May Phoebus, sender of the oracle, come with
106. it and be our saviour and deliverer!

The Chorus enter

Chorus

107. What message comes to famous Thebes from the
      Golden House?
108. What message of disaster from that sweet-throated
      Zeus?
109. What monstrous thing our fathers saw do the seasons
      bring?
110. Or what that no man ever saw, what new monstrous
      thing?
111. Trembling in every limb I raise my loud importunate
      cry,
112. And in a sacred terror wait the Delian God's reply.

113. Apollo chase the God of Death that leads no shouting
      men,
114. Bears no rattling shield and yet consumes this form
      with pain.
115. Famine takes what the plague spares, and all the crops are
      lost;
116. No new life fills the empty place—ghost flits after
      ghost

---

104. god . . . . **79.**
106. . . . deliverer. **79.**
109. What foul things that our . . . saw, do . . . ? **79.**
112. . . . god's . . . .
113. . . . god . . . death . . . ,
114. . . . pain, **79.**
116. . . . ghost. **79A.**

117. To that God-trodden western shore, as flit benighted
     birds.

118. Sorrow speaks to sorrow, but no comfort finds in
     words.

119. Hurry him from the land of Thebes with a fair wind
     behind

120. Out on to that formless deep where not a man can
     find

121. Hold for an anchor-fluke, for all is world-enfolding
     sea;

122. Master of the thunder-cloud, set the lightning free,

123. And add the thunder-stone to that and fling them on
     his head,

124. For death is all the fashion now, till even Death be
     dead.

125. We call against the pallid face of this God-hated God

126. The springing heel of Artemis in the hunting sandal
     shod,

127. The tousle-headed Maenads, blown torch and
     drunken sound,

128. The stately Lysian king himself with golden fillet
     crowned,

129. And in his hands the golden bow and the stretched
     golden string,

130. And Bacchus' wine-ensanguined face that all the
     Maenads sing.

131. *Oedipus.* You are praying, and it may be that your
132. prayer will be answered; that if you hear my words
133. and do my bidding you may find help out of all
134. your trouble. This is my proclamation, children of
135. Cadmus. Whoever among you knows by what man
136. Laius, son of Labdacus, was killed, must tell all he
137. knows. If he fear for himself and being guilty de-
138. nounce himself, he shall be in the less danger, suffer-

---

117. . . . god-trodden . . . .
118. . . . sorrow and finds no comfort in . . . . **79.**
121. . . . anchor fluke, . . . ;
122. . . . thundercloud, . . . ,
123. . . . head
124. . . . even death . . . .
125. . . . god-hated god **79.**

139. ing no worse thing than banishment. If on the other
140. hand there be one that knows that a foreigner did
141. the deed, let him speak, and I shall give him a reward
142. and my thanks: but if any man keep silent from fear
143. or to screen a friend, hear all what I will do to that
144. man. No one in this land shall speak to him, nor
145. offer sacrifice beside him; but he shall be driven
146. from their homes as if he himself had done the deed.
147. And in this I am the ally of the Pythian God and of
148. the murdered man, and I pray that the murderer's
149. life may, should he be so hidden and screened, drop
150. from him and perish away, whoever he may be,
151. whether he did the deed with others or by himself
152. alone: and on you I lay it to make—so far as man
153. may—these words good, for my sake, and for the
154. God's sake, and for the sake of this land. And even
155. if the God had not spurred us to it, it were a wrong
156. to leave the guilt unpurged, when one so noble, and
157. he your King, had perished; and all have sinned that
158. could have searched it out and did not: and now
159. since it is I who hold the power which he held once,
160. and have his wife for wife—she who would have
161. borne him heirs had he but lived—I take up this
162. cause even as I would were it that of my own father.
163. And if there be any who do not obey me in it, I
164. pray that the Gods send them neither harvest of the
165. earth nor fruit of the womb; but let them be wasted
166. by this plague, or by one more dreadful still. But
167. may all be blessed for ever who hear my words and
168. do my will!

169. *Chorus.* We do not know the murderer, and it were
170. indeed more fitting that Phoebus, who laid the task
171. upon us, should name the man.

172. *Oedipus.* No man can make the Gods speak against
173. their will.

---

154. god's . . .
155. . . . god . . . **79.**
157. . . . king, . . . **79.**
164. . . . gods . . . **79.**
168. . . . will. **79.**
172. . . . gods . . . **79.**

174. *Chorus.* Then I will say what seems the next best thing.

175. *Oedipus.* If there is a third course, show it.

176. *Chorus.* I know that our lord Tiresias is the seer most
177.   like to our lord Phoebus, and through him we may
178.   unravel all.

179. *Oedipus.* So I was advised by Creon, and twice already
180.   have I sent to bring him.

181. *Chorus.* If we lack his help we have nothing but vague
182.   and ancient rumours.

183. *Oedipus.* What rumours are they? I would examine
184.   every story.

185. *Chorus.* Certain wayfarers were said to have killed the
186.   King.

187. *Oedipus.* I know, I know. But who was there that
188.   saw it?

189. *Chorus.* If there is such a man, and terror can move
190.   him, he will not keep silence when they have told
191.   him of your curses.

192. *Oedipus.* He that such a deed did not terrify will not
193.   be terrified because of a word.

194. *Chorus.* But there is one who shall convict him. For
195.   the blind prophet comes at last—in whom alone of
196.   all men the truth lives.

Enter Tiresias, led by a boy

197. *Oedipus.* Tiresias, master of all knowledge, whatever
198.   may be spoken, whatever is unspeakable, whatever
199.   omens of earth and sky reveal, the plague is among
200.   us, and from that plague, Great Prophet, protect us
201.   and save us. Phoebus in answer to our question
202.   says that it will not leave us till we have found the

---

176. . . . lord, Tiresias, is . . . **79.**
186. king.
187. I know. I . . . **79.**

203. murderers of Laius, and driven them into exile or
204. put them to death. Do you therefore neglect neither
205. the voice of birds, nor any other sort of wisdom, but
206. rescue yourself, rescue the State, rescue me, rescue
207. all that are defiled by the deed. For we are in your
208. hands, and what greater task falls to a man than to
209. help other men with all he knows and has?

210. *Tiresias.* Aye, and what worse task than to be wise and
211. suffer for it? I know this well; it slipped out of mind,
212. or I would never have come.

213. *Oedipus.* What now?

214. *Tiresias.* Let me go home. You will bear your burden
215. to the end more easily, and I bear mine—if you but
216. give me leave for that.

217. *Oedipus.* Your words are strange and unkind to the
218. State that bred you.

219. *Tiresias.* I see that you, on your part, keep your lips
220. tight shut, and therefore I have shut mine that I may
221. come to no misfortune.

222. *Oedipus.* For God's love do not turn away—if you have
223. knowledge. We suppliants implore you on our knees.

224. *Tiresias.* You are fools—I will bring misfortune neither
225. upon you nor upon myself.

226. *Oedipus.* What is this? You know all and will say no-
227. thing? You are minded to betray me and Thebes?

228. *Tiresias.* Why do you ask these things? You will not
229. learn them from me.

230. *Oedipus.* What! Basest of the base! You would enrage
231. the very stones. Will you never speak out? Cannot
232. anything touch you?

233. *Tiresias.* The future will come of itself though I keep

---

209. . . . has. **79.**
211. . . . it. I . . . , **79.**
222. . . . god's . . . **79.**

234. silent.

235. *Oedipus.* Then seeing that come it must, you had best
236. speak out.

237. *Tiresias.* I will speak no further. Rage if you have a
238. mind to; bring out all the fierceness that is in your
239. heart.

240. *Oedipus.* That will I. I will not spare to speak my
241. thoughts. Listen to what I have to say. It seems to
242. me that you have helped to plot the deed; and, short
243. of doing it with your own hands, have done the deed
244. yourself. Had you eyesight I would declare that you
245. alone had done it.

246. *Tiresias.* So that is what you say? I charge you to obey
247. the decree that you yourself have made, and from
248. this day out to speak neither to these nor to me. You
249. are the defiler of this land.

250. *Oedipus.* So brazen in your impudence? How do you
251. hope to escape punishment?

252. *Tiresias.* I have escaped; my strength is in my truth.

253. *Oedipus.* Who taught you this? You never got it by your
254. art.

255. *Tiresias.* You, because you have spurred me to speech
256. against my will.

257. *Oedipus.* What speech? Speak it again that I may learn
258. it better.

259. *Tiresias.* You are but tempting me—you understood me
260. well enough.

261. *Oedipus.* No; not so that I can say I know it; speak it
262. again.

263. *Tiresias.* I say that you are yourself the murderer that
264. you seek.

265. *Oedipus.* You shall rue it for having spoken twice such

266.   outrageous words.

267. *Tiresias.* Would you that I say more that you may be
268.   still angrier?

269. *Oedipus.* Say what you will. I will not let it move me.

270. *Tiresias.* I say that you are living with your next of kin
271.   in unimagined shame.

272. *Oedipus.* Do you think you can say such things and
273.   never smart for it?

274. *Tiresias.* Yes, if there be strength in truth.

275. *Oedipus.* There is; yes—for everyone but you. But not
276.   for you that are maimed in ear and in eye and in wit.

277. *Tiresias.* You are but a poor wretch flinging taunts that
278.   in a little while everyone shall fling at you.

279. *Oedipus.* Night, endless night has covered you up so
280.   that you can neither hurt me nor any man that looks
281.   upon the sun.

282. *Tiresias.* Your doom is not to fall by me. Apollo is
283.   enough: it is his business to work out your doom.

284. *Oedipus.* Was it Creon that planned this or you your-
285.   self?

286. *Tiresias.* Creon is not your enemy; you are your own
287.   enemy.

288. *Oedipus.* Power, ability, position, you bear all burdens,
289.   and yet what envy you create! Great must that envy
290.   be if envy of my power in this town—a power put
291.   into my hands unsought—has made trusty Creon,
292.   my old friend Creon, secretly long to take that power
293.   from me; if he has suborned this scheming juggler,
294.   this quack and trickster, this man with eyes for his
295.   gains and blindness in his art. Come, come, where
296.   did you prove yourself a seer? Why did you say no-
297.   thing to set the townsmen free when the riddling

---

279.   Night—endless . . . **79.**

298. Sphinx was here? Yet that riddle was not for the
299. first-comer to read; it needed the skill of a seer. And
300. none such had you! Neither found by help of birds,
301. nor straight from any God. No, I came; I silenced
302. her, I the ignorant Oedipus, it was I that found
303. the answer in my mother-wit, untaught by any birds.
304. And it is I that you would pluck out of my place,
305. thinking to stand close to Creon's throne. But you
306. and the plotter of all this shall mourn despite your
307. zeal to purge the land. Were you not an old man, you
308. had already learnt how bold you are and learnt it to
309. your cost.

310. *Chorus.* Both this man's words and yours, Oedipus,
311. have been said in anger. Such words cannot help us
312. here, nor any but those that teach us to obey the
313. oracle.

314. *Tiresias.* King though you are, the right to answer when
315. attacked belongs to both alike. I am not subject to
316. you, but to Loxias; and therefore I shall never be
317. Creon's subject. And I tell you, since you have
318. taunted me with blindness, that though you have
319. your sight, you cannot see in what misery you stand,
320. nor where you are living, nor with whom, unknowing
321. what you do—for you do not know the stock you
322. come of—you have been your own kin's enemy be
323. they living or be they dead. And one day a mother's
324. curse and father's curse alike shall drive you from
325. this land in dreadful haste with darkness upon those
326. eyes. Therefore, heap your scorn on Creon and on my
327. message if you have a mind to; for no one of living
328. men shall be crushed as you shall be crushed.

329. *Oedipus.* Begone this instant! Away, away! Get you
330. from these doors!

331. *Tiresias.* I had never come but that you sent for me.

332. *Oedipus.* I did not know you were mad.

---

298. sphinx . . . **79.**
301. . . . god. . . . **79.**
303. . . . mother wit, ... **79.**
329. . . . ! Get thee **79.**

333. *Tiresias.* I may seem mad to you, but your parents
334.   thought me sane.

335. *Oedipus.* My parents! Stop! Who was my father?

336. *Tiresias.* This day shall you know your birth; and it
337.   will ruin you.

338. *Oedipus.* What dark words you always speak!

339. *Tiresias.* But are you not most skilful in the unravelling
340.   of dark words?

341. *Oedipus.* You mock me for that which made me great?

342. *Tiresias.* It was that fortune that undid you.

343. *Oedipus.* What do I care? For I delivered all this town.

344. *Tiresias.* Then I will go: boy, lead me out of this.

345. *Oedipus.* Yes, let him lead you. You take vexation with
346.   you.

347. *Tiresias.* I will go: but first I will do my errand. For
348.   frown though you may you cannot destroy me. The
349.   man for whom you look, the man you have been
350.   threatening in all the proclamations about the death
351.   of Laius, that man is here. He seems, so far as looks
352.   go, an alien; yet he shall be found a native Theban
353.   and shall nowise be glad of that fortune. A blind
354.   man, though now he has his sight; a beggar, though
355.   now he is most rich; he shall go forth feeling the
356.   ground before him with his stick; so you go in and
357.   think on that, and if you find I am in fault say that
358.   I have no skill in prophecy.

    [*Tiresias is led out by the boy. Oedipus enters the palace.*

Chorus

359. The Delphian rock has spoken out, now must a wicked
    mind,

---

350. . . . proclamation . . . **79A.**
359. . . . mind **79.**

360.   Planner of things I dare not speak and of this bloody
         wrack,

361.   Pray for feet that are as fast as the four hoofs of the
         wind:

362.   Cloudy Parnassus and the Fates thunder at his back.

363.   That sacred crossing-place of lines upon Parnassus'
         head,

364.   Lines that have run through North and South, and run
         through West and East,

365.   The navel of the world bids all men search the
         mountain wood,

366.   The solitary cavern, till they have found that in-
         famous beast.

Creon enters from the house

367.   *Creon.* Fellow-citizens, having heard that King Oedi-
368.   pus accuses me of dreadful things, I come in my
369.   indignation. Does he think that he has suffered
370.   wrong from me in these present troubles, or any-
371.   thing that could lead to wrong, whether in word or
372.   deed? How can I live under blame like that? What
373.   life would be worth having if by you here, and by
374.   my nearest friends, called a traitor through the town?

375.   *Chorus.* He said it in anger, and not from his heart
376.   out.

377.   *Creon.* He said it was I put up the seer to speak those
378.   falsehoods.

379.   *Chorus.* Such things were said.

380.   *Creon.* And had he his right mind saying it?

381.   *Chorus.* I do not know—I do not know what my
382.   masters do.

Oedipus enters

383.   *Oedipus.* What brought you here? Have you a face so

---

361.   . . . that run as . . . : **79.**
363.   . . . crossing place . . . ,
364.   Lines drawn through . . . South, and drawn through . . . , **79.**

384. brazen that you come to my house—you, the proved
385. assassin of its master—the certain robber of my
386. crown? Come, tell me in the face of the Gods what
387. cowardice, or folly, did you discover in me that you
388. plotted this? Did you think that I would not see what
389. you were at till you had crept upon me, or seeing it
390. would not ward it off? What madness to seek a
391. throne, having neither friends nor followers!

392. *Creon.* Now, listen, hear my answer, and then you
393. may with knowledge judge between us.

394. *Oedipus.* You are plausible, but waste words now that
395. I know you.

396. *Creon.* Hear what I have to say. I can explain it all.

397. *Oedipus.* One thing you will not explain away—that
398. you are my enemy.

399. *Creon.* You are a fool to imagine that senseless stubborn-
400. ness sits well upon you.

401. *Oedipus.* And you to imagine that you can wrong a
402. kinsman and escape the penalty.

403. *Creon.* That is justly said, I grant you; but what is
404. this wrong that you complain of?

405. *Oedipus.* Did you advise, or not, that I should send for
406. that notorious prophet?

407. *Creon.* And I am of the same mind still.

408. *Oedipus.* How long is it, then, since Laius—

409. *Creon.* What, what about him?

410. *Oedipus.* Since Laius was killed by an unknown hand?

---

384. . . .—you the . . . **79.**
386. crown. Come, . . . gods . . . **79.**
391. . . . followers. **79.**
403. . . . said I . . . **79.**
408. . . . it then since . . .— **79.**

411. *Creon.* That was many years ago.

412. *Oedipus.* Was this prophet at his trade in those days?

413. *Creon.* Yes; skilled as now and in equal honour.

414. *Oedipus.* Did he ever speak of me?

415. *Creon.* Never certainly when I was within earshot.

416. *Oedipus.* And did you enquire into the murder?

417. *Creon.* We did enquire but learnt nothing.

418. *Oedipus.* And why did he not tell out his story then?

419. *Creon.* I do not know. When I know nothing I say
420.   nothing.

421. *Oedipus.* This much at least you know and can say out.

422. *Creon.* What is that? If I know it I will say it.

423. *Oedipus.* That if he had not consulted you he would
424.   never have said that it was I who killed Laius.

425. *Creon.* You know best what he said; but now, question
426.   for question.

427. *Oedipus.* Question your fill—I cannot be proved guilty
428.   of that blood.

429. *Creon.* Answer me then. Are you not married to my
430.   sister?

431. *Oedipus.* That cannot be denied.

432. *Creon.* And do you not rule as she does? And with a like
433.   power?

434. *Oedipus.* I give her all she asks for.

---

414. . . . he speak of me at any time? **79.**
416. . . . you make inquiry into . . . ?
417. We made inquiry but . . . . **79.**
419-420. . . . know. Where I lack light I am silent. **79.**

435. *Creon.* And am not I the equal of you both?

436. *Oedipus.* Yes: and that is why you are so false a friend.

437. *Creon.* Not so; reason this out as I reason it, and first
438.   weigh this: who would prefer to lie awake amid terrors
439.   rather than to sleep in peace, granting that his power
440.   is equal in both cases? Neither I nor any sober-
441.   minded man. You give me what I ask and let me do
442.   what I want, but were I King I would have to do
443.   things I did not want to do. Is not influence and no
444.   trouble with it better than any throne, am I such a
445.   fool as to hunger after unprofitable honours? Now
446.   all are glad to see me, every one wishes me well, all
447.   that want a favour from you ask speech of me—
448.   finding in that their hope. Why should I give up these
449.   things and take those? No wise mind is treacherous.
450.   I am no contriver of plots, and if another took to
451.   them he would not come to me for help. And in
452.   proof of this go to the Pythian Oracle, and ask if
453.   I have truly told what the Gods said: and after that,
454.   if you have found that I have plotted with the Sooth-
455.   sayer, take me and kill me; not by the sentence of
456.   one mouth only—but of two mouths, yours and my
457.   own. But do not condemn me in a corner, upon some
458.   fancy and without proof. What right have you to
459.   declare a good man bad or a bad good? It is as bad a
460.   thing to cast off a true friend as it is for a man to
461.   cast away his own life—but you will learn these
462.   things with certainty when the time comes; for time
463.   alone shows a just man; though a day can show a
464.   knave.

465. *Chorus.* King! He has spoken well, he gives himself
466.   time to think; a headlong talker does not know what
467.   he is saying.

468. *Oedipus.* The plotter is at his work, and I must counter-
469.   plot headlong, or he will get his ends and I miss
470.   mine.

---

440.   . . . cases. Neither . . . **79.**
442.   . . . king . . . **79.**
446.   . . . , everyone . . . **79.**
453.   . . . gods . . ., **79.**
460.   . . . friend, as . . . **79.**

471.   *Creon.* What will you do then? Drive me from the
472.   land?

473.   *Oedipus.* Not so; I do not desire your banishment—
474.   but your death.

475.   *Creon.* You are not sane.

476.   *Oedipus.* I am sane at least in my own interest.

477.   *Creon.* You should be in mine also.

478.   *Oedipus.* No, for you are false.

479.   *Creon.* But if you understand nothing?

480.   *Oedipus.* Yet I must rule.

481.   *Creon.* Not if you rule badly.

482.   *Oedipus.* Hear him, O Thebes!

483.   *Creon.* Thebes is for me also, not for you alone.

484.   *Chorus.* Cease, princes: I see Jocasta coming out of
485.   the house; she comes just in time to quench the
486.   quarrel.

Jocasta enters

487.   *Jocasta.* Unhappy men! Why have you made this crazy
488.   uproar? Are you not ashamed to quarrel about your
489.   own affairs when the whole country is in trouble?
490.   Go back into the palace, Oedipus, and you, Creon,
491.   to your own house. Stop making all this noise about
492.   some petty thing.

493.   *Creon.* Your husband is about to kill me—or to drive
494.   me from the land of my fathers.

495.   *Oedipus.* Yes: for I have convicted him of treachery
496.   against me.

497.   *Creon.* Now may I perish accursed if I have done such

498. a thing!

499. *Jocasta.* For God's love believe it, Oedipus. First, for
500. the sake of his oath, and then for my sake, and for
501. the sake of these people here.

502. *Chorus [all].* King, do what she asks.

503. *Oedipus.* What would you have me do?

504. *Chorus.* Not to make a dishonourable charge, with no
505. more evidence than rumour, against a friend who
506. has bound himself with an oath.

507. *Oedipus.* Do you desire my exile or my death?

508. *Chorus.* No, by Helios, by the first of all the Gods,
509. may I die abandoned by Heaven and earth if I have
510. that thought! What breaks my heart is that our
511. public griefs should be increased by your quarrels.

512. *Oedipus.* Then let him go, though I am doomed thereby
513. to death or to be thrust dishonoured from the land;
514. it is your lips, not his, that move me to compassion;
515. wherever he goes my hatred follows him.

516. *Creon.* You are as sullen in yielding as you were vehe-
517. ment in anger, but such natures are their own
518. heaviest burden.

519. *Oedipus.* Why will you not leave me in peace and
520. begone?

521. *Creon.* I will go away; what is your hatred to me? In
522. the eyes of all here I am a just man.   [*He goes.*

523. *Chorus.* Lady, why do you not take your man in to the
524. house?

525. *Jocasta.* I will do so when I have learned what has

---

498. . . . thing.
499. . . . god's . . . **79.**
508. . . . gods, **79.**
510. . . . thought. What . . . **79.**
521. . . . me; in **79.**

526.   happened.

527. *Chorus.* The half of it was blind suspicion bred of talk;
528.   the rest the wounds left by injustice.

529. *Jocasta.* It was on both sides?

530. *Chorus.* Yes.

531. *Jocasta.* What was it?

532. *Chorus.* Our land is vexed enough. Let the thing alone
533.   now that it is over.   [*Exit leader of Chorus.*

534. *Jocasta.* In the name of the Gods, King, what put you
535.   in this anger?

536. *Oedipus.* I will tell you; for I honour you more than
537.   these men do. The cause is Creon and his plots
538.   against me.

539. *Jocasta.* Speak on, if you can tell clearly how this quarrel
540.   arose.

541. *Oedipus.* He says that I am guilty of the blood of Laius.

542. *Jocasta.* On his own knowledge, or on hearsay?

543. *Oedipus.* He has made a rascal of a seer his mouthpiece.

544. *Jocasta.* Do not fear that there is truth in what he says.
545.   Listen to me, and learn to your comfort that nothing
546.   born of woman can know what is to come. I will
547.   give you proof of that. An oracle came to Laius once,
548.   I will not say from Phoebus, but from his ministers,
549.   that he was doomed to die by the hand of his own
550.   child sprung from him and me. When his child was
551.   but three days old, Laius bound its feet together and
552.   had it thrown by sure hands upon a trackless moun-
553.   tain; and when Laius was murdered at the place
554.   where three highways meet, it was, or so at least the
555.   rumour says, by foreign robbers. So Apollo did not
556.   bring it about that the child should kill its father,

---

534.   . . . gods, king, . . . **79.**
551.   . . . old Laius . . . **79.**

557. nor did Laius die in the dreadful way he feared by
558. his child's hand. Yet that was how the message of
559. the seers mapped out the future. Pay no attention
560. to such things. What the God would show he will
561. need no help to show it, but bring it to light himself.

562. *Oedipus.* What restlessness of soul, lady, has come upon
563. me since I heard you speak, what a tumult of the
564. mind!

565. *Jocasta.* What is this new anxiety? What has startled
566. you?

567. *Oedipus.* You said that Laius was killed where three
568. highways meet.

569. *Jocasta.* Yes: that was the story.

570. *Oedipus.* And where is the place?

571. *Jocasta.* In Phocis where the road divides branching off
572. to Delphi and to Daulia.

573. *Oedipus.* And when did it happen? How many years
574. ago?

575. *Jocasta.* News was published in this town just before
576. you came into power.

577. *Oedipus.* O Zeus! What have you planned to do unto
578. me?

579. *Jocasta.* He was tall; the silver had just come into his
580. hair; and in shape not greatly unlike to you.

581. *Oedipus.* Unhappy that I am! It seems that I have laid
582. a dreadful curse upon myself, and did not know it.

583. *Jocasta.* What do you say? I tremble when I look on
584. you, my King.

585. *Oedipus.* And I have a misgiving that the seer can see
586. indeed. But I will know it all more clearly, if you

560. . . . god . . . **79.**
584. . . . king. **79.**

587.　tell me one thing more.

588.　*Jocasta.* Indeed, though I tremble I will answer what-
589.　ever you ask.

590.　*Oedipus.* Had he but a small troop with him; or did he
591.　travel like a great man with many followers?

592.　*Jocasta.* There were but five in all—one of them a
593.　herald; and there was one carriage with Laius in it.

594.　*Oedipus.* Alas! It is now clear indeed. Who was it brought
595.　the news, lady?

596.　*Jocasta.* A servant—the one survivor.

597.　*Oedipus.* Is he by chance in the house now?

598.　*Jocasta.* No; for when he found you reigning instead
599.　of Laius he besought me, his hand clasped in mine,
600.　to send him to the fields among the cattle that he
601.　might be far from the sight of this town; and I sent
602.　him. He was a worthy man for a slave and might
603.　have asked a bigger thing.

604.　*Oedipus.* I would have him return to us without delay.

605.　*Jocasta.* Oedipus, it is easy. But why do you ask this?

606.　*Oedipus.* I fear that I have said too much, and therefore
607.　I would question him.

608.　*Jocasta.* He shall come, but I too have a right to know
609.　what lies so heavy upon your heart, my King.

610.　*Oedipus.* Yes: and it shall not be kept from you now
611.　that my fear has grown so heavy. Nobody is more
612.　to me than you, nobody has the same right to learn
613.　my good or evil luck. My father was Polybus of
614.　Corinth, my mother the Dorian Merope, and I was
615.　held the foremost man in all that town until a thing

609.　. . . king.
610.　. . . you; now **79**.
614.　Corinth—my . . . **79**.

616. happened—a thing to startle a man, though not to
617. make him angry as it made me. We were sitting at
618. the table, and a man who had drunk too much cried
619. out that I was not my father's son—and I, though
620. angry, restrained my anger for that day; but the
621. next day went to my father and my mother and
622. questioned them. They were indignant at the taunt
623. and that comforted me—and yet the man's words
624. rankled, for they had spread a rumour through the
625. town. Without consulting my father or my mother
626. I went to Delphi, but Phoebus told me nothing of
627. the thing for which I came, but much of other things
628. —things of sorrow and of terror: that I should live
629. in incest with my mother, and beget a brood that
630. men would shudder to look upon; that I should be
631. my father's murderer. Hearing those words I fled
632. out of Corinth, and from that day have but known
633. where it lies when I have found its direction by the
634. stars. I sought where I might escape those infamous
635. things—the doom that was laid upon me. I came in
636. my flight to that very spot where you tell me this
637. king perished. Now, lady, I will tell you the truth.
638. When I had come close up to those three roads, I
639. came upon a herald, and a man like him you have
640. described seated in a carriage. The man who held
641. the reins and the old man himself would not give
642. me room, but thought to force me from the path,
643. and I struck the driver in my anger. The old man,
644. seeing what I had done, waited till I was passing
645. him and then struck me upon the head. I paid him
646. back in full, for I knocked him out of the carriage
647. with a blow of my stick. He rolled on his back, and
648. after that I killed them all. If this stranger were
649. indeed Laius, is there a more miserable man in the
650. world than the man before you? Is there a man more
651. hated of Heaven? No stranger, no citizen, may re-
652. ceive him into his house, not a soul may speak to
653. him, and no mouth but my own mouth has laid this
654. curse upon me. Am I not wretched? May I be swept
655. from this world before I have endured this doom!

656. *Chorus.* These things, O King, fill us with terror; yet

657.   hope till you speak with him that saw the deed, and
658.   have learnt all.

659.   *Oedipus.* Till I have learnt all, I may hope. I await the
660.   man that is coming from the pastures.

661.   *Jocasta.* What is it that you hope to learn?

662.   *Oedipus.* I will tell you. If his tale agrees with yours,
663.   then I am clear.

664.   *Jocasta.* What tale of mine?

665.   *Oedipus.* He told you that Laius met his death from
666.   robbers; if he keeps to that tale now and speaks of
667.   several slayers, I am not the slayer. But if he says one
668.   lonely wayfarer, then beyond a doubt the scale dips
669.   to me.

670.   *Jocasta.* Be certain of this much at least, his first tale
671.   was of robbers. He cannot revoke that tale—the city
672.   heard it and not I alone. Yet, if he should somewhat
673.   change his story, King, at least he cannot make the
674.   murder of Laius square with prophecy; for Loxias
675.   plainly said of Laius that he would die by the hand
676.   of my child. That poor innocent did not kill him,
677.   for it died before him. Therefore from this out I
678.   would not, for all divination can do, so much as
679.   look to my right hand or to my left hand, or fear
680.   at all.

681.   *Oedipus.* You have judged well; and yet for all that,
682.   send and bring this peasant to me.

683.   *Jocasta.* I will send without delay. I will do all that
684.   you would have of me—but let us come in to the
685.   house.   [*They go in to the house.*

Chorus

686.   For this one thing above all I would be praised as a man,
687.   That in my words and my deeds I have kept those laws in
       mind

---

667.   . . . slayers I . . . **79.**
673.   . . . , king, . . . **79.**
678.   . . . not for . . . do so . . . **79.**

688. Olympian Zeus, and that high clear Empyrean,
689. Fashioned, and not some man or people of mankind,
690. Even those sacred laws nor age nor sleep can blind.

691. A man becomes a tyrant out of insolence,
692. He climbs and climbs, until all people call him great,
693. He seems upon the summit, and God flings him thence;
694. Yet an ambitious man may lift up a whole State,
695. And in his death be blessed, in his life fortunate.

696. And all men honour such; but should a man forget
697. The holy images, the Delphian Sibyl's trance,
698. And the world's navel-stone, and not be punished for it
699. And seem most fortunate, or even blessed perchance,
700. Why should we honour the Gods, or join the sacred dance?

Jocasta enters from the palace

701. *Jocasta.* It has come into my head, citizens of Thebes,
702.   to visit every altar of the Gods, a wreath in my hand
703.   and a dish of incense. For all manner of alarms trouble
704.   the soul of Oedipus, who instead of weighing new
705.   oracles by old, like a man of sense, is at the mercy
706.   of every mouth that speaks terror. Seeing that my
707.   words are nothing to him, I cry to you, Lysian
708.   Apollo, whose altar is the first I meet: I come, a
709.   suppliant, bearing symbols of prayer; O, make us
710.   clean, for now we are all afraid, seeing him afraid,
711.   even as they who see the helmsman afraid.

Enter Messenger

712. *Messenger.* May I learn from you, strangers, where is
713.   the home of King Oedipus? Or better still, tell me
714.   where he himself is, if you know.

715. *Chorus.* This is his house, and he himself, stranger, is

---

697. . . . trance
698. . . . navel stone, . . . **79.**
700. . . . gods, . . . ? **79.**
702. . . . gods, . . . **79.**
709. . . . ; O make . . . **79.**

716.   within it, and this lady is the mother of his children.

717.   *Messenger.* Then I call a blessing upon her, seeing what
718.   man she has married.

719.   *Jocasta.* May God reward those words with a like bless-
720.   ing, stranger! But what have you come to seek or to
721.   tell?

722.   *Messenger.* Good news for your house, lady, and for your
723.   husband.

724.   *Jocasta.* What news? From whence have you come?

725.   *Messenger.* From Corinth, and you will rejoice at the
726.   message I am about to give you; yet, maybe, it will
727.   grieve you.

728.   *Jocasta.* What is it? How can it have this double power?

729.   *Messenger.* The people of Corinth, they say, will take
730.   him for king.

731.   *Jocasta.* How then? Is old Polybus no longer on the
732.   throne?

733.   *Messenger.* No. He is in his tomb.

734.   *Jocasta.* What do you say? Is Polybus dead, old man?

735.   *Messenger.* May I drop dead if it is not the truth.

736.   *Jocasta.* Away! Hurry to your master with this news.
737.   O oracle of the Gods, where are you now? This is the
738.   man whom Oedipus feared and shunned lest he
739.   should murder him, and now this man has died a
740.   natural death, and not by the hand of Oedipus.

Enter Oedipus

741.   *Oedipus.* Jocasta, dearest wife, why have you called me
742.   from the house?

---

719.   . . . god . . .
720.   . . . , stranger. But . . . **79.**
737.   . . . gods, . . . **79.**

743. *Jocasta*. Listen to this man, and judge to what the
744.   oracles of the Gods have come.

745. *Oedipus*. And he—who may he be? And what news has
746.   he?

747. *Jocasta*. He has come from Corinth to tell you that your
748.   father, Polybus, is dead.

749. *Oedipus*. How, stranger? Let me have it from your own
750.   mouth.

751. *Messenger*. If I am to tell the story, the first thing is
752.   that he is dead and gone.

753. *Oedipus*. By some sickness or by treachery?

754. *Messenger*. A little thing can bring the aged to their rest.

755. *Oedipus*. Ah! He died, it seems, from sickness?

756. *Messenger*. Yes; and of old age.

757. *Oedipus*. Alas! Alas! Why, indeed, my wife, should one
758.   look to that Pythian seer, or to the birds that scream
759.   above our heads? For they would have it that I was
760.   doomed to kill my father. And now he is dead—hid
761.   already beneath the earth. And here am I—who had
762.   no part in it, unless indeed he died from longing for
763.   me. If that were so, I may have caused his death;
764.   but Polybus has carried the oracles with him into
765.   Hades—the oracles as men have understood them—
766.   and they are worth nothing.

767. *Jocasta*. Did I not tell you so, long since?

768. *Oedipus*. You did, but fear misled me.

769. *Jocasta*. Put this trouble from you.

770. *Oedipus*. Those bold words would sound better, were
771.   not my mother living. But as it is—I have some
772.   grounds for fear; yet you have said well.

---

744. . . . gods . . . . **79.**

773. *Jocasta.* Yet your father's death is a sign that all is well.

774. *Oedipus.* I know that: but I fear because of her who
775.   lives.

776. *Messenger.* Who is this woman who makes you afraid?

777. *Oedipus.* Merope, old man, the wife of Polybus.

778. *Messenger.* What is there in her to make you afraid?

779. *Oedipus.* A dreadful oracle sent from Heaven, stranger.

780. *Messenger.* Is it a secret, or can you speak it out?

781. *Oedipus.* Loxias said that I was doomed to marry my
782.   own mother, and to shed my father's blood. For that
783.   reason I fled from my house in Corinth; and I did
784.   right, though there is great comfort in familiar faces.

785. *Messenger.* Was it indeed for that reason that you went
786.   into exile?

787. *Oedipus.* I did not wish, old man, to shed my father's
788.   blood.

789. *Messenger.* King, have I not freed you from that fear?

790. *Oedipus.* You shall be fittingly rewarded.

791. *Messenger.* Indeed, to tell the truth, it was for that I
792.   came; to bring you home and be the better for it—

793. *Oedipus.* No! I will never go to my parents' home.

794. *Messenger.* Ah, my son, it is plain enough, you do not
795.   know what you do.

796. *Oedipus.* How, old man? For God's love, tell me.

797. *Messenger.* If for these reasons you shrink from going

---

784. right though . . . . **79.**
794. Oh, my . . . **97A.**
796. . . . ? For the gods' . . . . **79.**

798.   home.

799. *Oedipus*. I am afraid lest Phoebus has spoken true.

800. *Messenger*. You are afraid of being made guilty through
801.   Merope?

802. *Oedipus*. That is my constant fear.

803. *Messenger*. A vain fear.

804. *Oedipus*. How so, if I was born of that father and
805.   mother?

806. *Messenger*. Because they were nothing to you in blood.

807. *Oedipus*. What do you say? Was Polybus not my father?

808. *Messenger*. No more nor less than myself.

809. *Oedipus*. How can my father be no more to me than
810.   you who are nothing to me?

811. *Messenger*. He did not beget you any more than I.

812. *Oedipus*. No? Then why did he call me his son?

813. *Messenger*. He took you as a gift from these hands of
814.   mine.

815. *Oedipus*. How could he love so dearly what came from
816.   another's hands?

817. *Messenger*. He had been childless.

818. *Oedipus*. If I am not your son, where did you get me?

819. *Messenger*. In a wooded valley of Cithaeron.

820. *Oedipus*. What brought you wandering there?

821. *Messenger*. I was in charge of mountain sheep.

822. *Oedipus*. A shepherd—a wandering, hired man.

823. *Messenger.* A hired man who came just in time.

824. *Oedipus.* Just in time—had it come to that?

825. *Messenger.* Have not the cords left their marks upon
826.   your ankles?

827. *Oedipus.* Yes, that is an old trouble.

828. *Messenger.* I took your feet out of the spancel.

829. *Oedipus.* I have had those marks from the cradle.

830. *Messenger.* They have given you the name you bear.

831. *Oedipus.* Tell me, for God's sake, was that deed my
832.   mother's or my father's?

833. *Messenger.* I do not know—he who gave you to me
834.   knows more of that than I.

835. *Oedipus.* What? You had me from another? You did
836.   not chance on me yourself?

837. *Messenger.* No. Another shepherd gave you to me.

838. *Oedipus.* Who was he? Can you tell me who he was?

839. *Messenger.* I think that he was said to be of Laius' house-
840.   hold.

841. *Oedipus.* The king who ruled this country long ago?

842. *Messenger.* The same—the man was herdsman in his
843.   service.

844. *Oedipus.* Is he alive, that I might speak with him?

845. *Messenger.* You people of this country should know that.

846. *Oedipus.* Is there any one here present who knows the

831.   . . . , for the gods' . . . **79.**
846.   . . . anyone . . . . **79.**

847.   herd he speaks of? Any one who has seen him in the
848.   town pastures? The hour has come when all must be
849.   made clear.

850. *Chorus.* I think he is the very herd you sent for but
851.   now; Jocasta can tell you better than I.

852. *Jocasta.* Why ask about that man? Why think about
853.   him? Why waste a thought on what this man has
854.   said? What he has said is of no account.

855. *Oedipus.* What, with a clue like that in my hands and
856.   fail to find out my birth?

857. *Jocasta.* For God's sake, if you set any value upon your
858.   life, give up this search—my misery is enough.

859. *Oedipus.* Though I be proved the son of a slave, yes,
860.   even of three generations of slaves, you cannot be
861.   made base-born.

862. *Jocasta.* Yet, hear me, I implore you. Give up this
863.   search.

864. *Oedipus.* I will not hear of anything but searching the
865.   whole thing out.

866. *Jocasta.* I am only thinking of your good—I have ad-
867.   vised you for the best.

868. *Oedipus.* Your advice makes me impatient.

869. *Jocasta.* May you never come to know who you are, un-
870.   happy man!

871. *Oedipus.* Go, some one, bring the herdsman here—and
872.   let that woman glory in her noble blood.

873. *Jocasta.* Alas, alas, miserable man! Miserable! That is

---

847. . . . ? Anyone . . .
848. . . . pastures. The . . . **79.**
851. now, Jocasta . . . . **79.**
861. . . . base born. **79.**
871. . . . , someone, . . . **79.**

V.E.P.Y.—2 E

874.   all that I can call you now or for ever.   [*She goes out.*

875. *Chorus.* Why has the lady gone, Oedipus, in such a
876.   transport of despair? Out of this silence will burst a
877.   storm of sorrows.

878. *Oedipus.* Let come what will. However lowly my origin
879.   I will discover it. That woman, with all a woman's
880.   pride, grows red with shame at my base birth. I
881.   think myself the child of Good Luck, and that the
882.   years are my foster-brothers. Sometimes they have
883.   set me up, and sometimes thrown me down, but he
884.   that has Good Luck for mother can suffer no dis-
885.   honour. That is my origin, nothing can change it, so
886.   why should I renounce this search into my birth?

Chorus

887.   Oedipus' nurse, mountain of many a hidden glen,
888.   Be honoured among men;
889.   A famous man, deep-thoughted, and his body strong;
890.   Be honoured in dance and song.

891.   Who met in the hidden glen? Who let his fancy run
892.   Upon nymph of Helicon?
893.   Lord Pan or Lord Apollo or the mountain Lord
894.   By the Bacchantes adored?

895. *Oedipus.* If I, who have never met the man, may ven-
896.   ture to say so, I think that the herdsman we await
897.   approaches; his venerable age matches with this
898.   stranger's, and I recognise as servants of mine those
899.   who bring him. But you, if you have seen the man
900.   before, will know the man better than I.

901. *Chorus.* Yes, I know the man who is coming; he was
902.   indeed in Laius' service, and is still the most trusted
903.   of the herdsmen.

904. *Oedipus.* I ask you first, Corinthian stranger, is this the

---

874. ... forever. .... **79.**
889. ..., deep thoughted, ... ; **79.**
[line 890, bottom of page; line 891, top of page] **84, 97E** ; [between 890 and
     891 no break] **97A.**
893. ... Lord, **79.**

905.   man you mean?

906.   *Messenger.* He is the very man.

907.   *Oedipus.* Look at me, old man! Answer my questions.
908.   Were you once in Laius' service?

909.   *Herdsman.* I was: not a bought slave, but reared up in
910.   the house.

911.   *Oedipus.* What was your work—your manner of life?

912.   *Herdsman.* For the best part of my life I have tended
913.   flocks.

914.   *Oedipus.* Where, mainly?

915.   *Herdsman.* Cithaeron or its neighbourhood.

916.   *Oedipus.* Do you remember meeting with this man
917.   there?

918.   *Herdsman.* What man do you mean?

919.   *Oedipus.* This man. Did you ever meet him?

920.   *Herdsman.* I cannot recall him to mind.

921.   *Messenger.* No wonder in that, master; but I will bring
922.   back his memory. He and I lived side by side upon
923.   Cithaeron. I had but one flock and he had two.
924.   Three full half-years we lived there, from spring to
925.   autumn, and every winter I drove my flock to my
926.   own fold, while he drove his to the fold of Laius.
927.   Is that right? Was it not so?

928.   *Herdsman.* True enough; though it was long ago.

929.   *Messenger.* Come, tell me now—do you remember giving
930.   me a boy to rear as my own foster-son?

931.   *Herdsman.* What are you saying? Why do you ask me
932.   that?

933.   *Messenger.* Look at that man, my friend, he is the child

934.   you gave me.

935.   *Herdsman.* A plague upon you! Cannot you hold your
936.   tongue?

937.   *Oedipus.* Do not blame him, old man; your own words
938.   are more blameable.

939.   *Herdsman.* And how have I offended, master?

940.   *Oedipus.* In not telling of that boy he asks of.

941.   *Herdsman.* He speaks from ignorance, and does not
942.   know what he is saying.

943.   *Oedipus.* If you will not speak with a good grace you
944.   shall be made to speak.

945.   *Herdsman.* Do not hurt me for the love of God, I am
946.   an old man.

947.   *Oedipus.* Some one there, tie his hands behind his back.

948.   *Herdsman.* Alas! Wherefore! What more would you
949.   learn?

950.   *Oedipus.* Did you give this man the child he speaks of?

951.   *Herdsman.* I did: would I had died that day!

952.   *Oedipus.* Well, you may come to that unless you speak
953.   the truth.

954.   *Herdsman.* Much more am I lost if I speak it.

955.   *Oedipus.* What! Would the fellow make more delay?

956.   *Herdsman.* No, no. I said before that I gave it to him.

957.   *Oedipus.* Where did you come by it? Your own child,
958.   or another?

959.   *Herdsman.* It was not my own child—I had it from

---

947.   Someone . . . .
948.   . . . ! Wherefore? What . . . **79.**

960. another.

961. *Oedipus.* From any of those here? From what house?

962. *Herdsman.* Do not ask any more, master; for the love
963. of God do not ask.

964. *Oedipus.* You are lost if I have to question you again.

965. *Herdsman.* It was a child from the house of Laius.

966. *Oedipus.* A slave? Or one of his own race?

967. *Herdsman.* Alas! I am on the edge of dreadful words.

968. *Oedipus.* And I of hearing: yet hear I must.

969. *Herdsman.* It was said to have been his own child. But
970. your lady within can tell you of these things best.

971. *Oedipus.* How? It was she who gave it to you?

972. *Herdsman.* Yes, King.

973. *Oedipus.* To what end?

974. *Herdsman.* That I should make away with it.

975. *Oedipus.* Her own child?

976. *Herdsman.* Yes: from fear of evil prophecies.

977. *Oedipus.* What prophecies?

978. *Herdsman.* That he should kill his father.

979. *Oedipus.* Why, then, did you give him up to this old
980. man?

981. *Herdsman.* Through pity, master, believing that he
982. would carry him to whatever land he had himself
983. come from—but he saved him for dreadful misery;
984. for if you are what this man says, you are the most
985. miserable of all men.

---

972. . . . , king. **79.**

986.   *Oedipus.* O! O! All brought to pass! All truth! Now,
987.   O light, may I look my last upon you, having been
988.   found accursed in bloodshed, accursed in marriage,
989.   and in my coming into the world accursed!

[*He rushes into the palace.*

Chorus.

990.   What can the shadow-like generations of man attain
991.   But build up a dazzling mockery of delight that under their
             touch dissolves again?
992.   Oedipus seemed blessed, but there is no man blessed amongst
             men.

993.   Oedipus overcame the woman-breasted Fate;
994.   He seemed like a strong tower against Death and first among
             the fortunate;
995.   He sat upon the ancient throne of Thebes, and all men called
             him great.

996.   But, looking for a marriage-bed, he found the bed of
             his birth,
997.   Tilled the field his father had tilled, cast seed into the same
             abounding earth;
998.   Entered through the door that had sent him wailing
             forth.

999.   Begetter and begot as one! How could that be hid?
1000.   What darkness cover up that marriage-bed? Time watches,
             he is eagle-eyed,
1001.   And all the works of man are known and every soul
             is tried.

1002.   Would you had never come to Thebes, nor to this
             house,
1003.   Nor riddled with the woman-breasted Fate, beaten off Death
             and succoured us,

---

986.   ... ! Now **79, 84.**
987.   ... Light, ... **79.**
995.   ... Thebes and .... **79.**
            [between 995 and 996 no break] **79A.**
996.   ... marriage bed, ... , **79.**
1000.   ... marriage bed? ... , **79.**
1003.   ... death ... , **79.**

1004.   That I had never raised this song, heartbroken Oedipus!

1005. *Second Messenger* [*coming from the house*]. Friends and kins-
1006.   men of this house! What deeds must you look upon,
1007.   what burden of sorrow bear, if true to race you still
1008.   love the House of Labdacus. For not Ister nor Phasis
1009.   could wash this house clean, so many misfortunes
1010.   have been brought upon it, so many has it brought
1011.   upon itself, and those misfortunes are always the
1012.   worst that a man brings upon himself.

1013. *Chorus.* Great already are the misfortunes of this house,
1014.   and you bring us a new tale.

1015. *Second Messenger.* A short tale in the telling: Jocasta, our
1016.   Queen, is dead.

1017. *Chorus.* Alas, miserable woman, how did she die?

1018. *Second Messenger.* By her own hand. It cannot be as
1019.   terrible to you as to one that saw it with his eyes,
1020.   yet so far as words can serve, you shall see it. When
1021.   she had come into the vestibule, she ran half crazed
1022.   towards her marriage-bed, clutching at her hair with
1023.   the fingers of both hands, and once within the
1024.   chamber dashed the doors together behind her. Then
1025.   called upon the name of Laius, long since dead,
1026.   remembering that son who killed the father and upon
1027.   the mother begot an accursed race. And wailed be-
1028.   cause of that marriage wherein she had borne a two-
1029.   fold race—husband by husband, children by her
1030.   child. Then Oedipus with a shriek burst in and
1031.   running here and there asked for a sword, asked
1032.   where he would find the wife that was no wife but
1033.   a mother who had borne his children and himself.
1034.   Nobody answered him, we all stood dumb; but
1035.   supernatural power helped him, for, with a dreadful

1004.   . . . Oedipus. **79.**
1015.   . . . telling; Jocasta, . . .
1016.   queen, ... **79.**
1022.   . . . marriage bed, . . . **79.**
1031.   rushing here . . . **79.**
1035.   . . . him for, . . . **79.**

1036.   shriek, as though beckoned, he sprang at the double
1037.   doors, drove them in, burst the bolts out of their
1038.   sockets, and ran into the room. There we saw the
1039.   woman hanging in a swinging halter, and with a
1040.   terrible cry he loosened the halter from her neck.
1041.   When that unhappiest woman lay stretched upon
1042.   the ground, we saw another dreadful sight. He
1043.   dragged the golden brooches from her dress and lift-
1044.   ing them struck them upon his eyeballs, crying out,
1045.   'You have looked enough upon those you ought
1046.   never to have looked upon, failed long enough to
1047.   know those that you should have known; henceforth
1048.   you shall be dark'. He struck his eyes, not once, but
1049.   many times, lifting his hands and speaking such or
1050.   like words. The blood poured down and not with a
1051.   few slow drops, but all at once over his beard in a
1052.   dark shower as it were hail.

[*The Chorus wails and he steps further on to the stage.*

1053.   Such evils have come forth from the deeds of those
1054.   two and fallen not on one alone but upon husband
1055.   and wife. They inherited much happiness, much good
1056.   fortune; but to-day, ruin, shame, death, and loud cry-
1057.   ing, all evils that can be counted up, all, all are theirs.

1058.   *Chorus.* Is he any quieter?

1059.   *Second Messenger.* He cries for some one to unbar the
1060.   gates and to show to all the men of Thebes his
1061.   father's murderer, his mother's—the unholy word
1062.   must not be spoken. It is his purpose to cast himself
1063.   out of the land that he may not bring all this house
1064.   under his curse. But he has not the strength to do it.
1065.   He must be supported and led away. The curtain
1066.   is parting; you are going to look upon a sight which
1067.   even those who shudder must pity.

Enter Oedipus

1068.   *Oedipus.* Woe, woe is me! Miserable, miserable that I
1069.   am! Where am I? Where am I going? Where am I
1070.   cast away? Who hears my words?

1071.   *Chorus.* Cast away indeed, dreadful to the sight of the

---

1038.   . . . , and rushed into . . . **79.**
1059.   . . . someone . . . **79, 97A.**

1072.   eye, dreadful to the ear.

1073.   *Oedipus.* Ah, friend, the only friend left to me, friend
1074.   still faithful to the blind man! I know that you are
1075.   there; blind though I am, I recognise your voice.

1076.   *Chorus.* Where did you get the courage to put out your
1077.   eyes? What unearthly power drove you to that?

1078.   *Oedipus.* Apollo, friends, Apollo, but it was my own
1079.   hand alone, wretched that I am, that quenched these
1080.   eyes.

1081.   *Chorus.* You were better dead than blind.

1082.   *Oedipus.* No, it is better to be blind. What sight is
1083.   there that could give me joy? How could I have
1084.   looked into the face of my father when I came among
1085.   the dead, aye, or on my miserable mother, since
1086.   against them both I sinned such things that no halter
1087.   can punish? And what to me this spectacle, town,
1088.   statue, wall, and what to me this people, since I,
1089.   thrice wretched, I, noblest of Theban men, have
1090.   doomed myself to banishment, doomed myself when
1091.   I commanded all to thrust out the unclean thing?

1092.   *Chorus.* It had indeed been better if that herdsman had
1093.   never taken your feet out of the spancel or brought
1094.   you back to life.

1095.   *Oedipus.* O three roads, O secret glen; O coppice and
1096.   narrow way where three roads met; you that drank
1097.   up the blood I spilt, the blood that was my own,
1098.   my father's blood: remember what deeds I wrought
1099.   for you to look upon, and then, when I had come
1100.   hither, the new deeds that I wrought. O marriage-

1075.   there blind . . . . **79.**
1076-1077.   [set as two lines of verse ending eyes? / that?] **79.**
1087.   . . . punish. And . . . , **79.**
1089.   . . . , I noblest . . . **79.**
1091.   . . . thing. **79.**
1093.   . . . the bonds or . . . **79.**
1098.   . . . blood; remember . . . **79.**
1100.   , , , marriage **79.**

1101.   bed that gave me birth and after that gave children
1102.   to your child, creating an incestuous kindred of
1103.   fathers, brothers, sons, wives, and mothers. Yes, all
1104.   the shame and the uncleanness that I have wrought
1105.   among men.

1106.   *Chorus.* For all my pity I shudder and turn away.

1107.   *Oedipus.* Come near, condescend to lay your hands upon
1108.   a wretched man; listen, do not fear. My plague can
1109.   touch no man but me. Hide me somewhere out of
1110.   this land for God's sake, or kill me, or throw me into
1111.   the sea where you shall never look upon me more.

Enter Creon and attendants

1112.   *Chorus.* Here Creon comes at a fit moment; you can
1113.   ask of him what you will, help or counsel, for he is
1114.   now in your place. He is King.

1115.   *Oedipus.* What can I say to him? What can I claim,
1116.   having been altogether unjust to him?

1117.   *Creon.* I have not come in mockery, Oedipus, nor to
1118.   reproach you. Lead him in to the house as quickly
1119.   as you can. Do not let him display his misery before
1120.   strangers.

1121.   *Oedipus.* I must obey, but first, since you have come
1122.   in so noble a spirit, you will hear me.

1123.   *Creon.* Say what you will.

1124.   *Oedipus.* I know that you will give her that lies within
1125.   such a tomb as befits your own blood, but there is
1126.   something more, Creon. My sons are men and can
1127.   take care of themselves, but my daughters, my two
1128.   unhappy daughters, that have ever eaten at my own
1129.   table and shared my food, watch over my daughters,
1130.   Creon. If it is lawful, let me touch them with my

1112.   ... moment, you ... **79.**
1114.   ... king. **79.**
1116.   ... him. **97A.**

1131.   hands. Grant it, Prince, grant it, noble heart. I would

1132.   believe, could I touch them, that I still saw them.

                 [Ismene and Antigone are led in by attendants.

1133.   But do I hear them sobbing? Has Creon pitied me

1134.   and sent my children, my darlings? Has he done this?

1135.   *Creon.* Yes, I ordered it, for I know how greatly you

1136.   have always loved them.

1137.   *Oedipus.* Then may you be blessed, and may Heaven be

1138.   kinder to you than it has been to me! My children,

1139.   where are you? Come hither—hither—come to the

1140.   hands of him whose mother was your mother; the

1141.   hands that put out your father's eyes, eyes once as

1142.   bright as your own; his who, understanding nothing,

1143.   seeing nothing, became your father by her that bore

1144.   him. I weep when I think of the bitter life that men

1145.   will make you live, and the days that are to come.

1146.   Into what company dare you go, to what festival,

1147.   but that you shall return home from it not sharing

1148.   in the joys, but bathed in tears? When you are old

1149.   enough to be married, what man dare face the re-

1150.   proach that must cling to you and to your children?

1151.   What misery is there lacking? Your father killed his

1152.   father, he begat you at the spring of his own being,

1153.   offspring of her that bore him. That is the taunt that

1154.   would be cast upon you and on the man that you

1155.   should marry. That man is not alive; my children,

1156.   you must wither away in barrenness. Ah, son of

1157.   Menoeceus, listen. Seeing that you are the only father

1158.   now left to them, for we their parents are lost, both

1159.   of us lost, do not let them wander in beggary—are

1160.   they not your own kindred?—do not let them sink

1161.   down into my misery. No, pity them, seeing them

1162.   utterly wretched in helpless childhood if you do not

1163.   protect them. Show me that you promise, generous

1164.   man, by touching me with your hand. *[Creon touches*

1131.   . . . , prince, . . .

1132.   believe could . . . them that . . . . **79.**

1138.   . . . me. My . . . , **79.**

1142.   . . . ; his, who understanding . . . , **79.**

1148.   . . . tears. When . . . **79.**

1165.　　*him.*] My children, there is much advice that I would
1166.　　give you were you but old enough to understand, but
1167.　　all I can do now is bid you pray that you may live
1168.　　wherever you are let live, and that your life be
1169.　　happier than your father's.

1170.　*Creon.* Enough of tears. Pass into the house.

1171.　*Oedipus.* I will obey, though upon conditions.

1172.　*Creon.* Conditions?

1173.　*Oedipus.* Banish me from this country. I know that
1174.　　nothing can destroy me, for I wait some incredible
1175.　　fate; yet cast me upon Cithaeron, chosen by my
1176.　　father and my mother for my tomb.

1177.　*Creon.* Only the Gods can say yes or no to that.

1178.　*Oedipus.* No, for I am hateful to the Gods.

1179.　*Creon.* If that be so you will get your wish the quicker.
1180.　　They will banish that which they hate.

1181.　*Oedipus.* Are you certain of that?

1182.　*Creon.* I would not say it if I did not mean it.

1183.　*Oedipus.* Then it is time to lead me within.

1184.　*Creon.* Come, but let your children go.

1185.　*Oedipus.* No, do not take them from me.

1186.　*Creon.* Do not seek to be master; you won the mastery
1187.　　but could not keep it to the end.

　　　　　[*He leads Oedipus into the palace, followed by Ismene, Antigone,
　　　　　and attendants.*

Chorus

1188.　　Make way for Oedipus. All people said,
1189.　　'That is a fortunate man';

1177.　. . . gods . . . .
1178.　. . . gods. **79.**
1188.　. . . said **79.**

1190. And now what storms are beating on his head!
1191. Call no man fortunate that is not dead.
1192. The dead are free from pain.

THE END

1190. . . . head? **79.**
1190a. 'That is a fortunate man'; **97A.**

NOTES

This version of Sophocles' play was written for Dublin players, for Dublin liturgical singers, for a small auditorium, for a chorus that must stand stock still where the orchestra are accustomed to put their chairs, for an audience where nobody comes for self-improvement or for anything but emotion. In other words, I put readers and scholars out of my mind and wrote to be sung and spoken. The one thing that I kept in mind was that a word unfitted for living speech, out of its natural order, or unnecessary to our modern technique, would check emotion and tire attention.

Years ago I persuaded Florence Farr to so train the chorus for a Greek play that the sung words were almost as intelligible and dramatic as the spoken; and I have commended that art of hers in *Speaking to the Psaltery*. I asked my Dublin producer Lennox Robinson to disregard that essay, partly because liturgical singers were there to his hand, but mainly because if a chorus stands stock still in half shadow music and singing should, perhaps, possess a variety of rhythm and pitch incompatible with dramatic intelligible words. The main purpose of the chorus is to preserve the mood while it rests the mind by change of attention. A producer who has a space below the level of the stage, where a chorus can move about an altar, may do well to experiment with that old thought of mine and keep his singers as much in the range of the speaking voice as if they sang 'The west's awake,' or sang round a binnacle. However, he has his own singers to think of and must be content with what comes to hand.

June 1st.   W. B. YEATS.
                                                    Preface to **79.**

*   *   *

Variant spellings

Cithaeron **97**; *Cythaeron* **79, 84.**
Istar **79, 84**; *Ister* **97.**
Labdacus **97**; *Labdicus* **79, 84.**
Loxias **79, 97**; *Loxius* **79** (both spellings), **84.**
Polybius **79, 84**; *Polybus* **97.**
tousel-headed **84**; *tousle-headed* **97**; *towsel-headed* **79.**

SOPHOCLES' OEDIPUS AT COLONUS

A Version for the Modern Stage

1934

Persons in the Play

Oedipus	Creon, King of Thebes, *brother-*
Antigone ⎱ *daughters of Oedipus*	*in-law of Oedipus*
Ismene ⎰	A Stranger
Polyneices, *son of Oedipus*	A Messenger
Theseus, King of Athens	Chorus
Servants and Soldiers	

SCENE

The neighbourhood of Athens, near a shrine

1. *Oedipus.* To what town or country have we come, Anti-
2. gone? Who to-day gives alms to the blind man, to
3. wandering Oedipus? I ask little and get less and am
4. content; where there is nobility of character suffer-
5. ing teaches patience, and we have been long enough
6. together to learn that lesson. Bring me, daughter,
7. to some place, to some sacred place perhaps, where
8. we can rest and speak to a passer-by, and find out
9. where we are and what we are to do. We must do
10. whatever they bid us.

11. *Antigone.* I can see the distant towers of a city, and this
12. place seems to be sacred; it is shaded with laurels,
13. olives and vines, and nightingales are singing. So sit
14. down upon this stone; you have travelled far for an
15. old man.

16. *Oedipus.* Seat me upon it and keep a watch over the
17. blind man.

18. *Antigone.* I have no need to learn that.

19. *Oedipus.* Where are we?

20. *Antigone*. I do not know this place, but the town I see
21.   is Athens.

22. *Oedipus*. Every passer-by has told us that.

23. *Antigone*. Shall I find somebody to tell us where we
24.   are?

25. *Oedipus*. Yes, child, if the place is inhabited.

26. *Antigone*. Inhabited it certainly is, but I need not
27.   search: somebody is coming.

28. *Oedipus*. Coming towards us?

29. *Antigone*. He is already beside us; ask whatever you
30.   want to know.

Enter Stranger, a man of Colonus

31. *Oedipus*. Stranger, this girl who has sight both for her-
32.   self and for me tells me that you are there. There is
33.   something I would ask.

34. *Stranger*. Get up from that seat before you ask it. You
35.   are in a place where no man is permitted to set his
36.   foot.

37. *Oedipus*. What place? And to what God sacred?

38. *Stranger*. A place where none may set his foot, for it
39.   belongs to the Dreadful Goddesses, daughters of the
40.   earth and of darkness.

41. *Oedipus*. I will pray to them if you tell me their names.

42. *Stranger*. We natives call them the Furies, but there
43.   are pleasanter names.

44. *Oedipus*. I beseech them to be gracious to me and to
45.   welcome me, for never will I leave this place.

46. *Stranger*. What do you mean by those words?

TEXT

27.   search; somebody . . . . **97A.**

47. *Oedipus.* My fate.

48. *Stranger.* I cannot remove you by force until I have
49.   reported to the authorities and got their warrant.

50. *Oedipus.* Seeing that I am an unlucky wanderer, do not
51.   for God's love refuse to answer my questions.

52. *Stranger.* Question and I will answer.

53. *Oedipus.* Into what manner of country have I come?

54. *Stranger.* The whole neighbourhood is sacred, sacred to
55.   Poseidon and to Prometheus the Firebringer; but the
56.   spot where you are seated protects Athens and is
57.   called the Brazen Threshold. And the first Lord of
58.   the Manor was named Colonus, and all his people
59.   bear his name as well as their own. Such is this
60.   neighbourhood. It is not famous in history, but it
61.   is dear to those that inhabit it.

62. *Oedipus.* So, then, there are inhabitants?

63. *Stranger.* Yes, all that bear the name of that settler.

64. *Oedipus.* Have they a king? Or do they decide every-
65.   thing for themselves?

66. *Stranger.* The King of Athens rules them.

67. *Oedipus.* What is his name?

68. *Stranger.* Theseus, son of Aegeus.

69. *Oedipus.* Could some one go to him with a message?

70. *Stranger.* With what object? To bring him here?

71. *Oedipus.* That he may win a great profit by doing a
72.   small service.

73. *Stranger.* What profit can he get from a blind man?

74. *Oedipus.* My words shall not be blind.

75. *Stranger.* Attend to what I say, friend. If I can judge
76.   by a man's looks and not by his clothes, you are

77. no common man. I would not have you get into
78. trouble. I will send no messenger to the town, but I
79. will say what you have said to the neighbours; and
80. so stay there where I found you until they decide
81. whether you may stay there or not.

[*The Stranger goes out.*

82. *Oedipus.* Is that man gone?

83. *Antigone.* He is gone: say whatever comes into your
84. head; no ear listens but mine.

85. *Oedipus.* Dreadful apparitions, Furies, Queens, your
86. shrine is the first in this land at which I have bent
87. my knees; therefore be gracious to me and gracious
88. to the God Phoebus. When he proclaimed my doom,
89. my countless sorrows, the God proclaimed that after
90. many years I should come to a shrine of yours and
91. find there rest, hospitality, and death, and bring
92. good fortune to those that did me good, and ruin
93. upon those that had driven me into wandering.
94. Furthermore, he warned me that thunder and light-
95. ning and earthquake would announce my death. If
96. I am not too base for your notice, Queens, I who
97. have borne the worst burden in the world, and if it
98. has been by your guidance, as I think, that I have
99. found this sacred wood, fulfil the words of Phoebus
100. and show me how to bring all to an end. Dear
101. daughters of ancient darkness, and Athens, most
102. honoured among cities, have mercy upon this ghost
103. of Oedipus, upon this ghost, for the man Oedipus
104. is dead, the man men knew.

105. *Antigone.* Hush. Some old men are coming, doubtless
106. to ask what we are doing here.

107. *Oedipus.* I will be silent, but lead me into the wood
108. and away from the road, till we have learnt what their
109. intentions are.

[*She leads him into the wood. The Elders of Colonus, the Chorus, enter as if searching for some one. At first there are confused voices, then one man speaks for all. Where the words are in rhyme all may join in the singing.*

110. *Chorus.* Where is he gone? Where has he hidden him-
111. self? Look carefully, search every place, for this must

112. be the most insolent man alive. He must be a
113. foreigner, a man from a distant country. No native
114. would dare to enter this untrodden wood, profane a
115. spot sacred to the apparitions whose very name we
116. dare not speak. A shrine which we pass turning our
117. eyes away, and pray to so silently that we dare not
118. even move our lips.

119. *Oedipus [led from his hiding-place by Antigone].* I am the
120.   man you are looking for. I can see with the mind's
121.   eye but have no other sight.

122. *Chorus.* O! O! Dreadful to look upon!

123. *Oedipus.* Do not consider me a lawless man.

124. *Chorus.* God protect us! Who is this old man?

125. *Oedipus.* Not so fortunate a man that you need envy
126.   him. This girl lets me walk with her strength and
127.   look through her eyes.

128. *Chorus.* Alas! Have you been blind from birth? Your
129.   life has indeed been accursed, and as it seems to me
130.   long, but do not add a new curse to the other. I can
131.   save you from that at any rate. Turn back from there
132.   before you have wandered into the silent depths of
133.   the wood where the sacred pool is. Come back.
134.   Come back. Do you not hear me, road-weary man?
135.   If you have anything to say to us, come first out of
136.   that forbidden spot, come to some place where it
137.   is lawful to speak, but keep silent until you have
138.   found it.

139. *Oedipus.* How shall we answer him, daughter?

140. *Antigone.* We must obey the customs of this place,
141.   listening to its people, and, as far as we can, doing
142.   what they ask.

143. *Oedipus.* Then give me your hand.

144. *Antigone.* I put it into yours.

---

112. . . . most insolent man . . . **97A.**
121. eye that have . . . . **97A.**

145. *Oedipus.* No one dare touch me while I stand upon this
146.   spot. Promise me, therefore, that when I leave it
147.   and put myself into your hands I shall not suffer
148.   injury.

149. *Chorus.* We promise that, old man.

               [Oedipus begins to move froward and then stops.

150. *Oedipus.* Further?

151. *Chorus.* Yes, still further.

152. *Oedipus.* Further yet?

153. *Chorus.* Lead him further yet, lady.

154. *Antigone.* Follow me as I lead.

155. *Chorus.* We would have you learn what our people hate
156.   that you may hate it also, and what we reverence
157.   that you may reverence it also.

158. *Oedipus.* Lead on, child, to some spot where I may
159.   speak and hear, for I would hear what is customary,
160.   and so not set myself up against fate.

    [Oedipus is brought to a ledge of rock at the edge of the road.

161. *Chorus.* Stay your feet at that edge of rock.

162. *Oedipus.* Have I gone far enough?

163. *Chorus.* I tell you that is far enough.

164. *Oedipus.* Shall I sit down?

165. *Chorus.* Move him sideways and put him down on the
166.   edge of the rock.

167. *Antigone.* This is my work; father, step carefully.

                        [Oedipus groans.

168. *Antigone.* Another step; lean your old body upon my
169.   arm.

170. *Oedipus.* It is a dreadful thing to be blind.

              [Antigone seats him upon the rock.

171. *Chorus.* Tell me now, unhappy man, what your name
172.   is, in what country you were born, and from what
173.   country you come.

174. *Oedipus.* I am an exile, strangers, but forbear.

175. *Chorus.* From what would you have us forbear, old
176.   man?

177. *Oedipus.* From asking my name, from asking anything.

178. *Chorus.* Why do you say that?

179. *Oedipus.* My birth was horrible.

180. *Chorus.* You must answer.

181. *Oedipus* [*to Antigone*]. My child, what am I to say?

182. *Chorus.* Who was your father, stranger? And of what
183.   family?

184. *Oedipus.* O misery, misery, what will become of me,
185.   my child?

186. *Antigone.* Speak: necessity compels it.

187. *Oedipus.* I will speak, if speak I must.

188. *Chorus.* You make a great delay between you; come,
189.   speak out.

190. *Oedipus.* I am the son of Laius—[*cry from the Chorus*]
191.   and my family the Labdacidae.

192. *Chorus.* O God!

193. *Oedipus.* And my name Oedipus.

194. *Chorus.* That man!

195. *Oedipus.* But why should my words make you afraid?
       [*The Chorus half turn away, cover their eyes with their cloaks, and
       cry out.*]

196. *Oedipus.* Miserable that I am! [*Clamour goes on.*]
197.　　Daughter, what is going to happen?

198. *Chorus.* Away with you, away out of this land!

199. *Oedipus.* And your promise? Will you not keep your
200.　　promise?

201. *Chorus.* The Gods do not punish any man for doing to
202.　　another what that other has done to him. You knew
203.　　I did not know your name; you let me promise in
204.　　ignorance of that, and so I but pay deceit by deceit.
205.　　Get you gone from this sacred spot, and gone from
206.　　this neighbourhood before you have brought a curse
207.　　upon it.

208. *Antigone.* Strangers, good honourable men, you will not
209.　　listen to my father because of what he did against
210.　　his will, but you should have compassion upon me;
211.　　there is nothing to set me apart from you! I can still
212.　　look at you with eyes that might be those of your
213.　　own kin, and I beseech you that you may have com-
214.　　passion also upon this old man. We come to you in
215.　　our misery as if you were a God—no, do not turn
216.　　away—we scarce dare hope; and yet grant our prayer.
217.　　I implore you by everything that you hold dear, by
218.　　wife, by child, by your home, by the God you
219.　　worship. My father was driven on by a God; how
220.　　could he help himself?

221. *Chorus.* We pity your father and you his daughter, we
222.　　pity both alike; you have shared misfortune to-
223.　　gether: but we dread the anger of the Gods and can-
224.　　not add anything to what we have already said.

225. *Oedipus.* It is said that Athens of all the cities of the
226.　　world has most will and power to succour and protect
227.　　the exile, but that is fame and therefore but a breath
228.　　of wind. You persuaded me to leave the rocky place
229.　　where none dared touch me that you might drive me
230.　　from your country. Was that succour and protection?
231.　　What are you afraid of? What can I do against you?
232.　　My life has been suffering, not doing. I need not tell
233.　　you that story of my father and my mother; you
234.　　know it already: it has put terror into you. But tell
235.　　me this, how does it prove my nature evil? Even had
236.　　I struck my father knowingly it would have been in

237.   self-defence, and I did it in ignorance; but the men
238.   that wronged me knew all that they did. Remember,
239.   strangers, that I left under a promise a place where the
240.   Gods protected me, and that if you do not keep your
241.   promise you do dishonour to those Gods, and the
242.   Gods know well how to separate those that do them
243.   honour from those that do not, and what man ever
244.   made them angry and prospered afterwards? Give the
245.   Gods their due, avoid what would blast the fair name
246.   of Athens. Do not despise me because my face is
247.   maimed and hideous. I came to you as a suppliant, I
248.   hold your pledge, fulfil that pledge. To you at any
249.   rate I should be sacred, for I can bring luck to all
250.   this neighbourhood if I have a mind to. When your
251.   master comes, whatever his name be, I shall explain
252.   my meaning; and as for the rest, see that you are not
253.   treacherous.

254. *Chorus.* You have spoken words that fill me with awe.
255.   I cannot understand, for they are full of hints and
256.   mysteries, but it is for my betters to find out their
257.   meaning.

258. *Oedipus.* Where is your master, strangers?

259. *Chorus.* At Athens, and the messenger who has brought
260.   us here has gone to fetch him. We sent him when
261.   you named yourself.

262. *Oedipus.* Do you think that he will come, that he will
263.   have respect enough for a blind man to come him-
264.   self?

265. *Chorus.* Yes, certainly; for he will hear your name.
266.   Your name has gone through all countries, and what-
267.   ever he is doing, resting or working, he will put it
268.   aside and come upon the instant.

269. *Oedipus.* May he act so that he may call down a blessing
270.   not upon me alone but upon his city! Only a fool is
271.   his own enemy.

272. *Antigone.* O God! Can I believe my own eyes? Can I
273.   be mistaken?

274. *Oedipus.* What is it, my child? What is it, Antigone?

275. *Antigone.* A girl in a Thessalian sunbonnet upon one of
276.   those young horses from Etna. But can it be she, or
277.   does my sight deceive me? Is it all my imagination?
278.   No, I cannot be certain, but it is, it is; she is waving
279.   her hand. She is flinging herself from her horse. She
280.   is here.

Enter Ismene

281. *Oedipus.* What are you saying, child?

282. *Antigone.* It is your daughter and my sister, Ismene.
283.   You will know in a moment, for she is going to
284.   speak.

285. *Ismene.* Father and sister, I had a long search before I
286.   found you—you who are more dear to me than any-
287.   body in the world,—and now can hardly see because
288.   of my tears.

289. *Oedipus.* You have come, my child.

290. *Ismene.* Old man, you have had a dreadful life.

291. *Oedipus.* But you are here, my child.

292. *Ismene.* Yes, after much toil.

293. *Oedipus.* Touch me, my daughter.

294. *Ismene.* A hand for both of you.

295. *Oedipus.* Children—sisters.

296. *Ismene.* Yes, child and sister, a twice wretched life.

297. *Oedipus.* Her life and mine.

298. *Ismene.* Mine also.

299. *Oedipus.* Child, what has brought you?

300. *Ismene.* Care for you, father.

---

285.   . . . had long . . . **97A.**

301. *Oedipus.* That you may see me?

302. *Ismene.* Yes, and because there is news that I cannot
303.   trust to any mouth but my own.

304. *Oedipus.* Your brothers might have brought it.

305. *Ismene.* They are—where they are. It is their dark hour.

306. *Oedipus.* Their dark hour? A true saying, for both in
307.   character and in life they are like those Egyptians
308.   who send out their wives to earn their daily bread
309.   but keep the house themselves. My daughters carry
310.   their father's burden while their brothers stay at
311.   home in comfort like women. One, since she came
312.   into a woman's strength, has been the guide of the
313.   old blind man. Often hungry and barefoot, often
314.   vexed by rain or summer's heat, often travel-weary
315.   amid waste places; and always that her father might
316.   have protection, indifferent to her own comfort. And
317.   you, my child, have been my messenger and my
318.   watcher, bringing, unknown to the men of Thebes,
319.   every oracle that touched upon my fate. And now
320.   what news, what message, what oracle have you
321.   brought? What words of terror? For you have not
322.   come empty-handed.

323. *Ismene.* I went through much before I found you, father,
324.   but let that pass, for I will not talk of myself but of
325.   the misfortunes that afflict your two sons. I have
326.   come to tell you of those misfortunes. At first they
327.   had only one thought, to save the city from the curse
328.   our family has brought upon it; that it might escape
329.   further pollution they made no claim upon the throne
330.   but let Creon have it. But now, driven mad by some
331.   God or stirred up by their own wickedness, they
332.   have both claimed the throne. The younger, and
333.   therefore the more excitable of the two, has seized
334.   it and driven the elder son Polyneices into banish-
335.   ment; but he, or so it has been rumoured, is in Argos,
336.   and has gathered soldiers there. He plans to bring
337.   Thebes under the rule of Argos. I have brought you
338.   an evil tale, father; when will the Gods have pity
339.   upon you?

340. *Oedipus.* You still hope that they will have pity?

341. *Ismene.* Yes, father, I have that hope. There have been
342.   new oracles.

343. *Oedipus.* What are they? What has been foretold that
344.   I can fix my hopes upon?

345. *Ismene.* A day will come when the men of Thebes will
346.   long for the living man that he may bequeath to them
347.   his bones.

348. *Oedipus.* So they know it at last, know that I am good
349.   still for something.

350. *Ismene.* You shall make them strong or weak as you
351.   please.

352. *Oedipus.* I have been made into nothing; am I to be
353.   made into a man once more?

354. *Ismene.* Yes, the Gods unmade you and the Gods re-
355.   make you.

356. *Oedipus.* A poor gift to a man to abase his youth and
357.   exalt his age.

358. *Ismene.* However that may be, Creon is coming to talk
359.   of these things and may be here sooner than you
360.   think.

361. *Oedipus.* What brings him, daughter?

362. *Ismene.* To set you somewhere outside the Theban
363.   border, yet near enough to be within their power.

364. *Oedipus.* What good can I do beyond the border?

365. *Ismene.* If an enemy's country possess your bones, they
366.   will bring it victory.

367. *Oedipus.* So the oracle has spoken at last.

368. *Ismene.* Yes, you must not be your own master, so they
369.   will have you for a neighbour but not for a Theban.

370. *Oedipus.* But if I die in that place, will they bury me
371.   in Theban earth?

372. *Ismene.* No, father, they dread pollution.

373. *Oedipus.* Then never shall they be my masters.

374. *Ismene.* A day is coming when that shall be a great
375.   grief to Thebes.

376. *Oedipus.* What do you know of that?

377. *Ismene.* They will come in arms and you will blast them
378.   from the tomb.

379. *Oedipus.* Where had you these things, child?

380. *Ismene.* I had them from the messengers of Delphi.

381. *Oedipus.* Yes; Apollo has said these things?

382. *Ismene.* Men went from Thebes to Delphi and brought
383.   back the news.

384. *Oedipus.* Do my sons know it?

385. *Ismene.* Both. They know it well.

386. *Oedipus.* Then they are base indeed not to have used
387.   the oracle for my recall.

388. *Ismene.* And not to the border but into the city itself.

389. *Oedipus.* They are afraid of offending; they think more
390.   of the kingship and of their struggle for it than of
391.   their own father.

392. *Ismene.* Your words fill me with grief, but I cannot
393.   contradict you.

394. *Oedipus.* Then may no God turn them from this war,
395.   may spear meet spear till I blast them from the tomb!
396.   I shall permit neither the son that now holds the
397.   throne to keep his throne, nor the son that is banished
398.   to return. They neither raised up their hands nor their
399.   voices to defend me driven out to shame and wander-
400.   ing. Say if you will that when the city drove me out
401.   it did the very thing I asked of it. No, I say, no!
402.   Upon that first day, when my soul was all in tumult
403.   and the dearest wish of my heart was to die, though

404. I were to be stoned to death, no man would grant me
405. my desire; but later on, when a long time had passed,
406. when the tumult in my soul had passed, when I
407. began to feel that in my anger against myself I had
408. asked for punishments beyond my deserts, the city
409. drove me out. My sons, who might have hindered,
410. did nothing, though one word could have changed
411. everything, and I their father was driven out to
412. wander through my whole life as a beggar and an
413. outcast. I owe my daily bread and whatever I have
414. found of care and shelter to my daughters, to these
415. two girls. Their brothers have preferred the mob's
416. favour; yes, they have trafficked with it and bartered
417. away their father for throne and sceptre. Never,
418. never shall Oedipus be ally of one or the other,
419. never shall the throne of Thebes be lucky to one or
420. the other. I meditate upon the new prophecies the
421. girl has brought, and when I speak, Phoebus Apollo
422. speaks. Nor shall I help the men of Thebes whether
423. it be Creon that they send or any other that may be
424. great amongst them. But, strangers, if you are willing
425. to help, if these Dreadful Goddesses are willing, I
426. shall deliver your country from all its enemies.

427. *Chorus.* Who could refuse compassion to Oedipus and
428. his daughters?—and you have added another claim
429. upon us, that you can deliver this country. Yet I have
430. advice to give, and you shall be the better for it.

431. *Oedipus.* Advise me, sir, and whatever that advice be I
432. shall take it.

433. *Chorus.* Make prayer and atonement to the Dark God-
434. desses, for you have trespassed upon their ground.

435. *Oedipus.* How shall I go about it, stranger?

436. *Chorus.* Draw water from the spring well over there.

437. *Oedipus.* And when I have drawn the water?

438. *Chorus.* There are three bowls made by a famous potter.

439. *Oedipus.* Yes; what must I do?

440. *Chorus.* Pour out three streams of water, facing to the
441. spot where the sun rises.

442. *Oedipus.* A stream from each bowl?

443. *Chorus.* Yes; and be careful to empty the last bowl
444.   completely.

445. *Oedipus.* And when the earth has drunk it?

446. *Chorus.* Put three times nine sprays from an olive-tree
447.   upon that earth, and pray.

448. *Oedipus.* What are the words that I must say? That is
449.   what chiefly matters.

450. *Chorus.* Remind them to be good to suppliants, seeing
451.   that they are called the Good People, and then pray
452.   for whatever you most need, but do not move your
453.   lips, or if you move your lips do not permit them to
454.   make any sound, and having prayed come from the
455.   place without looking behind you. Do this, and I will
456.   help you all I can.

457. *Oedipus.* These are men of the neighbourhood, daugh-
458.   ters; you have heard them.

459. *Antigone.* We have heard them; what would you have
460.   us do?

461. *Oedipus.* I cannot go, for I have neither sight nor
462.   strength, but let one of you two go, for I think that
463.   one can perform a rite of this kind. If it be done with
464.   goodwill, one can make an atonement for ten thou-
465.   sand men. Go quickly, but one must remain here,
466.   for I am helpless without a guide.

467. *Ismene.* I will go. I will perform the rite, but where
468.   shall I find the spot? Direct me.

469. *Chorus.* On the further side of the wood, lady, and
470.   there is a custodian of the shrine who has everything
471.   that you will want.

472. *Ismene.* Take care of our father, Antigone, until I re-
473.   turn.   [*She goes.*

474. *Chorus.* It is a terrible thing, stranger, to stir that old
475.   grief of yours, but there are things I long to know.

476. *Oedipus.* Must I tell all again?

477. *Chorus.* I am thinking of that heavy sorrow, that sorrow
478.   for which there is no cure, of all that heavy burden
479.   which you have borne.

480. *Oedipus.* You should be too considerate to probe into
481.   my shame; am I not your guest?

482. *Chorus.* I only speak of it because that tale has gone
483.   everywhere. I would know the true facts.

484. *Oedipus.* O misery!

485. *Chorus.* Do not deny me.

486. *Oedipus.* Misery! Misery!

487. *Chorus.* I have answered all your questions.

488. *Oedipus.* Every misfortune that I have suffered came
489.   from what I did in ignorance. I swear to God that I
490.   did nothing of my own will.

491. *Chorus.* How did that come about?

492. *Oedipus.* Thebes gave me the wife that brought the
493.   curse upon me. I knew nothing.

494. *Chorus.* Is it true then that you lay with your own
495.   mother?

496. *Oedipus.* O misery! For you have spoken words that are
497.   cruel as death, and those two girls that I begot—

498. *Chorus.* What is it that you say?

499. *Oedipus.* Those two daughters, those two curses.

500. *Chorus.* O God!

501. *Oedipus.* The womb that bore me bore them also.

502. *Chorus.* They are at once your children and—

503. *Oedipus.* My children and my sisters!

504. *Chorus.* O horror!

505. *Oedipus.* Horror indeed, every horror has again swept
506. back upon me; my soul is drowned.

507. *Chorus.* You have suffered.

508. *Oedipus.* Suffered dreadful things.

509. *Chorus.* But you have sinned.

510. *Oedipus.* Sinned without knowledge.

511. *Chorus.* I do not understand.

512. *Oedipus.* I tell you that Thebes gave her to me. Would
513. that I had never served that city, never been re-
514. warded by it, miserable that I am.

515. *Chorus.* But that is not all the tale; there was somebody
516. that you killed.

517. *Oedipus.* So you must still question?

518. *Chorus.* You killed your own father!

519. *Oedipus.* Another stab! Have I not suffered enough?

520. *Chorus.* You killed him!

521. *Oedipus.* Yes; but I can plead—

522. *Chorus.* What can you plead?

523. *Oedipus.* And plead justly.

524. *Chorus.* And what can you plead?

525. *Oedipus.* That those whom I slew would have taken my
526. own life, and that therefore I am innocent before the
527. law. No evil intent brought me into this misery.

528. *Chorus.* Our King Theseus comes, summoned by the
529. messenger. Theseus, son of Aegeus, will hear and
630. judge all that you have to say.

Enter Theseus

531. *Theseus.* Son of Laius, I have long known you by hear-
532. say and of the cruel putting out of your eyes, and
533. now you stand visible before me, a ragged man with
534. a disfigured face. I am full of compassion, Oedipus; I
535. have come to find out why you have taken up your
536. stand in this place, you and this luckless girl, and
537. what you would ask of Athens and of myself? I will
538. not refuse it, for I myself have been in exile, nor has
539. any living man been in greater peril of his life than
540. I. Never will I reject such a wanderer; what am I but
541. a man, and I may suffer to-morrow what you suffer
542. to-day.

543. *Oedipus.* Theseus, you have put great nobleness into a
544. few words, and why should I speak many words?
545. You have named me aright and named my father
546. aright, and you know from what land I come; I will
547. say what I must and so finish the tale.

548. *Theseus.* Say it, for I am all ears.

549. *Oedipus.* I offer you as a gift this battered body; though
550. hideous to look upon, it brings a blessing greater
551. than beauty.

552. *Theseus.* What blessing?

553. *Oedipus.* That you shall know later.

554. *Theseus.* But the blessing? When does it come?

555. *Oedipus.* When I am dead and you have given me a
556. grave.

557. *Theseus.* That is the last gift of all, the last service
558. hands can do. Is there nothing that you would have
559. between this and then?

560. *Oedipus.* Nothing. Give me that and I have all the rest.

561. *Theseus.* This is a trifling thing you ask.

562. *Oedipus.* It is no trifling thing. Weigh well what you
563. do; it will stir up rancour.

564. *Theseus.* What? Between your sons and me?

565. *Oedipus.* Yes, and before you bury me.

566. *Theseus.* How could that be?

567. *Oedipus.* They may come to carry me to Thebes.

568. *Theseus.* But if they come, why remain in exile?

569. *Oedipus.* When I would, they would not.

570. *Theseus.* It is folly to make ill-fortune worse by temper.

571. *Oedipus.* Blame me when you have heard my story, not
572.   before.

573. *Theseus.* Speak. I would not blame you from ignorance.

574. *Oedipus.* I have suffered an unheard-of wrong.

575. *Theseus.* You mean that ancient misery?

576. *Oedipus.* No. Who in all Hellas but knows that?

577. *Theseus.* What new grief is this that no man has seen
578.   the like of?

579. *Oedipus.* I have been driven from my country by my
580.   own children, banished by them as my father's
581.   murderer.

582. *Theseus.* Then why should they come to fetch you?

583. *Oedipus.* Compelled by an oracle from the God.

584. *Theseus.* Because of some misfortune it foretells?

585. *Oedipus.* That they shall be conquered if they do not,
586.   conquered by Athens.

587. *Theseus.* Why should Thebes and Athens fight? What
588.   can disturb the friendship between myself and
589.   Thebes?

590. *Oedipus.* Friendly son of Aegeus, the Gods neither grow
591.   old nor die, but all else is subject to change. Bodily
592.   strength and earth's fertility decay, man's trust in
593.   man dies out and enmity takes its place. Not even

594. the best of friends can keep in the same mood to-
595. ward one another, nor can city toward city, for be it
596. soon or late men find the bitter better than the sweet,
597. and then again, it may be, turn to the sweet. All is
598. sweet to-day between Thebes and you, but the known
599. goes and the unknown comes in its stead, and men
600. take to the spear for any trifle. My body shall be
601. asleep and buried, and yet, if Phoebus, son of God,
602. spoke truth and God be God, it shall, though cold
603. in death, drink hot Theban blood. But these are
604. mysteries I may not speak. Ask no more. I end the
605. tale where I began it—do that which you have
606. promised and you shall not, unless the God has
607. cheated me, make Oedipus welcome and get nothing
608. in return.

609. *Chorus*. From the first moment, King, he has promised
610. this or some like thing.

611. *Theseus*. Who would reject the friendship of such a
612. man? His house and mine are ancient allies, he pro-
613. mises great gifts to our city, and he is the suppliant
614. of the Gods. I cannot refuse what he asks. I admit
615. his claim and establish him as citizen amongst us.
616. Whatever choice you make, Oedipus, whether to
617. remain here under the protection of these men or to
618. live with me in my own house, your will shall be
619. my will.

620. *Oedipus*. The blessing of God upon such men as this!

621. *Theseus*. What is your decision? Will you come into my
622. house?

623. *Oedipus*. I would were it lawful—but this is the place.

624. *Theseus*. The place for what? I will not thwart you—

625. *Oedipus*. To vanquish those that drove me out, and to
626. blast them from the ground.

627. *Theseus*. Your presence may bring us a great destiny.

628. *Oedipus*. It shall—if you keep faith.

629. *Theseus*. Have no fear of that—I shall not fail you.

630. *Oedipus*. I will not bind you with an oath as we bind
631.   unworthy men.

632. *Theseus*. You would have gained nothing if you had;
633.   my word is my oath.

634. *Oedipus*. What will you do? How will you keep faith?

635. *Theseus*. What do you fear?

636. *Oedipus*. Men will come.

637. *Theseus*. There are those here who will see to that.

638. *Oedipus*. Beware—for if you leave me—

639. *Theseus*. It is not for you to teach me my business.

640. *Oedipus*. My fear drives me on.

641. *Theseus*. I see nothing to be afraid of.

642. *Oedipus*. You do not know what they have threatened.

643. *Theseus*. Let these Thebans threaten as they will, there
644.   shall be foul weather between the threat and the act.
645.   Be of good courage. If God sent you hither, you need
646.   no protection of mine, but God or no God my mere
647.   name will protect.   [*Theseus goes out.*

Chorus

648.   Come praise Colonus' horses, and come praise
649.   The wine-dark of the wood's intricacies,
650.   The nightingale that deafens daylight there,
651.   If daylight ever visit where,
652.   Unvisited by tempest or by sun,
653.   Immortal ladies tread the ground
654.   Dizzy with harmonious sound,
655.   Semele's lad a gay companion.

656.   And yonder in the gymnasts' garden thrives
657.   The self-sown, self-begotten shape that gives

658.   Athenian intellect its mastery,
659.   Even the grey-leaved olive-tree
660.   Miracle-bred out of the living stone;
661.   Nor accident of peace nor war
662.   Shall wither that old marvel, for
663.   The great grey-eyed Athene stares thereon.

664.   Who comes into this country, and has come
665.   Where golden crocus and narcissus bloom,
666.   Where the Great Mother, mourning for her daughter
667.   And beauty-drunken by the water
668.   Glittering among grey-leaved olive-trees,
669.   Has plucked a flower and sung her loss;
670.   Who finds abounding Cephisus
671.   Has found the loveliest spectacle there is.

672.   Because this country has a pious mind
673.   And so remembers that when all mankind
674.   But trod the road, or splashed about the shore,
675.   Poseidon gave it bit and oar,
676.   Every Colonus lad or lass discourses
677.   Of that oar and of that bit;
678.   Summer and winter, day and night,
679.   Of horses and horses of the sea, white horses.

680. *Antigone.* O country that all men praise, the time has
681.   come to pay for praise.

682. *Oedipus.* Why do you say that? What has happened,
683.   daughter?

684. *Antigone.* To pay with deeds—Creon approaches, with
685.   many at his heels.

686. *Oedipus.* Kind old men, prove that I am safe indeed.

687. *Chorus.* You shall have that proof. Put away all fear;
688.   though age has robbed me of my strength my country
689.   is as strong as ever.

Enter Creon with attendants

690. *Creon.* Sirs, worthy countrymen, my coming has alarmed
691.   you; I can see it by your eyes. Why do you shrink
692.   away? I have no hostile purpose. I come, an old man,
693.   to the strongest city in all Greece; I come, old as I
694.   am, to persuade that man there to return to Thebes.
695.   And I have been sent, not by any one man, but by the

696.   whole people, chosen for this embassy since being of
697.   his own blood I mourn for his misfortune as no other
698.   Theban can. Hear me, luckless Oedipus, come home.
699.   All the people call you hither, and I in chief, because I
700.   would be the basest of men if it did not grieve me
701.   more than it can any other to see you standing there,
702.   old man, a stranger and a wanderer, and to think that
703.   you have gone, one woman for attendant, hither and
704.   thither in beggary; and never did I think to see that
705.   woman sunk into such a state of misery, chained to
706.   your blindness and your penury, and she a ripe un-
707.   married girl at every brute's mercy. That such a
708.   thing should be is a public scandal, a shame that
709.   affects me and all our family. End this shame,
710.   Oedipus, by returning to your native city and to the
711.   house of your fathers; say goodbye in all friendship
712.   to this land, worthy though it be, for your own land
713.   has the first claim since you were born and bred there.

714.   *Oedipus.* Audacity, professing the highest motives that
715.   you may deceive! You would carry me away bound
716.   and shackled to that very place where captivity would
717.   be the most bitter. In old days, driven mad by all the
718.   evil that I had brought upon myself, I cried out that
719.   you should cast me out of the land, but you were deaf
720.   and would not grant me what I asked; and when the
721.   violence of grief had passed and the seclusion of the
722.   house grown dear to me, then, then it was that you
723.   cast me from the house and from the land. You did
724.   not remember that I was of your blood, but now you
725.   remember it. Now that I have been welcomed by
726.   Athens and her children you would drag me away,
727.   covering up your purpose with specious words. What
728.   good is kindness done against our will? If a man gave
729.   no help in need, no gift when you asked it, but
730.   offered help and gift when you had no need of either,
731.   would you take pleasure in that man? Or thank him?
732.   Yet that is what you offer me, and, therefore, though
733.   it looks good it is evil. I will tell you what that evil
734.   is and prove how false you are. You have come to

---

722.   ... me, then it was ... **97A.**

735. fetch me, but not that you may take me home, but
736. to plant me somewhere on the borders that you may
737. keep me in your power and therefore escape defeat in
738. war, defeat from this land. But you shall not escape,
739. that shall not be your portion, but this—the venge-
740. ance of my ghost; and for my two sons this heritage,
741. a place in Thebes where they may die, a place in my
742. kingdom just large enough for that. What do you
743. know of the fortune of that kindgom? But I know
744. it. My knowledge comes from Phoebus and his
745. father God most high, aye, from truth itself, while
746. you have come with fraudulent lips and between
747. them a tongue like a sword; yet plead however you
748. may, you shall not gain your case. What is the use
749. of words? No words of mine can alter you. Get you
750. gone; she and I live where we have chosen, and no
751. matter what a plight we are in, our life, so long as
752. we are contented with it, shall not be altogether
753. wretched.

754. *Creon.* Whom has this debate made the more wretched?
755. You who injure yourself thereby, or me that you
756. have injured?

757. *Oedipus.* I am well content with your part in it, for
758. you have moved neither me nor these that stand
759. beside us.

760. *Creon.* Do you want everybody to know, miserable
761. man, that age has not brought you sense? Do you
762. want to make yourself a byword?

763. *Oedipus.* Your tongue is too ready to be honest.

764. *Creon.* And you speak many words and nothing to the
765. point.

766. *Oedipus.* And yours, it seems, are to the point and few.

767. *Creon.* Who could speak to the point that had you for
768. a listener?

769. *Oedipus.* Begone, I tell you to be gone, in my own
770. name, and in the name of these others. And stop

---

769. ... you to be begone, in ... **97A.**

771. spying upon me in this place where I am predestined
772. to remain.

773. *Creon.* These others will bear me out in what I have
774. said, and as to the answer that you have sent to your
775. own kith and kin, if ever I take you—

776. *Oedipus.* Can you take me in spite of these?

777. *Creon.* No need to take you; I can make you smart
778. enough without that.

779. *Oedipus.* No matter how you bluster, what can you do?

780. *Creon.* One of your daughters has been seized and
781. sent hence, and now I shall seize the other and send
782. her after.

783. *Oedipus.* O misery!

784. *Creon.* You shall be more miserable yet.

785. *Oedipus.* You have taken my child.

786. *Creon.* And I shall take this one in a moment.

787. *Oedipus.* What will you do to help me, friends? Will
788. you forsake me, or will you drive away this godless
789. man?

790. *Chorus.* Get you gone, stranger; you have done a most
791. wicked act and plan another.

792. *Creon* [*to his attendants*]. Take that girl by force if she
793. will not come of her own will.

794. *Antigone.* What am I to do, miserable that I am? Where
795. shall I find help from Gods or men?

796. *Chorus* [*to Creon*]. What are you doing, stranger?

797. *Creon.* I will not touch that man, but his daughter is
798. mine.

799. *Oedipus.* Worthy old men—

800. *Chorus.* Stranger, what you do is unjust.

801. *Creon.* No. Just.

802. *Chorus.* How can it be just?

803. *Creon.* I take one of my own kin.

[Lays his hand on Antigone.

804. *Oedipus.* Hear me, Athens.

805. *Chorus.* Be careful, stranger, let her go. We shall soon
806.   find out whether you or we are the stronger.

[They gather round him, threatening.

807. *Creon.* Stand back.

808. *Chorus.* We shall not stand back unless you change
809.   your mind.

810. *Creon.* If you injure me it will be war between Thebes
811.   and Athens.

812. *Oedipus.* War. I said so.

813. *Chorus.* Take your hands from that girl.

814. *Creon.* You are not the master here.

815. *Chorus.* Leave hold, I tell you.

816. *Creon [to one of his guards who seizes Antigone].* Take her
817.   and begone.

818. *Chorus.* To the rescue, men of Colonus, to the rescue!
819.   The might of Athens is insulted. Help! Help!

820. *Antigone.* They are dragging me away—friends—
821.   friends—

822. *Oedipus [blindly seeking for her].* Where are you, my
823.   child?

824. *Antigone.* They are dragging me away.

825. *Oedipus.* Your hands, my child.

826. *Antigone.* I am helpless.

827. *Creon* [*to his guards*]. Away with you.

828. *Oedipus*. O misery!   [*Guards go out with Antigone.*

829. *Creon*. Never will those two crutches prop your steps
830.   again. It is your will to ruin friends and country,
831.   and I can do nothing to prevent you. I though a
832.   prince have been their messenger, and I have failed,
833.   but you have done yourself no good in giving way
834.   to anger, and you will know that in times to come.
835.   You have always given yourself up to anger, no
836.   friend could ever turn you from it, and that has
837.   been your curse.   [*He turns to follow his guard.*

838. *Chorus*. Stop! Stop!

839. *Creon*. Hands off!

840. *Chorus*. You shall not go until those two girls have
841.   been given back.

842. *Creon*. Then I shall take what is, it seems, dearer to
843.   Athens than those two girls.

844. *Chorus*. What are you planning now?

845. *Creon*. To take that man there captive.

846. *Chorus*. A brave threat!

847. *Creon*. It shall be made a deed upon the instant.

848. *Chorus*. Yes, unless the King of this country intervenes.

849. *Oedipus*. Will you dare to touch me?

850. *Creon*. Be silent.

851. *Oedipus*. No, no, but by permission of the powers of
852.   this place I speak yet one more curse. Wretch, I am
853.   blind, and you have taken by force the unhappy crea-
854.   ture who gave me sight. Therefore I call upon the
855.   Sun-God that sees all things, to give you an old age
856.   like mine.

857. *Creon*. Hear him, men of Colonus.

858. *Oedipus.* They hear both you and me, and they know
859.   that my wrongs can strike, that my revenge shall not
860.   be in words.

861. *Creon.* Then I will do what I threatened; alone and slow
862.   with age though I am, I will take that man by force.

                     [Approaches Oedipus to seize him.

863. *Oedipus.* O misfortune!

864. *Chorus.* You are a foolhardy man to think that you
865.   can do it.

866. *Creon.* I think it.

867. *Chorus.* If you do it there is no such city as Athens.

868. *Creon.* Even a weak man is strong in a good cause.

869. *Oedipus.* Hear what he is saying.

870. *Chorus.* Let him say what he likes. He cannot do it, by
871.   God, he cannot.

872. *Creon.* What do you know of God?

873. *Chorus.* Insolence!

874. *Creon.* Insolence that you must put up with.

Enter Theseus

875. *Theseus.* What is this quarrel? What is the trouble?
876.   High words have reached me at the altar of the Sea-
877.   God, the patron saint of your own Colonus. Speak
878.   out—you have interrupted the sacrifice.

879. *Oedipus.* Friend, I know your voice. That man there
880.   has done me a foul wrong.

881. *Theseus.* What wrong? What man? Speak out.

882. *Oedipus.* The man that is before your eyes—Creon. He
883.   has taken my children from me, all that I had.

884. *Theseus.* What is that you say?

885. *Oedipus.* My tale is finished.

886. *Theseus* [*to his attendants*]. Let one of you run to the
887.   altars, bid every one to leave the sacrifice and hurry
888.   to the cross-roads, whether upon foot or upon horse-
889.   back. Let the horsemen ride with a loose rein, for if
890.   they do not get there before the girls I shall be made
891.   a mockery. Away, away. [*Turning to Creon.*] As for
892.   this man, if I had not kept a tight hold upon myself
893.   he would already have had something to remember
894.   me by, but it is better to deal out to him the law that
895.   he dealt out to Oedipus. [*To Creon.*] You shall not
896.   leave this country until you have brought back those
897.   girls and set them there in my sight, for what you
898.   have done is a disgrace to me and to my people as
899.   it is to you and to your people. You have come to a
900.   city that observes justice, that does all things ac-
901.   cording to the law, and you have set aside the laws
902.   of that city, taken captives at your own pleasure,
903.   taken what you wanted by violence, as though my
904.   city were uninhabited, or inhabited by slaves, and I
905.   a mere nothing. Thebes never taught you this—her
906.   men are honourable—nor would Thebes approve an
907.   act of robbery against me, nor that you should com-
908.   mit an act of robbery against the Gods, and carry
909.   away their suppliants. Do you suppose that I, if I
910.   trod your soil, would take anything without licence
911.   from its ruler, even if my claim were of all claims
912.   the most just? I know better how to deport myself
913.   among the people of another nation. But you who
914.   are old and should have learnt wisdom, you have
915.   brought disgrace upon an honourable city. I there-
916.   fore repeat, unless those girls are brought to me you
917.   shall remain here, a captive in their stead, and do not
918.   think what I say mere words, for I say them with
919.   my whole heart and soul.

920. *Chorus.* Think where you stand, stranger; you come of
921.   a just race, but your actions have been weighed and
922.   they are unjust.

---

895. . . . dealt to . . . **97A.**
907. . . . me, not that . . . **97A.**
912. . . . know how . . . **97A.**

923. *Creon.* I have done what I have done, not because I
924.   thought this city lacked law, lacked men for its de-
925.   fence, as you have declared, but because I did not
926.   believe that its people were so much in love with my
927.   own kindred that they would keep them against my
928.   will. I thought they would not protect a parricide, a
929.   pollution, a man who had taken his own mother to
930.   wife. That is why I dared to act, nor had I done so
931.   even then, but that he called down curses upon my
932.   people and upon myself. I thought I could requite
933.   such wrong. Only the dead are free from anger,
934.   and anger does not grow less as a man grows old. I
935.   have a just cause, but I am in your power, so do
936.   what you think right, and yet remember that how-
937.   ever old I may be I can requite one deed with an-
938.   other.

939. *Oedipus.* Do such taunts disgrace most the man at
940.   whom they are aimed or the man that makes them?
941.   All that I am taunted with, parricide, incest, misery,
942.   I have borne indeed, but by no choice of mine, but at
943.   the pleasure of the Gods. Set me apart from these
944.   acts, apart from all that they, enraged, it may be,
945.   against my ancestors, have made me do against my
946.   family and myself, and there is nobody can accuse
947.   me of anything. They settled before my birth all that
948.   I was to do. The oracle had announced that my father
949.   was to die by the hand of his son. How then can I
950.   be blamed? I met my father not knowing who he was,
951.   and killed him not knowing what I did, but misery
952.   is not guilt. Are you not ashamed to have spoken of
953.   my mother, and to make me speak of my marriage
954.   with her, seeing that she was your own sister? You
955.   drive me to shameless speech and speak I must,
956.   whether I will or no—Misery! Misery! She was my
957.   mother indeed, and a mother bore children to her
958.   son, but one thing is plain as day, that what we did
959.   we did unknowingly, but that you knowingly have
960.   reviled her and me. You throw all that has happened
961.   in my teeth, and yet no man can judge me guilty
962.   either of that marriage or of my father's death.
963.   Answer this one question—if an armed man were to

964. start up before you now, would you out of your
965. righteousness ask before you drew to defend your-
966. self if he were, perchance, your father? I think that
967. you would have at him without further words and
968. not search here and there to find the rights of it,
969. seeing that you love your life. Yet that was how it
970. was with me; into that dilemma had the Gods led
971. me. If my father could come back to life he would
972. not contradict what I have said. Yet you in a frenzy
973. of speech, not caring what you say or do not say,
974. have accused me, and before these strangers. You
975. began with flattery, praising Theseus and Athens for
976. their justice, and then when you could not get your
977. way showed how little you thought of that justice
978. by stealing my daughters and by laying your hands
979. on me, yes, upon the old man and the suppliant.
980. And therefore I call upon those Goddesses whom this
981. land worships to fight upon my side, and I call upon
982. this land that you may learn what men serve it.

983. *Chorus.* King, he is a good man though under a curse,
984. and worthy of our help.

985. *Theseus.* Enough of words; the doers of the wrong are
986. in flight and we do nothing.

987. *Creon.* Well, what would you have me do? I am in
988. your power.

989. *Theseus.* Bring me to the girls if near at hand, put me
990. upon their track if your men have carried them away.
991. They will never cross the border. Come, set out, for
992. the robber has been robbed and the hunter taken in
993. the net. I will see to it that no accomplice helps you.
994. I am very certain that you would never have dared
995. to commit this outrage without some treachery
996. among my people. If you have any wits you will pay
997. more attention to my words than you paid to the
998. warnings these others spoke a while back.

999. *Creon.* You are in your own country, say what you
1000. will, but when I get home to mine I shall know how
1001. to act.

1002. *Theseus.* Threaten if you have a fancy for it, but set
1003. out. Oedipus, stay here in peace, be satisfied with

1004.   this pledge: I shall bring those children or die
1005.   attempting it.

1006.   *Oedipus.* May Heaven reward you, Theseus, for you are
1007.   a noble and faithful man.

[*Theseus, Creon, and attendants go out.*

Chorus

1008.   Would I were there when they turn and Theban robbers face,
1009.   Amid the brazen roar of shields, Colonus in chase;
1010.   Whether by the Pythian strand, or further away to the west
1011.   Where immortal spirits reveal the life of the blessed
1012.   To the living man that has sworn to let none living know;
1013.   Or it may be north and west amid Oea's desolate snow.
1014.   No matter how steep the climb Colonus follows the track,
1015.   No matter how loose the rein Theseus rides at their back;
1016.   And the captives turn in the saddle, turn their heads at his call.
1017.   Swords upon brazen shields and brazen helmets fall.
1018.   Creon is captured or slain, many are captured or slain.
1019.   Terrible the men of Colonus, terrible Theseus' men.
1020.   O glitter of bridle and bit; O lads in company
1021.   To the son of Rhea that rides upon the horses of the sea
1022.   Vowed, and to the Goddess Pallas Athene vowed!
1023.   O that I had seen it all mounted upon a cloud!
1024.   O that I had run thither, a bird upon the wind!
1025.   I have but imagined it all, seen it in the eye of the mind,
1026.   And cannot know what happened for all the words I say,
1027.   And therefore to God's daughter Pallas Athene pray
1028.   To bring the lads and the horses and the luckless ladies home,
1029.   And when that prayer is finished that a double blessing come
1030.   From the running ground of the deer, from the mountain land
            to this,
1031.   Pray to the brother and sister, Apollo and Artemis.
1032.   *Chorus.* I have not raised false hopes. The men return
1033.   with your daughters in the midst of them.

1034.   *Oedipus.* Where? Where? What is that you say?

Enter Antigone, Ismene, Theseus, and attendants

1035.   *Antigone.* O father, father! that God would restore
1036.   your sight that you might see how noble a man
1037.   stands there!

1038. *Oedipus.* My child, so you have come back to me.

1039. *Antigone.* Yes, thanks to the strong arms of Theseus
1040. 　and his men.

1041. *Oedipus.* Come to me, children; let me embrace you.
1042. 　I never thought to have touched you with my hands
1043. 　again.

1044. *Antigone.* We come, for we too long to embrace you.

1045. *Oedipus.* Where are you?

1046. *Antigone.* Here, approaching you together.

1047. *Oedipus.* My darlings—props of my old age.

1048. *Antigone.* We three are under the same curse.

1049. *Oedipus.* I draw my darlings to me, and now should I
1050. 　die I shall not be altogether wretched since you have
1051. 　come to me again. Come closer on either side,
1052. 　children; cling to your father; rest, for you are tired
1053. 　out after all that has happened. Tell me of it all;
1054. 　but no, you are young girls and so afraid to speak
1055. 　before such a crowd as this.

1056. *Antigone.* There is nothing we need say, for our de-
1057. 　liverer is there, and he can tell you all.

1058. *Oedipus.* Do not wonder, sir, that I have so much to
1059. 　say to these children lost and found when hope itself
1060. 　seemed lost,. I have not forgotten that by you and you
1061. 　alone were they rescued. May the Gods give you all
1062. 　the good that I wish, give it to you and to this land,
1063. 　for through you and through you alone, and here
1064. 　alone, here in this one place out of the whole world,
1065. 　have I found truth and piety and justice, and I have
1066. 　nothing to give you in return but words. Stretch out
1067. 　your hand towards me that I may take it in mine
1068. 　and kiss you upon the cheek. But what am I saying?
1069. 　I am miserable and sinful and polluted. I would not
1070. 　have you touch me; no, no, I dare not permit it
1071. 　even if you would. No one may touch me but those
1072. 　that lie under the same curse. Take my greeting

1073.   there where you stand, and be as favourable in the
1074.   future as in this hour.

1075.   *Theseus.* What more natural than to dwell upon your
1076.   joy and speak of it to these children; what more
1077.   natural than to think of these before you thought of
1078.   me? My fame comes from what I do and not from the
1079.   words of any man. Your daughters are there; I have
1080.   carried out my promise, old man, and all those
1081.   threats came to nothing; they will tell you all in
1082.   good time, for I will tell no tale and make no boast.
1083.   But as I returned here something happened that I must
1084.   speak of and get your advice about, for though no
1085.   great matter in itself I do not know what it may mean.

1086.   *Oedipus.* What is it, son of Aegeus? For I have heard
1087.   nothing of it.

1088.   *Theseus.* When the noise of the quarrel with Creon
1089.   reached me I was sacrificing at the altar of Poseidon,
1090.   and as I brought your daughters hither I passed that
1091.   altar and there I found a man who was, they told me,
1092.   a kinsman of yours, though not your countryman.

1093.   *Oedipus.* Of what country? What does he want?

1094.   *Theseus.* I know nothing but this one thing: he wants
1095.   to speak with you, but as he promises to be brief it
1096.   will not trouble you much.

1097.   *Oedipus.* What brings him? A man does not go to the
1098.   altar of Poseidon about nothing.

1099.   *Theseus.* All that he has asked of the God is that he
1100.   may speak with you and return home uninjured.

1101.   *Oedipus.* But who can this man be?

1102.   *Theseus.* He is of Argos. Have you a kinsman there?

1103.   *Oedipus.* Do not plead for that man, King.

1104.   *Theseus.* What ails you?

1105.   *Oedipus.* Do not ask me.

1106.   *Theseus.* Ask what?

1107.   *Oedipus.* I know that suppliant.

1108. *Theseus.* But what has he done that I should not plead
1109.   for him?

1110. *Oedipus.* My son, the hateful son whose voice would
1111.   vex me more than that of any living man.

1112. *Theseus.* Are you afraid that he will persuade you to
1113.   something against your will? It can do you no harm
1114.   to hear what he has to say.

1115. *Oedipus.* The voice of that son is hateful to his father;
1116.   do not compel me to give way.

1117. *Theseus.* Remember that he is a suppliant to the God
1118.   and that you have a duty to the God.

1119. *Antigone.* Father, let me speak, though I am too young
1120.   to advise anyone. Do what the King asks, seeing that
1121.   he asks it for his own sake and that of the God, and
1122.   let my brother come. He cannot force you to any-
1123.   thing against your will, nor will he be able to de-
1124.   ceive you. It is far more likely that he will betray his
1125.   own foolish plan. What harm, therefore, can come of
1126.   hearing what he has to say? You are his father, and
1127.   no matter what wrongs he may do against you, you
1128.   must not wrong him in return. Let him come. Other
1129.   men have been driven to anger by evil children and
1130.   have been none the worse when friends have talked
1131.   away their anger. Turn your eyes from the present
1132.   moment; think of all the evils that have come upon
1133.   you through your own father and mother; think what
1134.   you did in your anger against your own father and
1135.   against your own sight. What good ever came of in-
1136.   temperate anger? Give way because we all ask it of
1137.   you. It is not right to receive a favour and give
1138.   nothing in return, nor to keep a suppliant waiting.

1139. *Oedipus.* What you have asked goes bitterly against the
1140.   grain, my child, but let it be as you will. But promise
1141.   me this, my friend, that if this man comes hither
1142.   neither he nor any other shall be put over me as a
1143.   master.

1144. *Theseus.* No need to ask that, old man. I will not boast,

1145. but you may be certain that while God keeps me in
1146. the world no man shall be put over you as a master.

[*Theseus goes out.*

Chorus

1147. Endure what life God gives and ask no longer span;
1148. Cease to remember the delights of youth, travel-wearied aged
man;
1149. Delight becomes death-longing if all longing else be vain.

1150. Even from that delight memory treasures so,
1151. Death, despair, division of families, all entanglements of
mankind grow,
1152. As that old wandering beggar and these God-hated children
know.

1153. In the long echoing street the laughing dancers throng,
1154. The bride is carried to the bridegroom's chamber through
torchlight and tumultuous song;
1155. I celebrate the silent kiss that ends short life or long.

1156. Never to have lived is best, ancient writers say;
1157. Never to have drawn the breath of life, never to have looked
into the eye of day;
1158. The second best's a gay goodnight and quickly turn away.

1159. *Antigone.* Father, I can see the suppliant coming, a man
1160. without attendants, the tears pouring from his eyes.

1161. *Oedipus.* Who is he?

1162. *Antigone.* The man who was in your thoughts from the
1163. first—Polyneices.

Polyneices enters

1164. *Polyneices.* What shall I do or say? Must I mourn first
1165. for my own sorrow or first for my father, for that
1166. man there, that man lost among strangers, you two
1167. his only friends, his eyeballs blind, his clothing in
1168. squalid rags, his hair tossed by the wind, and his
1169. food—Heaven knows what scraps—in that old wallet?

1153. . . . streets . . . **97A.**
1169. . . . wallet. **84.**

1170. That is how I find him. I know now—now that it
1171. is too late—that I have proved myself, father, by
1172. neglect of you, the basest of living men. I proclaim
1173. it aloud, admit all that I am. And yet Mercy is the
1174. Queen of Heaven, and wherever God goes Mercy
1175. goes at His side, and that emboldens me to pray that
1176. she may stand at your side also. I have committed a
1177. great wrong, and yet all may be set right again. [*A*
1178. *pause.*] Why do you keep silent? Speak, father: do not
1179. turn away; will you not even answer? Will you drive
1180. me away with a contempt so great that you will not
1181. even explain why you are angry? Do what you can,
1182. sisters, to make our father speak to me; persuade
1183. him not to drive me away without even an answer.
1184. Remind him that I have come from the altar of the
1185. God.

1186. *Antigone.* Say why you come, my unhappy brother, for
1187. words full of emotion, joy, anger, tenderness, what-
1188. ever it is, can move a dumb man and make him
1189. speak.

1190. *Polyneices.* I will tell everything—you have given me
1191. good advice; but first put myself under the God's
1192. protection. The King of this country brought me
1193. from the altar and promised that I should say what-
1194. ever I had to say and suffer no wrong thereby, and I
1195. appeal to those here, to those who are strangers, and
1196. to my father and to my sisters, not to dishonour the
1197. King's word. And now, father, I will say what brings
1198. me here. I have been driven into exile, driven out of
1199. my own country, because being your eldest son I had
1200. claimed the throne. Eteocles, though younger than I,
1201. drove me into exile, though he neither worsted me
1202. in battle nor won the people from me by any sound
1203. argument. His cajolery and intrigue prevailed against
1204. me because of the curse that is upon your house; so
1205. at least do I think, and so I have been told by the
1206. oracle. And I am the more certain because when I
1207. reached Argos all went well. I married the daughter

1178. ..., father; do ... **97A.**
1182. ... me: persuade **97A.**

1208. of Adrastus, lately King there, gathered about me
1209. seven companies of spearmen, and all the men most
1210. famous in war, and all sworn to die or drive out my
1211. enemies. But why have I come? I come to entreat
1212. you, father, in my own name and in that of my allies.
1213. Seven leaders, each with his troop of spearmen,
1214. gathering against Thebes. Amphiaraus, incompar-
1215. able in war and divination alike; Tydeus the Aetolian;
1216. Eteoclus of Argos; Hippomedon, sent by Talaos his
1217. father; Capaneus, who boasts that he will burn
1218. Thebes to the ground; Parthenopaeus of Arcadia,
1219. son of Atalanta; and last of the seven, I, the son of
1220. Oedipus, but no, not his, but son of an accursed
1221. destiny. We seven who beleaguer Thebes and lead
1222. the men of Argos implore, pray, and beseech you.
1223. Remember your own children, remember your own
1224. exile, and turn away your anger. Do not let your
1225. anger follow when I march against the brother who
1226. has driven me out and stolen my inheritance. For
1227. victory, if truth be in the oracles, shall be with that
1228. party that you favour, and upon whatever side you
1229. claim to be your own. So by the Gods and by the
1230. founders of our race, I ask that you favour our party
1231. and our side. I too am a beggar and an exile—you
1232. and I eat the bread of strangers, and share a common
1233. doom, while he reigns as king, and strutting in our
1234. house mocks us both alike. With you to help, I shall
1235. conquer without toil or delay, and thereupon, my
1236. brother driven out, establish myself upon the throne
1237. and you in your own house once more. Favour our
1238. party, all shall be accomplished, but if you do not I
1239. shall not ever return alive.

1240. *Chorus*. Remember the man that brought him hither,
1241. Oedipus; say something, speak, speak to your son
1242. before you send him away.

1243. *Oedipus*. If I did not remember that Theseus brought
1244. him and begged me to speak, I would not speak a
1245. word. But now he shall hear words that shall bring
1246. no comfort to his heart, and after that let him be
1247. gone. Villain, when you had the throne that your
1248. brother has taken, when you had the sceptre in your

1249.   own hand, you drove me into exile, you made me a
1250.   nationless man, aye, clapped these rags upon my
1251.   back. And now that you are driven out in your turn
1252.   you cannot look upon these rags without tears, but
1253.   the time for tears is past. I bear my burden while I
1254.   live, and while I live think you my murderer, for it
1255.   was you that sent me wandering and begging for my
1256.   bread. And but for these, these daughters, my nurses
1257.   and preservers, these girls that have the strength of
1258.   a man, I had been dead by now. But you and your
1259.   brother are strangers and no sons of mine. Therefore
1260.   the eye of God has seen you; punishment has begun,
1261.   but it shall not ruin you utterly until your army
1262.   marches upon Thebes. You shall not overthrow that
1263.   city. No, but you shall fall and your brother fall,
1264.   each drowned in the other's blood. I have called
1265.   down that curse upon you, and now I call upon God
1266.   that you may learn before your death what it is to
1267.   mock a blind father. These are good, they are different,
1268.   altogether different. But you, throne and supplica-
1269.   tion alike, are in the power of my curse, if indeed
1270.   God's justice exists and his eternal law. Begone with
1271.   my abhorrence, son that I have made no son, vilest
1272.   of the vile, begone, orphan, begone, carry my curses
1273.   away—all that I have called down upon your head.
1274.   Never shall you vanquish your own country, your
1275.   own kin, never shall you return to Argos among its
1276.   hills, but find your death at the hand of kin and kill
1277.   the man that gives that death, aye, kill the brother
1278.   that drove you out of Thebes. And I call on the
1279.   ancestral Night, I, the blind man, to gather you into
1280.   itself, I call upon the spirits of this place and I call
1281.   upon that power that has put such fearful hatred
1282.   between brother and brother, I call upon the de-
1283.   stroying God himself. Go, carry away these words in
1284.   your ears; publish them abroad that the men of
1285.   Thebes and your faithful allies may know that
1286.   Oedipus pays as much honour to the one son as to
1287.   the other.

1288.   *Chorus.* Get you gone: as I do not approve of your
1289.   plottings I cannot wish you good luck.

1290. *Polyneices.* I mourn for my lost hope and for my useless
1291. journey, and I mourn for my comrades. What an
1292. end to all our plans; little did we think it when we
1293. marched from Argos. Misery, misery; such an end
1294. that I dare not speak of it to any, but must go in
1295. silence to this doom. Promise, you who are my sisters
1296. though his daughters, that if our father's curses be
1297. fulfilled, and if you be recalled to Thebes, you will
1298. give me fitting burial. Promise that my body suffer
1299. no dishonour; be praised among men for a double
1300. service—that done to a father, that done to a brother.

1301. *Antigone.* One thing I entreat of you, Polyneices.

1302. *Polyneices.* What is it, dear Antigone?

1303. *Antigone.* Order your army back to Argos. Do not de-
1304. stroy yourself and Thebes.

1305. *Polyneices.* No, it is impossible; I never could lead that
1306. army again once it were known that I had blenched.

1307. *Antigone.* So you would lead it again—why rage against
1308. Thebes? If you destroy your native city at last, how
1309. will you be the better?

1310. *Polyneices.* It is shameful to be an exile, an elder brother
1311. mocked at by a younger.

1312. *Antigone.* Then it is you that make all certain, you that
1313. bring about the fulfilment of his prophecies, the
1314. killing of a brother by a brother.

1315. *Polyneices.* Yes, that is what he wants, but I must not
1316. yield.

1317. *Antigone.* Alas! Alas! But who dare follow you when
1318. he has heard the prophecy?
1319. *Polyneices.* He will never hear it; no good leader brings
1320. bad news.

1321. *Antigone.* So, then, my brother, your decision is taken?

1293. ..., misery, such ... **97A.**
1321. So then, ... ? **97A.**

1322. *Polyneices.* Yes, taken. Do not delay me further. Hence-
1323.   forth I run my race followed by demons and my
1324.   father's curse; but I call down God's blessing upon
1325.   you, my sister, if after my death you do my will,
1326.   for while I live I am beyond your help. Take away
1327.   your arms. Good-bye, sisters, for never will you look
1328.   again upon my living body.

1329. *Antigone.* Alas!

1330. *Polyneices.* Do not mourn for me.

1331. *Antigone.* Who would not mourn you, brother, hurrying
1332.   away to a foreknown death?

1333. *Polyneices.* How can I help it if I am fated to die?

1334. *Antigone.* No, no; hear me, I beseech.

1335. *Polyneices.* You waste breath.

1336. *Antigone.* If wasted, then indeed am I wretched, for I
1337.   must lose you.

1338. *Polyneices.* Fortune will decide, but I pray to God that
1339.   only good fortune attend you two, for there is not
1340.   a man in the world but knows that you deserve it.

[*He goes out.*

Chorus

1341.   What is this portent? What does it shadow forth?
1342.   Have Heaven and Earth in dreadful marriage lain?
1343.   What shall the allotted season bring to birth?
1344.   This blind old ragged, rambling beggar-man
1345.   Calls curses upon cities, upon the great,
1346.   And scatters at his pleasure rich estate.

[*Thunder.*

1347. *Chorus.* What an uproar! God protect us!

1348. *Oedipus.* My children, my children, if there is any man
1349.   who can be sent, send to Theseus and summon him
1350.   hither.

1351. *Antigone.* Why should he be summoned, father?

1352. *Oedipus.* God's winged thunder comes to lead me down

1353.   to Hades; send for him, send for him upon the
1354.   instant.   [*A second peal of thunder.*

Chorus

1355.   Thunder has stirred the hair upon my head.
1356.   What horror comes to birth? What shall be found,
1357.   That travail finished, on the lowly bed?
1358.   Never in vain the dreadful thunder sounds,
1359.   Nor can the living lightning flash in vain;
1360.   Heaven has borne a child and shrieks from pain.

1361.   *Oedipus.* Daughters, your father comes to his pre-
1362.   destined end; he can no more turn away his face.

1363.   *Antigone.* How do you know it? What have you heard
1364.   or seen?

1365.   *Oedipus.* Enough that I know it. Let a man go quickly
1366.   and bring the lord of this country.   [*Thunder.*

Chorus

1367.   Once more that dreadful sound! God pity us
1368.   When all is finished on the bed of earth,
1369.   Nor hold us all unclean for Oedipus.
1370.   Whatever fate maternal sky bring forth,
1371.   Pity Colonus, nor lay us under ban
1372.   Because of Oedipus the beggar-man.

1373.   *Oedipus.* Has Theseus come? Will he find me living,
1374.   children? and with all my wits?

1375.   *Antigone.* What would you say to him? What are you
1376.   afraid of forgetting?

1377.   *Oedipus.* He has heaped benefits upon me. The time
1378.   has come to pay for all.

Chorus

1379.   Come, King of Athens, father of the land—
1380.   Whether at Poseidon's altars and the still
1381.   Unfinished sacrifice, or close at hand—
1382.   A blind old beggar-man proclaims God's will,
1383.   Proclaims a blessing on the land and us;
1384.   Come, King of Athens, come, King Theseus.

Enter Theseus

1385. *Theseus.* Why this sudden clamour? Why am I called
1386.   hither, called as it seems by this stranger and by my
1387.   own people alike? Have you been terrified by the
1388.   thunder? No wonder indeed if you are terrified by
1389.   such a storm.

1390. *Oedipus.* Welcome! God has sent you, King; good for-
1391.   tune waits you here.

1392. *Theseus.* What has happened, son of Laius?

1393. *Oedipus.* I am about to die, and before I die I would
1394.   accomplish for you and for this city what has been
1395.   foretold.

1396. *Theseus.* Why do you say you are about to die?

1397. *Oedipus.* The Gods have sent the signs that they pro-
1398.   mised.

1399. *Theseus.* What signs, old man?

1400. *Oedipus.* Prolonged loud thunder and abundant light-
1401.   ning.

1402. *Theseus.* You have foretold many things, and what you
1403.   have foretold has come true. Therefore I believe your
1404.   words and I ask what I must do.

1405. *Oedipus.* Son of Aegeus, I shall expound a mystery and
1406.   give your city that which time shall never take
1407.   away. First I shall lead you to my place of death, and
1408.   though blind I shall need no guiding hand. But that
1409.   place you must never show to any living man, for it
1410.   shall be, while it stays hidden, more protection than
1411.   a multitude of Athenian shields or than the bor-
1412.   rowed might of an ally; and there by that place mysteries
1413.   shall be revealed, revealed to you alone, things that
1414.   I dare not speak to my own daughters, much as I
1415.   love them, things it is not lawful to put into words;
1416.   and these you must guard in your heart and reveal
1417.   to your successor, and then only upon your death-
1418.   bed, that they may be revealed to his successor in
1419.   turn and so through all time. So shall this city and
1420.   countryside be kept unharmed from the dragon's
1421.   teeth and from the men of Thebes, but keep it
1422.   secret: while you keep all secret you shall be safe

1423. from your own citizens as from the enemy. Even
1424. the best-governed cities are turbulent, and though
1425. the Gods punish turbulence they are slow to act.
1426. But why should I warn you? the son of Aegeus knows
1427. how to guard himself. Now let us hurry to that
1428. place, for the heavens call and I dare not linger.
1429. Follow me, children, though but for a portion of the
1430. way. It is my turn to guide those that long have been
1431. their father's guide; come, come, but lay no hand upon
1432. me; all unhelped I shall discover my predestined
1433. plot of ground, my sacred tomb. Come this way, this
1434. way; Hermes guides and the Goddess of the Dead.
1435. O light bathing my body for the last time; O light,
1436. my light long ago, I tread the road to Hades; blessed
1437. be this land, blessed be its people, you, best of
1438. friends, be blessed, and when your fortune mounts,
1439. remember me in the tomb.

[*He goes out, followed by his daughters, Theseus, and attendants.*

Chorus.

1440. I call upon Persephone, queen of the dead,
1441. And upon Hades, king of night, I call;
1442. Chain all the Furies up that he may tread
1443. The perilous pathway to the Stygian hall
1444. And rest among his mighty peers at last,
1445. For the entanglements of God are past.

1446. Nor may the hundred-headed dog give tongue
1447. Until the daughter of Earth and Tartarus
1448. That even bloodless shades call Death has sung
1449. The travel-broken shade of Oedipus
1450. Through triumph of completed destiny
1451. Into eternal sleep, if such there be.

Enter Messenger

1452. *Messenger.* Fellow-countrymen, three words can sum up
1453. all I have to say—Oedipus is dead. But it all took
1454. time to happen and it will take time in the telling.

1455. *Chorus.* So that unhappy man is dead.

1456. *Messenger.* He is dead indeed.

1457. *Chorus.* How? In a God-appointed, painless way?

1458.   *Messenger.* There indeed you touch upon the wonder of
1459.   it. You saw with your own eyes how the man went
1460.   out from here, none to show him where to set his
1461.   feet, but he the guide of all. We followed to the
1462.   sacrificial hollow in the rock where the footpaths
1463.   cross and to the sacred threshold where brazen steps
1464.   go down into the earth, and there, midway between
1465.   the four sacred things, the basin of brass, the hollow
1466.   pear-tree, the marble tomb, the stone from Thoricus,
1467.   he sat upon the ground and began to loosen his
1468.   miserable rags. Then he bade his children find spring
1469.   water for washing and libation, and they climbed the
1470.   neighbouring hill, found spring water there, and
1471.   brought it to their father. They washed and dressed
1472.   him as we wash and dress the dead, and no sooner
1473.   had all been done according to his commands than
1474.   there came from under our feet, as if from the place
1475.   of shades, a sound of thunder. The two children
1476.   trembled, threw themselves down at their father's
1477.   knees, beat upon their breasts, wept and cried aloud.
1478.   And thereupon he cast his arms about them and said,
1479.   'From this day you are left without a father, and all
1480.   that is mine comes to an end. Your attendance upon
1481.   me has been a heavy burden, children; I know how
1482.   heavy, and yet it seemed to you light. A word, a
1483.   solitary word tells all, and that word is love. No
1484.   living man could have loved as I have loved. But now
1485.   I go, and never again shall you look upon me through
1486.   all your days of life.' After he had spoken all three
1487.   clung to one another, sobbing and crying out; but
1488.   presently they ceased to sob and to cry out and there
1489.   was silence, and then a voice spoke and summoned
1490.   Oedipus, and the hair stood up upon our heads, for
1491.   it was a God that spoke. It summoned Oedipus not
1492.   once but many times. 'Oedipus, Oedipus,' it said,
1493.   'what keeps you there? We must set out upon our
1494.   journey.' He, knowing what voice had spoken, called
1495.   King Theseus to his side and said, 'O best of friends,
1496.   put your right hand into the hands of my daughters;
1497.   promise to be their guardian and never forsake them.'

1476.   . . . down upon their . . . **97A.**

1498. King Theseus, that most magnanimous man, pro-
1499. mised and swore an oath, and yet fearing to wring
1500. the children's hearts anew spoke no word of grief.
1501. That oath being sworn, Oedipus groped for his
1502. daughters with blind hands and said, 'My children,
1503. be brave and go from this place, for there are things
1504. it is not lawful for you to see or hear. Go quickly,
1505. and let these others go, but let King Theseus stay and
1506. hear and see everything, for that is his right.' When
1507. he had spoken the children left and we followed with
1508. streaming eyes, but after a little time turned our heads.
1509. Oedipus had gone and the King stood there, a hand
1510. raised to shade his eyes as from some dreadful sight.
1511. Then, after a little, he bent down and kissed the
1512. earth, and after raised his arms to heaven praying, as
1513. it seemed, to heaven and earth in the same prayer.
1514. But by what death Oedipus died no man can say but
1515. Theseus. Neither did thunderbolt descend nor storm
1516. come up out of the sea, but some messenger carried
1517. him away or the foundations of the earth were riven
1518. to receive him, riven not by pain but by love. For I
1519. affirm, and care not if my words seem folly, that this
1520. man has gone without the pang of death and in a
1521. manner altogether wonderful.

1522. *Chorus.* But where are the others? And where are the
1523. two girls?

1524. *Messenger.* That sound of mourning tells where they are.

Enter Antigone, Ismene, and attendants

1525. *Ismene.* Where shall we wander, where find our daily
1526. bread? I dread what is to come.

1527. *Chorus.* Why should you, remembering the bitterness
1528. of your past, dread the future?

1529. *Ismene.* Things that were most bitter can seem most
1530. sweet in memory. How should those days seem bitter
1531. when we could take him in our arms? Our beloved is
1532. gone down under the earth.

1533. *Chorus.* He has found a blessed end.

1534. *Antigone.* Sister, I will go back there.

1535. *Ismene.* Why?

1536. *Antigone.* I have a great longing.

1537. *Ismene.* For what?

1538. *Antigone.* To find a bed under the earth.

1539. *Ismene.* What bed?

1540. *Antigone.* Our father's bed.

1541. *Ismene.* I thought you understood.

1542. *Antigone.* Understood what?

1543. *Ismene.* That he had no tomb, that nobody can tell
1544.   where he lies, that he went alone to his death.

1545. *Antigone.* Bring me to where we saw him last and kill
1546.   me there.

1547. *Ismene.* But if you died I should be friendless.

1548. *Chorus.* Do not be afraid, my children.

1549. *Antigone.* What refuge have we but our father's tomb?

1550. *Chorus.* A refuge has been found.

Enter Theseus

1551. *Theseus.* Your father is with the Powers under the
1552.   earth; you have his promise and their protection. Do
1553.   not vex them with lamentation. I bring you the pro-
1554.   tection of Athens.

1555. *Antigone.* Promise me, son of Aegeus.

1556. *Theseus.* What must I promise?

1557. *Antigone.* To bring me to my father's tomb.

1558. *Theseus.* The law forbids.

1559. *Antigone.* But you are King of Athens.

1560. *Theseus.* He laid a charge upon me that never human

1560.   He had a . . . **97A.**

1561.   foot approach that place.

1562. *Antigone.* If that be my father's will I must obey.

1563. *Theseus.* In all else it shall be as you will. I will omit
1564.   nothing that can profit you or gratify the dead.

1565. *Chorus.* Raise no funeral song. God's will has been
1566.   accomplished.

THE END

NOTE

. . . when I prepared 'Oedipus at Colonus' for the Abbey stage I saw that the wood of the Furies in the opening scene was any Irish haunted wood. No passing beggar or fiddler or benighted countryman has ever trembled or been awe-struck by nymph-haunted or Fury-haunted wood described in Roman poetry. Roman poetry is founded upon documents, not upon belief.

From 'Ireland after the Revolution', I, 93.

*   *   *

Variant spellings

Athena 84; *Athene* 97.
Labdacidae 97; *Labdicidae* 84.
Thorasus 84; *Thoricus* 97.

NOTE: Because of the marked differences between *The Adelphi* text and the texts in **81-97** the complete text from *The Adelphi* is given below and on succeeding verso pages. The collation of **81-97A** with the definitive text is on the recto pages. Similarities between *The Adelphi* text and the definitive text in **97E** are shown by bracketed line-numbers in the margin. Identities are shown by unbracketed line-numbers. Line lengths of *The Adelphi* text are the same as those in the magazine.

The Resurrection

Persons:

The Hebrew. / The Egyptian. / The Syrian. / Christ.

If this play is performed upon an ordinary stage, the songs at the beginning and end should be omitted, and the noise of drum and rattle made behind the scene. When played, as it will be in Dublin at its first performance, near one end of an ordinary room, three musicians enter with drum and rattle which they place at one or both sides of the stage. They will probably have their faces made up to resemble masks, and Christ, when he appears towards the end, may wear a mask. One musician, singing and carrying a black cloth, goes to the centre of the stage towards the front and stands motionless, the folded cloth hanging between his hands. Two musicians, after standing for a moment at either side of the stage, go towards him, and then slowly unfold the cloth, singing as they do so. They unfold the cloth moving backward until the stage is shut off from the audience that an actor may take his place unseen; they then fold up the cloth once more, singing as they do so.

THE RESURRECTION

To JUNZO SATO

1931

Persons in the Play

The Hebrew	The Syrian
The Greek	Christ

Three Musicians

Before I had finished this play I saw that its subject-matter might make it un-suited for the public stage in England or in Ireland. I had begun it with an ordinary stage scene in the mind's eye, curtained walls, a window and door at back, a curtained door at left. I now changed the stage directions and wrote songs for the unfolding and folding of the curtain that it might be played in a studio or a drawing-room like my dance plays, or at the Peacock Theatre before a specially chosen audience. If it is played at the Peacock Theatre the Musicians may sing the opening and closing songs, as they pull apart or pull together the proscenium curtain; the whole stage may be hung with curtains with an opening at the left. While the play is in progress the Musicians will sit towards the right of the audience; if at the Peacock, on the step which separates the stage from the audience, or one on either side of the proscenium.

PRINTINGS   *The Adelphi*, June 1927 [see opposite page]; **81, 83, 84, 97.**

DATE   [lacking] **81, 83.**

DEDICATION   [lacking] **81** ; . . . Sato / who gave me a sword **83.**

DRAMATIS PERSONAE   Characters: The Hebrew, The / Greek, The Syrian, and Christ. **81** ; . . . Play / Three Musicians / The Hebrew / . . . Christ **83.**

PROLOGUE AND STAGE DIRECTIONS   . . . *subject matter made it unsuited* . . . *Stage in* . . . *stage seen in the* . . . *played like my dance plays, in* . . . *drawing-room or at* . . . *Theatre and before* . . . *musicians* . . . *songs, each perhaps shortened by a verse, as* . . . *left. The song in the middle may be either spoken or sung, but must be accompanied by drum taps. If sung it may be shortened by a couple of verses. While* . . . *progress if played at the Peacock, the musicians* . . . *right of the proscenium on the steps* . . . *audience.* **81** ; . . . *right of the audience, if* . . . . **84.**

The Song of the Folding and Unfolding of the Cloth

[1]	1.	I saw that staring, virgin stand
2	2.	Where holy Dionysus died,
3	3.	And tear the heart out of his side,
[4]	4.	And lay the heart upon her hand,
5	5.	And bear that beating heart away;
[6]	6.	And then did all the muses sing
7	7.	Of Magnus Annus at the spring,
8	8.	As though God's death were but a play.
9	9.	Another Troy must rise and set,
10	10.	Another lineage feed the crow,
11	11.	Another Argo's painted prow
12	12.	Drive to a flashier bauble yet.
[13]	13.	The Roman Empire stood appalled;
[14]	14.	It dropped the reins of peace and war;
[15]	15.	When that fierce virgin and her star
16	16.	Out of the fabulous darkness called.

The stage represents an upper chamber in Jerusalem; there is a door at the right leading to an inner room and a door at the back leading by a stairway to the street, and windows at the back and left. When the play is performed in an ordinary room, neither door nor window need be represented, except by a curtain, that can be parted for a moment, and there should be no furniture. The Hebrew is discovered sitting or standing; the Egyptian enters from the street and is armed.

[39]	17.	*The Egyptian*: I have come because I heard you
	18.	were alone; why did the Syrian go?
	19.	*The Hebrew*: I heard that in spite of the Roman
	20.	Guard, people had taken the body of Jesus from the
[40]	21.	tomb and hidden it. I sent him up the mountain to
[41]	22.	find if it was true.
	23.	*The Egyptian*: They say that Judas has hanged
	24.	himself.
	25.	*The Hebrew*: Who told you that?

[Song for the unfolding and folding of the curtain]

I

1.	I saw a staring virgin stand
2.	Where holy Dionysus died,
3.	And tear the heart out of his side,
4.	And lay the heart upon her hand
5.	And bear that beating heart away;
6.	And then did all the Muses sing
7.	Of Magnus Annus at the spring,
8.	As though God's death were but a play.

II

9.	Another Troy must rise and set,
10.	Another lineage feed the crow,
11.	Another Argo's painted prow
12.	Drive to a flashier bauble yet.
13.	The Roman Empire stood appalled:
14.	It dropped the reins of peace and war
15.	When that fierce virgin and her Star
16.	Out of the fabulous darkness called.

[The Hebrew is discovered alone upon the stage; he has a sword or spear. The Musicians make faint drum-taps, or sound a rattle; the Greek enters through the audience from the left.

17.	*The Hebrew.* Did you find out what the noise was?
18.	*The Greek.* Yes, I asked a Rabbi.
19.	*The Hebrew.* Were you not afraid?
20.	*The Greek.* How could he know that I am called a
21.	Christian? I wore the cap I brought from Alexandria.
22.	He said the followers of Dionysus were parading the
23.	streets with rattles and drums; that such a thing had
24.	never happened in this city before; that the Roman

TEXT Title and date of first performance . . . Resurrection / First performed at the Abbey Theatre / on 30th July 1934 **83.**

    Directions before 1. The Unfolding . . . Folding . . . Curtain **81.**

2. . . . Holy . . . , **81.**

13. . . . appalled; **81.**

    Directions before 17. [. . . *drum taps,* . . . *audience.*] **81.**

21. Christian. I . . . . **81.**

[18]   26. *The Egyptian*: A Rabbi, without being asked.

19   27. *The Hebrew*: Were you not afraid?

[20]   28. *The Egyptian*: No, how could he know that I was
[21]   29.   a Christian? He was so full of his story that he could
            30.   not help telling it. I had seen him talking to a man
            31.   driving an ass with wine skins, and after I left him he
            32.   crossed the road to where some women were washing
            33.   clothes.

            34. *The Hebrew*: Did Judas take his own life out of
            35.   remorse?

            36. *The Egyptian*: Yes, and the Rabbi was angry that
            37.   a man should hang himself for doing what he called his
            38.   duty according to Hebrew Law. He said that it proved
            39.   the doctrine of Jesus, not only lawless but unwholesome.

                                   [*A distant sound of drum and rattle.*]

[17]   40. *The Hebrew*: I have heard that sound all morning,
            41.   now near, now distant.

            42. *The Egyptian*: I heard it when I was talking to the
[22, 23]   43.   Rabbi but I was afraid to ask what it was. People are
[22, 23]   44.   crowding into the streets.

[35]   45. *The Hebrew*: It is lucky that we are here to mount
[36]   46.   guard. If the crowd come, we can keep it off until the
[36]   47.   men in there escape over the roof.

[44, 45]   48. *The Egyptian*: What are the eleven doing now?

[46]   49. *The Hebrew*: A little while ago James took some
[47, 48]   50.   loaves out of a bag and laid them on the table and
[47, 48]   51.   Nathaniel found a skin of wine somewhere. It is a
[48, 49]   52.   long time since they have eaten anything; and then
                     they
[49, 50]   53.   began to speak in low voices and John spoke of the last
[50, 51]   54.   time they had eaten in that room.

25. authorities were afraid to interfere. The followers of
26. Dionysus have been out among the fields tearing a
27. goat to pieces and drinking its blood, and are now
28. wandering through the streets like a pack of wolves.
29. The mob was so terrified of their frenzy that it left
30. them alone, or, as seemed more likely, so busy hunt-
31. ing Christians it had time for nothing else. I turned
32. to go, but he called me back and asked where I lived.
33. When I said outside the gates, he asked if it was
34. true that the dead had broken out of the cemeteries.

35. *The Hebrew.* We can keep the mob off for some minutes,
36. long enough for the Eleven to escape over the roofs. I
37. shall defend the narrow stair between this and the
38. street until I am killed, then you will take my place.
39. Why is not the Syrian here?

40. *The Greek.* I met him at the door and sent him on a
41. message; he will be back before long.

42. *The Hebrew.* The three of us will be few enough for
43. the work in hand.

44. *The Greek* [*glancing towards the opening at the left*]. What
45. are they doing now?

46. *The Hebrew.* While you were down below, James brought
47. a loaf out of a bag, and Nathanael found a skin of
48. wine. They put them on the table. It was a long time
49. since they had eaten anything. Then they began to
50. speak in low voices, and John spoke of the last time
51. they had eaten in that room.

52. *The Greek.* They were thirteen then.

53. *The Hebrew.* He said that Jesus divided bread and wine
54. amongst them. When John had spoken they sat still,
55. nobody eating or drinking. If you stand here you
56. will see them. That is Peter close to the window.

---

32. ... go but .... **81.**
36. ... eleven ... **81.**
46. ... below James ... **81.**
50. ... voices and ... **81.**
55. ... or speaking. If ... **81.**

[52]   55. *The Egyptian*: They were thirteen then.

[53]   56. *The Hebrew*: He said that Jesus divided the bread
[53, 54]   57.   and wine amongst them and after he had said that, all
[55]   58.   sat still, nobody eating or speaking. If you stand here
[56-58]   59.   you will see them. Look at Peter with his head bowed
[56-58]   60.   on his breast, he has been quite motionless this long
[57]   61.   while.

[59]   62. *The Egyptian*: Is it true that when the soldier
[59, 60]   63.   asked if he were a follower of Jesus, he denied it?

[61]   64. *The Hebrew*: Yes, it is true. James told me that
[61, 62]   65.   he spoke about it himself; that it seemed he could not
[62]   66.   rest till he had told everything; but when the moment
[63]   67.   came they were all afraid. It is not for me to find fault,
[64]   68.   I might have been as great a coward. What are we all
[65]   69.   but dogs that have lost their master?

[66, 67]   70. *The Egyptian*: Yet, if the crowd come up that stair,
[66, 67]   71.   you and I will die rather than let it pass.

[68, 69]   72. *The Hebrew*: Ah, that is different. I am going to
[69]   73.   draw the curtain. They must not hear what I am going
[70]   74.   to say.

[71]   75. *The Egyptian*: I know what is in your mind.

72   76. *The Hebrew*: They are afraid because they do not
[73, 74]   77.   know what to believe. When Jesus was taken they
[74]   78.   could no longer believe that He was the Messiah.

            79. *The Egyptian*: Come further this way. Judas
            80.   doubted long ago; he has never been sure, that is why
            81.   he betrayed Him.

            82. *The Hebrew*: But are you and I any more sure?
            83.   Would it even be right for us to be so when the twelve,
            84.   when those men Jesus himself chose have denied or
            85.   doubted?

57. He has been quite motionless for a long time, his
58.   head upon his breast.

59. *The Greek.* Is it true that when the soldier asked him if
60.   he were a follower of Jesus he denied it?

61. *The Hebrew.* Yes, it is true. James told me. Peter told
62.   the others what he had done. But when the mo-
63.   ment came they were all afraid. I must not blame.
64.   I might have been no braver. What are we all but
65.   dogs who have lost their master?

66. *The Greek.* Yet you and I if the mob come will die
67.   rather than let it up that stair.

68. *The Hebrew.* Ah! That is different. I am going to draw
69.   that curtain; they must not hear what I am going to
70.   say. [*He draws curtain.*]

71. *The Greek.* I know what is in your mind.

72. *The Hebrew.* They are afraid because they do not know
73.   what to think. When Jesus was taken they could no
74.   longer believe him the Messiah. We can find con-
75.   solation, but for the Eleven it was always complete
76.   light or complete darkness.

77. *The Greek.* Because they are so much older.

78. *The Hebrew.* No, no. You have only to look into their
79.   faces to see they were intended to be saints. They
80.   are unfitted for anything else. What makes you
81.   laugh?

82. *The Greek.* Something I can see through the window.
83.   There, where I am pointing. There, at the end of the
84.   street. [*They stand together looking out over the heads of the audience.*]

85. *The Hebrew.* I cannot see anything.

86. *The Greek.* The hill.

---

61. Yes it . . . **81.**
69. the curtain; . . . **81.**
75. . . . eleven . . . **81.**

86. *The Egyptian*: I have not doubted. I was certain
87.   from the first moment. There was something in His
88.   manner—something that showed me—that showed . . .

89. *The Hebrew*: Oh, I know those Egyptian
90.   thoughts; you are about to say that He was a phantom
91.   or something of the kind and so has not died in reality,
92.   but that is only a thought. To-morrow you will go to
93.   Delos because the sacred ship went there when Socrates
94.   was condemned; you will find out if Socrates died at
95.   a full moon in March. Or you will go to Persia and
96.   talk about the Great Year and ask when we may expect
97.   another deluge and all that will keep you busy and happy
98.   after a fashion. Even I who am a Hebrew and know

[74, 75]   99.   what certainty is, will have my consolations. I know a
[74, 75]   100.   wine shop where I can court a girl between two skins of
[75, 76]   101.   wine. But with the twelve it has been altogether
[76]   102.   different.

[77]   103.   *The Egyptian*: You say that because they are so
[77]   104.   much older than we are.

[78]   105.   *The Hebrew*: No, I say it because you have only
[78, 79]   106.   to look in their faces to see that they were intended to
[79, 80]   107.   be saints and that they are unfitted to be anything else
           108.   Why else should I stand here to guard them at the risk
           109.   of my life?

110.   *The Egyptian*: You think that Judas had to be the
111.   best or worst of men?

112.   *The Hebrew*: I think that from the moment when
113.   his doubts were confirmed there was no need to offer
114.   him those silver pieces. He would have betrayed his
115.   master for a cup of wine.

116.   *The Egyptian*: I have seen him several times. He
117.   had red hair and mild eyes. I do not think he was a
118.   bad man.

119.   *The Hebrew*: But think of his discourage-

87. *The Hebrew.* That is Calvary.

88. *The Greek.* And the three crosses on the top of it. [*He laughs again.*]

89. *The Hebrew.* Be quiet. You do not know what you are
90.   doing. You have gone out of your mind. You are
91.   laughing at Calvary.

92. *The Greek.* No, no. I am laughing because they thought
93.   they were nailing the hands of a living man upon
94.   the Cross, and all the time there was nothing there
95.   but a phantom.

96. *The Hebrew.* I saw him buried.

97. *The Greek.* We Greeks understand these things. No
98.   god has ever been buried; no god has ever suffered.
99.   Christ only seemed to be born, only seemed to eat,
100.   seemed to sleep, seemed to walk, seemed to die. I did
101.   not mean to tell you until I had proof.

102. *The Hebrew.* Proof?

103. *The Greek.* I shall have proof before nightfall.

104. *The Hebrew.* You talk wildly, but a masterless dog can
105.   bay the moon.

106. *The Greek.* No Jew can understand these things.

107. *The Hebrew.* It is you who do not understand. It is I
108.   and those men in there, perhaps, who begin to under-
109.   stand at last. He was nothing more than a man, the
110.   best man who ever lived. Nobody before him had
111.   so pitied human misery. He preached the coming of
112.   the Messiah because he thought the Messiah would
113.   take it all upon himself. Then some day when he
114.   was very tired, after a long journey perhaps, he
115.   thought that he himself was the Messiah. He thought

---

94. . . . Cross and . . . **81.**
98. God . . . God . . . . **81.**
107. . . . I, **81.**
108. . . . there perhaps, . . . to see **81** ; . . . there perhaps who . . . **83.**
109. clearly at . . . **81.**

120. ment. When he became an apostle he thought his
121. Master was Solomon and David come again. He
122. thought that he would see the Roman driven out and
123. the Jew conquer the world in his place.

124. *The Egyptian*: Nobody can drive the Roman out,
125. but he eats too much and for that reason he cannot
126. think, and so he lets the Greeks, who are a lean race,
127. do it for him. Sooner or later somebody must control
128. his Empire. I would sooner it were a Jew than a
129. Greek. There are too many Greeks in Alexandria.
130. The Jews also are a lean race.

131. *The Hebrew*: Whatever He commanded I would
132. have done. I loved Him better than father or mother,
133. friend or sweetheart. But what was the good of it all?
134. The armed men but touched Him on the shoulder and
135. He no more thought of resisting than a man in a
        dream.

136. *The Egyptian*: Do not speak so loud. I would not
137. have Peter hear for the world.

138. *The Hebrew*: He deceived himself and us and I
139. think it was all because He loved mankind. Of course
140. I did not hear Him very often for I had my day's work,
141. but it seemed to me that at first He but spoke of
        Himself
142. as Son of God as all men are Sons of God, and that as
143. people flocked about Him there came a change. Per-
[110, 111] 144. haps He so brooded over our unhappiness that He
145. longed to be God for our sake, thought constantly per-
[112, 113] 146. haps that if He were our Judge at the last, He would
[112, 113] 147. know how to make allowances, and so through
        brooding
[114, 115] 148. always upon that one thought, became unhinged and
[115, 116] 149. called Himself "God's Only Son"—His Only Be-
150. gotten Son—and now He is dead and we shall never
151. look upon His face again and there is nothing
        more to
152. be said.

[155]   *[A sound of rattles and drums, but nearer now.]*
[165, 166] 153. There is that noise again. I can see them now. They

116.   it because of all destinies it seemed the most terrible.

117. *The Greek.* How could a man think himself the Messiah?

118. *The Hebrew.* It was always foretold that he would be
119.   born of a woman.

120. *The Greek.* To say that a god can be born of a woman,
121.   carried in her womb, fed upon her breast, washed as
122.   children are washed, is the most terrible blasphemy.

123. *The Hebrew.* If the Messiah were not born of a woman
124.   he could not take away the sins of man. Every sin
125.   starts a stream of suffering, but the Messiah takes it
126.   all away.

127. *The Greek.* Every man's sins are his property. Nobody
128.   else has a right to them.

129. *The Hebrew.* The Messiah is able to exhaust human
130.   suffering as though it were all gathered together in
131.   the spot of a burning-glass.

132. *The Greek.* That makes me shudder. The utmost pos-
133.   sible suffering as an object of worship! You are
134.   morbid because your nation has no statues.

135. *The Hebrew.* What I have described is what I thought
136.   until three days ago.

137. *The Greek.* I say that there is nothing in the tomb.

138. *The Hebrew.* I saw him carried up the mountain and
139.   the tomb shut upon him.

140. *The Greek.* I have sent the Syrian to the tomb to prove
141.   that there is nothing there.

142. *The Hebrew.* You knew the danger we were all in and

---

120. ... God ..., **81.**
131. ... burning glass. **81.**
135. What you have ... **81.**
137. ... Tomb. **81.**
139. ... Tomb ....
140. ... Tomb ... **81.**

[166]   154. are women and some carry on their shoulder a bier
[167]   155. with a dead man, while others shake rattles or beat
                 upon
           156. drums. Some of the crowd are angry but the Roman
           157. soldiers keep them back.

           158. *The Egyptian*: Are you certain that they are
[167, 168] 159. women and not men in women's clothes with rouged
           160. faces?

           161. *The Hebrew*: They are passing at the end of the
           162. street and the crowd obstructs the view. Now I can
[168]   163. see. I think you are right—they walk like men and
[172]   164. their cheeks and lips are vermilion—an impossible
           165. vermilion.

[167]   166. *The Egyptian*: Nor is that a dead man, but a
[169]   167. painted wooden image of a dead man. I have seen them
[171, 172] 168. in Alexandria—they are new arrivals here. They
[164]   169. worship a drunken God called among the Greeks
                 Diony-
[196, 197] 170. sus, and at the first full moon in March they gather in
[26]   171. some field outside the town, one of them with a live
           172. kid in his arms. The others stand in a circle and he
           173. throws the kid into the midst of them and they fall
           174. upon it tumbling over one another and seize it with
[27]   175. their teeth and their hands, and tear it asunder, and eat
[27, 28]   176. the raw flesh, their heads and garments all spotted with
[164]   177. blood. And all the while they keep crying out upon
[164]   178. the God Dionysus whose flesh they eat and whose
[27]   179. blood they drink.

           180. *The Hebrew*: Horrible—only a Greek could have
           181. such thoughts.

           182. *The Egyptian*: Then they go into the town and
[166, 167] 183. march hither and thither, some with a painted
                 image of
[166, 167] 184. a dead man upon their shoulders, some dancing and
           185. rending their clothes and calling upon their God to rise
           186. from the dead.

           187. *The Hebrew*: One of the priests has got separated
           188. from the rest and is among the crowd under the win-

143. yet you weakened our guard?

144. *The Greek.* I have risked the apostles' lives and our own.
145. What I have sent the Syrian to find out is more
146. important.

147. *The Hebrew.* None of us are in our right mind to-day. I
148. have got something in my own head that shocks me.

149. *The Greek.* Something you do not want to speak about?

150. *The Hebrew.* I am glad that he was not the Messiah;
151. we might all have been deceived to our lives' end, or
152. learnt the truth too late. One had to sacrifice every-
153. thing that the divine suffering might, as it were,
154. descend into one's mind and soul and make them
155. pure. [*A sound of rattles and drums, at first in short bursts that come between sentences, but gradually growing con-*
156. *tinuous.*] One had to give up all worldly knowledge,
157. all ambition, do nothing of one's own will. Only
158. the divine could have any reality. God had to take
159. complete possession. It must be a terrible thing when
160. one is old, and the tomb round the corner, to think
161. of all the ambitions one has put aside; to think,
162. perhaps, a great deal about women. I want to marry
163. and have children.

The Greek [who is standing facing the audience, and looking
164. *out over their heads].* It is the worshippers of Dionysus.
165. They are under the window now. There is a group
166. of women who carry upon their shoulders a bier
167. with an image of the dead god upon it. No, they are
168. not women. They are men dressed as women. I have
169. seen something like it in Alexandria. They are all
170. silent, as if something were going to happen. My

---

143. . . . guard. **81.**
147. . . . today. . . . **81**; . . . us is in . . . **83A.**
152. . . . truth when it was too . . .
153. . . . divine sufferer might, . . . , **81.**
Directions in 155-156. [. . . *drums at* . . . *continuous and drowning the voice.*] **81**; [. . . *drums at* . . . .] **83.**
159. . . . possession. I want to marry and have children. It . . . **81.**
161. . . . one had to put . . . ,
162. . . . women.
163. [lacking] **81.**

189.   dow. He is drunk and the crowd is making game of
190.   him pushing him about and laughing.

191.   *The Egyptian*: Some of the priests are always
192.   drunk. It is part of their piety to seem intoxicated by
193.   the blood of the God.

194.   *The Hebrew*: The drunken man has begun to sing.

Song of the Drunkard.

195.   The drunkard with the painted eyes
196.   Discovered thought is misery,
197.   Now, with drum and rattle, he
198.   Bids a drunken God arise.

[27]   199.   *The Hebrew*: They eat the flesh and drink the blood
200.   of their God. That is what you said.

201.   *The Egyptian*: Yes, it is their Sacrament. They
[201]   202.   say he died for the salvation of men. The Titans, as
203.   the story goes, were at war with the Gods and
climbed
[201]   204.   up Olympus, keeping in the woods' shadow. They
[199]   205.   came where the divine child was playing. They made
[202]   206.   him run towards them, by shaking rattles which they
[202, 203]   207.   had brought for the purpose. When the child had
[203, 215]   208.   come under the shadow of the trees, they tore him in
[215]   209.   pieces.

210.   *The Hebrew*: So that is why the priests have
211.   rattles?

[205, 206]   212.   *The Egyptian*: Certain loose women among the
[207]   213.   Titans, twelve it is said, twelve Titan women, tried to
[207]   214.   protect him and in commemoration of that, the
priests
215.   dress like women, rouge their lips and faces and
dance
216.   swaying their hips, like women enticing men.

217.   *The Hebrew*: Let them cry as loud as they please,
218.   even the Greeks cannot raise the dead.

171. God! What a spectacle! In Alexandria a few men
172. paint their lips vermilion. They imitate women that
173. they may attain in worship a woman's self-abandon-
174. ment. No great harm comes of it—but here! Come
175. and look for yourself.

176. *The Hebrew.* I will not look at such madmen.

177. *The Greek.* Though the music has stopped, some men
178. are still dancing, and some of the dancers have gashed
179. themselves with knives, imagining themselves, I sup-
180. pose, at once the god and the Titans that murdered
181. him. A little further off a man and woman are coup-
182. ling in the middle of the street. She thinks the
183. surrender to some man the dance threw into her
184. arms may bring her god back to life. All are from
185. the foreign quarter, to judge by face and costume,
186. and are the most ignorant and excitable class of
187. Asiatic Greeks, the dregs of the population. Such
188. people suffer terribly and seek forgetfulness in mon-
189. strous ceremonies. Ah, that is what they were waiting
190. for. The crowd has parted to make way for a singer.
191. It is a girl. No, not a girl; a boy from the theatre. I
192. know him. He acts girls' parts. He is dressed as a
193. girl, but his finger-nails are gilded and his wig is
194. made of gilded cords. He looks like a statue out of
195. some temple. I remember something of the kind in
196. Alexandria. Three days after the full moon, a full
197. moon in March, they sing the death of the god and
198. pray for his resurrection.

[*One of the Musicians sings the following song*]

---

171. ... spectacle. In ... **81.**
173. ... may obtain in ... **81, 83.**
174. ... it; but ... **81.**
177. Although the ... stopped some ... **81;** ... stopped some ... **84, 97A.**
179. ... knives, acting, I sup-
180. pose, the part of the Titans who killed
181. Dionysus. A little ... **81.**
185. ... quarter to ... , **83.**
193. ... finger nails ... **81.**
196. ... moon, the first full **81.**
Directions before 199. [... *song*;] **81.**

219. *The Egyptian*: Presently they hide the image and
220.   parade the streets again, crying out that he has arisen
221.   and pretend a great joy and excitement.

> [*He looks out of the window for a moment; the rattles and drums are now very distant.*]

222.   We can lay our weapons down. The street is
223.   empty now. The rabble have the priests of Dionysus
224.   to bait. [*They sit down.*] It is true as you said a
225.   while ago that I consider Jesus an appearance or a
226.   phantom. Once when I was a young lad I came upon
227.   a crowd of people at a street corner in Alexandria
228.   gathered round an Indian juggler. He had a table in
229.   front of him, and on the table a hen with a straw in
230.   its beak. I said: 'What are you all staring at?' and
231.   a woman answered: 'Cannot you see the hen with
232.   a great beam of wood in its beak?' Then I knew
233.   that the Indian juggler had enchanted them. From the
234.   first moment in which I heard Christ speak I knew that
235.   God had turned juggler and created the appearance
236.   that I called Christ. We think that He has been con-
237.   demned, that He has been tried, put to death, and
238.   buried, but all that may be but part of the appearance.

239. *The Hebrew*: You think that He cannot have been
240.   a man because of the miracles that He wrought.

241. *The Egyptian*: I think that if you Jews keep in
242.   mind all that you and I have seen, or seemed to see,
243.   you may become the masters of the dull Roman brain
244.   and drive out the Greeks.

245. *The Hebrew*: I once went on a trading ship to
246.   Gythium, with purple cloth from Tyre, and while the
247.   sailors were loading up with wine for the return journey,
248.   I rode to Sparta to see the sights. I saw there a great
249.   temple hung round with wax and wooden models of
250.   hands and feet, eyes and ears, and even of various parts
251.   of the inside of the human body. All had been hung
252.   there in gratitude for cures worked by the goddess.

199.	Astrea's holy child!
200.	A rattle in the wood
201.	Where a Titan strode!
202.	His rattle drew the child
203.	Into that solitude.
204.	Barrum, barrum, barrum [*Drum-taps accompany and follow the words*].
205.	We wandering women,
206.	Wives for all that come,
207.	Tried to draw him home;
208.	And every wandering woman
209.	Beat upon a drum.
210.	Barrum, barrum, barrum [*Drum-taps as before*].
211.	But the murderous Titans
212.	Where the woods grow dim
213.	Stood and waited him.
214.	The great hands of those Titans
215.	Tore limb from limb.
216.	Barrum, barrum, barrum [*Drum-taps as before*].
217.	On virgin Astrea
218.	That can succour all
219.	Wandering women call;
220.	Call out to Astrea
221.	That the moon stood at the full.
222.	Barrum, barrum, barrum [*Drum-taps as before*].
223.	*The Greek.* I cannot think all that self-surrender and
224.	self-abasement is Greek, despite the Greek name of
225.	its god. When the goddess came to Achilles in the
226.	battle she did not interfere with his soul, she took
227.	him by his yellow hair. Lucretius thinks that the
228.	gods appear in the visions of the day and night but
229.	are indifferent to human fate; that, however, is the
230.	exaggeration of a Roman rhetorician. They can be dis-

199.	. . . child; **81**.
	[between 203, 204; 209, 210; 215, 216; 221, 222 a break] **81, 83**.
	Directions in 204, 210, 216, 222. . . . [*Drum taps* . . . .] **81**; . . . ,
	barrum. [*Drum-taps* . . . .] **83**; Barrum Barrum Barrum [*Drum-taps*
	. . . .] **84**.
218.	. . . all, **81**.
226.	battle she took him by his yellow hair; she did not
227.	interfere with his soul. Lucretius . . . **81**.
229.	. . . fate, but that is . . . **81**.

253.   *The Egyptian*: God has given great power to His
254.   priests, but it was not of such miracles that I thought,
255.   but of what He was in Himself—an image of God's
256.   own incorruptible essence. If we but fix our faith
257.   upon that image, men in times to come will lay upon
258.   their altars, a splinter of the Cross whereon it seemed
259.   to have been nailed, and some Roman Emperor attri-
260.   bute his victories to the nail that he has made into the bit
261.   of his horse.

262.   *The Hebrew*: You think that if we can but keep our
263.   faith in a phantom, in an appearance, in an illusion, in
264.   some kind of a juggling trick, we can overcome the
265.   Greeks?

266.   *The Egyptian*: Did He not say that faith moved
267.   mountains?

268.   *The Hebrew*: I have not told you all that I saw in
269.   that temple. The guide—there is always a guide—
270.   showed me a piece of an old oar that had been used by
271.   Oddysseus, and there above the altar a great egg hung
272.   from the roof by a long gold chain, an unhatched egg
273.   of Leda's.

274.   *The Egyptian*: An egg of Leda, did you say? And
275.   unhatched? What frustrated destiny!

276.   *The Hebrew*: From another of her eggs came
277.   Helen. Helen and Odysseus will give the Greeks
278.   mastery of the human race for ever, for even I, at sight
279.   of that old piece of an oar and that egg, could hardly
280.   keep from prostrating myself before the altar. What
281.   phantom can prevail against the treasure of Sparta!
282.   Paris found a beating heart in Helen's breast.

283.   *The Egyptian*: Odysseus and Helen died; Christ
284.   only seemed to die.

285.   *The Hebrew*: What have you in your head now?
286.   Is it that we may see Him again? That being but dead

231.   covered by contemplation, in their faces a high keen
232.   joy like the cry of a bat, and the man who lives
233.   heroically gives them the only earthly body that they
234.   covet. He, as it were, copies their gestures and their
235.   acts. What seems their indifference is but their
236.   eternal possession of themselves. Man, too, remains
237.   separate. He does not surrender his soul. He keeps
238.   his privacy.

[*Drum-taps to represent knocking at the door*]

239. *The Hebrew.* There is someone at the door, but I dare
240.   not open with that crowd in the street.

241. *The Greek.* You need not be afraid. The crowd has begun
242.   to move away. [*The Hebrew goes down into the audience*
243.   *towards the left.*] I deduce from our great philosophers
244.   that a god can overwhelm man with disaster, take
245.   health and wealth away, but man keeps his privacy.
246.   If that is the Syrian he may bring such confirmation
247.   that mankind will never forget his words.

248. *The Hebrew* [*from amongst the audience*]. It is the Syrian.
249.   There is something wrong. He is ill or drunk.

[*He helps the Syrian on to the stage.*]

250. *The Syrian.* I am like a drunken man. I can hardly
251.   stand upon my feet. Something incredible has hap-
252.   pened. I have run all the way.

253. *The Hebrew.* Well?

254. *The Syrian.* I must tell the Eleven at once. Are they
255.   still in there? Everybody must be told.

256. *The Hebrew.* What is it? Get your breath and speak.

257. *The Syrian.* I was on my way to the tomb. I met the
258.   Galilean women, Mary the mother of Jesus, Mary
259.   the mother of James, and the other women. The
260.   younger women were pale with excitement and began

Directions after 238.   [*Drum taps . . . .*] **81.**
Directions in 242-243.   [*. . . audience.*] **81.**
254.   . . . eleven . . . **81.**
257.   . . . Tomb. . . . **81.**
259.   . . . James and . . . **81.**

287.   in seeming, He may show Himself again. [*Distant*
288.   *sound of drum and rattle.*] But, no, no, I will not let
289.   you put such thoughts into my head.

290.   *The Egyptian*: You said something about a heart—
291.   a beating heart, but it is the heart, that swirl of
      blood,
292.   that separates mankind from Divinity. What is the
293.   heart but corruption, change, death? It is gloomy,
294.   dark ignorant and terrible.

[248]   *The Hebrew* [*Who has been listening at the door*]:
[246]   295.   Hush, there is someone fumbling at the latch of the
[246]   296.   street door! Remember that, if we are very deter-
      mined,
297.   nobody can pass. I will go some steps down, but you
[248]   298.   must keep this door. It is all right—it is the Syrian—
[249]   299.   he looks as if he had heard something.

[250]   300.   *The Syrian* [*Who is out of breath*]: I am like a
[250-251]   301.   drunken man; I could hardly find the latch—such a
302.   strange thing has happened—such an incredible
[252]   303.   thing! I have run all the way.

[253]   304.   *The Hebrew*: Well, what is it?

[254]   305.   *The Syrian*: I must tell the eleven at once—are they
[255]   306.   still in there—everybody must be told—every-
[255]   307.   body—everybody!

[256]   308.   *The Hebrew*: Get your breath and speak!

[257]   309.   *The Syrian*: I was on my way to the tomb when I
[258]   310.   met the women from Galilee; Mary, the Mother of
[259]   311.   Jesus. Mary, the mother of James, and the other
[259-260]   312.   women. The younger women were pale with excite-
[261]   313.   ment. They began to speak all together, but Mary,
[262]   314.   the mother of James, silenced them and told me that
[263]   315.   they had gone to the tomb at daybreak and found it
[264, 268]   316.   empty. At the door stood a man, all shining, and
      cried
[269-270]   317.   out that Christ had arisen. [*Drums and rattles which*
[270]   318.   *are coming nearer.*] Then, as they came down the
[271]   319.   mountain, a Man stood suddenly at their side, and
      that

261. to speak all together. I did not know what they were
262. saying; but Mary the mother of James said that they
263. had been to the tomb at daybreak and found that it
264. was empty.

265. *The Greek.* Ah!

266. *The Hebrew.* The tomb cannot be empty. I will not
267. believe it.

268. *The Syrian.* At the door stood a man all shining, and
269. cried out that Christ had arisen. [*Faint drum-taps and*
270. *the faint sound of a rattle.*] As they came down the
271. mountain a man stood suddenly at their side; that
272. man was Christ himself. They stooped down and
273. kissed his feet. Now stand out of my way that I may
274. tell Peter and James and John.

The Hebrew [*standing before the curtained entrance of the*
275. *inner room*]. I will not stand out of the way.

276. *The Syrian.* Did you hear what I said? Our master has
277. arisen.

278. *The Hebrew.* I will not have the Eleven disturbed for
279. the dreams of women.

280. *The Greek.* The women were not dreaming. They told
281. you the truth, and yet this man is in the right. He is
282. in charge here. We must all be convinced before we
283. speak to the Eleven.

284. *The Syrian.* The Eleven will be able to judge better
285. than we.

286. *The Greek.* Though we are so much younger we know
287. more of the world than they do.

---

263. ... Tomb ... **81.**
265. [lacking]
266. ... Tomb ... **81.**
      Directions in 269-270. [... *drum taps* ....] **81.**
      Directions at 275. [... *of inner* ....] **81.**
278. ... eleven ... **81.**
283. ... eleven.
284. ... eleven ... **81.**

[272]   320.   Man was Christ Himself, and they stooped down and
[273]   321.   kissed His feet. And now make way that I may tell
[274]   322.   Peter and James and John.

[275]   323.   *The Hebrew*: I will not make way.

[276]   324.   *The Syrian*: But do you not understand? Our
[277]   325.   Master has risen from the dead.

[278-279]   326.   *The Hebrew*: I will not have the eleven disturbed
[279]   327.   for the dreams of women. The women are so wild
         328.   with grief they could persuade themselves of any-
                  thing.

[280]   329.   *The Egyptian*: I believe that what the women told
[281]   330.   you is true and yet he is in the right up to a certain
[282-283]   331.   point. We three must be convinced, before we speak
[283, 286]   332.   to the eleven. Though we are so much younger, we
[287]   333.   know more of the world than they do.

         334.   *The Syrian*: It is no dream if the tomb is empty—
         335.   and they say that it is empty.

         336.   *The Hebrew*: The Romans heard a rumour yester-
         337.   day that some of our people had planned to steal the
         338.   Body and put abroad a story that Christ had arisen.

[284]   339.   *The Syrian*: But the eleven will judge of all that
[284-285]   340.   better than we.

[288]   341.   *The Hebrew*: If you told your story they would
[289]   342.   judge of it as I do, but Peter's misery would be in-
[290]   343.   creased. I have known him longer than you and I
[291]   344.   know what would happen. Peter would remember that
[292]   345.   the women did not flinch, that not one amongst them
[293]   346.   denied her Master, that this dream but proved their
[294]   247.   love and confidence. Then he would think that he had
[295]   348.   lost both and he would imagine that John was looking
[295-297]   349.   at him, and he would turn away and bury his head in
[297]   350.   his hands.

         351.   *The Egyptian*: Before you came I was about to say
         352.   that Christ might appear again at any moment. I con-
         353.   trasted Him with Helen and Odysseus, who could
         354.   never so appear.

288. *The Hebrew.* If you told your story they would no more
289. believe it than I do, but Peter's misery would be in-
290. creased. I know him longer than you do and I know
291. what would happen. Peter would remember that the
292. women did not flinch; that not one amongst them
293. denied her master; that the dream proved their love
294. and faith. Then he would remember that he had
295. lacked both, and imagine that John was looking at
296. him. He would turn away and bury his head in his
297. hands.

298. *The Greek.* I said that we must all be convinced, but
299. there is another reason why you must not tell them
300. anything. Somebody else is coming. I am certain that
301. Jesus never had a human body; that he is a phantom
302. and can pass through that wall; that he will so pass;
303. that he will pass through this room; that he himself
304. will speak to the apostles.

305. *The Syrian.* He is no phantom. We put a great stone
306. over the mouth of the tomb, and the women say that
307. it has been rolled back.

308. *The Hebrew.* The Romans heard yesterday that some
309. of our people planned to steal the body, and to put
310. abroad a story that Christ had arisen; and so escape
311. the shame of our defeat. They probably stole it in
312. the night.

313. *The Syrian.* The Romans put sentries at the tomb. The
314. women found the sentries asleep. Christ had put
315. them asleep that they might not see him move the
316. stone.

317. *The Greek.* A hand without bones, without sinews, can-
318. not move a stone.

319. *The Syrian.* What matter if it contradicts all human
320. knowledge?—another Argo seeks another fleece, an-

300-301. . . . certain Jesus . . . **81.**
306. . . . Tomb, . . . **81.**
309. . . . body and . . . **81.**
312. that night.
313. . . . Tomb. . . . **81.**
320. knowledge: another . . . **81.**

355. *The Syrian*: Suddenly it came into my head—even
356.   while I was running—those priests of Dionysus had
357.   passed with all their noise—that all over Greece, all
358.   over Asia Minor and Magna Grecia, from generation
359.   to generation, men have celebrated the death and Re-
360.   surrection of Attis, or Adonis, or Dionysus, of God
361.   under some name or other, and now God Himself, that
362.   He might, as it were, sanctify man's tragedy, has turned
363.   all those songs and dances into prophesy, and that
364.   which we but dreamed has been accomplished, and
365.   God has become flesh.

366. *The Egyptian*: God has form but not body and,
367.   therefore, He is neither visible nor tangible, but God
368.   can communicate with mankind through an illusionary
369.   body, such a form as sculptors in my city make for
370.   Alexander the Great—no beating, suffering heart, all
371.   stone or bronze, as it were, perfect—exactly 6 ft. high,
372.   neither more nor less—nothing can be added, nothing
373.   taken away and perfect maturity. Christ when he
374.   began to preach was exactly thirty years old.

375. *The Syrian*: If Christ were but a phantom, whom
376.   was she I met but now and heard called 'Mary, the
377.   Mother of Jesus'?

378. *The Egyptian*: God made her believe that she had
379.   carried Him upon her knees, that we might not discover
380.   the truth till the right time had come. This Jew said
381.   a moment ago that women will believe anything.

382. *The Syrian*: But . . . .

383. *The Egyptian*: Listen to me. There can be no
384.   contact, Hermes, the Thrice Great has said, between
[120]   385.   the corruptible and the incorruptible, and to suggest
              that
[120-121] 386.   God was born of a woman, that He lay in her womb,
[121]   387.   that she fed Him upon her breast, that she washed
[121-122] 388.   Him as other children are washed, is the most terrible
[122]   389.   blasphemy.

390. *The Syrian*: You mean that God has not really
391.   died for us?

321.   other Troy is sacked.

322.   *The Greek.* Why are you laughing?

323.   *The Syrian.* What is human knowledge?

324.   *The Greek.* The knowledge that keeps the road from
325.   here to Persia free from robbers, that has built the
326.   beautiful humane cities, that has made the modern
327.   world, that stands between us and the barbarian.

328.   *The Syrian.* But what if there is something it cannot
329.   explain, something more important than anything
330.   else?

331.   *The Greek.* You talk as if you wanted the barbarian
332.   back.

333.   *The Syrian.* What if there is always something that lies
334.   outside knowledge, outside order? What if at the
335.   moment when knowledge and order seem complete
336.   that something appears?   [*He has begun to laugh.*

337.   *The Hebrew.* Stop laughing.

338.   *The Syrian.* What if the irrational return? What if the
339.   circle begin again?

340.   *The Hebrew.* Stop! He laughed when he saw Calvary
341.   through the window, and now you laugh.

342.   *The Greek.* He too has lost control of himself.

343.   *The Hebrew.* Stop, I tell you.   [*Drums and rattles.*]

344.   *The Syrian.* But I am not laughing. It is the people out
345.   there who are laughing.

346.   *The Hebrew.* No, they are shaking rattles and beating
347.   drums.

---

332.   back? **81.**
        Directions in 336.   [lacking] **81.**
342.   . . . too, has . . . .
343.   Stop I . . . . **81.**

392. *The Egyptian*: A God cannot die.

393. *The Syrian* [*To the Hebrew*]: You will understand
394. me; this Egyptian cannot because he is almost a Greek.
395. We are all humiliated by life; we think that we are
396. nothing and that it is no use behaving well. But what
397. if God said to himself, 'I will share all the humiliation
398. and let them know that I have done it out of love. If
399. I do that they will no longer think that they are
400. nothing.' What if He came down for that reason and
401. was born and died, not in seeming but in reality. Why
402. should I care for a phantom or a shadow which only
403. seemed to suffer [*drums and rattles but very near now*].

404. *The Egyptian*: What you say is impossible, but I
405. cannot make myself understood with all that noise
406. outside.

407. *The Hebrew*: One is as impossible as the other.
408. You with your phantom that appears from nowhere.
409. You with your God that needs to be fed and washed.
410. There is only one sensible thing to say; He deceived
411. Himself and us, maddened by His love—and He is
412. dead. [*He goes to window; he may stand, perhaps,
        as though the window were in front of the stage, where*

[351]   413. *the audience are.*] The priests of Dionysus are on the
[352]   414. other side of the house, but they have hidden the image
[353-354] 415. of the dead man, and from that I judge that they have
[353-354] 416. raised their lunatic cry 'God has arisen, God has
[354-356] 417. arisen!' They will cry that through every street of
[356-357] 418. the city, making their God live and die as they please.
[357]   419. But why are they silent—is it because they are hoarse
[358]   420. that they dance silently, or is it some part of the play
[358]   421. to seem, speechless at last, poor effeminate crack-pated
[358-359] 422. men, with their imaginary joy? They are coming
[359]   423. nearer and nearer, dancing all the while some kind of
[360]   424. elaborate step, like steps of an old Syrian dance. Look
[365-366] 425. how they roll their painted eyes, as the dance grows
[366]   426. quicker and quicker. Did ever man show such abandon
[361, 366-
367]   427. in the expression of a real emotion? They are almost
[361, 366-
367]   428. under the window now. [*A loud sound of drums and*

348. *The Syrian.* I thought they were laughing. How
349.   horrible!

350. *The Greek [looking out over heads of audience].* The wor-
351.   shippers of Dionysus are coming this way again.
352.   They have hidden their image of the dead god, and
353.   have begun their lunatic cry, 'God has arisen! God
354.   has arisen!'
       [The Musicians who have been saying 'God has arisen!' *fall
       silent.*
355.   They will cry 'God has arisen!' through all the
356.   streets of the city. They can make their god live and
357.   die at their pleasure; but why are they silent? They
358.   are dancing silently. They are coming nearer and
359.   nearer, dancing all the while, using some kind of
360.   ancient step unlike anything I have seen in Alex-
361.   andria. They are almost under the window now.

362. *The Hebrew.* They have come back to mock us, because
363.   their god arises every year, whereas our god is dead
364.   for ever.

365. *The Greek.* How they roll their painted eyes as the
366.   dance grows quicker and quicker! They are under
367.   the window. Why are they all suddenly motionless?
368.   Why are all those unseeing eyes turned upon this
369.   house? Is there anything strange about this house?

370. *The Hebrew.* Somebody has come into the room.

371. *The Greek.* Where?

372. *The Hebrew.* I do not know; but I thought I heard a
373.   step.

374. *The Greek.* I knew that he would come.

375. *The Hebrew.* There is no one here. I shut the door at
376.   the foot of the steps.

---

353. . . . cry 'God . . . **81.**
      Directions after 354. [. . . *arisen' fall* . . . .] **81.**
359. nearer dancing . . . **81, 84.**
364. forever. **81.**
366. . . . quicker. They . . . **81.**

rattles through which one hears the drunken man singing.]

Song of the Drunkard.

429.   The drunkard with the painted eyes
430.   Discovered thought is misery,
431.   Now, with drum and rattle, he
432.   Bids a drunken God arise.

[*The drums and rattles are silent.*]

[367]   433.   *The Hebrew*: Why are they all suddenly silent and
[367]   434.   raise their arms above their head and stand motionless,
[368]   435.   all their unseeing eyes turned upon this house?

[370]   436.   *The Egyptian*: There is someone in the room.

[371]   437.   *The Hebrew*: Where?

[372]   438.   *The Egyptian*: I do not know but I thought I heard
[373]   439.   someone breathing.

[375]   440.   *The Hebrew*: There is no one here. No one could
[375]   441.   get in without our knowing, and the door is still
[375]   442.   fastened.

[377]   443.   *The Egyptian*: The curtain over there is moving.

[378]   444.   *The Hebrew*: No, it is quite still and, besides, there
[378-379] 445. is nothing behind the curtain but a blank wall.

[380]   446.   *The Egypian:* Look! Look.

[381]   447.   *The Hebrew*: Yes, it has begun to move!

[382]   448.   *The Egyptian*: O God of Egypt! There is some-
[382]   449.   one coming through it! [*They cower away from curtain, the Syrian towards the door of inner room, the
Hebrew towards the back of the stage. The figure of
[383]   450.   Christ enters through curtain.*] It is the figure of Christ.
[383-384] 451. Why are you afraid? Seeing that he was not buried or
[384-385] 452. crucified in reality, it is natural that He should
appear.
[386]   453.   But there is nothing but an appearance, a phantom—

377. *The Greek.* The curtain over there is moving.

378. *The Hebrew.* No, it is quite still, and besides there is
379.   nothing behind it but a blank wall.

380. *The Greek.* Look, look!

381. *The Hebrew.* Yes, it has begun to move. [*During what follows he
    backs in terror towards the left-hand corner of the stage.*]

382. *The Greek.* There is someone coming through it.
    [*The figure of Christ wearing a recognisable but stylistic mask enters
    through the curtain. The Syrian slowly draws back the curtain that
    shuts off the inner room where the apostles are. The three young men
    are towards the left of the stage, the figure of Christ is at the back
    towards the right.*

383. *The Greek.* It is the phantom of our master. Why are
384.   you afraid? He has been crucified and buried, but
385.   only in semblance, and is among us once more. [*The
386.   Hebrew kneels.*] There is nothing here but a phantom,
387.   it has no flesh and blood. Because I know the truth
388.   I am not afraid. Look, I will touch it. It may be
389.   hard under my hand like a statue—I have heard of
390.   such things—or my hand may pass through it—but
391.   there is no flesh and blood. [*He goes slowly up to the
392.   figure and passes his hand over its side.*] The heart of a
393.   phantom is beating! The heart of a phantom is beat-
394.   ing! [*He screams. The figure of Christ crosses the stage and passes into
    the inner room.*]

395. *The Syrian.* He is standing in the midst of them. Some
396.   are afraid. He looks at Peter and James and John.
397.   He smiles. He has parted the clothes at his side. He

---

380. . . . , Look! **81.**
    Directions at 381. [. . . *left hand* . . . .] **81.**
385. . . . semblance and . . .
386. . . . phantom.
387. It . . .
388. . . . . Look I . . .
389. . . . statue; I . . .
390. . . . things; or . . . it; but **81.**
394. ing. [*He* . . . **81.**
397. . . . the grave clothes from his side. There **81.**

[387]	454.	there is no flesh, there is no blood. Because I know
[387-388]	455.	the truth I am not afraid—look, I will touch the form.
[388-390]	456.	It may be hard under my hand, I have heard of such
[390-391]	457.	things, or my hand may pass through it, but there is no
[391-392]	458.	blood. [*He goes up to the phantom slowly and touches*
[392-393]	459.	*the side and then cries out.*] The Heart of the Phan-
[393-394]	460.	tom is beating—the Heart of the Phantom is beating!

[*He shrinks back as the phantom passes. It goes into the inner room, the Syrian passing in before it, the Hebrew is cowering against the back of the stage.*]

	461.	Something terrible has happened; I thought my hand
[395]	462.	would have passed through Him. He is standing in
[396]	463.	the midst of them now—some of them are afraid—He
[396-397]	464.	looks at Peter and James and John and He smiles.
[397]	465.	Thomas is saying something and He answers. He has
[397-398]	466.	pulled the grave clothes from His side and there is a
[398-399]	467.	wound, a great wound in His side—Thomas has put
[399-400]	468.	his hand into the wound. Now they are all gathering
	469.	round. He speaks again and there in the street the
	470.	priests of Dionysus are still standing, perhaps, with
	471.	their arms lifted. [*Going to window.*] Yes, they are
	472.	standing there and they look up in a kind of stupor,
	473.	and that drunkard is still dancing, turning round like a
	474.	top, and they and he know nothing. . . . And there
	475.	are the Galilæan women, Mary, the Mother of Jesus,
	476.	and Mary, the mother of James, and the rest coming
	477.	from the mountain to tell what they have seen—they
	478.	know, but they do not know how terrible it is. Never
	479.	before did the Heart of a Phantom beat. How terrible!
[401]	480.	Reason itself is dead. [*In a loud voice.*] Rome,
[401-402]	481.	Greece, Egypt—it has come, the miracle, that which
[402]	482.	must destroy you, irrational force. The Heart of a
[402-403]	483.	Phantom is beating!

Song of the Unfolding and Folding of the Cloth

406	484.	In pity for man's darkening thought
407	485.	He walked that room and issued thence
408	486.	In Galilæan turbulence;
[409]	487.	The Babylonian star-light brought
410	488.	A fabulous, formless darkness in;
411	489.	Odour of blood when Christ was slain
[412]	490.	Made Plato's tolerance in vain,
[413]	491.	And vain the Doric discipline.

THE END

398. shows them his side. There is a great wound there.
399. Thomas has put his hand into the wound. He has put
400. his hand where the heart is.

401. *The Greek.* O Athens, Alexandria, Rome, something
402. has come to destroy you. The heart of a phantom is
403. beating. Man has begun to die. Your words are clear
404. at last, O Heraclitus. God and man die each other's
405. life, live each other's death.

[*The Musicians rise, one or more singing the following words. If the performance is in a private room or studio, they unfold and fold a curtain as in my dance plays; if at the Peacock Theatre, they draw the proscenium curtain across.*]

I

406. In pity for man's darkening thought
407. He walked that room and issued thence
408. In Galilean turbulence;
409. The Babylonian starlight brought
410. A fabulous, formless darkness in;
411. Odour of blood when Christ was slain
412. Made all Platonic tolerance vain
413. And vain all Doric discipline.

II

414. Everything that man esteems
415. Endures a moment or a day:
416. Love's pleasure drives his love away,
417. The painter's brush consumes his dreams;
418. The herald's cry, the soldier's tread
419. Exhaust his glory and his might:
420. Whatever flames upon the night
421. Man's own resinous heart has fed.

THE END

---

398. is a . . . . **81.**
401. Oh! Athens, . . . **81.**
402. . . . you! The . . .
403. beating! Man . . . **83.**
       Directions after 405.   [. . . *studio they . . . Theatre they* . . . .] **81.**
410. . . . fabulous formless . . . ; **81.**
412. Made Plato's tolerance in vain;
413. In vain the Doric . . . . **81.**
415. . . . day; **81** ; . . . day. **83.**

NOTES

I

This play, or the first sketch of it, more dialogue than play, was intended for my drawing-room, where my *Hawk's Well* had just been played.

For years I have been preoccupied with a certain myth that was itself a reply to a myth. I do not mean a fiction, but one of those statements our nature is compelled to make and employ as a truth though there cannot be sufficient evidence. When I was a boy everybody talked about progress, and rebellion against my elders took the form of aversion to that myth. I took satisfaction in certain public disasters, felt a sort of ecstasy at the contemplation of ruin, and then I came upon the story of Oisin in Tir-nan-oge and reshaped it into my *Wanderings of Oisin*. He rides across the sea with a spirit, he passes phantoms, a boy following a girl, a hound chasing a hare, emblematical of eternal pursuit, he comes to an island of choral dancing, leaves that after many years, passes the phantoms once again, comes to an island of endless battle for an object never achieved, leaves that after many years, passes the phantoms once again, comes to an island of sleep, leaves that and comes to Ireland, to S. Patrick and old age. I did not pick these images because of any theory, but because I found them impressive, yet all the while abstractions haunted me. I remember rejecting, because it spoilt the simplicity, an elaborate metaphor of a breaking wave intended to prove that all life rose and fell as in my poem. How hard it was to refrain from pointing out that Oisin after old age, its illumination half accepted, half rejected, would pass in death over another sea to another island. Presently Oisin and his islands faded and the sort of images that come into *Rosa Alchemica* and *The Adoration of the Magi* took their place. Our civilization was about to reverse itself, or some new civilization about to be born from all that our age had rejected, from all that my stories symbolised as a harlot, and take after its mother; because we had worshipped a single god it would worship many or receive from Joachim de Flora's Holy Spirit a multitudinous influx. A passage in *La Peau de chagrin* may have started me, but because I knew no ally but Balzac, I kept silent about all I could not get into fantastic romance. So did the abstract ideas persecute me that *On Baile's Strand*, founded upon a dream, was only finished when, after a struggle of two years, I had made the Fool and Blind Man, Cuchulain and Conchubar whose shadows they are, all image, and now I can no longer remember what they meant except that they meant in some sense those combatants who turn the wheel of life. Had I begun *On Baile's Strand* or not when I began to imagine, as always at my left side just out of the range of the sight, a brazen winged beast[1] that I associated with laughing, ecstatic destruction?

[1] Afterwards described in my poem 'The Second Coming.'

Then I wrote, spurred by an external necessity, *Where There is Nothing*, a crude play with some dramatic force, since changed with Lady Gregory's help into *The Unicorn from the Stars*. A neighbourhood inflamed with drink, a country house burnt down, a spiritual anarchy preached! Then after some years came the thought that a man always tried to become his opposite, to become what he would abhor if he did not desire it, and I wasted some three summers and some part of each winter before I had banished the ghost and turned what I had meant for tragedy into a farce: *The Player Queen*. Then unexpectedly and under circumstances described in *A Packet to Ezra Pound* came a symbolical system displaying the conflict in all its forms:

> Where got I that truth?
> Out of a medium's mouth,
> Out of nothing it came,
> Out of the forest loam,
> Out of dark night where lay
> The crowns of Nineveh.

II

> And then did all the Muses sing
> Of Magnus Annus at the spring.

In 1894 Gorky and Lunacharsky tried to correct the philosophy of Marxian socialism by the best German philosophy of their time, founding schools at Capri and Bologna for the purpose, but Lenin founded a rival school at Paris and brought Marxian socialism back to orthodoxy: 'we remain materialist, anything else would lead to religion.' Four or five years later Pius X saw a Commission of Catholic scholars considering the text of the Bible and its attribution to certain authors and dissolved the Commission: 'Moses and the Four Evangelists wrote the Books that are called by their names; any other conclusion would lead to scepticism.' In this way did two great men[1] prepare two great movements, purified of modernism, for a crisis when, in the words of Archbishop Downey, they must dispute the mastery of the world.

So far I have the sympathy of the Garrets and Cellars, for they are, I am told, without exception Catholic, Communist, or both! Yet there is a third myth or philosophy that has made an equal stir in the world. Ptolemy thought the precession of the equinoxes moved at the rate of a degree every hundred years, and that somewhere about the time of Christ and Caesar the equinoctial sun had returned to its original place in the constellations,

---

[1] It is not true, according to Prince Mirsky, that Marxian socialism denies the existence of great men. 'Great men are the embodiment of great social movements, and it is natural that the greater the movement the greater the "great man" produced by it.'

completing and recommencing the thirty-six thousand years, or three hundred and sixty incarnations of a hundred years apiece, of Plato's man of Ur. Hitherto almost every philosopher had some different measure for the Greatest Year, but this Platonic Year, as it was called, soon displaced all others; it was a Christian heresy in the twelfth century, and in the East, multiplied by twelve as if it were but a month of a still greater year, it became the Manvantra[1] of 432,000 years, until animated by the Indian jungle it generated new noughts and multiplied itself into Kalpas.

It was perhaps obvious, when Plotinus substituted the archetypes of individual men in all their possible incarnations for a limited number of Platonic Ideas, that a Greatest Year for whale and gudgeon alike must exhaust the multiplication table. Whatever its length, it divided, and so did every unit whose multiple it was, into waxing and waning, day and night, or summer and winter. There was everywhere a conflict like that of my play between two principles or 'elemental forms of the mind,' each 'living the other's life, dying the other's death.' I have a Chinese painting of three old sages sitting together, one with a deer at his side, one with a scroll open at the symbol of yen and yin, those two forms that whirl perpetually, creating and re-creating all things. But because of our modern discovery that the equinox shifts its ground more rapidly than Ptolemy believed, one must, somebody says, invent a new symbolic scheme. No, a thousand times no; I insist that the equinox does shift a degree in a hundred years; anything else would lead to confusion.

All ancient nations believed in the re-birth of the soul and had probably empirical evidence like that Lafcadio Hearn found among the Japanese. In our time Schopenhauer believed it, and McTaggart thinks Hegel did, though lack of interest in the individual soul had kept him silent. It is the foundation of McTaggart's own philosophical system. Cardinal Mercier saw no evidence for it, but did not think it heretical; and its rejection compelled the sincere and noble Von Hügel to say that children dead too young to have earned Heaven suffered no wrong, never having heard of a better place than Limbo. Even though we think temporal existence illusionary it cannot be capricious; it is what Plotinus called the characteristic act of the soul and must reflect the soul's coherence. All our thought seems to lead by antithesis to some new affirmation of the supernatural. In a few years perhaps we may have much empirical evidence, the only evidence that moves the mass of men to-day that man has lived many times; there is some not yet perfectly examined—I think of that Professor's daughter in Palermo. This belief held by Plato and Plotinus, and supported by weighty argument, resembles the mathematical doctrines of Einstein before the experimental proof of the curvature of light.

---

[1] This explanation of the Manvantra comes from an Arab who visited India at the beginning of the tenth century. He is quoted in Pierre Duhem, *Système du Monde*, vol. i, pp. 67 and 68.

We may come to think that nothing exists but a stream of souls, that all knowledge is biography, and with Plotinus that every soul is unique; that these souls, these eternal archetypes, combine into greater units as days and nights into months, months into years, and at last into the final unit that differs in nothing from that which they were at the beginning: everywhere that antinomy of the One and the Many that Plato thought in his *Parmenides* insoluble, though Blake thought it soluble 'at the bottom of the graves.' Such belief may arise from Communism by antithesis, declaring at last even to the common ear that all things have value according to the clarity of their expression of themselves, and not as functions of changing economic conditions or as a preparation for some Utopia. There is perhaps no final happy state except in so far as men may gradually grow better; escape may be for individuals alone who know how to exhaust their possible lives, to set, as it were, the hands of the clock racing. Perhaps we shall learn to accept even innumerable lives with happy humility—'I have been always an insect in the roots of the grass'—and putting aside calculating scruples be ever ready to wager all upon the dice.

Even our best histories treat men as function. Why must I think the victorious cause the better? Why should Mommsen think the less of Cicero because Caesar beat him? I am satisfied, the Platonic Year in my head, to find but drama. I prefer that the defeated cause should be more vividly described than that which has the advertisement of victory. No battle has been finally won or lost; 'to Garret or Cellar a wheel I send.'

III

'What if there is always something that lies outside knowledge, outside order? . . . What if the irrational return? What if the circle begin again?' Years ago I read Sir William Crookes' *Studies in Psychical Research*. After excluding every possibility of fraud, he touched a materialised form and found the heart beating. I felt, though my intellect rejected what I read, the terror of the supernatural described by Job. Just before the war a much respected man of science entering a room in his own house found there two girl visitors—I have questioned all three—one lying asleep on the table, the other sitting on the end of the table screaming, the table floating in the air, and 'immediately vomited.' I took from the beating heart, from my momentary terror, from the shock of a man of science, the central situation of my play: the young man touching the heart of the phantom and screaming. It has seemed to me of late that the sense of spiritual reality comes whether to the individual or to crowds from some violent shock, and that idea has the support of tradition.

'The Resurrection,' Introduction, **83.**

* * *

THE WORDS UPON THE WINDOW-PANE

1934

IN MEMORY OF
LADY GREGORY
IN WHOSE HOUSE IT WAS WRITTEN

Persons in the Play

Dr. Trench	Cornelius Patterson
Miss Mackenna	Abraham Johnson
John Corbet	Mrs. Mallet

Mrs. Henderson

A lodging-house room, an armchair, a little table in front of it, chairs on either side. A fireplace and window. A kettle on the hob and some tea-things on a dresser. A door to back and towards the right. Through the door one can see an entrance hall. The sound of a knocker. Miss Mackenna passes through and then she re-enters hall together with John Corbet, a man of twenty-two or twenty-three, and Dr. Trench, a man of between sixty and seventy.

1. *Dr. Trench* [*in hall*]. May I introduce John Corbet, one
2. of the Corbets of Ballymoney, but at present a
3. Cambridge student? This is Miss Mackenna, our

PRINTINGS   **82, 83, 84, 89, 97.**

DATE   [lacking] **82, 83.**

DRAMATIS PERSONAE   Persons of the Play / Doctor[1] Trench / . . . **82.**

STAGE DIRECTIONS   . . . *lodging house . . . door at back . . . passes the door, returns bringing with her John Corbet,* . . . *twenty two* . . . *twenty three,* . . . . **82;** . . . *re-enters the hall* . . . . **83.**

TEXT   Title . . . Window Pane **82.**
Title and Date of First Performance . . . Window-Pane / First performed at the Abbey Theatre / on 17th November 1930 **83.**

3.   . . . Mackenna our **82.**

[1] Spelled thus throughout **82.**

4.   energetic secretary. [*They come into room, take off their coats.*]

5.   *Miss Mackenna.* I thought it better to let you in myself.
6.   This country is still sufficiently medieval to make
7.   spiritualism an undesirable theme for gossip. Give
8.   me your coats and hats, I will put them in my own
9.   room. It is just across the hall. Better sit down; your
10. watches must be fast. Mrs. Henderson is lying down,
11. as she always does before a séance. We won't begin
12. for ten minutes yet. [*She goes out with hats and coats.*]

13. *Dr. Trench.* Miss Mackenna does all the real work of
14. the Dublin Spiritualists' Association. She did all the
15. correspondence with Mrs. Henderson, and persuaded
16. the landlady to let her this big room and a small
17. room upstairs. We are a poor society and could not
18. guarantee anything in advance. Mrs. Henderson has
19. come from London at her own risk. She was born
20. in Dublin and wants to spread the movement here.
21. She lives very economically and does not expect a
22. great deal. We all give what we can. A poor woman
23. with the soul of an apostle.

24. *John Corbet.* Have there been many séances?

25. *Dr. Trench.* Only there so far.

26. *John Corbet.* I hope she will not mind my scepticism.
27. I have looked into Myer's *Human Personality* and a
28. wild book by Conan Doyle, but am unconvinced.

29. *Dr. Trench.* We all have to find the truth for ourselves.
30. Lord Dunraven, then Lord Adare, introduced my
31. father to the famous David Home. My father often
32. told me that he saw David Home floating in the air
33. in broad daylight, but I did not believe a word of it.
34. I had to investigate for myself, and I was very hard

---

4.   enthusiastic secretary. [. . . *room, and take* . . . **82**; enthusiastic secretary.
     [. . . . **84, 89.**
9.   . . . down, your **82, 84, 89.**
11. . . . wont . . . **82.**
14. . . . Spiritualists . . .
15. . . . Henderson and . . . **82.**
27. . . . 'Human Personality' . . . **82.**

35.   to convince. Mrs. Piper, an American trance medium,
36.   not unlike Mrs. Henderson, convinced me.

37. *John Corbet.* A state of somnambulism and voices com-
38.   ing through her lips that purport to be those of dead
39.   persons?

40. *Dr. Trench.* Exactly: quite the best kind of medium-
41.   ship if you want to establish the identity of a spirit.
42.   But do not expect too much. There has been a hostile
43.   influence.

44. *John Corbet.* You mean an evil spirit?

45. *Dr. Trench.* The poet Blake said that he never knew a
46.   bad man that had not something very good about
47.   him. I say a hostile influence, an influence that dis-
48.   turbed the last séance very seriously. I cannot tell
49.   you what happened, for I have not been at any of
50.   Mrs. Henderson's séances. Trance mediumship has
51.   nothing new to show me—I told the young people
52.   when they made me their President that I would
53.   probably stay at home, that I could get more out of
54.   Emanuel Swedenborg than out of any séance. [*A*
55.   *knock.*] That is probably old Cornelius Patterson; he
56.   thinks they race horses and whippets in the other
57.   world, and is, so they tell me, so anxious to find
58.   out if he is right that he is always punctual. Miss
59.   Mackenna will keep him to herself for some minutes.
60.   He gives her tips for Harold's Cross.
      [*Miss Mackenna crosses to hall door and admits Cornelius Patterson.*
      She brings him to her room across the hall.

61. *John Corbet* [*who has been wandering about*]. This is a
62.   wonderful room for a lodging-house.

63. *Dr. Trench.* It was a private house until about fifty
64.   years ago. It was not so near the town in those days,
65.   and there are large stables at the back. Quite a

---

51. . . . me. I . . . **82.**
57. world and . . . **82.**
62. . . . lodging house. **82.**
64. . . . days **82.**

66.   number of notable people lived here. Grattan was
67.   born upstairs; no, not Grattan, Curran perhaps—
68.   I forget—but I do know that this house in the early
69.   part of the eighteenth century belonged to friends of
70.   Jonathan Swift, or rather of Stella. Swift chaffed her
71.   in the *Journal to Stella* because of certain small sums
72.   of money she lost at cards probably in this very room.
73.   That was before Vanessa appeared upon the scene.
74.   It was a country-house in those days, surrounded by
75.   trees and gardens. Somebody cut some lines from
76.   a poem of hers upon the window-pane—tradition
77.   says Stella herself. [*A knock.*] Here they are, but you
78.   will hardly make them out in this light. [*They stand in the window.*
        Corbet stoops down to see better. Miss Mackenna and Abraham
        Johnson enter and stand near door.]

79. *Abraham Johnson.* Where is Mrs. Henderson?

80. *Miss Mackenna.* She is upstairs; she always rests before
81.   a séance.

82. *Abraham Johnson.* I must see her before the séance. I
83.   know exactly what to do to get rid of this evil
84.   influence.

85. *Miss Mackenna.* If you go up to see her there will be
86.   no séance at all. She says it is dangerous even to
87.   think, much less to speak, of an evil influence.

88. *Abraham Johnson.* Then I shall speak to the President.

89. *Miss Mackenna.* Better talk the whole thing over first in
90.   my room. Mrs. Henderson says that there must be
91.   perfect harmony.

92. *Abraham Johnson.* Something must be done. The last
93.   séance was completely spoiled. [*A knock.*]

---

67.   ... upstairs, no, ...— **82** ; ... upstairs—no, ...— **84, 89.**
74.   ... country house ... days surrounded ... **82** ; ... country house
     ... **84, 89.**
77.   ... are but ... **82.**
80.   ... upstairs, she ... **82.**
87.   ... speak of, an .... **84, 89.**
93.   ... spoilt. [.... **82, 83.**

94. *Miss Mackenna.* That may be Mrs. Mallet; she is a very
95. experienced spiritualist. Come to my room, old
96. Patterson and some others are there already. [*She brings him to
the other room and later crosses to hall door to admit Mrs. Mallet.*]

97. *John Corbet.* I know those lines well—they are part of
98. a poem Stella wrote for Swift's fifty-fourth birthday.
99. Only three poems of hers—and some lines she added
100. to a poem of Swift's—have come down to us, but
101. they are enough to prove her a better poet than
102. Swift. Even those few words on the window make
103. me think of a seventeenth-century poet, Donne or
104. Crashaw. [*He quotes*]

105.   'You taught how I might youth prolong
106.   By knowing what is right and wrong,
107.   How from my heart to bring supplies
108.   Of lustre to my fading eyes.'

109. How strange that a celibate scholar, well on in life,
110. should keep the love of two such women! He met
111. Vanessa in London at the height of his political
112. power. She followed him to Dublin. She loved him
113. for nine years, perhaps died of love, but Stella loved
114. him all her life.

115. *Dr. Trench.* I have shown that writing to several persons,
116. and you are the first who has recognised the lines.

117. *John Corbet.* I am writing an essay on Swift and Stella
118. for my doctorate at Cambridge. I hope to prove that
119. in Swift's day men of intellect reached the height

---

94. . . . Mallet, she . . . **82.**
    Directions at 96. [. . . *hall-door* . . . .]
97. . . . know these lines . . . **82.**
99. . . . hers and . . .
100. . . . Swift's have . . . **84, 89.**
103. . . . seventeenth century . . .
    Directions in 104. [. . . *quotes*]: **82.**
107. . . . from the heart . . .
108. . . . eyes' **82.**
110. . . . women. He . . . **82.**
113. . . . love; but . . . **82.**
115. . . . persons **82, 84, 89.**

120.   of their power—the greatest position they ever at-
121.   tained in society and the State, that everything great
122.   in Ireland and in our character, in what remains of
123.   our architecture, comes from that day; that we have
124.   kept its seal longer than England.

125.   *Dr. Trench.* A tragic life: Bolingbroke, Harley, Or-
126.   monde, all those great Ministers that were his
127.   friends, banished and broken.

128.   *John Corbet.* I do not think you can explain him in that
129.   way—his tragedy had deeper foundations. His ideal
130.   order was the Roman Senate, his ideal men Brutus
131.   and Cato. Such an order and such men had seemed
132.   possible once more, but the movement passed and
133.   he foresaw the ruin to come, Democracy, Rousseau,
134.   the French Revolution; that is why he hated the
135.   common run of men,—'I hate lawyers, I hate doctors,'
136.   he said, 'though I love Dr. So-and-so and Judge So-
137.   and so'—that is why he wrote *Gulliver*, that is why he
138.   wore out his brain, that is why he felt *saeva indignatio*,
139.   that is why he sleeps under the greatest epitaph in
140.   history. You remember how it goes? It is almost finer
141.   in English than in Latin: 'He has gone where fierce
142.   indignation can lacerate his heart no more.'

      [*Abraham Johnson comes in, followed by Mrs. Mallet and Cornelius Patterson.*

143.   *Abraham Johnson.* Something must be done, Dr. Trench,
144.   to drive away the influence that has destroyed our
145.   séances. I have come here week after week at con-
146.   siderable expense. I am from Belfast. I am by profes-

---

121.   . . . Society . . . State—that . . . **82**.
125.   . . . life, Ormonde, Harley, Bo- **82** ; . . . life; Bolingbroke, . . . **83**.
126.   lingbroke, all . . . **82**.
129.   . . . foundations, his . . . **84, 89**.
131.   . . . Cato; such . . .
132.   . . . more; but . . . **82**.
133.   . . . come. Democracy, . . . , **97A**.
134.   . . . Revolution, that . . . **82**.
135.   . . . doctors' **82** ; . . . men—'I . . . ,' **84, 89**.
136.   . . . said 'though . . . **82**.
137.   and-so',—that . . . Gulliver, . . . **82** ; and-so'—that . . . **83, 97A**.
141.   . . . Latin:—'He . . . **82**.

147. sion a minister of the Gospel, I do a great deal of
148. work among the poor and ignorant. I produce con-
149. siderable effect by singing and preaching, but I know
150. that my effect should be much greater than it is. My
151. hope is that I shall be able to communicate with the
152. great Evangelist Moody. I want to ask him to stand
153. invisible beside me when I speak or sing, and lay his
154. hands upon my head and give me such a portion of
155. his power that my work may be blessed as the work
156. of Moody and Sankey was blessed.

157. *Mrs. Mallet.* What Mr. Johnson says about the hostile
158. influence is quite true. The last two séances were
159. completely spoilt. I am thinking of starting a tea-
160. shop in Folkestone. I followed Mrs. Henderson to
161. Dublin to get my husband's advice, but two spirits
162. kept talking and would not let any other spirit say
163. a word.

164. *Dr. Trench.* Did the spirits say the same thing and go
165. through the same drama at both séances?

166. *Mrs. Mallet.* Yes—just as if they were characters in
167. some kind of horrible play.

168. *Dr. Trench.* That is what I was afraid of.

169. *Mrs. Mallet.* My husband was drowned at sea ten
170. years ago, but constantly speaks to me through Mrs.
171. Henderson as if he were still alive. He advises me
172. about everything I do, and I am utterly lost if I
173. cannot question him.

174. *Cornelius Patterson.* I never did like the Heaven they
175. talk about in churches: but when somebody told me
176. that Mrs. Mallet's husband ate and drank and went
177. about with his favourite dog, I said to myself, 'That
178. is the place for Corney Patterson'. I came here to
179. find out if it was true, and I declare to God I have

152. ... Evangelist Sankey. I ... **82, 84, 89.**
166. ... character ... **82.**
170. ... ago but ... **82.**
175. ... churches, but ... **82 ;** ... churches; but ... **83.**
179. ... true and ... **82.**

180.   not heard one word about it.

181.   *Abraham Johnson.* I ask you, Dr. Trench, as President
182.   of the Dublin Spiritualists' Association, to permit
183.   me to read the ritual of exorcism appointed for such
184.   occasions. After the last séance I copied it out of an
185.   old book in the library of Belfast University. I have
186.   it here.   *[He takes paper out of his pocket.*

187.   *Dr. Trench.* The spirits are people like ourselves, we
188.   treat them as our guests and protect them from dis-
189.   courtesy and violence, and every exorcism is a curse
190.   or a threatened curse. We do not admit that there are
191.   evil spirits. Some spirits are earth-bound—they think
192.   they are still living and go over and over some action
193.   of their past lives, just as we go over and over some
194.   painful thought, except that where they are thought
195.   is reality. For instance, when a spirit which has died
196.   a violent death comes to a medium for the first time,
197.   it re-lives all the pains of death.

198.   *Mrs. Mallet.* When my husband came for the first time
199.   the medium gasped and struggled as if she was
200.   drowning. It was terrible to watch.

201.   *Dr. Trench.* Sometimes a spirit re-lives not the pain of
202.   death but some passionate or tragic moment of life.
203.   Swedenborg describes this and gives the reason for it.
204.   There is an incident of the kind in the *Odyssey*, and
205.   many in Eastern literature; the murderer repeats his
206.   murder, the robber his robbery, the lover his serenade,
207.   the soldier hears the trumpet once again. If I were a
208.   Catholic I would say that such spirits were in Purga-
209.   tory. In vain do we write *requiescat in pace* upon the
210.   tomb, for they must suffer, and we in our turn must
211.   suffer until God gives peace. Such spirits do not
212.   often come to séances unless those séances are held in
213.   houses where those spirits lived, or where the event
214.   took place. This spirit which speaks those incompre-
215.   hensible words and does not answer when spoken to
216.   is of such a nature. The more patient we are, the more

---

182.   . . . Spiritualist . . . **82.**
197.   . . . relives . . . . **83A.**
215.   . . . words, and . . . to, **82.**

217.   quickly will it pass out of its passion and its remorse.

218. *Abraham Johnson.* I am still convinced that the spirit
219.   which disturbed the last séance is evil. If I may not
220.   exorcise it I will certainly pray for protection.

221. *Dr. Trench.* Mrs. Henderson's control, Lulu, is able
222.   and experienced and can protect both medium and
223.   sitters, but it may help Lulu if you pray that the
224.   spirit find rest.
         [*Abraham Johnson sits down and prays silently, moving his lips.
         Mrs. Henderson comes in with Miss Mackenna and others. Miss
         Mackenna shuts the door.*

225. *Dr. Trench.* Mrs. Henderson, may I introduce to you
226.   Mr. Corbet, a young man from Cambridge and a
227.   sceptic, who hopes that you will be able to convince
228.   him?

229. *Mrs. Henderson.* We were all sceptics once. He must
230.   not expect too much from a first séance. He must
231.   persevere. [*She sits in the armchair, and the others begin to seat them-
         selves. Miss Mackenna goes to John Corbet and they remain stand-
         ing.*]

232. *Miss Mackenna.* I am glad that you are a sceptic.

233. *John Corbet.* I thought you were a spiritualist.

234. *Miss Mackenna.* I have seen a good many séances, and
235.   sometimes think it is all coincidence and thought-
236.   transference. [*She says this in a low voice.*] Then at
237.   other times I think as Dr. Trench does, and then I
238.   feel like Job—you know the quotation—the hair of
239.   my head stands up. A spirit passes before my face.

240. *Mrs. Mallett.* Turn the key, Dr. Trench, we don't want
241.   anybody blundering in here. [*Dr. Trench locks door.*]
242.   Come and sit here, Miss Mackenna.

         Directions after 224. [*. . . silently moving . . . .*] **82.**
228.   him. **82, 84, 89.**
         Directions at 231. [*. . . armchair and . . . .*] **84, 89.**
234.   . . . séances and **82.**
238.   feel as Job—. . .
239.   . . . passed . . . . **82.**

243. *Miss Mackenna.* No, I am going to sit beside Mr. Corbet.

                 [*Corbet and Miss Mackenna sit down.*

244. *John Corbet.* You feel like Job to-night?

245. *Miss Mackenna.* I feel that something is going to happen,
246.   that is why I am glad that you are a sceptic.

247. *John Corbet.* You feel safer?

248. *Miss Mackenna.* Yes, safer.

249. *Mrs. Henderson.* I am glad to meet all my dear friends
250.   again and to welcome Mr. Corbet amongst us. As
251.   he is a stranger I must explain that we do not call up
252.   spirits, we make the right conditions and they come.
253.   I do not know who is going to come; sometimes
254.   there are a great many and the guides choose between
255.   them. The guides try to send somebody for every-
256.   body but do not always succeed. If you want to speak
257.   to some dear friend who has passed over, do not be
258.   discouraged. If your friend cannot come this time,
259.   maybe he can next time. My control is a dear little
260.   girl called Lulu who died when she was five or six
261.   years old. She describes the spirits present and tells
262.   us what spirit wants to speak. Miss Mackenna, a
263.   verse of a hymn, please, the same we had last time,
264.   and will everyone join in the singing.

      [*They sing the following lines from Hymn* 564, *Irish Church Hymnal.*

265.   'Sun of my soul, Thou Saviour dear,
266.   It is not night if Thou be near:
267.   O may no earth-born cloud arise
268.   To hide Thee from Thy servant's eyes.'

      [*Mrs. Henderson is leaning back in her chair asleep.*

---

246.   . . . glad you . . . . **82.**
252.   spirits; we . . . . **82** ; spirits: we . . . . **83.**
259.   may-be . . . **82.**
264.   . . . singing? **83.**
      Directions after 264. [. . . *Hymn,* 564, *Dublin Church Hymnal, Tune Stillorgan.*] **82** ; [. . . 564, *Dublin Church* . . . .] **83-89.**
266.   . . . Thou art near: **82.**

269. *Miss Mackenna* [*to John Corbet*]. She always snores like
270.   that when she is going off.

271. *Mrs. Henderson* [*in a child's voice*]. Lulu so glad to see all
272.   her friends.

273. *Mrs. Mallet.* And we are glad you have come, Lulu.

274. *Mrs. Henderson* [*in a child's voice*]. Lulu glad to see new
275.   friend.

276. *Miss Mackenna* [*to John Corbet*]. She is speaking to you.

277. *John Corbet.* Thank you, Lulu.

278. *Mrs. Henderson* [*in a child's voice*]. You mustn't laugh at
279.   the way I talk.

280. *John Corbet.* I am not laughing, Lulu.

281. *Mrs. Henderson* [*in a child's voice*]. Nobody must laugh.
282.   Lulu does her best but can't say big long words.
283.   Lulu sees a tall man here, lots of hair on face [*Mrs.*
284.   *Henderson passes her hands over her cheeks and chin*], not
285.   much on the top of his head [*Mrs. Henderson passes*
286.   *her hand over the top of her head*], red necktie, and such
287.   a funny sort of pin.

288. *Mrs. Mallet.* Yes. . . . Yes. . . .

289. *Mrs. Henderson* [*in a child's voice*]. Pin like a horseshoe.

290. *Mrs Mallet.* It's my husband.

291. *Mrs. Henderson* [*in a child's voice*]. He has a message.

292. *Mrs. Mallet.* Yes.

293. *Mrs. Henderson* [*in a child's voice*]. Lulu cannot hear.
294.   He is too far off. He has come near. Lulu can hear
295.   now. He says . . . he says, 'Drive that man away!' He
296.   is pointing to somebody in the corner, that corner
297.   over there. He says it is the bad man who spoilt
298.   everything last time. If they won't drive him away,

298.   . . . wont . . . , 82.

299.   Lulu will scream.

300.   *Miss Mackenna.* That horrible spirit again.

301.   *Abraham Johnson.* Last time he monopolised the séance.

302.   *Mrs. Mallet.* He would not let anybody speak but him-
303.   self.

304.   *Mrs. Henderson* [*in a child's voice*]. They have driven that
305.   bad man away. Lulu sees a young lady.

306.   *Mrs. Mallet.* Is not my husband here?

307.   *Mrs. Henderson* [*in a child's voice*]. Man with funny pin
308.   gone away. Young lady here—Lulu thinks she must
309.   be at a fancy dress party, such funny clothes, hair all
310.   in curls—all bent down on floor near that old man
311.   with glasses.

312.   *Dr. Trench.* No, I do not recognize her.

313.   *Mrs. Henderson* [*in a child's voice*]. That bad man, that
314.   bad old man in the corner, they have let him come
315.   back. Lulu is going to scream. O. . . . O. . . . [*In*
316.   *a man's voice*]. How dare you write to her? How dare
317.   you ask if we were married? How dare you question
318.   her?

319.   *Dr. Trench.* A soul in its agony—it cannot see us or
320.   hear us.

    Mrs. Henderson [*upright and rigid, only her lips moving, and*
321.   *still in a man's voice*]. You sit crouching there. Did
322.   you not hear what I said? How dared you question
323.   her? I found you an ignorant little girl without in-
324.   tellect, without moral ambition. How many times
325.   did I not stay away from great men's houses, how
326.   many times forsake the Lord Treasurer, how many
327.   times neglect the business of the State that we might
328.   read Plutarch together!

---

325.   . . . houses,' . . .
326.   . . . Treasurer's, . . . **82.**
328.   . . . together. **82 ;** . . . together? **84, 89.**

[*Abraham Johnson half rises. Dr. Trench motions him to remain seated.*

329. *Dr. Trench.* Silence!

330. *Abraham Johnson.* But, Dr. Trench . . .

331. *Dr. Trench.* Hush—we can do nothing.

332. *Mrs. Henderson* [*speaking as before*]. I taught you to think
333. in every situation of life not as Hester Vanhomrigh
334. would think in that situation, but as Cato or Brutus
335. would, and now you behave like some common slut
336. with her ear against the keyhole.

337. *John Corbet* [*to Miss Mackenna*]. It is Swift, Jonathan
338. Swift, talking to the woman he called Vanessa. She
339. was christened Hester Vanhomrigh.

340. *Mrs. Henderson* [*in Vanessa's voice*]. I questioned her,
341. Jonathan, because I love. Why have you let me spend
342. hours in your company if you did not want me to
343. love you? [*In Swift's voice.*] When I rebuilt Rome in
344. your mind it was as though I walked its streets. [*In
345. Vanessa's voice.*] Was that all, Jonathan? Was I no-
346. thing but a painter's canvas? [*In Swift's voice.*] My
347. God, do you think it was easy? I was a man of strong
348. passions and I had sworn never to marry. [*In Van-
349. essa's voice.*] If you and she are not married, why
350. should we not marry like other men and women? I
351. loved you from the first moment when you came to
352. my mother's house and began to teach me. I thought
353. it would be enough to look at you, to speak to you,
354. to hear you speak. I followed you to Ireland five
355. years ago and I can bear it no longer. It is not enough
356. to look, to speak, to hear. Jonathan, Jonathan, I am
357. a woman, the women Brutus and Cato loved were
358. not different. [*In Swift's voice.*] I have something in
359. my blood that no child must inherit. I have constant
360. attacks of dizziness; I pretend they come from a surfeit

---

329. Silence.
330. . . . Trench. **82.**
334. . . . situation but . . . **82.**
343. . . . re-built . . . **82, 84, 89.**
345. . . . all Jonathan? . . . **82.**

361.   of fruit when I was a child. I had them in London. . . .
362.   There was a great doctor there, Dr. Arbuthnot; I told
363.   him of those attacks of dizziness, I told him of
364.   worse things. It was he who explained. There is a line
365.   of Dryden's. . . . [*In Vanessa's voice.*] O, I know—'Great
366.   wits are sure to madness near allied'. If you had chil-
367.   dren, Jonathan, my blood would make them healthy.
368.   I will take your hand, I will lay it upon my heart—
369.   upon the Vanhomrigh blood that has been healthy
370.   for generations. [*Mrs. Henderson slowly raises her left*
371.   *hand.*] That is the first time you have touched my
372.   body, Jonathan. [*Mrs. Henderson stands up and remains*
373.   *rigid. In Swift's voice.*] What do I care if it be healthy?
374.   What do I care if it could make mine healthy? Am
375.   I to add another to the healthy rascaldom and
376.   knavery of the world? [*In Vanessa's voice.*] Look at me,
377.   Jonathan. Your arrogant intellect separates us. Give
378.   me both your hands. I will put them upon my breast.
        [*Mrs. Henderson raises her right hand to the level of her*
379.   *left and then raises both to her breast.*] O, it is white—
380.   white as the gambler's dice—white ivory dice. Think
381.   of the uncertainty. Perhaps a mad child—perhaps a
382.   rascal—perhaps a knave—perhaps not, Jonathan. The
383.   dice of the intellect are loaded, but I am the common
384.   ivory dice. [*Her hands are stretched out as though drawing*
385.   *somebody towards her.*] It is not my hands that draw
386.   you back. My hands are weak, they could not draw
387.   you back if you did not love as I love. You said that
388.   you have strong passions; that is true, Jonathan—
389.   no man in Ireland is so passionate. That is why you
390.   need me, that is why you need children, nobody has
391.   greater need. You are growing old. An old man with-
392.   out children is very solitary. Even his friends, men
393.   as old as he, turn away, they turn towards the young,
394.   their children or their children's children. They can-
395.   not endure an old man like themselves. [*Mrs. Hender-*

---

361.   . . . London— **82.**
362.   there was . . . Arbuthnot, I . . . **82, 84, 89.**
364.   . . . explained.—there . . . **82.**
379.   . . . O it . . .— **82.**
382.   rascal—Perhaps . . . **84, 89.**

son moves away from the chair, her movements gradually

396. *growing convulsive.*] You are not too old for the dice,
397. Jonathan, but a few years if you turn away will make
398. you an old miserable childless man. [*In Swift's voice.*]
399. O God, hear the prayer of Jonathan Swift, that
400. afflicted man, and grant that he may leave to posterity
401. nothing but his intellect that came to him from
402. Heaven. [*In Vanessa's voice.*] Can you face solitude
403. with that mind, Jonathan? [*Mrs. Henderson goes to the*
404. *door, finds that it is closed.*] Dice, white ivory dice. [*In*
405. *Swift's voice.*] My God, I am left alone with my
406. enemy. Who locked the door, who locked me in
407. with my enemy? [*Mrs. Henderson beats upon the door,*
408. *sinks to the floor and then speaks as Lulu.*] Bad old man!
409. Do not let him come back. Bad old man does not
410. know he is dead. Lulu cannot find fathers, mothers,
411. sons that have passed over. Power almost gone. [*Mrs.*
       Mallet leads Mrs. Henderson, who seems very exhausted,
       back to her chair. She is still asleep. She speaks again as
412. *Lulu.*] Another verse of hymn. Everybody sing.
413. Hymn will bring good influence.

[*They sing*]

414. 'If some poor wandering child of Thine
415. Have spurned to-day the voice divine,
416. Now, Lord, the gracious work begin;
417. Let him no more lie down in sin.'

[*During the hymn Mrs. Henderson has been murmuring 'Stella',*
but the singing has almost drowned her voice. The singers draw one
another's attention to the fact that she is speaking. The singing stops.]

418. *Dr. Trench.* I thought she was speaking.

419. *Mrs. Mallet.* I saw her lips move.

420. *Dr. Trench.* She would be more comfortable with a
421. cushion, but we might wake her.

---

399. . . . God hear . . . **82.**
408. . . . man. **82.**
       Directions at 411. [. . . *Henderson who . . . exhausted back* . . . .] **82.**
415. . . . today . . . , **82.**
       Directions after 417. [. . . *'Stella' but* . . . .] **82.**
421. cushion but . . . . **82.**

422. *Mrs. Mallet.* Nothing can wake her out of a trance like
423.   that until she wakes up herself. [*She brings a cushion and she and*
          Dr. Trench put Mrs. Henderson into a more comfortable position.]

424. *Mrs. Henderson* [*in Swift's voice*]. Stella.

425. *Miss Mackenna* [*to John Corbet*]. Did you hear that? She
426.   said 'Stella'.

427. *John Corbet.* Vanessa has gone, Stella has taken her place.

428. *Miss Mackenna.* Did you notice the change while we
429.   were singing? The new influence in the room?

430. *John Corbet.* I thought I did, but it must have been
431.   fancy.

432. *Mrs. Mallet.* Hush!

433. *Mrs. Henderson* [*in Swift's voice*]. Have I wronged you,
434.   beloved Stella? Are you unhappy? You have no chil-
435.   dren, you have no lover, you have no husband. A
436.   cross and ageing man for friend—nothing but that.
437.   But no, do not answer—you have answered already
438.   in that poem you wrote for my last birthday. With
439.   what scorn you speak of the common lot of women
440.   'with no endowments but a face—'
441.   'Before the thirtieth year of life
442.   A maid forlorn or hated wife.'
443.   It is the thought of the great Chrysostom who wrote
444.   in a famous passage that women loved according to
445.   the soul, loved as saints can love, keep their beauty
446.   longer, have greater happiness than women loved
447.   according to the flesh. That thought has comforted
448.   me, but it is a terrible thing to be responsible for
449.   another's happiness. There are moments when I
450.   doubt, when I think Chrysostom may have been

Directions at 423. [. . . *cushion, and* . . . .] **83.**
426. . . . Stella. **82.**
430. . . . must, have . . . **84A.**
440. '. . . no adornment but . . . face— **82-89.**
441. Before . . . **82.**
443. . . . Chrysostom, who . . . **83.**

451.   wrong. But now I have your poem to drive doubt
452.   away. You have addressed me in these noble words:

453.   'You taught how I might youth prolong
454.   By knowing what is right and wrong;
455.   How from my heart to bring supplies
456.   Of lustre to my fading eyes;
457.   How soon a beauteous mind repairs
458.   The loss of chang'd or falling hairs;
459.   How wit and virtue from within
460.   Can spread a smoothness o'er the skin.'

461.   *John Corbet.* The words upon the window-pane!

462.   *Mrs. Henderson* [*in Swift's voice*]. Then, because you
463.   understand that I am afraid of solitude, afraid of
464.   outliving my friends—and myself—you comfort me
465.   in that last verse—you overpraise my moral nature
466.   when you attribute to it a rich mantle, but O how
467.   touching those words which describe your love:

468.   'Late dying may you cast a shred
469.   Of that rich mantle o'er my head;
470.   To bear with dignity my sorrow,
471.   One day alone, then die to-morrow.'

472.   Yes, you will close my eyes, Stella. O, you will live
473.   long after me, dear Stella, for you are still a young
474.   woman, but you will close my eyes. [*Mrs. Henderson*
475.   *sinks back in chair and speaks as Lulu.*] Bad old man gone.
476.   Power all used up. Lulu can do no more. Good-bye,
477.   friends. [*Mrs. Henderson, speaking in her own voice.*] Go
478.   away, go away! [*She wakes.*] I saw him a moment ago,
479.   has he spoilt the séance again?

480.   *Mrs. Mallet.* Yes, Mrs. Henderson, my husband came,

---

452. . . . words— **82.**
454. . . . right or wrong; **82.**
458. . . . hairs, **82.**
461. . . . words on the window-pane. **82.**
467. . . . love— **82.**
468. '. . . dying, may . . . **83-89.**
471. . . . tomorrow.'
472. . . . , Stella, but you . . . **82.**
476. . . . more. Goodbye, **82.**
    Directions in 477. [. . . *Henderson speaking* . . . .] **82, 83.**

481.   but he was driven away.

482.   *Dr. Trench.* Mrs. Henderson is very tired. We must
483.   leave her to rest. [*To Mrs. Henderson.*] You did your
484.   best and nobody can do more than that. [*He takes out money.*]

485.   *Mrs. Henderson.* No. . . . No. . . . I cannot take any
486.   money, not after a séance like that.

487.   *Dr. Trench.* Of course you must take it, Mrs. Hender-
488.   son. [*He puts money on table, and Mrs. Henderson gives a furtive
        glance to see how much it is. She does the same as each sitter lays
        down his or her money.*]

489.   *Mrs. Mallet.* A bad séance is just as exhausting as a good
490.   séance, and you must be paid.

491.   *Mrs. Henderson.* No. . . . No. . . . Please don't. It is
492.   very wrong to take money for such a failure.
                                            [*Mrs. Mallet lays down money.*

493.   *Cornelius Patterson.* A jockey is paid whether he wins
494.   or not. [*He lays down money.*]

495.   *Miss Mackenna.* That spirit rather thrilled me. [*She lays down
        money.*]

496.   *Mrs. Henderson.* If you insist, I must take it.

497.   *Abraham Johnson.* I shall pray for you to-night. I shall
498.   ask God to bless and protect your séances. [*He lays down money.*]
                            [*All go out except John Corbet and Mrs. Henderson.*

499.   *John Corbet.* I know you are tired, Mrs. Henderson, but
500.   I must speak to you. I have been deeply moved by
501.   what I have heard. This is my contribution to prove
502.   that I am satisfied, completely satisfied. [*He puts a note on the
        table.*]

503.   *Mrs. Henderson.* A pound note—nobody ever gives me
504.   more than ten shillings, and yet the séance was a

Directions at 488. [. . . *table and . . . .*] **82, 83.**
497.   . . . tonight. . . . **82.**

505.   failure.

506.   *John Corbet* [*sitting down near Mrs. Henderson*]. When I
507.   say I am satisfied I do not mean that I am convinced
508.   it was the work of spirits. I prefer to think that you
509.   created it all, that you are an accomplished actress
510.   and scholar. In my essay for my Cambridge doctorate
511.   I examine all the explanations of Swift's celibacy
512.   offered by his biographers and prove that the ex-
513.   planation you selected was the only plausible one.
514.   But there is something I must ask you. Swift was
515.   the chief representative of the intellect of his epoch,
516.   that arrogant intellect free at last from superstition.
517.   He foresaw its collapse. He foresaw Democracy, he
518.   must have dreaded the future. Did he refuse to beget
519.   children because of that dread? Was Swift mad? Or
520.   was it the intellect itself that was mad?

521.   *Mrs. Henderson.* Who are you talking of, sir?

522.   *John Corbet.* Swift, of course.

523.   *Mrs. Henderson.* Swift? I do not know anybody called
524.   Swift.

525.   *John Corbet.* Jonathan Swift, whose spirit seemed to be
526.   present to-night.

527.   *Mrs. Henderson.* What? That dirty old man?

528.   *John Corbet.* He was neither old nor dirty when Stella
529.   and Vanessa loved him.

530.   *Mrs. Henderson.* I saw him very clearly just as I woke
531.   up. His clothes were dirty, his face covered with
532.   boils. Some disease had made one of his eyes swell
533.   up, it stood out from his face like a hen's egg.

534.   *John Corbet.* He looked like that in his old age. Stella
535.   had been dead a long time. His brain had gone, his

---

515.   . . . epoch
516.   free at last . . . .
517.   . . . democracy, . . . **82.**
526.   . . . tonight. **82.**
535.   . . . gone his **82.**

536.   friends had deserted him. The man appointed to
537.   take care of him beat him to keep him quiet.

538.   *Mrs. Henderson.* Now they are old, now they are young.
539.   They change all in a moment as their thought
540.   changes. It is sometimes a terrible thing to be out of
541.   the body, God help us all.

542.   *Dr. Trench [at doorway].* Come along, Corbet, Mrs.
543.   Henderson is tired out.

544.   *John Corbet.* Good-bye, Mrs. Henderson. [*He goes out with Dr.
        Trench. All the sitters except Miss Mackenna, who has returned to
        her room, pass along the passage on their way to the front door. Mrs.
        Henderson counts the money, finds her purse, which is in a vase on the
        mantelpiece, and puts the money in it.*]

545.   *Mrs. Henderson.* How tired I am! I'd be the better of a
546.   cup of tea. [*She finds the teapot and puts kettle on fire, and then as she
        crouches down by the hearth suddenly lifts up her hands and counts
        her fingers, speaking in Swift's
547.   voice.*] Five great Ministers that were my friends are
548.   gone, ten great Ministers that were my friends are
549.   gone. I have not fingers enough to count the great
550.   Ministers that were my friends and that are gone.
                [*She wakes with a start and speaks in her own voice.*]
551.   Where did I put that tea-caddy? Ah! there it is. And
552.   there should be a cup and saucer. [*She finds the saucer.*]
553.   But where's the cup? [*She moves aimlessly about the stage and then,
        letting the saucer fall and break, speaks in Swift's
554.   voice.*] Perish the day on which I was born!

THE END

---

542.   ..., Corbet. Mrs. **82, 83.**
        Directions at 544. [*. . . purse which . . . mantelpiece and . . . .*] **82.**
        Directions at 546. [*. . . counting her fingers, speaks in . . . .*] **82**; [*. . .
        counting . . . .*] **84, 89.**
550.   ministers . . . . **82.**
554.   . . . born. **82.**

NOTES

I

Somebody said the other night that Dublin was full of clubs—he himself knew four—that met in cellars and garrets and had for their object our general improvement. He was scornful, said that they had all begun by drawing up a programme and passing a resolution against the censorship and would never do anything else. When I began my public life Dublin was full of such clubs that passed resolutions and drew up programmes, and though the majority did nothing else some helped to find an audience for a school of writers. The fall of Parnell had freed imagination from practical politics, from agrarian grievance and political enmity, and turned it to imaginative nationalism, to Gaelic, to the ancient stories, and at last to lyrical poetry and to drama. Political failure and political success have had the same result except that to-day imagination is turning full of uncertainty to something it thinks European, and whether that something will be 'arty' and provincial, or a form of life, is as yet undiscoverable. Hitherto we have walked the road, but now we have shut the door and turned up the lamp. What shall occupy our imagination? We must, I think, decide among these three ideas of national life: that of Swift; that of a great Italian of his day; that of modern England. If the Garrets and the Cellars listen I may throw light upon the matter, and I hope if all the time I seem thinking of something else I shall be forgiven. I must speak of things that come out of the common consciousness, where every thought is like a bell with many echoes.

My little play *The Words upon the Window-pane* came to me amidst considerations such as these, as a reward, as a moment of excitement. John O'Leary read, during an illness, the poems of Thomas Davis, and though he never thought them good poetry they shaped his future life, gave him the moral simplicity that made him so attractive to young men in his old age, but we can no longer permit life to be shaped by a personified ideal, we must serve with all our faculties some actual thing. The old service was moral, at times lyrical; we discussed perpetually the character of public men and never asked were they able and well-informed, but what would they sacrifice? How many times did I hear on the lips of J. F. Taylor these words: 'Holy, delicate white hands'? His patriotism was a religion, never a philosophy. More extreme in such things than Taylor and O'Leary, who often seemed to live in the eighteenth century, to acknowledge its canons alone in literature and in the arts, I turned from Goldsmith and from Burke because they had come to seem a part of the English system, from Swift because I acknowledged, being a romantic, no verse between Cowley and Smart's *Song to David*, no prose between Sir Thomas Browne and the *Conversations* of Landor. But now I read Swift for months together, Burke and Berkeley less often but always with excitement, and Goldsmith lures and waits. I collect materials for my thought and work, for some identification of my beliefs with the nation itself, I seek an image of the modern mind's discovery of itself, of its own permanent form, in that one Irish century that escaped from darkness and confusion. I would that our fifteenth, sixteenth, or even our seventeenth century had been the clear mirror, but fate decided against us.

Swift haunts me; he is always just round the next corner. Sometimes it is a thought of my great-great-grandmother, a friend of that Archbishop King who sent him to England about the 'First Fruits,' sometimes it is S. Patrick's, where I have gone to wander and meditate, that brings him to mind, sometimes I remember something hard or harsh in O'Leary or in Taylor, or in the public speech of our statesmen, that reminds me by its style of his verse or prose. Did he not speak, perhaps, with just such an intonation? This instinct for what is near and yet hidden is in reality a return to the sources of our power, and therefore a claim made upon the future. Thought seems more true, emotion more deep, spoken by someone who touches my pride, who seems to claim me of his kindred, who seems to make me a part of some national mythology, nor is mythology mere ostentation, mere vanity if it draws me onward to the unknown; another turn of the gyre and myth is wisdom, pride, discipline. I remember the shudder in my spine when Mrs. Patrick Campbell said, speaking words Hofmannsthal put into the mouth of Electra, 'I too am of that ancient race':

> Swift has sailed into his rest:
> Savage indignation there
> Cannot lacerate his breast.
> Imitate him if you dare,
> World-besotted traveller; he
> Served human liberty.

'In Swift's day men of intellect reached the height of their power, the greatest position they ever attained in society and the State. . . . His ideal order was the Roman Senate, his ideal men Brutus and Cato; such an order and such men had seemed possible once more.' The Cambridge undergraduate into whose mouth I have put these words may have read similar words in Oliver, 'the last brilliant addition to English historians,' for young men such as he read the newest authorities; probably Oliver and he thought of the influence at Court and in public life of Swift and of Leibniz, of the spread of science and of scholarship over Europe, its examination of documents, its destruction of fables, a science and a scholarship modern for the first time, of certain great minds that were medieval in their scope but modern in their freedom. I must, however, add certain thoughts of my own that affected me as I wrote. I thought about a passage in the Grammont *Memoirs* where some great man is commended for his noble manner, as we commend a woman for her beauty or her charm; a famous passage in the *Appeal from the New to the Old Whigs* commending the old Whig aristocracy for their intellect and power and because their doors stood open to like-

minded men; the palace of Blenheim, its pride of domination that expected a
thousand years, something Asiatic in its carved intricacy of stone.

'Everything great in Ireland and in our character, in what remains of
our architecture, comes from that day . . . we have kept its seal longer than
England.' The overstatement of an enthusiastic Cambridge student, and
yet with its measure of truth. The battle of the Boyne overwhelmed a civilisation full of religion and myth, and brought in its place intelligible laws
planned out upon a great blackboard, a capacity for horizontal lines, for
rigid shapes, for buildings, for attitudes of mind that could be multiplied
like an expanding bookcase: the modern world, and something that
appeared and perished in its dawn, an instinct for Roman rhetoric, Roman
elegance. It established a Protestant aristocracy, some of whom neither
called themselves English[1] nor looked with contempt or dread upon conquered Ireland. Indeed the battle was scarcely over when Molyneux,
speaking in their name, affirmed the sovereignty of the Irish Parliament.[2]
No one had the right to make our laws but the King, Lords and Commons
of Ireland; the battle had been fought to change not an English but an Irish
Crown; and our Parliament was almost as ancient as that of England. It
was this doctrine[3] that Swift uttered in the fourth *Drapier Letter* with such
astringent eloquence that it passed from the talk of study and parlour to
that of road and market, and created the political nationality of Ireland.
Swift found his nationality through the *Drapier Letters*, his convictions came
from action and passion, but Berkeley, a much younger man, could find it
through contemplation. He and his fellow-students but knew the war
through the talk of the older men. As a boy of eighteen or nineteen he called
the Irish people 'natives' as though he were in some foreign land, but two
or three years later, perhaps while still an undergraduate, defined the
English materialism of his day in three profound sentences, and wrote after
each that 'we Irishmen' think otherwise—'I publish . . . to know whether
other men have the same ideas as we Irishmen'—and before he was twenty-
five had fought the Salamis of the Irish intellect. The Irish landed aristo-

[1] Nor were they English: the newest arrivals soon intermarried with an older stock, and
that older stock had intermarried again and again with Gaelic Ireland. All my childhood the
Coopers of Markree, County Sligo, represented such rank and fashion as the County knew,
and I had it from my friend the late Bryan Cooper that his supposed Cromwellian ancestor
being childless adopted an O'Brien; while local tradition thinks that an O'Brien, promised
the return of her confiscated estate if she married a Cromwellian soldier, married a Cooper
and murdered him three days after. Not, however, before he had founded a family. The
family of Yeats, never more than small gentry, arrived, if I can trust the only man among us
who may have seen the family tree before it was burnt by Canadian Indians, 'about the time
of Henry VII.' Ireland, divided in religion and politics, is as much one race as any modern
country.
[2] 'Until 1691 Roman Catholics were admitted by law into both Houses of Legislature in
Ireland' (MacNeill's *Constitutional and Parliamentary History of Ireland*, p. 10.)
[3] A few weeks ago the hierarchy of the Irish Church addressed, without any mandate from
Protestant Ireland, not the Irish people as they had every right to, even in the defence of
folly, but the Imperial Conference, and begged that the Irish Courts might remain sub-
servient to the Privy Council. Terrified into intrigue where none threatened, they turned
from Swift and Molyneux. I remind them that when the barons of the Irish Court of Ex-
chequer obeyed the English Privy Council in 1719 our ancestors clapped them into gaol.
(1931.)

cracy, who knew more of the siege of Derry and the battle of the Boyne delineated on vast tapestries for their House of Lords by Dublin Huguenots than of philosophy, found themselves masters of a country demoralised by generations of war and famine and shared in its demoralisation. In 1730 Swift said from the pulpit that their houses were in ruins and no new building anywhere, that the houses of their rack-ridden tenants were no better than English pigsties, that the bulk of the people trod barefoot and in rags. He exaggerated, for already the Speaker, Connolly, had built that great house at Celbridge where slate, stone and furniture were Irish, even the silver from Irish mines; the new Parliament House had perhaps been planned; and there was a general stir of life. The old age of Berkeley passed amid art and music, and men had begun to boast that in these no country had made such progress; and some dozen years after Berkeley's death Arthur Young found everywhere in stately Georgian houses scientific agriculturalists, benefactors of their countryside, though for the half-educated, drunken, fire-eating, impoverished lesser men he had nothing but detestation. Goldsmith might have found likeable qualities, a capacity for mimicry[1] perhaps, among these lesser men, and Sir Jonah Barrington made them his theme, but, detestable or not, they were out of fashion. Miss Edgeworth described her *Castle Rackrent* upon the title-page of its first edition as 'the habits of the Irish squirearchy before 1782.' A few years more and the country people would have forgotten that the Irish aristocracy was founded like all aristocracies upon conquest, or rather, would have remembered, and boasted in the words of a medieval Gaelic poet, 'We are a sword people and we go with the sword.' Unhappily the lesson first taught by Molyneux and Swift had been but half learnt when the test came—country gentlemen are poor politicians—and Ireland's 'dark insipid period' began. During the entire eighteenth century the greatest land-owning family of the neighbourhood I best knew in childhood sent not a single man into the English army and navy, but during the nineteenth century one or more in every generation; a new absenteeism, foreseen by Miss Edgeworth, began; those that lived upon their estates bought no more fine editions of the classics; separated from public life and ambition they sank, as I have heard Lecky complain, 'into grass farmers.' Yet their genius did not die out; they sent everywhere administrators and military leaders, and now that their ruin has come—what resolute nation permits a strong alien class within its borders?—I would, remembering obscure ancestors that preached in their churches or fought beside their younger sons over half the world, and despite a famous passage of O'Grady's, gladly sing their song.

'He foresaw the ruin to come, Democracy, Rousseau, the French Revolution; that is why he hated the common run of men,—"I hate lawyers, I hate doctors," he said, "though I love Dr. So-and-so and Judge So-and-so," —that is why he wrote *Gulliver*, that is why he wore out his brain, that is why he felt *saeva indignatio*, that is why he sleeps under the greatest epitaph

---

[1] He wrote that he had never laughed so much at Garrick's acting as at somebody in an Irish tavern mimicking a Quaker sermon.

in history.' The *Discourse of the Contests and Dissensions between the Nobles and the Commons in Athens and Rome*, published in 1703 to warn the Tory Opposition of the day against the impeachment of Ministers, is Swift's one philosophical work. All States depend for their health upon a right balance between the One, the Few, and the Many. The One is the executive, which may in fact be more than one—the Roman republic had two Consuls—but must for the sake of rapid decision be as few as possible; the Few are those who through the possession of hereditary wealth, or great personal gifts, have come to identify their lives with the life of the State, whereas the lives and ambitions of the Many are private. The Many do their day's work well, and so far from copying even the wisest of their neighbours affect 'a singularity' in action and in thought; but set them to the work of the State and every man Jack is 'listed in a party,' becomes the fanatical follower of men of whose characters he knows next to nothing, and from that day on puts nothing into his mouth that some other man has not already chewed and digested. And furthermore, from the moment of enlistment thinks himself above other men and struggles for power until all is in confusion. I divine an Irish hatred of abstraction likewise expressed by that fable of Gulliver among the inventors and men of science, by Berkeley in his *Commonplace Book*, by Goldsmith in the satire of *The Good-Natured Man*, in the picturesque, minute observation of *The Deserted Village*, and by Burke in his attack upon mathematical democracy. Swift enforced his moral by proving that Rome and Greece were destroyed by the war of the Many upon the Few; in Rome, where the Few had kept their class organisation, it was a war of classes, in Greece, where they had not, war upon character and genius. Miltiades, Aristides, Themistocles, Pericles, Alcibiades, Phocion, 'impeached for high crimes and misdemeanours . . . were honoured and lamented by their country as the preservers of it, and have had the veneration of all ages since paid justly to their memories.' In Rome parties so developed that men born and bred among the Few were compelled to join one party or the other and to flatter and bribe. All civilisations must end in some such way, for the Many obsessed by emotion create a multitude of religious sects but give themselves at last to some one master of bribes and flatteries and sink into the ignoble tranquillity of servitude. He defines a tyranny as the predominance of the One, the Few, or the Many, but thinks that of the Many the immediate threat. All States at their outset possess a ruling power seated in the whole body as that of the soul in the human body, a perfect balance of the three estates, the king some sort of chief magistrate, and then comes 'a tyranny: first either of the Few or the Many; but at last infallibly of a single person.' He thinks the English balance most perfect in the time of Queen Elizabeth, but that in the next age a tyranny of the Many produced that of Cromwell, and that, though recovery followed, 'all forms of government must be mortal like their authors,' and he quotes from Polybius, 'those abuses and corruptions, which in time destroy a government, are sown along with the very seeds of it' and destroy it 'as rust eats away iron, and worms devour wood.' Whether the final tyranny is created by the

Many—in his eyes all Caesars were tyrants—or imposed by foreign power, the result is the same. At the fall of liberty came 'a dark insipid period through all Greece'—had he Ireland in his mind also?—and the people became, in the words of Polybius, 'great reverencers of crowned heads.'

Twenty-two years later Giambattista Vico published that *Scienza Nuova* which Mr. James Joyce is expounding or symbolising in the strange fragments of his *Work in Progress*. He was the opposite of Swift in everything, an humble, peaceful man, son of a Neapolitan bookseller and without political opinions; he wrote panegyrics upon men of rank, seemed to admire all that they did, took their gratuities and yet kept his dignity. He thought civilisation passed through the phases Swift has described, but that it was harsh and terrible until the Many prevailed, and its joints cracked and loosened, happiest when some one man, surrounded by able subordinates, dismissed the Many to their private business, that its happiness lasted some generations until, sense of the common welfare lost, it grew malicious and treacherous, fell into 'the barbarism of reflection,' and after that into an honest, plain barbarism accepted with relief by all and started upon its round again. Rome had conquered surrounding nations because those nations were nearer than it to humanity and happiness; was not Carthage already almost a democratic state when destruction came? Swift seemed to shape his narrative upon some clairvoyant vision of his own life, for he saw civilisation pass from comparative happiness and youthful vigour to an old age of violence and self-contempt, whereas Vico saw it begin in penury like himself and end as he himself would end in a long inactive peace. But there was a greater difference; Swift, a practical politician in everything he wrote, ascribed its rise and fall to virtues and vices all could understand, whereas the philosophical Vico ascribed them to 'the rhythm of the elemental forms of the mind,' a new idea that would dominate philosophy. Outside Anglo-Saxon nations where progress, impelled by moral enthusiasm and the Patent Office, seems a perpetual straight line, this 'circular movement,' as Swift's master, Polybius, called it, has long been the friend and enemy of public order. Both Sorel and Marx, their eyes more Swift's than Vico's, have preached a return to a primeval state, a beating of all down into a single class that a new civilisation may arise with its Few, its Many, and its One. Students of contemporary Italy, where Vico's thought is current through its influence upon Croce and Gentile, think it created, or in part created, the present government of one man surrounded by just such able assistants as Vico foresaw. Some philosopher has added this further thought: the classes rise out of the matrix, create all mental and bodily riches, sink back, as Vico saw civilisation rise and sink, and government is there to keep the ring and see to it that combat never ends. These thoughts in the next few generations, as elaborated by Oswald Spengler, who has followed Vico without essential change, by Flinders Petrie, by the German traveller Frobenius, by Henry Adams, and perhaps by my friend Gerald Heard, may affect the masses. They have already deepened our sense of tragedy and somewhat checked the naïver among those creeds and parties who push their way to power by flattering our moral hopes. Pascal thought there was evidence for and against the existence of God, but that if a man kept his mind in suspense about it he could not live a rich and active life, and I suggest to the Cellars and Garrets that though history is too short to change either the idea of progress or the eternal circuit into scientific fact, the eternal circuit may best suit our preoccupation with the soul's salvation, our individualism, our solitude. Besides we love antiquity, and that other idea— progress—the sole religious myth of modern man, is only two hundred years old.

Swift's pamphlet had little effect in its day; it did not prevent the impeachment and banishment a few years later of his own friends; and although he was in all probability the first—if there was another 'my small reading cannot trace it'—to describe in terms of modern politics the discord of parties that compelled revolutionary France, as it has compelled half a dozen nations since the war, to accept the 'tyranny' of a 'single person,' it was soon forgotten; but for the understanding of Swift it is essential. It shows that the defence of liberty boasted upon his tombstone did not come from political disappointment (when he wrote it he had suffered none); and what he meant by liberty. Gulliver, in those travels written twenty years later, calls up from the dead 'a sextumvirate to which all the ages of the world cannot add a seventh': Epaminondas and Socrates, who suffered at the hands of the Many; Brutus, Junius Brutus, Cato the Younger, Thomas More, who fought the tyranny of the One; Brutus with Caesar still his inseparable friend, for a man may be a tyrant without personal guilt.

Liberty depended upon a balance within the State, like that of the 'humours' in a human body, or like that 'unity of being' Dante compared to a perfectly proportioned human body, and for its sake Swift was prepared to sacrifice what seems to the modern man liberty itself. The odds were a hundred to one, he wrote, that 'violent zeal for the truth' came out of 'petulancy, ambition, or pride.' He himself might prefer a republic to a monarchy, but did he open his mouth upon the subject would be deservedly hanged. Had he religious doubts he was not to blame so long as he kept them to himself, for God had given him reason. It was the attitude of many a modern Catholic who thinks, though upon different grounds, that our civilisation may sink into a decadence like that of Rome. But sometimes belief itself must be hidden. He was devout; had the Communion Service by heart; read the Fathers and prayed much, yet would not press the mysteries of his faith upon any unwilling man. Had not the early Christians kept silent about the divinity of Christ; should not the missionaries to China 'soften' it? He preached as law commanded; a man could save his soul doubtless in any religion which taught submission to the Will of God, but only one State could protect his body; and how could it protect his body if rent apart by those cranks and sectaries mocked in his *Tale of a Tub*? Had not French Huguenots and English Dissenters alike sinned against the State? Except at those moments of great public disturbance, when a man must choose his creed or his king, let him think his own thoughts in silence.

What was this liberty bought with so much silence, and served through all his life with so much eloquence? 'I should think,' he wrote in the *Discourse*, 'that the saying, *vox populi, vox dei* ought to be understood of the universal bent and current of a people, not of the bare majority of a few representatives, which is often procured by little arts, and great industry and application; wherein those who engage in the pursuits of malice and revenge are much more sedulous than such as would prevent them.' That *vox populi* or 'bent and current,' or what we even more vaguely call national spirit, was the sole theme of his *Drapier Letters*; its right to express itself as it would through such men as had won or inherited general consent. I doubt if a mind so contemptuous of average men thought, as Vico did, that it found expression also through all individual lives, or asked more for those lives than protection from the most obvious evils. I remember J. F. Taylor, a great student of Swift, saying 'individual liberty is of no importance, what matters is national liberty.'

The will of the State, whether it build a cage for a dead bird or remain in the bird itself, must always, whether interpreted by Burke or Marx, find expression through some governing class or company identified with that 'bent and current,' with those 'elemental forms,' whether by interest or training. The men of Swift's day would have added that class or company must be placed by wealth above fear and toil, though Swift thought every properly conducted State must limit the amount of wealth the individual could possess. But the old saying that there is no wisdom without leisure has somewhat lost its truth. When the physical world became rigid; when curiosity inherited from the Renaissance, and the soul's anxiety inherited from the Middle Ages, passed, man ceased to think; his work thought in him. Spinoza, Leibniz, Swift, Berkeley, Goethe, the last typical figure of the epoch, recognised no compulsion but the 'bent and current' of their lives; the Speaker, Connolly, could still call out a posse of gentlemen to design the facade of his house, and though Berkeley thought their number too great, that work is still admired; Swift called himself a poor scholar in comparison with Lord Treasurer Harley. Unity of being was still possible though somewhat over-rationalised and abstract, more diagram than body; whereas the best modern philosophers are professors, their pupils compile notebooks that they may be professors some day; politicians stick to their last or leave it to plague us with platitudes; we poets and artists may be called, so small our share in life, 'separated spirits,' words applied by the old philosophers to the dead. When Swift sank into imbecility or madness his epoch had finished in the British Isles, those 'elemental forms' had passed beyond him; more than the 'great Ministers' had gone. I can see in a sort of nightmare vision the 'primary qualities' torn from the side of Locke, Johnson's ponderous body bent above the letter to Lord Chesterfield, some obscure person somewhere inventing the spinning-jenny, upon his face that look of benevolence kept by painters and engravers, from the middle of the eighteenth century to the time of the Prince Consort, for such as he, or, to simplify the tale—

Locke sank into a swoon;
The Garden died;
God took the spinning-jenny
Out of his side.

'That arrogant intellect free at last from superstition': the young man's overstatement full of the unexamined suppositions of common speech. I saw Asia in the carved stones of Blenheim, not in the pride of great abstract masses, but in that humility of flower-like intricacy—the particular blades of the grass; nor can chance have thrown into contiguous generations Spinoza and Swift, an absorption of the whole intellect in God, a fakir-like contempt for all human desire; 'take from her,' Swift prayed for Stella in sickness, 'all violent desire whether of life or death'; the elaboration and spread of Masonic symbolism, its God made in the image of a Christopher Wren; Berkeley's declaration, modified later, that physical pleasure is the *Summum Bonum*, Heaven's sole reality, his counter-truth to that of Spinoza.

In judging any moment of past time we should leave out what has since happened; we should not call the Swift of the *Drapier Letters* nearer truth because of their influence upon history than the Swift who attacked in *Gulliver* the inventors and logicians; we should see certain men and women as if at the edge of a cliff, time broken away from their feet. Spinoza and the Masons, Berkeley and Swift, speculative and practical intellect, stood there free at last from all prepossessions and touched the extremes of thought; the Gymnosophists of Strabo close at hand, could they but ignore what was harsh and logical in themselves, or the China of the Dutch cabinet-makers, of the *Citizen of the World*: the long-settled rule of powerful men, no great dogmatic structure, few great crowded streets, scattered unprogressive communities, much handiwork, wisdom wound into the roots of the grass.

'I have something in my blood that no child must inherit.' There have been several theories to account for Swift's celibacy. Sir Walter Scott suggested a 'physical defect,' but that seems incredible. A man so outspoken would have told Vanessa the truth and stopped a tragic persecution, a man so charitable have given Stella the protection of his name. The refusal to see Stella when there was no third person present suggests a man that dreaded temptation; nor is it compatible with those stories still current among our country people of Swift sending his servant out to fetch a woman, and dismissing that servant when he woke to find a black woman at his side. Lecky suggested dread of madness—the theory of my play—of madness already present in constant eccentricity; though, with a vagueness born from distaste of the theme, he saw nothing incompatible between Scott's theory and his own. Had Swift dreaded transmitting madness he might well have been driven to consorting with the nameless barren women of the streets. Somebody else suggests syphilis contracted doubtless between 1799 when he was engaged to Varina and some date soon after Stella's arrival in Ireland.

Mr. Shane Leslie thinks that Swift's relation to Vanessa was not platonic,[1] and that whenever his letters speak of a cup of coffee they mean the sexual act; whether the letters seem to bear him out I do not know, for those letters bore me; but whether they seem to or not he must, if he is to get a hearing, account for Swift's relation to Stella. It seems certain that Swift loved her though he called it by some other name, and she him, and that it was platonic love.

> Thou, Stella, wert no longer young,
> When first for thee my harp was strung,
> Without one word of Cupid's darts,
> Of killing eyes or bleeding hearts;
> With friendship and esteem possest,
> I ne'er admitted Love a guest.
> In all the habitudes of life,
> The friend, the mistress, and the wife,
> Variety we still pursue,
> In pleasure seek for something new;
> Or else comparing with the rest,
> Take comfort that our own is best;
> The best we value by the worst,
> As tradesmen show their trash at first;
> But his pursuits are at an end,
> Whom Stella chooses for a friend.

If the relation between Swift and Vanessa was not platonic there must have been some bar that affected Stella as well as Swift. Dr. Delaney is said to have believed that Swift married Stella in 1716 and found in some exchange of confidences that they were brother and sister, but Sir William Temple was not in Ireland during the year that preceded Swift's birth, and so far as we know Swift's mother was not in England.

There is no satisfactory solution. Swift, though he lived in great publicity, and wrote and received many letters, hid two things which constituted perhaps all that he had of private life: his loves and his religious beliefs.

'Was Swift mad? Or was it the intellect itself that was mad?' The other day a scholar in whose imagination Swift has a pre-eminence scarcely possible outside Ireland said: 'I sometimes feel that there is a black cloud about to overwhelm me, and then comes a great jet of life; Swift had that black cloud and no jet. He was terrified.' I said, 'Terrified perhaps of everything but death,' and reminded him of a story of Dr. Johnson's.[2] There was a reward of £500 for the identification of the author of the *Drapier Letters*. Swift's butler, who had carried the manuscript to the printer, stayed

---

[1] Rossi and Hone take the same view, though uncertain about the coffee. When I wrote, their book had not appeared.

[2] Sheridan has a different version, but as I have used it merely to illustrate an argument I leave it as Dr. Johnson told it.

away from work. When he returned Swift said, 'I know that my life is in your hands, but I will not bear, out of fear, either your insolence or negligence.' He dismissed the butler, and when the danger had passed he restored him to his post, rewarded him, and said to the other servants, 'No more Barclay, henceforth Mr. Barclay.' 'Yes,' said my friend, 'he was not afraid of death but of life, of what might happen next; that is what made him so defiant in public and in private and demand for the State the obedience a Connacht priest demands for the Church.' I have put a cognate thought into the mind of John Corbet. He imagines, though but for a moment, that the intellect of Swift's age, persuaded that the mechanicians mocked by Gulliver would prevail, that its moment of freedom could not last, so dreaded the historic process that it became in the half-mad mind of Swift a dread of parentage: 'Am I to add another to the healthy rascaldom and knavery of the world?' Did not Rousseau within five years of the death of Swift publish his *Discourse upon Arts and Sciences* and discover instinctive harmony not in heroic effort, not in Cato and Brutus, not among impossible animals—I think of that noble horse Blake drew for Hayley—but among savages, and thereby beget the sans-culottes of Marat? After the arrogance of power the humility of a servant.

II

When I went into the theatre café after the performance a woman asked a question and I replied with some spiritualistic anecdote. 'Did that happen with the medium we have seen to-night?' she said: and yet May Craig who played the part had never seen a séance. I had, however, assisted her by self-denial. No character upon the stage spoke my thoughts. All were people I had met or might have met in just such a séance. Taken as a whole, the man who expected to find whippet-racing beyond the grave, not less than the old man who was half a Swedenborgian, expresses an attitude of mind of millions who have substituted the séance-room for the church. At most séances there is somebody who finds symbol where his neighbour finds fact, but the average man or woman thinks that the dead have houses, that they eat and sleep, hear lectures, or occasionally talk with Christ as though He were a living man; and certainly the voices are at times so natural, the forms so solid, that the plain man can scarce think otherwise.

If I had not denied myself, if I had allowed some character to speak my thoughts, what would he have said? It seems to me that after reading many books and meeting many phenomena, some in my own house, some when alone in my room, I can see clearly at last. I consider it certain that every voice that speaks, every form that appears, whether to the medium's eyes and ears alone or to someone or two others or to all present, whether it remains a sight or sound or affects the sense of touch, whether it is confined to the room or can make itself apparent at some distant place, whether it can or cannot alter the position of material objects, is first of all a secondary personality or dramatisation created by, in, or through the medium.

Perhaps May Craig, when alone in her room after the play, went, without knowing what she was doing, through some detail of her performance. I once saw an Abbey actor going up the stairs to his dressing-room after playing the part of a lame man and saw that he was still limping. I see no difference except one of degree between such unconscious movements and the strange powerful grotesque faces imprinted by the controls of Eusapia Palladino upon paraffin wax. The Polish psychologist Ochorowicz, vexed by the mischievous character of his medium's habitual control, created by suggestion a docile and patient substitute that left a photograph of its hand and arm upon an unopened coil of film in a sealed bottle. But at most séances the suggestions come from sub-conscious or unspoken thought. I found the preacher who wanted Moody's help at a séance where the mind of an old doting general turned all into delirium. We sat in the dark and voices came about us in the air; crowned head after crowned head spoke until Cromwell intervened and was abused by one of the sitters for cutting off the head of 'Charles the Second,' while the preacher kept repeating, 'He is monopolising the séance, I want Mr. Moody, it is most important I should get Mr. Moody.' Then came a voice, 'King George is here.' I asked which of the Georges, and the sitter who hated Cromwell said, 'King George, our George; we should all stand up,' but the general thought it would be enough if we sang 'God save the King.' We sang, and then there was silence, and in the silence from somewhere close to the ceiling the clear song of a bird. Because mediumship is dramatisation: even honest mediums cheat at times either deliberately or because some part of the body has freed itself from the control of the waking will, and almost always truth and lies are mixed together. But what shall we say of their knowledge of events, their assumption of forms and names beyond the medium's knowledge or ours? What of the arm photographed in the bottle?

The Indian ascetic passing into his death-like trance knows that if his mind is not pure, if there is anything there but the symbol of his God, some passion, ambition, desire, or phantasy will confer upon him its shape or purpose, for he is entering upon a state where thought and existence are the same. One remembers those witches described by Glanvil who course the field in the likeness of hares while their bodies lie at home, and certain mediumistic phenomena. The ascetic would say, did we question him, that the unpurified dead are subject to transformations that would be similar were it not that in their case no physical body remains in cave or bed or chair, all is transformed. They examine their past if undisturbed (past undisturbed **83A**) by our importunity, tracing events to their source, and as they take the form their thought suggests, seem to live backward through time; or if incapable of such examination, creatures not of thought but of feeling, renew as shades certain detached events of their past lives, taking the greater excitements first. When Achilles came to the edge of the blood-pool (an ancient substitute for the medium) he was such a shade. Tradition affirms that, deprived of the living present by death, they can create nothing, or, in the Indian phrase, can originate no new Karma. Their aim, like that of the ascetic in meditation, is to enter at last into their own archetype, or into all being: into that which is there always. They are not, however, the personalities which haunt the séance-room: these when they speak from, or imply, supernormal knowledge, when they are more than transformations of the medium, are, as it were, new beings begotten by spirit upon medium to live short but veritable lives, whereas the secondary personalities resemble those eggs brought forth without the assistance of the male bird. They, within their narrow limits, create; they speak truth when they repeat some message suggested by the past lives of the spirit, remembered like some prenatal memory, or when, though such instances must be few, begotten by some spirit obedient to its source, or, as we might say, blessed; but when they neither repeat such message nor were so begotten they may justify passages in Swedenborg that denounce them as the newspapers denounce cheating mediums, seeing that they find but little check in their fragmentary knowledge or vague conscience.

Let images of basalt, black, immovable,
Chiselled in Egypt, or ovoids of bright steel
Hammered and polished by Brancusi's hand,
Represent spirits. If spirits seem to stand
Before the bodily eyes, speak into the bodily ears,
They are not present but their messengers.
Of double nature these, one nature is
Compounded of accidental phantasies.
We question; it but answers what we would
Or as phantasy directs—because they have drunk the blood.

I have not heard of spirits in a European séance-room re-enacting their past lives; our séances take their characteristics from the desire of those present to speak to, or perhaps obtain the counsel of, their dead; yet under the conditions described in my play such re-enacting might occur, indeed most hauntings are of that nature. Here, however, is a French traveller's account of a séance in Madagascar, quoted by César de Vesme:

... One, Taimandebakaka, of the Bara race, and renowned in the valley of the Menamaty as a great sorcerer, evoked one day in my presence in his village the souls of Captain Flayelle and of Lieutenant Montagnole, both killed at Vohingheso in a fight with the Baras four years before. Those present—myself and some privileged natives—saw nothing when Taimandebakaka claimed to see the two persons in question; but we could hear the voices of officers issuing orders to their soldiers, and these voices were European voices which could not be imitated by natives. Similarly, at a distance we could hear the echoes of firing and the cries of the wounded and the lowing of frightened cattle—oxen of the Fahavalos.

III

It is fitting that Plotinus should have been the first philosopher to meet his daimon face to face, though the boy attendant out of jealousy or in convulsive terror strangled the doves, for he was the first to establish as sole source the timeless individuality or daimon instead of the Platonic Idea, to prefer Socrates to his thought. This timeless individuality contains archetypes of all possible existences whether of man or brute, and as it traverses its circle of allotted lives, now one, now another, prevails. We may fail to express an archetype or alter it by reason, but all done from nature is its unfolding into time. Some other existence may take the place of Socrates, yet Socrates can never cease to exist. Once a friend of mine was digging in a long-neglected garden and suddenly out of the air came a voice thanking her, an old owner of the garden, she was told later, long since reborn, yet still in the garden. Plotinus said that we should not 'baulk at this limitlessness of the intellectual; it is an infinitude having nothing to do with number or part' (*Ennead* V. 7. 1.); yet it seems that it can at will re-enter number and part and thereby make itself apparent to our minds. If we accept this idea many strange or beautiful things become credible. The Indian pilgrim has not deceived us; he did hear the bed where the sage of his devotion slept a thousand years ago creak as though someone turned over in it, and he did see—he himself and the old shrine-keeper—the blankets all tossed about at dawn as if someone had just risen; the Irish country-woman did see the ruined castle lit up, the bridge across the river dropping; those two Oxford ladies did find themselves in the garden of the Petit Trianon with Marie Antoinette and her courtiers, see that garden as those saw it; the gamekeeper did hear those footsteps the other night that sounded like the footsteps of a stag where stag has not passed these hundred years. All about us there seems to start up a precise inexplicable teeming life, and the earth becomes once more, not in rhetorical metaphor, but in reality, sacred.   1931.

'The Words upon the Window-pane,' Introduction. **83.**

I

Somebody . . . that in Dublin were many clubs—he . . . four—that . . . programmes and, though the majority stopped there, some did much to find . . . enmity and . . . we but walked . . . life; that . . . consciousness where . . . echoes.

II

My . . . *The Words upon the Window Pane* came . . . Davis and . . . public men; we never . . . well-informed but . . . Swift because, being a romantic, I acknowledged no verse . . . the dialogues of Landor. But . . . , sixteenth or . . . against us.

III

Swift . . . Saint Patrick's, . . . deep spoken . . . , pride discipline. I . . . Electra 'I . . . race'
. . . liberty.

IV

'In . . . position they had reached in society . . . state. . . . [T] His . . .
Oliver 'The . . . Leibnitz, . . . *Grammont Memoirs* . . . stone.

'. . . Ireland, in our character, . . . civilization . . . blackboard; a . . .
shapes; buildings, attitudes . . . bookcase; the . . . aristocracy some . . .
contempt nor dread . . . fellow students . . . twenty five . . . aristocracy who
knew more of the battle of the Boyne . . . Huguenots, than . . . exaggerated
for . . . ; the Parliament . . . half-educated drunken, . . . for mimicry [foot-
note 1 lacking **82**] . . . title page of . . . as the . . . 1728. A . . . 'dark, insipid
. . . song.

V

'He . . . , democracy, . . . Revolution, that . . . doctors' he said 'though
. . . *Gulliver* that . . . *Dissensions of Athens and Rome* published . . . hereditary
. . . well and . . . state and every man's Jack is 'listed to a party' becomes
. . . abstraction expressed likewise by . . . it and have . . . way, for the many
obsessed . . . defines a tyrant as . . . Elizabeth but . . . Polybius 'those . . .
eats iron or worms wood? Whether . . . power the . . . because in . . . heads?'

Twenty-two . . . Scienza Nuova . . . man surrounded . . . subordinates
dismissed . . . reflection and . . . difference, Swift . . . wrote ascribed . . .
movement' as . . . it has . . . traveller Frobenius, . . . naiver . . . change the
idea of progress or that of the eternal . . . fact, that of the eternal . . . idea,
progress, the . . . old.

VI

Swift's . . . seventh'; Epaminondas . . . guilt.

Liberty . . . state, . . . itself: The . . . blame, for God had given him reason,
so long as he kept them to himself. It was . . . state could . . . state? . . .
silence.

What . . . eloquence? 'I think' he . . . Discourse 'that . . . arts and application wherein . . . pursuit . . . than those who would . . . lives or . . . liberty.'

VII

The will . . . , Leibnitz, . . . comparison to Lord . . . 'Great . . . engravers
from . . . Consort for
. . . side.

VIII

'That . . . superstition at last': A young . . . grass;—nor . . . of Sir Christopher . . . reality: his counter truth . . . Spinoza.

In . . . Gmnosophists . . . *World*; the . . . grass.

IX

'I have . . . celibacy; Sir . . . play, of . . . ; though with . . . platonic [footnote 1 lacking **82**] and . . . know, for that excited bluestocking bores . . . birth and . . . beliefs.

X

'Was . . . mad? or . . . said 'I . . . said 'Terrified . . . death' and . . . Johnson's. [footnote 1 lacking **82**] There . . . of five hundred pounds for . . . butler who . . . printer stayed . . . said 'I . . . butler and . . . him and . . . the servants 'No . . . friend, 'He . . . Connaught . . . half mad . . . savages and . . . Marat: after . . . servant.

XI

When . . . had however assisted . . . grave not . . . Swedenborgian, they express the attitude . . . scéance room . . . Church. At . . . otherwise.

If . . . thoughts what . . . house, some of it when . . . some one . . . dramatisation of the medium's. Perhaps . . . play went, . . . man, and . . . no necessary difference except of degree . . . and the powerful grotesque . . . Paladino . . . subconscious . . . wanted Sankey's help . . . voice 'King . . . George's, . . . said 'King . . . George, we . . . medium's . . . together. Swedenborg, lacking our experimental proof of the complicity of medium and sitter, denounced all spirits that had not reached their final rest for jugglers and cheats. But what . . . bottle?

The . . . , desire or fantasy . . . purpose for . . . say did . . . him that . . past, if . . . feeling, renew, as shades, detached events . . . excitement first.

When Achilles comes to . . . blood pool . . . that deprived . . . death they . . . own timeless being, into the whole of being, that which . . . not however the . . . séance room, these . . . , or imply supernormal . . . medium, are, as . . . were, new . . . bird. They within . . . limits create, they . . . pre-natal . . . , or, when, . . . find in their . . . conscience but little check upon invention.

> . . . spirits; if . . .
> . . . ears
> . . . these; one . . . is,
> . . . phantasies;
> . . . blood.

I have . . . an European séance room . . . to or . . . of their . . . nature. Here however is . . . Vesme: 'One, . . . Fahavalos?'

XII

It is . . . strangled the sacrificial dove, for . . . daimon, instead . . . existence . . . or brute, . . . traverses its 'period' or series of lives, . . . archetype, or . . . time. In that sense the dramatisation that kept the actor lame though the curtain had fallen, and some apparition that describes its suicide, are both spirits. Another existence . . . long neglected . . . garden she . . . reborn, but still . . . garden. Plotinus thought that . . . (*Ennead* V. 7. I.) yet . . . bed, where . . . ago, creak . . . see the blankets . . . courtiers and . . . as she saw it; . . . precise, inexplicable, teeming . . . reality, sacred.

Introduction, **82.**

I

Somebody . . . clubs that met . . . garrets, he himself knew four, and had . . . programmes and . . . majority stopped there some did much to find . . . enmity and . . . life; that . . . else I should be . . . consciousness where . . . echoes.

II

My . . . Davis and . . . O'Leary who . . . because, I acknowledged, . . . the Dialogues of Landor. But . . . , sixteenth or . . . us.

III

Swift . . . St. Patrick's where . . . deep spoken . . . unknown, another . . . Electra 'I . . . race'

> Jonathan Swift's at rest:
> . . . dare
> World besotted . . .
> . . . liberty.

IV

'In . . . state . . . Cats, such . . . Oliver 'the . . . Leibnitz, . . . shapes, attitudes of mind, buildings, that could . . . bookcase, the . . . contempt nor dread . . . fellow students . . . undergraduate defined . . . otherwise 'I . . . Irishmen' and . . . aristocracy who . . . Huguenots, found themselves . . . pig-styes, . . . mines, the . . . , fire-eating impoverished . . . mimicry [footnote I lacking **DM**] . . . title page . . . the . . . 1782. A . . . poet 'We . . . 'dark, insipid . . . song.

VI [numbered incorrectly **DM**]

'He . . . , democracy, . . . Revolution, that . . . doctors' he said 'though . . . *Dissensions of Athens and Rome* published . . . Tory government of . . . ministers, . . . states . . . Few and . . . state, . . . well and . . . thought, but . . . state . . . man's Jack is 'listed to a party' becomes . . . Commonplace book, . . . Good Natured . . . , Phocean, . . . of it and . . . states . . . Elizabeth but . . . Polybius 'those . . . corruptions; which . . . seed . . . eats iron or worms wood.' . . . power the . . . also—and . . . became in . . . Polybius 'great . . . heads.'

Twenty-two . . . Giambetta . . . Scienza Nuova which . . . 'Work in Transition.' He . . . man surrounded . . . subordinates dismissed . . . reflection' and . . . difference, Swift a . . . wrote ascribed . . . movement' as . . . it has . . . created the . . . thought; the . . . naiver . . . solitude. Beside we . . . old.

VII [numbered incorrectly **DM**]

Swift's . . . first, if . . . it,' to . . . disappointment; when . . . none; and . . . sexumvirate . . . seventh'; Epaminondas . . . quiet.

Liberty . . . state, . . . itself: The . . . blame, for God had given him reason, so long . . . himself. It was . . . state . . . Hugenots . . . state? . . . silence.

What . . . eloquence? 'I think' he . . . Discourse 'that . . . arts and . . . application wherein . . . pursuit . . . than those who would . . . men, thought as . . . lives or . . . liberty.'

VIII [numbered incorrectly **DM**]

The will . . . forms' whether . . . thought every . . . of wealth . . . , passed man . . . , Leibnitz, . . . comparison to Lord . . . over rationalised . . . 'Great . . . engravers for such as he from the . . . Consort, or, to

. . . swoon;

. . . died;

. . . side.

IX [numbered incorrectly **DM**]

'That . . . grass;—nor . . . her' Swift . . . sickness 'all . . . Spinoza.

In . . . hand could . . . grass.

X [numbered incorrectly **DM**]

'I . . . celibacy; Sir . . . ; though with . . . Varenna . . . Ireland. Mr. Shaun Leslie . . . platonic [footnote 1 lacking **DM**] and . . . know for that excited blue-stocking bores . . . birth and . . . beliefs.

XI [numbered incorrectly **DM**]

'Was . . . mad? or . . . preeminence . . . said 'I . . . said 'Afraid perhaps of . . . death' and . . . butler who . . . printer stayed . . . said 'I . . . hands, but I will not from cowardice be the slave of any man's insolence or inattention.' He dismissed the butler and . . . him and said to the servants 'No . . . next,

that . . . Connaught . . . half mad . . . discover the wisdom instinct not in
. . . savages and . . . Marat: after . . . servant.
November, 1930.   'A Commentary.' *The Dublin Magazine*,
                                                  October–December 1931.

Part II [collated with II and III in **83**;
XI and XII in **82**]

When . . . seance. I had assisted . . . seance. Taken . . . whippet racing
. . . grave not . . . express . . . seance room . . . Church. At . . . seances . . .
otherwise.

If . . . thoughts what . . . meeting much phenomena, some of it in . . . ,
some of it when . . . , I see . . . some one . . . dramatisation of the medium's.
Perhaps . . . Craig when . . . play went, . . . seances . . . subconscious . . .
seance . . . Second' while . . . repeating 'He . . . seance, . . . voice 'King . . .
George's, . . . said 'King George, our George, we . . . together. Swedenborg,
lacking our experimental proof of the complicity of medium and sitter,
denounced all spirits that had not reached their final rest for jugglers and
cheats. But what . . . or ours? Must that not be more than dramatisation?

I cannot say with Flournoy 'as a philosopher I affirm the immortality of
the soul, as a man of science I deny it.' There is something within a man or
enclosing him that Leibnitz called a monad, and that I prefer to call a
daimon. That daimon is timeless, it has present before it his past and future,
or it has no present and is that past and future, and as the dramatisations
recede from his waking mind and from the dreams that reproduce his
waking desires they begin to express that knowledge. But the mirror-like
daimon reflects all other daimons; the dramatisation or the medium can as
it were pass from daimon to daimon. Nor do I deny that these daimons
which give a book of words or a scenario have volition as well as knowledge.
Dramatisation or medium passes from daimon to daimon at the suggestion
of some spoken word, or some association in the unconscious mind of some
sitter. I take a letter from my pocket and ask the medium about its writer
who was perhaps some dead friend, and she talks about somebody else of
whom I know nothing but whose letter has lain next to it in my pocket; she
is in contact with some knowledge that any trifle may as it were discharge.

Is dramatisation necessary because we cannot imagine knowledge of
the past reaching us without testimony? Do our occasional previsions of the
future reach us without it because so extraordinary that our subconscious-
ness gives up the problem? There are seances where the past seems present
without dramatisation. A French traveller quoted by Cesar de Vesmes,[1]
[footnote 1 reads: 'A History of Experimental Spiritualism' Vol. 1. p. 144.
English Edition.] describes such a seance in Madagascar.

'. . . . One, . . . Fahavalos.'

In my play, Swift and Vanessa are obviously dramatisations; the medium thinks and speaks what they say, and it seems natural for Dr. Trench to talk of them as condemned to re-enact the past. His explanation is traditional, one finds it in Japanese plays and in Swedenborg, and we may think it more than a necessary substitution for unintelligible reality; we may say, perhaps even must say, that before the spirit identify itself with its own timeless Daimon it substitutes for our living present a dead present made out of some passionate past moment. Such a spirit is seen by the living continually to re-enact such a moment and all the more so if the medium's dramatisation permit it to answer or seem to answer our question. It may even be in need of something—some act upon our part that can set it free and itself incite the dramatisation. It is in part because the shades can so answer that a seance, whether that of Ulysses and his blood pool, or that of the witch of Endor or some modern medium, so seldom resembles Taimandebakaka's invocation. Mrs. Wriedt's voices said that they must fade out if we did not question, and it is perhaps only because of the necessity of answering that the shades can separate themselves from our desires, attain to spiritual objectivity, identify themselves with a timeless daimon.

Theologians and mystics generally give more importance to those apparitions which occur without apparent intervention of thaumaturgist or medium, which seem spontaneous although they are still dramatisations: St. Michael has his sword, the Madonna resembles statue or picture. But the dramatist seems less the individual than the Church; though the difference is one of degree alone, the Egyptian priest who made Plotinus see his daimon had his traditional ritual, his sacrifice of doves, the daimon probably wore some traditional form or garb, and even when our seances do not start with some popular hymn there is a vague sense of something at rest and immaterial that resembles prayer. Theologian and mystic object to the seance because its traffic with human passion makes error easy, and yet error or no error experiment cannot cease. A peasant girl's vision of some holy person harms none and encourages many innocent lives but is incapable of verification. If an apparition tells me that it drowned itself at Richmond Bridge eighty years ago I can go to Somerset House.

It is fitting . . . source the daimon or spiritual individuality instead . . . thought. The spiritual individuality . . . traverses its 'period' or series of lives, . . . archetype, or . . . into time. In that sense the dramatisation that kept the actor lame though the curtain had fallen, and the apparition that described its suicide, were both spirits. Some other existence . . . Socrates yet . . . long neglected . . . garden she was told. She said 'Have you not been reborn?' 'Yes,' was the answer, 'but I am still in the garden.' Plotinus thought that . . . (*Ennead* V. 7. I.). If we accept . . . over in it and . . . shrine-keeper being somewhat mediumistic—the blankets . . . courtiers and see . . . as they saw . . . sacred.

November, 1931.   'A Commentary.' *The Dublin Magazine*,
                                                January–March, 1932.

*   *   *

Variant spellings

saeva **83-97** ; *saevo* **82.**
séance **83-97** ; *seance, séance* **82.**

* * *

[See *Preface to 83*, p. 1308.]

A FULL MOON IN MARCH

1935

Persons in the Play

First Attendant   The Queen
Second Attendant   The Swineherd

The Swineherd wears a half-savage mask covering the upper part of his face. He is bearded. When the inner curtain rises for the second time the player who has hitherto taken the part of the Queen is replaced by a dancer.

When the stage curtain rises, two Attendants, an elderly woman and a young man, are discovered standing before an inner curtain.

1. *First Attendant.* What do we do?
2.   What part do we take?
3.   What did he say?

4. *Second Attendant.* Join when we like,
5.   Singing or speaking.

6. *First Attendant.* Before the curtain rises on the play?

7. *Second Attendant.* Before it rises.

PRINTINGS   *Poetry* (Chicago), March 1935; **87, 91, 97.**
DATE   [lacking] **P, 87, 91.**
DRAMATIS PERSONAE   [lacking] **P** ; Characters / First . . . **87, 91.**
STAGE DIRECTIONS   [lacking] **P.**
Directions before 1.   [*Enter Three Attendants*] **P.**
TEXT

1.   What are we to do? What part do
2.   we take in the Play? Did he tell you that?
3.   [lacking]
4.   He said we were to join in wher-
5.   ever we thought it necessary, singing or speaking.
6.   But what are we to do before the
6a.   Play begins?
7.   We are to sing, of course. **P.**

8. *First Attendant.* What do we sing?

9. *Second Attendant.* 'Sing anything, sing any old thing,' said he.

10. *First Attendant.* Come then and sing about the dung of swine.
>   [*They slowly part the inner curtain. The Second Attendant sings—the First Attendant may join in the singing at the end of the first or second verse. The First Attendant has a soprano, the Second a bass voice.*

11. *Second Attendant.* Every loutish lad in love
12.   Thinks his wisdom great enough,
13.   *What cares love for this and that?*
14.   Tó make all his parish stare,
15.   As though Pythagoras wandered there.
16.   *Crown of gold or dung of swine.*

17.   Should old Pythagoras fall in love
18.   Little may he boast thereof.
19.   *What cares love for this and that?*
20.   Days go by in foolishness.
21.   O how great their sweetness is!
22.   *Crown of gold or dung of swine.*

23.   Open wide those gleaming eyes,
24.   That can make the loutish wise.
25.   *What cares love for this and that?*
26.   Make a leader of the schools
27.   Thank the Lord, all men are fools.
28.   *Crown of gold or dung of swine.*

---

8. But what? **P.**
9. At first he said any love song I
9a. could remember. And then he said that I must sing
9b. that song with the line: 'Crown of gold, dung of
9c. swine.'
10. [lacking]
    Directions before 11. [*Second Attendant sings, unfolding and folding a cloth as in The Hawk's Well. The First . . . in singing the burden at . . . verse; the . . . a tenor voice; the Second Attendant a . . . .*] **P.**
14. To . . . , **97A.**
21. Oh, how . . . is. **P.**
    Name of singer repeated before 23. *Second Attendant.* **P.**

[They sit at one side of stage near audience. If they are musicians, they have beside them drum, flute and zither. The Queen is discovered seated and veiled.

29.　*The Queen [stretching and yawning].* What man is at the door?

Second Attendant. Nobody, Queen.

30.　*The Queen.*[1] Some man has come, some terrifying man,
31.　　For I have yawned and stretched myself three times.
32.　　Admit him, Captain of the Guard. . . .

Second Attendant [speaking as Captain of the Guard]. He comes.

Enter the Swineherd

33.　*The Swineherd.* The beggars of my country say that he
34.　　That sings you best shall take you for a wife.

35.　*The Queen.* He that best sings his passion.

The Swineherd.　　　　　　　　　And they say
36.　　The kingdom is added to the gift.

The Queen.　　　　　　　　　I swore it.

Directions before 29.　*[When the cloth has been folded the Three Attendants sit at one or both sides of the stage, where it is nearest to the stage. They may find there, or have placed there at their first entrance, gong, drum, ...]* **P;**
[*. . . of the stage . . . .*] **91.**
29.　. . . door?
First Attendant. Nobody, ...
32.　. . . Guard . . . [T]
First Attendant. He . . . . **P.**
34.　. . . best, shall . . . . **P.**
36.　. . . gift.
　　　　　So have I sworn. **P.**

[1] 'Queen' for 'The Queen' from here on. **P.**

37. *The Swineherd.*[1] But what if some blind aged cripple sing
38.   Better than wholesome men?

      The Queen.   Some I reject.
39.   Some I have punished for their impudence.
40.   None I abhor can sing.

      The Swineherd.   So that's the catch.
41.   Queen, look at me, look long at these foul rags,
42.   At hair more foul and ragged than my rags;
43.   Look on my scratched foul flesh. Have I not come
44.   Through dust and mire? There in the dust and mire
45.   Beasts scratched my flesh; my memory too is gone,
46.   Because great solitudes have driven me mad.
47.   But when I look into a stream, the face
48.   That trembles upon the surface makes me think
49.   My origin more foul than rag or flesh.

50. *The Queen.* But you have passed through perils for my sake;
51.   Come a great distance. I permit the song.

52. *The Swineherd.* Kingdom and lady, if I sing the best?
53.   But who decides?

      The Queen.   I and my heart decide.
54.   We say that song is best that moves us most.
55.   No song has moved us yet.

      The Swineherd.   You must be won

---

37.   . . . crippled man
37a.   Or some base beggar in his famine sing **P.**
39.   No man abhorrent to these eyes can sing,
40.   Some I have punished for their impudence.
41.   *Swineherd.* So that's the catch.
                    Look well upon me, Queen.
42.   My hair is foul and matted—here and there
43.   My flesh seems scarce less ragged than my rags.
44.   I have crossed many forests and the beasts
45.   Have torn me with their claws—my memory's gone
46.   . . . mad,
47.   . . . stream the . . . **P.**
49.   . . . origin was fouler than my rags. **P.**
53.   . . . decide **P.**

      [1] 'Swineherd' for 'The Swineherd' from here on. **P.**

56.   At a full moon in March, those beggars say.
57.   That moon has come, but I am here alone.

58.   *The Queen.* No other man has come.

    The Swineherd.   The moon is full.

59.   *The Queen.* Remember through what perils you have come;
60.   That I am crueller than solitude,
61.   Forest or beast. Some I have killed or maimed
62.   Because their singing put me in a rage,
63.   And some because they came at all. Men hold
64.   That woman's beauty is a kindly thing,
65.   But they that call me cruel speak the truth,
66.   Cruel as the winter of virginity.
67.   But for a reason that I cannot guess
68.   I would not harm you. Go before I change.
69.   Why do you stand, your chin upon your breast?

70.   *The Swineherd.* My mind is running on our marriage night,
71.   Imagining all from the first touch and kiss.

72.   *The Queen.* What gives you that strange confidence? What makes
73.   You think that you can move my heart and me?

74.   *The Swineherd.* Because I look upon you without fear.

75.   *The Queen.* A lover in railing or in flattery said

---

56. ... Moon ... say,
57. ... Moon ... come but ....
58. [lacking] **P.**
59. ... come. **P** ; ... come: **87, 91.**
60. But I ... , **P.**
62. ... rage **P.**
64. ... thing. **P.**
68. ... change; **P.**
70. ... night **P.**
72. ... confidence. What ... **P.**
74. ... fear
75. [lacking] **P.**

76.   God only looks upon me without fear.

77. *The Swineherd*. Desiring cruelty, he made you cruel.
78.   I shall embrace body and cruelty,
79.   Desiring both as though I had made both.

80. *The Queen*. One question more. You bring like all the rest
81.   Some novel simile, some wild hyperbole
82.   Praising my beauty?

The Swineherd.   My memory has returned.
83.   I tended swine, when I first heard your name.
84.   I rolled among the dung of swine and laughed.
85.   What do I know of beauty?

The Queen.   Sing the best
86.   And you are not a swineherd, but a king.

87. *The Swineherd*. What do I know of kingdoms?
                    [*Snapping his fingers*] That for kingdoms!

88. *The Queen*. If trembling of my limbs or sudden tears
89.   Proclaim your song beyond denial best,
90.   I leave these corridors, this ancient house,
91.   A famous throne, the reverence of servants—
92.   What do I gain?

The Swineherd.   A song—the night of love,
93.   An ignorant forest and the dung of swine.
                    [*Queen leaves throne and comes down stage.*

94. *The Queen*. All here have heard the man and all have judged.

---

76. *Swineherd*. I know the thought of God.
    Queen.   What is that thought? **P.**
78. . . . cruelty **P.**
79a. *Queen*. You cannot help but yield to such desire.
80. Another question. You . . . **P.**
84. . . . laughed **P.**
88. If by the trembling . . .
89. I should proclaim . . . denial
90. More moving than the rest, I leave this throne
91. These corridors, the . . . servants, **P.**

95.   I led him, that I might not seem unjust,
96.   From point to point, established in all eyes
97.   That he came hither not to sing but to heap
98.   Complexities of insult upon my head.

99.   *The Swineherd.* She shall bring forth her farrow in the dung.
100.   But first my song—what nonsense shall I sing?

101.   *The Queen.* Send for the headsman, Captain of the Guard.

102.   *Second Attendant* [*speaking as Captain of the Guard*]. I have already
         sent. He stands without.

103.   *The Queen.* I owe my thanks to God that this foul wretch,
104.   Foul in his rags, his origin, his speech,
105.   In spite of all his daring has not dared
106.   Ask me to drop my veil. Insulted ears
107.   Have heard and shuddered, but my face is pure.
108.   Had it but known the insult of his eyes
109.   I had torn it with these nails.

         The Swineherd [*going up stage*]. Why should I ask?
110.   What do those features matter? When I set out
111.   I picked a number on the roulette wheel.
112.   I trust the wheel, as every lover must.

113.   *The Queen.* Pray, if your savagery has learnt to pray,
114.   For in a moment they will lead you out

---

95.   . . . him that . . . unjust
96.   . . . point established . . . eyes.
97.   He has brought hither insult and not love.
98.   [lacking] **P.**
102.   *First Attendant.* I have sent already, Queen. He . . . .
103.   . . . wretch **P.**
110.   . . . matter. When . . .
111.   . . . wheel, **P.**
113.   Pray if . . . , **P.**

115. Then bring your severed head.

The Swineherd. My severed head.

[*Laughs.*

116. There is a story in my country of a woman
117. That stood all bathed in blood—a drop of blood
118. Entered her womb and there begat a child.

119. *The Queen.* A severed head! She took it in her hands;
120. She stood all bathed in blood; the blood begat.
121. O foul, foul, foul!

The Swineherd. She sank in bridal sleep.

122. *The Queen.* Her body in that sleep conceived a child.
123. Begone! I shall not see your face again.
[*She turns towards him, her back to the audience, and slowly drops her veil.*
The Attendants close the inner curtain.

124. *Second Attendant.* What do we sing?

First Attendant. An ancient Irish Queen
125. That stuck a head upon a stake.

Second Attendant. Her lover's head;

---

115. ... head! [*laughs*] **P.**
119. [lacking]
120. Oh, foul, foul, foul—I shall be quit of him.
121. I shall not touch his blood.
   Swineherd. She ... in sleep,
122. *Swineherd.* Her ... in the bridal sleep, conceived. **P.**
   Directions after 123. [... *Attendants unfold the cloth.*]
124. What are you to sing?
   The song of that ancient ... **P.**
124, 125. [set as four lines] **87, 91.**
125. Who put her lover's head ... stake. **P.**

126.   But that's a different queen, a different story.

127. *First Attendant*. He had famished in a wilderness,
128.   Braved lions for my sake,
129.   And all men lie that say that I
130.   Bade that swordsman take
131.   His head from off his body
132.   And set it on a stake.

133.   He swore to sing my beauty
134.   Though death itself forbade.
135.   They lie that say, in mockery
136.   Of all that lovers said,
137.   Or in mere woman's cruelty
138.   I bade them fetch his head.
                                   [*They begin to part the inner curtain.*
139.   O what innkeeper's daughter
140.   Shared the Byzantine crown?
141.   Girls that have governed cities,
142.   Or burned great cities down,
143.   Have bedded with their fancy-man
144.   Whether a king or clown;

145.   Gave their bodies, emptied purses
146.   For praise of clown or king,
147.   Gave all the love that women know!
148.   O they had their fling,
149.   But never stood before a stake
150.   And heard the dead lips sing.

---

126.   *Second Attendant*. But that has nothing to do with this Play. **P**; [set
       as two lines ending queen, / story.] **87, 91.**
126a. That was quite a different Queen. **P.**
134.   . . . forbade,
135.   . . . say in . . . **P.**
       Directions after 138.   [lacking] **P.**
140.   . . . crown! **P.**
146.   . . . king. **P.**
148.   . . . fling **P.**

[The Queen is discovered standing exactly as before, the dropped veil at her side, but she holds above her head the severed head of the Swineherd. Her hands are red. There are red blotches upon her dress, not realistically represented: red gloves, some pattern of red cloth.

151. *First Attendant.* Her lips are moving.

Second Attendant.   She has begun to sing.

152. *First Attendant.* I cannot hear what she is singing.
153.   Ah, now I can hear.

[singing as Queen]
154.   Child and darling, hear my song,
155.   Never cry I did you wrong;
156.   Cry that wrong came not from me
157.   But my virgin cruelty.
158.   Great my love before you came,
159.   Greater when I loved in shame,
160.   Greatest when there broke from me
161.   Storm of virgin cruelty.

[The Queen dances to drum-taps and in the dance lays the head upon the throne.

162. *Second Attendant.* She is waiting.

First Attendant.   She is waiting for his song.

Directions after 150. [*When the cloth has been folded up again the Queen ... represented; red ... cloth are sufficient.*] **P.**
151. [set as two lines] **P-91.**
151. *Second Attendant.* Her ....
      First Attendant. She ....
152. *Second Attendant.* I .... **P.**
      Speaker and Directions before 154. *First Attendant* [*Singing ... Queen*]: **P.**
155. ... wrong, **P.**
      [between 157 and 158, a break] **P.**
      Directions after 161. [... *dances and* ....] **P.**
162. [set as two lines] **P-91.**

163.   The song he has come so many miles to sing.

164.   She has forgotten that no dead man sings.

165.   *Second Attendant* [*laughs softly as Head*]. He has begun to laugh.

    First Attendant.   No; he has begun to sing.

    Second Attendant [*singing as Head*].

166.   I sing a song of Jack and Jill.

167.   Jill had murdered Jack;

168.   *The moon shone brightly;*

169.   Ran up the hill, and round the hill,

170.   Round the hill and back.

171.   *A full moon in March.*

172.   Jack had a hollow heart, for Jill

173.   Had hung his heart on high;

174.   *The moon shone brightly;*

175.   Had hung his heart beyond the hill,

176.   A-twinkle in the sky.

177.   *A full moon in March.*

    [*The Queen in her dance moves away from the head, alluring and refusing.*

    First Attendant [*laughs as Queen*].

178.   *Second Attendant.* She is laughing. How can she laugh,
                   Loving the dead?

---

163.   . . . come such a long way to . . . .
164.   . . . that the dead cannot sing. **P.**
165.   [. . . *head*]. He . . . laugh.
               He has . . . . **P** ; [set as 2 lines] **87, 91.**
    Directions before 166.   [. . . *head*]:
166.   . . . Jill,
167.   . . . Jack,
168.   . . . *brightly,* **P.**
170.   . . . back, **P, 91.**
172.   . . . heart for . . .
173.   . . . high,
174.   . . . *brightly,* **P.**
175.   . . . hill. **87, 91.**
176.   A twinkle . . . sky, (sky. **87, 91**) **P-91.**
178.   . . . . laugh if she loves the . . . ? **P,**

179. *First Attendant.* She is crazy. That is why she is laughing.

> [*Laughs again as Queen.*
> [*Queen takes up the head and lays it upon the ground. She dances before it—a dance of adoration. She takes the head up and dances with it to drum-taps, which grow quicker and quicker. As the drum-taps approach their climax, she presses her lips to the lips of the head. Her body shivers to very rapid drum-taps. The drum-taps cease. She sinks slowly down, holding the head to her breast. The Attendants close inner curtain, singing, and then stand one on either side while the stage curtain descends.*

180. *Second Attendant.* Why must those holy, haughty feet descend
181.   From emblematic niches, and what hand
182.   Ran that delicate raddle through their white?
183.   My heart is broken, yet must understand.
184.   What do they seek for? Why must they descend?

185. *First Attendant.* For desecration and the lover's night.

186. *Second Attendant.* I cannot face that emblem of the moon
187.   Nor eyelids that the unmixed heavens dart,
188.   Nor stand upon my feet, so great a fright
189.   Descends upon my savage, sunlit heart.
190.   What can she lack whose emblem is the moon?

191. *First Attendant.* But desecration and the lover's night.

192. *Second Attendant.* Delight my heart with sound; speak yet again.
193.   But look and look with understanding eyes
194.   Upon the pitchers that they carry; tight
195.   Therein all time's completed treasure is:
196.   What do they lack? O cry it out again.

197. *First Attendant.* Their desecration and the lover's night.

THE END

Directions in 179.   [*He laughs . . .*] **P.**
Directions after 179.   [*. . . drum taps, . . . drum taps . . . drum taps . . . drum taps . . . breast.*]; **P**; [*. . . curtain singing and . . . .*] **87, 91.**
Directions before 180.   *Song | The Folding and Unfolding of the Cloth* **P.**
181.   . . . *niches and . . .* **P.**

NOTE

[See *Prefaces to 87, 91,* pp. 1310, 1311.]

THE KING OF THE GREAT CLOCK TOWER[1]

First performed at the Abbey Theatre on the
thirtieth of June, nineteen thirty-four.

The Persons of the Play

The King (Dressed in red)
The Queen (Dressed in orange with details in black or red)
Stroller (Dressed in black with details in red)
First Attendant (Dressed in black. Bass Voice)
Second Attendant (Dressed in black. Tenor Voice)

[*When the stage curtain rises it shows an inner curtain, pale
purple in colour. It may have a stencilled pattern of dancers. At the right and left sides of the proscenium are a
drum and gong.*
*The Queen should wear a beautiful impassive mask, the
Stranger, a wild half-savage mask. It should cover the
upper part of his face, the lower part being hidden by his
red beard.*
*The Attendants stand by drum and gong; they slowly part the
curtains, singing.*

1   1. *Second Attendant.* They dance all day that dance in Tir-nan-
oge.

PRINTINGS   *Life and Letters*, November 1934; **85, 86.**

PERFORMANCE NOTE   [lacking] **LL.**

STAGE DIRECTIONS   [*The Queen . . . mask. The Stroller: a wild . . . face. The
lower . . . beard. When the stage curtain rises it shows an inner curtain, pale purple
in colour. It may have a stencilled pattern of dancers. At the right and left side of
the proscenium are a drum and a gong. The Attendants . . . curtain, singing as
follows*:—] **LL.**

1.   . . . Tir-na-nogue. **LL.**

[1] **LL, 85,** and **86** are in verse and prose; **87, 91,** and **97** in verse. Because of the difficulty of
making an intelligible collation of both versions, the prose-and-verse texts are collated with
86 on the verso pages. Line-lengths are from **86.** The verse texts are collated on the recto
pages. Identities between **86** and **97E** are shown by unbracketed line-numbers in the margin
of **86**; similarities by bracketed line-numbers.

THE KING OF THE GREAT CLOCK TOWER

1935

TO

NINETTE DE VALOIS

ASKING PARDON FOR COVERING

HER EXPRESSIVE FACE WITH A MASK

Persons in the Play

First Attendant	The King
Second Attendant	The Queen
	The Stroller

When the stage curtain rises it shows an inner curtain whereon is perhaps a stencilled pattern of dancers. At the right and left sides of the proscenium are a drum and gong. The Queen should wear a beautiful impassive mask; the Stroller a wild half-savage mask. It should cover the upper part of his face, the lower part being hidden by his red beard. The Attendants stand by drum and gong; they slowly part the curtains, singing.

1. *Second Attendant.* They dance all day that dance in Tir-nan-oge.

2. *First Attendant.* There every lover is a happy rogue;
3.   And should he speak, it is the speech of birds.
4.   No thought has he, and therefore has no words,
5.   No thought because no clock, no clock because
6.   If I consider deeply, lad and lass,
7.   Nerve touching nerve upon that happy ground,
8.   Are bobbins where all time is bound and wound.

9. *Second Attendant.* O never may that dismal thread run loose;

PRINTINGS **87, 91, 97.**

DATE [lacking] **87, 91.**

DRAMATIS PERSONAE Characters / First . . . **87, 91.**

STAGE DIRECTIONS . . . *mask; the Stranger, a* . . . . **87, 91.**

2	2.	*First Attendant.* There every lover is a happy rogue;
3	3.	And should he speak, it is the speech of birds.
4	4.	No thought has he, and therefore has no words,
5	5.	No thought because no clock, no clock because
6	6.	If I consider deeply, lad and lass,
7	7.	Nerve touching nerve upon that happy ground,
8	8.	Are bobbins where all time is bound and wound.
9	9.	*Second Attendant.* O never may that dismal thread run loose;
10	10.	*First Attendant.* For there the hound that Oisin saw pursues
11	11.	The hornless deer that runs in such a fright;
[12]	12.	And there the woman clasps an apple tight,
[13]	13.	For all the clamour of a famished man;
[14]	14.	They run in foam, and there in foam they ran
15	15.	Nor can they stop to take a breath that still
[16]	16.	Here in the foam, the beating of a bell.

> [*When the curtains are parted one sees to left the King
> and Queen upon two thrones, which may be two cubes.
> There should be two cubes upon the opposite side to
> balance them. The background and the cubes are a rich
> blue. The background may be a curtain hung in a semi-
> circle, or a semi-circle of one foot Craig screens, so
> painted that the blue is darker below than above.
> The two Attendants sit down by drum and gong, they re-
> main facing the audience at either side of the stage,
> but a little in the shadow.*

[17-18]	17.	*The King.* A year ago this night, you walked into
[18-19]	18.	my house. I made you my Queen, yet neither I, nor
[19-20]	19.	any other man, know from what Country you came.
[21]	20.	And now before our friends and courtiers here assem-
[21, 23, 24]	21.	bled, I ask you, not for the first time, where that
[24]	22.	Country is, who and what you were before you be-
[25]	23.	came my Queen? You have kept silence long enough,
[25, 28]	24.	sat there an image of stone or wood. That silence has
[28]	25.	become unendurable to these others, and to me.

---

2. . . . rogue. **LL.**   19. . . . country . . . . **LL.**

10. . . . Hound . . . **LL.**   22. country . . .

14. . . . ran, **LL, 85.**   23. . . . enough.

16. Hear . . . . **LL, 85.**   24. Sat . . . **LL.**

10. *First Attendant.* For there the hound that Oisin saw pursues
11.   The hornless deer that runs in such a fright;
12.   And there the woman clasps an apple tight
13.   For all the clamour of a famished man.
14.   They run in foam, and there in foam they ran,
15.   Nor can they stop to take a breath that still
16.   Hear in the foam the beating of a bell.

> [*When the curtains are parted one sees to the left the King and Queen upon two thrones, which may be two cubes. There should be two cubes upon the opposite side to balance them. The background may be a curtain hung in a semicircle, or a semicircle of one-foot Craig screens.*
>
> *The two Attendants sit down by drum and gong. They remain facing the audience at either side of the stage, but a little in the shadow.*

17. *The King.* A year ago you walked into this house,
18.   A year ago to-night. Though neither I
19.   Nor any man could tell your family,
20.   Country or name, I put you on that throne.
21.   And now before the assembled court, before
22.   Neighbours, attendants, courtiers, men-at-arms,
23.   I ask your country, name and family,
24.   And not for the first time. Why sit you there
25.   Dumb as an image made of wood or metal,
26.   A screen between the living and the dead?
27.   All persons here assembled, and because
28.   They think that silence unendurable,
29.   Fix eyes upon you.

> [*There is a pause. The Queen neither speaks nor moves. First Attendant strikes the drum three times.*

Captain of the Guard!

30.   Some traveller strikes a blow upon the gate.
31.   Open. Admit him.

First Attendant [*speaking as Captain of the Guard, without turning his head*]. I admit him, King.

The Stroller enters

TEXT

Directions after 16.   [*. . . semi-circle, . . . semi-circle . . . .*] **87, 91.**

[*There is a pause. The Queen neither speaks nor moves.
First Attendant strikes the drum three times.*

[29]   26. *The King.* Captain of the Guard.

            First Attendant [*speaking as Captain of the Guard*
    27.   *without turning his head*]. King, I am here.

30]   28. *King.* Someone has struck three times upon the great
[31]   29.   door. Admit him!

[31]   30. *First Attendant* [*speaking as before*]. I will admit
[31]   31.   him.
                  [*The Stroller enters.*

[32]   32. *The King.* What is your name?

[32-33]   33. *Stroller.* It is enough that I am a stroller and a
[33-34]   34.   fool, and that you are the King of the Great Clock
[34]   35.   Tower.

[34]   36. *The King.* I am that King. What do you want?

[35-36]   37. *Stroller.* A year ago somebody told me that you
[36-37]   38.   had married the most beautiful woman in the world,
[38]   39.   and from that moment I have had her image in my
[39]   40.   head, and month by month, it has grown more and
[37-39]   41.   more beautiful. I have made poems about her and
                sung
[40-42]   42.   them everywhere, but I have never seen her.

[42-43]   43. *The King.* Have you no wife or sweetheart of your
           44.   own?

[44-45]   45. *Stroller.* I had a wife, but she was so much uglier
[44-45, 47]   46.   than the image in my head, that I left her. The other
[47-49]   47.   night I was eating my dinner in a tavern; I am a man
[49-50]   48.   of no account, and so must eat my meals amongst
[50]   49.   servants and boors; a man there said I was a fool, be-
[53]   50.   cause I was in love with a woman I had never seen.

[54]   51. *The King.* But what have I to do with it?

[54]   52. *Stroller.* I do not want to be called a fool. Send
[54-55]   53.   for the Queen that I may look at her.

---

26. . . . Guard! **LL.**
    Directions in 27. [. . . *Guard, without* . . . .] **LL, 85.**
47. . . . tavern: I . . . **LL.**

32.   *The King.* What is your name?

The Stroller.   Enough that I am called

33.   A stroller and a fool, that you are called
34.   King of the Great Clock Tower.

The King.   What do you want?

35.   *The Stroller.* A year ago I heard a brawler say
36.   That you had married with a woman called
37.   Most beautiful of her sex. I am a poet.
38.   From that day out I put her in my songs,
39.   And day by day she grew more beautiful.
40.   Hard-hearted men that plough the earth and sea
41.   Sing what I sing, yet I that sang her first
42.   Have never seen her face.

The King.   Have you no wife,

43.   Mistress or friend to put into a song?

44.   *The Stroller.* I had a wife. The image in my head
45.   Made her appear fat, slow, thick of the limbs,
46.   In all her movements like a Michaelmas goose.
47.   I left her, but a night or two ago
48.   I ate my sausage at a tavern table—
49.   A stroller and a man of no account
50.   I dine among the ganders—a gander scoffed,
51.   Said I would drink myself to sleep, or cry
52.   My head among the dishes on the table,
53.   Because of a woman I had never seen.

54.   *The King.* But what have I to do with it?

The Stroller.   Send for the Queen.

55.   The ganders cannot scoff when I have seen her.

56.   *The King.* He seems a most audacious brazen man,
57.   Not caring what he speaks of, nor to whom,
58.   Nor where he stands.

The Stroller.   But never have I said

59.   Brazen, audacious, disrespectful words
60.   Of the image in my head. Summon her in
61.   That I may look on its original.

---

33.   ... Stroller ... **87, 91.**

[56]	54.	*The King.* You seem to be a brazen, audacious man,
[57-58]	55.	not caring where you stand, nor of whom, nor to
[58]	56.	whom you speak.
[58-59]	57.	*Stroller.* I have never shown disrespect to the
[59-61]	58.	image in my head, yet I must see the woman herself.
[62]	59.	*The King.* She is at my side.
[62]	60.	*Stroller.* Is this the Queen of the Great Clock
[62]	61.	Tower?
[63]	62.	*The King.* She is that Queen.

           [The Stroller stands in front of the Queen.

[64-65]	63.	*Stroller.* She is not so tall as I had thought, not so
[65-66]	64.	white and red, but what does it matter, I shall pro-
[66-67]	65.	claim everywhere that she is the most beautiful woman
	66.	in the world.
[67]	67.	*The King.* Then go! You have seen her.
[68]	68.	*Stroller.* Not yet. I was a little drunk that night
[68-69]	69.	when they mocked me, and I swore that not only
[69-70]	70.	would I see the Queen, but that—O, I must have been
[70-71]	71.	very drunk—that she would dance for me.
[71]	72.	*The King.* What!
[71-72]	73.	*Stroller.* When she has danced, I shall be grateful,
[72]	74.	and I shall sing.
[74]	75.	*The King.* I shall have you flogged.
[74]	76.	*Stroller.* Then you will flog a sacred man.
[75]	77.	*The King.* How? A sacred man?
[75]	78.	*Stroller.* I will tell you a great secret. I went to
[77-78]	79.	the Boyne where the old Gods live. I lay there for a
[78-79]	80.	month eating nothing. Then I saw Aengus and all
[79-80]	81.	the Gods. I told them of my oath and all the Gods
[81]	82.	shouted. After that there was silence and then Aen-

Directions after 62. [. . . *Queen.*]— **85.**
64.   . . . matter? I . . . **LL.**
77.   How! A . . . ? **LL.**
81.   . . . oath, and . . . **LL.**

62. *The King.* She is at my side.

The Stroller.   The Queen of the Great Clock Tower?

63. *The King.* The Queen of the Great Clock Tower is at my side.

64. *The Stroller.* Neither so red, nor white, nor full in the breast
65.   As I had thought. What matter for all that
66.   So long as I proclaim her everywhere
67.   Most beautiful!

The King.   Go now that you have seen!

68. *The Stroller.* Not yet, for on the night the gander gabbed
69.   I swore that I would see the Queen, and that—
70.   My God, but I was drunk—the Queen would dance
71.   And dance to me alone.

The King.   What?

Stroller.   Dance, and dance
72.   Till I grow grateful, and grown grateful sing.

73. *The King.* Sing out you may, but not from gratitude.
74.   Guard, flog this man!

The Stroller.   What, flog a sacred man?

75. *The King.* A sacred man?

The Stroller.   I ran to the Boyne Water
76.   And where a sea-mew and the salt sea wind
77.   Yelled Godhead, on a round green hillock lay;
78.   Nine days I fasted there—but that's a secret
79.   Between us three—then Aengus and the Gods
80.   Appeared, and when I said what I had sworn
81.   Shouted approval. Then great Aengus spoke—
82.   O listen, for I speak his very words—
83.   'On stroke of midnight when the old year dies,
84.   Upon that stroke, the tolling of that bell,
85.   The Queen shall kiss your mouth,'—his very words—
86.   Your Queen, my mouth, the Queen shall kiss my mouth.

[81-82]	83.	gus spoke; and listen well for these were his very
[82]	84.	words:—
[83-84]	85.	'Upon the last night of the year, when the Great
[84-85]	86.	Clock strikes the last note of midnight, the Queen
[85]	87.	shall kiss you upon the mouth.'
[87]	88.	*The King.* Captain of the Guard!

First Attendant [*speaking as Captain and as be-*

[87]	89.	*fore*]. I am here!
[88]	90.	*The King.* I give this man to you. He has said that
	91.	the Queen will kiss him upon the mouth at the last
[89]	92.	stroke of the clock. Take him therefore and strike his
[89]	93.	head from his body.

First Attendant [*speaking as Captain of the*

[89]	94.	*Guard*]. I will strike his head from his body.
[90]	95.	*Stroller.* I go, but this is what will happen. First
[90-91]	96.	[*counting on his fingers*] the Queen will dance; sec-
[91]	97.	ond, I shall sing—
[92]	98.	*The King.* What with your head off?
[92-93]	99.	*Stroller.* When I am grateful, I sing. The Queen,
[93]	100.	being grateful, will give me a kiss.

[*He goes right.*

[94-95]	101.	*The King.* Stop! You have told us nothing but lies.
[96-97]	102.	*King* [*to Queen*]. Speak! Who is this man? Per-
[97-98]	103.	haps if you will answer my questions, I shall spare
[98]	104.	his life.

[*The Queen remains silent and immovable.*

	105.	*The King.* So be it. Whether his tale be true or not,
	106.	it is plain that he wishes to sacrifice his life, to lay it
[99]	107.	down at your feet. Take him Captain of the Guard.

First Attendant [*speaking as Captain of the*

[99]	108.	*Guard*]. I take him.

[*The King thrusts the Stroller out to right.*

83.	. . . well, for . . . **LL.**
86.	. . . midnight. the . . . **85.**
98.	What, with . . . ? **LL.**
107.	. . . him, Captain . . . . **LL.**

87. *The King.* Come, Captain of the Guard.

First Attendant [*speaking as Captain of the Guard*]. King, I am here.

88. *The King.* This man insults me and insults the Queen.
89.   Take him and bring me his head.

First Attendant [*speaking as Captain of the Guard*]. I take him, King.

90. *The Stroller.* I go; but this must happen:
                    [*Counting on his fingers*] First the Queen
91.   Will dance before me, second I shall sing.

92. *The King.* What, sing without a head?

     The Stroller.   Grateful I sing,
93.   Then, grateful in her turn, the Queen will kiss
94.   My mouth because it sang.

     The King.   Stand where you are!
95.   Stand! All from the beginning has been lies,
96.   Extravagance and lies. Who is this man?
97.   Perhaps if you will speak, and speak the truth,
98.   I may not kill him. What? You will not speak?
99.   Then take him, Captain of the Guard.

First Attendant [*speaking as Captain of the Guard*]. I take him.

100. *The King.* And bring his head as evidence of his death.
101.   If he was not your lover in that place
102.   You come from, if the nothing that he seems,
103.   A stroller and a fool, a rambling rogue
104.   That has insulted you, laugh, dance or sing,
105.   Do something, anything, I care not what
106.   So that you move—but why those staring eyes?

     Second Attendant [*singing as Queen in a low voice*].
107.   O, what may come
108.   Into my womb?

---

105. . . . , anything. I . . . **97A.**
107. O what . . . **87, 91.**
      V.E.P.Y.—2 K

[100]	109.	*The King.* Bring me his head that I may know
[100]	110.	that he is dead. [*He now stands looking off stage.*]
[101-102]	111.	If he was not your lover before you came into this
[102]	112.	country. If he is nothing to you if he is nothing but
[103-104]	113.	a stroller and fool, if he is nothing but a man who has
[104-105]	114.	insulted you, laugh or sing, I do not care which it is.

[*The Queen moves for the first time. Turning her head
slowly and looking at the King.*]

| | 115. | *The King.* Why do you fix your eyes upon me? |

Second Attendant [*singing as Queen in a low voice*].

| [107] | 116. | O what may come |
| [108] | 117. | Into my womb! |

| [109] | 118. | *The King.* Ah, that is better. But sing out loud that |
| [110] | 119. | all here may know that you rejoice in his death. |

[*The Queen rises.*

Second Attendant [*singing as Queen*].

111	120.	He longs to kill
112	121.	My body, until
113	122.	That sudden shudder
114	123.	And limbs lie still.
115	124.	O, what may come
[116]	125.	Into my womb,
117	126.	What caterpillar
[118]	127.	My beauty consume!

| [119] | 128. | *The King.* I do not know what those words mean, |
| [120] | 129. | but they sound scornful. |

[*The King goes out right and returns with the head of
the Stroller, and lays it upon the cubical throne
to right, nearest audience.*]

| [121] | 130. | *The King.* Now I shall know if those lips can sing. |

[*He sits on the other cubical throne to right.*]

| [120] | 131. | You have our attention. Sing Stroller and fool. |

[*The Queen begins to dance.*

| [122] | 132. | *The King.* That is a good thought. Dance! Turn |
| [122-123] | 133. | him into mockery with a dance. O, a good thought. |

---

112.   . . . you, if . . . **LL, 85.**
131.   . . . . Sing, Stroller . . . . **LL.**

109.   *The King.* Ah! That is better. Let the voice ring out
110.   Let everybody hear that song of joy.

    Second Attendant [*singing as Queen*].
111.   He longs to kill
112.   My body, until
113.   That sudden shudder
114.   And limbs lie still.

115.   O, what may come
116.   Into my womb,
117.   What caterpillar
118.   My beauty consume?

119.   *The King.* I do not know the meaning of those words
120.   That have a scornful sound.
    [*The King goes to right and returns with the head of the Stroller,
and lays it upon the cubical throne to the right nearest audience.*
                Sing, Stroller and fool.
121.   Open that mouth, my Queen awaits a song.
                 [*The Queen begins to dance.*
122.   Dance, turn him into mockery with a dance!
123.   No woman ever had a better thought.
124.   All here applaud that thought. Dance, woman, dance!
125.   Neither so red, nor white, nor full in the breast,
126.   That's what he said! Dance, give him scorn for scorn,
127.   Display your beauty, spread your peacock tail.
    [*The Queen dances, then takes up the severed head and stands in
centre of the stage facing audience, the severed head upon her shoulder.*

128.   *The King.* His eyelids tremble, his lips begin to move.

    First Attendant [*singing as Head in a low voice*].
129.   Clip and lip and long for more—

130.   *The King.* O, O, they have begun to sing.

    First Attendant [*singing as Head*].
131.   Clip and lip and long for more,
132.   Mortal men our abstracts are;

---

109.   . . . out. **87, 91.**
    [between 114 and 115 no break] **91.**

		[*He laughs. The Queen lays the head on the ground at the centre of the stage, stands motionless looking at*
[125]	134.	*the head.*] Dance! Dance! If you are nothing to him
[125]	135.	but an image, a body in his head, he is nothing to
[126-127]	136.	you but a head without a body. What is the good of
	137.	a lover without a body? Dance! He thought you were
	138.	not so fine as the image in his head, nor so tall, nor
	139.	so red nor so white. Dance! Display your beauty!

[*The Queen dances. Then stands in the centre of the stage, facing audience, the head upon her shoulder.*

| [128] | 140. | *The King.* The lips are opening. The eyes are mov- |
| [128] | 141. | ing. |

First Attendant [*singing as head in a low voice*].

| | 142. | Images ride, I heard a man say— |
| [130] | 143. | *The King.* O, terror, it has begun to sing! |

[*He cowers down covering his face.*

First Attendant [*singing as head*].

[168]	144.	Images ride, I heard a man say,
[169]	145.	Out of Benbulben and Knocknareagh,
170	146.	*What says the Clock in the Great Clock Tower?*
[171]	147.	Out of the grave. Saddle and ride
172	148.	But turn from Rosses' crawling tide,
173	149.	The meet's upon the mountain side.
174	150.	*A slow low note and an iron bell.*
[175]	151.	What made them mount and what made them come,
[176]	152.	Cuchulain that fought night long with the foam;
[177]	153.	*What says the Clock in the Great Clock Tower.*
178	154.	Niam that rode on it; lad and lass
179	155.	That sat so still and played at the chess?
[180]	156.	What but heroic wantonness
181	157.	*A slow low note and an iron bell.*
182	158.	Aleel, his Countess; Hanrahan

Directions at 134.   [. . . *lays head . . . stage; stands* . . . .] **LL** ; [. . . *lays head* . . . .] **85.**

139.   . . . red, nor . . . ! **LL.**
Directions after 139.   [. . . *audience the* . . . .] **85.**
Directions after 143.   [. . . *down, covering* . . . .] **LL, 85.**
[between 150 and 151 a break] **LL.**

153.   . . . *Tower?* **LL.**
155.   . . . chess— **LL.**
156.   . . . wantonness. **LL, 85.**

133.	*What of the hands on the Great Clock face?*
134.	All those living wretches crave
135.	Prerogatives of the dead that have
136.	Sprung heroic from the grave.
137.	*A moment more and it tolls midnight.*
138.	Crossed fingers there in pleasure can
139.	Exceed the nuptial bed of man;
140.	*What of the hands on the Great Clock face?*
141.	A nuptial bed exceed all that
142.	Boys at puberty have thought,
143.	Or sibyls in a frenzy sought.
144.	*A moment more and it tolls midnight.*
145.	What's prophesied? What marvel is
146.	Where the dead and living kiss?
147.	*What of the hands on the Great Clock face?*
148.	Sacred Virgil never sang
149.	All the marvel there begun,
150.	But there's a stone upon my tongue.
151.	*A moment more and it tolls midnight.*

[*When the song has finished, the dance begins again, the Clock strikes. The strokes are represented by blows on a gong struck by Second Attendant. The Queen dances to the sound, and at the last stroke presses her lips to the lips of the head. The King has risen and drawn his sword. The Queen lays the head upon her breast, and fixes her eyes upon him. He appears about to strike, but kneels, laying the sword at her feet. The two Attendants rise singing, and slowly close the inner curtain.*]

152.	*First Attendant.* O, but I saw a solemn sight;
153.	*Said the rambling, shambling travelling-man;*
154.	Castle Dargan's ruin all lit,
155.	Lovely ladies dancing in it.
156.	*Second Attendant.* What though they danced! Those days are gone,
157.	*Said the wicked, crooked, hawthorn tree;*
158.	Lovely lady or gallant man
159.	Are blown cold dust or a bit of bone.

183	159.	That seemed but a wild wenching man;
184	160.	*What says the Clock in the Great Clock Tower?*
185	161.	And all alone comes riding there
186	162.	The King that could make his people stare,
187	163.	Because he had feathers instead of hair.
188	164.	*A slow low note and an iron bell.*

[*When the song has finished, the dance begins again, the Clock strikes. The strokes are represented by blows on a gong struck by second Attendant. The Queen dances to the sound, and at the last stroke presses her lips to the lips of the head. The King has risen and drawn his sword. The Queen lays the head upon her breast, and fixes her eyes upon him. He appears about to strike, but kneels, laying the sword at her feet. The two Attendants rise singing, and slowly close the inner curtain:*

152	165.	*First Attendant.* O, but I saw a solemn sight;
153	166.	*Said the rambling, shambling travelling-man;*
154	167.	Castle Dargan's ruin all lit,
155	168.	Lovely ladies dancing in it.
[156]	169.	*Second Attendant.* What though they danced; those days are gone;
157	170.	*Said the wicked, crooked, hawthorn tree;*
158	171.	Lovely lady or gallant man
159	172.	Are blown cold dust or a bit of bone.
[160]	173.	*First Attendant.* O, what is life but a mouthful of air;
161	174.	*Said the rambling, shambling travelling-man;*
162	175.	Yet all the lovely things that were
163	176.	Live, for I saw them dancing there.

[*The Queen has come down stage and now stands framed in the half closed curtains.*

[164]	177.	*Second Attendant.* Nobody knows what may befall;
165	178.	*Said the wicked, crooked, hawthorn tree.*
166	179.	I have stood so long by a gap in the wall
[167]	180.	May be I shall not die at all.

[*The inner curtain is closed; the two Attendants stand upon either side singing.*

Directions after 164. [. . . *clock* . . . *gong struck off stage. The Queen* . . . *sound of the gong, and* . . . *curtain. Their song is as follows:*—] **LL.**
Directions after 176. [. . . *half-closed* . . . .] **LL.**
179.   . . . have stopped so long a . . . **LL.**

160. *First Attendant.* O, what is life but a mouthful of air?
161.   *Said the rambling, shambling travelling-man;*
162.   Yet all the lovely things that were
163.   Live, for I saw them dancing there.

[*The Queen has come down stage and now stands framed in the half-closed curtains.*

164. *Second Attendant.* Nobody knows what may befall,
165.   *Said the wicked, crooked, hawthorn tree.*
166.   I have stood so long by a gap in the wall
167.   Maybe I shall not die at all.

[*The outer curtains descends*]

ALTERNATIVE SONG FOR
THE SEVERED HEAD[1]

168.   Saddle and ride, I heard a man say,
169.   Out of Ben Bulben and Knocknarea,
170.   *What says the Clock in the Great Clock Tower?*
171.   All those tragic characters ride
172.   But turn from Rosses' crawling tide,
173.   The meet's upon the mountain side.
174.   *A slow low note and an iron bell.*

175.   What brought them there so far from their home,
176.   Cuchulain that fought night long with the foam,
177.   *What says the Clock in the Great Clock Tower?*
178.   Niam that rode on it; lad and lass
179.   That sat so still and played at the chess?
180.   What but heroic wantonness?
181.   *A slow low note and an iron bell.*

182.   Aleel, his Countess; Hanrahan
183.   That seemed but a wild wenching man;
184.   *What says the Clock in the Great Clock Tower?*
185.   And all alone comes riding there

Alternative Song for the Severed Head   [lacking] **87.**

[1] The title in **91** is 'Alternative . . . Head in The King of the Great Clock Tower.'

181. *Second Attendant.* Why must those holy, haughty feet descend
182. From emblematic niches and what hand
183. Ran that delicate raddle through their white?
184. My heart is broken, yet must understand.
185. What do they seek for? why must they descend?

186. *First Attendant.* For desecration and the lover's night.

187. *Second Attendant.* I cannot face that emblem of the moon,
188. Nor eyelids that the unmixed heavens dart,
189. Nor stand upon my feet, so great a fright
190. Descends upon my savage, sunlit heart.
191. What can she lack whose emblem is the moon?

192. *First Attendant.* But desecration and the lover's night.

193. *Second Attendant.* Delight my heart with sound; speak yet again;
194. But look and look with understanding eyes
195. Upon the pitchers that they carry; tight
196. Therein all time's completed treasure is:
197. What do they lack? O cry it out again.

198. *First Attendant.* Their desecration and the lover's night.
 [*I prefer the stanza in this form, but the musician may substitute
 the following as he may prefer something resembling a stop at the end
 of every line, nothing resembling a stop before the last word of any
 line, believing in spite of evidence that the words of the singer will
 be heard, even enjoyed, as words, if rhythm and punctuation be
 obvious. It might however be better to omit in performance this last
 song. I thought on the first night, though we left out one stanza that
 there was too much music between the end of the dance and the descent
 of the curtain.*]

199. *First Attendant.* Delight my heart with sound, speak it again;
200. I look on feet but not upon a face;
201. Cry it again but understand the sight,
202. All time's completed treasure in one place;
203. What do they lack O cry it all again.

204. *Second Attendant.* Their desecration and the lover's night.
 [*The stage curtain descends.*

---

185. [lacking] **LL.**
187. . . . moon. **LL.**
 Directions after 198. [*The stage curtain descends.*] **LL.**
199-204. [lacking] **LL.**

186.   The King that could make his people stare,
187.   Because he had feathers instead of hair.
188.   *A slow low note and an iron bell.*

THE END

I

When I was a young man I said to singers, 'If you want to sing unintelligible sounds sing a receipt from a cookery book, anything you want to get by heart'; but singing has changed—I can hear the words—I put my fingers in my ears to keep them out. The singer, shrill from conflict with the violins, loud from the strain of great concert halls, trained by some voice-producer to turn language into honey and oil, cannot sing poetry; that art died centuries ago, hardly perhaps survived, the unknown thirteenth century Italian poet who wrote upon 'true and false singing'.

> A little wild bird sometimes at my ear
> Sings his own verses very clear;
> Others sing louder that I do not hear
> For singing loudly is not singing well,
> But ever by the song that's soft and low
> The mastersinger's voice is plain to tell
> Few have it and yet all are masters now.
> And each of them can thrill out what he calls
> His ballads, canzonettes and madrigals.

(My wife says 'Had you heard Elena Gerhardt or Campbell McInnes or Gervase Elwes you would know that's all nonsense'. 'But I have heard so and so' I say 'and so and so and their words although audible were more bloodless than veal'. 'O', my wife says, 'if you think they can sing'.)

II

I am not musical; I have the poet's exact time sense, only the vaguest sense of pitch; yet I get the greatest pleasure from certain combinations of singing, acting, speaking, drum, gong, flute, string, provided that some or all the words keep their natural passionate rhythm. Thirty years ago I persuaded Florence Farr, beautiful woman, incomparable elocutionist, to rediscover with the help of Arnold Dolmetsch, what seemed the ancient art of singing or speaking poetry to notes: Greek music if Greek music was, as some authorities think, 'regulated declamation.' Many people came to learn but she had only one successful pupil—I think her name was Taylor, I have not heard of her for many years—all others had the sense of pitch without the understanding of words or the understanding of words without the sense of pitch. I gave a number of lectures; Miss Farr spoke or sang to her psaltery passages from Homer, Shelley, Keats or from my own writings. When one spoke to members of the audience they seemed divided like her pupils into musicians who said that she was out of tune and into well (tune and well **85**) satisfied readers of poetry. I remember a famous war-corre-spondent saying, in an aggressive voice as he left the hall, (hall **85**) 'singing is a decadent art.' It seemed that in the twelfth century everybody had but one set of ears and that it is now possible to have two sets that cannot be pleased at the same time. I was puzzled, sometimes doubtful, but en-couraged now and again when some acknowledged authority—I remember a long notice by the musical critic of the *Manchester Guardian*—said that we had discovered a great lost beauty. I, at any rate, keep among my most vivid memories a moment when, during the performance of a Greek play translated by Gilbert Murray, Florence Farr and her one pupil sang or spoke about 'the daughters of the sunset' with alternating voices; so I thought, so I still think, did the ancient world where the poets 'I sing' seemed but literal truth, hear poetry.

When I had enough knowledge to discover some dramatic form to give her the opportunity she lacked Florence Farr had accepted a post in a Cingalese girls' (girls **85**) school that she might hide her ageing beauty. I have the psaltery Arnold Dolmetsch designed for her, certain strings are broken, probably nobody will play on it again, but that I may not injure it by exposure to the air I do not hang it upon the wall to revive old memories.

I did find one or two others. Sarah Allgood, could do, though in a different way, exactly what I wanted. I doubt if she could do so now for she sings in opera. The dirge in my *Deirdre*—'Eagles have gone into their cloudy bed'—sung by her and somebody else, perhaps her sister, preserved the utmost poignancy of speech. Her method was 'folk-singing' or allied to it, beautifully humble and simple, whereas Florence Farr's was Greek and arrogant.

III

I gave up the fight, began writing little dance plays, founded upon a Japanese model, that need no scenery, no properties, and can be performed in studio or drawingroom, thinking that some group of students might make a little money playing them and gradually elaborate a technique that would respect literature and music alike. Whenever I produced one of these plays I asked my singers for no new method, did not even talk to them upon the subject. When The Abbey School of Ballet was founded I tried these plays upon the stage where they seemed out of place. Why should musician or actor fold and unfold a cloth when the proscenium curtain was there, why carry on to the stage drum, gong, and flute when the orchestra was there. *Fighting the Waves* and the present play so far imitate the Japanese model that they climax in a dance, substitute suggestion for representation, but like the Japanese plays themselves they are stage plays.

The orchestra brings more elaborate music and I have gone over to the enemy. I say to the musician 'Lose my words in patterns of sound as the name of God is lost in Arabian arabesques. They are a secret between the singers, myself, yourself. The plain fable, the plain prose of the dialogue, Ninette de Valois' dance are there for the audience. They can find my words in the book if they are curious, but we will not thrust our secret upon them. I can be as subtle or metaphysical as I like without endangering the clarity necessary for dramatic effect. The Elizabethan singer, according to Edmund Spenser, and his music was simpler than yours, read out his song before he sang it. We will adopt no such arbitrary practice; our secret is our religion.'

IV

The dance with the severed head, suggests the central idea of Wilde's *Salome*. Wilde took it from Heine who has somewhere described Salome in hell throwing into the air the head of John the Baptist. Heine may have found it in some Jewish religious legend for it is part of the old ritual of the year: the mother goddess and the slain god. In the first edition of *The Secret Rose* there is a story based on some old Gaelic legend. A certain man swears to sing the praise of a certain woman, his head is cut off and the head sings. A poem of mine called, (called 85) 'He Gives His Beloved Certain Rhymes' was the song of the head. In attempting to put that story into a dance play I found that I had gone close to Salome's dance in Wilde's play. But in his play the dance is before the head is cut off.

> He had famished in a wilderness,
> Braved lions for my sake,
> And all men lie that say that I
> Bade that swordsman take
> His head from off his body
> And set it on a stake.
>
> He swore to sing my beauty
> Though death itself forbade,
> They lie that say in mockery
> Of all that lovers said,
> Or in mere woman's cruelty
> I bade them fetch his head.
>
> O what innkeeper's daughter
> Shared the Byzantine crown!
> Girls that have governed cities,
> Or burned great cities down,
> Have bedded with their fancy-man
> Whether a king or clown;
>
> Gave their bodies, emptied purse
> For praise of clown or king,

Gave all the love that women know!
O they had their fling
But never stood before a stake
And heard the dead lips sing.
Commentary on 'The Great Clock Tower' **85, 86.**

* * *

[See also *Prefaces to 85, 86, 87, 91*, pp. 1309, 1310, 1311.]

THE HERNE'S EGG

1938

Persons in the Play

Congal, *King of Connacht*
Aedh, *King of Tara*
Corney, *Attracta's servant*
Mike, Pat, Malachi, Mathias, Peter,
John, *Connacht soldiers*

Attracta, *A Priestess*
Kate, Agnes, Mary, *Friends
of Attracta*
A Fool
Soldiers of Tara

Scene I

*Mist and rocks; high up on backcloth a rock, its base hidden in mist; on this rock
stands a great herne. All should be suggested, not painted realistically. Many men
fighting with swords and shields, but sword and sword, shield and sword, never
meet. The men move rhythmically as if in a dance; when swords approach one
another cymbals clash; when swords and shields approach drums boom. The
battle flows out at one side; two Kings are left fighting in the centre of the stage;
the battle returns and flows out at the other side. The two Kings remain, but are
now face to face and motionless. They are Congal, King of Connacht, and Aedh,
King of Tara.*

1. *Congal.* How many men have you lost?

2. *Aedh.* Some five-and-twenty men.

3. *Congal.* No need to ask my losses.

4. *Aedh.* Your losses equal mine.

5. *Congal.* They always have and must.

PRINTINGS **90, 91, 97.**

DATE [lacking] **90, 91.**

DRAMATIS PERSONAE [the listing of 'James,' a soldier, is omitted from the
Dramatis Personae in all printings (see Directions after line 12, Scene II)];
Persons / Congal, . . . of Attracta / Soldiers . . . / A Fool **90, 91.**

6. *Aedh.* Skill, strength, arms matched.

7. *Congal.* Where is the wound this time?

8. *Aedh.* There, left shoulder-blade.

9. *Congal.* Here, right shoulder-blade.

10. *Aedh.* Yet we have fought all day.

11. *Congal.* This is our fiftieth battle.

12. *Aedh.* And all were perfect battles.

13. *Congal.* Come, sit upon this stone,
14.   Come and take breath awhile.

15. *Aedh.* From daybreak until noon,
16.   Hopping among these rocks.

17. *Congal.* Nothing to eat or drink.

18. *Aedh.* A story is running round
19.   Concerning two rich fleas.

20. *Congal.* We hop like fleas, but war
21.   Has taken all our riches.

22. *Aedh.* Rich, and rich, so rich that they
23.   Retired and bought a dog.

24. *Congal.* Finish the tale and say
25.   What kind of dog they bought.

26. *Aedh.* Heaven knows.

     Congal.   You must have thought
27.   What kind of dog they bought.

28. *Aedh.* Heaven knows.

     Congal.   Unless you say,

TEXT
15. ... day-break ..., **90, 91.**
27. ... bought **97A.**

29. I'll up and fight all day.

30. *Aedh.* A fat, square, lazy dog,
31. No sort of scratching dog.

Scene II

The same place as in previous scene. Corney enters, leading a Donkey, a donkey on wheels like a child's toy, but life-size.

1. *Corney.* A tough, rough mane, a tougher skin,
2. Strong legs though somewhat thin,
3. A strong body, a level line
4. Up to the neck along the spine.
5. All good points, and all are spoilt
6. By that rapscallion Clareman's eye!
7. What if before your present shape
8. You could slit purses and break hearts,
9. You are a donkey now, a chattel,
10. A taker of blows, not a giver of blows.
11. No tricks, you're not in County Clare,
12. No, not one kick upon the shin.
     [*Congal, Pat, Mike, James, Mathias, Peter, John, enter, in the dress and arms of the previous scene but without shields.*

13. *Congal.* I have learned of a great hernery
14. Among these rocks, and that a woman,
15. Prophetess or priestess, named Attracta,
16. Owns it—take this donkey and man,
17. Look for the creels, pack them with eggs.

18. *Mike.* Manners!

     Congal.   This man is in the right.
19. I will ask Attracta for the eggs
20. If you will tell how to summon her.

21. *Corney.* A flute lies there upon the rock
22. Carved out of a herne's thigh.
23. Go pick it up and play the tune

24.   My mother calls 'The Great Herne's Feather'.

25.   If she has a mind to come, she will come.

26. *Congal.* That's a queer way of summoning.

27. *Corney.* This is a holy place and queer;

28.   But if you do not know that tune,

29.   Custom permits that I should play it,

30.   But you must cross my hand with silver.

> [*Congal gives money, and Corney plays flute.*

31. *Congal.* Go pack the donkey creels with eggs.

> [*All go out except Congal and Mike. Attracta enters.*

32. *Attracta.* For a thousand or ten thousand years,

33.   For who can count so many years,

34.   Some woman has lived among these rocks,

35.   The Great Herne's bride, or promised bride,

36.   And when a visitor has played the flute

37.   Has come or not. What would you ask?

38. *Congal.* Tara and I have made a peace;

39.   Our fiftieth battle fought, there is need

40.   Of preparation for the next;

41.   He and all his principal men,

42.   I and all my principal men,

43.   Take supper at his principal house

44.   This night, in his principal city, Tara,

45.   And we have set our minds upon

46.   A certain novelty or relish.

47. *Mike.* Herne's eggs.

Congal.   This man declares our need;

48.   A donkey, both creels packed with eggs,

49.   Somebody that knows the mind of a donkey

50.   For donkey-boy.

Attracta.   Custom forbids:

51.   Only the women of these rocks,

52.   Betrothed or married to the Herne,

53.   The god or ancestor of hernes,

54.   Can eat, handle, or look upon those eggs.

55. *Congal.* Refused! Must old campaigners lack

56.   The one sole dish that takes their fancy,

57.   My cooks what might have proved their skill,

58. Because a woman thinks that she
59. Is promised or married to a bird?

60. *Mike.* Mad!

Congal.   Mad! This man is right,
61. But you are not to blame for that.
62. Women thrown into despair
63. By the winter of their virginity
64. Take its abominable snow,
65. As boys take common snow, and make
66. An image of god or bird or beast
67. To feed their sensuality:
68. Ovid had a literal mind,
69. And though he sang it neither knew
70. What lonely lust dragged down the gold
71. That crept on Danae's lap, nor knew
72. What rose against the moony feathers
73. When Leda lay upon the grass.

74. *Attracta.* There is no reality but the Great Herne.

75. *Mike.* The cure.

Congal.   Why, that is easy said;
76. An old campaigner is the cure
77. For everything that woman dreams—
78. Even I myself, had I but time.

79. *Mike.* Seven men.

Congal.   This man of learning means
80. That not a weather-stained, war-battered
81. Old campaigner such as I,—
82. But seven men packed into a day
83. Or dawdled out through seven years—
84. Are needed to melt down the snow
85. That's fallen among these wintry rocks.

86. *Attracta.* There is no happiness but the Great Herne.

79a. That seven men packed into a day
79b. Or dawdled out through seven years
 80. And not . . .
 81. . . . I, **90, 91.**
82-83. [lacking] **90, 91.**

87. *Congal*. It may be that life is suffering,
88.   But youth that has not yet known pleasure
89.   Has not the right to say so; pick,
90.   Or be picked by seven men,
91.   And we shall talk it out again.

92. *Attracta*. Being betrothed to the Great Herne
93.   I know what may be known: I burn
94.   Not in the flesh but in the mind;
95.   Chosen out of all my kind
96.   That I may lie in a blazing bed
97.   And a bird take my maidenhead,
98.   To the unbegotten I return,
99.   All a womb and a funeral urn.
      [*Enter Corney, Pat, James, Mathias, etc., with Donkey. A creel packed with eggs is painted upon the side of the Donkey.*

100. *Corney*. Think of yourself; think of the songs:
101.   Bride of the Herne, and the Great Herne's bride,
102.   Grow terrible: go into a trance.

103. *Attracta*. Stop!

    Corney.   Bring the god out of your gut;
104.   Stand there asleep until the rascals
105.   Wriggle upon his beak like eels.

106. *Attracta*. Stop!

    Corney.   The country calls them rascals,
107.   I, sacrilegious rascals that have taken
108.   Every new-laid egg in the hernery.

109. *Attracta*. Stop! When have I permitted you
110.   To say what I may, or may not do?
111.   But you and your donkey must obey
112.   All big men who can say their say.

113. *Congal*. And bid him keep a civil tongue.

114. *Attracta*. Those eggs are stolen from the god.
115.   It is but right that you hear said
116.   A curse so ancient that no man

117.   Can say who made it, or any thing at all
118.   But that it was nailed upon a post
119.   Before a herne had stood on one leg.

120.   *Corney.* Hernes must stand on one leg when they fish
121.   In honour of the bird who made it.

122.   'This they nailed upon a post,
123.   On the night my leg was lost,'
124.   *Said the old, old herne that had but one leg.*

125.   'He that a herne's egg dare steal
126.   Shall be changed into a fool,'
127.   *Said the old, old herne that had but one leg.*

128.   'And to end his fool breath
129.   At a fool's hand meet his death,'
130.   *Said the old, old herne that had but one leg.*

131.   I think it was the Great Herne made it,
132.   Pretending that he had but the one leg
133.   To fool us all; but Great Herne or another
134.   It has not failed these thousand years.

135.   *Congal.* That I shall live and die a fool,
136.   And die upon some battlefield
137.   At some fool's hand, is but natural,
138.   And needs no curse to bring it.

        Mike.   Pickled!

139.   *Congal.* He says that I am an old campaigner,
140.   Robber of sheepfolds and cattle trucks,
141.   So cursed from morning until midnight
142.   There is not a quarter of an inch

---

117.   ... it, any ...
118a.   And has not failed these thousand years.
118b.   Maybe it was the Great Herne who made it.
119.   [lacking] **90, 91.**
        [between 121 and 122 no break] **91.**
122.   ... post **90, 91.**
131-134.   [lacking] **90, 91.**
139.   ... campaigner **90, 91.**
141.   So, cursed ... midnight, **90, 91.**

143. To plaster a new curse upon.

    Corney. **Luck!**

144. *Congal.* Adds that your luck begins when you
145.   Recall that though we took those eggs
146.   We paid with good advice; and then
147.   Take to your bosom seven men.
        [*Congal, Mike, Corney, Mathias, James, and Donkey go out.
        Enter timidly three girls, Kate, Agnes, Mary.*

148. *Mary.* Have all those fierce men gone?

149. *Attracta.* All those fierce men have gone.

150. *Agnes.* But they will come again?

151. *Attracta.* No, never again.

152. *Kate.* We bring three presents.
        [*All except Attracta kneel.*

153. *Mary.* This is a jug of cream.

154. *Agnes.* This is a bowl of butter.

155. *Kate.* This is a basket of eggs.
        [*They lay jug, bowl and basket on the ground.*

156. *Attracta.* I know what you would ask.
157.   Sit round upon these stones.
158.   Children, why do you fear
159.   A woman but little older,
160.   A child yesterday?
161.   All, when I am married,
162.   Shall have good husbands. Kate
163.   Shall marry a black-headed lad.

164. *Agnes.* She swore but yesterday
165.   That she would marry black.

166. *Attracta.* But Agnes there shall marry
167.   A honey-coloured lad.

---

143. . . . curse on.
    Luck! **90, 91.**

168. *Agnes.* O!

     Attracta.   Mary shall be married
169.   When I myself am married
170.   To the lad that is in her mind.

171. *Mary.* Are you not married yet?

172. *Attracta.* No. But it is almost come,
173.   May come this very night.

174. *Mary.* And must he be all feathers?

175. *Agnes.* Have a terrible beak?

176. *Kate.* Great terrible claws?

177. *Attracta.* Whatever shape he choose,
178.   Though that be terrible,
179.   Will best express his love.

180. *Agnes.* When he comes—will he?—

181. *Attracta.* Child, ask what you please.

182. *Agnes.* Do all that a man does?

183. *Attracta.* Strong sinew and soft flesh
184.   Are foliage round the shaft
185.   Before the arrowsmith
186.   Has stripped it, and I pray
187.   That I, all foliage gone,
188.   May shoot into my joy—
         [*Sound of a flute, playing 'The Great Herne's Feather'.*

189. *Mary.* Who plays upon that flute?

190. *Agnes.* Her god is calling her.

191. *Kate.* Look, look, she takes
192.   An egg out of the basket.
193.   My white hen laid it,
194.   My favourite white hen.

---

180. . . . he— **97A.**

195. *Mary*. Her eyes grow glassy, she moves
196.   According to the notes of the flute.

197. *Agnes*. Her limbs grow rigid, she seems
198.   A doll upon a wire.

199. *Mary*. Her human life is gone
200.   And that is why she seems
201.   A doll upon a wire.

202. *Agnes*. You mean that when she looks so
203.   She is but a puppet?

204. *Mary*. How do I know? And yet
205.   Twice have I seen her so,
206.   She will move for certain minutes
207.   As though her god were there
208.   Thinking how best to move
209.   A doll upon a wire.
210.   Then she will move away
211.   In long leaps as though
212.   He had remembered his skill.
213.   She has still my little egg.

214. *Agnes*. Who knows but your little egg
215.   Comes into some mystery?

216. *Kate*. Some mystery to make
217.   Love-loneliness more sweet.

218. *Agnes*. She has moved. She has moved away.

219. *Kate*. Travelling fast asleep
220.   In long loops like a dancer.

221. *Mary*. Like a dancer, like a hare.

222. *Agnes*. The last time she went away
223.   The moon was full—she returned
224.   Before its side had flattened.

225. *Kate*. This time she will not return.

226. *Agnes*. Because she is called to her marriage?

227. *Kate*. Those leaps may carry her where
228.   No woman has gone, and he

229.   Extinguish sun, moon, star.
230.   No bridal torch can burn
231.   When his black midnight is there.

232. *Agnes.* I have heard her claim that they couple
233.   In the blazing heart of the sun.

234. *Kate.* But you have heard it wrong!
235.   In blue-black midnight they couple.

236. *Agnes.* No, in the sun.

     Kate.   Blue-black!

237. *Agnes.* In the sun!

     Kate.   Blue-black, blue-black!

238. *Mary.* All I know is that she
239.   Shall lie there in his bed.
240.   Nor shall it end until
241.   She lies there full of his might,
242.   His thunderbolts in her hand.

Scene III

Before the gates of Tara, Congal, Mike, Pat, Peter, James, Mathias, etc.,
soldiers of Congal, Corney, and the Donkey.

1.   *Congal.* This is Tara; in a moment
2.   Men must come out of the gate
3.   With a great basket between them
4.   And we give up our arms;
5.   No armed man can enter.

6. *Corney.* And here is that great bird
7.   Over our heads again.

8. *Pat.* The Great Herne himself

———————————————————————

239.   . . . bed, **90, 91.**
241.   . . . might **90, 91.**
               Scene III
4.   . . . arms, **90, 91.**

9.   And he in a red rage.

10. *Mike.* Stones.

Congal.   This man is right.
11. Beat him to death with stones.
     [*All go through the motion of picking up and throwing stones. There are no stones except in so far as their gestures can suggest them.*

12. *Pat.* All those stones fell wide.

13. *Corney.* He has come down so low
14. His legs are sweeping the grass.

15. *Mike.* Swords.

Congal.   This man is right.
16. Cut him up with swords.

17. *Pat.* I have him within my reach.

18. *Congal.* No, no, he is here at my side.

19. *Corney.* His wing has touched my shoulder.

20. *Congal.* We missed him again and he
21. Rises again and sinks
22. Behind the wall of Tara.
     [*Two men come in carrying a large basket slung between two poles. One is whistling. All except Corney, who is unarmed, drop their swords and helmets into the basket. Each soldier when he takes off his helmet shows that he wears a skull-cap of soft cloth.*

23. *Congal.* Where have I heard that tune?

24. *Mike.* This morning.

Congal.   I know it now,
25. The tune of 'The Great Herne's Feather'.
26. It puts my teeth on edge.

---

12. All our stones . . . . **90, 91.**

Scene IV

Banqueting hall. A throne painted on the backcloth. Enter Congal, alone, drunk, and shouting.

1. *Congal.* To arms, to arms! Connacht to arms!
2. Insulted and betrayed, betrayed and insulted.
3. Who has insulted me? Tara has insulted.
4. To arms, to arms! Connacht to arms!
5. To arms—but if you have not got any
6. Take a table-leg or a candlestick,
7. A boot or a stool or any odd thing.
8. Who has betrayed me? Tara has betrayed!
9. To arms, to arms! Connacht to arms!
    > [*He goes out to one side. Music, perhaps drum and concertina, to suggest breaking of wood. Enter, at the other side, the King of Tara, drunk.*

10. *Aedh.* Where is that beastly drunken liar
11. That says I have insulted him?

Congal enters with two table-legs

12. *Congal.* I say it!

    Aedh.   What insult?

    Congal.   How dare you ask?
13. When I have had a common egg,
14. A common hen's egg put before me,
15. An egg dropped in the dirty straw
16. And crowed for by a cross-bred gangling cock,
17. And every other man at the table
18. A herne's egg.   [*Throws a table-leg on the floor.*
    There is your weapon. Take it!
19. Take it up, defend yourself.
20. An egg that some half-witted slattern
21. Spat upon and wiped on her apron!

Scene IV

STAGE DIRECTIONS   [. . . *back-cloth.* . . . .] **91.**

Directions after 9.   [. . . . *Enter at* . . . .] **90, 91** ; [*Goes* . . . . *Music, as drum* . . . *concertina, suggests breaking* . . . , *at other side, King* . . . .] **97A.**

22. *Aedh.* A servant put the wrong egg there.

23. *Congal.* But at whose orders?

    Aedh.   At your own.

24.   A murderous drunken plot, a plot
25.   To put a weapon that I do not know
26.   Into my hands.

    Congal.   Take up that weapon.
27.   If I am as drunken as you say,
28.   And you as sober as you think,
29.   A coward and a drunkard are well matched.

    [*Aedh takes up the table-leg. Connacht and Tara soldiers come in,
they fight, and the fight sways to and fro. The weapons, table-legs,
candlesticks, etc., do not touch. Drum-taps represent blows. All go out
fighting. Enter Pat, drunk, with bottle.*

30. *Pat.* Herne's egg, hen's egg, great difference.
31.   There's insult in that difference.
32.   What do hens eat? Hens live upon mash,
33.   Upon slop, upon kitchen odds and ends.
34.   What do hernes eat? Hernes live on eels,
35.   On things that must always run about.
36.   Man's a high animal and runs about,
37.   But mash is low, O, very low.
38.   Or, to speak like a philosopher,
39.   When a man expects the movable
40.   But gets the immovable, he is insulted.

    Enter Congal, Peter, Malachi, Mathias, etc.

41. *Congal.* Tara knew that he was overmatched;
42.   Knew from the start he had no chance;
43.   Died of a broken head; died drunk;
44.   Accused me with his dying breath
45.   Of secretly practising with a table-leg,
46.   Practising at midnight until I
47.   Became a perfect master with the weapon.
48.   But that is all lies.

    Pat.   Let all men know
49.   He was a noble character
50.   And I must weep at his funeral.

Directions after 29.   [*. . . up table-leg. . . . fight. The fight . . . .*] **97A.**

51. *Congal.* He insulted me with a hen's egg,
52. Said I had practised with a table-leg,
53. But I have taken kingdom and throne
54. And that has made all level again
55. And I can weep at his funeral.
56. I would not have had him die that way
57. Or die at all, he should have been immortal.
58. Our fifty battles had made us friends;
59. And there are fifty more to come.
60. New weapons, a new leader will be found
61. And everything begin again.

62. *Mike.* Much bloodier.

    Congal.   They had, we had
63. Forgotten what we fought about,
64. So fought like gentlemen, but now
65. Knowing the truth must fight like the beasts.
66. Maybe the Great Herne's curse has done it.
67. Why not? Answer me that; why not?

68. *Mike.* Horror henceforth.

    Congal.   This wise man means
69. We fought so long like gentlemen
70. That we grew blind.
      [*Attracta enters, walking in her sleep, a herne's egg in her hand. She stands near the throne and holds her egg towards it for a moment.*]

    Mathias.   Look! Look!
71. She offers that egg. Who is to take it?

72. *Congal.* She walks with open eyes but in her sleep.

73. *Mathias.* I can see it all in a flash.
74. She found that herne's egg on the table
75. And left the hen's egg there instead.

76. *James.* She brought the hen's egg on purpose
77. Walking in her wicked sleep.

78. *Congal.* And if I take that egg, she wakes,

---

58. . . . friends. **90, 91.**
    Directions after 70. [. . . *near throne . . . holds egg . . . it a* . . . .] **97A.**
73. . . . flash, **97A.**

79. Completes her task, her circle;
80. We all complete a task or circle,
81. Want a woman, then all goes—pff.

[*He goes to take the egg.*

82. *Mike.* Not now.

    Congal.   This wise man says 'not now'.
83. There must be something to consider first.

84. *James.* By changing one egg for another
85. She has brought bloodshed on us all.

86. *Pat.* He was a noble character,
87. And I must weep at his funeral.

88. *James.* I say that she must die, I say;
89. According to what my mother said,
90. All that have done what she did must die,
91. But, in a manner of speaking, pleasantly,
92. Because legally, certainly not
93. By beating with a table-leg
94. As though she were a mere Tara man,
95. Nor yet by beating with a stone
96. As though she were the Great Herne himself.

97. *Mike.* The Great Herne's bride.

    Congal.   I had forgotten
98. That all she does he makes her do,
99. But he is god and out of reach;
100. Nor stone can bruise, nor a sword pierce him,
101. And yet through his betrothed, his bride,
102. I have the power to make him suffer;
103. His curse has given me the right,
104. I am to play the fool and die
105. At a fool's hands.

    Mike.   Seven men.
[*He begins to count, seeming to strike the table with the table-leg, but table and table-leg must not meet, the blow is represented by the sound of the drum.*

---

88. ... say, **90, 91.**
93. ... table-leg.
94-96. [lacking] **90, 91.**

106.   One, two, three, four,
107.   Five, six, seven men.

108.   *Pat.* Seven that are present in this room,
109.   Seven that must weep at his funeral.

110.   *Congal.* This man who struck those seven blows
111.   Means that we seven in the name of the law
112.   Must handle, penetrate, and possess her,
113.   And do her a great good by that action,
114.   Melting out the virgin snow,
115.   And that snow image, the Great Herne;
116.   For nothing less than seven men
117.   Can melt that snow, but when it melts
118.   She may, being free from all obsession,
119.   Live as every woman should.
120.   I am the Court; judgement has been given.
121.   I name the seven: Congal of Tara,
122.   Patrick, Malachi, Mike, John, James,
123.   And that coarse hulk of clay, Mathias.

124.   *Mathias.* I dare not lay a hand upon that woman.
125.   The people say that she is holy
126.   And carries a great devil in her gut.

127.   *Pat.* What mischief can a Munster devil
128.   Do to a man that was born in Connacht?

129.   *Malachi.* I made a promise to my mother
130.   When we set out on this campaign
131.   To keep from women.

        John.   I have a wife that's jealous
132.   If I but look the moon in the face.

133.   *James.* I am promised to an educated girl.
134.   Her family are most particular,
135.   What would they say—O my God!

136.   *Congal.* Whoever disobeys the Court
137.   Is an unmannerly, disloyal lout,
138.   And no good citizen.

        Pat.   Here is my bottle.

---

129.   . . . mother. **97A.**

139.   Pass it along, a long, long pull;

140.   Although it's round like a woman carrying,

141.   No unmannerly, disloyal bottle,

142.   An affable, most loyal bottle.   *[All drink.*

143.   *Mathias.* I first.

        Congal.   That's for the Court to say.

144.   A Court of Law is a blessed thing,

145.   Logic, Mathematics, ground in one,

146.   And everything out of balance accursed.

147.   When the Court decides on a decree

148.   Men carry it out with dignity.

149.   Here where I put down my hand

150.   I will put a mark, then all must stand

151.   Over there in a level row.

152.   And all take off their caps and throw.

153.   The nearest cap shall take her first,

154.   The next shall take her next, so on

155.   Till all is in good order done.

156.   I need a mark and so must take

157.   The herne's egg, and let her wake.

        [He takes egg and lays it upon the ground. Attracta stands motionless,
        looking straight in front of her. She sings. The seven standing in a
        row throw their caps one after another.

158.   *Attracta.* When I take a beast to my joyful breast,

159.   Though beak and claw I must endure,

160.   *Sang the bride of the Herne, and the Great Herne's bride,*

161.   No lesser life, man, bird or beast,

162.   Can make unblessed what a beast made blessed,

163.   Can make impure what a beast made pure.

164.   Where is he gone, where is that other,

165.   He that shall take my maidenhead?

166.   *Sang the bride of the Herne, and the Great Herne's bride,*

167.   Out of the moon came my pale brother,

168.   The blue-black midnight is my mother.

169.   Who will turn down the sheets of the bed?

170.   When beak and claw their work begin

171.   Shall horror stir in the roots of my hair?

---

171.   . . . hair, **90, 91.**

172.   *Sang the bride of the Herne, and the Great Herne's bride,*
173.   And who lie there in the cold dawn
174.   When all that terror has come and gone?
175.   Shall I be the woman lying there?

Scene V

Before the Gate of Tara. Corney enters with Donkey.

1.   *Corney.* You thought to go on sleeping though dawn was up,
2.   Rapscallion of a beast, old highwayman.
3.   That light in the eastern sky is dawn,
4.   You cannot deny it; many a time
5.   You looked upon it following your trade.
6.   Cheer up, we shall be home before sunset.

Attracta comes in

7.   *Attracta.* I have packed all the uneaten or unbroken eggs
8.   Into the creels. Help carry them
9.   And hang them on the donkey's back.

10. *Corney.* We could boil them hard and keep them in the larder,
11.   But Congal has had them all boiled soft.

12. *Attracta.* Such eggs are holy. Many pure souls,
13.   Especially among the country-people,
14.   Would shudder if herne's eggs were left
15.   For foul-tongued, bloody-minded men.

Congal, Malachi, Mike, etc., enter

16. *Congal.* A sensible woman; you gather up what's left,
17.   Your thoughts upon the cupboard and the larder.

Scene V

8.   . . . creels, help . . . **90, 91.**
12. . . . souls
13. . . . country-people **90, 91.**
16. . . . woman, you . . . , **90, 91.**

18.   No more a herne's bride—a crazed loony
19.   Waiting to be trodden by a bird—
20.   But all woman, all sensible woman.

21. *Mike.* Manners.

    Congal.   This man who is always right
22.   Desires that I should add these words,
23.   The seven that held you in their arms last night
24.   Wish you good luck.

    Attracta.   What do you say?
25.   My husband came to me in the night.

26. *Congal.* Seven men lay with you in the night.
27.   Go home desiring and desirable,
28.   And look for a man.

    Attracta.   The Herne is my husband.
29.   I lay beside him, his pure bride.

30. *Congal.* Pure in the embrace of seven men?

31. *Mike.* She slept.

    Congal.   You say that though I thought,
32.   Because I took the egg out of her hand,
33.   That she awoke, she did not wake
34.   Until day broke upon her sleep—
35.   Her sleep and ours—did she wake pure?
36.   Seven men can answer that.

37. *Corney.* King though you are, I will not hear
38.   The bride of the Great Herne defamed—
39.   A king, a king but a Mayo man.
40.   A Mayo man's lying tongue can beat
41.   A Clare highwayman's rapscallion eye,
42.   Seven times a liar.

    Mike.   Seven men.

43. *Congal.* I, Congal, lay with her last night.

---

18. ... bride, a ...
19. ... bird, **90, 91.**
39-41. [lacking] **90, 91.**

44. *Mathias.* And I, Mathias.

Mike. And I.

James. And I.

45. *Peter.* And I.

John. And I.

Pat. And I; swear it;

46. And not a drop of drink since dawn.

47. *Corney.* One plain liar, six men bribed to lie.

48. *Attracta.* Great Herne, Great Herne, Great Herne,
49. Your darling is crying out,
50. Great Herne, declare her pure,
51. Pure as that beak and claw,
52. Great Herne, Great Herne, Great Herne,
53. Let the round heaven declare it.
    [*Silence. Then low thunder growing louder. All except Attracta and Congal kneel.*

54. *James.* Great Herne, I swear that she is pure;
55. I never laid a hand upon her.

56. *Mathias.* I was a fool to believe myself
57. When everybody knows that I am a liar.

58. *Pat.* Even when it seemed that I covered her
59. I swear that I knew it was the drink.

60. *Attracta.* I lay in the bride-bed,
61. His thunderbolts in my hand,
62. But gave them back, for he,
63. My lover, the Great Herne,
64. Knows everything that is said
65. And every man's intent,
66. And every man's deed; and he
67. Shall give these seven that say
68. That they upon me lay
69. A most memorable punishment.
    [*It thunders. All prostrate themselves except Attracta and Congal. Congal had half knelt, but he has stood up again.*

---

50. ... pure 91.

70. *Attracta.* I share his knowledge, and I know
71.   Every punishment decreed.
72.   He will come when you are dead,
73.   Push you down a step or two
74.   Into cat or rat or bat,
75.   Into dog or wolf or goose.
76.   Everybody in his new shape I can see,
77.   But Congal there stands in a cloud
78.   Because his fate is not yet settled.
79.   Speak out, Great Herne, and make it known
80.   That everything I have said is true.
     [*Thunder. All now, except Attracta, have prostrated themselves.*

81. *Attracta.* What has made you kneel?

Congal.   This man
82.   That's prostrate at my side would say,
83.   Could he say anything at all,
84.   That I am terrified by thunder.

85. *Attracta.* Why did you stand up so long?

86. *Congal.* I held you in my arms last night,
87.   We seven held you in our arms.

88. *Attracta.* You were under the curse, in all
89.   You did, in all you seemed to do.

90. *Congal.* If I must die at a fool's hand,
91.   When must I die?

Attracta.   When the moon is full.

92. *Congal.* And where?

Attracta.   Upon the holy mountain,
93.   Upon Slieve Fuadh, there we meet again
94.   Just as the moon comes round the hill.
95.   There all the gods must visit me,
96.   Acknowledging my marriage to a god;
97.   One man will I have among the gods.

---

93. . . . we shall meet . . . **90, 91.**
97. I would have one man among those gods. **90, 91.**

98. *Congal.* I know the place and I will come,
99.   Although it be my death, I will come.
100.   Because I am terrified, I will come.

Scene VI

A mountain-top, the moon has just risen; the moon of comic tradition, a round smiling face. A cauldron lid, a cooking-pot, and a spit lie together at one side of the stage. The Fool, a man in ragged clothes, enters carrying a large stone; he lays it down at one side and goes out. Congal enters carrying a wine-skin, and stands at the other side of the stage. The Fool re-enters with a second large stone which he places beside the first.

1. *Congal.* What is your name, boy?

Fool.   Poor Tom Fool.
2.   Everybody knows Tom Fool.

3. *Congal.* I saw something in the mist,
4.   There lower down upon the slope,
5.   I went up close to it and saw
6.   A donkey, somebody's stray donkey.
7.   A donkey and a Fool—I don't like it at all.

8. *Fool.* I won't be Tom the Fool after to-night.
9.   I have made a level patch out there,
10.   Clearing away the stones, and there
11.   I shall fight a man and kill a man
12.   And get great glory.

Congal.   Where did you get
13.   The cauldron lid, the pot and the spit?

14. *Fool.* I sat in Widow Rooney's kitchen,
15.   Somebody said, 'King Congal's on the mountain
16.   Cursed to die at the hands of a fool'.
17.   Somebody else said 'Kill him, Tom'.
18.   And everybody began to laugh
19.   And said I should kill him at the full moon,

Scene VI

STAGE DIRECTIONS   *. . . moon is about to rise; the moon of . . . .* **90, 91.**

20.   And that is to-night.

Congal.   I too have heard
21.   That Congal is to die to-night.
22.   Take a drink.

Fool.   I took this lid,
23.   And all the women screamed at me.
24.   I took the spit, and all screamed worse.
25.   A shoulder of lamb stood ready for the roasting—
26.   I put the pot upon my head.
27.   They did not scream but stood and gaped.
       [*Fool arms himself with spit, cauldron lid and pot, whistling 'The
       Great Herne's Feather'.*

28.   *Congal.* Hush, that is an unlucky tune!
29.   And why must you kill Congal, Fool?
30.   What harm has he done you?

Fool.   None at all.
31.   But there's a Fool called Johnny from Meath,
32.   We are great rivals and we hate each other,
33.   But I can get the pennies if I kill Congal,
34.   And Johnny nothing.

Congal.   I am King Congal,
35.   And is not that a thing to laugh at, Fool?

36.   *Fool.* Very nice, O very nice indeed,
37.   For I can kill you now, and I
38.   Am tired of walking.

Congal.   Both need rest.
39.   Another drink apiece—that is done—
40.   Lead to the place you have cleared of stones.

41.   *Fool.* But where is your sword? You have not got a sword.

42.   *Congal.* I lost it, or I never had it,
43.   Or threw it at the strange donkey below,

Directions after 27.   [. . . , *cauldron, lid* . . . .] **97A.**
28.   [lacking]
29.   But why . . . ? **90, 91.**

44.   But that's no matter—I have hands.

[They go out at one side. Attracta, Corney and Donkey come in. Attracta sings.

45. *Attracta.* When beak and claw their work began
46.   What horror stirred in the roots of my hair?
47.   *Sang the bride of the Herne, and the Great Herne's bride.*
48.   But who lay there in the cold dawn,
49.   When all that terror had come and gone?
50.   Was I the woman lying there?

[They go out. Congal and Tom the Fool come. Congal is carrying the cauldron lid, pot and spit. He lays them down.

51. *Congal.* I was sent to die at the hands of a Fool.
52.   There must be another Fool on the mountain.

53. *Fool.* That must be Johnny from Meath.
54.   But that's a thing I could not endure,
55.   For Johnny would get all the pennies.

56. *Congal.* Here, take a drink and have no fear;
57.   All's plain at last; though I shall die
58.   I shall not die at a Fool's hand.
59.   I have thought out a better plan.
60.   I and the Herne have had three bouts,
61.   He won the first, I won the second,
62.   Six men and I possessed his wife.

63. *Fool.* I ran after a woman once.
64.   I had seen two donkeys in a field.

65. *Congal.* And did you get her, did you get her, Fool?

66. *Fool.* I almost had my hand upon her.
67.   She screamed, and somebody came and beat me.
68.   Were you beaten?

Congal.   No, no, Fool.
69.   But she said that nobody had touched her,
70.   And after that the thunder said the same,
71.   Yet I had won that bout, and now
72.   I know that I shall win the third.

73. *Fool.* If Johnny from Meath comes, kill him!

74. *Congal.* Maybe I will, maybe I will not.

75. *Fool.* You let me off, but don't let him off.

76. *Congal.* I could not do you any harm,
77.   For you and I are friends.

    Fool.   Kill Johnny!

78. *Congal.* Because you have asked me to, I will do it,
79.   For you and I are friends.

    Fool.   Kill Johnny!
80.   Kill with the spear, but give it to me
81.   That I may see if it is sharp enough.

                                                           [Fool takes spit.

82. *Congal.* And is it, Fool?

    Fool.   I spent an hour
83.   Sharpening it upon a stone.
84.   Could I kill you now?

    Congal.   Maybe you could.

85. *Fool.* I will get all the pennies for myself.
    [He wounds Congal. The wounding is symbolised by a movement of
    the spit towards or over Congal's body.

86. *Congal.* It passed out of your mind for a moment
87.   That we are friends, but that is natural.

88. *Fool [dropping spit].* I must see it, I never saw a wound.

89. *Congal.* The Herne has got the first blow in;
90.   A scratch, a scratch, a mere nothing.
91.   But had it been a little deeper and higher
92.   It would have gone through the heart, and maybe
93.   That would have left me better off,
94.   For the Great Herne may beat me in the end.
95.   Here I must sit through the full moon,
96.   And he will send up Fools against me,
97.   Meandering, roaring, yelling,
98.   Whispering Fools, then chattering Fools,
99.   And after that morose, melancholy,
100.   Sluggish, fat, silent Fools;
101.   And I, moon-crazed, moon-blind,
102.   Fighting and wounded, wounded and fighting.

103.   I never thought of such an end.

104.   Never be a soldier, Tom;

105.   Though it begins well, is this a life?

106.   If this is a man's life, is there any life

107.   But a dog's life?

  Fool.   That's it, that's it;

108.   Many a time they have put a dog at me.

109.   *Congal.* If I should give myself a wound,

110.   Let life run away, I'd win the bout.

111.   He said I must die at the hands of a Fool

112.   And sent you hither. Give me that spit!

113.   I put it in this crevice of the rock,

114.   That I may fall upon the point.

115.   These stones will keep it sticking upright.

      [*They arrange stones, he puts the spit in.*

116.   *Congal* [*almost screaming in his excitement*]. Fool! Am I myself a Fool?

117.   For if I am a Fool, he wins the bout.

118.   *Fool.* You are King of Connacht. If you were a Fool

119.   They would have chased you with their dogs.

120.   *Congal.* I am King Congal of Connacht and of Tara,

121.   That wise, victorious, voluble, unlucky,

122.   Blasphemous, famous, infamous man.

123.   Fool, take this spit when red with blood,

124.   Show it to the people and get all the pennies;

125.   What does it matter what they think?

126.   The Great Herne knows that I have won.

   [*He falls symbolically upon the spit. It does not touch him. Fool takes the spit and wine-skin and goes out.*

127.   It seems that I am hard to kill,

128.   But the wound is deep. Are you up there?

129.   Your chosen kitchen spit has killed me,

130.   But killed me at my own will, not yours.

     Attracta and Corney enter

131.   *Attracta.* Will the knot hold?

  Corney.   There was a look

132.   About the old highwayman's eye of him

---

118.   . . . fool **90, 91.**
   Directions after 130. [. . . *enter. The moon rises.*] **90, 91.**

133.   That warned me, so I made him fast
134.   To that old stump among the rocks
135.   With a great knot that he can neither
136.   Break, nor pull apart with his teeth.

137.   *Congal.* Attracta!

    Attracta.   I called you to this place,
138.   You came, and now the story is finished.

139.   *Congal.* You have great powers, even the thunder
140.   Does whatever you bid it to do.
141.   Protect me, I have won my bout,
142.   But I am afraid of what the Herne
143.   May do with me when I am dead.
144.   I am afraid that he may put me
145.   Into the shape of a brute beast.

146.   *Attracta.* I will protect you if, as I think,
147.   Your shape is not yet fixed upon.

148.   *Congal.* I am slipping now, and you up there
149.   With your long leg and your long beak.
150.   But I have beaten you, Great Herne,
151.   In spite of your kitchen spit—seven men—

                                                   [He dies.

152.   *Attracta.* Come lie with me upon the ground,
153.   Come quickly into my arms, come quickly, come
154.   Before his body has had time to cool.

155.   *Corney.* What? Lie with you?

    Attracta.   Lie and beget.
156.   If you are afraid of the Great Herne,
157.   Put that away, for if I do his will,
158.   You are his instrument or himself.

159.   *Corney.* The thunder has me terrified.

160.   *Attracta.* I lay with the Great Herne, and he,
161.   Being all a spirit, but begot
162.   His image in the mirror of my spirit,
163.   Being all sufficient to himself

---

155.   . . . beget, **90, 91.**

164.   Begot himself; but there's a work
165.   That should be done, and that work needs
166.   No bird's beak nor claw, but a man,
167.   The imperfection of a man.

                              [*The sound of a donkey braying.*

168. *Corney.* The donkey is braying.
169.   He has some wickedness in his mind.

170. *Attracta.* Too late, too late, he broke that knot,
171.   And there, down there among the rocks
172.   He couples with another donkey.
173.   That donkey has conceived. I thought that I
174.   Could give a human form to Congal,
175.   But now he must be born a donkey.

176. *Corney.* King Congal must be born a donkey!

177. *Attracta.* Because we were not quick enough.

178. *Corney.* I have heard that a donkey carries its young
179.   Longer than any other beast,
180.   Thirteen months it must carry it.

                                          [*He laughs.*

181.   All that trouble and nothing to show for it,
182.   Nothing but just another donkey.

                    THE END

___

166.   [lacking] **90, 91.**

                    NOTES

                 *   *   *

                Variant Spelling

Connacht **97** ; *Connaught* **90, 91.**

                 *   *   *

    [See *Preface to 91*, p. 1311.]

PURGATORY

1939

Persons in the Play

A Boy   An Old Man

Scene.—A ruined house and a bare tree in the background.

1. *Boy.* Half-door, hall door,
2.   Hither and thither day and night,
3.   Hill or hollow, shouldering this pack,
4.   Hearing you talk.

   Old Man.   Study that house.
5.   I think about its jokes and stories;
6.   I try to remember what the butler
7.   Said to a drunken gamekeeper
8.   In mid-October, but I cannot.
9.   If I cannot, none living can.
10.   Where are the jokes and stories of a house,
11.   Its threshold gone to patch a pig-sty?

12. *Boy.* So you have come this path before?
13. *Old Man.* The moonlight falls upon the path,
14.   The shadow of a cloud upon the house,
15.   And that's symbolical; study that tree,
16.   What is it like?

   Boy.   A silly old man.

PRINTINGS   **92, 93, 94, 97.**

DATE [lacking] **92**; April, 1938. **93**; 1938–1939 [This date under fly-title of 'Last Plays'] **94.**

DRAMATIS PERSONAE [lacking] **92, 93.**

STAGE DIRECTIONS [*A ruined . . . .*] **92, 93.**

TEXT

1. Half door, . . . door **92** ; . . . door **93.**
2. . . . night
3. . . . pack. **92, 93.**
4. . . . house **93.**
8. . . . cannot, **92, 93.**
10. . . . house **92.**
14. ,,, house **92, 93.**

17. *Old Man.* It's like—no matter what it's like.
18.   I saw it a year ago stripped bare as now,
19.   So I chose a better trade.
20.   I saw it fifty years ago
21.   Before the thunderbolt had riven it,
22.   Green leaves, ripe leaves, leaves thick as butter,
23.   Fat, greasy life. Stand there and look,
24.   Because there is somebody in that house.

             [*The Boy puts down pack and stands in the doorway.*

25. *Boy.* There's nobody here.

     Old Man.   There's somebody there.

26. *Boy.* The floor is gone, the windows gone,
27.   And where there should be roof there's sky,
28.   And here's a bit of an egg-shell thrown
29.   Out of a jackdaw's nest.

     Old Man.   But there are some
30.   That do not care what's gone, what's left:
31.   The souls in Purgatory that come back
32.   To habitations and familiar spots.

33. *Boy.* Your wits are out again.

     Old Man.   Re-live
34.   Their transgressions, and that not once
35.   But many times; they know at last
36.   The consequence of those transgressions
37.   Whether upon others or upon themselves;
38.   Upon others, others may bring help,
39.   For when the consequence is at an end
40.   The dream must end; if upon themselves,
41.   There is no help but in themselves

---

19. [lacking] **92.**
     [between 19 and 20 a break] **93.**
21. . . . thunder-bolt . . . , **92.**
30. . . . left; **92, 93.**
35. . . . times, they . . . **92.**
37. . . . others, or . . . ;
38. . . . help **92.**
40. . . . end; upon themselves **92-94.**

42.   And in the mercy of God.

       Boy.   I have had enough!
43.   Talk to the jackdaws, if talk you must.

44. *Old Man.* Stop! Sit there upon that stone.
45.   That is the house where I was born.

46. *Boy.* The big old house that was burnt down?

47. *Old Man.* My mother that was your grand-dam owned it,
48.   This scenery and this countryside,
49.   Kennel and stable, horse and hound—
50.   She had a horse at the Curragh, and there met
51.   My father, a groom in a training stable,
52.   Looked at him and married him.
53.   Her mother never spoke to her again,
54.   And she did right.

       Boy.   What's right and wrong?
55.   My grand-dad got the girl and the money.

56. *Old Man.* Looked at him and married him,
57.   And he squandered everything she had,
58.   She never knew the worst, because
59.   She died in giving birth to me,
60.   But now she knows it all, being dead.
61.   Great people lived and died in this house;
62.   Magistrates, colonels, members of Parliament,
63.   Captains and Governors, and long ago
64.   Men that had fought at Aughrim and the Boyne.
65.   Some that had gone on Government work
66.   To London or to India came home to die,
67.   Or came from London every spring

---

42. ... God
       I ... ! **92.**
     [between 49 and 50 a break] **93.**
51. ... stable; **93.**
     [between 57 and 58 a break] **93.**
     [between 60 and 61 a break] **93.**
65. ... government ... **92, 93.**
66. ... India, came ... , **92.**

68. To look at the may-blossom in the park.
69. They had loved the trees that he cut down
70. To pay what he had lost at cards
71. Or spent on horses, drink and women;
72. Had loved the house, had loved all
73. The intricate passages of the house,
74. But he killed the house; to kill a house
75. Where great men grew up, married, died,
76. I here declare a capital offence.

77. *Boy.* My God, but you had luck! Grand clothes,
78. And maybe a grand horse to ride.

79. *Old Man.* That he might keep me upon his level
80. He never sent me to school, but some
81. Half-loved me for my half of her:
82. A gamekeeper's wife taught me to read,
83. A Catholic curate taught me Latin.
84. There were old books and books made fine
85. By eighteenth-century French binding, books
86. Modern and ancient, books by the ton.

87. *Boy.* What education have you given me?

88. *Old Man.* I gave the education that befits
89. A bastard that a pedlar got
90. Upon a tinker's daughter in a ditch.
91. When I had come to sixteen years old
92. My father burned down the house when drunk.

93. *Boy.* But that is my age, sixteen years old,
94. At the Puck Fair.

   Old Man.   And everything was burnt;
95. Books, library, all were burnt.

96. *Boy.* Is what I have heard upon the road the truth,
97. That you killed him in the burning house?

---

68. ... May-blossom .... **92, 93.**
77. ... luck. Grand ... , **92.**
81. ... her, **92.**
85. ... eighteenth century ... **92, 93.**
93. ... old. **92** ; ... old **93.**

98. *Old Man.* There's nobody here but our two selves?

99. *Boy.* Nobody, Father.

    Old Man.   I stuck him with a knife,

100.   That knife that cuts my dinner now,

101.   And after that I left him in the fire.

102.   They dragged him out, somebody saw

103.   The knife-wound but could not be certain

104.   Because the body was all black and charred.

105.   Then some that were his drunken friends

106.   Swore they would put me upon trial,

107.   Spoke of quarrels, a threat I had made.

108.   The gamekeeper gave me some old clothes,

109.   I ran away, worked here and there

110.   Till I became a pedlar on the roads,

111.   No good trade, but good enough

112.   Because I am my father's son,

113.   Because of what I did or may do.

114.   Listen to the hoof-beats! Listen, listen!

115. *Boy.* I cannot hear a sound.

    Old Man.   Beat! Beat!

116.   This night is the anniversary

117.   Of my mother's wedding night,

118.   Or of the night wherein I was begotten.

119.   My father is riding from the public-house,

120.   A whiskey-bottle under his arm.

                  [A window is lit showing a young girl.

121.   Look at the window; she stands there

122.   Listening, the servants are all in bed,

123.   She is alone, he has stayed late

124.   Bragging and drinking in the public-house.

125. *Boy.* There's nothing but an empty gap in the wall.

126.   You have made it up. No, you are mad!

127.   You are getting madder every day.

---

101. . . . fire; **92, 93.**

114. . . . hoof beats! . . . , Listen! **92** ; . . . hoof beats! . . . ! **93.**

119. . . . public house,

120. . . . whiskey bottle . . . . **92, 93.**

124. . . . public house. **92** ; . . . publichouse. **93.**

128. *Old Man.* It's louder now because he rides

129.   Upon a gravelled avenue

130.   All grass to-day. The hoof-beat stops,

131.   He has gone to the other side of the house,

132.   Gone to the stable, put the horse up.

133.   She has gone down to open the door.

134.   This night she is no better than her man

135.   And does not mind that he is half drunk,

136.   She is mad about him. They mount the stairs.

137.   She brings him into her own chamber.

138.   And that is the marriage-chamber now.

139.   The window is dimly lit again.

140.   Do not let him touch you! It is not true

141.   That drunken men cannot beget,

142.   And if he touch he must beget

143.   And you must bear his murderer.

144.   Deaf! Both deaf! If I should throw

145.   A stick or a stone they would not hear;

146.   And that's a proof my wits are out.

147.   But there's a problem: she must live

148.   Through everything in exact detail,

149.   Driven to it by remorse, and yet

150.   Can she renew the sexual act

151.   And find no pleasure in it, and if not,

152.   If pleasure and remorse must both be there,

153.   Which is the greater?

                       I lack schooling.

154.   Go fetch Tertullian; he and I

155.   Will ravel all that problem out

156.   Whilst those two lie upon the mattress

157.   Begetting me.

                  Come back! Come back!

158.   And so you thought to slip away,

---

130. . . . hoof beat . . . , **92, 93.**

131. . . . house **93.**

136. . . . stairs **92-94** ; . . . stairs, **97A.**

138. . . . marriage chamber . . . . **92, 93.**

     [between 139 and 140 no break] **93.**

141. . . . beget **92, 93.**

145. . . . or stone . . . ; **92.**

152. . . . there **92, 93.**

159. My bag of money between your fingers,
160. And that I could not talk and see!
161. You have been rummaging in the pack.

[*The light in the window has faded out*

162. *Boy.* You never gave me my right share.

163. *Old Man.* And had I given it, young as you are,
164. You would have spent it upon drink.

165. *Boy.* What if I did? I had a right
166. To get it and spend it as I chose.

167. *Old Man.* Give me that bag and no more words.

168. *Boy.* I will not.

Old Man. I will break your fingers.
[*They struggle for the bag. In the struggle it drops, scattering the money. The Old Man staggers but does not fall. They stand looking at each other. The window is lit up. A man is seen pouring whiskey into a glass.*

169. *Boy.* What if I killed you? You killed my grand-dad,
170. Because you were young and he was old.
171. Now I am young and you are old.

172. *Old Man* [*staring at window*]. Better-looking, those sixteen years—

173. *Boy.* What are you muttering?

Old Man. Younger—and yet
174. She should have known he was not her kind.

175. *Boy.* What are you saying? Out with it!
[*Old Man points to window.*

---

163. . . . are **92, 93.**
Directions after 168. [. . . *other.*] **92**; [. . . *other. Window* . . . *up, a* . . . .] **93.**
169. . . . grand-dad **92.**
170. . . . old; **93.**
Directions after 171. [*A window is lit up, a man is seen pouring whiskey into a glass.*] **92.**
172. Better looking, . . .— **92, 93.**

176.   My God! The window is lit up
177.   And somebody stands there, although
178.   The floorboards are all burnt away.

179. *Old Man.* The window is lit up because my father
180.   Has come to find a glass for his whiskey.
181.   He leans there like some tired beast.

182. *Boy.* A dead, living, murdered man!

183. *Old Man.* 'Then the bride-sleep fell upon Adam':
184.   Where did I read those words?
                                    And yet
185.   There's nothing leaning in the window
186.   But the impression upon my mother's mind;
187.   Being dead she is alone in her remorse.

188. *Boy.* A body that was a bundle of old bones
189.   Before I was born. Horrible! Horrible!
                                    [*He covers his eyes.*

190. *Old Man.* That beast there would know nothing, being nothing,
191.   If I should kill a man under the window
192.   He would not even turn his head.
                                    [*He stabs the Boy.*

193.   My father and my son on the same jack-knife!
194.   That finishes—there—there—there—
                    [*He stabs again and again. The window grows dark.*

195.   'Hush-a-bye baby, thy father's a knight,
196.   Thy mother a lady, lovely and bright.'
197.   No, that is something that I read in a book,
198.   And if I sing it must be to my mother,

---

199. And I lack rhyme.
  [The stage has grown dark except where the tree stands in white light.
       Study that tree.
200. It stands there like a purified soul,
201. All cold, sweet, glistening light.
202. Dear mother, the window is dark again,
203. But you are in the light because
204. I finished all that consequence.
205. I killed that lad because had he grown up
206. He would have struck a woman's fancy,
207. Begot, and passed pollution on.
208. I am a wretched foul old man
209. And therefore harmless. When I have stuck
210. This old jack-knife into a sod
211. And pulled it out all bright again,
212. And picked up all the money that he dropped,
213. I'll to a distant place, and there
214. Tell my old jokes among new men.
     [He cleans the knife and begins to pick up money.
215. Hoof-beats! Dear God,
216. How quickly it returns—beat—beat—!
217. Her mind cannot hold up that dream.
218. Twice a murderer and all for nothing,
219. And she must animate that dead night
220. Not once but many times!
      O God,
221. Release my mother's soul from its dream!
222. Mankind can do no more. Appease
223. The misery of the living and the remorse of the dead.

       THE END

---

202. . . . again **92, 93.**
205. . . . lad for he was growing up, **92** ; . . . because he had grown up, **93, 94.**
206. . . . would soon take some woman's . . . ,
207. Beget and pass pollution . . . . **92.**
212. . . . dropped **92, 93.**
215. Hoof beats! . . . God
216. . . .—beat—beat— **92, 93.**
217. [speaker's name repeated] **93.**
  [between 216 and 217 no break] **92.**
220. . . . God! **92** ; . . . God **93.**

NOTES

Purgatory was first produced at the Abbey Theatre, Dublin, on August 10, 1938, with Michael Dolan as the Old Man and Liam Redmond as the Boy.

w. b. yeats, October, 1938.
From 'Preface,' **93**.

* * *

[See also *Preface to 93*, p. 1312.]

THE DEATH OF CUCHULAIN

1939

Persons in the Play

Cuchulain	An Old Man
Eithne Inguba	A Blind Man
Aoife	A Servant
Emer	A Singer, a Piper, and
The Morrigu, *Goddess of War*	a Drummer

Scene.—*A bare stage of any period. A very old man looking like something out of mythology.*

a. *Old Man.* I have been asked to produce a play called
b. *The Death of Cuchulain.* It is the last of a series of
c. plays which has for theme his life and death. I have
d. been selected because I am out of fashion and out of
e. date like the antiquated romantic stuff the thing is
f. made of. I am so old that I have forgotten the name
g. of my father and mother, unless indeed I am, as I
h. affirm, the son of Talma, and he was so old that his
i. friends and acquaintances still read Virgil and Homer.
j. When they told me that I could have my own way, I
k. wrote certain guiding principles on a bit of news-
l. paper. I wanted an audience of fifty or a hundred, and
m. if there are more, I beg them not to shuffle their feet
n. or talk when the actors are speaking. I am sure that
o. as I am producing a play for people I like, it is not
p. probable, in this vile age, that they will be more in
q. number than those who listened to the first perform-
r. ance of Milton's *Comus*. On the present occasion
s. they must know the old epics and Mr. Yeats' plays

PRINTINGS **92, 94, 97.**

DATE [lacking] **92**; 1938–1939 [This date under fly-title of 'Last Plays'] **94.**

DRAMATIS PERSONAE [lacking] **92.**

STAGE DIRECTIONS [*A bare . . . .*] **92.**

b. 'The Death of Cuchulain.' It . . . **92.**
j. . . . me I . . . **92.**
m. . . . more I . . . **92.**
o. . . . like it . . .
p. probable in . . **92.**

t.   about them; such people, however poor, have libraries

u.   of their own. If there are more than a hundred I

v.   won't be able to escape people who are educating

w.   themselves out of the Book Societies and the like,

x.   sciolists all, pickpockets and opinionated bitches.

y.   Why pickpockets? I will explain that, I will make it

z.   all quite clear.

[Drum and pipe behind the scene, then silence.

aa.   That's from the musicians; I asked them to do that

bb.   if I was getting excited. If you were as old you would

cc.   find it easy to get excited. Before the night ends you

dd.   will meet the music. There is a singer, a piper, and a

ee.   drummer. I have picked them up here and there about

ff.   the streets, and I will teach them, if I live, the music

gg.   of the beggar-man, Homer's music. I promise a

hh.   dance. I wanted a dance because where there are no

ii.   words there is less to spoil. Emer must dance, there

jj.   must be severed heads—I am old, I belong to mytho-

kk.   logy—severed heads for her to dance before. I had

ll.   thought to have had those heads carved, but no, if the

mm. dancer can dance properly no wood-carving can look

nn.   as well as a parallelogram of painted wood. But I was

oo.   at my wit's end to find a good dancer; I could have

pp.   got such a dancer once, but she has gone; the tragi-

qq.   comedian dancer, the tragic dancer, upon the same

rr.   neck love and loathing, life and death. I spit three

ss.   times. I spit upon the dancers painted by Degas.

tt.   I spit upon their short bodices, their stiff stays,

uu.   their toes whereon they spin like peg-tops, above

vv.   all upon that chambermaid face. They might have

ww. looked timeless, Rameses the Great, but not the

xx.   chambermaid, that old maid history. I spit! I spit!

yy.   I spit!

---

t.   . . . people however poor have . . . **92.**

w. . . . book societies . . . , **92.**

dd. . . . piper and . . . **92, 94.**

gg. . . . beggarman, . . . **92.**

rr. . . . death, I . . . **97A.**

[The stage is darkened, the curtain falls. Pipe and drum begin and continue until the curtain rises on a bare stage. Half a minute later Eithne Inguba enters.

1. *Eithne.* Cuchulain! Cuchulain!

Cuchulain enters from back

I am Emer's messenger,

2. I am your wife's messenger, she has bid me say
3. You must not linger here in sloth, for Maeve
4. With all those Connacht ruffians at her back
5. Burns barns and houses up at Emain Macha:
6. Your house at Muirthemne already burns.
7. No matter what's the odds, no matter though
8. Your death may come of it, ride out and fight.
9. The scene is set and you must out and fight.

10. *Cuchulain.* You have told me nothing. I am already armed,
11. I have sent a messenger to gather men,
12. And wait for his return. What have you there?

13. *Eithne.* I have nothing.

Cuchulain.   There is something in your hand.

14. *Eithne.* No.

Cuchulain. Have you a letter in your hand?

15. *Eithne.* I do not know how it got into my hand.
16. I am straight from Emer. We were in some place.
17. She spoke. She saw.

Cuchulain.   This letter is from Emer,

18. It tells a different story. I am not to move
19. Until to-morrow morning, for, if now,
20. I must face odds no man can face and live.
21. To-morrow morning Conall Caernach comes

Directions after yy. [. . . *continue, until* . . . .] **92.**

TEXT

1. . . . ! Cuchulain'

Cuchulain . . . back

Eithne.   I . . . , **92.**

3. . . . sloth for . . . **92.**

10. . . . armed **92.**

13, 14. [set as four lines ending nothing. / hand. / No. / hand?] **94A.**

22.　　　With a great host.

　　　Eithne.　　　　　　　I do not understand.
23.　　　Who can have put that letter in my hand?

24.　*Cuchulain.* And there is something more to make it certain
25.　　　I shall not stir till morning; you are sent
26.　　　To be my bedfellow, but have no fear,
27.　　　All that is written, but I much prefer
28.　　　Your own unwritten words. I am for the fight,
29.　　　I and my handful are set upon the fight;
30.　　　We have faced great odds before, a straw decided.

　　　　　The Morrigu enters and stands between them

31.　*Eithne.* I know that somebody or something is there,
32.　　　Yet nobody that I can see.

　　　Cuchulain.　　　　　　　There is nobody.

33.　*Eithne.* Who among the gods of the air and upper air
34.　　　Has a bird's head?

　　　Cuchulain.　　　　　Morrigu is headed like a crow.

35.　*Eithne* [*dazed*]. Morrigu, war goddess, stands between.
36.　　　Her black wing touched me upon the shoulder, and
37.　　　All is intelligible.　　　　　　[*The Morrigu goes out.*
　　　　　　　Maeve put me in a trance.
38.　　　Though when Cuchulain slept with her as a boy
39.　　　She seemed as pretty as a bird, she has changed,
40.　　　She has an eye in the middle of her forehead.

41.　*Cuchulain.* A woman that has an eye in the middle of her forehead!
42.　　　A woman that is headed like a crow!
43.　　　But she that put those words into your mouth

25.　. . . morning: you . . . **94.**
27.　. . . written but . . .
28.　. . . fight
29.　. . . fight, **92.**
31.　. . . there **92.**
36.　. . . , and now
37.　. . . intelligible. [*Morrigu* . . . .]
　　　　　Maeve . . . trance, **92.**

44. Had nothing monstrous; you put them there yourself;
45. You need a younger man, a friendlier man,
46. But, fearing what my violence might do,
47. Thought out these words to send me to my death,
48. And were in such excitement you forgot
49. The letter in your hand.

Eithne.   Now that I wake
50. I say that Maeve did nothing out of reason;
51. What mouth could you believe if not my mouth?

52. *Cuchulain.* When I went mad at my son's death and drew
53. My sword against the sea, it was my wife
54. That brought me back.

Eithne   Better women than I
55. Have served you well, but 'twas to me you turned.

56. *Cuchulain.* You thought that if you changed I'd kill you for it,
57. When everything sublunary must change,
58. And if I have not changed that goes to prove
59. That I am monstrous.

Eithne.   You're not the man I loved,
60. That violent man forgave no treachery.
61. If, thinking what you think, you can forgive,
62. It is because you are about to die.

63. *Cuchulain.* Spoken too loudly and too near the door;
64. Speak low if you would speak about my death,
65. Or not in that strange voice exulting in it.
66. Who knows what ears listen behind the door?

67. *Eithne.* Some that would not forgive a traitor, some
68. That have the passion necessary to life,
69. Some not about to die. When you are gone
70. I shall denounce myself to all your cooks,

---

44. . . . yourself, **92.**
46. But fearing . . . do **92.**
56. . . . it **92.**
61. If thinking . . . think you . . . forgive **92.**
70. . . . cooks. **92.**

71.   Scullions, armourers, bed-makers and messengers,
72.   Until they hammer me with a ladle, cut me with a knife,
73.   Impale me upon a spit, put me to death
74.   By what foul way best please their fancy,
75.   So that my shade can stand among the shades
76.   And greet your shade and prove it is no traitor.

77.   *Cuchulain.* Women have spoken so, plotting a man's death.

Enter a Servant

78.   *Servant.* Your great horse is bitted. All wait the word.

79.   *Cuchulain.* I come to give it, but must ask a question.
80.   This woman, wild with grief, declares that she
81.   Out of pure treachery has told me lies
82.   That should have brought my death. What can I do?
83.   How can I save her from her own wild words?

84.   *Servant.* Is her confession true?

    Cuchulain.   I make the truth!
85.   I say she brings a message from my wife.

86.   *Servant.* What if I make her swallow poppy-juice?

87.   *Cuchulain.* What herbs seem suitable, but protect her life
88.   As if it were your own, and should I not return
89.   Give her to Conall Caernach because the women
90.   Have called him a good lover.

    Eithne.   I might have peace that know
91.   The Morrigu, the woman like a crow,
92.   Stands to my defence and cannot lie,
93.   But that Cuchulain is about to die.

---

71.   . . . , bed-makers, and . . . , **92, 94E.**
80.   . . . woman wild . . . **92.**
86.   . . . poppy juice? **92.**
90.   [set as two lines ending lover. / know] **94A.**
91.   . . . crow **92.**

[Pipe and drum. The stage grows dark for a moment. When it lights up again, it is empty. Cuchulain enters wounded. He tries to fasten himself to a pillar-stone with his belt. Aoife, an erect white-haired woman, enters.

94. *Aoife.* Am I recognised, Cuchulain?

Cuchulain. You fought with a sword,
95. It seemed that we should kill each other, then
96. Your body wearied and I took your sword.

97. *Aoife.* But look again, Cuchulain! Look again!

98. *Cuchulain.* Your hair is white.

Aoife. That time was long ago,
99. And now it is my time. I have come to kill you.

100. *Cuchulain.* Where am I? Why am I here?

Aoife. You asked their leave,
101. When certain that you had six mortal wounds,
102. To drink out of the pool.

Cuchulain. I have put my belt
103. About this stone and want to fasten it
104. And die upon my feet, but am too weak.
105. Fasten this belt. *[She helps him to do so.*
And now I know your name,
106. Aoife, the mother of my son. We met
107. At the Hawk's Well under the withered trees.
108. I killed him upon Baile's Strand, that is why
109. Maeve parted ranks that she might let you through.
110. You have a right to kill me.

Aoife. Though I have,
111. Her army did not part to let me through.
112. The grey of Macha, that great horse of yours
113. Killed in the battle, came out of the pool

Directions after 93. [. . . *woman enters.*] **92.**
98. . . . ago **92.**
105. . . . belt
     [*She* . . . . **92.**
107. . . . trees **92.**

114.   As though it were alive, and went three times
115.   In a great circle round you and that stone,
116.   Then leaped into the pool; and not a man
117.   Of all that terrified army dare approach,
118.   But I approach.

   Cuchulain.   Because you have the right.

119. *Aoife.* But I am an old woman now, and that
120.   Your strength may not start up when the time comes
121.   I wind my veil about this ancient stone
122.   And fasten you to it.

   Cuchulain.   But do not spoil your veil.

123.   Your veils are beautiful, some with threads of gold.

124. *Aoife.* I am too old to care for such things now.

                           [*She has wound the veil about him.*

125. *Cuchulain.* There was no reason so to spoil your veil:
126.   I am weak from loss of blood.

   Aoife.   I was afraid,
127.   But now that I have wound you in the veil
128.   I am not afraid. But—how did my son fight?

129. *Cuchulain.* Age makes more skilful but not better men.

130. *Aoife.* I have been told you did not know his name
131.   And wanted, because he had a look of me,
132.   To be his friend, but Conchubar forbade it.

133. *Cuchulain.* Forbade it and commanded me to fight;
134.   That very day I had sworn to do his will,
135.   Yet refused him, and spoke about a look;
136.   But somebody spoke of witchcraft and I said
137.   Witchcraft had made the look, and fought and killed him.
138.   Then I went mad, I fought against the sea.

---

116.   . . . pool and . . . **92** ; . . . pool, and . . . **94.**
117.   . . . approach; **92, 94.**
125.   . . . veil **92.**
127.   . . . veil,
128.   . . . . But how . . . ? **92.**
130.   . . . name, **92.**

139. *Aoife*. I seemed invulnerable; you took my sword,
140.   You threw me on the ground and left me there.
141.   I searched the mountain for your sleeping-place
142.   And laid my virgin body at your side,
143.   And yet, because you had left me, hated you,
144.   And thought that I would kill you in your sleep,
145.   And yet begot a son that night between
146.   Two black thorn-trees.

    Cuchulain.   I cannot understand.

147. *Aoife*. Because about to die!
                       Somebody comes,
148.   Some countryman, and when he finds you here,
149.   And none to protect him, will be terrified.
150.   I will keep out of his sight, for I have things
151.   That I must ask questions on before I kill you.
    [She goes. The Blind Man of 'On Baile's Strand' comes in. He
moves his stick about until he finds the standing stone; he lays his
stick down, stoops and touches Cuchulain's feet. He feels the legs.

152. *Blind Man*. Ah! Ah!

    Cuchulain.   I think you are a blind old man.

153. *Blind Man*. A blind old beggar-man. What is your name?

154. *Cuchulain*. Cuchulain.

    Blind Man.   They say that you are weak with wounds.
155.   I stood between a Fool and the sea at Baile's Strand

---

141. . . . sleeping place **92**.
143. . . . yet because . . . you
144. . . . sleep **92**.
146. . . . thorn trees. . . . .
147. . . . comes.
148. . . . countryman; and . . . here **92**.
150. . . . sight for . . . **92**.
      Directions after 151. [. . . *goes, the* . . . *of Baile's Strand comes* . . . .]
      92 ; [. . . *of On* . . . *Strand comes* . . . .] **94**.
152. [set as two lines ending Ah! / man.] **94A**.
153. . . . beggar man. . . . ? **92**.

156.   When you went mad. What's bound about your hands
157.   So that they cannot move? Some womanish stuff.
158.   I have been fumbling with my stick since dawn
159.   And then heard many voices. I began to beg.
160.   Somebody said that I was in Maeve's tent,
161.   And somebody else, a big man by his voice,
162.   That if I brought Cuchulain's head in a bag
163.   I would be given twelve pennies; I had the bag
164.   To carry what I get at kitchen doors,
165.   Somebody told me how to find the place;
166.   I thought it would have taken till the night,
167.   But this has been my lucky day.

     Cuchulain.   Twelve pennies!

168.   *Blind Man.* I would not promise anything until the woman,
169.   The great Queen Maeve herself, repeated the words.

170.   *Cuchulain.* Twelve pennies! What better reason for killing a man?
171.   You have a knife, but have you sharpened it?

172.   *Blind Man.* I keep it sharp because it cuts my food.
     [*He lays bag on ground and begins feeling Cuchulain's body, his
     hands mounting upward.*

173.   *Cuchulain.* I think that you know everything, Blind Man.
174.   My mother or my nurse said that the blind
175.   Know everything.

     Blind Man.   No, but they have good sense.
176.   How could I have got twelve pennies for your head
177.   If I had not good sense?

     Cuchulain.   There floats out there
178.   The shape that I shall take when I am dead,
179.   My soul's first shape, a soft feathery shape,
180.   And is not that a strange shape for the soul

---

166.   . . . night 92.
169.   . . . queen . . . . 92.
173.   . . . everything Blind . . . . 92.
180.   . . . for a soul 92.

181. Of a great fighting-man?

Blind Man. Your shoulder is there,
182. This is your neck. Ah! Ah! Are you ready, Cuchulain!

183. *Cuchulain.* I say it is about to sing.

[*The stage darkens.*

Blind Man. Ah! Ah!
[*Music of pipe and drum, the curtain falls. The music ceases as the curtain rises upon a bare stage. There is nobody upon the stage except a woman with a crow's head. She is the Morrigu. She stands towards the back. She holds a black parallelogram, the size of a man's head. There are six other parallelograms near the backcloth.*

184. *The Morrigu.* The dead can hear me, and to the dead I speak.
185. This head is great Cuchulain's, those other six
186. Gave him six mortal wounds. This man came first;
187. Youth lingered though the years ran on, that season
188. A woman loves the best. Maeve's latest lover,
189. This man, had given him the second wound,
190. He had possessed her once; these were her sons,
191. Two valiant men that gave the third and fourth:
192. These other men were men of no account,
193. They saw that he was weakening and crept in;
194. One gave him the sixth wound and one the fifth;
195. Conall avenged him. I arranged the dance.

---

181. . . . fighting man? . . . , 92.
182. . . . ready Cuchulain? 92 ; . . . , Cuchulain? 94.
183. . . . say, it . . . ! 92.
Directions after 183. [. . . *back cloth.*] 92 ; [. . . *back-cloth.*] 94.
184. . . . me and . . . . 92.
186. . . . wounds; this . . . first, 92.
191. . . . fourth; 92, 94.
193. . . . in 92.
195. . . . him, I . . . . 94A.

[*Emer enters. The Morrigu places the head of Cuchulain upon the ground and goes out. Emer runs in and begins to dance. She so moves that she seems to rage against the heads of those that had wounded Cuchulain, perhaps makes movements as though to strike them, going three times round the circle of the heads. She then moves towards the head of Cuchulain; it may, if need be, be raised above the others on a pedestal. She moves as if in adoration or triumph. She is about to prostrate herself before it, perhaps does so, then rises, looking up as if listening; she seems to hesitate between the head and what she hears. Then she stands motionless. There is silence, and in the silence a few faint bird notes. The stage darkens slowly. Then comes loud music, but now it is quite different. It is the music of some Irish Fair of our day. The stage brightens. Emer and the head are gone. . . . There is no one there but the three musicians. They are in ragged street-singers' clothes; two of them begin to pipe and drum. They cease. The Street-Singer begins to sing.*]

196.	*Singer.*	The harlot sang to the beggar-man.
197.		I meet them face to face,
198.		Conall, Cuchulain, Usna's boys,
199.		All that most ancient race;
200.		Maeve had three in an hour, they say.
201.		I adore those clever eyes,
202.		Those muscular bodies, but can get
203.		No grip upon their thighs.
204.		I meet those long pale faces,
205.		Hear their great horses, then
206.		Recall what centuries have passed
207.		Since they were living men.
208.		That there are still some living
209.		That do my limbs unclothe,
210.		But that the flesh my flesh has gripped
211.		I both adore and loathe.

Directions after 195. [. . . *Cuchulain, it . . . be, raised . . . or in triumph. . . . it. Perhaps . . . so. Then . . . as though listening; . . . silence and . . . gone. There is none there . . . street singers' clothing; two . . . to play the pipe . . . street singer . . . .*] **92**; [. . . *silence and . . . street-singer . . . .*] **94E**; [. . . *does so. Then . . . silence and . . . street-singer . . . .*] **94A**.

196.	. . . beggarman.
197.	. . . face **92**.
200.	. . . hour they . . . . **92**.
204.	. . . faces **92**.

[Pipe and drum music.

212.   Are those things that men adore and loathe
213.   Their sole reality?
214.   What stood in the Post Office
215.   With Pearse and Connolly?
216.   What comes out of the mountain
217.   Where men first shed their blood?
218.   Who thought Cuchulain till it seemed
219.   He stood where they had stood?

220.   No body like his body
221.   Has modern woman borne,
222.   But an old man looking on life
223.   Imagines it in scorn.
224.   A statue's there to mark the place,
225.   By Oliver Sheppard done.
226.   So ends the tale that the harlot
227.   Sang to the beggar-man.

[Music from pipe and drum.

THE END

217. . . . blood, **92, 94E.**
221. . . . borne. **92.**
222. . . . looking back on . . . **92, 94.**
224. . . . place
225. . . . done, **92.**
227. . . . beggarman. **92.**

WHERE THERE IS NOTHING

Paul Ruttledge, a Country Gentleman.
Thomas Ruttledge, his Brother.
Mrs. Thomas Ruttledge.
Mr. Dowler,
Mr. Algie,
Colonel Lawley, } Magistrates.
Mr. Joyce,
Mr. Green, a Stipendiary Magistrate.
Sabina Silver,
Molly the Scold,
Charlie Ward,
Paddy Cockfight, } Tinkers.
Tommy the Song,
Johneen, etc.
Father Jerome,
Father Aloysius,
Father Colman, } Friars.
Father Bartley,
Other Friars, and a crowd of countrymen.

ACT I.

Scene: *A lawn with croquet hoops, garden chairs and tables. Door into house at left. Gate through hedge at back. The hedge is clipped into shapes of farmyard fowl. Paul Ruttledge is clipping at the hedge in front. A table with toys on it.*

Printings   9, 10, 10a, 11.[1]

Date   October 30, 1902 9.[2]

Dramatis Personae   ...Brother. / Mr. Dowler, ... Ward, / Jimmy Head, / Paddy ... / Other Friars. / Mrs. Thomas Ruttledge. 9; Dramatis Personae / Paul ... *Brother*. / Mr. Dowler ... *Magistrate*. / Mrs. Thomas Ruttledge. / Sabina ... Scold, &c. (Scold 10a) / Charlie Ward / Jimmy Head / Paddy ... Johneen, &c. / Brother Jerome / Brother Aloysius / Brother Colman / Brother Bartley / Other (Bartley / Superior / Other 10a) Friars / [these priests designated *Franciscan Friars*] / A Mob. 10, 10a.

[1] The basic text is 11E.
[2] See Wade, *op. cit.*, item 41.

1. *Thomas Ruttledge.* [*Coming out on steps.*] Paul, are you
2.   coming in to lunch?

3. *Paul Ruttledge.* No; you can entertain these people
4.   very well. They are your friends: you understand
5.   them.

6. *Thomas Ruttledge.* You might as well come in. You have
7.   been clipping at that old hedge long enough.

8. *Paul Ruttledge.* You needn't worry about me. I should
9.   be bored if I went in, and I don't want to be bored
10.   more than is necessary.

11. *Thomas Ruttledge.* What is that creature you are clip-
12.   ping at now? I can't make it out.

13. *Paul Ruttledge.* Oh, it is a Cochin China fowl, an
14.   image of some of our neighbours, like the others.

15. *Thomas Ruttledge.* I don't see any likeness to anyone.

16. *Paul Ruttledge.* Oh, yes there is, if you could see
17.   their minds instead of their bodies. That comb now—

STAGE DIRECTIONS. Scene—*A . . . through clipped hedge to path at back. Paul is sitting on a garden chair. A table . . . .* 9;
    Scene.—*A . . . hoops, garden chairs,* (*hoops. Garden chairs* 10a) *and . . . left gate* (*left. Gate* 10a) *through clipped hedge to path at back. Paul sitting on a garden chair. A table . . . .* 10, 10a.

TEXT Title . . . Nothing: / A Play in Five Acts by W. B. Yeats. / (All rights reserved by the Author) 9.

1. . . . . Paul, won't you
2. come in . . . ? 9¹-10a².
4. . . . : you asked 9; . . . friends; you asked 10, 10a.
6. . . . in; I don't
7. like to think you are sitting out here.
8. . . . about that. I . . . 9-10a.
    Directions after 10. [*Paul yawns, takes up a cup and ball from table, and sways it. Mrs. Ruttledge* (*Ruttledge,* 10a) *comes out on steps.*] 9-10a.
11-17. [lacking] 9-10a.

  ¹ Wherever possible the basic line-length in the variants is from 9.
  ² After line 1, 'Ruttledge' is omitted from Thomas Ruttledge and Paul Ruttledge in names of speakers. 9-10a.

18. *Mrs. Ruttledge.* [*Coming out on steps.*] Thomas, are
19.   you coming in?

20. *Thomas Ruttledge.* Yes, I'm coming; but Paul won't
21.   come.
      [*Thomas Ruttledge goes out.*

22. *Mrs. Ruttledge.* Oh! this is nonsense, Paul; you must
23.   come. All these men will think it so strange if you
24.   don't. It is nonsense to think you will be bored. Mr.
25.   Green is talking in the most interesting way.

26. *Paul Ruttledge.* Oh! I know Green's conversation very
27.   well.

28. *Mrs. Ruttledge.* And Mr. Joyce, your old guardian.
29.   Thomas says he was always so welcome in your father's
30.   time, he will think it so queer.

31. *Paul Ruttledge.* Oh! I know all their virtues. There's
32.   Dowler, who puts away thousands a year in Consols,
33.   and Algie, who tells everybody all about it. Have I
34.   forgotten anybody? Oh, yes! Colonel Lawley, who used
35.   to lift me up by the ears, when I was a child, to see
36.   Africa. No, Georgina, I know all their virtues, but
37.   I'm not coming in.

38. *Mrs. Ruttledge.* I can't imagine why you won't come in
39.   and be sociable.

---

18.   *Mrs. Ruttledge.* Thomas, . . . **9-10a.**
20.   . . . coming, but . . . **10, 10a.**
     Directions after 21. [*Exit Thomas.*] **9-10a.**
22.   Oh, this . . .
23.   . . . it is so . . . **10, 10a.**
26.   Oh, I . . . **10, 10a.**
28.   . . . Joyce— **10, 10a.**
30.   time. He . . . .
31.   Oh, I . . .
32.   Dowler, (Dowler **10a**) who . . . away three thousand a . . . consols,
    9-10a.
32a. and boasts of the appetites of his young pheasants;
33.   . . . , who eats them—I mean, shoots them—when they are fat. Have
    . . . **10, 10a.**
34.   . . . ? Oh! yes; Colonel . . . **9** ; . . . , yes, Colonel . . . **10, 10a.**
35.   . . . ears when . . . **9, 10.**
38.   . . . come **10, 10a.**

40. *Paul Ruttledge.* You see I can't. I have something to
41.   do here. I have to finish this comb. You see it is a
42.   beautiful comb; but the wings are very short. The
43.   poor creature can't fly.

44. *Mrs. Ruttledge.* But can't you finish that after lunch?

45. *Paul Ruttledge.* No, I have sworn.

46. *Mrs. Ruttledge.* Well, I am sorry. You are always
47.   doing uncomfortable things. I must go in to the
48.   others. I wish you would have come.   *[She goes in.*

    Jerome. [*Who has come to gate as she disappears.*]
49.   Paul, you there! that is lucky. I was just going to
50.   ask for you.

    Paul Ruttledge. [*Flinging clipper away, and jumping*
51.   *up.*] Oh, Father Jerome, I am delighted to see you. I
52.   haven't seen you for ever so long. Come and have a
53.   talk; or will you have some lunch?

---

40.   *Paul* [*beginning to throw ball and catch it*]. You . . . can't; I . . .
41.   . . . here.
41a.   *Mrs. Ruttledge.* What have you to do?
41b.   *Paul.* I have to catch this ball twenty times without missing.
41c.   I have set myself that task. I have sworn not to leave this
41d.   chair till I have done it. See, (See,—**10, 10a**) four, five—Ah! (five,—
      ah, **10, 10a**) I missed the
41e.   sixth. Now, (Now **10, 10a**) I must begin it all over again.
41f.   *Mrs. Ruttledge.* Well, I don't know what you are at: (at. **10, 10a**) I
41g.   don't know why you should want to catch that ball.
41h.   *Paul.* It is because, (because **10, 10a**) when I have caught it twenty
      times in
41i.   the cup, (cup **10, 10a**) I may learn to catch it on the small end. Ask
      Green
41j.   if he can catch it on the small end.
41k.   *Mrs. Ruttledge.* I don't understand you in the least. I **9-10a**.
42-47.   [lacking] **9-10a**.
48.   must go in now— (now; **10**; now. **10a**) I . . . .
49.   *Father Jerome*[1] [*who* . . .]. . . . there! that (there? That **10, 10a**) . . .
      lucky; I . . . **9-10a**.
51.   *Paul* [*flinging cup and ball away,* . . .] Oh! (Oh, **10, 10a**) Brother Jerome
      . . . **9-10a**.
53.   talk,—or . . .? **10, 10a**.

[1] The friars are usually 'Father' in **9**; 'Brother' in **10** and **10a**.

54. *Jerome.* No, thank you; I will stay a minute, but I
55. won't go in.

56. *Paul Ruttledge.* That is just as well, for you would be
57. bored to death. There has been a meeting of magis-
58. trates in the village, and my brother has brought
59. them all in to lunch.

60. *Jerome.* I am collecting for the Monastery, and my
61. donkey has gone lame; I have had to put it up in the
62. village. I thought you might be able to lend me one
63. to go on with.

64. *Paul Ruttledge.* Of course, I'm delighted to lend you
65. that or anything else. I'll go round to the yard with
66. you and order it. But sit down here first. What have
67. you been doing all this time?

68. *Jerome.* Oh, we have been very busy. You know we are
69. going to put up new buildings.

70. *Paul Ruttledge.* [*Absent-mindedly.*] No, I didn't know
71. that.

72. *Jerome.* Yes, our school is increasing so much we are
73. getting a grant for technical instruction. Some of
74. the Fathers are learning handicrafts. Father Aloysius
75. is going to study industries in France; but we are
76. all busy. We are changing with the times, we are be-
77. ginning to do useful things.

78. *Paul Ruttledge.* Useful things. I wonder what you have
79. begun to call useful things. Do you see those marks
80. over there on the grass?

---

60. ... monastery, ... **10a, 11A.**
64. ... course; I'm ... **10, 10a.**
68. Oh! we ... **9.**
  Directions in 70. [*absently*]. **9-10a.**
74. the brothers are ... handicrafts. Brother Aloysius **10, 10a.**
75. ... France. **9-10a.**
76. *Paul.* Building building, you (building! You **10, 10a**) are just like the
  rest; there (rest. There **10a**) is
77. too much building. **9-10a.**
78-101. [lacking] **9-10a.**

81. *Jerome.* What marks?

82. *Paul Ruttledge.* Those marks over there, those little
83.   marks of scratching.

Jerome. [*Going over to the place Paul Ruttledge has*
84.   *pointed out.*] I don't see anything.

85. *Paul Ruttledge.* You are getting blind, Jerome. Can't
86.   you see that the poultry have been scratching there?

87. *Jerome.* No, the grass is perfectly smooth.

88. *Paul Ruttledge.* Well, the marks are there, whether
89.   you see them or not; for Mr. Green and Mr. Dowler
90.   and Mr. Algie and the rest of them run out of their
91.   houses when nobody is looking, in their real shapes,
92.   shapes like those on my hedge. And then they begin
93.   to scratch, they scratch all together, they don't
94.   dig but they scratch, and all the time their mouths
95.   keep going like that.
    [*He holds out his hand and opens and shuts his fingers like a bird's bill.*

96. *Jerome.* Oh, Paul, you are making fun of me.

97. *Paul Ruttledge.* Of course I am only talking in para-
98.   bles. I think all the people I meet are like farm-
99.   yard creatures, they have forgotten their freedom,
100.   their human bodies are a disguise, a pretence they
101.   keep up to deceive one another.

102. *Jerome.* [*Sitting down.*] What is wrong with you?

103. *Paul Ruttledge.* Oh, nothing of course. You see how
104.   happy I am. I have a good house and a good property,
105.   and my brother and his charming wife have come to
106.   look after me. You see the toys of their children
107.   here and everywhere. What should be wrong with me?

---

103.   Oh! nothing . . . **9** ; . . . , nothing, of . . . **10, 10a.**
104.   . . . am: (am; **10, 10a**) I . . . , **9-10a.**
106.   . . . me; you (me. You **10, 10a**) . . . their charming children **9-10a.**
107a. *Father Jerome.* Perhaps you want change? (change. **10, 10a**).
107b. *Paul.* There is nothing wrong with me that change could
107c. put right (right, **10, 10a**) unless I could get away from everybody.
    9-10a.

108. *Jerome.* I know you too well not to see that there is
109.   something wrong with you.

110. *Paul Ruttledge.* There is nothing except that I have
111.   been thinking a good deal lately.

112. *Jerome.* Perhaps your old dreams or visions or whatever
113.   they were have come back. They always made you rest-
114.   less. You ought to see more of your neighbours.

115. *Paul Ruttledge.* There's nothing interesting but human
116.   nature, and that's in the single soul, but these
117.   neighbours of mine they think in flocks and roosts.

118. *Jerome.* You are too hard on them. They are busy men,
119.   they hav'n't much time for thought, I daresay.

120. *Paul Ruttledge.* That's what I complain of. When I hear
121.   these people talking I always hear some organized or
122.   vested interest chirp or quack, as it does in the
123.   newspapers. Algie chirps. Even you, Jerome, though
124.   I have not found your armorial beast, are getting a
125.   little monastic; when I have found it I will put it

107d. *Father Jerome.* But are you not interested in your friends
107e. and neighbours?
107f. *Paul.* I don't see anything interesting about them.
107g. *Father Jerome.* I have always heard that Mr. Green is a
107h. very well read (well-read **10a**) man. He took a good degree. **9-10a.**
108-114.   [lacking] **9-10a.**
  116. nature, but (and **10, 10a**) that is in . . . soul. These (There's **10,
      10a**) **9-10a.**
  117. people [*with a wave of his hand towards the house*] think **9, 10a**; people
      [*with a wave of his hand towards the house*] **10.**
117a. like newspapers, (newspapers— **10, 10a**) they think in packs.
118. . . . hard to please. They . . . men; **9-10a.**
119. . . . haven't time for much thought, ... **9-10a** ; . . . haven't. . . . **11A.**
120. But that is just it. When . . . **9-10a.**
121. . . . organised and **9** ; . . . talking, I . . . organised and **10, 10a.**
122. . . . interest giving tongue,
123. and that is not human life. Even you, Brother Jerome,
124. are . . .
125. . . . monastic.
125a. *Father Jerome.* I have often thought you would come to the
125b. Monastery (monastery **10a**) yourself in the end. You were the most
      pious
125c. of us all at school. You would be happy in a monastery. Some-
      9-10a.

126. among others. There is a place for it there, but
127. the worst of it is that it will take so long getting
128. nice and green.

129. *Jerome.* I don't know what creature you could make for
130. me.

131. *Paul Ruttledge.* I am not sure yet; I think it might
132. be a pigeon, something cooing and gentle, and always
133. coming home to the dovecot; not to the wild woods
134. but to the dovecot.

135. *Jerome.* I wonder what creature you yourself are like.

136. *Paul Ruttledge.* I daresay I am like some creature or
137. other, for very few of us are altogether men; but if
138. I am, I would like to be one of the wild sort. You
139. are right about my dreams. They have been coming
140. back lately. Do you remember those strange ones I
141. had at college?

142. *Jerome.* Those visions of pulling something down?

143. *Paul Ruttledge.* Yes, they have come back to me lately.
144. Sometimes I dream I am pulling down my own house, and
145. sometimes it is the whole world that I am pulling
146. down. [*Standing up.*] I would like to have great iron
147. claws, and to put them about the pillars, and to pull
148. and pull till everything fell into pieces.

149. *Jerome.* I don't see what good that would do you.

150. *Paul Ruttledge.* Oh, yes it would. When everything was

125d. thing is always happening there.
125e. *Paul.* I have no joy in anything.
125f. *Father Jerome.* But what do you think of doing? **9-10a.**
126-142. [lacking] **9-10a.**
143. *Paul.* It is not religion I want. I'm not even sure that I am
144. a Christian. I don't love anything. I want to pull down all
145. this—what do you call it— (it?— **10**; it . . . [T] **10a**) the thing,
   the building of the world
146. —to (world. To **10**) put a crowbar under the gates and a grappling-
   iron over
147. the towers and uproot it all.
148. [lacking] **9-10a.**
149. . . . see that that would . . . you any particular good.
150. Oh! (Oh, **10**) yes, it . . . . When the stones are out of the **9-10a.**

151.   pulled down we would have more room to get drunk in,
152.   to drink contentedly out of the cup of life, out of
153.   the drunken cup of life.

154. *Jerome.* That is a terribly wild thought. I hope you
155.   don't believe all you say.

156. *Paul Ruttledge.* Perhaps not. I only know that I want
157.   to upset everything about me. Have you not noticed
158.   that it is a complaint many of us have in this coun-
159.   try? and whether it comes from love or hate I don't
160.   know, they are so mixed together here.

161. *Jerome.* I wish you would come and talk to our Supe-
162.   rior. He has a perfect gift for giving advice.

163. *Paul Ruttledge.* Well, we'll go to the yard now.

[*He gets up.*

164. *Jerome.* I have often thought you would come to the

---

151.   way there will be more . . . in— (in,— **10, 10a**) not with wine,
152.   for that has never amused me, though it may suit other people
153.   —I (people. I **10, 10a**) want to get drunk with life, (life; **10, 10a**)
        and I don't care whether it is
153a.   good or bad so long as it is life. **9-10a.**
155.   don't mean all . . . .
156.   . . . I hate
157.   everything . . . noticed,
158.   Brother Jerome, that is . . .
159.   try?
160.   [lacking] **9-10a.**
162.   rior (rior, **10, 10a**) some day; he . . . . **9-10a.**
163.   . . . yard (yard, **10**) now. [*Puts his hand on*
163a.   *Father Jerome's shoulder and they go up garden.*] How well
163b.   you and I used to think, Jerome, when we were students.
163c.   There is so much fire in the soul, (soul,— **10, 10a**) in your's, in mine,
        in the soul
163d.   of any old apple-woman in the market (market,— **10, 10a**) that if
        one could get it
163e.   out it would consume the world.   [*Turning towards the house.*]
163f.   Do you think anybody could change those people?
163g.   *Father Jerome.* No, Paul.
163h.   *Paul.* You are right. They have never had a dangerous
163i.   thought, never a dangerous thought. [*Exeunt. (They go out.* **10, 10a**)]
        9-10a.
164-171.   [lacking] **9-10a.**

165. Monastery yourself in the end. You were so much the
166. most pious of us all at school. You would be happy
167. in a Monastery. Something is always happening there.

Paul Ruttledge. [*As they go up the garden.*]
168. I daresay, I daresay; but I am not even sure that I am
169. a Christian.

170. *Jerome.* Well, anyway, I wish that you would come and
171. talk to our Superior. [*They go out.*

Charlie Ward and Boy enter by the path beyond the hedge and stand at gate.

172. *Charle Ward.* No use going up there, Johneen, it's
173. too grand a place, it's a dog they might let loose
174. on us. But I'll tell you what, just slip round to
175. the back door and ask do they want any cans mended.

176. *Johneen.* Let you take the rabbit then we're after
177. taking out of the snare. I can't bring it round with
178. me.

179. *Charlie Ward.* Faith, you can't. They think as bad of
180. us taking a rabbit that was fed and minded by God as
181. if it was of their own rearing; give it here to me.
182. It's hardly it will go in my pocket, it's as big as

---

165. monastery . . . 11A.
167. . . . monastery. . . . . 11A.
Directions before 172. [. . . *enter along the* . . . .] 10, 10a.
172. . . . , Johneen; it's
173. . . . place; it's . . . 10, 10a.
174. . . . . But, I'll . . . 9.
176. . . . the duck, then. 9 ; . . . the duck, then; 10, 10a.
177. I . . . it along with 9-10a.
179. . . . can't. The (can't; the 10, 10a) cook might know it
180. was one of her own feeding. I wonder is she the girl I put the
181. comether on (on, 10, 10a) and she at the corner of the road yesterday. (yesterday? 10, 10a) If
181a. she is, I (I'll 10, 10a) engage she won't let me go home empty if I get as far 9-10a.
182. as her. This divil of a duck won't fit in . . . 9-10a.

183.   a hare. It's next my skin I'll have to put it, or it

184.   might be noticed on me.   [*Boy goes out.*
      [*Charlie Ward is struggling to put rabbit inside his coat when Paul Ruttledge comes back.*

185. *Paul Ruttledge.* Is there anything I can do for you?

186.   Do you want to come in?

187. *Charlie Ward.* I'm a tinker by trade, your honour. I

188.   wonder is there e'er a tin can the maids in the house

189.   might want mended or any chairs to be bottomed?

190. *Paul Ruttledge.* A tinker; where do you live?

191. *Charlie Ward.* Faith, I don't stop long in any place.

192.   I go about like the crows; picking up my way of

193.   living like themselves.

194. *Paul Ruttledge.* [*Opening gate.*] Come inside here.

195.   [*Charlie Ward hesitates.*] Come in, you are welcome.
      [*Puts his hand on his shoulder. Charlie Ward tries to close his shirt over rabbit.*

196. *Paul Ruttledge.* Ah, you have a rabbit there. The

197.   keeper told me he had come across some snares in my

198.   woods.

199. *Charlie Ward.* If he did, sir, it was no snare of mine

200.   he found. This is a rabbit I bought in the town of

---

183.   a goose. It's . . . it (it, **10**) or . . . **9-10a.**
      Directions in 184.   [*Boy goes.*] **9.**
      Directions after 184.   [. . . *put duck inside* . . . .] **9-10a.**

188.   . . . 'ere . . .

189.   . . . mended, or . . . ? **10, 10a.**

192.   I'm everywhere, like the birds; picking . . . **10, 10a.**

194.   . . . inside, here.

195.   . . . in; you . . . . **10, 10a.**
      Directions after 195.   [. . . *over duck.*] **9-10a.**

196.   Ah! you . . . duck. I (Ah, you have something there; I **10, 10a**) think I recognise one of my own

197.   Aylesburys. **9-10a.**

198.   [lacking] **9.**

199.   Not at all, sir, it was a little boy (the divil **9**; Not at all, sir; it was a little boy—the divil **10, 10a.**

200.   fly away with him) gave it to me yesterday in Derrykeel, and **9**; fly away with him!—gave it to me yesterday in Ballybuie, and **10, 10a.**

201. Garreen early this morning. Sixpence I was made give
202. for it, and to mend a tin can along with that.

203. *Paul Ruttledge.* [*Touching rabbit.*] It's warm still,
204. however. But the day is hot. Never mind; you are
205. quite welcome to it. I daresay you will have a cheery
206. meal of it by the roadside; my dinners are often
207. tiresome enough. I often wish I could change—look
208. here, will you change clothes with me?

209. *Charlie Ward.* Faith, I'd swap soon enough if you
210. weren't humbugging me. It's I that would look well
211. with that suit on me! The peelers would all be touch-
212. ing their caps to me. You'd see them running out for
213. me to sign summonses for them.

214. *Paul Ruttledge.* But I am not humbugging. I am in
215. earnest.

216. *Charlie Ward.* In earnest! Then when I go back I'll
217. commit Paddy Cockfight to prison for hitting me
218. yesterday.

219. *Paul Ruttledge.* You don't believe me, but I will ex-
220. plain. I'm dead sick of this life; I want to get
221. away; I want to escape—as you say, to pick up my
222. living like the crows for a while.

223. *Charlie Ward.* To make your escape. Oh! that's dif-
224. ferent. [*Coming closer.*] But what is it you did? You

---

201. that's (that **10**) fifteen miles away. The old grandmother sent it to me
202. for mending two tin cans and a kettle. I'm carrying it ever since.
      9-10a.
203. [lacking] **9.**
204. *Paul.* But even if it is one of my own ducks that had flown **9-10a.**
205. to Derrykeel (Ballybuie, **10, 10a**) you are quite . . . it.
206. [lacking] **9-10a.**
207. I often . . . **9**; I often . . . change—Look **10, 10a.**
208. here! will . . . ? **10, 10a.**
209. . . . swop . . . **10, 10a.**
210. . . . me. Faith, it's . . . **9-10a.**
217. commit Tommy the Song to . . . for wanting to box me **9-10a.**
220. . . . life. I . . . **10a.**
221. . . . escape—to . . . **9**; away, (away. **10a**) I . . . escape— **10, 10a.**
222. [lacking]
223. . . . escape! Oh, that's . . . **10, 10a.**

225. don't look like one that would be in trouble. But
226. sometimes a gentleman gets a bit wild when he has a
227. drop taken.

228. *Paul Ruttledge.* Well, never mind. I will explain bet-
229. ter while we are changing. Come over here to the
230. potting shed. Make haste, those magistrates will be
231. coming out.

232. *Charlie Ward.* The magistrates! Are they after you?
233. Hurry on, then! Faith, they won't know you with this
234. coat. [*Looking at his rags.*] It's a pity I didn't
235. put on my old one coming out this morning.
       [*They go out through the garden. Thomas Ruttledge comes down
       steps from house with Colonel Lawley and Mr. Green.*

236. *Mr. Green.* Yes, they have made me President of the
237. County Horticultural Society. My speech was quite a
238. success; it was punctuated with applause. I said I
239. looked upon the appointment not as a tribute to my
240. own merits, but to their public spirit and to the
241. Society, which I assured them had come to stay.

242. *Colonel Lawley.* What has become of Paul and Father
243. Jerome? I thought I heard their voices out here, and
244. now they are conspicuous by their absence.

245. *Thomas Ruttledge.* He seems to have no friend he cares
246. for but that Father Jerome.

247. *Mr. Green.* I wish he would come more into touch with
248. his fellows.

249. *Colonel Lawley.* What a pity he didn't go into the
250. army. I wish he would join the militia. Every man

---

230. . . . , those blessed magistrates are **9-10a.**
      Directions in 234. [. . . *at its rags.*] **9.**
234. coat [*looking at its rags.*] . . . **10** ; . . . did'nt **11A.**
      Directions after 235. [. . . *go up garden and exeunt. Thomas* . . . .]
      9-10a.
236. Yes; they . . . **10, 10a.**
239. . . . appointment, not . . .
240. . . . merits, but as a token of their well known (well-known **10a**)
      public spirit. **10, 10a.**
241. society, ... **9**; [lacking] **10, 10a.**
250. army! I . . . **10.**

251.   should try to find some useful sphere of employment.

252.   *Mr. Green.* Thomas, your brother will never come to see
253.   me, though I often ask him. He would find the best
254.   people—people worth meeting—at my house. I wonder
255.   if he would join the Horticultural Society? I know I
256.   voice the sentiments of all the members in saying
257.   this. I spoke to a number of them at the function the
258.   other day.

259.   *Thomas Ruttledge.* I wish he would join something.
260.   Joyce wants him to join the Masonic Lodge. It is not
261.   a right life for him to keep hanging about the place
262.   and doing nothing.

263.   *Mr. Green.* He won't even come and sit on the Bench.
264.   It's not fair to leave so much of the work to me. I
265.   ought to get all the support possible from local men.
      [Mrs. Ruttledge comes down steps with Mr. Dowler, Mr. Algie,
      and Mr. Joyce. She is walking in front.

266.   *Mrs. Ruttledge.* [*To Thomas Ruttledge.*] Oh! Thomas,
267.   isn't it too bad, Paul has lent the donkey to that
268.   friar. I wanted Mr. Joyce to see the children in
269.   their panniers. Do speak to him about it.

270.   *Thomas Ruttledge.* Well, the donkey belongs to him,
271.   and for the matter of that so does the house and the
272.   place. It would be rather hard on him not to be able
273.   to use things as he likes.

274.   *Mr. Algie.* What a pleasure it must be to Paul to have
275.   you and the little ones living here. He certainly
276.   owes you a debt of gratitude. Man was not born to

---

252.   Your ... **10, 10a.**
253.   me though ... **9;** ... find **10, 10a.**
254.   people worth meeting, the best people, at ... **10, 10a.**
      Directions after 265. [..., *Mr. Algie and* ....] **11A.**
266.   *Mrs. Ruttledge.* [*Comes down steps with Mr. Joyce, Mr. Dowler, and Mr.*
      Algie. She ... *front. To Thomas.*] Oh, Thomas,
267.   ... bad? Paul ... **10, 10a.**
271.   and, for ... that, so ... **10, 10a.**
275.   ... here!
276.   Man ... **10.**

277.   live alone.

278.   *Mrs. Ruttledge.* Well, I think we have done him good.
279.   He hasn't done anything for years, except mope about
280.   the house and cut the bushes into those absurd shapes,
281.   and now we are trying to make him live more like
282.   other people.

283.   *Colonel Lawley.* He was always inclined to be a bit of
284.   a faddist.

285.   *Mrs. Ruttledge.* [*To Mr. Algie.*] Do let me give you a
286.   lesson in croquet. I have learned all the new rules.
287.   [*To Mr. Joyce.*] Please bring me that basket of balls.
288.   [*To Colonel Lawley.*] Will you bring me the mallets?
289.   Yes, I am afraid he is a faddist. We have done our
290.   best for him, but he ought to be more with men.

291.   *Mr. Algie.* Yes, Mr. Dowler was just saying he ought
292.   to try and be made a director of the new railway.

293.   *Colonel Lawley.* The militia—the militia.

294.   *Mr. Joyce.* It's a great help to a man to belong to a
295.   Masonic Lodge.

296.   *Mr. Green.* The Horticultural Society is in want of
297.   new members.

298.   *Mrs. Ruttledge.* Well, I wish he would join something.

> *Enter Paul Ruttledge in tinker's clothes, carrying a rabbit in his hand. Charlie Ward follows in Paul's clothes. All stand aghast.*

---

279.   He shut himself up so much before we came,
280.   [lacking] **9–10a**.
288.   . . . mallets. **9** ; . . . mallets?— **10, 10a**.
288a.   they are just inside the door. (door.— **10a**) **10, 10a**.
289.   *Mrs. Ruttledge.* Yes, . . . **10**.
292.   . . . Director . . . . **10**.
293.   . . . Militia! the Militia! **10** ; . . . militia, the . . . . **10a**.
        Directions after 298. [. . . , *carrying duck in . . . hand, Charlie Ward following him in his clothes.* . . . .] **9** ; [. . . , *carrying duck in . . . follows (following **10a**) him in his clothes.* . . . .] **10, 10a**.

299. *Mr. Joyce.* Good God!

    [*Drops basket. Colonel Lawley, who has mallets in his hand, at sight of Paul Ruttledge drops them, and stands still.*

300. *Mrs. Ruttledge.* Paul! are you out of your mind?

301. *Thomas Ruttledge.* For goodness sake, Paul, don't make
302.   such a fool of yourself.

303. *Mrs. Ruttledge.* What on earth has happened, and who
304.   on earth is that man?

    Paul Ruttledge. [*Opens gate for tinker. To Charlie*
305.   *Ward.*] Wait for me, my friend, down there by the
306.   cross-road.   [*Charlie Ward goes out.*

307. *Mr. Green.* Has he stolen your clothes?

308. *Paul Ruttledge.* Oh! it's all right; I have changed
309.   clothes with him. I am going to join the tinkers.

310. *All.* To join the tinkers!

311. *Paul Ruttledge.* Life is getting too monotonous; I
312.   would give it a little variety. [*To Mr. Green.*] As
313.   you would say, it has been running in grooves.

314. *Mr. Joyce.* [*To Mrs. Ruttledge.*] This is only his hum-
315.   bugging talk; he never believes what he says.

    [*Paul Ruttledge goes towards the steps.*

316. *Mrs. Ruttledge.* Surely you are not going into the

Directions after 299. [. . . *Lawley comes out of door with mallets; at*
(*mallets. At* 10a) . . . *them and* . . . .] 10, 10a.
300. . . . mind! 10, 10a.
302. . . . yourself!
303. . . . happened and . . . 10, 10a.
306. crossroad. [. . . .] 10, 10a.
308. Oh, it's . . . right. I . . . 10, 10a.
311. . . . monotonous. As
312. you would say, Mr. Green, it has been running in
313. grooves. I would give it a little variety.
314. . . . only hum-
315. . . . talk. He . . . . 10, 10a.

317.   house with those clothes?

318. *Paul Ruttledge.* You are quite right. Thomas will go
319.   in for me. [*To Thomas Ruttledge.*] Just go to my
320.   study, will you, and bring me my despatch-box; I want
321.   something from it before I go.

322. *Thomas Ruttledge.* Where are you going to? I wish you
323.   would tell me what you are at.

324. *Paul Ruttledge.* The despatch-box is on the top of the
325.   bureau.   [*Thomas Ruttledge goes out.*

326. *Mr. Joyce.* What does all this mean?

327. *Paul Ruttledge.* I will explain. [*Sits down on the edge*
328.   *of iron table.*] Did you never wish to be a witch, and
329.   to ride through the air on a white horse?

330. *Mr. Joyce.* I can't say I ever did.

331. *Paul Ruttledge.* Never? Only think of it—to ride in
332.   the darkness under the stars, to make one's horse
333.   leap from cloud to cloud, to watch the sea glittering
334.   under one's feet and the mountain tops going by.

335. *Colonel Lawley.* But what has this to do with the
336.   tinkers?

337. *Paul Ruttledge.* As I cannot find a broomstick that
338.   will turn itself into a white horse, I am going to
339.   turn tinker.

340. *Mr. Dowler.* I suppose you have some picturesque idea
341.   about these people, but I assure you, you are quite
342.   wrong. They are nothing but poachers.

343. *Mr. Algie.* They are nothing but thieves.

344. *Mr. Joyce.* They are the worst class in the country.

---

317.   . . . clothes! **10.**
320.   . . . despatch-box; I . . . **10, 10a.**
321.   . . . go? **9.**
      Directions in 325.   [*Exit Thomas.*] **9**; [*Thomas goes.*] **10, 10a.**
332.   . . . darkness, under . . . **10, 10a.**
334.   . . . feet, and . . . by— **10, 10a.**
341.   . . . people; but . . . **10, 10a.**

345. *Paul Ruttledge.* Oh, I know that; they are quite law-
346. less. That is what attracts me to them. I am going to
347. be irresponsible.

348. *Mr. Green.* One cannot escape from responsibility by
349. joining a set of vagabonds.

350. *Paul Ruttledge.* Vagabonds—that is it. I want to be a
351. vagabond, a wanderer. As I can't leap from cloud to
352. cloud I want to wander from road to road. That little
353. path there by the clipped edge goes up to the high-
354. road. I want to go up that path and to walk along the
355. highroad, and so on and on and on, and to know all
356. kinds of people. Did you ever think that the roads
357. are the only things that are endless; that one can
358. walk on and on and on, and never be stopped by a
359. gate or a wall? They are the serpent of eternity.
360. I wonder they have never been worshipped. What are
361. the stars beside them? They never meet one another.
362. The roads are the only things that are infinite.
363. They are all endless.

364. *Mrs. Ruttledge.* But they must stop when they come to
365. the sea?

366. *Paul Ruttledge.* Ah! you are always so wise.

367. *Mr. Joyce.* Stop talking nonsense, Paul, and throw
368. away those filthy things.

369. *Paul Ruttledge.* That would be setting cleanliness be-
370. fore godliness. I have begun the regeneration of my

---

345. Oh! I . . . **9** ; . . . that. They . . . **10, 10a.**
351. . . . I cannot leap . . . **10, 10a.**
352. . . . to hobble from . . . **9** ; cloud, I . . . **10, 10a.**
353. . . . clipped hedge goes . . . **11A.**
355. . . . so on, and . . . **9.**
357. . . . thing that is endless; . . . **10a.**
358. walk on and on, and never . . .
359. . . . wall. They . . . serpents (serpent **10a**) . . . . **10, 10a.**
362. . . . infinite;
363. they . . . . **10, 10a.**
365. . . . sea.
366. Ah, you . . . . **10, 10a.**
367. . . . , and go
368. under the pump. **9-10a.**

371.   soul.

372.   *Mr. Dowler.* I don't see what godliness has got to do
373.   with it.

374.   *Mr. Algie.* Nor I either.

375.   *Paul Ruttledge.* There was a saint who said, 'I must
376.   rejoice without ceasing, although the world shudder
377.   at my joy.' He did not think he could save his soul
378.   without it. I agree with him, and as I was discon-
379.   tented here, I thought it time to make a change. Like
380.   that worthy man, I must be content to shock my
381.   friends.

382.   *Mr. Dowler.* But you had everything here you could want.

383.   *Paul Ruttledge.* That's just it. You who are so wealthy,
384.   you of all people should understand that I want to get
385.   rid of all that responsibility, answering letters and
386.   so on. It is not worth the trouble of being rich if
387.   one has to answer letters. Could you ever understand,
388.   Georgina, that one gets tired of many charming things?
389.   There are family responsibilities [*to Mr. Joyce*], but
390.   I can see that you, who were my guardian, sympathize
391.   with me in that.

392.   *Mr. Joyce.* Indeed I do not.

393.   *Mrs. Ruttledge.* I should think you could be cheerful
394.   without ceasing to be a gentleman.

395.   *Paul Ruttledge.* You are thinking of my clothes. We

---

372.   . . . godliness has to . . . **10, 10a.**
374.   . . . I, either. **10.**
375.   . . . said: 'I . . .
376.   . . . ceasing although . . . **10, 10a.**
378.   . . . was getting more and more discon- **10, 10a.**
380.   . . . man I . . . **9** ; . . . man, Ruysbreck, the admirable, (Ruysbroeck, the Admirable, **10a**) I . . . **10, 10a.**
385.   . . . letters, and **10, 10a.**
386.   . . . on.
387.   Could . . . , **9-10a.**
388.   . . . things. **9.**
389.   Then there . . . **10** ; . . . responsibilities, [*to Mr. Joyce*] but **10a, 11A.**
390.   . . . , sympathise **9** ; . . . you who . . . guardian sympathise **10, 10a.**
391.   . . . that! **10, 10a.**

396.   must feel at ease with the people we live amongst.
397.   I shall feel at ease with the great multitude in
398.   these clothes. I am beginning to be a man of the
399.   world. I am the beggarman of all the ages—I have
400.   a notion Homer wrote something about me.

401.   *Mr. Dowler.* He is either making fun of us or talking
402.   great rot. I can't listen to any more of this non-
403.   sense. I can't see why a man with property can't let
404.   well alone. Algie are you coming my way?
        [They both go into the house, and come out presently with umbrella and coat.

405.   *Mr. Green.* Depend upon it, he's going to write a book.
406.   There was a man who made quite a name for himself by
407.   sleeping in a casual ward.

408.   *Paul Ruttledge.* Oh! no, I'm not going to write about
409.   it; if one writes one can do nothing else. I am
410.   going to express myself in life. *[To Thomas Ruttledge*
411.   *who has returned with box.]* I hope soon to live by
412.   the work of my hands, but every trade has to be
413.   learned, and I must take something to start with.
414.   *[To Mrs. Ruttledge.]* Do you think you will have any
415.   kettles to mend when I come this way again?
        [He has taken box from Thomas Ruttledge and unlocked it.

416.   *Thomas Ruttledge.* I can't make head or tail of what
417.   you are at.

418.   *Colonel Lawley.* What he is at is fads.

419.   *Mr. Green.* I don't think his motive is far to seek.

---

397.   . . . with great multitudes . . . **10, 10a.**
399.   . . . ages. I . . . **10, 10a.**
    Directions after 400. *[Thomas comes out with box and gives it to Paul, who begins to open it.]* **10, 10a.**
404.   . . . . Algie, are . . . ? **9-10a, 11A.**
    Directions after 404. [. . . *house and* . . . .] **10, 10a.**
408.   Oh, no, . . . **10.**
409.   . . . writes, one . . . **10** ; it. If . . . writes, one . . . **10a.**
    Directions in 410-411. [*To Thomas.*] **10, 10a.**
413.   learned and . . . . **10a.**
    Directions after 415. [lacking] **10, 10a.**
419.   [lacking] **10.**

420.   He has some idea of going back to the dark ages.

421.   Rousseau had some idea of the same kind, but it

422.   didn't work.

423. *Paul Ruttledge.* Yes; I want to go back to the dark

424.   ages.

425. *Mr. Green.* Do you want to lose all the world has

426.   gained since then?

427. *Paul Ruttledge.* What has it gained? I am among those

428.   who think that sin and death came into the world the

429.   day Newton eat the apple. [*To Mrs. Ruttledge, who is*

430.   *going to speak.*] I know you are going to tell me he

431.   only saw it fall. Never mind, it is all the same

432.   thing.

433. *Mrs. Ruttledge.* [*Beginning to cry.*] Oh! he is going

434.   mad!

435. *Mr. Joyce.* I'm afraid he is really leaving us.

    Paul Ruttledge. [*Who has been looking at papers, tear-*
    ing one or two, etc., takes out a packet of notes,

436.   *which he puts in his breast.*] I daresay this will

437.   last me long enough, Thomas. I am not robbing you of

438.   very much. Well, good-bye. [*Pats him gently on the*

439.   *shoulder.*] I mustn't forget the rabbit, it may be my

440.   dinner to-night; I wonder who will skin it. Good-bye,

441.   Colonel, I think I've astonished you to-day. [*Slaps*

442.   *his shoulder.*] That was too hard, was it? Forgive it,

443.   you know I'm a common man now. [*Lifts his hat and*
    goes out of gate. Closes it after him and stands with
    his hands on it, and speaks with the voice of a common

---

420.   *Mr. Green.* He . . . Dark Ages. **10.**

423.   Yes, I . . . Dark

424.   Ages. **10.**

429.   . . . Newton ate the apple. . . . [T] [*To* . . . **10, 10a** ; . . . Newton ate
    the . . . **11A.**

433.   Oh, he . . . **10, 10a.**

437.   . . . enough Thomas. . . . **9** ; . . . , Thomas; I . . . **10.**

438.   . . . , good-by. . . . **11A.**

439.   . . . the duck, it . . . **9** ; . . . the duck. Maybe it will be . . . **10, 10a.**

440.   . . . will pluck it. . . . , **9-10a.**

441.   Colonel. I . . . **10a.**

443.   . . . know, I'm . . . **10.**
    Directions at 443.   [. . . *on it.*] **9-10a.**

444.   *man.*] Go on, live in your poultry-yard. Scratch straw
445.   and cluck and cackle at everything that you take for
446.   a fox.   [*Exit.*

Mr. Joyce. [*Goes to Mrs. Ruttledge, who has sat down*
447.   *and is wiping her eyes.*] I am very sorry for this,
448.   for his father's sake, but it may be as well in the
449.   end. If it comes to the worst, you and Thomas will
450.   keep up the family name better than he would have
451.   done.

452. *Mr. Dowler.* He'll find the poor very different from
453.   what he thinks when they pick his pocket.

454. *Colonel Lawley.* To think that a magistrate should have
455.   such fads!

456. *Mr. Green.* I venture to say you will see him here in a
457.   very different state of mind in a week.

458. *Mr. Algie.* [*Who has been in a brown study.*] He has
459.   done for himself in this world and the next. Why, he
460.   won't be asked to a single shoot if this is heard of.

461. *Thomas Ruttledge.* [*Turning from the gate.*] Here are
462.   the children, Georgina. Don't say anything before the
463.   nurse.

464. *Mr. Green.* Well, I must be off.   [*Goes in for stick.*

465. *Mr. Joyce.* Just bring me out my coat, Green.
      [*They all prepare to go. Mrs. Ruttledge has gone to open gate and
      children come in, one in a perambulator. All gather round them
      admiringly.*

---

444. . . . on; live . . . poultry yard. . . . **10, 10a.**
445. and cackle at every strong spirit that goes by, at
446. everything that seems to you a fox. [*More solemnly.*]
446a. I am going to mix myself with the multitudes of men and women.
      [*Exit.*]
447. . . . this **9-10a.**
448. . . . well. **10, 10a.**
449. . . . worst you . . . **9**; If . . . **10, 10a.**
450. . . . name much better . . . **10.**
455. . . . fads. **9, 10a.**
459. . . . next; why, ... **10.**
460. . . . to shoots . . . . **10, 10a.**

466. *Mr. Joyce.* Have you a kiss for god-father to-day?

467. *Mrs. Ruttledge.* The poor darlings! I hope they will
468.   never know what has happened.

469. *Colonel Lawley.* Thank goodness, they have no nonsense
470.   in their heads. We know where we are with them.

---

466.   ... godfather ... ? **9** ; ... Godfather ... ? **10.**
468.   ... know that has .... **9.**
470.   ... goodness they ... **9.**

ACT II

Scene: *By the roadside. A wall of unmortared stone in the background. Tinkers'
encampment. Men, women, and children standing round. Paul Ruttledge
standing by a fire.*

1. *Paul Ruttledge.* What do you mean by 'tinning' the
2. soldering iron?

3. *Charlie Ward.* If the face of it is not well tinned it
4. won't lift the solder. Show me here.
   [*Takes soldering iron from Paul Ruttledge's hand.*

   Paul Ruttledge. [*Sitting down and drawing a tin can*
5. *to him.*] Now, let me see how you mend this hole. It
6. seems easy. I'm sure I will be able to learn it as
7. well as any of you.
   [*Two tinkers come and stand over him.*

8. *Charlie Ward.* [*Pointing to one of them.*] This, sir,
9. is Tommy the Song. He's the best singer we have, but
10. the divil a much good he is only that. He's a great
11. warrant to snare hares.

12. *Tommy the Song.* Is the gentleman going to join us?

13. *Paul Ruttledge.* Indeed I am, if you'll let me. There's
14. nothing I'd like better.

15. *Tommy the Song.* But are you going to learn the trade?

16. *Paul Ruttledge.* Yes, if you'll teach me. I'm sure I'll
17. make a good tinker. Look at that now, see how I've
18. stopped that hole already.

STAGE DIRECTIONS   Scene—*By . . .* , *women and . . . .* **9** ; Scene.—*By . . . .
Tinker's . . . .* **10, 10a** ; *. . . , women and . . . .* **11A**.

2. soldering-iron? **10, 10a**.
3. *. . .* well-tinned *. . .* **9** ; *. . .* well tinned, it **10, 10a**.
   Directions after 4. [*. . . soldering-iron . . . .*] **9-10a**.
5. *. . . .*] Now let *. . .* **10, 10a**.
10. *. . .* that. And here [*pointing*
10a. *to the other man*] is Jimmy Head, but we mostly call him Jimmy
10b. Heels, (Heel's **10a**) for no bailiff nor peeler was ever able to catch
     him. He's a great **9-10a**.
15. *Jimmy Heels.* But *. . .* ? **9** ; *Jimmy Head.* But *. . .* ? **10, 10a**.
17. *. . .* now; see *. . .* **10, 10a**.

Charlie Ward. [*Taking the can from him and looking at*
19.   *it.*] If every can had a little hole in the middle like
20.   that, I think you *would* be able to mend them; but
21.   there's the straight hole, and the crooked hole, the
22.   round hole, the square hole, the angle hole, the bot-
23.   tom hole, the top hole, the side leak, the open leak,
24.   the leak-all-round, but I won't frighten you with the
25.   names of them all, only this I will say, that, when
26.   you've learned to mend all the leakages in a can—and
27.   that should take you a year—you're only in the first
28.   day of the tinker's week.

29.   *Tommy the Song.* Don't believe him. He's only humbug-
30.   ging you. It's not the hardness of the work will
31.   daunt you.

32.   *Paul Ruttledge.* Thank you. I was not believing him at
33.   all. I'm quite sure I'll be able to mend any can at
34.   the end of a week, but the bottoming of them will
35.   take longer. I can see that's not so easy. When will
36.   you start to teach me that, Charlie?

37.   *Charlie Ward.* [*As another tinker comes up.*] Paddy,
38.   here's the gentleman I was telling you about. He's
39.   going to join us for good and all. [*To Paul Rutt-*
40.   *ledge.*] Wait till we have time and some quiet place,
41.   and he'll show you as good a cockfight as ever you
42.   saw. [*A woman comes up.*] This is his wife; Molly the
43.   Scold we call her; faith, she is a better fighter
44.   than any cock he ever had in a basket; he'd find it
45.   hard to shut the lid on her.

46.   *Molly the Scold.* The gentleman seems foolish. Is he
47.   all there?

---

21.   the straight . . . **10, 10a.**
24.   . . . leak-all-round—but . . .
25.   . . . all; only . . . , that when **10, 10a.**
30.   . . . you. You have a nice hand yourself at the iron.
31.   I see by you (by it **10, 10a**) that it's you that will make the grand tinker.
       9-10a.
32.   . . . you; I . . . believing Charlie at
33.   . . . can at all at **10, 10a.**
41.   . . . cock-fight . . . **9.**
42.   . . . wife, Molly . . . **9 ;** . . . wife—Molly . . . **10, 10a.**
43.   . . . her. Faith, . . .
44.   . . . basket. He'd . . . **10a.**

48. *Paddy Cockfight.* Stop your chat, Molly, or I'll hit
49.   you a welt.

50. *Charlie Ward.* Keep your tongue quiet, Molly. If the
51.   gentleman has reasons for keeping out of the way it
52.   isn't for us to be questioning him. [*To Paul Rutt-*
53.   *ledge.*] Don't mind her, she's cross enough, but maybe
54.   your own ladies would be cross as well if they saw
55.   their young sons dying by the roadside in a little
56.   kennel of straw under the ass-cart the way she did;
57.   from first to last.

58. *Paul Ruttledge.* I suppose you have your troubles like
59.   others. But you seem cheerful enough.

60. *Charlie Ward.* It isn't anything to fret about. Some
61.   of us go soon, and some travel the roads for their
62.   lifetime. What does it matter when we are under the
63.   nettles if it was with a short rope or a long one we
64.   were hanged?

65. *Paul Ruttledge.* Yes, that is the way to take life.
66.   What does the length of our rope matter?

67. *Charlie Ward.* We haven't time to be thinking of
68.   troubles like people that would be shut up in a
69.   house. We have the wide world before us to make our
70.   living out of. The people of the whole world are be-
71.   grudging us our living, and we make it out of them
72.   for all that. When they will spread currant cakes and
73.   feather beds before us, it will be time for us to sit
74.   down and fret.

75. *Tommy the Song.* It's likely you'll think the life too
76.   hard. Would you like to be passing by houses in the

---

53. ... her; she's ... **10, 10a.**
55. ... son ... **10, 10a.**
56. ... did
57. last week. **9-10a.**
58. ... troubles, like **10, 10a.**
59. ... you all seem very cheerful. **9-10a.**
61. ... soon and ... **10, 10a.**
65-74. [lacking] **9-10a.**
75. *Jimmy Heels.* It's ... **9**; *Jimmy Head.* It's ... **10, 10a.**

77. night-time, and the fire shining out of them, and you
78. hardly given the loan of a sod to light your pipe,
79. and the rain falling on you?

80. *Paul Ruttledge.* Why are the people so much against
81. you?

82. *Tommy the Song.* We are not like themselves. It's lit-
83. tle we care about them or they about us. If their
84. saint did curse us itself—

85. *Charlie Ward.* Stop. I won't have you talking about
86. that story here. Why would they think so much of the
87. curse of one saint, and saints so plenty?

88. *Paddy Cockfight.* Where's the good of a gentleman being
89. here? He'll be breaking down on the road. It's on the
90. ass-cart he'll be wanting to sit.

91. *Tommy the Song.* Indeed, I don't think he'll stand the
92. hardship.

93. *Paul Ruttledge.* Oh, I'll stand it well enough.

94. *Tommy the Song.* You're not like us that were reared
95. to it. You were not born like us with wandering in
96. the heart.

97. *Paul Ruttledge.* Oh yes, I have wandering in the heart.

---

77. night time, . . . **10, 10a.**
80. Are they so unkind as that? I thought the country- (country **10, 10a**).
81. people were always good to one another.
82. *Jimmy Heels.* That (*Jimmy.* That **10, 10a**) may be, but we . . . **9-10a.**
83. . . . them, or . . . **10, 10a.**
84. . . . itself. **10.**
85. Stop; I . . . **10, 10a.**
87. . . . plenty. **10a.**
88-90. [lacking] **9-10.**
91. *Jimmy Heels* [*to Paddy*]. I . . .
92. hardship of the roads. **9-10a.**
93. Oh! I'll . . . . **9.**
94. *Jimmy Heels.* You're . . . **9**; *Jimmy.* You're . . . **10, 10a.**
95. . . . it.
96. [lacking] **9-10a.**
97. Well, I couldn't stand the old life anyhow. **9-10a**; Oh, yes, ... **11A.**

98. I got sick of these lighted rooms you were talking of
99.   just now.

100. *Charlie Ward.* That might be so. It's the dark is wel-
101.   come to a man sometimes.

102. *Paul Ruttledge.* The dark. Yes, I think that is what I
103.   want. [*Stands up.*] The dark, where there is nothing
104.   that is anything, and nobody that is anybody; one
105.   can be free there, where there is nothing. Well, if
106.   you let me stay with you, I don't think you will hear
107.   any complaints from me. Charlie Ward, Paddy, and the
108.   rest of you, I want you to understand that from this
109.   out I am one of yourselves. I'll live as you live and
110.   do as you do.

                     [*Johneen and other children come running in.*

111. *Johneen.* I was on the top of the bank and I seen a
112.   priest coming down the cross-road with his ass. It's
113.   collecting he is. We're going to set ourselves here
114.   to beg something from him.

115. *Another Child.* [*Breathlessly.*] And he has a whole lot
116.   of things on the ass. A whole lot of things up behind
117.   him.

118. *Another Child.* O boys, O boys, we'll have our dealing
119.   trick out of them yet. The best way'll be—[*He sud-
120.   denly catches sight of Paul Ruttledge.*] Whist, ye
121.   divils ye, don't you see the new gentleman?

---

98. . . . of those lighted . . . **9-10a.**
102. . . . dark—yes, . . .
103. . . . dark where . . . **10, 10a.**
104. . . . anybody, one **9, 10**; . . . anybody. One **10a.**
105. . . . there—where . . . **10, 10a.**
107. . . . Ward, Jimmy Head, Paddy, and . . . **9-10a**; . . . , Paddy and . . .
   11A.
   Directions after 110. [. . . *and three or four boys come running in.*] **10,
   10a.**
111. . . . was in the top of the (a **10, 10a**) tree and . . . **9-10a.**
112. . . . . Its **9**; . . . crossroad . . . **10, 10a.**
113. collecting, he . . . **10.**
119. . . . be [*he* . . .
120. . . . *Paul*], whist ye
121. . . . gentleman. **9.**

122. *Paul Ruttledge.* Speak out, boys; don't be afraid of
123.   me; I'm one of yourselves now.

124. *Child.* Oh! but we were going to—But I won't tell
125.   you. [*To the other children.*] Come away here, and
126.   we'll not tell him what we'll do.

127. *Paul Ruttledge.* [*To Charlie Ward.*] What are they going
128.   to do? They're putting their heads together.

129. *Charlie Ward.* They're going to put a bush across the
130.   road, and when the friar gets down to pull it out of
131.   the way they'll snap what they can off the ass, and
132.   away with them.

133. *Paul Ruttledge.* And why wouldn't they tell me that?
134.   Am I not one of yourselves?

135. *Charlie Ward.* Ah! It's likely they'll never trust you.

136. *Paul Ruttledge.* But they will soon see that I am one
137.   of themselves.

138. *Charlie Ward.* No; but that's the very thing, you're
139.   not one of ourselves. You were not born on the road,
140.   reared on the road, married on the road like us.

141. *Paul Ruttledge.* Well, it's too late for me to be
142.   reared on the road, but I don't see why I shouldn't
143.   marry on the road like you. I certainly would do it
144.   if it would make me one of you.

145. *Charlie Ward.* It might make you one of us, there's no
146.   doubt about that. It's the only thing that would do
147.   it.

---

122. . . . , boys, don't . . . **10, 10a.**
123. me. I'm . . . . **10a.**
124. . . . to—, but . . . **9** ; Oh, but . . .—but . . . **10, 10a.**
129. . . . to pull a . . . **10, 10a.**
135. Ah! (Ah, **10, 10a**) I misdoubt me they'll . . . . **9-10a.**
138. No, but . . . thing; you're **10, 10a.**
140. . . . road, like . . . . **10, 10a.**
141. . . . , its . . . **9.**
143. . . . road, like . . . **10, 10a.**
145. It would make . . . **9-10a.**
146. . . . that It's . . . **9.**

148. *Paul Ruttledge.* Well, find a wife for me.

149. *Charlie Ward.* Faith, you haven't far to go to find
150. one. Paddy there will give you over his wife quick
151. enough; he won't make a hard bargain over her.

152. *Paul Ruttledge.* But I am in earnest. I want to cut my-
153. self off from my old life.

154. *Charlie Ward.* Oh! I was forgetting that.

155. *Sabina Silver.*[1] [*To Molly.*] I wonder what was it he
156. did? I wonder had he the misfortune to kill anybody?

157. *Charlie Ward.* [*Calling Sabina over.*] Here's a girl
158. should make a good wife, Sabina Silver her name is.
159. Her father is just dead; he didn't treat her over
160. well.

161. *Sabina Silver.* [*Coming over.*] What is it?

162. *Charlie Ward.* This gentlemen wants to speak to you. I
163. think he's looking out for a wife.

164. *Sabina Silver.* [*Hanging her head.*] Don't be humbugging
165. me.

166. *Paul Ruttledge.* Indeed he's not, Sabina.

167. *Sabina Silver.* You're only joking a poor girl. Sure,
168. what would make you think of me at all?

169. *Paul Ruttledge.* Sabina, have you been always on the
170. road with Charlie Ward and the others?

171. *Sabina Silver.* I have, indeed.

---

150. . . . . Paddy, there, will . . . **10.**
154. Oh, I . . . . **10, 10a.**
     Directions in 157. [*Beckoning Sabina . . . .*]
158. . . . wife; Sabina . . . . **10, 10a.**
159. . . . father's just . . . **10 ;** . . . father's just dead. He . . . **10a.**
167. . . . . Sure **9-10a.**

[1] *Sabina Silver* is *Sabina* in **9-10a.**

172. *Paul Ruttledge.* And you'd make a good tinker's wife?

173. *Sabina Silver.* You're joking me, but I would be a bet-
174. ter wife for a tinker than for anyone else.

175. *Paul Ruttledge.* Sabina, will you marry me?

176. *Sabina Silver.* Oh! but I'd be afraid.

177. *Paul Ruttledge.* Why, Sabina?

178. *Sabina Silver.* I'd be afraid you'd beat me.

179. *Charlie Ward.* You see her father used to beat her.
180. She's afraid of the look of a man now.

181. *Paul Ruttledge.* I would not beat you, Sabina. How can
182. you have got such an idea?

183. *Sabina Silver.* Will you promise me that you won't beat
184. me? Will you swear it to me?

185. *Paul Ruttledge.* Of course I will.

186. *Sabina Silver.* [*To Charlie Ward.*] Will you make him
187. swear it? Haven't you a little book in your pack?
188. Bring it out and make him swear to me on it, and
189. you'll be my witness.

190. *Charlie Ward.* I think, Sibby, you need not be afraid.

191. *Sabina Silver.* What's your name, gentleman?

192. *Paul Ruttledge.* My name is Paul. Do you like it?

193. *Sabina Silver.* Then I won't marry you, Mr. Paul, till
194. you swear to me upon the book that you will never
195. beat me with any stick that you could call a stick,
196. and that you will never strike a kick on me from be-
197. hind.

---

174. . . . any one . . . . **10, 10a.**
176. Oh, but . . . . **10, 10a.**
179. *Charlie Ward* [*With explanatory gesture*]. You . . . . **10, 10a.**
187. . . . your budget? **10, 10a.**

198. *Paul Ruttledge.* Charlie, go and bring out that book to
199.   satisfy her. Of course I swear that; it is absurd.
                    [Charlie Ward brings the book out of his pack.

200. *Paul Ruttledge.* I swear, Sabina, that I will never
201.   strike you with any stick of any kind, and that I
202.   will never kick you. There, will that do? [*He takes
      book and kisses it.*

203. *Sabina Silver.* I misdoubt you. Kiss the book again.
                            [Paul Ruttledge kisses it.

204. *Charlie Ward.* That's all right.

205. *A Child.* [*Crying from a distance.*] He's coming now,
206.   the priest's coming!

207. *Paul Ruttledge.* Then the priest will marry us. That
208.   comes in very handy.

209. *Charlie Ward.* [*Scornfully.*] A priest marry you, indeed
210.   he'll do nothing of the kind. I hate priests and
211.   friars. It's unlucky to get talking to them at all.
212.   You never know what trouble you're in for.

213. *A Child.* [*Coming up.*] That's true, indeed. The last
214.   time I spoke to a priest it's what he leathered me
215.   with a stick; may the divil fly away with him.

216. *Paul Ruttledge.* But somebody must marry us.

217. *Charlie Ward.* Of course. You'll lep over the tinker's
218.   budget the usual way. You'll just marry her by lep-
219.   ping over the budget the same as the rest of us marry.

---

199. . . . absur. **10.**
     Directions after 199. [*Charlie brings . . . .*] **10, 10a.**
     Directions at 202. [*Kisses book.*] **10, 10a.**
     Directions after 204. [*One of the children cries from a distance.*] **10, 10a.**
205. [Speaker and directions lacking] **10, 10a.**
209. . . . you! Indeed, **10, 10a.**
213. . . . true indeed. . . . **10a.**
214. . . . priest, it's . . . **10.**
215. . . . stick. May (stick, may **10a**) . . . devil . . . him! **10, 10a.**
217. . . . the **10, 10a.**
218. . . . way. I'll not let the old customs be changed for any one. You'll
    . . . **9-10a.**

220. *Paul Ruttledge*. That's all I want to know. Please
221.   marry me in whatever is your usual way.

> *Jerome enters, leading the ass. He carries a pig's cheek, some groceries, a string of onions, etc., on the ass, which still has its nursery trappings. He goes up to Charlie Ward thinking he is Paul Ruttledge.*

222. *Jerome*. Paul, what are you doing here?

223. *Charlie Ward*. [*Turning.*] What do you want?

224. *Jerome*. Oh! I'm mistaken. I thought—

225. *Paul Ruttledge*. I am here, Father Jerome, but you're
226.   talking to the wrong man.

227. *Jerome*. Good God, Paul, what has happened?

228. *Paul Ruttledge*. Nothing has happened that need sur-
229.   prise you. Don't you remember what we talked of to-
230.   day? You told me I was too much by myself. After you
231.   went away I thought I would make a change.

232. *Jerome*. But a change like this!

233. *Paul Ruttledge*. Why should you find fault with it? I
234.   am richer now than I was then. I only lent you that
235.   donkey then, now I give him to you.

236. *Jerome*. What has brought you among such people as
237.   these?

238. *Paul Ruttledge*. I find them on the whole better com-
239.   pany than the people I left a little while ago. Let
240.   me introduce you to—

Directions after 221.   [. . . *enters leading* . . . .] **9**; [. . . *Ward, thinking*
. . . .] **10, 10a**.
224. Oh, I'm . . .— **10, 10a**.
226. . . . man **9**.
227. . . . , Paul! What . . . ? **10**.
230. day? Did I not tell you I wanted a change?
231. [lacking] **9-10a**.
233. . . . it. I **9**.

241. *Jerome.* What can you possibly gain by coming here? Are
242.   you going to try and teach them?

243. *Paul Ruttledge.* Oh! no, I am going to learn from them.

244. *Jerome.* What can you learn from them?

245. *Paul Ruttledge.* To pick up my living like the crows,
246.   and to solder tin cans. Just give me that one I
247.   mended a while ago.   [*Holds it out to Father Jerome.*

248. *Jerome.* That is all nonsense.

249. *Paul Ruttledge.* I am happy. Do not your saints put all
250.   opponents to the rout by saying they alone of all man-
251.   kind are happy?

252. *Jerome.* I suppose you will not compare the happiness
253.   of these people with the happiness of saints?

254. *Paul Ruttledge.* There are all sorts of happiness. Some
255.   find their happiness like Thomas à Kempis, with a
256.   little book and a little cell.

257. *Paddy Cockfight.* I would wonder at anybody that could
258.   be happy in a cell.

259. *Paul Ruttledge.* These men fight in their way as your
260.   saints fought, for their hand is against the world.
261.   I want the happiness of men who fight, who are hit
262.   and hit back, not the fighting of men in red coats,
263.   that formal, soon-finished fighting, but the endless
264.   battle, the endless battle. Tell me, Father Jerome,

---

243. Oh, no, ... **10, 10a.**
245. Don't you see, I am learning to
246. solder . . . **10, 10a.**
247. . . . awhile . . . . **11A.**
249. But if I . . . happy? Do . . . **9**; Do . . . **10, 10a.**
254. Oh, there . . . **10, 10a.**
255. . . . Thomas a Kempis, . . . **9**; . . . happiness, like . . . **10, 10a.**
256. . . . book in a . . . . **10, 10a.**
257. *Jimmy Heels.* I . . . anyone (any one **10, 10a**) . . . **9-10a.**
259-260. [lacking] **9-10a.**
262. . . . red-coats, **9**; . . . back; not . . . , **10, 10a.**
263. that soon finished . . . **9-10a.**
264. . . . endless battle! [*He stands up.*] Tell . . . , **10, 10a.**

265.   did you ever listen in the middle of the night?

266. *Jerome.* Listen for what?

267. *Paul Ruttledge.* Did you ever, when the monastery was
268.   silent, and the dogs had stopped barking, listen till
269.   you heard music?

270. *Jerome.* What sort of music do you mean?

271. *Paul Ruttledge.* Not the music we hear with these ears
272.   [*touching his ears*], but the music of Paradise.

273. *Jerome.* Brother Colman once said he heard harps in the
274.   night.

275. *Paul Ruttledge.* Harps! It was because he was shut in a
276.   cell he heard harps, maybe it sounds like harps in a
277.   cell. But the music I have heard sometimes is made of
278.   the continual clashing of swords. It comes rejoicing
279.   from Paradise.

280. *Jerome.* These are very wild thoughts.

281. *Tommy the Song.* I often heard music in the forths.
282.   There is many of us hear it when we lie with our
283.   heads on the ground at night.

284. *Jerome.* That was not the music of Paradise.

285. *Paul Ruttledge.* Why should they not hear that music,
286.   although it may not set them praying, but dancing.

287. *Jerome.* How can you think you will ever find happiness
288.   amongst their devils' mirth?

289. *Paul Ruttledge.* I have taken to the roads because
290.   there is a wild beast I would overtake, and these

---

267. ... Monastery ... **10.**
268. silent and ... **10, 10a.**
276. ... harps; maybe ... **10;** ... harps. Maybe ... **10a.**
277. ... I spoke of is ... **9, 10.**
281. ... heard of people that heard music in (of **10**) the forts. (forths. **10,**
       10a)
282. *Charlie Ward.* Long Mike heard music coming from the
283. bush one night that was as loud as a brass band. **9-10a.**
286. ... dancing? **10;** ... praying but dancing? **10a.**
288. ... devil's ... ? **10.**

291.   people are good snarers of beasts. They can help me.

292.   *Charlie Ward.* What kind of a wild beast is it you want?

293.   *Paul Ruttledge.* Oh! it's a very terrible wild beast,
294.   with iron teeth and brazen claws that can root up
295.   spires and towers.

296.   *Charlie Ward.* It's best not to try and overtake a
297.   beast like that, but to cross running water and leave
298.   it after you.

299.   *Tommy the Song.* I heard one coming after me one night;
300.   very big and shadowy it was, and I could hear it
301.   breathing. But when it came up with me I lifted a
302.   hazel rod was in my hand, and it was gone on the
303.   moment.

304.   *Paul Ruttledge.* My wild beast is Laughter, the
305.   mightiest of the enemies of God. I will outrun it and
306.   make it friendly.

307.   *Jerome.* That is your old wild talk. Do have some sense
308.   and go back to your family.

309.   *Paul Ruttledge.* I am never going back to them. I am
310.   going to live among these people. I will marry among
311.   them.

312.   *Jerome.* That is nonsense; you will soon change your
313.   mind.

314.   *Paul Ruttledge.* Oh! no, I won't; I am taking my vows
315.   as you made yours when you entered religion. I have
316.   chosen my wife; I am going to marry before evening.

---

291.   . . . beasts. **10.**
293.   Oh, it's . . . ,
294.   . . . and iron claws . . .
295.   . . . towers— **10, 10a.**
299-303.   [lacking] **9-10a.**
302.   . . . rod that was . . . **11A.**
304.   That wild . . . **9**; That wild . . . laughter, . . . **10, 10a.**
312.   . . . nonsense, you . . . **9**; . . . nonsense. You . . . **10, 10a.**
314.   Oh, no, . . . won't. I . . . **10, 10a.**
316.   . . . wife. I . . . . **10, 10a.**

317. *Jerome.* Thank God, you will have to stop short of
318.   that, the Church will never marry you.

319. *Paul Ruttledge.* Oh! I am not going to ask the help of
320.   the Church. But I am to be married by what may be as
321.   old a ceremony as yours. What is it I am to do,
322.   Charlie?

323. *Charlie Ward.* To lep a budget, sir.

324. *Paul Ruttledge.* Yes, that is it, the budget is there
325.   by the wall.

326. *Jerome.* I command you, in the name of the Holy Church
327.   and of the teaching you have received from the Church,
328.   to leave this folly, this degradation, this sin!

329. *Paul Ruttledge.* You forget, Jerome, that I am on the
330.   track of the wild beast, and hunters in all ages have
331.   been a bad people to preach to. When I have tamed the
332.   beast, perhaps I will bring him to your religious
333.   house to be baptized.

334. *Jerome.* I will not listen to this profanity. [*To*
335.   *Charlie Ward.*] It is you who have put this madness
336.   on him as you have stolen his clothes!

337. *Charlie Ward.* Stop your chat, ye petticoated preacher.

338. *Paul Ruttledge.* I think, Father Jerome, you had better
339.   be getting home. This people never gave in to the
340.   preaching of S. Patrick.

---

318.   that. The . . . .
319.   Oh, I . . .
320.   . . . Church. I . . . **9-10a.**
323.   . . . , Sir. **9.**
324.   . . . it. The . . . **10, 10a.**
326.   . . . you in . . . **10, 10a.**
327.   . . . Church **9** ; . . . teachings . . . Church **10, 10a.**
336.   . . . him, as . . . !
337.   . . . preacher!
338-340.   [lacking] **10, 10a.**
339.   . . . home. **9.**
340.   [lacking] **9.**

341. *Paddy Cockfight.* I'll send you riding home with your
342.   face to the tail of the ass!

343. *Tommy the Song.* No, stop till we show you that we can
344.   make as good curses as yourself. That you may never
345.   be warm in winter or cold in summer time—

346. *Charlie Ward.* That's the chat! Bravo! Let him have it.

347. *Tinkers.* Be off! be off out of this!

348. *Molly the Scold.* Now curse him, Tommy.

349. *Tommy the Song.* A wide hoarseness on you—a high hang-
350.   ing to you on a windy day; that shivering fever may
351.   stretch you nine times, and that the curses of the
352.   poor may be your best music, and you hiding behind
353.   the door.   [*Jerome goes out.*

354. *Molly the Scold.* And you hiding behind the door, and
355.   squeezed between the hinges and the wall.

356. *Other tinkers.* Squeezed between the hinges and the
357.   wall.   [*They follow Jerome.*

358. *Paul Ruttledge.* [*Crying after them.*] Don't harm that
359.   gentleman; he is a friend of mine.
        [*He goes to the wall, and stands there silently, looking upward.*

360. *Sabina Silver.* It was grand talk, indeed: I didn't

---

342.   head to . . . ass. **10, 10a.**
343-345.   [lacking] **9-10a.**
346.   *Jimmy Heels.* That's . . . chat! (chat. **10, 10a**).
346a.   *Tommy the Song.* Bravo! Let him have it. **9-10a.**
346b.   *Paul.* I think, Brother Jerome, you had better
346c.   be getting home. **10, 10a.**
347.   . . . off, be . . . this. **9** ; . . . off, out . . . ! **10.**
        Directions after 347. [*Exit Jerome, most of the tinkers follow him,
        mocking him.*] **9** ; [*Exit Jerome.*] **10, 10a.**
348-357.   [lacking] **9-10a.**
358.   *Paul.* Don't . . .
359.   . . . mine. Well, Sabina, what
359a.   did you think of all that?
        Directions before 360.   [lacking]
360.   . . . , indeed. I . . . **10, 10a.**

361.   understand a word of it.

362. *Paul Ruttledge.* The crows are beginning to fly home.
363.   There is a flock of them high up under that cloud. I
364.   wonder where their nests are.

365. *Charlie Ward.* A long way off, among those big trees
366.   about Tillyra Castle.

367. *Paul Ruttledge.* Yes, I remember. I have seen them com-
368.   ing home there on a windy evening, tossing and whirl-
369.   ing like the sea. They may have seen what I am looking
370.   for, they fly so far. A sailor told me once that he
371.   saw a crow three hundred miles from land, but maybe
372.   he was a liar.

373. *Charlie Ward.* Well, they fly far, anyway.

374. *Paul Ruttledge.* They tell one another what they have
375.   seen, too. That is why they make so much noise. Maybe
376.   their news goes round the world. [*He comes towards the*
377.   *others.*] I think they have seen my wild beast, Laugh-
378.   ter. They could tell me if he has a face smoky from
379.   the eternal fires, and wings of brass and claws of
380.   brass—claws of brass. [*Holds out his hands and moves*
381.   *them like claws.*] Sabina, would you like to see a
382.   beast with eyes hard and cold and blue, like sap-
383.   phires? Would you, Sabina? Well, it's time now for
384.   the wedding. So what shall we get for the wedding
385.   party? What would you like, Sabina?

386. *Sabina Silver.* I don't know.

387. *Paul Ruttledge.* What do you say, Charlie? A wedding
388.   cake and champagne. How would you like champagne?
                                 [*Tinkers begin to return.*

362-382. [lacking] **10, 10a.**
365. . . . off among . . . **9.**
367. . . . them **9.**
368. there . . . **9.**
379. . . . brass, and . . . **9.**
383. *Paul.* Now, boys, for the wedding. What
384. shall . . . **10, 10a.**
387. . . . say Charlie? . . . **9;** . . . wedding- **10, 10a.**
388. . . . champagne? How . . . ?
    Directions after 388. [lacking] **10, 10a.**

389. *Charlie Ward.* It might be middling.

390. *Paul Ruttledge.* What would you say to a——

> *One of the Boys runs in carrying a pig's cheek. The rest of the Tinkers return with him.*

391. *Boy.* I knew I could do it. I told you I'd have my
392.   dealing trick out of the priest. I took a hold of
393.   this, and Johneen made a snap at the onions.

394. *Paul Ruttledge.* And he didn't catch you?

395. *Boy.* He'd want to be a lot smarter than he is to do
396.   that.

397. *Paul Ruttledge.* You are a smart lad, anyway. What do
398.   you say we should have for our wedding party?

399. *Boy.* Are you rich?

400. *Paul Ruttledge.* More or less.

401. *Boy.* I seen a whole truck full of cakes and bullseyes
402.   in the village below. Could you buy the whole of them?

403. *Charlie Ward.* Stop talking nonsense. What we want is
404.   porter.

405. *Paul Ruttledge.* All right. How many public-houses are
406.   there in the village?

407. *Tommy the Song.* Twenty-four.

408. *Paul Ruttledge.* Is there any place we can have barrels
409.   brought to?

Directions after 390. [. . . *in, carrying . . . cheek.*] **10, 10a.**
392. . . . . I nobbled **9-10a.**
393. . . . onions, (onions **10a**) but he missed them. **10, 10a.**
395. You bet, we (bet! We **10, 10a**) cut away like blazes. (blazes! **10, 10a**) **9-10a.**
396. [lacking] **9-10a.**
397. . . . lad. What . . . **9-10a.**
403. . . . we would like is **9-10a.**
405. . . . publichouses . . . **9** ; . . . public houses . . . **10, 10a.**

410. *Charlie Ward*. There's a shed near seems to be empty.
411.   We might go there.

412. *Paul Ruttledge*. Then go and order as many barrels as
413.   we can make use of to be brought there.

414. *Paddy Cockfight*. We will; and we'll stop till we've
415.   drunk them out.

416. *Paul Ruttledge*. [*Taking out money*.] I have more money
417.   than will pay for that. Sabina, we'll treat the whole
418.   neighbourhood in honour of our wedding. I'll have all
419.   the public-houses thrown open, and free drinks going
420.   for a week!

421. *Tinkers*. Hurrah! hurrah! hurrah!

422. *Charlie Ward*. Three cheers more, boys.

423. *All*. Hurrah! hurrah! hurrah!

424. *The Boys*. Now here's the budget.

425. *Paul Ruttledge*. [*Taking Sabina Silver's hand*.] Now,
426.   Sabina, one, two, three!

---

414. *Jimmy Heels*. We will; (will, **10, 10a**) and . . . **9-10a.**
418. . . . wedding; I'll . . . **9.**
419. . . . publichouses . . . **9** ; . . . public houses . . . open and . . . **10, 10a.**
424. Now, here's . . . . **10, 10a.**

Scene: *A large shed. Some sheepskins hanging up. Irons and pots for branding sheep, some pitchforks, etc. Tinkers playing cards, Paul Ruttledge sitting on an upturned basket.*

1. *Charlie Ward.* Stop that melodeon, now will ye, and
2. we'll have a taste of the cocks. Paul didn't see them
3. yet what they can do. Where's Tommy? Where in the
4. earthly world is Tommy the Song?

5. *Paddy Cockfight.* He's over there in the corner.

6. *Charlie Ward.* What are you doing there, Tommy?

7. *Tommy the Song.* Taking a mouthful of prayers, I am.

8. *Charlie Ward.* Praying! did anyone ever hear the like
9. of that? Pull him out of the corner.
   [*Paddy Cockfight pulls Tommy the Song out of the corner.*

10. *Charlie Ward.* What is it you were praying for, I would
11. like to know?

12. *Tommy the Song.* I was praying that we might all soon
13. die.

14. *Paddy Cockfight.* Die, is it?

15. *Charlie Ward.* Is it die and all that porter about?
16. Well! You have done enough praying, go over there
17. and look for the basket. Who was it set him praying,
18. I wonder? I am thinking it is the first prayer he
19. ever said in his life.

20. *Sabina Silver.* It's likely it was Paul. He's after
21. talking to him through the length of an hour.

STAGE DIRECTIONS   Scene—(Scene.—**10, 10a**) *A* .... *Tinkers dancing,*
   (*dancing.* **10, 10a**) *Paul sitting* .... **9-10a.**
1. ... melodion, now, will ... **10, 10a.**
3. yet (yet, **10a**) ... do. Now Paddy (Now, Paddy, **10, 10a**) we'll have
   real
4. sport. I want to see that new speckled bird of yours play. **9-10a.**
5-39. [lacking] **9-10a.**

22. *Paul Ruttledge.* Maybe it was. Don't mind him. I said
23. just now that when we were all dead and in heaven it
24. would be a sort of drunkenness, a sort of ecstasy.
25. There is a hymn about it, but it is in Latin. 'Et
26. calix meus inebrians quam praeclarus est.' How
27. splendid is the cup of my drunkenness!

28. *Charlie Ward.* Well, that is a great sort of a hymn.
29. I never thought there was a hymn like that, I never
30. did.

31. *Paddy Cockfight.* To think, now, there is a hymn like
32. that. I mustn't let it slip out of my mind. How
33. splendid is the cup of my drunkenness, that's it.

34. *Charlie Ward.* Have you found that old bird of mine?

Tommy the Song. [*Who has been searching among the*
35. *baskets.*] Here he is, in the basket and a lot of
36. things over it.

37. *Charlie Ward.* Get out that new speckled bird of yours,
38. Paddy, I've been wanting to see how could he play for
39. a week past.

40. *Paul Ruttledge.* Where do you get the cocks?

41. *Paddy Cockfight.* It was a man below Mullingar owned
42. this one. The day I first seen him I fastened my two
43. eyes on him, he preyed on my mind, and next night, if
44. I didn't go back every foot of nine miles to put him
45. in my bag.

46. *Paul Ruttledge.* Do you pay much for a good fighting
47. cock?

48. *Sabina Silver.* [*Laughs.*] Do you pay much, Paddy?

49. *Paul Ruttledge.* Perhaps you don't pay anything.

---

41. . . . Millingar . . . **10.**
42. . . . him, I . . .
43. . . . him. He . . . **10, 10a.**
46. . . . fighting- **10, 10a.**
49. . . . anything? **10, 10a.**

50. *Sabina Silver.* I think Paddy gets them cheap.

51. *Charlie Ward.* He gets them cheaper than another man
52.   would, anyhow.

53. *Paddy Cockfight.* He's the best cock I ever saw before
54.   or since. Believe me, I made no mistake when I pitched
55.   on him.

56. *Tommy the Song.* I don't care what you think of him.
57.   I'll back the red; it's he has the lively eye.

58. *Molly the Scold.* Andy Farrell had an old cock, and it
59.   bent double like himself, and all the feathers flit-
60.   tered out of it, but I hold you he'd leather both
61.   your red and your speckled cock together. I tell ye,
62.   boys, that was the cock!
                                [Uproarious shouts and yells heard outside.

63. *Charlie Ward.* Those free drinks of yours, Paul, is
64.   playing the devil with them. Do you hear them now
65.   and every roar out of them? They're putting the
66.   cocks astray. [*He takes out a cock.*] Sure they think
67.   it's thunder.

68. *Molly the Scold.* There's not a man of them outside
69.   there now but would be ready to knock down his own
70.   brother.

71. *Tommy the Song.* He wouldn't know him to knock him
72.   down. They're all blind. I never saw the like of it.

73. *Paul Ruttledge.* You in here stood it better than that.

74. *Charlie Ward.* When those common men drink it's what
75.   they fall down. They haven't the heads. They're not
76.   like us that have to keep heads and heels on us.

77. *Paddy Cockfight.* It's well we kept them out of this,

---

58. *Jimmy Heels.* Andy . . . **9-10a.**
60. . . . it; but . . . you, he'd . . . **10, 10a.**
64. . . . . Do ye hear . . . **9** ; . . . divil . . . Do ye hear . . ., **10, 10a.**
68. *Tommy the Song.* There's . . . **9-10a.**
71. *Jimmy Heels.* He . . . **9-10a.**
74. . . . drink, it's . . . **10, 10a.**

78.   or they'd be lying on the floor now, and there'd be
79.   no place for my poor bird to show himself off. Look
80.   at him now! Isn't he the beauty!   [*Takes out the cock.*

81.   *Charlie Ward.* Now boys, settle the place, put over
82.   those barrels out of that. [*They push barrels into a*
83.   *row at back.*] Paul, you sit on the bin the way you'll
84.   get a good view.
      [*A loud knock at the door. An authoritative voice outside.*

85.   *Voice.* Open this door.

86.   *Paddy Cockfight.* That's Green, the Removable; I know
87.   his voice well!

88.   *Charlie Ward.* Clear away, boys. Back with those cocks.
89.   There, throw that sack over the baskets. Quick, will
90.   ye!

91.   *Colonel Lawley.* [*Outside.*] Open this door at once.

92.   *Mr. Green.* [*Outside.*] I insist on this door being
93.   opened.

94.   *Molly the Scold.* What do they want at all? I wish we
95.   didn't come into a place with no back door to it.

96.   *Paul Ruttledge.* There's nothing to be afraid of. Open
97.   the door, Charlie.   [*Charlie Ward opens the door.*

Enter Mr. Green, Colonel Lawley, Mr. Dowler, Mr. Joyce, Mr. Algie
and Thomas Ruttledge.

---

81.   Now, boys, . . . place; put . . . **10, 10a.**
83.   . . . sit up on . . . **10, 10a.**
85.   . . . door! **10, 10a.**
86.   *Jimmy Heels.* That's . . . **9**; *Jimmy Heels.* That's . . . Removable. I . . .
     10.
87.   . . . well **10**; . . . well. **10a, 11A.**
88.   . . . , boys! Back . . . cocks! **10.**
91.   *Colonel Lawley's Voice.* Open . . . once. (once! **10**) **9-10a.**
92.   *Mr. Green's Voice.* I . . .
93.   opened! **10.**
94.   *Jimmy Heels.* What . . . **9-10a.**
97 and Directions.   . . . door, Jimmy. [*Jimmy opens the door.* (*opens door.* **10,**
     10a) . . . *Algie, and* . . . .] **9-10a.**

98. *Paddy Cockfight.* All J.P.'s; I have looked at every
99.   one of them from the dock!

100. *Mr. Green.* Mr. Ruttledge, this is very sad.

101. *Mr. Joyce.* This is a disgraceful business, Paul; the
102.   whole countryside is demoralized. There is not a man
103.   who has come to sensible years who is not drunk.

104. *Mr. Dowler.* This is a flagrant violation of all pro-
105.   priety. Society is shaken to its roots. My own ser-
106.   vants have been led astray by the free drinks that
107.   are being given in the village. My butler, who has
108.   been with me for seven years, has not been seen for
109.   the last two days.

110. *Paul Ruttledge.* I am sure you will echo Mr. Dowler,
111.   Algie.

112. *Mr. Algie.* Indeed I do. I endorse his sentiments com-
113.   pletely. There has not been a stroke of work done for
114.   the last week. The hay is lying in ridges where it has
115.   been cut, there is not a man to be found to water the
116.   cattle. It is impossible to get as much as a horse
117.   shod in the village.

118. *Paul Ruttledge.* I think you have something to say,
119.   Colonel Lawley?

120. *Colonel Lawley.* I have undoubtedly. I want to know when
121.   law and order are to be re-established. The police
122.   have been quite unable to cope with the disorder.
123.   Some of them have themselves got drunk. If my advice
124.   had been taken the military would have been called in.

125. *Mr. Green.* The military are not indispensable on occa-

---

 98. .... P.'s. I . . . **10, 10a.**
101. . . . , Paul. The **10, 10a.**
102. . . . country side . . . demoralised. . . . **10, 10a.**
104. It is . . . **10, 10a.**
105. priety—Society . . . **9.**
107. . . . butler who . . .
108. . . . years has . . . **10a.**
111. Algie! **9**; Algie? **10, 10a.**
112. Indeed, I . . . . I echo his . . . **10, 10a.**
115. . . . cut. There . . . **10, 10a.**
120. . . . have, undoubtedly. . . . **10, 10a.**
124. . . . taken, the . . . . **10, 10a.**

126.   sions like the present. There are plenty of police
127.   coming now. We have wired to Dublin for them, they
128.   will be here by the four o'clock train.

129.   *Paul Ruttledge.* [*Gets down from his bin.*] But you have
130.   not told me what you have come here for? Is there any-
131.   thing I can do for you?

132.   *Thomas Ruttledge.* Won't you come home, Paul? The chil-
133.   dren have been asking for you, and we don't know what
134.   to say.

135.   *Mr. Green.* We have come to request you to go to the
136.   public-houses, to stop the free drinks, to send the
137.   people back to their work. As for those tinkers, the
138.   law will deal with them when the police arrive.

139.   *Thomas Ruttledge.* Oh, Paul, why have you upset the
140.   place like this?

141.   *Paul Ruttledge.* Well, I wanted to give a little
142.   pleasure to my fellow-creatures.

143.   *Mr. Dowler.* This seems rather a low form of pleasure.

144.   *Paul Ruttledge.* I daresay it seems to you a little
145.   violent. But the poor have very few hours in which to
146.   enjoy themselves; they must take their pleasure raw;
147.   they haven't the time to cook it.

148.   *Mr. Algie.* But drunkenness!

    Paul Ruttledge. [*Putting his hand on the shoulders of two of*
149.   *the magistrates.*] Have we not tried sobriety? Do you
150.   like it? I found it very dull? [*A yell from outside.*]
151.   There is not one of those people outside but thinks
152.   that he is a king, that he is riding the wind. There

---

127.   . . . them. They **10, 10a** ; . . . them; they **11A.**
130.   . . . for. Is . . . **11A.**
133.   . . . you. We . . . **10.**
136.   publichouses, . . . **9** ; public houses, . . . **10, 10a.**
139.   Oh! Paul, . . . **9.**
143.   *Mr. Algie.* This . . . . **10, 10a.**
145.   violent, but . . . **10.**
146.   . . . themselves. They . . . ; **10, 10a.**
150.   . . . dull. [*A* . . . .] **10, 10a, 11A.**
152.   he . . . king,—that . . . **10, 10a.**

153. is not one of them that would not hit the world a
154. slap in the face. Some poet has written that exuber-
155. ance is beauty, and that the roadway of excess leads
156. to the palace of wisdom. But I forgot—you do not
157. read the poets.

158. *Mr. Dowler.* What we want to know is, are you going to
159. send the people back to their work?

160. *Paul Ruttledge.* Oh, work is such a little thing in
161. comparison with experience. Think what it is to them
162. to have their imagination like a blazing tar-barrel
163. for a whole week. Work could never bring them such
164. blessedness as that.

165. *Mr. Dowler.* Everyone knows there is no more valuable
166. blessing than work.

167. *Mr. Algie.* Idleness is the curse of this country.

168. *Paul Ruttledge.* I am prejudiced, for I have always
169. been an idler. Doubtless, the poor must work. It was,
170. no doubt, of them you were speaking. Yet, doesn't the
171. Church say, doesn't it describe heaven as a place
172. where saints and angels only sing and hold branches
173. and wander about hand in hand. That must be changed.
174. We must teach the poor to think work a thing fit for
175. heaven, a blessed thing. I'll tell you what we'll do,
176. Dowler. Will you subscribe, and you, and you, and
177. we'll send lecturers about with magic lanterns show-
178. ing heaven as it should be, the saints with spades
179. and hammers in their hands and everybody working. The

154. slap on the . . . **10, 10a.**
155. . . . that a roadway . . . **9.**
157. . . . poets? **9.**
160. Oh! work . . . **9.**
162. . . . imaginations . . . tar barrel **10, 10a.**
163. through a . . . week! Work . . . **10.**
164. . . . that!
165. Every one . . . **10, 10a.**
169. . . . . Doubtless the . . . , **10, 10a.**
171. . . . say—doesn't . . . **10, 10a.**
172. . . . sing; and . . . **9.**
173. . . . hand? That . . . . **10, 10a.**
176. Dowler, will . . . subscribe, and you, and you—and **10, 10a.**
179. . . . hands, and . . . **10, 10a.**

180. poor might learn to think more of work then. Will you
181.   join in that scheme, Dowler?

182. *Mr. Dowler.* I think you'd better leave these subjects
183.   alone. It is obvious you have cut yourself off from
184.   both religion and society.

185. *Mr. Green.* The world could not go on without work.

186. *Paul Ruttledge.* The world could not go on without work!
187.   The world could not go on without work! I must think
188.   about it. [*Gets up on bin.*] Why should the world go
189.   on? Perhaps the Christian teacher came to bring it to
190.   an end. Let us send messengers everywhere to tell the
191.   people to stop working, and then the world may come
192.   to an end. He spoke of the world, the flesh, and the
193.   devil. Perhaps it would be a good thing to end these
194.   one by one.

195. *Colonel Lawley.* Come away out of this. He has gone mad.

196. *Paul Ruttledge.* Ah! I thought that would scare them.

197. *Mr. Joyce.* I wish, Paul, you would come back and live
198.   like a Christian.

199. *Paul Ruttledge.* Like a Christian?

200. *Mr. Joyce.* Come away, there's no use stopping here any
201.   longer.

202. *Paul Ruttledge.* [*Sternly.*] Wait, I have something to
203.   say to that. [*To Charlie Ward.*] Do not let anyone

---

183. . . . off both
184. from religion . . . . **10, 10a.**
186. . . . work—
187. the . . . not get on . . . work. I (work . . . . [T] I **10a**) . . . **10, 10a.**
192. . . . flesh and . . . **9.**
193. . . . to bring these,
194. . . . by one, to an end. **10, 10a.**
196. Ah, I . . . them! **10, 10a.**
199. . . . Christian! **10, 10a.**
203. . . . any one **10, 10a.**

204.   leave this place.

> [*Tinkers close together at the door.*

205. *Mr. Green.* [*To Tinkers.*] This is nonsense. Let me
206.   through.   [*Tinker spreads out his arms before him.*

207. *Paul Ruttledge.* You have come into a different kingdom
208.   now; the old kingdom of the people of the roads, the
209.   houseless people. We call ourselves tinkers, and you
210.   are going to put us on our trial if you can. You call
211.   yourselves Christians and we will put you on your
212.   trial first. I will put the world on its trial, and
213.   myself of yesterday. [*To a Boy.*] Run out, Johneen,
214.   keep a watch, and tell us when the train is coming.
215.   Sabina, that rope; we will set these gentlemen on
216.   those barrels.   [*Tinkers take hold of them.*

217. *Colonel Lawley.* Keep your hands off me, you drunken
218.   scoundrel!
> [*Strikes at Charlie Ward, but Tinkers seize his arms behind.*

219. *Paul Ruttledge.* Tie all their hands behind them.

220. *Mr. Dowler.* We'd better give in, there's no saying how
221.   many more of them there are.

222. *Mr. Algie.* I'll be quiet, the odds are too great
223.   against us.

Directions after 204. [. . . *at door.*] **10, 10a.**
205. . . . nonsense; let . . .
Directions in 206. [*A tinker* . . . .] **10, 10a.**
208. now, the . . . **10, 10a.**
211. . . . Christians, and . . . **9, 11A** ; . . . Christians. We . . . **10, 10a.**
212. . . . first. [*To a Boy.*] Run out, Johneen, (Johneen; **10, 10a**) **9-10a.**
213. [lacking] **9.**
215. [*To the others.*] Set . . . **9-10a.**
Directions in 216. [lacking] **10, 10a.**
Directions after 218. [. . . *arms, and tie his hands quickly behind him.*]
9-10a.
219. [lacking] **9-10a.**
220. . . . in. There's . . . **10, 10a.**
222. . . . quiet. The . . . **10, 10a.**

224. *Mr. Green.* The police will soon be here; we may as
225.   well stay quietly.

226. *Paddy Cockfight.* Here, give it to me, I'll put a good
227.   twist in it. Don't be afraid, sir, it's not about
228.   your neck I'm putting it—. There now, sit quiet and
229.   easy, and you won't feel it at all.

230. *Paul Ruttledge.* Are all their hands tied? Now then,
231.   heave them up on to the barrels.
      [*Slight scuffle, during which all are put on the barrels in a semi-
      circle.*]

232. *Paul Ruttledge.* Ah! yes, you are on my barrels now;
233.   last time I saw you you were on your own dunghill.
234.   Let me see, is there anyone here who can write?

235. *Charlie Ward.* Nobody.

236. *Paul Ruttledge.* Never mind, you can keep count on your
237.   fingers. The rest must sit down and behave themselves
238.   as befits a court. They say they are living like
239.   Christians. Let us see.

240. *Thomas Ruttledge.* Oh, Paul, don't make such a fool of
241.   yourself.

242. *Paul Ruttledge.* The point is not wisdom or folly, but
243.   the Christian life.

244. *Mr. Dowler.* Don't answer him, Thomas. Let us preserve

---

224. . . . here. We . . . **10, 10a.**
226-229. [lacking] **9-10a.**
230. Tie their hands behind them. **9** ; Tie their hands behind them and
   put **10, 10a.**
231. [lacking] **9** ; them on the . . . . **10, 10a.**
   Directions after 231. [. . . *all have their hands tied (tied, 10) and are . . .
   semi-circle.*] **9-10a.**
232. Ah, yes, . . . now.
233. Last . . . you, you . . . .
234. . . . see. Is . . . any one . . . ? **10, 10a.**
236. . . . mind; you . . . **10, 10a.**
237. fingers.
238. They . . . **9-10a.**
240. Oh! Paul, . . . **9.**

245.   our dignity.

246.   *Mr. Algie.* Yes, let us keep a dignified attitude—we
247.   won't answer these ruffians at all.

248.   *Paul Ruttledge.* Respect the court! [*Turns to Colonel*
249.   *Lawley.*] You have served your Queen and country in
250.   the field, and now you are a colonel of militia.

251.   *Colonel Lawley.* Well, what is there to be ashamed of
252.   in that? Answer me that, now.

253.   *Paul Ruttledge.* Yet there is an old saying about turn-
254.   ing the other cheek, an old saying, a saying so im-
255.   possible that the world has never been able to get it
256.   out of its mind. You have helped to enlist men for
257.   the army, I think? Some of them have fought in the
258.   late war, and you have even sent some of your own
259.   militia there.

260.   *Colonel Lawley.* If I did I'm proud of it.

261.   *Paul Ruttledge.* Did they think it was a just war?

262.   *Colonel Lawley.* That was not their business. They had
263.   taken the Queen's pay. They would have disgraced
264.   themselves if they had not gone.

265.   *Paul Ruttledge.* Is it not the doctrine of your Chris-
266.   tian Church, of your Catholic Church, that he who
267.   fights in an unjust war, knowing it to be unjust,

---

246.   . . . attitude. We **10, 10a.**
248.   . . . court! [*To* . . .
249.   . . . queen . . . **10, 10a.**
252.   . . . me that now. **10, 10a.**
253.   It was written, 'To him that smiteth thee on the one **9**; Perhaps not,
         perhaps not. But surely **10, 10a.**
253a.   it was written: (written **10a**) 'To him that smiteth thee on the one
         10, 10a.
254.   cheek (cheek, **10**) offer also the other.' **9-10a.**
255.   [lacking] **9-10a.**
256.   You (And you **10, 10a**) have . . . **9-10a.**
258.   . . . have sent . . . **10, 10a.**
260.   . . . did, I'm . . . . **10, 10a.**
265.   It is the . . . **10, 10a.**

268.   loses his own soul?

269.   *Colonel Lawley.* I should like to know what would
270.   happen to the country if there weren't soldiers to
271.   protect it.

272.   *Paul Ruttledge.* We are not discussing the country, we
273.   are discussing the Christian life. Has this gentleman
274.   lived the Christian life?

275.   *All the Tinkers.* He has not!

276.   *Paddy Cockfight.* His sergeant tried to enlist me,
277.   giving me a shilling, and I drunk.

        Tommy the Song. [*Singing.*]
278.   She bid me take love easy, as the leaves grow on the tree,
279.   But I, being young and foolish, with her would not agree.

280.   *Charlie Ward.* Stop your mouth, Tommy, This is not
281.   your show. [*To Paul Ruttledge.*] Are you going to put
282.   a fine on the Colonel? If so I'd like his cloak.

283.   *Paul Ruttledge.* Now we'll try Mr. Dowler, the rich
284.   man. [*Holds up his fingers in a ring.*] Mr. Dowler,
285.   could you go through this?

286.   *Mr. Algie.* Don't answer him, Dowler; he's going be-
287.   yond all bounds.

288.   *Paul Ruttledge.* I was a rich man and I could not, and
289.   yet I am something smaller than a camel, and this is
290.   something larger than a needle's eye.

---

268. . . . soul! **10, 10a.**
272. . . . country; we **10, 10a.**
278.   'Oh! ('O **10, 10a**) Biddy Donahoe,
279.   I'll tell you what you'll do;
279a.   You'll take the name of Patterson,
279b.   And I'll be Donahoe!' **9-10a.**
280. . . . , Tommy. This . . . **11A.**
       Directions in 284. [. . . *fingers on a* . . . .] **10, 10a.**
286. . . . , Dowler. He's . . . **10a.**
288. I see you cannot, and
289. yet you are something . . . **9-10a.**

291. *Mr. Joyce.* Don't answer this profanity.

292. *Charlie Ward.* But what about the cloak?

293. *Paul Ruttledge.* Oh! go and take it.
        [*Charlie Ward goes and takes cloak off the Colonel.*

294. *Colonel Lawley.* You drunken rascal, I'll see you in
295.   the dock for this.

296. *Mr. Joyce.* You're encouraging robbery now.

297. *Paul Ruttledge.* Remember the commandment, 'Give to
298.   him that asketh thee'; and the hard commandment goes
299.   even farther, 'Him that taketh thy cloak forbid not
300.   to take thy coat also.' [*Holding out his rags.*] Have
301.   I not shown you what Mr. Green would call a shining
302.   example. Charlie, ask them all for their coats.

303. *Charlie Ward.* I will, and their boots, too.

304. *All the Tinkers.* [*Uproariously.*] Give me your coat;
305.   I'll have your boots, etc.

306. *Mr. Green.* Wait till the police come. I'll turn the
307.   tables on you; you may all expect hard labour for
308.   this.

309. *Paul Ruttledge.* [*To the Tinkers.*] Stand back, the
310.   trial is not over. Mr. Green, these friends of yours
311.   have been convicted of breaking the doctrine they
312.   boast of. They do not love their enemies; they do not

---

293. Oh, go . . . . **10.**
      Directions after 293.   [*Charlie goes . . . .*] **9**; [*Charlie goes . . . cloak.*]
      10, 10a.
294. . . . rascal! I'll . . . **10.**
297. . . . the command: (command, **10, 10a**) 'Give . . .
298. . . . thee,' and the text goes
299. . . . farther: (farther, **10a**) 'Him ('him **10, 10a**) . . .
300. . . . also.' **9-10a.**
301. [lacking] **9-10a.**
302. Charlie, ... **9-10a.**
304. . . . coat, **9**; . . . coat! **10, 10a.**
305. . . . boots! [*Etc.*] **10, 10a.**
307. . . . you. You may expect . . . **10, 10a.**
309. . . . back! the **10.**
312. . . . enemies, they . . . **10, 10a.**

313.   give to every man that asks of them. Some of them,
314.   Mr. Dowler, for instance, lay up treasures upon earth;
315.   they ask their goods again of those who have taken
316.   them away. But you, Mr. Green, are the worst of all.
317.   They break the Law of Christ for their own pleasure,
318.   but you take pay for breaking it. When their goods
319.   are taken away you condemn the taker; when they are
320.   smitten on one cheek you punish the smiter. You en-
321.   courage them in their breaking of the Law of Christ.

322.   *Tommy the Song.* He does, indeed. He gave me two months
323.   for snaring rabbits.

324.   *Paddy Cockfight.* He tried to put a fine on me for a
325.   cock I had, and he took five shillings off Molly for
326.   hitting a man.

327.   *Paul Ruttledge.* Your evidence is not wanted. His own
328.   words are enough. [*Stretching out his arms.*] Have any
329.   of these gentlemen been living the Christian life?

330.   *All.* They have not.

331.   *Johneen.* [*Coming in.*] Ye'd best clear off now. I see
332.   the train coming in to the station.

333.   *Paddy Cockfight.* The police will find plenty to do in
334.   the village before they come to us; that's one good
335.   job.

336.   *Paul Ruttledge.* One moment. I have done trying the
337.   world I have left. You have accused me of upsetting
338.   order by my free drinks, and I have showed you that

---

313.   . . . them—
314.   . . . instance—lay . . . ; **10, 10a.**
315.   . . . have always taken **10.**
317.   . . . law . . . , **10, 10a.**
319.   . . . away, you . . .
320.   . . . cheek, you . . . **10, 10a.**
322.   *Jimmy Heels.* He . . . **9-10a.**
325.   . . . off Tommy the
326.   Song one time for hitting . . . . **9-10a.**
331.   . . . off, now. . . . **10, 10a.**
334.   . . . us, that's . . . **10, 10a.**

339. there is a more dreadful fermentation in the Sermon
340. on the Mount than in my beer-barrels. Christ thought
341. it in the irresponsibility of His omnipotence. [*Get-*
342. *ting from his bin.*] Charlie, give me that cloak.

[*He flings it back.*

343. *Charlie Ward.* Aren't you going to punish them anyway?

344. *Paul Ruttledge.* No, no, from this out I would punish
345. nobody but myself.　　　[*Some of the Tinkers have gone out.*

346. *Charlie Ward.* We'd best be off while we can. Come
347. along, Paul, Sibby's gone.
　　　[*As they go out Tommy the Song is singing,*

348.　　　Down by the sally garden my love and I did stand,
349.　　　And on my leaning shoulder she laid her milk-white hand;
350.　　　She bade me take love easy, as the leaves grow on the tree,
351.　　　But I, being young and foolish, with her would not agree.
　　　[*All go out except Paul Ruttledge.*

352. *Paul Ruttledge.* Well, good-bye, Thomas; I don't sup-
353. pose I'll see you again. Use all I have; spend it on
354. your children; I'll never want it.　　　[*To the others.*]
355. Will you come and join us? We will find rags for you
356. all. Perhaps you will give up that dream that is
357. fading from you, and come among the blind, homeless
358. people; put off the threadbare clothes of the Apostles
359. and run naked for awhile.　　　[*Is going out.*

360. *Thomas Ruttledge.* You have nothing against me, have
361. you, Paul?

---

340. . . . beer barrels. . . .
341. . . . his . . . **10, 10a.**
343. . . . any way? **10, 10a.**
344. . . . , no, we are here to judge but not
345. to punish. [*Some* . . . .] **9-10a.**
347. . . . , Paul; Sibby's . . . . **10, 10a.**
　　　Directions after 347. [*All go out.*] **9**; [*Tinkers go out.*] **10, 10a.**
348-Directions after 351. [lacking] **9-10a.**
352. . . . , Thomas. I . . . **10, 10a.**
353. . . . have. Spend . . . **10a.**
354. . . . children. I'll . . . . **10, 10a.**
358. . . . people, put . . . **10, 10a.**
359. . . . a while. [*Is* . . . .] **9-10a.**

362. *Paul Ruttledge.* Oh, yes, I have; a little that I have
363.   said against all these, and a worse thing than all,
364.   though it is not in the book.
365. *Thomas Ruttledge.* What is it?
366. *Paul Ruttledge.* [*Looking back from the threshold.*] You
367.   have begotten fools.

---

363. ... these and ..., **10, 10a.**

Scene 1.—*Great door in the middle of the stage under a stone cross, with flights of steps leading to door. Enter Charlie Ward, Paddy Cockfight, Tommy the Song, and Sabina Silver. They are supporting Paul Ruttledge, who is bent and limping.*

1. *Charlie Ward.* We must leave you here. The monks will
2.   take you in. We're very sorry, Paul. It's a heart-
3.   scald to us to leave you and you know that, but what
4.   can we do? [*They lead Paul Ruttledge to steps.*

5. *Paul Ruttledge.* Ah! that was a bad stitch! [*Gasps.*]
6.   Take care now; put me down gently.

7. *Sabina Silver.* Oh! can't we keep him with us anyway;
8.   he'll find no one to care him as well as myself.

9. *Tommy the Song.* What way can you care him, Sibby? It's
10.   no way to have him lying out on the roadside under
11.   guano bags, like ourselves, and the rain coming down
12.   on him like it did last night. It's in hospital he'll
13.   be for the next month.

14. *Charlie Ward.* We'd never leave you if you could even
15.   walk. If we have to give you to the monks itself,
16.   we'd keep round the place to encourage you, only for
17.   the last business. We'll have to put two counties at

STAGE DIRECTIONS . . . *Cockfight, Jimmy Heels, Tommy . . . Sabina. They* . . . .
9; Scene 1.—*A great . . . of stage under stone cross. A flight . . . steps up to . . .*
Cockfight, Jimmy Heels, Tommy . . . . **10, 10a**; Scene: *Great . . .* **11A**

1. . . . . The friars will **10, 10a**.
3. . . . you, and . . . **10, 10a**.
5. Ah—that . . . stitch. [*Gasps.*] **10, 10a**.
6. . . . now, put . . . . **9-10a**.
7. Oh, can't . . . anyway.
8. He'll . . . one care . . . . **10, 10a**.
9. . . . you cure him, . . . **9**.
10. . . . the roadway under
11. . . . bags like . . .
12. . . . him as it . . . **9-10a**.
15. . . . the friars itself, **10, 10a**.

18.   least between us and Gortmore after what we're after
19.   doing.

20.   *Paul Ruttledge.* Never mind, boys, they'll never insult
21.   a tinker again in Gortmore as long as the town's a
22.   town.

23.   *Charlie Ward.* Dear knows! it breaks my heart to think
24.   of the fine times we had of it since you joined us.
25.   Why the months seemed like days. And all the fine
26.   sprees we had together! Now you're gone from us we
27.   might as well be jailed at once.

28.   *Paddy Cockfight.* And how you took to the cocks! I be-
29.   lieve you were a better judge than myself. No one but
30.   you would ever have fancied that black-winged cock—
31.   and he never met his match.

32.   *Paul Ruttledge.* Ah! Well, I'm doubled up now like
33.   that old cock of Andy Farrell's.

34.   *Paddy Cockfight.* No, but you were the best warrant to
35.   set a snare that ever I came across.

       Paul Ruttledge. [*Sitting down with difficulty on the*
36.   *steps.*] Yes; it was a grand time we had, and I
37.   wouldn't take back a day of it; but it's over now,
38.   I've hit my ribs against the earth and they're aching.

39.   *Sabina Silver.* Oh! Paul, Paul, is it to leave you we
40.   must? And you never once struck a kick or a blow on
41.   me all this time, not even and you in pain with the

---

20.   . . . , boys; they'll . . . **10, 10a.**
23.   Dear God! It (it **10, 10a**) . . . **9-10a.**
25.   Why, the . . .
26.   . . . us, we **10, 10a.**
32.   Ah, well, . . . now, like
33.   Andy Farrell's old cock! **10, 10a.**
34.   *Jimmy Heels.* No, . . . **9**; *Jimmy Head.* No, . . . **10, 10a.**
       Directions before 36. [. . . *down on steps with difficulty*].
36.   Yes, but it . . . **10, 10a.**
37.   . . . it, but . . . , **9**; . . . it, but . . . now. **10, 10a**; . . . now; **11A.**
39.   Oh, Paul, . . . **10, 10a.**
40.   must! . . . **9-10a.**

42. rheumatism.   *[A clock strikes inside.*

43. *Charlie Ward.* There's the clock striking. The monks
44.   will be getting up. We'd best be off after the
45.   others. I hear some noise inside; they'd best not
46.   catch us here. I'll stop and pull the bell. Be off
47.   with you, boys!

48. *Paul Ruttledge.* Good-bye, Sabina. Don't cry! you'll
49.   get another husband.

50. *Sabina Silbver.* I'll never lep the budget with another
51.   man; I swear it.

52. *Paul Ruttledge.* Good-bye, Paddy. Good-bye, Tommy. My
53.   mother Earth will have none of me and I will go look
54.   for my father that is in heaven.

55. *Paddy Cockfight.* Come along, Sibby.
                     [Takes her hand and hurries off.

56. *Charlie Ward.* [*Rings bell.*] Are they sure to let you
57.   in, Paul? Have you got your story ready?

58. *Paul Ruttledge.* No fear, they won't refuse a sick man.
59.   No one knows me but Father Jerome, and he won't tell
60.   on me.

61. *Charlie Ward.* There's a step inside. I'll cut for it.
                  [He goes out. Paul is left sitting on steps.

---

42. rheumatics. . . . .
43. . . . . The friars **10, 10a.**
46. . . . here. Jimmy will stop . . . bell. Come
47. along, boys! (boys. **10, 10a**) **9-10a.**
48. . . . cry. You'll **10, 10a.**
51. . . . it! **9**; man,—I . . . . **10, 10a.**
52-54. [lacking] **10, 10a.**
55. *Charlie Ward.* Come . . . . **10, 10a.**
56. *Jimmy Heels* (*Head* **10, 10a**) [*rings bell*]. Are . . . **9-10a.**
57. . . . your sorty ready?
58. . . . fear; they . . . . **10, 10a.**
61. *Jimmy Heels.* There's . . . inside, I'll . . . . **9**; *Jimmy Head.* There's . . . .
10, 10a.
Directions after 61. [*Exit. Paul* . . . .] **9-10a.**

Scene 2.—*The crypt under the Monastery church. A small barred window high up in the wall, through which the cold dawn is breaking. Altar in a niche at the back of stage; there are seven unlighted candles on the altar. A little hanging lamp near the altar. Paul Ruttledge is lying on the altar steps. Friars are dancing slowly before him in the dim light. Father Aloysius is leaning aganist a pillar. Some Friars come in carrying lanterns.*

STAGE DIRECTIONS Scene II.—*After five years. Chapel in the monastery.* (*Monastery.* **10**) *Altar steps at right. A bench against wall at back, a little to the left, with flowers and seven great altar candlesticks on it. Paul kneeling in prayer. Father Colman standing looking at him. Father Jerome enters.* **9-10a**; Scene 2: *The . . . monastery . . . .* **11A.**

a.[1]   *Father Jerome.* Where is Father Paul?
b.   *Father Colman.* He is praying there by the altar. He has
c.   been praying there for the last hour (hour, **10, 10a**) though he is worn out
d.   with fasting.
e.   *Father Jerome.* What could have put these wild ideas into
f.   his head after he had been for years the most holy among us,
g.   almost a saint. (saint? **10, 10a**) He might have become our Superior in time, **9-10a.**
h.   after rising so quickly from step to step, novice to lay brother, **9**; after rising so quickly from step to step, from lay brother to novice, **10, 10a.**
i.   from lay brother to friar. **9**; from novice to friar. **10, 10a.**
j.   *Father Colman.* My cell is next to his. (next his. **10, 10a**) I think he has
k.   seen God.
l.   *Father Jerome.* I am afraid you are on his side. Leave me
m.   now; the Superior has asked me to use my influence with him,
n.   now that he is come to absolute rebellion.
               [*Father Colman goes out.*] **9-10a.**
o.   *Father Jerome.* Paul! (Paul, **10, 10a**) Paul!
        [*Paul stands up. Passes his hands (hand* **10,10a**) *over his eyes like one bewildered.*] **9-10a.**
p.   *Paul.* Have I been long here? (here long? **10, 10a**) I seem to have come from
q.   a long way off.
r.   *Father Jerome.* The Superior has sent me to you. He is
s.   getting very angry. You are upsetting the whole monastery (Monastery **10**)
t.   with your ideas. The monks (friars **10, 10a**) begin to laugh suddenly in the **9-10a.**

[1] Many of the lines a-rrr are similar to lines located elsewhere in this scene in **II.**

u. middle of the night. As I came through the passages I could

v. hear them dancing. Now, (Now **10, 10a**) it has come to absolute rebellion; you (rebellion. You **10, 10a**)

w. have forbidden your followers among them to go up to (go to **10**) the

x. technical school at the proper hour. They say you have bidden

y. them to come to you here. The Superior demands obedience.

z. *Paul.* I would obey him if I could. But I have had orders

aa. from beyond him. I have been given certain truths to tell, and

bb. I must tell them at this moment (moment, **10**) or they may begin to slip from me.

cc. *Father Jerome.* I cannot understand your ideas. You tell

dd. them impossible things—(things, **10, 10a**) things that are against the order of

ee. nature.

ff. *Paul.* One needs a religion that is wholly supernatural, that

gg. is so opposed to the order of nature that the world can never

hh. capture it.

ii. *Father Jerome.* Paul, I did you a service when you came

jj. here. I had you brought in (in, **10, 10a**) and I did not tell who you really

kk. were. I did not tell about that wild business.

ll. *Paul.* Were you not pleased to see me? We like our pro-

mm. phesies (prophecies **10, 10a**) to be fulfilled, and you have always said I would turn

nn. friar in the end.

oo. *Father Jerome.* I have done penance for that deceit. (that little deceit. **10**) Make

pp. some little return to me now, and submit yourself.

qq. *Paul.* My poor Jerome! [*Taking his hand.*] I know how

rr. this goes to your heart, but I cannot. I know I owe every-

ss. thing to you, for it was here that sickness and silence and

tt. fasting taught me to pray. I prayed and fasted (and I fasted **10a**) till at last one

uu. night in my cell a sudden light enfolded me, and I had thoughts

vv. that were (that yet were **10**; that were yet **10a**) not thoughts, (thoughts. **10, 10a**) I seemed to rise above law and number.

ww. I became king and priest in my own house, and learned, I know

xx. not how, the meditations that liberate the soul (soul, **10, 10a**) and unite it to

yy. the lawless unity.

zz. *Father Jerome.* I am afraid the restless fit is on you again.

aaa. I hoped you had done with that now.

bbb. *Paul.* I thought so, too. I kept the truth to myself for (myself a **10**; myself for a **10a**) **9-10a**.

1.   *First Friar.* What are they doing? Dancing?

2.   *Second Friar.* I told you they were dancing, and you
3.   would not believe me.

4.   *First Friar.* What on earth are they doing it for?

5.   *Third Friar.* I heard them saying Father Paul told them
6.   to do it if they ever found him in a trance again. He
7.   told them it was a kind of prayer and would bring joy
8.   down out of heaven, and make it easier for him to
9.   preach.

10.   *Second Friar.* How still he is lying; you would nearly
11.   think him to be dead.

12.   *A Friar.* It is just a twelvemonth to-day since he was
13.   in a trance like this.

14.   *Second Friar.* That was the time he gave his great
15.   preaching. I can't blame those that went with him,
16.   for he all but persuaded me.

---

ccc.   years. And then one day when I was praying on this very spot **9**; long time. And then, one day, (then one day **10a**) when I was praying on this very spot, **10, 10a.**

ddd.   the light came again and I heard the sound of clashing swords (swords, **10, 10a**) **9-10a.**

eee.   and I saw angels (saw the angels **10, 10a**) riding upon unicorns. They stood there, (stood up there, **10, 10a**) a

fff.   host of them, and they called out, (out: **10**) 'Teach, teach while there is

ggg.   time, Brother Paul.' [*Some of the friars begin to come in,* (*in;* **10, 10a**)
hhh.   *they carry green branches in their hands.*] Here they are **9-10a.**

iii.   coming. I must light the candles. Some of them are come **9**; coming. [*He rises.*] I must light the candles. Some of them are come **10, 10a.**

jjj.   to hear me now. Will you not stay and believe. Hear **9**; to hear me now. Will you not stay and hear **10, 10a.**

kkk.   what has been put into my mouth? [*He begins to light*
lll.   *candles.*] I have told them to bring green boughs, for I am
mmm.   going to teach them joyful thoughts.

nnn.   *Father Jerome.* I will not stay. I will not listen to you any
ooo.   more. We are separated. Separated (separated—separated **10, 10a**) in this world and in the next.

ppp.   *Paul.* We shall be together in Paradise, for God is joy, and
qqq.   will accomplish all joyful things.

rrr.   *Father Jerome* [*going out*]. Paul, Paul, we are separated for ever.
     [*Paul remains* (*remains,* **10, 10a**) *leaning against a pillar.*] **9-10a.**

1-231.   [lacking] **9-10a.**

17. *First Friar.* They think he is going to preach again
18.   when he awakes, that's why they are dancing. When he
19.   wakes one of them will go and call the others.

20. *Third Friar.* We were all in danger when one so pious
21.   was led away. It's five years he has been with us
22.   now, and no one ever went so quickly from lay brother
23.   to novice, and novice to friar.

24. *First Friar.* The way he fasted too! The Superior bade
25.   me watch him at meal times for fear he should starve
26.   himself.

27. *Third Friar.* He thought a great deal of Brother Paul
28.   then, but he isn't so well pleased with him now.

29. *Second Friar.* What is Father Aloysius doing there?
30.   standing so quiet and his eyes shut.

31. *Third Friar.* He is meditating. Didn't you hear Brother
32.   Paul gives meditations of his own.

33. *First Friar.* Colman was telling me about that. He
34.   gives them a joyful thought to fix their minds on.
35.   They must not let their minds stray to anything else.
36.   They must follow that single thought and put every-
37.   thing else behind them.

38. *Third Friar.* Colman fainted the other day when he was
39.   at his meditation. He says it is a great labour to
40.   follow one thought always.

41. *Second Friar.* What do they do it for?

42. *First Friar.* To escape what they call the wandering
43.   of nature. They say it was in the trance Brother Paul
44.   got the knowledge of it. He says that if a man can
45.   only keep his mind on the one high thought he gets
46.   out of time into eternity, and learns the truth for
47.   itself.

48. *Third Friar.* He calls that getting above law and num-
49.   ber, and becoming king and priest in one's own house.

---

32.   . . . give . . . own? **11A.**
45.   . . . thought, he . . . **11A.**

V.E.P.Y.—2 O

50. *Second Friar.* A nice state of things it would be if
51.   every man was his own priest and his own king.

52. *First Friar.* I wonder will he wake soon. I thought I
53.   saw him stir just now. Father Aloysius, will he wake
54.   soon?

55. *Aloysius.* What did you say?

56. *First Friar.* Will he wake soon?

57. *Aloysius.* Yes, yes, he will wake very soon now.

58. *Second Friar.* What are they going to do now; are they
59.   going to dance?

60. *Third Friar.* He was too patient with him. He would
61.   have made short work of any of us if we had gone so
62.   far.

63. *First Dancer.* Nam, et si ambulavero in medio umbrae mortis,
64.   Non timebo mala, quoniam tu mecum es.

65. *First Friar.* They are singing the twenty-second Psalm.
66.   What madness to sing!

67. *Second Dancer.* Virga tua, et baculus tuus,
68.   Ipsa me consolata sunt.

69. *First Dancer.* Parasti in conspectu meo mensam
70.   Adversus eos qui tribulant me.

71. *Second Dancer.* Impinguasti in oleo caput meum;
72.   Et calix meus inebrians quam praeclarus est.

73. *Second Friar.* Here is the Superior. There'll be bad
74.   work now.

         Superior comes in.

75. *Superior.* [*Holding up his hand.*] Silence!
                [*They stop singing and dancing.*

---

71.   Inpinguasti . . . ; 11A.

76. *First Dancer.* It's the Superior.

77. *Superior.* Stop this blasphemy! Leave the chapel at
78. once! I will deal with you by-and-by.

> [*Dancing Friars go out.*

79. *Jerome.* [*Stooping over Paul.*] He has not wakened from
80. the trance yet.

    Aloysius. [*Who still remains perfectly motionless.*]
81. Not yet, but he will soon awake—Paul!

82. *Superior.* It is hardly worth while being angry with
83. those poor fools whose heads he has turned with his
84. talk. [*Stoops and touches his hand.*] It is quite
85. rigid. I will wait till he is alive again, there is
86. no use wasting words on a dead body.

87. *Jerome.* [*Stooping over him.*] His eyes are beginning to
88. quiver. Let me be the first to speak to him. He may
89. say some wild things when he awakes, not knowing who
90. is before him.

91. *Superior.* He must not preach. I must have his submis-
92. sion at once.

93. *Jerome.* I will do all I can with him. He is most likely
94. to listen to me. I was once his close friend.

95. *Superior.* Speak to him if you like, but entire submis-
96. sion is the only thing I will accept. [*To the other*
97. *Monks.*] Come with me, we will leave Father Jerome
98. here to speak to him. [*Superior and Friars go to the*
99. *door.*] Such desecration, such blasphemy. Remember,
100. Father Jerome, entire submission, and at once.

> [*Superior and Friars go out.*

101. *Jerome.* Where are the rest of his friends, Father
102. Aloysius? Bartley and Colman ought to be with him
103. when he is like this.

104. *Aloysius.* They are resting, because, when he has given
105. his message, they may never be able to rest again.

---

78. . . . by and by. **11A.**

106. *Jerome.* [*Bending over him.*] My poor Paul, this will
107.   wear him out; see how thin he has grown!

108. *Aloysius.* He is hard upon his body. He does not care
109.   what happens to his body.

110. *Jerome.* He was like this when he was a boy; some wild
111.   thought would come on him, and he would not know day
112.   from night, he would forget even to eat. It is a
113.   great pity he was so hard to himself; it is a pity he
114.   had not always someone to look after him.

115. *Aloysius.* God is taking care of him; what could men
116.   like us do for him? We cannot help him, it is he who
117.   helps us.

118. *Jerome.* [*Going on his knee and taking his hand.*] He is
119.   awaking. Help me to lift him up.

> [*They lift him into a chair.*

120. *Aloysius.* I will go and call the others now.

121. *Jerome.* Do not let them come for a little time, I must
122.   speak to him first.

123. *Aloysius.* I cannot keep them away long. One cannot
124.   know when the words may be put in his mouth.

> [*Aloysius goes out. Jerome stands by Paul Ruttledge, holding his hand.*

125. *Paul Ruttledge.* [*Raising his head.*] Ah, you are there,
126.   Jerome. I am glad you are there. I could not get up
127.   to drive away the mouse that was eating the wax that
128.   dropped from the candles. Have you driven it away?

129. *Jerome.* It is not evening now. It is almost morning.
130.   You were on your knees praying for a great many hours,
131.   and then I think you fainted.

132. *Paul Ruttledge.* I don't think I was praying. I was
133.   among people, a great many people, and it was very
134.   bright—I will remember presently.

135. *Jerome.* Do not try to remember. You are tired, you
136.   must be weak, you must come and have food and rest.

137. *Paul Ruttledge.* I do not think I can rest. I think

138. there is something else I have to do, I forget what
139. it is.

140. *Jerome.* I am afraid you are thinking of preaching
141. again. You must not preach. The Superior says you
142. must not. He is very angry; I have never seen him so
143. angry. He will not allow you to preach again.

144. *Paul Ruttledge.* Did I ever preach?

145. *Jerome.* Yes. It was in the garden you got the trance
146. last time. We found you like this, and we lifted you
147. to the bench under the yew tree, and then you began
148. to speak. You spoke about getting out of the body
149. while still alive, about getting away from law and
150. number. All the friars came to listen to you. We had
151. never heard such preaching before, but it was very
152. like heresy.

153. *Paul Ruttledge.* [*Getting up.*] Jerome, Jerome, I remem-
154. ber now where I was. I was in a great round place,
155. and a great crowd of things came round me. I couldn't
156. see them very clearly for a time, but some of them
157. struck me with their feet, hard feet like hoofs, and
158. soft cat-like feet; and some pecked me, and some bit
159. me, and some clawed me. There were all sorts of
160. beasts and birds as far as I could see.

161. *Jerome.* Were they devils, Paul, were they the deadly
162. sins?

163. *Paul Ruttledge.* I don't know, but I thought, and I
164. don't know how the thought came to me, that they were
165. the part of mankind that is not human; the part that
166. builds up the things that keep the soul from God.

167. *Jerome.* That was a terrible vision.

168. *Paul Ruttledge.* I struggled and I struggled with them,
169. and they heaped themselves over me till I was unable
170. to move hand or foot; and that went on for a long,
171. long time.

172. *Jerome.* [*Crossing himself.*] God have mercy on us.

173. *Paul Ruttledge.* Then suddenly there came a bright
174. light, and all in a minute the beasts were gone, and

175.   I saw a great many angels riding upon unicorns, white
176.   angels on white unicorns. They stood all round me,
177.   and they cried out, 'Brother Paul, go and preach; get
178.   up and preach, Brother Paul.' And then they laughed
179.   aloud, and the unicorns trampled the ground as though
180.   the world were already falling in pieces.

181. *Jerome.* It was only a dream. Come with me. You will
182.   forget it when you have had food and rest.

183. *Paul Ruttledge.* [*Looking at his arm.*] It was there one
184.   of them clawed me; one that looked at me with great
185.   heavy eyes.

186. *Jerome.* The Superior has been here; try and listen to
187.   me. He says you must not preach.

188. *Paul Ruttledge.* Great heavy eyes and hard sharp claws.

189. *Jerome.* [*Putting his hands on his shoulders.*] You must
190.   awake from this. You must remember where you are. You
191.   are under rules. You must not break the rules you are
192.   under. The brothers will be coming in to hear you,
193.   you must not speak to them. The Superior has forbid-
194.   den it.

195. *Paul Ruttledge.* [*Touching Jerome's hand.*] I have al-
196.   ways been a great trouble to you.

197. *Jerome.* You must go and submit to the Superior. Go and
198.   make your submission now, for my sake. Think of what
199.   I have done for your sake. Remember how I brought you
200.   in, and answered for you when you came here. I did
201.   not tell about that wild business. I have done pen-
202.   ance for that deceit.

203. *Paul Ruttledge.* Yes, you have always been good to me,
204.   but do not ask me this. I have had other orders.

205. *Jerome.* Last time you preached the whole monastery was
206.   upset. The Friars began to laugh suddenly in the mid-
207.   dle of the night.

208. *Paul Ruttledge.* If I have been given certain truths to
209.   tell, I must tell them at once before they slip away
210.   from me.

211. *Jerome.* I cannot understand your ideas; you tell them
212.   impossible things. Things that are against the order

213. of nature.

214. *Paul Ruttledge.* I have learned that one needs a re-
215. ligion so wholly supernatural, that is so opposed to
216. the order of nature that the world can never capture
217. it.

[*Some Friars come in. They carry green branches in their hands.*]

218. *Paul Ruttledge.* They are coming. Will you stay and
219. listen?

220. *Jerome.* I must not stay. I must not listen.

221. *Paul Ruttledge.* Help me over to the candles. I am weak,
222. my knees are weak. I shall be strong when the words
223. come. I shall be able to teach. [*He lights a taper at the hanging
lamp and tries to light the candles with a shaking hand. Jerome takes
the taper from him and*
224. *lights the candles.*] Why are you crying, Jerome?

225. *Jerome.* Because we that were friends are separated
226. now. We shall never be together again.

227. *Paul Ruttledge.* Never again? The love of God is a very
228. terrible thing.

229. *Jerome.* I have done with meddling. I must leave you to
230. authority now. I must tell the Superior you will not
231. obey. [*He goes out.*

232. *First[1] Friar.* Father Jerome had a very dark look going
233. out.

234. *Second Friar.* He was shut up with the Superior this
235. morning. I wonder what they were talking about.

236. *First Friar.* I wonder if the Superior will mind our
237. taking the branches. They are only cut on Palm Sunday
238. other years. What will he tell us, I wonder? It seems

---

238. . . . years.
238a. *Third Friar.* It (*Aloysius.* It **10, 10a**) is likely he will be vexed we did
not go to
238b. the school. I had a mind to go, but I could not stop away from
9-10a.

[1] *First, Second,* etc., *Friar* are 1*st,* 2*nd,* etc. *Friar* in **10.**

239.   as if he was going to tell us how to do some great
240.   thing. Do you think he will teach us to do cures like
241.   the friars used at Esker?

242.   *Second Friar.* Those were great cures they did there,
243.   and they were not strange men, but just the same as
244.   ourselves. I heard of a man went to them dying on a
245.   cart, and he walked twenty miles home to Burren hold-
246.   ing the horse's head.

247.   *First Friar.* Maybe we'll be able to see visions the
248.   same as were seen at Knock. It's a great wonder all
249.   that was seen and all that was done there.

250.   *Third Friar.* I was there one time, and the whole place
251.   was full of crutches that had been thrown away by
252.   people that were cured. There was a silver crutch
253.   there some rich man from America had sent as an of-
254.   fering after getting his cure. Speak to him, Brother
255.   Colman. He seems to be in some sort of a dream.
256.   Ask if he is going to speak to us now.

257.   *Colman.* We are all here, Brother Paul.

258.   *Paul Ruttledge.* Have you all been through your medita-
259.   tions?   [*They all gather round him.*

238c.   here when I knew Father Paul was going to speak.
238d.   *First Friar.* What will he tell us, I wonder? It seems
  239.   as . . . **9-10a.**
  240.   things . . . . **10, 10a.**
  244.   . . . man who went . . . .
  245.   . . . Burren, hold- **10, 10a.**
  248.   . . . great number all **10, 10a.**
  253.   . . . some man (some rich man **10a**) . . . had got made as . . . **10, 10a.**
  254.   . . . cure.
254a.   *Father Colman* [*Coming in*]. Am I in time? I was afraid I
254b.   would be late.
254c.   *First Friar.* He hasn't said anything yet. He seems to be
254d.   in some sort of a dream.
254e.   *Father Colman.* I haven't got a branch. I was afraid to go
254f.   for it at the last, for fear I should miss a word.
  255.   *Third Friar.* Speak to him, Brother Colman. **9-10a.**

260. *Bartley.* We have all tried; we have done our best; but
261.   it is hard to keep our mind on the one thing for long.

262. *Paul Ruttledge.* 'He ascended into heaven.' Have you
263.   meditated upon that? Did you reject all earthly
264.   images that came into your mind till the light began
265.   to gather?

266. *Third Friar.* I could not fix my mind well. When I put
267.   out one thought others came rushing in.

268. *Colman.* When I was meditating, the inside of my head
269.   suddenly became all on fire.

270. *Aloysius.* While I was meditating I felt a spout of
271.   fire going up between my shoulders.

272. *Paul Ruttledge.* That is the way it begins. You are
273.   ready now to hear the truth. Now I can give you the
274.   message that has come to me. Stand here at either
275.   side of the altar. Brother Colman, come beside me
276.   here. Lay down your palm branches before this altar;
277.   you have brought them as a sign that the walls are
278.   beginning to be broken up, that we are going back to
279.   the joy of the green earth. [*Goes up to the candles*
280.   *and speaks.*] Et calix meus inebrians quam praeclarus
281.   est. For a long time after their making men and women
282.   wandered here and there, half blind from the drunken-

---

260. ... tried. We ... best, but **10, 10a.**
264. ... mind, till ... **10, 10a.**
267. ... thought, others .... **10, 10a.**
268-269. [lacking] **10.**
268. ... meditating the ... **10a.**
270. *Brother Colman.* When I ... meditating, I ... **10**; ... meditating, I ... **11A.**
275. ... of me. Brother ...
276. ... altar.
277. You ... **10, 10a.**
    Directions in 279. [*Paul goes* ... **9**; [*Standing on the altar,* **10, 10a.**
280. ... *speaks.*] In the first days of the world when men **9**; *speaks*] In the first days of the world, (world **10a**) when men **10, 10a.**
281. came freshly from God (God, **10**) they lived as God meant them to live.
282. They were full of faith and hope and love and anger, for he (anger; for He **10, 10a**) had **9-10a.**

283.   ness of Eternity; they had not yet forgotten that the
284.   green Earth was the Love of God, and that all Life
285.   was the Will of God, and so they wept and laughed and
286.   hated according to the impulse of their hearts. [*He takes up the*
       green boughs and presses them to his
287.   *breast.*] They gathered the green Earth to their
288.   breasts and their lips, as I gather these boughs to
289.   mine, in what they believed would be an eternal kiss.

                               [*He remains a little while silent.*

290. *Second Friar.* I see a light about his head.

291. *Third Friar.* I wonder if he has seen God.

292. *Paul Ruttledge.* It was then that the temptation began.
293.   Not only the Serpent who goes upon his belly, but all
294.   the animal spirits that have loved things better than
295.   life, came out of their holes and began to whisper.
296.   The men and women listened to them, and because when
297.   they had lived according to the joyful Will of God in

---

283.   made them entirely living (living, **10, 10a**) and living with every
       kind of life, and
284.   all life was the will of God. And in those days they lived
285.   in the woods and by the side of the woods, (woods **10a**) and they
       slept on
286.   the bare ground, (ground; **10**) and whatever they set their hands to,
       (to **10a**) they had
286a.   always about them dark and dawn (dawn, **10**) and evening twilight
       (twilight, **10**) and
286b.   the green things. They lived always under the shelter of God's
286c.   love, for the changing heaven and the many coloured fields are
286d.   God's love. They had within them, therefore, (them therefore **10a**)
       the will of God and
286e.   His love was over them and about them. [*He takes flowers*
287.   *from his altar and* (*from the bunch* (*bench* **10a**) *and* **10, 10a**) *presses them*
       upon his heart.] And as I
288.   gather these flowers to my heart (heart, **10a**) they gathered all His
       love into
289.   their hearts. **9-10a.**
       Directions after 289. [. . . *remains silent for a little.*] **10, 10a.**
291.   . . . God? **10, 10a.**
292.   Then men eat (ate **10, 10a**) the fruit of the tree of knowledge. And
       9-10a.
293-295.   [lacking] **9-10a.**
296.   because (because, **10**) when
297.   they lived . . . the will . . . **9-10a.**

298. mother wit and natural kindness, they sometimes did
299. one another an injury, they thought that it would be
300. better to be safe than to be blessèd, they made the
301. Laws. The Laws were the first sin. They were the
302. first mouthful of the apple, the moment man had made
303. them he began to die; we must put out the Laws as I
304. put out this candle.

[*He puts out the candle with an extinguisher, still holding the boughs with his left hand. Two orthodox Friars have come in.*

305. *First Orthodox Friar.* You had better go for the Su-
306. perior.

307. *Second Orthodox Friar.* I must stop and listen.

[*The First Orthodox Friar listens for a minute or two and then goes out.*

308. *Paul Ruttledge.* And when they had lived amidst the
309. green Earth that is the Love of God, they were some-
310. times wetted by the rain, and sometimes cold and
311. hungry, and sometimes alone from one another; they
312. thought it would be better to be comfortable than to
313. be blessèd. They began to build big houses and big
314. towns. They grew wealthy and they sat chattering at
315. their doors; and the embrace that was to have been
316. eternal ended, lips and hands were parted. [*He lets*

---

298. ... kindness (kindness, **10**) they ... **9-10a.**
299. ... thought it ... **10, 10a.**
300. ... blessed, and they ... **10.**
301. laws. ... laws ...
302. ... apple.
303. We ... laws ... **9-10a.**
Directions after 304. [... *out the (a* **10, 10a**) *candle ... extinguisher. Two ....*] **9-10a.**
305. *The First Friar.* ... **9**; *The First.* ... **10, 10a.**
307. *The Second Friar.* ... **9**; *The Second.* ... **10, 10a.**
Directions after 307. [... *first listens ... two, and ....*] **9-10a.**
308. And then (the **10, 10a**) men began to make cities and build villages,
309. because, (because **10, 10a**) when they lived in the midst of the love of God, (God— **10**) that
309a. is (is, **10**) the changing heavens and the many-coloured (many coloured **10, 10a**) fields, they were **9-10a.**
310. sometimes ... **9**; sometimes ... rain and ... **10, 10a.**
311. ... another. They **9**; hungry and ... another. They **10, 10a.**
313. ... blessed. **9-10a.**
314-Directions in 317. [lacking] **9-10a.**

317.   *the boughs slip out of his arms.*] We must put out the
318.   towns as I put out this candle.

                                   [*Puts out another candle.*

319.   *A Friar.* Yes, yes, we must uproot the towns.

320.   *Paul Ruttledge.* But that is not all, for man created
321.   a worse thing, yes, a worse defiance against God.
322.   [*The Friars groan.*] God put holiness into everything
323.   that lives, for everything that desires is full of
324.   His Will, and everything that is beautiful is full
325.   of His Love; but man grew timid because it had been
326.   hard to find his way amongst so much holiness, and
327.   though God had made all time holy, man said that only
328.   the day on which God rested from life was holy, and
329.   though God had made all places holy, man said, 'no
330.   place but this place that I put pillars and walls
331.   about is holy, this place where I rest from life';
332.   and in this and like ways he built up the Church. We
333.   must destroy the Church, we must put it out as I put

---

317.   We . . . **9-10a.**
318.   cities as . . . . **9**; cities as we put . . . . . **10, 10a.**
319.   . . . the cities. **9, 10.**
321.   . . . defiance of God. **9**; . . . thing; yes, . . . defiance of God. **10.**
322.   [. . . .] God made everything holy, (holy **10a**)
323.   because everything that is full of life is . . . **9-10a.**
324.   . . . will, (will **10a**) . . . beautiful is an **9-10a.**
325.   image of . . . love. But . . . timid, (timid **10, 10a**) and called some things holy
325a.   and some things unholy, because it had been
326.   . . . among . . . holiness. He grew timid and bold, and
327.   . . . had put holiness into every day He (day, he **10**; day he **10a**) said only one should be holy. **9-10a.**
328.   [lacking] **9, 10a.**
329.   And though . . . had put holiness into all places (places, **10**) he said, (said: **10**)
330.   'This little place . . .
331.   about, (about **10a**) and a roof above (above, **10, 10a**) is alone holy.' God has (had **10, 10a**) put holiness into
331a.   all passions, but man said, being bold and timid: (timid, **10a**) 'Only this little
331b.   number of passions (passions, **10**) that I count as I count the rings on my hand (hand, **10**)
332.   have holiness.' And from these (these, **10**) and from like things, (things **10a**) he . . .
333.   . . . Church. We . . . **9-10a.**

334. out this candle.   [*Puts out another candle.*

335. *Friars.* [*Clasping one another's hands.*] He is right,
336. he is right. The Church must be destroyed.

            [*The Superior comes in.*

337. *First Friar.* Here is the Superior.

338. *A Friar.* He has been saying——

339. *Superior.* Hush! I will hear him to the end.

340. *Paul Ruttledge.* That is not all. These things may be
341. accomplished and yet nothing be accomplished. The
342. Christian's business is not reformation but revela-
343. tion, and the only labours he can put his hand to can
344. never be accomplished in Time. He must so live that
345. all things shall pass away. [*He stands silent for a moment and then cries, lifting his hand above his*
346. *head.*] Give me wine out of thy pitchers; oh, God,
347. how splendid is my cup of drunkenness. We must become
348. blind, and deaf, and dizzy. We must get rid of every-
349. thing that is not measureless eternal life. We must
350. put out hope as I put out this candle. [*Puts out a*
351. *candle.*] And memory as I put out this candle. [*As be-*
352. *fore.*] And thought, the waster of Life, as I put out
353. this candle. [*As before.*] And at last we must put
354. out the light of the Sun and of the Moon, and all

---

335. *A Friar* [*clasping another's hands*]. . . . , **10, 10a.**
336. . . . destroyed! **9-10a.**
338. *An Orthodox Friar* [*goes to him*]. He . . .—
339. *The Superior.*/ Hush, (Hush! **10**) I . . . .
340. But that . . . **9-10a.**
341. accomplished, and . . . **9.**
342. . . . reformation, but . . . **10.**
343. . . . labour (labours **10, 10a**) he will put . . . hands to are
344. those than can never . . . time. . . .
345. . . . away. He will so live
345a. that he will put out the body. [*Puts out a candle.*] He will so live **9-10a.**
346-353. [lacking] **9-10a.**
347. . . . drunkenness! We . . . **11A.**
354. that he will put out the moon and stars. [*Puts out a candle.*] He **9-10a.**

---

¹ *Superior* is *The Superior* in **9.**

355.   the light of the World and the World itself. [*He now puts out the last candle, the chapel is very dark. The only light is the faint light of morning coming*

356.   *through the window.*] We must destroy the World; we
357.   must destroy everything that has Law and Number, for
358.   where there is nothing, there is God.

        [*The Superior comes forward. One of Paul's Friars makes as if to speak to him. The Superior strikes at him with the back of his hand*

359.   *Superior.* [*To Paul Ruttledge.*] Get out of this, rebel,
360.   blasphemous rebel!

361.   *Paul Ruttledge.* Do as you like to me, but you cannot
362.   silence my thoughts. I learned them from Jesus Christ,
363.   who made a terrible joy, and sent it to overturn
364.   governments, and all settled order.

        [*Paul's Friars rush to save him from the Superior.*

365.   *Paul Ruttledge.* There is no need for violence. I am
366.   ready to go.

367.   *Colman.* [*Taking his hand.*] I will go with you.

368.   *Aloysius.* I will go with you too.

369.   *Several other Friars.* And I, and I, and I.

370.   *Superior.* Whoever goes with this heretic goes straight
371.   into the pit.

372.   *Bartley.* Do not leave us behind you. Let us go with

---

355.   will so live that he will put out the whole world. [*Puts out last (out a* **10a**)
356.   *candle.*] We . . . world. We **9-10a.**
357.   . . . law . . . number, . . . **9** ; . . . has form and law . . . number, . . . **10, 10a.**
358.   . . . nothing there . . . . **9, 10** ; . . . nothing there . . . God. [*Puts out last candle.*] **10a.**
364.   governments and . . . . **10, 10a.**
        Directions after 364. [. . . *Superior. Paul motions them back.*] **10, 10a.**
366.   . . . go. [*To his friars.*] Who is coming with me? **9-10a.**
        [*All come towards him.*] **9-10a.**
367-369.   [lacking] **9-10a.**
370.   . . . heretic, goes . . . **10, 10a.**
371.   to everlasting death.
371a.   *Paul.* Who will come with me to the life that is outside
371b.   walls and laws and numbers? **9-10a.**
372-Directions after 405.   [lacking] **9-10a.**

373. you.

374. *Colman*. Teach us! teach us! we will help you to teach
375.   others.

376. *Paul Ruttledge*. Let me go alone, the one more, the one
377.   nearer falsehood.

378. *Bartley*. We will go with you! We will go with you! We
379.   must go where we can hear your voice.

380. *A Friar*. [*Who stands behind the Superior*.] God is
381.   making him speak against himself.

382. *Paul Ruttledge*. No, the time has not come for you. You
383.   would be thinking of your food at midday and listen-
384.   ing for bells at prayer time. You have not yet
385.   heard the voices and seen the faces.

386. *Superior*. A miracle! God is making the heretic speak
387.   against himself. Listen to him!

388. *Aloysius*. We will not stay behind, we will go with
389.   you.

390. *Bartley*. We cannot live without hearing you!

391. *Paul Ruttledge*. I am led by hands that are colder than
392.   ice and harder than diamonds. They will lead me where
393.   there will be hard thoughts of me in the hearts of all
394.   that love me, and there will be a fire in my heart
395.   that will make it as bare as the wilderness.

396. *Aloysius*. We will go with you. We too will take those
397.   hands that are colder than ice and harder than dia-
398.   monds.

399. *Several Monks*. We too! we too!

400. *Patrick*. Bring us to the hands that are colder than
401.   ice and harder than diamonds.

402. *Other Monks*. Pull them away! pull them away from him!
      [*They are about to seize the Monks who are with Paul Ruttledge.*

403. *Superior*. [*Going between them.*] Back! back! I will

404.　　have no scuffling here. Let the devil take his chil-
405.　　dren if he has a mind to. God will call His own.
　　　　[*The Monks fall back. Superior goes up to altar, takes the cross from
　　　　it and turns, standing on the steps.*

406.　*Superior.* Father Aloysius, come to me here. [*Aloysius*
407.　　*takes Paul Ruttledge's hand.*] Father Bartley, Father
408.　　Colman. [*They go nearer to Paul Ruttledge.*] Father
409.　　Patrick! [*A Friar comes towards him.*] Kneel down!
410.　　[*Father Patrick kneels.*] Father Clement, Father Nes-
411.　　tor, Father James . . . leave the heretic—you are
412.　　on the very edge of the pit. Your shoes are growing
413.　　red hot.

414.　*A Friar.* I am afraid, I am afraid.　　　　　　　　[*He kneels.*

415.　*Superior.* Kneel down; return to your God.

　　　　　　　　　　　　　　　　　　　　[*Several Monks kneel.*

416.　*Colman.* They have deserted us.

417.　*Paul Ruttledge.* Many will forsake the truth before the
418.　　world is pulled down. [*Stretching out his arms over
419.　　his head.*] I pulled down my own house, now I go out
420.　　to pull down the world.

406.　*The Superior* [*going up to the altar-steps* (*altar steps* **10, 10a**)]. I demand
407-408.　[lacking]
409.　obedience in the name of the Church! (Church. **10, 10a**) Down on
　　　your knees! (knees. **10, 10a**)
410.　[*One or two kneel.*] Down on your knees! (knees. **10, 10a**) You are on
　　　the
411.　[lacking]　　　.
412.　brink of death; (death— **10, 10a**) on the brink of hell! (Hell. **10,
　　　10a**) Your . . . are already
413.　becoming red-hot; (red hot. **10, 10a**) [*Lifts a Cross.* (*Lifts Cross.* **10**)]
　　　Return to your God!
　　　　[*All the friars kneel down but three,* (*three* **10a**) *who go over to Paul.*]
414-Directions after 415.　[lacking]
416.　*Father Colman* [*pointing to kneeling friars*]. They have forsaken us.
417.　*Paul.* Do not reproach them. Who knows how many may
418.　fail before the world is put down. (down? **10, 10a**) Come you with
　　　me. **9-10a.**
419-420.　[lacking] **9-10a.**

421. *Superior.* Strip off those holy habits.
422. *Paul Ruttledge.* [*Taking off his habit.*] One by one I
423.   am plucking off the rags and tatters of the world.

---

421. *The Superior* [*from altar steps*]. Strip . . . habits! **9-10a.**
422. Here, (Here **10a**) I gladly
423. take off another covering of . . . . **10, 10a.**

ACT V.

Scene: *Smooth level grass near the Shannon. Ecclesiastical ruins, a part of which have been roofed in. Rocky plain in the distance, with a river. Father Colman sorting some bundles of osiers.*
Aloysius enters with an empty bag.

STAGE DIRECTIONS   Scene—*Smooth*, (Scene.—*Smooth* **10, 10a**) *level . . . river.*
Father Bartley, (*Bartley* **10, 10a**) *on a short ladder, mending roof. Paul weaving baskets.* **9-10a.**

a.[1]   *Father Aloysius [laying down an armful of osiers].* I think

b.   there are enough there to finish this day's work.

c.   *Paul.* Did you see anything of Father Colman (Colman, **10**) when you

d.   were at the river?

e.   *Father Aloysius.* There was no sign of him on the road. I

f.   went as far as the corner to look.

g.   *Paul.* I hope nothing has happened to him. The last time I

h.   was preaching at Shanaglish the people were not as glad to see

i.   me as before. The priests had (have **10, 10a**) been speaking against us. Yet

j.   if one does not go on market days (days, **10**) it is hard to find the people

k.   gathered together.

l.   *Father Aloysius.* It will be my turn to go out to-morrow;

m.   the baskets will be ready to sell then. I have a mind to go as

n.   far as Athlone. Do you think, Brother Paul, we might have

o.   done better to begin with the towns? I used to think I

p.   preached better to a big congregation.

q.   *Paul.* No, Aloysius, the towns will fall of themselves some **9-10a.**

r.   day; we must fight an impossible battle that we may have a **9;** day. The work has to be done in the villages, for the shell is **10, 10a.**

s.   perfect joy. **9;** hardest there. **10, 10a.**

t.   *Father Aloysius.* We have been working a good time now,

u.   and we don't seem to have done much yet.

v.   *Paul.* Have you begun to doubt, Brother Aloysius? If one

w.   has faith in God (God, **10**) one cannot help being certain that He (he **10, 10a**) will

x.   accomplish at last all that He (he **10**) has shown to us of perfection.

y.   *Father Aloysius.* I don't doubt, (doubt; **10, 10a**) but one gets a little tired

z.   sometimes when nothing comes of one's preaching. **9-10a.**

---

[1] Some of the lines a-ggg are similar to lines located elsewhere in this act in **11.**

aa. *Paul.* Many and many a one will have to dig under the
bb. foundations before the walls begin to crack. But it will happen **9-10a.**
cc. at last, the joyful individual life will return, everything will
dd. become sacred, the laws will come to an end, and everyone will
ee. walk about upon the hand of God.
ff. *Father Bartley* [*from the roof*]. I see five herons standing
gg. in the water.
hh. *Father Aloysius.* I saw them, but I kept quiet that I might
ii. not scare them. They were quite close to me.
jj. *Father Bartley.* They have no master.
kk. *Father Aloysius.* They looked so wise and peaceful, they
ll. made me think of the rest that remaineth to the people of God.
mm. *Father Bartley.* I heard an otter splash into the water
nn. yesterday. No wonder we got (get **10, 10a**) so few fish.
oo. *Paul.* We will not depend on fish so much after a while,
pp. when our own little garden begins to give us something, and
qq. when we are able to cut those cabbages.
rr. *Father Aloysius.* If we sell all those baskets to-morrow (to-morrow, **10, 10a**) we
ss. can buy some potatoes against the winter. (winter . . . [T] **10a**) Do you hear the
tt. curlews calling; (calling?— **10, 10a**) they make me sad.
uu. *Father Bartley.* They make me sad, too. **9-10a.**
vv. *Paul.* Those sad cries are God lamenting over the fall of **9**; I sometimes think that those sad cries, the cry **10, 10a.**
ww. man, but it is better to listen to His rejoicings when a soul **9**; of the curlew and the plover, are Jesus Christ lamenting **10, 10a.**
xx. ascends into heaven. The crows are my darlings! I like their **9**; over the fall of man and over the sins of man. **10, 10a.**
yy. harsh merriment better than those sad cries. I often saw them **9.**
zz. coming home in a storm when I was a child, whirling hither and **9.**
aaa. thither, drunk with the wind, crying out to one another as the **9.**
bbb. witches do when their white horses dance upon the clouds. **9.**
ccc. *Father Bartley.* What a great noise the wind made last
ddd. night. (night! **10, 10a**) I wonder it did not tear away the whole roof, instead
eee. of this little corner. **9-10a.**
fff. *Paul.* That is a good noise, too. The wind tears down **9**; There is a great deal of trouble in nature, but it is a good trouble. **10, 10a.**
ggg. everything before it trying to get back to the place it came from. **9**; Everything alive is striving to destroy all that is in its way that it may get back to the place it came from. **10, 10a.**

1. *Colman.* You are the first to come back Aloysius. Where
2.   is Brother Bartley?

3. *Aloysius.* He parted from me at the cross roads and
4.   went on to preach at Shanaglish. He should soon be
5.   back now.

6. *Colman.* Have you anything in the bag?

7. *Aloysius.* Nothing. [*Throws the bag down.*] It doesn't
8.   seem as if our luck was growing. We have but food
9.   enough to last till to-morrow. We have hardly that.
10.   The rats from the river got at the few potatoes I
11.   gathered from the farmers at Lisheen last week, in
12.   the corner where they were.

13. *Colman.* This is the first day you got nothing at all.
14.   Maybe you didn't ask the right way.

15. *Aloysius.* I asked for alms for the sake of the love
16.   of God. But the first place where I asked it, the man
17.   of the house was giving me a handful of meal, and the
18.   woman came and called out that we were serving the
19.   devil in the name of God, and she drove me from the
20.   door.

21. *Colman.* It is since the priests preached against us
22.   they say that. Did you go on to Lisheen. They used
23.   always to treat us well there.

24. *Aloysius.* I did, but I got on no better there.

25. *Colman.* That is a wonder, after the woman that had the
26.   jaundice being cured with prayers by Brother Paul.

27. *Aloysius.* That's just it. If he did cure her, they say
28.   the two best of her husband's bullocks died of the
29.   blackwater the next day, and he was no way thankful
30.   to us after that.

31. *Colman.* Did you try the houses along the bog road?

32. *Aloysius.* I did, and the children coming back from
33.   school called out after me and asked who was it did

1-89. [lacking] **9-10a.**

34.   away with the widow Cloran's cow.

35. *Colman*. The widow Cloran's cow?

36. *Aloysius*. That was the cow that died after grazing in
37.   the ruins here.

38. *Colman*. If it did, it was because of an old boot it
39.   picked up and ate, and that never belonged to us.

40. *Aloysius*. I wish we had something ourselves to eat.
41.   They should be sitting down to their dinner in the
42.   monastery now. They will be having a good dinner to-
43.   day to carry them over the fast to-morrow.

44. *Colman*. I am thinking sometimes, Brother Paul should
45.   give more thought to us than he does. It is all very
46.   well for him, he is so taken up with his thoughts and
47.   his visions he doesn't know if he is full or fasting.

48. *Aloysius*. He has such holy thoughts and visions no one
49.   would like to trouble him. He ought not to be in the
50.   world at all, or to do the world's work.

51. *Colman*. So long as he is in the world, he must give
52.   some thought to it. There must be something wrong in
53.   the way he is doing things now. I thought he would
54.   have had half Ireland with him by this time with his
55.   great preaching, but someway when he preaches to the
56.   people, they don't seem to mind him much.

57. *Aloysius*. He is too far above them; they have not edu-
58.   cation to understand him.

59. *Colman*. They understand me well enough when I give my
60.   mind to it. But it is harder to preach now than it
61.   was in the monastery. We had something to offer then;
62.   absolution here, and heaven after.

63. *Aloysius*. Isn't it enough for them to hear that the
64.   kingdom of heaven is within them, and that if they
65.   do the right meditations——

66. *Colman*. What can poor people that have their own
67.   troubles on them get from a few words like that they
68.   hear at a cross road or a market, and the wind maybe
69.   blowing them away? If we could gather them together

70.   now. . . . Look, Aloysius, at these sally rods; I
71.   have a plan in my mind about them.

   [*He has stuck some of the rods in the ground, and begins weaving
   others through them.*]

72. *Aloysius.* Are you going to make baskets like you did
73.   in the monastery schools?

74. *Colman.* We must make something if we are to live. But
75.   it is more than that I was thinking of; we might coax
76.   some of the youngsters to come and learn the basket
77.   making; it would make them take to us better if we
78.   could put them in the way of earning a few pence.

   Aloysius. [*Taking up some of the osiers and beginning
79.   to twist them.*] That might be a good way to come at
80.   them; they could work through the day, and at evening
81.   we could tell them how to repeat the words till the
82.   light comes inside their heads. But would Paul think
83.   well of it? He is more for pulling down than building
84.   up.

85. *Colman.* When I explain it to him I am sure he will
86.   think well of it; he can't go on for ever without
87.   anyone to listen to him.

88. *Aloysius.* I suppose not, and with no way of living.
89.   But I don't know, I'm afraid he won't like it.

90. *Colman.* Hush! Here he is coming.

91. *Aloysius.* If one had a plan now for doing some destruc-
92.   tion——

93. *Colman.* Hush! don't you see there is somebody with him.

---

90.   *Father Bartley.* I think I see Father Colman. Oh! (Oh, **10, 10a**) no,
      it's
91-92. [lacking] **9-10a.**
93.   noth im; there (him; it **10, 10a**) is a man on the road; he (road.
      He **10, 10a**) is a stranger. **9-10a ;** . . . him? **11A.**
93a.   *Paul.* Whoever he is (is, **10, 10a**) he is welcome. Come down and
93b.   light the fire inside. [*Father Bartley comes down.*] Maybe
93c.   he will want something to eat.
93d.   *Father Bartley.* We have a few eggs I gathered up this
93e.   morning. I wish the hens didn't lay so far astray. **9-10a.**

Paul Ruttledge comes in with Charlie Ward.

94. *Paul Ruttledge.* This is Charlie Ward, my old friend.

95. *Aloysius.* The Charlie Ward you lived on the roads with?

96. *Paul Ruttledge.* Yes, when I went looking for the
97.   favour of my hard mother, Earth, he helped me. He is
98.   her good child and she loves him.

99. *Colman.* He is welcome. How did he find you out?

100. *Paul Ruttledge.* I don't know. How did you find me out,
101.   Charlie?

102. *Charlie Ward.* Oh, I didn't lose sight of you so much
103.   as you thought. I had to stop away from Gortmore a
104.   good while after we left you at the gate, but I sent
105.   Paddy Cockfight one time to get news, and he mended
106.   cans for the laundry of the monastery, and they told
107.   him you were well again, and a monk as good as the
108.   rest. But a while ago I got word there was a monk had
109.   gone near to break up the whole monastery with his
110.   talk and his piety, and I said to myself, 'That's
111.   Paul!' And then I heard there was a monk had been
112.   driven out for not keeping the rules, and I said to

93f.   *Paul.* We'll make a shed for them some of these days. **9-10a.**
      [*Enter Charlie Ward.*]

93g.   *Charlie Ward.* So I thought. This is that merry chap (chap, **10, 10a**)
      Paul.

93h.   *Paul.* Charlie! Is that you yourself! Oh! (yourself? Oh, **10, 10a**) I
      am delighted

94.   to see you! Aloysius, Bartley, this . . . Charlie Ward (Ward,— **10**)
      that I told you about.

95.   *Father Bartley.* The . . . Ward that you lived with? **9-10a.**

96-99.   [lacking] **9-10a.**

100.   *Paul.* How . . . out?

101.   [lacking] **9-10a.**

102.   Oh! I . . . **9.**

105.   Tommy the Song one . . . **9-10a.**

106.   . . . laundry at the . . . **9, 10a ;** . . . laundry at the Monastery, . . . **10.**

107.   . . . again, (again **10a**) and a friar as . . . **10, 10a.**

108.   . . . . But long ago . . . **9 ;** . . . . But long ago . . . a friar had **10, 10a ;**
      . . . awhile . . . **11A.**

109.   . . . Monastery . . . **10.**

110.   . . . myself 'That's **9 ;** . . . myself: 'That's **10.**

111.   . . . a friar had . . . **10, 10a.**

113. myself, 'That's Paul!' And the other day when what's
114. left of us came to Athlone, I heard talk of some dis-
115. frocked monks that were upsetting the whole neighbour-
116. hood, and I said, 'That's Paul.' To Sabina Silver I
117. said that. 'That merry chap Paul,' I said.

118. *Paul Ruttledge*. I'm afraid you have a very bad opinion
119. of me, Charlie. Well, maybe I earned it.

120. *Aloysius*. You cannot know much of him if you have a
121. bad opinion of him. He will be made a saint some day.

122. *Charlie Ward*. He will, if there's such a thing as a
123. saint of mischief.

124. *Paul Ruttledge*. A saint of mischief? Well, why not
125. that as well as another? He would upset all the bee-
126. hives, he would throw them into the market-place. Sit
127. down now, Charlie, and eat a bit with us.

---

113. myself (myself: **10**) 'That's . . . day, when . . . **9, 10**.
115. frocked friars that . . . **10, 10a**.
116. . . . said (said: **10**) 'That's Paul!' To . . . **9, 10**.
117. . . . that. **9-10a**.
118. . . . afraid you've a . . .
119. . . . , maybe, (maybe **10**) I . . . it. Sit down now, and stop to eat a
    bit with us.
    [*Charlie sits down.*] **9-10a**.
119a. *Father Aloysius*. Maybe he could tell us what is putting
119b. the people against us. Is it only what the priest has been saying?
119c. *Charlie Ward*. Well, indeed, you seem to have no better
119d. name among the people than if you were of my own tribe!
119e. You might as well have stopped along with us, Paul; you had
119f. the makings of a good tinker in you.
119g. *Paul*. But what are they accusing us of?
119h. *Charlie Ward*. Every sort of thing. Some bad luck they
119i. say you brought on the neighbourhood. Some hag you cured
119j. with a prayer, and if you did, a blood murrain came on the
119k. husband's cattle the next day, and faith he was no way thank-
119l. ful to you. And there was a milch cow belonging to a widow
119m. died after grazing about the ruins here.
119n. *Father Bartley*. If she did, it was because of an old brogue
119o. she picked up and eat, and that never belonged to us.
119p. *Charlie Ward*. Well, whether or not, I'd advise you to be
119q. like myself, (myself **10a**) and not stop too long in one place. **9-10a**.
120-132. [lacking] **9**.
120-265. [lacking] **10, 10a**.

128. *Colman.* You are welcome, indeed, to all we can give
129.   you, but we have not a bit of food that is worth
130.   offering you. Aloysius got nothing at all in the
131.   villages to-day, Brother Paul. The people are getting
132.   cross.

133. *Paul Ruttledge.* Well, sit down, anyway. The country
134.   people liked me well enough once, there was no man
135.   they liked so much as myself when I gave them drink
136.   for nothing. Didn't they, Charlie?

137. *Charlie Ward.* Oh, that was a great time. They were
138.   lying thick about the roads. I'll be thinking of it
139.   to my dying day.

140. *Paul Ruttledge.* I have given them another kind of
141.   drink now.

142. *Charlie Ward.* What sort of a drink is that?

143. *Paul Ruttledge.* We have rolled a great barrel out of
144.   a cellar that is under the earth. We have rolled it
145.   right into the midst of them. [*He moves his hand
146.   about as if he were moving a barrel.*] It's heavy, and
147.   when they have drunk what is in it, I would like to
148.   see the man that would be their master.

149. *Charlie Ward.* That would be a great drink, but I
150.   wouldn't be sure that you're in earnest.

151. *Paul Ruttledge.* Colman and Aloysius will tell you all
152.   about it. It was made in a good still, the barley was
153.   grown in a field that's down under the earth.

---

133. *Paul.* The country- **9.**
135. . . . drinks
136. . . . nothing.
137. Oh! that . . . **9.**
140. I am giving them . . . **9.**
142. I didn't know that; they never told me that.
143. We are rolling a . . .
144. . . . . We are rolling it **9.**
     Directions in 145. [. . . *hands*
     Directions in 146. . . . *were rolling a* . . . .] **9.**
149. . . . be the grand drink, . . . **9.**
151. Aloysius and Bartley will . . . **9.**

154. *Charlie Ward.* That's likely enough. I often heard of
155.   places like that.

156. *Paul Ruttledge.* And when they have drunk from my bar-
157.   rel, they will break open the door, they will put law
158.   and number under their two feet; and they will have a
159.   hot palm and a cold palm, for they will put down the
160.   moon and the sun with their two hands.

161. *Charlie Ward.* There's no mistake but you're the same
162.   Paul still; nice and plain and simple, only for your
163.   hard talk. And what about the rheumatism? It's hardly
164.   you got through that fit you had, and you don't look
165.   as if much hardship would agree with you now.

166. *Aloysius.* He does not, indeed, and if he doesn't kill
167.   himself one way he will another. Wait now till I tell
168.   you the way he is living. I don't think he tasted bit
169.   or sup to-day, and all he had last night was a couple
170.   of dry potatoes.

171. *Charlie Ward.* Is that so? [*Takes Paul Ruttledge's arm.*]
172.   You haven't much more flesh on you than a crane in
173.   moonlight. They don't seem to have much notion of
174.   minding you here, you that were reared soft. It would
175.   be better for you to come back to us; bad as our
176.   lodging is, there'd be a bit in the pot for you and
177.   Sabina to care you. It's she would give you a good
178.   welcome.

179. *Colman.* [*Starting up.*] We can mind him well enough
180.   here. I have a plan. We haven't been getting on the
181.   way we ought with the people. It's no way to be get-
182.   ting on with people to be asking things of them al-
183.   ways, they have no opinion at all of us seeing us the
184.   way we are. They have no notion of the respect they

---

154.   *Father Bartley.* We are teaching them that the Kingdom of
155.   Heaven is within them.
156.   Yes; and . . .
157.   rel they . . . **9.**
162.   still, nice . . .
163.   . . . talk.
163a.   *Father Bartley.* If you would stay with us I would explain it all
163b.   to you; I will be preaching at Athlone to-morrow. Christ said— **9.**
164-265.   [lacking] **9.**
164.   got . . . **11A.**

185.   should show to Brother Paul, and the way all the
186.   Brothers used to be listening to his preaching, and
187.   the townspeople as well. And I, myself, the time I
188.   preached in Dublin——

189. *Aloysius.* Yes, indeed, Paul, think of the great crowds
190.   used to come when you preached in the Abbey church,
191.   and all the money that was gathered that time of the
192.   Mission.

193. *Paul Ruttledge.* Yes, I used to like once to see all
194.   faces looking up at me. But now all that is gone
195.   from me. Now I think it is enough to be a witness for
196.   the truth, and to think the thoughts I like. God will
197.   bring the people to me. He will make of my silence a
198.   great wind that will shatter the ships of the world.

199. *Colman.* That is all very well, but the people are not
200.   coming.

201. *Aloysius.* And more than that, they are driving us away
202.   from their doors now, Paul.

203. *Charlie Ward.* The way they do to us. But Paul was not
204.   born on the roads.   *[Lights his pipe.*

205. *Colman.* It's no use stopping waiting for a wind; if
206.   we have anything to say that's worth the people
207.   listening to, we must bring them to hear it one way
208.   or another. Now, it is what I was saying to Aloysius,
209.   we must begin teaching them to make things, they
210.   never had the chance of any instruction of the sort
211.   here.

212. *Paul Ruttledge.* To make things? This sort of things?
                     [Takes the half-made basket from Colman.

213. *Colman.* Those and other things, we got a good training
214.   in the old days. And we'll get a grant from the Tech-
215.   nical Board. The Board pays up to four hundred pounds
216.   to some of its instructors.

217. *Paul Ruttledge.* And then?

218. *Aloysius.* Oh, then we'll sell all the things we make.

---

209.   . . . things; they **11A.**
213.   . . . things; we . . . **11A.**

219.   I'm sure we'll get a market for them.

220.   *Paul Ruttledge.* Oh, I understand; you will sell them.

221.   And what about the dividing of the money? You will
222.   need to make laws about that.

223.   *Colman.* Of course; we will have to make rules, and to
224.   pay according to work.

225.   *Paul Ruttledge.* Oh, we will grow quite rich in time.
226.   What are we to do then? we can't go on living in this
227.   ruin?

228.   *Colman.* Of course not. We'll build workshops and
229.   houses for those who come to work from a distance,
230.   good houses, slated, not thatched.

    Paul Ruttledge. [*Turning to Aloysius and Charlie Ward.*]
231.   Yes, you see his plan. To gather the people together,
232.   to build houses for them; to make them rich too, and
233.   to keep their money safe. And the Kingdom of God too?
234.   What about that?

235.   *Colman.* Oh, I'm just coming to that. They will think
236.   so much more of our teaching when we have got them
237.   under our influence by other things. Of course we
238.   will teach them their meditations, and give them a
239.   regular religious life. We must settle out some lit-
240.   tle place for them to pray in—there's a high gable
241.   over there where we could hang a bell——

242.   *Paul Ruttledge.* Oh yes, I understand. You would weave
243.   them together like this [*weaves the osiers in and
244.   out*], you would add one thing to another, laws and
245.   money and church and bells, till you had got every-
246.   thing back again that you have escaped from. But it
247.   is my business to tear things asunder like this [*tears
248.   pieces from the basket*], and this, and this——

249.   *Aloysius.* I told him you'd never agree to it. He ought
250.   to have known that himself.

251.   *Colman.* We must have something to offer the people.

252.   *Paul Ruttledge.* You say that because you got nothing
253.   today. Aloysius has got nothing in his sack. [*Taking
254.   sack and turning it upside down.*] It is quite empty.
255.   Every religious teacher before me has offered some-
256.   thing to his followers, but I offer them nothing.

257. [*Plunging his arm down into the sack.*] My sack is
258. quite empty. I will never dip my hand into nature's
259. full sack of illusions; I am tired of that old con-
260. juring bag.   [*He walks up and down muttering.*

261. *Charlie Ward.* [*To Colman.*] You may as well give up
262. trying to settle him down to anything. He was a
263. tinker once, and he'll be a tinker always; he has got
264. the wandering into his blood. Will you come back to
265. the roads, Paul, to your old friends and to Sabina?

266. *Paul Ruttledge.* [*Sitting down beside him.*] Ah, my old
267. friends, they were very kind to me; but these friends
268. too are very kind to me.

269. *Charlie Ward.* Well, come and see them anyway; they'll
270. be glad to see you, those that are left of us.

271. *Paul Ruttledge.* Those that are left of you? Where are
272. the others?

273. *Charlie Ward.* Some are dead, and some are jailed, and
274. some are on the roads here and there. Sabina is with
275. us always, and Johneen is a great hand with the tools
276. now, but Tommy the Song——

277. *Paul Ruttledge.* Oh, Tommy the Song, does he pray still?
278. He was beginning to pray. Did he ever get an answer?

---

266. *Paul* [*interrupting him*]. We'll talk of that some other time. **9**; No,
Charlie; I've had enough of adventures. I think I'll stop in **10, 10a.**
267. Tell me, how is Sabina? **9**; this little corner till I die. Tell me: How
(me, how **10a**) is Sabina? **10, 10a.**
268. *Charlie Ward.* Sure she's not far off, the poor thing! (thing. **10, 10a**)
I'll
269. go for her now. It's she will be glad to see you again. She
270. fretted a good time after you. [*He gets up.*]
271. *Paul.* And all the others, are they with you?
272. [lacking]
273. Indeed (Indeed, **10, 10a**) the most of them aren't in it now; (now.
10, 10a)
274. didn't (Didn't **10, 10a**) you hear poor Jimmy Heels got two years
for taking a
275. bred mare; that's (mare?——that's **10**; mare? That's **10a**) four years
ago, and we never saw a sight of
276. him since, so I'm laying out that's the (out that's the **10, 10a**)
last of him.
277. And where are Tommy the Song and Paddy
278. Cockfight? **9-10a.**

279. *Charlie Ward.* Well, I don't know about an answer, but
280. I believe he heard something one night beside an old
281. thorn tree, some sort of a voice it was.

282. *Paul Ruttledge.* A voice? What did it say to him? Did
283. he see anything? We have learned too much, our minds
284. are like troubled waters—we get nothing but broken
285. images. He who knew nothing may have seen all. Is he
286. praying still?

287. *Charlie Ward.* If he is, it's in Galway gaol he's pray-
288. ing, with or without a thorn tree.

289. *Paul Ruttledge.* Did he tell no one what the voice said
290. to him?

291. *Charlie Ward.* He did not, unless he might have told
292. Johneen or some other one.

293. *Paul Ruttledge.* I will go with you and see them.

            [Gets up.

 Colman. [*To Aloysius, with whom he has been whisper-*
294. *ing.*] Take care, but if he goes back to his old
295. friends, he'll stop with them and leave us.

 Aloysius. [*Putting his hand on Paul Ruttledge's arm.*]
296. Don't go, Brother Paul, till I talk to you awhile.

297. *Paul Ruttledge.* Do you want me? Well, Charlie, I will
298. stay here, I won't go; but bring all the rest to see
299. me, I want to ask them about that vision.

---

279. Oh, my poor Paddy! That was the worst
280. of all! He got too hard a hit from a blackthorn at the last
281. election in Athenry, and he did no good after. It's under the
281a. nettles he is now. What business had he meddling in elec-
281b. tions, and he not knowing the name of any of the candidates.
   (candidates? **10, 10a**)
281c. And as to Tommy the Song, he joins us now and again, but
281d. since we lost Jimmy he got someway restless. I didn't see him
281e. this long time; (time. **10, 10a**) I hope it's not jailed he is.
282. I'm sorry for Paddy. He would be a help to me now, (now. **10, 10a**)
283. I could put him to keep the hens from straying. **9-10a.**
284-299. [lacking] **9-10a.**

300. *Charlie Ward.* I'll bring one of them, anyway. [*Exit.*

301. *Aloysius.* Brother Paul, it is what I am thinking; now
302.   the tinkers have come back to you, you could begin to
303.   gather a sort of an army; you can't fight your battle
304.   without an army. They could call to the other tinkers,
305.   and the tramps and the beggars, and the sieve-makers
306.   and all the wandering people. It would be a great
307.   army.

308. *Paul Ruttledge.* Yes, that would be a great army, a
309.   great wandering army.

310. *Aloysius.* The people would be afraid to refuse us then;
311.   we would march on——

312. *Paul Ruttledge.* Yes, we could march on. We could march
313.   on the towns, and we could break up all settled order;
314.   we could bring back the old joyful, dangerous, indi-
315.   vidual life. We would have banners, we would each
316.   have a banner, banners with angels upon them—we will
317.   march upon the world with banners——

318. *Colman.* We would not be in want of food then, we could
319.   take all we wanted.

320. *Aloysius.* We could take all we wanted, we would be too
321.   many to put in gaol; all the people would join us in
322.   the end; you would be able to persuade them all,
323.   Brother Paul, you would be their leader; we would
324.   make great stores of food——

---

300. Well, I'll go look for Sabina. I left her just **9**; I'll go and look for
     Sabina. I left her just **10, 10a.**
300a. beyond the bend of the river. We have our little place made there.
     [*Exit.*]
300b. *Father Bartley.* Do you think they will join us here?
300c. *Paul.* I don't know, (know; **10, 10a**) they might get tired of the life.
     And
300d. we haven't many pots or chairs to mend. But I daresay they
300e. could spend a good deal of time in confessing their sins.
300f. *Father Aloysius.* The Lord have mercy on them. (them! **10**) I dare-
300g. say they never went to confession since they were born. **9-10a.**
301-356. [lacking] **9-10a.**

325. *Paul Ruttledge.* We will have one great banner that
326.   will go in front, it will take two men to carry it,
327.   and on it we will have Laughter, with his iron claws
328.   and his wings of brass and his eyes like sapphires——

329. *Aloysius.* That will be the banner for the front, we
330.   will have different troops, we will have captains to
331.   organize them, to give them orders——

332. *Paul Ruttledge.* [*Standing up.*] To organize? That is to
333.   bring in law and number? Organize—organize—that is
334.   how all the mischief has been done. I was forgetting,
335.   we cannot destroy the world with armies, it is inside
336.   our minds that it must be destroyed, it must be con-
337.   sumed in a moment inside our minds. God will accom-
338.   plish his last judgment, first in one man's mind and
339.   then in another. He is always planning last judgments.
340.   And yet it takes a long time, and that is why he la-
341.   ments in the wind and in the reeds and in the cries
342.   of the curlews.

343. *Colman.* I think we had better go down to the river
344.   and see are there any eels on the lines we set. We
345.   must find something for supper. It is near sunset;
346.   see how the crows are flying home.

347. *Paul Ruttledge.* [*Looking up.*] The crows are my dar-
348.   lings! I like their harsh merriment better than those
349.   sad cries of the wind and the rushes. Look at them,
350.   they are tossing about like witches, tossing about on
351.   the wind, drunk with the wind.

352. *Colman.* Well, I'll go look at the lines, anyhow. Put
353.   turf on the fire, Aloysius; Bartley should soon be
354.   home from Shanaglish.

355. *Aloysius.* I wonder why he isn't home by this. I'm un-
356.   easy till I see him, after the way the people treated
357.   me to-day. [*Shades his eyes to look out.*] Here he is!
358.   He's running!

359. *Colman.* [*Coming over to him.*] He is running hard! He
360.   must be in some danger——

---

357.   *Father Bartley.* Here is Brother Colman coming; he (coming. He **10a**) is
358.   running.   [*Enter Father Colman.*]
359-Directions after 360.   [lacking] **9-10a.**

Enter Bartley out of breath.

361. *Bartley.* Run, run, come away, there's not a minute to
362.   lose.

363. *Colman.* What is the matter? what has happened?

364. *Bartley.* The people are coming up the road! They at-
365.   tacked me in the market! They followed me, they are
366.   on the road. I slipped away across the fields. Run,
367.   run!

368. *Colman.* What is it? What are they going to do to us?

369. *Bartley.* You would know that if you saw them! They
370.   have stones and sticks. Raging they are, and calling
371.   for our lives. They say we brought witchcraft and
372.   ill-luck on the place! Come to the boat, it's in
373.   the rushes; they won't see us, we'll get to the is-
374.   land. Hurry, hurry!   [*He runs out.*

375. *Aloysius.* Come, Brother Paul, hurry, hurry!

376. *Paul Ruttledge.* I am going to stay.

377. *Colman.* They will kill us if we stay! Brother Bartley
378.   said they have stones and sticks; I think I hear them!

379. *Paul Ruttledge.* You are afraid because you have been
380.   shut up so long. I am not afraid because I have lived

---

361. *Father Colman.* Run, . . . **9**; *Brother Colman.* Run! (Run, **10a**) run!
     Come away! There's . . . **10, 10a.**
362. lose! **10, 10a.**
363. *Father Bartley.* What . . . matter; what . . . ? **9** ; . . . ? What . . . ? **10, 10a.**
364. *Father Colman.* The . . . **9-10a.**
365. . . . me; they . . .
366. . . . road! I . . . field. . . . , **10, 10a.**
368. *Father Bartley.* What . . . ?
369. *Father Colman.* You . . . **9-10a.**
372. ill luck . . . boat; it's . . .
373. . . . rushes. They . . . us; we'll . . . **10, 10a.**
374. . . . , hurry. [*He* . . . .] **9** ; . . . . Hurry! hurry! **10.**
375. . . . Paul! Hurry! hurry! **10, 10a.**
377. *Father Bartley.* They . . . ! Brother Colman **9-10a.**
378. . . . sticks. I . . . ! **10, 10a.**
380. . . . up among walls so . . . afraid (afraid, **10**) . . . **9-10a.**

381. upon the roads, where one is ready for anything that
382. may happen. One has to learn that, like any other
383. thing. I will stay.

384. *Aloysius.* He wants the crown!

385. *Paul Ruttledge.* Where is Bartley?

386. *Colman.* He is gone. Come, you must go too, we can't
387. leave you here. You have too much to do to throw your
388. life away, we have all too much to do.

389. *Paul Ruttledge.* No, no. There is nothing to do; I am
390. going to stay.

391. *Aloysius.* I will stay with you. [*Takes his hand.*

392. *Paul Ruttledge.* Death is the last adventure, the first
393. perfect joy, for at death the soul comes into posses-
394. sion of itself, and returns to the joy that made it.

[*A great shout outside.*

395. *Colman.* [*Seizing Aloysius.*] Come, come, Aloysius! come,
396. Paul! We haven't a moment, here they are.

[*Drags Aloysius away.*

---

384. *Father Bartley.* He . . . !
384a. *Father Aloysius.* Let us stay with him. **9-10a.**
385. . . . is Colman? **9 ;** . . . is Brother Colman? **10, 10a.**
386. *Father Bartley.* He has gone. **9 ;** *Brother Bartley.* . . . gone. **10, 10a.**
386a. *Paul.* Is he gone? Give me your hands, (hands; **10, 10a**) that may give you
386b. more courage. [*He takes their hands.*] Do you not know that **9-10a.**
387-391. [lacking] **9-10a.**
392. death . . .
393. . . . joy; for . . .
394. . . . itself and . . . it. [*A great shout outside.*] Ah! (Ah, **10, 10a**) you are trembling, (trembling; **10** ; trembling. **10a**)
394a. you (You **10a**) had better go. And you know everything that I have **9-10a.**
394b. learned, everything that I have seen. I can teach you no more; **9 ;** learned, everything that I have seen. I have nothing more to teach you. **10, 10a.**
394c. don't (Don't **10, 10a**) get discouraged. Keep a pick going at the foundations
394d. of the world.
395-Directions after 398. [lacking] **9-10a.**

397. *Paul Ruttledge.* Good-bye, Aloysius, good-bye, Colman.
398.   Keep a pick going at the foundations of the world.

                       [Colman and Aloysius run on.

399. *One of the Mob outside.* They are here in the ruins!

400. *Another Voice.* This way! This way!

401. *Paul Ruttledge.* I will not go. I have a little reason
402.   for staying, but no reason is too little to be the
403.   foundation of martyrdom. People have been martyred
404.   for all kinds of reasons, and my reason that is not
405.   worth a rush will do as well as any other. [*Looks*
406.   *round.*] Ah! they are gone. A little reason, a little
407.   reason. I have entered into the second freedom—the
408.   irresponsibility of the saints.

                            Sings.

409.   Parasti in conspectu meo mensam
410.   Adversus eos qui tribulant me.
411.   Impinguasti in oleo caput meum,
412.   Et calix meus inebrians quam praeclarus est.

                [People rush in with sticks uplifted.

413. *One of the Mob.* Where are the heretics?

414. *Another.* We'll make an end of their witchcraft!

415. *Another.* Here is the worst of them!

416. *Another.* Give me back my cattle you put the sickness
417.   on!

418. *Another.* We'll have no witchcraft here! Drive away the
419.   unfrocked priest!

    Directions after 400. [*The two Friars (monks* 10, 10a) *slip away.*]
    9-10a.
403. . . . Martyrdom. . . . **10, 10a.**
405. . . . other . . . [T] [*Looks* **10a.**
406. . . . .] Ah, they . . .
407. . . . have come to the . . . freedom, the **10, 10a.**
    Directions before 409-412. [lacking] **9-10a.**
413. . . . heretics! **9.**
    Directions after 415. [*They hesitate.*] **10, 10a.**
415a. *Paul.* What are you afraid of? I have no stick. I am
415b. not going to pick up a stone. **10, 10a.**

420. *Another.* Make an end of him when we have the chance!

421. *Paul Ruttledge.* Yes, make an end of me. I have tried
422.   hard to live a good life; give me a good death now.

423. *One of the Crowd.* Quick, don't give him time to put
424.   the evil eye on us!
      [*They rush at him. His hands are seen swaying about above the crowd.*

425. *Paul Ruttledge.* I go to the invisible heart of flame!

426. *One of the Crowd.* Throw him there now! Where are the
427.   others?

428. *Another.* They must be among the rocks.

429. *Another.* They are not; they are gone down the road!

430. *Another.* I tell you it's in the rocks they are! It's
431.   in the rocks they're hiding!

432. *Another.* They are not; they couldn't run in the rocks;
433.   they're running down the road.

434. *Several Voices.* They're on the road; they're on the
435.   road.
      [*They all rush out, leaving Paul Ruttledge lying on the ground. It grows darker. Fathers Colman and Aloysius creep up.*

436. *Colman.* Paul, Paul, come; we have still time to get to
437.   the boat.

438. *Aloysius.* Oh! they have killed him; there is a wound

---

422.   . . . life. Give . . . . **10, 10a.**
429.   . . . not. They . . . ! **10, 10a.**
431.   . . . hiding. **11A.**
432.   . . . not! They . . . rocks.
433.   They're . . . road!
434.   . . . road! They're . . .
435.   road! **10, 10a.**
        Directions after 435.   [. . . . *Fathers Bartley and* . . . .] **9-10a.**
436.   *Father Bartley.* Paul, . . . have no time . . . **9**; *Brother Bartley.* . . . . , Paul!
        Come, we have time . . . **10, 10a.**
438.   *Brother Aloysius.* Oh, they . . . **10, 10a.**

439. in his neck! Oh! he has been the first of us to get
440. the crown!

441. *Colman.* There are voices! They must be coming back!
442. Come to the boat, maybe we can bury him to-morrow!
[*They go out. Paul Ruttledge half rises and sinks back.*

Enter Charlie Ward and Sabina Silver.

443. *Charlie Ward.* They have done for him. I thought they
444. would.

445. *Sabina Silver.* Oh, Paul, I never thought to find you
446. like this! He's not dead; he'll come round yet.

Charlie Ward. [*Opens his shirt and puts in his hand on*
447. *his heart.*] Paul!

448. *Paul Ruttledge.* Ah! Charlie, give me the soldering
449. iron—no, bring me the lap anvil—I'm as good a tinker
450. as any of you.

451. *Charlie Ward.* He thinks he's back on the roads with
452. us! He is done for.

453. *Sabina Silver.* I knew he'd have to come back to me to
454. die after all; it's a lonesome thing to die among
455. strangers.

456. *Paul Ruttledge.* That is right, that is right, take me
457. up in your brazen claws. But no—no—I will not go

---

439. . . . ! Oh, he . . . **10, 10a.**
441. *Father Bartley.* There . . . ! **9.**
442. . . . boat! Maybe . . . !
443. . . . him! I . . . **10, 10a.**
445. Oh! Paul, . . . **9.**
446. . . . dead. He'll . . . . **10, 10a.**
448. . . . soldering- **9**; Ah, Charlie, . . . soldering- **10, 10a.**
449. . . . lap-anvil—. . . **9-10a.**
450. . . . you— **10, 10a.**
452. . . . for! **10, 10a.**
454. die, after all. It's . . . **10, 10a.**
456. *Paul* [*half raises himself*]. First, (First **10, 10a**) the circle of the moon, then
457. the circle of Mercury, then the circle of Venus. (Venus . . . [T] **10a**) But it's not **9-10a.**

458.   out beyond Saturn into the dark. Take me down—down
459.   to that field under the earth, under the roots of the
460.   grave.

461.   *Sabina Silver.* I don't know what he is saying. I never
462.   could understand his talk.

463.   *Paul Ruttledge.* O plunge me into the wine barrel, into
464.   the wine barrel of God.

465.   *Sabina Silver.* Won't you speak to me, Paul? Don't you
466.   know me? I am Sibby; don't you remember me, Sibby,
467.   your wife?

468.   *Charlie Ward.* He sees you now; I think he knows you.
        [*Paul Ruttledge has raised himself on his elbow and is looking at
        Sabina Silver.*

469.   *Sabina Silver.* He knows me. I was sure he would know
470.   me.

471.   *Paul Ruttledge.* Colman, Colman, remember always where
472.   there is nothing there is God.   [*He sinks down again.*

        One of the Crowd. [*Coming back with two or three
473.   others.*] I knew they must be in the rocks.

474.   *Charlie Ward.* Well, he's gone! There'll soon be none
475.   of us left at all. And I never knew what it was he
476.   did that brought him to us.

---

458.   till we get beyond Jupiter that we get beyond law and number.
        (number . . . [T] **10a**)
459.   Ah! (Ah, **10, 10a**) there is Cassiel, the angel of Saturn; how cold
        his hand is. (is—**10, 10a**)
460.   [lacking]
461.   . . . what he's saying. . . . **9-10a.**
463.   Cassiel, I will not go out beyond the fixed stars to **9-10a**; . . . wine-
        barrel, . . . **11A.**
464.   that dark nothing. (nothing . . . [T] **10a**) I will go into the sun, for
        God is in the **9-10a**; . . . wine-barrel . . . . **11A.**
464a.   heart of it, where the flame burns up everything. **9-10a.**
466.   . . . Sibby. Don't . . . , Sibby, (Sibby **10a**) **10, 10a.**
468.   . . . now. I . . . .
        Directions after 468. [. . . *elbow, and* . . . .] **10, 10a.**
471.   Brother Colman, Brother Colman, Brother Colman, . . .
472.   . . . God!
        Directions in 472. [lacking] **10, 10a.**

477. *Sabina Silver.* Oh, Paul, Paul!
          [*Begins to keen very low, swaying herself to and fro.*

478. *One of the Crowd.* [*To Charlie Ward.*] Was he a friend
479.   of yours?

480. *Charlie Ward.* He was, indeed. I must do what I can for
481.   him now.

482. *One of the Crowd.* That's natural, that's natural. It's
483.   a pity they did it. They'd best have left him alone.
484.   We'd best be going back to the town.
          [*Sabina Silver raises the keen louder. The Strangers and Charlie
          Ward take off their hats.*

THE END

---

477. Oh! Paul, . . . ! **9;** . . . , Paul! Paul! **10, 10a.**
482. *Man.* That's . . . **10, 10a.**

NOTES

[The following letter of John Quinn's, that includes an extract from a letter of Yeats to Quinn, is printed verbatim and is self-explanatory.]

ALEXANDER & COLBY,

Attorneys and Counsellors at Law,
Equitable Building, 120 Broadway.

Cable Address: Lexby, New York.   New York, Feby. 18, 1903.

My dear Sir:

The boy from my office tells me that you had gone before he got to your office last night. I am very sorry that he was delayed. I had put the MS. in his hands in ample time for him to reach you by 4 or 4:30 and am very sorry that he was delayed. I send you herewith enclosed that part of Mr. Yeats' letter to myself referring to the play. I hope that you will agree with me in thinking that it is a fine and beautiful play. Not only is there fine poetry in the play, but I think it would be a splendid acting play and I am sure that all persons interested in Yeats' work or in fine drama and poetry will be greatly interested in the play. It has not only a poetic but a philosophical and human interest—the story of a soul's struggle for truth and the history of the hard knocks it gives the poor body along the journey to the end.

I do not want you to think that this is mere unreasoning enthusiasm. I feel that I am fairly well acquainted with modern literature and believe that this is as fine a play as any published these ten years and much more poetical and striking than several of Ibsen's plays.

You will recall that I told you that it was duly copyrighted in the United States in December—a few weeks ago. I have all the copyright documents and if your house decides to take the play they will be turned over to you. The dramatic rights Mr. Yeats would want to reserve or else make some arrangement with you about them. You recall that I told you it is to be acted by the Stage Society in London next month and it is quite possible that it may be performed here in the spring or next fall by Mr. Sothern or another actor whom I have in mind. But these are details that can be discussed between us if you are interested in the play.

Very truly yours,

Mr. Booth,   John Quinn
    c/o The Macmillan Company,
        66 Fifth Avenue,
            New York City.

(Extract from letter of W. B. Yeats to John Quinn with reference to the play 'Where There is Nothing'):

'I think when you read it you will find that we have made a new man of Paul. In the old version he did rather ram his ideas down people's throats

1166

and was not I think a very lovable person. I was anxious to get him for a little while away from opinions that I might make him more emotional, more merely passionate. I think you will be struck with the fourth act as it now stands; it is I think the most changed of all. In it and indeed throughout I have tried to show Paul's magnetic quality, his power of making people love him and of carrying them away. I don't think he himself would have been in the ordinary sense sympathetic. I think he was a man like William Morris, who was too absorbed and busy to give much of himself to persons. Edmond Gosse told me that he once got a letter from Burne-Jones which began by saying that Morris was the noblest man he had ever known. He said also that Burne-Jones felt that if he was to die it would not make much difference to Morris. But he added that Morris's death would kill him. People love Paul because they find in him a certain strength, a certain abundance. This abundance comes from him in the first three acts with a kind of hard passion, but his five years in the monastery as I understand him fills him with dreams, mad reverie, and detaches him from the things about which men are passionate.

'Nobody here has as yet seen the new version, but the old one has had quite a success. Miss Edith Craig, Ellen Terry's daughter, got hold of a copy by chance and persuaded the Stage Society to undertake its production. And now Gordon Craig, her brother, wants to produce it with elaborate scenery instead of the Maeterlinck which they had asked him to do. He is the great innovator here in the matter of scenery and has begun experiments which may perhaps revolutionize the whole art. . . .'

From the files of The Macmillan Company (New York)

* * *

Variant spellings

baptised **9-10a** ; *baptized* **11**.
demoralised **9-10a** ; *demoralized* **11**.
good-by **11A** ; *good-bye* **9-10a, 11E**.
melodeon **9, 11** ; *melodion* **10, 10a**.
organise **9-10a** ; *organize* **11**.

* * *

[See also notes on *The Unicorn from the Stars*, p. 712, *The Resurrection*, p. 932; *Dedication to 10, 10a*, p. 1292; and *Preface to 29*, p. 1295.]

DIARMUID AND GRANIA

A Play in Three Acts

By

George Moore

And

W. B. Yeats

Now first printed

With an introductory note

By

William Becker

[*The Dublin Magazine*, April–June, 1951]

1168

INTRODUCTORY NOTE

Written partly in London, partly in Dublin, and partly at Coole, DIARMUID AND GRANIA was finished in December, 1900. Neither Yeats nor Moore thought the play worthy of publication at the time of its original (and only) production, though both have left long and amusing accounts of its composition (see Moore's AVE and Yeats's DRAMATIS PERSONAE 1896–1902). And subsequently, the few complete typescripts used by the actors disappeared, leaving only a stack of haphazard manuscript notes and incomplete drafts among Yeats's private papers. Thus until the discovery of the typescript on which the present version is based, the play was commonly thought to be lost. This typescript, although it contains various manuscript corrections by both men, seems to have been Moore's and was given to its present owner by Lady Cunard shortly before her death.

How much of the writing is Yeats's and how much Moore's is now impossible to tell. In fact, there is every possibility that Lady Gregory and Arthur Symons also had their fingers in the pie in a small way. Lady Gregory, at least, prepared the original synopsis of the Diarmuid and Grania legend from which Yeats and Moore worked, and seems to have refereed a good many of their quarrels. For nearly two years, work on the play proceeded in a factious and wayward fashion before a version finally emerged that was satisfactory to both men. Yet there does seem to have been a set of principles behind the collaboration, even a rather strict set, and tempers frequently flared over infringements and demands for concessions. The following hitherto unpublished draft of a letter from Yeats to Moore gives a clear indication of their procedure:

My dear Moore : You say both should make concessions. I think so too, but I have so far made them. I have recognized that you have a knowledge of the stage, a power of construction, a power of inventing a dramatic climax far beyond me, and I have given way again and again. I have continually given up motives and ideas that I preferred to yours, because I admitted your authority to be greater than mine. On the question of style however I will make no concessions. Here you need give way to me. Remember our original compact was that the final words were to be mine. I would never have begun the play at all, but for this compact. It is no use going on with the work at all if we are not clear on this point. I send you what seems to me a sufficient version of Act I. I will listen to any suggestions you make, or consider any emendations of language as I have always done, but the final version must be in words of mine or in such words of yours as I may accept. Remember that this is the original compact. If I hear that you have accepted this Act I, I will go on to Act II. It will be a pity if we fall out over a few phrases after so much planned work together.

There is only one alternative and this is the alternative I offered you some weeks ago. I will accept any form of words of yours that Arthur Symons approves of. I have perfect trust in his judgment and so should you as you have got him to revise a novel. This was no part of our compact but it seems to me reasonable.

In later years, a sizeable rift came to separate Yeats and Moore; and Yeats was outraged by the original publication of certain attacks on himself and Lady Gregory which later appeared in a softened form in HAIL AND FAREWELL. A note in Yeats's 1909 Diary reads as follows:

> *On George Moore:*
>
> > *Moore once had visits from the muse*
> > *But fearing that she would refuse*
> > *An ancient lecher took to geese*
> > *He now gets novels at his ease.*
>
> *Made long ago but written now because it comes up into memory, and it may amuse me in some moment of exasperation with that artless man.*

On completion, the play was shown to Forbes-Robertson and to Mrs. Patrick Campbell before F. R. Benson finally agreed to produce it in Dublin. In a letter to Lady Gregory dated 27 December 1900, Yeats gives an amusing and apropos account of the interview with Mrs. Pat:

> *The shields are the success of the play with her. Moore told her they were my work and she said almost the moment she saw me: 'O Mr. Yeats the opening of Act I is wonderful. Why did you not do the whole play?' I then of course explained how essential Moore had been. She went on 'I am sure I know what part you have done and what part he has done for sometimes the words are beautiful and sometimes they are like a French Novel and spoil everything.' She then quoted the part about 'your eyes are grey' as beautiful and said 'It would make an actress crazy with excitement merely to have such things spoken over her' and she took up the play and read them out to somebody who was there. She has begged me to read the play to her right through that she may point out places where she thinks it needs some verbal improvement. This is a delicate matter—I don't quite know how Moore will like it but she is right. When one has to give up one's own standard as I have had to do in this play, one rather loses the power of judging at all. I told her that I was just a lyric poet and that Moore was a very considerable dramatist and she answered 'Well you have made a very great work between you' and quoted Max Beerbohm who had said 'But where do they begin to come together?' I gave her 'The Shadowy Waters' but her chief interest seemed to be, had I written 'a beautiful inscription' to her but alas I had only written 'Mrs. Patrick Campbell from W. B. Yeats' and slurred over the word 'Campbell' because I was not sure of the spelling.*

Final arrangements with the Bensons for the production were left entirely to Moore, who evidently undertook the task with considerable relish. On August 8th 1901, he wrote to Yeats:—

> *I have spent the day with the Bensons and a very satisfactory day it was. We went through the play and they will begin to rehearse it at Brighton and will continue rehearsing it. They evidently think very highly of it and will (I think) play it all the week. They will be obliged to for Forbes Robertson will be in Dublin for the same week and with Robertson in Dublin Benson will I think feel it would be*

useless for him to play Shakespeare. He is very much taken with the idea of the sheep shearing. He says he will carry in a sheep. I told him a sheep is a difficult animal to carry but he says there will be no difficulty for him. The stage will show fleeces hung about, there will be branding irons and crooks; Cormac will watch the shearing and when Diarmuid and the shepherd have carried out the kicking animal Cormac will out with his lament. I cannot tell you how pleased I am; I walk about the streets thinking of the fleeces and the sheep. The shearing will take the audience back to the beginning of things. Man has shorn sheep since the beginning and the wars and the strive [sic] will break in upon Arcady as they always have done. I cannot tell you how pleased I am, I am only sorry that you are not here to rejoice with me . . . If you were to send a couple of paragraphs to the Irish papers about the piece you would be doing good work—the sheep-shearing would make a nice paragraph, Benson as an athlete carrying out the bleating beast. I don't mind if the audience laughs, better that it should laugh—the scene will put them in good humour to listen to the act.

The play was first performed 21 October, 1901, at the Gaiety Theatre, Dublin, by the F. R. Benson Company at the request of the Irish Literary Theatre. Music for the play was specially composed by Edward Elgar. The cast was as follows:

King Cormac	. . . Alfred Brydone
Finn MacCoole	. . . Frank Rodney
Diarmuid	. . . F. R. Benson
Goll	. . . Charles Bibby
Usheen	. . . Henry Ainley
Caoelte	. . . E. Harcourt Williams
Fergus	. . . G. Wallace Johnstone
Fathna	. . . Walter Hampden
Griffan	. . . Stuart Edgar
Niall	. . . Matheson Lang
Conan the Bald	. . . Arthur Whitby
An Old Man	. . . H. O. Nicholson
A Shepherd	. . . Mr. Owen
A Boy	. . . Ella Tarrant
A Young Man	. . . Jean Mackinlay
Grania	. . . Mrs. F. R. Benson
Laban	. . . Lucy Franklein

For permission to publish the play and the letters included in this note, I am indebted to Mrs. Yeats and to Mr. C. D. Medley, George Moore's literary executor. I should also like to express my gratitude to Mr. J. Millward, owner of the original typescript from which this version of the play is taken, for his kind and unfailing patient co-operation.

W. B.

Oxford, *November,* 1950.

[The text is from *The Dublin Magazine*, April–June 1951.
No other printing.]

DIARMUID AND GRANIA

DRAMATIS PERSONAE

King Cormac	The High King.
Finn MacCoole	The Chief of the Fianna.
Diarmuid Goll Usheen Caoelte	His chief men.
Conan the Bald	One of the Fianna.
Niall	A head servant.
Fergus Fathna Griffan	Spearmen.
Grania	The King's daughter.
Laban	A druidess.
An Old Man	
A Boy	
A Young Man	
A Shepherd	
The Four Troops of the Fianna	
Serving Men	

ACT I.

*The banqueting hall in Tara. A table at the back of the stage on a dais.
Pillars in front. There are doors to the right and left. A number of Serving Men
are laying the table for the feast. Niall is directing them. There is a spinning
wheel to left.*

1. Niall: Do not put the salmon there; put it in front of the chief man
2.   at the feast.

3. Boy: Is not the King the chief man at a feast?

4. Niall: Not at a wedding feast; the chief man at a wedding feast is
5.   the man comes to be wed.

6. Boy: Where shall I put the boar's head?

7. Niall: Put it where the old King used to sit, Art, King Cormac's
8.   father, Art the Melancholy they used to call him. He was deaf
9.   at the left ear, and he was always complaining that the meat was
10.   hard, and that the wind came under the door. Yes, Boy, under
11.   this roof a hundred kings have sat, right back to Ollam Fodla

12. that made the laws. What meals they have eaten! What ale they
13. have drunk! Before Cormac there was Art, and before Art there
14. was Conn.

15. Boy: Was that Conn the Hundred Fighter?

16. Niall: Yes, Conn the Hundred Fighter they used to call him and he
17. knew a hare was put before him if the fire had been bright behind
18. it; and he knew if the swine's flesh had been dried in the smoke
19. of a whitehorn tree. Put the curds over there; it is not the
20. curds but the trotters and cow-heel that used to be put there,
21. for that was the place of the king's fool. One day he flouted
22. the Fianna on the high road, and they hanged him on an apple tree.

23. Boy: Did they hang the king's fool in time of peace?

24. Niall: Fool, or wise man, war or peace, it's all one to them when
25. their pride is up. But they are great men. Bring the dishes
26. quickly, it is time for their messenger to be here. Put the
27. bread there, Art's wife, Queen Maeve, used to sit there, Maeve
28. the Half Ruddy they called her, and she liked thin barley cakes,
29. and six men got their death because of her. [*To the Servants*].
30. Bring in the flagons; put them here, where Art's hound used to
31. lie. [*A knocking at the door*]. Here is the messenger of the
32. Fianna. I knew we should not get done in time. Bring in the
33. flagons. [*To the Servants*]. Where are the drinking horns? [*More
knocking. He goes to the door and opens it. Conan comes in. He is a fat
rough man and is much out of breath. He is followed by three men, who
carry bundles of shields on their backs*].

34. Conan: Well, here are the shields. I must tell you the order they
35. have to be hung in; and you will want to know the deeds of all
36. these boasters, that you may tell them to the horse boys and the
37. scullions . . . but no, I have seen you before. Yes, now I re-
38. member, you have been in Tara fifty years and have hung them
39. many a time. Come, the sooner we bring the Fianna, the sooner
40. we shall eat. [*He turns to go out, coming back*]. Well, there is good
41. food on this table and all for the marriage of Finn and Grania.
42. This boar was a fine beast, they fatten well on the acorns of Tara,
43. and you have good big salmon in your river. Many a time I have
44. had nothing but badger's flesh and otter's flesh when I have been
45. in the woods with the Fianna, and the war about us. Give me a
46. horn of ale. [*He is given a horn of ale but the horn is not a big one
47. and he flings it away in disgust. He is given a larger one*]. Ah,
48. you have a good life of it here, but I am tired running the mes-

49. sages of the Fianna. Have I not legs to grow weary, and a body to
50. sweat like another? I am hungry too, but I dare not put a knife
51. in the meat till the Fianna are here.

52. Niall: You are one of the Fianna and have just left them. You will
53. be able to tell us when they will be here.

54. Conan: I left them at the foot of the hill. A shepherd's wife fol-
55. lowed Diarmuid and Diarmuid laughed at her. Goll took her part
56. and Finn took Diarmuid's part for Finn and Diarmuid always
57. stand together. Well, come, let us go hurry them. I will tell them
58. about the boar's head and the salmon. Yes, you have fine salmon
59. in Tara. [*They go out*].

60. Boy: The Fianna have a rough messenger.

61. Niall: I would have none say that I have said it, but he is a man
62. of little account among them.

63. Boy: Men wear sheep-skins in my country, but I had thought that
64. the Fianna wore fine clothes.

65. Niall: I will tell you why the Fianna made him wear it one of
66. these days, and why Finn made him one of the Fianna. Would
67. you be one of them?

68. Boy: Yes, if I might be Finn, or Diarmuid, or Caoelte.

69. Niall: They are famous for their battles; they are great men, but
70. would you not be Conan the Bald if you could?

71. Boy: That man with the sheep skin?

72. Niall: Well, he eats when he is hungry, and sleeps when he is
73. sleepy and rails at whomever displeases him. Those great men
74. have the best seats at the table, and the fairest women for
75. their bed-fellows, and yet I would not . . . [*He rushes across
    the stage to keep one of the men from hanging Goll's shield at
76. the lower end of the table.*] Would you put Goll son of Morna's
77. shield below Alvin's and Fergus's; would you have the roof tree
78. burnt over our heads? It is the third shield from Finn's. Let me
79. see now, let me think, it was Cool Finn's father who made this
80. custom of the hanging up of every man's shield above his place.
81. No quarreling, everything settled. I was going to tell you who
82. made the Fianna, Boy; it was Cool. He took a thousand men out of
83. every kingdom, and made them into an army, and set them to watch
84. the shores. No one is old enough except myself to remember those
85. times. The men of Lochland and the men of Mona, and the men of

86.   Alba carrying off women here and sheep there, and leaving smoke
87.   and fire behind them, and nobody to meet them but men taken
88.   from the sheep-fold, and from the plough and from the smithy. Yes,
89.   that is where Caoelte's shield hangs. I told you its place last
90.   time and you remembered it. [*Returning to the Boy*]. But I was
91.   telling you how the Fianna saved the women and sheep. They
92.   fight well, but they are proud. Ah, they are very proud. I was
93.   telling you Boy, how they hanged the king's fool, and many and
94.   many a time they have made war on the king himself. Finn's
95.   father, Cool, died fighting against Cormac's father, Art the
96.   Melancholy, and it was for that death Finn kept out of the
97.   battle Cormac fought against the men of Mona. It has been this
98.   way always, and sometimes Eri has been like a shaking sod be-
99.   tween them; but this marriage mends all. [*Enter Grania and
      Laban*].

100. Boy: There is old Laban and the King's daughter.

101. Niall: Quick, quick put up the rest of the shields—Come away.

102. Boy: I have heard that there are women who live seven hundred
103.   years in the woods, spinning the threads of the long lived
104.   people of the woods, and then seven hundred years spinning for
105.   men. She is one of them. She has come back after these many
106.   years an old witch; they say she has more shapes than one.
      [*Niall and the Boy go out, and are followed by other serving men*].

107. Grania: You cannot persuade me. I will not marry Finn.

108. Laban: Hush! Hush!

109. Grania: But the Fianna are coming too; you will tell me about
110.   them, about the young men. Yes, their shields are here already.

111. Laban: Conan has brought them.

112. Grania: You have promised to tell me about the Fianna. If you
113.   will, not, Niall will.

114. Laban: You have been in the woods with Niall lately, and he has
115.   shown you where bees make their nests, and you have come home
116.   with honeycomb and flowers.

117. Grania: But it was you who taught me the magic there is in the
118.   herbs. You took me to a place where Earth breathes out of a cave.

119. Laban: I am too old to go far now.

120. Grania: Mother, there are some that say you will never be older
121.   than you are. And now we will go over to the shields, because
122.   you will not refuse me anything I ask. Niall would not refuse
123.   me anything.

124. Laban: Do not call him. Let nobody know what is in your mind.

125. Grania: [*Going to the table*]. My father sits here, Finn son of
126.   Cool sits next to him, and here is my place next to Finn . . .
127.   but it will be empty.

128. Laban: Hush! no man matters to you now but Finn.

129. Grania: You told me his hair was grey. Grey hair and brown hair
130.   were the same to me a month ago. A month ago I was in the
131.   woods . . .

132. Laban: It was spring time when the young find many things among
133.   the woods.

134. Grania: I had climbed a little path, and stood on the hill, where
135.   the trees grow sparer, looking into the mist.

136. Laban: And it was then that you thought about a young man.

137. Grania: The mist was hanging on the brow of the hill, and some-
138.   thing seemed to be moving over the world and to come out of the
139.   mist. It was beautiful, mother. The world was singing and the
140.   singing came into my breasts. But come to the shields and tell
141.   me of the men who are to sit under them.

142. Laban: I dare not, I dare not.

143. Grania: But you said that to-night would not be my marriage night.

144. Laban: No, no child I never said such a thing. Hush, lest they
145.   should hear you.

146. Grania: They who are wiser than you said it, Mother. The thread
147.   that you spun yesterday, the stars that we watched last night,
148.   the pebbles that we threw into the well this morning.

149. Laban: Hush, your father will be here; there is no time now. I saw
150.   you talking to King Cormac this morning, why did you not tell
151.   him of this change.

152. Grania: I took his hands in mine, and thought to tell him.

153. Laban: You should have told him.

154. Grania: But he would have sent a messenger, and I should not have
155.   seen the Fianna together.

156. Laban: So that you might pick a man who would carry you away. It
157.   will be long before men come to the end of this mischief. The
158.   Fianna shall be broken in two because of it. Oh, why did Cormac
159.   shut his ears to what I told him? There will be flights and
160.   battles, ruin on ruin, and neither you nor I can do anything.

161. Grania: I would not be a trouble if I could help it. I would not
162.   set Finn against any man. I would have Finn and my man friends.
163.   I would stand between them. I would hand them their ale. Whose
164.   shield is that, mother? That one with the red otter painted upon
165.   it.

166. Laban: That shield with the red otter is the shield of Fergus. He
167.   is taller than all the others, his hair and his beard are brown,
168.   and he wears a crimson cloak over a white tunic.

169. Grania: Is he strong and stately? Would he make my heart beat?

170. Laban: He is strong and stately, but there is grey in his beard.
171.   That red shield with the white deer's head painted upon it is
172.   the shield of Usheen. He has yellow hair, and he has long white
173.   hands, with fingers hard at the tips from plucking of harp
174.   strings, and they say that no woman has refused him her love.

175. Grania: Is he young?

176. Laban: There are younger than he. That grey shield with the raven
177.   painted upon it, is the shield of Goll, the son of Morna. He is
178.   a great hunter, and his arms and legs are as strong as the posts
179.   of a door.

180. Grania: Is there mirth in his eyes?

181. Laban: He has the quiet of the woods in his eyes. But I see your
182.   mind is not set upon one that is strong, but one that is young.
183.   That white shield with the green fish is the shield of Caoelte.
184.   They call him Caoelte the Swift-Footed, and he is young and a
185.   teller of battle tales. But that silver shield with the flying
186.   white heron upon it is the shield of Diarmuid. He is the young-
187.   est and comeliest of all. He has brown hair and blue eyes, and
188.   light limbs, and his skin is white but for freckles. He is
189.   courteous and he is merry with women. It is said of him that he

190.   will not be remembered for deeds of arms but as a true lover,
191.   and that he will die young.

192.   Grania: Diarmuid, Diarmuid, a pleasant sounding name . . .
193.   Diarmuid a sweet sounding name.

194.   Laban: But, child, how think you that these things will come about?

195.   Grania: I believe in your soothsaying, Mother, that a man as young
196.   as I am will come and carry me away.

197.   Laban: No, no, Diarmuid will not break his oath to Finn. Diarmuid
198.   has saved Finn's life three times and Finn has saved Diarmuid's
199.   life once. They always stand together.

200.   Grania: You said his hair was brown, and his eyes blue, and his
201.   limbs light, and his skin white but for freckles. It was for
202.   such a man that I looked into the mist. But thinking of love
203.   makes the brain giddy.

204.   Laban: What can he do? He cannot overthrow Finn and his army.

205.   Grania: [*Waking from a reverie*]. You must find a way, Mother, it
206.   is for you to find a way.

207.   Laban: They would hang me from the rafters, child, they would
208.   hang me.

209.   Grania: You would baffle them: it would not be difficult for you.
210.   But how shall I escape from Finn's marriage bed? Shall I run
211.   into the woods?

212.   Laban: The woods are full of wolves.

213.   Grania: I do not fear the wolves.

214.   Laban: They would follow you. You could not escape them. They
215.   would tear you to pieces.

216.   Grania: If you would not have me go into the woods, find a way of
217.   escape.

218.   Laban: Why will you not marry Finn? You would be the greatest
219.   woman in Eri.

220.   Grania: I will not marry Finn; and you, mother, who has taken care
221.   of me since you could carry me in your arms, you would not have

222. me run alone into the woods.

223. Laban: The woods are lonely, Grania, you must not go.

224. Laban: Hush! [*Taking her aside*]. Child, love has made you wise as
225. the bird in the wood that seeks a mate. There is a way, listen!
226. The greatest among the Fianna sit at table with Cormac and Finn;
227. and Niall and another serving man will wait upon them . . . But
228. do you say that you will pour out their ale for them, and let
229. them not deny you this. You must say that there could be no
230. denying you anything on your marriage night. Then come to me
231. and I will find a way. Then I will bewitch the ale, and I will
232. put a pale dust into it, and will make a spell over it. [*Enter
233. Cormac with two Councillors*]. Hush, here is your father. [*Laban
      sits down and begins to spin*].

234. Cormac: This is the wisest marriage, though I might have made a
235. greater one. I might have married her to the King of Alba, but
236. this marriage will keep our kingdom safe. [*He turns and sees
237. Grania*]. My dear daughter, I have been looking for you. Let us
238. sit together and talk to one another. To-night you go away from
239. me, but you go with the chief man in Eri. [*The Councillors with-
240. draw*]. Come, dear daughter, let us sit together. Why do you
241. stand with fixed eyes, and I see you have not an ornament upon
242. you.

243. Grania: I have forgotten them.

244. Cormac: I should have wished to have seen you in your bracelets
245. and your clasp with the emeralds. Will you wear them?

246. Grania: I can send for them and wear them for you, but I am not
247. minded to wear them.

248. Cormac: Why are you not minded to wear them? [*Pause*]. What has
249. Laban told you? She was telling you something when I came in.

250. Grania: Father you have often see me wear my bracelets, and my
251. clasp, and can love me without them, as can any other man.
252. Father, listen, let us sit together, or let us talk as we walk
253. hither and thither. I am going from this house where my mother
254. lived and where I have always lived, with one you call the chief
255. man in Eri, but whom I have never seen, so I have been question-
256. ing her spindle, and you know all that she finds in her spindle
257. is true.

258. Cormac: And she has told you?

259. Grania: Only that I am going away into the woods.

260. Cormac: You are troubled, my daughter, a woman is always troubled
261.   when her marriage is at hand. Maybe you think Finn too rough a
262.   man to marry—I might have married you to the King of Alba who
263.   is a man of peace: he sent messengers, but Finn is more worthy
264.   to be your husband.

265. Grania: I have not seen Finn.

266. Cormac: The enemies of Eri have seen him; you know how he has
       held
267.   its borders against them. Finn and his Fianna have made Eri
268.   great, as when the Red Branch was at Emain Macha.

269. Grania: You wish me to marry as kings and queens marry, but I . . .

270. Cormac: [*Suspiciously*]. You have set your heart upon some boy.

271. Grania: The Fianna are coming. I shall wed this night him who is
272.   the chief man among them in my eyes.

273. Cormac: That is well, Finn is the chief man of Eri after the high
274.   king. [*A sound of trumpets outside. The Councillors of Cormac
       and the servants enter. The servants open the door. Niall stands by
       the door*].

275. Niall: Way for Finn and his Council. [*Enter Finn, Usheen, Caoelte,
       Diarmuid etc.*].

276. Cormac: Finn is welcome to my house.

277. Finn: As the marriage law is, I declare the bride price upon the
278.   threshold. I give my word to guard this kingdom against all
279.   cattle spoilers, that are of the kingdom of Eri, and to guard it
280.   before my own country from the men of Lochland and the men of
281.   Mona; and I give my word to overthrow all kings of Eri that
282.   raise their hand against the high king. I cannot give a king's
283.   gift for the Fianna have neither sheep nor cattle, nor towns nor
284.   villages, nor great store of silver and gold.

285. Cormac: The bride price is worthy of Finn and of my daughter.
       [*Cormac takes Finn across the stage and presents him to Grania*].

286. Diarmuid: [*At the door*]. And this is Grania.

287. Usheen: Do not look at her, Diarmuid, king's daughters are not for
288.   us.

289. Niall: [*In a loud voice*]. Let the hot meats be brought in, way for
290.   the heads of the four troops of the Fianna . . . [*Enter a number
       of men, they stand about the door, Cormac leaves Finn and Grania and
       goes towards the door to welcome the Fianna*].

291. Grania: There is a scar upon your cheek. That is the scar made by
292.   the sword of Forgael, when you overthrew the men of Aidne.

293. Finn: Has the tale of that battle come so far?

294. Grania: I have listened all my life to tales of your battles.
295.   [*Taking his hand in both her hands*]. This hand has overthrown
296.   many kings.

297. Finn: Grania must not praise me if she would not take my luck away

298. Grania: Some day you will tell me about your battles. [*She turns
       away as if already weary of him*].

299. Finn: Are my battles more to you than my love? [*Cormac brings
       Caoelte, Usheen and Diarmuid towards Grania—Cormac and Finn go
       up the stage*].

300. Grania: Ah, this is Usheen, I knew him by his harp of red yew.
301.   Will you sing us love songs to-night?

302. Caoelte: I am Caoelte, and this is Diarmuid.

303. Grania: Welcome Caoelte, teller of battle tales. There is a tale
304.   you tell . . . [*She stands looking at Diarmuid, forgetful of
305.   everything*]. And this is Diarmuid. Has Diarmuid nothing to say
306.   to me?

307. Diarmuid: What should I say to you. I see you on your wedding
308.   night, Grania.

309. Grania: The wedding feast is spread and I shall be wedded and
310.   bedded before dawn if someone does not carry me away.

311. Diarmuid: If someone does not carry you away!

312. Grania: I know your shield Diarmuid. It has a flying white heron
313.   upon it, and this is your sword. [*He gives her his sword and they
       stand looking at each other*].

314. Usheen: Diarmuid! [*Grania gives back Diarmuid's sword*].

315. Niall: The King and Finn son of Cool are seated, the guests at
316. this table are Usheen, Caoelte, Goll son of Morna, Diarmuid,
317. Fergus, Fathna. The tables for the rest of the Fianna are spread
318. beyond the arras of the western hall. [*The Fianna and serving men
withdraw leaving Niall and one serving man to wait at the king's table.*]

319. Cormac: My daughter, why do you not take your place beside Finn
320. son of Cool?

321. Grania: Every night, father, I have poured out your ale, I would
322. do so this the last time, and this night pour out my husband's
323. for the first time.

324. Cormac: Grania must not pour out our ale.

325. Finn: But if this be her wish?

326. Grania: It is the firs (*sic*) favour I have asked.

327. Finn: All here will remember this as an honour. [*The King signs to
the serving men to withdraw, Grania returns to Laban*].

328. Grania: Has this been done well? Give me the ale.

329. Laban: Here are two flagons that I have made sleepy . . . but no,
330. I will make a spell over them.
331.   Do all that I bid you
332.   Pour sleep in the ale horns
333.   That all that have drunk them
334.   May sleep as on pillows
335.   Till cock crow at morning.
336. Give them this ale and they will sleep till cockcrow. Give it to
337. all but Caoelte and Usheen and Diarmuid. [*Laban goes out, Grania
passes along the table filling the cups and horns. Caoelte and Usheen
are the last who should be served. When she comes to Diarmuid she
stands looking at him*].

338. Cormac: Why do you not fill Diarmuid's cup? [*Grania drops the
flagon*].

339. Grania: The ale is all spilled; I will bring another flagon.

340. Cormac: Daughter, I do not like the spilling of ale at a marriage
341. feast.

342. Conan: It never happens but it brings ill luck.

343. Diarmuid: Conan sees ill luck everywhere. When will Finn take away
344.   his favour from Conan, and let the Fianna give him his deserts?

345. Finn: Tell us a story Caoelte, and put the spilling of the ale out
346.   of our minds. [*Caoelte rises from his place, and takes his harp.
      He stands touching his harp as if uncertain what story he is
347.   going to tell*]. Tell us the story of the house of the quicken
348.   trees.

349. Caoelte: Yes, I will tell you the story of the house of the
350.   quicken trees. [*A pause*]. It is gone, it went out of my mind of
351.   a sudden. A new story is coming to me . . . it is coming to me
352.   . . . I see a man lying dead and his wife going away with
353.   another.

354. Finn: What quarrel have you with me Caoelte, that you tell such a
355.   story at my marriage?

356. Caoelte: There is fear on me Finn, for I saw beyond the world
357.   suddenly and clearly.

358. Usheen: Let us hear the story of the quicken trees. Tell it to us,
359.   Caoelte. Or shall we ask Goll to tell it to us? [*He tries to
360.   rouse Goll*]. Goll is sleepy.

361. Conan: You have no need to tell your stories to make men sleepy.
362.   The names of them are enough.

363. Finn: Let us drink and forget our thoughts of ill luck.

364. Conan: The Fianna have had their share of good luck. To-day the
365.   ale has been spilt, and a strange tale put into Caoelte's mind.

366. Diarmuid: I am weary of Conan's bitter tongue, Finn. I would beat
367.   him from the table.

368. Finn: It would be worst of all for blows to be struck at my mar-
369.   riage feast. Conan and Diarmuid, I will have peace.

370. Cormac: [*Trying to rouse himself*]. Let Conan tell his story or let
371.   Usheen tell us a story; I am growing sleepy.

372. Usheen: I cannot remember any story—I too have had my thoughts
373.   taken away.

374. Conan: Diarmuid, Caoelte, and Usheen have forgotten their boast-
375.   ing stories, but Conan has many a pleasant story and no one asks
376.   him for one. I will tell a pleasant story. I will tell of the death
377.   of Diarmuid.

378. Finn: I will have no tale of death at my marriage feast. To speak
379.   of Diarmuid's death may be to bring death upon him. Be silent or
380.   you may take his luck away.

381. Grania: [*Coming nearer to the table*]. Will Diarmuid die by sword
382.   or will he be made captive?

383. Finn: I forbid this story.

384. Diarmuid: The story of my death is an old story, and it no longer
385.   makes me afeared. Tell on.

386. Conan: [*Obsequiously. Coming from the table*]. Oh, my beautiful
387.   Grania, this is the way it was. Diarmuid was put out to foster
388.   with a shepherd, and no one was so beautiful as Diarmuid when
389.   he was a child, except the shepherd's son. The shepherd's son was
390.   much more beautiful than Diarmuid and his beauty made
391.   Diarmuid's father jealous and one day he crushed the shepherd's
392.   son to death between his knees.

393. Grania: Tell me of Diarmuid, tell me of Diarmuid.

394. Conan: The shepherd wept and wept. Oh, how he wept. And after
395.   a while he took his second son into the woods, and made a spell
396.   over him with a Druid hazel stick, and changed him into a black
397.   and bristless (*sic*) boar. And some day that boar is to break out of
398.   the woods and to kill many men and many women. All the Fianna
399.   are to gather for the hunting of him; they are to hunt him round
400.   Eri and through Eri and from kingdom to kingdom. Oh what a
401.   hunting, oh, what a hunting!

402. Grania: Tell me more of Diarmuid. Tell me quickly.

403. Conan: I must drink again, I am thirsty again. [*He drinks*].
404.   Diarmuid must go out against that boar and must be killed. It
405.   was to kill him that the shepherd made the spell over his second
406.   son. He shall be torn by the tusks, and his face shall be foul,
407.   because it will be bloody. I would that the women of Eri could
408.   see him when he is foul and bloody. [*He staggers*]. I am growing
409.   sleepy, because I have to run the messages of the Fianna . . .
410.   [*He recovers himself*]. I shall live to see him when the tusks
411.   have torn him, for it has been foretold of him also that he shall

412.   not live long. He shall not be remembered for the deeds of arms
413.   but as a lover of women. He shall live as a lover of women, and
414.   his life will soon be over. Who has put witchcraft in my ale?
415.   Who among the Fianna has done this? [*He falls*].

416.   Usheen: He said there was witchcraft in the ale, and look, they
417.   are all sleeping. Who was it that put witchcraft into the ale,
418.   Grania?

419.   Grania: Laban, the Druidess has done this for me. I had never a
420.   mind to marry Finn. But why does not Diarmuid come to us?
421.   [*Diarmuid comes from the table*]. It was for you that I ordered
422.   witchcraft to be put into the ale.

423.   Diarmuid: For me, Grania?

424.   Grania: I had never a mind to marry Finn. I am going away with
425.   you to-night, we shall be far away before they awake.

426.   Diarmuid: You and I, and you did not see me before this night!

427.   Grania: I desired you and you were in my thoughts before I saw
428.   you, Diarmuid. You were in my thoughts, Diarmuid. [*She takes
        him in her arms*]

429.   Diarmuid: I too desired you and you were in my thoughts—oh
430.   beautiful woman! You were in my thoughts, Grania. Let me look
431.   at you. Let me put back your hair. Your eyes are grey, Grania,
432.   your eyes are grey and your hands . . . But Finn, but Finn . . .
433.   Grania wife of Finn, why have you played with me?

434.   Grania: I am not the wife of Finn [*She goes towards Diarmuid*]. And
435.   now I cannot be Finn's wife for you have held me in your arms
436.   and you have kissed me.

437.   Diarmuid: What is this madness, Grania? Here, here this night and
438.   Finn sleeping there.

439.   Grania: If he had loved me, his love would have been stronger than
440.   witchcraft. [*A pause*]. But why do you go away? Is not my hair
441.   soft, are not my cheeks red, is not my body shapely? You held my
442.   hair in your hands but now, and your lips were on my cheek and
443.   lips. Were not my lips soft? You see that he shrinks from me.
444.   It may be that no man will take me because he wants me, but only
445.   because I am a king's daughter. Would you shrink from me
446.   Caoelte, if it were you I had asked to go away with me. Would
        you Usheen?

447. Caoelte: Look, Grania, at the sleeping man whose ale you have be-
448. witched.

449. Usheen: If Finn were to wake, he would take some terrible ven-
450. geance for this.

451. Grania: What is his vengeance to me now? I will go into the woods
452. and will wander alone there till I die.

453. Finn: [*In his sleep*]. Diarmuid! Diarmuid!

454. Diarmuid: When I looked into your eyes, Grania, it was as though I
455. had come out of a cave into the dawn. But I cannot, I cannot, we
456. have sworn an oath to Finn. We swore it upon the rock where the
457. earth screamed under Con son of Filmy. If the oath were broken
458. the earth would send famine, the corn would wither, the Fianna
459. would be divided, an enemy would come.

460. Usheen: Take down your shield and begone from her Diarmuid.

461. Grania: He looks at me because it has been foretold.

462. Diarmuid: [*Disengaging himself from Usheen and Caoelte*]. What has
463. been foretold? Who has foretold it?

464. Usheen: [*Putting his hand on Diurmid's shoulder*]. Diarmuid!

465. Caoelte: You will be the first of the Fianna to break his oath.

466. Diarmuid: The fortune teller has lied, if she has said that I will
467. break my oath to Finn. What did she tell you? What has she said?
468. Has she said this?

469. Grania: She spoke of a woman pledged to marry a man whom she
470. did not love, and of a man who would come and take her away
471. from that marriage bed. She foretold that the man would leave
472. all things and that the woman would leave all things for love's
473. sake. She foretold that they would go away in the middle of the
474. marriage feast, and wander in the unpeopled woods, and be
475. happy by the rushy margin of many streams.

476. Diarmuid: And the man is I; and the woman is you.

477. Grania: She foretold that it shall seem as if all men had for-
478. gotten them, but the wild creatures shall not fly from them.
479. They shall be happy under green boughs and become wise in all
480. woodland wisdom, and as she spoke I too seemed to see them wan-

481.   dering on paths untrodden by the feet of the deer, where there
482.   are sudden odours of wild honey, and where they will often throw
483.   their arms about one another and kiss one another on the mouth.
484.   [*She goes nearer to him*]. And she told me, Diarmuid, that we
485.   should make our beds with the skins of deer under cromlechs and
486.   in caves, and awake from sleep we know not why, as though the
487.   dwarfs in the rocks had called to us, that we might see the
488.   starlight falling through the leaves. She told me the dwarfs of
489.   the rocks and the secret people of the trees should watch over
490.   us, and though all the men of Eri were our enemies they should
491.   not pluck us out of one another's arms.

492.   Diarmuid: I must not listen or I will take her in my arms. I will
493.   awake Finn—Finn, Finn awake!

494.   Grania: What would you tell him?

495.   Diarmuid: That the world vanishes, that I see nothing but you.

496.   Grania: Is it not said that Diarmuid never refused help to a woman,
497.   and who is more helpless than I?

498.   Diarmuid: Had you not told me that you loved me, I would have
499.   helped you.

500.   Grania: Help me, Diarmuid.

501.   Diarmuid: Caoelte and Usheen have seen my trouble; they will tell
502.   Finn of my trouble. She has asked me for help and I must give it.

503.   Grania: [*Standing at the door which she has thrown open*]. Come,
504.   Diarmuid, to the woods, the birds of Aognhus, the birds of love,
505.   the birds that the eye cannot see, sing joyously, sing fiercely,
506.   they clap their wings and sing.

507.   Diarmuid: She asks for my help and I must give it.

508.   Usheen: From this night the Fianna are broken in two.

509.   Caoelte : And the kingdom that was to be made safe is in danger,
510.   and Diarmuid's oath is broken.

511.   Diarmuid: My oath is not broken, tell Finn that. Tell him that
512.   this sword shall guard her by day, and will lie between us by
513.   night. Tell him I will send some messenger, some token that shall
514.   say to him—Finn, I bring you word that so many hours or so
515.   many moons have passed by and that Diarmuid's oath is
         unbroken.

516. Grania: The woods are sad with their summer sadness, and the
517.   birds of love have become silent, but they are not sleeping, their
518.   eyes are bright among the boughs . . . [*She goes out*].

519. Diarmuid: I must follow her. Upon whose face shall I after this
520.   look in friendship again? [*He takes his shield from the wall and*
        goes out].

521. Usheen: [*Goes to the door and looks after them*]. They have gone
522.   westward to the woods.

523. Caoelte: When Finn wakes, we must tell him that they have gone
524.   eastward towards the sea.

[End Act I].

ACT II.

Diarmuid's house. A spinning wheel to left. Walls made of roughly hewed timber. Laban sitting before the spinning wheel. Cormac sitting near her. The twilight is slowly deepening. Enter Diarmuid and a shepherd carrying fleeces.

1. Diarmuid: We have not yet finished our shearing. There are a few
2.   more sheep and we shall be done. [*Diarmuid and shepherd go out*].

3. Cormac: Every kind of sorrow has come upon this land: the Fianna
4.   are divided, and the galleys of our enemies are drawn up upon
5.   the shore. Our kingdom will be over-run by the Lochlanders and
6.   the hunting of Diarmuid and Grania will begin again.

7. Laban: Have your long talks with Diarmuid come to no better end
8.   than that?

9. Cormac: I talked with Diarmuid late into the night and I could not
10.   persuade him. Old woman who has spoken nothing but lies, I told
11.   him that the kingdom I had given him would be taken from him,
12.   and that I could not save him from Finn, or Eri from the invader.

13. Laban: I heard your voices, but I did not hear Grania's voice.

14. Cormac: He said "Tell Finn to begone from my valley, let the sod
15.   be blown into flame again and the pursuit of Diarmuid and Grania
16.   begin again."

17. Laban: And Grania stood by the door post watching the moon
18.   shining down the valley, looking to where Diarmuid's cattle were
19.   feeding and towards the encampment of Finn.

20. Cormac: Yes, she stood there saying nothing. I turned to her often,
21.   saying, "If I take this message to Finn, you will have to fly
22.   into the woods again."

23. Laban: And she answered nothing?

24. Cormac: Only this: "Where will Laban go if we are driven from this
25.   valley?" She said, "Father, you brought her here to be near me
26.   and if we are driven into the woods you will see that no harm
27.   comes to her." But remember how near the Fianna were to hang-
28.   ing you from a rafter that night at Tara, and if I bring Diarmuid's
29.   message to Finn I may not know how to save you from them.

30. Laban: They did not dare. The rope fell out of Goll's hand; and

31.   Conan told them they could not hang me but with a rope that I
32.   had spun, and they tried to make me spin one.

33. Cormac: Yes, yes, but Finn has waited for three days. [*Going to*
34.   *the door*]. This sunset ends the third day. The horses are wait-
35.   ing and Niall is at their heads. Speak if you have found any
36.   meaning in the thread.

37. Laban: The thread keeps breaking as it runs from the distaff.

38. Cormac: Then the end of somebody is near; the end of Diarmuid or
39.   of Grania or of Finn . . . or the end of Eri. You must tell me
40.   before I go for I cannot wait any longer.

41. Laban: The thread is breaking; I cannot find a whole thread in the
42.   flax.

43. Cormac: You have lied to me, old woman. You brought me this long
44.   way that you might be near Grania. [*She gets up from the wheel,*
45.   *Cormac puts her back again*]. But spin since there is flax in
46.   the distaff, the earth knows all things and the flax comes out
47.   of the earth.

48. Laban: What would you know? If there be forgiveness in Finn's
49.   heart?

50. Cormac: The men of Lochland have dragged up 70 galleys on to the
51.   beach of Rury.

52. Laban: You are troubled, being afraid that Caoelte and Usheen may
53.   not fight against the men of Lochland because they are angry
54.   with Finn. You are afraid that Finn may begin the hunting of
55.   Diarmuid and Grania again? You are afraid that Diarmuid and
56.   Grania . . .

57. Cormac: Old woman full of wisdom about everything but the danger
58.   that waits us, I have to carry Diarmuid's answer to Finn and I
59.   would know what will happen to Diarmuid and to my daughter.
60.   You sit silent. Will you answer me? [*A long pause, the King walks*
      up the stage slowly and when he turns Laban rises from the wheel].

61. Laban: I see Diarmuid standing by Finn with his hand on Finn's
62.   shoulder.

63. Cormac: Then they are friends.

64. Laban: I see Diarmuid drawing his sword.

65. Cormac: Against whom, Laban? And then . . . .

66. Laban: I can see Finn drawing his dagger.

67. Cormac: His dagger—his sword—look again.

68. Laban: It is a dagger that I see.

69. Cormac: Now wind the thread tightly round the forefinger. Now
70.   hold the thread tightly and look, for the earth knows all and her
71.   knowledge is in the flax.

72. Laban: The vision has passed from me, I see nothing else.

73. Cormac: Spin again, spin another thread.

74. Laban: I cannot see more than once, and the thread is broken again,
75.   you have broken it.

76. Cormac: Then is ill luck in my hands. If the thread had not broken
77.   we should know all. You say you saw Finn pull out his dagger,
78.   but was not Diarmuid standing by his side with his hand on Finn's
79.   shoulder? What is the meaning of this? If you do not tell me I
80.   will have you beaten and your wheel thrown into the lake. [*Enter
    Grania*].

81. Grania: Ah, my father, she can tell you nothing if you speak so
82.   loud.

83. Cormac: She has told me strange things, things without meaning.

84. Grania: You never believe her words, father, when she speaks them,
85.   but afterwards you find out that she had spoken truly.

86. Cormac: True or false it matters not since they do not help me.
87.   Where is Diarmuid? Does he speak to-day as he spoke last night?

88. Grania: He has said nothing to me. But a day and night have gone
89.   since you have spoken to him. His mind may have changed. [*Going
90.   up the stage*]. This is the hour when the flock comes home.
91.   Diarmuid is thinking of the folding of his sheep. You will find
92.   him with the shepherd. Or shall I send Laban to bring him?
93.   [*Laban gets up and goes out*]. The fold is not far from the house,
94.   It was brought nearer for the wolves carried off three of our
95.   sheep last week . . . Ah, I see him coming up the path, Laban is

96. 　going to meet him. [*Grania comes down the stage to Cormac*]. But,
97. 　dear father, three days are not a long while to see you in,
98. 　after seven years. You will come here again and forget the
99. 　troubles that kingdom brings. You are lonely at Tara. I used to
100. 　sing for you. Shall I come to Tara and sing for you again?

101. 　Cormac: But Diarmuid and Finn—you cannot come to Tara until
102. 　they have made peace. I have persuaded Finn to make peace and
103. 　I have brought him here . . . But we go on saying this one thing
104. 　again and again.

105. 　Grania: How will it all end? What a broil it has been since that
106. 　night at Tara.

107. 　Cormac: Never did men sleep as we slept that night over our ale.
108. 　We sat at that table like stones till the cock crew. We woke
109. 　together at the crowing of the cock, and Finn cried out, "Grania
110. 　has been taken from me."

111. 　Grania: I thought that Finn did not love me, that you made the
112. 　marriage that you might be stronger than any other king or than
113. 　any invader.

114. 　Cormac: Ah, Grania, you have you (*sic*) mother's eyes. Your mother
115. 　was very beautiful, Grania.

116. 　Grania: I thought nothing but this: that a man should love me
117. 　among the woods, far among the woods.

118. 　Cormac: And Diarmuid has loved this fair face very dearly.

119. 　Grania: But in this valley love has become terrible and we are
120. 　sometimes afraid of one another. And now I would have Diarmuid
121. 　arm the shepherds and lead them against the Lochlanders and
122. 　drive them into their galleys.

123. 　Cormac: If you think like this, why did you stand looking down the
124. 　valley and saying nothing? Diarmuid asked you, and I asked you.

125. 　Grania: If I had said "yes" to you, I should have said "no" to
126. 　Diarmuid. I would say nothing but leave things to work out,
127. 　whatever will may be in them. [*Enter Niall and the King's councillors. Councillors stand in the background. Niall advances*].

128. 　Cormac: Yes, Niall, I have delayed too long.

129. 　Grania: [*Going to Niall*]. You are going now, Niall, and I have had

130. little time to speak with you, and I would have spoken to you
131. about the days at Tara, when you were my only playfellow. How
132. well I remember going with you, one spring morning to a little
133. pool at the edge of the wood. We sat on the high bank fishing
134. for roach. Have you forgotten?

135. Niall: No, Princess, I have not forgotten. That same day I showed
136. you a blackbird sitting on her nest. You had never seen a bird
137. sitting on her nest before. But how many things have happened
138. since then: you know the woodland now better than I.

139. Grania: Shall I ever see Tara again? I have wandered a long way.

140. Cormac: Five days' journey from here, Grania. We must hurry,
141. neither Nial nor I can keep the saddle for many hours at a
142. time: Diarmuid's cattle are coming this way and their sides are
143. heavy with the rich grass of the valley which I have given you,
144. and the rooks are flying home. [Enter Diarmuid].

145. Cormac: I shall be with Finn in half an hour and I would not say
146. to him the words you bade me say last night. Do not send me to
147. the man you wronged with the words you spoke last night.

148. Diarmuid: Tell him to be gone out of my valley.

149. Cormac: Then farewell, dear daughter.

150. Grania: Father stay with us, Diarmuid do you not hear? Do you not
151. understand?

152. Cormac: Diarmuid knows how great Finn's anger will be when I
153. bring him this answer.

154. Diarmuid: I have fought Finn and overthrown him. Did I not
155. break out of the house with the seven doors when he had set a
156. watch at all doors? I went out of the door where he himself held
157. the watch and my sword struck the sword out of his hand.

158. Cormac: If you will send me with this answer, so be it. I can say
159. no more. Farewell to all here. [Exeunt Cormac, Niall and Coun-
cillors].

160. Diarmuid: We thought we should weary of the silence of this valley
161. but it is of their voices that we weary. Why should we listen to
162. anything except one another. But they are gone at last, and care
163. is gone with them, and we are alone again with ourselves and our
164. flocks and herds. Come to the door Grania and see my black bull

165.   in the meadow. [*Coming down the stage to her*]. Do you not be-
166.   lieve that care is gone with them?

167. Grania: You saw my father's face as he went out. His look has put
168.   a deep care into my heart.

169. Diarmuid: These northern raiders will not dare to move from their
170.   galleys. They will soon sail away, and should we give up our
171.   happiness because we fear they may carry off a few score of
172.   cattle?

173. Grania: Let it be as you wish it, Diarmuid.

174. Diarmuid: But oath upon oath is broken. I broke my oath to Finn,
175.   and now I break the oath which binds me to take up arms against
176.   all invaders. Grania, you would like to see Tara again. You
177.   would like to see Finn again.

178. Grania: I gave up Tara for your sake, Diarmuid, and that was
179.   easier than to live in this valley.

180. Diarmuid: Ah, you are weary of this valley. But Finn and I are
181.   divided, Grania, as by the sea, and if the peace your father has
182.   made between us is not to be broken, Finn must leave my valley.
183.   It is for your sake, Grania, that he would have me among his
184.   Fianna again.

185. Grania: He has not seen me for seven years.

186. Diarmuid: To see you once is enough, Grania.

187. Grania: I think that it is for Eri's sake he would have you among the
188.   Fianna again. He does not think of women. Why should a woman
189.   think of him? Have I not loved you for seven years, Diarmuid?
190.   And my father has told you that Finn is bound by an oath and
191.   that he has said, "Diarmuid has his love; let him keep her."

192. Diarmuid: He will not break his oath, but he will find some way
193.   out of it. There is always treachery behind his peacemaking.

194. Grania: He made peace with Goll and that peace is still unbroken.
195.   Yet it was Goll's father who plundered Finn's country and mur-
196.   dered his people.

197. Diarmuid: Goll does Finn's bidding although he might be chief
198.   man himself. But Finn has not forgiven. Usheen saw a look in his
199.   eyes at Tara.

200. Grania: Ah, how well you remember. That was seven years ago.

201. Diarmuid: And when I am dead it will be Goll's turn.

202. Grania: Unhappy brooding man, you will neither believe in Finn's
203. oath nor in my love.

204. Diarmuid: Here we have everything we sought for. But in return for
205. this kingdom your father would have me among the Fianna again.
206. I thought we should live and die here, I thought our children would
207. grow up about us here, if the gods accept my offering and give us
208. children. [*He goes up the stage*]. Come, look at the sleepy even-
209. ing. These evenings are better than the evenings of battle long
210. ago, and were I among my old companions again, Usheen, Goll,
211. Caoelte, I should look back upon these quiet evenings when the
212. flock came home and you gave me my supper in the dusk. [*Comes
213. down the stage*]. If I were to die, Grania, would you be Finn's
214. wife?

215. Grania: How did such a thought come into your mind?

216. Diarmuid: My life began with you and it ends with you. Oh, that
217. these breasts should belong to another, and the usage of this
218. body. Life of my life, I new (*sic*) you before I was born, I made a
219. bargain with this brown hair before the beginning of time and it
220. shall not be broken through unending time. And yet I shall sit
221. alone upon that shore that is beyond the world—though all the
222. gods are there, the shore shall be empty because one is not
223. there, and I shall weep remembering how we wandered among
224. the woods. But you say nothing Grania. You are weary of the
225. shadows of these mountains and of the smell of the fold. It is many
226. days since you came to my bed and it is many weeks since I have
227. seen an ornament upon you. Your love is slipping from me, it
228. slips away like the water in the brook. You do not answer. These
229. silences make me afraid.

230. Grania: Then, Diarmuid, go to your old companions.

231. Diarmuid: My old companions? What shall I say to them?

232. Grania: You will fight shoulder to shoulder with Finn and Caoelte.
233. You will listen to Usheen's harp playing, and I shall love you
234. better when you come to me with the reek of battle upon you.

235. Diarmuid: We shall be again what we were to one another. You are
236. not that Grania I wandered with among the woods.

237. Grania: You are no longer that Diarmuid who overthrew Finn at
238.   the house of the seven doors.

239. Diarmuid: You speak the truth, Grania. I should have gone to the
240.   Fianna. Now it is too late.

241. Grania: Cormac cannot have reached the ford, you will overtake
          him. [*She goes to her chest and takes out an ornament*].

242. Diarmuid: Who is the shepherd, Grania? I have never seen him be-
243.   for. Where has he come from?

244. Grania: What shepherd do you speak of?

245. Diarmuid: There, there in the doorway.

246. Grania: There is nobody there.

247. Diarmuid: He beckons me—I must follow—[*He goes towards the*
248.   *door*]. I see him no longer. A mist must have come in my eyes. I
249.   see clearer now and there is no one. But I must follow.

250. Grania: Whom would you follow?

251. Diarmuid: I see no one now and yet there was a sudden darkening
252.   of the light and a shepherd carrying a hazel stick came into the
253.   doorway and beckoned me.

254. Grania: No, Diarmuid, nobody has come into that doorway.

255. Diarmuid: Nobody came for you, but one came for me. Let me go,
256.   Grania.

257. Grania: No, no, it is a warning that you must not go.

258. Diarmuid: That is not how I understand the warning. I am bidden
259.   to leave this valley. He beckoned me. I am bidden to the Fianna.
          [*They go out. Enter Laban, who sits down at her wheel and begins
          to spin. Grania enters shortly after, she stands by the door looking after
          Diarmuid*].

260. Grania: He is like one whose mind is shaken. His thoughts are far
261.   away and I do not know what they are.

262. Laban: He is brooding over that story Conan told him at Tara—it
263.   has been in his mind all day.

264. Grania: And before he left me he saw a shepherd where there was
265.   nobody.

266. Laban: A shepherd with a Druid hazel stick.

267. Grania: It is better that he should live among his old companions.
268.   He talks one moment of Finn's crookedness; and at another of my
269.   love as if it were waning . . . In a few minutes, Diarmuid and
270.   Finn will meet.

271. Laban: In a few minutes, Finn will stand with his hand on Diar-
272.   muid's shoulder.

273. Grania: Then I have done well in sending him to Finn. I did it for
274.   Diarmuid's sake, and for my father's sake and for the sake of my
275.   father's kingdom. I chose Diarmuid because he was young and
276.   comely, but oh, how can I forget the greatness of Finn. He has
277.   gone to bring Finn to me. In a few minutes Finn and his Fianna
278.   will stand under this roof.

279. Laban: That is true, my daughter, sit beside me here and tell me
280.   what happened to you when you left Tara.

281. Grania: When we left Tara we came to a little glade on the hill-
282.   side and we heard there a sudden and a beautiful singing of
283.   birds, and we saw a red fox creeping in the grass.

284. Laban: And then?

285. Grania: And then we saw a young man sitting in the long grass.

286. Laban: What did he say?

287. Grania: He was but a herdsman's son seeking a master and so Diar-
288.   muid took him into his service, and yet, Mother, I think that he
289.   was greater than Diarmuid or I, for he gave us much good service,
290.   and so much good counsel. He never put us in a cave that had not
291.   two mouths, or let us take refuge in an island that had not two
292.   harbours, nor eat our food where we had cooked it, nor sleep
293.   where we had eaten it. He never let us lie for many hours in one
294.   place, and he often changed our sleeping places in the middle of
295.   the night.

296. Laban: What name did he bid you call him?

297. Grania: He bid us call him, Mudham. But I think he had some great
298.   and beautiful name did we but know it. Have you ever seen him,

299.   Mother?

300. Laban: It is said that none who have seen him have been long con-
301.   tent with any mortal lover.

302. Grania: I have been content with Diarmuid nigh on seven years.

303. Laban: Did you ever hear that beautiful singing of birds again?

304. Grania: Yes, I heard them sing by the banks of a river; I heard
305.   them when Diarmuid broke his oath to Finn. We had wandered
306.   by the banks of a river nine days, and Mudham fished for us, and
307.   every day we hung an uncooked salmon, on a tree as a token to
308.   Finn. On the tenth day we hung a cooked salmon, for on the
309.   ninth night a sword had not lain between us—but Mother, I can
310.   tell you no more. I would have you tell me, you who know all
311.   things, what is passing in the valley. Have Finn and Diarmuid
312.   made friends? Has Diarmuid passed the fires of the Fianna
313.   without speaking?

314. Laban: They have spoken, and they are on their way hither, so
315.   forget them for a while, and tell me if you are happy in this
316.   valley.

317. Grania: I stand by the door of this house, seeing the hours wane,
318.   waiting for Diarmuid to come home from his hunting. Nothing
319.   has happened until to-day, and now Diarmuid and Finn are
320.   walking up the valley together, reconciled at last. I had come to
321.   think I should never look on a stirring day again, and I had
322.   thought to send all the thread you would spin to be woven into a
323.   grass green web on which to embroider my wanderings with
324.   Diarmuid among the woods. I should have been many years em-
325.   broidering it, but when it was done and hung round this room, I
326.   should have seen birds, beasts, and leaves which ever way I
327.   turned, and Diarmuid and myself wandering among them.

328. Laban: But now you have thrown the doors wide open and the days
329.   are streaming in upon you again.

330. Grania: Yes, yes, have I done rightly? Had I not sent Diarmuid to
331.   Finn, the broil would have begun again . . . I must put on my
332.   jewels. The Fianna will be here in a moment, and Finn has never
333.   seen me in my jewels. Spin for me, Mother, spin for me; tell me
334.   I have done rightly. But no, they are coming I can hear their
335.   footsteps. Go to the serving men and bid them take the drinking
336.   horns and the flagons from the cupboard. [*Exit Laban. Grania*
    stands before a long brazen mirror that hangs upon the wall, and

puts the gold circlet about her head and the heavy bracelets upon her
arm, and the great many-coloured cloak upon her which she fastens
with an emerald clasp. She puts a gold girdle about her waist. Enter
Cormac, Finn, Caoelte, Diarmuid and others of the Fianna. Diarmuid
is talking to Finn. Enter servants with

337. *flagons of ale, drinking horns and torches*]. Welcome Usheen, welcome
338. Caoelte, welcome Goll and all the noble Fianna into my house.
339. I am happy that such men shall stand under my roof. The shep-
340. herds of Ben Bulben will tell each other many years after we are
341. dead that Finn, Usheen, Caoelte, and Goll stood under this roof.
342. [*Grania goes to her father and leads him to a high seat*]. You
343. cannot go from us now, for I am too glad for leave taking.

344. Cormac: I will stay a little while, and will drink a horn of ale
345. with this noble company who will defend Eri against the men of
346. Lochland.

347. Diarmuid: We have been here but three moons and have not had
348. time to build a house great enough for ourselves and for our
349. people. This winter we shall build a house of oak wood great
350. enough for two hundred people to sleep under its pillars. All the
351. Fianna who come shall sleep under our roof.

352. Grania: When you speak of their coming, you make us think of their
353. leave-taking, and I would forget that they shall ever leave us.

354. Cormac: Eri is safe now that her great men are united.

355. Caoelte: For a long while when we lighted our fires at night,
356. there was no fire at which some did not side with Finn, some
357. with Diarmuid. But at last those that were of Finn's party and
358. those that were of Diarmuid's party gathered about different
359. fires. And this year the fires were lighted far apart.

360. Usheen: And time wore on until one day the swords were out and
361. the earth red underfoot.

362. Finn: If all Eri were red under foot, it was but Grania's due that
363. men in coming times might know of the love she had put into
364. men's hearts. [*He puts his hand on Diarmuid's shoulder. Two serving*
men go round with ale. Grania stops them and takes the flagons from
them].

365. Grania: It is right that I should serve the ale on such a day as
366. this.

367. Cormac: My daughter must not pour out the ale.

368. Usheen: If Grania pours out the ale we shall sleep sound to-night.

369. Cormac: You have spoken folly, Usheen . . . I, I spoke out of a
370.   dream. Grania, since you have taken the flagons from your serv-
371.   ing men, serve us. But I would you had not done this. [*Grania*
        goes round filling each one's horn with ale. Diarmuid and Finn are
        still standing together on the right. She pauses, considering for an instant,
        and then fills Finn's horn].

372. Caoelte: Diarmuid, we have not spoken to you nor seen you these
373.   seven years.

374. Goll: Have you no word for us?

375. Usheen: We would drink with you. [*Diarmuid goes up the stage and*
        joins the group who are standing half way up the stage, near to where
        the King is sitting].

376. Grania: In this ale you will not drink sleep, but you will drink
377.   forgetfulness of me, and friendship for Diarmuid.

378. Finn: Had I known that you would speak like this I would not have
379.   come to your house.

380. Grania: But you have come here for this.

381. Usheen: It is not enough for Finn and Diarmuid to drink together;
382.   they must be bound together by the blood bond. They must be
383.   made brothers before the gods. They must be bound together.

384. Caoelte: Yes, yes, one of you there by the door—you Finmole—cut
385.   a sod of grass with your sword. They must be bound together.

386. Diarmuid: [*As he comes down the stage, he draws his sword*]. Finn,
387.   draw blood out of your hand as I draw blood out of mine. [*Finn*
        pricks his hand with his dagger and goes towards Diarmiud and lets
        blood from his hand drop into Diarmuid's cup. Diarmuid lets the
        blood from his hand drop into the cup also. He gives the cup to Finn].
388.   Speak the holy words, Finn.

Finn: [*Having drunk out of the cup*].
389.   This bond has bound us
390.   Like son to father
391.   Let him who breaks it
392.   Be driven from the thresholds
393.   Of God-kind and man-kind.

[*Diarmuid takes the cup and drinks*].

394.	Diarmuid:	Let the sea bear witness,
395.		Let the wind bear witness,
396.		Let the earth bear witness,
397.		Let the fire bear witness,
398.		Let the dew bear witness,
399.		Let the stars bear witness.

[*Finn takes the cup and drinks*].

400.	Finn:	Six that are deathless
401.		Six holy creatures
402.		Have witnessed the binding.

[*A sod of grass is handed in through the door and from man to man till it comes to Usheen and Caoelte who hold it up one on each side. First Finn and then Diarmuid pass under it*].

403. Caoelte. They are of one blood.

404. Usheen: They have been born again out of the womb of the earth.

405. Caoelte. Give back the sod to the ground. Give the holy sod to the
406.   Goddess. [*The Fianna pass the sod from one to another and out through the door, each one speaking these words over it in a monotonous and half audible muttering: "Blessed is the Goddess. May the ground be blessed."*].

407. Goll: This bond has shown that Finn can forgive. It has been said
408.   falsely that he never forgives although he has forgiven me. Finn
409.   has forgiven Goll. [*Finn turns to Goll effusively*].

410. Cormac: Now my errand is done and I shall bid Grania and Diar-
411.   muid and all this goodly company farewell. [*He rises but lingers, talking with certain of his councillors*].

412. Diarmuid: I have done this though you have followed me and
413.   hunted me through the woods of Eri for seven years.

414. Finn: I forgave you because we had need of you, Diarmuid.
415.   [*Turning away*]. Although you left the Fianna for a woman.

416. Diarmuid: Grania, pour out the ale for Finn.

417. Finn: It is right for a man to have a time for love, but now you
418.   are with your old companions again.

419. Diarmuid: I did not accept the peace you offered me at once, be-
420.   cause I had taken Grania from you.

421. Finn: [*Looking at Grania*]. It seems a long while ago, Grania. You
422.   should have been my wife seven years ago.

423. Grania: Then it was not for me that you followed Diarmuid so
424.   many years. Why did you follow him? What reason could you
425.   have had, if it all seems so long ago.

426. Finn: Our marriage was to have mended an old crack in the land. It
427.   was to have joined the Fianna to the High King for ever, but it
428.   was not for this marriage's sake that I followed Diarmuid. I fol-
429.   lowed him because he had broken his oath.

430. Diarmuid: I shall make atonement for the breaking of my oath with
431.   fifty heads of cattle, and I will give you my black bull. Come
432.   to the door, and you will see him in the valley. He is grazing
433.   on the edge of the herd and you will see what a noble stride he
434.   has. But who is this with two of the Fianna, this fat man in the
435.   sheep skin. It is my enemy Conan. I shall be glad to drink a
436.   horn of ale with him to the forgetfulness of all enemity (*sic*). [*To the
437.   others*]. I have not seen you for seven years and seven years
438.   have changed some here a little. I would drink with every one of
439.   you. I would that you had but a single hand that I might hold it
440.   this day, this happy day. [*Enter Conan with Griffan and Fergus
       and a shepherd*].

441. Conan: Keep your spears in your hands. We are only just in time
442.   . . . a great beast . . . come . . . come . . . we will be in
443.   front of him before he can run into the wood. [*Exeunt Conan and
       all the Fianna except Finn*].

444. Diarmuid: I thought I had driven off the last of the wolves.
       [*Diarmuid goes out. There are only Cormac, Finn, Grania and a
       shepherd on the stage*].

445. Shepherd: He is a not (*sic*) wolf! He is not a wolf! He has gored
446.   twenty of my sheep. He broke out by the stepping stones. [*He goes
       out*].

447. Grania: The shepherd said it was not a wolf, ask him.

448. Finn: He said it has gored twenty of his sheep. It must be the
449.   boar I heard of as I came hither. It has come out of a dark wood
450.   to the eastward . . . a wood men are afraid of.

451. Grania: Then Diarmuid must not go to this hunting. I will call him.
452.   [*She goes to the door*]. He is standing on the hillside. He is
453.   coming towards us. That is well. [*Coming down the stage to Finn*].
454.   So it was not for my sake that you followed Diarmuid. This flight

455. and this pursuit for seven years were for no better reason than
456. the breaking of an oath.

457. Finn: I followed Diarmuid because I hated him.

458. Grania: But now you have forgiven him. You are friends again. Yes,
459. Finn, I would have you friends but my wish can be nothing to
460. you. I was proud to think you followed Diarmuid for me, but you
461. have said it was to avenge the breaking of an oath. This is a
462. man's broil. No woman has part in it.

463. Finn: Cormac told me that it was you who persuaded Diarmuid to
464. bring me to this house, and but for this, I would not have come.

465. Grania: It was well that you came. Men who are so great as Finn
466. and Diarmuid must be friends. My father fears a landing of the
467. men of Lochlann, and I am weary of this valley where there is
468. nothing but the rising and the setting of the sun and the grazing
469. of flocks and herds.

470. Finn: Did you send for me because you are weary of this valley?

471. Grania: I wanted to see you because of your greatness. I loved
472. Diarmuid . . . he was young and comely and you seemed to me to
473. be old, you were grey.

474. Finn: I am seven years older now, and my hair is greyer. I must
475. seem very old to you now.

476. Grania: No, you seem younger. As you stand there, as you lean upon
477. your spear, you seem to me a young man. I do not think of your
478. grey hair any longer.

479. Finn: That day in Tara you would not wear your ornaments, but
480. now you wear them. [*Diarmuid comes slowly down the stage*].

481. Diarmuid: What have you to say to one another; what were you
482. saying to Grania, Finn? I can see by Grania's face that she is but
483. little pleased to see me again.

484. Grania: Why do you say this? What has happened, Diarmuid?
485. That shepherd said the wolf had killed twenty sheep.

486. Diarmuid: There is no wolf in the thicket; they do not know what
487. they are hunting. [*Enter Conan*]. No matter whether it be a wolf
488. or a boar that is hiding there, I have come in to find you and
489. Finn talking together in a way that is not to my liking. [*Cormac*

and the Fianna enter].

490. Finn: Was it to watch me, Diarmuid, that you came back again?
491.   And would you not have me speak to Grania? As you will, then.
492.   [*Turning to Conan*]. Conan is listening. What has he to say about
493.   this beast that has gored twenty sheep?

494. Conan: And Diarmuid has come back again because he saw it was a
495.   boar and not a wolf, and he remembered that day in Tara, when
496.   I told him he is to go out hunting a boar and be killed by it, and
497.   Diarmuid is to be torn by the tusks, he is to be bloody, his
498.   face shall be foul because it shall be bloody. I told him these
499.   things in Tara, and he remembers them, that is why he has not
500.   gone out hunting.

501. Diarmuid: Finn has contrived the trap for me, but I shall not fall
502.   into it. There can be no peace between Finn and me. [*He draws
       his sword*].

503. Finn: [*Who draws his sword*]. By the drawing of his sword, Diarmuid
504.   has broken the peace I gave him, and the sight of Grania has
505.   brought to mind all the wrongs he has done me.

506. Grania: To you, Finn, I say that I would not have sent for you had
507.   I thought that the broil would begin again. To you, Diarmuid, I
508.   say that I will speak to what man I please, that no man shall
509.   thwart me. Where is my father? [*Turning suddenly towards them*].
510.   No, I will not have you fight for me. Forbid them, father. [*She
       goes to Cormac*].

511. Diarmuid: Our swords shall decide between us, I shall slay you,
512.   Finn.

513. Finn: One of us two shall die. [*They draw their swords, and the Fianna
       rush between them*].

514. Goll: Finn and Diarmuid cannot fight—fling up their swords,
515.   thrust the spear between them. Has Finn forgotten the blood
516.   bond? He who raises his hand against the blood bond raises his
517.   hand against the gods.

518. Conan: [*Coming towards them*]. If Finn and Diarmuid cannot fight
519.   with one another, let them hunt the boar, and let Grania be
520.   given to him who kills it. Aognhus, who watches over lovers and
521.   hunters shall decide between them. [*Diarmuid lifts his sword to
       strike. Leaving her father, Grania comes forward*].

522. Grania: He is not worthy enough for you to strike him—give me
523.   your sword.

524. Finn: [*Standing in front of Conan*]. No, Grania, he shall not die,
525.   he has spoken the truth. Finn and Diarmuid love the one woman.

526. Conan: A tale I once told him has given him no stomach for the
527.   hunting of a boar.

528. Fergus: The boar is bigger than any beast I ever saw.

529. Griffan: It is certainly no mortal beast.

530. Diarmuid: What was its colour, was it covered with bristles?

531. Conan: I saw it; it was black and bristless (*sic*). [*He goes over and stands
532.   by Diarmuid*]. Finn, Caoelte, Usheen look at us; there is one
533.   terror in the heart of Diarmuid and Conan.

534. Griffan: I saw it too, it was dark like the sea, and it made a
535.   noise like the sea in a storm.

536. Finn: We listen to the idle tales of spearmen. Whatever the colour
537.   of the beast may be, we shall slay it. [*The Fianna move up the
538.   stage*]. Conan has spoken well. Diarmuid has little stomach for
539.   this hunting. Why did he ask for the blood bond? It was not I
540.   who went to him . . . it was he who came to me with his hand
541.   pricked with his dagger. These are the only wounds he will dare.
542.   This blood bond keeps him from my sword and he speaks of an
543.   old tale that he may not go to the hunt. Diarmuid is craven.

544. Diarmuid: Finn lies; he knows why I will not go to this hunt. He
545.   seeks my death because he loves Grania.

546. Fergus: If Diarmuid does not go to this hunt, Diarmuid is craven.

547. Griffan: Finn has said it, he is craven.

548. Caoelte: Diarmuid must not go to this hunt. You have done
549.   wickedly this day, Conan, and after your kind.

550. Fathna: He has a hare's heart. The gods have given him a hare's
551.   heart.

552. Finn: Take up your spears we will go against this beast, let him
553.   who will stay behind.

554. Diarmuid: Go against the boar, but it shall be as if you hunted
555. the sea or the wind. Your spears shall break, and your hounds
556. fly and whimper at your heels. [*Exeunt all except Grania, Cormac,
and Diarmuid. After a moment's pause a horn is heard in the distance.
Diarmuid takes a spear from the wall*].

557. Grania: Why do you take your spear . . . you will not go to this
558. hunt?

559. Diarmuid: This beast came to slay us. This hunt will sweep over us (*sic*)
560. It is coming through the woods, and I shall be caught up like a
561. leaf. [*They bar the door and stand listening*].

562. Grania: They said the bear (*sic*) ran into the woods—it will have gone
563. into the mountain before this.

564. Diarmuid: The things to come are like the wind; they could sweep
565. this house away. This image of death is coming like the wind—
566. who knows what enchantment has called it out of the earth? It
567. was not here yesterday; it was not here at noon. I have hunted
568. deer in these woods and have not seen the slot of natural or
569. unnatural swine. No, it will not bear thinking of. I am caught
570. in this valley like a wolf in a pit . . . [*Pause*]. Cormac, you sit
571. there like a stone, why did you do this? You came here with
572. a tale about the men of Lochlann, but you were on the gods'
573. business.

574. Cormac: I gave you this valley to be happy in.

575. Diarmuid: When we are about to die, the gods give us more than we
576. ask. There has been too much happiness here for our hunger, and
577. I would roll up the broken meats in a sack for you to carry them
578. away.

579. Grania: That tale has shaken your mind.

580. Diarmuid: Then you do not believe in it.

581. Grania: We believe, we disbelieve, and there is a time when we do
582. not know what we think.

583. Diarmuid: We are always on the gods' business. Cormac in crafti-
584. ness, you in lust; they put lust into women's bodies that men
585. may not defy the gods who made them. I, too, shall be on their
586. business in this hunting.

587. Grania: You are not going to this hunting.

588. Diarmuid: I see many ornaments upon you. How long is it since
589.   you have worn them for me? You have not worn them . . . we are
590.   common to one another night and day.

591. Grania: Take your Broad Edge, your heavy spear. Take your heavy
592.   shield.

593. Diarmuid: No man shall say Diarmuid went to this hunting with
594.   his battle gear upon him. [*Exit*].

595. Grania: He is gone to this hunting . . . he is gone that he may give
596.   me to Finn. [*She turns her face towards the wall and weeps*].

597. Cormac: Have you ceased to love him? [*Grania walks a few steps
            towards her father as if she were going to speak but her emotion
598.   overpowers her, and she returns to the same place*]. If you have not
599.   ceased to love him, follow him and bring him back.

600. Grania: I will follow him in the woods; he will take the path
601.   under the oak trees. [*Exit Grania*].

602. Cormac: [*Coming down the stage*]. Laban! Laban! [*Going to the door
603.   at the side*]. They have all followed the hunters . . . there is
604.   nobody in the house . . . but Laban must be here. Laban! Laban!
605.   [*He goes to the wheel and takes the distaff in his hand*]. There
606.   is no more flax in the distaff. [*Exit*.]

Curtain

[End Act II]

ACT III.

The wooded slopes of Ben Bulben, Diarmuid is sleeping under a tree. It is night but the dawn is beginning to break. Enter two peasants].

1. Old Man: There has been no such night as this these fifty years.

2. Young Man: How the wind rages, like the dragon or maybe it is the
3.   dragon himself. Listen, a tree has fallen.

4. Old Man: It is only the wind, I have seen wind like this before,
5.   and then the sheep were lost in the torrent.

6. Young Man: I met a herdsman whose cattle had broken out of their
7.   byres, and fifty drowned themselves in the lake.

8. Old Man: The Fianna frightened them ... the Fianna came into the
9.   forest at midnight sounding their horns.

10. Young Man: And at midnight I saw two hosts fighting, one host fly-
11.   ing and one following, and among them that were flying an old
12.   one armed man.

13. Old Man: That was Diarmuid's grandfather; he has been dead this
14.   fifty years.

15. Young Man: But I saw something more.

16. Old Man: What did you see, boy?

17. Young Man: A gaunt grey ragged man, and he was driving this
18.   beast the Fianna are hunting. He drove it along the edge of the
19.   mountain prodding it before him with a spear.

20. Old Man: That was the god Aognhus. He watches over Diarmuid.
21.   The deaths of all these great men are foretold, and the end of the
22.   Fianna. They will perish as their forefathers did when Cairbre
23.   Cathead called the folk together and broke their power for two
24.   hundred years.

25. Young Man: Tell me about Cairbre Cathead.

26. Old Man: Not now; we must go in search for our sheep. If I have
27.   lost my ram, my ewes will be useless to me. We must go now, for
28.   at daybreak the Fianna will be sounding their horns. They were
29.   sounding them till the moon went down; it was they who fright-
30.   ened my sheep.

31. Young Man: But this hunting, will the boar be killed?

32. Old Man: It is no great matter to us, maybe a little less damage,
33.   to our fields that is all. The seasons will be none the better,
34.   the cows will have no more milk in their udders; and my lambs,
35.   there will be no lambs next year.

36. Young Man: When the Fianna have killed the boar they will give us
37.   some parts of it.

38. Old Man: The Fianna have no thoughts for such as we. All that they
39.   do not eat of the boar they will throw to their dogs; they would
40.   not think it well for us to taste meat. They beat back the invader
41.   when they can and it is more than our lives are worth to pick
42.   up a dead hare from the path.

43. Young Man: Hush, there is a man sleeping under the tree. If we do
44.   not wake him the beast may come upon him sleeping.

45. Old Man: Better do nothing, we must not do anything against the
46.   gods. The god Aognhus will save him if it be pleasing to him to
47.   do so, or he may call him away. Let us begone, boy, let us find
48.   our sheep. [*Exit.*]

49. Diarmuid: They croak like ravens over carrion—croak, croak,
    croak. [*Enter Grania*].

50. Grania: I have sought you all night. I have been wandering in the
51.   woods since the moon went down.

52. Diarmuid: What have you come for?

53. Grania: I was afraid and have been running; give me time to draw
54.   my breath.

55. Diarmuid: Your hair is down and your hands are torn with brambles.

56. Grania: Yes, look at my hands, and I am so weary, Diarmuid. I am
57.   so weary that I could lie down nd die here. That mossy bank is
58.   like a bed; lay me down there. Oh, I have come to bring you home
59.   with me.

60. Diarmuid: And you show me torn hands, and you hold out to me wet
61.   hair, and would have me go home. You talk of dying too, and
62.   would have me lay you on this bank. But what good is there in
63.   all this, Grania, for I have no time to listen.

64. Grania: Give up this hunting for I have had warning that you will
65. die if you do not turn back. Turn before we lose ourselves in
66. the darkness of the woods.

67. Diarmuid: I am in a little way that leads to darkness, but what
68. does that matter to you, Grania? Your way home winds along the
69. hill and down into the valley; my way is a different way, a
70. shorter way, and the morrows that men live frighten me more than
71. this short way. I have no heart for that crooked road of morrows.

72. Grania: [*Wringing her hands*]. Come to our home, Diarmuid, come to
73. our house.

74. Diarmuid: All the roads, the straight road and the crooked road,
75. lead to blackness. If blackness be the end and there is no light
76. beyond it? But what have such questions to do with me? Whatever
77. road I am on, I will walk firmly with my sword out. [*He draws
78. his sword*]. But you have come to tell me something. What is it?
79. Out with it quickly for the day is breaking, and when it is
80. broken there will be no hunting.

81. Grania: I have come to ask you to go home with me.

82. Diarmuid: You would have me in the straight road, and so you have
83. come to tell me that I am in it. For it is certain that a man walks
84. where he thinks he walks. The mind makes all; we will talk
85. of that some day. I tell you that you are lying to me. I am not
86. in the road that leads on and on, and then shatters under one's
87. feet, and becomes flying bits of darkness.

88. Grania: Diarmuid, you are going straight upon your death, if you
89. do not come back with me.

90. Diarmuid: What do you know of all this that you come like a sooth-
91. sayer? Who has been whispering in your ear? Who has sent you to
92. me?

93. Grania: I had a warning last night.

94. Diarmuid: From that old woman who spins? I tell you I have had
95. enough of her warnings. I saw her last night carrying a bundle
96. of new flax through the woods.

97. Grania: No, Diarmuid, I left her in the house.

98. Diarmuid: I tell you I saw her. She is going somewhere on some
99. evil work. But where is she going with the new flax? What have

100.   you come to tell me about her?

101.   Grania: I have come to tell you of a dream that came to me last
102.   night.

103.   Diarmuid: Well, what did the dream tell you?

104.   Grania: I dreamt I was sitting by Finn.

105.   Diarmuid: I do not think much of that dream, for I saw you yester-
106.   day walking with Finn and holding his hands.

107.   Grania: But I dreamed I was sitting by Finn, and that your shield
108.   was hanging among the shields of the slain over our heads.

109.   Diarmuid: Did you not say it was a bad dream? I have heard worse
110.   dreams than that. Ah, foolish gods, can you find nothing better
111.   than the dreams of an unfaithful wife to vex and shake my will.

112.   Grania: Do not blaspheme against the gods for they are near to us
113.   now. I have been praying to them to spare you. I have been pray-
114.   ing to them all night, while I looked for you.

115.   Diarmuid: Yes, every man is a god in heaven, and on earth we are
116.   the hurly balls they drive hither and thither—oh, they are
117.   great hurly players. The camauns are never out of their hands.
118.   All night I have heard them laughing. I tell you I have heard
119.   them laughing. Do you not hear me? Do you not hear me?

120.   Grania: I heard, but oh, Diarmuid, take my hands and touch my
121.   hair. They may bring some memory to your mind, some softness
122.   to your heart.

123.   Diarmuid: Yes, yes, I remember well enough. Your hands and your
124.   hair were sweet to me long ago. No, no, yesterday, even yester-
125.   day. Let me see your hands. They are beautiful hands, torn as
126.   they are. No wonder I love them; and this hair too. You loved
127.   me once, Grania, you loved me better than Finn. I remember it
128.   all the day before yesterday.

129.   Grania: I love you still, Diarmuid.

130.   Diarmuid: My dear one, why did you send me to Finn? It may be
131.   that my words have been a little wild. Speak quickly, do not be
132.   afraid.

133.   Grania: I sent you to Finn, because I wanted you to live among the

134.   Fianna as before you saw me.

135.   Diarmuid: All you say is true.

136.   Grania: I wanted you to be friends with Finn, because your love
137.   had become a sickness, a madness.

138.   Diarmuid: Yes, yes, it has become a madness. But it is a long while,
139.   Grania, since we were alone together.

140.   Grania: No, Diarmuid not long.

141.   Diarmuid: Yesterday is a long while and there may be no other time
142.   for wringing this secret from you. There was a thought of Finn
143.   in your mind when you sent me to him.

144.   Grania: There is no secret in me; I have told you everything. And
145.   I come through this wood by night, to bring you from this hunt,
146.   as a wife comes to her husband.

147.   Diarmuid: Grania was not meant to sit by the fireside with chil-
148.   dren on her knees. The gods made her womb barren because she
149.   was not meant to hold children on her knees. The gods gave her a
150.   barren womb, hungry and barren like the sea. She looked from
151.   the red apple in her hand to the green apple on the bough. She
152.   looked from me to Finn, even when she first lusted for me, and
153.   after Finn there will be some other. The malignant gods made
154.   your beauty, Grania. Your hand is very weak, your arm is weak
155.   and fragile. Your hair is very soft. [*He takes her by the hair*]. I
156.   could kill you as easily as I could kill a flower by the wayside.

157.   Grania: Kill me if you will, kill me with your sword, here in my
158.   breast.

159.   Diarmuid: You would have me kill you. Maybe if I killed you, all
160.   would be well.

161.   Grania: Hold fast my hair, draw back my head and kill me. I would
162.   have you do it . . . [*Pause*]. Why do you not do it? If you would
163.   go to this hunting, you must do it; for while I live, you shall
164.   not go.

165.   Diarmuid: Let go my spear, I say; let go my spear, if you would
166.   have your life. I see that you are thinking of Finn this very
167.   moment. I see thoughts of Finn in your eyes. Let me go, or I
168.   will let the lust out of you with this sword point.

169.   Grania: Kill me, Diarmuid, I would have you do it.

170. Diarmuid: And leave this white body like a cut flower on the way-
171.   side.

172. Grania: Kill me, Diarmuid.

173. Diarmuid: I have heard the gods laugh, and I have been merry, but
174.   if I killed you I would remember everything. And I should wan-
175.   der in the woods seeing white and red flowers—after killing you I
176.   might kill myself—oh, that would be a good thing to do. But
177.   seeing you there, your soft hair spattered with blood, and your
178.   white hands stained with blood, I might not remember to do it. I
179.   might remember nothing but yesterday and to-day. I cannot kill
180.   you. I would not see your blood nor touch your hands. Your lips
181.   and teeth, and all this beauty I have loved seem in my eyes no
182.   better than a yellow pestilence. Grania, Grania, out of my sight.
        [*He goes out driving her before him. A moment after he returns alone*].
183.   That is over, let me think. Yes, yes, there is a beast coming
184.   that I am to kill. I should take him so, upon my spear. The
185.   spear will be my best weapon, but the land must be steady
186.   beneath it. If the point slipped he would be upon me. Maybe it
187.   will be better to let him run upon my shield and kill him with
188.   my sword, while he digs his tusks into my shield. My danger will
189.   be the darkness, for the darkness makes the hand shake, and day
190.   breaks but slowly. Higher up in the woods there is a little more
191.   light. [*He goes out. Enter Caoelte and Usheen*].

192. Caoelte: We have hardly escaped with our lives. The branches
193.   touched me as the tree fell.

194. Usheen: What made that great ash tree fall?

195. Caoelte: The wind had lulled and yet it crashed across our way as
196.   if it would kill us.

197. Usheen: I heard a thud and a crackling of branches before it fell,
198.   as though a great rock had been thrown against it, though I saw
199.   nothing, and for some time I had heard crashings in the woods. I
200.   think that hosts have been hurling rocks at one another. All
201.   night there has been fighting on the earth, and in the air, and
202.   in the water.

203. Caoelte: Never was there such a night before. As I came by the
204.   river I saw swans fighting in the air, and three fell screaming
205.   into the tree tops.

206. Usheen: Have you seen how Finn's hounds whimper at his heels?

207. Caoelte: They whimper and cry till the touch of his hand gives
208.　　them courage for a moment. They would not follow him at all
209.　　were they not afraid of being left alone ... [*They walk to and fro—*
210.　　*a pause*]. That light must be the beginning of the day. A pale
211.　　foolish light that makes the darkness worse. The sky and earth
212.　　would turn to their old works again but they have been palsy
213.　　struck. Let us put this darkness out of our minds. Find us some-
214.　　thing to talk of, Usheen. Where is Diarmuid?

215. Diarmuid: [*Coming forward*]. Diarmuid is here, waiting whatever
216.　　may befall him. Tell Finn that though the mountain arose like an
217.　　ox from sleep, and came against me, and though the clouds came
218.　　like eagles, and the sea upon its feet that are without number, I
219.　　would not turn from this hunting.

220. Caoelte: We have been seeking you. We would have you leave this
221.　　hunting.

222. Diarmuid: It may be that you fear, and that Finn fears, because of
223.　　the falling of trees and the screaming of swans, but I do not
224.　　fear.

225. Caoelte: Turn from this hunting, Diarmuid.

226. Diarmuid: I would not, had I nothing but a reason no bigger than
227.　　a pea, and I have weighty reasons.

228. Caoelte: It were no wonder if even we, whose death at a hunt like
229.　　this has not been foretold, should turn from this hunting. For
230.　　we are following no mortal beast. A man who had been trapping
231.　　otters followed the footmarks last night, not knowing what they
232.　　were, and as he followed they grew greater and greater and fur-
233.　　ther and further apart.

234. Diarmuid: The night is dark.

235. Caoelte: But the footmarks were deep. Deeper than any made by a
236.　　mortal beast.

237. Diarmuid: It came yesterday out of the woods like a blight, like a
238.　　flood, like a toad stool, and now it grows bigger and bigger.
239.　　But so much more the need for hunters. Goodbye, comrades.
240.　　Goodbye. [*Exit*].

241. Caoelte: I would not follow where he has gone. He is among those
242.　　broken rocks where I heard screams, and sounds as of battle.
243.　　They say that dwarfs and worse things have their homes among
244.　　those rocks.

245. Usheen: He is the only one among us who has not been shaken by
246.   this night of terror. Look, look something is coming this way.

247. Caoelte: A tall staff in his hand, and he moves noiselessly, and
248.   there is another following him.

249. Usheen: Draw your sword, Caoelte.

250. Caoelte: It will not come out of its sheath. It is but a shepherd.
251.   We are craven and no better than Conan. [*Enter two peasants*].

252. Old Man: Be of good heart, great deliverer of Eri. I am but a
253.   shepherd looking for his sheep, and not, as well might be, some
254.   bad thing out of the rocks.

255. Young Man: Can you tell me, noble sirs, of any strayed sheep, or
256.   what is troubling the water and the air over our heads?

257. Caoelte: We have been wandering in the dark all night. We are as
258.   blind as you are.

259. Old Man: We must go, sirs, we must find our sheep or starve. [*Exit
    peasants*].

260. Usheen: Maybe he was laughing at us because he was afraid. We
261.   must wait here till we hear Finn's horn. If we were to seek him we
262.   would lose him, and it may be never come alive out of the woods.

263. Caoelte: We had better go further up the hill. Who is this coming?
264.   Since dawn began, the wood has been full of shadows and sound.
265.   They are coming out of the rocks: they rise out of the rocks.

266. Usheen: There is one who seems to be pushed along, and if it is
267.   but a shadow it is a heavy one. It is Conan. I can see the sheep-
268.   skin. I am glad he has not seen our fear. [*Enter Goll, Conan,
    Griffan, Fathna and two of the Fianna*].

269. Goll: The night is over at last.

270. Conan: The night is over, and the last day has begun. Give me a
271.   drink for I can go no further without one.

272. Caoelte: We must go further up the hill. We must hurry on if we
273.   would find Finn again. Have you seen him? Have you heard his
274.   horn?

275. Goll: No, he has not sounded it, but the beast will be stirring.

276. Fathna: The last time I saw Finn he was standing on the rock
277.   yonder. He stood facing the dawn and shouting to his hounds.
278.   When he saw us he shouted that we were to climb up to him. He
279.   bellowed like a bull for its heifer.

280. Griffan: But I had had climbing enough.

281. Conan: Sit down; I will go no further. When a man has got to die,
282.   is it not better for him to die sitting down than walking about,
283.   and better to die on clean ground than in the mire, or up to his
284.   middle in water. Give me your ale skin, Caoelte.

285. Caoelte: I will not, Conan; you have been asking for it all night.

286. Conan: Give me your ale skin Usheen, it is the last drink I shall
287.   ever drink.

288. Usheen: I will give him a drink; he will not move until we do.
289.   [*Usheen gives Conan his ale skin*]. Drink and think no more of
290.   death.

291. Conan: All the disasters that have come to Diarmuid have come to
292.   him because of the spilling of the ale out of the flagon; but I
293.   have lost both ale and ale skin and must therefore die.

294. Caoelte: [*To Fathna*]. We might light a fire, there must be dry
295.   leaves under these rocks. [*Fathna and Griffan go together to collect
        dry leaves and sticks, and they return a moment after with them*].

296. Conan: We are shivering since we crossed that river; and it was in
297.   that river I lost my ale skin; some one plucked it from behind.

298. Caoelte: I too am shivering; the day is bleaker than the night.

299. Conan: Ah, be careful with the tinder, be careful, for the first
300.   leaves are the dry ones—bring the fire a little nearer, I would
301.   die warm though I have to get cold after. Make room for me by
302.   the fire. Do you not understand that I am going to die—that
303.   Conan the Bald is going to die—you will never flout me for my
304.   great belly again, Caoelte.

305. Caoelte: You are not going to die, Conan. Here I will give you a
306.   drink.

307. Conan: Yellow ale, bitter on the tongue, tasting a little of the
308.   vat of red yew that it came from . . . the last drink Conan will

309. ever drink. [*Caoelte and the others talk among themselves*]. They
310. think that all this hurly burly is for Diarmuid, but I know
311. better; you are my friends and I will tell you about it.

312. Caoelte: Give me my ale skin, Conan.

313. Conan: Not yet, I must drink a little more—and now this is the
314. way it was—it was not the loss of the ale skin that told me I
315. was going to die, that only showed me that some great evil was
316. going to happen—it was a swan screaming in the trees that told
317. me I was going to die. Before I was born, and when yet my mother
318. was carrying with me, towards the seventh month she was one day
319. washing clothes in the river, and she saw three geese swimming;
320. and while one was cackling and billing with its mate, an otter
321. caught it by the leg and dragged it under the water; so my
322. mother knew something was to happen to the child under her
323. belt, and she told me never to cross a river when there were geese
324. about.

325. Caoelte: They were swans that screamed in the trees.

326. Conan: Are not swans a kind of geese; but how do I know it was not
327. swans my mother saw.

328. Caoelte: Conan, give me my ale skin.

329. Conan: Why did I keep Finn and Diarmuid from killing one
330. another? They could have done it so easily in Diarmuid's house.
331. Why did I bring them to this hunt? Conan has brought his own
332. death upon him. [*Enter Finn*].

333. Finn: We have come upon the slot of a boar in the hills; he can
334. only just have passed by; if we go to the bend of the stream we
335. should come upon him. [*To Conan*]. Why are you lying there? We
336. want every man. Get up, we will put you in the gap yonder. The
337. boar shall not escape unless he escapes through you.

338. Caoelte: Conan is in terror; he thinks he is going to die.

339. Finn: Conan, get up or you may have to face this beast alone.

340. Conan: Do not believe them; it is not Diarmuid this pig is looking
341. for, it is for me.

342. Finn: If Conan will not go, let him stay there. Here is a handful
343. more leaves to warm your shins. [*Finn throws some wet leaves on
the fire and quenches it*].

344. Conan: You have thrown wet leaves on the fire; now I shall die of
345.   cold. But are you leaving me? They all go because Finn has bid-
346.   den them. You leave me, Goll, yet some day Finn who has put out
347.   my fire will put out your life. Is it not the oath of the Fianna
348.   to protect one another? Caoelte, Usheen, do you not hear me?
349.   [*They go out laughing*]. They are an evil stony-hearted proud
350.   race . . . Rot in the ear wheat, frogs spawn in the pool,
351.   yellow sickness in one's body, henbane in one's drink, lice in
352.   my beard, fleas in my sheep skin . . . A stony-hearted proud
353.   race. [*He follows them out. Enter Grania and Finn*].

354. Finn: You are cold and tired, Grania, and have stumbled through
355.   the wood, you are all bruised.

356. Grania: I am bruised and full of wretchedness, and I am very cold;
357.   and the dawning of the day frightens me. However, cold as it is,
358.   I do not wish to see the sun—but I am cold, oh, the cold.

359. Finn: There has been a fire here; I will blow the ashes to a blaze.

360. Grania: [*Sitting down*]. Why did you not leave me to die where I had
361.   chosen.

362. Finn: The beast we are hunting might have run upon you and you
363.   would have been trampled and gored by it. I could not have left
364.   you there. The blaze is already beginning; hold your hands to it.

365. Grania: I would that you had left me to be killed by it. You have
366.   planned that the death of this boar is to put me on one side or
367.   the other, to give me to Diarmuid or to give me to you. But I am
368.   no man's spoil. [*Standing up*]. You have planned it all between
369.   you; your plans are not mine. Go from me, Finn, go to this hunt
370.   and kill the boar, make the fire or go where you will.

371. Finn: Although I lose my chance of killing this beast I must stay
372.   with you. I will protect you.

373. Grania: It does not matter. Stay with me here or go to this hunt.

374. Finn: I will not leave you, if it were to spring upon you from the
375.   thicket.

376. Grania: It might be better, for I have done mischief enough. I
377.   wished that you and Diarmuid could have made peace and all
378.   would have been well, had not this evil thing broken out of the
       earth.

379. Finn: Diarmuid and I could not be at peace. The peace we made

380. was a false peace. [*Hunting horns heard in the distance*]. The hounds
381. are at the boar's heels now. I can hear my hounds. Yes, it is
382. Bran. Now it is Skealon. They have found their courage and are
383. driving him from cover to cover. [*Going up the stage*]. Listen—
384. now it is Lomair.

385. Grania: Finn, I beseech you to put the desire of me out of your
386. heart. Be Diarmuid's friend and save him. Kill the boar and save
387. him.

388. Finn: If I kill the boar, will you belong to me?

389. Grania: Not because you kill the boar.

390. Finn: If I were there, and Diarmuid here, and this boar coming
391. against me, would Diarmuid save me?

392. Grania: You have fought side by side. Will you let him die?

393. Finn: Why do you wish me to do this?

394. Grania: It was I who sent Diarmuid to you; and by the blood bond,
395. you are brothers.

396. Finn: Should not a woman's breast be more to me than a man's
hand?

397. Grania: But the blood bond—he who breaks it shall be cast out by
398. God-kind and man-kind.

399. Finn: I cannot save Diarmuid, his end has been foretold. I cannot
400. change it. The deaths of everyone of us and the end of the
401. Fianna have been foretold. Many will die in a great battle,
402. Oscar who is but a child will die in it, but I shall die long
403. after by a spear thrust, and Diarmuid by the tusk of a boar, and
404. Usheen will go far away, and Caoelte storm the house of the gods
405. at Assaroe. [*A cry is heard close by, Finn plunges into the thicket and
returns with Diarmuid who has been mortally wounded by the boar.
Diarmuid struggles to his feet, and leans against a rock*].

406. Diarmuid: Water, is there no water? My life is ebbing out with my
407. blood. [*Finn goes to a well and comes back with water in his hand,
but as he holds up his hand the water drips through his fingers*].
408. If I had water I might not die.

409. Grania: Finn, bring him water in your helmet. [*Diarmuid looks from
one to the other*].

410. Diarmuid: Grania and Finn. [*When Finn returns with his helmet filled
         with water, Diarmuid looks from one to the other, and then whether by
         accident or design he overturns the helmet*].

411. Grania: Why have you done this? Why will you not drink the water
412.   that Finn brought you? [*She takes up the helmet and fetches the water
         herself. Again Diarmuid looks from one to another and puts the water
413.   away*]. For my sake, for the sake of Grania, I beseech you
414.   to drink it.

415. Diarmuid: It is growing lighter. There is a light coming out of
416.   the hill.

417. Finn: Let me bind up your wounds or in a moment you'll be gone.

418. Diarmuid: They're about me, they're about me. They were always
419.   about me though I could not see them.

420. Finn: He is dying, they are coming for him.

421. Diarmuid: There is somebody there by the trees . . . move me a
422.   little that I may see him. [*Finn helps Diarmuid and slightly changes
         his position. He begins swaying his hand as if to music*].

423. Finn: He hears the harp-playing of Aognhus; it is by music that he
424.   leads the dead.

425. Grania: Diarmuid, oh, Diarmuid! Do not look at them. If you do
426.   not look at them you will not die. Do not die. You said once that
427.   you would be lonely without me among the immortals.

428. Diarmuid: I cannot hear the harp playing; there is so much noise
429.   about me.

430. Grania: He has forgotten me.

431. Finn: Henceforth his business is with them.

432. Grania: Oh, Diarmuid! Oh, Diarmuid! Oh, Diarmuid!

433. Diarmuid: Someone spoke to me; No, not the harp player, some
434.   other. It was you Finn, who spoke to me. No, no, who was it who
435.   spoke to me? [*He falls back dead*].

436. Finn: He is dead: he has died as the son of the gods should die. A
437.   friend against whom I have made war is dead. I warred against

438. him for you, Grania. [*They stand looking at each other for a moment and then Grania goes away and weeps. Enter a young man*].

439. Young Man: The beast you have been hunting is dead, killed by a
440. spear thrust. Here is the spear.

441. Finn: The spear is mine; give it to me. [*Walking towards Grania*].
442. We must send for men to carry the body to the house. [*To the*
443. *young man*]. Go fetch King Cormac, bring him here. [*Exit shepherd*].

444. Grania: [*Trying to overcome her emotion*]. What did you say, and
445. what are you saying? That spear with the blood upon it in your
446. hand, where did it come from?

447. Finn: It is the spear that killed the boar—a thrust behind the
448. shoulder did it. We must send for help.

449. Grania: A great man is dead. Ah, why did I send him to you, Finn?
450. I thought that two who were so great should be friends.

451. Finn: The gods chose you, Grania, to give him love and death.

452. Grania: [*Wringing her hands*]. Finn, we must mourn him. You have
453. to go against the Lochlanders, and this one that I have taken from
454. you will not be by your side. Before the Fianna go against the
455. Lochlanders they must mourn him, all his comrades must mourn
456. him. [*The hunters begin to come in from the wings*]. All the
457. Fianna must mourn him, and the shepherds of his valley. [*She
      goes towards the body of Diarmuid. They make way for her, and
      when she reaches Diarmuid's body a shepherd coming in from the
      back gives her Diarmuid's shield and his broken spear*]. His shield
458. with the flying white heron upon it shall be laid upon his
459. breast and I will lay beside him the Broad Edge that I bade
460. him take instead of this spear I warned him not to take. Where is
461. my father? Where is King Cormac? He shall see that Diarmuid's
462. burning be worthy of him. [*Enter King Cormac*]. Here is my father
463. [*She goes to her father*]. Father, he is dead, one of the great
464. men of Eri is dead. I am telling all these people that you will
465. see to his burning that it may be worthy of him.

466. Cormac: My daughter has lost a husband and Eri a defender. The
467. Fianna must mourn him, and all the shepherds of this valley.
468. Finn son of Cool, you too shall watch over this mourning. [*Finn
      goes over and stands by her*].

469. Grania: There are birch trees upon the mountain that the summer

470. has made ready for the flame. Every shepherd shall bring a tree
471. and they shall be heaped to a great height. Diarmuid shall be
472. laid upon them and when they are lighted all people that are on
473. the western shore shall see the blaze.

474. Caoelte: I will send messengers to gather the swift runners, and
475. the swift riders, and the boxers, and the throwers of the weight,
476. that the funeral games be worthy of him.

477. Usheen: I shall send messengers who will gather the harpers and
478. gather the women that his funeral songs may be well sung. Many
479. queens shall mourn him to the sound of harps, for when he lived
480. there was none that would not have taken Grania's place, and
481. wandered with him in her stead. It may be that he will come with
482. Aonghus out of the heart of some hill and stand invisible among
483. us and know that he is not forgotten.

484. Finn: The best of my horses shall be killed with his own horse
485. that he may have noble horses when he awakes. [*Turning to the*
486. *men who have brought in the litter*]. Carry him gently for he was
487. well-beloved when alive. [*They lay Diarmuid's body upon the litter.*
488. *Finn turns to Grania*]. Lay his shield upon his breast. [*Grania*
walks again to the body and lays the shield upon Diarmuid. The men
lift the litter and carry it slowly to the wood].

489. Cromac: Diarmuid is dead, but the Fianna are united and the
490. Lochlanders shall be driven into the sea. [*Finn, Cormac, an*
Grania go up the stage, following the procession. Conan remains warming
his shins by the fire].

491. Conan: Grania makes great mourning for Diarmuid, but her wel-
492. come to Finn shall be greater.

THE END

[The text is from *The Dublin University Review*]

THE ISLAND OF STATUES

An Arcadian Faery Tale—in Two Acts.

DRAMATIS PERSONAE

Naschina,	. . . . .	*Shepherdess.*
Colin, .	. . . .	*Shepherd.*
Thernot,	. . .	*Shepherd.*
Almintor,	. . . .	*A Hunter.*
Antonio,	. . . .	*His Page.*
Enchantress of the Island.		

And a company of the Sleepers of the Isle.

Act I

Scene I

Before the cottage of Naschina. *It is morning; and away in the depth of the heaven the moon is fading.*

Enter Thernot *with a lute.*

1. *Thernot.* Maiden, come forth: the woods keep watch for thee;
2. Within the drowsy blossom hangs the bee;
3. 'Tis morn: thy sheep are wandering down the vale—
4. 'Tis morn: like old men's eyes the stars are pale,
5. And thro' the odorous air love-dreams are winging—
6. 'Tis morn, and from the dew-drench'd wood I've sped
7. To welcome thee, Naschina, with sweet singing.

[*Sitting on a tree-stem, he begins to tune his lute.*

Enter Colin, *abstractedly.*

8. *Colin.* Come forth: the morn is fair; as from the pyre
9. Of sad Queen Dido shone the lapping fire
10. Unto the wanderer's ships, or as day fills
11. The brazen sky, so blaze the daffodils;
12. As Argive Clytemnestra saw out-burn
13. The flagrant signal of her lord's return,
14. Afar, clear-shining on the herald hills,
15. In vale and dell so blaze the daffodils;
16. As when upon her cloud-o'er-muffled steep
17. Oenone saw the fires of Troia leap,
18. And laugh'd, so, so along the bubbling rills
19. In lemon-tinted lines, so blaze the daffodils.
20. Come forth, come forth, my music flows for thee,
21. A quenchless grieving of love melody.

[*Raises his lute.*

PRINTINGS The entire play was printed in *The Dublin University Review,* April–July 1885 [April, act I, scene I; May, act I, scenes II and III; June, act II, scenes I and II; July, act II, scene III] and in **98.** Act II, scene III was reprinted in **2.** Lines 1-15 and 248-263 of this scene had been printed in *The Dublin University Review,* March 1885; lines 1-15 were printed again in **5,** etc., and were retained as a separate poem to the definitive edition of the poems. Lines 22-29, 32-39, 42-49, 51-62, 64-80, from act I, scene I; lines 60-79 from act I, scene II; and lines 1-19 from act I, scene III, were reprinted in 'A Celtic Christmas' (Christmas number of *The Irish Homestead*), December 1899. For textual variants see the appropriate acts and scenes.

22. *Thernot.* [*Sings*] Now her sheep all browsing meet
23.   By the singing waters' edge,
24.   Tread and tread their cloven feet
25.   On the ruddy river sedge,
26.   For the dawn the foliage fingereth,
27.   And the waves are leaping white,
28.   She alone, my lady, lingereth
29.   While the world is roll'd in light.

30. *Colin.* Shepherd, to mar the morning hast thou come?
31.   Hear me, and, shepherd, hearing me, grow dumb.
32. [*Sings*] Where is the owl that lately flew
33.   Flickering under the white moonshine?
34.   She sleeps with owlets two and two,
35.   Sleepily close her round bright eyne;
36.   O'er her nest the lights are blending:
37.   Come thou, come, and to this string—
38.   Though my love-sick heart is rending,
39.   Not a sad note will I sing.

40. *Thernot.* I am not dumb: I'd sooner silent wait
41.   Within the fold to hear the creaking gate—
42. [*Sings*] The wood and the valley and sea
43.   Awaken, awaken to new-born lustre;
44.   A new day's troop of wasp and bee
45.   Hang on the side of the round grape-cluster;
46.   Blenching on high the dull stars sicken
47.   Morn-bewildered, and the cup

Title before 22. Lyrics from 'The Island of / Statues' / The Shepherds' Contest of Song **CC.**

22. *Thernot.* Now . . . **CC.**
26. . . . dawn of foliage . . . , **CC.**
30, 31. [lacking]
32. *Colin.* Where . . . **CC.**
40, 41. [lacking]
42. *Thernot.* The . . . **CC.**

48.   Of the tarn where young waves quicken

49.   Hurls their swooning lustre up.

50.   *Colin.* I'll silence this dull singer—

51.   [*Sings*] Oh, more dark thy gleaming hair is

52.   Than the peeping pansy's face,

53.   And thine eyes more bright than faery's,

54.   Dancing in some moony place,

55.   And thy neck's a poisèd lily;

56.   See, I tell thy beauties o'er,

57.   As within a cellar chilly

58.   Some old miser tells his store;

59.   And thy memory I keep,

60.   Till all else is empty chaff,

61.   Till I laugh when others weep,

62.   Weeping when all others laugh.

63.   *Thernot.* I'll quench his singing with loud song—

64.   [*Sings wildly*] Come forth, for in a thousand bowers

65.   Blossoms open dewy lips;

66.   Over the lake the water-flowers

67.   Drift and float like silver ships;

68.   Ever ringing, ringing, ringing,

69.   With unfaltering persistence,

70.   Hundred-throated morn is singing,

71.   Joy and love are one existence.

72.   *Colin.* [*Sings*] Lone, and wanting thee, I weep;

73.   Love and sorrow, one existence,

74.   Sadness, soul of joy most deep,

75.   Is the burthen and persistence

76.   Of the songs that never sleep.

---

50. [lacking]

51. *Colin.* Oh, . . . **CC.**

53. . . . faery's **CC.**

63. [lacking] **CC.**

72. *Colin.* Lone, . . . ; **CC.**

77. Love from heaven came of yore
78. As a token and a sign,
79. Singing o'er and o'er and o'er
80. Of his death and change malign.

81. *Thernot.* With fiery song I'll drown yon puny voice.

[*Leaping to his feet.*

82. [*Sings*] Passeth the moon with her sickle of light,
83. Slowly, slowly fadeth she,
84. Weary of reaping the barren night
85. And the desolate shuddering sea.

86. *Colin.* [*Sings*] Loud for thee the morning crieth,
87. And my soul in waiting dieth,
88. Ever dieth, dieth, dieth.

89. *Thernot.* [*Sings*] Far the morning vapours shatter,
90. As the leaves in autumn scatter.

91. *Colin.* [*Sings*] In the heart of the dawn the rivers are singing,
92. Over them crimson vapours winging.

93. *Thernot.* [*Sings*] All the world is ringing, ringing;
94. All the world is singing, singing.

95. *Colin.* [*Sings*] Lift my soul from rayless night—

96. *Thernot.* [*Sings*] Stricken all the night is past—

97. *Colin.* [*Sings*] Music of my soul and light—

98. *Thernot.* [*Sings*] Back the shadows creep aghast—

[*They approach one another, while singing, with angry gestures.*

Enter Naschina

99. *Naschina.* Oh, cease your singing! wild and shrill and loud,
100. On my poor brain your busy tumults crowd.

101. *Colin.* I fain had been the first of singing things
102. To welcome thee, when o'er the owlet's wings
103. And troubled eyes came morning's first-born glow:
104. But yonder thing, yon idle noise, yon crow,
105. Yon shepherd—

    Thernot.   Came your spirit to beguile

106.   With singing sweet as e'er round lake-lulled isle

107.   Sing summer waves. But yonder shepherd vile,

108.   All clamour-clothed—

    Colin.   Was't clamour when *I* sung,

109.   Whom men have named Arcadia's sweetest tongue.

                                  [A horn sounds.

110.   A horn! some troop of robbers winding goes

111.   Along the wood with subtle tread and bended bows.

                            [An arrow passes above.

112.   Fly!

    Thernot. Fly!

                            [Colin and Thernot *go.*

    Naschina. So these brave shepherds both are gone;

113.   Courageous miracles!

        Enter Almintor *and* Antonio, *talking together.*

    Almintor.   The sunlight shone

114.   Upon his wings. Thro' yonder green abyss

115.   I sent an arrow.

    Antonio.   And I saw you miss;

116.   And far away the heron sails, I wis.

117. *Almintor.* Nay, nay, I miss'd him not; his days

118.   Of flight are done.

                    [Seeing Naschina, *and bowing low.*

               Most fair of all who graze

119.   Their sheep in Arcady, Naschina, hail!

120.   Naschina, hail!

    Antonio. [*Mimicking him*] Most fair of all who graze

121.   Their sheep in Arcady, Naschina, hail!

122.   Naschina, hail!

    Almintor.   I'd drive thy woolly sheep,

123.   If so I might, along a dewy vale,

124.   Where all night long the heavens weep and weep,

125.   Dreaming in their soft odour-laden sleep;
126.   Where all night long the lonely moon, the white
127.   Sad Lady of the deep, pours down her light;
128.   And 'mong the stunted ash-trees' drooping rings,
129.   All flame-like gushing from the hollow stones,
130.   By day and night a lonely fountain sings,
131.   And there to its own heart for ever moans.

132. *Naschina.* I'd be alone.

      Almintor.   We two, by that pale fount,
133.   Unmindful of its woes, would twine a wreath
134.   As fair as any that on Ida's mount
135.   Long ere an arrow whizzed or sword left sheath
136.   The shepherd Paris for Oenone made,
137.   Singing of arms and battles some old stave,
138.   As lies dark water in a murmurous glade,
139.   Dreaming the live-long summer in the shade,
140.   Dreaming of flashing flight and of the plumèd wave.

141. *Antonio.* Naschina, wherefore are your eyes so bright
142.   With tears?

      Naschina.   I weary of ye. There is none
143.   Of all on whom Arcadian suns have shone
144.   Sustains his soul in courage or in might.
145.   Poor race of leafy Arcady, your love
146.   To prove what can ye do? What things above
147.   Sheep-guiding, or the bringing some strange bird,
148.   Or some small beast most wonderfully furr'd,
149.   Or sad sea-shells where little echoes sit?
150.   Such quests as these, I trow, need little wit.

151. *Antonio.* And the great grey lynx's skin!

      Naschina.   In sooth, methinks
152.   That I myself could shoot a great grey lynx.

                      [Naschina *turns to go.*

153. *Almintor.* Oh stay, Naschina, stay!

154. *Naschina.* Here, where men know the gracious woodland joys,

155. Joy's brother, Fear, dwells ever in each breast—
156. Joy's brother, Fear, lurks in each leafy way.
157. I weary of your songs and hunter's toys.
158. To prove his love a knight with lance in rest
159. Will circle round the world upon a quest,
160. Until afar appear the gleaming dragon-scales:
161. From morn the twain until the evening pales
162. Will struggle. Or he'll seek enchanter old,
163. Who sits in lovely splendour, mail'd in gold,
164. And they will war, 'mid wondrous elfin-sights:
165. Such may I love. The shuddering forest lights
166. Of green Arcadia do not hide, I trow,
167. Such men, such hearts. But, uncouth hunter, thou
168. Know'st naught of this.

[She goes.

Antonio.   And, uncouth hunter, now—

169. Almintor. Ay, boy.

Antonio.   Let's see if that same heron's dead.
[The boy runs out, followed slowly by Almintor.

<h2 style="text-align:center">Scene II</h2>

Sundown.—A remote forest valley.

Enter Almintor, followed by Antonio.

1. Antonio. And whither, uncouth hunter? Why so fast?
2. So! 'mid the willow-glade you pause at last.

3. Almintor. Here is the place, the cliff-encircled wood;
4. Here grow that shy, retiring sisterhood,
5. The pale anemones. We've sought all day,
6. And found.

Antonio.   'Tis well!—another mile of way
7. I could not go.

[They sit down.

Almintor.   Let's talk, and let's be sad,
8.   Here in the shade.

Antonio.   Why? Why?

Almintor.   For what is glad?
9.   For, look you, sad's the murmur of the bees,
10.   Yon wind goes sadly, and the grass and trees
11.   Reply like moaning of imprisoned elf:
12.   The whole world's sadly talking to itself.
13.   The waves in yonder lake where points my hand
14.   Beat out their lives lamenting o'er the sand;
15.   The birds that nestle in the leaves are sad,
16.   Poor sad wood-rhapsodists.

Antonio.   Not so: they're glad.

17. *Almintor.* All rhapsody hath sorrow for its soul.

18. *Antonio.* Yon eager lark, that fills with song the whole
19.   Of this wide vale, embosomed in the air,
20.   Is sorrow in his song, or any care?
21.   Doth not yon bird, yon quivering bird, rejoice?

22. *Almintor.* I hear the whole sky's sorrow in one voice.

23. *Antonio.* Nay, nay, Almintor, yonder song is glad.

24. *Almintor.* 'Tis beautiful, and therefore it is sad.

25. *Antonio.* Have done this phrasing, and say why, in sooth,
26.   Almintor, thou hast grown so full of ruth,
27.   And wherefore have we come?

Almintor.   A song to hear.

28. *Antonio.* But whence, and when?

Almintor.   Over the willows sere
29.   Out of the air.

Antonio.   And when?

Almintor.   When the sun goes down
30.   Over the crown of the willows brown.
31.   Oh, boy, I'm bound on a most fearful quest;
32.   For so she willed—thou heard'st? Upon the breast
33.   Of yonder lake, from whose green banks alway
34.   The poplars gaze across the waters grey,
35.   And nod to one another, lies a green,
36.   Small island, where the full soft sheen
37.   Of evening and glad silence dwelleth aye,
38.   For there the great Enchantress lives.

Antonio.   And there
39.   Groweth the goblin flower of joy, her care,
40.   By many sought, and 'tis a forest tale,
41.   How they who seek are ever doomed to fail.
42.   Some say that all who touch the island lone
43.   Are changed for ever into moon-white stone.

44. *Almintor.* That flower I seek.

Antonio.   Thou never wilt return.

45. *Almintor.* I'll bring that flower to her, and so may earn
46.   Her love: to her who wears that bloom comes truth,
47.   And elvish wisdom, and long years of youth
48.   Beyond a mortal's years. I wait the song
49.   That calls.

Antonio.   O evil starred!

Almintor.   It comes along
50.   The wind at evening when the sun goes down
51.   Over the crown of the willows brown.
52.   See, yonder sinks the sun, yonder a shade
53.   Goes flickering in reverberated light.
54.   There! There! Dost thou not see?

Antonio.   I see the night,
55.   Deep-eyed, slow-footing down the empty glade.

56. *A Voice* [*sings.*] From the shadowy hollow
57.   Arise thou and follow!

58. *Almintor.* Sad faery tones.

Antonio.   'Tis thus they ever seem,
59.   As some dead maiden's singing in a dream.

60. *Voice.* When the tree was o'er-appled
61.   For mother Eve's winning
62.   I was at her sinning.
63.   O'er the grass light-endappled
64.   I wandered and trod,
65.   O'er the green Eden-sod;
66.   And I sang round the tree
67.   As I sing now to thee:
68.   Arise from the hollow,
69.   And follow, and follow!

70.   Away in the green paradise,
71.   As I wandered unseen,
72.   (How glad was her mien!),
73.   I saw her as you now arise;
74.   Before her I trod
75.   O'er the green Eden-sod,
76.   And I sang round the tree,
77.   As I sing now to thee:
78.   From the shadowy hollow
79.   Come follow! Come follow!

[*Almintor goes.*

Title before 60.   Lyrics from 'The Island of / Statues' / The Fairy's Call
    CC.
60.   [the word 'Voice' lacking]
61.   . . . winning, **CC.**
68.   . . . hollow **CC.**
70.   . . . Paradise, **CC.**
78.   . . . hollow, **CC.**
    Direction after 79.   [lacking] **CC.**

[*The Voice sings, dying away.*]
80. And I sang round the tree,
81. As I sing now to thee:
82. From the green shaded hollow
83. Arise, worm, and follow!

84. *Antonio.* I, too, will follow for this evil-starred one's sake
85. Unto the dolorous border of the fairy lake.

[*Goes.*

Scene III

The Birth of Night.—The Island.—*Far into the distance reach shadowy ways, burdened with the faery flowers. Knee-deep amongst them stand the immovable figures of those who have failed in their quest.*

1. *First Voice.* See! oh, see! the dew-drowned bunches
2. Of the monk's-hood how they shake,
3. Nodding by the flickering lake,
4. There where yonder squirrel crunches
5. Acorns green, with eyes awake.

6. *Second Voice.* I followed him from my green lair,
7. But wide awake his two eyes were.

8. *First Voice.* Oh, learnèd is each monk's-hood's mind,
9. And full of wisdom is each bloom,
10. As, clothed in ceremonial gloom,
11. They hear the story of the wind,
12. That dieth slow with sunsick doom.

13. *Second Voice.* The south breeze now in dying fears
14. Tells all his sinning in their ears.

Directions before 1.   [lacking] **CC.**
Title before 1.   Lyrics from 'The Island of / Statues' / **The Fairy Voices CC.**
8.   . . ., learned . . ., **CC.**
13.   . . . fears,
14.   . . . all her sinning . . . . **CC.**

15. *First Voice.* He says 'twas he, and 'twas no other,
16.   Blew my crimson cap away
17.   O'er the lake this very day.
18.   Hark! he's dead—my drowsy brother,
19.   And has not heard *Absolvo te.*

                                       [A pause.

20. *First Voice.* Peace, peace, the earth's a-quake. I hear
21.   Some barbarous, un-faery thing draw near.

Enter Almintor

22. *Almintor.* The evening gleams are green and gold and red
23.   Along the lake. The crane has homeward fled.
24.   And flowers around in clustering thousands are,
25.   Each shining clear as some unbaffled star;
26.   The skies more dim, though burning like a shield,
27.   Above these men whose mouths were sealed
28.   Long years ago, and unto stone congealed.
29.   And, oh! the wonder of the thing! each came
30.   When low the sun sank down in clotted flame
31.   Beyond the lake, whose smallest wave was burdened
32.   With rolling fire, beyond the high trees turbaned
33.   With clinging mist, each star-fought wanderer came
34.   As I, to choose beneath day's dying flames;
35.   And they are all now stone, as I shall be,
36.   Unless some pitying god shall succour me
37.   In this my choice.

                         [Stoops over a flower, then pauses.

            Some god might help; if so
38.   Mayhap 'twere better that aside I throw
39.   All choice, and give to chance for guiding chance
40.   Some cast of die, or let some arrow glance
41.   For guiding of the gods. The sacred bloom
42.   To seek not hopeless have I crossed the gloom,

---

15.   . . . other **CC.**

43.   With that song leading where harmonic woods
44.   Nourish the panthers in dim solitudes;
45.   Vast greenness, where eternal Rumour dwells,
46.   And hath her home by many-folded dells.
47.   I passed by many caves of dripping stone,
48.   And heard each unseen Echo on her throne,
49.   Lone regent of the woods, deep muttering,
50.   And then new murmurs came new uttering
51.   In song, from goblin waters swaying white,
52.   Mocking with patient laughter all the night
53.   Of those vast woods; and then I saw the boat,
54.   Living, wide wingèd, on the waters float.
55.   Strange draperies did all the sides adorn,
56.   And the waves bowed before it like mown corn,
57.   The wingèd wonder of all Faery Land.
58.   It bore me softly where the shallow sand
59.   Binds, as within a girdle or a ring,
60.   The lake-embosomed isle. Nay, this my quest
61.   Shall not so hopeless prove: some god may rest
62.   Upon the wind, and guide mine arrow's course.
63.   From yonder pinnacle above the lake
64.   I'll send mine arrow, now my one resource;
65.   The nighest blossom where it falls I'll take.

                [*Goes out, fitting an arrow to his bow.*

66.   *A Voice.* Fickle the guiding his arrow shall find!
67.   Some goblin, my servant, on wings that are fleet,
68.   That nestles alone in the whistling wind,
69.   Go pilot the course of his arrow's deceit!

                [*The arrow falls. Re-enter* Almintor.

70.   *Almintor.* 'Tis here the arrow fell: the breezes laughed
71.   Around the feathery tip. Unto the shaft
72.   This blossom is most near. Statue! Oh, thou
73.   Whose beard a moonlight river is, whose brow
74.   Is stone: old sleeper! this same afternoon
75.   O'er much I've talked: I shall be silent soon,
76.   If wrong my choice, as silent as thou art.
77.   Oh! gracious Pan, take now thy servant's part.
78.   He was our ancient god. If I speak low,
79.   And not too clear, how will the new god know

80.   But that I called on him?

       [*Pulls the flower, and becomes stone. From among the flowers a sound as of a multitude of horns.*

81.   *A Voice.* Sleeping lord of archery,
82.   No more a-roving shalt thou see
83.   The panther with her yellow hide,
84.   Of the forests all the pride,
85.   Or her ever burning eyes,
86.   When she in a cavern lies,
87.   Watching o'er her awful young,
88.   Where their sinewy might is strung
89.   In the never-lifting dark.
90.   No! Thou standest still and stark,
91.   That of old wert moving ever,
92.   But a mother panther never
93.   O'er her young so eagerly
94.   Did her lonely watching take
95.   As I my watching lest you wake,
96.   Sleeping lord of archery.

Act II

Scene I

The wood in the early evening.

Enter Antonio *and* Naschina.

1.   *Naschina.* I, as a shepherd dressed, will seek and seek
2.   Until I find him. What a weary week,
3.   My pretty child, since he has gone, oh say
4.   Once more how on that miserable day
5.   He passed across the lake.

  Antonio.   **When we two came**
6.   From the wood's ways, then, like a silver flame,

7. We saw the dolorous lake; and then thy name
8. He carved on trees, and with a sun-dry weed
9. He wrote it on the sands (the owls may read
10. And ponder it if they will); then near at hand
11. The boat's prow grated on the shallow sand,
12. And loudly twice the living wings flapt wide,
13. And, leaping to their feet, far Echoes cried,
14. Each other answering. Then between each wing
15. He sat, and then I heard the white lake sing,
16. Curving beneath the prow; as some wild drake
17. Half lit, so flapt the wings across the lake—
18. Alas! I make you sadder, shepherdess.

19. *Naschina.* Nay, grief in feeding on old grief grows less.

20. *Antonio.* Grief needs much feeding then. Of him I swear
21. We've talked and talked, and not a whit more rare
22. Your weeping fits!

Naschina.   Look you, so very strait
23. The barred woodpecker's mansion is and deep,
24. No other bird may enter in.

Antonio.   Well?

Naschina.   Late—
25. Aye, very lately, sorrow came to weep
26. Within mine heart; and naught but sorrow now
27. Can enter there.

Antonio.   See! See! above yon brow
28. Of hill two shepherds come.

Naschina.   Farewell! I'll don
29. My shepherd garments, and return anon.

             [Goes.

Enter Colin *and* Thernot.

30. *Thernot.* Two men who love one maid have ample cause
31. Of war. Of yore, two shepherds, where we pause,

32.   Fought once for self-same reason on the hem
33.   Of the wide woods.

Colin.   And the deep earth gathered them.

34. *Thernot.* We must get swords.

Colin.   Is't the only way? Oh, see,
35.   Yon is the hunter's, Sir Almintor's, page;
36.   Let him between us judge, for he can gauge
37.   And measure out the ways of chivalry.

38. *Thernot.* Sir Page, Almintor's friend, and therefore learned
39.   In all such things, pray let thine ears be turned,
40.   And hear, and judge.

Antonio.   My popinjay, what now?

41. *Colin.* This thing we ask: must we two fight?—Judge thou.
42.   Each came one morn, with welcoming of song,
43.   Unto her door; for this, where nod the long
44.   And shoreward waves, we nigh have fought; waves bring
45.   The brown weed burden, so the sword brings fear
46.   To us.

Thernot.   Oh wise art thou in such a thing,
47.   Being Almintor's page. Now judge you here.
48.   We love Naschina both.

Antonio.   Whom loves *she* best?

49. *Colin.* She cares no whit for either, but has blest
50.   Almintor with her love.

       Enter Naschina, *disguised as a shepherd boy.*

Colin.   Who art thou?—speak,
51.   As the sea's furrows on a sea-tost shell,
52.   Sad histories are lettered on thy cheek.

53. *Antonio.* It is the shepherd Guarimond, who loveth well
54.   In the deep centres of the secret woods.
55.   Old miser hoards of grief to tell and tell:
56.   Young Guarimond he tells them o'er and o'er,
57.   To see them drowned by those vast solitudes,
58.   With their unhuman sorrows.

Naschina.   Cease! no more!
59.   Thou hast an over-nimble tongue.

Colin.   Thy grief,
60.   What is it, friend?

Antonio.   He lost i' the woods the chief
61.   And only sheep he loved of all the troop.

62. *Colin.* More grief is mine. No man shall ever stoop
63.   Beneath the weight of greater grief than I;
64.   I like you, and, in sooth I know not why.
65.   Now, judge, must shepherd Thernot there and I
66.   For this thing fight—we love one maid?

Naschina.   Her name?

67. *Colin.* Naschina.

Naschina.   Oh, I know her well—a lame,
68.   Dull-witted thing, with face red squirrel-brown.

69. *Antonio.* A long, brown grasshopper of maids!

Naschina.   Peace, sir!

70. *Colin.* 'Tis clear that you have seen her not. The crown
71.   Is not more fair and joyous than she is
72.   Of beams a-flicker on yon lonely fir,
73.   Nor faeries in the honey-heart of June astir.
74.   By bosky June I swear, and by the bee, her minister.

75. *Naschina.* There is no way but that ye fight I wis,
76.   If *her* ye love.

Thernot.   Aye, Colin, we must fight.

77. *Colin.* Aye, fight we must.
                    [Antonio *and* Naschina *turn to go.*

Naschina.   Tell me, Antonio, might
78.   They get them swords, and both or either fall?

79. *Antonio.* No, no; when that shall be, then men may call
80.   Down to their feet the stars that shine alone,
81.   Each one at gaze for aye upon his whirling throne.
                                        [*They go.*

Scene II

A remote part of the forest.—Through black and twisted trees the lake is shining under the red evening sky.

Enter Naschina, *as a shepherd-boy, and* Antonio.

1. *Antonio.* Behold, how like a swarm of fiery bees
2.   The light is dancing o'er the knotted trees,
3.   In busy flakes; re-shining from the lake,
4.   Through this night-vested place the red beams break.

5. *Naschina.* From the deep earth unto the lurid sky
6.   All things are quiet in the eve's wide eye.

7. *Antonio.* The air is still above, and still each leaf,
8.   But loud the grasshopper that sits beneath.

9. *Naschina.* And, boy, saw you, when through the forest we
10.   Two came, his name and mine on many a tree
11.   Carved; here, beyond the lake's slow-muffled tread,
12.   In sand his name and mine I've also read.

13. *Antonio.* Yonder's the isle in search whereof we came;
14.   The white waves wrap it in a sheet of flame,

15.   And yonder huddling blackness draweth nigh—
16.   The faery ship that swims athwart the sky.

17. *Naschina.* Antonio, if I return no more,
18.   Then bid them raise my statue on the shore;
19.   Here where the round waves come, here let them build,
20.   Here, facing to the lake, and no name gild;
21.   A white, dumb thing of tears, here let it stand,
22.   Between the lonely forest and the sand.

23. *Antonio.* The boat draws near and near. You heed me not!

24. *Naschina.* And when the summer's deep, then to this spot
25.   The Arcadians bring, and bid the stone be raised
26.   As I am standing now—as though I gazed,
27.   One hand brow-shading, far across the night,
28.   And one arm pointing thus, in marble white.
29.   And once a-year let the Arcadians come,
30.   And 'neath it sit, and of the woven sum
31.   Of human sorrow let them moralize;
32.   And let them tell sad histories, till their eyes
33.   All swim with tears.

     Antonio.   The faery boat's at hand;
34.   You must be gone; the rolling grains of sand
35.   Are 'neath its prow, and crushing shells.

36. *Naschina* [*turning to go*]. And let the tale be mournful each one tells.
                          [Antonio *and* Naschina *go out.*

                    Re-enter Antonio.

37. *Antonio.* I would have gone also; but far away
38.   The faery thing flew with her o'er the gray
39.   Slow waters, and the boat and maiden sink
40.   Away from me where mists of evening drink
41.   To ease their world-old thirst along the brink
42.   Of sword-blue waves of calm; while o'er head blink
43.   The mobs of stars in gold and green and blue,

44.   Piercing the quivering waters through and through,
45.   The ageless sentinels who hold their watch
46.   O'er grief. The world drinks sorrow from the beams
47.   And penetration of their eyes.

[Starting forward.

Where yonder blotch

48.   Of lilac o'er the pulsing water gleams,
49.   Once more those shepherds come. Mayhap some mirth
50.   I'll have. Oh, absent one, 'tis not for dearth
51.   Of grief. And if they say, 'Antonio laughed,'
52.   Say then,—'A popinjay before grief's shaft
53.   Pierced through, chattering from habit in the sun,
54.   Till his last wretchedness was o'er and done.'

55.   *A Voice from among the trees.* Antonio!

Enter Colin and Thernot.

Thernot.   We have resolved to fight.

56.   *Antonio.* To yonder isle, where never sail was furled,
57.   From whose green banks no living thing may rove,
58.   And see again the happy woodland light,
59.   Naschina's gone, drawn by a thirst of love,
60.   And that was strange; but *this* is many a world
61.   More wonderful!

Thernot.   And we have swords.

Antonio.   O night
62.   Of wonders! eve of prodigies!

Colin.   Draw! draw!

63.   *Antonio* [*aside*] He'll snap his sword.

Thernot.   Raised is the lion's paw.

[Colin and Thernot fight.

64.   *Antonio.* Cease! Thernot's wounded, cease! They will not heed,
65.   Fierce thrust! A tardy blossom had the seed,

66.   But heavy fruit. How swift the argument
67.   Of those steel tongues! Crash, swords! Well thrust! Well bent
68.   Aside!—

                                           [*A far-off multitudinous sound of horns.*

            The wild horns told Almintor's end,

69.   And of Naschina's now they tell—rend! rend!
70.   Oh, heart! Her dirge! With rushing arms the waves
71.   Cast on the sound, on, on. This night of graves,
72.   The spinning stars—the toiling sea—whirl round
73.   My sinking brain!—Cease!—Cease! Heard ye yon sound?
74.   The dirge of her ye love. Cease!—Cease!

     [*An echo in a cliff in the heart of the forest sends mournfully back the blast of the horns.* Antonio *rushes away, and the scene closes on* Colin *and* Thernot *still fighting.*

<h2 style="text-align:center">Scene III*</h2>

Between title and words 'Scene III.' Summary of Previous Scenes.—Two shepherds at dawn meet before the door of the shepherdess Naschina and sing to her in rivalry. Their voices grow louder and louder as they try to sing each other down. At last she comes out, a little angry. An arrow flies across the scene. The two shepherds fly, being full of Arcadian timidity. Almintor, who is loved by Naschina, comes in, having shot the arrow at a heron. Naschina receives him angrily. 'No one in Arcadia is courageous,' she says. Others, to prove their love, go upon some far and dangerous quest. They but bring Arcadian gifts, small birds and beasts. She goes again angrily into her cottage. Almintor seeks the enchanted island, to find for her the mysterious flower, guarded there by the Enchantress and her spirits. He is led thither by a voice singing in a valley. The island is full of flowers and of people turned into stone. They chose the wrong flower. He also chooses wrong, and is turned into stone. Naschina resolves to seek him disguised as a shepherd. On her way she meets with the two shepherds of Scene I; they do not recognize her, but like to be near her. They tell her they love one maid; she answers, if that be so, they must clearly settle it by combat. She, not believing they will do so, passes on and comes to the edge of the lake in which is the enchanted island, and is carried over in a boat with wings. The shepherds also come to the edge of the lake. They fight fiercely, made courageous by love. One is killed. The scene quoted gives the adventures of Naschina on the island. 2.

    Ed.'s notes: 1. For 'Printings' of Scene III see act I, scene I, above.
2.   The textual variants are from 2.

The Island.—*Flowers of manifold colour are knee-deep before a gate of brass, above which, in a citron-tinctured sky, glimmer a few stars. At intervals come mournful blasts from the horns among the flowers.*

1. *First Voice.* What do you weave so fair and bright?

2. *Second Voice.* The cloak I weave of sorrow.
3.   Oh, lovely to see in all men's sight
4.   Shall be the cloak of sorrow,
5.   In all men's sight.

6. *Third Voice.* What do you build with sails for flight?

7. *Fourth Voice.* A boat I build for sorrow.
8.   O swift on the seas all day and night
9.   Saileth the rover sorrow,
10.   All day and night.

11. *Fifth Voice.* What do you weave with wool so white?

12. *Sixth Voice.* The sandals these of sorrow.
13.   Soundless shall be the footfall light
14.   In each man's ears of sorrow,
15.   Sudden and light.

> Naschina, *disguised as a shepherd-boy, enters with the*
> Enchantress, *the beautiful familiar of the Isle.*

16. *Naschina.* What are the voices that in flowery ways
17.   Have clothed their tongues with song of songless days?

18. *Enchantress.* They are the flowers' guardian sprights;

TEXT   Title. Island of Statues / A Fragment
18.   . . . sprites;

19.   With streaming hair as wandering lights
20.   They passed a-tip-toe everywhere,
21.   And never heard of grief or care
22.   Until this morn. As adder's back
23.   The sky was banded o'er with wrack.
24.   They were sitting round a pool,
25.   At their feet the waves in rings
26.   Gently shook their moth-like wings;
27.   For there came an air-breath cool
28.   From the ever-moving pinions
29.   Of the happy flower minions.
30.   But a sudden melancholy
31.   Filled them as they sat together;
32.   Now their songs are mournful wholly
33.   As they go with drooping feather.

34.   *Naschina.* O, Lady, thou whose vestiture of green
35.   Is rolled as verdant smoke! O thou whose face
36.   Is worn as though with fire. Oh, goblin queen,
37.   Lead me, I pray thee, to the statued place!

38.   *Enchantress.* Fair youth, along a wandering way
39.   I've led thee here, and as a wheel
40.   We turned around the place alway,
41.   Lest on thine heart the stony seal
42.   As on those other hearts were laid.
43.   Behold the brazen-gated glade!

> [*She partially opens the brazen gates; the statues are seen within; some are bending, with their hands among the flowers; others are holding withered flowers.*

---

20. . . . a-tiptoe . . . ,
22. . . . morn. The sky with wrack
23. Was banded as an adder's back,
24. And they . . . pool.
34. O Lady, . . .
36. . . . fire! O goblin . . . ,
    Directions before 44.]   [. . . *gates. The* . . . *within. Some* . . . .

44. *Naschina.* O let me pass! the spells from off the heart
45. Of my sad hunter-friend will all depart
46. If on his lips the enchanted flower be laid;
47. O let me pass!

[Leaning with an arm upon each gate.

Enchantress. That flower none
48. Who seek may find, save only one,
49. A shepherdess long years foretold;
50. And even she shall never hold
51. The flower, some thing be found
52. To die for her in air or ground.
53. And none there is; if such there were,
54. E'en then, before her shepherd hair
55. Had felt the island breeze, my lore
56. Had driven her forth, for ever more
57. To wander by the bubbling shore.
58. Laughter-lipped, but for her brain
59. A guerdon of deep-rooted pain,
60. And in her eyes a lightless stare,
61. For if severed from the root
62. The enchanted flower were,
63. From my wizard island lair,
64. And the happy wingéd day,
65. I, as music that grows mute,
66. On a girl's forgotten lute,
67. Pass away—

---

44. Oh, let . . .
46. . . . laid.
47. Oh, let . . .
55. Had left the . . .
56. . . . evermore
57. . . . shore,
60. . . . stare;
61. For, if . . .
62. . . . were;
65. . . . mute

68. *Naschina.* Your eyes are all a-flash. She is not here.

69. *Enchantress.* I'd kill her if she were. Nay, do not fear!
70.   With you I am all gentleness; in truth,
71.   There's little I'd refuse thee, dearest youth.

72. *Naschina.* It is my whim! bid some attendant sprite
73.   Of thine cry over wold and water white,
74.   That one shall die, unless one die for her.
75.   'Tis but to see if anything will stir
76.   For such a call. Let the wild word be cried
77.   As though she whom you fear had crossed the wide
78.   Swift lake.

       Enchantress. A very little thing that is,
79.   And shall be done, if you will deign to kiss
80.   My lips, fair youth.

    Naschina.   It shall be as you ask.

81. *Enchantress.* Forth! forth! O spirits, ye have heard your task!

82. *Voices.* We are gone!

    Enchantress [*sitting down by* Naschina].
83.   Fair shepherd, as we wandered hither,
84.   My words were all: 'Here no loves wane and wither,
85.   Where dream-fed passion is and peace encloses,
86.   Where revel of fox-glove is and revel of roses.'
87.   My words were all: 'O whither, whither, whither
88.   Wilt roam away from this rich island rest?
89.   I bid thee stay, renouncing thy mad quest.'
90.   But thou wouldst not, for then thou wert unblest

---

68.   ... aflash. . . . .
78.   ... is
86.   ... foxglove . . . .'
88.   ... rest?'
89.   ... quest,

91. And stony-hearted; now thou hast grown kind,
92. And thou wilt stay. All thought of what they find
93. In the far world will vanish from thy mind,
94. Till thou rememberest only how the sea
95. Has fenced us round for all eternity.
96. But why art thou so silent? Did'st thou hear
97. I laughed?

Naschina.   And why is that a thing so dear?

98. *Enchantres.* From thee I snatched it; e'en the fay that trips
99. At morn, and with her feet each cobweb rends,
100. Laughs not. It dwells alone on mortal lips:
101. Thou'lt teach me laughing, and I'll teach thee peace,
102. Here where laburnum hangs her golden fleece;
103. For peace and laughter have been seldom friends.
104. But, for a boy, how long thine hair has grown!
105. Long citron coils that hang around thee, blown
106. In shadowy dimness. To be fair as thee
107. I'd give my faery fleetness, though I be
108. Far fleeter than the million-footed sea.

109. *A Voice.* By wood antique, by wave and waste,
110. Where cypress is and oozy pine,
111. Did I on quivering pinions haste,
112. And all was quiet round me spread,
113. As quiet as the clay-cold dead.
114. I cried the thing you bade me cry.
115. An owl, who in an alder tree
116. Had hooted for an hundred years,
117. Up-raised his voice, and hooted me.
118. E'en though his wings were plumeless stumps,
119. And all his veins had near run dry,
120. Forth from the hollow alder trunk
121. He hooted as I wandered by.

---

101.   . . . peace
117.   Upraised . . . .

122.   And so with wolf, and boar, and steer.
123.   And one alone of all would hark,
124.   A man who by a dead man stood.
125.   A star-lit rapier, half blood-dark,
126.   Was broken in his quivering hand.
127.   As blossoms, when the winds of March
128.   Hold festival across the land,
129.   He shrank before my voice, and stood
130.   Low bowed and dumb upon the sand.
131.   A foolish word thou gavest me!
132.   For each within himself hath all
133.   The world, within his folded heart,
134.   His temple and his banquet hall;
135.   And who will throw his mansion down
136.   Thus for another's bugle call!

137.   *Enchantress.* But why this whim of thine? A strange unrest,
138.   As alien as a cuckoo in a robin's nest,
139.   Is in thy face, and lips together pressed;
140.   And why so silent? I would have thee speak.
141.   Soon wilt thou smile, for here the winds are weak
142.   As moths with broken wings, and as we sit
143.   The heavens all star-throbbing are a-lit.

144.   *Naschina.* But art thou happy?

     Enchantress.   Let me gaze on thee
145.   At arm's length, thus till dumb eternity
146.   Has rolled away the stars and dried the sea
147.   I could gaze, gaze upon thine eyes' clear grey;

---

132.   . . . all;
133.   . . . world within . . . heart—
138.   Alien as cuckoo . . . ,
143.   . . . alit.
144.   . . . thee,
145.   . . . length thus; till . . .
147.   . . . eyes of grey;

148.   Gaze on till ragged time himself decay.
149.   Ah! you are weeping; here should all grief cease.

150.   *Naschina.* But art thou happy?

    Enchantress.   Youth, I am at peace.

151.   *Naschina.* But art thou happy?

    Enchantress.   Those grey eyes of thine
152.   Have they ne'er seen the eyes of lynx or kine,
153.   Or aught remote; or hast thou never heard
154.   Mid bubbling leaves a wandering song-rapt bird
155.   Going the forest through, with flutings weak;
156.   Or hast thou never seen, with visage meek,
157.   A hoary hunter leaning on his bow,
158.   To watch thee pass? Yet deeper than men know
159.   These are at peace.

160.   *A Voice.* Sad lady, cease!
161.   I rose, I rose
162.   From the dim wood's foundation—
163.   I rose, I rose
164.   Where in white exultation
165.   The long lily blows,
166.   And the wan wave that lingers
167.   From flood-time encloses
168.   With infantine fingers
169.   The roots of the roses.
170.   Thence have I come winging;
171.   I there had been keeping
172.   A mouse from his sleeping,
173.   With shouting and singing.

---

148.   . . . Time . . . .
151.   . . . thine,
154.   Mid babbling leaves . . .
170.   Now here I . . . ;

174. *Enchantress.* How sped thy quest? This prelude we'll not hear it.
175.   I' faith thou ever wast a wordy spirit!

176. *The Voice.* A wriggling thing on the white lake moved,
177.   As the canker-worm on a milk-white rose;
178.   And down I came as a falcon swoops
179.   When his sinewy wings together close.
180.   I lit by the thing, 'twas a shepherd-boy,
181.   Who, swimming, sought the island lone;
182.   Within his clenchèd teeth a sword.
183.   I heard the deathful monotone,
184.   The water-serpent sings his heart
185.   Before a death. O'er wave and bank
186.   I cried the words you bid me cry.
187.   The shepherd raised his arms and sank,
188.   His rueful spirit fluttered by.

189. *Naschina* [*aside*]. I must bestir myself. Both dead for me!
190.   Both dead!—No time to think.
     [*Aloud.*]   I am she,
191.   That shepherdess; arise, and bring to me,
192.   In silence, that famed flower of wizardry,
193.   For I am mightier now by far than thee,
194.   And faded now is all thy wondrous art.

                    [*The* Enchantress *points to a cleft in a rock.*

195. *Naschina.* I see within a cloven rock dispart
196.   A scarlet bloom. Why raisest thou, pale one,
197.   Oh famous dying minion of the sun,

---

180. I 'lit . . . ,
183. . . . monotone
190. . . . time for thinking.
                    I . . . ,
191. . . . shepherdess: arise, . . . ,
195. ['*Naschina*' lacking]
197. O . . . ,

198.   Thy flickering hand? What mean the lights that rise
199.   As light of triumph in thy goblin eyes—
200.   In thy wan face?

  Enchantress. Hear thou, O daughter of the days,
201.   Behold the loving loveless flower of lone ways,
202.   Well nigh immortal in this charmèd clime,
203.   Thou shalt outlive thine amorous happy time,
204.   And dead as are the lovers of old rime
205.   Shall be the hunter-lover of thy youth.
206.   Yet ever more, through all thy days of ruth,
207.   Shall grow thy beauty and thy dreamless truth,
208.   As an hurt leopard fills with ceaseless moan,
209.   And aimless wanderings the woodlands lone,
210.   Thy soul shall be, though pitiless and bright
211.   It is, yet shall it fail thee day and night
212.   Beneath the burthen of the infinite,
213.   In those far years, O daughter of the days.
214.   And when thou hast these things for many ages felt,
215.   The red squirrel shall rear her young where thou hast dwelt—
216.   Ah, woe is me! I go from sun and shade,
217.   And the joy of the streams where long-limbed herons wade;
218.   And never any more the wide-eyed bands
219.   Of the pied panther-kittens from my hands
220.   Shall feed. I shall not in the evenings hear
221.   Again the woodland laughter, and the clear
222.   Wild cries, grown sweet with lulls and lingerings long.
223.   I fade, and shall not see the mornings wake,

---

200.   . . . ?
   Hear, daughter . . . days.
202.   Well-nigh . . . clime;
204.   . . . rhyme
206.   . . . evermore, . . . ,
207.   . . . truth;
208.   As a hurt . . . moan
212.   . . . burden . . . ,
213.   . . . those fair years, ...
214.   . . . for ages . . . ,

224.   A-fluttering the painted populace of lake
225.   And sedgy stream, and in each babbling brake
226.   And hollow lulling the young winds with song.
227.   I dream!—I cannot die!—No! no!
228.   I hurl away these all unfaery fears.
229.   Have I not seen a thousand seasons ebb and flow
230.   The tide of stars? Have I not seen a thousand years
231.   The summers fling their scents? Ah, subtile and slow,
232.   The warmth of life is chilling, and the shadows grow
233.   More dark beneath the poplars, where yon owl
234.   Lies torn and rotting. The fierce kestrel birds
235.   Slew thee, poor sibyl: comrades thou and I;
236.   For, ah, our lives were but two starry words
237.   Shouted a moment 'tween the earth and sky.
238.   Oh death is horrible! and foul, foul, foul!

239.   *Naschina.* I know not of the things you speak. But what
240.   Of him on yonder brazen-gated spot,
241.   By thee spell-bound?

            Enchantress.   Thou shalt know more:
242.   Meeting long hence the phantom herdsman, king
243.   Of the dread woods; along their russet floor
244.   His sleuth-hounds follow every faery thing.

                              [*Turns to go.* Naschina *tries to prevent her.*

245.   Before I am too weak, fierce mortal, let me fly,
246.   And crouch in some far stillness of the isle, and die.

                                                    [*Goes.*

---

227.   . . . die!—not die! No! . . . !
236.   For ah, . . .
238.   Oh, death . . . !
244.   . . . fairy . . . .
245.   . . . weak, oh let . . . ,
245a. Fierce mortal, and crouched low beside the lake
246.   In a far . . . the island die.

247. *Naschina* [*following*]. Will he have happiness? Great sobs her
     being shake.

248. *Voices* [*sing*]. A man has a hope for heaven,
249.   But soulless a faery dies,
250.   As a leaf that is old, and withered, and cold,
251.   When the wintry vapours rise.

252.   Soon shall our wings be stilled,
253.   And our laughter over and done:
254.   So let us dance where the yellow lance
255.   Of the barley shoots in the sun.

256.   So let us dance on the fringèd waves,
257.   And shout at the wisest owls
258.   In their downy caps, and startle the naps
259.   Of the dreaming water-fowls,

260.   And fight for the black sloe-berries,
261.   For soulless a faery dies,
262.   As a leaf that is old, and withered, and cold,
263.   When the wintry vapours rise.

Re-enter Naschina.

264. *Naschina.* I plucked her backwards by her dress of green.
265.   To question her—oh no, I did not fear,
266.   Because St. Joseph's image hangeth here
267.   Upon my necklace. But the goblin queen
268.   Faded and vanished, nothing now is seen,
269.   Saving a green frog dead upon the grass.
270.   As figures moving mirrored in a glass,
271.   The singing shepherds, too, have passed away.
272.   O Arcady, O Arcady, this day
273.   A deal of evil and of change hath crossed

---

268.   . . . vanished: nothing . . . ,

274.   Thy peace. Ah, now I'll wake these sleepers, lost
275.   And woe-begone. For them no evil day!

                              [*Throws open the brazen gates.*

276.   *To Almintor.* O wake! wake! wake! for soft as a bee sips
277.   The faery flower lies upon thy lips.

278.   *Almintor.* I slept, 'twas sultry, and scarce circling shook
279.   The falling hawthorn bloom. By mere and brook
280.   The otters dreaming lay.

Naschina.   Aye!
281.   Behold the hapless sleepers standing by.
282.   I will dissolve away the faeries' guile;
283.   So be thou still, dear heart, a little while!

[*To the Second Sleeper.*]

284.   Old warrior, wake! for soft as a bee sips,
285.   The faery blossom lies upon thy lips.

286. *Sleeper.* Have I slept long?

Naschina.   Long years.

The Sleeper.   With hungry heart
287.   Doth still the Wanderer rove? With all his ships
288.   I saw him from sad Dido's shores depart,
289.   Enamoured of the waves' impetuous lips.

---

277.   . . . fairy . . . .
280.   . . . lay. Naschina!
             Ay!
284.   . . . sips
285.   . . . fairy . . . .

290. *Naschina.* Those twain are dust. Wake! Light as a bee sips
291.   The faery blossom lies upon thy lips;
292.   Seafarer, wake!

Third Sleeper.   Was my sleep long?

Naschina.   Long years.

293. *The Sleeper.* A rover I, who come from where men's ears
294.   Love storm; and stained with mist the new moons flare.
295.   Doth still the Man whom each stern rover fears,
296.   The austere Arthur, rule from Uther's chair?

297. *Naschina.* He is long dead.
                                Wake! soft as a bee sips
298.   The goblin flower lieth on thy lips.

299. *Fourth Sleeper.* Was my sleep long, oh, youth?

Naschina.   Long, long and deep.

300. *The Sleeper.* As here I came I saw god Pan. He played
301.   An oaten pipe unto a listening fawn,
302.   Whose insolent eyes unused to tears would weep.
303.   Doth he still dwell within the woody shade,
304.   And rule the shadows of the eve and dawn?

305. *Naschina.* Nay, he is gone. Wake! wake! as a bee sips
306.   The faery blossom broods upon thy lips.
307.   Sleeper, awake!

---

291.   . . . fairy . . . ;
293.   . . . I who . . .
294.   . . . storm and . . . moon's . . . .
295.   . . . man . . . fears—
296.   . . . Arthur—rule . . . ?
299.   . . . , O youth? . . . .
301.   . . . faun,
306.   . . . fairy . . . .

  Fifth Sleeper. How long my sleep?

  Naschina.   Unnumbered
308. The years of goblin sleep.

  The Sleeper.   Ah! while I slumbered,
309. How have the years in Troia flown away?
310. Are still the Achaians' tented chiefs at bay?
311. Where rise the walls majestical above
312. The plain, a little fair-haired maid I love.

313. *The Sleepers all together.* She is long ages dust.

  The Sleeper.   Ah, woe is me!

314. *First Sleeper.* Youth, here will we abide, and be thou king
315. Of this lake-nurtured isle!

  Naschina.   Let thy king be
316. Yon archer, he who hath the halcyon's wing
317. As flaming minstrel-word upon his crest.

318. *All the Sleepers.* Clear-browed Arcadian, thou shalt be our king!

319. *Naschina.* O, my Almintor, noble was thy quest;
320. Yea, noble and most knightly hath it been.

321. *All the Sleepers.* Clear-browed Arcadian, thou shalt be our king!

322. *Almintor.* Until we die within the charmed ring
323. Of these star-shuddering skies, you are the queen.

   [*The rising moon casts the shadows of* Almintor *and the Sleepers
   far across the grass. Close by* Almintor's *side,* Naschina *is standing,
   shadowless.*

        THE END

---

311. . . . above,
312. There dwells a little . . . .
322. . . . charmed . . .

THE SEEKER

A Dramatic Poem—in Two Scenes.

Scene I.

A woodland valley at evening. Around a wood fire sit three Shepherds.

1. *First Shepherd.* Heavy with wool the sheep are gathered in,
2. And through the mansion of the spirit rove
3. My dreams round thoughts of plenty, as in gloom
4. Of desert-caves the red-eyed panthers rove
5. And rove unceasing round their dreadful brood.

6. *Second Shepherd.* O brother, lay thy flute upon thy lips;
7. It is the voice of all our hearts that laugh.
   [*The first* Shepherd *puts the flute to his lips; there comes from it a piercing cry. He drops it.*

8. *First Shepherd.* It is possessed.

   Second Shepherd.   A prophesying voice.

9. *Third Shepherd.* Nay, give it me, and I will sound a measure;
10. And unto it we'll dance upon the sward.
    [*Puts it to his lips. A voice out of the flute still more mournful.*

11. *First Shepherd.* An omen!

    Second Shepherd. An omen!

12. *Third Shepherd.* A creeping horror is all over me.

PRINTINGS   *The Dublin University Review,* September 1885; **2,** 98.
Ed's. note: The variants are from *The Dublin University Review.*
TEXT   Stage directions.   *A . . . wood-fire . . . shepherds; without a curve rises the smoke.*

3.   . . . dreams o'er thoughts . . . , as the red-
4.   Eyed panthers in their desert caverns rove
6.   . . . lips,
8.   [the words '*Second Shepherd.* A prophesying voice.' lacking]

Enter an Old Knight. *They cast themselves down before him.*

13. *Knight.* Are all things well with you and with your sheep?

14. *Second Shepherd.* Yes, all is very well.

    First Shepherd.   Whence comest thou?

15. *Knight.* Shepherds, I came this morning to your land
16.   From three score years of dream-led wandering
17.   Where spice-isles nestle on the star-trod seas,
18.   And where the polar winds and waters wrestle
19.   In endless dark, and by the weedy marge
20.   Of Asian rivers, rolling on in light.
21.   But now my wandering shall be done, I know.
22.   A voice came calling me to this your land,
23.   Where lies the long-lost forest of the sprite,
24.   The sullen wood. But many woods I see
25.   Where to themselves innumerable birds
26.   Make moan and cry.

    First Shepherd.   Within yon sunless valley,
27.   Between the hornèd hills—

    Knight.   Shepherds, farewell!
28.   And peace be with you, peace and wealth of days.

29. *Second Shepherd.* Seek not that wood, for there the goblin snakes
30.   Go up and down, and raise their heads and sing
31.   With little voices songs of fearful things.

32. *Third Shepherd.* No shepherd foot has ever dared its depths.

33. *First Shepherd.* The very squirrel dies that enters there.

34. *Knight.* Shepherds, farewell!   *[Goes.*

---

20.   Of India's rivers, ...
21.   But soon my . . . done I . . . .
22.   . . . voice has told me how within this land
23.   There lies . . . ,
26.   . . . valley
27.   . . . horned . . . !
33.   . . . enters it.

Second Shepherd.   He soon will be—

First Shepherd.   Ashes

35.   Before the wind.

Third Shepherd.   Saw you his eyes a-glitter?

36.   His body shake?

Second Shepherd.   Ay, quivering as yon smoke

37.   That from the fire is ever pouring up

38.   Among the boughs, blue as the halcyon's wing,

39.   Star-envious.

Third Shepherd. He was a spirit, brother.

40.   *Second Shepherd.* The blessèd God was good to send us such,

41.   To make us glad with wonder as we sat

42.   Weary of watching round the fire at night.

Scene II.

*A ruined palace in the forest. Away in the depth of
the shadow of the pillars a motionless* Figure.

Enter the Old Knight.

43.   *Knight.* Behold, I bend before thee to the ground

44.   Until my beard is in the twisted leaves

45.   That with their fiery ruin fill the hall,

46.   As words of thine through fourscore years have filled

47.   My echoing heart. Now raise thy voice and speak!

48.   Even from boyhood, in my father's house,

49.   That was beside the waterfall, thy words

50.   Abode, as banded adders in my breast.

51.   Thou knowest this, and how from 'mid the dance

52.   Thou called'st me forth.

                              And how thou madest me

---

35.   . . . a-glitter,
36.   . . . ?
                    Aye, . . .
37.   . . . up,
38.   Within the woodways, blue . . . ,
40.   . . . blessèd . . . ,
43.   Behold I . . .
51.   . . . mid . . .
52.   . . . forth,
                    And . . .

53. A coward in the field; and all men cried:
54. 'Behold the Knight of the waterfall, whose heart
55. The spirits stole, and gave him in its stead
56. A peering hare's;' and yet I murmured not,
57. Knowing that thou hadst singled me with word
58. Of love from out a dreamless race for strife,
59. Through miseries unhuman ever on
60. To joys unhuman, and to thee—Speak! Speak!

[*He draws nearer to the* Figure. *A pause.*

61. Behold, I bend before thee to the ground;
62. Thou wilt not speak, and I with age am near
63. To Death. His darkness and his chill I feel.
64. Were all my wandering days of no avail,
65. Untouched of human joy or human love?
66. Then let me see thy face before I die.
67. Behold, I bend before thee to the ground!
68. Behold, I bend! Around my beard in drifts
69. Lie strewn the yellow leaves—the clotted leaves.

[*He gathers up the leaves and presses them to his breast.*

70. I'm dying! Oh, forgive me if I touch
71. Thy garments' hem, thou visionary one!

---

54. Behold . . . Waterfall, . . .
56. . . . hare's; and . . . ,
60. . . . ! Speak
61. Behold I . . . ;
63. . . . Death. His lips are glued, with quivering touch,
63a. To mine, and he is slowly sucking forth
63b. My soul. His darkness and his chill I feel.
64. . . . avail
67. Behold I bow before . . . !
68. Behold I bow! Around . . .
69. . . . strewn the clotted leaves—the dead old leaves.
69a. Thou wilt not speak, Oh cruel art thou yet!
69b. Mine heart-strings are all broken saving one,
69c. That trembles and resounds with hymns to thee,
69d. That fill the blazing hollows of my heart.
70. . . . ! Oh forgive . . .
71. . . . garment's . . . !

[*He goes close to the* Figure. *A sudden light bursts over it.*

72. A bearded witch, her sluggish head low bent
73. On her broad breast! Beneath her withered brows
74. Shine dull unmoving eyes. What thing art thou?
75. I sought thee not.

    Figure.   Men call me Infamy.
76. I know not what I am.

    Knight.   I sought thee not.

77. *Figure.* Lover, the voice that summoned thee was mine.

78. *Knight.* For all I gave the voice, for all my youth,
79. For all my joy—ah, woe!
    [*The* Figure *raises a mirror, in which the face and the form of the*
    Knight *are shadowed. He falls.*
    Figure [*bending over him and speaking in his ear*].
80. What, lover, die before our lips have met?

81. *Knight.* Again, the voice! the voice!   [*Dies.*

                THE END

    Directions after 71. [*He approaches close* . . . .
72. *Knight.* A . . .
73. . . . ! beneath . . .
79. . . . joy.—Ah, . . . !
    Directions after 79. [. . . *falls forward.*
    Directions before 80.   *The figure bending* . . . *him, and* . . . *ear.*
80. What! Lover, . . . ?

[The text is from 2]

MOSADA

'And my Lord Cardinal hath had strange days in his youth.'
    —*Extract from a Memoir of the Fifteenth Century.*

        Mosada, *a Moorish lady.*
        Ebremar, *a monk.*
        Cola, *a lame boy.*
        Monks and Inquisitors.

PRINTINGS   *The Dublin University Review,* June 1886 (**D**); **1, 2, 95, 98.**

Scene I.

A little Moorish room in the village of Azubia. In the centre of the room a chafing-dish.

Mosada *alone*

1.	*Mosada.* Three times the roses have grown less and less,
2.	And thrice the peaches flushed upon the walls,
3.	And thrice the corn around the sickles flamed,
4.	Since 'mong my people, tented on the hills,
5.	Where they all summer feed their wandering flocks,
6.	He stood a messenger. In April's prime
7.	(Swallows were flashing their white breasts above
8.	Or perching on the tents, a-weary still
9.	From waste seas cross'd, yet ever garrulous)
10.	Along the velvet vale I saw him come—
11.	Feet of dark Gomez, where now wander ye?
12.	In autumn, when far down the mountain slopes
13.	The heavy clusters of the grapes were full,
14.	I saw him sigh and turn and pass away;
15.	For I and all my people were accurst
16.	Of his sad God; and down among the grass
17.	Hiding my face, I cried long, bitterly.
18.	'Twas evening, and the cricket nation sang
19.	Around my head and danced among the grass;
20.	And all was dimness, till a dying leaf
21.	Slid circling down and softly touched my lips

TEXT   Stage directions.   *A Little* . . . *Room* . . . *Village* . . . *chafing dish.* **D, 1 ;**
    . . . chafing dish. **95.**

1a.	As slowly Autumn climbed the golden throne
1b.	Where sat old Summer fading into song, **D, 1.**
10.	. . . come:
11.	[lacking]
12.	. . . Autumn, . . . **D, 1.**
18.	Twas . . . **1.**
20.	. . . dimness till . . . **D, 1.**

22.   With dew, as though 'twere sealing them for death.
23.   Yet somewhere in the footsore world we meet,
24.   We two, before we die; for Azolar,
25.   The star-taught Moor, said thus it was decreed
26.   By those wan stars that sit in company
27.   Above the Alpujarras on their thrones:
28   That when the stars of our nativity
29   Draw star to star, as on that eve he passed
30.   Down the long valleys from my people's tents,
31.   We meet—we two. [*She opens the casement. A sound of laughter floats in.*] How merry all these are
32.   Among the fruit! But there, lame Cola crouches
33.   Away from all the others. Now the sun
34.   Sinks, shining on the little crucifix
35.   Hung on his doublet—dear and mournful child,
36.   Seër of visions! Now eve falls asleep,
37.   The hour of incantation comes a-tiptoe,
38.   And Cola, seeing, knows the sign and comes.
39.   Thus do I burn these precious herbs, whose smoke
40.   Pours up and floats in fragrance round my head
41.   In coil on coil of azure.

---

22.   . . . dew as . . . .
23.   . . . meet
24.   . . . two before . . . die, for Azolar
25.   . . . Moor said . . . **D, 1.**
27.   . . . thrones, **D, 1.**
      Directions in 31. [. . . *casement—the mingled sound of the voices and laughter of the apple gatherers floats in*] **D, 1.**
32.   . . . fruit. But yon, lame . . .
33.   . . . sun—
34.   A-shining on . . .
35.   Of silver hanging round lame Cola's neck— **D, 1.**
36.   Sinks down at last with yonder minaret, **D, 1** ; Seer . . . , **95.**
37.   Of the Alhambra black athwart his disk; **D, 1.**
38.   . . . Cola seeing, ... **D, 1** ; . . . sign and rises. **95.**
39.   . . . herbs whose . . .
40.   . . . fragrance o'er my . . . **D, 1.**
41.   . . . ready **D.**

Enter Cola.

All is ready.

42. *Cola.* I will not share your sin.

Mosada.   This is no sin.
43.   No sin to see in coil on coil of azure
44.   Pictured, where wander the beloved feet
45.   Whose footfall I have longed for, three sad summers.
46.   Why these new fears?

Cola.   The great monk Ebremar,
47.   The dark still man, has come and says 'tis sin.

48. *Mosada.* They say the wish itself is half the sin;
49.   Then has this one been sinned full many times.
50.   Yet 'tis no sin; my father taught it me.
51.   He was a man most learned and most mild,
52.   Who, dreaming to a wondrous age, lived on,
53.   Tending the roses round his lattice door.
54.   For years his days had dawned and faded thus
55.   Among the plants; the flowery silence fell
56.   Deep in his soul, like rain upon a soil
57.   Worn by the solstice fierce, and made it pure.
58.   Would he teach any sin?

Cola.   Gaze in the cloud
59.   Yourself.

Mosada.   None but the innocent can see.

60. *Cola.* They say I am all ugliness; lame-footed
61.   I am; one shoulder turned awry—why then
62.   Should I be good? But you are beautiful.

41a.   *Cola.* Mosada, it is then so much the worse; (worse. 1) **D, 1.**
  42.   . . . sin.
                   It is . . . sin
  43.   That you shall see on yonder glowing cloud **D, 1.**
  45.   . . . summers— D, 1 ; . . . summers **95.**
  46.   . . . fears?
                   The servant of the Lord,
  47.   . . . come, and . . . .
  48.   . . . sin.
  49.   . . . times,
  50.   . . . sin—my . . . . **D, 1.**
  52.   . . . on **D, 1.**

63. *Mosada.* I cannot see.

    Cola.   The beetles, and the bats,
64.   And spiders are my friends; I'm theirs, and they are
65.   Not good; but you are like the butterflies.

66. *Mosada.* I cannot see! I cannot see! but you
67.   Shall see a thing to talk on when you're old,
68.   Under a lemon tree beside your door;
69.   And all the elders sitting in the sun
70.   Will wondering listen, and this tale shall ease
71.   For long the burthen of their talking griefs.

72. *Cola.* Upon my knees I pray you, let it sleep,
73.   The vision.

    Mosada.   You are pale and weeping. Child,
74.   Be not afraid, you'll see no fearful thing.
75.   Thus, thus I beckon from her viewless fields—
76.   Thus beckon to our aid a Phantom fair
77.   And calm, robed all in raiment moony white.
78.   She was a great enchantress once of yore,
79.   Whose dwelling was a tree-wrapt island, lulled
80.   Far out upon the water world and ringed
81.   With wonderful white sands, where never yet
82.   Were furled the wings of ships. There in a dell,
83.   A lily-blanchèd place, she sat and sang,
84.   And in her singing wove around her head
85.   White lilies, and her song flew forth afar
86.   Along the sea; and many a man grew hushed
87.   In his own house or 'mong the merchants grey,
88.   Hearing the far-off singing guile, and groaned,
89.   And manned an argosy and sailing died.

---

64. . . . spiders, are . . . friends, I'm . . . **D, 1.**
69. . . . sun, **D, 1.**
71. . . . long, the . . . . **D, 1.**
73. . . . vision.
         You're pale . . . weeping, child. **D, 1.**
81. . . . sand, where . . .
82. . . . dell
83. . . . lily blanched . . . , **D, 1.**
88. . . . far off . . . guile and . . . , **D, 1.**

90.   In the far isle she sang herself asleep,
91.   But now I wave her hither to my side.

92. *Cola.* Stay, stay, or I will hold your white arms down.
93.   Ah me! I cannot reach them—here and there
94.   Darting you wave them, darting in the vapour.
95.   Heard you? Your lute hung in the window sounded!
96.   I feel a finger drawn across my cheek!

97. *Mosada.* The phantoms come; ha! ha! they come, they come!
98.   I wave them hither, my breast heaves with joy.
99.   Ah! now I'm Eastern-hearted once again,
100.   And, while they gather round my beckoning arms,
101.   I'll sing the songs the dusky lovers sing,
102.   Wandering in sultry palaces of Ind,
103.   A lotus in their hands—   [*The door is flung open.*

Enter the Officers of the Inquisition.

First Inquisitor.   Young Moorish girl
104.   Taken in magic, in the Church's name
105.   I here arrest thee.

Mosada.   It was Allah's will.
106.   Touch not this boy, for he is innocent.

107. *Cola.* Forgive! for I have told them everything.
108.   They said I'd burn in hell unless I told.
                [*She turns away—he clings to her dress.*

---

90.   . . . asleep
91.   At last. But . . . her to my side. **D, 1.**
93.   . . . me, I . . . **D, 1.**
95.   . . . lute upon the wall has sounded! **D, 1.**
97.   . . . ; ha ha! . . . ! **D, 1** ; . . . phantoms come; they come, they come, they come! **95.**
99.   . . . eastern-hearted . . . , **D, 1.**
100. And while . . . , **D, 1, 95.**
104. . . . magic. In . . .
105. . . . . It is Allah's . . . . **D, 1.**
108. . . . told **D, 1.**
108a. Them all, and let them find you in the vapour. **D, 1.**

109.   Forgive me!

Mosada.   It was Allah's will.

Second Inquisitor.   The cords.

110.   *Mosada.* No need to bind my hands. Where are ye, sirs?
111.   For ye are hid with vapour.

Second Inquisitor.   Round the stake
112.   The vapour is much thicker.

Cola.   God! the stake!
113.   Ye said that ye would fright her from her sin—
114.   No more; take me instead of her, great sirs.
115.   She was my only friend; I'm lame, you know—
116.   One shoulder twisted, and the children cry
117.   Names after me.

First Inquisitor. Lady—

Mosada.   I come.

Cola [*following*].   Forgive,
118.   Forgive, or I will die.

Mosada [*stooping and kissing him*]. 'Twas Allah's will.

---

109.   . . . will.
    Now cords.
110.   . . . , sirs,
111.   . . . with vapours?
    Round . . . **D, 1.**
115.   . . . lame you . . .— **D, 1.**
117.   . . . . Forgive. **D, 1.**

Scene II.

A room in the building of the Inquisition of Granada, lighted by a stained window, picturing St. James of Spain.

Monks *and* Inquisitors.

1. *First Monk.* Will you not hear my last new song?

First Inquisitor.   Hush, hush!

Stage directions.   . . . *Room, the building* . . . *Granada, lit by a stained* (*by stained* 1) . . . . **D, 1.**

2.   So she must burn, you say?

Second Inquisitor.   She must in truth.

3. *First Inquisitor.* Will he not spare her life? How would one matter
4.   When there are many?

Second Monk.   Ebremar will stamp
5.   This heathen horde away. You need not hope;
6.   And know you not she kissed that pious child
7.   With poisonous lips, and he is pining since?

8. *First Monk.* You're full of wordiness. Come, hear my song.

9. *Second Monk.* In truth, an evil race. Why strive for her,
10.   A little Moorish girl?

Second Inquisitor.   Small worth.

First Monk.   My song—

11. *First Inquisitor.* I had a sister like her once, my friend.
                    [*Touching the first* Monk *on the shoulder.*
12.   Where is our brother Peter? When you're nigh,
13.   He is not far. I'd have him speak for her.
14.   I saw his jovial mood bring once a smile
15.   To sainted Ebremar's sad eyes. I think
16.   He loves our brother Peter in his heart.
17.   If Peter would but ask her life—who knows?

18. *First Monk.* He digs his cabbages. He brings to mind
19.   That song I've made. 'Tis of an Irish tale.
20.   A saint of Munster, when much fasting, saw
21.   This vision of Peter and the burning gate.
22. [*Sings*]   I saw a stranger tap and wait
23.   By the door of Peter's gate,

---

2. . . . burn you say.
          She . . . . **D** ; . . . burn you . . . . **1.**
9. . . . truth an . . . race; why . . . , **D, 1.**
11. . . . once my friend, **D, 1.**
19. . . . made—is of a Russian tale
20. Of Holy Peter of the Burning Gate:
21. A saint of Russia in a vision saw
22. A stranger new arisen wait **D, 1.**
23. Beside the . . . gate. **95.**

24.	Then he shouted, 'Open wide
25.	Thy sacred door;' but Peter cried,
26.	'No, thy home is deepest hell,
27.	Deeper than the deepest well.'
28.	Then the stranger softly crew—
29.	'Cock-a-doodle-doodle-do!'
30.	Answered Peter: 'Enter in,
31.	Friend; but 'twere a deadly sin
32.	Ever more to speak a word
33.	Of any unblessed earthly bird.'

34. *First Inquisitor.* Be still; I hear the step of Ebremar.
35.   Yonder he comes; bright-eyed, and hollow-cheeked
36.   From fasting—see, the red light slanting down
37.   From the great painted window wraps his brow,
38.   As with an aureole.

Ebremar enters. They all bow to him.

First Inquisitor. My suit to you—

39. *Ebremar.* I will not hear; the Moorish girl must die.
40.   I will burn heresy from this mad earth,
41.   And—

First Inquisitor. Mercy is the manna of the world.

42. *Ebremar.* The wages of sin is death.

Second Monk.   No use. No good.

43. *First Inquisitor.* My lord, if it must be, I pray descend
44.   Yourself into the dungeon 'neath our feet

---

24. And he shouted Open . . . **D, 1**; The stranger shouted, . . . **95.**
25. . . . door, but . . . ,
26. No, . . . ,
27. . . . well.
28. . . . crew
29. Cock-a-doodle-doodle-doo!
30. . . . : Enter in **D, 1.**
33. . . . bird.
34. . . . still, I . . . . **D, 1.**
    Directions in 38. . . . *enters—they* . . . . **D, 1.**
42. . . . use. **D, 1**; The wage of . . . death.
                No use. No use. **95.**

45.   And importune with weighty words this Moor,
46.   That she forswear her heresies and save
47.   Her soul from seas of endless flame in hell.

48.   *Ebremar.* I speak alone with servants of the Cross
49.   And dying men—and yet—But no, farewell.

50.   *Second Monk.* No use.

       Ebremar.   Away! [*They go.*] Hear, thou enduring God,
51.   Who giveth to the golden-crested wren
52.   Her hanging mansion. Give to me, I pray,
53.   The burthen of Thy truth. Reach down Thy hands
54.   And fill me with Thy rage, that I may bruise
55.   The heathen. Yea, and shake the sullen kings
56.   Upon their thrones. The lives of men shall flow
57.   As quiet as the little rivulets
58.   Beneath the sheltering shadow of Thy Church;
59.   And Thou shalt bend, enduring God, the knees
60.   Of the great warriors whose names have sung
61.   The world to its fierce infancy again.

---

46.   ... foreswear ... **D, 1.**
49.   ... yet—but ....
50.   .... Hear oh! thou ... , **D, 1.**
53.   ... thy truth. ... thy ...
54.   ... thy ... **D, 1.**
58.   ... thy Church, **D, 1.**
59.   ... thou ... **D, 1 ;** ... Thou shall bend, ... **95.**

Scene III.

The dungeon of the Inquisition. The morning of the auto-da-fé dawns dimly through a barred window. A few faint stars are shining. Swallows are circling in the dimness without.

Mosada, *alone.*

Stage directions.   ... *Auto-da-Fe* .... **D, 1.** [The words 'Mosada, *alone.*'
lacking] **D.**

1. *Mosada.* Oh, swallows, swallows, swallows, will ye fly
2.   This eve, to-morrow, or to-morrow night
3.   Above the farm-house by the little lake
4.   That rustles in the reeds with patient pushes,
5.   Soft as the whispering of a long-lost footstep
6.   Circling the brain? My brothers will pass down
7.   Quite soon the cornfield, where the poppies grow,
8.   To their farm work; how silent all will be!
9.   But no, in this warm weather, 'mong the hills,
10.   Will be the faint far thunder-sound, as though
11.   The world were dreaming in its summer sleep;
12.   That will be later, day is scarcely dawning.
13.   And Hassan will be with them—he was so small,
14.   A weak, thin child, when last I saw him there.
15.   He will be taller now—'twas long ago.

16.   The men are busy in the glimmering square.
17.   I hear the murmur as they raise the beams
18.   To build the circling seats, where high in air
19.   Soon will the churchmen nod above the crowd.
20.   I'm not of that pale company whose feet
21.   Ere long shall falter through the noisy square,
22.   And not come thence; for here in this small ring—
23.   Hearken, ye swallows!—I have hoarded up

---

1. Oh! swallows, . . . **D, 1.**
2. . . . , to-morrow—, or . . . **95.**
4. That's rustling in . . . ,
5. . . . as a long dead footstep whispering through **D, 1 ;** . . . a lost footstep **95.**
6. The brain. My . . . will be passing down **D, 1 ;** . . . brain? my brothers now pass . . . **95.**
7. Along the cornfield, . . . , **95.**
8. . . . farm-work; . . . be. **D, 1.**
10. . . . thunder-sound as . . . **D, 1 ;** Will move the . . . **95.**
12. . . . is dawning.
13. Hassan is with them too—he . . . , **95.**
22. . . . thence—for . . . ring.
23. . . . swallows! I . . . **D, 1.**

24.   A poison drop. A toy, a fancy once,
25.   A fashion with us Moorish maids, begot
26.   Of dreaming and of watching by the door
27.   The shadows pass; but now, I love my ring,
28.   For it alone of all the world will do
29.   My bidding. [*Sucks poison from the ring.*] Now 'tis done, and I am
          glad
30.   And free—'twill thieve away with sleepy mood
31.   My thoughts, and yonder brightening patch of sky
32.   With three bars crossed, and these four walls my world,
33.   And yon few stars grown dim, like eyes of lovers
34.   The noisy world divides. How soon a deed
35.   So small makes one grow weak and tottering!
36.   Where shall I lay me down? That question is
37.   A weighty question, for it is the last.
38.   Not there, for there a spider weaves her web.
39.   Nay here, I'll lay me down where I can watch
40.   The burghers of the night fade one by one.
41.   . . . Yonder a leaf
42.   Of apple-blossom circles in the gloom,
43.   Floating from yon barred window. Small new-comer,
44.   Thou'rt welcome. Lie there close against my fingers.
45.   I wonder which is whitest, they or thou.
46.   'Tis thou, for they've grown blue around the nails.
47.   My blossom, I am dying, and the stars
48.   Are dying too. They were full seven stars;
49.   Two only now they are, two side by side.

---

24.   . . . drop. The toy of fancy . . . , **D, 1.**
27.   . . . now I . . . , **95.**
33.   . . . stars, grown dim like . . . **D, 1.**
35.   . . . tottering. **D, 1.**
40.   . . . one, **D, 1.**
41.   [lacking] **95.**
42.   . . . apple blossom . . . , **D, 1;** An apple blossom . . . , **95.**
43.   . . . window. New comer, **D, 1.**
          [between 49 and 50 no break] **D, 1.**

50. Oh, Allah! it was thus they shone that night
51. When my lost lover left these arms. My Gomez
52. We meet at last, the ministering stars
53. Of our nativity hang side by side,
54. And throb within the circles of green dawn.
55. Too late, too late, for I am near to death.
56. I try to lift mine arms—they fall again.
57. This death is heavy in my veins like sleep.
58. I cannot even crawl along the flags
59. A little nearer those bright stars. Tell me,
60. Is it your message, stars, that when death comes
61. My soul shall touch with his, and the two flames
62. Be one? I think all's finished now and sealed.

After a pause enter Ebremar.

63. *Ebremar.* Young Moorish girl, thy final hour is here;
64. Cast off thy heresies, and save thy soul
65. From the undying worm. She sleeps— [*Starting.*] Mosada—
66. Oh, God!—awake! thou shalt not die. She sleeps,
67. Her head cast backward in her unloosed hair.
68. Look up, look up, thy Gomez is by thee.
69. A fearful paleness creeps across her breast
70. And out-spread arms. [*Casting himself down by her.*]
　　　　　　Be not so pale, dear love.
71. Oh, can my kisses bring a flush no more
72. Upon thy face? How heavily thy head
73. Hangs on my breast! Listen, we shall be safe.

---

50. Oh! Allah, it . . . night, **D, 1.**
51. . . . . My Vallence, **D, 1 ;** . . . Gomez, **95.**
63. . . . here, **D, 1.**
64. . . . heresies and . . . **1.**
65. From dateless pain. She sleeps—
　　　　　　　[*Starting.*]
　　　　　　Mosada—thou—
66. Oh God!—awake, thou . . . sleeps. **D, 1.**
68. . . . , thy Vallence is . . . . **D, 1.**
71. Oh! can . . .
72. . . . face. How . . .
73. . . . breast. Listen, ... **D, 1.**

74.   We'll fly from this before the morning star.
75.   Dear heart, there is a secret way that leads
76.   Its paven length towards the river's marge
77.   Where lies a shallop in the yellow reeds.
78.   Awake, awake, and we will sail afar,
79.   Afar along the fleet white river's face—
80.   Alone with our own whispers and replies—
81.   Alone among the murmurs of the dawn.
82.   Once in thy nation none shall know that I
83.   Was Ebremar, whose thoughts were fixed on God,
84.   And heaven, and holiness.

Mosada.   Let's talk and grieve,
85.   For that's the sweetest music for sad souls.
86.   Day's dead, all flame-bewildered, and the hills
87.   In list'ning silence gazing on our grief.
88.   I never knew an eve so marvellous still.

89. *Ebremar.* Her dreams are talking with old years. Awake,
90.   Grieve not, for Gomez kneels beside thee—

Mosada.   Gomez,
91.   'Tis late, wait one more day; below the hills
92.   The foot-worn way is long, and it grows dark.
93.   It is the darkest eve I ever knew.

94. *Ebremar.* I kneel by thee—no parting now—look up.
95.   She smiles—is happy with her wandering griefs.

96. *Mosada.* So you must go; kiss me before you go.
97.   Oh, would the busy minutes might fold up
98.   Their thieving wings that we might never part.
99.   I never knew a night so honey-sweet.

100. *Ebremar.* There is no leave-taking. I go no more.

---

76.   . . . marge, **D, 1.**
82.   Among thy . . . **D, 1.**
90.   . . . , for Vallence kneels . . . thee—
                              Vallence, **D, 1 ;**
       . . . —
              Gomez **95.**
92.   . . . footworn . . . . **95.**
97.   Oh! would . . . **D, 1.**
99.   . . . honey sweet.
100.   . . . leave taking. . . . . **D, 1.**

101. Safe on the breast of Gomez lies thy head,
102. Unhappy one.

Mosada.   Go not, go not, go not;
103. For night comes fast. Look down on me, my love,
104. And see how thick the dew lies on my face.
105. I never knew a night so dew-bedrowned.

106. *Ebremar.* Oh, hush the wandering music of thy mind.
107. Look on me once. Why sink your eyelids thus?
108. Why do you hang so heavy in my arms?
109. Love, will you die when we have met? One look
110. Give to thy Gomez.

Mosada.   Gomez—he has gone
111. From here, along the shadowy way that winds
112. Companioning the river's pilgrim torch.
113. I'll see him longer if I stand out here
114. Upon the mountain's brow. [*She tries to stand and totters. Ebremar*
        supports her, and she stands as if pointing down into a valley.]
                              Yonder he treads
115. The path o'er-muffled with the leaves—dead leaves,
116. Like happy thoughts grown sad in evil days.
117. He fades among the mists; how fast they come,
118. And pour upon the world! Ah! well-a-day!
119. Poor love and sorrow, with their arms thrown round
120. Each other's necks, and whispering as they go,
121. Still wander through the world. He's gone, he's gone.
122. I'm weary—weary, and 'tis very cold.

---

101. . . . of Vallence is thy head **D, 1 ;** . . . Gomez is thy . . . , **95.**
102. . . . not. Go not. Go not.
103. . . . fast; look . . . , **D, 1.**
106. Oh! hush . . . . **D, 1.**
107. . . . eyelids so? **D ;** . . . once Why . . . eyelids so? **1.**
110. . . . thy Vallence.
                    Vallence—he . . . **D, 1.**
      Directions in 114. [. . . *stands pointing down as if into a visionary valley.*]
      D, 1.
115. . . . o'er muffled . . . , **95.**
118. . . . ! well a day!
119. . . . sorrow with . . . **D, 1.**

123.   I'll draw my cloak around me; it is cold.
124.   I never knew a night so bitter cold.   [*Dies.*

Enter Monks *and* Inquisitors.

125.   *First Inquisitor.* My lord, you called?

Ebremar.   Not I. This maid is dead.

126.   *First Monk.* From poison; for you cannot trust these Moors.
127.   You're pale, my lord.

First Inquisitor [*aside*]. His lips are quivering;
128.   The flame that shone within his eyes but now
129.   Has flickered and gone out.

Ebremar.   I am not well.
130.   'Twill pass. I'll see the other prisoners now,
131.   And importune their souls to penitence,
132.   So they escape from hell. But, pardon me,
133.   Your hood is threadbare—see that it be changed
134.   Before we take our seats above the crowd.

                                        [*They go out.*

THE END

124a. *Ebremar.* Mosada! Oh, Mosada! **D, 1.**
125.   . . . called.
                Not . . . .
126.   . . . poison, for . . . .
127.   . . . quivering. **D, 1.**
132.   . . . . But pardon . . . , **D, 1.**
       Directions after 134.   [lacking] **D, 1.**
134a. *First Monk.* I always said you could not trust these Moors.
                                        [*They go.*] **D, 1.**

TIME AND THE WITCH VIVIEN

*A marble-flagged, pillared room. Magical instruments
in one corner. A fountain in the centre.*

1. *Vivien* [*looking down into the fountain*]. Where moves there any beauti-
     ful as I,
2. Save, with the little golden greedy carp,
3. Gold unto gold, a gleam in its long hair,
4. My image yonder? [*Spreading her hand over the water.*] Ah, my
     beautiful,
5. What roseate fingers! [*Turning away.*] No; nor is there one
6. Of equal power in spells and secret rites.
7. The proudest or most coy of spirit things,
8. Hide where he will, in wave or wrinkled moon,
9. Obeys.
               Some fierce magician flies or walks
10. Beyond the gateway—by the sentries now—
11. Close and more close—I feel him in my heart—
12. Some great one. No; I hear the wavering steps
13. Without there of a little, light old man;
14. I dreamt some great one. [*Catching sight of her image, and spreading
     her hand over the water.*]
                              Ah, my beautiful,
15. What roseate fingers!

     Enter Time *as an old pedlar, with a scythe, an hour-glass,
                    and a black bag.*
                        Ha, ha! ha, ha, ha!
16. The wrinkled squanderer of human wealth.
17. Come here. Be seated now; I'd buy of you.
18. Come, father.

     Time.   Lady, I nor rest nor sit.

19. *Vivien.* Well then, to business; what is in your bag?

20. *Time* [*putting the bag and hour-glass on the table and resting on his scythe*].
          Grey hairs and crutches, crutches and grey hairs,
21. Mansions of memories and mellow thoughts

PRINTINGS   **2, 98.**

22. Where dwell the minds of old men having peace,
23. And—

Vivien. No; I'll none of these, old Father Wrinkles.

24. *Time.* Some day you'll buy them, maybe.

Vivien.   Never!

Time [*laughing*].   Never?

25. *Vivien.* Why do you laugh?

Time.   I laugh the last always.
[*She lays the hour-glass on one side.* Time *rights it again.*

26. *Vivien.* I do not need your scythe. May that bring peace
27. To those your 'mellow' wares have wearied out.
28. I'd buy your glass.

Time.   My glass I will not sell.
29. Without my glass I'd be a sorry clown.

30. *Vivien.* Yet whiter beard have you than Merlin had.

31. *Time.* No taste have I for slumber 'neath an oak.

32. *Vivien.* When were you born?

Time.   Before your grandam Eve.

33. *Vivien.* Oh, I am weary of that foolish tale.
34. They say you are a gambler and a player
35. At chances and at moments with mankind.
36. I'll play you for your old hour-glass. [*Pointing to the instruments of magic.*] You see
37. I keep such things about me; they are food
38. For antiquarian meditation.   [*Brings dice.*

Time.   Ay,
39. We throw three times.

40. *Vivien.* Three-six.

41. *Time.* Four-six.

42. *Vivien.* Five-six. Ha, time!

43. *Time.* Double sixes!

44. *Vivien.* I lose! They're loaded dice. Time always plays
45.   With loaded dice. Another chance! Come, father;
46.   Come to the chess, for young girls' wits are better
47.   Than old men's any day, as Merlin found.

          [Places the chess-board on her knees.

48.   The passing of those little grains is snow
49.   Upon my soul, old Time.

          [She lays the hour-glass on its side.

    Time.   No; thus it stands. *[Rights it again.*

50.   For other stakes we play. You lost the glass.

51. *Vivien.* Then give me triumph in my many plots.

52. *Time.* Defeat is death.

    Vivien.   Should my plots fail I'd die.   *[They play.*
53.   Thus play we first with pawns, poor things and weak;
54.   And then the great ones come, and last the king.
55.   So men in life and I in magic play;
56.   First dreams, and goblins, and the lesser sprites,
57.   And now with Father Time I'm face to face.

          [They play.

58.   I trap you.

    Time.   Check.

    Vivien.   I do miscalculate.
59.   I am dull to-day, or you were now all lost.
60.   Chance, and not skill, has favoured you, old father!

          [She plays.

61. *Time.* Check.

    Vivien.   Ah! how bright your eyes. How swift your moves.
62.   How still it is! I hear the carp go splash,
63.   And now and then a bubble rise. I hear
64.   A bird walk on the doorstep.   *[She plays.*

    Time.   Check once more.

65. *Vivien.* I must be careful now. I have such plots—
66.   Such war plots, peace plots, love plots—every side;
67.   I cannot go into the bloodless land
68.   Among the whimpering ghosts.

    Time.   Mate thus.

    Vivien.   Already?
69.   Chance hath a skill!   *[She dies.*

THE END

Appendix I

GENERAL NOTES

The Pronunciation of the Irish Words. **6, 7, 18, 31, 49, 51, 52, 61, 62, 66, 67, 72, 74, 78, 80.**

When I wrote the greater number of these poems I had hardly considered the question seriously. I copied at times somebody's perhaps fanciful phonetic spelling, and at times the ancient spelling as I found it in some literal translation, pronouncing the words always as they were spelt. I do not suppose I would have defended this system at any time, but I do not yet know what system to adopt. The modern pronounciation, which is usually followed by those who spell the words phonetically, is certainly unlike the pronunciation of the time when classical Irish literature was written, and, so far as I know, no Irish scholar who writes in English or French has made that minute examination of the way the names come into the rhythms and measures of the old poems which can alone discover the old pronunciation. A French Celtic scholar gave me the pronunciation of a few names, and told me that Mr. Whitley Stokes had written something about the subject in German, but I am ignorant of German. If I ever learn the old pronunciation, I will revise all these poems, but at present I can only affirm that I have not treated my Irish names as badly as the mediaeval writers of the stories of King Arthur treated their Welsh names. In the following glossary [see pp. 1284-7] I give the old spelling in parentheses wherever I have adopted somebody's phonetic spelling in the poems. The glossary is very inadequate, but I have written of many of the things it speaks of at some length in the notes to *The Wind Among the Reeds.* **6, 7.**

The . . . Words. When . . . treated their Welsh names. **18-51, 61-74.**

The . . . Words. When . . . pronunciation of a few names, and I understand that Mr. Whitley Stokes . . . subject in German. If I ever learn the old pronunciation, I may revise these poems, . . . Welsh names. **52.**

The . . . Words. When . . . always as they were spelt. I can only affirm that I did not even in my youth treat Irish names as badly as the mediaeval writers . . . Welsh names. **78, 80.**

*   *   *

The Legendary and Mythological Foundation of the Plays and Poems

Almost every story I have used or person I have spoken of is in one or other of Lady Gregory's 'Gods and Fighting Men' and 'Cuchulain of Muirthemne.' If my present small Dublin audience for poetical drama grows and spreads beyond Dublin, I shall owe it to these two books, masterpieces of prose, which can but make the old stories as familiar to Irishmen everywhere as are the stories of Arthur and his knights to all readers of books. I cannot believe that it is from friendship that I weigh these books with Mallory and feel no discontent at the tally, or that it is the wish to make the circumstantial origin of my own art familiar, that would make me give them before all other books to Irish boys and girls. I wrote for the most part before they were written, but all or all but all is there, Oisin wandering, Cuchulain killing his son and fighting the sea, Maeve and her children, Baile and Aillin, Angus and his fellow-immortals, all literally translated, though with much condensation and selection, from the old writings. A few of my stories are not hers also. I took the story of 'The Ballad of the Old Fox Hunter' from 'Knocknagow,' and the story of 'The Ballad of Father Hart' from a Sligo county history; that of 'The Ballad of Moll Magee' from a sermon preached in the chapel at Howth if I remember rightly, that of 'The Countess Cathleen' from a story told as Irish by Léo Lespès in 'Les Matinées de Timothé Trimm,'—there is a Donegal story resembling it in its principal incident in Larmonie's 'West Irish Folk Tales,'—and the story of the 'King's Threshold' from a middle Irish account of the fantastic demands of the poet at the court of King Guaire; but I have revised the moral of this last story to let the poet have the best of it. One of my fellow-playwrights is going, I have good hope, to take the other side and make a play that can be played after it, as in Greece the farce followed the tragedy. 'The Shadowy Waters' and 'The Land of Heart's Desire' have a good deal of incidental Irish folklore and mythology but are not founded on any particular story. Here and there, specially in 'The Wind among the Reeds,' I have used fragments of ancient mythology common to all lands. 'The Deer with no Horns' and the 'Flying Fawn' are certainly Irish symbols of the desire of the man which is for the woman, and the desire of the woman which is for the desire of the man, as Coleridge said; but it is only the speculation of Celtic scholars that makes the 'Death-pale Deer' and 'The Boar without Bristles' not mere creatures of romance, but symbols of the end of all things. For a long time symbols of this kind had for me a very intense, a very personal importance, and they are too much woven into the fabric of my work for me to give a detailed account of them one by one.

Appendix 1, 28, 48.

* * *

The Legendary and Mythological Foundation of the Plays

The greater number of the stories I have used, and persons I have spoken of, are in Lady Gregory's *Gods and Fighting Men* and *Cuchulain of Muirthemne*. If my small Dublin audience for poetical drama grows to any size, whether now or at some future time, I shall owe it to these two books, masterpieces of prose, which can but make the old stories as familiar to Irishmen at anyrate as are the stories of Arthur and his Knights to all readers of books. I cannot believe that it is from friendship that I weigh these books with Malory, and feel no discontent at the tally, or that it is the wish to make the substantial origin of my own art familiar, that would make me give them before all other books to young men and girls in Ireland. I wrote for the most part before they were written, but all, or all but all, is there. I took the Aengus and Edain of *The Shadowy Waters* from poor translations of the various Aengus stories, which, new translated by Lady Gregory, make up so much of what is most beautiful in both her books. They had, however, so completely become a part of my own thought that in 1897, when I was still working on an early version of *The Shadowy Waters*, I saw one night with my bodily eyes, as it seemed, two beautiful persons, who would, I believe, have answered to their names. The plot of the play itself has, however, no definite old story for its foundation, but was woven to a very great extent out of certain visionary experiences.

The foundations of *Deirdre* and of *On Baile's Strand* are stories called respectively the 'Fate of the Sons of Usnach' and 'The Son of Aoife' in *Cuchulain of Muirthemne*.

The King's Threshold is, however, founded upon a middle-Irish story of the demands of the poets at the Court of King Guaire of Gort, but I have twisted it about and revised its moral that the poet might have the best of it. It owes something to a play on the same subject by my old friend Edwin Ellis, who heard the story from me and wrote of it long ago.

Appendix III, **32**.

The greater . . . all, is there.

The foundations of *Deirdre* . . . *Muirthemne*. *The Green Helmet* is founded upon an old Irish story, *The Feast of Bricriu*, given in that work also, and is meant as an introduction to *On Baile's Strand*.

The King's Threshold is founded . . . friend Mr. Edwin . . . ago.

I took the Aengus . . . answered to those names. The plot . . . experiences.

The Hour-Glass is founded upon a story—*The Priest's Soul*—recorded by Lady Wilde in *Ancient Legends of Ireland*, 1887, vol. i, pp. 60-67.

Notes, **45.**

The greater . . . any rate . . . make the circumsubstantial origins [follows the version in **45** with the following exceptions:] . . . saw one night standing at my bedside, as it seemed, two . . . believed, have answered . . . certain dream experiences.

The foundations. . ., pp. **60-67.**   Notes, **69.**

Glossary

Adene. Adene was a famous legendary queen who went away from the world and dwelt among the 'shee,' as the fairies are called in the old poems and in contemporary folk lore. **3 ;** *Adene.*—Adene was a famous legendary

---

[1] This passage about 'The Shadowy Waters' follows 'The greater . . . all, is there.' in **32**.

queen who went away and lived among the Shee. **5**; *Adene (Etain)*.—A famous legendary queen who was lured away by Meder, (Mider **7**) King of the Shee. **6, 7.**

Angus.—The god of youth, beauty, and poetry. He reigned in Tirnan-Oge, the country of the young. **5**; *Angus (Aengus)*.—The . . . . **6, 7.**

Ardroe.—A Ballyshannon faery ruler. **5**; *Ardroe (Aedh Ruadh)*.—A . . . . **6.**

Balor.—The Irish Chimaera, the leader of the hosts of darkness at the great battle of good and evil, life and death, light and darkness, which was fought out on the strands of Moytura, near Sligo. **5-7.**

Barach.—Barach enticed Fergus away to a feast, that the sons of Usna might be killed in his absence. Fergus had made an oath never to refuse a feast from him, and so was compelled to go, though all unwillingly. **5**; *Barach (Borrach)*.—Barach . . . go, though unwilling. (unwillingly. **7**) **6, 7.**

Bonyeen. A 'bonyeen, is a little pig. **3**; *Bonyeen*.—A little pig. **5-7, 18, 31.**

Brig or *Brigit*.—The goddess of spring, whether in the fields and woods or in the mind of the poet. **7.**

Cailitin.—The Druid Cailitin and his sons warred upon Cuhoollin with magical arts. **5-7.**

Clauber is a Sligo word for thick and clinging mud. **3**; *Clauber*.—A Sligo word for clinging mud. **5-7, 18, 31.**

Conhor or *Concobar*.—He was King of all Ireland in the time of the Red Branch kings. **5**; *Conhor (Concobar)*.—He . . . . **6, 7.**

Cuhoollin.—The great hero of the Red Branch cycle. **5**; *Cuhoollin (Cuchullainn)*.—The . . . . **6, 7.**

Danaan. 'Danaan' is a common abbreviation of Tuatha-de-Danaan, the name of the gods of Celtic Ireland in old days, and of the fairies in medieval literature, and modern folk lore. **3**; *Danaan*.—See *Tuath De Danaan*. **5-7.**

Dectera.—The mother of Cuhoollin. **5**; *Dectera (Dechtere)*.—The . . . . **6, 7.**

Deirdre.—The heroine of the most tender (pathetic **7**) of old Gaelic stories. She was loved by Concobar, but fled from him with Naisi, only to be recaptured by treachery. She is the sad and beautiful woman of the Red Branch cycle, just as Grania is the sad and beautiful woman of the Fenian cycle. **5-7.**

Emen. The capital of the Red Branch kings. **5**; *Emen (Emhain)*.—The chief town of . . . . **6, 7.**

Feacra.—A sea faery. **5**; *Feacra*.—An ancient hero, now, I think, a sea faery. **6, 7.**

The Fenians.—The great military order of which Finn was chief. **5-7.**

Fergus. Fergus, poet of the Conorian age, had been king of all Ireland, but gave up his throne that he might live at peace hunting in the forest. **3**; *Fergus*.—He was the poet of the Red Branch cycle as Usheen (Oisin **6, 7**) was of the Fenian. He was once King of all Ireland, but gave (Ireland, and, as the legend is shaped by Ferguson, gave **6, 7**) up his throne that . . . the woods. **5-7.**

Fin (Fion).—A very famous hero, and chief of the heroes of Ireland in his time. **6, 7.**

Finvarra.—The king of the faeries of Connaught. **5-7, 18, 31** ; *Finvarra (Finbar).*—The . . . . **49, 51, 61, 62, 66, 67, 72, 74.**

Fomoroh.—Fomoroh means from under the sea, and is the name of the gods of night and death and cold. The Fomoroh were misshapen and had now the heads of goats and bulls, and now but one leg, and one arm that came out of the middle of their breasts. They were the ancestors of the evil faeries and, according to one Gaelic writer, of all misshapen persons. The giants and the leprecauns are expressly mentioned as of the Fomoroh. **5** ; *Fomoroh (Fomori or Fomoraig).*—. . . cold. The Fomoroh are often described as misshapen, now with the heads . . . now with but . . . as of them. **6, 7.**

Horned Owl. The horned owl is associated in popular belief with evil fairies. **3.**

Maive.—A famous queen of the Red Branch cycle. She is rumoured to be buried under the cairn on Knocknarea. Ferguson speaks of 'the shell-heaped cairn of Maive high up on haunted Knocknarea,' but inaccurately, for the cairn is of stones. **5** ; *Maive (Medb).*—A . . . Knocknarea,' but the cairn . . . . **6, 7.**

Mythological Gods and Heroes.—I refer the reader for such names as Balor and Finn and Oisin to Lady Gregory's 'Cuchulain of Muirthemne' and to her 'Gods and Fighting Men.' **18, 31** ; *Mythological* . . . Usheen . . . .' **49, 51, 61, 62, 66, 67, 72, 74.**

Naisi.—The lover of Deirdre. He was treacherously killed by Concobar. **5** ; *Naisi (Naoise).*—The . . . . **6, 7.**

Nuala.—The wife of Finvarra. **5-7, 18, 31, 49, 51, 61, 62, 66, 67, 72, 74.**

Oisin. Oisin, the poet of the Finian age, and son to Fin-ma-cool, crossed the sea on an enchanted horse with Niam, his fairy bride, and lived three hundred years in Tier-nan-oge, or fairyland. **3** ; *Oisin.*—The poet of the Fenian cycle of legend, as Fergus was the poet of the Red Branch cycle. **6, 7.** [see Usheen]

Orchil.—A Fomorian sorceress. **5** ; *Orchil.*—A Fomoroh and a sorceress, if I remember rightly. I forget whatever I may have once known about her. **6, 7.**

Pooka. The Pooka is a spirit that rarely takes human form, but appears commonly as a bull, horse, goat, eagle, or ass. **3** ; *Pooka.*—A spirit which takes the form now of a dog, now of a horse, now of an ass, now of an eagle. **5, 18, 31** ; *Pooka (Puca).*—A spirit [as 5]. **6, 7.**

Red Branch. 'Red Branch' was the name of the circle of warriors who preceded the Finian circle by about two hundred years, according to bardic chronology, and gathered round 'Concobar' or 'Conor,' as the later circle gathered round Fin. **3.**

Shannachus. 'Shannachus' is a Gaelic word meaning 'stories.' It is, or was a common word among the peasantry, both Gaelic and English speaking. **3** ; *Shannachus.*—A Gaelic word for stories, which is common even among the English-speaking peasantry. **5** ; *Shannachus (Seanachus).*—A Gaelic [as 5]. **6, 7, 18, 31.**

Shee.—The Shee are the faery people. The word is said to mean also the wind. 5 ; *Shee (Sidhe).*—The . . . word means also . . . . 6, 7.

Sheogue. A 'sheogue' is a diminutive, and means 'a little fairy.' 3 ; *Sheogue.*—A diminutive of Shee, meaning a little faery. 5 ; *Sheogue (Sidheog).*—A [as 5]. 6.

Sowlth. A formless, luminous apparition. (phantom. 5) 3, 5 ; *Sowlth.*—A . . . phantom for which Father O'Hanlon was, I think, my authority. 6.

Sualtam.—The father of Cuhoollin. 5-7.

Tevish. A 'tevish' is an earth-bound and earth-wandering ghost. 3 ; *Thivish.*—An earth-bound . . . . 5 ; *Thivish (Taibhse).*—An earth-bound . . . ghost, or so I thought. 6.

Tuath De Danaan.—Tuath De Danaan means the Race of the Gods of Dana. Dana was the mother of all the ancient gods of Ireland. They were the powers of light and life and warmth, and did battle with the Fomoroh, or powers of night and death and cold. Robbed of offerings and honour, they have gradually dwindled in the popular imagination until they have become the Faeries. 5 ; . . . Dana. They were . . . become Faeries. 6, 7.

Usheen.—The poet of the Fenian cycle of legend, as Fergus was the poet of the Red Branch cycle. 5. [see *Oisin*]

Usna.—The father of Naisi, the lover, and Ardan and Anly, the friends of Deirdre. Deirdre's beautiful lament over their bodies has been finely translated by Sir Samuel Ferguson. 5 ; *Usna (Usnach).*—The . . . Ainle, the . . . . 6, 7.

PREFACES AND DEDICATIONS

THESE are from those volumes in the bibliography whose contents, with some exceptions, are primarily plays.

Preface to 3.

The greater number of the poems in this book, as also in 'The Wanderings of Oisin,' are founded on Irish tradition. The chief poem is an attempt to mingle personal thought and feeling with the beliefs and customs of Christian Ireland; whereas the longest poem in my earlier book endeavoured to set forth the impress left on my imagination by the Pre-Christian cycle of legends. The Christian cycle being mainly concerned with contending moods and moral motives needed, I thought, a dramatic vehicle. The tumultous and heroic Pagan cycle, on the other hand, having to do with vast and shadowy activities and with the great impersonal emotions, expressed itself naturally—or so I imagined—in epic and epic-lyric measures. No epic method seemed sufficiently minute and subtle for the one, and no dramatic method elastic and all-containing enough for the other.

Ireland having a huge body of tradition behind her in the depths of time, will probably draw her deepest literary inspiration from this double fountainhead if she ever, as is the hope of all her children, make for herself a great distinctive poetic literature. She has already many moving songs and ballads which are quite her own. 'The Countess Kathleen,' like 'The Wanderings of Oisin,' is an attempt to unite a more ample method to feeling not less national, Celtic, and distinctive.

A number of the 'legends and lyrics' originally appeared in *The National Observer*, and I have to thank the proprietors for leave to reprint them here.

W. B. YEATS.

3.

* * *

Prefaces to 5, 6, 7, 18, 31, 33, 49, 51, 61, 62, 66, 67, 72, 74, 78, 80.

This book contains all the writer cares to preserve out of his previous volumes of verse. He has revised, and to a large extent re-written, *The Wanderings of Usheen* and the lyrics and ballads from the same volume, and expanded and, he hopes, strengthened *The Countess Cathleen*. He has, however, been compelled to leave unchanged many lines he would have gladly re-written, because his present skill is not great enough to separate them from thoughts and expressions which seem to him worth preserving. He has printed the ballads and lyrics from the same volume as *The Wanderings of Usheen*, and two ballads written at the same time, though published later, in a section named *Crossways*, because in them he tried many pathways; and those from the same volume as *The Countess Cathleen* in a section named *The Rose*, for in them he has found, he believes, the only pathway

whereon he can hope to see with his own eyes the Eternal Rose of Beauty
and of Peace.

W. B. YEATS.

Sligo, *March 24th*, 1895. **5.**

The writer revised, and, to a great extent, re-wrote 'The Wanderings of
Oisin' and certain lyrics and ballads from the same volume, and revised
and expanded 'The Countess Cathleen' for the first edition of this book;
and he has still further revised these and other poems for the present edition.
Other revisions are necessary, and he hopes to make them when he is further
from the mood in which the poems were written, and has more leisure.
He has printed the lyrics and ballads written about the same time as 'The
Wanderings of Oisin' in a section called 'Crossways,' for in these he tried
many pathways; and those written about the same time as 'The Countess
Cathleen' in a section called 'The Rose,' for in them he found, as he believes,
the only pathway from which he may hope to see beauty and wisdom with
his own eyes.

This book and *The Wind Among the Reeds* contain all of his published
poetry which he cares to preserve.

W. B. YEATS.

February 24, 1899. **6.**

I have added some passages to 'The Land of Heart's Desire,' and a new
scene of some little length, besides passages here and there, to 'The Countess
Cathleen.' The goddess has never come to me with her hands so full that I
have not found many waste places after I had planted all that she had
brought me. The present version of 'The Countess Cathleen' is not quite
the version adopted by the Irish Literary Theatre a couple of years ago,
for our stage and scenery were capable of little; and it may differ still more
from any stage version I make in future, for it seems that my people of the
waters and my unhappy dead, in the third act, cannot keep their supernatural essence, but must put on too much of our mortality, in any ordinary
theatre. I am told that I must abandon a meaning or two and make my
merchants carry away the treasure themselves. The act was written long
ago, when I had seen so few plays that I took pleasure in stage effects.
Indeed, I am not yet certain that a wealthy theatre could not shape it to
an impressive pageantry, or that a theatre without any wealth could not
lift it out of pageantry into the mind, with a dim curtain, and some dimly
robed actors, and the beatified voices that should be as important in poetical
as in musical drama. The Elizabethan stage was so little imprisoned in
material circumstances that the Elizabethan imagination was not strained
by god or spirit, nor even by Echo herself—no, not even when she answered,
as in 'The Duchess of Malfi,' in clear, loud words which were not the words
that had been spoken to her. We have made a prison-house of paint and
canvas, where we have as little freedom as under our own roofs, for there is

no freedom in a house that has been made with hands. All art moves in the cave of the Chimaera, or in the garden of the Hesperedes, or in the more silent house of the gods, and neither cave, nor garden, nor house can show themselves clearly but to the mind's eye.

Besides re-writing a lyric or two, I have much enlarged the note on 'The Countess Cathleen,' as there has been some discussion in Ireland about the origin of the story, but the other notes are as they have always been. They are short enough, but I do not think that anybody who knows modern poetry will find obscurities in this book. In any case, I must leave my myths and symbols to explain themselves as the years go by and one poem lights up another, and the stories that friends, and one friend in particular, have gathered for me, or that I have gathered myself in many cottages, find their way into the light. I would, if I could, add to that majestic heraldry of the poets, that great and complicated inheritance of images which written literature has substituted for the greater and more complex inheritance of spoken tradition, some new heraldic images, gathered from the lips of the common people. Christianity and the old nature faith have lain down side by side in the cottages, and I would proclaim that peace as loudly as I can among the kingdoms of poetry, where there is no peace that is not joyous, no battle that does not give life instead of death; I may even try to persuade others, in more sober prose, that there can be no language more worthy of poetry and of the meditation of the soul than that which has been made, or can be made, out of a subtlety of desire, an emotion of sacrifice, a delight in order, that are perhaps Christian, and myths and images that mirror the energies of woods and streams, and of their wild creatures. Has any part of that majestic heraldry of the poets had a very different fountain? Is it not the ritual of the marriage of heaven and earth?

These details may seem to many unnecessary; but after all one writes poetry for a few careful readers and for a few friends, who will not consider such details very unnecessary. When Cimabue had the cry it was, it seems, worth thinking of those that run, but to-day, when they can write as well as read, one can sit with one's companions under the hedgerow contentedly. If one writes well and has the patience, somebody will come from among the runners and read what one has written quickly, and go away quickly, and write out as much as he can remember in the language of the highway.

*   *

*

'The Wanderings of Oisin' was published with the lyrics now collected under the title 'Crossways' in 1888, 'The Countess Cathleen' with the lyrics now collected under the title 'The Rose' in 1891, and 'The Land of Heart's Desire' by itself in 1894. They were revised and reprinted in one volume in 1895, and again revised and reprinted in 1898. w. b. yeats. *January*, 1901. **7.**

I have added some passages . . . 1895, again revised . . . 1898, and again reprinted in 1901 and 1904. *May*, 1904. **18.**

I have added some passages . . . 1895, again revised . . . 1898, and again reprinted in 1901, 1904, and 1908. **31.**

The present version of *The Countess Cathleen* is . . . the beautiful voices . . . circumstance . . . *The Duchess of Malfi*, . . . Hesperides, . . . eye.

Besides . . . *The Countess Cathleen*, . . . other notes* [Yeats's note reads: I have left them out of this edition as Lady Gregory's *Cuchulain of Muirthemne* and *Gods and Fighting Men* have made them unnecessary. When I began to write, the names of the Irish heroes were almost unknown even in Ireland.] are as . . . , add to that great and complicated inheritance . . . tradition, to that majestic heraldry of the poets some new heraldic images gathered . . . earth?

These details . . . run; but . . . highway.

January, 1901.   W. B. YEATS.

The Countess Cathleen. Preface to the Fourth Edition. Appendix, **33.**

During the last year I have spent much time altering 'The Countess Cathleen' and 'The Land of Heart's Desire' that they might be a part of the repertory of the Abbey Theatre. I had written them before I had any practical experience, and I knew from the performance of the one in Dublin in 1899 and of the other in London in 1894 that they were full of defects. But in their new shape—and each play has been twice played during the winter—they have given me some pleasure, and are, I think, easier to play effectively than my later plays, depending less upon the players and more upon the producer, both having been imagined more for variety of stage-picture than variety of mood in the player. It was, indeed, the first performance of 'The Countess Cathleen,' when our stage-pictures were made out of poor conventional scenery and hired costumes, that set me writing plays where all would depend upon the player. The first two scenes are wholly new, and though I have left the old end in the body of this book I have given in the notes an end less difficult to producer and audience, and there are slight alterations elsewhere in the poem. 'The Land of Heart's Desire,' besides some mending in the details, has been thrown back in time because the metrical speech would have sounded unreal if spoken in a country cottage now that we have so many dialect comedies. The shades of Mrs. Fallan and Mrs. Dillane and of Dan Bourke and the Tramp would have seemed too boisterous or too vivid for shades made cold and distant with the artifice of verse.

I have not again retouched the lyric poems of my youth, fearing some stupidity in my middle years, but have changed two or three pages that I always knew to be wrong in 'The Wanderings of Usheen.' W. B. YEATS. *June*, 1912.

Preface to the Third Edition. I have added some passages . . . language of the highway. W. B. YEATS. *January*, 1901. **49-74.**

This volume contains what is, I hope, the final text of the poems of my youth; and yet it may not be, seeing that in it are not only the revisions from my 'Early Poems and Stories,' published last year, but quite new revisions on which my heart is greatly set. One is always cutting out the dead wood.

I have enclosed in brackets those passages in 'The Land of Heart's Desire' which are omitted when it is played at the Abbey Theatre, Dublin, and I hope the amateurs, who perform this play more often than any other of mine, will accept my guidance and omit them also.   W. B. YEATS.
January, 1927.

Preface to the Seventh Edition. During the last year [follows the preface in **49-74**, immediately above, to 'depend upon the player.'] The first two scenes of the present version of the play are wholly new, [follows **49-74** to 'artifice of verse.' where it ends. The *Preface to the Third Edition is omitted*.] **78, 80.**

*   *   *

Dedication to 10, 10a.

To Lady Gregory:

I offer you a book which is in part your own. Some months ago, when our Irish dramatic movement took its present form, I saw that somebody must write a number of plays in prose if it was to have a good start. I did not know what to do, although I had my dramatic fables ready and a pretty full sketch of one play, for my eyes were troubling me, (me **10a**) and I thought I could do nothing but verse, which one can carry about in one's head for a long time, and write down, as De Musset put it, with a burnt match. You said I might dictate to you, and we worked in the mornings at Coole, and I never did anything that went so easily and quickly, for when I hesitated, you had the right thought ready, and it was always (was almost always **10a**) you who gave the right turn to the phrase and gave it the ring of daily life. We finished several plays, of which this is the longest, in so few weeks, that if I were to say how few, (few **10a**) I do not think anybody would believe me. I have spent a year at a play of no great length, and yet I do not think I could better these plays by taking time over them. We have the pleasure of knowing that our little Irish Theatre has found our work useful.   W. B. YEATS.
September 19, 1902.   **10, 10a.**

Mr. Yeats says in dedicating it [Where There Is Nothing] to me:

'I offer . . . quickly; for . . . hesitated you . . . ready and it was almost always you . . . believe me.' Lady Gregory, *Our Irish Theatre*. New York and London, 1913, pp. 80-81.

*   *   *

[For *Dedication to 11* see Notes on *Cathleen ni Houlihan*, p. 232.]

Preface to 23 [in part].

'The Shadowy Waters,' 'The King's Threshold,' and 'On Baile's Strand' are not at all as they were when first printed, for they have been rewritten and rewritten until I feel I can do no better with my present subjects and experiences. I am the least confident about 'The Shadowy Waters,' for it is so unlike what it was when last played that it is a new play, and I have but tried it at rehearsal, and without its scenery and its costumes, and that harp which is to burn with a faint fire. It is to be judged, like all my plays, as part of an attempt to create a national dramatic literature in Ireland, and it takes upon itself its true likeness of a Jack-a-Lantern among more natural and simple things, when set among the plays of my fellow-workers. What I have done is but a form and colour in an elaborate composition, where they have painted the other forms and colours. The extravagance, the joyous irony, the far-flying phantasy, the aristocratic gaiety, the resounding and rushing words of the comedy of the countryside, of the folk as we say, is akin to the elevation of poetry, which can but shrink even to the world's edge from the harsh, cunning, traditionless humour of the towns. I write of the tragic stories told over the fire by people who are in the comedies of my friends, and I never see my work played with theirs that I do not feel that my tragedy heightens their comedy and tragi-comedy, and grows itself more moving and intelligible from being mixed into the circumstance of the world by the circumstantial art of comedy. Nor is it only the stories and the country mind that have made us one school, for we have talked over one another's work so many times, that when a play of mine comes into my memory I cannot always tell how much even of the radical structure I may not owe to the writer of 'The Lost Saint,' or of 'The Shadow of the Glen,' or more than all, to the writer of 'Hyacinth Halvey'; or that I would have written at all in so heady a mood if I did not know that one or the other were at hand to throw a bushel of laughter into the common basket.

I have printed the plays and poems in the order of their first publication, but so far as the actual writing of verse is concerned, 'The Shadowy Waters' and 'On Baile's Strand' have been so much rewritten that they are later than 'The King's Threshold.' I have put no explanatory notes to the poems and very few to the plays, for impatient readers do not read even the shortest notes, and the patient would cry out upon an arid summary, for they can read the legends in those strange and beautiful books, canonical with most of us in Ireland now, Lady Gregory's 'Gods and Fighting Men' and 'Cuchulain of Muirthemne.'

W. B. YEATS.

In the Seven Woods;
    18 May 1906.

*   *   *

Preface to 28, 48.

The first two plays in this book were written before I had any adequate knowledge of the stage, but all were written to be played. I have always looked upon the play written to be read only as an imperfect form, even for the reader who would find it the more exciting for the vigorous structure, the working to a climax, that had made it hold some fitting audience.

A writer of drama must observe the form as carefully as if it were a sonnet, but he must always deny that there is any subject-matter which is in itself dramatic—any especial round of emotion fitted to the stage, or that a play has no need to await its audience or to create the interest it lives by. Dramatic art is a method of expression, and neither an hair-breadth escape nor a love affair more befits it than the passionate exposition of the most delicate and strange intuitions; and the dramatist is as free as the painter of good pictures and the writer of good books. All art is passionate, but a flame is not the less flame because we change the candle for a lamp or the lamp for a fire; and all flame is beautiful.

A lover is subtle about his mistress's eyebrow, and I have found in Dublin a small audience so much interested in Ireland that they have not complained too loudly that my fellow-dramatists at the Abbey Theatre or I myself write of difficult and unfamiliar things. I have chosen all of my themes from Irish legend or Irish history, and my friends have made joyous, extravagant, and, as I am certain, distinguished comedy out of the common life of the villages, or out of a phantasy trained by the contemplation of that life and of the tales told by its firesides. This theatre cannot but be the more interesting to people of other races because it is Irish and, therefore, to some extent, stirred by emotions and thoughts not hitherto expressed in dramatic form, for the arts have always gained by their limitations, and I look forward to a day when a company will carry its plays into other lands,—above all, where there are Irish people,—and when I close my eyes I can see all clearly. It will play principally comedy, for the day of tragedy will return slowly, but of an extravagant, abounding kind that is half poetry; the inspiration of a muse that, although she is a little drunken, her lips still wet from the overflowing cup of life, is ready, as in old days, to abate her voice when her sister has carried a taper among the tombs that she may tell strange stories of the deaths of kings. Above all, for one imagines as one pleases when the eyes are closed, it will be a theatre of speech; the speech of the country-side, the eloquence of poets, of rhythm, of style, of proud, living, unwasted words, and among its players there may be some who can sing like a poet of Languedoc stories and songs where the music shall be as simple as in a sailor's chanty, for I would restore the whole ancient art of passionate speech, and would no more let a singer spoil a word or the poet's rhythm for the musician's sake than I would let an actor who, as Colley Cibber said, 'should be tied to time and tune like a singer,' spoil the poet's rhythm that he might give to a word what seemed to him a greater weight of drama. The labour of two players, Miss Florence Farr and Mr. Frank Fay, have done enough to show that all is possible, if the summer be lucky and the corn ripen.

December, 1906.

The first . . . sister carrying a taper among the tombs would tell . . . corn ripen.

Since I wrote these words I have in the light of what is now a considerable dramatic experience greatly altered 'The Land of Heart's Desire,' and so greatly altered 'The Countess Cathleen' that it is all but a new play. Both plays are now, like the other plays in the book, a part of the repertory of the Abbey Theatre.

February, 1912. **W. B. YEATS.**

48.

* * *

Preface to 29.

About seven years ago I began to dictate the first of these Plays to Lady Gregory. My eyesight had become so bad that I feared I could henceforth write nothing with my own hands but verses, which, as Theophile Gautier has said, can be written with a burnt match. Our Irish Dramatic movement was just passing out of the hands of English Actors, hired because we knew of no Irish ones, and our little troop of Irish amateurs—as they were at the time—could not have too many Plays, for they would come to nothing without continued playing. Besides, it was exciting to discover, after the unpopularity of blank verse, what one could do with three Plays written in prose and founded on three public interests deliberately chosen,— religion, humour, patriotism. I planned in those days to establish a dramatic movement upon the popular passions, as the ritual of religion is established in the emotions that surround birth and death and marriage, and it was only the coming of the unclassifiable, uncontrollable, capricious, uncompromising genius of J. M. Synge that altered the direction of the movement and made it individual, critical, and combative. If his had not, some other stone would have blocked up the old way, for the public mind of Ireland, stupefied by prolonged intolerant organisation, can take but brief pleasure in the caprice that is in all art, whatever its subject, and, more commonly, can but hate unaccustomed personal reverie.

I had dreamed the subject of 'Cathleen ni Houlihan,' but found when I looked for words that I could not create peasant dialogue that would go nearer to peasant life than the dialogue in 'The Land of Heart's Desire' or 'The Countess Cathleen.' Every artistic form has its own ancestry, and the more elaborate it is, the more is the writer constrained to symbolise rather than to represent life, until perhaps his ladies of fashion are shepherds and shepherdesses, as when Colin Clout came home again. I could not get away, no matter how closely I watched the country life, from images and dreams which had all too royal blood, for they were descended like the thought of every poet from all the conquering dreams of Europe, and I wished to make that high life mix into some rough contemporary life without ceasing to be itself, as so many old books and Plays have mixed it and so few modern, and to do this I added another knowledge to my own. Lady

Gregory had written no Plays, but had, I discovered, a greater knowledge of the country mind and country speech than anybody I had ever met with, and nothing but a burden of knowledge could keep 'Cathleen ni Houlihan' from the clouds. I needed less help for the 'Hour-Glass,' for the speech there is far from reality, and so the Play is almost wholly mine. When, however, I brought to her the general scheme for the 'Pot of Broth,' a little farce which seems rather imitative to-day, though it plays well enough, and of the first version of 'The Unicorn,' 'Where there is Nothing,' a five-act Play written in a fortnight to save it from a plagiarist, and tried to dictate them, her share grew more and more considerable. She would not allow me to put her name to these Plays, though I have always tried to explain her share in them, but has signed 'The Unicorn from the Stars,' which but for a good deal of the general play and a single character and bits of another is wholly hers. I feel indeed that my best share in it is that idea, which I have been capable of expressing completely in criticism alone, of bringing together the rough life of the road and the frenzy that the poets have found in their ancient cellar,—a prophecy, as it were, of the time when it will be once again possible for a Dickens and a Shelley to be born in the one body.

The chief person of the earlier Play was very dominating, and I have grown to look upon this as a fault, though it increases the dramatic effect in a superficial way. We cannot sympathise with the man who sets his anger at once lightly and confidently to overthrow the order of the world, for such a man will seem to us alike insane and arrogant. But our hearts can go with him, as I think, if he speak with some humility, so far as his daily self carry him, out of a cloudy light of vision; for whether he understand or not, it may be that voices of angels and archangels have spoken in the cloud, and whatever wildness came upon his life, feet of theirs may well have trod the clusters. But a man so plunged in trance is of necessity somewhat still and silent, though it be perhaps the silence and the stillness of a lamp; and the movement of the Play as a whole, if we are to have time to hear him, must be without hurry or violence.   **29.**

* * *

Preface to 45.

In poetical drama there is, it is held, an antithesis between drama and lyric poetry, for lyric poetry however much it move you when read out of a book can, as these critics think, but encumber the action. Yet when we go back a few centuries and enter the great periods of drama, character grows less and sometimes disappears, and there is much lyric feeling, and at times a lyric measure will be wrought into the dialogue, a flowing measure that had well befitted music, or that more lumbering one of the sonnet. Suddenly it strikes us that character is continuously present in comedy alone, and that there is much tragedy, that of Corneille, that of Racine, that of Greece and Rome, where its place is taken by passions and motives, one person being jealous, another full of love or remorse or pride or anger. In writers of tragi-comedy (and Shakespeare is always a writer of tragi-comedy) there is indeed character, but we notice that it is in the moments of comedy that character is defined, in Hamlet's gaiety let us say; while amid the great moments, when Timon orders his tomb, when Hamlet cries to Horatio 'Absent thee from felicity awhile', when Anthony names 'Of many thousand kisses the poor last' all is lyricism, unmixed passion, 'the integrity of fire'. Nor does character ever attain to complete definition in these lamps ready for the taper, no matter how circumstantial and gradual the opening of events, as it does in Falstaff who has no passionate purpose to fulfil, or as it does in Henry the Fifth whose poetry, never touched by lyric heat, is oratorical; nor when the tragic reverie is at its height do we say 'How well that man is realised! I should know him were I to meet him in the street', for it is always ourselves that we see upon the stage, and should it be a tragedy of love we renew, it may be, some loyalty of our youth, and go from the theatre with our eyes dim for an old love's sake.

I think it was while rehearsing a translation of *Les Fourberies de Scapin* in Dublin, and noticing how passionless it all was, that I saw what should have been plain from the first line I had written, that tragedy must always be a drowning and breaking of the dykes that separate man from man, and that it is upon these dykes comedy keeps house. But I was not certain of the site (one always doubts when one knows no testimony but one's own); till somebody told me of a certain letter of Congreve's. He describes the external and superficial expressions of 'humour' on which farce is founded and then defines 'humour' itself, the foundation of comedy, as 'a singular and unavoidable way of doing anything peculiar to one man only, by which his speech and actions are distinguished from all other men' and adds to it that 'passions are too powerful in the sex to let humour have its course', or as I would rather put it, that you can find but little of what we call character in unspoiled youth, whatever be the sex, for, as he indeed shows in another sentence, it grows with time like the ash of a burning stick, and strengthens towards middle life till there is little else at seventy years.

Since then I have discovered an antagonism between all the old art and our new art of comedy and understand why I hated at nineteen years Thackeray's novels and the new French painting. A big picture of cocottes sitting at little tables outside a Café, by some follower of Manet's, was exhibited at the Royal Hibernian Academy while I was a student at a life class there, and I was miserable for days. I found no desirable place, no man I could have wished to be, no woman I could have loved, no Golden Age, no lure for secret hope, no adventure with myself for theme out of that endless tale I told myself all day long. Years after I saw the Olympia of Manet at the Luxembourg and watched it without hostility indeed, but as I might some incomparable talker whose precision of gesture gave me pleasure, though I did not understand his language. I returned to it again and again at intervals of years, saying to myself 'some day I will understand'; and yet it was not until Sir Hugh Lane brought the Eva Gonzales to Dublin, and I had said to myself 'How perfectly that woman is realized as distinct from all other women that have lived or shall live!' that I understood I was carrying on in my own mind that quarrel between a tragedian and a comedian which the Devil on Two Sticks showed to the young man who had climbed through the window.

There is an art of the flood, the art of Titian when his Ariosto and his Bacchus and Ariadne give new images to the dreams of youth, and of Shakespeare when he shows us Hamlet broken away from life by the passionate hesitations of his reverie. And we call this art poetical, because we must bring more to it than our daily mood if we would take our pleasure; and because it delights in picturing the moment of exaltation, of excitement, of dreaming (or the capacity for it, as in that still face of Ariosto's that is like some vessel soon to be full of wine). And there is an art that we call real, because character can only express itself perfectly in a real world, being that world's creature, and because we understand it best through a delicate discrimination of the senses, which is but entire wakefulness, the daily mood grown cold and crystalline.

We may not find either mood in its purity, but in mainly tragic art one distinguishes devices to exclude or lessen character, to diminish the power of that daily mood, to cheat or blind its too clear perception. If the real world is not altogether rejected it is but touched here and there, and into the places we have left empty we summon rhythm, balance, pattern, images that remind us of vast passions, the vagueness of past times, all the chimeras that haunt the edge of trance; and if we are painters, we shall express personal emotion through ideal form, a symbolism handled by the generations, a mask from whose eyes the disembodied looks, a style that remembers many masters, that it may escape contemporary suggestion; or we shall leave out some element of reality as in Byzantine painting, where there is no mass, nothing in relief; so it is that in the supreme moment of tragic art there comes upon one that strange sensation as though the hair of one's head stood up. And when we love, if it be in the excitement of youth, do we not also, that the flood may find no wall to narrow, no stone to convulse it, exclude character or the signs of it by choosing that beauty which seems unearthly because the individual woman is lost amid the labyrinth of its lines as though life were trembling into stillness and silence, or at last folding itself away? Some little irrelevance of line, some promise of character to come, may indeed put us at our ease, 'give more interest' as the humour of the old man with the basket does to Cleopatra's dying; but should it come as we had dreamed in love's frenzy to our dying for that woman's sake, we would find that the discord had its value from the tune.

Certainly we have here the Tree of Life and that of the Knowledge of Good and Evil which is rooted in our interests and if we have forgotten their differing virtues, it is surely because we have taken delight in a confusion of crossing branches. Tragic art, passionate art, the drowner of dykes, the confounder of understanding, moves us by setting us to reverie, by alluring us almost to the intensity of trance. The persons upon the stage, let us say, greaten till they are humanity itself. We feel our minds expand convulsively or spread out slowly like some moon-brightened image-crowded sea. That which is before our eyes perpetually vanishes and returns again in the midst of the excitement it creates, and the more enthralling it is the more do we forget it. When I am watching my own *Deirdre* I am content with the players and myself, if I am moved for a while not by the contrasted sorrows of Deirdre and Naisi, but because the words have called up before me the image of the sea-born woman so distinctly that Deirdre seems by contrast to those unshaken eyelids that had but the sea's cold blood what I had wished her to seem, a wild bird in a cage.

It was only by watching my own plays that I came to understand that this reverie, this twilight between sleep and waking, this bout of fencing, alike on the stage and in the mind, between man and phantom, this perilous path as on the edge of a sword, is the condition of tragic pleasure, and to understand why it is so rare and so brief. If an actor becomes over emphatic, picking out what he believes to be the important words with violence, and running up and down the scale, or if he stresses his lines in wrong places, or even if an electric lamp that should have cast but a reflected light from sky or sea, shows from behind the post of a door, I discover at once the proud fragility of dreams.

At first I was driven into teaching too statuesque a pose, too monotonous a delivery, that I might not put 'vitality' in the place of the sleep walking of passion, and for the rest became a little deaf and blind.

But alas! it is often my own words that break the dream. Then I take the play from the stage and write it over again, perhaps many times. At first I always believed it must be something in the management of events, in all that is the same in prose or verse, that was wrong, but after I had reconstructed a scene with the messenger in *Deirdre* in many ways, I discovered that my language must keep at all times a certain even richness. I had used 'traitor', 'sword', 'suborned', words of a too traditional usage, without plunging them into personal thought and metaphor, and I had forgotten in a moment of melodrama that tragic drama must be carved out of speech as a statue is out of stone.

But train our players and our mechanists as we will and if we have not thought out the art of stage decoration afresh every brush stroke of our scene painter will mix into the reverie the meretricious or the irrelevant. We shall have hired some journeyman to accompany the poet's description with a painted landscape which, because it must give all to the first glance and yet copy nature, will alone copy what is obvious, and which even if it could keep the attention and give it pleasure could but keep it to the poet's loss:—

> 'A vapour, sometimes, like a bear, or lion,
> A tower'd citadel, a pendant rock,
> A forked mountain, or blue promontory
> With trees upon't that nod unto the world
> And mock our eyes with air.'

I have heard Anthony speak those lines before a painted cloth that, though it could not make them nothing, left in the memory the sensation of something childish, theatrical as we say. Words as solemn, and having more for the mind's eye than those of the Book of Common Prayer are spoken where no reformer has cast out the idolatrous mummery and no tradition sanctified.

In no art can we do well unless we keep to those effects that are peculiar to it or it can show better than the other arts. We no longer paint wood with a grain that is not its own, but are content that it should display itself or be covered with paint that pretends to be but paint, and if we make a design for a vase or a plate, we are careful not to attempt something that can be better done in an easel picture. But in the art of the theatre we imitate an easel picture even though we ignore or mar for its sake the elements we should have worked in, the characteristics of the stage, light and shadow, speech, the movement of the players. Our tree-wings . . . let us say . . . can only be given mass and detail by painted light and shadow and these will contradict, or be in no relation to the real light, and this real light will be so cut up and cut off by wings and borders arranged for effects of painting that we shall be content to use it in but a few obvious ways. Then too our background will be full of forms and colours, instead of showing an even or almost even surface whereon the players are outlined clearly that we may see their movements and feel their importance; and all the while the background, even if it were fine painting and had no false light and shadow and did not reduce the players to a picturesque group in the foreground of a water colour painting by my grandmother, could but insist on the unreality we are anxious to forget, for every time a player stood close to that garden scene we would but feel over again on how flat a surface they had painted that long garden walk dwindling away into the distance.

If we would give our theatre the dignity of a church, of a Greek open air theatre, of an Elizabethan platform stage, and cannot be content with any of these, we must have a scene where there is no painted light and shade, and that is but another way of saying, no realism, no objects represented in mass (unless they can be copied exactly as we can sometimes copy an interior), and the mechanism of this scene must as little as possible prevent the free and delicate use of light and shadow.

When we have made this change in obedience to a logic which has been displayed in the historical development of all the other arts, we shall have created a theatre that will please the poet and the player and the painter. An old quarrel will be ended, the stage will be beautifully decorated, every change will be full of meaning and yet never create a competing interest, or set bounds to the suggestions of speech and motion. At last liberated from the necessity of an always complete realization, the producer, recovering caprice, will be as free as a modern painter, as Signor Mancini let us say, to give himself up to an elliptical imagination. Gloster will be able to fall but from his own height and think that he has fallen from Dover cliff, and Richard's and Richmond's tents can face one another again. We shall have made possible once more a noble, capricious, extravagant, resonant, fantastic art.

All summer I have been playing with a little model, where there is a scene capable of endless transformation, of the expression of every mood that does not require a photographic reality. Mr. Craig—who has invented all this—has permitted me to set up upon the stage of the Abbey another scene that corresponds to this, in the scale of a foot for an inch, and henceforth I shall be able, by means so simple that one laughs, to lay the events of my plays amid a grandeur like that of Babylon; and where there is neither complexity nor compromise nothing need go wrong, no lamps become suddenly unmasked, no ill-painted corner come suddenly into sight. Henceforth I can all but 'produce' my play while I write it, moving hither and thither little figures of cardboard through gay or solemn light and shade, allowing the scene to give the words and the words the scene. I am very grateful for he has banished a whole world that wearied me and was undignified and given me forms and lights upon which I can play as upon some stringed instrument.

W. B. YEATS.

P.S.

Two of Mr. Craig's designs, 'The Heroic Age—Morning', and 'The Heroic Age—Evening', are impressions worked out in Mr. Craig's scene, of the world my people move in, rather than exact pictures of any moment of a play. The one, however, suggests to me *On Baile's Strand*, and the other *Deirdre*. The design for *The Hour-Glass* shows the scene as it was used in Dublin, and 'The Fool'—who belongs to *The Hour-Glass* and *On Baile's Strand*—is as he was in Dublin in the first play, except that we have found no one who can make us a mask of leather, and we do not yet know how to make it ourselves.

W. B. Y.

45.

I noticed in all but all the printed criticisms of Synge's 'Deirdre of the Sorrows' that none of the things that made certain moments seem to me the noblest tragedy were written of, but that the play was judged by things that seemed to me but wheels and pulleys necessary to the effect, but in themselves nothing.

Upon the other hand, those who spoke to me of the play never spoke of these wheels and pulleys, but if they cared at all for the play, cared for the things I cared for. One's own world of painters, of poets, of good talkers, of ladies who delight in Ricard's portraits or Debussy's music, all those whose senses feel instantly every change in imagination, in our mother the moon, saw the stage in one way; and those others who look at plays every night, who tell the general playgoer whether this play or that play is to his taste, saw it in a way so different that there is certainly some body of dogma whether in the instincts or in the memory, pushing the ways apart. A printed

criticism for instance found but one dramatic moment, that when Deirdre
in the second act overhears her lover say that he may grow weary of her;
and not one, if I remember rightly, chose for praise or explanation the third
act which alone had satisfied the author, or contained in any abundance
those sentences that were quoted at the fall of the curtain and for days after.

Deirdre and her lover, as Synge tells the tale, returned to Ireland though
it was nearly certain they would die there, because death was better than
broken love, and at the side of the open grave that had been dug for one
and would serve for both, quarreled, losing all they had given their life to
keep. 'Is it not a hard thing that we should miss the safety of the grave and
we trampling its edge?' That is Deirdre's cry at the outset of a reverie
of passion that mounts and mounts till grief itself has carried her beyond
grief into pure contemplation. Up to this the play had been a Master's
unfinished work, monotonous and melancholy, ill arranged, little more than
a sketch of what it would have grown to, but now I listened breathless to
sentences that may never pass away, and as they filled or dwindled in their
civility of sorrow, the player, whose art had seemed clumsy and incomplete,
like the writing itself, ascended into that tragic ecstacy which is the best
that art . . . . . [T] perhaps that life . . . . . [T] can give. At last when Deirdre,
in the paroxysm before she took her life, touched with compassionate fingers
him that had killed her lover, we knew that the player had become, if but
for a moment, the creature of that noble mind which had gathered its art
in waste islands, and we too were carried beyond time and persons to where
passion living through its thousand purgatorial years, as in the wink of an
eye, becomes wisdom; and it was as though we too had touched and felt
and seen a disembodied thing.

One dogma of the printed criticism is that if a play does not contain
definite character, its constitution is not strong enough for the stage, and
that the dramatic moment is always the contest of character with character.
In poetical drama . . . between character and lyric poetry, . . . however
beautiful when read out of a book can but, as . . . think, encumber . . .
music, or that laboured one . . . say; but that in the great . . . awhile,' when
Cleopatra names . . . oratorical like a speech at a general election, like an
article in some daily paper; nor when . . . realised, I . . . sake.

I think . . . site; (one . . . sex, for as . . . as one might . . . gave one pleasure,
though one did . . . understand' and . . . live' that I . . . window.

There is . . . Ariadne gave new . . . dreaming (or in the . . . crystalline.

We may . . . relief, and so . . . dying. But . . . tune.

When we look at the faces of the old tragic paintings, whether it is in
Titian or in some painter of medieval China, we find there sadness and
gravity, a certain emptiness even as of a mind that waited the supreme crisis
(and indeed it seems at times as if the graphic art, unlike poetry which sings
the crisis itself, were the celebration of waiting). Whereas in modern art,
whether in Japan or in Europe, 'vitality' (is not that the great word of the
studios?) the energy that is to say that is under the command of our common
moments, sings, laughs, chatters or looks its busy thoughts.

Have we not here then the Tree of Life and that of the knowledge . . . interests, and . . . differing forms of leaf and fruit, it is surely . . . dykes, the compounder of understanding, . . . image crowded . . . myself, when I . . . Naoise, . . . distinctly, that her unshaken . . . had not the sea's cold blood seem by contrast what I . . . cage.

It was . . . phantoms, . . . dreams.

At first . . . passion in these things, and for . . . blind.

But alas! . . . that our language . . . , 'suborned' words in a too . . . stone.

It is certain therefore that should suggestion run thin, should some one move violently, should there be a sudden noise, any one out of a thousand accidents that would hardly trouble the robust pleasure of comedy, the climbing shoulders will come from under the stone. Perhaps there is in tragic art something womanish come from the continual presence of the Muses who have given Comedy a later and a slighter love, and we know that men can have their day's work amid the abrupt, the common, the foolish even without utter loss, but that women cannot keep their fineness lacking a fine company.

But train . . . scene painters will . . . reverie the monotonous or the irrelevant. We will hire some . . . loss:—

       . . . vapour, sometimes, like . . . ,

       . . .

       . . . world.

       . . . air.

I have . . . Prayer must be spoken . . . sanctified.

In no . . . to it or that it . . . if we paint a design upon a vase . . . in easel painting. But . . . imitate easel painting, even . . . distance.

If we . . . these we . . . mass unless . . . interior, and . . . shadow.

When we . . . yet it will never . . . motion, and liberated . . . art.

'The Tragic Theatre,' *The Mask* (Florence), October, 1910.

*   *   *

Preface to 52.

The plays in this volume of selections that I have made for Baron Tauchnitz, are part of the repertory of the Abbey Theatre, Dublin, and with the exception of 'The Countess Cathleen' are printed as they are played. I have left an end to 'The Countess Cathleen' that is not played, because the new end, as given in the notes, was not made for dramatic or poetic reasons, but to suit audiences that, even in Dublin, know little of Irish mythology. The rest of the play, which differs from any published version, is as it has been shaped after many rehearsals and performances. I have spent so much of my time in the theatre, that what gives me displeasure there, gives me displeasure when in print, seeming as though it were something unshapely in a woman's body. It seems to me that what plays best before a worthy audience, will read best, and with this conviction, which may be but a false light of the theatre, I have left out passages that used to please me.

If I had but music enough to make settings that had but enough music to adorn the words yet leave them natural and audible, I should have written lyrics to be sung, for it is speaking or singing before an audience that makes us tell our stories well, and put our thoughts into some lasting order and set our emotions clambering to some arduous climax, but as it is, lacking music but that of words I have chosen the lyrics not out of singers' mouths but from little books published at Stratford-on-Avon, or in London, or by my sisters at the hand-press worked by the village of Dundrum, in Ireland.

W. B. YEATS.

October, 1912.   52.

*   *   *

[For *A Preface to the New Version* (The Hour-Glass), see text, p. 577.]

*   *   *

Preface to 60.

In a note at the end of my last book 'The Wild Swans at Coole' (Cuala Press.) I explained why I preferred this kind of drama, and where I had found my models, and where and how my first play after this kind was performed, and when and how I would have it performed in the future. I can but refer the reader to the note or to the long introduction to 'Certain Noble Plays of Japan'[1] (Cuala Press.)

W. B. YEATS. October 11th, 1918.

P.S. That I might write 'The Dreaming of the Bones,' Mr. W. A. Henderson with great kindness wrote out for me all historical allusions to Dervorgilla.

60.

*   *   *

Preface to 64; Preface in 71 to 'Four Plays for Dancers.'

Two of these plays must be opened by the unfolding and folding of the cloth, a substitute for the rising of the curtain, and all must be closed by it. The others, 'The Dreaming of the Bones' and 'Calvary,' should have the same opening, unless played after plays of the same kind, when it may seem a needless repetition. All must be played to the accompaniment of drum and zither and flute, but on no account must the words be spoken 'through music' in the fashionable way; and the players must move a little stiffly and gravely like marionettes and, I think, to the accompaniment of drum taps. I felt, however, during the performance of 'The Hawk's Well,' the only one played up to this, that there was much to discover. Should I make a serious attempt, which I may not, being rather tired of the theatre, to arrange and supervise performances, the dancing will give me most trouble, for I know but vaguely what I want. I do not want any existing form of stage dancing, but something with a smaller gamut of expression, something

---

[1] Reprinted in *The Cutting of an Agate*. London, 1919; *Essays*. London, 1924; New York, 1924; and *Essays and Introductions*. London, 1961; New York, 1961.

more reserved, more self-controlled, as befits performers within arm's reach of their audience.

The designs by Mr. Dulac represent (Mr. Edmund Dulac designed **71**) the masks and costumes used in the first performance of 'The Hawk's Well.' The beautiful mask of Cuchulain may, I think, serve for Dervorgilla, and if I write plays and organize performances on any scale and with any system, I shall hope for a small number of typical masks, each capable of use in several plays. The face of the speaker should be as much a work of art as the lines that he speaks or the costume that he wears, that all may be as artificial as possible. Perhaps in the end one would write plays for certain masks. If some fine sculptor should create for my 'Calvary,' for instance, the masks of Judas, of Lazarus, and of Christ, would not this suggest other plays now, or many generations from now, and possess one cannot tell what philosophical virility? The mask, apart from its beauty, may suggest new situations at a moment when the old ones seem exhausted; 'The Only Jealousy of Emer' was written to find what dramatic effect one could get out of a mask, changed while the player remains upon the stage to suggest a change of personality. At the end of this book there is some music by Mr. Rummel, which my friends tell me is both difficult and beautiful (beautiful, **71**) for 'The Dreaming of the Bones.' It will require, I am told, either a number of flutes of which the flute-player will pick now one, now another, or an elaborate modern flute (flute, **71**) which would not look in keeping. I prefer the first suggestion. I notice that Mr. Rummel has written no music for the dance, and I have some vague memory that when we talked it over in Paris he felt that he could not without the dancer's help. There is also music for 'The Hawk's Well' by Mr. Dulac, which is itself an exposition of method, for it was written after a number of rehearsals and for instruments that have great pictorial effect.

'The Dreaming of the Bones' and 'The Only Jealousy of Emer,' bound together as *Two Plays for Dancers*, were printed on my sister's hand-press at Dundrum, County Dublin, and published in a limited edition in the spring of 1919, while 'At the Hawk's Well' makes a part of the edition of *The Wild Swans at Coole*, printed at the same press in 1917, though not of the later edition of that book published by Macmillan. 'At the Hawk's Well' and 'The Only Jealousy of Emer' are the first and last plays of a series of four dealing with Cuchulain's life. The others are my 'Green Helmet' and 'Baile's Strand.' 'Calvary' has not hitherto been published. [This paragraph 'The Dreaming . . . published.' omitted in **71**.]

That I might write 'The Dreaming of the Bones' (Bones,' **71**) Mr. W. A. Henderson with great kindness wrote out for me all historical allusions to 'Dervorgilla'; but neither that nor any of these plays could have existed if Mr. Edmond (Edmund **71**) Dulac had not taught me the value and beauty of the mask and rediscovered how to design and make it.

W. B. YEATS.

July 1920.   **64, 71.**

*   *   *

Preface to 69.

In this book are all Plays of mine played at the Abbey Theatre, Dublin, except 'The Land of Heart's Desire' and 'The Countess Cathleen,' which are in *Poems* (T. Fisher Unwin). I (*Poems* 169A) have also written *Four Plays for Dancers*, but I leave them under separate cover as they were written for private performances in studio or drawing-room, and are a different form of art. 'On Baile's Strand,' though produced for the first time at the opening of the Abbey Theatre in December 1904, was planned when I had no hope of that, or any, theatre, and the characters walk on to an empty stage at the beginning and leave that stage empty at the end, because I thought of its performance upon a large platform with a door at the back and an exit through the audience at the side, and no proscenium, (proscenium 69A) or curtain; and being intended for a platform and a popular audience—no other audience at the time caring a straw about us—is full of what I thought to be good round speeches. It makes one of a series of plays upon events in the life of Cuchulain, and if placed in the order of those events the plays would run: 1. 'The Hawk's Well' (*Four Plays for Dancers*); 2. 'The Green Helmet'; 3. 'On Baile's Strand'; 4. 'The Only Jealousy of Emer' (*Four Plays for Dancers*): but they were so little planned for performance upon one evening that they should be at their best on three different kinds of stage.

'The Player Queen' is the only work of mine, not mere personal expression, written during these last twenty years, which is not avowedly Irish in its subject matter, being all transacted in some No-Man's-Land. I wrote it, my head full of fantastic architecture invented by myself upon a miniature stage, which corresponds to that of the Abbey in the proportion of one inch to a foot, with a miniature set of Gordon Craig screens and a candle; and if it is gayer than my wont it is that I tried to find words and events that would seem well placed under a beam of light reflected from the ivory-coloured surface of the screens.

No verse play of mine requires much more than an hour for its performance; and most, being intended for a theatre where every evening winds up with comedy or satire, are much shorter.

'Deirdre,' 'The King's Threshold,' 'The Hour-Glass,' in its verse form, are more difficult to play than 'The Green Helmet' or 'The Countess Cathleen' because in each some one personage is upon the stage through the whole, or all but the whole play, and should not be attempted where the principal player lacks subjectivity and variety.

I have explained at the end of this book how often Lady Gregory has collaborated with me. I have sometimes asked her help because I could not write dialect and sometimes because my construction had fallen into confusion. To the best of my belief 'The Unicorn from the Stars,' but for fable and chief character, is wholly her work. 'The Green Helmet' and 'The Player Queen' alone perhaps are wholly mine.   W. B. YEATS.

Thoor Ballylee, *May* 1, 1922.   **69.**

*   *   *

Preface to 71.

I have gathered into this book two plays, written before the foundation
of the Irish Theatre though much corrected since, and four plays written
but the other day and intended for performance in drawing-room and
studio, and a long series of dramatic notes. I begin the book with these
notes, which are taken for the most part from an occasional publication
called *Samhain*, started in the third year of 'The Irish Dramatic Movement'
to defend that movement, and long out of print. In a little while Dail
Eireann and our Dublin newspapers will consider, as I hope, the foundation
of an Irish State Theatre; and I would put these old notes into evidence.
Though often about foolish quarrels, or plays but little better, they may
keep their use even when that occasion passes; being passionately written,
and at a moment when Ireland was preparing, in that dark portion of the
mind which is like the other side of the moon, for insurrection and anarchic
violence; and all in some measure a plea for intellectual spontaneity against
unyielding, mechanical, abstract principles. I ask indulgence if I over-
rate their value, for it may be that I cannot judge sentences that call up
memories of the time when I was most alive, having most friends and
enemies. All needful explanations are in Lady Gregory's book, *Our Irish
Theatre.*

The plays are so abundantly annotated and prefaced that I need say
nothing more except that the first was planned and partly written when
I was little more than a boy, and that it gives me more pleasure in the
memory than any of my plays. It was all thought out in the first fervour of
my generation's distaste for Victorian rhetoric; that rhetoric once away,
every poetical virtue seemed possible.

W. B. YEATS.

Dublin,
February 1923.

*   *   *

[For Preface to 'The Land of Heart's Desire' in **71,** see p. 212.]

*   *   *

Preface to 75.

To Lady Gregory

I dedicate this book to you because of a thought that has been in my head
all day. When some years ago we produced my 'Baile's Strand,' with scenes and
costumes designed by Mr. Charles Ricketts, my imagination was greatly
stirred, and I wanted to take up my theme once more, but to make it more
mythological, more indefinite. I began to play with the idea of inventing
for Cuchullain some youthful sojourn in the forest, and writing for him
many love poems like those Indian poets have put into the mouth of Krishna,
but addressed, not to girls who herd the cows, but to girls who herd the
swine. I do not know why I preferred swine to cows except that our old

legends speak so often of swineherds. Now that I have just read through the poems in this little book, I renew an impression, especially from the 'Cat and the Moon,' which I have received much more powerfully from the last act of Synge's 'Well of the Saints' and from your 'Gaol Gate' and as powerfully from 'The Grasshopper' by Mr. Padraic Colum, and from a play of Mr. Daniel Corkery's—an odour, a breath, that suggests to me Indian or Japanese poems and legends. I get no such impression from the powerful art of Mr. T. C. Murray, nor from that of Mr. Macnamara, or of Shiels, or of Mr. Lennox Robinson, nor from that of any other Irish dramatist, poet or novelist that I can remember. Why has our school, which has perhaps come to an end, been interested mainly in something in Irish life so old that one can no longer say this is Europe, that is Asia? It cannot be because of the books we have read, for we have all read such different books. Will poets and novelists and dramatists, younger than Mr. Lennox Robinson or Mr. Macnamara, take up our theme again, urged thereto by some change in the world's thought too subtle to be attributed to any book? Perhaps; for the other day when I read that strange 'Waste Land' by Mr. T. C. Eliot I thought of your work and of Synge's; and he is American born, and Englishman bred, and writes but of his own mind. That is the kind of insoluble problem that makes the best conversation, and if you will come and visit me, I will call the Dublin poets together, and we will discuss it until midnight.

w. b. YEATS, 25th February, 1924.

75

*   *   *

[For *Preface to 79* see notes on 'Sophocles' King Oedipus', p. 851.]

*   *   *

Preface to 83.

All these plays have been played at the Abbey Theatre, Dublin. *The Words upon the Window-pane* has been revived several times, *The Cat and the Moon* once, but *Fighting the Waves*, which drew large audiences, not at all, because Mr. George Antheil's most strange, most dramatic music requires a large expensive orchestra. A memory of that orchestra has indeed roused a distinguished Irish lyric poet to begin a dance play which he assures me requires but a tin whistle and a large expensive concertina. *The Resurrection* was played for the first time at the Abbey a few days ago. Like *The Cat and the Moon* it was not intended for the public theatre. I permitted it there after great hesitation. Owing perhaps to a strike which has prevented the publication of the religious as well as of the political newspapers and reviews, all is well.

w. b. y.

4th August 1934.

83.

*   *   *

Preface to 84.

The plays in this book are intended for hearers and for readers; all have been played at the Abbey Theatre, Dublin, except *Calvary*, which has not yet been played anywhere. The dates in the list of Contents, and under the title of each play, refer to the year of their publication. Those who think of producing any particular play should seek for it in *Plays and Controversies*, *Plays*[1], and *Wheels and Butterflies*. The Note on *The Countess Cathleen*, for instance, in *Plays and Controversies* contains a simplified version of the last scene, and when I have known of appropriate music for some play I have given it in Note or Appendix. The version of *The Hour-Glass* in the present book has been but once played at the Abbey Theatre and once elsewhere, whereas the prose version in *Plays* has been played a great many times; speakers of verse are rare. I do not include in the present book *Fighting the Waves*, a prose version of *The Only Jealousy of Emer* so arranged as to admit of many dancers and to be immediately intelligible to an average theatrical audience; it can be found in *Wheels and Butterflies*. In *Plays* and *Plays and Controversies* I have explained my indebtedness to Lady Gregory. If I could have persuaded her, she would have signed *The Unicorn from the Stars*, her share in it is so great. She had generally some part wherever there is dialect, and often where there is not.

W. B. Y.
84.

*   *   *

Preface to 85, 86.

A year ago I found that I had written no verse for two years; I had never been so long barren; I had nothing in my head, and there used to be more than I could write. Perhaps Coole Park where I had escaped from politics, from all that Dublin talked of, when it was shut, shut me out from my theme; or did the subconscious drama that was my imaginative life end with its owner? but it was more likely that I had grown too old for poetry. I decided to force myself to write, then take advice. In 'At Parnell's Funeral' I rhymed passages from a lecture I had given in America; a poem upon mount Meru came spontaneously, but philosophy is a dangerous theme; then I was barren again. I wrote the prose dialogue of *The King of the Great Clock Tower* that I might be forced to make lyrics for its imaginary people. When I had written all but the last lyric I went a considerable journey partly to get the advice of a poet not of my school who would, as he did some years ago, say what he thought. I asked him to dine, tried to get his attention. 'I am in my sixty ninth (sixty-ninth **86**) year' I said, 'probably I should stop writing verse, I want your opinion upon some verse I have written lately.' I had hoped he would ask me to read it but he would not speak of art, or of literature, or of anything related to them. I had however been talking to his latest disciple and knew that his opinions had not changed: Phidias had corrupted sculpture, we had nothing of true Greece but certain

---

[1] *Plays in Prose and Verse.*—Ed.

Nike dug up out of the foundations of the Parthenon, and that corruption ran through all our art; Shakespeare and Dante had corrupted literature, Shakespeare by his too abounding sentiment, Dante by his compromise with the Church.

He said, apropos (said apropos **86**) of nothing 'Arthur Balfour was a scoundrel,' and from that on would talk of nothing but politics. All the other modern statesmen were more or less scoundrels except 'Mussolini and that hysterical imitator of his Hitler.' When I objected to his violence he declared that Dante considered all sins intellectual, even sins of the flesh, he himself refused to make the modern distinction between error and sin. He urged me to read the works of Captain Douglas who alone knew what caused our suffering. He took my manuscript and went away denouncing Dublin as 'a reactionary hole' because I had said that I was re-reading Shakespeare, would go on to Chaucer, and found all that I wanted of modern life in 'detection and the wild west.' Next day his judgment came and that in a single word 'Putrid.'

Then I took my verses to a friend of my own school, and this friend said 'go on just like that. Plays like *The Great Clock Tower* always seem unfinished but that is no matter. Begin plays without knowing how to end them for the sake of the lyrics. I once wrote a play and after I had filled it with lyrics abolished the play.' Then I brought my work to two painters and a poet until I was like Panurge consulting oracles as to whether he should get married and rejecting all that did not confirm his own desire.

[Yeat's Poem 'A Prayer for Old Age,' follows.]

> God guard me from those thoughts men think
> In the mind alone,
> He that sings a lasting song
> Thinks in a marrow bone;
>
> From all that makes a wise old man
> That can be praised of all;
> O what am I that I should not seem
> For the song's sake a fool.
>
> I pray—for fashion's word is out
> And prayer comes round again—
> That I may seem though I die old
> A foolish, passionate man.   **85, 86.**

*   *   *

Preface to 87.

I wrote *The King of the Great Clock Tower* in prose; a friend, whose judgment I have trusted in the past, denounced it in violent language; but produced in the Abbey Theatre some months ago—McCormick, 'King,' Ninette de

Valois, 'Queen'—it was more successful than any recent play of mine. A friend I had asked to read *The Resurrection*, that preceded it on the same night, and decide if that play were theologically dangerous, sought me out at the fall of the curtain full of enthusiasm, but said, 'When I tried to read it I was so bored that I could not get beyond the second page.' I came to the conclusion that prose dialogue is as unpopular among my studious friends as dialogue in verse among actors and playgoers. I have therefore rewritten *The King of the Great Clock Tower* in verse, but if anybody is inclined to play it, I recommend the prose version published by the Cuala Press last October. In *The King of the Great Clock Tower* there are three characters, King, Queen and Stroller, and that is a character too many; reduced to the essentials, to Queen and Stroller, the fable should have greater intensity. I started afresh and called the new version *A Full Moon in March*.

The dance with the severed head suggests the central idea in Wilde's *Salome*. Wilde took it from Heine, who has somewhere described Salome in Hell throwing into the air the head of John the Baptist. Heine may have found it in some Jewish religious legend, for it is part of the old ritual of the year: the mother goddess and the slain god. In the first edition of *The Secret Rose* there is a story based on some old Gaelic legend. A man swears to sing a woman's praise; his head is cut off and the head sings. In attempting to put this story into a dance play I found that I had gone close to Salome's dance in Wilde's play. But in his play the dance is before the head is cut off.

The hermit Ribh in 'Supernatural Songs' is an imaginary critic of St. Patrick. His Christianity, come perhaps from Egypt like much early Irish Christianity, echoes pre-Christian thought.

May 30, 1935.   **87.**

*   *   *

Preface to 91.

'The Herne's Egg' was written in the happier moments of a long illness that had so separated me from life that I felt irresponsible; the plot echoes that of Samuel Ferguson's 'Congal,' and in one form or another had been in my head since my early twenties.

I first wrote 'The King of the Great Clock Tower' in prose; a friend who is temperamentally violent denounced it in characteristic language, but when I produced it at the Abbey Theatre (MacCormick 'King,' Ninette de Valois 'Queen'), it was more successful than any recent play of mine. After a similar experience with another play I came to the conclusion that prose dialogue is as unpopular among my studious friends as dialogue in verse among actors and playgoers. I have therefore re-written 'The King of the Great Clock Tower' in verse. But if anybody is inclined to play it I recommend the prose version, published by The Macmillan Company a few years ago. In 'The King of the Great Clock Tower' there are three characters, King, Queen and stroller, and that is a character too many; reduced to the essentials, Queen and Stroller, the fable should have greater intensity. I started afresh and called the new version 'A Full Moon in March.'

The dance with the severed head suggests the central idea in Wilde's 'Salome.' Wilde took it from Heine, who has somewhere described Salome in Hell throwing into the air the head of John the Baptist. Heine may have found it in some Jewish religious legend, for it is part of the old ritual of the year: the mother-goddess and the slain god. In the first edition of 'The Secret Rose' there is a story based on some old Gaelic legend. A man swears to sing a woman's praise; his head is cut off and the head sings. In attempting to put this story into a dance play I found that I had gone close to Salome's dance in Wilde's play. But in his play the dance is before the head is cut off. **91.**

* * *

Preface to 93.

Many years ago I brought out an occasional publication called, according to the season, 'Beltaine' or 'Samhain'; it contained my defence of the Abbey Theatre, its actors and its plays. Though I wrote most of it, Synge's 'Riders to the Sea,' some of Lady Gregory's little comedies, as well as my 'Cathleen ni Houlihan,' appeared first in its pages. In this new publication I shall write whatever interests me at the moment, trying, however, to keep some kind of unity, and only including poem or play that has something to do with my main theme. 'Purgatory' was first produced at the Abbey Theatre, Dublin, on August 10, 1938, with Michael Dolan as the Old Man and Liam Redmond as the Boy.

W. B. YEATS, October, 1938. **93.**

DATES, PLACES OF PERFORMANCE, AND CASTS OF CHARACTERS OF FIRST PRODUCTIONS

[This information is mainly from Yeats's notes to the plays. I have ignored his variant spellings of proper names.]

The Countess Cathleen. Produced by the Irish Literary Theatre at the Ancient Concert Rooms, Dublin, 8 May 1899.

First Demon .	.	. Marcus St. John
Second Demon .	.	. Trevor Lowe
Shemus Rua .	.	. Valentine Grace
Teig .	.	. Charles Sefton
Mary .	.	. Madame San Carolo
Kevin (Aleel) .	.	. Florence Farr
Oona .	.	. Anna Mather
Herdsman .	.	. Charles Holmes
Gardener .	.	. Jack Wilcox
Peasant .	.	. Mr. Walford
Spirit .	.	. Dorothy Paget
Peasant Woman .	.	. Miss M. Kelly
Servant .	.	. T. E. Wilkinson
Countess Kathleen .	.	. May Whitty

7-80.

See also Lennox Robinson, *Ireland's Abbey Theatre.* London, 1951, p. 12.

The Land of Heart's Desire. Produced at the Avenue Theatre, London, 29 March 1894.

Maurteen Bruin .	.	. James Welch
Shawn Bruin .	.	. A. E. W. Mason
Father Hart .	.	. G. R. Foss
Bridget Bruin .	.	. Charlotte Morland
Maire Bruin .	.	. Winifred Fraser
A Faery Child .	.	. Dorothy Paget

4-33, 47-67, 71-76, 78, 80.

Cathleen ni Houlihan. Produced by the Irish National Dramatic Company at St. Teresa's Hall, Clarendon Street, Dublin, 2 April 1902.

Cathleen ni Houlihan .	.	. Miss Maud Gonne
Delia Cahel .	.	. Miss Maire nic Sheublagh
Bridget Gillan .	.	. Miss M. T. Quinn
Patrick Gillan .	.	. Mr. C. Caufield
Michael Gillan .	.	. Mr. T. Dudley Digges
Peter Gillan .	.	. Mr. W. G. Fay

34, 45, 69.

See Robinson, *op. cit.,* p. 31.

The Pot of Broth. Produced by the Irish National Dramatic Company at the Ancient Concert Rooms, Dublin, 30 October 1902.

For cast see Robinson, *op. cit.*, p. 31.

The King's Threshold. Produced by the Irish National Theatre Society at Molesworth Hall, Dublin, 7 [8[1]] October 1903.

Seanchan	F. Fay
King Guaire	P. Kelly
Lord High Chamberlain	Shamus O'Sullivan
Soldier	William Conroy
Monk	S. Sheridan-Neill
Mayor	William Fay
A Cripple	Patrick Columb
A Court Lady	Honor Saville
Another Court Lady	Dora Melville
A Princess	Sara Allgood
Another Princess	Dora Gunning
Fedelm	Maire MacShiubhlaigh
A Servant	P. MacShiubhlaigh
Another Servant	P. Josephs
A Pupil	G. Roberts
Another Pupil	Cartia McChormac

23-32, 45, 48, 69.

The Shadowy Waters. Produced by the Irish National Theatre Society at Molesworth Hall, Dublin, 14 January 1904.

Forgael	F. Fay
Aibric	Shamus O'Sullivan
Dectora	Maire MacShiubhlaigh

23, 28-69.

See Robinson, *op. cit.*, p. 41.

Deirdre. Produced by the National Theatre Society, Ltd., at Molesworth Hall, Dublin, 24 November 1906.

Musicians	Sara Allgood
	Maire O'Neill
	Brigit O'Dempsey
Fergus	Arthur Sinclair
Naisi	F. J. Fay
Deirdre	Miss Darragh
A Dark-faced Messenger	U. Wright
Conchubar	J. M. Kerrigan
Dark-faced Executioner	A. Power

27-32, 45-52, 63, 69.

[1] Appendix IV, **34**; and Robinson, *op. cit.*, p. 33.

At the Hawk's Well. Produced privately in Lady Cunard's drawing-room, Cavendish Square, London, 2 April 1916.

The Young Man	.	.	Henry Ainley
The Old Man		.	Allan Wade
The Guardian of the Well	.	Mr. Ito
The Three Musicians		.	Mr. Dulac
		.	Mrs. Mann
		.	Mr. Foulds

HB-71.

The Golden Helmet. Produced by the National Theatre Society, Ltd., at the Abbey Theatre, 19 March 1908.

Cuchulain	.	.	J. M. Kerrigan
Conal .		.	Arthur Sinclair
Leagerie	.	.	Fred. O'Donovan
Laeg .	.	.	Sydney Morgan
Emer .	.	.	Sara Allgood
Conal's Wife .	.	.	Maire O'Neill
Leagerie's Wife	.	.	Eileen O'Doherty
Red Man	.	.	Ambrose Power

Horseboys, Scullions, and Black Men, S. Hamilton, T. J. Fox, U. Wright, D. Robertson, T. O'Neill, I. A. O'Rourke, P. Kearney.

34, 45, 69.

The Green Helmet. Produced by the National Theatre Society, Ltd., at the Abbey Theatre, 10 February 1910.

[The cast was different from *The Golden Helmet* cast in these parts:

Laegaire's Wife	.	Miss Magee

Horseboys, Scullions, and Black Men, Eric Gorman, J. A. O'Rourke, John Carrick, F. R. Harford, T. Moloney, T. Durkin, P. Byrne.]

See Robinson, *op. cit.*, p. 103.

On Baile's Strand. Produced by the Irish National Theatre Society at the Abbey Theatre, 27 December 1904.

Cuchulain	.	.	Frank Fay
Conchubar	.	.	George Roberts
Daire (an old King)	.	.	G. MacDonald
The Blind Man	.	.	Seumas O'Sullivan
The Fool	.	.	William Fay
The Young Man	.	.	P. MacShiubhlaigh
Old Kings and Young Kings		R. Nash, N. Power,

U. Wright, E. Kegan, Emma Vernon, Doreen Gunning, Sara Allgood.

23, 28, 45-69.

See Robinson, *op. cit.*, p. 46.

The Only Jealousy of Emer. See p. 567, above: '. . . somebody put it on a public stage in Holland . . . .' [No other information available.]

Fighting the Waves. Produced by the National Theatre Society, Ltd., at the Abbey Theatre, 13 August 1929.   **83.**

For cast see Robinson, *op. cit.*, p. 143.

The Hour-Glass (Prose). Produced by the Irish National Theatre Society at Molesworth Hall, Dublin, 14 March 1903.

The Wise Man .	J. W. Digges
Bridget, his wife.	Maire T. Quinn
Her children .	Eithne and Padragan ni Shiubhleigh
Pupils . .	P. I. Kelly, Seumas O'Sullivan, P. Colum, P. MacShiubhlaigh
The Angel .	Maire ni Shiubhlaigh
The Fool. .	F. J. Fay

See Robinson, *op. cit.*, p. 33.   **29-69.**

The Hour-Glass (Verse). Produced by the National Theatre Society, Ltd., at the Abbey Theatre, 21 November 1912.

The Wise Man . .	Mr. Nugent Monck.

[Yeats gives but this one character. Robinson, *op. cit.*, p. 108, lists another play for this date.]   **69.**

The Unicorn from the Stars. Produced by the National Theatre Society, Ltd., at the Abbey Theatre, 23 [21[1]] November 1907.

Father John . .	Ernest Vaughan
Thomas Hearne . .	Arthur Sinclair
Andrew Hearne . .	J. A. O'Rourke
Martin Hearne .	F. J. Fay
Johnny Bacach .	W. G. Fay
Paudeen . .	J. M. Kerrigan
Biddy Lally . .	Maire O'Neill
Nanny. . .	Bridget O'Dempsey

29-69.

The Player Queen. Produced by the London Stage Society at King's Hall, Covent Garden, 25 May 1919.

Decima . .	Maire O'Neill
Septimus . .	Nicholas Hannen
Nona . .	Edith Evans[2]

[1] Robinson, *op. cit.*, p. 80.
[2] Allan Wade, *The Letters of W. B. Yeats.* London, 1954, p. 654. For complete cast of first presentation at the Abbey Theatre on 9 December 1919 see Robinson, *op. cit.*, p. 130.

The Dreaming of the Bones. Produced by the National Theatre Society, Ltd., at the Abbey Theatre, 6 December 1931.

For cast see Robinson, *op. cit.*, p. 146.

Calvary. No record.

The Cat and the Moon. Produced by the National Theatre Society, Ltd., at the Abbey Theatre, 9 May 1926 [21 September 1931[1]]. **83.**

Sophocles' King Oedipus. Produced by the National Theatre Society, Ltd., at the Abbey Theatre, 7 December 1926.

Oedipus . . .	F. J. McCormick
Jocasta . . .	Eileen Crowe
Creon . . .	Barry Fitzgerald
Priest . . .	Eric Gorman
Tiresias . . .	Michael J. Dolan
Boy . . .	D. Breen
First Messenger .	Arthur Shields
Herdsman .	Gabriel J. Fallon
Second Messenger	P. J. Carolan
Nurse . . .	May Craig
Children . . .	Raymond and Edna Fardy
Servants . .	Tony Quinn, Michael Scott, C. Haughton
Leader of the Chorus .	J. Stevenson
Chorus . . .	Peter Nolan, Walter Dillon, T. Moran, M. Finn, D. Williams

79.

Sophocles' Oedipus at Colonus. Produced by the National Theatre Society, Ltd., at the Abbey Theatre, 12 September 1927.

For cast see Robinson, *op. cit.*, p. 141.

The Resurrection. Produced by the National Theatre Society, Ltd., at the Abbey Theatre, 30 July 1934.

For cast see Robinson, *op. cit.*, p. 159.

The Words upon the Window-Pane. Produced by the National Theatre Society, Ltd., at the Abbey Theatre, 17 November 1930.

83.

For cast see Robinson, *op. cit.*, p. 145.

[1] Robinson, *op. cit.*, p. 146. For cast see Robinson, *ibid.*

A Full Moon in March. No record.

The King of the Great Clock Tower. Produced by the National Theatre Society, Ltd., at the Abbey Theatre, 30 June [30 July[1]] 1934.

84, 85.

The Herne's Egg. No record.

Purgatory. Produced by the National Theatre Society, Ltd., at the Abbey Theatre, 10 August 1938.

Old Man . . .	Michael Dolan
Boy	Liam Redmond

93.

The Death of Cuchulain. Produced by Austin Clarke's Lyric Theatre at the Abbey Theatre, 13 August 1949.[2]

Where There is Nothing. Produced by the London Stage Society at the Royal Court Theatre on 26 June 1904.

Paul Ruttledge .	Lyall Swete[3]

Diarmuid and Grania. Produced for the Irish Literary Theatre at the Gaiety Theatre, Dublin, on 21 October 1901.

King Cormac . . .	Alfred Brydone
Finn MacCoole . .	Frank Rodney
Diarmuid . .	F. R. Benson
Goll . . .	Charles Bibby
Usheen . .	Henry Ainley
Caoelte . .	E. Harcourt Williams
Fergus . . .	G. Wallace Johnstone
Fathna . .	Walter Hampden
Griffan . .	Stuart Edgar
Niall . . .	Matheson Lang
Conan the Bald .	Arthur Whitby
An Old Man . .	H. O. Nicholson
A Shepherd . .	Mr. Owen
A Boy . .	Ella Tarrant
A Yaung Man .	Jean Mackinley
Grania . .	Mrs. F. R. Benson
Laban . .	Lucy Franklein

---

[1] Robinson, *op. cit.*, p. 159. For cast see Robinson, *ibid.*
[2] Birgit Bjersby, *The Interpretation of the Cuchulain Legend in the Works of W. B. Yeats*. Upsala, 1950; Dublin, 1950, p. 23.
[3] Wade, *op. cit.*, pp. 382n-383n.

The Island of Statues. No record.

The Seeker. No record.

Mosada. No record.

Time and the Witch Vivien. No record.

INDEX

PART I

PART I records the characters in the plays with a notation of the line in the basic text and in the variants where each character first speaks. These play-abbreviations are used:

* The character appears but does not speak.